The Law of Clean Energy

Efficiency and Renewables

Michael B. Gerrard, Editor

For updates: http://www.columbiaenergylaw.com

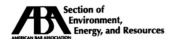
Section of
Environment,
Energy, and Resources
AMERICAN BAR ASSOCIATION

Cover design by Catherine Zaccarine.

The materials contained herein represent the views of each chapter author in his or her individual capacity and should not be construed as the views of the author's firms, employers, or clients, or of the editor or other chapter authors, or of the American Bar Association or the Section of Environment, Energy, and Resources unless adopted pursuant to the bylaws of the Association.

Nothing contained in this book is to be considered as the rendering of legal advice, either generally or in connection with any specific issue or case. Readers are responsible for obtaining advice from their own lawyers or other professionals. This book is intended for educational and informational purposes only.

Printed in the United States of America

15 14 13 12   5 4 3

Library of Congress Cataloging-in-Publication Data

The law of clean energy : efficiency and renewables / edited by Michael B. Gerrard—1st ed.
   p. cm.
   Includes bibliographical references and index.
   ISBN 978-1-61438-008-5 (alk. paper)
1. Energy conservation—Law and legislation—United States. 2. Power resources—Law and legislation—United States. I. Gerrard, Michael.
   KF2120.L39 2011
   346.7304'67916—dc23

                                    2011019079

Discounts are available for books ordered in bulk. Special consideration is given to state bars, CLE programs, and other bar-related organizations. Inquire at Book Publishing, ABA Publishing, American Bar Association, 321 North Clark Street, Chicago, Illinois 60654-7598.

www.ShopABA.org

Summary of Contents

PART III
Energy Use Sectors

Contents

PART II
Financing, Pricing, and Taxation

Chapter Six
Government Purchasing of Efficient Products and Renewable Energy. 117
Geraldine E. Edens, Peter L. Gray, and Stephen E. Ruscus

Chapter Eight
Government Nontax Incentives for Clean Energy

John A. Herrick

PART III
Energy Use Sectors

Chapter Eleven
Conservation of Energy in Agriculture and Forestry 263
Thomas P. Redick and A. Bryan Endres

Chapter Twelve
Appliances, Lighting, Computers, Data Centers, and Computer Servers 277
John A. Hodges

Chapter Eighteen
Geothermal Resources 423
Sylvia Harrison

Chapter Nineteen

Biofuels. 445

James M. Van Nostrand and Anne Marie Hirschberger

Preface and Acknowledgments

A major portion of the solution to today's environmental problems, led by global climate change, must lie in a transition to an economy that uses energy efficiently and relies as much as possible on renewable sources. This transition is also likely to be a major source of jobs and economic growth in the coming decades.

This book is an explication of the legal issues involved in the transition to a clean energy economy, especially in the United States.

Though this book is entitled *The Law of Clean Energy: Efficiency and Renewables*, only so much meaning can be crammed into eight words, and here is the place to indicate more precisely what the book does and does not cover. Discussion of energy conservation as well as efficiency is included; the law is generally more pertinent to efficiency, but some legal techniques are being applied to conservation as well. (The distinction between the two is covered in chapter 1.) Many people will argue that nuclear power is clean and (with fuel reprocessing) renewable; without getting into that debate, the legal and policy issues with nuclear power are much different than those with conventional renewables, and those issues are left to other books. Carbon capture and sequestration may someday allow coal to be burned cleanly, but this technology is not yet in commercial application, and it does not address many of the other problems of fossil fuels. Thus it is not covered either.[1]

Though examples from around the world are used, the focus of this book is on U.S. law. Its editor and its chapter authors are U.S. lawyers; it is published by the American Bar Association (ABA); to cover the laws of other countries in any detail would involve multiple volumes. It is relevant here to note that the United States has long been the world's largest consumer of energy, though around 2007 it was overtaken by China. In 2008 the United States generated 19 percent of the world's carbon dioxide (CO_2) emissions, despite having less than 5 percent of the global population; China contributed about 22 percent of the world's CO_2 emissions but had 20 percent of the world's population; and India, with 17 percent of the world's population, contributed less than 5 percent of the emissions.[2]

Most of the credit for this book belongs with the chapter authors, each of whom devoted considerable time and expertise to this joint effort. I am also very grateful to Julia Errea Ciardullo, who helped edit and refine the final manuscript; Leslie Keros of ABA Publishing, whose skilled, patient, and meticulous hand was invaluable; Alexsandra Guerra, who prepared the list of abbreviations; the Book Publishing Board of the ABA's Section of Environment, Energy, and Resources (SEER), headed by Peter Wright, for its guiding hand and for organizing the peer review process; and David Hodas and several anonymous reviewers, who greatly improved the book's quality. I also greatly benefited from the support and encouragement of my colleagues at Columbia Law School and Arnold & Porter LLP.

Most of all, I am perpetually grateful for the love and support of my wonderful family, Barbara, David, and William.

Each chapter in this book represents the views of each chapter author in his or her individual capacity. It does not necessarily reflect the views of the authors' firms, employers, or clients, nor of the editor or the authors of the other chapters, nor of the ABA or SEER. This book does not provide legal advice, which should be sought from the reader's own lawyers.

M.B.G.

New York, New York

February 2011

Notes

1. This topic is covered in David J. Hayes and Joel C. Beauvais, "Carbon Sequestration," GLOBAL CLIMATE CHANGE AND U.S. LAW ch. 19 (Michael B. Gerrard ed., ABA 2007).

2. INTERNATIONAL ENERGY AGENCY, CO_2 EMISSIONS FROM FUEL COMBUSTION: HIGHLIGHTS 11 (2010).

About the Editor

Michael B. Gerrard is Andrew Sabin Professor of Professional Practice and Director of the Center for Climate Change Law at Columbia Law School. He teaches courses in environmental law, energy law, and climate change law. He has practiced environmental law in New York since 1979. Until 2008 he was managing partner of the New York office of Arnold & Porter LLP; he is now Senior Counsel to the firm. Mr. Gerrard formerly chaired the American Bar Association's Section of Environment, Energy, and Resources; the New York State Bar Association's Environmental Law Section; and the New York City Bar Association's Executive Committee. He is author or editor of eight books, two of which were named Best Law Book of the Year by the Association of American Publishers. Among his books for the ABA are *Global Climate Change and U.S. Law* (2007) and *The Law of Green Buildings* (2010). Mr. Gerrard received his BA from Columbia University and his JD from New York University School of Law, where he was a Root Tilden Scholar.

About the Authors

John C. Dernbach is distinguished professor of law at Widener University in Harrisburg, Pennsylvania, and director of Widener's Law Center. He has written more than forty articles for law reviews and peer-reviewed journals, and has authored, coauthored, or contributed chapters to thirteen books. Professor Dernbach's scholarship focuses on environmental law, climate change, sustainable development, and legal writing. He is the editor of *Agenda for a Sustainable America* (Environmental Law Institute 2009) and *Stumbling Toward Sustainability* (Environmental Law Institute 2002), comprehensive assessments of U.S. sustainable development activities that include recommendations for future efforts. Professor Dernbach coauthored an amicus brief to the U.S. Supreme Court on behalf of eighteen prominent climate scientists in *Massachusetts v. Environmental Protection Agency*. He is a member of the National Academy of Sciences Committee on Incorporating Sustainability in the U.S. Environmental Protection Agency. He is past chair (now a vice chair) of the American Bar Association's Section of Environment, Energy, and Resources Climate Change, Sustainable Development, and Ecosystems Committee. He also worked in a variety of positions at the Pennsylvania Department of Environmental Protection, most recently as director of policy, and is the primary drafter of three major Pennsylvania waste laws.

Michael Dworkin is professor of law at Vermont Law School, where he directs the Institute for Energy and the Environment. Professor Dworkin chaired the Vermont Public Service Board from 1999 to 2005; in 2003, on behalf of the board, he received the Innovations in American Government Award from Harvard University's Kennedy School of Government for helping oversee the development of Efficiency Vermont, a statewide energy efficiency utility, into one of America's five most innovative and effective public service programs. Professor Dworkin is also the former chair of the National Association of Regulatory Utility Commissioners (NARUC) Committee on Energy Resources and the Environment. In 2008 he received the Mary Kilmarx Award from NARUC for his achievements in promoting good government, clean energy, and the environment. Professor Dworkin serves on the board of directors for the Electric Power Research Institute, the Vermont Energy Investment Corporation, and the American Council for an Energy-Efficient Economy. He is a graduate of Middlebury College and Harvard Law School.

Geraldine E. Edens is a partner in the law firm McKenna Long & Aldridge LLP, specializing in environmental and energy law. She leads the firm's cross-practice Climate, Energy, and Sustainability Initiative. Ms. Edens has extensive experience counseling clients and litigating issues under the Clean Air Act, as well as issues involving climate change and indoor air pollution. She provides strategic advice to companies and foreign governments on emerging U.S. climate change law and regulation and assists companies to develop projects eligible for offset credits under existing and emerging law. Ms. Edens' practice also focuses heavily on alternative energy projects and technologies, assisting clients with funding opportunities through federal grants and incentives, as well as with project siting and permitting. She counsels and litigates issues under the National Environmental Policy Act and related statutes, including the Endangered Species Act, the Marine Mammal Protection Act, and the Clean Water Act. She currently represents Cape Wind Associates in its efforts to construct the first offshore wind project in the United States.

A. Bryan Endres is an associate professor of agricultural law in the Department of Agricultural and Consumer Economics at the University of Illinois and Director of the European Union Center. He also holds research appointments with the Business, Economics and Law program and the Energy Biosciences Institute within the university's Institute for Genomic Biology. Professsor Endres has taught courses in agricultural law, food law, biotechnology law, and renewable energy law. Current research interests include renewable energy, land use, carbon sequestration, agricultural biotechnology, sustainable agriculture, and local food networks. He formerly chaired the Illinois State Bar Association's Agricultural Law Section Council and currently serves on the board of directors of the American Agricultural Law Association. Professor Endres earned a BS in mathematical economics from the United States Military Academy at West Point, an MS in administrative management from the European Division of Bowie State University, and a JD from the University of Illinois.

Steven Ferrey is professor of law at Suffolk University Law School in Boston, and also has served as visiting professor of law at Harvard University Law School and Boston University Law School. In addition to his teaching, he has served over the past two decades as a principal legal advisor to the World Bank and to the United Nations on their projects in developing countries on renewable power and climate change, working in Indonesia, Thailand, India, Sri Lanka, Vietnam, Uganda, and Tanzania. He also advises energy clients in the United States. Between 2007 and 2011, he has served as vice chair of two energy subcommittees of the American Bar Association's Section of Environment, Energy, and Resources. He is the author of seven books and has contributed chapters to a dozen other books. His books include *The Law of Independent Power* (28th ed. 2010); *Unlocking the Global Warming Toolbox* (2010); *The New Rules: A Guide to Electric Market Regulation* (2000); and *Renewable Power in Developing Countries: Winning the War on Global Warming* (2006). In 2009–2010, he published articles on energy and environmental law and policy appearing in law reviews at Stanford, University of California at Berkeley, Duke, University of Vermont, Lewis & Clark, University of Minnesota, University of Missouri, Fordham, Boston College, and Notre Dame.

Joshua P. Fershee is associate professor of law and Faculty Development Fellow for Research & Scholarship at the University of North Dakota School of Law. He writes and teaches in the areas of energy law and policy, business law and corporate governance, and labor and employment law. Before joining UND, he served as a visiting assistant professor of law at Penn State University's Dickinson School of Law in State College, Pennsylvania, and practiced in New York City and Washington, D.C. In his practice he represented energy clients in matters before state and federal regulators, analyzed state and federal legislation, and advised clients on mergers and acquisitions, climate change issues, and renewable portfolio standards. Recent articles have appeared in a variety of journals, including the Harvard Journal on Legislation, Energy Law Journal, Connecticut Law Review, and Environmental Law. Professor Fershee received his JD magna cum laude from Tulane Law School, where he was elected Order of the Coif and editor in chief of the Tulane Law Review.

Jeremy Firestone is associate professor, College of Earth, Ocean, and Environment, and senior research scientist, Center for Carbon-free Power Integration, University of Delaware. He teaches courses on offshore wind power, ocean and coastal law, climate change policy, and international environmental policy. In 2010, Professor Firestone served as conference chair of the Philadelphia Offshore Wind Forum, and on the Planning Committee of the National Academy of Sciences Marine Board's Offshore Wind Power Workshop. He has published the results of his wind research in leading journals, including Wind Energy, Energy Policy, Land Economics and Environmental Law. Professor Firestone was the lead citizen participant in separate administrative proceedings leading to the United States' first offshore wind power purchase agreement and to explicit consideration of externalities in long-term energy planning in Delaware and lead faculty member in project development of a jointly owned and operated (with the manufacturer, Gamesa) 2 MW wind turbine on UD's coastal campus. He received his JD from University of Michigan Law School and PhD in public policy analysis from University of North Carolina at Chapel Hill.

Paul Foley has practiced environmental and energy law since he became a member of the New York bar in 2001. He has made numerous appearances before the New York Supreme Court, the New York Public Service Commission, the California Environmental Commission, the California Public Utilities Commission, the New York City Environmental Control Board, and several local planning boards. Mr. Foley previously served on the Cambridge, New York, Planning Board and on the Board of the Battenkill Conservancy. Most recently he was an LLM global energy fellow at Vermont Law School's Institute for Energy and the Environment. Mr. Foley received a JD from the University of Maine School of Law and a Master of Community Planning and Development from the University of Southern Maine's Muskie School of Public Service. He currently resides in Budapest, Hungary.

Clay Francis is the Clean Energy Advocate for the Vermont Public Interest Research Group (VPIRG). Before joining VPIRG, Mr. Francis was a research associate at the Institute for Energy and the Environment at Vermont Law School. While at the Institute, he wrote a monthly e-publication on Chinese energy policy and contributed to a book describing the environmental design of energy security. Prior to coming to Vermont, Mr. Francis taught advanced Spanish at a private boarding school in Tennessee and was an associate professor of international relations at the Tennessee Governor's School for International Studies at the University of Memphis. Mr. Francis holds a BA in Spanish and political science from Middle Tennessee State University and a Master of Environmental Law and Policy from Vermont Law School. At VPIRG, Mr. Francis conducts policy research and advocacy on energy issues, with a focus on the home heating and energy efficiency aspects of Vermont's clean energy future.

Frederick R. Fucci is a partner in the New York City office of Arnold & Porter LLP, where he focuses his practice on the development and financing of infrastructure projects in the United States and in emerging markets with a focus on energy. He has advised on the installation of numerous distributed generation facilities (on-site) using combined heat and power (CHP) or cogeneration technologies. He also advises energy services companies (ESCOs) on energy efficiency projects carried out under energy performance contracts or demand-side management programs. He is the author of two chapters, on alternative energy options and energy performance contracting for buildings, in *The Law of Green Buildings* (J. Cullen Howe and Michael B. Gerrard eds., 2010).

Javier García-Lomas Gago is an attorney specializing in renewable energy law at Perez Moreno LLP in Seville, Spain, a firm that represents developers, utilities, and environmental organizations. Mr. García-Lomas is also an adjunct professor at the University of Seville, where he teaches administrative law. He earned his BA and JD from the University of Seville and his LLM from Vermont Law School, where he served as a research associate for the Institute for Energy and the Environment. While working at the Institute, Mr. Garcia-Lomas developed and maintained the Institute's blog and helped to design model legislation for energy efficiency. He teaches a summer course on comparative energy law at Vermont Law School and has developed a website devoted to the subject, www.energylawtoday.com.

Peter L. Gray serves as national chair of McKenna Long & Aldridge LLP's Environment, Energy and Product Regulation Department. Since joining the firm in 1985, he has worked on a broad range of environmental litigation and counseling matters. Mr. Gray helped to form the firm's climate change practice, which assists clients with a number of climate-related projects, including developing climate change strategies and policies; identifying and capturing value through carbon emission reduction strategies; complying with SEC disclosure obligations implicated by climate risks or impacts on business; and monitoring climate and energy legislation and conceptualizing legislative strategies. Mr. Gray cofounded and launched the Association of Climate Change Officers, the first organization dedicated to advancing the knowledge and skills of climate change professionals. He launched the Climate Change Insights blog, a forum for critical analyses of climate law and policy. Mr. Gray also participates as a commentator in broadcast media, having appeared on Fox Business News and Bloomberg Radio.

Sylvia Harrison is a partner in the law firm of McDonald Carano Wilson, LLP in Reno, Nevada, where she practices primarily in the fields of environmental law, energy law, and natural resources law. Ms. Harrison holds an MS degree in earth sciences and a PhD in geology. Prior to attending law school, she worked as a geologist in the minerals industry. Ms. Harrison received her JD from the University of Montana, where she was editor of the Public Land Law Review. Representative publications include: *Disposition of the Mineral Estate on United States Public Lands: A Historical Perspective*, 10 PUBLIC LAND L. REV. 131; *Environmental Due Diligence in Real Property Transactions: Practice Pointers*, NEVADA LAWYER, Vol. 5, No. 1, January 1997; *The Historical Development of Nevada Water Law*, UNIVERSITY OF DENVER WATER L. REV., Vol. 5, Issue 1, fall 2001. Her current practice focuses largely on the development of commercial-scale renewable energy projects on public lands.

John K. Harting obtained his bachelor of science degree in environmental sciences, policies, and management from the University of Minnesota in 2008, and expects to obtain his JD degree from the University of Minnesota Law School in 2011. While in law school Mr. Harting conducted significant research on environmental law and energy topics in connection with law review articles and a major environmental law textbook. Upon graduation, John will join the Robins, Kaplan, Miller & Ciresi law firm in Minneapolis as an associate attorney.

John A. Herrick is senior counsel in the Denver office of Brownstein Hyatt Farber Schreck, where he specializes in the clean technology practice area. Mr. Herrick has over thirty years' experience in assisting private companies and public entities in developing clean energy, including wind, solar, geothermal, smart grid, and equipment manufacturing projects. He has helped structure new energy production facilities totaling over $5 billion, structured the federal financing for the nation's first cellulosic biorefinery, and helped form research and development partnerships with private industry, academia, and the National Renewable Energy Laboratory (NREL) in Golden, Colorado, and the Department of Energy's Office of Energy Efficiency and Renewable Energy, where he helped structure the DOE loan guarantee program, the DOE clean energy grant programs, and federal energy performance contracting. He is one of America's leading practitioners in assisting companies in entering into public and private partnerships in clean energy financing. An adjunct professor of law at the University of Denver Sturm College of Law, Mr. Herrick teaches Renewable Energy & Energy Project Finance, the first law course in the nation concentrating on renewable energy, and is an avid speaker on these topics to the general public.

Anne Marie Hirschberger is the Climate Change Law and Policy Advisor at the Pace Energy and Climate Center. She received her JD and Certificate in environmental law as well as her LLM in climate change law from Pace Law School. She has been at the Center since spring 2009, where she began as an intern and then served as the first Ottinger energy research fellow while completing her LLM degree. During her time at the Center, she has researched state and federal energy policies, in particular renewable portfolio standards, emissions trading, and biomass policy, and has also supported the Center's involvement in various utility proceedings. She contributed to the *Renewable Fuels Roadmap and Sustainable Biomass Feedstock Supply for New*

York State, an extensive state-funded report on the potential for a biofuels industry in New York State, and authored *Appendix N: Inventory of Existing Relevant State and Federal Policies*.

John A. Hodges is a partner with Wiley Rein LLP in Washington, DC. He has been practicing energy efficiency law for thirty years. His practice includes counseling clients on standards, test procedures, certification, labeling, waivers, enforcement, Energy Star, and other matters. His practice includes representation before federal agencies, such as the Department of Energy, EPA, and the FTC, state agencies such as the California Energy Commission, the courts, and Congress. He has negotiated and drafted amendments to the Energy Policy and Conservation Act. He is admitted to practice in the District of Columbia and is a member of the District of Columbia Bar Association and the American Bar Association's Section of Environment, Energy, and Resources. He received his AB from Harvard and his LLB from Columbia Law School, where he graduated with honors, was a Stone Scholar, and was managing editor of the Columbia Journal of Law and Social Problems. He was a judicial clerk to Judge Edwin D. Steel, Jr., United States District Court for the District of Delaware.

J. Cullen Howe is an environmental law specialist in Arnold & Porter LLP's environmental practice group and a LEED AP. He is the managing editor of *Environmental Law in New York*, a monthly newsletter, and edits the *Environmental Law Practice Guide, Brownfields Law and Practice*, and *Environmental Impact Review in New York*. He is an adjunct professor at Pace University School of Law, where he teaches a course on the legal aspects of green buildings. Mr. Howe is the coeditor of *The Law of Green Buildings* (with Michael B. Gerrard, 2010) and has coauthored chapters on climate change and green buildings for the *Environmental Law Practice Guide* as well as a chapter on green building financing for the *Real Estate Financing Guide*.

Jeffrey P. Kehne is a founding member of Hill & Kehne, LLC. He has practiced environmental and administrative law in Washington, DC, since 1989. Until 2003, he served at the Department of Justice, first as an appellate litigator in the Environment and Natural Resources Division and then as an attorney-advisor in the Office of Legal Counsel. Since founding Hill & Kehne, his work has focused principally on renewable energy and brownfield redevelopment projects. He currently serves as counsel to the Offshore Wind Development Coalition and advises a range of renewable energy and brownfield redevelopment firms. Mr. Kehne received his BA from Haverford College and his JD from Yale Law School, where he was a notes editor of the Yale Law Journal.

Alexandra B. Klass is a professor of law, associate dean for academic affairs, and the Solly Robins distinguished research fellow at the University of Minnesota Law School. She teaches and writes in the areas of environmental law, natural resources law, tort law, and property law. Her scholarly work includes publications in William & Mary Law Review, Minnesota Law Review, University of Illinois Law Review, Iowa Law Review, University of Colorado Law Review, Harvard Environmental Law

Review, and Ecology Law Quarterly. Her recent scholarship includes federalism issues associated with state energy efficiency laws, the role of property rights in encouraging wind and solar development, and an analysis of property rights and tort liability associated with the use of carbon capture and sequestration technology as a means to address climate change. Prior to her teaching career, Professor Klass was a partner at Dorsey & Whitney LLP in Minneapolis, where she specialized in environmental law and land use litigation. She received her BA from the University of Michigan and her JD from the University of Wisconsin Law School. She was a law clerk to the Honorable Barbara B. Crabb, U.S. District Court, Western District of Wisconsin. She is a member scholar at the Center for Progressive Reform and a resident fellow at the University of Minnesota's Institute on the Environment.

Craig M. Kline is a partner in the New York office of Troutman Sanders and a co-practice leader of the Project Development and Finance practice group. He also co-chairs the firm's interdisciplinary Renewable Energy Team. His practice is focused on domestic and cross-border project finance transactions, renewable energy transactions, structured finance, and leveraged leasing. Mr. Kline has represented a wide variety of commercial and public institutions, including developers, utilities, lenders, issuers, lessors, lessees, credit support providers, and trustees. He also has experience with the securitization of financial assets, synthetic leasing, secured lending, and bankruptcy. He has advised in matters involving power and energy generation and distribution facilities (including over 150 renewable energy transactions: solar, wind, and biomass facilities), aircraft, rolling stock and other rail equipment, vessels and other maritime assets, telecommunications equipment, real estate, waste facilities, and manufacturing plants. In addition to U.S. domestic transactions, he has closed cross-border transactions in connection with assets or counterparties located in, among other jurisdictions, Australia, Austria, Belgium, France, Germany, Hong Kong, Mexico, the Netherlands, Portugal, South Korea, and the United Kingdom.

Roberta F. Mann is professor of law and dean's distinguished faculty fellow at the University of Oregon Law School. She teaches several tax law courses. She has extensive government practice experience with the Office of Chief Counsel of the Internal Revenue and the Joint Committee on Taxation. Professor Mann has been active with the American Bar Association's Section of Taxation, currently serving as the vice chair of the Tax Policy and Simplification Committee. She has authored numerous articles and book chapters about the intersection of tax policy and environmental issues. Professor Mann received her BS, MBA, and JD cum laude from Arizona State University. She received her LLM in taxation from Georgetown University Law Center, with distinction.

Jonathan S. Martel is a partner at Arnold & Porter LLP. He concentrates his practice on Clean Air Act matters and environmental litigation and counseling. Mr. Martel's recent work includes representation of electric utilities, consumer products, automotive, nonroad equipment, and other diversified manufacturers in Clean Air Act regulatory, permitting, and enforcement matters, as well as other environmental litigation and regulatory matters. From 1991 to 1994, Mr. Martel served at the Office of General Counsel of the U.S. Environmental Protection Agency, primarily involved in the implementation of the Clean Air Act Amendments of 1990. He has contributed a chapter on the Clean Air Act to *Global Climate Change and U.S. Law* (Michael B. Gerrard ed., 2007) and a chapter on the fuels provisions of the Clean Air Act to the *Clean Air Act Handbook* (Julie R. Domike and Alec C. Zacaroli eds., 3d ed. 2011). Mr. Martel received his BA from Dartmouth College and his JD from Yale Law School.

Shahin Milani earned his LLM in environmental law, cum laude, from Vermont Law School and his JD from Howard University School of Law. While at Vermont Law School, he was a research associate at Vermont Law School's Institute for Energy and the Environment, where he researched and wrote on renewable portfolio standards, energy security, and energy justice. He was also a student clinician at Vermont Law School's Environmental and Natural Resources Law Clinic, where he worked on an appellate brief for a groundwater contamination case going before the Second Circuit Court of Appeals. He also interned at the Environmental Protection Agency's Office of Enforcement and Compliance Assurance and the Natural Resources Defense Council.

Braden W. Penhoet is a research fellow at the Berkeley Center for Law, Business and the Economy, at the University of California, Berkeley Law School. His current interests include federal fiscal policy in connection with applied research and commercialization activities. He has practiced corporate and securities law at major law firms, and has served as a strategic consultant to nonprofit, government, and startup company enterprises. Mr. Penhoet holds degrees from Stanford University, the UCLA School of Law, and UC Berkeley's Haas School of Business.

Thomas P. Redick has a solo practice in environmental law as Global Environmental Ethics Counsel in St. Louis, Missouri, advising high-technology and agricultural biotechnology clients on product liability prevention and compliance with complex regulatory frameworks, including the Cartagena Protocol on Biosafety and the Basel Convention on Hazardous Waste. He recently coauthored three books, *Innovation and Liability in Biotechnology: Transnational and Comparative Perspectives* (2010 Edward Elgar), *Thwarting Consumer Choice: The Case against Mandatory Labeling for Genetically Modified Foods* (2010 American Enterprise Institute), and *Products Liability: Design and Manufacturing Defects* (The West Group). Before establishing a solo practice in 2005, he was a partner with Gallop, Johnson & Neuman, L.C. in St. Louis, Missouri. He has held many leadership positions in the American Bar Association's Section of Environment, Energy, and Resources and is currently its newsletter coordinator. In 2008, the ABA Board of Governors appointed him to represent the ABA on the board of the Council for Agricultural Science and Technology (CAST), which elected him president in 2010. He studied international environmental law at the University of Michigan (JD 1985, BA high honors 1982).

E. Margaret Rowe is a research associate at the Ocean & Coastal Law Center at the University of Oregon. She was a 2009 Energy Law & Policy fellow at the University of Oregon Bowerman Center for Environmental Law. Ms. Rowe is the author of *Distributed Generation and Renewable Energy Payments: Stimulants for a Renewable Energy Economy*, published in the Western Environmental Law Update (spring 2009). She received her JD from the University of Oregon School of Law with a Certificate in Environment & Natural Resource Law, an MFA from the Art Institute of Chicago, and a BA in psychology from the University of Montana.

Stephen E. Ruscus is a partner in the Washington office of McKenna Long & Aldridge LLP and a member of the firm's Government Contracts-Climate Change Initiative. His experience includes litigation of complex statutory and contractual issues, including those arising out of the design, financing, construction, and operation of privatized cogeneration facilities as well as disposal of spent nuclear fuel. He regularly counsels clients on a variety of government contract law issues involving federal contract funding, claims, and terminations. Mr. Ruscus also conducts internal investigations for his clients and prepares all necessary reports under the Department of Defense, Department of State, and Department of Veterans Affairs Voluntary Disclosure programs. Mr. Ruscus lectures on privatization, outsourcing, and federal compliance issues. He received his JD from the Catholic University of America Columbus School of Law.

Patricia E. Salkin is the Raymond & Ella Smith distinguished professor of law, associate dean and director of the Government Law Center at Albany Law School. She is the author and editor of numerous books and treatises, including the five-volume *American Law of Zoning* (5th ed. (West) and *Climate Change and Sustainable Development Law in a Nutshell* (with Nolon) (West). She has also written many law review and journal articles on land use, green development, land use, alternative energy, and sustainable development. Professor Salkin is a past chair of the American Bar Association's Section of State and Local Government Law and is currently the chair of the New York State Bar Association's Municipal Law Section and the American Association of Law Schools' Section of State and Local Government Law. She is an appointed member of National Environmental Justice Advisory Council, a federal advisory body to the EPA. Professor Salkin earned a BA from the University at Albany and a JD from Albany Law School.

Charles R. Sensiba is a member at Van Ness Feldman in Washington, DC. His practice focuses on energy and natural resources issues with a particular emphasis on the regulation of hydroelectric facilities under the Federal Power Act, the National Historic Preservation Act, the National Environmental Policy Act, Clean Water Act, and other federal statutes affecting energy and water development. Mr. Sensiba is actively involved in several organizations within the hydroelectric industry. He currently serves as chairman of the American Bar Association's Section of Environment, Energy, and Resources Hydro Power Committee and vice chair of the National Hydropower Association's (NHA) Regulatory Affairs Committee. In addition, Mr. Sensiba has authored many articles and is a regular speaker at conferences and seminars on issues facing the hydroelectric industry, including water quality, federal water policies, annual charges programs, and other environmental and regulatory issues affecting water power development. Mr. Sensiba received his BS from the University of Utah and his JD from the University of Colorado School of Law, where he served as a casenote and comment editor for the University of Colorado Law Review.

Anna Skubikowski is currently an attorney-advisor in the Office of General Counsel of the Federal Energy Regulatory Commission (FERC). Before joining FERC, Ms. Skubikowski was a JD student at Vermont Law School and a research associate at the law school's Institute for Energy and the Environment; it was in this capacity that she contributed to this book. As a JD candidate, Ms. Skubikowski won a USAID-funded fellowship to study and present a paper in China on the privatization of sewage treatment in the United States and in China, and interned for a semester at the United Nations Framework Convention on Climate Change Secretariat in Bonn, Germany. She also interned at the U.S. State Department's Office of Ocean and Polar Affairs. Prior to obtaining her JD, Ms. Skubikowski was a World Bank Junior Professional Associate at the Global Environment Facility. Ms. Skubikowski holds a BA in comparative literature from Barnard College and an MA in Italian literature from Harvard University. The opinions and views expressed in chapter 22 do not necessarily represent the views of the United States, the Federal Energy Regulatory Commission (FERC), individual FERC commissioners, or FERC staff.

Marianne Tyrrell is a Global Energy fellow in Vermont Law School's Institute for Energy and the Environment (IEE) and an adjunct professor in Marlboro College's MBA in Managing for Sustainability. Before joining Vermont Law, Professor Tyrrell worked as a consultant serving such clients as the British Consulate General, Boston; ICF International; and the Center for Climate Strategies. Since 2004, Professor Tyrrell has served as a vice chair of the American Bar Association's Section of Environment, Energy, and Resources Climate Change, Sustainable Development, and Ecosystems Committee. She received her BA from Bryn Mawr College and her JD from Widener University School of Law, Harrisburg, where she served as editor in chief of the Law Review.

James M. Van Nostrand is executive director of the Energy and Climate Center at Pace Law School in White Plains, New York. Before coming to Pace in spring 2008, he was a partner in the environmental and natural resources practice group of Perkins Coie LLP in Seattle and Portland, and was also a partner in the energy practice group at Stoel Rives LLP in Portland. In his last year in private practice, Professor Van Nostrand was recognized by the Energy Bar Association as its 2007 State Regulatory Practitioner of the Year. He teaches Energy Law and Eco Markets & Trading as a member of the adjunct faculty at Pace Law School. He received his JD from the University of Iowa College of Law, an MA in economics from SUNY at Albany, and a BA in economics from the University of Northern Iowa. Professor Van Nostrand is currently enrolled in the Climate Change track of Pace's graduate law program, and will receive his LLM in environmental law in May 2011.

Judith Wallace is an associate in the Environmental Practice Group at Carter Ledyard and Milburn LLP in New York, where she has represented public agencies and power authorities, private developers, and private parties in connection with environmental review for conventional and renewable energy generation and other development and infrastructure projects, compliance with energy efficiency requirements, and other environmental and land use regulatory and permitting requirements. She is a former secretary of the Energy Committee of the New York City Bar Association and the author of numerous articles on issues in alternative energy development. Ms. Wallace received her BA from New York University and her JD cum laude from Georgetown University Law Center.

Kristen Klick White is an environmental attorney in the Office of the General Counsel at Chrysler Group LLC. She previously served as an associate at Arnold & Porter LLP, where her practice focused on regulatory compliance counseling and litigation under the Clean Air Act, Clean Water Act, Resource Conservation and Recovery Act, the Comprehensive Environmental Response, Compensation and Liability Act, and other state and federal environmental laws. Prior to joining Arnold & Porter LLP, Ms. White was law clerk to the Honorable Beth P. Gesner, United States Magistrate Judge for the District of Maryland. Ms. White graduated with honors from the University of Maryland School of Law, where she was an articles editor for the Maryland Law Review. She received her BA, with honors, from Lehigh University.

Abbreviations

AB 32	California Global Warming Solutions Act of 2006
ACEEE	American Council for an Energy-Efficient Economy
ACES	American Clean Energy and Security Act
ACHP	Advisory Council on Historic Preservation
ACHRI	Air-Conditioning, Heating and Refrigeration Institute
ACP	alternative compliance payments
AFV	alternative fuel vehicle
AHRI	Air-Conditioning, Heating, and Refrigeration Institute
ANOPR	Advance Notice of Proposed Rulemaking
APA	Administrative Procedure Act
ARPA–E	Advanced Research Projects Agency–Energy
ARRA	American Recovery and Reinvestment Act
ASHRAE	American Society of Heating, Refrigerating, and Air-Conditioning Engineers
AWEA	American Wind Energy Association
BACT	best available control technology
BCAP	Biomass Crop Assistance Program
BETC	Business Energy Tax Credit
BLM	Bureau of Land Management
BOD	biochemical oxygen demand
BOEMRE	Bureau of Ocean Energy Management, Regulation, and Enforcement (formerly known as MMS)
BOMA	Building Owners and Managers Association
BPA	Bonneville Power Administration
BRE	Building Research Establishment
BTU	British Thermal Unit
C&D	construction and demolition
CAA	Clean Air Act
CAFE	Corporate Average Fuel Efficiency
CAISO	California ISO
CARB	California Air Resources Board
CARS	Consumer Assistance to Recycle and Save
CBES	Commercial Building Energy Standards
CCS	Carbon Capture and Storage
CCX	Chicago Climate Exchange
CEC	California Energy Commission
CEQ	U.S. Council on Environmental Quality

Prepared by Alexsandra Guerra, Columbia University Earth and Environmental Engineering (class of 2012).

CFC	chlorofluorocarbon
CFL	compact fluorescent lamps
CHP	combined heat and power
CO_2	carbon dioxide
CPUC	California Public Utilities Commission
CRADAs	Cooperative Research and Development Agreements
CREB	Clean Energy Renewable Bonds
CRS	Congressional Research Service
CSP	concentrated solar power
CWA	Clean Water Act
CZMA	Coastal Zone Management Act
DARPA	Defense Advanced Research Projects Agency
DC	direct current
DG	distributed generation
DLA	Defense Logistics Agency
DOD	U.S. Department of Defense
DOE	U.S. Department of Energy
DOI	U.S. Department of the Interior
DOT	U.S. Department of Transportation
DSIRE	Database of State Incentives for Renewables and Efficiency
DSM	Demand Side Management
EA	Environmental Assessment
ECB	energy conservation bonds
EECBG	Energy Efficiency and Conservation Block Grant
EERE	The Department of Energy's Office of Energy Efficiency and Renewable Energy
EERS	Energy Efficiency Resource Standards
EIA	Energy Information Administration
EIEA	Energy Improvement and Extension Act
EIS	environmental impact statement
EISA	Energy Independence and Security Act
EPA	U.S. Environmental Protection Agency
EPAct92	Energy Policy Act of 1992
EPAct05	Energy Policy Act of 2005
EPCA	Energy Policy and Conservation Act
EPRI	Electric Power Research Institute
ERCOT	Electric Reliability Council of Texas
ESA	Endangered Species Act
ESCO	energy service company
ESPC	energy savings performance contract
EU	European Union
FAA	Federal Aviation Administration

FAR	Federal Acquisition Regulation
FARA	Federal Acquisition Reform Act
FCRA	Federal Credit Reform Act
FEA	Federal Energy Administration
FEMP	Federal Energy Management Program
FERC	Federal Energy Regulatory Commission
FFVs	flexible fuel vehicles
FONSI	Finding of No Significant Impact
FPA	Federal Power Act
FPC	Federal Power Commission
FSS	Federal Supply Schedule
FTC	Federal Trade Commission
FTCA	Federal Trade Commission Act
FWPA	Federal Water Power Act
FWS	U.S. Fish & Wildlife Service
FY	fiscal year
GAO	Government Accountability Office
GHG	greenhouse gas
GSA	General Services Administration
GW	gigawatt
GWh	gigawatt hours
HUD	Department of Housing and Urban Development
IRS	Internal Revenue Service
IBLA	Interior Board of Land Appeals
ICC	International Code Council
ICTA	International Center for Technology Assessment
IEA	International Energy Agency
IECC	International Energy Conservation Code
IGCC	International Green Construction Code
IOU	investor-owned utilities
IPO	initial public offering
IPP	independent power producers
IRC	Internal Revenue Code
ISO	International Organization for Standardization or Independent System Operator
ITC	investment tax credits
LCA	life cycle analysis
LCFS	low carbon fuel standard
LED	light-emitting diode
LEED	The U.S. Green Building Council's Leadership in Energy and Environmental Design
LEED-CI	LEED certifications for commercial interiors

LEED-CS	LEED certifications for core and shell design
LEED-EBOM	LEED certifications for existing buildings operation and maintenance
LEED-NC	LEED certifications for new construction and major renovations
LEED-ND	LEED certifications for neighborhood development projects
LPG	liquefied petroleum gas
MBTA	Migratory Bird Treaty Act
MEC	Model Energy Code
MET	metrological testing tower
MGA	Midwestern Governors Association
MGGRA	Midwestern Greenhouse Gas Reduction Accord
MISO	Midwest ISO
MMPA	Marine Mammals Protection Act
MMS	Minerals Management Service (now BOEMRE)
MMT	million metric tons
MOU	Memorandum of Understanding
MSW	municipal solid waste
MW	megawatt
MWh	megawatt-hour
MY	model year
NAECA	National Appliance Energy Conservation Act
NAS	National Academy of Science
NECPA	National Energy Conservation Policy Act
NEPA	National Environmental Policy Act
NESCAUM	Northeast States for Coordinated Air Use Management
NFMA	National Forest Management Act
NHPA	National Historic Preservation Act
NHTSA	National Highway Traffic Safety Administration
NIETC	National Interest Electric Transmission Corridor
NIMBY	"Not in my backyard"
NIST	National Institute of Standards and Technology
NMFS	National Marine Fisheries Service
NOAA	National Oceanic and Atmospheric Administration
NOPR	Notice of Proposed Rulemaking
NRCS	Natural Resources and Conservation Service
NREL	National Renewable Energy Laboratory
NUG	non-utility generators
NYISO	New York ISO
NYSDEC	New York State Department of Environmental Conservation
NYSERDA	New York State Energy Research and Development Authority
O&M	operation and maintenance
OATT	open access transmission tariffs

OCS	Outer Continental Shelf
OCSLA	Outer Continental Shelf Lands Act
OHPGB	Office of High-Performance Green Buildings
OPEC	Organization of the Petroleum Exporting Countries
OTEC	Ocean Thermal Energy Conversion
PACE	Property Assisted Clean Energy
PEIS	programmatic environmental impact study
PHEV	plug-in hybrid electric vehicles
PIPE	private investment in public equity
PMA	Power Marketing Administrations
PPA	power purchase agreements
PSC	Public Service Commission
PSD	prevention of significant deterioration
PTC	production tax credits
PUE	Power Usage Effectiveness
PUHCA	Public Utility Holding Company Act
PURPA	Public Utilities Regulatory Policies Act
PV	photovoltaics
QEC	qualified energy conservation
QECB	qualified energy conservation bonds
QF	qualified facility
R&D	research and development
RBES	Residential Building Energy Standard
RCRA	Resource Conservation and Recovery Act
REA	Renewable Energy Act
REAP	Rural Energy for America Program
REC	renewable energy credits
RES	Renewable Electricity Standard
RETC	Residential Energy Tax Credit
RFI	Request for Interest
RFRA	Religious Freedom Restoration Act
RFS	renewable fuel standard
RFS2	second renewable fuel standard
RGGI	Regional Greenhouse Gas Initiative
RPS	renewable portfolio standards
RTO	Regional Transmission Organizations
RVO	renewable volume obligation
SBC	system benefit charges
SEC	Securities and Exchange Commission
SEP	State Energy Program
SES	sustainable energy standard
SHPO	State Historic Preservation Officer
SSL	solid-state lighting

SSP	Southwest Power Pool RTO
ST&T	Supporting Research and Testing
SUV	sport utility vehicle
TEC	typical energy consumption
TRECs	tradable renewable energy credits
TVA	Tennessee Valley Authority
UCC	Uniform Commercial Code
UESC	utility energy service contract
UPS	uninterruptible power supply
USDA	U.S. Department of Agriculture
USFS	U.S. Forest Service
USFWS	U.S. Fish and Wildlife Service
USGBC	U.S. Green Building Council
USGS	United States Geological Survey
VEETC	Volumetric Ethanol Excise Tax Credit
VMT	vehicle miles traveled
WAPA	Western Area Power Administration
WCI	Western Climate Initiative
WRPA	Water Resources Planning Act
ZEV	Zero Emission Vehicle

chapter one

Introduction and Overview

Michael B. Gerrard

Plentiful supplies of energy are essential to modern civilization. However, 83 percent of the energy consumed in the United States[1] and 85 percent of the energy consumed in the world[2] are from fossil fuels. This leads to many problems, but four stand out:

1. Fossil fuel combustion creates 81 percent of the United States'[3] and 67 percent of the world's[4] emissions of greenhouse gases (GHGs), the primary cause of anthropogenic climate change.
2. Fossil fuel combustion is the principal source of urban air pollution, which leads to something like eight hundred thousand deaths worldwide every year (mostly in developing countries).[5]
3. Much oil and gas are located in unstable or hostile nations, a central feature of geopolitics today and the source of much global tension and some wars.[6] It also distorts international trade; in 2008 the United States imported $488 billion worth of fossil fuels,[7] accounting for 70 percent of its trade deficit.[8]
4. There is debate about when the planet's exhaustible supply of fossil fuels will run out,[9] but much of the fuel that is easiest to remove is already gone, and removing the rest poses increasing environmental perils.

Two main ways exist to address all four of these problems simultaneously: use less energy, and increase the share of nonfossil energy.

Most techniques to use less energy can be grouped into two categories. Energy *conservation* reduces the unnecessary use of energy services; it largely involves changes in behavior. Energy *efficiency* involves doing more with less by increasing the ratio of energy output to energy input; it largely involves technology. If I turn out the lights when I leave a room, that's energy conservation; if I replace an incandescent bulb with a fluorescent bulb, that's energy efficiency. Either way, I have lowered my electric bill.[10]

Increasing the share of nonfossil energy involves a switch from the fuels that took tens of millions of years to form under the ground, to sources that are constantly renewed.[11] These renewable energy sources (with the exception of geothermal) derive from the constant influx of solar energy, and (with the exception of certain uses of biofuels) they emit little by way of GHGs and other air pollutants, come from local sources, and are inexhaustible. Of course, energy that is not used at all, thanks to either conservation or efficiency, has zero emissions, zero imports, and zero exhaustion of resources, though it may take some up-front financial and physical cost to reduce usage.

The growth of clean energy looks as if it will be one of the major economic engines of the coming decades. One 2010 estimate projected that annual global expenditure on renewable energy projects and energy efficiency will increase from US$90 billion in 2009 to $150 billion in 2020 and $200 billion by 2030.[12] Another global estimate from the same year was that there are about three million direct jobs in renewable energy industries, about half of them in the biofuels industry. However, the United States is lagging behind: in 2009, China produced 40 percent of the world's solar photoelectric supply, 30 percent of the world's wind turbines (up from 10 percent in 2007), and 77 percent of the world's solar hot water collectors.[13] A 2008 estimate found seven hundred fifty thousand green jobs in the United States, rising to 2.5 million in 2018, 3.5 million in 2028, and 4.2 million in 2038, under various scenarios and assumptions.[14]

Purpose and Plan of the Book

This book aims to explicate the U.S. laws that govern energy efficiency and renewable energy as of late 2010. The picture that emerges is one of fragmentation across levels of government, regions of the country, types of energy resources, regulatory techniques, and policy objectives. Hundreds of laws are in place (statutes, regulations, and official policies); each emerged from its own historical, economic, political, and technological circumstances, and many of them work at cross purposes to each other. For example, many laws encourage the development of wind energy, and many others make that quite difficult. The same thing applies to coal and to virtually every other kind of energy source. Moreover, each of the major types of energy sources is governed by its own legal regime and has its own constituencies.

To the extent that generalities are possible, it is that the energy laws—for the most part those administered by the Federal Energy Regulatory Commission, the U.S. Department of Energy, and the state public utility commissions—aim primarily to keep the price of energy low and to assure reliable supplies, and do so with heavy reliance on large-scale, centralized facilities. The environmental laws—those administered by the U.S. Environmental Protection Agency and other federal resource agencies, and by the state environmental and resource agencies—attempt to preserve precious elements of the natural world, to protect public health, and to reduce despoliation and pollution, often to the disadvantage of energy production and use. The energy laws and environmental laws are thus often in tension, with different origins, objectives, mechanisms, and implementing agencies.[15]

Lawyers, and their clients, who attempt to navigate through these various laws and accomplish a substantive objective, such as building a project, must be prepared to dive into a broad range of disparate, uncoordinated provisions that may apply to the specific kind of facility and the particular place where it would be built. This book aims to describe the most important provisions and help readers work with them. It is not a prescription for reform (though many ideas for reform will emerge from a close reading).

Part 1 of the book discusses the energy efficiency laws that exist at the federal, state, and local levels, as well as the mandates and goals written into law for renewable energy. It also covers the siting and permitting of renewable energy facilities.

Part 2 is concerned with financial issues. It covers tax and nontax incentives for efficiency and renewables, relevant aspects of the sale of electricity and rate-making, the various ways that transactions for the financing of efficiency and renewables are structured, and government consumption and purchase of energy.

The use of energy and how it can be saved in particular sectors are covered in part 3. The sectors covered are agriculture and forestry; appliances, lighting and computers; buildings; motor vehicles; and distributed generation.

The different kinds of renewable energy are covered in part 4. Separate chapters are devoted to wind, solar, geothermal, biofuels, hydropower, and tides, waves, and ocean currents. Energy transmission and storage also receive a chapter.

The book closes with a fifty-state survey of the state laws on energy efficiency and renewables. Much more detail about each state is presented, and frequently updated, on the website www.columbiaclimatelaw.com.

The balance of this introductory chapter is devoted to laying out some of the basic facts and statistics about energy use and energy supplies, primarily in the United States, and also the obstacles to achieving a clean energy economy. This factual predicate is important to understanding the chapters that follow and to gauging the relative significance of the various technologies that are or may become available.

Energy Use and Efficiency

Patterns of Energy Use

The two most important factors in determining a country's energy consumption are population and affluence. Thus it was no surprise that China's immense size and soaring economy drove its energy consumption above that of the United States, though the crossover point occurred much earlier than had been projected just a few years before. Today both China and the United States are making major efforts to improve the efficiency of their energy use, the third most important factor that determines a country's energy consumption.

As table 1 shows, transportation is by far the largest total user of primary energy in the United States; almost all of transportation's energy use is in the form of gasoline and diesel fuel. However, in total energy used, it is behind industrial use when electricity is included. Residential and commercial uses are far ahead of industrial in their consumption of electricity. Electricity is generated mostly by burning coal, natural

Table 1
Total U.S. Energy Consumption in 2009 (trillion BTU)

	Primary	Electricity*	Total
Residential	6,606	14,601	21,207
Commercial	3,974	14,174	18,148
Industrial	18,751	9,448	28,199
Transportation	26,951	82	27,033
Electricity	38,304	—	—
Total	94,586	94,578	

Source: U.S. ENERGY INFO. ADMIN., ANNUAL ENERGY REVIEW 2009, at 40 table 2.1a (Aug. 2010).

Note: The two columns do not exactly balance because of sector-specific conversion factors for natural gas and coal.

*This column includes both electricity retail sales and electrical system energy losses.

gas, and (to a much lesser extent) oil, but also in nuclear power plants and renewable sources such as hydro, wind, solar, geothermal energy, and biomass such as wood. Industrial use, other than electricity, is primarily natural gas, but also includes some oil and coal for process heating. In the residential and commercial sectors, nonelectric energy is primarily from natural gas, and to a lesser extent, oil for heating buildings.

As shown in figure 1, energy consumption in the United States has been rising since at least 1950. The United States was self-sufficient in energy until the late 1950s, when energy consumption began to outpace domestic production and the United States began to rely heavily on energy imports.

The growth of energy consumption in the United States over the past thirty years is due in considerable part to population growth. As illustrated by figure 2, per capita energy use in the United States was climbing until the early 1970s, when the price shocks of the OPEC oil embargo in 1973, followed by those of the Iranian revolution in 1978 and the first Gulf War in 1990, largely flattened out the per capita demand. To the extent that population growth has increased the demand for energy services, by one count, about three-quarters of this increased demand has been met by increased energy efficiency and by structural changes in the economy, and only one-quarter by conventional energy resources.[16] However, it should also be pointed out that between 1980 and 2007, when the U.S. population rose about 32 percent,[17] residential energy consumption rose 37 percent, transportation consumption rose 48 percent, commercial consumption rose 73 percent, and manufacturing consumption was very slightly lower.[18] In other words, over the past nearly three decades, though the overall per capita consumption was about flat, commercial consumption per capita rose considerably (due largely to increased computer use) and manufacturing consumption per capita dropped (due largely to the movement of much U.S. heavy manufacturing capacity to other countries).

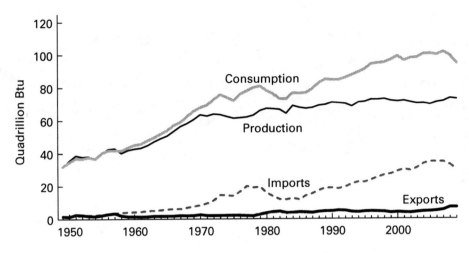

Figure 1
Primary energy overview

The United States was self-sufficient in energy until the late 1950s. At that point energy consumption outpaced domestic production, and the nation began to import more energy to meet its needs. In 2009, net imported energy accounted for 24 percent of all energy consumed. *Source:* U.S. ENERGY INFO. ADMIN., ANNUAL ENERGY REVIEW 2009, at xix figure 1 (Aug. 2010).

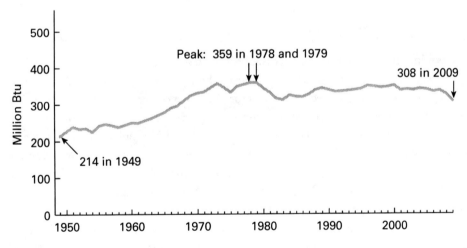

Figure 2
Energy consumption per person

Energy use per person stood at 214 million British thermal units (BTU) in 1949. The rate generally increased until the oil price shocks of the mid-1970s and early 1980s, when the trend reversed for a few years. From 1988 on, the rate held fairly steady until the 2008–2009 economic downturn. In 2009, 308 million BTU of energy were consumed per person, 44 percent above the 1949 rate. *Source:* U.S. ENERGY INFO. ADMIN., ANNUAL ENERGY REVIEW 2009, at xix figure 2 (Aug. 2010).

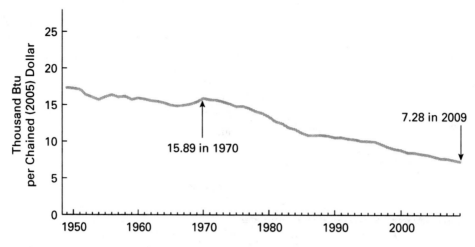

Figure 3
Energy consumption per real dollar of gross domestic product

After 1970, the amount of energy consumed to produce a dollar's worth of the nation's output of goods and services declined as a result of efficiency improvements and structural changes in the economy. The level in 2009 was 54 percent below that of 1970. *Note:* Chained dollars are used to express real prices based on the average weights of goods and services in successive pairs of years. They are "chained" because the second year in each pair, with its weights, becomes the first year of the next pair. *Source:* U.S. ENERGY INFO. ADMIN., ANNUAL ENERGY REVIEW 2009, at xix figure 3, 389 (Aug. 2010).

Improving Energy Efficiency

As shown in figure 3, energy intensity (i.e., energy consumption per unit of economic output) has been declining since 1970, mostly because of improvements in energy efficiency in the industrial sector (the sector that is most sensitive to energy price changes) but also because of the shift of some energy-intensive manufacturing activity overseas. This effect has been counteracted somewhat by population shifts toward warmer regions (requiring more air conditioning); more dispersed dwellings (leading to greater automobile travel); increasing home size; and more use of computers and other electronic appliances.[19] Most of the other major industrialized countries have also achieved overall gains in energy efficiency.[20]

Much potential remains for further improvements in U.S. energy efficiency. According to the Lawrence Livermore National Laboratory, only 42 percent of the energy used in the United States actually provides energy services; the rest is lost.[21] The National Academies of Science have concluded that the United States could reduce its energy use by 17 to 22 percent by 2020 and 25 to 31 percent by 2030, mostly by using existing technologies that are already in commercial use, and delivering the same services as their less efficient counterparts.[22] The buildings sector (including both private housing and commercial buildings) offers the greatest potential for saving energy through efficiency gains, through such actions as lighting, reflective roof products, advanced window coatings, natural ventilation, and smart heating and air conditioning control systems.[23] Along similar lines, the Electric Power Research Institute (EPRI) has concluded that the energy uses with the greatest potential savings are, in descending order: commercial lighting, industrial machine drives, residential electronics, and residential cooling.[24]

Almost all commentators agree with the conclusion of the National Academies of Science that "[c]ost-effective energy improvements are the cheapest and quickest way to move toward a sustainable energy future with lower greenhouse gas emissions."[25] Returns on energy efficiency have been calculated at 20 to 30 percent for many actions, while their relative invulnerability to price fluctuations enhances their reliability as investments.[26] In a series of well-known reports, the McKinsey consulting firm has found that just by using measures with a positive net present value (defined to include direct energy, operating, and maintenance cost savings over the equipment's useful life, net of equipment and installation costs), end-use energy consumption in the United States could be reduced by roughly 23 percent of projected demand by 2020.[27]

Impediments to Energy Efficiency

If energy efficiency measures are so cost-effective and environmentally sound, why aren't many more of them undertaken? There are several reasons; below are some of the most prominent.[28]

Split incentives   Often the party that would have to pay for energy efficiency improvements is different from the party that would benefit. For example, the builder of a commercial office tower has little incentive to spend extra on window insulation that would lower the utility bills of the building's future tenants.[29] Likewise, in an apartment complex where the landlord pays for the electricity, tenants may leave the air conditioning on all day so they can come home to an already cooled apartment.[30] In one especially egregious example, cable television boxes can consume up to 40 watts of electricity continuously; cable subscribers cannot choose which box they get (even if they pay for the electricity), and cable companies have no incentive to make the boxes more efficient.[31]

Low energy prices   One of the central objectives of U.S. energy policy for a century or longer has been to keep energy prices low.[32] Low energy prices reduce the incentive to spend money on energy efficiency by, for example, buying appliances that cost more up front but yield energy savings over time.[33] Moreover, while the many benefits of energy are mostly reflected in their market prices, the negative effects of the production, distribution, and use of energy are all negative externalities that are rarely reflected in pricing.[34] One analysis found that the negative externalities of an average coal-fired power plant—mostly health effects, and not considering climate impacts at all—are $156 million, compared to $1.49 million for a natural-gas-fired plant (and presumably almost nothing for energy efficiency measures that would render some such plants unnecessary altogether).[35]

Capital budgeting Energy efficiency measures typically require capital expenditures and yield reductions in operating expenses. Many organizations (both governmental and private) have separate capital and operating budgets, and they are not always well coordinated. Moreover, many entities have little ability to borrow capital money, even for projects with an assured return. High transaction costs and high internal discount rates also discourage investments.[36] A number of government programs have begun providing grants, loans and loan guarantees, and other subsidies to help provide the missing capital, and energy service companies (ESCOs) have emerged to provide the capital to commercial and industrial users and reap some of the operating expense rewards.[37]

Capital stock turnover Some energy-consuming devices, such as laptop computers, are replaced every few years, and thus new energy-saving characteristics can quickly be disseminated. Many other devices, such as refrigerators (which often have a second life as a place for surplus beverages in the basement) and industrial motors (which are often embedded in complex production lines), stay in service for many years, even though much more efficient equipment has become available.

Utility rate systems[38] Cost-of-service rate-making, the traditional means by which utility rates have been set in the United States, and regional wholesale electricity markets both reward utilities for making and selling more electricity and natural gas. These companies have had little incentive to encourage their customers to use less energy. "Decoupling" legislation that separates utility revenues from the amount of electricity sold has severed this linkage in some states. Other states have adopted a "shared savings" model in which utilities receive a financial return on reductions in energy consumption.

Invisibility of waste Energy conservation is inhibited because people are often not aware that they are using energy unnecessarily. There is no warning sign that an electronic appliance is still gobbling energy while in the "standby" mode. Except in certain automobiles, no alarm sounds when someone leaves without turning off the lights. Some "smart meter" programs are beginning to address this problem with real-time displays of energy consumption by each appliance in a home.

In sum, though saving energy will often lead to saving money, various institutional arrangements and other factors mean that these energy and money savings are often not realized.

Sources of Energy

Patterns of Energy Sources

Table 2 shows the sources of primary energy production and consumption in the United States in 2009.

The principal difference between the production and consumption columns is that most crude oil consumed in the United States is produced elsewhere and imported

Table 2
U.S. Primary Energy Production and Consumption by Source, 2009 (trillion BTU)

Source	Production	Consumption
Coal	21,578	19,751
Natural gas (dry)	21,500	23,362
Crude oil	11,241	35,268
Nuclear	8,349	8,349
Biomass	3,900	3,883
Hydroelectric	2,682	2,682
Natural gas plant liquids	2,541	
Wind	697	697
Geothermal	373	373
Solar/PV	109	109
Total	72,970	94,578

Source: U.S. ENERGY INFO. ADMIN., ANNUAL ENERGY REVIEW 2009, at 7 table 1.2, 9 table 1.3 (Aug. 2010).

into the United States. Table 2 also does not reflect electricity flows; most important, a considerable amount of hydroelectric power is imported into the United States from Canada, but it does not appear here.

It is evident from the above that biomass and hydroelectricity are the only forms of renewable energy that, so far, are more than a blip in the overall U.S. energy picture. Wind energy production, for example, is 3.2 percent of coal energy production.

Table 3 provides an overview of what portions of the economy consume what kinds of energy.

Several observations can be made from this table. All the nuclear energy and wind, and almost all the coal, hydro, and geothermal, go to make electricity for sale. The great bulk of the petroleum is used for transportation. Natural gas is the only energy source that is widely used across all sectors. Table 3 further highlights the relative insignificance of renewables other than hydro in today's energy mix.

However, this is changing rapidly. Construction of new coal-fired power plants has greatly slowed, largely due to uncertainty about GHG regulation and other environmental issues. Wind power has soared ahead and together with natural gas is now experiencing the fastest growth rate of all energy sources in North America, with capacity growing 30 percent per year over the last five years.[39] Table 4 shows the total capacity of new electricity-generating units in the United States by energy source.

Outside of the United States, the pattern is very similar. In Europe, renewable energy accounted for 62 percent of the energy from new electric power installations in 2009.[40] Indeed, there has been rapid growth in renewables all around the world. During the period 2005 to 2009, wind power capacity grew an average of 27 percent annually; solar hot water, 19 percent annually; ethanol production, 20 percent

Table 3
U.S. Energy Consumption, 2009 (trillion BTU)

	Residential	Commercial	Industrial	Transportation	Electric
Coal	7	61	1,396	—	18,296
Natural gas	4,874	3,187	7,584	687	7,039
Petroleum	1,162	600	7,775	25,342	390
Nuclear	—	—	—	—	8,349
Hydroelectric	—	1	18	—	2,663
Geothermal	33	17	4	—	320
Solar/PV	101	—	—	—	8
Wind	—	—	—	—	697
Biomass	430	108	1,977	922	426
Electricity sales	4,650	4,514	3,009	26	—
Electricity system energy losses	9,950	9,659	6,439	56	—
Electricity net imports	—	—	—	—	117
Total	**21,207**	**18,148**	**28,199**	**27,033**	**38,304**

Source: U.S. ENERGY INFO. ADMIN., ANNUAL ENERGY REVIEW 2009, at 41–45 tables 2.1b, 2.1c, 2.1d, 2.1e, and 2.1f (Aug. 2010).

Table 4
Planned Nameplate Capacity Additions from New Generators—U.S. 2009 (megawatts)

Natural gas	10,760
Wind	9,581
Coal	2,021
Other biomass	278
Geothermal	199
Wood and wood-derived fuels	99
Petroleum	93
Solar thermal and photovoltaic	88
Hydroelectric conventional	26
Other	
Total	**23,144**

Source: U.S. ENERGY INFO. ADMIN., ELECTRIC POWER INDUSTRY 2009, at 19 table 1.5 (Jan. 2011).

annually. Grid-connected solar photovoltaic (PV) has grown by an average of 60 percent every year for the past decade, increasing one-hundred-fold since 2000.[41]

Naturally, investments are also soaring. Worldwide, new investment in sustainable energy began rising steadily in early 2004, and reached $173 billion in 2008; it slumped to $162 billion amid the global recession in 2009, but by early 2010 had come back.[42]

Impediments to Growth in Renewables

As with efficiency, renewable energy sources offer many advantages over fossil fuels, but there are also numerous impediments.

Intermittency The largest single impediment to growth in renewables is that most of them are intermittent. The wind does not always blow and the sun does not always shine. Thus renewables have been thought of as unsuitable for providing baseload power—the irreducible minimum of electricity that must be available without fail. For that, fossil fuels, plus nuclear and some hydro, seemed essential. This problem is addressed in several ways:[43]

(1) Storage—It is easy to store fossil fuels, and much harder to store electricity. The most widespread energy storage system used at the utility scale is pumped storage: surplus electricity (usually at night) is used to pump water up to an elevated reservoir; when there is a peak in power demand (or a drop in supply, such as when the wind calms), the water is released and spins a generator to produce electricity. Other storage technologies under development are compressed air storage, flywheels, and various advanced batteries. If plug-in hybrid vehicles become widespread, they can become a dispersed type of electricity storage. Surplus electricity can also be used to hydrolyze water; the resulting hydrogen can be stored for use in fuel cells.

(2) Transmission—With enough transmission capacity to and from the right places, power can be brought in from remote locations to fill in for gaps in generation.

(3) Energy efficiency and conservation—These lower the peaks in power demand, softening the impact of unavailable generation resources.

(4) Demand response—Many large commercial and industrial customers of electricity enter into interruptible power contracts with their utilities; in exchange for a substantial reduction in their electric bills, they agree to be on call to reduce their power demand in an emergency. In residential settings, this can be done automatically by, for example, sending out a signal to lower the air conditioning or delay the operation of the dishwasher at times of peak electric load.

Fossil subsidies The federal government has long provided numerous subsidies (whether in the form of direct spending or foregone revenues) to the fossil fuel industry. More recently it has also begun heavily subsidizing renewables. According to a study by the Environmental Law Institute, for the period 2002–2008, federal subsidies to fossil fuels totaled approximately $72 billion; those to renewables totaled $29 billion, but almost half of that was for corn-based ethanol.[44] Most of the largest subsidies for fossil fuels are written into the tax code as permanent provisions; many subsidies for renewables are implemented through temporary enactments and only last for a few years (sometimes only one year), greatly reducing their usefulness as a spur to investment.

Around the world, many countries offer considerable subsidies to producers and consumers of fossil fuels. Several studies have shown that global reform of fossil fuel subsidies could lead to a decrease in global GHG emissions in the 4 to 5 percent range (though other studies, using different assumptions, came to much higher or lower figures).[45] A study by Bloomberg New Energy Finance found that in 2009, governments around the world gave $43–46 billion to support renewable energy through various kinds of credits and guaranteed electricity prices. This is compared to $557 billion that went to subsidizing fossil fuels in 2008.[46] On the other hand, this does not reflect the amount of subsidy per unit of energy generated (which is much higher for renewables than for fossil energy), or the fact that much of the fossil subsidy is for fuel subsidies for poor people in developing countries.[47]

Capital availability Most renewables have low operating costs because their source of energy is free. (Biofuels are the notable exception.) In the words of Geoffrey Heal:

> If we build a wind (or other renewable) power station today, we are providing free electricity to its users for the next forty years: if we build a coal-fired power station today, we are meeting the capital costs but leaving our successors over its forty year life to meet the large fuel costs and the external costs associated with its pollution. When we build a renewable power station we are effectively pre-paying for the next forty years of electricity from it.[48]

Thus most of the costs of renewables are for up-front capital; users do not have to pay for fuel. A corresponding advantage of renewables, of course, is that they are largely immune from the price fluctuations of oil and natural gas, allowing greater certainty in planning. (These characteristics of renewables are also shared by efficiency gains—the costs are at the beginning, the benefits are long lasting, and energy price fluctuations matter little.)

Turnover rate of capital plant Most capital facilities in the energy system have a lifetime of twenty-five to fifty years. That means only 2 to 4 percent of existing equipment needs replacing in a given year. Companies are reluctant to retire their equipment before the end of its useful life unless compelled by regulatory requirements, or unless the total cost of the new technology (capital and operating costs) falls below the operating cost of the old.[49] The average age of U.S. generating plants is forty years for coal, twenty-two years for natural gas, and thirty years for nuclear.[50] Until these plants are no longer economical to operate, they are unlikely to be replaced by renewables. (Closure of these plants could be accelerated if their owners had to pay for GHG emissions, as through a carbon tax or the purchase of allowances under a cap-and-trade system, but the ability to pass these costs through to captive customers dampens the effect.)

Scale and timing   Some alternative energy technologies are still in the demonstration phase. It is a major step to move to commercial scale. Once a technology has reached a commercial scale—such as wind turbines have—it takes quite a bit of time to build so many units as to make a notable difference in the overall energy supply picture.[51] The new energy sources cannot simply be plugged into the transmission grid; extensive changes may be needed to the grid system to accommodate them.[52] Moreover, some specialized minerals and other materials are needed for certain renewable technologies, and their availability in the necessary quantities is uncertain.[53]

Siting and environmental impacts   Though renewables (other than biofuels) have minimal GHG emissions, they all have certain other environmental impacts. As the chapters in this book devoted to particular kinds of renewables show, each presents its own concerns. Wind turbines (chapter 16) elicit aesthetic objections as well as concerns over avian impacts and noise. Solar collectors (chapter 17) cover large areas of land and require much water to keep the pipes cool and the reflectors clean. Geothermal facilities (chapter 18) may use large quantities of water. The life cycles of biofuels (chapter 19) raise numerous issues in the growing, processing, and transportation of crops. Hydropower (chapter 20) harms aquatic life. Tidal, wave, and ocean current energy (chapter 21) may have uncertain aquatic effects. All of these facilities need to be connected to the users of the energy by a transmission grid (chapter 22), which usually involves crossing large swaths of land with overhead wires. New energy generation facilities (whether renewable or fossil) all require approval from at least one and often several levels of government, based on a variety of environmental and other laws. As shown in chapter 5, considerable litigation has arisen, typically from neighbors, seeking to prevent the siting of facilities by blocking these required approvals, using whatever laws and arguments are available, and this has often impeded construction.

It is difficult to compare the environmental impacts of different kinds of renewables because (other than GHGs) there are so many incommensurable considerations. One such effort was made, using twelve impact categories: resource abundance, GHG emissions, mortality from air pollution, footprint, required spacing around facilities, water consumption, effects on wildlife, thermal pollution, water use, chemical pollution/radioactive waste, energy supply disruption, and normal operating reliability. The author ranked the resources in order, from best to worst: wind, concentrated solar power, geothermal, tidal, solar photovoltaic, wave, hydroelectric, nuclear and fossil with carbon capture and sequestration (tied), corn-based ethanol, and cellulosic ethanol.[54] Others have come up with much different rankings.[55] One subject of particular debate is the extent to which the need for fossil back-up negates the air pollution advantages of intermittent renewables.[56]

In sum, existing economic and legal mechanisms as well as physical constraints significantly inhibit the growth of renewable energy resources.

Legal Techniques to Improve Efficiency and Increase Renewables

Several legal techniques have been developed to meet the objectives of reducing energy consumption and of reducing the carbon content of the energy sources we still need. Some apply only to efficiency and some only to renewables, but we will start with those that apply to both.

Techniques for Both Efficiency and Renewables

Portfolio standards Each electric utility satisfies customer demand through its own portfolio of measures, typically including a mix of various kinds of generation sources, the purchase of power from outside its service territory, and actions to reduce or change the time of electricity use. As detailed in chapter 4, many states have begun requiring their regulated utilities to include in their portfolios a certain amount of renewable energy. These are often called renewable portfolio standards (RPSs). A common feature of RPSs is that companies can satisfy some of their obligation to generate power from renewables by paying someone else who uses renewables, even if they do not buy the power themselves. This is often carried out through the purchase and sale of renewable energy credits (RECs).

More recent variations on RPSs involve energy efficiency resource standards, under which utilities must spend certain amounts of money on energy efficiency measures or achieve a certain amount of demand reduction.[57] Variations also involve clean energy portfolio standards, under which credit is given not only for renewables and efficiency but also for low-GHG generation such as from nuclear power, and fossil fuel coupled with carbon capture and sequestration.[58]

These portfolio standards have been adopted at the state level. A national portfolio standard has been included in several of the energy and climate bills that have been considered by Congress, but as of February 2011, none of the bills have been enacted into law.

Carbon price Burning fossil fuels creates negative externalities, including the accumulation of GHGs in the atmosphere. Being able to do so for free can be seen as a subsidy. To correct this and to impose a price on emitting GHGs (for which "carbon" is shorthand), two methods have been intensely debated in recent years—a carbon tax and cap-and-trade policy. Under a carbon tax, a charge is imposed on the extraction, importation, or combustion of fossil fuels (different proposals have different design details). Under cap-and-trade, a finite amount of GHG emissions is allowed nationwide. The legal ability to emit a certain amount (typically a ton) is called an allowance. If a power plant emits one million tons of GHGs in a year, it must obtain one million allowances. Allowances can be bought and sold in the market; they are initially sold by the government (though under some variations, many of them are given away at the start). Over time, the total number of available allowances (the "cap") declines, so the price of allowances should go up.[59] GHG emitters thus have an incentive to reduce emissions so that they do not have to buy so many allowances (or so that they can sell some of the allowances they already have but no longer need).

Either a carbon tax or a cap-and-trade system would generate many billions of dollars of revenue for the government each year. Under some variations, all of this money would be immediately given back to the public, often in the form of tax rebates, so that it is revenue neutral. Under other variations, the money is used for all manner of purposes, such as subsidizing energy efficiency and renewables, providing fuel and electricity price relief to low-income households, and helping industries that would be especially hard hit by climate regulation (or that have particularly effective lobbies).

The leading climate legislation considered by Congress in recent years has involved cap-and-trade, on the theory that this is more politically acceptable than a carbon tax. It was not politically acceptable enough, however, and to date, neither has been adopted. Except for some very limited state and local experiments with carbon taxes, the only carbon pricing mechanism used in the United States today is the Regional Greenhouse Gas Initiative (RGGI), in which ten northeastern and mid-Atlantic states have imposed a cap-and-trade system on carbon dioxide emissions from electric power plants. As of December 2010, RGGI had generated $777.5 million in revenues from the sale of allowances; most of this money has gone toward energy efficiency programs.[60] However, the price of allowances is so low that RGGI has had little direct impact on energy use. California is now developing a cap-and-trade program to take effect in 2012.[61]

One of the most important developments in the energy world in recent years has been the emergence of technologies to extract natural gas from shale formations using hydraulic fracturing and horizontal drilling. Largely as a result, natural gas prices have fallen and are likely to remain low.[62] Compared to a power plant burning coal, a plant burning natural gas produces about half as much carbon dioxide, less than a third as much nitrogen oxides, and about 1 percent as much sulfur oxides.[63] The low prices of natural gas pose a real threat to the future of coal and nuclear power and may also inhibit the growth of renewables. Natural gas is emerging as a major pathway to reducing GHG emissions, mostly by displacing coal.[64]

Tax incentives A broad range of special tax provisions aim to encourage some kinds of activities, discourage others, and (for various economic and political reasons) subsidize still others. The tax incentives for efficiency and renewables are detailed in chapter 7.

Nontax incentives In addition to the subsidies provided by tax incentives, the government provides a wide array of direct incentives and subsidies for efficiency and renewables, as discussed in chapter 8. Especially prominent is the American Recovery and Reinvestment Act, signed into law by President Obama in 2009, which provided some $80 billion for various kinds of clean energy (though this includes substantial funding for nuclear power and carbon capture and sequestration in addition to efficiency and renewables).[65]

Government procurement   The U.S. federal government spends more than $24 billion a year on energy purchases and is the largest volume purchaser of energy-consuming products in the world.[66] Chapter 6 describes the extensive efforts undertaken by the federal government and some state and local governments to purchase renewable energy and energy-efficient products.

Research and development (R&D)   The sun and the wind are freely available to everyone, and energy efficiency would save a lot of people a little money (as opposed to making a few people a lot of money); it has been suggested that this is largely why R&D for renewables and efficiency have lagged behind R&D for oil and gas.[67] The American Recovery and Reinvestment Act and other sources are providing substantial funding for R&D for renewables and efficiency.

Techniques for Efficiency and Conservation[68]

Technology standards   Beginning with the Energy Policy and Conservation Act of 1975, Congress has required manufacturers of certain kinds of products to achieve minimum standards of energy efficiency or fuel consumption. Chapter 2 presents the history of federal technology standards of energy efficiency and conservation. The greatest impact on national energy consumption has been achieved by the federal standards for appliances and lighting (discussed in chapter 12), and the Corporate Average Fuel Efficiency (CAFE) standards and other requirements for motor vehicles (the topic of chapter 14). As covered in chapter 3, some state and local governments are imposing their own efficiency standards, to the extent they are not preempted by federal law.

More recently, buildings—which consume about 40 percent of all energy used and 75 percent of all electricity generated in the United States[69]—have become the subject of intense regulation, mostly at the state and local levels, as well as under voluntary standards that have achieved significant recognition in the marketplace. Regulation of energy consumption by buildings is covered in chapter 13.[70]

The American Clean Energy and Security Act of 2009 (also known as the Waxman-Markey bill after its sponsors, Reps. Henry Waxman and Edward Markey), which passed the House of Representatives in June 2009 but died in the Senate, proposed extensive additional technology standards. In the absence of climate legislation, the U.S. Environmental Protection Agency (EPA) has been utilizing its authority under the existing Clean Air Act. In developing a permitting program for GHG emissions from stationary sources under this law, EPA is encouraging energy efficiency measures under the rubric of the best available control technology (BACT) requirements.[71]

Retrofitting   Most technology standards apply to new products, vehicles, and buildings. However, buildings in particular may have a very long life, and there are many opportunities to retrofit them to improve their energy efficiency. Weatherization (to reduce heating and cooling loads) and changes in lighting are in some places either required or subsidized (or both), as discussed in chapter 13.

Information   The government still allows many energy-guzzling appliances and vehicles to be manufactured. As shown in chapter 12, for some of these products, the government requires labeling of energy or fuel consumption so that consumers can at least make informed purchasing decisions.[72]

System benefit charges   Many state public utility commissions require regulated electric and gas utilities to set aside a certain amount of money every year from "system benefit charges" for use in energy efficiency programs and other purposes that benefit the public. This practice is discussed in more detail in chapter 9.

Urban density   GHG emissions from motor vehicles are mostly a product of three factors: the fuel economy of the vehicles (as regulated by CAFE standards), the carbon content of the fuels (as regulated by the biofuel standards discussed in chapter 19), and the number of vehicle miles traveled (VMT). VMT, in turn, is inversely proportional to urban density: the more densely populated an area, the more likely it is to be served by mass transit and the shorter the trips that are not taken by mass transit.[73] Apartment buildings, with their vertical and horizontal stacking of dwellings, also tend to use less energy per occupant for heating and cooling than single-family homes.[74] Encouraging urban density and discouraging sprawl are central to energy conservation, as they reduce the demand for energy services.

Urban land use is primarily a matter of state and local regulation. Federal programs, such as federal assistance for highways, sewers, and various housing types, have a significant effect on land use development patterns, but federal efforts to overtly determine land use patterns have been met with ferocious resistance.[75] Some states, led by California, have taken tentative steps to regulate this linkage.[76]

Techniques for Renewables

Most of the legal techniques to increase the use of renewable energy were discussed above in the listing of measures that increase both efficiency and renewables. However, there are two that are unique to renewables.

Mandatory utility purchases   RPSs were discussed previously. An additional technique is to require electric utilities to purchase renewable energy from those who offer it, thereby removing one of the chief risks in building a new facility (that it will not have enough customers). As explained in more detail in chapter 15, the Public Utility Regulatory Policies Act of 1978 (PURPA)[77] requires electric utilities to interconnect with and purchase excess power from "qualifying facilities" (a category that includes many independent producers of renewable energy) at the price the utility would pay to generate or purchase the power.

Several European countries have gone further by instituting "feed-in tariffs," which involve long-term contracts under which utilities must purchase wholesale power from renewable energy suppliers at prices that are attractive to the suppliers. Feed-in tariffs are the centerpiece of Germany's successful policy to greatly expand its production of renewable energy,[78] and many have advocated their adoption in

the United States[79] However, as laid out in chapter 9, imposing this requirement on investor-owned utilities raises difficulties due to the exclusive jurisdiction of the Federal Energy Regulatory Commission to set wholesale electricity rates.

Renewable fuel standards Congressional enactments in 2005 and 2007 require motor vehicle fuels to include large and increasing content from renewable sources, most prominently corn-based ethanol. Chapter 19 describes these requirements.

Role of Efficiency and Renewables in Combating Climate Change

There is consensus that increasing energy efficiency and use of renewable energy are the most important actions that can be taken to combat climate change. The International Energy Agency declared in 2010 that "[i]ncreasing energy efficiency, much of which can be achieved through low-cost options, offers the greatest potential for reducing CO_2 emissions over the period to 2050. It should be the highest priority in the short term . . . . Decarbonising the power sector [is] the second-largest source of emissions reductions."[80] The United Nations Foundation has calculated that if the G8 countries (United States, Canada, France, Germany, Italy, Japan, Russia, and the United Kingdom) doubled their historical rate of energy efficiency improvement, that would avoid the need for two thousand coal-fired power stations and would make it possible to keep CO_2 concentrations in the atmosphere below 550 parts per million.[81]

The central role of energy efficiency and renewable energy in addressing the climate change problem has been similarly affirmed (and, by several of them, quantified) by the Intergovernmental Panel on Climate Change,[82] the U.S. National Research Council,[83] the Union of Concerned Scientists,[84] the American Solar Energy Society,[85] the European Renewable Energy Council and Greenpeace,[86] and such noted commentators as Stephen Pacala and Robert Socolow,[87] Mark C. Jacobson and Mark A. Delucci,[88] and Lester Brown.[89] The National Petroleum Council has shown the tremendous potential for energy efficiency in future fleets of motor vehicles,[90] and the Federal Energy Regulatory Commission has calculated how peak power demand could be greatly reduced through demand response measures.[91] One study has shown the potential to meet all of the GHG emission reduction goals for 2020 under the Waxman-Markey bill through energy efficiency measures.[92]

As this is written in February 2011, there appear to be no immediate prospects for comprehensive climate and energy legislation in the United States. The tension between energy law and environmental law remains. However, as this book attempts to demonstrate, an abundance of legal techniques are available at the federal, state and municipal levels that cumulatively could accomplish a great deal in cutting energy use, increasing the share of energy that is provided by low-carbon sources, lowering U.S. reliance on foreign sources of fuel, and reducing GHG emissions and the other adverse environmental impacts of energy production.

Notes

1. U.S. Energy Info. Admin., Annual Energy Review 2009, at 9 tbl. 1.3 (Aug. 2010).

2. U.S. Energy Info. Admin., International Energy Statistics database, www.eia.gov/emeau/international.

3. U.S. Energy Info. Admin., Emissions of Greenhouse Gases Report (Dec. 8, 2009).

4. World Resources Inst., World Greenhouse Gas Emissions 2005, *available at* http://www.wri.org/chart/world-greenhouse-gas-emissions-2005.

5. World Health Org., the World Health Report 2002, annex tbl.9.

6. *See* John Deutch, *Oil and Gas Energy Security Issues*, Resources for the Future, June 2010.

7. U.S. Energy Info. Admin., Annual Energy Review 2009, at 81 tbl. 3.7 (Aug. 2010).

8. U.S. Bureau of Econ. Analysis, U.S. International Trade in Goods and Services exh. 1 (June 10, 2010).

9. *See* David Goodstein, Out of Gas: The End of the Age of Oil (2004).

10. For estimates of the savings in energy costs due to energy efficiency and conservation, see Mark Cooper, Consumer Fed'n of Am., Building on the Success of Energy Efficiency Programs to Ensure an Affordable Energy Future: State-by-State Savings on Residential Utility Bills from Aggressive Energy Efficiency Policies (Feb. 2010); and Alliance to Save Energy et al., Reducing the Cost of Addressing Climate Change through Energy Efficiency (Feb. 2009).

11. *See* David Hodas, *Ecosystem Subsidies for Fossil Fuels*, 22 J. Land Use & Envtl. L. 599 (2007).

12. Press Release, Bloomberg New Energy Finance, Bloomberg New Energy Finance Model Projects Clean Energy Investment at $200 Billion per Year by 2030 (Mar. 17, 2010), http://bnef.com/Download/pressreleases/113/pdffile/.

13. REN21: Renewable Energy Pol'y Network for the 21st Century, Renewables 2010 Global Status Report 9 (2010).

14. U.S. Conference of Mayors, Oct. 2008, *Global Insight, U.S. Metro Economies: Current and Potential Green Jobs in the U.S. Economy.* Other estimates of current and future job creation in renewable energy and energy efficiency are discussed in Gary Gereffi et al., Ctr. for Globalization, Governance & Competitiveness, Duke University, Manufacturing Climate Solutions: Carbon-Reducing Technologies and U.S. Jobs (Nov. 2008); and Karen Ehrhardt-Martinez & John A. "Skip" Laitner, Am. Council for an Energy-Efficient Economy, The Size of the U.S. Energy Efficiency Market: Generating a More Complete Picture 27 (May 2008).

15. *See generally* Lincoln L. Davies, *Alternative Energy and the Energy-Environment Disconnect*, 46 Idaho L. Rev. 473 (2010).

16. John A. "Skip" Laitner, Am. Council for an Energy-Efficient Economy, The Positive Economics of Climate Change Policies: What the Historical Evidence Can Tell Us 3 (July 2009).

17. U.S. Bureau of the Census, Statistical Abstract of the United States § 1 tbl. 2 (2010).

18. U.S. Energy Info. Admin., Annual Energy Review 2009, at 40 tbl. 2.1a (Aug. 2010).

19. McKinsey Global Energy & Materials, Unlocking Energy Efficiency in the U.S. Economy 17 (July 2009); Nat'l Research Council, Limiting the Magnitude of Future Climate Change 39 (2010).

20. Int'l Energy Agency, Progress with Implementing Energy Efficiency Policies in the G8 (2009).

21. Lawrence Livermore Nat'l Laboratory, Americans Using Less Energy, More Renewables (Aug 23. 2010).

22. Nat'l Academies of Science, Real Prospects for Energy Efficiency in the United States: Report in Brief (2009).

23. Nat'l Research Council, *supra* note 19, at 44.

24. Electric Power Research Inst., Assessment of Achievable Potential from Energy Efficiency and Demand Response Programs in the U.S. (2010–2030) 12–13 (Jan. 2009).

25. Nat'l Academies of Science, *supra* note 22.

26. Ehrhardt-Martinez & Laitner, *supra* note 14, at 29.

27. McKinsey Global Energy & Materials, *supra* note 21, at iii–v.

28. Various lists of impediments to energy efficiency can be found in Neil Peretz, *Growing the Energy Efficiency Market through Third-Party Financing*, 30 Energy L.J. 377 (2009); McKinsey Global Energy & Materials, *supra* note 19, at 22–27 Richard L. Ottinger et al., *Renewable Energy in National Legislation: Challenges and Opportunities, in* Donald N. Zillman et al., Beyond the Carbon Economy: Energy Law in Transition 183–206 (2008).

29. Peretz, *supra* note 28, at 386.

30. *See* Sam Dolnick, *Air-Conditioners That Run When Nobody's Home*, N.Y. Times, Aug. 15, 2010.

31. Dan Charles, *Leaping the Efficiency Gap*, 325 Science 804, 808 (Aug. 14, 2009).

32. *See generally* Michael J. Graetz, The End of Energy (forthcoming Apr. 2011).

33. Kenneth Gillingham et al., *Energy Efficiency Economics and Policy*, 1 Ann. Rev. Resource Econ. 597, 601 (2009).

34. Nat'l Research Council, Hidden Costs of Energy: Unpriced Consequences of Energy Production and Use 3 (2010).

35. *Id.* at 6, 8.

36. David Hodas, *Imagining the Unimaginable: Reducing U.S. Greenhouse Gas Emissions by 40%*, 26 Va. Envtl. L.J. 271, 288–89 (2008).

37. Gillingham et al., *supra* note 33, at 607.

38. *See* Noah M. Sachs, *Greening Demand: Energy Consumption and U.S. Climate Policy*, 19 Duke Envtl. L. & Pol'y F. 296 (2009); Nat'l Action Plan for Energy Efficiency, Aligning Utility Incentives with Investment in Energy Efficiency (2007).

39. North Am. Elec. Reliability Corp., Reliability Impacts of Climate Change Initiatives: Technology Assessment and Scenario Development 34 (July 2010).

40. Hans Bloem et al., European Comm'n, Joint Research Centre, Inst. for Energy, Renewable Energy Snapshots (2010).

41. REN21: Renewable Energy Pol'y Network for the 21st Century, Renewables 2010 Global Status Report 9 (2010).

42. United Nations Env't Programme, Global Trends in Sustainable Investment 2010: Analysis of Trends and Issues in the Financing of Renewable Energy and Energy Efficiency, Bloomberg New Energy Finance 10, 15 (2010). "Sustainable energy" is defined in this report to include all biomass, geothermal, and wind generation projects of more than 1 MW; hydro projects between 0.5 and 50 MW; all solar projects more than 0.5 MW; all marine energy projects; energy efficiency investment including financial investment in technology, plus corporate and government research and development, but excluding investment in energy efficiency projects by governments, companies, and public financing institutions. *Id.* at 8.

43. The following discussion draws heavily on North Am. Elec. Reliability Corp., *supra* note 39, and David Lindley, *The Energy Storage Problem*, 463 Nature 18 (Jan. 7, 2010).

44. Envtl. Law Inst., Estimating U.S. Government Subsidies to Energy Sources: 2002–2008 (Sept. 2009). *See also* Richard W. Caperton & Sima J. Gandhi, Center for Am. Progress, American's Hidden Power Bill: Examining Federal Energy Tax Expenditures (Apr. 2010).

45. Jennifer Ellis, Int'l Inst. for Sustainable Dev., Assessing the Impacts of Fossil-Fuel Subsidies 31 (Dec. 2009). *See also* Organisation for Econ. Cooperation and Dev., Cost-Effective Actions to Tackle Climate Change 2 (Aug. 2009) (removing subsidies for energy consumption and production would reduce global emissions by 10 percent).

46. Alex Morales, Fossil Fuel Subsidies Are 12 Times Support for Renewables, Study Shows, Bloomberg New Energy Finance (July 29, 2010).

47. Int'l Energy Agency et al., Analysis of the Scope of Energy Subsidies and Suggestions for the G-20 Initiative (June 16, 2010).

48. Geoffrey Heal, Nat'l Bureau of Econ. Research, The Economics of Renewable Energy 4 (June 2009).

49. Gert Jan Kramer & Martin Haigh, *No Quick Switch to Low-Carbon Energy*, 462 Nature 568 (Dec. 3, 2009).

50. North Am. Elec. Reliability Corp., *supra* note 39, at 51.

51. *See* Richard A. Kerr, *Do We Have the Energy for the Next Transition?*, 329 Science 780 (Aug. 13, 2010).

52. Timothy P. Duane, *Greening the Grid: Implementing Climate Change Policy through Energy Efficiency, Renewable Portfolio Standards, and Strategic Transmission System Investments*, 34 Vt. L. Rev. 711 (2010).

53. David Fridley, *Nine Challenges of Alternative Energy*, *in* The Post Carbon Reader: Managing the 21st Century's Sustainability Crises (Richard Heinberg & Daniel Lerch eds., 2010).

54. Mark Z. Jacobson, *Review of Solutions to Global Warming, Air Pollution, and Energy Security*, 2 Energy & Envtl. Sci. 148 (2009). The author ranked cellulosic ethanol lower than corn ethanol primarily due to its potentially larger land footprint and its higher upstream air pollution emissions.

55. *E.g.*, Jesse H. Ausubel, *Renewable and Nuclear Heresies*, 1 Int'l J. Nuclear Governance, Econ. & Ecology 229 (2007).

56. *See* Warren Katzenstein & Jay Apt, *Air Emissions Due to Wind and Solar Power*, 43 Envtl. Sci. Tech. 253 (2009); Andrew Mills et al., *Comment on Air Emissions Due to Wind and Solar Power*, 43 Envtl. Sci. Tech. 6106 (2009).

57. Laura A. Furrey et al., Am. Council for an Energy-Efficient Economy, Laying the Foundation for Implementing a Federal Energy Efficiency Resource Standard (Mar. 2009).

58. Alan J. Krupnick et al., Nat'l Energy Pol'y Inst. and Resources for the Future, Toward a New National Energy Policy: Assessing the Options (June 2010).

59. Allowance prices under cap-and-trade systems have often been volatile, which reduces their impact in encouraging investment in low-GHG technologies. A number of techniques have been proposed to reduce this volatility. *See* The Brattle Group, CO2 Price Volatility: Consequences and Cures (Jan. 2009).

60. Regional Greenhouse Gas Initiative, *RGGI Benefits*, http://www.rggi.org/rggi_benefits (last visited Feb. 6, 2010).

61. *See* California Air Resources Board, *Cap-and-Trade*, http://www.arb.ca.gov/cc/capandtrade/capandtrade.htm (last visited Feb. 6, 2011).

62. Mass. Inst. of Tech., The Future of Natural Gas: An Interdisciplinary MIT Study (2010).

63. U.S. Envtl. Prot. Agency, *Clean Energy: Natural Gas* (undated), *available at* http://epa.gov/cleanenergy/energy-and-you/affect/natural-gas.html.

64. DB Climate Change Advisors, Natural Gas and Renewables: A Secure Low Carbon Future Energy Plan for the United States (Nov. 2010).

65. Memorandum for the President from the Vice President, *Progress Report: The Transformation to a Clean Energy Economy* (Dec. 15, 2009), *available at* http://www.whitehouse.gov/sites/default/files/administration-official/vice_president_memo_on_clean_energy_economy.pdf.

66. Statement of Richard Kidd, Program Manager, Fed. Energy Mgmt. Program, Office of Energy Efficiency & Renewable Energy, U.S. Dep't of Energy, *Before the Senate Subcomm. on Federal Financial Management, Government Information, Federal Services and International Security, Committee on Homeland Security and Government Affairs*, 111th Cong. (Jan. 27, 2010).

67. Gillingham et al., *supra* note 33, at 608.

68. For a worldwide survey of energy efficiency measures, see Int'l Confederation of Energy Regulators, A Description of Current Regulatory Practices for the Promotion of Energy Efficiency (June 21, 2010).

69. Chapter 13 *infra*, at 301.

70. Greater detail may be found in The Law of Green Buildings: Regulatory and Legal Issues in Design, Construction, Operations, and Financing (J. Cullen Howe & Michael B. Gerrard eds., 2010).

71. U.S. Envtl. Prot. Agency, Office of Air and Radiation, PSD and Title V Permitting Guidance for Greenhouse Gases, Nov. 2010.

72. *See* Hunt Allcott & Sendhil Mullainathan, *Behavior and Energy Policy*, 327 Science 1204 (Mar. 5, 2010); Abhijit Banerjee & Barry D. Solomon, *Eco-labeling for Energy Efficiency and Sustainability: A Meta-evaluation of US Programs*, 31(2) Energy Pol'y 109 (2003).

73. *See* Reid Ewing et al., Urban Land Institute, Growing Cooler: The Evidence on Urban Development and Climate Change (2008).

74. *See generally* David Owen, Green Metropolis: Why Living Smaller, Living Closer, and Driving Less are the Keys to Sustainability (2009).

75. *See* Stephen M. Esposito, *State Plans for Clean Air: Have the Section 179 Sanction Provisions Become the Achilles Heel of the Clean Air Act?*, 15 Temp. Envtl. L. & Tech. J. 241 (1996).

76. *See* Henry Stern, *A Necessary Collision: Climate Change, Land Use, and the Limits of A.B. 32*, 35 Ecology L.Q. 611 (2008); Patricia Salkin, *Sustainability and Land Use Planning: Greening State and Local Land Use Plans and Regulations to Address Climate Change Challenges and Preserve Resources for Future Generations* 34 Wm. & Mary Envtl. L. & Pol'y Rev. 121 (2009).

77. 16 U.S.C. § 824-a-3(e), 824(m); *see* 18 C.F.R. § 292.602.

78. Frank N. Laird & Christoph Stefes, *The Diverging Paths of German and United States Policies for Renewable Energy: Source of Difference*, 37 Energy Pol'y 2619 (2009).

79. *See* DB Climate Change Advisors, "Paying for Renewable Energy: TLC at the Right Price—Achieving Scale through Efficient Policy Design," Dec. 2009.

80. Int'l Energy Agency, Energy Technology Perspectives 2010—Scenarios & Strategies to 2050, at 49 (2010).

81. United Nations Found., Realizing the Potential of Energy Efficiency: Targets, Policies, and Measures for G8 Countries (2007).

82. Intergovernmental Panel on Climate Change, Climate Change 2007: Mitigation of Climate Change, in Contribution of Working Group III to the Fourth Assessment Report of the Intergovernmental Panel on Climate Change 627–41 (2007); *see also* Diane Urge-Vorsatz & Bert Metz, *Energy Efficiency: How Far Does It Get Us in Controlling Climate Change?*, 2 Energy Efficiency 87 (2009).

83. Nat'l Research Council, Limiting the Magnitude of Future Climate Change 43 (2010).

84. Rachel Cleetus et al., Union of Concerned Scientists, Climate 2030: A National Blueprint for a Clean Energy Economy (May 2009).

85. Am. Solar Energy Soc'y, Tackling Climate Change in the U.S.: Potential Carbon Emissions Reductions from Energy Efficiency and Renewable Energy by 2030 (Jan. 2007).

86. European Renewable Energy Council & Greenpeace Int'l, Energy [r]evolution: A Sustainable Energy Outlook (2010).

87. Stephen Pacala & Robert Socolow, *Stabilization Wedges: Solving the Climate Problem for the Next 50 Years with Current Technologies*, 305 Science 968 (Aug. 13, 2004).

88. Mark Z. Jacobson & Mark A. Delucchi, *A Path to Sustainable Energy by 2030*, Sci. Am., Nov. 2009, at 58.

89. Lester R. Brown, Plan B 4.0: Mobilizing to Save Civilization 136, 139 (2009).

90. Nat'l Petroleum Council, Facing the Hard Truths about Energy: A Comprehensive View to 2030 of Global Oil and Natural Gas 42, 85 (2007).

91. Fed. Energy Regulatory Comm'n, Staff Report, A National Assessment of Demand Response Potential x, xii, 27–28 (June 2009).

92. Priya Sreedharan, Energy & Envtl. Econ. (E3), Energy Efficiency Potential in the U.S.: A Review and Comparison of Recent Estimates (June 29, 2010).

Part I

Laws Governing Efficiency, Renewables, and Siting

chapter two

Federal Energy Efficiency and Conservation Laws

John C. Dernbach and Marianne Tyrrell

Energy efficiency and conservation are the cleanest forms of energy. The kilowatt of electricity or gallon of electricity that is not used is also the cheapest form of energy. And we have known for generations that we can (and should) use less energy. We can do that through energy efficiency, which involves doing the same amount of work or producing the same amount of goods or services with less energy.[1] Or we can do that through energy conservation, which involves using less energy regardless of whether energy efficiency has changed.[2] Energy efficiency and conservation are better than renewable energy for delivering significant and reliable short-term results and improving national security and economic competitiveness.[3]

Yet energy efficiency and conservation policy has a Groundhog Day[4] aspect, in which the same or similar arguments are made year after year, decade after decade, and often (it appears) to little effect. In 1974, in its then-famous report, *A Time to Choose*, the Energy Policy Project of the Ford Foundation concluded that the United States could achieve zero energy growth within a decade.[5] United States energy consumption, however, did not flatten; it is about one-third higher than it was then.[6] In 2010, the National Research Council issued a comprehensive report, *Real Prospects for Energy Efficiency in the United States*, which concluded that the United States could, through the "full deployment of cost-effective, energy-efficient technologies," *reduce* its annual energy consumption by about 10 percent by 2020 and even more after that.[7]

Energy conservation policy has a Groundhog Day aspect for a variety of reasons.[8] Not least of these is the ambivalent attitude many Americans have toward conservation. Many people associate greater energy consumption with higher quality of life and reduced energy consumption with deprivation. Indeed, the traditional purposes of U.S. energy policy have been to supply plentiful energy at low prices with appropriate environmental and public health protections. Energy law has been more focused on protecting, supporting, and encouraging industries that produce energy and fossil fuels than on

Ed Sonenberg, research librarian at Widener University Law School; Stephen Kramer, Widener University Law School Class of 2011; and Guillermo Cuevas, Columbia University Law School Class of 2011 were very helpful in finding information for this chapter.

realizing the benefits that could be gained by reducing energy consumption. Low energy prices and widespread availability, in turn, reduce the incentive to conserve energy.

Thus, while the United States has had energy efficiency and conservation legislation in place for more than three decades, the effect of these laws has been mixed. According to the U.S. Energy Information Administration's *2010 Annual Energy Outlook*, primary energy consumption is projected to increase by 14 percent between 2008 and 2035. Yet the annual growth rate for energy consumption, about .5 percent, is less than a quarter of the projected annual GDP growth rate of 2.4 percent for the same period. Because of these laws, as well as structural changes in the economy (more services, less industry), energy consumption grows at a much slower rate than the economy.[9] The United States has not yet decoupled economic growth from increased energy consumption—that is, achieved economic growth while *reducing* overall energy consumption.

In recent years, policy makers are treating efficiency and conservation with greater seriousness, spurred by a newer set of reasons. These include the threat of climate change; a desire to move the economy in a greener and more job-creating direction; global economic competition; growing global demand for energy resources; and the environmental effects of fossil fuels, an old issue made new by the BP Gulf of Mexico oil disaster in 2010. Reducing energy consumption, in short, is needed to move the United States in a more sustainable direction.[10] And studies continue to identify a great many cost-effective energy efficiency and conservation opportunities.[11]

Still, energy efficiency and conservation are not coherently reflected in the goals or structure of U.S. law.[12] United States law and policy concerning energy efficiency and conservation can broadly be divided into two opposing categories. The first is comprised of laws and policies that are expressly intended to improve energy conservation. The second is laws and policies that have the effect, if the not the intent, of encouraging energy consumption and, in many. cases, reducing energy conservation. The laws in this second category offset, to some degree, the improvements that are being pursued by energy efficiency and conservation laws.

Moreover, energy efficiency and conservation are often easier to support in principle than they are to achieve in real life. In spite of numerous existing "cost-effective energy efficiency opportunities," there is a complex "behavior gap" impeding the use of those opportunities. Among other things, consumers often give more weight to higher up-front costs and less weight to the much greater but later savings; they may not be aware of the benefits; and cost savings are only one of many reasons for a consumer purchasing decision.[13] Relatively low energy prices are still another barrier. And the lack of an existing economic and legal infrastructure for many energy efficiency improvements means that many interested homeowners or businesses lack a reliable and relatively easy way to make those improvements.

This chapter provides an overview of U.S. law and policy concerning energy efficiency and conservation. The first part of this chapter discusses supportive and antagonistic laws and policies. Subsequent parts focus on ways these laws may change in the future as well as international influences on these laws, describing energy efficiency and conservation features of proposed climate change and clean energy legislation, and discussing energy conservation under the Framework Convention on Climate Change and in the European Union. Readers who are interested in state energy efficiency and conservation efforts should consult chapter 3.

Laws and Policies That Affect Energy Efficiency and Conservation

Overview

Brief History of Energy Efficiency and Conservation Law

While a great many statutes have in one way or another expressed some intent to increase energy efficiency or conservation,[14] the first prominent statute—the Energy Policy and Conservation Act of 1975—was enacted in the wake of the 1973 and 1974 oil embargoes by the Organization of the Petroleum Exporting Countries.[15] The legislation required the Department of Transportation (DOT) to establish corporate average fuel efficiency (CAFE) standards for automobiles and required the adoption of energy performance standards for household appliances.[16] In 1976, the Energy Conservation and Production Act[17] required states to set energy efficiency standards for new commercial and residential buildings. In 1978, Congress passed the National Energy Conservation Policy Act, which set up an energy audit and state planning process for saving energy in buildings, as well as an energy efficiency labeling and testing program for industrial equipment such as pumps.[18]

The Reagan Administration in the 1980s brought legislation that cut back on some of these laws. For example, Congress repealed the mandatory requirements for buildings in the 1976 legislation, making those standards voluntary.[19] In response to the Department of Energy's (DOE's) slow implementation of appliance standards in the 1975 legislation, however, the National Appliance Energy Conservation Act of 1987 actually set performance standards for appliances.[20]

The Energy Policy Act of 1992 completely revised the rules for residential and commercial buildings, requiring states to consider adopting the current private energy efficiency building code for residential buildings (by the Council of American Building Officials) and to adopt the current standard (by the American Society of Heating, Refrigerating, and Air-Conditioning Engineers) for commercial buildings.[21] The act also set efficiency standards for air conditioners and electric motors.[22]

Energy efficiency and conservation received less congressional attention during the Clinton and George W. Bush administrations, although attention grew at the end of the last decade. Two laws—one adopted in 2005 and the other in 2007—together are projected to reduce U.S. energy use by 6 percent from its projected level in 2020.[23] The Energy Policy Act of 2005—the first significant energy efficiency legislation adopted since 1992—requires new or more stringent standards for a variety of products[24] as well as commercial and industrial equipment.[25] The Act also instructs the Federal Trade Commission to consider improvements in product labeling.[26] The Act provides a set of tax credits and deductions for energy efficiency in new and existing homes as well as commercial buildings, appliances, heating and air conditioning systems, and hybrid vehicles.[27] The Energy Independence and Security Act of 2007 raises CAFE standards for passenger automobiles and light trucks to at least 35 miles per gallon (mpg) for model year 2020.[28] This legislation also sets energy efficiency standards for electric lights, including incandescent and fluorescent lights.[29]

More recently, Congress has used economic stimulus legislation to provide greater support for fuel-efficient infrastructure and energy efficiency. In the Emergency Economic Stabilization Act of 2008, Congress included a handful of provisions relating to efficiency and conservation, including extension of the life of several tax credits and deductions for energy-efficient homes and commercial buildings, and added a tax credit for new plug-in electric drive motor vehicles.[30] The American Recovery and Reinvestment Act of 2009 (ARRA) authorized more money for energy efficiency than had previously been authorized, including $5 billion for home weatherization grants to low- and middle-income families;[31] $1 billion for energy efficiency upgrades to federally supported and public housing, including new insulation, windows, and frames;[32] and $8 billion for investments in high-speed rail (which is more energy-efficient than cars).[33]

Role of Environmental Law in Energy Efficiency and Conservation

Environmental law has not played a prominent role in fostering energy efficiency and conservation because that is not its primary objective. Rather, our air, water, and waste laws are primarily intended to reduce the emission or discharge of pollutants to safe levels and limit exposure of pollutants and wastes to humans and the environment. There has never been a serious federal effort to integrate energy law and environmental law, much less integrate energy efficiency and conservation with environmental law.

The environmental statute with perhaps the greatest effect on efficiency and conservation is the Clean Air Act.[34] Most of the criteria air pollutants long regulated by the Act—including sulfur dioxide, carbon monoxide, nitrogen oxides—come from "a single class of activities: burning fossil fuels."[35] Because the Act imposes costs—in the form of pollution controls—on those who emit regulated amounts of these pollutants, it creates an incentive for facilities to use fuel more efficiently and to make industrial and other processes more fuel efficient. To some degree, the Act leads to such improvements.[36]

Perhaps the most prominent initial effort under the Clean Air Act to foster energy efficiency and conservation occurred with the 1990 amendments, which established an emissions trading system for sulfur dioxide emissions for major coal-fired power plants.[37] The Act reduced sulfur dioxide emissions from those plants by about 50 percent between 1990 and 2000. The reduction was implemented through an emissions cap or limit for each covered facility, and the level of this cap declined over time. Covered facilities could meet this cap more or less as they saw fit—by, for example, becoming more energy efficient, switching to a less carbon-intensive fuel (for example, from coal to natural gas), or using more renewable energy. Another option for covered facilities was trading or purchasing emissions allowances. Some facilities were able to reduce their greenhouse gas emissions—on a per-ton basis—more cheaply than others. Those that could were allowed to trade or sell their "excess" reductions—in the form of allowances that are equal to one ton of sulfur dioxide—to facilities whose control costs were greater. Many observers hoped a significant increase in energy efficiency and conservation would result from this incentive to employ the lowest-cost option to meet the required reduction; the Act even identifies energy conservation as one of its purposes.[38] The Act also set a special reserve of bonus allowances in a Conservation and Renewable Energy Reserve; utilities could earn these allowances through efficiency and renewable energy projects.[39] Yet the main choices of utilities were instead conventional pollution controls (scrubbers) and switching from high-sulfur coal to low-sulfur coal.[40] Utilities made very little use of the Conservation and Renewable Allowance Reserve.[41] Among other reasons, the lower-than-expected market price for allowances was not high enough to justify investment in efficiency, it was difficult for utilities to demonstrate emissions reductions due to efficiency, and utility interest in efficiency declined because of state deregulation of utility prices.[42]

The role of the Clean Air Act in achieving energy efficiency and conservation appears to be growing after the U.S. Supreme Court's 2007 decision in *Massachusetts v. EPA* that greenhouse gases are "air pollutants" under the Clean Air Act.[43] Greenhouse gas regulation under the Clean Air Act can lead to greater energy efficiency in a variety of ways.[44] As more fully explained below, the Environmental Protection Agency (EPA) and DOT in 2010 adopted combined greenhouse gas and fuel efficiency regulations for light-duty motor vehicles. In so doing, EPA expressly recognized that there is only a "single pool of technologies" for reducing tailpipe emissions of greenhouse gases and improving fuel economy—"those that reduce fuel consumption and thereby reduce carbon dioxide emissions as well."[45]

The motor vehicle regulations also mean that greenhouse gases are "regulated pollutants" at stationary sources (such as factories and power plants) under the Clean Air Act.[46] In late 2010, EPA issued guidance emphasizing the importance of energy efficiency in meeting the new greenhouse gas requirements for stationary sources.[47] After January 2, 2011, the effective date of the motor vehicle rule, new stationary sources or modifications to those sources that increase greenhouse gas emissions (generally by more than seventy-five thousand or one hundred thousand tons of carbon dioxide equivalent) are subject to permitting under two Clean Air Act programs (Title V and Prevention of Significant Deterioration).[48] As a result, greenhouse gas emissions from such sources will be subject to best available control technology (BACT) limits, which are determined on a case-by-case basis. The guidance emphasizes the importance of determining BACT based on consideration of "options that improve the overall energy efficiency of the source or modification—through technologies, processes and practices at the emitting unit."[49] Because stationary source emissions are overwhelmingly based on combustion of fossil fuel, and because energy efficiency can save money, it seems likely that energy efficiency also will be integrated into other EPA actions under the Clean Air Act.

Conservation and Efficiency Laws and Policies
for Specific Economic Sectors

Energy legislation tends to address many different economic sectors at once. This section summarizes the development of the law for each of the following sectors: appliances; motor vehicles; residential and commercial buildings; federal buildings and operations; energy-efficient infrastructure; and research, development, and demonstration. Readers who are interested in detail on several of these sectors should consult chapters 6 (government purchasing), 12 (appliances), 13 (buildings), or 14 (motor vehicles).

The evolution of the law for these sectors shows a tendency for greater stringency and broader scope over time, periods of indifference (especially for automobiles), and a lack of focus on certain existing parts of the problem (especially existing residential and commercial buildings). The United States has not realized maximum achievable energy efficiency and conservation because it has not even tried. Still, in recent years, it appears to be trying harder.

Motor Vehicles

The quest for greater efficiency in motor vehicles began in earnest in 1975, stalled in 1990, and has now been restarted in a serious way. Light-duty motor vehicles (cars and light trucks, such as sport utility vehicles) account for 40 percent of U.S. oil consumption and 23 percent of U.S. greenhouse gas emissions.[50] A significant new development is the combination of fuel efficiency standards and greenhouse gas emission standards for motor vehicles.

As discussed above, the 1975 Energy Policy and Conservation Act directs DOT to adopt CAFE standards for automobiles.[51] Each standard is to be based on the "maximum feasible fuel economy" that the Secretary of Transportation determines can be achieved for a particular year.[52] In determining what the maximum feasible fuel economy is, the Secretary is required to consider "technological feasibility, economic practicability, the effect of other motor vehicle standards of the Government on fuel economy, and the need of the United States to conserve energy."[53] Regulations adopted under the Act increased average fuel economy for automobiles from 18.0 mpg in 1978 to 27.5 mpg in 1990.[54] Automobile dealers are also obliged to attach a label in a prominent place on each new car offered for sale, stating the fuel economy of that car.[55] Congress also authorized DOT to set fuel economy standards for light trucks, which include sport utility vehicles, minivans, and pickup trucks. These standards began at 17.2 mpg in 1979 and rose to 20.7 mpg for the 1996 to 2004 model years.[56]

Fuel efficiency for cars and light trucks increased rapidly at first, from 13.2 mpg in 1975 to 22 mpg in 1987. Fuel efficiency then slowly dropped until 2004, and has been growing slightly since then.[57] As light trucks gained market share, they began to slowly pull the mpg-combined-average rating for cars and light trucks below the 1987 peak.

The Energy Independence and Security Act of 2007 changed the CAFE standards. The Act requires that the Secretary of Transportation prescribe a separate average fuel economy standard for passenger automobiles and a separate average fuel economy standard for light trucks to achieve a combined standard for model year 2020 of at least 35 mpg for the total fleet manufactured for sale in the United States.[58] The Act also establishes a new fuel economy program for commercial medium- and heavy-duty on-highway vehicles and work trucks.[59]

The Obama administration combined fuel efficiency in motor vehicles with regulation of greenhouse gases from motor vehicles. In 2007, when the Supreme Court held that greenhouse gases are "air pollutants" under the Clean Air Act, it remanded to EPA for further consideration a petition to regulate greenhouse gases from motor vehicles under that Act.[60] On May 7, 2010, EPA and DOT published a final regulation increasing CAFE standards for light-duty motor vehicles to a combined average emissions level of 250 grams of carbon dioxide per mile by 2016. These standards are equivalent to 35.5 mpg if manufacturers meet them entirely with fuel efficiency improvements.[61] The 2016 deadline is four years ahead of the schedule Congress laid out in the 2007 Act. The regulation applies to passenger cars, light-duty trucks, and medium-duty passenger vehicles (60 percent of U.S. transportation-related greenhouse gas emissions), and covers model years 2012 through 2016. The government estimates that "these standards will cut greenhouse gas emissions by an estimated 960 million metric tons and 1.8 billion barrels of oil over the lifetime of the vehicles sold under the program."[62] These are the standards that petitioners sought in *Massachusetts v. EPA*.

And there is more to come. EPA and DOT have also announced their intent to jointly propose even more stringent standards for light-duty vehicles for the 2017 to 2025 model years—standards that could raise CAFE standards to as high as 62 mpg by 2025.[63] In addition, EPA and DOT have proposed the first national fuel efficiency and greenhouse gas emission standards for heavy-duty trucks and buses.[64] In a May 2010 memorandum directing these further improvements in fuel efficiency, President Obama noted that "large tractor trailers, representing half of all greenhouse gas emissions from this sector, can reduce greenhouse gas emissions by as much as twenty percent and increase their fuel efficiency by as much as twenty-five percent with the use of existing technologies."[65]

Finally, the federal government has also begun to find ways to retire old and less efficient vehicles. The Consumer Assistance to Recycle and Save (CARS) Act of 2009[66] (better known as the "Cash for Clunkers" law) created the first national fleet modernization program ever implemented in the United States. The legislation was an effort to stimulate new car sales, create jobs, and boost the economy. But it also addressed a longstanding weakness in the CAFE program. Cars and light trucks are used for an average of sixteen years before they are scrapped,[67] which means long delays in the full effectiveness of new fuel efficiency standards.

CARS provided rebates to less fuel-efficient vehicles that were traded in for more fuel-efficient vehicles.[68] Qualifying vehicles could be traded in for new vehicles with a retail price of less than $45,000 that had a fuel efficiency rating of 22 mpg or more.[69] Depending on improvement in fuel efficiency, the rebate reduced the price of the qualifying cars by either $3,500 or $4,500. The National Highway Traffic Safety Administration (NHTSA) reimbursed the dealer for that amount.[70] One billion dollars was originally allocated for the program, which was exhausted in less than a month. Congress then appropriated an additional $2 billion to CARS[71] that was also fully consumed in less than a month.[72]

The CARS program stimulated the economy by significantly increasing the sales of automobiles in the short term[73] without decreasing future sales.[74] Furthermore, 49 percent of the cars sold under the program were manufactured in the United States, thereby boosting the struggling economy, contributing $4 to $7 billion to GDP, and saving or creating more than sixty thousand jobs in automobile manufacturing and sales as well as related industries.[75] By replacing older vehicles with new vehicles, CARS reduced emissions of criteria pollutants such as carbon monoxide and hydrocarbons,[76] and increased fuel efficiency.[77] CARS also caused a relatively modest reduction in greenhouse gas emissions. When measured against the $3 billion cost of CARS, these reductions may have cost as much as $600 per ton, much more than the $13 per ton estimated cost of greenhouse gas reductions under federal climate change legislation.[78] Such assessments, however, do not address the other benefits of CARS. Few if any prior federal energy efficiency programs have achieved the intense (if brief) level of public attention that CARS did. In fact, "Cash for Clunkers" provided a basis for "Cash for Clunker Appliances" legislation and has prompted second-generation proposals for "Cash for Caulkers."

Appliances and Equipment

Appliance and equipment efficiency standards have enjoyed considerable long-term success in reducing energy use. Energy Star, perhaps the nation's most effective "voluntary" program, is based to a considerable extent on those standards. Because these standards have been implemented with relatively little public controversy, however, their scope and effectiveness are likely not fully known or appreciated.

The Energy Policy and Conservation Act of 1975, as amended most recently by the Energy Independence and Security Act of 2007,[79] requires DOE to adopt testing procedures for the standardized determination of energy efficiency, energy use, and estimated annual operating cost for particular products.[80] The Federal Trade Commission is required to adopt labeling rules based on energy use stating the estimated annual operating cost of the particular product and the range of annual estimated operating costs for such products.[81] These rules are intended to inform consumers about a product's energy use and costs at the time of purchase.

The Act also establishes energy efficiency standards for certain consumer products and authorizes DOE to set new or amended energy and water conservation standards for these products.[82] (Water conservation saves energy because it reduces the amount of water that needs to be pumped, treated for use, heated or cooled, and then pumped again and treated for discharge or disposal.) New or amended standards are to be based on the "maximum improvement in energy efficiency, or, in the case of showerheads, faucets, water closets, or urinals, water efficiency, which the Secretary determines is technologically feasible and economically justified."[83] As a consequence, standards have been established (and often subsequently made more stringent) for new refrigerators, refrigerator-freezers, freezers, central air conditioners and central air conditioning heat pumps, water heaters, furnaces, dishwashers, clothes washers, clothes dryers, fluorescent lamp ballasts, general service fluorescent lamps and incandescent reflector lamps, fluorescent lamp ballasts, washing machines, clothes dryers, faucets, showerheads, ceiling fans, and ceiling fan light kits.[84] Recently revised regulations include those for residential water heaters, direct heating equipment, and pool heaters.[85] (Manufacturers of energy-efficient appliances may also be eligible for tax credits.[86])

Recently adopted standards for electric lighting, which go into effect in 2012, require 30 percent greater efficiency than current lights.[87] As a result, the familiar incandescent light bulb is likely to be replaced by the much more efficient compact fluorescent light, which is already widely sold, and the light-emitting diode (LED) bulb, which will likely be on the market by 2012.[88]

In general, federal standards for a particular product preempt state standards for the same product, unless the state files a petition with DOE and convinces the agency that the state's interests are substantially different from, or greater than, those in the United States generally, and that the state regulation is preferable or necessary based on "costs, benefits, burdens, and reliability of energy or water savings."[89] As of this writing, Massachusetts and California are the only states that have petitioned DOE for a waiver.[90] State appliance efficiency regulations and preemption are discussed in greater detail in chapter 3.

A somewhat similar set of testing, labeling, and standard setting requirements exists for commercial and industrial equipment.[91] DOE has adopted efficiency standards for electric motors and a variety of other equipment.[92]

As a result of standards in place in 2009, U.S. electricity use in 2020 is projected to be 11.5 percent lower than it would have been, with attendant reductions in greenhouse gas emissions.[93] Energy use and greenhouse gas emissions would have been reduced even further had DOE adopted required standards on a timely basis.[94] In the Energy Policy Act of 2005, Congress directed DOE to establish a plan for expeditiously concluding the energy efficiency standards that Congress had required in the 1975 Energy Policy and Conservation Act.[95] In 2006, in response to a suit by fourteen states, two state agencies, the city of New York, and the Natural Resources Defense Council, DOE entered into a consent decree to finalize new or revised standards for twenty-two types of products by no later than 2011.[96] In February 2009, noting that DOE had not yet issued regulations for fifteen of these twenty-two product categories, President Obama requested DOE to expeditiously conclude all of the needed rulemakings.[97]

Until recently, these standards have been primarily important to manufacturers, and very little formal enforcement has occurred.[98] In 2009, that began to change. DOE's Office of General Counsel issued guidance

> to make clear that under existing DOE regulations, a manufacturer's failure to properly certify a covered product and retain records in accordance with DOE regulations may be subject to enforcement action, including the assessment of civil penalties. In addition, DOE announces its intent to exercise this enforcement authority more rigorously, beginning this fall, with a program to randomly select and review manufacturers' compliance with these certification requirements.[99]

DOE later announced a thirty-day amnesty program for manufacturers that corrected or revised their certifications by January 8, 2010.[100] DOE has now brought more than a dozen energy efficiency enforcement actions[101] and is actively seeking information on how to improve its energy efficiency enforcement program.[102]

The Energy Star program builds on the federal standards. Energy Star is a government-industry energy efficiency partnership involving more than seventeen thousand public and private entities. It was begun by EPA in 1992 "as a voluntary labeling program designed to identify and promote energy-efficient products to reduce greenhouse gas emissions." It now covers a variety of office and residential equipment as well as homes and commercial and industrial buildings.[103] After more than a decade of existence by administrative fiat, Congress formally authorized Energy Star as part of the Energy Policy Act of 2005.[104]

The widely recognized Energy Star label can be placed on products that meet certain efficiency standards. This is no small thing: "The American public trusts Energy Star as the national symbol for energy efficiency to guide their purchasing decisions, save them money, and protect the environment."[105] Energy Star criteria ordinarily represent more stringent voluntary targets that manufacturers commit to when they participate in the program. This typically requires appliances to be 10 to 25 percent more efficient than applicable minimum requirements.[106] Energy Star criteria also apply to appliances and equipment for which no standards have been set, including personal computers and computer monitors.

Energy Star has grown steadily in scope and effectiveness. In 2009 alone, Energy Star helped Americans prevent 45 million metric tons of greenhouse gas emissions—"equivalent to the annual emissions from 30 million vehicles"—and "saved nearly $17 billion on their utility bills."[107] Energy Star's 2009 energy savings were more than three times those achieved in 2000.[108] In addition, "Americans purchased over 300 million Energy Star qualified products in 2009 across more than 60 product categories for a cumulative total of about 3 billion products since 2000."[109]

The success of Energy Star has prompted Congress to include it in new legislation. These laws include procurement requirements for the Department of Defense[110] and public housing agencies,[111] requirements for development of the Small Business Administration's energy efficiency assistance program,[112] federal procurement requirements for energy efficient products[113] and leasing,[114] and energy efficiency test procedures for certain appliances.[115]

Energy Star also provides the basis for a substantial energy efficiency rebate program known as the "Cash for Clunker Appliances" program.[116] This program, which is funded through ARRA, provides $300 million of rebates to consumers who replace old appliances with new, more energy-efficient household devices that contain the Energy Star seal.[117] Unlike CARS, the age of the old appliance does not matter nor does the old appliance necessarily need to be in working order. Also unlike CARS, the Cash for Clunker Appliances program is run by the states. The Cash for Clunker Appliances program is discussed in greater detail in chapter 3. The Energy Star program and appliances in general are discussed in greater detail in chapter 12.

Residential and Commercial Buildings

While energy efficiency standards for buildings are primarily a matter of state law, federal legislation has prompted adoption or improvement of such standards for *new* buildings. The Energy Policy Act of 1992 required each state to review the energy efficiency provisions of its residential building codes and to determine within two years whether it should adopt the 1992 Model Energy Code published by the Council of American Building Officials.[118] For commercial building codes, the Act requires states to adopt the current American Society of Heating, Refrigerating, and Air-Conditioning Engineers (ASHRAE) Code.[119] Both of these codes are revised periodically. Whenever either code is revised, the Act requires states to consider or adopt updated provisions that the DOE determines "would improve energy efficiency" in residential or commercial buildings.[120] To bolster state performance, the Energy Policy Act of 2005 authorizes DOE to provide $25 million annually to states to improve existing energy efficiency codes and to improve compliance with such codes.[121] This legislation has been only modestly successful. As of summer 2010, only one state (Vermont) had adopted the most recent (2009) energy efficient residential code, twenty-four had adopted the next most recent code (2006), and ten appeared to have no energy efficiency building code at all.[122] For commercial buildings, the story is similar. Only two states had adopted the 2009 code (Florida and Massachusetts), twenty-six had adopted the 2006 code, and nine did not even have a very outdated commercial efficiency code.[123] Whether a state has an up-to-date building code or not, owners of residential buildings may be eligible for tax credits of up to $1,500 for energy efficiency improvements in the building envelope (roof, windows, walls) or heating and cooling equipment.[124] In addition, energy conservation subsidies provided by public utilities to homeowners do not count as taxable income.[125] Builders of energy-efficient homes, including manufactured homes, may also be eligible for a tax credit of up to $2,000 per home.[126]

In 2007, as part of the Energy Independence and Security Act, Congress set a goal of zero net energy use for all new commercial buildings by 2030 and for half of existing commercial building stock by 2040, and established the Zero-Net-Energy Commercial Buildings Initiative to achieve those goals.[127] Further improvements in federal building requirements are possible in the future. For example, the Waxman-Markey bill, which passed the House of Representatives in June 2009 but died in the Senate, would have required the establishment of national energy efficiency codes for commercial and residential buildings. These national codes would have been 30 percent more efficient than the baseline codes (which were, for this bill, the 2006 residential and 2004 commercial codes), 50 percent more efficient by 2014 (residential) or 2015 (commercial), and 5 percent more efficient every three years after then until 2029 and 2030.[128]

As is the case with appliances, the Energy Star program supplements the existing regulatory program for new homes. To be certified for Energy Star, a home needs to be 20 to 30 percent more energy-efficient than homes designed to a standard energy efficiency code. This determination is based both on the building's shell (including windows and insulation) and its heating, ventilation, and air conditioning systems, lighting, and various appliances.[129] More than one million Energy Star homes have been built in the United States, including more than one hundred thousand in 2009. A similar program exists for commercial buildings, but with much lower participation.[130]

There is no federal regulatory program requiring that *existing* residential and commercial buildings be renovated or upgraded for energy efficiency, or requiring that states make this happen. While this is understandable, the opportunities for greater energy efficiency and reduced greenhouse gas emissions are considerable. Existing residential and commercial buildings are responsible for 38 percent of U.S. carbon dioxide emissions.[131] Yet 60 percent of residences are not well insulated, and 70 percent or more of commercial buildings lack roof or wall insulation.[132]

The federal government encourages energy efficiency upgrades and renovation through tax credits for certain home energy efficiency improvements[133] and advice to homeowners under the Energy Star program.[134] A tax deduction is also available for commercial buildings that achieve a 50 percent energy savings target.[135]

The federal government is also trying to help develop a national infrastructure for energy efficiency upgrades and renovation in existing buildings. Energy efficiency retrofits in the nation's 130 million homes could reduce home energy use by as much as 40 percent and reduce energy bills by $21 billion per year.[136] Yet the lack of "straightforward and reliable information," large up-front costs, and the lack of businesses and skilled workers to do retrofits all prevent the existence of a large-scale effective market.[137] To overcome these barriers, DOE has awarded $508 million under ARRA to forty-one states, local governments, and other organizations for pilot programs to "ramp-up energy efficiency building retrofits in their communities." DOE plans to make the lessons learned from these programs available to other communities as part of its effort to scale up retrofits across the country.[138]

Legislation has also been proposed to increase retrofits. The Obama administration's proposed Home Star Program to fund energy-efficient retrofits of U.S. homes ("Cash for Caulkers") would provide two types of incentives to homeowners. The Silver Star program would offer rebates for specified energy-saving measures for up to $3,000 or 50 percent of total project cost. The Gold Star program would include a comprehensive energy audit and provide rebates for up to $8,000 or 50 percent of total project cost based on energy savings achieved through efficiency measures.[139] The Practical Energy and Climate Plan Act (S. 3464), sponsored by Senator Richard Lugar and others, provides another approach. It would set annual targets for retrofits of existing buildings (5 percent for homes and 2 percent for commercial buildings).[140] The bill would also authorize DOE to provide a variety of forms of financial assistance for building owners, including loan guarantees, letters of credit, and loans. In addition, the bill would authorize DOE to create new financial instruments to aggregate the retrofit debts of many building owners to facilitate private financing.[141]

Energy efficiency can be especially helpful to the poor, particularly by reducing the amount of money to be spent on household energy.[142] Low-income persons tend to live in the least efficient housing; they spend about 14 percent of their income on energy, as opposed to 3.5 percent spent by other households.[143] Congress authorized a Weatherization Assistance Program for low-income persons in 1976 "to increase the energy efficiency of dwellings owned or occupied by low-income persons, reduce their total residential energy expenditures, and improve their health and safety."[144] DOE administers the program, which provides funding to states and Indian tribal governments. More than 6.4 million homes have been weatherized under the program, which reduces annual energy bills by $350 per home.[145] About 28 million households are eligible.[146] While the weatherization program began with a focus on insulation and caulking, it now includes a range of energy efficiency services for "whole house weatherization," including improved heating and cooling systems and more efficient appliances.[147]

ARRA provides about $5 billion for low-income energy assistance for 590,000 residences over three years, compared to $450 million appropriated for this program in fiscal year 2009.[148] Congress and the administration believed that use of this money for a preexisting program would quickly create a significant number of new jobs. Yet by February 2010, the one-year anniversary of ARRA, DOE's Inspector General found that less than 8 percent of the money awarded to grantees had been spent on weatherization and that "only 2 of the 10 highest funded recipients completed more than two percent of planned units."[149] Among other things, state hiring freezes and furloughs brought on by the recession, as well as the need to train new people, contributed to delays in scaling up the program. DOE said it was smoothing out these implementation difficulties and accelerating program implementation.[150]

Investment in Energy-Efficient Infrastructure

Much energy is wasted because U.S. infrastructure—including the transportation system as well as the electric grid—is inefficient. Congress has shown greater interest in making U.S. infrastructure more energy efficient. Most recently, for example, ARRA provided $8 billion for high-speed rail investments,[151] $1.5 billion for public transit improvements and infrastructure investments,[152] and $3.4 billion for modernization of the electric grid.[153] Most observers see such funding as a small positive step toward a much more energy-efficient infrastructure.

Federal Buildings and Operations

The federal government is the nation's largest single user of energy.[154] Requirements for energy efficiency in federal buildings have become more ambitious over time. The Energy Policy Act of 1992 required new federal buildings to meet energy efficiency requirements specified in then-current commercial and residential industry standards.[155] In 2005, Congress revised the law to require new federal buildings to meet updated industry efficiency standards and, "if life cycle cost effective for new Federal buildings," an energy consumption level at least 30 percent below the industry standards.[156] In 2007, Congress revised the standard again, requiring new federal buildings and federal buildings "undergoing major renovations" to be designed to reduce fossil fuel consumption by sixty-five percent by 2015 and one hundred percent by 2030 compared to a similar building in 2003.[157] The legislation also requires that "sustainable design principles" be applied "to the siting, design, and construction of such buildings."[158] In May 2010, DOE issued a notice of proposed rulemaking setting out specific requirements for energy efficiency, water conservation, sustainable design, and green building certification for federal buildings.[159]

An October 2009 Executive Order by President Obama puts in place a set of requirements for federal agencies to "lead by example" in increasing energy efficiency, reporting and reducing their greenhouse gas emissions, and improving water use efficiency and reducing waste.[160] The executive order requires agencies to set a percentage target for an absolute reduction in greenhouse gas emissions by considering, among other things, "reducing energy intensity in agency buildings" and to reduce the agency vehicle fleet's petroleum consumption by at least 2 percent annually from 2005 levels until 2020.[161] The order also requires recycling and waste reduction, water conservation, and consideration of new building locations in areas "that are pedestrian friendly, near existing employment centers, and accessible to public transit."[162] Finally, the order requires that nearly all new contracts for products and services be energy efficient (e.g., meet Energy Star standards) and water efficient.[163] Each agency's plan for meeting these commitments must be integrated with its duties under the Government Performance and Results Act,[164] which means that the executive order requirements will be incorporated into each agency's overall strategic plan and budget process.

Research, Development, and Demonstration

The federal government administers a variety of grant programs for research, development, and demonstration of energy efficiency technologies. These include programs for buildings, energy efficiency inventions and innovations, industrial technologies, and vehicle technologies.[165] In addition, the Advanced Research Projects Agency–Energy was created to fund research and development projects that "(1) translate scientific discoveries and cutting-edge inventions into technological innovations and (2) accelerate transformational technological advances in areas that industry by itself is not likely to undertake because of high technical or financial risk."[166] These include, but are not limited to, energy efficiency projects. The potential impact of breakthrough or game-changing technologies is suggested by Amory Lovins's famous argument that we could improve the efficiency with which we use energy by a factor of ten, which would mean reducing energy use by 90 percent without any loss of productivity.[167]

Laws and Policies Fostering Energy Inefficiency and Energy Consumption

Few if any federal laws are explicitly *intended* to increase energy consumption or energy inefficiency. As a result, these laws cannot be identified by their purpose or their title. But many laws have had the *effect* of increasing energy use and making energy use less efficient. These laws have received growing attention in recent years, and there have been growing federal efforts to address these effects. The most significant of these federal laws include the following.

Transportation laws. Since the 1950s, when construction of the federal interstate highway system began, federal transportation laws have favored the building of highways over other forms of transportation. When coupled with state and municipal zoning laws favoring single-use zoning and state transportation laws that are similar to federal laws, federal transportation law contributes to overdependence on personal automobile travel and sprawl—all of which cause greater energy consumption. The last two reauthorizations of federal transportation laws—in 1991 and 2005—have focused more on repair of existing roads than the building of new roads and have focused more on the development of alternatives to driving.[168] In 2009, EPA, DOT, and the Department of Housing and Urban Development entered an interagency agreement on sustainable communities. The agreement is intended, among other things, to redirect federal funding toward greater choice and lower costs in transportation—which should reduce driving and therefore energy use.[169]

Tax laws. The federal mortgage interest tax deduction appears to create a major incentive for sprawl and therefore greater energy consumption.[170] "Because of increasing lot sizes, home sizes, and correspondingly larger mortgage financing packages, and because the deduction is indexed to income, the deduction is worth more to borrowers in the suburbs and newer areas than in central cities and older areas."[171] To be sure, a 1997 amendment to the Internal Revenue Code, which permits homeowners to purchase less expensive homes in cities without incurring capital gains tax for the sale of the more expensive home in the suburbs[172] was a step toward reduced energy use.[173] But the overall structure of these federal tax incentives has not changed.

Subsidies for fossil fuel production. A variety of direct and indirect subsidies exists for the production of energy, particularly oil, natural gas, and coal.[174] Because these subsidies are greater than those for energy conservation and efficiency, they tend to give fossil fuels a competitive edge in the marketplace.[175] More broadly, fossil fuel production and use are subsidized by the failure of federal law to internalize all of the costs associated with these forms of energy, including but not limited to greenhouse gas emissions. The resulting lower price for fossil fuels makes energy and conservation measures less cost-effective for energy users. These direct and indirect subsidies are offset, to some degree, by state and federal taxes on the sale of gasoline and diesel fuel.[176]

Proposed Climate Change and Energy Conservation Legislation

Cap-and-Trade Legislation

Comprehensive climate change legislation, based on cap and trade, was seriously considered in Congress in 2009 and 2010 but did not pass, and prospects for future climate change legislation are uncertain. On June 26, 2009, the House of Representatives passed the American Clean Energy and Security Act (H.R. 2454). The Senate considered a somewhat similar bill, the Clean Energy Jobs and American Power Act (S. 1733), but it was ultimately not adopted. While these bills, or bills like them, would likely encourage energy efficiency and conservation, such legislation is not likely to be successful by itself in significantly reducing energy use.

The heart of these bills was a cap-and-trade program for greenhouse gas emissions. This system would have functioned very much like the program for sulfur dioxide reduction created by the 1990 Clean Air Act Amendments, except it would have applied to a broader range of facilities. Each of the bills would have required a steady reduction of greenhouse gas emissions, with the ultimate requirement for an 83 percent cut from 2005 levels by 2050 (which equates to a 69 percent cut from 1990 emissions levels by 2050). The bills also would have created a cap-and-trade program as the primary means of achieving that result.

A cap-and-trade system such as that contained in these bills should lead to a price on carbon that would have ripple effects throughout an economy. (Though politically less likely, a carbon tax would have the same effect.) The price would be reflected in the market price for allowances. According to conventional economic wisdom, the economic pressure created by a cap-and-trade program should lead to more energy efficiency and energy conservation.

Because of market imperfections, though, this pressure will not always have the desired result. Consumers often do not purchase more energy-efficient products because they undervalue the economic savings of those products.[177] Thus, even higher prices do not necessarily stimulate greater efficiency and conservation. In addition, the person with the ability to achieve greater energy efficiency (e.g., landlord) is frequently not the person who pays the energy bills (e.g., tenant). The incentive, in other words, is not directed at the person with the ability to make decisions that will reduce energy use.[178] Indeed, the proverbial "low-hanging fruit" of energy efficiency is based on actions that are already cost-effective based on existing technology.

In addition, there is considerable evidence that higher prices alone do not motivate individuals. A wealth of data on individual behavior indicates that the most effective approaches use multiple policy tools (including information, incentives, and requirements); communicate in many ways (e.g., mass-media and community-based appeals); and address many audiences (e.g., individuals, businesses).[179] Moral, ethical, and religious principles may also encourage reduced energy consumption.[180]

Moreover, while a cap-and-trade program can surely reduce the costs of emissions control, it is less likely to lead to more immediate environmental, social, and economic co-benefits than a performance standard of equivalent stringency. Buyers of emissions allowances are primarily interested in reducing their costs, not in fostering or capturing the co-benefits (other benefits such as cost savings, reduction in other air pollutants, and job creation) that may come from a use of a particular policy or measure.[181] These limitations in a stand-alone cap-and-trade program strengthen the case for energy efficiency policies and measures, for policies and measures that would drive greater levels of private investment, and for policies and measures that would generate substantial co-benefits.

Finally, the distribution of allowances under the cap-and-trade program may or may not be another limiting factor, depending on how the allowances (or proceeds from the sale of allowances) are distributed and required to be spent. To a significant degree, each of the bills would have diluted the market signal created by a higher carbon price in order to protect consumers and low-income persons. They would have done so by distributing a large share of allowances to utilities for the express purpose of protecting utility customers from the price impact of the cap-and-trade program. From the perspective of traditional U.S. energy policy, as well as the economic hardship caused or exacerbated by the recession that began in 2008, keeping prices relatively low is both sensible and necessary. Yet the effectiveness of cap-and-trade is premised on the existence of that same price signal. On the other hand, cap-and-trade legislation can require that allowances or proceeds from the sale of allowances be spent by utilities or states for energy efficiency and conservation purposes. The cap-and-trade bills would have done that to some degree; a more ambitious program for using funds from allowances for efficiency and conservation could do even more.[182]

The Congress that was elected on November 2, 2010, has many members and a Republican House majority that are opposed to cap and trade. Thus, the immediate future for such a mechanism at the federal level is murky at best.

Supplemental Energy Efficiency Measures

Climate change bills typically include additional energy efficiency measures.[183] Another group of bills, which tends to focus more on clean energy than cap and trade, also includes specific energy efficiency measures. These proposed measures, which are in addition to those described above for motor vehicles and buildings, include the following. While the climate change bills are unlikely to pass in the immediate future, similar measures may appear in other legislation.

Energy efficiency resource standard. An energy efficiency resource standard may be the tool with the greatest energy efficiency potential. This tool formed the basis for several bills introduced in the House and Senate in early 2009.[184] An energy efficiency resource standard requires electricity and natural gas utilities "to achieve a particular percentage of energy savings relative to their average energy sales" in prior years.[185] These energy savings are achieved by helping residential, commercial, and industrial customers reduce their energy use "through utility efficiency programs, building energy codes, appliance standards, and related efficiency measures."[186] The proposed federal bills would require electricity distributors to achieve a savings of 1 percent in 2012 that rises steadily and reaches 15 percent in 2020, and would require natural gas distributors to achieve a 0.75 percent energy savings in 2012 that increases to 10 percent in 2020.[187] These bills, in turn, are based on recently enacted laws in at least twenty states—including California, Texas, Pennsylvania, and Vermont—which require varying percentages of energy savings over time.[188]

The energy and cost savings of these standards, if applied at the national level, could be considerable. The American Council for an Energy-Efficient Economy estimated that the federal bills would "save American consumers and businesses almost $170 billion, create over 220,000 jobs" and eliminate "the need to build 390 power plants." In addition, the legislation would reduce projected 2020 U.S. greenhouse gas emissions by 4 percent. These impacts would be in addition to those achieved by existing state laws.[189]

National energy efficiency goals. The Waxman-Markey bill would have established a national goal of improving energy productivity (GDP per unit of energy input) by at least 2.5 percent annually by 2012 and maintain that level through 2030. DOE would have been required to develop a strategic plan for doing so, to receive public comment, and to update the plan biennially.[190]

Federal support and encouragement for state energy efficiency programs. The Waxman-Markey bill would have allocated a substantial number of allowances to each state for a State Energy and Environment Development (SEED) Account.[191] Under this program, states and Indian tribes would have provided loans, grants, and other financial support for renewable energy and energy efficiency purposes. Energy efficiency programs funded under SEED would have included adoption and implementation of new energy efficiency building codes, building energy performance labeling programs, low-income community energy efficiency programs, a Retrofit for Energy and Environmental Performance (REEP) program (that would pay up to 50 percent of energy efficiency retrofit costs for buildings), and mass transit.[192]

Congress has other options for encouraging or prompting the states to do more on energy efficiency. It could allocate greater funding to state and federal energy efficiency programs. Congress could also require that states adopt comprehensive climate change action plans identifying a range of cost-effective measures, including energy efficiency and conservation measures, and then implement them.[193]

Deployment goals for energy efficiency technologies. It is one thing to invent and fine-tune a new technology; it is quite another to get that technology broadly used or deployed. The Waxman-Markey bill would have required DOE to publish near-, medium-, and long-term goals for deployment of clean energy technologies to promote, among other things, transformation of U.S. building stock to zero net energy consumption. It would have also required sufficient availability of financial products to enable building owners and users to make energy efficiency and distributed generation technology investments with reasonable payback periods.[194] The bill would have also established a "best-in-class" appliance deployment program.[195] This program is discussed in greater detail in chapter 12.

Watersense. The Waxman-Markey bill and S. 1733 would have required EPA "to identify and promote water efficient products, buildings and landscapes, and services" to save energy and water. EPA would have done so through "voluntary labeling of, or other forms of communications about, products, buildings and landscapes, and services that meet the highest water efficiency and performance standards." The bills would have required EPA to provide funds to states for rebates or vouchers for purchase of residential water-efficient products or services.[196]

Energy efficiency in transportation. The Waxman-Markey bill and S. 1733 would have required each state and metropolitan planning organization to develop targets and strategies for reduction of transportation-related greenhouse gases. In both bills, targets and strategies were required to include, among other things, efforts to increase public transportation ridership and programs to increase walking, bicycling, and other forms of nonmotorized transportation.[197] In the Senate bill, these targets and strategies were also required to include zoning and land use changes to promote infill and travel demand management programs.[198]

Product carbon disclosure program. Under the Waxman-Markey bill and S. 1733, EPA would have been required to study the feasibility of establishing a "national program for measuring, reporting, publicly disclosing, and labeling products or materials sold in the United States for their carbon content." Then, EPA would have been required to establish a national voluntary product carbon disclosure program.[199] Because the carbon content of a product is based on both the type and amount of energy used to produce it, this program could encourage improvements in energy efficiency in the design, manufacture, and transportation of products or materials.

Comprehensive effort to engage individuals. In the past half century, the U.S. economy has shifted from industry to services, and individuals and households use more (and more energy-consuming) electronic devices and have more cars (and drive them more) than they did fifty years ago. About one-third of the energy consumed in the United States "is directly controlled by households."[200] Many existing energy efficiency programs, as well as those being proposed, are intended to encourage individuals to reduce their energy consumption. Congress could put existing pieces (including tax credits and public information) together with new pieces to form a comprehensive, long-term campaign that directly and fully engages individuals on behalf of energy efficiency and conservation.[201]

International and Comparative Law Perspective

International climate change negotiations will, to some degree, influence the development of U.S. policies for energy efficiency and conservation. So will legal developments in other countries, and particularly in the European Union.

Energy Efficiency and the Convention on Climate Change

While the United Nations Framework Convention on Climate Change and the Kyoto Protocol say little about energy efficiency and conservation, nations generally realize that efficiency and conservation will need to play a central role in reducing greenhouse gas emissions. The objective of the United Nations Framework Convention on Climate Change is "stabilization of greenhouse gas concentrations in the atmosphere at a level that would prevent dangerous anthropogenic interference with the climate system."[202] The Convention requires all parties, both developed and developing, to establish, implement, and periodically update national programs to mitigate climate change.[203]

Energy efficiency and conservation are mentioned only once. Energy consumption in developing countries "will need to grow," the preamble states, but that growth should take into account "the possibilities for achieving greater energy efficiency."[204]

Because developed countries have greater financial and technological resources and greater historic responsibility for increased atmospheric greenhouse gas concentrations, the Framework Convention anticipates that they will take the lead in reducing emissions. Under the Kyoto Protocol, developed countries agreed to reduce their net greenhouse gas emissions by at least 5 percent from 1990 levels by 2008–2012.[205] A key feature of the Kyoto Protocol is its use of market mechanisms, particularly different forms of emissions trading, to achieve the required reductions.[206] The Protocol does not identify any other policies that developed countries are to use to achieve its purposes, but it does provide an illustrative list of "policies and measures" that national governments may employ. The first listed option is "[e]nhancement of energy efficiency in relevant sectors of the national economy."[207]

Negotiations for a post-Kyoto protocol or agreement have become more urgent as we approach the end of the 2008–2012 Kyoto Protocol commitment period. Parties were unable to reach agreement on such a protocol in December 2009 in Copenhagen at their fifteenth annual conference. Still, most countries agreed to a "Copenhagen Accord." The Accord recognizes "the scientific view that the increase in global temperature should be below 2 degrees Celsius" but does not adopt that limit as a goal. It also calls upon developed countries to submit "quantified economy-wide emission targets for 2020" and developing countries to submit "nationally appropriate mitigation actions" that they would then achieve by 2020.[208] Both developed and developing countries submitted commitments.[209] An analysis of the developed country submissions by the World Resources Institute shows they would reduce developed country emissions by 12 to 19 percent below 1990 levels. As impressive as that reduction may be, it is far short of the 25 to 40 percent commitment needed to ensure that temperatures will not rise more than 2 degrees Celsius.[210]

In contrast to developed countries, which submitted an overall quantitative goal, developing countries identified specific policies and measures, or types of policies and measures, that tended to implicitly or explicitly include energy efficiency and conservation. China and India stated goals in terms of greenhouse gas intensity—greenhouse gas emissions per unit of GDP—a measure that implicitly includes energy efficiency. China said it would "endeavor to lower its carbon dioxide emissions per unit of GDP by 40–45% by 2020 compared to the 2005 level."[211] India said it would "endeavour to reduce the emissions intensity of its GDP by 20–25% by 2020 in comparison to the 2005 level."[212] Brazil was more explicit: it committed to use energy efficiency to reduce its greenhouse gas emissions by 2020 by 12 to 15 million tons of carbon dioxide equivalent.[213]

Worldwide, the potential for energy efficiency continues to be both enormous and underutilized. The International Energy Agency's 2009 edition of *World Energy Outlook* analyzed the policies and measures that would be needed by 2030 to keep global greenhouse gas levels below 450 parts per million of greenhouse gas equivalent, a level that reduces below 50 percent the likelihood of a temperature increase of more than 2 degrees Celsius. It found that half of the required reduction could come from energy efficiency.[214] A 2010 report by the Organization for Economic Cooperation and Development noted "signs of energy efficiency policy innovations, including the development of markets to trade energy savings and innovative financial instruments to encourage energy efficiency investment," but added that "[u]ntapped energy efficient potential is hidden across all sectors (e.g. buildings, industries and transport)" in OECD countries.[215]

Energy efficiency opportunities in developing countries are also considerable. Despite their low per capita greenhouse gas emissions, the greenhouse gas intensity of developing countries is nearly double that of developed countries.[216] With 57 percent of the gross world product, developed countries have a greenhouse gas intensity of 0.68 kilograms of carbon dioxide equivalent per U.S. dollar in GDP.[217] Developing countries, with 43 percent of the gross world product, have a greenhouse gas intensity of 1.06 kilograms of carbon dioxide equivalent per U.S. dollar of GDP.[218]

A variety of international organizations conduct research, policy analysis, and other work relating to energy consumption and energy efficiency. These include:

- The International Energy Agency (IEA), which produces *World Energy Outlook*, is a Paris-based intergovernmental organization that essentially operates as an energy policy advisor to twenty-eight member countries.[219] The IEA has analyzed global energy efficiency trends and issued energy efficiency policy recommendations for G-8 countries that would significantly reduce energy consumption by 2030.[220]

- The International Partnership for Energy Efficiency Cooperation was created in June 2008 as a partnership with the International Energy Agency to "to facilitate those actions that yield high energy efficiency gains."[221] The partnership, which includes sixteen nations (including the United States) and the European Community, spent $1.6 million in 2009 to share best energy efficiency practices to "better leverage financing from domestic sources, such as commercial banks" and to develop indicators for energy efficiency performance.[222]

- The International Organization for Standardization (ISO), a nongovernmental organization comprised of the standards institutes in 162 countries, "is the world's largest developer and publisher of International Standards."[223] In 2008, ISO issued a standard for assessing energy efficiency in new buildings (ISO 23045).[224] ISO is also developing a standard for energy management (ISO 50001), which is intended to help organizations continually improve energy performance and energy efficiency.[225]

European Union

The European Union has the world's first fully functioning cap-and-trade system for the reduction of greenhouse gas emissions. That system should, to some degree, also foster energy efficiency and conservation. Partly because the EU was working on energy efficiency before adopting this program, and partly because cap-and-trade programs by themselves are not likely to capture all cost-effective energy efficiency opportunities, the EU has adopted supplemental measures to increase energy efficiency.

The EU has both an energy efficiency goal and a strategy for achieving energy efficiency. European leaders have agreed to "increase energy efficiency in the EU so as to achieve the objective of saving 20% of the EU's energy consumption compared to projections for 2020."[226] In 2006, the European Commission adopted an action plan for achieving energy efficiency. The strategy calls for labeling and energy efficiency requirements for fourteen categories of appliances and equipment, strengthening existing requirements for energy performance in buildings, improving efficiency in new and existing power generating facilities, improving fuel efficiency in new cars to meet a target of 120 grams of carbon dioxide/kilometer by 2012 (equivalent to 46 mpg for internal combustion engine vehicles and 53 mpg for diesel vehicles),[227] facilitating energy efficiency financing for small and medium businesses, encouraging energy efficiency in new member states, improving the ability of the taxation system to encourage and reward energy efficiency, raising public awareness of energy efficiency, encouraging energy efficiency in major cities, and supporting and encouraging energy efficiency around the globe.[228]

Two directives encompassed by this strategy are illustrative of both the ambitiousness of the EU's approach to energy efficiency and the challenges that energy efficiency policy faces. In EU parlance, a directive requires member countries to take a particular action, but requires implementing legislation within each member country.

A 2006 directive requires each member country to submit and implement an Energy Efficiency Action Plan to achieve, at a minimum, an energy savings target of 9 percent within nine years.[229] The directive also requires member countries to repeal or amend many laws that impede energy efficiency, to "ensure the availability of efficient, high-quality energy audit schemes that are designed to identify potential energy efficiency improvement measures," and to make information available to consumers that will enable them to compare their current energy use with the previous year's energy use and energy use in the same user category.[230] A 2009 review of the Energy Efficiency Action Plans submitted by all twenty-seven member countries found that, while a few countries were planning to fully realize the economic and energy savings potential provided by energy efficiency, most were not.[231]

A 2002 directive, which notes that residential and commercial buildings account for about 40 percent of EU energy consumption, was strengthened in 2010. The 2002 directive requires member countries to set minimum energy performance standards for new buildings, to ensure that major renovations of buildings with more than 1,000 square meters of floor space include an energy efficiency upgrade, and to ensure that the prospective buyer or tenant of a property has access to an energy performance certificate for the property.[232] Initial implementation was disappointing but suggested the value of modifying the directive to improve its workability.[233] In May 2010, a "recast" directive for energy performance in buildings was issued, eliminating the 1,000 square meter threshold for energy efficiency upgrades in renovated buildings, strengthening the energy efficiency requirements of the 2002 directive, and requiring that new buildings built in the EU after 2020 be "nearly zero-energy" buildings.[234] The EU calculates that the recast directive will yield an additional energy savings of 5 to 6 percent of EU energy consumption.[235]

Conclusion

The United States has had energy efficiency and conservation legislation in place for more than three decades, and yet the effect has been mixed. This mixed result expresses the ambivalence that exists in the United States about energy efficiency and conservation. Americans appear torn between two narratives—one expressing the abundant demonstrated opportunities provided by energy savings and the other based on a fear of deprivation from using less energy. Rather than choosing between the two, as this chapter has shown, we have split the difference—embracing efficiency and conservation more or less halfheartedly.

In recent years, the federal government has strengthened the nation's commitment to efficiency and conservation. These actions, by both Congress and the President, may signal the beginning of a much more serious embrace of the narrative based on opportunity and sustainability. If so, we may also see the end of Groundhog Day.

Notes

1. NAT'L COMM'N ON ENERGY POL'Y, ENDING THE ENERGY STALEMATE: A BIPARTISAN STRATEGY TO MEET AMERICAN'S ENERGY CHALLENGES 30 (2004) (defining energy efficiency as "doing more with less, as opposed to suffering hardships or closing businesses"). *See also* 42 U.S.C. § 6291(5) (defining energy efficiency as "the ratio of the useful output of services from a consumer product to the energy use of such product)."

2. NAT'L ENERGY POL'Y DEVELOPMENT GROUP, NATIONAL ENERGY POLICY 1–3 (2001).

3. PIETRO S. NIVOLA, THE POLITICS OF ENERGY CONSERVATION 1 (1986).

4. After the 1993 film by that name, starring Bill Murray and Andie MacDowell, in which a "weatherman finds himself living the same day over and over again." GROUNDHOG DAY (Columbia Pictures 1993); *see* http://www.imdb.com/title/tt0107048/ (last visited Feb. 6, 2011).

5. ENERGY POLICY PROJECT, FORD FOUNDATION, A TIME TO CHOOSE: AMERICAN'S ENERGY FUTURE 326 (1974).

6. U.S. ENERGY INFORMATION ADMIN., ANNUAL ENERGY REVIEW 2008, Table 1.5 Energy Consumption, Expenditures, and Emissions Indicators, Selected Years, 1949–2008 (2008), *available at* http://www.eia.doe.gov/emeu/aer/pdf/pages/sec1_13.pdf (2008 consumption of approximately 99 quadrillion BTUs compared to 1974 consumption of about 74 quadrillion BTUs).

7. NAT'L ACADEMY OF SCIENCES, REAL PROSPECTS FOR ENERGY EFFICIENCY IN THE UNITED STATES 2 (2009) (prepublication copy). *See also* Noah Sachs, *Greening Demand: Energy Consumption and U.S. Climate Policy,* 19 DUKE ENVTL. L. & POL'Y F. 295 (2009); David Hodas, *Imagining the Unimaginable: Reducing U.S. Greenhouse Gas Emissions by Forty Percent,* 26 VA. ENVTL. L.J. 271 (2008); John Dernbach & the Widener University Law School Seminar on Energy Efficiency, *Stabilizing and Then Reducing U.S. Energy Consumption: Legal and Policy Tools for Efficiency and Conservation,* 37 ENVTL. L. REP. (Envtl. L. Inst.) 10,003 (2007) (all drawing similar conclusions).

8. NAT'L ACADEMY OF SCIENCES et al., AMERICA'S ENERGY FUTURE: TECHNOLOGY AND TRANSFORMATION 136–37 (2009).

9. U.S. ENERGY INFORMATION ADMIN., ANNUAL ENERGY OUTLOOK 2010, 2 (2010), *available at* http://www.eia.doe.gov/oiaf/aeo/pdf/0383(2010).pdf.

10. Mark D. Levine & Nathaniel T. Aden, *Sustainable and Unsustainable Developments in the U.S. Energy System, in* AGENDA FOR A SUSTAINABLE AMERICA 145, 153–54, 156 (John C. Dernbach ed., 2009).

11. MCKINSEY & COMPANY, REDUCING U.S. GREENHOUSE GAS EMISSIONS: HOW MUCH AT WHAT COST? (2007), *available at* http://www.mckinsey.com/clientservice/ccsi/pdf/us_ghg_final_report.pdf.

12. Hank Schilling, *Energy Efficiency, in* SUSTAINABLE ENVIRONMENTAL LAW: INTEGRATING NATURAL RESOURCE AND POLLUTION ABATEMENT LAW FROM RESOURCES TO RECOVERY § 10.5(B) (Celia Campbell-Mohn et al. eds., 1993).

13. AMERICA'S ENERGY FUTURE, *supra* note 8, at 136–37 (listing ten reasons energy efficiency opportunities are not more attractive).

14. See Schilling, *supra* note 12, § 10.1(B), for a summary of these many statutes.

15. Pub. L. No. 94-163, 89 Stat. 871 (codified as amended at 42 U.S.C. §§ 6201–6422 and in scattered sections of 15 U.S.C.). See also Schilling, *supra* note 12, describing act as "first concerted attempt by Congress to address issues of energy conservation.").

16. Pub. L. No. 94-163, *supra* note 15, at tit. III.

17. Pub. L. No. 94-385, 90 Stat. 1142 (codified in scattered sections of 12, 15b, & 42 U.S.C.).

18. Pub. L. No. 95-619, 92 Stat. 3206 (codified as amended at 42 U.S.C. §§ 8201–8284 and in scattered sections of 12, 15, & 42 U.S.C.).

19. Pub. L. No. 97-35, 95 Stat. 621 (codified at 42 U.S.C. § 6836).

20. Pub. L. No. 100-12, 101 Stat. 103 (codified in scattered sections of 42 U.S.C.).

21. Pub. L. No. 102-486 (codified at 42 U.S.C. § 6833).

22. *Id.* § 122.

23. Brian T. Castelli, Alliance to Save Energy, *Key Energy Efficiency Provisions in the Energy Independence and Security Act* (2008) (paper copy on file with Professor Dernbach).

24. Energy Policy Act of 2005 § 135; 42 U.S.C. §§ 6291–6297. For an overview of the act, see Brad Sherman, *Note: A Time to Act Anew: A Historical Perspective on the Energy Policy Act of 2005 and the Changing Electrical Energy Market,* 31 WM. & MARY ENVTL. L. & POL'Y REV. 211 (2006).

25. Energy Policy Act of 2005 § 136; 42 U.S.C. §§ 6311–6316.

26. *Id.* § 137, 42 U.S.C. § 6294(a)(2)(F).

27. For a summary and explanation, see STEVEN NADEL ET AL., AM. COUNCIL FOR AN ENERGY-EFFICIENT ECONOMY, THE ENERGY POLICY ACT OF 2005: ENERGY EFFICIENCY PROVISIONS AND IMPLICATIONS FOR FUTURE POLICY EFFORTS 8-205 to 8-209 (2006), *available at* http://www.aceee.org/sites/default/files/publications/proceedings/SS06_Panel8_Paper17.pdf.

28. Energy Independence and Security Act of 2007, Pub. L. No. 110-140, § 102(a)(2)(b)(2)(A) (codified at 49 U.S.C. § 32902).

29. *Id.* §§ 321–325 (codified at 42 U.S.C. §§ 6291–6294 & 6295).

30. *Id.* §§ 205, 303 & 304 (codified at 26 U.S.C. §§ 30D, 45L(g) & 179D(h)).

31. American Recovery and Reinvestment Act of 2009, Pub. L. No. 111-5, 123 Stat. 138.

32. *Id.* at 123 Stat. 214. Other allocations in the Act, which are reported to total $6.3 billion, support related efficiency measures. *See, e.g.,* http://s.wsj.net/public/resources/documents/WSJ_Stimulus_021209.pdf (last visited Feb. 6, 2011).

33. American Recovery and Reinvestment Act of 2009, *supra* note 31, 123 Stat. at 208.

34. 42 U.S.C. §§ 7401–7671p.

35. David M. Driesen, *Air Quality: The Need to Replace Basic Technologies With Cleaner Alternatives, in* AGENDA FOR A SUSTAINABLE AMERICA, *supra* note 10, at 239, 240.

36. For a comprehensive discussion of the various ways in which energy efficiency and conservation may be employed to comply with Clean Air Act requirements, *see* Regulating Greenhouse Gas Emissions Under the Clean Air Act: Proposed Rule, 73 Fed. Reg. 44,354 (July 30, 2008).

37. 42 U.S.C. §§ 7651–7651o.

38. *Id.* § 7651(b).

39. *Id.* § 7651c(f).

40. Dallas Burtraw et al., *Economics of Pollution Trading for SO$_2$ and NO$_x$*, 30 ANN. REV. ENV'T & RESOURCES 253 (2005).

41. DAN YORK, AMERICAN COUNCIL FOR AN ENERGY-EFFICIENT ECONOMY, ENERGY EFFICIENCY AND EMISSIONS TRADING: EXPERIENCE FROM THE CLEAN AIR ACT AMENDMENTS OF 1990 FOR USING ENERGY EFFICIENCY TO MEET AIR POLLUTION REGULATIONS 10–11 (2003), *available at* http://www.aceee.org/sites/default/files/publications/researchreports/u034.pdf.

42. *Id.* at 11.

43. Mass. v. EPA, 549 U.S. 497 (2007).

44. Regulating Greenhouse Gas Emissions Under the Clean Air Act; Proposed Rule, *supra* note 36.

45. Light-Duty Vehicle Greenhouse Gas Emission Standards and Corporate Average Fuel Economy Standards, 75 Fed. Reg. 25,324, 25,327 (May 7, 2010) (to be codified at 40 C.F.R. pts. 85, 86 & 600; 49 C.F.R. pts. 531, 533 & 536).

46. Reconsideration of Interpretation of Regulations that Determine Pollutants Covered by Clean Air Act Permitting Programs, 75 Fed. Reg. 17,004 (Apr. 2, 2010).

47. PSD and Title V Permitting Guidance for Greenhouse Gases, 75 Fed. Reg. 70,254 (Nov. 17, 2010) (notice of availability and public comment period); U.S. ENVIRONMENTAL PROTECTION AGENCY, PSD AND TITLE V PERMITTING GUIDANCE FOR GREENHOUSE GASES (2010), *available at* http://www.eenews.net/assets/2010/11/10/document_gw_04.pdf.

48. Prevention of Significant Deterioration and Title V Greenhouse Gas Tailoring Rule, 75 Fed. Reg. 31,514 (June 3, 1010) (to be codified at 40 C.F.R. pts. 50, 51, 70, & 71).

49. PSD and Title V Permitting Guidance for Greenhouse Gases, *supra* note 47, at 22.

50. Light-Duty Vehicle Greenhouse Gas Emission Standards and Corporate Average Fuel Economy Standards, *supra* note 45, at 25,326–27.

51. Energy Policy and Conservation Act of 1975, 42 U.S.C. §§ 32901–32919.

52. *Id.* § 32902(a).

53. *Id.* § 32902(f).

54. 40 C.F.R. § 531.5(a).

55. 42 U.S.C. 39, § 32908(b)(1)A).

56. 40 C.F.R. § 533.5(a), Table IV.

57. U.S. ENVTL. PROTECTION AGENCY, LIGHT-DUTY AUTOMOTIVE TECHNOLOGY, CARBON DIOXIDE EMISSIONS, AND FUEL ECONOMY TRENDS: 1975 THROUGH 2009—EXECUTIVE SUMMARY, at i (Nov. 2009), *available at* http://www.epa.gov/oms/cert/mpg/fetrends/420s09001.pdf (last visited Mar. 9, 2011).

58. H.R. 6 §102; *see also* CRS REPORT FOR CONGRESS, ENERGY INDEPENDENCE AND SECURITY ACT OF 2007: A SUMMARY OF MAJOR PROVISIONS (Dec. 21, 2007), CRS-4-5, *available at* http://energy.senate.gov/public/_files/RL342941.pdf.

59. *Id.*

60. Section 202(a) of the Clean Air Act states: EPA "shall by regulation prescribe . . . standards applicable to the emission of any air pollutant from any class or classes of new motor vehicles or new motor vehicle engines, which in his judgment cause, or contribute to, air pollution which may reasonably be anticipated to endanger public health or welfare." 42 U.S.C. § 7521(a).

61. Light-Duty Vehicle Greenhouse Gas Emission Standards and Corporate Average Fuel Economy Standards, *supra* note 45.

62. U.S. ENVTL. PROTECTION AGENCY, TRANSPORTATION AND CLIMATE: REGULATIONS & STANDARDS, http://www.epa.gov/oms/climate/regulations.htm (last visited Feb. 7, 2011).

63. 2017 and Later Model Year Light Duty Vehicle GHG Emissions and CAFE Standards; Notice of Intent, 75 Fed. Reg. 62,739 (Oct. 13, 2010).

64. Greenhouse Gas Emission Standards and Fuel Efficiency Standards for Medium- and Heavy-Duty Engines and Vehicles, 75 Fed. Reg. 74,152 (Nov. 30, 2010).

65. Barack H. Obama, Memorandum for the Secretary of Transportation et al., Improving Energy Security, American Competitiveness and Job Creation, and Environmental Protection Through a Transformation of Our Nation's Fleet of Cars and Trucks (May 21, 2010), *available at* http://www.faqs.org/periodicals/201005/2053837941.html.

66. Consumer Assistance to Recycle and Save Act of 2009, Pub. L. 111-32, 123 Stat. 1859 (June 24, 2009).

67. U.S. Dep't of Transportation, Report to Congress, Transportation's Role in Reducing U.S. Greenhouse Gas Emissions ES-5 (Apr. 2010), *available at* http://ntl.bts.gov/lib/32000/32700/32779/DOT_Climate_Change_Report_-_April_2010_-_Volume_1_and_2.pdf.

68. The trade-in vehicles had to be less than twenty-five years old, in drivable condition, registered and insured for the prior twelve months, and with a fuel efficiency rating of 18 miles per gallon or less. 49 C.F.R. § 599.300.

69. *Id.*

70. Consumer Assistance to Recycle and Save Act of 2009, *supra* note 66, § 1302(b).

71. 49 U.S.C. 32901 (2009).

72. U.S. Dep't of Transportation, Consumer Assistance to Recycle and Save Act of 2009: Report to the House Comm. on Energy and Commerce, the Senate Comm. on Commerce, Science, and Transportation and the House and Senate Committees on Appropriations—Report to Congress 1 (Dec. 2009), *available at* http://www.cars.gov/files/official-information/CARS-Report-to-Congress.pdf [hereinafter Report to Congress].

73. The Department of Transportation reported that the CARS program resulted in 690,114 dealer transactions submitted, requesting a total of $2.85 billion in rebates. *Id* at 2.

74. A 2010 analysis shows the program did not decrease sales in the long term but, instead, generated "halo sales" of another quarter of a million vehicles. PR Newswire, *Maritz Research Findings: Cash for Clunkers Created Significantly More Incremental Automobile Sales Than Previously Reported,* (2010), http://www.prnewswire.com/news-releases/maritz-research-findings-cash-for-clunkers-created-significantly-more-incremental-automobile-sales-than-previously-reported-87118097.html (last visited Dec. 5, 2010).

75. Report to Congress, *supra* note 72, at 56.

76. *Id.*

77. The Department of Transportation estimated a 58 percent increase in the fuel economy of the cars purchased under CARS compared to those traded in. *See id.* at 43. Moreover, a University of Michigan study concluded that the CARS program improved the average fuel economy of all vehicles purchased by 0.6 mpg in July 2009 and by 0.7 mpg in August 2009. Michael Sivak & Brandon Schoettle, Univ. of Mich. Transportation Research Inst., The Effect of the "Cash for Clunkers" Program on the Overall Fuel Economy of Purchased New Vehicles (Sept. 2009), *available at* http://deepblue.lib.umich.edu/bitstream/2027.42/64025/1/102323.pdf.

78. Shoshanna M. Lenski, *The Impact of 'Cash for Clunkers' on Greenhouse Gas Emissions: A Life Cycle Perspective*, 5 Envtl. Research Letters 044003 (2010). NHTSA estimated that the increased fuel efficiency will result in a fuel consumption reduction of 33 million gallons annually (or 824 million gallons in twenty-five years), which will lead to greenhouse gas emissions reductions of 9 million metric tons in twenty-five years. Report to Congress, *supra* note 72, at 2.

79. Energy Independence and Security Act of 2007, 42 U.S.C. §§ 6291–6309.

80. *Id.* § 6293. For showerheads, faucets, water closets, and urinals, the test procedures are required to cover water use. *Id.* § 6293(b).

81. *Id.* § 6294(c)(1).

82. *Id.* § 6295.

83. *Id.* § 6295(o)(2)(A).

84. 10 C.F.R. § 430.32. There are also water conservation standards for water closets and urinals, which do not ordinarily involve heating or cooling of water. *Id.* § 430.32(q) & (r).

85. *See, e.g.*, Energy Conservation Program: Energy Conservation Standards for Residential Water Heaters, Direct Heating Equipment, and Pool Heaters, 75 Fed. Reg. 20,112 (Apr. 16, 2010).

86. 26 U.S.C. §§ 38(b)(24) & 45M(a).

87. Energy Conservation Program: Energy Conservation Standards and Test Procedures for General Service Fluorescent Lamps and Incandescent Reflector Lamps, 74 Fed. Reg. 34,080 (July 14, 2009).

88. Eric A. Taub, *LED Bulbs Strong Enough for Reading Are Imminent*, N.Y. TIMES, May 17, 2010, at B8.

89. 42 U.S.C. § 6297(d)(1).

90. U.S. DEP'T OF ENERGY, APPLIANCES & COMMERCIAL EQUIPMENT STANDARDS: STATE PETITIONS, http://www1.eere.energy.gov/buildings/appliance_standards/state_petitions.html#ca (last visited Feb. 7, 2011).

91. 42 U.S.C. §§ 6311–6317.

92. 10 C.F.R. pt 431.

93. MAX NEUBAUER ET AL., AM. COUNCIL FOR AN ENERGY-EFFICIENT ECONOMY & APPLIANCE STANDARDS AWARENESS PROJECT, KA-BOOM! THE POWER OF APPLIANCE STANDARDS: OPPORTUNITIES FOR NEW FEDERAL APPLIANCE AND EQUIPMENT STANDARDS 9 (2009), *available at* http://www.aceee.org/sites/default/files/publications/researchreports/a091.pdf (projecting reduction for 2010).

94. *Id.*

95. President Barack Obama, Memorandum for the Secretary of Energy: Appliance Efficiency Standards, 74 Fed. Reg. 6,537 (Feb. 9, 2009).

96. Consent Decree, New York v. Bodman, Nos. 05 Civ. 7807 (JES) & 05 Civ. 7808 (JES) (S.D.N.Y. Nov. 6, 2006), *available at* http://www.ag.ca.gov/globalwarming/pdf/2-27-08 consent_decree_NYvBodman.pdf.

97. Memorandum for the Secretary of Energy, *supra* note 95, at 6,537.

98. Thomas G. Echikson, *Upping the Ante on Energy Efficiency Standards*, LAW 360 (Apr. 23, 2010) (paper copy on file with Professor Dernbach).

99. Guidance on Energy-Efficiency Enforcement Regulations, 74 Fed. Reg. 52,793, 52,794 (Oct. 14, 2009).

100. Grace Period From Enforcement of Energy-Efficiency Certification for Residential Products, 74 Fed. Reg. 65,105 (Dec. 9, 2009).

101. Echikson, *supra* note 98.

102. Revisions to Energy Efficiency Enforcement Regulations, 75 Fed. Reg. 25,121 (May 7, 2010).

103. U.S. ENVTL. PROTECTION AGENCY & U.S. DEP'T OF ENERGY, ENERGY STAR, HISTORY OF ENERGY STAR, http://www.energystar.gov/index.cfm?c=about.ab_history (last visited Feb. 7, 2011).

104. Energy Policy Act of 2005, Pub. L. No. 109-58, § 131, 119 Stat. 594, 620 (2005) (codified at 42 U.S.C. § 6294a).

105. *Id.*

106. GOVERNMENT ACCOUNTABILITY OFFICE, ENERGY STAR PROGRAM: COVERT TESTING SHOWS THE ENERGY STAR PROGRAM CERTIFICATION PROCESS IS VULNERABLE TO FRAUD AND ABUSE 1 (2010), *available at* http://www.gao.gov/new.items/d10470.pdf.

107. U.S. ENVTL. PROTECTION AGENCY & U.S. DEP'T OF ENERGY, ENERGY STAR, ENERGY STAR OVERVIEW OF 2009 ACHIEVEMENTS 1, *available at* http://www.energystar.gov/ia/partners/annualreports/2009_achievements.pdf.

108. *Id.* (191 billion kWh saved in 2009 versus 59 billion kWh saved in 2000).

109. *Id.* at 2.

110. 10 U.S.C. § 2915(e)(2)(A).

111. 42 U.S.C. § 15841.

112. 15 U.S.C. § 657h(b)(2) & 42 U.S.C. § 6307(d).

113. 40 U.S.C. § 3313(d) & 42 U.S.C. § 8259b.

114. 42 U.S.C. § 17091.

115. *Id.* § 6293(b).

116. *Id.* § 15821. *See also* U.S. DEP'T OF ENERGY, REBATES, TAX CREDITS, & FINANCING, http://www.energysavers.gov/financial/70020.html (last visited Feb. 6, 2011).

117. U.S. DEP'T OF ENERGY, REBATES FOR ENERGY STAR® APPLIANCES, http://www.energysavers.gov/financial/70020.html (last viewed Feb. 6, 2011).

118. 42 U.S.C. §§ 6832(15), 6833(a).

119. *Id.* at §§ 6832(16), 6833(b).

120. *Id.* at §§ 6833(a)(5), (b)(2).

121. *Id.* at § 6833(e).

122. Pew Center on Global Climate Change, Residential Building Energy Codes, http://www.pewclimate.org/what_s_being_done/in_the_states/res_energy_codes.cfm (last visited Feb. 7, 2011).

123. Pew Center on Global Climate Change, Commercial Building Energy Codes, http://www.pewclimate.org/what_s_being_done/in_the_states/comm_energy_codes.cfm (last visited Feb. 7, 2011).

124. 26 U.S.C. § 25C.

125. *Id.* § 136.

126. Energy Policy Act of 2005, Pub. L. No. 1009-58, Aug. 8, 2005, 119 Stat. 594 (codified as 42 U.S.C. § 15801). *See also* IR-2006-32, Treasury and IRS Provide Guidance on Energy Credit to Home Builders (Feb. 21, 2006), http://www.irs.gov/newsroom/article/0,,id=154658,00.html.

127. 42 U.S.C. § 17082.

128. American Clean Energy and Security Act, H.R. 2454, 111th Cong. § 304(a) & (b) (passed by House of Representatives June 26, 2009).

129. U.S. Envtl. Protection Agency & U.S. Dep't of Energy, How New Homes Earn the Energy Star, http://www.energystar.gov/index.cfm?c=new_homes.nh_verification_process (last visited Feb. 7, 2011).

130. U.S. Envtl. Protection Agency & U.S. Dep't of Energy, Energy Star® Overview of 2009 Achievements 2 (2010), *available at* http://www.energystar.gov/ia/partners/annual reports/2009_achievements.pdf. Energy Star designs for about one hundred commercial building designs were approved in 2009. *Id.*

131. U.S. Dep't of Energy, 2009 Buildings Energy Data Book 2–24 & 3–18 (2009), *available at* http://buildingsdatabook.eren.doe.gov/docs/DataBooks/2009_BEDB_Updated.pdf.

132. Marilyn A. Brown et al., Oak Ridge Nat'l Laboratory, Pew Center on Global Climate Change, Towards a Climate-Friendly Built Environment 14 (June 2005), *available at* http://www.pewclimate.org/docUploads/Buildings_FINAL.pdf.

133. 26 U.S.C. § 25C(c)(1) (roofs), 26 U.S.C. § 25D(d)(5)(B)(ii) (geothermal heat pumps), 26 U.S.C. § 45L(c)(3)(B) (manufactured homes).

134. U.S. Envtl. Protection Agency & U.S. Dep't of Energy, Home Improvement: Improve Your Home's Energy Efficiency with ENERGY STAR, http://www.energystar.gov/index.cfm?c=home_improvement.hm_improvement_index (last visited Feb 7, 2011); Energy Star Overview of 2009 Achievements, *supra* note 130, at 2.

135. 26 U.S.C. § 179D.

136. Middle Class Task Force & Council on Environmental Quality, Recovery Through Retrofit 1 (Oct. 2009), *available at* http://www.whitehouse.gov/assets/documents/Recovery_Through_Retrofit_Final_Report.pdf.

137. *Id.*

138. U.S. Dep't of Energy, BetterBuildings, http://www.eere.energy.gov/betterbuildings/ (last visited Feb. 7, 2011).

139. H. R. 5019, 111th Cong. (2010); Home Star, RESNET Conference Presentation, Creating Jobs & Delivering Energy Efficiency (Feb. 24, 2010), *available at* www.resnet.us/conference/2010/presentations/HOME_STAR.pdf (last viewed Feb. 7, 2011).

140. Practical Energy and Climate Plan Act, S. 3464, 111th Cong. § 222(a) (2010).

141. *Id.* § 222(c).

142. Envtl. Law Centre, University of Victoria, Conserving the Planet Without Hurting Low-Income Families: Options for Fair Energy-Efficiency Programs for Low-Income Households (2010), *available at* http://www.elc.uvic.ca/press/documents/Conserving-planet-without-hurting-low-income-families-April2010-FINAL.pdf.

143. Towards a Climate-Friendly Built Environment, *supra* note 132, at 50.

144. 42 U.S.C. § 6861(b). For the statutory authority for the program, see 42 U.S.C. §§ 6862–6873.

145. U.S. Dep't of Energy, Weatherization Assistance Program, http://www1.eere.energy.gov/wip/wap.html (last visited Feb. 7, 2011).

146. Towards a Climate-Friendly Built Environment, *supra* note 132, at 50–51.

147. U.S. Dep't of Energy, Weatherization Services, *supra* note 145.

148. Office of Inspector General, U.S. Dep't of Energy, Special Report: Progress in Implementing the Department of Energy's Weatherization Assistance Program Under the American Recovery and Reinvestment Act 1 (2010), *available at* http://www.ig.energy.gov/documents/OAS-RA-10-04.pdf.

149. *Id.* at 2.

150. *Id.* at 3–5.

151. American Recovery and Reinvestment Act of 2009, *supra* note 31.

152. *Id.* at 123 Stat. 203. Other allocations in the Act, which are reported to total $8.4 billion, support related efficiency measures. *See, e.g.*, s.wsj.net/public/resources/documents/WSJ_Stimulus_021209.pdf (last visited Feb. 7, 2011).

153. American Recovery and Reinvestment Act of 2009, *supra* note 31, at 123 Stat. 138.

154. Press Release, Office of the Press Secretary, The White House, President Obama Sets Greenhouse Gas Emissions Reduction Target for Federal Operations (Jan. 29, 2010), http://www.whitehouse.gov/the-press-office/president-obama-sets-greenhouse-gas-emissions-reduction-target-federal-operations.

155. 42 U.S.C. § 6834(a)(2)(a) (referencing Council of American Building Officials (CABO) Model Energy Code, 1992 (for residential buildings) and American Society of Heating, Refrigerating and Air-Conditioning Engineers (ASHRAE) Standard 90.1-1989 (for commercial buildings)).

156. *Id.* § 6834(a)(2) & 6834(a)(3)(A)(i).

157. *Id.* § 6834(a)(3)(D)(i)(I).

158. *Id.* § 6834(a)(3)(D)(i)(III).

159. Energy Efficiency and Sustainable Design Standards for New Federal Buildings, 75 Fed. Reg. 29,933 (May 28, 2010).

160. Exec. Order No. 13,514, § 1, 74 Fed. Reg. 52,217, 52,217 (Oct. 8, 2009).

161. *Id.* § 2(a) & (b).

162. *Id.* § 2(d)–(f).

163. *Id.* § 2(h).

164. Exec. Order 13,514, 74 Fed. Reg. 52,117 at § 8(c) (Oct. 8, 2009).

165. Richard J. Campbell et al., Congressional Research Service, Renewable Energy and Energy Efficiency Program Incentives: A Summary of Federal Programs 6–13 (2009).

166. *Id.* at 15–16.

167. Rocky Mountain Institute, Factor Ten Engineering, http://www.10xe.org/ (last visited Feb. 7, 2011).

168. Trip Pollard, *Transportation: Challenges and Choices, in* Agenda for a Sustainable America, *supra* note 10, at 365, 368.

169. U.S. Envtl. Protection Agency, HUD-DOT-EPA Interagency Partnership for Sustainable Communities, http://www.epa.gov/dced/partnership/index.html (last visited Feb. 7, 2011).

170. Roberta F. Mann, *The (Not So) Little House on the Prairie: The Hidden Costs of the Home Mortgage Interest Deduction*, 32 Ariz. St. L.J. 1347 (2000). See also Jonathan D. Weiss, *Local Governance, in* Stumbling Toward Sustainability 683, 689 (John C. Dernbach ed., 2009) (The "federal mortgage deduction favors wealthier home buyers over those who are less wealthy, renters, multi-family property owners, and people who rehabilitate existing structures.").

171. John C. Dernbach & Scott Bernstein, *Pursuing Sustainable Communities: Looking Back, Looking Forward*, 35 Urb. Law. 495, 505 (2003).

172. Pub. L. 105-34 (Aug. 5, 1997), § 312, 111 Stat. 836-841 (codified at 26 U.S.C. § 121).

173. James M. McElfish, Jr. & Eric Feldman, Environmental Law Institute, Linking Tax Law and Sustainable Urban Development: The Taxpayer Relief Act of 1997 (1998).

174. Environmental Law Institute, Estimating U.S. Government Subsidies to Energy Sources: 2002–2008 (Sept. 2009), *available at* http://www.elistore.org/Data/products/

d19_07.pdf; Roberta Mann, *Subsidies, Tax Policy and Technological Innovation, in* GLOBAL CLIMATE CHANGE AND U.S. LAW 565, 576–83 (Michael Gerrard ed., 2007); DAVID SANDALOW, FREEDOM FROM OIL: HOW THE NEXT PRESIDENT CAN END THE UNITED STATES' OIL ADDICTION 125 & n.11 (2007) (describing "large literature on externalities related to oil use, as well as on government subsidies that promote oil use"); Doug Koplow & John Dernbach, *Federal Fossil Fuel Subsidies and Greenhouse Gas Emissions: A Case Study of Increasing Transparency for Fiscal Policy,* 26 ANN. REV. ENERGY & ENV'T 361 (2001).

175. *Id.*

176. John C. Dernbach & the Widener University Law School Seminar on Energy Efficiency, *Stabilizing and Then Reducing U.S. Energy Consumption: Legal and Policy Tools for Efficiency and Conservation,* 37 ENVTL. L. REP. (Envtl. L. Inst.) 10,003, 10,023 (2007).

177. ROBERT N. STAVINS, THE HAMILTON PROJECT, THE BROOKINGS INST., PROPOSAL FOR A U.S. CAP-AND-TRADE SYSTEM TO ADDRESS GLOBAL CLIMATE CHANGE: A SENSIBLE AND PRACTICAL APPROACH TO REDUCE GREENHOUSE GAS EMISSIONS 30 (July 22, 2007), *available at* http://ksghome.harvard.edu/~rstavins/Papers/Stavins_Hamilton_Working_Paper_on_Cap-and-Trade.pdf.

178. *Id.*

179. Thomas Dietz et al., *Household Actions Can Provide a Behavioral Wedge to Rapidly Reduce U.S. Carbon Emissions,* 106 PROC. NAT'L ACAD. SCI. 18,452, 18,453 (2009).

180. John C. Dernbach & Donald A. Brown, *The Ethical Responsibility to Reduce Energy Consumption,* 37 HOFSTRA L. REV. 985 (2009).

181. David M. Driesen, *Sustainable Development and Market Liberalism's Shotgun Wedding: Emissions Trading Under the Kyoto Protocol,* 83 IND. L.J. 21, 52–57 (2008).

182. Marc B. Mihaly, *Recovery of a Lost Decade (or is it Three?): Developing the Capacity in Government Necessary to Reduce Carbon Emissions and Administer Energy Markets,* 88 OR. L. REV. 405 (2009).

183. These additional measures may not capture all of the efficiency improvements that are possible. RACHEL GOLD ET AL., ENERGY EFFICIENCY IN THE AMERICAN CLEAN ENERGY AND SECURITY ACT OF 2009: IMPACTS OF CURRENT PROVISIONS AND OPPORTUNITIES TO ENHANCE THE LEGISLATION, ACEEE Report EO96 (Sept. 2009), *available at* http://cdn.publicinterestnetwork.org/assets/fSkoF8k05pgplRHQJpvbjA/FINAL-ACEEE-Report.pdf.

184. Save American Energy Act, S. 485, 111th Cong. (2009); H.R. 1889, 111th Cong. (2009).

185. John A. "Skip" Laitner et al., *The National Energy Efficiency Resource Standard as an Energy Productivity Tool* (Feb. 1, 2009), *available at* http://www.aceee.org/energy/national/EERS_article09.pdf. *See also* Laura A. Furrey, *Laying the Foundation for Implementing a Federal Energy Efficiency Resource Standard* (2009), *available at* http://www.aceee.org/files/pdf/white-paper/EERS_article09.pdf.

186. H.R. 1889 §2(a) (adding §610(a) to Public Utility Regulatory Polices Act of 1978 (PURPA)).

187. *See, e.g., id.* (adding §610(d)(2) to PURPA).

188. PEW CENTER FOR GLOBAL CLIMATE CHANGE, ENERGY EFFICIENCY STANDARDS AND TARGETS, http://www.pewclimate.org/what_s_being_done/in_the_states/efficiency_resource.cfm (last visited Feb. 7, 2010).

189. *Energy Efficiency Resource Standards: Hearing on S. 548 Before S. Comm. on Energy and Natural Resources,* 111th Cong. (Apr. 22, 2009) (statement by Steven Nadel, Exec. Director, American Council for an Energy Efficient Economy).

190. H.R. 2454 §272.

191. *Id.* §131.

192. *Id.* §§132 & 133. A REEP program was also authorized in S. 1733 §164.

193. John C. Dernbach et al., *Making the States Full Partners in a National Climate Change Effort: A Necessary Element for Sustainable Economic Development,* 40 ENVTL. L. REP. (Envtl. L. Inst.) 10,597 (2010).

194. H.R. 2454 § 185.

195. *Id.* § 214.

196. H.R. 2454, § 215 (state residential water efficiency and conservation incentives program); S. 1733 §§ 141–143 (authorizing financial incentives for residential consumers).

197. H.R. 2454 § 841; S. 1733 § 831.

198. S. 1733 § 831(e)(6)(C)(iv)(V)(cc).

199. H.R. 2454 § 274.

200. Paul C. Stern & Gerald T. Gardner, *Psychological Research and Energy Policy*, AMERICAN PSYCHOLOGIST, Apr. 1981, at 332, 336.

201. *See, e.g.*, Hope M. Babcock, *Assuming Personal Responsibility for Improving the Environment: Moving Toward a New Environmental Norm*, 33 HARV. ENVTL. L. REV. 117, 121 (2009); Michael P. Vandenbergh & Ann C. Steinemann, *The Carbon-Neutral Individual*, 82 N.Y.U. L. REV. 1673 (2007); John C. Dernbach, *Overcoming the Behavioral Impetus for Greater Energy Consumption*, 20 PAC. MCGEORGE GLOBAL BUS. & DEV. L.J. 15 (2007).

202. United Nations Framework Convention on Climate Change, art. 3, U.N. Doc. A/AC.237/18 (1992), *reprinted in* 31 I.L.M. 849 (1992).

203. *Id.* art. 4.1(b).

204. *Id.* preamble (penultimate paragraph).

205. Kyoto Protocol to the United Nations Framework Convention on Climate Change, art 3.1, Dec. 10, 1997, U.N. Doc. FCCC/CP/197/L.7/Add. 1, reprinted in 37 I.L.M. 22 (1998).

206. These are Joint Implementation (*id.* art. 6), the Clean Development Mechanism (*id.* art. 12), and emissions trading (*id.* art. 17).

207. *Id.* art. 2(a)(i).

208. Conference of the Parties of the United Nations Framework Convention on Climate Change, Copenhagen Accord, FCCC/CP/2009/L.7 (Dec. 18, 2009), *available at* http://unfccc .int/resource/docs/2009/cop15/eng/l07.pdf.

209. United Nations Framework Convention on Climate Change, Appendix I—Quantified economy-wide emissions targets for 2020, http://unfccc.int/home/items/5264.php (last visited Feb. 7, 2011) (developed country commitments); United Nations Framework Convention on Climate Change, Appendix II—Nationally appropriate mitigation actions of developing country Parties, http://unfccc.int/home/items/5265.php (last visited Feb. 7, 2011) (developing country commitments).

210. Kelly Levin & Rob Bradley, *Comparability of Annex I Emission Reduction Pledges* 2 (World Resources Inst. Working Paper 2010), *available at* http://pdf.wri.org/working_papers/ comparability_of_annex1_emission_reduction_pledges_2010-02-01.pdf.

211. Letter from S. U. Wei to Yvo de Boer (Jan. 28, 2010), *available at* http://unfccc.int/files/ meetings/application/pdf/chinacphaccord_app2.pdf.

212. Letter from Rajani Ranjan Rashmi to Yvo de Boer (Jan. 30, 2010), *available at* http:// unfccc.int/files/meetings/application/pdf/indiacphaccord_app2.pdf.

213. Letter from Embassy of the Federated Republic of Brazil to Yvo de Boer (Jan. 29, 2010), *available at* http://unfccc.int/files/meetings/application/pdf/brazilcphaccord_app2.pdf.

214. INT'L ENERGY AGENCY, WORLD ENERGY OUTLOOK 2009 EXECUTIVE SUMMARY 7–8 (2009), *available at* http://www.iea.org/Textbase/npsum/weo2009sum.pdf.

215. ORGANIZATION FOR ECONOMIC COOPERATION & DEVELOPMENT, INTERIM REPORT OF THE GREEN GROWTH STRATEGY: IMPLEMENTING OUR COMMITMENT FOR A SUSTAINABLE FUTURE 48 (2010), *available at* http://www.oecd.org/dataoecd/42/46/45312720.pdf.

216. INTERGOVERNMENTAL PANEL ON CLIMATE CHANGE, CONTRIBUTION OF WORKING GROUP III TO THE FOURTH ASSESSMENT REPORT OF THE INTERGOVERNMENTAL PANEL ON CLIMATE CHANGE, CLIMATE CHANGE 2007: MITIGATION 30 (Bert Metz et al. eds. 2007).

217. *Id.*

218. *Id.*

219. INT'L ENERGY AGENCY, ABOUT THE IEA, http://www.iea.org/about/index.asp (last visited June 3, 2010).

220. Int'l Energy Agency, Worldwide Trends in Energy Use and Efficiency (2008), *available at* http://www.iea.org/Papers/2008/cd_energy_efficiency_policy/1-Croos-sectoral/1-Indicators_2008.pdf; Int'l Energy Agency, Energy Efficiency Policy Recommendations (2008), *available at* http://www.iea.org/Papers/2008/cd_energy_efficiency_policy/1-Croos-sectoral/1-G8_EE_2008.pdf.

221. Canada et al., Declaration: International Partnership for Energy Efficiency Cooperation [IPEEC] (2009), *available at* http://www.enecho.meti.go.jp/topics/g8/ipeecsta_eng.pdf; Secretary Chu Joins with World Leaders to Sign International Partnership for Energy Efficiency Cooperation (May 24, 2009), http://www.energy.gov/news/7420.htm.

222. Int'l Partnership for Energy Efficiency Cooperation holds first global policy meeting (May 12, 2010), http://www.newenergyworldnetwork.com/renewable-energy-news/by_technology/energy_efficiency/international-partnership-for-energy-efficiency-cooperation-holds-first-global-policy-meeting.html.

223. Int'l Organization for Standardization, About ISO, http://www.iso.org/iso/about.htm (last visited June 3, 2010).

224. Int'l Organization for Standardization, ISO 23045:2008, http://www.iso.org/iso/catalogue_detail.htm?csnumber=45694 (last visited Feb. 7, 2011).

225. Edwin Piñero, *Future ISO 50001 for Energy Management Systems*, ISO Focus, Sept. 2009, at 18, *available at* http://www.iso.org/iso/pinero_focus_sept09.pdf.

226. Council of the European Union, Brussels European Council 8/9 March 2007: Presidency Conclusions para. 6, 7224/1/07, REV 1 (2007).

227. Thanks to Rob Altenburg for the calculation.

228. European Commission, Action Plan for Energy Efficiency: Realizing the Potential 3, {SEC(2006)1173}, {SEC(2006)1174}, & {SEC(2006)1175}.

229. Council and European Parliament Directive 2006/32/EC, arts. 4.1 & 4.2, 2006 O.J. (L 114) 64 (E.C.).

230. *Id.* arts. 9, 10, 12.1, & 13.3.

231. Commission Staff Working Document, *Synthesis of the Complete Assessment of all 27 National Energy Efficiency Action Plans as Required by Directive 2006/32/EC on Energy End-use Efficiency and Energy Services* 51–52, SEC(2009)889 final (June 23, 2009).

232. Council and European Parliament Directive 2002/91/EC, arts. 5, 6, & 7, 2003 O.J. (L 1) 65 (E.C.).

233. Wouter Vandorpe, *Recent Energy Efficiency Developments at the EU Level, in* EU Energy Law and Policy Issues 245, 255–64 (Bram Delvaux et al. eds., 2008).

234. Council and European Parliament Directive 2010/31/EU, arts. 7, 9–20, 27, 2010 O.J. (L 153) 13 (E.C.).

235. European Commission Directorate-General for Energy and Transport, *EU Energy Policy for Buildings after the recast* (2009), *available at* http://ec.europa.eu/energy/efficiency/doc/buildings/presentation_general_short.pdf.

chapter three

State and Municipal Energy Efficiency Laws

Alexandra B. Klass and John K. Harting

Introduction

While the federal government has now begun efforts to address climate change on a national level, states and local governments have historically been and still remain key players in efforts to achieve measurable reductions in greenhouse gas (GHG) emissions and energy use. Despite the inherent difficulties associated with states and local governments attempting to address a problem that is national and international in scope, these units of government have continued to take the lead, responding to citizen demand by instituting progressive policies to address energy use, energy efficiency, and reduction of GHG emissions.

As of October 2010, all fifty states had adopted some law or policy addressing energy efficiency and/or climate change.[1] States have used a wide variety of policy options in their attempts to increase efficiency from traditional sources of energy production and use while also reducing GHG emissions. These include energy efficiency tax incentives, rebates for purchasing energy-efficient appliances, utility recovery for energy efficiency expenditures, incentives for electric utilities to pursue energy efficiency, energy efficiency resource standards (EERS), energy-efficient building codes for both private and public buildings, energy audit requirements, and mandatory appliance efficiency standards. Similar to how a money manager invests in multiple stocks or funds, states often employ a battery of these options to achieve their goals. For example, Virginia has enacted energy standards for public buildings, building energy codes, a renewable portfolio standard, construction and design policies for renewable energy, and mandatory green power purchasing.

As a procedural matter, states enact energy generation and use legislation (which generally encompasses energy efficiency) in order to address issues that are either anticipated to arise in the future or that have already arisen. Besides the ever-present ecological and societal problems presented by global climate change, other examples of such issues include existing energy shortages, such as the rolling blackouts that have occurred in California, rising energy costs, and increasing demand for energy production. Once proposed, the bills are generally submitted to state legislative committees; however, the specific committee to which a bill is submitted can vary greatly from state to state. Such legislative committees include commerce, finance, environment, or even ways and means.

Moreover, in the area of appliance efficiency, some states, particularly California, are becoming more aggressive in setting efficiency standards for appliances not yet regulated at the federal level. For instance, in September 2009, the California Energy Commission proposed a new rule (Docket # 09-AAER-1C) aimed at improving the energy efficiency of flat-screen televisions. The rule would go into effect in two phases (referred to as "Tiers"). Tier I would result in an estimated 33 percent energy savings from affected televisions, while Tier II would result in estimated savings of 49 percent. As expected, both electronics producers and consumer groups opposed the proposed rule based on fears that the associated cost increase would be too substantial. After incorporating comments and suggestions, the agency ultimately adopted the rule, which took effect in January 2011.[2]

As discussed in greater detail later in this chapter, such action by one state generally creates a ripple effect. This ripple effect begins when other states adopt the same or similar appliance efficiency standards and often ends with product manufacturers seeking a national standard that preempts state standards. Sometimes this process results in greater energy efficiency for the particular product nationwide; other times it leads to a more relaxed national standard that preempts state efforts to obtain greater energy efficiency in the product. In a partial response to industry concerns regarding economies, scale, and uniformity, states are beginning to work together to set the same or similar standards to increase uniformity and reduce redundancy. The most striking example of this effort is the Multi-State Appliance Standards Collaborative, which includes California, Connecticut, Oregon, Rhode Island, and Washington, all of which have adopted the same or similar standards to those of California for certain appliances such as DVD players and commercial refrigerators. Meanwhile though, at least under current federal law, federal preemption stands as an obstacle for states that wish to take the lead on increasing energy efficiency through the regulation of appliances.

This chapter will review the range of primary policy tools states and local governments have adopted as part of their response to energy use and global climate change, with a specific focus on energy efficiency. It will describe the overall structure of such policies and provide examples of their implementation. Chapters 2, 7, 8, and 13 of this book describe the use of some of these policy tools at the federal level.

Energy Efficiency Tax Incentives

Various tax incentives are used by state and local governments to increase energy efficiency. Many of them apply to renewable energy sources as well. Tax incentives for renewables are discussed in further detail in chapter 7. Energy efficiency tax incentives include incentives relating to personal taxes, corporate taxes, sales taxes, and property taxes.

Personal Energy Efficiency Tax Incentives

Personal taxes aimed at improving energy efficiency can take the form of either personal income tax credits or deductions, as both have the same goal of reducing expenses associated with purchasing and installing energy efficiency systems and equipment. According to the Database of State Incentives for Renewables and Efficiency (DSIRE), as of October 2010, fourteen states currently provide personal tax incentives for energy efficiency.[3] For example, Idaho residents with homes built or under construction before 1976, or who had a building permit issued before 1976, qualify for an income tax deduction for 100 percent of the costs of installing new insulation. However, any insulation added must be in addition to—not a replacement of—existing insulation. The amount charged for labor is also deductible.[4]

While the eligible technologies and the percentage of the credit or deduction vary by state, in most cases there is a maximum limit on the dollar amount of the credit or deduction. For example, Kentucky allows for a 30 percent state income tax credit for taxpayers who install certain energy efficiency measures on their principal residence or residential rental property. This credit applies to efficient appliances such as water heaters, heat pumps, and central air conditioners, along with weatherization measures such as windows, storm doors, and added insulation. The credit for each improvement contains a cap, such as one hundred dollars for insulation.[5]

Corporate Energy Efficiency Tax Incentives

While in recent years the federal government has begun to offer corporate tax incentives for improved energy efficiency, nine states currently provide corporate tax incentives for energy efficiency in the form of tax credits, deductions, or exemptions.[6] Depending on the state, tax incentives are available for corporate actions such as the purchase and installation of eligible energy efficiency equipment or the construction of green buildings. However, just like personal tax incentives, states that have chosen to implement corporate tax incentives have also placed restrictions on the amounts by which a corporation may benefit. In some cases, such restrictions are based on the minimum amount of economic resources that must be invested in a project and also include a maximum limit on the monetary amount of the deduction or credit.

For example, Georgia provides credits for energy efficiency systems installed on property used for any purpose other than single-family residential. The maximum credit available is equal to 35 percent of the cost of the system (including installation), and is calculated according to the following options: $0.60/square foot for lighting retrofit projects, $1.80/square foot for energy-efficient products installed during construction, or a flat 35 percent of a renewable energy system. The credit is capped at different levels ranging from $100,000 to $500,000, depending upon the technology used.[7] New Mexico has also devised a corporate tax credit for sustainable buildings that applies to both commercial and residential buildings. Commercial buildings must be registered and certified by the U.S. Green Building Council at LEED Silver or higher for new construction, existing buildings, core and shell, or commercial interiors. The amount of the credit varies in accordance with the square footage of the building and the level of certification achieved.[8]

Energy Efficiency–Based Sales Taxes

Ten states currently provide sales tax incentives for energy efficiency.[9] Such sales tax incentives generally provide consumers with an exemption from state sales tax (or sales and use tax) when they purchase energy-efficient appliances or other energy efficiency measures. For example, Connecticut enacted legislation exempting from state sales tax compact fluorescent light bulbs; certain residential weatherization products including programmable thermostats, window film, caulking, window and door weather strips, and insulation; water heater blankets; water heaters; natural gas and propane furnaces and boilers that meet the federal Energy Star standard; windows and doors that meet the federal Energy Star standard; oil furnaces and boilers that are not less than 84 percent efficient; and ground-source heat pumps that meet the minimum federal energy efficiency rating.[10]

States have also begun to implement "sales tax holidays," which are specific calendar days when certain energy-efficient products are exempt from sales tax. For instance, in 2009, Missouri began offering consumers a seven-day exemption from sales taxes on certain Energy Star-certified new appliances with purchase prices up to $1,500. The sales tax holiday will last from April 19 to April 25 each year for clothes washers and dryers, water heaters, trash compactors, furnaces, freezers, refrigerators, dishwashers, and conventional ovens, ranges, and stoves.[11]

Energy Efficiency–Based Property Taxes

Five states and five units of local government currently provide property tax incentives for energy efficiency.[12] These tax incentives, which include exemptions, exclusions, and credits, are all applied to a property owner's tax bill and operate by excluding the value of an energy-efficient system from the overall valuation of the property. For example, if a central air conditioning system that uses renewable energy costs more to install than a conventional air conditioning system, the additional cost of the energy-efficient system is excluded from the property's valuation. Arizona has created a similar property tax exemption for solar energy devices as well as for combined heat and power systems, and energy-efficient building components.[13] For assessment purposes, these appliances are deemed to add no value to the property.

Additionally, states are beginning to allow property tax incentives to apply to the added up-front costs associated with a green building. Some states have granted local taxing authorities the ability to choose whether to allow their own property tax incentive for energy conservation measures.[14] For example, Maryland's property tax code allows county governments the option of providing property tax credits for buildings equipped with solar, geothermal, or qualifying energy conservation devices.[15] The device must be used to heat or cool the structure, to generate electricity to be used in the structure, or to provide hot water for use in the structure.

Rebates for Purchasing Energy-Efficient Appliances

Similar to tax or other efficiency-based incentives, many states have begun to use rebate programs in further efforts to spur the sales of energy-efficient appliances and building materials. Local governments and individual utilities can also offer such rebates. DSIRE estimates that as of October 2010, there were 1,039 different energy efficiency–based rebate programs (along with an additional 443 rebate programs for renewable energy) in effect at varying state and local government levels throughout the country. Some states have relied upon local utilities to provide their own uniquely tailored rebates, thus increasing the total number of rebates offered. For instance, in Minnesota, 104 different local governments and utilities offer rebates in addition to two statewide programs. By contrast, other states such as Virginia (which has four statewide and two local rebates) have implemented fewer rebates, but such rebates generally apply statewide.

These programs commonly provide funding for rebates on purchases of energy-efficient appliances such as those that achieve certain Energy Star ratings. The Energy Star program is discussed in further detail in chapter 12. As noted above, utilities administer most rebate programs that support energy efficiency. While rebate amounts vary widely based on technology and program administrator, they have the potential to play a significant role in reducing total U.S. GHG emissions. That is because it is estimated that approximately 70 percent of the emissions generated in commercial, residential, and industrial buildings come from lighting, heating, cooling, and ventilation systems, and other appliances.[16]

Rebate programs have also greatly increased in use and visibility as a result of the State Energy Efficient Appliance Rebate Program, otherwise known as the "Cash for Clunkers Appliance" program.[17] This program, which was originally authorized under Section 124 of the Energy Policy Act of 2005, received $300 million in funding from the American Recovery and Reinvestment Act of 2009, to be divided among the states based on their population and used as rebates for consumers purchasing new Energy Star–rated appliances to replace older, outdated models. The law requires each state to design a rebate program that fits their citizen base and specifically choose the monetary value of the rebates they will provide and the appliances to which the rebates will apply. After designing their programs, the states submitted them to the Department of Energy (DOE) in October 2009 for approval. Once the programs were approved, the funding was provided. As an example of an approved program, Wisconsin, which received $5.4 million in funding, created rebates ranging from $25 for a dishwasher up to $150 for a water heater and $200 for a furnace or boiler.[18] The program went into effect in January 2010. Similarly, Arizona, which received $6.2 million for its program, designed rebates ranging from $75 to $425, which apply to dishwashers, washing machines, and refrigerators. The program, which began in March 2010, was expected to benefit over thirty thousand Arizona citizens.[19]

The popularity of such rebate programs has been mixed. For example, in Minnesota, which received $5 million for its program, the entire fund was gone within twenty-four hours of becoming available to the public.[20] Similarly, Iowa disposed of its entire $2.8 million in one day. However, after being available for over two months, Wisconsin had used only 20 percent of the $5.4 million it received, and New York and Michigan were forced to extend the duration of their programs in order to use the entirety of their funds.[21]

Utility Cost and Revenue Recovery for Energy Efficiency Expenditures

Just as it is important for corporations and individual consumers to be able to recover some of the costs associated with implementing energy efficiency measures, it is likewise important for utilities to recover similar costs. Accordingly, the ability of utilities to recover costs they incur in establishing renewable energy programs or through offering rebates on energy-efficient appliances has become a major focus for legislatures and regulators. This is due to the economic fact that because a utility's income increases proportionately with the level of electricity sold, traditional utility rate-making acts as a disincentive for utilities to provide energy efficiency programs for customers.[22]

Thus, state legislatures have found it necessary to enact cost recovery programs to address this problem and help to "align company financial objectives with societal energy resource objectives."[23] Examples of such cost recovery programs include tariff riders, rate case recovery, and system benefits charges.[24] "Tariff riders" are special rate schedules that create an additional rate charged to all customers used to fund demand-side energy conservation programs.[25] "Rate case recovery" allows utilities to include prudently incurred costs of management programs in the rates charged to customers.[26] "System benefits charges" are designed to fund certain public benefits such as renewable energy or energy efficiency programs that may be placed at risk in a competitive marketplace.[27]

However, research conducted by the American Council for an Energy-Efficient Economy (ACEEE) has also shown that while a *cost* recovery programs is a "necessary condition" for achieving supply-side energy efficiency, such cost recovery programs alone generally are not sufficient to align utility incentives and efficiency goals.[28] Rather, *revenue* recovery programs are also often required to achieve such an alignment.[29]

Historically, there were two options states could use to address lost revenues: (1) simply compensating the utility for its lost revenues, or (2) decoupling revenues from sales (breaking the link between sales volume and profit).[30] Simply compensating utilities for lost revenues was heavily employed by states in the early 1990s, but has since been mostly abandoned as it does not truly address the disincentive to provide the energy efficiency or renewable energy programs described above.[31] As of 2006, the second of these approaches, decoupling revenues from sales, was in use by seven states,[32] while another five states were considering it.[33] As an example, California Public Utilities Code Section 739.10 requires that the California Public Utilities Commission resume a decoupling program that was abandoned in the mid-1990s in favor of a deregulated market. California's current decoupling program combines revenue decoupling with performance incentives for meeting or exceeding energy efficiency targets.[34]

Shareholder Incentives for Electric Utilities to Pursue Energy Efficiency

In addition to enacting legislation requiring electric utilities to improve energy efficiency and provide cost and revenue recovery payments, states have developed other types of shareholder incentives for utilities, both positive and negative, to spur energy efficiency improvements.[35] As part of its research, ACEEE found that utility rate-setting statutes that provide shareholder incentives can actually provide both cost and revenue recovery mechanisms.[36] Examples of shareholder incentive programs include allowing utilities to earn a rate of return on energy efficiency investments equal to supply-side and other capital investments, allowing utilities to earn an overall increased return on energy efficiency investments, providing utilities with specific monetary rewards for meeting certain set targets, and providing utilities with monetary rewards representing a certain portion of the net benefits provided by the program.[37]

Overall, ACEEE's research found eight states with various forms of shareholder incentive programs in place, while California's was then under development.[38] Earlier research by the now-defunct U.S. Office of Technology Assessment also identified Massachusetts, Rhode Island, and New Hampshire as having tied positive incentives directly to clear performance goals, often specifically tailored to identified customer segments.

Such shareholder incentive legislation is designed to reward program outcomes that are under the control of the utilities, not those that are highly influenced by outside factors such as customer demand and energy prices. Additionally, some states have developed "bonus" systems that increase a utility's return on investment for achieving its demand-side management goals.[39]

One example of such a positive incentive is commonly referred to as a "bounty." It assures a utility of a predetermined payment that it will receive upon exceeding a specifically set goal, usually measured in terms of reduced energy such as a percentage of power saved. For example, in Massachusetts 5 percent of energy efficiency expenditures related to electricity is refunded to utilities that meet specific goals.[40] Similarly, a state could provide a utility with a certain amount of money per kilowatt-hour saved.

Shared savings programs are another positive incentive various states employ. Savings programs are designed to provide utilities with a predetermined percentage of savings, as calculated by a statutory sharing formula. The utility can recover the savings if it exceeds program goals by anywhere from 10 percent to 50 percent. The savings are often subject to a cap, generally at 5 to 10 percent of the savings.[41] Thus, an added benefit for utilities is that they can readily calculate the amount of cost recovery they can expect based on the reductions they achieve or plan to achieve. However, under such a regulation, it is very important that the savings be accurately quantified, which can require a high level of regulatory oversight.[42]

While not entirely unheard of, negative incentives are less common than the positive incentives described above. This is likely because using penalties for not meeting mandated requirements may be economically ineffective unless set at a high level, and penalties are less palatable politically than incentives. As discussed above, the profits utility companies earn are directly tied to the amount of electricity they generate and supply; and as their output increases, the accompanying increase in revenues from sales has the potential ability to offset any penalty.[43]

Energy Efficiency Resource Standards

An Energy Efficiency Resource Standard (EERS) is another commonly used policy tool for energy efficiency. An EERS requires energy providers to meet a specific portion of their electricity demand through improved energy efficiency. An EERS is a market-based mechanism used to increase efficiency in the generation, transmission, and use of electricity and natural gas. State public utility commissions or other regulatory bodies set electric and/or gas energy savings targets which are applied to utility companies. An EERS will often contain flexible market-based trading systems, allowing companies with greater ability to increase efficiency to do so while other companies compensate them for the effort.

By establishing explicit requirements that ensure cost-effective energy efficiency measures are used to help offset growing electricity demand, an EERS is able to overcome existing barriers to investing in cost-effective energy efficiency. As of May 2010 twenty-two states had enacted an EERS, and New Jersey, Massachusetts, Utah, and Wisconsin had legislation pending.[44] The first state to establish an EERS was Texas, which, beginning in 1999, required electric utilities to offset 10 percent of their load growth (increase in electricity produced) through improved end-use energy efficiency. Thus, rather than produce an extra 10 percent of electricity to meet consumer demand, the utility companies had to design improved transmission methods that would reduce loss between the power plants and the consumer's home. Ultimately, this would ensure that the necessary electricity reached consumers without utilities actually increasing their output. Since its original enactment, the requirement was increased to 20 percent by 2010.

As described, the market-based approach of an EERS allows for trading similar to that commonly discussed under a cap-and-trade system. Within an EERS, those utilities that are able improve the efficiency of their energy production and transmission at a lower cost (thereby reducing overall electricity produced) are allowed to sell excess reductions to other companies that face greater costs associated with such improvements. While trading under an EERS creates many benefits by allowing for the market to minimize costs associated with achieving appropriate reductions, scholars also point out that allowing trading among states may have some negative consequences, including the potential for providing an incentive for states to *not* adopt or to *dismantle* other reduction strategies, such as tougher building codes.[45] Further, if the EERS is weak, there will likely be a surplus of credits in the market, thus further weakening the regulation's ability to improve overall efficiency.[46] No interstate trading system for EERS yet exists, and thus no basis for these concerns has materialized. States have continued to utilize EERS as an energy efficiency policy tool with success.[47]

As detailed in chapter 4, Renewable Portfolio Standards generally require utilities to ensure that a certain percentage of the total electricity they sell is generated through the use of renewable energy sources. Currently, forty-one states have established Renewable Portfolio Standards, with an additional five local units of government having established their own requirements.[48] While a Renewable Portfolio Standard is a different policy tool from energy efficiency incentives and standards, state and local governments often use the policy options in tandem, particularly in connection with an EERS, and thus they warrant a brief mention in this chapter. For example, Minnesota, which has enacted legislation requiring 25 percent of the electricity generated within the state to come from renewable resources by 2025,[49] has also created rebates for purchasing energy-efficient appliances, utility recovery for efficiency expenditures, and energy-efficient building codes.[50] Additionally, some states allow energy efficiency improvements to be counted toward their Renewable Portfolio Standard, thereby providing utilities with another option to meet state-mandated targets.[51]

Energy-Efficient Building Codes

As discussed above, appliance-related emissions account for a significant percentage of the emissions of those buildings that house them. Yet further, according to DOE, the total emissions from residential, commercial, and industrial buildings account for approximately 40 percent of *total U.S. emissions*.[52] While other reports suggest the percentage may be lower (between 30 and 40 percent), either way these emissions account for approximately 8 percent of the total *worldwide* anthropogenic emissions.[53] Compounding the problem is the fact that the United States is expected to add over 15 million households and 11 billion square feet of commercial space by 2015,[54] and based on current use, experts estimate emission levels from commercial and residential appliances will respectively increase by 1.9 percent and 1.3 percent annually through 2030.[55] While this is certainly a significant increase, research has indicated that improving energy efficiency in buildings could offset some 85 percent of the projected incremental demand for electricity by 2030.[56] These numbers have caused states and local governments to embrace "green building" initiatives to help decrease the GHG emissions associated with new and existing buildings.

States and municipalities first began using green building codes in the 1970s in order to provide a method for overcoming the split incentives that are created when builders bear the costs of installing higher-efficiency equipment while consumers reap the benefits of lower energy bills.[57] Today such building codes are often specific to either the private or public sectors, with more stringent requirements placed on new and existing buildings in the public sector and limiting requirements in the private sector to primarily new buildings or major renovations of existing buildings. One exception to this public/private split, however, is New York City, which enacted legislation in 2010 requiring, among other things, energy audits, lighting and other energy-related improvements, and public disclosure of energy use for existing and new buildings of a certain size and type in both the public and private sectors.[58]

A typical green building code will specify requirements for "thermal resistance" in building shells and windows, minimum air leakage in ventilation systems and through shell orifices, and minimum heating and cooling equipment efficiencies. Other requirements include specifications for lighting and insulation.[59] In addition to creating the codes, certain local governments such as Austin, Texas, are starting to actively enforce their codes through the use of Energy Inspectors. In Austin, each newly constructed building or home must pass an Energy Audit (energy audits are discussed in further detail below), which includes a visit from the Energy Inspector and a test of each regulated component of the structure to ensure it passes code. Due to the resulting increase in energy savings, the city was able to avoid building a coal-fired power plant that had been in the planning stage.[60]

States and municipalities often rely in part on model codes in adopting their own green building codes. One of the primary examples of such a code is the International Energy Conservation Code (IECC). Created by the International Code Council, the IECC was last revised in 2008 and took effect in 2009.[61] The IECC is designed to provide up-to-date energy conservation provisions for both residential and commercial construction. The code specifically addresses building envelope requirements for thermal performance and air leakage, as well as the installation of energy-efficient mechanical, lighting, and power systems, while also providing regulations that will help result in the optimal utilization of fossil fuels and nondepletable resources. A study completed by an independent consulting firm estimates that new homes built under "the 2009 IECC standards will save 12.2% [of their total energy use] under the simple 'prescriptive' method and could save 14.7% or more using the more complicated 'performance-based' method."[62] Further, the 2009 IECC standard is generally viewed as at least 15 percent more efficient than its 2006 predecessor as it improves efficiency for windows, lighting, and doors, increases required insulation levels, and improves testing for envelope and duct air leakage.[63]

Beyond being adopted by numerous states and municipalities across the county,[64] the federal government has also utilized the IECC. The Energy Policy Act of 1992 established the code as a basis for federal tax credits for energy-efficient homes, energy efficiency standards for federal residential buildings and manufactured housing, and state energy code determinations.[65] More recently, the passage of the American Recovery and Reinvestment Act of 2009 (ARRA)[66] resulted in many additional states adopting the IECC's requirements for energy efficiency. For example, Idaho, which received $9,593,500 in funding under ARRA, has allocated a portion of the money to go toward helping cities and counties adopt the 2009 IECC. Specifically, Idaho will award scholarships to code enforcement officials to receive training and provide grants to cities and counties to support code adoption and enforcement.[67]

Other similar codes and provisions, including the International Green Construction Code (IGCC), the American Society of Heating, Refrigerating and Air-Conditioning Engineers (ASHRAE) 90.1 Standard, the LEED and Energy Star standards, and other aspects of green buildings, are discussed in chapter 13.[68]

Energy Audit Requirements

As evidenced by the requirements put in place by the city of Austin, Texas, energy audits are quickly becoming one of the primary methods through which interested parties are able to recognize areas where efficiency can be improved. Energy audits can identify areas of leakage, inefficient appliances or products, and more important, they are able to ensure that required efficiency improvements are actually implemented and are achieving their intended results. Examples include legislation in the state of New York, which provides that upon the request of either an eligible customer or a landlord, each utility must conduct one free energy audit of the customer's residential premises or the landlord's multiple dwelling.[69] In Florida, the Public Service Commission requires each utility to offer, or to contract to offer, energy audits to its residential customers, as provided by statute.[70] The Commission also has the option to extend the requirement to some or all commercial customers. Likewise, New York City's green building legislation requires energy audits for "any building that exceeds 50,000 gross square feet."[71] The use of energy audits for residential or commercial properties has also led to discussions of requiring industrial energy audits. Such audits would be aimed at improving overall efficiency within the high-energy use sector responsible for producing America's goods.

State Appliance Efficiency Standards

In the early 1970s, the United States began to realize the significance of its dependence on foreign energy sources. In response, a call went out for improved self-reliance, which included attempts to improve the energy efficiency of appliances. States were the first to react, with California creating the nation's first appliance efficiency standards in 1974. California's regulation, which was aimed at reducing wasteful or uneconomical energy use, and ultimately at reducing energy consumption and saving natural resources, applied to refrigerators, freezers, and air conditioning systems. This was followed in the early to mid-1980s by other states, including Florida, Kansas, Massachusetts, and New York, which began to adopt the same or similar standards.

While the federal government enacted the first national energy efficiency legislation as part of the Energy Policy and Conservation Act of 1975 (EPCA), the provisions relating to appliance efficiency were voluntary and generally imposed only labeling and reporting requirements.[72] The continued increase in state activity regarding appliance efficiency requirements, however, led national industry groups to begin pushing the federal government to enact uniform national standards to avoid a patchwork of state regulation that would allegedly reduce economies of scale and increase costs that would be passed on to consumers.[73] This resulted in DOE adopting national standards for many of the products that states had begun to regulate. Since then, there has been a history of states adopting appliance efficiency standards for products not regulated by DOE, followed by DOE using those state standards to develop federal standards for the product. For instance, in the late 1980s and early 1990s, states such as Colorado, Connecticut, Delaware, Florida, Georgia, Massachusetts, New Jersey, New York,

Rhode Island, Texas, Vermont, and Washington adopted standards for showerheads and for fluorescent lamp ballasts and other types of lamp products. Soon after, in the Energy Policy Act of 1992, Congress added standards for light bulbs, electric motors, heating and cooling equipment, plumbing fittings, and other appliances.[74]

State Appliance Efficiency Regulations and Preemption

In response to industry's desire for uniform standards, ever since 1987, EPCA has preempted (i.e., prohibited) states from setting appliance efficiency standards if a federal standard exists for the product in question.[75] Federal preemption occurs when (1) Congress preempts state law by saying so in express terms (express preemption); (2) Congress and federal agencies create a sufficiently comprehensive federal regulatory structure in an area where the federal interest is so dominant that it requires the inference that Congress left no room for state law (implied field preemption); or (3) Congress does not completely displace state regulation, but the state law actually conflicts with federal law or "stands as an obstacle" to achieving the full purposes and objectives of Congress (implied conflict preemption).[76]

EPCA's preemption provision allows states to regulate appliances at any level until a federal standard goes into place, at which point states are expressly prohibited from imposing regulations "concerning the energy efficiency, energy use, or water use" of a product or appliance covered by a federal efficiency standard.[77] While states may request preemption waivers, such waivers must be based on "unusual and compelling state or local energy or water interests" that are "substantially different in nature or magnitude than those prevailing in the United States generally."[78] Further, the proposed state regulation must be such that the "costs, benefits, burdens, and reliability of energy or water savings resulting from the State regulation make such regulations preferable or necessary [relative to other approaches]."[79]

To date, DOE has never granted a preemption waiver. Only two states, California and Massachusetts, have ever applied for a preemption waiver, and states generally have viewed such a waiver as impossible to obtain. Although DOE denied Massachusetts's petition for a preemption waiver for energy conservation standards for residential nonweatherized gas furnaces in 2010,[80] other events show that both DOE and the courts may make future preemption waivers more achievable. In 2006, DOE denied the California Energy Commission's petition for a preemption waiver for California's water conservation standards for residential clothes washers. DOE found that the Commission had failed to provide sufficient data to determine whether the petition met EPCA requirements regarding whether the state had "unusual and compelling water interests" to justify granting the petition under the statute.[81] In October 2009, however, the U.S. Court of Appeals for the Ninth Circuit held that DOE's rejection of the petition was arbitrary and capricious and remanded the matter to DOE for reconsideration on grounds that California had in fact provided sufficient data and analysis for DOE to make a decision on the petition.[82]

Moreover, in 2006, DOE issued a Notice of Proposed Rulemaking on energy efficiency standards for residential boilers in which it responded to comments regarding whether the agency could set different standards for furnaces and boilers in different regions of the country.[83] DOE stated that EPCA did not allow it to set regional standards, only national standards, but that the states could rely on regional differences as evidence of the need for a preemption waiver.[84] Specifically, DOE stated that in the context of residential boilers and furnaces, "where regional climactic effects can have significant impact on whether a specified energy conservation standard would be technologically feasible and economically justified in that region, such regional climactic effects will be important in DOE's assessment of whether there are 'unusual and compelling State or local energy interests.'"[85] Likewise, the Energy Independence and Security Act of 2007 now expressly grants DOE authority to create regional standards for climate-sensitive products.[86] These developments provide at least some additional legal support for states or groups of states that wish to establish stricter efficiency standards for appliances, even when a federal standard is in place.

Current State Efforts to Set Appliance Efficiency Standards

Outside of obtaining a preemption waiver, the only other option state and local governments have under EPCA to impose appliance efficiency standards that are stricter than established federal standards is through the use of building codes. When creating such a strategy, a state is allowed to design building codes for new construction that contain multiple paths to compliance, one or more of which, but not all, may contain requirements for the installation of products that have energy efficiency ratings above the federal standard.[87] As this option is limited to new construction, however, it applies almost exclusively to "space conditioning" appliances that are built into a building, such as boilers, furnaces, air conditioners, and water heaters. For instance, Minnesota and Oregon have pursued this compliance option by creating statewide building codes that ensure that the least expensive path to compliance is to install a natural gas furnace that achieves a 90 percent AFUE rating (as compared to the nationwide standard of 80 percent) in exchange for a relaxed requirement for building shell elements, such as insulation and duct work.[88]

As noted earlier, when there is no national standard regarding a certain product, states are generally free to regulate the product's energy efficiency level as they wish.[89] For these products, states have begun to adopt standards similar to those enacted by other states. One example of such a formal state collaboration is the Multi-State Appliance Standards Collective, in which California, Connecticut, Massachusetts, New York, Oregon, Rhode Island, and Washington are participating. The alliance was formed under the leadership of the Appliance Standards Awareness Project and is intended to facilitate the adoption of similar, if not identical, energy efficiency standards for products that do not yet have federal standards in place. Appliances currently without federal standards include commercial ice makers, compact audio players, distribution transformers, DVD players and recorders, hot food holding cabinets, metal halide lamp fixtures, pool heaters, portable electric spas, commercial refrigerators and freezers, unit heaters and duct furnaces, and water dispensers.[90] Examples of states adopting similar or the same standards include both California and Oregon setting the same standards for DVD players[91] and California, Connecticut, Oregon, Rhode Island, and Washington all setting similar standards for energy efficiency in commercial refrigerators.[92]

Preemption Litigation

Not surprisingly, in light of EPCA's preemption provisions, state and local action intended to increase energy efficiency of buildings and appliances has sometimes prompted legal challenges by industry groups. For instance, the Air-Conditioning, Heating, and Refrigeration Institute (ACHRI), an industry trade group, challenged California regulations that required labeling and submission of energy efficiency testing data for certain consumer appliances on grounds that EPCA preempted such requirements. When the case reached the U.S. Court of Appeals for the Ninth Circuit in 2005, the court found that EPCA did not preempt any of the challenged provisions.[93]

In evaluating the preemption claim, the court considered the purposes of the statute as a whole, and then interpreted § 6297(a) of EPCA narrowly to find that: (1) the federal statute addressed only disclosure on labels directed to consumers at the point of sale or use—as opposed to the California regulations, which required disclosure to the state;[94] (2) the federal statute addressed only disclosure of information with respect to energy consumption or water use and thus did not apply to the additional information California required be included on the label;[95] (3) the state provision mandating compliance with federal marking requirements merely provided appliance manufacturers with another reason to comply with existing requirements under federal law and did not conflict with federal law;[96] and (4) the federal statute did not address energy performance labeling, and there was no evidence Congress's silence on that issue exhibited an express intent to preclude state law requiring such labeling.[97]

In 2008, the ACHRI challenged the City of Albuquerque's green building code (the Code) on preemption grounds.[98] The Code provisions applied to new residential and commercial buildings and to additions and alterations to existing buildings. The Code generally provided for three compliance paths: (1) LEED certification at the silver level; (2) 30 percent efficiency improvement; and (3) compliance with prescriptive standards for individual components of a building such as its HVAC system or water heaters. On a motion for preliminary injunction, the U.S. District Court for the District of New Mexico agreed with the plaintiffs that the Code's prescriptive alternatives were regulations that "concern" the energy efficiency of products for which DOE had set standards and were thus expressly preempted under EPCA.

The court found that in EPCA, Congress had meant to expressly preempt such regulations in order to establish a uniform national standard for the products at issue. The court reasoned that even though the Code provided alternatives for compliance, each alternative itself was not a regulation subject to EPCA's preemption provision. The court stated that some of the elements of the Code might be valid, but that enough of its provisions were in violation of EPCA's preemption provision to justify an injunction while the case went forward on its merits. In September 2010, the court partially granted the plaintiffs' motion for summary judgment and entered a permanent injunction prohibiting enforcement of the Code's prescriptive alternatives. The court denied the plaintiffs' motion for summary judgment on the nonprescriptive portions of the Code and requested further information from the parties regarding whether those portions were severable from the portions subject to the permanent injunction.[99]

Experts have opined that as a result of this case, "we will definitely see more challenges to mandatory green building regulations over time on a variety of theories, including preemption. . . ."[100] However, as discussed above with regard to the Minnesota and Oregon regulations, which ensure that the least expensive path to compliance results in the highest efficiency level, there are other models of building codes or energy efficiency standards that may not violate the current preemption provisions in EPCA.[101] Indeed, in February 2011, the U.S. District Court for the Western District of Washington dismissed an industry challenge to the Washington state building energy code, rejecting the plaintiffs' contention that EPCA preempted the law[102] while specifically acknowledging the fact that the least expensive path to compliance was by installing appliances with energy efficiency ratings that exceeded the federal standards.[103]

Such potential for litigation and other negative incentives created by the current EPCA preemption provisions has led to a call by scholars for a new approach to preemption in this area based on a "dynamic" or "polyphonic" system of federalism that would allow states greater leeway in setting the standards in order to meet localized or regional demands created by climate and political differences across the country.[104] Granting states such authority could be accomplished through amending EPCA's preemption provision to allow states to obtain a preemption waiver more easily or simply through a more generous application of the current standard by DOE, as has been suggested in recent DOE rulemaking in certain circumstances.[105]

Conclusion

In the absence of comprehensive federal requirements for energy efficiency, state and local governments have been left to develop statutes and regulations of their own to meet the demands of their local citizenry. These efforts include energy efficiency tax incentives, rebates for purchasing energy-efficient appliances, utility recovery for energy efficiency expenditures, incentives for electric utilities to pursue energy efficiency, EERSs, energy-efficient building codes for both private and public buildings, energy audit requirements, and mandatory appliance efficiency standards. Congress and federal agencies will undoubtedly continue to work on energy policy and appliance efficiency standards, thus increasing the federal presence in the energy efficiency arena. Continued initiatives by states and cities, however, such as the recent efforts by New York City and Austin, Texas, provide reason to believe energy efficiency will remain high on state and local agendas, thereby ensuring continued advancements and providing templates for future federal action.

Notes

1. This statement is based upon a review of the applicable information contained online on the Database of State Incentives for Renewables & Efficiency (DSIRE) website. For more information, see http://www.dsireusa.org/.

2. CAL. CODE REGS. tit. 20, §§ 1601–08. *See also* http://www.energy.ca.gov/appliances/2009_tvregs/index.html.

3. DSIRE, Financial Incentives for Energy Efficiency, http://www.dsireusa.org/summarytables/finee.cfm (last visited Feb. 7, 2011).

4. Idaho Code § 63-3022B (2008).

5. Ky. Rev. Stat. §§ 141.435 et seq. (2008).

6. DSIRE, Financial Incentives for Energy Efficiency, http://www.dsireusa.org/summarytables/finee.cfm (last visited Feb. 7, 2011).

7. Ga. Code. § 48-7-29.14 (2008).

8. N.M. Stat. Ann. § 7-2A-21 (2007).

9. DSIRE, Financial Incentives for Energy Efficiency, http://www.dsireusa.org/summarytables/finee.cfm (last visited Feb. 7, 2011).

10. Conn. Gen. Stat. § 12-412k (2006).

11. Mo. Rev. Stat. § 144.526 (2008).

12. DSIRE, Financial Incentives for Energy Efficiency, http://www.dsireusa.org/summarytables/finee.cfm (last visited Feb. 7, 2011).

13. Ariz. Rev. Stat. § 42-11054; H.B. 2332 (2009) (amending the original statute to include additional technologies).

14. DSIRE, Financial Incentives for Energy Efficiency, http://www.dsireusa.org/summarytables/finee.cfm (last visited Feb. 7, 2011).

15. Md. Code: Property Tax § 9-203 (2010) (of note, this program was originally enacted in 1985).

16. See Office of Energy Efficiency & Renewable Energy, U.S. Dep't of Energy, Buildings Energy Data Book 1–21 (2009) (citing to data from 2006). Included in the "other appliances" category are refrigerators, basic electronics, motors, swimming pool heaters, and hot tub heaters.

17. American Clean Energy and Security Act, H.R. 2454, 111th Cong. § 146 (2009).

18. Thomas Content, *Cash for Appliances Begins, Program Offers Rebates for an Array of Energy Saving Household-Products*, Milwaukee Journal Sentinel, Jan. 5, 2010, at D1.

19. Max Jarman, *Cash for Appliances Rebate Program to Launch in March Will Help Consumers Save Water, Energy, Money*, The Ariz. Republic, Dec. 30, 2009, at D1.

20. Kara McGuire, *A Quick Cycle for Appliance Rebates*, Minneapolis Star Tribune, Mar. 2, 2010, at D1.

21. *Id*. For further information on the Smart Appliance Rebate Program, visit its website at http://www.energysavers.gov/financial/70020.html.

22. See Martin Kushler et al., American Council for an Energy-Efficiency Economy, Aligning Utility Interests with Energy Efficiency Objectives: A Review of Recent Efforts at Decoupling and Performance Incentives 3 (Oct. 2006).

23. *Id*. at 15.

24. *Id*. at 7–8 (citing to programs in Arizona, Idaho, Minnesota, Washington, and Wisconsin).

25. See Lowe E. Alt, Jr., Energy Utility Rate Setting 97 (2006).

26. *Id*. at 28.

27. For an example of a system benefits charge, see New York State's Public Service Commission's Opinion No. 96-12 (Cases 94-E-0953, et al.) (2006). System benefits charges are discussed in greater detail in chapter 8.

28. Kushler et al., *supra* note 22, at 8; *see also* Nat'l Regulatory Research Inst., How Regulators Can Help to Increase the Benefits from Utility Energy-Efficiency Initiatives 4 (July 2009) (identifying (1) cost recovery of utility energy efficiency actions; (2) utility recovery of lost margins from energy efficiency; and (3) explicit utility-performance incentives for cost-effective energy efficiency actions as factors regulators should consider regarding utility energy efficiency programs).

29. Kushler et al., *supra* note 22, at 8.

30. *Id*.

31. *Id*.

32. *Id.* at 8–9 (identifying California, Maryland, Oregon, North Carolina, Ohio, Utah, and New Jersey as states with approved decoupling mechanisms).

33. *Id.* at 9 (identifying Idaho, New Mexico, New York, Vermont, and Washington as states pursuing decoupling mechanisms).

34. For more information on California's decoupling program and decoupling programs in general, see PEW CENTER ON GLOBAL CLIMATE CHANGE, DECOUPLING POLICIES, *available at* http://www.pewclimate.org/what_s_being_done/in_the_states/decoupling (last visited Feb. 7, 2011).

35. KUSHLER ET AL., *supra* note 22, at 8–9.

36. *Id.*

37. *Id.* at 9–10.

38. *Id.* (identifying Arizona, Connecticut, Massachusetts, Minnesota, Nevada, New Hampshire, Rhode Island, and Wisconsin as providing shareholder incentive programs for at least one of its utility providers).

39. OFFICE OF TECHNOLOGY ASSESSMENT, U.S. CONGRESS, ENERGY EFFICIENCY: CHALLENGES AND OPPORTUNITIES FOR ELECTRIC UTILITIES 137 (1993).

40. *Id.*

41. *Id.* at 138.

42. *Id.*

43. *Id.*

44. PEW CENTER ON GLOBAL CLIMATE CHANGE, ENERGY EFFICIENCY STANDARDS AND TARGETS, *available at* http://www.pewclimate.org/what_s_being_done/in_the_states/efficiency_resource.cfm (last visited Feb. 7, 2011).

45. JOE LOPER ET AL., ALLIANCE TO SAVE ENERGY, DEAL OR NO DEAL? PROS AND CONS OF TRADING UNDER AN ENERGY EFFICIENCY RESOURCE STANDARD 8–9 (2008) *available at* http://ase.org/content/article/detail/5211.

46. *Id.* at 3–5.

47. For a further description of specific EERSs put in place by different states around the country, see STEVEN NADEL, ENERGY EFFICIENCY RESOURCE STANDARDS: EXPERIENCE AND RECOMMENDATIONS, ACEEE Report E063 (Mar. 2006) *available at* http://www.epatechforum.org/documents/2005-2006/2006-05-16/2006-05-16-ACEEE%20Report%20on%20EE%20Portfolio%20Standards.pdf.

48. DSIRE, RULES, REGULATIONS & POLICIES FOR RENEWABLE ENERGY, http://www.dsireusa.org/summarytables/rrpre.cfm (last visited Feb. 7, 2011).

49. MINN. STAT. § 216B.1691 (2009). The legislation allows for the use of the following renewable resources: solar thermal electric, photovoltaics, landfill gas, wind, biomass, hydroelectric, municipal solid waste, hydrogen, co-firing, anaerobic digestion.

50. *See supra* notes 16–20 and 23–27 and *infra* notes 57–59 and 65–66.

51. *See* NADEL, *supra* note 47, at 3 (specifically noting Nevada, which allows for up to 25 percent of the total portfolio standard to be met through improved efficiency, and Hawaii, which allows for the entirety of a 20 percent transition from traditional electricity generation to renewables to come from improved efficiency).

52. *See* OFFICE OF ENERGY EFFICIENCY & RENEWABLE ENERGY, U.S. DEP'T OF ENERGY, BUILDINGS ENERGY DATA BOOK 1–21 (2009) (citing to data from 2006).

53. Based on current estimates, the United States accounts for approximately 20 percent of the total worldwide carbon dioxide emissions. *See* INT'L ENERGY AGENCY, CO_2 EMISSIONS FROM FUEL COMBUSTION 44 (2010) *available at* http://www.iea.org/co2highlights/CO2highlights.pdf. Since 40 percent of the U.S. emissions are generated by buildings, approximately 8 percent of the worldwide emissions are generated by U.S. buildings.

54. U.S. DEP'T OF ENERGY, BUILDINGS ENERGY DATA BOOK § 1.1.3 (2006).

55. MCKINSEY & COMPANY, REDUCING U.S. GREENHOUSE GAS EMISSIONS: HOW MUCH AT WHAT COST? 7 (2007).

56. *Id.* at xv.

57. Envtl. Protection Agency, EPA Clean Energy–Environment Guide to Action: Policies, Best Practices and Action Steps for States 4–37 (Apr. 2006), *available at* http://www.epa.gov/cleanenergy/documents/gta/guide_action_full.pdf.

58. David J. Freeman & Jesse Hiney, *New York City Adds to Growing Tide of Green Building Legislation*, 39 Daily Env't Rep. (BNA), at B-1 (Mar. 2, 2010).

59. *Id.*

60. Clifford Krauss, *New Enforcer in Buildings, the Energy Inspector*, N.Y. Times, July 18, 2009, at A1.

61. For a current version of the IECC, see the International Code Council's website at www.iccsafe.org.

62. Energy Efficiency Codes Coalition, Energy & Cost Savings Analysis of 2009 IECC Efficiency Improvements 1 (Sept. 2008) (citing to a report issued by independent consulting firm ICF International).

63. *Id.*

64. Marilyn A. Brown et al., Oak Ridge Nat'l Laboratory, Pew Center on Global Climate Change, Towards a Climate-Friendly Built Environment 46 (June 2005).

65. *See* 42 U.S.C. § 6834(a) (2006).

66. Pub. L. No. 111-5 (Feb. 17, 2009).

67. *See Obama Administration Delivers Nearly $72 Million for Energy Efficiency and Conservation Projects in 7 States and Territories*, Transmission & Distribution World (Oct. 7, 2009), *available at* http://tdworld.com/business/doe-recovery-awards-1009/.

68. *See also* The Law of Green Buildings: Regulatory and Legal Issues in Design, Construction, Operations, and Financing (J. Cullen Howe & Michael B. Gerrard eds., 2010).

69. N.Y. Pub. Serv. Law § 135-f(1) (2009).

70. F.S.A. § 366.82 (2008).

71. *See* Freeman & Hiney, *supra* note 58, at 2.

72. Pub. L. No. 94-163, Dec. 22, 1975, 89 Stat. 871 (codified as amended in scattered sections of 42 U.S.C.). For a good summary of the development of energy efficiency standards within EPCA and the related action by government agencies such as DOE and EPA, see *Natural Resources Defense Council, Inc. v. Herrington*, 768 F.2d 1355 (D.C. Cir. 1985).

73. The DOE maintains a listing of the efficiency standards for products/appliances that are regulated under EPCA. See http://www1.eere.energy.gov/buildings/appliance_standards/. The current federal standards are discussed in more detail in chapter 12.

74. *See* Steven Nadel et al., Leading the Way: Continued Opportunities for New State Appliance and Equipment Efficiency Standards 2–4, ACEEE Report ASAP-6/A062 (Mar. 2006), *available at* http://www.standardsasap.org/documents/a062.pdf; Ann E. Carlson, Commentary, *Energy Efficiency and Federalism*, 107 Mich. L. Rev. First Impressions 63, 65 (2008), *available at* http://www.michiganlawreview.org/assets/fi/107/carlson.pdf (discussing the congressional response to state regulatory activity setting appliance efficiency standards).

75. 42 U.S.C. § 6297(c) (2006).

76. *See* Hillsborough County v. Automated Medical Laboratories, Inc., 471 U.S. 707, 713 (1985) (citing Hines v. Davidowitz, 312 U.S. 52, 67 (1941)); Caleb Nelson, *Preemption*, 86 Va. L. Rev. 225, 226–28 (2000) (describing the three types of preemption). The doctrine of federal preemption is based on the Supremacy Clause in the U.S. Constitution, which states that the Constitution and U.S. laws "shall be the supreme law of the Land" notwithstanding any state law to the contrary. U.S. Const. art. VI, cl. 2.

77. 42 U.S.C. § 6297(c) (2006).

78. 42 U.S.C. § 6297(d)(1) (2006).

79. 42 U.S.C. § 6297(d)(1)(C)(ii) (2006).

80. 75 Fed. Reg. 62115 (Oct. 7, 2010).

81. *See* Energy Efficiency Program for Consumer Products: California Energy Commission Petition for Exemption from Federal Preemption of California's Water Conservation Standards for Residential Clothes Washers, 71 Fed. Reg. 78,157 (Dec. 28, 2006).

82. *See* Cal. Energy Comm'n v. Dep't of Energy, 585 F.3d 1143 (9th Cir. 2009).

83. *See* U.S. Dep't of Energy, Notice of Proposed Rulemaking and Public Meeting, Energy Conservation Program for Consumer Products: Energy Conservation Standards for Residential Furnaces and Boilers, 71 Fed. Reg. 59,204, 59,209 (Oct. 6, 2006).

84. *Id*. at 59,209–59,210.

85. *Id*. at 59,209.

86. Pub. L. No. 110-140, 121 Stat. 1492 (2007) (to be codified at 42 U.S.C. § 17001).

87. *See* 42 U.S.C. § 6297(f)(3)(E) (2006).

88. *See* 10 C.F.R. § 430.32 (2007); MINN. R. pt. 1322.1102 (2009); OREGON DEP'T OF ENERGY, BUILDING CODES DIV., SIMPLE OVERVIEW OF 2008 RESIDENTIAL ENERGY CODE REQUIREMENTS (2008), *available at* http://www.oregon.gov/ENERGY/CONS/Codes/docs/Overview_0208.pdf.

89. For an overview of state standards for products not regulated by the federal government, please see the Multi-State Appliance Standards Collaborative's website at http://appliancestandards.org/states/.

90. Multi-State Appliance Standards Collaborative, http://appliancestandards.org/states/ (last visited Feb. 7, 2011).

91. CAL. CODE REGS. tit. 20, § 1605.3(u) (2010); OR. REV. STAT. § 469.233 (2009).

92. CAL. CODE REGS. tit. 20, § 1605.3(a)(7) (2010); CONN. AGENCIES REGS. § 16a-48-4(B) (2010); OR. REV. STAT. § 469.233(4)(a) (2009); R.I. GEN. LAWS § 39-27-5 (2010); WASH. REV. CODE. § 19-260-020-.050 (2010).

93. Air Conditioning & Refrigeration Inst. v. Energy Res. Conservation & Dev. Comm'n, 410 F.3d 492 (9th Cir. 2005).

94. *Id*. at 497–98.

95. *Id*. at 502.

96. *Id*.

97. *Id*. at 503.

98. Air Conditioning, Heating & Refrigeration Inst. v. City of Albuquerque, Civ. No. 08-633, 2008 WL 5586316 at *2–3 (D.N.M. Oct. 3, 2008).

99. *See* Air Conditioning, Heating & Refrigeration Inst. v. City of Albuquerque, Civ. No. 08-633, 2010 U.S. Dist. LEXIS 141814 (D.N.M. Sept. 30, 2010).

100. *See* Leslie Guevarra, *Federal Judge Puts Albuquerque's Green Building Code on Hold*, GREENBIZSITE (Oct. 6, 2008), http://www.greenbiz.com/news/2008/10/06/federal-judge-puts-albuquerques-green-building-code-hold?page=0%2C0.

101. *Court Issues Injunction on Energy Efficiency Codes*, 17(10) ENVTL. DUE DILIGENCE GUIDE (BNA) (Oct. 16, 2008) (quoting Harvey Sachs, senior fellow at American Council for an Energy-Efficient Economy).

102. *See* Bldg. Indus. Ass'n of Wash. v. Wash. State Bldg. Code Council, 2011 WL 485895 (W.D. Wash. Feb. 7, 2011).

103. *Id*. at *12–13.

104. *See* Alexandra B. Klass, *State Standards for Nationwide Products Revisited: Federalism, Green Building Codes, and Appliance Efficiency Standards*, 34 HARV. ENVTL. L. REV. 335 (2010) (arguing for the adoption of federal policies that allow states to play a larger role in the regulation of appliance efficiency standards); Carlson, *supra* note 74 (discussing the ramifications of allowing for an iterative federalism system with regards to energy efficiency).

105. *See* U.S. Dep't of Energy, Notice of Proposed Rulemaking and Public Meeting, Energy Conservation Program for Consumer Products: Energy Conservation Standards for Residential Furnaces and Boilers, 71 Fed. Reg. 59,204, 59,209 (Oct. 6, 2006).

chapter four

Renewables Mandates and Goals

Joshua P. Fershee

Introduction

Renewable goals and mandates are potentially powerful mechanisms to encourage the construction and use of renewable energy-generating facilities. For a quarter century, the most significant renewable mandate was the Public Utility Regulatory Policies Act of 1978 (PURPA),[1] passed in the wake of the oil crisis in the 1970s. PURPA is discussed in chapter 15. Since the mid-2000s, that role has largely been supplanted by state renewable energy mandates.[2] Such renewable energy mandates are often known as renewable portfolio standards (RPSs) or renewable electricity standards (RESs).[3]

Renewable Portfolio Standards

Overview

The most common method for requiring the use of renewable fuel sources is the imposition of a renewable electricity mandate, usually in the form of an RPS or an RES (these terms are generally used interchangeably). Comparable programs for the transportation sector have been imposed through renewable fuel standards, which are discussed in chapter 19.

Basic RPS Structure

An RPS requires covered electricity suppliers to procure a certain percentage of their electricity from renewable resources or purchase renewable energy credits (RECs) from other sources to meet the statutory (or regulatory) standard.[4] Such plans typically set a mid- to long-range goal, then phase in the mandate over time. For example, an RPS might begin with a requirement of 2.75 percent renewable energy beginning in 2011, increasing gradually (but significantly) through 2020 up to 15 percent.[5] Some programs will also permit a covered utility to comply (or achieve a portion of the compliance requirement) through efficiency programs, as described in chapter 3.[6]

Because an RPS is a mandate, the law typically prescribes the use of sanctions and/or waivers (permission for temporary noncompliance)[7] for shortfalls (i.e., failures to meet the RPS requirements).[8] The RPS imposes a reporting requirement on the covered electricity supplier, and the supplier then reports compliance via the delivery of RECs, which are earned through electricity generation from qualified renewable sources.[9] (RECs are described in more detail below.) If a covered supplier cannot acquire the required number of RECs, programs usually offer the option of making alternative compliance payments.[10] Such alternative payments are usually offered at a cost in excess of the REC market price.[11] If the supplier does not comply with the RPS requirements, the supplier may be liable for civil fines and penalties.[12]

A small number of states have decided to promote renewable energy via laws similar to RPSs that lack mandates, which are often known as renewable portfolio goals (RPGs). RPGs generally mirror RPS programs, minus the mandates.

An RPS covers any entity stated in the statute. The scope of RPS coverage could be as broad as all retail sellers or limited to private investor-owned utilities (IOUs). Many RPS programs exempt municipalities and rural electric cooperatives. Similarly, an RPS will also provide specifically what constitutes "renewable energy," as discussed below.

An RPS, of course, is only one part of bringing renewable energy online. The RPS provides the mandate, but the process requires assistance in other areas. For example, it is one thing to construct a renewable electricity generating unit; it is quite another to bring that renewable electricity to market. Renewable resources, such as wind, are often a significant distance from the transmission infrastructure needed to bring the power to market. Transmission infrastructure issues are discussed in detail in chapter 22.

Similarly, there are several financing issues related to renewable energy projects. Renewable projects are often dependent upon tax credits and tax incentives to compete with other energy forms. Chapter 10 discusses the financial issues related to clean energy projects, and chapter 7 discusses tax issues.

RPS plans are often proposed along with other programs; cap-and-trade programs to reduce greenhouse gas emissions are especially common.[13] The motivation for such programs has significant overlap, and there are those who believe that proper energy policy would pursue one or the other, but not both. Others believe that such programs are complementary, and even essential, to achieving the goals of both programs. However, the primary goals and execution of such policies can often differ greatly.

RPS programs are focused primarily on increasing the mix of renewable sources of electricity; cap-and-trade programs are focused on emissions reduction strategies (whether to reduce pollution, climate-impacting emissions, or both). Thus, sources like wind and solar energy satisfy the goals of (and can be used to comply with the requirements of) both an RPS and a cap-and-trade program. However, electricity generated by nuclear energy would serve as a great source of electricity in a cap-and-trade program, but it would not comply with any current RPS program.

Renewable Energy Credits and Certificates

Under most RPS systems, covered electricity retailers are required to hold RECs in the specified proportion to the amount of retail energy they sell. RECs can be self-generated (i.e., generating electricity using qualifying renewable resources) or purchased from other qualifying renewable generators.

The organization responsible for the RECs tracking system (as discussed below) issues RECs to the generators of renewable energy. The RECs can then be sold to a purchaser along with the electricity used to create them or sold separately to another purchaser. RPS statutes require a program to verify and issue the RECs, which are generally issued directly to renewable energy generators. These programs must also track the sale, exchange, and retirement of RECs to ensure that compliance can be measured and that no double counting occurs. Thus, as an example, if an RPS were set at 10 percent, and a generator sold 100,000 kilowatt-hours that year, the generator would need to acquire ten thousand RECs before that year's compliance deadline, if one REC were issued per kilowatt-hour under that RPS.[14]

The RPS statute will specify how much power is needed to generate one REC. For example, some programs issue one REC for each kilowatt-hour of renewable electric energy generated, although this is by no means the only system. Other statutes may provide one REC per megawatt-hour, for instance. In addition, the RPS can provide incentives for particular types of renewable energy. Thus, a plan could provide a premium (i.e., additional RECs) in certain especially desirable circumstances. For example, a recently proposed federal RPS provided that two RECs would be issued per kilowatt-hour of renewable energy generated on Indian land, and that three RECs would be issued for renewable energy used to offset all or part of the customer's electricity requirements if that renewable energy was generated at an on-site facility.

One of the unique facets of renewable energy under an RPS is the separation (or unbundling) of the renewable or "green" attribute of the energy from the generated electricity itself. That is, when renewable energy is used to generate electricity under an RPS, the energy creates two saleable products: (1) the electricity and (2) the RECs. Traditional fuel sources, as always, simply produce electricity. The sale of RECs and some related concerns are discussed below. RECs are also discussed in chapter 17.

Eligible Energy Sources

As mentioned above, what constitutes "renewable" under any RPS is determined by the RPS statute. This includes electricity generated from qualified renewable generators, and typically, this will mean electric energy that is generated from renewable energy sources such as "solar (including solar water heating), wind, ocean, tidal, geothermal energy, biomass, landfill gas, or incremental hydropower."[15] However, the statute can, at least theoretically, include any thing the drafter wishes to include. The qualifying RPS resources vary from state to state.

The state of Maine provides a good example of how RPS-eligible resources are dictated by, and evolve under, state RPS rules. Maine passed its first RPS in 1997 with what seemed to be an aggressive renewable energy mandate.[16] The plan required that

Maine utilities provide at least 30 percent of all retail power sold in the state from "renewable" sources.[17] However, the definition of "renewable" in Maine's first RPS included all existing hydroelectric and biomass power plants.[18] Maine utilities were able to meet the 30 percent requirement the day the RPS went into effect with already existing power plants.[19] The Maine RPS thus did not require a single new renewable generation facility to meet the mandate.[20]

In 2007, Maine added a second mandatory RPS, which was designed specifically to increase development of new renewable resources.[21] This second RPS required all covered electricity suppliers to show that at least 1 percent of their total kilowatt-hour sales in Maine came from "new renewable resources" in 2008, with the total going up 1 percent each year until 2017 (and beyond), when 10 percent of such sales from renewable resources would be required.[22] In this case, existing hydropower (as an example) was not sufficient. The second RPS statute requires that any renewable resources used to comply with the new RPS come from new or additional sources, and not already-existing production facilities.

However, the statutory definition of what is renewable can be beyond the scope of what most people consider, at least conceptually, renewable. Although coal is plainly not a "renewable" resource, Michigan adopted an RPS in 2008 that allows coal-fired plants that both capture and store 85 percent of carbon dioxide emissions to satisfy the requirements.[23] Similarly, Ohio[24] and Pennsylvania[25] also added clean coal to their RPS programs, further muddying the mix as to what is "renewable" in the RPS context. As such, the scope of some renewable energy mandates has evolved to include other forms of (at least arguable) clean energy. Such standards might better be considered sustainable energy standards, rather than RPSs.

State-Level RPSs

Thirty states and the District of Columbia have implemented an RPS at some level.[26] Most RPSs require covered utilities to secure a specific percentage of their electricity from renewable sources. These ranges can be quite broad. For example, just 8 percent of electricity from renewable sources by 2020 is required under the Pennsylvania RPS, while the New York plan requires utilities to obtain 30 percent by 2015. Other states have instead implemented specific megawatt mandates, with equally varied expectations. For example, Iowa, which was the first RPS implemented, still requires only 105 megawatts of renewable energy per year under its RPS,[27] a requirement that has long been met. Texas, on the other hand, requires that utilities procure 5,880 megawatts of renewable energy per year by 2015.[28]

In addition to the RPS programs implemented across the country, six other states have implemented renewable electricity goals, commonly known as renewable portfolio goals (RPGs), which mirror other state-level RPSs, but lack the enforcement mechanisms found in the mandatory laws. The RPG states—North Dakota, South Dakota, Utah, Vermont, Virginia, and West Virginia—have all passed nonbinding goals or objectives to promote renewable energy generation,[29] but have not enacted compliance enforcement mechanisms.[30] Although nonbinding goals of this sort may promote renewable electricity generation, mandates are expected to be more effective.[31]

Some states, such as Missouri, have shifted from renewable energy goals to mandates. The Missouri legislature in 2007 created a voluntary renewable energy and energy-efficiency objective that applied to IOUs (municipal utilities and electric cooperatives were exempt).[32] Each such covered utility in the state was "compelled" to make a "good-faith effort" to use renewable-sourced electricity equal to 4 percent of total retail electric sales by 2012, increasing to 11 percent by 2020. Effective efficiency measures were also permitted toward the goal. However, little more than a year later, a ballot initiative repealed the Missouri RPG and replaced it with a mandatory renewable electricity standard, which required covered utilities (still excluding municipal utilities and electric cooperatives) to obtain 15 percent of their energy from renewable sources by 2021.[33] The standard also uniquely included a solar-specific electricity mandate of 2 percent of each year's requirement.[34]

Impediments to Implementation

At least initially, there was some fear that state RPS programs might run afoul of PURPA.[35] As explained in chapter 15, PURPA (like RPS programs) was created to encourage development of renewable resources, which was to be accomplished by requiring each covered utility to purchase electricity from "qualified facilities" (QFs) at the utility's "avoided cost." In 1997, the Federal Energy Regulatory Commission (FERC) determined that state agencies were preempted by PURPA from requiring utilities to purchase power generated by QFs at rates above avoided costs.[36] However, state mandates requiring utilities to procure renewable resources do not violate PURPA in and of themselves.[37]

Representative State RPS Programs[38]

California

California first passed RPS legislation in 2002, and the renewable requirements have been raised through amendments requiring that the state's IOUs provide 20 percent of their retail sales from renewable generation by 2010.[39] That level was subsequently increased through executive order, which raised the renewable mandate to 33 percent of all retail sales by 2020 and expanded the scope to include all utilities.[40]

In March 2010, the California Public Utilities Commission (CPUC) authorized RPS compliance through the use of tradable renewable energy credits (TRECs), which are renewable energy credits that are unbundled from the associated renewable energy used to produce the attribute (i.e., a REC that is not delivered with the associated electricity).[41] Prior to that decision, the CPUC had not authorized the use of unbundled RECs for RPS compliance.[42] (Note that the nature of RECs and the related concepts of attributes and unbundling are discussed in detail below.) As part of the approval, the CPUC implemented a price cap of $50 per TREC and limited TREC use to 25 percent of California's three largest utilities' annual RPS requirements. These provisions sunset on December 31, 2011, unless the CPUC determines they should be retained or adjusted.

New York

Rather than through direct legislative action, the New York Public Service Commission (PSC) adopted an RPS in 2004 and issued related implementation rules the following year.[43] In January 2010, the PSC issued an order expanding the RPS to 30 percent by 2015 from the original RPS mandate of 25 percent by 2013.[44]

The New York RPS program allows as eligible resources biomass, liquid biofuels, fuel cells, hydroelectric, solar (photovoltaics), ocean, tidal, and wind power. Although the goal is to facilitate additional renewable generation sources, existing renewable energy facilities that began operation on or after January 1, 2003, are also eligible. Renewable generators for certain types of facilities in operation before that date may also be eligible, if financial need is demonstrated. In addition to an RPS, New York has also adopted an energy efficiency standard.[45]

Minnesota

In 2007, Minnesota enacted legislation that created a utility-specific RPS for Xcel Energy, added a separate RPS for other electric utilities, and modified the state's then-existing RPG.[46] Eligible energy sources included power generated by solar, wind, hydroelectric facilities generating less than 100 megawatts of power, and biomass. Hydrogen is also eligible, but only if it is generated by other eligible renewable energy sources.

The RPS that applies to other (non-Xcel Energy) Minnesota utilities requires that renewable energy make up 25 percent of retail electricity sales to retail customers by 2025. Xcel Energy, by 2020, is required to account for 30 percent of its total retail electricity from renewable source sales in Minnesota. The Xcel Energy RPS is also more source-specific than the other RPS program. At least 25 percent of the RPS mandate must be satisfied by wind energy or solar energy systems, and solar energy must contribute no more than 1 percent of the overall Xcel RPS mandate.

Minnesota uses the Midwest Renewable Energy Tracking System (M-RETS) for registering and tracking RECs. Although the state RECs are generally tradable, Xcel Energy is not permitted to sell RECs to other Minnesota utilities until 2021.

Possible Constitutional Challenges

There are three primary areas in which state RPS programs could face constitutional challenges: (1) Commerce Clause claims, (2) Fifth and Fourteenth Amendment takings claims; and (3) substantive due process claims.

First, some state RPS programs may be subject to constitutional challenges under the "dormant" or "negative" Commerce Clause. The Commerce Clause of Article I of the United States Constitution provides that Congress has the ability "[t]o regulate Commerce with foreign Nations, and among the several States, and with the Indian Tribes."[47] As interpreted by the United States Supreme Court, in addition to a grant of authority, this clause also has a negative implication that prohibits states from enacting laws designed to exact benefits for in-state businesses.[48]

Nonetheless, some state-level RPSs favor in-state renewable resources. Both Ohio[49] and Arizona,[50] for example, have provisions that provide benefits to in-state resources that are not available for other sources. Minnesota, on the other hand, treats all eligible renewable sources equally, and expressly will not allow an increase or decrease in the amount of RECs granted based on the electricity's origin state or the renewable source to generate that electricity.

To rectify Commerce Clause concerns, some have called for a national RPS to moot this possible claim.[51] To date, no state RPS has been overturned for violating the dormant Commerce Clause, but many believe that, absent federal action, this is only a matter of time.[52] In fact, such a challenge was filed in April 2010 as an objection to two provisions of the Massachusetts RPS: (1) a program requiring and soliciting long-term renewable energy contracts with in-state generators and (2) a requirement that retail suppliers buy a portion of the solar energy required under the RPS from in-state generators.[53] The parties settled the solar energy issue without resolving the constitutionality of the provision.[54] The constitutionality of the long-term contracts provision remains pending.[55]

Next, the U.S. Constitution, through the Fifth Amendment, does not permit the U.S government to convert private property to a public use without providing the property owner "just compensation." This prohibition was extended to state and local governments through the due process clause of the Fourteenth Amendment.

An RPS program that destroys an existing property right or that leads to unjust rates could conceivably lead to problems under the Takings Clause, although there are no current RPS programs that obviously raise these issues. In addition, takings claims are not likely to prevail in cases where an RPS creates new property rights, as discussed more fully below.

Finally, the due process clause of the Fourteenth Amendment provides "substantive due process" protections against economic legislation that impacts individual property interests.[56] However, the protection here is "very limited,"[57] requiring only that the economic legislation "be rationally related to a legitimate government interest."[58] Thus, unless the compliance costs of the renewables mandates were disproportionately large, compared to other fees and profits related to electricity generation, it is unlikely that such a challenge would prevail.[59]

Federal RPS

As of February 2011, there is not a federal RPS in place. Although some have argued that the broad scope of state RPS programs eliminates the need for a federal program,[60] a national RPS has benefits beyond those obtained through state-level programs.

Overview

A federal RPS could provide value through economies of scale gained via a broader mandate. By requiring national compliance, the federal RPS would increase the amount of renewable energy that retailers would need to purchase, requiring larger bulk equipment purchases, which could, in turn, allow for lower prices as manufacturing facilities increase and expand production.

Furthermore, as discussed in more detail below, a national RPS would create a national market for RECs, providing incentives for rapid expansion of renewable energy generation in areas where it is most readily available. Under the current market system, even if there is renewable energy available, if there is not an RPS, or the RPS is met by current production, there is not an incentive to build. This would change almost immediately with a national RPS.

A national RECs market would also operate more efficiently than state-by-state systems by linking buyers and sellers across the country. It would provide a uniform market for the sale of RECs, making compliance easier and more predictable. This would help stabilize the market for RECs, and thus renewable energy, providing further incentives for expanding renewable energy facilities.

Federal RPS proposals have regularly been proposed in both houses of Congress, but thus far have not passed. Legislation that would implement a national RPS has passed the Senate three times since 2002,[61] and the House of Representatives has passed such a proposal in 2007 and 2009.

Federal RPS proposals are generally proposed as amendments to Title VI of PURPA.[62] Recent proposals have required that "retail electric supplier[s]" obtain between 15 percent and 20 percent of their energy sold from renewable sources by the year 2020.[63] Thus, the target percentage of each covered retail electricity supplier's energy would either need to be generated from renewable energy resources or the supplier would be compelled to purchase or exchange RECs.[64] As is often the case, recent proposals have also allowed a portion of the RPS compliance to come from efficiency measures.[65]

Some proposals provide that some of the funds generated via RPS compliance be shared with states.[66] These funds come from proceeds related to alternative compliance payments, which are fees paid by electricity sellers unable to acquire the RECs needed to satisfy the RPS (as discussed above). These proceeds are to be used for investments in renewable energy and efficiency projects.[67]

Federal RPS legislation has, to date, provided that state RPS programs would be allowed to coexist with the federal plan. Thus, states would be allowed, but not required, to revise, reduce, or repeal existing state RPS compliance requirements consistent with (i.e., at least as stringent as) the federal RPS. More stringent state programs would not be preempted, allowing states to require more (but not less) renewable energy than prescribed under the federal mandate.

Potential Impacts of a National RPS

A national RPS would impact a broad group of constituencies, including the covered utilities/electricity providers, state and federal regulators, and consumers. Each would bear a portion of the implementation burden, but some of that burden may be offset in each case by corresponding benefits flowing from the national RPS.

Impact on Electricity Suppliers

For covered retail electricity suppliers, a national RPS would have significant impacts on their investment decision-making process (and ultimate decisions), and would add administrative and operational requirements. Even without a national RPS, decisions to make capital-intensive investments, like construction of new generation facilities, are always difficult; a national RPS would provide an additional layer of complexity to an already multifaceted analysis. Under a national RPS, each supplier would need to determine whether it was preferable to invest in new generation infrastructure, directly or indirectly, or purchase the required RECs from other generators.[68] However, the ability to implement efficiency measures and buy RECs from others would help retail electric suppliers push some investment decisions down the road, allowing ample time for careful consideration of their capital investments.[69]

Impact on Regulators

A national RPS would likely require that state and federal regulators take on new or expanded obligations. Regulators would first be charged with developing a tracking program for RECs, and state and federal regulators would each have an enforcement function under a national RPS.

Any national RPS would require development of a program to verify and issue federal RECs to renewable energy generators; track REC sales, exchanges, and retirement; and enforce RPS compliance.[70] Most legislation has contemplated the use of existing and emerging state- or regional-level RECs tracking systems for implementation at the federal level.[71] Approximately thirty-six states have some form of RECs tracking systems for RPS, so there are ample options.

A federal RECs tracking program cannot simply adopt an existing state RECs tracking program, however, because each state program has its own special features.[72] A federal RPS would certainly have differences as well.[73] The biggest difference is likely to be in what constitutes "renewable energy" under the RPS.

Ultimately, regulators will need to deal with coordinating such issues, which will add time and effort, but the process should be manageable. Regional programs that track multiple state RECs, such as PJM's[74] Generation Attributes Tracking System (GATS), are already in place. Thus, adding federal RECs should not be overly onerous.[75] GATS records the generation attributes and related ownership as the RECs are traded or used for compliance.[76] GATS also creates generator-specific records that identify the attributes that electricity suppliers need to satisfy state policies.[77] Such tracking systems will gather data such as megawatt-hours produced, emissions, fuel source, and generator location, in addition to noting which state programs the energy meets and who owns the attributes for each tracked megawatt-hour of electricity.[78]

Similar REC tracking programs are in place around the country. The programs are run by the Independent System Operators (ISOs) and Regional Transmission Organizations (RTOs), which were organized to provide nondiscriminatory access to transmission mandated as part of electricity deregulation that occurred in the 1990s. The ISOs and RTOs running such programs include the Michigan Renewable Energy Certifications System, Midwest (M-RETS), Electric Reliability Council of Texas (ERCOT),[79] ISO New England,[80] and the Western Electricity Coordinating Council (WECC).[81] In fact, all of these RECs tracking programs use systems created by a single developer. As such, the addition of a national tracking system would not be effortless, but it should be manageable and efficient.

Consumer Impacts

Despite the fact that more than 50 percent of the country (both in terms of population and number of states) is already subject to an RPS, one of the most contested issues raised by possible national RPS legislation surrounds the likely impact on consumers. As is to be expected, small variances in RPS proposals can lead to a broad range of projected impacts. The chosen RPS mandate can mean significant differences in estimated outcomes. For example, an Energy Information Administration (EIA) analysis determined that a 15 percent national RPS would lead to an increase in retail electricity prices roughly 1 percent over the 2005 to 2030 period and that RECs under the same scenario would cost 1.9 cents per kilowatt-hour between 2020 and 2030 (see table on page 87).[82]

EIA analysis of a proposed 25 percent national RPS determined that the average retail electricity price would be 6.2 percent higher in 2030 and that REC prices of 3.8 cents and 4.8 cents per kilowatt-hour would be expected between 2025 and 2030.[83] These estimated differences of approximately 1 to 6 percent, at least when taking into account past increases caused by natural gas price spikes, mean that the consumer impacts of a national RPS would likely be relatively modest.[84] With more than half the country subject to some form of RPS, the issue is not whether an RPS will apply to most consumers; the question instead is whether all of the United States will be subject to an RPS or just some parts.[85]

Project Financing

If a national RPS were implemented, it would provide some incentive for all covered utilities to invest in renewable generation because of the two markets available for the output: the electricity market and the RECs market.[86]

However, depending on how confident investors are that the RECs market will last (and at what price), power projects under an RPS may require "more equity, less debt, and shorter debt repayment periods."[87] Energy developers can be expected to sign (or try to sign) contracts with market participants (utilities, industrial users, marketers, aggregators, etc.), but REC price volatility may cause contract terms to end up shorter than they were traditionally, adding additional uncertainty.[88] Some states have acted to address such concerns, but these concerns would remain for at least some time under a national RPS.[89] As such, a national RPS could have a significant impact on capital-intensive electricity investments.

Estimated RPS Costs

RPS Level	15%	25%
Est. retail price increase	1% between 2005 and 2030	Up to 6.2% by 2030
REC prices	1.9 cents between 2020 and 2030	3.8 to 4.8 cents between 2025 and 2030

Source: U.S. ENERGY INFORMATION ADMINISTRATION, IMPACTS OF A 15-PERCENT RENEWABLE PORTFOLIO STANDARD, at iv (June 2007).

Current State of Renewable Energy Credits and Certificates and Related Markets

The implementation of RPS programs led to some unforeseen consequences. Contracts created prior to state RPS legislation have led to litigation over the ownership of the newly created commodity, RECs, which were not contemplated at the time the original agreement was ratified. Additional litigation has followed with regard to how utilities can, and should, recover costs related to securing RECs in their efforts to comply with RPS mandates.

In *Wheelabrator Lisbon, Inc. v. Department of Public Utility Control*, the Connecticut Supreme Court was asked to determine whether the utility or the generator was the proper owner of RECs created pursuant to an entire output contract.[90] Because the state RPS, and thus state RECs, did not exist when the contract was drafted, the contract never mentioned who would own the later-created RECs.[91] The utility in the case entered a contract in 1991 to purchase all of a generation facility's output.[92] The Department of Public Utility Control (PUC) reviewed the contract and considered the issue, determining that the term "electricity" in the contract included the renewable attribute generated by the electricity purchased under the agreement. Thus, the PUC decided, the utility had purchased the RECs that were created by the RPS.[93] The court agreed.

As part of the rationale for this interpretation, the court explained that "unbundling" (separating) the renewable attributes from the generated electricity, rendering the possibility of the sale of each as a separate commodity, "implies that the renewable attribute of the energy generated by renewable energy sources is an inherent attribute of the energy." Thus, the court determined, when the RPS created the RECs, the RPS "did not result in an entirely new commodity"; instead, the result was the division of "a preexisting commodity," which the utility purchased under the contract.[94]

Not all reviewers have agreed with this determination. Some feel that RECs are an entirely new commodity[95] because they did not exist before the RPS, and thus came into existence with the passage of the RPS legislation. The Federal Energy Regulatory Commission (FERC), for example, determined the fact that the states have created RECs that are unbundled and tradeable "indicates that the environmental attributes do not inherently convey pursuant to an avoided cost contract to the purchasing utility."[96]

In fact, when *Wheelabrator Lisbon* was decided, FERC had clearly stated that contracts such as the one at issue in that case do not automatically grant ownership of the later-resulting RECs to the purchasing utility unless there is an express contract provision doing so.[97] FERC noted that unless otherwise specified, states were free to decide that power sales automatically transfer RECs to the purchaser; however, that authority must be found under state law.[98] Therefore, automatic transfer of RECs was a state law issue that was not inherently part of a wholesale power contract. Nonetheless, even where the RPS law is silent, states have generally determined that the purchasing utility in such cases, and not the renewable energy generator, is the owner of unanticipated RECs.[99]

State utility commissions and courts have also grappled with how to deal with recovery of costs related to RECs under power purchase contracts. For example, in *New Mexico Industrial Energy Consumers v. New Mexico Public Regulation Commission*, the New Mexico Supreme Court held that the costs for RECs could not be recovered through a utility's "automatic adjustment clause" because RECs are not "purchased power."[100] Instead, traditional rate case procedures must be used for the utility to recover costs for RECs.[101]

The New Mexico RPS is found in the state's Renewable Energy Act (REA). The RPS required that, as of 2006, at least 5 percent of retail energy sold by IOUs come from renewable sources, with an additional 1 percent annual increase through 2020 (up to 20 percent).[102] The statutory language allows for the recovery of reasonable costs of RPS compliance via the "rate-making process."[103] The New Mexico Public Utility Act, which also applied, had a fast-track recovery provision for certain costs that could be recovered via an "automatic adjustment clause."[104] Items recovered under the automatic adjustment clause are not required to go through the traditional process utilities normally use to change rates, which requires the full notice, hearing, and approval process.[105] The relevant provision provides that a utility can recover "taxes or cost of fuel, gas or purchased power" through the automatic adjustment clause.[106]

The New Mexico Public Regulation Commission (NMPRC) decided that RECs were required as part of the utility's "energy supply mix," and were thus a "purchased power cost" (or were "closely related to purchased power"), which could be included for recovery in the automatic adjustment clause.[107] The court agreed with NMPRC's determination that the automatic adjustment clause was part of the "rate-making process," as required by the REA, but determined that NMPRC did not have the authority to permit recovery of RECs costs through the automatic adjustment clause.[108]

The automatic adjustment clause was designed to "flow through" increases or decreases in costs of "delivered energy" to electricity customers.[109] The court found that RECs did not satisfy the "delivered" energy requirement because the energy generated to create the RECs was not also purchased and delivered to the utility's customers.[110] The court stated that although the automatic adjustment clause provided an efficient and cost-effective mechanism for RECs cost recovery, state law did not permit that method of recovery.[111]

Conclusion

Renewable energy laws, including RPS programs, are designed to encourage investment in new renewable energy infrastructure, with the hope of facilitating broader energy and economic policy goals. Renewable energy programs have been advanced to reduce environmental harm, stimulate job growth, improve national security, and address climate change concerns. A national RPS would help facilitate a national market for RECs and minimize or eliminate constitutionally related litigation concerns, as well as harmonize inconsistent state rulings on renewable energy issues.

Regardless, renewable energy mandates, whether state or federal, do not stand alone, and require support and assistance in a multitude of areas. Project financing, tax incentives, subsidies, transmission infrastructure, and even parallel environmental and climate change legislation (e.g., a cap-and-trade program) are essential to facilitating renewable energy projects, meeting renewable energy mandates, and ultimately achieving the lofty goals of the mandates themselves.

Notes

1. Pub. L. No. 95-617, § 2, 92 Stat. 3117, 3119 (codified as amended in scattered sections of 7, 15, 16, and 30 U.S.C.).

2. *Cf.* Gunnar Birgisson & Erik Petersen, *Renewable Energy Development Incentives: Strengths, Weaknesses and the Interplay*, 19 Elec. J. 40, 45 (Apr. 2006) (explaining that PURPA operated as the early option for renewable energy mandates and that state renewable energy mandates are the "most significant current example").

3. *See* Joshua P. Fershee, *Changing Resources, Changing Market: The Impact of a National Renewable Portfolio Standard on the U.S. Energy Industry*, 29 Energy L.J. 49, 50 & n.4 (2008).

4. *See, e.g.*, Renewable Energy and Energy Conservation Tax Act of 2007, H.R. 3221, 110th Cong. (as passed by the House, Aug. 4, 2007).

5. *See id.* § 9611(a).

6. *See id.*

7. *See, e.g.*, Mont. Code § 69-3-20 (11) ("A public utility or competitive electricity supplier may petition the commission for a short-term waiver from full compliance with the [RPS] and the [related] penalties.")

8. *Id.*

9. *Id.*

10. *See id.*

11. *See id.* ("The Secretary shall accept payment equal to 200 percent of the average market value of Federal renewable energy credits and Federal energy efficiency credits for the applicable compliance period or 3.0 cents per kilowatt hour. . . .").

12. *Id.*

13. American Clean Energy and Security Act of 2009, H.R. 2454, 111th Cong. (2009).

14. Nancy Rader, The Mechanics of a Renewable Portfolio Standard Applied at the Federal Level (1997) (on file with author).

15. *Id.*

16. *See* Me. Rev. Stat. Ann. tit. 35-A, § 3210 (1997).

17. *Id.* § 3210(3).

18. *See* Union of Concerned Scientists, Maine Renewable Portfolio Standard Summary I (2008), *available at* http://www.ucsusa.org/assets/documents/clean_energy/maine.pdf.

19. *See id.*

20. *Id.*

21. *See* Me. Rev. Stat. Ann. tit. 35-A, § 3210(3-A) (2010).

22. *Id.* § 3210(3-A)(A).

23. 2008 Mich. Pub. Acts 143, § 3(c)(3)z (enrolled S. Bill 213).

24. Ohio Pub. Util. Comm., Alternative Energy Portfolio Standard, 4901:1-40-01(F), *available at* http://www.puc.state.oh.us/emplibrary/files/legal/rules/chapters/4901$1-40.doc.

25. 73 P.S. § 1648.1 *et seq.*

26. *See generally* Database of State Incentives for Renewables and Efficiency, Rules, Regulations, & Policies for Renewable Energy, http://www.dsireusa.org/summarytables/reg1.cfm?&CurrentPageID=7&EE=0&RE=1 (last visited Apr. 22, 2010) (providing state-by-state laws relating to renewable and efficient energy policy).

27. Iowa Code § 476.41 *et seq.* (2010).

28. Tex. Util. Code § 39.904 (2010).

29. *See, e.g.,* Va. Code § 56-585.2(C) ("It is in the public interest for utilities to achieve . . . [this statute's] 'RPS Goals.' Accordingly, the Commission, in addition to providing recovery of incremental RPS program costs . . . , shall increase the fair combined rate of return on common equity for each utility participating in such program. . . .").

30. *See, e.g.,* N.D. Century Code § 49-02-28 ("This [renewable energy] objective is voluntary and there is no penalty or sanction for a retail provider of electricity that fails to meet this objective.").

31. *See* Headwaters Economics, Clean Energy Leadership in the Rockies: Competitive Positioning in the Emerging Green Economy 63 (June 2010), *available at* http://www.headwaterseconomics.org/greeneconomy/CleanEnergyLeadership.pdf ("Utah is one of few states in the country that has a Renewable Portfolio Goal that offers utility [*sic*] a 'cost-effectiveness' exit strategy, rather than a mandate backed up with penalties for noncompliance. In the absence of an enforcement mechanism, it is questionable how well the policy will succeed.").

32. Mo. Senate Bill 54 (2007), *available at* http://www.senate.mo.gov/07info/pdf-bill/comm/SB54.pdf.

33. Mo. Rev. Stat. §§ 393.1020–393.1030 (2010).

34. *Id.*

35. Pub. L. No. 95-617, § 2, 92 Stat. 3117, 3119 (codified, as amended, in various sections of 7, 15, 16, and 30 U.S.C.).

36. *Midwest Power Systems Inc.*, 78 FERC ¶ 61,067 (Jan. 29, 1997).

37. S. Cal. Edison Co. and San Diego Gas & Elec. Co., 70 FERC ¶ 61,215 (Feb. 23, 1995) ("Our decision here simply makes clear that the State can pursue its policy choices concerning particular generation technologies consistent with the requirements of PURPA and our regulations, so long as such action does not result in rates above avoided cost.").

38. For an excellent resource regarding renewable energy legislation, see the website, Database of State Incentives for Renewables & Efficiency (DSIRE): http://www.dsireusa.org.

39. Cal. Pub. Util. Code § 399.11 et seq.

40. Cal. Exec. Order, S-21-09 (Sept. 15, 2009), http://gov.ca.gov/executive-order/13269.

41. Proposed Decision Authorizing Use of Renewable Energy Credits for Compliance with the California Renewables Portfolio Standard, issued Oct. 29, 2008 in CPUC Rulemaking 06-02-012.

42. *See id.*

43. N.Y. Pub. Serv. Comm'n, Order, Case 03-E-0188 (Sept. 24, 2004), *available at* http://www3.dps.state.ny.us/pscweb/WebFileRoom.nsf/Web/85D8CCC6A42DB86F85256F1900533518/$File/301.03e0188.RPS.pdf?OpenElement.

44. N.Y. Pub. Serv. Comm'n, Order, Case 03-E-0188 (Jan. 8, 2010), *available at* http://documents.dps.state.ny.us/public/Common/ViewDoc.aspx?DocRefId={30CFE590-E7E1-473B-A648-450A39E80F48}.

45. N.Y. State Dep't of Pub. Serv. Comm'n, Order Establishing Energy Efficiency Portfolio Standard and Approving Programs, Case 07-M-0548 (June 23, 2008).

46. Minn. Stat. § 216B.1691 (2010).

47. U.S. Const. art. 1, § 8.

48. *E.g.*, Bacchus Imports, Ltd. v. Dias, 468 U.S. 263 (1984); New England Power Co. v. New Hampshire, 455 U.S. 331 (1982); Wyoming v. Oklahoma, 502 U.S. 437 (1992).

49. OHIO REV. CODE ANN. § 4928.64(B)(3).

50. ARIZ. ADMIN. CODE R14-2-1806(D), (E).

51. *See, e.g.*, Benjamin Sovacool & Christopher Cooper, *Congress Got it Wrong: The Case for a National Renewable Portfolio Standard and Implications for Policy*, 3 ENVTL. & ENERGY L. & POL'Y J. 85, 89 (2008) ("We suggest that a national RPS can help prevent 'free riders,' create a more equitable electricity marketplace, and avoid legal challenges related to the dormant Commerce Clause.").

52. Trevor D. Stiles, *Renewable Resources and the Dormant Commerce Clause*, 4 ENVTL. & ENERGY L. & POL'Y J. 33, 63 (2009) ("Any requirement that the energy used to meet the RPS threshold must be generated within the state itself would almost certainly be found to violate the Dormant Commerce Clause."); *cf.* Lincoln L. Davies, *Power Forward: The Argument for a National RPS*, 42 CONN. L. REV. 1339, 1368 (2010) (stating that the "most prominent" jurisdictional concerns created by the lack of a national RPS "are dormant Commerce Clause concerns"); Benjamin K. Sovacool, *The Best of Both Worlds: Environmental Federalism and the Need for Federal Action on Renewable Energy and Climate Change*, 27 STAN. ENVTL. L.J. 397, 458 (2008) ("The growing tension between state and federal electricity regulators may mean that a Commerce Clause challenge is impending."); Joel B. Eisen, *Realizing the Promise of Electricity Deregulation: Regulatory Linearity, Commerce Clause Brinksmanship, and Retrenchment in Electric Utility Deregulation*, 40 WAKE FOREST L. REV. 545, 572 (2005) ("Electricity involves a national marketplace . . . [and] is perhaps the clearest case of unfettered Commerce Clause jurisdiction extant today (at least in a situation where some parties believe the federal government does not have it).").

53. Complaint at ¶¶ 18–46, TransCanada Power Mktg. v. Bowles, Civ. Action No. 4:10-cv-40070-FDS (C.D. Mass. filed Apr. 17, 2010).

54. *See* Erin Ailworth, *Deal Reached in State Energy Suit*, BOSTON GLOBE, May 29, 2010, http://www.boston.com/business/articles/2010/05/29/deal_reached_in_state_energy_suit/ ("TransCanada plans to drop claims against the state's solar program in return for an agreement to grandfather electricity supply contracts[, which] would allow suppliers with existing contracts to escape the higher fee imposed for being out of compliance with the state's renewable energy goals.").

55. *Id.*

56. *See* Robin Kundis Craig, *Constitutional Contours for the Design and Implementation of Multistate Renewable Energy Programs and Projects*, 81 U. COLO. L. REV. 771, 776 (2010).

57. *Id.*

58. *See* Star Scientific Inc. v. Beales, 278 F.3d 339, 348 (4th Cir. 2002).

59. *See* Craig, *supra* note 56, at 800–01.

60. Mary Ann Ralls, *Congress Got It Right: There's No Need to Mandate Renewable Portfolio Standards*, 27 ENERGY L.J. 451, 451 (2006) ("When the sum of other federal, state, regional, local, and utility-specific activities in the renewable arena is calculated, [it is clear that other efforts] supplant the need for a federal RPS.").

61. Energy Policy Act of 2005, H.R. 6, 109th Cong. (as passed by the Senate, June 28, 2005); Energy Policy Act of 2003, H.R. 6, 108th Cong. (as passed by the Senate, July 31, 2003); Energy Policy Act of 2002, H.R. 4, 107th Cong. (as passed by the Senate, Apr. 24, 2002).

62 . H.R. 969, 110th Cong. § 9611(a) (2007) (proposing to add by amendment a new section 610 to the end of Title VI of PURPA).

63. H.R. 3221 § 9611(a).

64. *Id.*

65. *Id.*

66. *See* NAT'L RENEWABLE ENERGY LABORATORY. FEDERAL RPS BILL COMPARISON 5 (2009), *available at* http://www.cleanenergystates.org/JointProjects/RPS/Bird_april7_Presentation.pdf (comparing four federal RPS proposals).

67. *Id.*

68. *See* Thomas W. Kaslow & Robert S. Pindyck, *Valuing Flexibility in Utility Planning*, 7 ELEC. J. 60 (Mar. 1994).

69. David Berry, *The Market for Tradable Renewable Energy Credits*, 42 ECOLOGICAL ECON. 369, 371 (2002) ("By being able to defer an investment decision, the utility may be able to get additional information on its investment options or negotiate more favorable contracts to purchase renewable generating equipment." (citation omitted)).

70. Renewable Energy and Energy Conservation Tax Act of 2007, H.R. 3221 § 9611(a), 110th Cong. (as passed by the House, Aug. 4, 2007).

71. *Id.*

72. Karlynn S. Cory & Blair G. Swezey, *Renewable Portfolio Standards in the States: Balancing Goals and Rules*, 40 ELEC. J. 21, 24 (Apr. 2007) ("REC tracking platforms have been designed for the specific state or regional circumstances. As more states employ REC tracking systems to monitor RPS compliance, the trading of RECs between systems with divergent definitions and tracking structures will have to be addressed.").

73. Response from Edison Electric Institute (EEI) to Rep. John Dingell & Rep. Rick Boucher 13, http://energycommerce.house.gov/Climate_Change/RSP%20feedback/EEI%2006%2009%2007.pdf (last visited Feb. 9, 2008) (stating that nine of the then twenty-four existing state RPS plans would have failed to meet a federal RPS target of 15 percent by 2020).

74. PJM is a Regional Transmission Organization that serves approximately 51 million people and "that coordinates the movement of wholesale electricity in all or parts of Delaware, Illinois, Indiana, Kentucky, Maryland, Michigan, New Jersey, North Carolina, Ohio, Pennsylvania, Tennessee, Virginia, West Virginia and the District of Columbia." *See* PJM, WHO WE ARE, http://www.pjm.com/about-pjm/who-we-are.aspx (last visited Apr. 22, 2010).

75. *See* Press Release, PJM/EIS, PJM EIS Launches Environmental Tracking System (Apr. 15 2005), http://www.pjm-miso.com/contributions/news-releases/2005/20050415-GATS-launched.pdf.

76. *Id.*

77. *Id.*

78. *Id.*

79. ERCOT, the Electric Reliability Council of Texas, is the program administrator of the REC trading program in Texas. *See* ENERGY RELIABILITY COUNCIL OF TEXAS, RENEWABLE ENERGY CREDIT, http://www.ercot.com/services/programs/rec/ (last visited Feb. 7, 2011).

80. ISO New England is an RTO serving Connecticut, Maine, Massachusetts, New Hampshire, Rhode Island, and Vermont. *See* ISO NEW ENGLAND, OVERVIEW, http://www.iso-ne.com/aboutiso/co_profile/overview/index.html (last visited Feb. 7, 2011).

81. The WECC was formed by a merger of several groups in the West and Southwest, and "WECC's interconnection-wide focus is intended to complement current efforts to form Regional Transmission Organizations (RTO) in various parts of the West." WESTERN ELECTRICITY COORDINATING COUNCIL, ABOUT WECC, http://www.wecc.biz/About/Pages/default.aspx (last visited Feb. 7, 2011).

82. ENERGY INFO. ADMIN., OFFICE OF INTEGRATED ANALYSIS & FORECASTING, U.S. DEP'T OF ENERGY, IMPACTS OF A 15-PERCENT RENEWABLE PORTFOLIO STANDARD, at iv (2007), http://www.eia.doe.gov/oiaf/servicerpt/prps/index.html.

83. ENERGY INFO. ADMIN., OFFICE OF INTEGRATED ANALYSIS & FORECASTING, U.S. DEP'T OF ENERGY, ENERGY AND ECONOMIC IMPACTS OF IMPLEMENTING BOTH A 25-PERCENT RENEWABLE PORTFOLIO STANDARD AND A 25-PERCENT RENEWABLE FUEL STANDARD BY 2025, at xi (2007), http://www.eia.doe.gov/oiaf/servicerpt/eeim/index.html.

84. *See* Karen Palmer & Dallas Burtraw, *The Environmental Impacts of Electricity Restructuring: Looking Back and Looking Forward*, 1 ENVTL. & ENERGY L. & POL'Y J. 171, 196 & fig. 8 (2005) ("The resulting effect of the run up in natural gas prices in 2001 on wholesale electricity prices is evident in the retail price spike in 2001. . . .").

85. *See* Benjamin K. Sovacool & Christopher Cooper, Letter to the Editor, *Messrs. Sovacool and Cooper Respond*, 19 ELEC. J. 4 (Dec. 2006) ("The true question is whether a federal

RPS mandate is a better intervention than a patchwork of 50 inconsistent, state–based RPS mandates.").

86. RYAN WISER & STEVEN PICKLE, FINANCING INVESTMENTS IN RENEWABLE ENERGY: THE ROLE OF POLICY DESIGN AND RESTRUCTURING, at xvi (Mar. 1997), http://eetd.lbl.gov/EA/EMP/reports/39826.pdf (stating that under RPS programs, renewable energy generation owners can create revenue "from two 'commodity' markets: the power market and the REC market").

87. *Cf. id.* at xv.

88. *Id.*

89. RYAN H. WISER & GALEN BARBOSE, ENVTL. ENERGY TECHS. DIV., LAWRENCE BERKELEY NAT'L LABORATORY, RENEWABLES PORTFOLIO STANDARDS IN THE UNITED STATES: A STATUS REPORT WITH DATA THROUGH 2007, at 30 (Apr. 2008), *available at* http://eetd.lbl.gov/ea/ems/reports/lbnl-154e.pdf ("Renewable projects are capital intensive, and concerns about the challenges of project financing with REC price variability has spurred some states to adopt provisions to help projects secure financing."). At least fifteen states have adopted such provisions. *See id.*

90. 931 A.2d 159, 163 (Conn. 2007).

91. *See id.* at 170.

92. *Id.* at 163, 166.

93. *Id.* at 176.

94. *Id.*

95. See *In re* Ownership of Renewable Energy Certificates, 913 A.2d 825, 827 (N.J. Super. Ct. App. Div. 2007) (stating that the issue in the case was the ownership of RECs, "a commodity created" by the state the electric power industry); CAROL SUE TOMBARI, POWER OF THE PEOPLE: AMERICA'S NEW ELECTRICITY CHOICES 273 (2008) (considering RECs as "New Financial Instruments and Tools"); *cf.* David Hurlbut, A *Look Behind the Texas Renewable Portfolio Standard: A Case Study*, 48 NAT. RES. J. 129, 150 (2008) (discussing the "separate" values of both the power and the green attributes created by generating electricity from renewable resources).

96. American Ref-Fuel Co., 107 F.E.R.C. ¶ 61,016, at 61,044 (2004).

97. American Ref-Fuel Co., 105 F.E.R.C. ¶ 61,004, at 61,005 (2003), *reh'g denied*, 107 F.E.R.C. ¶ 61,016 (2004).

98. *Id.*

99. *Wheelabrator Lisbon.*, 931 A.2d at 174 (reporting that at least nine states have made such a determination).

100. 168 P.3d 105, 116 (N.M. 2007).

101. *See id.*

102. N.M. STAT. § 62-16-4(A)(1).

103. N.M. STAT. § 62-16-6(A).

104. *Id.* § 62-8-7(E).

105. *N.M. Indus.*, 168 P.3d at 108.

106. N.M. STAT. § 62-8-7(E).

107. *N.M. Indus.*, 168 P.3d at 109–10.

108. *See id.* at 111–16.

109. *Id.* at 114 (quoting N.M. PUB. REG. COMM'N R. 550).

110. *Id.*

111. *Id.* at 116.

chapter five

Facility Siting and Permitting

Patricia E. Salkin

Introduction

The manner in which governments approve facility siting and permitting for renewable energy projects is a key consideration in both project design and the cost-benefit analysis of project feasibility. A variety of federal, state, and local laws may be implicated depending upon the magnitude of the project and the geographic location of the project site. In addition to the application of a suite of environmental review–related statutes for proposed clean energy projects, public participation issues as well as land acquisition issues may be present. At times, federal and state preemption may factor into the siting and permitting analysis, and local zoning and building code laws and regulations may also affect projects. This chapter is designed to provide an overview of whether and how these laws apply to siting and permitting applications.

The National Environmental Policy Act and State Environmental Review Laws

The National Environmental Policy Act (NEPA) was enacted in 1969 to establish a process for federal agencies to identify and consider the environmental impacts of their programs and activities before making key decisions.[1] If it is determined that a federal action will have significant impacts of the human environment, the responsible federal agency, known as the "lead agency," must prepare an environmental impact statement, or "EIS."[2] The EIS should include analysis of the direct, indirect, and cumulative environmental impacts, as well as project alternatives (including the no-action alternative), other reasonable courses of action, and mitigation measures.[3] NEPA is a procedural statute and does not require agencies to refrain from actions that will have environmental impacts or choose alternatives with fewer negative impacts; "once an agency has made a decision subject to NEPA's procedural requirements, the

The author thanks Albany Law School student Robin Wheeler '10 and staff attorney Amy Lavine for their assistance in the preparation of this chapter.

only role for a court is to insure that the agency has considered the environmental consequences; it cannot 'interject itself within the area of discretion of the executive as to the choice of the action to be taken.'"[4]

Renewable energy projects often require federal approvals that trigger NEPA review. The Bureau of Land Management (BLM), for example, must conduct NEPA reviews before granting easements or leases for federal lands sought to be developed with solar, wind, or geothermal projects.[5] The Bureau of Ocean Energy Management, Regulation and Enforcement (BOEMRE) (also known as the Bureau of Ocean Energy (BOE) and formerly known as the Minerals Management Service (MMS)) has a similar role in leases of offshore land for wind farms,[6] and NEPA reviews of hydrokinetic projects on the outer continental shelf are led by the Federal Energy Regulatory Commission (FERC).[7] The Department of Energy may also issue NEPA documents for renewable energy projects.[8]

If a project is not subject to an EIS under NEPA, it may still be required to go through a similar state-level environmental review process.[9] In New York, for example, wind projects not requiring any federal approvals will nevertheless be subject to review under the State Environmental Quality Review Act.[10] For the most part, state environmental review statutes (sometimes called "mini-NEPAs" or SEPAs) mirror NEPA and require state agencies and local governments to assess environmental impacts, mitigations, and alternatives before approving actions with significant environmental impacts. Unlike NEPA, however, some of the state environmental review acts impose mitigation requirements. Thus, the New York State Environmental Quality Review Act (SEQRA) provides that "[w]hen an agency decides to carry out or approve an action which has been the subject of an environmental impact statement, it shall make an explicit finding that . . . to the maximum extent practicable, adverse environmental effects revealed in the environmental impact statement process will be minimized or avoided."[11]

Under NEPA and state counterparts, if an agency determines that a project (including a clean energy project) will not have significant environmental impacts, and if the agency has followed the proper procedures, its decision will generally be upheld if it is reasonable and supported by the evidence.[12] However, the courts may overturn an agency's decision if it fails to take a "hard look" at the project's impacts. For example, in a case decided under the New York State Environmental Quality Review Act, a town's determination that its wind turbine law would not have any significant environmental impacts was overturned. The court concluded that even though the town board had identified "the relevant areas of environmental concern" in arriving at its conclusion, it failed to take a "hard look" at those environmental concerns and did not set forth a "reasoned elaboration" for its determination. The fact that the new law was more restrictive than the prior law in terms of setbacks and noise standards did not support the negative declaration.[13]

Assuming that a project may have significant environmental impacts and an EIS is prepared, the designated lead agency is held to the hard-look standard of review regarding its analysis of the project's impacts, mitigation strategies, and possible alternatives. Impacts required to be addressed in the EIS will vary based on the specifics of the project. For wind projects, they may include impacts to the water supply, bird and bat mortality, noise, ice throw, property values, and scenic views.[14] Similarly, the alternatives that must be considered will differ on a case-to-case basis, but may include different site locations, smaller projects, alternate site layouts, different technologies, and alternative construction phasing.[15]

Courts applying the hard-look standard of review acknowledge that the demands of the environmental review process must be "viewed in the light of the rule of reason"[16] and "bounded by some notion of feasibility."[17] The Supreme Court of Washington explained that an "FEIS does not violate the 'rule of reason' merely because it does not list 'moving turbines away from every possible viewpoint' as a potential mitigation measure. The FEIS served its function of presenting 'decisionmakers with a "reasonably thorough discussion"' of the visual impact of the project."[18] In a case involving the construction of a hydroelectric plant, the District of Columbia Circuit Court applied the rule of reason and held that although purchasing power from an existing supplier was an "alternative" that had to be considered under NEPA, the lead agency did not need to explore the possibility of purchasing power from out-of-state suppliers.[19] And in a case decided under the California Environmental Quality Act, it was held that the EIS for exploratory geothermal wells did not need to include an analysis of the impacts of commercial geothermal development because such development was speculative and the approval of the exploratory wells did not commit the county to approve any more intensive geothermal development in the future.[20]

When NEPA or state NEPAs are used by environmental organizations to delay or halt renewable energy projects because of their impacts on endangered species or water quality, among other things, the results can seem contrary to the environmental protection purposes of these laws. Environmental review laws, however, have not evolved to ease the burden on facilities with *positive* environmental impacts like reducing emissions and pollution from more traditional power plants.[21] One suggestion to address this problem has been to waive NEPA review for renewable energy facilities.[22] The better position, and the one taken by many environmental organizations, is that NEPA should be applied in a more nuanced way so as to evaluate positive environmental impacts alongside negative impacts.[23] This analysis would consider as part of the no-action alternative the emissions impacts that would result if the renewable project did not go forward, and it would also "cover a geographic scope that is adequate to allow full consideration of emission reductions."[24] Agencies involved in environmental reviews have recently begun to incorporate the negative impacts of greenhouse gas emissions into the review process,[25] and as they become more skilled in making these evaluations, the positive impacts of clean energy projects should begin to fit more easily within the NEPA process.

Specific Environmental Issues

Protected Areas

The environmental review process will address impacts to critical habitat areas and other natural environments, but separate approvals may be needed for projects proposed for protected lands. In 2009, for example, the U.S. Forest Service refused to grant permits for three meteorological data towers that were to be used to explore the possibility of developing a large-scale wind project. The Forest Service cited as reasons for its denial the need to construct new roads, visual impacts on forest landscapes, impacts on recreational opportunities, habitat degradation, and wildlife impacts.[26]

On the other hand, the Adirondack Park Agency (New York) has proposed a streamlined and expedited process for the siting of small-scale residential and commercial wind turbines up to a height of 125 feet. Among the requirements in the proposal are that the turbines blend in with the surroundings so as to be "substantially invisible," consistent with the agency's policy on the siting of telecommunications towers. The proposal also limits blade diameter to no more than 25 feet, and it would impose setbacks of at least 150 feet. Under the review criteria, permits would be issued only for projects that would not have any undue adverse impact upon the natural, scenic, aesthetic, ecological, wildlife, historic, recreational, or open space resources of the park.[27]

Protected Species and Wildlife Impacts

Energy projects proposed on lands containing endangered species habitats may be subject to the Endangered Species Act (ESA).[28] The ESA was enacted in 1973, and it prohibits the "taking" (a broadly defined term) of species listed as endangered,[29] except pursuant to an incidental take permit.[30] ESA violations have arisen in the context of hydroelectric projects,[31] and as wind development becomes more widespread they are likely to arise with increasing frequency in relation to turbine projects, which can have fatal impacts on birds and bats.[32] The District Court for the District of Maryland has held that a wind farm was in violation of the ESA for insufficiently studying and disclosing the potential impacts on endangered Indiana bats. The court enjoined the developer from constructing any additional turbines or operating any turbines (except during the winter, when the bats hibernate) until it obtains an incidental take permit from the Fish and Wildlife Service (FWS).[33]

The Migratory Bird Treaty Act of 1918 (MBTA) covers hundreds of species of birds and may also be implicated in the siting and approval of renewable energy projects, especially wind farms and transmission lines.[34] Like the ESA, the MBTA prohibits the taking of covered species, but unlike the ESA, there is no process to obtain an incidental take permit. Instead, regulations are promulgated and selectively enforced by the U.S. Fish and Wildlife Service.[35] The Service's Wind Turbine Guidelines Advisory Committee issued voluntary guidelines in 2010 (covering bats and other species as well as migratory birds),[36] and turbine operators that follow them are unlikely to be prosecuted by the FWS. As illustrated in *United States v. Moon Lake Electric Association*, a case where the MBTA was enforced only after FWS gave advance warning to the company requiring it to install inexpensive technology to prevent bird electrocutions, FWS is unlikely to enforce the MBTA against renewable energy facilities that implement measures to prevent reasonably foreseeable bird takings.[37]

Even if a renewable energy project will not take any protected species or encroach on their habitat, a project's effects on wildlife will be considered as part of the environmental review process. As a result, for example, the New York Department of Environmental Conservation issued guidelines for evaluating the potential impacts of commercial wind farms on birds and bats. The guidelines are intended to provide comparability of data collection among sites and between years so that the information from each site contributes to a statewide understanding of the ecological effects of wind energy generation.[38] Under the New York State Environmental Quality Review Act, adverse project impacts must be mitigated to the maximum extent practicable, and measures that might be taken to reduce bird and bat mortality include pre-construction avian surveys, the avoidance of high-value habitat areas, buffer zones, placing transmission lines underground, and post-construction monitoring are now common techniques used to minimize impacts on bird and bat populations.[39]

Since hydroelectric projects can have negative impacts on aquatic species, these will also be assessed during the environmental review process. Additionally, geothermal energy projects may have significant adverse environmental impacts, including "thermal and mineral stream pollution from plant discharge, loss of thermophile biodiversity and geologic record, unknown groundwater depletion and subsidence, and tectonic effects of injection and re-injection of water into geothermal reservoirs."[40]

Visual Impacts

In 2005, prominent environmental activist Robert F. Kennedy, Jr., authored a controversial op-ed piece in the New York Times opposing the Cape Wind project. His opposition was based primarily on the visual impacts the development would have on Cape Cod, where his family owns property, though he also cited impacts on marine life.[41] Indeed, visual impacts are often one of the most controversial aspects of wind farm projects.[42] Community members have also opposed wind turbines out of the belief that wind turbine aesthetics could harm tourism.[43] Though entirely subjective, aesthetic effects can be minimized somewhat by "painting [turbines] a neutral color, arranging them in a visually pleasing manner, and designing each turbine uniformly."[44] For offshore projects, visual impacts can also be minimized by locating turbines farther out to sea.

Aesthetic impacts alone will generally be insufficient to invalidate the approval of a proposed wind project. In a Texas case involving a nuisance claim brought against a wind farm, the court acknowledged that "[u]nobstructed sunsets, panoramic landscapes, and starlit skies have inspired countless artists and authors and have brought great pleasure to those fortunate enough to live in scenic rural settings. The loss of this view has undoubtedly impacted Plaintiffs." This emotional toll, however, is not enough to support a nuisance claim. As the Texas court explained, an aesthetically rooted nuisance claim must be accompanied by some invasion of the plaintiff's property to be actionable.[45] However, aesthetic interests may be considered in zoning matters. The Supreme Court of Kansas, for example, upheld a county-wide ban on commercial wind farms, explaining that the "Board's findings [relating to aesthetics] could reasonably have been found to justify its decision: that the commercial wind farms would adversely, if not dramatically, affect the aesthetics of the county and for that reason should be prohibited."[46]

The visual impacts associated with wind farms and other aspects of their regulation are discussed in greater detail in chapter 16.

Cultural and Historic Impacts

The National Historic Preservation Act (NHPA)

The National Historic Preservation Act (NHPA),[47] enacted in 1966, requires federal agencies to consider the impacts of their "undertakings"[48] on property listed on or eligible for listing on the National Register of Historic Places.[49] As with NEPA, review under NHPA is mostly procedural, and an agency need not adopt mitigations or abandon an undertaking, so long as it follows the process established by the Act. A federal agency undertaking a construction project must consult with the State Historic Preservation Officer and other appropriate parties to help it determine whether there are any historic properties in the area potentially affected by the project, and if there are, whether the project will have any adverse effects on them. If the agency identifies likely adverse impacts, a consultation process ensues that ideally leads to agreed-upon measures to eliminate or mitigate these adverse effects.[50]

In a case involving the extension of a federal lands lease for the development of geothermal resources, the Ninth Circuit Court of Appeals found an NHPA violation where the agencies failed to consult with appropriate persons or consider the possible impacts on historic and cultural sites. The lease extension did not continue the status quo because it did not preserve the agencies' authority to prevent surface disturbances related to geothermal development, and it was not saved by a later NHPA consultation made in relation to approval of the company's geothermal plant because that consultation did not address whether the lease should have been granted at all.[51] On the other hand, no NHPA violation was found in a case involving the Army Corps' approval of a hydroelectric facility upgrade because the Corps provided the plaintiffs with adequate opportunity to receive information and express their views, it adequately considered the project's impacts on prehistoric cultural resources, and it agreed to mitigations with the State Historic Preservation Officer.[52]

The Religious Freedom Restoration Act (RFRA)

The Religious Freedom Restoration Act (RFRA) prohibits federal agencies from imposing any "substantial burden" on religious exercise unless the burden is supported by compelling governmental interests and is the least restrictive means of furthering that interest.[53] The substantial burden standard is also used under the Religious Land Use and Institutionalized Persons Act (RLUIPA), which is limited in the renewable energy context to zoning and landmarking laws.[54]

RFRA has arisen in the context of renewable energy facility siting where a project will impact sacred Native American sites. *Snoqualmie Indian Tribe v. FERC*[55] involved the relicensing of a hydroelectric facility located on a waterfall considered sacred by the tribe's members. The tribe claimed that the project substantially burdened its members' free exercise by depriving them of access to the falls, eliminating the mist necessary for their religious experience, and altering the natural and sacred flow of water over the falls. The court rejected these arguments, explaining that to prove a "substantial burden," the tribe would have needed to show that the federal action "forced [its members] to choose between following the tenets of their religion and receiving a government benefit . . . or . . . coerced [them] to act contrary to their religious beliefs by the threat of civil or criminal sanctions."[56] A similar result was reached in a case where Pele practitioners claimed that geothermal development tapping a volcano's heat source would desecrate the body of the goddess Pele and interfere with their religious exercise.[57] Tribal members have also voiced opposition to the Cape Wind project in Nantucket Sound. They claim that the turbines will interfere with their view of the rising sun and that it will desecrate land where their ancestors are buried. Despite these concerns, the project was approved by Interior Secretary Ken Salazar in 2010. He explained that "The need to preserve the environmental resources and rich cultural heritage of Nantucket Sound must be weighed in the balance with the importance of developing new renewable energy sources and strengthening our nation's energy security while battling climate change and creating jobs[.]"[58]

Public Participation Issues

NEPA and state-level environmental review statutes provide opportunities for public participation in the approval of renewable energy projects. Some state siting laws provide additional opportunities for public participation. Under the Minnesota statute, for example, affected landowners and local governments receive a copy of permit applications and have at least thirty days to submit comments. The state then holds a public comment meeting for each application, and it may hold a contested case meeting if requested by the public.[59] The California Energy Commission follows an environmental justice policy and the "cornerstone of [its] approach is based on wide-reaching public outreach efforts by the Siting, Transmission & Environmental Protection Division, the Hearing Office, Media & Public Communications Office, in addition to the Public Adviser's Office, to notify, inform and involve community members, including non-English speaking people."[60]

A notable example of a project that went above and beyond minimal public participation requirements is the Bluewater wind farm development being planned off the shore of Delaware.[61] To head off local opposition, Bluewater hired consultants to prepare visual models of what the wind farm would look like and to respond to concerns about bird kills and wind availability. The company held public meetings, and its director of communications regularly appeared on a local talk show to respond to the community's questions about wind turbines and to explain why wind power was preferable to coal and natural gas. Eventually, when the Public Service Commission solicited comments, they came in ten to one in favor of Bluewater's project. A poll taken by the University of Delaware showed that 91 percent of Delaware residents supported the proposal. Even the coastal tourist towns that relied on the view more than other parts of the state came to support the project.[62]

Land Acquisition

Eminent Domain

Some of the earliest Supreme Court and state high court cases adopting a broad interpretation of the public use requirement for eminent domain involved hydroelectric projects.[63] In the 1916 case *Mt. Vernon-Woodberry Cotton-Duck Company v. Alabama Interstate Power Company*, the Court upheld the condemnation of downstream owners' water rights in order to allow the power company to dam the river. As the Court explained, "to gather the streams from waste and to draw from them energy, labor without brains, and so to save mankind from toil that it can be spared, is to supply what, next to intellect, is the very foundation of all our achievements and all our welfare. If that purpose is not public, we should be at a loss to say what is."[64] Accordingly, energy generation has long been considered to be a public use sufficient to support the use of eminent domain. The additional benefits to be obtained from renewable energy projects only strengthen the justification for such takings.

Dudley v. Town Board of Prattsburgh, a recent New York case, involved the condemnation of an easement to enable placement of underground electricity lines for a wind project. The court concluded that the petitioners failed to meet their burden of establishing that the board's determination of public use was "without foundation and baseless," because the board's findings stated that the easement and wind project would "create jobs, provide infrastructure, and possibly stimulate new private sector economic development."[65]

Offshore Siting Issues

Siting industrial-scale wind farms offshore allows energy producers to install larger turbines to take advantage of more powerful winds.[66] However, offshore turbines are more expensive than land-based wind farms because weather, waves, and tides require more complex and durable designs.[67] For a discussion of offshore wind project siting issues, see chapter 16.

Brownfields

The U.S. Environmental Protection Agency (EPA) encourages "renewable energy development of current and formerly contaminated land and mining sites." To facilitate renewable energy projects on brownfields, EPA identifies sites with potential for solar, wind, biomass, geothermal, and landfill gas development and then provides assistance to communities, developers, and state and local governments interested in reusing the sites.[68] As part of this project, EPA has partnered with the DOE's National Renewable Energy Laboratory.[69] The New Mexico Energy, Minerals and Natural Resources Department has a similar program to redevelop brownfields with renewable energy projects.[70]

Federal Preemption of Siting and Permitting

While siting decisions are generally made at the state or local level, under the Energy Act of 2005, FERC has the authority to site electric transmission lines in designated national interest electric transmission corridors.[71] Areas qualify as "natural interest electric transmission corridors" if they are "experiencing electric energy transmission capacity constraints or congestion that adversely affects consumers."[72] Under the legislation, FERC has the authority to consider an application and issue a permit to construct an energy transmission line "if a state either withholds approval for more than one year, does not have the authority to site transmission facilities, or cannot consider interstate project benefits of a proposed to project located in a National Corridor."[73]

Even if the federal government has a limited ability to preempt state and local siting decisions, federal agencies are often involved in approving renewable energy projects. These agencies include FERC,[74] the Army Corps,[75] FWS,[76] BLM,[77] the Forest Service,[78] the Department of Energy,[79] the Federal Aviation Administration,[80] the Department of Defense,[81] and the National Park Service.[82]

State Siting Processes

Beyond the need in some cases to obtain federal permits, siting decisions for renewable energy projects are subject to state and/or local approvals. Some states preempt local governments' ability to apply zoning and land use regulations to energy facilities, although preemption may not apply to small projects.[83]

The Supreme Court of Washington applied its state siting law to a wind power project in a 2008 case.[84] In Washington, state siting permits preempt local restrictions on energy facilities, but regulations in force when the facts of the case arose required an energy project applicant to make all reasonable efforts to resolve noncompliance with local laws. The court held that preemption in the case was warranted because the developer acted in good faith to meet the county's requirements by actively participating in numerous hearings, submitting various reports and expert testimony, and making substantial changes to its plans in response to the county's concerns.[85]

Some state laws apply specifically to renewable energy facilities or specific types of renewable energy facilities. A 2009 New Jersey law, for example, declares that renewable energy facilities are permitted uses when located on industrially zoned properties of at least twenty acres,[86] and local restrictions on solar panels are preempted by state law in California and Florida.[87] In Minnesota, large wind energy conversion systems need only obtain a state site permit.[88] Although counties are authorized to adopt more stringent regulations, the state commission need not apply county standards so long as it has good cause.[89] Under Wisconsin law, municipalities can restrict solar and wind energy systems only to protect the public health or safety. An appellate court, interpreting the state provision, held that a county could not enact across-the-board restrictions for wind energy systems; rather, the court determined that "political subdivisions must rely on the facts of an individual situation to make case-by-case restrictions."[90]

A number of states have also enacted regulations to expedite the approval of renewable energy projects. In California, Governor Arnold Schwarzenegger issued an executive order "direct[ing] state agencies to create comprehensive plans to prioritize regional renewable projects based on an area's renewable resource potential and the level of protection for plant and animal habitat" and directed the California Energy

Commission and the Department of Fish and Game to create a "one-stop" permitting process to implement the executive order.[91] Local governments in Arizona are authorized to establish renewable energy incentive districts, and within these districts they may expedite zoning and rezoning decisions, as well as plan and permit approvals. They can also waive zoning and processing fees, development standards, and procedural requirements.[92] Hawaii's Department of Land and Natural Resources has similarly been directed by statute to "[w]ork with electric utility companies and with other renewable energy developers on all applicable planning and permitting processes to expedite the development of renewable energy resources."[93]

Local Zoning and Building Codes

Solar

Many states do not preempt municipal restrictions on the siting of renewable energy projects.[94] Allowing purely local control, however, can create barriers to the siting of renewable energy facilities due to residents' concerns (whether they are characterized as valid environmental objections or related to more subjective aesthetic concerns) and the increased costs of obtaining multiple regulatory approvals.[95] In other cases, local regulations may simply be counterproductive. For example, screening requirements for roof-mounted solar panels, which are intended to shield unsightly equipment from view, "can shade the panels and impair their effectiveness."[96]

Most local governments require at least an electrical permit for the installation of rooftop solar panels.[97] Building permits, design review, or other planning approvals may also be required.[98] Homeowners associations,[99] historic district regulations,[100] and maximum height limits[101] may impose further restrictions on solar panels. Ground-mounted solar energy systems may be subject to additional requirements, such as minimum lot sizes and setbacks.[102] While local regulations are often burdensome,[103] some local governments have attempted to encourage solar energy use by designating solar panels as uses permitted as of right,[104] or by exempting them from height limits and historic district regulations.[105]

Solar energy systems are discussed in greater detail in chapter 17.

Wind

Zoning ordinances regulating wind energy facilities tend to be more complicated than ordinances regulating solar energy systems, covering such varied issues as visual impacts, shadow flicker, noise, ice throw, setbacks, and decommissioning. Wind turbines may be specifically permitted in some districts and prohibited from others, or they may be allowed only in wind overlay zones.[106] Some type of special permit is typically required, often in conjunction with site design and environmental review.[107] Wind ordinances may include separate provisions for building-mounted turbines,[108] turbines intended to generate energy primarily for on-site use,[109] and larger wind energy facilities intended to supply energy to the grid.[110]

Local wind laws typically impose height restrictions on wind towers, although these limits may vary substantially.[111] Setback requirements are another regulation commonly found in wind laws, and they serve to mitigate aesthetic impacts as well as to protect adjacent property from turbine dangers such as ice throws and collapses.[112] Nearly all local wind laws require wind turbines to be set back from residences, power lines, public roads, and property lines, although setbacks may be calculated using different formulas.[113]

Height restrictions and setbacks are only two of the ways local governments have attempted to mitigate the visual impacts of wind turbines. Other common provisions require turbines and blades to be painted in neutral, nonreflective colors,[114] transmission lines to be placed underground,[115] and noise limits to be observed.[116] For safety reasons, most ordinances require turbines to have automatic and/or manual braking systems.[117] Signs generally have to be posted to warn any passersby of high voltages and ice throws, although the number and placement of signs vary among local governments.[118]

Wind energy facilities are discussed in greater detail in chapter 16.

Geothermal

Geothermal energy systems have the potential to deplete or pollute groundwater supplies, and for this reason they are typically subject to local well excavation or health ordinances,[119] or more specific geothermal ordinances. Many geothermal ordinances prohibit open loop systems, which pump and discharge water, as opposed to closed loop systems, which use pipes containing a heat transfer liquid.[120] Geothermal energy system ordinances may also require environmental impact analyses,[121] submission of site plans depicting the system,[122] or screening.[123]

Geothermal energy systems are discussed in greater detail in chapter 18.

Conclusion

The siting and permitting of clean energy projects are subject to myriad intergovernmental environmental and land use reviews, and they may implicate various state and local laws relating to nuisance actions, zoning, and condemnation. Which level(s) of government may be involved and which agencies and regulations may be implicated depend upon the project location and scope. While strong public policy generally supports the siting and permitting of these projects, navigating through the regulatory morass can be time-consuming and result in legal challenges, both delaying the projects and driving up the cost of the projects, and risking the overall sustainability of the project implementation. There are many opportunities for developers to build upon best practices, however, as well as opportunities for government to facilitate the siting process and incorporate the benefits of renewable energy projects into the application process.

Notes

1. Pub. L. No. 91-190, 83 Stat. 852 (1970) (codified at 42 U.S.C. §§ 4321 *et seq.*). This section is not intended to be a comprehensive discussion of NEPA or the environmental review process, and will not discuss generic, programmatic, or supplemental environmental impact

statements or other more technical aspects of the environmental review process. For a more detailed discussion of environmental review statutes and climate change impacts, see Caleb W. Christopher, *Success by a Thousand Cuts: The Use of Environmental Impact Assessment in Addressing Climate Change*, 9 Vt. J. Envtl. L. 549 (2007–2008); Michael B. Gerrard, *Climate Change and Environmental Impact Assessment*, Nat. Resources & Env't, Winter 2008, at 20.

2. 42 U.S.C. § 4332(1). An Environmental Impact Statement (EIS) does not need to be prepared for federal actions that qualify for a categorical exclusion (i.e., they have no significant environmental impact), or when a preliminary environmental assessment (EA) indicates that an EIS is unnecessary. *See* 40 C.F.R. § 1501.4; Mich. Gambling Opposition v. Kempthorne, 525 F.3d 23 (D.C. Cir. 2008) (upholding the Department of the Interior's decision not to prepare an EIS, based on the EA it prepared for a casino that was proposed to be built on 147 acres that would be taken into trust for an Indian tribe)

3. 40 C.F.R. § 1508.25. *See also* 40 C.F.R. §§ 1502.1–1502.25 (regulations pertaining to EISs). *See generally* Environmental Law Practice Guide § 1.09.

4. Strycker's Bay Neighborhood Council, Inc. v. Karlen, 444 U.S. 223, 227–28 (1980) (quoting Kleppe v. Sierra Club, 427 U.S. 390, 410 n.21 (1976)).

5. Tom Mounteer & Jeff Almon, *Treasury Can Award Renewable Energy Grants Without Environmental Review*, 78 Daily Env't Rep. (BNA), at B4 (Apr. 27, 2009).

6. *Id.*

7. Press Release, U.S. Dep't of the Interior, Secretary Salazar, FERC Chairman Wellinghof Sign Agreement to Spur Renewable Energy on the U.S. Outer Continental Shelf (Apr. 9, 2009), http://www.doi.gov/news/pressreleases/2009_04_09_releaseA.cfm.

8. *See, e.g.*, MNS Wind Co., LLC v. United States, 87 Fed. Cl. 167 (2009) (finding the Department of Energy liable for failing to complete the NEPA process for a wind project proposed for a former nuclear weapons site, as provided for in a contract between it and a wind energy developer); http://www.gc.energy.gov/NEPA/documents/Select_DOE_Renewable_EIS_EA_Table_ 02_02_10.pdf (listing DOE environmental review documents for wind, solar, and geothermal projects).

9. More than a dozen states have enacted their own environmental review statutes. *See, e.g.*, California Environmental Quality Act, Cal. Pub. Res. Code §§ 21000 et seq.; Hawaii Environmental Policy Act, Haw. Rev. Stat. §§ 343-1 et seq.; Massachusetts Environmental Policy Act, Mass. Gen. Laws ch. 30, §§ 61 et seq.; Minnesota Environmental Policy Act, Minn. Stat. §§ 116D.01 et seq.; New York State Environmental Quality Review Act, Envtl. Conserv. Law §§ 8-0101 et seq.; State Environmental Policy Act, Wash. Rev. Code §§ 43.21C.010 et seq. *See* American Planning Association, Growing Smart Legislative Guidebook 12-6(2002).

10. *See* http://www.dec.ny.gov/docs/permits_ej_operations_pdf/decwindprojrev.pdf.

11. N.Y. Envtl. Conserv. Law § 8-0109(8). *See also* Minn. Stat. § 116D.04 (6) ("No state action significantly affecting the quality of the environment shall be allowed, nor shall any permit for natural resources management and development be granted, where such action or permit has caused or is likely to cause pollution, impairment, or destruction of the air, water, land or other natural resources located within the state, so long as there is a feasible and prudent alternative consistent with the reasonable requirements of the public health, safety, and welfare and the state's paramount concern for the protection of its air, water, land and other natural resources from pollution, impairment, or destruction. Economic considerations alone shall not justify such conduct.").

12. *See, e.g.*, Alliance to Protect Nantucket Sound, Inc. v. U.S. Dep't of the Army, 398 F.3d 105 (1st Cir. 2005) (upholding the Army Corps's environmental assessment and finding of no significant impacts for a data tower for Cape Wind); Sierra Club v. Hathaway, 579 F.2d 1162 (9th Cir. 1978) (holding that geothermal exploration leases did not require an EIS because they permitted only casual use); Pit River Tribe v. U.S. Forest Serv., 469 F.3d 768 (9th Cir. 2006) (holding that the agencies violated NEPA because they did not prepare an EIS before extending geothermal leases; an EIS was required because the extensions did not reserve to the agencies the right to preclude geothermal surface-disturbing activity and did not merely preserve the status quo); Friends of Ompompanoosuc v. FERC, 968 F.2d 1549 (2d Cir. 1992) (upholding

FERC's finding of no significant impact regarding a hydroelectric project because it considered the project's impacts and proposed measures to minimize certain impacts).

13. Hamlin Preservation Group v. Town Bd., Index No. 2008/11217 (Monroe Cnty., N.Y. Jan. 5, 2009).

14. *See* Matter of Advocates for Prattsburgh, Inc. v. Steuben County Indus. Dev. Agency, 859 N.Y.S.2d 892 (N.Y. App. Div., Monroe Cnty. 2007), *aff'd*, 48 A.D.3d 1160 (N.Y. App. Div., 4th Dep't 2008).

15. *See, e.g.*, Matter of Brander v. Town of Warren Town Bd., 847 N.Y.S.2d 450 (N.Y. App. Div., Onondaga Cnty. 2007) (holding that the town failed to comply with SEQRA because it did not assess project alternatives that were identified by commenters and mentioned in the draft and final EIS); Friends of River v. Fed. Energy Regulatory Comm'n, 720 F.2d 93, 105 (D.C. Cir. 1983) (where hydroelectric project was proposed to create independent energy source, holding that agency adequately assessed the alternative of continuing to purchase power from another supplier).

16. Matter of Brander v. Town of Warren Town Bd., 847 N.Y.S.2d 450, 453 (N.Y. App. Div., Onondaga Cnty. 2007) (citing Matter of Jackson v. N.Y.S. Urban Dev. Corp., 67 N.Y.2d 400 (1986)).

17. Vt. Yankee Nuclear Power Corp. v. NRDC, 435 U.S. 519, 551 (1978).

18. Residents Opposed to Kittitas Turbines v. State Energy Facility Site Evaluation Council, 197 P.3d 1153 (Wash. 2008).

19. Friends of River v. Fed. Energy Regulatory Comm'n, 720 F.2d 93, 105 (D.C. Cir. 1983).

20. Lake Cnty. Energy Council v. County of Lake, 139 Cal. Rptr. 176 (Cal. Ct. App. 1977). *See also* Mo. Coalition for Env't v. FERC, 544 F.3d 955 (8th Cir. 2008) (holding that EIS did not need to assess impacts of relicensed operation of a hydroelectric plant because FERC's approval was for reconstruction, and any future relicensing was speculative); Abenaki Nation of Mississquoi v. Hughes, 805 F. Supp. 234 (D. Vt. 1992) (upholding the Army Corps's decision not to issue a new environmental assessment for the reissuance of a hydroelectric permit that was substantially similar to prior permit, and upholding the decision not to issue an EIS for an upgrade allowed under the permit when the Army Corps determined that it would not have significant impacts because it was conditioned on completion of a mitigation plan for cultural and biological impacts).

21. *See, e.g.*, Frederick R. Anderson & Geraldine E. Edens, *Alternative Energy and the Rebirth of NEPA*, 23 NAT. RESOURCES & ENV'T 22 (2009) ("current NEPA analysis presents a very top-sided picture of the overall balance by emphasizing the downside at the expense of the upside of greener energy development. The preferred alternative for a green energy project can no longer be the one with the fewest environmental impacts. Rather, the preferred alternative should be the one that confers the greatest environmental benefits."); Dorothy W. Bisbee, *NEPA Review of Offshore Wind Farms: Ensuring Emission Reduction Benefits Outweigh Visual Impacts*, 31 B.C. ENVTL. AFF. L. REV. 349, 354–58 (2004) (discussing NEPA's lack of guidance regarding the balancing of positive and negative impacts, and the balancing of local and regional impacts).

22. *See, e.g.*, Quarles & Brady LLP, *Stimulus Bill May Expedite NEPA Review, But Waiver Unlikely*, ENVTL. L. UPDATE, Feb. 2009, *available at* http://www.quarles.com/Publications/detail.aspx?publication=470 (discussing Senator Barrasso's (D-WY) attempt to waive NEPA for renewable energy projects, and Senator Boxer's (D-CA) response, which merely expedited the procedure; the Boxer amendment was later passed); *see also* Jonathan Tolman, *Renewable Energy Jobs Will Have to Wait*, Feb. 2, 2009, http://www.openmarket.org/2009/02/02/renewable-energy-jobs-will-have-to-wait/.

23. *See* Letter from Bill Snape, Senior Counsel, Center for Biological Diversity et al., to the Hon. Nancy Sutley, Chair, White House Council on Environmental Quality (Sept. 10, 2009), *available at* http://wilderness.org/files/CEQ-Renewable-Energy-NEPA.pdf; Frederick R. Anderson & Geraldine E. Edens, *Alternative Energy and the Rebirth of NEPA*, 23 NAT. RESOURCES & ENV'T 22 (2009).

24. *See* Dorothy W. Bisbee, *NEPA Review of Offshore Wind Farms: Ensuring Emission Reduction Benefits Outweigh Visual Impacts*, 31 B.C. ENVTL. AFF. L. REV. 349, 382–84 (2004).

25. New York DEC guidance, California, Massachusetts, Seattle/King County, CEQ guidance.

26. Letter from Maureen Hyzer, Forest Supervisor, to Timothy Williamson, Freedomworks, LLC (Apr. 2, 2009), *available at* http://www.windaction.org/documents/20686.

27. *See* Adirondack Park Agency, *General Permit 2009G-1, Installation of Certain New Small-Scale Wind Turbines,* (Staff Draft, Mar. 3, 2009), *available at* http://www.apa.state .ny.us/Mailing/0903/Regulatory/GP%202009G-1%20Permit%20for%20Small%20Scale%20 Wind%20Turbines%203-3-09.pdf.

28. Pub. L. No. 93-205, 87 Stat. 884 (1973) (codified at 16 U.S.C. §§ 1531 et seq.). Information about the ESA can be found at Fish and Wildlife Service's web page, http://www.fws .gov/endangered/. For a detailed analysis, see ENDANGERED SPECIES ACT: LAW, POLICY, AND PERSPECTIVES (Donald C. Baur & Wm. Robert Irvin eds., 2d ed. 2009). Other statutes protecting species or habitats may also apply to renewable energy projects, such as the Marine Mammals Protection Act, 16 U.S.C. §§ 1361 et seq., and the Wild and Scenic Rivers Act, 16 U.S.C. § 1278. For further discussion of wildlife impacts caused by wind energy developments, see chapter 16.

29. 16 U.S.C. § 1538(a)(1). The term "take" "means to harass, harm, pursue, hunt, shoot, wound, kill, trap, capture, or collect, or to attempt to engage in any such conduct." 16 U.S.C. § 1532(19). The term can also encompass habitat modification. *See* Babbitt v. Sweet Home Chapter of Cmtys. for a Great Oregon, 515 U.S. 687 (1995).

30. 16 U.S.C. § 1539. In order to obtain an incidental take permit, the taking must be incidental to an otherwise lawful activity, and the applicant must submit a conservation plan that specifies the impacts that are likely to result from the taking, mitigation steps, the reasons alternatives cannot be utilized, and other measures deemed appropriate. *Id.*

31. *See, e.g.,* Nat'l Wildlife Fed'n v. Nat'l Marine Fisheries Serv., 422 F.3d 782 (9th Cir. 2005); Pac. Coast Fed'n of Fishermen's Ass'n v. Gutierrez, 606 F. Supp. 2d 1122 (E.D. Cal. 2008); Am. Rivers v. U.S. Army Corps of Eng'rs, 271 F. Supp. 2d 230 (D.D.C. 2003).

32. Bird and bat mortality caused by wind turbines has proven to be a controversial issue, often pitting emission-reductions-environmentalists against wildlife-preservation-environmentalists. These wildlife concerns can be traced back to the Altamont Pass wind farm in California, one of the oldest and largest in the United States, with more than five thousand turbines located on about 150 square kilometers of land. In a suit challenging the project, the Center for Biological Diversity claimed that: "Since the 1980's, the ... generators ... have killed tens of thousands of birds, including between 17,000 and 26,000 raptors—more than a thousand Golden Eagles, thousands of hawks, and thousands of other raptors." Ctr. for Biological Diversity v. FPL Group, Inc., 83 Cal. Rptr. 3d 588, 592 (Cal. Ct. App. 2008) (alteration and in original). When the project was constructed, the avian impacts were somewhat unexpected, and they led to increased concerns over the effects of wind development on bird populations. SUSAN ORLOFF & ANNE FLANNERY, CAL. ENERGY COMM'N, WIND TURBINE EFFECTS ON AVIAN ACTIVITY, HABITAT USE, AND MORTALITY IN ALTAMONT PASS AND SOLANO COUNTY WIND RESOURCE AREAS 1989–1991, at 1-1, 1-4 (1992), available at http://www.energy.ca.gov/ windguidelines/documents/2006-12-06_1992_FINAL_REPORT_1989-1991.PDF. Today, the high rate of bird mortality at Altamont Pass is understood to be an "anomaly" caused by poor siting choices and outdated technology. MICK SAGRILLO, ADVICE FROM AN EXPERT: PUTTING WIND POWER'S EFFECT ON BIRDS IN PERSPECTIVE (2001), http://www.awea.org/smallwind/ sagrillo/swbirds.html (last visited Jan. 18, 2010). The effects of wind turbines on birds and bats are discussed in greater detail in chapter 16.

33. Animal Welfare Inst. v. Beech Ridge Energy LLC, 675 F. Supp. 2d 540 (D. Md. 2009).

34. 16. U.S.C. §§ 703-712. Additional protections are contained in the Bald and Golden Eagle Protection Act, 16 U.S.C. §§ 668–668d (1940).

35. *See generally* John Arnold McKinsey, *Regulating Avian Impacts Under the Migratory Bird Treaty Act and Other Laws: The Wind Industry Collides With One of Its Own, the Environmental Protection Movement,* 28 ENERGY L.J. 71, 77–78 (2007); Meredith Blaydes Lilley & Jeremy Firestone, *Wind Power, Wildlife, and the Migratory Bird Treaty Act: A Way Forward,* 38 ENVT'L L. 1167 (2008).

36. REPORT OF THE U.S. FISH & WILDLIFE SERVICE WIND TURBINE GUIDELINES ADVISORY COMMITTEE (Mar. 4, 2010), *available at* http://www.fws.gov/habitatconservation/windpower/ Wind_Turbine_Guidelines_Advisory_Committee_Recommendations_Secretary.pdf. *See also*

U.S. Fish & Wildlife Service Interim Guidance on Avoiding and Minimizing Wildlife Impacts from Wind Turbines (May 13, 2003), *available at* http://www.fws.gov/habitat conservation/Service%20Interim%20Guidelines.pdf.

37. Meredith Blaydes Lilley & Jeremy Firestone, *Windpower, Wildlife, and the Migratory Bird Treaty Act: A Way Forward*, 38 Envt'l L. 1167, 1197–98 (2008) (discussing United States v. Moon Lake Elec. Ass'n, Inc., 45 F. Supp. 2d 1070 (D. Colo. 1999)).

38. N.Y. Dep't of Envt'l Conservation, Wind Power (July 2009), http://www.dec .ny.gov/energy/40966.html; N.Y. Dep't of Envt'l Conservation, Review of Wind Energy Generation Products (July 16, 2009), http://www.dec.ny.gov/docs/permits_ej_operations_ pdf/decwindprojrev.pdf.

39. *See, e.g.*, Fish & Wildlife Serv., U.S. Dep't of the Interior, Draft: Voluntary Guidelines for Wind Energy Development in Texas, http://www.fws.gov/habitatconservation/windpower/ Subcommittee/Existing_Guidelines/Reports/FAC_DRAFT_Framework_July08.pdf (recommending measures to reduce impact of wind projects on wildlife); Joseph Caputo, Can Wind Power Be Wildlife Friendly, Smithsonian Mag., Feb. 27, 2009, http://www.smithsonianmag.com/ specialsections/ecocenter/Can-Wind-Power-Be-Wildlife-Friendly.html ("By curtailing production during low wind conditions, and increasing the wind speed threshold required to jumpstart the turbines, bat fatalities dropped between 56 and 92 percent."); Press Release, Ctr. for Biological Diversity, Lawsuit Seeks Redress for Massive Illegal Bird Kills at Altamont Pass, CA, Wind Farms (Jan. 12, 2003), http://www.biologicaldiversity.org/news/press_releases/ birdkills1-12-04.htm (describing measures that could be used to reduce bird deaths); Suzanne Goldenberg, Texas Wind Farm Pioneers Radar Technology to Protect Migrating Birds, Guardian (London), May 1, 2009, http://www.guardian.co.uk/environment/2009/may/01/windfarm-bird-radar (describing use of radar technology to avoid bird deaths).

40. Donald J. Kochan & Tiffany Grant. In the Heat of the Law, It's Not Just Steam: Geothermal Resources and the Impacts on Thermophile Biodiversity, 13 Hastings W.-NW. J. Envtl. L. & Pol'y 35, 49 (2007). Thermophiles are microbes that have adapted to extreme habitats, and their ability to withstand high temperatures and chemical environments toxic to other organisms has made them an important subject of medical and scientific study. Because species are often confined and specially adapted to isolated sites, geothermal projects can pose an extinction threat to these species. *Id.* at 36–38.

41. Robert F. Kennedy, Jr., Op-Ed., *An Ill Wind Off Cape Cod*, N.Y. Times, Dec. 16, 2005, at A41.

42. Avi Brisman, *The Aesthetics of Wind Energy Systems*, 13 N.Y.U. Envtl. L.J. 1, 74–80 (2005) (describing aesthetic opposition to wind turbines); *Ecogen, LLC v. Town of Italy, 438 F. Supp. 2d 149, 153 (W.D.N.Y. 2006)* (where residents expressed concern that wind turbines would negatively impact the aesthetics of the town); *Zimmerman v. Bd. of Comm'rs, 218 P.3d 400 (Kan. 2009)* (upholding ban on commercial wind farms due to aesthetic impact and local opposition); In re Halnon, 811 A.2d 161, 162 (Vt. 2002) (where, for aesthetic reasons, residents opposed their neighbors' application to erect a wind turbine).

43. *See, e.g.*, *Wind Turbines Could Hurt Tourism in Ocean County, Study Finds*, Star-Ledger (Newark, N.J.), Sept. 9, 2008, *available at* http://www.nj.com/news/index.ssf/2008/09/ wind_turbines_could_hurt_touri.html. While particularly scenic or historic areas may see some drop in tourism due to wind turbines, some studies have found turbines' effects on tourism to be negligible. *See* British Wind Energy Ass'n, Wind Farms and Tourism, http://www .bwea.com/ref/tourism.html ("[W]here studies have been carried out investigating the impact of wind farms on tourism, the results demonstrate that the effect is negligible at worst, with many respondents taking a positive view of wind farms, and saying that it would not affect their liklihood [sic] of returning to an area. . . .").

44. Windustry, The Benefits of Wind Energy and Community Wind, http://www .windustry.org/policy-amp-research/benefits-of-wind-and-community-wind/the-benefits-of-wind-energy-and-community-wi; *see also* Brisman, *supra* note 42, at 77–78.

45. Rankin v. FPL Energy, LLC, 266 S.W.3d 506, 512–13 (Tex. App. 2008) *See also* Burch v. Nedpower Mount Storm, LLC, 647 S.E.2d 879 (W. Va. 2007) (ruling that a wind power electric generating facility with about two hundred wind turbines in close proximity to residential property could constitute a nuisance, but that the wind farm at issue was not a nuisance).

46. Zimmerman v Bd. of Comm'rs, 218 P.3d 400, 418 (Kan. 2009).

47. 80 Stat. 915 (codified at 16 U.S.C. §§ 470 et seq.).

48. An undertaking is defined as "a project, activity, or program funded in whole or in part under the direct or indirect jurisdiction of a Federal agency, including those carried out by or on behalf of a Federal agency; those carried out with Federal financial assistance; and those requiring a Federal permit, license or approval." 36 C.F.R. § 800.16(y).

49. 16 U.S.C. § 470(f). Related regulations are located at 36 C.F.R. §§ 800.1 et seq.

50. See ANDERSONS AMERICAN LAW OF ZONING § 27:2. When a renewable energy project impacts Native American cultural properties, a federal agency must consult with the affected Tribe under NHPA regulations. 36 C.F.R. § 800.2(c)(2). However, in order for the requirement to apply, the tribe must be federally recognized. Snoqualmie Indian Tribe v. FERC, 545 F.3d 1207, 1216 (9th Cir. 2008); Abenaki Nation of Mississquoi v. Hughes, 805 F. Supp. 234, 250 (D. Vt. 1992). Even where not required under the NHPA, however, federal agencies should consult with tribes on projects affecting tribal trust assets on federal land.

51. Pit River Tribe v. U.S. Forest Serv., 469 F.3d 768, 787 (9th Cir. 2006). For further details about this case, see chapter 18.

52. Abenaki Nation of Mississquoi v. Hughes, 805 F. Supp. 234 (D. Vt. 1992).

53. 42 U.S.C. § 2000bb.

54. 42 U.S.C. § 2000cc. RFRA was held to be unconstitutional as applied to the states in *City of Boerne v. Flores*, 521 U.S. 507 (1997), but it is still applied to federal agency actions. In 2000, Congress enacted the Religious Land Use and Institutionalized Persons Act (RLUIPA) to restore some of the protection that RFRA was intended to confer on religious practitioners. 42 U.S.C. § 2000cc. RLUIPA uses the same substantial burden test as RFRA, but it applies only to actions involving institutionalized persons (mainly prisoners) and zoning and landmarking laws affecting houses of worship. In the clean energy context, it would apply to local zoning ordinances regulating energy facilities siting, if such regulations imposed a substantial burden on religious exercise. However, no such challenges have yet been brought.

55. 545 F.3d 1207 (9th Cir. 2008).

56. *Id.* at 1214 (quoting Navajo Nation v. U.S. Forest Serv., 535 F.3d 1058, 1068 (9th Cir. 2008)).

57. Dedman v. Bd. of Land & Natural Res., 740 P.2d 28 (Haw. 1987), *cert. denied*, 485 U.S. 1020 (1988). This case was brought under the First Amendment free exercise clause, but in 1990 the Supreme Court held that free exercise claims are subject to rational basis review if they are religion-neutral and generally applicable. Employment Div. v. Smith. 444 U.S. 872 (1990). RFRA was enacted in response to this doctrinal shift, and thus pre-*Smith* free exercise cases are more similar to RFRA cases than they are to post-*Smith* free exercise cases.

58. U.S. DEP'T OF INTERIOR, SECRETARY SALAZAR ANNOUNCES APPROVAL OF CAPE WIND ENERGY PROJECT ON OUTER CONTINENTAL SHELF OFF MASSACHUSETTS, April 28, 2010; Gale Courey Toensing, *Salazar Approves Cape Wind; Multiple Lawsuits to Follow*, INDIAN COUNTRY TODAY, Apr. 30, 2010.

59. MINN. R. 7854.0900.

60. CAL. ENERGY COMM'N, ENVIRONMENTAL JUSTICE (last modified Nov. 5, 2009), http://www.energy.ca.gov/public_adviser/environmental_justice_faq.html.

61. See Mark Svenvold, *Wind-Power Politics*, N.Y. TIMES, Sept. 12, 2008, http://www.nytimes.com/2008/09/14/magazine/14wind-t.html?pagewanted=1&_r=1.

62. *See id.; see also* UNIVERSITY OF DELAWARE, COLLEGE OF EARTH, OCEAN, AND ENVIRONMENT, OFFSHORE WIND POWER: DELAWARE OFFSHORE WIND PROJECT, http://www.ocean.udel.edu/Windpower/deproject.html (last visited Feb. 13, 2011).

63. *See, e.g.*, Bd. of Hudson River Regulating Dist. v. Fonda, Johnstown & Gloversville R.R. Co., 249 N.Y. 445 (1928) (rejecting a claim that a dam said to be needed for flood control purposes was actually intended to benefit private power producers; even if there was a profit motive, the public use was sufficient); Hendersonville Light & Power Co. v. Blue Ridge Interurban Ry. Co., 243 U.S. 563, 569–70 (1917) (upholding a condemnation of downstream water rights for the purpose of generating electricity to use for a railway despite the fact that excess

electricity might be sold for a profit; even if such sales were to occur, they would be merely a "possible incident, necessary to prevent waste, of the primary public use.").

64. Mt. Vernon-Woodberry Cotton Duck Co. v. Ala. Interstate Power Co., 240 U.S. 30, 32 (1916).

65. Dudley v. Town Bd. of Prattsburgh, 872 N.Y.S.2d 614 (N.Y. App. Div. 2009).

66. Bureau of Ocean Energy Management, Regulation and Enforcement, Offshore Wind Energy, http://ocsenergy.anl.gov/guide/wind/index.cfm.

67. Elisa Wood, *Offshore Awakening: U.S. Investment Flows to Offshore Wind*, RENEWABLE ENERGY WORLD, Mar. 22, 2010, *available at* http://www.renewableenergyworld.com/rea/news/article/2010/03/offshore-awakening.

68. U.S. ENVT'L PROTECTION AGENCY, SITING RENEWABLE ENERGY ON POTENTIALLY CONTAMINATED LANE AND MINE SITES, http://www.epa.gov/oswercpa/.

69. News Release, U.S. Envt'l Protection Agency, EPA, NREL Partner to Develop Renewable Energy on Potentially Contaminated Sites: Clean Energy Project Aims to Benefit Local Economies and Create Jobs (Feb. 23, 2010), http://yosemite.epa.gov/opa/admpress.nsf/d0cf6618525a9efb85257359003fb69d/b35339fd1c4175b9852576d30058b278!OpenDocument.

70. http://www1.eere.energy.gov/wip/solutioncenter/pdfs/tap_webinar_20090422_johnson.pdf.

71. 16 U.S.C. § 824p(a).

72. *Id.* § 824p(a)(2).

73. FED. ENERGY REGULATORY COMM'N, A GUIDE TO THE FERC ELECTRIC TRANSMISSION FACILITIES PERMIT PROCESS 3, *available at* http://www.ferc.gov/for-citizens/citizen-guides/electric/guide-transmission.pdf. *See also* Jim Rossi, *The Trojan Horse of Electric Transmission Line Siting Authority*, 39 ENVT'L L. 1015 (2009).

74. *See, e.g.*, FED. ENERGY REGULATION COMM'N, STAFF BRIEFING PAPER: ASSESSING THE STATE OF WIND ENERGY IN WHOLESALE ELECTRICITY MARKETS (Nov. 2004), *available at* http://www.ferc.gov/legal/maj-ord-reg/land-docs/11-04-wind-report.pdf.

75. *See, e.g.*, U.S. Army Corps of Eng'rs, New England District, Project Information Page, Cape Wind Energy Project Permit Application, http://www.nae.usace.army.mil/projects/ma/ccwf/windfarm.htm (explaining that the Army Corps is a cooperating agency in the environmental review); U.S. Army Corps of Eng'rs, Headquarters, Hydropower, http://www.usace.army.mil/cecw/planningcop/pages/hydropower.aspx.

76. *See, e.g.*, Memorandum from Deputy Director, Fish & Wildlife Serv. to Regional Directors (May 13, 2003) (providing guidance on avoiding/minimizing impacts on wildlife and habitats), *available at* http://www.fws.gov/habitatconservation/windpower/wind_turbine_advisory_committee.html; http://www.fws.gov/habitatconservation/Service%20Interim%20Guidelines.pdf; http://www.fws.gov/habitatconservation/windpower/Second_Release_Draft_One_Text_FAC_Briefing_3_13_09.pdf.

77. In June, 2009, the BLM launched an initiative to designate twenty-four tracts of federal lands as Solar Energy Study Areas, with the objective of providing "landscape-scale planning and zoning for solar projects . . . , allowing a more efficient process for permitting and siting responsible solar development." News Release, Bureau of Land Mgmt., Secretary Salazar, Senator Reid Announce "Fast Track" Initiatives for Solar Energy Development on Western Lands (June 29, 2009), *available at* http://www.blm.gov/wo/st/en/info/newsroom/2009/june/NR_0629_2009.html. Several months later, the BLM opened Renewable Energy Coordination Offices in four western states, and established renewable permitting teams in another six western states, to "help to swiftly complete application reviews on the most ready-to-go and environmentally appropriate solar, wind, and geothermal projects on U.S. public lands." http://www.blm.gov/wo/st/en/info/newsroom/2009/october/NR_10_12A_2000.html. *See also* BUREAU OF LAND MGMT., WIND ENERGY http://www.blm.gov/wo/st/en/prog/energy/wind_energy.html.

78. *See, e.g.*, Letter from Maureen Hyzer, Forest Supervisor, to Timothy Williamson, Freedomworks, LLC (Apr. 2, 2009), http://www.windaction.org/documents/20686; Wind Energy, Proposed Forest Service Directive, 72 Fed. Reg. 54233 (Sept. 24, 2007), *available at* http://www.fs.fed.us/recreation/permits/documents/federal_register_wind.pdf.

79. *See, e.g.,* http://www.windpoweringamerica.gov/pdfs/wpa/county_commissioners.pdf; http://www1.eere.energy.gov/windandhydro/federalwindsiting/.

80. *See, e.g.,* FED. AVIATION ADMIN., OBSTRUCTION EVALUATION/AIRPORT AIRSPACE ANALYSIS (OE/AAA), https://oeaaa.faa.gov/oeaaa/external/portal.jsp; Clark County, Nev. v. Fed. Aviation Admin., 522 F.3d 437 (D.C. Cir. 2008) (finding that the FAA failed to provide evidence in the record to support its determination that the proposed wind project would not exceed federal obstruction standards, and that instead, evidence in the record suggested that indeed, 400-foot high wind turbines in close proximity to a proposed new airport could significantly interfere with radar systems at the airport).

81. *See, e.g.,* Office of the Secretary of Defense, Policy Board on Federal Aviation, Policy Letter, Department of Defense Policy on Proposed Wind Farm Locations, Jan. 29, 2007, http://www1.eere.energy.gov/windandhydro/federalwindsiting/pdfs/windmill_policy_letter_012907.pdf; DOD/DHS Joint Program Office, Memorandum, July 10, 2006, http://www1.eere.energy.gov/windandhydro/federalwindsiting/pdfs/ windmill_policy_letter_071006.pdf; DOD/DHS Joint Program Office, Memorandum, Mar. 21, 2006, http://www1.eere.energy.gov/windandhydro/federalwindsiting/pdfs/windmill_policy_letter_032106.pdf.

82. *See, e.g.,* Abby Goodnough, For Cape Cod Wind farm, New Hurdle Is Spiritual, N.Y. Times, Jan. 4, 2010, at A11, *available at* http://www.nytimes.com/2010/01/05/science/earth/05wind.html?emc=eta1.

83. *See* Patricia E. Salkin & Ashira Pelman Ostrow, *Cooperative Federalism and Wind: A New Framework for Achieving Sustainability*, 37 HOFSTRA L. REV. 1049, 1065 (2009). An example is Connecticut, where the state Siting Council regulates all electric generators over one megawatt. CONN. GEN. STAT. §§ 16-50(g)–50(k).

84. Residents Opposed to Kittitas Turbines v. State Energy Facility Siting Evaluation Council, 197 P.3d 1153 (Wash. 2008).

85. *Id.* at 1175.

86. N.J. STAT. § 40:55D-66.11, L. 2009, c. 35, § 1.

87. CAL. CIV. CODE § 714; FLA. STAT. § 163.04. *See also* Arterberry v. County of San Diego, 106 Cal. Rptr. 3d 743 (Cal. Ct. App. 2010) (discussing the California statutes involving solar energy systems and holding that a local government is not liable for damages where it unreasonably limits use of a solar energy system).

88. MINN. STAT. § 216F.07. Large wind energy systems are defined as those producing 5,000 kilowatts or more. MINN. STAT. § 216F.01.

89. MINN. STAT. § 216F.081.

90. Ecker Bros. v. Calumet Cnty., 2009 WI App. 112, 321 Wis. 2d 51, 772 N.W.2d 240.

91. Arnold Schwarzenegger, Exec. Order No. S-14-08 (Nov. 17, 2008), *available at* http://gov38.ca.gov/index.php?/executive-order/11072/.

92. ARIZ. REV. STAT. . § 9-499.14 (cities and towns); ARIZ. REV. STAT. § 11-254.07 (counties). *See also* H.F. No. 810, 2009 Leg., XXX Sess. (Iowa 2009). To target the installation of residential wind turbines in the state, the Iowa law allows municipalities to establish small wind energy innovation zones to optimize local, regional, and state benefits from wind energy and to facilitate and expedite interconnection of small wind energy systems with electric utilities throughout the state. The Iowa League of Cities, the Iowa Association of Counties, the Iowa Environmental Council, the Iowa Wind Energy Association, and representatives from the utility industry are tasked with developing a model local ordinance that contains an expedited small wind system approval process. The model law must be adopted by municipalities that desire to qualify as a small wind energy innovation zone. *Id.*

93. HAW. REV. STAT. § 196-41.

94. States in which siting decisions are left to local governments include Idaho, Illinois, Kansas, New York, Texas, and Utah. *See* Salkin & Pelman Ostrow, *supra* note 83.

95. *See, e.g.,* Salkin & Pelman Ostrow, *supra* note 83; Michael L. Pisauro, Jr., *Renewables and Land Use Law*, 23 NAT. RESOURCES & ENV'T 39 (2008); DAMIAN PITT, TAKING THE RED TAPE OUT OF GREEN POWER (Sept. 2008), http://www.newenergychoices.org/uploads/redTape-rep.pdf; AM. PLANNING ASS'N, POLICY GUIDE ON PLANNING AND CLIMATE CHANGE, *Specific Policy #19.4: Eliminate Regulatory Barriers to the Use of Renewable Energy Systems.*

96. Michael L. Pisauro, Jr., *Renewables and Land Use Law*, 23 Nat. Resources & Env't 39 (2008).

97. Pitt, *supra* not 95, at 16–18.

98. *Id.* at 17–18.

99. *Id.* at 25–28. However, ten states prohibit private covenant restrictions that unreasonably restrict the use of solar panels. *Id.* at 27.

100. *See, e.g.*, Kate Galbraith, *Historic Architecture vs. Clean Energy*, New York Times Green Blog, May 27, 2009, http://greeninc.blogs.nytimes.com/2009/05/27/historic-architecture-vs-clean-energy/; Cameron Scott, *No Blood for . . . Solar?*, San Francisco Chronicle, the Thin Green Line Blog, Oct. 22, 2009, http://www.sfgate.com/cgi-bin/blogs/green/detail?entry_id=50115.

101. *See, e.g.*, Woodbury, Minn., Alternative Energy Systems Ordinance § 24-406(b)(3) (Sept. 2009), http://www.ci.woodbury.mn.us/environ/altenergyord.pdf.

102. *Id.* § 24-406(b)(2), (b)(4), (b)(5).

103. *See* Pitt, *supra* note 95, at 19–25.

104. *See, e.g.*, Albany City Code art. XIV, § 375-9, http://www.ecode360.com/?custId=AL0934; Woodbury, Minn., Alternative Energy Systems Ordinance § 24-406(a) (Sept. 2009), http://www.ci.woodbury.mn.us/environ/altenergyord.pdf.

105. *See, e.g.*, Northampton, Mass. City Code: Chapter 195, http://www.ecode360.com/?custId=NO2226; Berlin, N.J. Borough Code, http://www.ecode360.com/?custId=BE0276.

106. *See generally* N.Y. State Energy Research & Development Auth., Power Naturally, Wind Energy Model Ordinance Options 3, http://www.powernaturally.org/Programs/Wind/toolkit/2_windenergymodel.pdf; *see also* Plaxton v. Lycoming Cnty. Zoning Hearing Bd., 986 A.2d 199 (Pa. Commw. Ct. 2009) (upholding ordinance that permitted turbines as of right in certain districts because "the goal of the ordinance amendments, to harvest wind as a natural resource and to convert it to energy as a source of power to provide electricity to the public, promotes public health, safety or welfare").

107. N.Y. State Energy Research & Development Auth., Power Naturally, Wind Energy Model Ordinance Options 3, http://www.powernaturally.org/Programs/Wind/toolkit/2_windenergymodel.pdf.

108. *See, e.g.*, Town of Ithaca, Local Law No. 13 of 2007; Woodbury, Minn., Alternative Energy Systems Ordinance (Sept. 2009), http://www.ci.woodbury.mn.us/environ/altenergyord.pdf (roof-mounted turbines not permitted).

109. *See, e.g., id.*; Town of South Bristol, N.Y. (residential windmills); Woodbury, Minn., Alternative Energy Systems Ordinance § 24-405 (Sept. 2009), http://www.ci.woodbury.mn.us/environ/altenergyord.pdf (residential windmills).

110. *See, e.g.*, Cohocton, N.Y. (restricting large wind facilities to the agricultural-residential district); Martinsburg, N.Y. (definition of wind power generating facility); South Bristol, N.Y. § 170-42 (prohibits industrial windmills); Zimmerman v. Bd. of Wabaunsee Cnty. Comm'rs, 218 P.3d 400 (Kan. 2009) (upholding ordinance that prohibited commercial wind energy conversion systems based on the county's interests in aesthetics, preserving its rural and scenic character, and complying with the wishes of residents).

111. *See, e.g.*, Town of Bethany, Local Law No. 1 of 2008 (80 feet if located on parcels smaller than five acres, and to 150 feet on larger parcels); Town of Cohocton, Windmill Local Law (maximum 500 feet); Woodbury, Minn., Alternative Energy Systems Ordinance (Sept. 2009), http://www.ci.woodbury.mn.us/environ/altenergyord.pdf (60 feet in R-1 district, with up to 120 feet permissible as an interim conditional use; 45 feet, with up to 75 feet permissible as an interim conditional use in the R-2, R-4, B-2, and I-1 districts). For safety reasons, wind ordinances often specify the lowest minimum distance permitted between the ground and the tips of the blades. In Ithaca, New York, for example, the lowest part of the turbine blade must pass no closer to the ground than 30 feet, and for building mounted turbines, Ithaca requires the blades to be at least 15 feet above any "outdoor surfaces intended for human occupancy . . . that are located directly below the facility." Town of Ithaca, Local Law No. 13 of 2007.

112. *See generally* N.Y. State Energy Research & Development Auth., Power Naturally, Wind Energy Model Ordinance Options 9–10, http://www.powernaturally.org/

Programs/Wind/toolkit/2_windenergymodel.pdf (discussing setbacks); N.Y. STATE ENERGY RESEARCH & DEVELOPMENT AUTH., POWER NATURALLY, ASSESSING AND MITIGATING VISUAL IMPACTS, http://www.powernaturally.org/Programs/Wind/toolkit/6_visualimpactupfront.pdf (discussing visual impacts); GE ENERGY, ICE SHEDDING AND ICE THROW—RISK AND MITIGATION, http://www.gepower.com/prod_serv/products/tech_docs/en/downloads/ger4262.pdf (discussing ice throw mitigation).

113. *See generally* N.Y. STATE ENERGY RESEARCH & DEVELOPMENT AUTH., POWER NATURALLY, WIND ENERGY MODEL ORDINANCE OPTIONS 4, http://www.powernaturally.org/Programs/Wind/toolkit/2_windenergymodel.pdf; *see also* Town of South Bristol, LOCAL LAW NO. 2 OF 2003, § 170-40(B)(1) (residential), § 170-41(B)(1) (commercial). Roberts v. Manitowoc Cnty. Bd. of Adjustment, 2006 WI App 169, 295 Wis. 2d 522, 721 N.W.2d 499 (2006) (upholding the board's approval of a smaller setback because it was specifically permitted in the ordinance).

114. Town of Bethany, LOCAL LAW NO. 1 OF 2008, p. 9; Town of Ellington, N.Y., WIND ENERGY CONVERSION SYSTEMS LOCAL LAW 16 (2008) (on file with authors) (nonreflective matte color or camouflage); Woodbury, Minn., ALTERNATIVE ENERGY SYSTEMS ORDINANCE 7 (Sept. 2009), http://www.ci.woodbury.mn.us/environ/altenergyord.pdf (nonreflective, nonobtrusive color).

115. *See, e.g.*, Town of Bethany, LOCAL LAW NO. 1 OF 2008 (providing that all wiring is to be underground or on existing wires, except for tie-in lines and by permission of the town board for reasons relating to the terrain); Woodbury, Minn., ALTERNATIVE ENERGY SYSTEMS ORDINANCE 7 (Sept. 2009), http://www.ci.woodbury.mn.us/environ/altenergyord.pdf.

116. *See, e.g.*, Town of Ellington, N.Y., WIND ENERGY CONVERSION SYSTEMS LOCAL LAW 21 (2008) (on file with authors).

117. *See, e.g.*, Town of Ellington, N.Y., WIND ENERGY CONVERSION SYSTEMS LOCAL LAW 18–20 (2008) (on file with authors).

118. In Ellington, warning signs must include a local phone number for a 24-hour hotline, and in Bethany, warning signs must be located at a height of 5 feet (eye-level) on the base of any turbine.

119. *See* Mich. Dept. of Envtl. Quality, Water Bureau Guidance, Geothermal Heat Pump Systems 4 (May 2007), http://www.michigan.gov/documents/deq/deq-wd-gws-wcu-ghpsguidance_195216_7.pdf (explaining that "A local health department permit may be required for the discharge well, depending on the local well permitting ordinance."); Hendricks County, Ind., GROUND WATER WELL ORDINANCE NO. 2003-26, http://www.co.hendricks.in.us/departmentwebfiles/health/ordinances/well.pdf.

120. *See, e.g.*, Barton Hills Village, Mich., AN ORDINANCE TO REGULATE GEOTHERMAL SYSTEMS (Apr. 2009), http://vil-bartonhills.org/ordinances/active_ordinances/Ord29.pdf; City of Hiawatha, Iowa, GEOTHERMAL WELL STANDARDS ORDINANCE § 9 (July 2008), http://www.hiawatha-iowa.com/mod/press/documents/Ordinance%20622.pdf; Home Rule Borough of Edinboro, Pa., GROUND SOURCE HEAT PUMPS ORDINANCE, http://www.edinboro.net/Ordinances/Ordinance%20569.htm; Woodbury, Minn., ALTERNATIVE ENERGY SYSTEMS ORDINANCE § 24-404(b)(1) (Sept. 2009), http://www.ci.woodbury.mn.us/environ/altenergyord.pdf.

121. *See, e.g.*, City of Hiawatha, Iowa, GEOTHERMAL WELL STANDARDS ORDINANCE (July 2008), http://www.hiawatha-iowa.com/mod/press/documents/Ordinance%20622.pdf; Pete Fowler, *Hot Springs Aims to Protect Aquifer*, GLENWOOD SPRINGS POST INDEPENDENT, Nov. 1, 2007, http://www.postindependent.com/article/20071101/VALLEYNEWS/111010043.

122. City of Hiawatha, Iowa, GEOTHERMAL WELL STANDARDS ORDINANCE (July 2008), http://www.hiawatha-iowa.com/mod/press/documents/Ordinance%20622.pdf.

123. Woodbury, Minn., ALTERNATIVE ENERGY SYSTEMS ORDINANCE § 24-404(b)(5) (Sept. 2009), http://www.ci.woodbury.mn.us/environ/altenergyord.pdf.

Part II

Financing, Pricing, and Taxation

chapter six

Government Purchasing of Efficient Products and Renewable Energy

Geraldine E. Edens, Peter L. Gray, and Stephen E. Ruscus

The federal government is the single largest user of energy in the nation. In fiscal year (FY) 2008, the government consumed 1.6 quadrillion British thermal units (BTUs), which is approximately equal to 1.5 percent of the total U.S. energy consumption.[1] The government's energy bill for energy delivered to federal sites was $24.5 billion—about 0.8 percent of total federal expenditures.[2] Of the $24.5 billion, over $7 billion was spent on energy to operate federal buildings.[3] The government is also the largest volume purchaser of energy-consuming products in the world.

This chapter discusses the laws and executive orders that have directed federal agencies to reduce their energy consumption, increase their use of renewable energy, make federal buildings more energy efficient, purchase energy-efficient goods and services, and increase the use of alternative fuels. Overall, the government has made progress in each of these areas. For example, in FY 2008, federal agencies decreased their energy consumption, produced or purchased 1,903.6 gigawatt hours (GWh) of renewable energy—equivalent to 3.4 percent of their total electricity use,[4] and invested significantly in making federal facilities more energy efficient. Nevertheless, agencies face significant challenges in meeting many of the ambitious goals that have been set by the administration.

Basic Principles of Government Procurement

Federal agencies rely on third-party contractors to provide energy-related goods and services. This includes the purchase of energy-efficient products and renewable energy, as well as a wide range of energy-saving services. All of these goods and services are procured in accordance with long-standing government contract laws and regulations.

The sections that follow discuss unique aspects of government contracting that shape the ability of Congress and the Executive Branch to increase procurement and utilization of energy-efficient products and services as well as renewable energy.

These policies include the required purchase of energy-efficient products/renewable energy, outright prohibition on the use of appropriated funds to purchase non-energy-efficient products, and inclusion of evaluation criteria favoring energy-efficient products in contract solicitations. Such policies may be targeted at specific agencies or specific products or product types, or may be of general applicability to all federal procurements.

Primary Procurement Statutes and Regulations

Federal agencies possess inherent authority under their enabling statutes to enter into contracts for supplies and services necessary to fulfill their designated missions. Not surprisingly, however, Congress has placed constraints on the manner in which agencies may acquire these supplies and services. First, Congress, through the Anti-Deficiency Act,[5] has prohibited agencies from both (1) committing the government to any contract or obligation for the payment of money before a sufficient congressional appropriation is made and (2) accepting voluntary services from contractors. Second, Congress has, through the Federal Property and Administrative Services Act of 1949 (applicable to procurements by civilian agencies)[6] and the Armed Services Procurement Act of 1947 (applicable to procurements by the U.S. Armed Services),[7] set forth requirements for agency purchases using appropriated funds. These statutes provide direction to agencies in many areas including planning and solicitation requirements, requirements for competition, limitations on contract duration, and requirements applicable to specific types of contracts.

In the mid-1990s, Congress significantly altered the procurement landscape, amending the procurement statutes through passage of the Federal Acquisition Streamlining Act of 1994 (FASA) and the Federal Acquisition Reform Act of 1995 (FARA).[8] Together, these legislative enactments streamlined the cumbersome federal procurement process, particularly for low-dollar procurements (under $100,000) and for the procurement of commercial items,[9] and reduced administrative burdens and compliance obligations imposed on contractors. Specifically, FASA and FARA eliminated contractor certification requirements not required by law and exempted commercial supply and service contracts from certain regulations relating to cost accounting and the provision of cost and pricing data to the government. These changes are significant for contractors selling commercial energy-efficient or renewable energy-related products and services to the government because they significantly reduce entry barriers to, and the cost of participation in, government markets.

All procurement laws noted above are implemented through the Federal Acquisition Regulation (FAR).[10] The FAR is the deskbook for all contractors seeking to do business with the federal government. Agencies issue supplemental FAR regulations, such as the Department of Defense FAR supplement, to implement agency-specific laws and programs. The FAR and agency FAR supplements, rooted as they are in legislation, have the force and effect of law.[11] They mandate inclusion of many specific clauses in government contracts. Commercial item vendors new to the federal marketplace should be aware that, unlike contract clauses in the commercial world, many of these mandatory government contract clauses are non-negotiable.

Competitive Bidding

One of the bedrock principles of government contracting is the requirement for "full and open competition" as established in the Competition in Contracting Act of 1984 (CICA).[12] Thus, contractors seeking to sell energy-efficient and renewable energy-related products and services to the government will find that federal sales often entail a lengthy competitive procurement process involving public notice of the proposed contract action, solicitation and evaluation of proposals, and contract award.

Several important CICA exceptions exist. First, Congress has explicitly reserved the right to place certain types of procurements outside the scope of CICA's competition requirements.[13] However, it has not specifically exempted procurements specific to energy-related goods and services.

Second, CICA and the implementing FAR regulations provide limited exceptions to the full and open competition requirement. These include circumstances in which there is only one source of supply and no other supplies or services will satisfy agency requirements; unusual and compelling urgency; preservation of the industrial base; agreement between the United States and a foreign government or international organization; national security; as well as a blanket "public interest" exception.[14] For contractors seeking federally funded development of innovative, energy-efficient or renewable energy-related products and services, such products and services may be deemed available from only one source (and thus exempted from competition) if that contractor submits an unsolicited proposal in accordance with specific procedures provided in the FAR that demonstrates a unique and innovative concept or capability to provide a concept or a service not otherwise available to the government that does not resemble the substance of an ongoing competitive acquisition.[15]

Third, Congress has deemed the award of certain multiple award schedule (MAS) contracts (also known as Federal Supply Schedule (FSS) contracts) as satisfying the requirement for full and open competition, even though contractors do not compete against each other for the award of these contracts.[16] Competitive pricing for MAS contracts is established through negotiation based on contractor disclosures of commercial sales practices and pricing. These contracts are critical tools for contractors seeking to sell energy efficient or renewable energy-related products and services to the government. The federal government purchases over $40 billion in supplies and services listed on MAS contracts each year. The MAS program will be discussed in more detail below.

Bid Protests

One unique aspect of government contract law that continually surprises new entrants into government markets is the bid protest, which may lead to the government's cancellation of contracts only days after they are awarded. A bid protest is a challenge either to the propriety of a solicitation (pre-award) or to a contract allegedly awarded in violation of procurement laws and regulations or in such a manner as to deprive a bidder/offeror a fair opportunity to compete for a contract. Bid protests may be brought by an interested party defined as "an actual or prospective bidder or offeror whose direct economic interest would be affected by the award of a contract or by the failure to award a contract."[17] Bid protests may be filed with the procuring agency, the General Accountability Office (GAO), or the United States Court of Federal Claims (CFC).

The rules for bid protests balance government interests in having a lawful, level playing field in procurements so that competition can produce best value for the government, while minimizing delays in the procurement process caused by bid protests.[18] When an agency receives notice of a protest from the GAO prior to award, it is prohibited from awarding the contract. If the contract has been awarded and the agency receives notice of a protest from the GAO within ten days of award or five days of a required debriefing, the agency must suspend performance of the contract. Agencies have limited authority to avoid such suspensions. The bid protest rules also require that, to be heard, bidders/offerors must file protests—and GAO must resolve protests—on strict schedules. Protests regarding defects in a solicitation must be filed *before* the bid opening date or the closing date for receipt of proposals. Protests after award of a contract must be filed *within ten days* after the basis of the protest is known or should have been known.[19] GAO is required to resolve protests within one hundred days of filing. If a protest is sustained, the GAO may recommend remedies including reevaluation of proposals, re-competition of the contract, termination and re-award of the contract as necessary, and payment of bid protest costs to the protestor. Common bases for protest focus on failures to evaluate proposals in accordance with the solicitation's stated evaluation terms.

Types of Contracts and Associated Contract Risks

Congress has permitted agencies wide latitude in choosing the contract type most appropriate to a particular procurement. Permitted contract types fall generally into the category either of fixed-price or cost-reimbursement contracts, both of which are used to procure energy-related goods and services. Fixed-price contracts can be firm, or the price may be adjusted based on factors such as changes in specified index prices or agreed-upon incentives. In general, fixed-price contracts are appropriate when the risk to the contractor is low and predictable so that the proposed price, including profit, appropriately can reflect risk. Fixed-price contracts nonetheless do have financial risk to the contractor as the contractor is required to perform for a fixed price even if its total costs ultimately exceed contract price.[20] The government views fixed-price contracts as safeguarding its interests in efficient use of taxpayer funds since the risk of cost overruns resulting from inefficient performance is borne by the contractor, and fixed-price contractors are therefore highly motivated to perform efficiently and on time. FAR § 16.201 specifically requires that contracting officers use firm fixed-price or fixed price with economic price adjustment contract forms when contracting for commercial items. Firm fixed-price commercial item contracts are commonly viewed as imposing a more limited compliance burden than other fixed-price contracts because procurements for commercial items themselves are streamlined with reduced obligations on contractors.

Cost-reimbursement contracts provide for reimbursement of allowed costs. Certain types of cost-reimbursement contracts do not allow for the payment of profits (fee). Others provide for a fixed or incentive fee. In general, cost-reimbursement contracts are appropriate when performance-related uncertainties prevent the reliable estimate of cost needed to use a fixed-price contract vehicle. Cost-reimbursement contracts pose little financial risk to the contractor as the contractor is reimbursed all allowable costs. However, profits on cost-reimbursement-type contracts are statutorily limited to 15 percent on research and development contracts and 10 percent on all others and may be negotiated lower. Also, cost-reimbursement contracts generally are viewed as having significantly higher compliance risks as the government protects its monies by requiring the tracking of actual costs incurred in performance, approval of accounting systems as adequate for the accounting of costs, increased surveillance over contract performance, detailed cost reporting, and related certifications. Fee on cost-type contracts typically is fixed at contract award based upon estimated costs, not as a percentage but as a fixed dollar amount. Federal law specifically prohibits award of cost plus percentage of cost contracts. It should be noted that FAR § 16.301-3 expressly forbids the use of cost-reimbursement contract forms when contracting for commercial items.

Other important contract types include time and materials contracts, which reimburse materials at cost, and time at negotiated fixed hourly rates—including wages, overhead, general and administrative (home office) expenses, and profit—and labor hour contracts, a variant of the time and materials contract in which materials are not supplied by the contractor.

Finally, Indefinite Delivery Indefinite Quantity (IDIQ) contracts are binding contracts that order work on a task order basis. No specific delivery dates or specified quantities beyond a guaranteed nominal amount are established at time of award. Instead, the government issues task orders within the scope of the contract for supplies (or task orders for the delivery of services). This contract type affords the government significant flexibility in the timing, magnitude, and content of its orders. IDIQ contracts may be single award (one contractor receives all the work) or multiple award (several contractors receive contracts and compete for task orders).

Federal Supply Schedule Contracts

MAS/FSS contracts are IDIQ contracts mostly for commercial items that are entered into under special statutory authority vested in the General Services Administration (GSA) to administer the Multiple Award Schedule (MAS) Program. To implement the program, GSA establishes "schedules" for categories of products or services.[21] GSA then negotiates IDIQ contracts with multiple contractors for the provision of products and services within the scope of each separate schedule. Once an FSS IDIQ contract is negotiated by GSA, all executive agencies and other eligible entities are entitled to place orders (either directly or competitively) and purchase products and services from contractors under the various contracts. GSA imposes a user fee on each sale that is collected by the FSS contractor from the agency using the contract. Contractors are required to remit collected fees quarterly to the GSA. As noted above, the government currently purchases over $40 billion in commercial products and services annually under the schedule program, which includes over 11 million products and services.

One critical aspect of FSS contracts is that they are not competitive. Rather, the GSA negotiates with each contractor separately to establish a fair and reasonable price. These prices are based on commercial sales practices and data the contractor is required to disclose accurately and completely prior to conclusion of negotiations. Pricing is subject to downward adjustment over the life of the contract through the operation of the mandatory Price Reductions Clause. Under this clause, contractors monitor an agreed-upon commercial customer price/discount level and implement proportionate changes in FSS prices when the commercial price is reduced (or the discount is increased). Contractors may request price increases (generally annually) under the Equitable Price Adjustment Clause. The data and tracking requirements of GSA schedules are somewhat burdensome, and contractors often incur penalties for compliance errors. The schedules are nonetheless the most preferred vehicle for agencies seeking to procure commercial items, as it is far simpler for them to issue FSS orders than to conduct full and open competitions of their own. Either party to the FSS contract may cancel all or part of the contract on thirty days' notice.

Terminations for Convenience

Unlike commercial contractors, whenever it is in the government's interests to do so, the government is permitted to walk away from any deal without paying the contractor its expected profit. This right is embodied in the FAR termination for convenience clauses that are required to be inserted in virtually every type of government contract. So fundamental is the right to walk away when taxpayers' best interests are no longer served that courts have held that the termination for convenience clause will be read into government contracts, even if both the contractor and the contracting officer have agreed to leave it out.[22]

Under the termination for convenience clauses, the contractor is entitled to costs incurred as of the termination, as well as contract closeout costs, and a fair profit, but only on the costs incurred. Recovery of anticipatory profits is prohibited. Accordingly, a contractor considering investment in performance of government contracts should consider the risk of termination for convenience when making investment/contracting decisions.

Long-Term Contracts for Facilities and Infrastructure

Contractors wishing to construct energy-efficient buildings or renewable power production facilities on government land for the benefit of the government face unique procurement issues if the government is unwilling, or lacks the appropriated funds necessary, to purchase such facilities outright. Long-term facility leases or long-term contracts for the purchase of power at rates that amortize design, construction, operation, and maintenance costs, as well as a fair rate of return on investment, are options but are accompanied by unique challenges.

Because contractors are usually unwilling or unable to carry the cost of the acquisition for long periods, contractors in such situations typically look to third-party capital sources. While the financial community seeks as much certainty as possible when financing capital projects, the government, on the other hand, typically commits funding only in short increments (e.g., one-year funds), generally cannot promise payment in excess of appropriated funds, and, in addition, retains unilateral exit rights in the form of the termination for convenience clause discussed above. The success of these long-term contracts as an alternative financing vehicle in government procurements therefore depends on the financial community's ability to understand the limitations under which the government must operate and the government's ability to use the legal tools it has available to reduce uncertainty for the financial community.

To be enforceable, such long-term government contracts must be authorized either generally or specifically by Congress and must not violate the Anti-Deficiency Act's prohibition against obligation of funds in excess of appropriated funds unless otherwise authorized by law.[23] Examples of congressional authorizations include provisions authorizing the Department of Defense (DOD) to enter into contracts for up to thirty years for the provision and operation of energy production facilities on private property or real property under DOD's jurisdiction and the purchase of energy produced from such facilities,[24] and provisions authorizing DOD to enter into leases for up to twenty years for military housing to be constructed or rehabilitated to residential use near military installations.[25] This latter authorization, however, requires leases authorized by the statute to contain provisions stating that the obligation of the United States to make payments under the contract in any fiscal year is subject to appropriations being provided specifically for that fiscal year and specifically for that project; that the government commits to obligate the necessary amount for each fiscal year covered by the contract when and to the extent that funds are appropriated for that project for that fiscal year; and that such a commitment does not constitute an obligation of the United States to appropriate necessary funds.

Financial institutions participating in government leases typically rely upon the payment stream from the underlying lease agreement rather than any interest in the goods themselves as security, especially if construction has occurred on government land where the facility in question likely has little commercial value. Consequently, the remedies available to an institution in the event of a termination for convenience or of failure to appropriate funds typically must be addressed before a long-term contract can go forward.

One method of accomplishing this is to include termination liability provisions. However, these provisions must comply with the Anti-Deficiency Act by not promising termination payments for which no funds have been appropriated or by being statutorily exempted from coverage by the Act, and must comply with the related "bona fide needs" rule prohibiting the use of one fiscal year's appropriated money to be used for another year's needs. If adequate funds have been appropriated, one method by which an agency may satisfy the bona fide needs rule is through a showing that the contractor was unwilling to make the necessary construction investment to provide the service without assurances of recovery, and that, thus, inclusion of a termination liability provision is the only way to obtain the necessary services.[26] In this way, the contingent future liability properly may be viewed as a bona fide need of the contract in the current year, and available funds may be used to pay termination liability charges.[27]

Policy Tools for Implementing Preferences for Energy-Efficient Products

As discussed in the sections that follow, federal statutes and executive orders require purchases of renewable energy using products for certain kinds of acquisitions. For example, Congress has required that agency federal fleet purchases consist of no less than 75 percent alternatively fueled vehicles.[28] Federal statutes also require that, beginning January 1, 2010, each federal fleet fueling center have at least one renewable fuel pump, thereby permitting executive agencies to better utilize renewable fuel vehicles.[29] Similarly, agencies are required to purchase Energy Star or Federal Energy Management Program (FEMP) products in product categories covered by either program, unless these products are not cost-effective taking into account life-cycle costs, including energy cost, or do not satisfy agency functional requirements.[30]

Congress also prohibits the purchase of specific, energy-inefficient products. For example, 42 U.S.C. § 17141 specifically prohibits the United States Coast Guard from purchasing incandescent lights with limited exceptions. Congress also prohibits any agency from purchasing any renewable alternative or synthetic fuel for mobility-related use unless the life-cycle greenhouse gas emissions associated with both the production and combustion of the fuel are less than or equal to emissions from conventional fuels.[31]

Further, Congress has imposed mandates on agencies to require certain types of contractors to use energy-efficient products in performance of their contracts. For example, 42 U.S.C. § 8259b requires that agencies incorporate criteria for energy efficiency into specifications and evaluation criteria for all procurements involving energy-consuming products and systems, including construction, renovation, and services contracts that include provision of energy-consuming products and systems.

Given the recent U.S. policy focus on the reduction of greenhouse gases, use of all of these policy tools to increase purchases of energy-efficient, renewable energy-related products and services almost certainly will increase. Accordingly, contractors should expect to see both solicitations seeking such products and services and government contract clauses requiring use of such products and services in contract performance. Contractors also should expect to see inclusion of contract provisions requiring contractors to report on their own use of energy-efficient products and services and to execute related certifications.

Federal Efforts to Promote Use and Purchase of Energy-Efficient Products

The federal government is the largest volume purchaser of energy-consuming products in the world, spending approximately $10 billion per year.[32] Although the government is often the largest single customer for a given product, the federal market share is only 1 to 2 percent of national sales for most products.[33] Nevertheless, there is a clear recognition that the federal government can move the entire market toward greater efficiency. There are also significant energy, cost, and GHG emissions savings that can be achieved through energy-efficient products. One study found that in 2010 for a specified group of products, the federal sector could save 11 to 42 tons BTU per year, which represents a cost savings of $160 to $620 million per year.[34] These savings equate to a 3 to 12 percent savings in annual energy use.

Federal Procurement Policy for Energy-Efficient Products

Federal policy for the purchase of energy-efficient products was established by the Energy Policy Act of 1992 (EPAct92)[35] and by Executive Order (EO) 12902, issued by President Clinton in 1994.[36] EPAct92 directed the GSA, DOD, and the Defense Logistics Agency (DLA),[37] in consultation with the Secretary of Energy, to "identify and designate those energy efficient products that offer significant potential savings."[38] It also encouraged "the acquisition and use by all federal agencies of [the energy efficient] products identified." The EO went a step further and directed federal agencies to purchase products identified in accordance with EPAct92. In addition, to encourage a market for highly energy-efficient products, the EO directed agencies to increase purchases of products that are in the upper 25 percent of energy efficiency for all similar products, or products that are at least 10 percent more efficient than the minimum level that meets federal standards.

The EO further directed DOE, in cooperation with other agencies, to issue a "Federal Procurement Challenge," inviting each agency to commit a specified fraction of their purchases within a certain time period to energy-efficient products. The challenge was initiated by the Federal Energy Management Program (FEMP)[39] and was cosponsored by the Council on Environmental Quality and the Office of Management and Budget Office of Federal Procurement Policy. More than twenty-one agencies, representing 95 percent of the buying power of the federal government, agreed to participate in the challenge. FEMP estimated that the agencies' commitment to specify and purchase "best practice" energy products would result in a cost savings of $900 million per year and would reduce GHG emissions by as much as 11 million metric tons of CO_2.[40]

In 1999, President Clinton issued a second EO (Executive Order 13123) addressing energy efficiency and titled "Greening the Government Through Efficient Energy Management." Section 403(b) directed federal agencies to select "Energy Star and other energy-efficient products when acquiring energy-using products."[41] If Energy Star labels were not yet available, the EO directed agencies to select FEMP designated products that are in the upper 25 percent of energy efficiency. EPA and DOE were directed to expedite the process of designating Energy Star products.

The Energy Policy Act of 2005 and Implementing Regulations

Section 104 of the Energy Policy Act of 2005 (EPAct05) codified the requirements set forth in EO 13123 requiring that federal agencies purchase only Energy Star and FEMP-designated energy-consuming products.[42] Federal agencies are also required to incorporate into all procurements involving energy-consuming products criteria for energy efficiency that are consistent with the criteria used for rating Energy Star and FEMP designated products.[43] Further, the GSA and the DLA are required to clearly and predominantly identify Energy Star and FEMP designated products in their inventory of products. GSA and DLA are also required to supply only Energy Star and FEMP-designated products in all covered product categories, unless the head of an agency ordering a product specifies in writing that an exemption applies.[44]

Agencies are exempt from purchasing Energy Star or FEMP-designated products if the head of an agency justifies in writing that: (1) Energy Star or FEMP-designated products are not life-cycle cost-effective taking energy cost savings into account; (2) no Energy Star or FEMP-designated product is reasonably available that meets the functional requirements of the agency; or (3) the product is being purchased for combat-related activities.

The EPAct05 also formalized the Energy Star program as a joint program within EPA and DOE "to identify and promote energy-efficient products."[45] The agencies were directed to (1) promote Energy Star–compliant technologies as the preferred technologies in the marketplace; (2) enhance public awareness of the Energy Star label; (3) preserve the integrity of the Energy Star label; (4) regularly update Energy Star product criteria for product categories; and (5) solicit public comments prior to establishing or revising an Energy Star product category, specification, or criterion.

In 2007, FAR § 23.204 was revised to reflect the requirements of § 104 of EPAct05.[46] In 2009, DOE finalized regulations to provide guidance to federal agencies implementing the EPAct05 requirements to purchase Energy Star and FEMP designated products.[47]

Executive Order 13514 and Procurement

On October 5, 2009, President Obama signed Executive Order 13514, entitled "Federal Leadership in Environmental, Energy, and Economic Performance."[48] The EO mandates that each federal agency develop and implement a plan to reduce greenhouse gas (GHG) emissions that fall into three categories (Scopes 1, 2 and 3) by 2020. They are as follows:

- Direct GHG emissions from sources that are owned or controlled by the federal agency (Scope 1);

- Direct GHG emissions resulting from the generation of electricity, heat, or steam that a federal agency purchases (Scope 2); and
- GHG emissions from sources not owned or directly controlled by a federal agency but related to agency activities, such as vendor supply chains, delivery services, and employee travel and commuting (Scope 3).

In recognition that improved energy efficiency decreases GHGs, the EO requires that agencies

> ensure that 95 percent of new contract actions, including task and delivery orders, for products and services, with the exception of acquisition of weapons systems, are energy efficient . . . , water-efficient, biobased, environmentally preferable . . . , non-ozone depleting, contain recycled content, or are non-toxic or less-toxic alternatives, where such products and services meet agency performance requirements.

Energy efficient products are defined as Energy Star or FEMP-designated products. Thus, the mandate to purchase energy efficient products is now directly related to the government's efforts to significantly decrease GHG emissions.

FEMP-Designated and Energy Star Products

Currently, Energy Star–qualified and FEMP-designated products cover sixty-two types of products in the following categories: (1) lighting; (2) commercial and industrial equipment; (3) food service equipment; (4) office equipment; (5) home electronics; (6) appliances; (7) residential equipment; (8) plumbing; and (9) construction. Unlike the Energy Star label that is applied to specific products, FEMP-designated products are not product-specific. Rather, FEMP identifies required purchasing specifications and performance requirements for a category of products, which are typically an energy consumption level within the upper 25 percent of the product category. As FEMP explains,

> In the category for "widgets," if there are some widgets that consume 1 kilowatt hour (kWh) per year and others that consume 100 kWh per year, the required consumption level for FEMP-designated widgets will be set at 25 kWh per year. Any widget that uses less than 25 kWh per year will meet FEMP-designated Federal purchasing specifications for widgets.[49]

FEMP will create new product categories if it can be shown that there is (1) a standard test procedure to determine annual energy consumption, including standby energy consumption, for all products within the category, (2) an outside data source for consumers to access annual energy consumption information for all category products sold within the United States, and (3) data showing the use of a particular product category within the federal government or the annual number of products within that category purchased by the federal sector.[50] FEMP will not designate a product category that does not have significant energy savings potential for the federal government based both on the volume of federal purchases and the difference in energy use between a "base" model and a more efficient one.[51] If no federal agencies purchase the product, or if the difference in energy performance among products within the same category is minor, FEMP will not designate performance specifications for the product category.[52]

Federal Compliance with Energy-Efficient Procurement Laws and Regulations

With support from FEMP, in 2007, the Alliance to Save Energy examined 164 federal procurement solicitations of $25,000 or more that included at least one product or piece of equipment subject to Energy Star or FEMP specifications to determine if they contained any reference to the energy efficiency procurement requirements of EPAct05.[53] The Alliance found that only 7 percent of the solicitations complied with the law. The Alliance also surveyed twenty-five government procurement officials, only two of which knew in detail the energy efficiency procurement requirements. The high unawareness rate may be attributed to there not being in place at the time a mandatory FAR contract clause that could be inserted into solicitations. The FAR regulations promulgated in December 2007 added such a clause.[54] Finally, the Alliance found that GSA and DLA failed to sell energy-efficient models in 65 percent and 80 percent of the covered product categories, respectively. The Alliance makes a number of recommendations for improving compliance, including training procurement officials, redesigning purchasing websites, tracking compliance, and taking enforcement measures, some of which have been implemented.

Federal Building Energy Management and Greening Federal Buildings

As discussed in chapter 2, lowering our energy consumption through deployment of energy-efficient equipment and buildings is the fastest, cheapest way for the United States to reduce GHG emissions. Over 40 percent of energy in the United States is consumed by buildings, and the largest owner of buildings, by a wide margin, is the federal government. The U.S. government owns approximately 445,000 buildings with total floor space of over 3 billion square feet. In addition, the U.S. government leases an additional 57,000 buildings comprising 374 million square feet of floor space.[55] As the owner of nearly 3 percent of commercial buildings in the United States, the federal government has a vital role to play in reducing GHG emissions. In recognition of its significant contribution to U.S. GHG emissions and consistent with U.S. policy of encouraging energy efficiency and use of green energy, the federal government has imposed a number of green building requirements on federal agencies. These requirements are summarized below.

Section 109 of the Energy Policy Act of 2005

Section 109 of the EPAct05 directed the Secretary of Energy to establish energy standards for new federal buildings. Within one year of enactment of EPAct05, the Secretary of Energy was to establish standards requiring that new federal buildings "be designed to energy consumption levels that are at least 30 percent below the levels established" by American Standard of Heating, Refrigerating and Air Conditioning Engineers (ASHRAE) Standard 90.1-2004 (which applies to commercial and high-rise residential buildings) or the 2004 International Energy Conservation Code (which applies to low-rise residential buildings). These standards are to apply provided they are determined to be "life-cycle cost-effective" as defined under 10 C.F.R. Part 436.[56]

EPAct05 also requires that sustainable building design principles be applied to siting, design, and construction of "new and replacement" buildings; and that water conservation technologies be applied whenever water is used to achieve energy efficiency, so long as the technologies are life-cycle cost-effective.

Federal Leadership in High Performance and Sustainable Buildings Memorandum

In 2006, nearly two dozen federal agencies signed a Memorandum of Understanding (MOU) reinforcing the EPAct05 energy efficiency performance standards. Titled the "Federal Leadership in High Performance and Sustainable Buildings,"[57] the MOU signatories committed to establishing a common set of guiding principles for planning, acquiring, siting, designing, building, operating and maintaining "High Performance and Sustainable Buildings." Among the standards under the MOU:

- For new construction, reduce the energy cost budget by 30 percent compared to the baseline building performance rating per ASHRAE Standard 90.1-2004.
- For major renovations, reduce the energy cost budget by 20 percent below pre-renovations 2003 baseline.
- Consistent with DOE guidelines, install building utility meters to track and continuously optimize energy performance and to evaluate performance against energy design targets.
- Enter data and lessons learned from sustainable buildings into the High Performance Building Database.
- Employ strategies to use at least 20 percent less drinking water than the baseline calculated for the building.
- Use efficient low-irrigation landscaping to reduce outdoor water consumption by 50 percent as compared to consumption expected with conventional landscaping.
- Buildings must be designed to earn the Energy Star label for new construction and major renovation.

DOE Regulations for New Federal Building Construction

On December 31, 2007, the Department of Energy promulgated regulations[58] that established energy efficiency standards for new federal buildings, i.e., federal buildings which began design for construction on or after January 3, 2007. These regulations also apply to buildings leased by federal agencies. Many of the standards contained in the "Federal Leadership in High Performance and Sustainable Buildings" MOU are now codified in the DOE regulations (such as ASHRAE Standard 90.1-2004).

In May 2010, DOE proposed additional regulations that would require new federal buildings and major renovations of existing buildings to incorporate sustainable principles in design, siting, and construction, taking into account life-cycle costs.[59] They would also require the use of solar water heaters to provide at least 30 percent of the demand for hot water and that federal agencies install on-site facilities to generate power from renewable energy sources. The regulations would largely implement the requirements set forth in the EPAct05 and the Energy Independence and Security Act of 2007 (EISA).

Energy Independence and Security Act of 2007

EISA[60] created new future energy efficiency performance standards for federal buildings. By fiscal year 2010, buildings were to be designed to reduce fossil fuel–generated consumption by 55 percent. The percent reduction increases every five years until fiscal year 2030, when no fossil fuel–generated energy may be consumed ("zero-fossil-fuel" building). The baseline for this requirement is a similar building in fiscal year 2003, as measured by the Commercial Buildings Energy Consumption Survey (CBECS) or the Residential Energy Consumption Survey (RECS) data. These new requirements are generally consistent with the goals of the Architecture 2030 Challenge, and at least in later years are more stringent than the "30 percent below model energy code" requirements of the EPAct05.

The American Recovery and Reinvestment Act

On February 17, 2009, President Obama signed into law the American Recovery and Reinvestment Act (ARRA),[61] a $787 billion stimulus package that contains nearly $72 billion in direct investments and $22 billion in tax incentives for energy efficiency, renewable energy, green vehicles, green job training, and smart grid projects. Of relevance to this chapter are the provisions creating incentives for development of green, energy-efficient federal buildings.

Specifically, ARRA allocated $5.55 billon, of which $4.5 billion is for measures necessary to convert GSA buildings to High Performance Green Buildings. GSA was required to, and did, submit a detailed plan to the House and Senate Committees on Appropriation that detailed by project the use of the funds.[62] GSA must provide the Committees with fifteen days' prior notice of any changes/reallocations to the use of the funds and must submit quarterly reports on the obligation of the funds.

Executive Order 13514 and Federal Buildings

As discussed above, on October 5, 2009, President Obama issued EO 13514 mandating that federal agencies take a sweeping series of steps to address GHG management, renewable energy use, water efficiency, pollution prevention, regional and local transportation planning, sustainable facility development, and electronics stewardship. EO 13514 also strengthens the federal government's commitments for green buildings. Federal agencies must enhance efforts toward sustainable buildings and communities. Specific requirements include:

- Implementing high-performance sustainable federal building design, construction, operation and management, maintenance, and deconstruction by:
  - Ensuring all new federal buildings, entering the design phase in 2020 or later, are designed to achieve zero net energy by 2030.
  - Ensuring all new construction, major renovations, or repair or alteration of federal buildings complies with the Guiding Principles of Federal Leadership in High Performance and Sustainable Buildings.
  - Ensuring at least 15 percent of existing agency buildings and leases (above 5,000 gross square feet) meet the Guiding Principles by 2015 and that the agency makes annual progress toward 100 percent compliance across its building inventory.
  - Pursuing cost-effective, innovative strategies (e.g., highly reflective and vegetated roofs) to minimize consumption of energy, water, and materials.
  - Managing existing building systems to reduce the consumption of energy, water, and materials, and identifying alternatives to renovation that reduce existing asset-deferred maintenance costs.
  - When adding assets to agency building inventories, identifying opportunities to consolidate and eliminate existing assets, optimize the performance of portfolio property, and reduce associated environmental impacts.
  - Ensuring that rehabilitation of federally owned historic buildings utilizes best practices and technologies in retrofitting to promote long-term viability of the building.
- Advancing regional and local integrated planning by:
  - Participating in regional transportation planning and recognizing existing community transportation infrastructure.
  - Aligning federal policies to increase the effectiveness of local planning for energy choices such as locally generated renewable energy.
  - Ensuring that planning for new federal facilities and leases considers sites that are pedestrian friendly, near existing employment centers, and accessible to public transport and emphasizes existing central cities and, in rural communities, existing or planned town centers.
  - Identifying and analyzing impacts from energy usage and alternative energy sources in all environmental impact statements and environmental assessments for proposals covering new or expanded federal facilities under the amended National Environmental Policy Act (NEPA) of 1969.

Federal Efforts to Decrease Energy Consumption and Increase Renewable Energy Use

Efforts to Decrease Energy Consumption

Over the past two decades, the federal government has worked to reduce its overall energy consumption. In 2007, primary energy use decreased 16 percent from 1985,

3.7 percent from 2003, and 0.6 percent from 2006.[63] In 2007, primary energy use was 1.6 quadrillion BTU. That is 16 percent less than consumption in 1985 (1.9 quadrillion BTU), 3.7 percent less than consumption in 2003 (1.66 quads BTU), and 0.6 percent *more* than consumption in 2006 (1.59 quads BTU).

The National Energy Conservation Policy Act (NECPA), as amended, requires federal agencies to improve energy management in their facilities and operations.[64] Amendments to NECPA made by the Federal Energy Management Improvement Act of 1988 required each agency to achieve a 10 percent reduction in energy consumption by FY 1995, measured against a 1985 baseline on a BTU-per-gross-square-foot basis (BTU-GSF). Section 102 of EPAct05 set an energy reduction goal of 20 percent by 2015 from a 2003 baseline.[65]

On January 24, 2007, President George W. Bush issued EO 13423, the goal of which was to strengthen federal goals for energy consumption, efficiency, and sustainability.[66] The EO directs the head of each agency to improve energy efficiency and reduce GHG emissions by 3 percent annually through 2015 (for a total reduction of 30 percent relative to the agency's baseline energy use in 2003). The EO also directs the heads of federal agencies to (1) ensure that half of their agency's energy comes from renewable sources, (2) reduce water consumption by 2 percent annually (for a total 16 percent by 2015), and (3) acquire goods and services that are produced in a sustainable manner ("bio-based, environmentally preferable, energy-efficient, water efficient, and recycled content products").

These EO energy and efficiency goals were codified by EISA. To assist federal agencies in achieving these goals, EISA requires agencies to identify facilities that together consume at least 75 percent of total agency energy use and to appoint an energy manager for each of those facilities.

According to FEMP, the federal government as a whole was on track to meet its energy intensity reduction targets of 9 percent for FY 2008 (October 1, 2008 through September 30, 2009).[67] Collectively, all federal agencies reduced their energy intensity by 9.3 percent. However, overall government performance improved only 1.2 percent from the previous year, less than half of the EISA prescribed target of 3 percent.

Agency progress in FY 2009 is not yet available, but a recent survey of agency officials with purchasing authority commissioned by the Alliance to Save Energy suggests that agencies face several obstacles in achieving energy efficiency goals.[68] While 79 percent of those surveyed recognize that energy efficiency is among the most effective ways to meet energy needs, reduce energy costs, and lower greenhouse gas emissions, many believe that the biggest obstacle to achieving energy goals is a lack of funding. The struggling economy and the potential tightening of agency budgets will likely impact their ability to pursue energy efficiency projects. Nevertheless, about two-thirds of the respondents believe their agency has a culture that encourages energy efficiency practices throughout all levels and across all departments, and about half report that the significance of energy efficiency in their operations has increased in the last two years.

Efforts to Increase Renewable Energy Use

Section 203 of the EPAct05 directed that Department of Energy (i.e., FEMP) ensure, to the extent economically feasible and technically practicable, that the total amount of electric energy the federal government consumes during any fiscal year include the following amounts of renewable energy: (1) not less than 3 percent in fiscal years 2007 through 2009; (2) not less than 5 percent in fiscal years 2010 through 2012; and (3) not less than 7.5 percent in fiscal year 2013 and each fiscal year thereafter.[69] Renewable energy is defined as electric energy generated from solar, wind, biomass,[70] landfill gas, ocean (including tidal, waves, current, and thermal), geothermal, municipal solid waste, or new hydroelectric generation capacity achieved from increased efficiency or additions of new capacity at an existing hydroelectric project. For purposes of determining compliance with EPAct05, the amount of renewable energy consumed is doubled if it is produced and used on site at a federal facility or is produced on Indian land and used at a federal facility.

EO 13423 directed federal agencies to:

> ensure that (i) at last half of the statutorily required renewable energy consumed by the agency in a fiscal year comes from new renewable sources, and (ii) to the extent feasible, the agency implements renewable energy generation projects on agency property for agency use.[71]

Thus, EPAct05 and EO 13423 place a strong emphasis on federal agencies consuming "new" renewable energy and on developing renewable energy projects on federal facilities.[72]

Agencies have made progress in meeting the renewable energy goals established by EPAct05 and EO 13423. According to FEMP, as of 2008, nine agencies had met EPAct05's renewable energy goal of 5 percent for fiscal years 2010 through 2012.[73] Sixteen agencies achieved more than 3 percent total energy consumption from renewable sources. In total, federal agencies reported purchasing or producing 1,895.1 gigawatt-hours of renewable electric energy in FY 2008, equivalent to 3.4 percent of the federal government's electricity use.

In addition to the renewable energy goals established for all federal agencies, the National Defense Authorization Act of 2007 established a goal for DOD to "produce or procure" not less than 25 percent of its total facility energy consumption from renewable energy sources by 2025.[74] In April 2010, the GAO reported that DOD had 454 renewable energy initiatives producing energy or under development.[75] Solar photovoltaic or thermal projects accounted for 68 percent of the reported initiatives. Other technologies included geothermal heat pumps (12 percent), wind (5 percent), and daylighting (3 percent). While DOD is making progress, the Deputy Under Secretary of Defense for Installations and Environment testified before Congress in February 2010 that DOD was "not even close to meeting the interim target" established for meeting the goal to produce or procure 25 percent of its total energy consumption from renewable sources.[76] On July 22, 2010, DOD entered into an MOU with DOE to strengthen coordination between the agencies related to energy efficiency, renewable energy, alternative fuels, and other energy-related efforts to enhance national energy security and transition to a low-carbon economy.[77]

Financing Mechanisms Available to Achieve Federal Energy Goals

There are three principal methods by which federal agencies can finance energy efficiency and renewable energy projects: (1) direct appropriated funding, (2) energy savings performance contracts (ESPCs), and (3) utility energy service contracts (UESCs). In 2007, funding from these three sources totaled approximately $640 million.[78]

Direct Appropriations

NECPA requires that the President identify in each budget submitted to Congress the funds requested for energy conservation measures.[79] In 2007, federal agencies spent $335.3 million on energy-related projects, compared with $287 million in 2006. Some agencies increased their direct spending significantly, e.g., U.S. Postal Service (40.2 percent increase); Department of Homeland Security (1,005 percent increase), and U.S. Department of Agriculture (321 percent increase).

Energy Savings Performance Contracts

Recognizing that funding for energy efficiency improvements can be difficult to obtain because of budget constraints and competing agency priorities, in 1986 Congress authorized agencies to use Energy Savings Performance Contracts (ESPCs) to finance energy savings projects.[80] An ESPC is a contract between a federal agency and an energy service company (ESCO), whereby the ESCO identifies, designs, and constructs facility energy improvements, e.g., energy-efficient lighting, automated controls, updated heating, ventilation, air conditioning equipment, and so forth. The federal agency repays the ESCO for its capital investment over a period of years from the savings generated. The ESCO is responsible for maintaining the equipment, as well as measuring the energy consumption and savings. The aggregate annual amount of payments to the ESCO and payments for utilities cannot exceed the amount that the agency would have paid for utilities without an ESPC.

The EPAct92 expanded agency authority to execute guaranteed-savings ESPCs that require ESCOs to guarantee the energy savings to be realized.[81] It also required that the energy savings be measured and verified, and set a maximum twenty-five-year contract term. DOE implementing regulations establish a list of qualified ESCOs and specify procurement procedures and criteria for selecting ESCOs.[82] They also provide standard ESCO contract terms and conditions, define conditions of payment, and address annual measurement and verification requirements.

EISA permanently reauthorized agency ESPC authority and authorized agencies to use any combination of appropriated funds and private financing for federal ESPCs. It also prohibited agencies from establishing policies that would limit the maximum contract term to less than twenty-five years or limit the total amount of private financing under a contract. Agencies were also authorized to sell or transfer renewable energy generated on federal sites in excess of federal needs to utilities or nonfederal energy users. Finally, EISA directed DOE to study the potential application of ESPCs to reduce energy consumption in nonbuilding applications (i.e., vehicles, devices, equipment, etc.).[83]

In 2007, twenty-one ESPC contracts or delivery orders were awarded at eight agencies, providing the government with the opportunity to save more than 1.1 trillion BTU each year.[84] DOD awarded the largest number of contracts covering projects and equipment, such as new thermal storage systems, chillers, boilers, lights, motors, and energy management control systems. In December 2009, DOE awarded sixteen special umbrella ESPCs (Super ESPCs), with a combined ceiling of $80 billion that can be used by all federal agencies for facilities worldwide.[85] As of April 2009, DOE had sixteen active ESPC orders with a combined value of $473 million.

In 2004 and 2005 reports, the GAO questioned the effectiveness of the ESPC program.[86] In September 2009, the DOE Inspector General (IG) released a report that examined four ESPCs at the department valued at $256 million.[87] The IG found that DOE had not always effectively used ESPC orders to achieve energy savings and that it had not ensured that the government's interests were adequately protected in the process. As a result, the IG found that DOE risked spending up to $17.3 million more that it would realize in energy savings from the four ESPC contracts reviewed. In response, the DOE has implemented a number of measures to strengthen DOE's management of ESPC contracts. These measures include increased competition during the selection process, accelerated timeline to award, enhanced training for all personnel, regular on-site reviews, and increased technical support.

Utility Energy Services Contracts

Under a Utility Energy Services Contract (UESC), a utility company agrees to provide a federal agency with services or products (or both) to make the agency's facilities more energy efficient. During the contract period, the agency pays for the cost of services or products from the "avoided-costs-savings" resulting from the energy efficiency improvements.

The EPAct92 authorized and encouraged federal agencies to participate in utility energy efficiency programs. The Act expressly authorizes federal agencies to enter contracts with utilities for energy conservation, accepting "financial incentives, goods, or services."[88] According to the legislative history of this provision, Congress contemplated that agencies would be permitted to participate in utility incentive programs "to the same extent permitted other customers of the utility."[89]

In fiscal year 2007, federal agencies awarded thirty-five UESCs that yielded an estimated annual energy savings of 1.1 trillion BTUs.[90] Twenty-five of the contracts were awarded by DOD to implement a range of energy and water efficiency improvements. Equipment purchased with UESCs included HVAC and steam system upgrades, chillers, boilers, lights, motors, EMCS systems, and water-reducing devices.[91]

Management of the Federal Fleet

The federal government's efforts to reduce its energy consumption and increase its renewable energy use have focused largely on stationary sources of energy use, i.e., buildings and facilities. However, about 45 percent of the government's primary energy use and about one-half of its GHG emissions are attributable to fuel used in transportation vehicles and mobile equipment. In FY 2007, the government consumed 693.2 trillion BTUs of energy in vehicles and equipment, with DOD consuming about 93 percent of all vehicles and equipment energy used.[92]

Alternative Fuel Vehicles

To address vehicles and equipment energy use, EPAct92 directed federal agencies with fleets of twenty or more in metropolitan areas to acquire alternative fuel vehicles (AFVs).[93] Beginning in 2000, 75 percent of all new vehicle acquisitions were to be light-duty vehicles.[94] Agency compliance with EPAct92 is measured by AFV acquisition credits, which are granted on the number of AFVs acquired and the quantity of biodiesel fuel used.[95] In FY 2006, federal agencies acquired 18,307 AFVs and earned 3,446 additional credits, for a total of 21,753 credits or 119 percent of covered acquisitions.[96]

Alternative Fuels

Executive Order 13423, issued by President Bush in 2007 and later codified in EISA, requires that federal agencies reduce petroleum use by federal fleet vehicles by 2 percent per year and increase annual alternative fuel use by 10 percent each year through fiscal year 2015 relative to a fiscal year 2005 baseline.[97] It also requires federal agencies to use plug-in hybrid electric vehicles (PHEVs) when commercially available at a cost reasonably comparable, on the basis of life-cycle cost, to non-PHEVs. Currently no PHEVs are commercially available.

Similarly, EO 13123, issued by President Obama in 2009, directed federal agencies to reduce the use of fossil fuels by using low GHG-emitting vehicles and by reducing petroleum use by federal fleet vehicles by 2 percent per year through 2020 relative to a 2005 baseline. These are relatively modest goals, since they only apply to federal fleet vehicles of twenty or more and thus exclude many military uses. In FY 2007, alternatives fuels comprised only 0.2 percent of the government's energy consumption in vehicles and equipment. This is because DOD—the largest consumer of energy related to vehicles and equipment—is largely exempt from EPAct92, EISA, and EO requirements.

DOD Efforts to Reduce Vehicle Energy Consumption

DOD has begun an earnest effort to reduce its overall energy use. With respect to energy consumption in vehicles and equipment, the army, which accounts for 36 percent of total DOD energy use, plans to transition to four thousand electric vehicles that will cut the use of fossil fuels by more than 11 million gallons by 2013.[98] The navy, which accounts for approximately 25 percent of DOD's total use of petroleum, intends to reduce petroleum use by 50 percent by 2015, largely through the use of alternative fuels.[99] The navy is conducting tests to certify algae and camelina-based biofuels for use in jet aircraft fuel and as shipboard diesel fuel. It is also conducting aircraft test flights of F/A-18 Super Hornet jets powered by biofuels. The Air Force, DOD's largest consumer of energy, has established a goal of obtaining 50 percent of its aviation fuels from biofuel blends by 2016.[100]

Greening the Federal Supply Chain

President Obama's Executive Order 13514 directed GSA to develop, in coordination with other agencies, recommendations to measure and reduce supply chain GHG emissions by the federal supplier community. The EO directed GSA to consider four questions concerning the feasibility of:

1. requiring vendors and contractors to register with a voluntary registry or organization for reporting GHG emissions;
2. requiring contractors to develop and make available their GHG inventory and a description of efforts to mitigate GHG emissions;
3. using federal purchasing preferences or other incentives for products manufactured using processes that minimize GHG emissions; and
4. pursuing other options for encouraging sustainable practices and reducing GHG emissions.[101]

On July 8, 2010, GSA published its recommendations.[102] GSA found that it is feasible for federal agencies to work with suppliers to voluntarily disclose and reduce Scope 3 GHG emissions, but that any such program should be implemented in phases.[103] Calculating GHG inventories and collecting emissions data is an emerging area that not all suppliers, particularly small businesses, have the ability to accomplish. GSA therefore recommended that there should be outreach and coordination with key industry groups.

GSA also found that it is technically feasible to use purchasing incentives or other incentives for low GHG suppliers, but that it is not feasible to implement such a program until a sufficient number of suppliers are reporting data and there is a reliable process for incorporating that data into the acquisition system. Instead, GSA recommends that federal agencies use suppliers' GHG emissions reporting data as an evaluation factor. This would allow agencies to trade the price of a given procurement against the GHG emissions associated with that procurement and thereby enable Scope 3 emissions reductions through the acquisition system.

In November 2010, GSA took a first step toward implementing the recommendations by creating the GreenGov Supply Chain Partnership. The Partnership is a voluntary program by which suppliers will measure and report their GHG emissions. They will share with GSA their experiences collecting the data, which will assist GSA in further developing a comprehensive program for agencies to reduce Scope 3 emissions. The Partnership also includes a small-business pilot program whereby small businesses will receive technical assistance from GSA to measure, report, and reduce GHG emissions. The pilot will enable GSA to assess the benefits and challenges of having small businesses report GHG emissions.

A Brief Word about State and Local Governments

Together, state and local governments spend more than $12 billion annually for energy consumption and purchase $50 to $70 million on energy-related products.[104] In the absence of a comprehensive national energy policy, states and local governments are moving ahead with strategies to be more energy efficient, to use more renewable energy, and to make choices that are more environmentally sustainable.

In 2009, states budgeted about $4.3 billion for energy efficiency programs, more than double the expenditures made in 2006.[105] About 75 percent of these investments are concentrated in fifteen states. Local and regional efforts for energy efficiency are also expanding. ARRA provided $3.2 billion in grants to help local governments improve their energy planning capacity and implement new energy efficiency programs.[106] These "Energy Efficiency and Conservation Block Grants" are being used by local governments to:

- develop energy efficiency and conservation strategies,
- incentivize energy efficiency through energy savings performance contracting, on-bill financing, or revolving loan funds,
- develop building codes,
- install distributed energy technologies, including combined heat and power and district heating and cooling systems,
- implement conservation programs, and
- reduce and capture GHG emissions from landfills or similar waste sources.

In addition, almost half of the states have established Energy Efficiency Resource Standards (EERS) that require electric or natural gas utilities to meet a percentage of their energy sales through efficiency savings.[107] An EERS, or energy efficiency target, is similar to a Renewable Portfolio Standard (RPS) in that an EERS requires utilities to reduce energy use by a specified and increasing percentage or amount each year.

Many states also have "public benefit funds" that are dedicated to energy efficiency and renewable energy projects, such as low-income household energy assistance, weatherization programs, investment in renewable technologies, and subsidies for efficient appliances.[108] To date, eighteen states with publicly managed clean energy funds have formed the Clean Energy States Alliance to coordinate public benefit fund investments in renewable energy. In 2008, state clean energy funds supported the installation of more than 12,500 new renewable generation projects—a 13 percent increase over the number of projects installed in 2007.[109]

Finally, many states, local agencies, and schools have adopted energy-efficient purchasing policies and practices similar to those in place at the federal level. For example, twenty-one states and the District of Columbia have mandated that state agencies purchase Energy Star–labeled products.[110] Other purchasing initiatives, such as LED traffic signals, vary widely by state and local jurisdiction.

Notes

1. *Cutting the Federal Government's Energy Bill: An Examination of the Sustainable Federal Government Executive Order: Hearing before the S. Subcomm. on Federal Financial Management, Government Information, Federal Services and International Security, Committee on Homeland Security and Government Affairs*, 111th Cong. (Jan. 27, 2010) (statement of Richard Kidd, Program Manager, Federal Energy Management Program, Office of Energy Efficiency and renewable Energy, Department of Energy).

2. *Id.*

3. *Id.*

4. *Id.*

5. Anti-Deficiency Act, 31 U.S.C. §§ 1341–1342 (2006).

6. Federal Property and Administrative Services Act of 1949, 41 U.S.C. §§ 255 et seq. (2006).

7. Armed Services Procurement Act of 1947, 10 U.S.C. §§ 2301–2314 (2006).

8. Federal Acquisition Streamlining Act of 1994, Pub. L. No. 103-355, Stat. 1587 (codified in scattered sections of 10 U.S.C. and 41 U.S.C.); Federal Acquisition Reform Act of 1995, Pub. L. No. 103-337, 108 Stat. 2663.

9. Many energy-efficient and renewable energy-related products and services that the federal government is purchasing and will purchase in the future will be "commercials items," making federal commercial item contracts a virtual certainty for contractors supplying these products and services. Federal Acquisition Regulation (FAR) § 2.101 defines "commercial item" in part as

> (1) Any item, other than real property, that is a type customarily used by the general public or by non-governmental entities for purposes other than governmental purpose, and (i) Has been sold, leased, or licensed to the general public; or (ii) Has been offered for sale, lease, or license to the general public. . . .
>
> (6) Services of a type offered and sold competitively in substantial quantities in the commercial marketplace based on established catalog or market prices for specific tasks performed or specific outcomes to be achieved and under standard commercial terms and conditions.

10. *See* 48 C.F.R. pts. 1–99 (many of which are reserved).

11. Dyncorp Info. Sys., L.L.C. v. United States, 58 Fed. Cl. 446, 452 (Fed. Cl. 2003).

12. Competition in Contracting Act of 1984, 41 U.S.C. § 251 (2006).

13. 41 U.S.C. § 253 (2006).

14. 41 U.S.C. § 253(c) (2006); FAR 6.302 (2009).

15. FAR 6.302 (2009); FAR subpart 15.6 (Unsolicited Proposals) (2009).

16. Competition in Contracting Act of 1984, 41 U.S.C. § 259(b) (2006); FAR 6.102 (2009).

17. 4 C.F.R. § 21.0 (2009).

18. 4 C.F.R. § 21.2.

19. For "protests challenging a procurement conducted on the basis of competitive proposals under which a debriefing is requested and, when requested, is required[,] the initial protest [with respect to any protest basis which is known or should have been known either before or as a result of the debriefing] shall not be filed before the debriefing date offered to the protester, but shall be filed not later than 10 days after the date on which the debriefing is held." 4 C.F.R. § 21.2(a)(2) (2009).

20. As with commercial contracts, federal law provides a way to recover increased costs caused by government action or breach. Barring breach, excusable delay, or a change under the contract's changes clause, however, contractors will find contract pricing inflexible.

21. As the GSA's delegee of authority for healthcare-related items, the U.S. Department of Veterans Affairs often assists in the implementation of the MAS program.

22. *See* G.L. Christian & Assocs. v. United States, 312 F.2d 418 (Ct. Cl.), *cert. denied*, 375 U.S. 954 (1963).

23. *See* 31 U.S.C. § 1341.

24. 10 U.S.C. § 2922a (permitting the costs of the resulting contracts for any year may be paid from annual appropriations for that year).

25. 10 U.S.C. § 2835.

26. *See* 37 Comp. Gen. 155 (1957).

27. Burroughs Corp., 56 Comp. Gen. 142 (1976).

28. *See* 42 U.S.C. § 6374 (emergency, police, and certain military uses excluded); 42 U.S.C. § 13212; and Exec. Order No. 13031.

29. Energy Independence and Security Act of 2007, Pub. L. No. 110-140, § 246, 42 U.S.C. § 17053.

30. Energy Policy Act of 1992, Pub. L. No. 102-486, § 553, 42 U.S.C. § 8259b (2006).

31. Energy Independence and Security Act of 2007, Pub. L. No. 110-140, § 522; 42 U.S.C. § 17142.

32. Dep't of Energy, Energy Efficiency and Renewable Energy, Fed. Energy Mgmt. Program, Selling Energy-Efficient Products to the Federal Government (Mar. 2008), http://www1.eere.energy.gov/femp/pdfs/selling_eeproducts_to_gov.pdf. Approximately 25 percent of the $10 billion is spent on building-related equipment and appliances, such as lighting, office equipment, heating and cooling equipment, and residential appliances.

33. *Id.*

34. Jeffrey Harris & Francis Johnson, Potential Energy, Cost, and CO_2 Savings from Energy Efficient Government Purchasing (Aug. 2002), *available at* http://www1.eere.energy.gov/femp/pdfs/government_purchasing.pdf.

35. The Energy Policy Act of 1992, as it amends the National Energy Conservation Policy Act (codified at 42 U.S.C. §§ 8251 et seq. (2006)).

36. Exec. Order 12902 was titled "Energy Efficiency and Water Conservation at Federal Facilities."

37. The Defense Logistics Agency is the military's major purchasing channel, supplying almost 90 percent of DOD's consumable items.

38. The Energy Policy Act of 1992, Pub. L. No. 102-486, § 161; 42 U.S.C. § 8259b (2006).

39. The Federal Energy Management Program (FEMP) resides within the Department of Energy's Office of Energy Efficiency and Renewable Energy (EERE). Established in 1973, FEMP facilitates the federal government's implementation of sound, cost-effective energy management practices to enhance energy security and environmental stewardship. Among other things, FEMP assists federal agencies to evaluate and procure energy-efficient products by specifying energy efficiency requirements, purchasing tips, and cost data.

40. Fed. Energy Mgmt. Program, Office of Energy Efficiency & Renewable Energy, U.S. Dep't of Energy, "You Have Power," 1997 FEMP Program Report.

41. The Environmental Protection Agency (EPA) introduced Energy Star in 1992 as a voluntary labeling program designed to identify and promote energy-efficient products to reduce greenhouse gas emissions. Computers and monitors were the first such labeled products. Through 1995, the products expanded to include office equipment products and residential heating and cooling equipment. In 1996, EPA partnered with DOE to set criteria for particular product categories, such as exit signs, insulation, and boilers.

42. *See* 42 U.S.C. § 8259b(b)(1). Like its predecessor, the EPAct05 amends the National Energy Conservation Policy Act. The Energy Independence and Security Act of 2007 (EISA) clarified that the procurement requirement applies only to products covered by the Energy Star and FEMP programs (*see* Pub. L. No. 110-140, § 525 (Dec. 19, 2007).

43. Energy Policy Act of 2005, § 104(b)(3); 42 U.S.C. § 8259b(b)(3) (2006).

44. *Id.*

45. Energy Policy Act of 2005, § 104(b)(2); 42 U.S.C. § 6294a (2006).

46. Fed/ Acquisition Regulation; Final Rules & Small Entity Compliance Guide, 72 Fed. Reg. 65868 (Nov. 23, 2007). FAR § 23.204 provides in relevant part:

> (a) Unless exempt as provided at 23.204, (1) When acquiring energy-consuming products listed in the Energy Star Program or Federal Energy Management Program (FEMP), (i) Agencies shall purchase Energy Star or FEMP-designated products; . . . (2) When contracting for services or construction that will include the provision of energy-consuming products, agencies shall specify products that comply with the applicable requirements in paragraph (a)(1) of this section.

47. Fed. Procurement of Energy Efficient Products, 74 Fed. Reg. 10830 (Mar. 13, 2009).

48. *See* 74 Fed. Reg. 52117 (Oct. 8, 2009). Implementation of EO 13514 is overseen by the Office of the Federal Executive (OFE), which is housed within the Executive Office of the President, Council on Environmental Quality. The OFE was created by executive order in 1993 to promote sustainability and environmental stewardship throughout federal government operations.

49. U.S. DEPARTMENT OF ENERGY, FEDERAL ENERGY MANAGEMENT PROGRAM, PRODUCT DESIGNATION PROCESS, http://www1.eere.energy.gov/femp/technologies/eep_fempdesignated-products.html (last updated Nov. 22, 2010).

50. *Id.*

51. *Id.*

52. *Id.*

53. STEVE CAPANNA ET AL., ALLIANCE TO SAVE ENERGY, FACT SHEET: IMPROVING FEDERAL ENERGY MANAGEMENT (June 2008), *available at* http://ase.org/sites/default/files/file_FEMP_Fact_Sheet_2008_08.pdf.

54. The FAR provides:

> 23.206 Contract clause.
>
> Unless exempt pursuant to 23.204, insert the clause at 52.223–15, Energy Efficiency in Energy-Consuming Products, in solicitations and contracts when energy-consuming products listed in the Energy Star Program or FEMP will be— (a) Delivered; (b) Acquired by the contractor for use in performing services at a federally controlled facility; (c) Furnished by the contractor for use by the Government; or (d) Specified in the design of a building or work, or incorporated during its construction, renovation, or maintenance.

55. ALLIANCE TO SAVE ENERGY, ENERGY-EFFICIENT NEW FEDERAL BUILDINGS: AWARENESS AND IMPLEMENTATION OF FEDERAL BUILDING STANDARDS & CASE STUDIES (Apr. 2008).

56. Life-cycle costs are the "total cost of owning, operating and maintaining a building over its useful life (including its fuel and water, energy, labor, and replacement components), determined on the basis of a systematic evaluation and comparison of alternative building systems, except that in the case of leased buildings, the life cycle cost shall be calculated over the effective remaining term of the lease." 10 C.F.R. § 436.11. A building is life-cycle cost-effective if the proposed building has a lower life-cycle cost than the life-cycle costs of the baseline building, as described by 10 C.F.R. § 436.19; or has a positive estimated net savings, as described by 10 C.F.R. § 436.20; or has a savings-to-investment ratio estimated to be greater than one, as described by 10 C.F.R. § 436.21; or has an adjusted internal rate of return, as described by 10 C.F.R. § 436.22, that is estimated to be greater than the discount rate as listed in OMB Circular No. A–94, GUIDELINES AND DISCOUNT RATES FOR BENEFIT-COST ANALYSIS OF FEDERAL PROGRAMS (Oct. 29, 1992), available at http://webcache.googleusercontent.com/search?q=cache:qYqXTGYPruQJ:www.whitehouse.gov/omb/circulars_a094/+%22Guidelines+and+Discount+Rates+for+Benefit-Cost+Analysis+of+Federal+Programs%22&cd=1&hl=en&ct=clnk&gl=us&source=www.google.com.

57. DEP'T OF DEFENSE ET AL., FEDERAL LEADERSHIP IN HIGH PERFORMANCE AND SUSTAINABLE BUILDINGS: MEMORANDUM OF UNDERSTANDING (Jan. 2006), *available at* http://www.epa.gov/oaintrnt/documents/sustainable_mou_508.pdf.

58. 10 C.F.R. § 433 (2009).

59. 75 Fed. Reg. 29933 (May 28, 2010).

60. The Energy Independence and Security Act of 2007, Pub. L. No. 110-140, 121 Stat. 1492 (2007).

61. The American Reinvestment and Recovery Act, Pub. L. No. 111-5, 123 Stat. 115 (2009).

62. U.S. Gen. Servs. Admin.-Pub. Bldgs. Serv., Federal Building Fund, Revised ARRA Spending Plan (Mar. 5, 2010), *available at* http://www.gsa.gov/graphics/pbs/GSA_Spend_Plan_Update_3_030510_FINAL.pdf.

63. U.S. Dep't of Energy: Energy Efficiency & Renewable Energy, Fed. Energy Mgmt. Program, Annual Report to Congress on Federal Government Energy Management and Conservation Programs, Fiscal Year 2007 (Jan. 27, 2010), *available at* http://www.eere.energy.gov/femp/pdfs/annrep07.pdf.

64. 42 U.S.C. § 8253 (2006).

65. EPAct05 § 102 provides:

> (a) ENERGY REDUCTION GOALS.—
>
> (1) AMENDMENT.—Section 543(a)(1) of the National Energy Conservation Policy Act (42 U.S.C. 8253(a)(1)) is amended by striking "its Federal buildings so that" and all that follows through the end and inserting "the Federal buildings of the agency (including each industrial or laboratory facility) so that the energy consumption per gross square foot of the Federal buildings of the agency in fiscal years 2006 through 2015 is reduced, as compared with the energy consumption per gross square foot of the Federal buildings of the agency in fiscal year 2003, by the percentage specified in the following table:"

Fiscal Year	Percentage Reduction
2006	2
2007	4
2008	6
2009	8
2010	10
2011	12
2012	14
2013	16
2014	18
2015	20

66. EO 13423 was titled "Strengthening Federal Environmental, Energy, and Transportation Management."

67. U.S. Dep't of Energy, Energy Efficiency & Renewable Energy, 2008 Federal Energy Management Program (FEMP) Market Report (July 2009), *available at* http://www.nrel.gov/docs/fy09osti/46021.pdf.

68. Ronnie Kweller, Alliance to Save Energy, Poll: Energy Efficiency Key to Reducing Costs in Federal Government Buildings (Nov. 9, 2010), *available at* http://ase.org/efficiencynews/poll-energy-efficiency-key-reducing-costs-federal-government-buildings.

69. Energy Policy Act of 2005 § 203, 42 U.S.C. § 15852 (2006).

70. Biomass is defined by section 203 of EPAct05 as any lignin waste material that is segregated from other waste materials and is determined to be nonhazardous by the Administrator of the Environmental Protection Agency and any solid, nonhazardous, cellulosic material that is derived from—

> (A) any of the following forest-related resources: mill residues, precommercial thinnings, slash, and brush, or nonmerchantable material;
>
> (B) solid wood waste materials, including waste pallets, crates, dunnage, manufacturing and construction wood wastes (other than pressure-treated, chemically-treated, or painted wood wastes), and landscape or right-of-way tree trimmings, but not including municipal solid waste (garbage), gas derived from the biodegradation of solid waste, or paper that is commonly recycled;

(C) agriculture wastes, including orchard tree crops, vineyard, grain, legumes, sugar, and other crop by-products or residues, and livestock waste nutrients; or

(D) a plant that is grown exclusively as a fuel for the production of electricity.

71. Exec. Order 13423, § 2(b), 70 Fed. Reg. 3919 (Jan. 24, 2007).

72. In 2008, FEMP developed guidance for implementing EPAct05 and EO 13423. The guidance defines "new" renewable energy as energy sources placed into service after January 1, 1999. However, sources that are significantly refurbished, rebuilt, or modified may also qualify as new. *See* FEMP, Renewable Energy Requirement Guidance for EPACT05 and Executive Order 13423 (Jan. 28, 2008).

73. *See* Chandra Shah, Fed. Energy Mgmt. Program, Introduction to Federal Renewable Energy Goals and FEMP Services, *available at* http://www1.eere.energy.gov/femp/pdfs/re_webinar_110410.pdf.

74. *See* 10 U.S.C. § 2911(e) (2006).

75. GAO, Defense Infrastructure: Department of Defense's Renewable Energy Initiatives (Apr. 26, 1010), *available at* http://www.gao.gov/new.items/d10681r.pdf.

76. *See* Testimony of Dr. Dorothy Robyn, Deputy Under Secretary for Defense for Installations and Environment before the Subcomm. on Readiness, House Armed Servs. Comm. (Feb. 24, 2010), *available at* http://www.acq.osd.mil/ie/download/robyn_testimony022410.pdf.

77. Memorandum of Understanding Between U.S. Department of Energy and U.S. Department of Defense Concerning Cooperation in a Strategic Partnership to Enhance National Energy Security (July 22, 2010), *available at* http://www.energy.gov/news/documents/Enhance-Energy-Security-MOU.pdf.

78. FEMP, Annual Report to Congress on Federal Government Energy Management and Conservation Programs Fiscal Year 2007 (Jan. 27, 2010).

79. 42 U.S.C. § 8255 (2006).

80. ESPCs were first introduced under the Comprehensive Omnibus Budget Reconciliation Act of 1985, Pub. L. No. 99-272, which amended the National Energy Conservation Policy Act.

81. DOD's authority to enter ESPCs derives from provisions contained in the national Defense Authorization Act of 1991 and EPAct92. 10 U.S.C. § 2865 (1994).

82. 10 C.F.R. pt. 436. DOD also issued rules governing ESPCs that are nearly identical to the DOE regulations. *See* Office of the Under Secretary of Defense, Department of Defense, Defense Energy Program Policy Memorandum 94-2, Energy Savings Performance Contracting (1994), *available at* http://www.wbdg.org/ccb/DEP/dep94_2.pdf.

83. The Energy Independence and Security Act of 2007, Pub. L. No. 110-140, §§ 511-516, 121 Stat. 1658–1659 (2007).

84. FEMP, Annual Report to Congress on Federal Government Energy Management and Conservation Programs Fiscal Year 2007 (Jan. 27, 2010).

85. The 16 DOE "Super ESPC" awardees were Ameresco, Inc., Chevron Energy Solutions, Clark Realty Builders, Consolidated Edison Solutions, Inc., Constellation Energy Projects & Services Group, Inc., FPL Energy Services, Inc., Honeywell International, Inc., Johnson Controls Government Systems, LLC, Lockheed Martin Services, Inc., McKinstry Essention, Inc., NORESCO, LLC, Pepco Energy Services, Siemens Government Services, Inc., TAC Energy Solutions, The Benham Companies, LLC, and Trane U.S., Inc.

86. *See* GAO, Capital Financing: Partnerships and Energy Savings Performance Contracts Raise Budgeting and Monitoring Concerns (Dec. 2004), *available at* http://www.gao.gov/new.items/d0555.pdf; GAO, Energy Savings Performance Contracts Offer Benefits, but Vigilance is Needed to Protect Government Interests (June 2005), *available at* http://www.gao.gov/new.items/d05340.pdf.

87. DOE Office of Inspector General, Audit Report: Management of Energy Savings Performance Contract Delivery Orders at the Department of Energy (Sept. 10, 2009), *available at* http://www.ig.energy.gov/documents/IG-0822.pdf.

88. *See* 42 U.S.C. § 8256(c)(2) (2006).

89. H.R. Rep. No. 474(V), 102d Cong., 2d Sess. 42 (1992), *reprinted in* 1992 U.S.C.C.A.N. 2224.

90. FEMP, Annual Report to Congress on Federal Government Energy Management and Conservation Programs Fiscal Year 2007 (Jan. 27, 2010).

91. Id.

92. FEMP, Annual Report to Congress on Federal Government Energy Management and Conservation Programs Fiscal Year 2007 (Jan. 27, 2010).

93. Alternative fuel vehicles are discussed in greater detail in chapter 14.

94. Vehicles that weigh less than 8,500 pounds are considered LDVs.

95. Federal fleets earn one credit for every bi- or flexible-fuel AFV acquired. An additional credit can be earned by acquiring dedicated AFVs that operate exclusively on alternative fuels. Three credits are earned for dedicated medium-duty vehicles. Four credits are earned for dedicated heavy-duty vehicle acquisitions. Fleets also earn one credit for every 450 gallons of biodiesel (B100) or 2,250 gallons of B20 (20 percent biodiesel and 80 percent petroleum diesel) used.

96. FEMP, Federal Fleet Compliance with EPACT and E.O. 13149, Fiscal year 2006 (2006), *available at* http://www.afdc.energy.gov/afdc/pdfs/ff22_federal_fleet_report.pdf.

97. Alternative fuels are discussed in greater detail in chapter 19.

98. PEW Project on Nat'l Sec., Energy, & Climate, Reenergizing America's Defense (Apr. 20, 2010), *available at* http://www.pewtrusts.org/our_work_report_detail.aspx?id=58542.

99. Id.

100. Id.

101. 74 Fed. Reg. 52117, 52124 (Oct. 8, 2009).

102. GSA, Executive Order 13514 Section 13: Recommendations for Vendor and Contractor Emissions (Apr. 2010), *available at* http://www.gsa.gov/graphics/admin/GSA_Section13_FinalReport_040510_v2.pdf.

103. As noted above, Scope 3 emissions are GHG emissions from sources not owned or directly controlled by a federal agency but related to agency activities, such as vendor supply chains, delivery services, and employee travel and commuting.

104. *See* Consortium for Energy Efficiency, State and Local Government Purchasing Initiative, http://www.cee1.org/gov/purch/purch-main.php3 (last visited Feb. 14, 2011).

105. *See id.*

106. American Recovery and Reinvestment Act, Pub. L. No. 111-5, 123 Stat. 115 (2009).

107. *See* American Council on an Energy Efficient Economy, State Energy Efficiency Resource Standards (Aug. 2010), *available at* http://www.aceee.org/files/pdf/State%20EERS%20Summary%20Aug%202010.pdf.

108. *See* PEW Center on Global Climate Change & Pew Center on the States, Climate Change 101: State Action (Jan. 2009), *available at* http://www.pewclimate.org/docUploads/Climate101-State-Jan09_1.pdf.

109. Clean Energy States Alliance, 2010 Report: State Efforts to Advance Clean Energy (2010), *available at* http://www.cleanenergystates.org/Publications/CESA_Members_Report_2010-Final_LR.pdf.

110. EPA Energy Star Program, List of States With Mandated Energy Star Purchasing Efforts, *available at* http://www.energystar.gov/ia/business/bulk_purchasing/StatesPurchasingRequirements.pdf. The states are: Alabama, Arizona, California, Colorado, Connecticut, Delaware, Hawaii, Illinois, Kentucky, Louisiana, Maryland, Massachusetts, Michigan, Nevada, New Hampshire, New Jersey, New York, North Carolina, Texas, Vermont, and Virginia.

chapter seven

Taxation

Roberta F. Mann and
E. Margaret Rowe

Introduction

This chapter addresses the effect of U.S. federal and state tax policy on the development and implementation of clean energy sources. Tax incentives encourage clean energy by reducing the tax liability of businesses and consumers who engage in the qualifying activities. Qualifying activities include production of energy, investment in energy equipment, or investment in a variety of conservation and efficiency measures. Tax incentives reduce tax liability either directly via tax credits, or indirectly by enhanced deductions or income exclusions.

U.S. federal energy tax policy shifted significantly in 2007. Before 2007, fossil-based fuels received the majority of tax support.[1] According to an analysis by economist Gilbert E. Metcalf, after 2007, on a BTU basis, renewable energy sources now receive the largest tax subsidy.[2] The Obama administration has recommended repealing tax incentives for oil and gas, which would further the tax shift to renewable fuels.[3] Tax expenditures for energy have more than tripled since 1999, rising from $3.2 billion to more than $10.4 billion in 2007.[4] Federal legislation in 2008 and 2009 continued to increase tax support for renewable energy.[5] These developments highlight the changing environment for federal energy tax incentives. Many of the federal tax incentives for renewable energy are at least nominally temporary. This chapter will note when particular tax incentives expire. Some of these incentives may have expired by the date of publication. However, readers should be aware that renewable energy tax incentives are frequently reinstated by Congress after their expiration. For example, the tax incentives for generation of wind energy have expired and been reinstated multiple times.[6] At the state and local level, tax incentives can enhance the competitiveness of the business environment, but budget constraints have caused some states to reassess their portfolios of clean energy tax incentives.

This chapter begins with a look at the federal energy tax incentives for businesses. We then examine federal business tax incentives for renewable energy; federal tax incentives for energy conservation; and federal tax incentives directed at consumers, including energy conservation, production of renewable energy for residential use, and alternative fuel vehicle credits. We also addresses federal tax incentives for alternative transportation fuels; state and local tax incentive programs for both business and consumers, focusing on best practices at the state and local level in conservation and renewable energy generation; and potential state-federal synergies or conflicts. We conclude by discussing some general concerns about tax incentives for renewable energy, noting that using an all-incentive policy is less likely to cause a significant energy shift toward renewable sources than using a balanced policy, including carbon pricing as well as incentives.

Federal Business Tax Incentives for Renewable Energy

Tax provisions create incentives for activity by reducing the tax cost of the activity. In the renewable energy sector, the bulk of the tax incentives come in the form of either production tax credits (PTCs) or investment tax credits (ITCs). PTCs provide a tax credit that is measured by the unit of electricity generated by the qualifying project over a period of years. ITCs provide a tax credit based on the cost of building the qualifying project. Other tax incentives for renewable energy include advantageous depreciation rules, the energy research credit, the credit for advanced energy equipment, and renewable fuels income tax and excise credits.

Energy projects frequently operate at a loss in the early years of development, in part because of the nature of new businesses and in part because of favorable tax depreciation treatment for renewable energy projects. Energy projects are eligible for accelerated depreciation deductions, which provide larger deductions in the early years of the project.[7] Businesses must have a positive net income to have tax liability, and the renewable energy tax credits operate by reducing tax liability. Congress does not allow "sale" of tax credits, but energy projects can be structured so as to share the tax credits with investors that have positive tax liability. To reap the benefits of tax credits, project developers enter into partnership or sale-leaseback transactions with corporate investors with income to shelter.[8] In a so-called partnership flip transaction, one or more tax equity investors are brought in as partners to own a project with the developer. The partnership tax provisions are designed to allow partnerships to allocate tax characteristics to particular partners, so long as those allocations have substantial economic effect.[9] The Internal Revenue Service (IRS) allows PTCs attributable to the partnership to be passed through and allocated among the partners, and has provided guidance on how to structure the transaction.[10] As commonly structured, the partnership may allocate as much as 99 percent of the tax benefits and other economic returns to the tax equity investors until they reach a target return, after which their interest drops usually to 5 percent and the developer has an option to buy out the remaining 5 percent interest of the investors for the fair market value determined when the option is exercised.

In a sale-leaseback transaction, the energy project is sold to the tax investor and leased back to the project developer, thus transferring the tax benefits to the investor/

owner. The IRS has provided guidance on how sale-leaseback transactions can be structured.[11] Sale-leaseback transactions may only be used with ITCs, not with PTCs, because the PTC rules require the owner of the facility to be the operator of the facility.[12] A sale-leaseback structure may be preferable to a partnership flip structure for both developers and investors because it provides 100 percent financing and can transfer 100 percent of the tax benefits to the equity investor. To effectively transfer the tax benefits, the sale-leaseback must be put in place within three months after the project is placed in service.[13] The lease may not run longer than 80 percent of the expected life and value of the project.[14] If the developer wants to continue using the project after the lease ends, then it must either negotiate an extension at then-current market rent or buy the project at fair market value.

Developers may prefer to use an inverted pass-through lease to avoid the cost of buying the entire project back after the end of the lease to the tax equity investors. In an inverted pass-through lease, the developer owns the project and leases it to the tax equity investor. The developer elects to pass through the tax credits to the lessee/investor.[15] Unlike in a sale-leaseback transaction, the developer retains the depreciation deductions, which may be used to offset the income from the rent payments under the lease. The tax equity investor claims the ITC and deductions for rent under the lease. At the end of the lease, the developer owns the project without any additional cash outlay.

Before the financial crisis of late 2008, banks were willing investors in renewable energy projects. However, the decline in the financial sector had eliminated demand for tax credits, as financial institutions and investors lacked cash for investment and had current tax losses of their own. Wanting to stimulate renewable energy projects and recognizing that investors had become scarce, Congress added grants in lieu of ITCs in the American Recovery and Reinvestment Act of 2009 (ARRA 2009).[16] Congress also allowed a one-time, irrevocable election to convert PTC property into ITC property, thus qualifying converted PTC property for the direct grant option.[17]

Electricity Production Tax Credits—I.R.C. § 45

The production tax credit is calculated by multiplying the credit amount by the amount of electricity generated. The PTC is paid each year during the credit period. The credit amount and credit period may vary, depending on the type of electricity production activity, although for projects placed in service after August 8, 2005 (the date of enactment of the Energy Policy Act of 2005[18]), the credit period is ten years. The credit amount is generally 1.5 cents per kilowatt-hour generated by the qualifying activity, adjusted for inflation. Certain types of renewable energy receive only half that amount. (The sources receiving half of the general credit are marked with an asterisk in the list below.) To qualify for the credit, the electricity must be sold to an unrelated purchaser. The IRS has held that electricity will be treated as sold to an unrelated person if the ultimate purchaser of the electricity is not related to the person that produces the electricity.[19] The amount of credit that may be claimed by the taxpayer phases out if the market price of electricity exceeds the statutory threshold.[20] The PTC applies to the following types of electricity production activity:

- Wind
- Closed-loop biomass
- Open-loop biomass*
- Geothermal
- Small irrigation power*
- Municipal solid waste*
- Qualified hydropower*
- Marine and hydrokinetic.*

A wind energy facility is a facility that uses wind to produce electricity. To qualify, the wind energy facility must be placed in service before January 1, 2013. The IRS has ruled that wind turbines are treated as being placed in service on the date the turbines are placed in a condition or state of readiness and are available to produce electricity.[21] Wind power production increased 51 percent from 2007 to 2008.[22]

A closed-loop biomass facility is a facility that uses any organic material from a plant that is planted exclusively for the purpose of being used at a qualifying facility to produce electricity.[23] Certain facilities may qualify if they have been modified to use closed-loop biomass co-fired with other biomass or coal.

An open-loop biomass facility produces electricity using any agricultural livestock waste nutrients or any solid, nonhazardous, cellulosic waste material or any lignin material that is segregated from other waste materials and that is derived from:

- forest-related resources, including mill and harvesting residues, precommercial thinnings, slash, and brush;
- solid wood waste materials, including waste pallets, crates, dunnage, manufacturing and construction wood wastes, and landscape or right-of-way tree trimmings; or
- agricultural sources, including orchard tree crops, vineyard, grain, legumes, sugar, and other crop by-products or residues.

Open-loop biomass receives only half of the general 1.5 cent per kilowatt-hour credit.

A geothermal facility uses geothermal energy to produce electricity. A small irrigation facility generates electric power through an irrigation system canal or ditch without any dam.

Municipal solid waste facilities can be either landfill gas facilities or trash combustion facilities. A landfill gas facility uses methane gas derived from the biodegradation of municipal solid waste to generate electricity. A trash combustion facility uses garbage to produce steam to drive a turbine to generate electricity.

Electricity produced by hydropower is eligible for the PTC if it is incremental electricity created by efficiency improvements or additions to capacity made after August 8, 2005, to a preexisting hydropower facility, or if it is produced by a dam that did not produce electricity before August 8, 2005.

A marine and hydrokinetic energy facility produces electricity from energy derived (1) from waves, tides, and currents in oceans, estuaries, and tidal areas; (2) from free-flowing waters in rivers, lakes, and streams; (3) from free-flowing water in an irrigation system, canal, or other man-made channel; or (4) by ocean thermal energy conversion (created by differentials in ocean temperature).

Investment Tax Credits—I.R.C. § 48

The ITC provides a tax credit for a percentage of the cost of eligible renewable energy projects. Qualified projects include solar energy property, geothermal heat pump property, and small wind property. In addition, a taxpayer may make an irrevocable election to take the ITC instead of the PTC for PTC eligible facilities placed in service between 2009 and 2013.[24] For solar energy, small wind energy, and converted PTC facilities, the credit percentage is 30 percent. For geothermal energy, it is 10 percent. Any subsidized energy financing must be excluded from the cost used to calculate the ITC.[25]

ITCs vest at the rate of 20 percent per year. If an ITC project or an interest in an ITC project is sold within five years, a portion of the credit must be recaptured; that is, the taxpayer will have an increase in tax liability in the amount of the recaptured credit. Thus, although an ITC project has additional flexibility in that it can be structured as a sale-leaseback or an inverted pass-through lease, investors must be willing to accept a loss of liquidity in their tax equity investment. Using the ITC also limits the value of tax depreciation, as the depreciable basis of the project must be reduced by one-half of the credit claimed.[26] The taxpayer may apply for a direct grant in lieu of the ITC.[27] The amount of the grant is not included in the taxpayer's gross income.[28]

Solar energy property is new equipment that uses solar energy to generate electricity, to heat or cool a structure (other than a swimming pool), to provide solar process heat, or to illuminate the inside of a structure using fiber-optic distributed sunlight. The ITC for solar energy property is discussed in greater detail in chapter 17.

Geothermal heat pump property is equipment that uses the ground or groundwater as a thermal energy source to heat a structure or as a thermal energy sink to cool a structure.

Qualified small wind energy property is property that uses a wind turbine of 100 kilowatts-rated energy or less to generate electricity. As noted above, PTC projects may be converted to ITC projects using a one-time irrevocable election. Thus, larger wind projects are also eligible for the ITC through the election.

Federal Tax Incentives for Energy Conservation

"The gallon of gas or the kilowatt of electricity that is not used is the cleanest of all."[29] Conceptually, renewable energy generation, energy conservation, and energy efficiency may overlap. Tax benefits for products and projects for renewable energy, energy conservation, and energy efficiency may overlap as well, although generally a project that receives one kind of tax benefit will be ineligible for other tax benefits, or will have those other benefits reduced. The tax benefits for energy conservation accrue to manufacturers that produce advanced energy property, energy-efficient appliances, and energy-efficient new homes. Taxpayers who invest in energy research and make expenditures for energy-efficient commercial buildings receive immediate deductions. Tax credit bonds may fund energy conservation projects. Energy conservation subsidies provided by public utilities to commercial and industrial (as well as residential) customers are exempt from the customer's gross income.[30]

Credit for Advanced Energy Property—I.R.C. § 48C

Congress allocated $2.3 billion under ARRA 2009 for the credit for advanced energy property.[31] This incentive expands the traditional ITC to cover not only renewable energy generation, but also projects that manufacture equipment for renewable energy generation. A 30 percent tax credit is available to a certified project that re-equips, expands, or establishes a manufacturing facility for the production of advanced energy equipment. Qualifying advanced energy property includes equipment for renewable energy generation as well as for energy conservation technologies. The Secretary of the Treasury, acting in consultation with the Secretary of Energy, must certify the property. The selection criteria include:

- domestic job creation;
- greenhouse gas reduction;
- potential for technological innovation and commercial deployment;
- lowest levelized cost of generated or stored energy;
- shortest time from certification to completion.

On January 8, 2010, President Obama announced that 183 projects had been selected to receive the advanced energy property tax credit, including residential smart meters, advanced membranes for building efficiency and energy management, and more efficient wind turbines.

Energy Efficient Appliance Credit—I.R.C. § 45M

Manufacturers of energy-efficient appliances are eligible for a myriad of credits, which vary in amount depending on the type and energy efficiency of the appliance.[32] The eligible appliances are dishwashers, clothes washers, and refrigerators. The credit amounts range from $45 for a dishwasher using no more than 324 kilowatt-hours and 5.8 gallons of water per cycle to $250 for a residential or commercial clothes washer that meets or exceeds a 2.2 modified energy factor and does not exceed a 4.5 water consumption factor. The modified energy factor is established by the Department of Energy (DOE) for compliance with the federal energy conservation standard. The water consumption factor means the total weighted per-cycle water consumption divided by the cubic capacity of the clothes washer. The energy efficient appliance credit is one of only two federal tax benefits for saving water.[33]

Energy Efficient Home Credit—I.R.C. § 45L

Several of the federal tax incentives for energy conservation that expired as of the end of 2009 were extended until the end of 2011, including the energy efficient home construction credit and the energy research credit.[34] An eligible contractor that constructs a qualified new energy-efficient home is eligible for the energy efficient home construction credit.[35] Manufactured homes certified to achieve a 30 percent reduction in heating and cooling consumption compared to a comparable dwelling are eligible for a $1,000 credit, and other homes must be certified to meet a 50 percent reduction in heating and cooling consumption to receive a $2,000 tax credit.

Energy Research Credit—I.R.C. § 41

The energy research credit is a tax credit for 20 percent of the amount paid to an energy research consortium that is either a § 501(c)(3) corporation organized and operated to conduct energy research or any other organization organized and operated primarily to conduct energy research in the public interest.[36]

Energy Efficient Commercial Buildings Deduction—I.R.C. § 179D

When a taxpayer makes an investment in a commercial building, the taxpayer usually has to wait up to thirty-nine years to fully recover the investment through depreciation deductions.[37] The energy efficient commercial buildings deduction allows immediate recovery of up to $1.80 per square foot for property installed as part of a plan designed to reduce the total annual energy and power costs by 50 percent or more with respect to the interior lighting systems, heating, cooling, ventilation, and hot water systems of the building, in comparison to a reference building meeting certain requirements set by the American Society of Heating, Refrigerating, and Air Conditioning Engineers and the Illuminating Engineering Society of North America. The basis of the property is reduced by the amount of the deduction. If the property is installed in a public building like a school, the deduction may go to the designer of the project.

Qualified Energy Conservation Bonds—I.R.C. § 54D

State or local governments issue qualified energy conservation (QEC) bonds, which are tax credit bonds, but instead of only interest, the bond payments to the investors include federal tax credits. QEC bonds are discussed in greater detail in chapter 8.

Federal Tax Incentives for Consumers

The Internal Revenue Code contains several tax incentives targeting consumers rather than businesses. These incentives apply to taxpayers' homes and vehicles. The incentives may apply to both energy efficiency and renewable energy expenditures. However, the provisions limit the amount of the benefit, and the type of expenditures are strictly defined.

Nonbusiness Energy Property Credit—I.R.C. § 25C

The nonbusiness energy property credit provides a 30 percent tax credit for the cost of qualified energy efficiency improvements and residential energy property installed in the taxpayer's principal residence, up to an aggregate lifetime credit amount of $1,500. ARRA 2009 increased the credit from a 10 percent to a 30 percent credit, increased the aggregate lifetime credit amount from $500 to $1,500, and extended the availability of the credit through the end of 2010.[38] At the end of 2010, Congress further extended the credit through the end of 2011, but reduced the credit to its pre-2009 amounts.[39]

Qualified energy efficiency improvements mean energy-efficient building envelope components, such as insulation, exterior doors, metal roofs, and exterior windows—provided that such components meet the 2000 International Energy Conservation Code. The use of the component must originate with the taxpayer, and the component must reasonably be expected to remain in use for at least five years.

Residential energy property expenditures include the following equipment, provided that it meets certain efficiency standards:

- electric heat pumps;
- geothermal heat pumps;
- central air conditioner;
- natural gas, propane, or oil furnace or hot water boiler;
- biomass fuel stove; and
- advanced main air circulating fan.

Residential Energy Efficiency Property Credit—I.R.C. § 25D

The residential energy efficiency property credit provides a 30 percent tax credit for the cost of certain property that either generates electricity, heats water, or heats or cools a residence. The qualified property eligible for an unlimited credit uses renewable energy, such as solar, geothermal, and wind. Fuel cell property is eligible for a credit limited to $500 per half-kilowatt of capacity.[40] Fuel cell property must be installed on the taxpayer's principal residence, while the other eligible property need only be installed in a residence of the taxpayer, which could include the taxpayer's vacation home. The qualified property must be placed in service by December 31, 2016.

Qualified property includes:

- solar electric property;
- solar water heating property (that must be used exclusively for heating water other than swimming pools or hot tubs);
- small wind energy property; and
- geothermal heat pump property.

Alternative Motor Vehicle Credit—I.R.C. § 30B

The alternative motor vehicle credit applies to vehicles that save fuel based on four different technologies:

- hybrid gas-electric;

- advanced lean-burn;
- fuel cell; and
- alternative fuel.

The total credit available for a hybrid motor vehicle or an advanced lean burn technology vehicle is the sum of the fuel economy credit and the conservation credit. The fuel economy credit varies according to how much the fuel economy of the qualifying vehicle exceeds the base fuel economy of a comparable 2002 model year conventionally powered vehicle. The conservation credit is based on estimated lifetime fuel savings over a comparable 2002 model year conventionally powered vehicle, assuming a 120,000-mile vehicle life. The comparison is based on the weight of the vehicle. The credits for hybrid and advanced lean burn vehicles are phased out as each manufacturer sells its 60,000th car or light truck. Credits for Toyota and Honda phased out with the 2008 model year. For the 2010 model year, credits are available for certain vehicles manufactured by GM, Ford, BMW, Mercedes, and Nissan.[41]

The U.S. DOE reports that no fuel cell vehicles are commercially available.[42] Honda reports that it will be leasing a limited number of its FCX Clarity fuel cell vehicles over the next three years, mostly in Southern California, where refueling stations are available.[43] To obtain the credit, the vehicle must be purchased by December 31, 2014. Assuming that any such vehicles become available before then, the amount of the credit will depend on the weight class of the vehicle and on the rated fuel economy based on a comparable 2002 model vehicle.

Taxpayers purchasing an alternative fuel vehicle can get a credit of 50 percent of the incremental cost of the vehicle over the cost of a comparable conventionally fueled vehicle. Alternative fuels include:

- compressed natural gas;
- liquified natural gas;
- hydrogen; and
- any liquid fuel that is at least 85 percent methanol.

Plug-In Electric Drive Motor Vehicle Credit—I.R.C. § 30D

Owners or lessors of qualified vehicles acquired after December 31, 2009, are eligible for a tax credit of up to $7,500. A qualified plug-in electric drive vehicle is a motor vehicle that:

- has at least four wheels,
- is manufactured for use on public roads,
- meets certain emissions standards,
- draws propulsion using a traction battery with at least four kilowatt-hours of capacity, and
- is capable of being recharged from an external source of electricity.

The base amount of the credit is $2,500, plus $417 for each kilowatt-hour of battery capacity in excess of four kilowatt-hours. The credit for plug-in vehicles is phased out as each manufacturer sells its 200,000th vehicle. As of this writing, the only qualified plug-in electric drive motor vehicle certified eligible for the credit is the Tesla Roadster, which is eligible for a $7,500 credit.[44] The base sticker price of the Tesla Roadster is $109,000.[45] More moderately priced plug-in vehicles are expected to be available in the coming years.

I.R.C. § 30B provides a 10 percent tax credit for the cost of converting any motor vehicle to a plug-in electric. The credit is capped at $4,000, and the conversion must be completed by December 31, 2011.

Electric Drive Low-Speed Vehicle Credit—I.R.C. § 30

Purchasers or lessors of new electric drive low-speed vehicles, motorcycles, and three-wheeled vehicles may receive a 10 percent tax credit, capped at $2,500. Low speed means 25 miles per hour or less, on a paved, level surface.[46] The vehicle must be placed in service by December 31, 2011.

Federal Tax Incentives for Alternative Fuels— I.R.C. §§ 40, 40A, 6426, 6427(e)

Domestically produced biofuels receive either an income tax credit or a credit against the gasoline excise tax. The credit amounts for various biofuels are detailed in the table on the next page.

In addition to the biofuel production credits, taxpayers investing in fuel equipment that dispenses at least 85 percent ethanol (E85) are eligible for accelerated cost recovery under the alternative refueling stations tax credit.[47] This credit is intended to increase the number of alternative fuel gas stations, as currently only 1,120 stations (of 170,000 stations nationwide) dispense E85.[48] Taxpayers installing alternative fuel refueling property are eligible for a credit of up to 30 percent of the property cost. The credit is capped at $30,000 per taxable year per location.[49]

Critics of biofuel incentives, particularly ethanol, have observed that biofuel consumption may not produce a net increase in petroleum use, that it can create environmental problems such as pesticide run-off, and that using crops to generate motor fuel may exacerbate worldwide food shortages.[50] Biofuels are discussed in greater detail in chapter 19.

State and Local Incentive Programs

In the decades since the energy crisis of the 1970s, states have consistently surpassed the federal government in enacting innovative clean energy policies and in their spending commitments.[51] This section will focus on six incentive types relating to renewable energy and alternative fuel vehicles: personal income tax credits and deductions; corporate income tax incentives, including tax credits, deductions, and exemptions; local property tax abatements; sales and use tax incentives; utility-based incentives; and incentives for vehicle purchase.[52] This section will also review the research on the efficacy of various incentive structures, followed by a discussion of state best

Fuel	Credit Amount	Type of Credit	Expiration Date
Alcohol mixture	$0.45/gal	Income or excise	12/31/2011
Alcohol (neat)	$0.45/gal	Income only	12/31/2011
Small producer ethanol	$0.10/gal	Income or excise	12/31/2011
Cellulosic biofuel	$1.01/gal	Income only	12/31/2012
Biodiesel mixture	$1.00/gal	Income or excise	12/31/2011
Small agri-biodiesel producer	$0.10/gal	Income only	12/31/2011
Renewable diesel	$1.00/gal	Income or excise	12/31/2011

practices, using Oregon as an example of policy implementation. Chapter 3 of this book provides a discussion of state and municipal energy efficiency laws, including corporate and individual tax incentives for energy efficiency.

Renewable Energy

Forty-seven of the fifty states have at least one state or local tax incentive for renewable energy.[53] Tax credits for renewable energy production are designed for both corporate and individual taxpayers. Incentive types include production tax credits, based on a per kilowatt-hour for energy generated and sold by eligible entities, and investment tax credits for individual or corporate taxpayers, based on the cost of residential or commercial alternative energy systems, with specific limits set based on the technology installed.

Personal Tax Incentives

Personal income tax incentives use tax credits or deductions to reduce the expense of purchase and installation of residential renewable energy systems. As of December 2010, twenty-four states provided for personal income tax incentives.[54] The amount varies by program, and in most cases there is a maximum dollar amount of the credit or deduction. Some states permit carryover or structured application of the credit over a set number of years.

Corporate Tax Incentives

Corporate income tax incentives include tax credits, deductions, and exemptions for the purchase and installation of eligible renewable energy equipment. As of December 2010, twenty-five states provided for corporate income tax incentives.[55] Most programs establish a maximum limit on the dollar amount of the credit or deduction, and some states permit the tax credit only if a corporation has invested a minimum amount in an eligible project.

Local Property Tax Incentives

Property tax incentives are exemptions, exclusions, abatements, and credits that exclude the added value of the upgrade or renewable energy system from the valuation of the property for taxation purposes. As of a 2009 report, thirty-three states offered property tax incentives, as did a number of localities.[56] Honolulu, New York City, Cincinnati, and five counties in Maryland offer property tax reductions for renewable energy.

Sales and Use Tax Incentives

Sales tax incentives characteristically provide a refund of or an exemption from the state sales tax (or sales and use tax) for the purchase of a renewable energy system, in full or partial amount.

According to the 2009 NREL report, sales and use tax incentives were then employed in twenty-two states.[57] In 2009, Colorado enacted a policy to provide a "sales and use tax" exemption for a comprehensive list of equipment used to produce alternative current electricity from a renewable energy source, including photovoltaic systems, solar thermal electric systems, small wind systems, biomass systems, or geothermal systems.[58] Both commercial and residential taxpayers are eligible.

Tax-Exempt Utility Incentives

Incentives provided by utilities to customers for the purchase or installation of any energy conservation measure are excluded from the customer's federal taxable income.[59] Utility rebates for installation of renewable energy equipment, if they are a reduction in the purchase price of energy, are also nontaxable under general income tax principles. This is a popular incentive form: thirty-eight states have one or more utility-based rebate programs, in total offering 338 individual programs; twenty-five states have one or more utility-based loan program, for a total of 163 individual programs.[60]

Vehicle Purchase Incentives

In state programs, incentives for purchase of gasoline-electric hybrid vehicles are or have been phased out, with some hybrid-electric incentives at or near sunset dates while electric and alternative fuel vehicles are gaining prominence in state policy strategies. Forty-three states and the District of Columbia have some tax incentive policy to encourage the purchase of hybrid and/or alternative fuel vehicles. For example, Oregon's credit for the purchase of gasoline-electric hybrid vehicles sunset on December 31, 2009, but the state still offers the credit for the purchase of a new qualifying, alternative fuel vehicle,[61] conversion of vehicles to an alternative fuel, and the purchase of charging/fueling systems. The credit is 25 percent of the cost up to $750. The maximum tax credit is $1,500 for both the vehicle and the fueling/charging station.[62] The 2010 Oregon Legislature added electric all-terrain vehicles to the list of eligible vehicles.[63]

Policy Efficacy

Assessments of the effectiveness of individual policies are uncommon, dispersed, and difficult to locate. There is a wealth of analysis and academic debate over the economic impact of different tax policies,[64] but there is less research focused on the efficacy (e.g., the effect on consumer behavior) of specific policies post-implementation.

A 2008 Harvard study explored the extent to which the increase in consumer purchases of hybrid vehicle technology can be fairly attributed to three factors: government incentives, increased gas prices, and social preferences (concern for environment and energy security).[65] The authors found that, nationally, 6 percent of the increase in high-economy hybrid vehicle sales from 2000 to 2006 could be attributed to government tax incentives.[66] Researchers further distinguished between types of policies and found that at a state level, sales tax incentives had a much larger impact on demand than state income tax credits.[67] This appears to be true even when taking into account the amount of each incentive.[68] The authors conclude that the immediacy and the automatic nature of the sales tax incentive had a positive impact on consumer behavior.[69] They suggest that other policies designed to incentivize energy-efficient consumer choices should be designed with immediacy and ease of benefit as a central feature.[70]

Iowa established a program within the Department of Revenue in 2005 to track tax credit awards and claims and periodically evaluate the various tax credit programs. A one-year study of the impacts of four tax incentive programs used by biofuel producers indicates that state tax credits may have induced up to 25 percent of the state's ethanol production capacity.[71] A portion of the increase in corn prices can be attributed to the increased ethanol production induced by tax credits, and that that in turn led to an increase in the average farmland prices, accompanied by an increase in farming input costs.[72] The authors determined that the operation of an ethanol plant in a town increased the average household income only $822, suggesting a weak correlation between the construction of a new plant and a change in local retail sales.[73]

Initiatives for evaluation and accountability, such as the Iowa tracking program and Oregon's analysis of economic impacts of the BETC/RETC programs discussed *infra*, are vital tools in crafting and refining state tax policy to advance renewable energy production and the dissemination of the most effective solutions.

Best Practices

"Best" practices are hard to quantify due to lack of baseline data and the challenge of identifying how much energy savings may be attributed to which policy. Potential savings may be estimated, but actual savings from implementation of a given policy are challenging to gather and quantify. The "best practices" here are drawn from the 2009 State Energy Efficiency Scorecard,[74] the DSIRE database, and state energy departments' websites.

Idaho

Idaho offers a notable personal tax credit for residential alternative energy systems and conservation. Taxpayers who install a qualifying system[75] can deduct 40 percent of the cost the first year and 20 percent of the cost each year thereafter for three years. The maximum deduction in any one year is $5,000, and the total maximum deduction is $20,000.[76]

South Dakota

South Dakota has implemented numerous policies designed to incentivize commercial-scale wind development.[77] The state provides an alternative tax assessment method in lieu of all taxes on real and personal property levied by the state or by local governance units.[78] The tax method has two components: an annual tax equal to $3 per kilowatt (kW) of capacity of the wind farm; and a 2 percent annual tax assessment on the gross receipts of the wind farm. Gross receipts are measured as the number of kilowatt-hours (kWh) produced, multiplied by a base electricity rate of $0.0475/kWh in 2008, with the base rate increasing by 2.5 percent annually thereafter.[79]

The Case of Oregon's BETC/RETC

Oregon's Business Energy Tax Credit (BETC) and its sister Residential Energy Tax Credit (RETC) were designed to stimulate commercial and consumer investment in renewable energy resources, as well as energy conservation and sustainable resource use.

Under the BETC, any Oregon business with taxable income[80] can take a 35 percent tax credit for qualifying energy efficiency/conservation projects, taken over five years—10 percent in the first and second years, and 5 percent each year thereafter. For qualifying renewable energy, high-efficiency combined heat and power, and renewable energy equipment manufacturing facilities, the credit is 50 percent of eligible project costs.[81] The maximum credit is $10 million, taken over five years—10 percent each year; unused credit may be carried forward up to eight years. Taxpayers with eligible project costs[82] of $20,000 or less may take the tax credit in one year.[83]

In 2008, approximately 65 percent of the BETC program tax credits went to renewable energy projects; 25 percent went to conservation and energy efficiency projects; and 9 percent went to the manufacturing program designed to identify, attract, and retain manufacturing operations in Oregon in the green energy sector.[84]

Eligible conservation projects include energy efficiency equipment, transportation projects that reduce miles traveled to work or invest in efficient truck technology, and construction of LEED-certified homes and home-builder-installed renewable energy facilities.[85]

Renewable energy projects make up the largest sector of the BETC program. These include: high-efficiency combined heat and power projects; facilities that manufacture renewable energy resource equipment; renewable energy resource generation; solar thermal; and biomass infrastructure projects. Analysis indicates that in 2008, renewable projects represented 74 percent of the project credits and accounted for 65 percent of the energy savings dollars.[86]

The RETC is available to Oregon taxpayers who purchase qualifying conservation and renewable energy projects for their primary or secondary residence.[87] Conservation projects include "premium-efficiency" appliances that exceed the federal Energy Star standards,[88] heating and air conditioning systems,[89] and alternative-fuel vehicles.

Purchase and installation of renewable energy systems (Alternative Energy Devices or AEDs)[90] are eligible for up to $1,500 per year per project.[91] Project classifications include:

- solar energy systems, including photovoltaic, passive solar space heating;
- wind;
- geothermal heat pumps;
- groundwater heat pump or ground loop device;
- fuel cell systems; and
- premium efficiency biomass combustion devices.

Credit amounts vary based on project type, but are capped at $1,500.

The high utilization of the program and the accompanying increase in economic activity come with the disadvantage of decreased tax revenue. For example, the cost of the BETC increased from $68 million in the 2007–2009 biennium to an estimated $167 million in the 2009–2011 biennium.[92] Projections anticipate an increase to $243 million in 2011–2013.[93] Escalating costs of the programs lead to public criticism in difficult economic times when budget constraints require reduced public services and legislators discuss raising taxes.

The Oregon Department of Energy (ODOE) commissioned an analysis of the economic effects of the BETC and RETC programs.[94] The authors considered data from 2007 and 2008, assessing each program individually by year and producing an aggregate analysis.[95] The aggregate data indicate that the effect of the credits, combined with spending by the taxpayers benefiting from the credit, had substantial positive net impacts on Oregon's economy.[96] Both programs combined produced $185 million in net economic output, $20.7 million in wages, and nine hundred jobs.[97] State and local tax revenues increased $6.1 million,[98] and energy costs decreased by $102 million through conservation or renewable energy generation.[99]

The environmental impacts of the credits are also notable. Carbon dioxide emissions were reduced by 712,000 tons as a result of the two programs.[100] According to the report, "the energy savings realized from the RETC and BETC programs generate significant reductions in carbon emissions that move Oregon closer to its 2020 [greenhouse gas reduction] goal."[101]

Oregon, like the rest of the country, struggled to balance state budgets after the market collapse of 2008. Concern over lost revenue and media investigation into potential fraud and misuse led to calls for repeal or modification.[102] A bill introduced in the 2009 session of the state legislature would have markedly rolled back the BETC/RETC, reducing the cap on credits from $10 million to $3.5 million.[103] The bill passed but was vetoed by the governor, who stated the rollback went too far and would adversely impact Oregon's growing renewable energy sector, resulting in fewer jobs.[104] The governor then instructed the ODOE to perform an evaluation of program incentive levels; study and implement rule changes, including ensuring Oregon's permitting and license laws are addressed; examine job creation; and determine how BETC incentives align with actual output of power generation realized by renewable energy facilities.[105] The resulting report made recommendations to increase accountability;[106] cap the renewable program growth while maintaining ability to attract jobs;[107] implement conservation programs;[108] and initiate a new alternative funding model for large scale wind.[109]

Reforms passed in the February 2010 Special Session of the legislature, capping credits for renewable energy generation facilities at $300 million for the 2009–2011 biennium and $150 million for the 2011–2013 biennium.[110] The reforms are likely to have the largest effect on "big wind" projects, reducing the credit cap for wind generation facilities greater than 10 MW to $3.5 million in 2010, $2.5 million in 2011 and $1.5 million in 2012. Credits for manufacturing facilities are capped at $200 million through the 2009–2011 and 2011–2013 biennia and $50 million for the second half of 2013.

Significantly, the law established a broad series of measures to ensure increased program accountability.[111] ODOE director Mark Long estimated that the reforms would save the state an estimated $53 million in the 2009–2010 budget and $97 million in the budgets two years thereafter.[112]

The Other Side of the Coin: Excise Tax on Wind Energy Development

Wyoming Governor Dave Freudenthal signed House Bill 101 on March 5, 2010, making Wyoming the first state to impose a state excise tax on wind production. The law levies an excise tax of $1 per megawatt-hour on wind energy production at facilities over 500 WM per twenty-four-hour period. Power generated for personal use generates less than 500 MW in a twenty-four-hour period. The law provides a three-year grace period from first production for sale. Revenue is projected at a minimum of $4 million annually, to be divided between affected counties (60 percent) and the state general fund (40 percent).[113] Wyoming produces more coal than any other state,[114] and some might view this tax as evidence of legislative protection of the coal industry. A 2010 study shows that the Wyoming wind tax would impose the highest tax burden on the wind industry in the Rocky Mountain states.[115] However, Wyoming also imposes a significant severance tax on coal. The coal severance tax raised $800 million in 2007, making the $8 million annual wind tax revenues small in comparison.[116]

Conclusion

U.S. energy tax policy relies solely on tax incentives to encourage conservation, efficiency, and the substitution of renewable energy sources for fossil energy sources.

This model has a number of disadvantages. First, the effectiveness of tax incentives depends on the market price of fossil energy. Tax incentives reduce the relative price of renewable energy, and if fossil energy costs decline, tax incentives lose effectiveness. In addition, fossil energy prices depend on factors beyond U.S. control and are notoriously volatile.

Second, the demand for tax incentives depends on the strength of the economy. As discussed in the beginning of this chapter, profitable businesses like banks invested in renewable energy projects to harvest the tax credits. During the financial crisis of 2008 and 2009, banks had generated their own tax losses, and the market for renewable energy tax credits evaporated. Renewable energy projects cannot get stable financing from the tax credit model, particularly when tax credits expire and there is no guarantee that Congress will extend their availability.

Third, the tax system continues to subsidize fossil fuels. While President Obama has proposed repealing tax incentives for oil and gas, it seems likely that Congress will continue to support fossil fuels, including coal. Even renewable energy incentives may subsidize oil use. The tax credit for fuels blended with ethanol reduces the price of motor fuel and encourages use.[117] Energy tax policy has historically been motivated by the goal of enhancing U.S. energy security.[118] President Obama's proposal reflects a shift in energy tax policy from one of energy security to one that discourages the use of fossil fuels, regardless of their nation of origin.

Finally, no matter how carefully drafted, federal and state tax incentives can be used in unintended ways. Two examples, one federal and one state, illustrate this problem. The paper industry has been burning a highly toxic pulp by-product known as black liquor since the 1930s.[119] As black liquor is produced from biomass, it qualifies for the alternative fuels credit, which was intended primarily to increase the use of biofuels in cars and trucks.[120] One paper company alone, International Paper, received $1.5 billion in alternative fuel credits in the first three quarters of 2009. The credits accounted for more than 60 percent of the company's pretax earnings. The tax extenders legislation considered by Congress in 2010 contains provisions limiting the black liquor tax benefits. The Joint Committee on Taxation estimates that the provisions will raise over $21 billion between 2010 and 2020.[121] Oregon's BETC, described above, was designed to conserve energy and promote green job growth in Oregon. Reporters discovered that a Texas trucking company with minimal ties to Oregon received 752 separate Oregon tax credits worth $4.5 million to upgrade its truck fleet with fuel-saving technology.[122] The company, Mesilla Valley Transportation, sold the tax credits as part of the BETC's pass-through program, netting $3.9 million at the Oregon taxpayers' expense. As noted above, Oregon restricted the availability of the BETC for 2010 and subsequent years.

While encouraging a shift to renewable energy may provide benefits in energy security and climate change mitigation, renewable energy tax incentives may exacerbate other environmental issues. Wind farms raise land use issues and may endanger wildlife. Production of biomass transportation fuel uses much more water than production of fossil transportation fuel, with the most significant emerging resource issue being scarcity of clean water: water is the new oil.[123] Renewable tax incentives fail to take water usage into account.

A balanced policy mix for renewable energy and conservation should include a price on carbon emissions, via either a cap-and-trade program or a carbon tax.[124] This would control the price volatility of fossil fuels by putting a floor on the price, thereby assuring the competitiveness of renewable sources.

Notes

1. U.S. ENERGY INFO. ADMIN., FEDERAL FINANCIAL INTERVENTIONS AND SUBSIDIES IN ENERGY MARKETS 2007, at xi, (April 2008) [hereinafter SUBSIDIES], *available at* http://www .eia.doe.gov/oiaf/servicerpt/subsidy2/index.html.

2. GILBERT E. METCALF, ENERGY POLICY AND THE ENVIRONMENT REPORT, TAXING ENERGY IN THE UNITED STATES: WHICH FUELS DOES THE TAX CODE FAVOR? 4 (Jan. 2009), *available at* http://www.manhattan-institute.org/html/eper_04.htm.

3. *See* Joint Committee on Taxation, *Oil and Gas Tax Provisions: A Consideration of the President's Fiscal Year 2010 Budget Proposal*, JCX-34-09 (Sept. 9, 2009), *available at* http:// www.jct.gov/publications.html?func=select&id=7.

4. SUBSIDIES, *supra* note 1, at xi.

5. The Emergency Economic Stabilization Act of 2008, Pub. Law No. 110-343, added $10.8 billion in energy tax incentives from 2009 to 2018, although over 10 percent of the total applied to clean coal provisions. JCX-78-08. The American Recovery and Reinvestment Act of 2009, Pub. Law No. 111-9, added $20 billion in energy tax incentives from 2009 to 2019. Joint Committee on Taxation, *Estimated Budget Effects of the Revenue Provisions Contained in the Conference Agreement to the "American Recovery and Reinvestment Act of 2009*, JCX-19-09 (Feb. 12, 2009).

6. *See* Jeffry S. Hinman, *The Green Economic Recovery: Wind Energy Tax Policy After Financial Crisis and the American Recovery and Reinvestment Act of 2009*, 24 J. ENVTL. L. & LITIG. 35, 60–63 (2009).

7. I.R.C. § 168(e)(3)(vi).

8. *See* Howard A. Cooper, *Tax Credit for Electricity from Renewables—Updated*, TAX NOTES 221, 226 (Oct. 12, 2009). Partnership flip and sale-leaseback transactions are also discussed in chapter 17.

9. I.R.C. § 704.

10. Rev. Proc. 2007-65, 2007-2 C.B. 967.

11. Rev. Proc. 2001-28, 2001-1 C.B. 38.

12. I.R.C. § 45(a)(2)(A), (d).

13. I.R.C. § 50(d)(4), referring to § 48(b)(2) and (3) prior to amendment by the Revenue Reconciliation Act of 1990, Pub. Law No. 101-508, § 11813(a). Section 48(b)(2)(b) required that the property be sold and leased back within three months after the date the property was originally placed in service. *See* Revenue Act of 1964, Pub. Law No. 88-272, § 203(c).

14. I.R.C. § 50(d)(5), referring to § 48(d) prior to amendment by the Revenue Reconciliation Act of 1990, Pub. Law No. 101-508, § 11813(a). Section 48(d)(2) provided a special rule for certain short-term leases. Section 48(d)(4) defined property to which § 48(d)(2) applies as, inter alia, property that is "leased for a period that is less than 80% of its class life." *See* Tax Reform Act of 1969, Pub. Law No. 91-172, § 401(e)(3).

15. Treas. Reg. § 1.48-4.

16. ARRA 2009, Pub. Law 111-5, § 1603. The grant program was extended for an additional year, until the end of 2011, under the Tax Relief, Unemployment Insurance Reauthorization, and Job Creation Act of 2010, Pub. Law 111-312, § 707. For further details, see chapter 17.

17. ARRA 2009 Pub. Law 111-5, § 1102(a) (codified at I.R.C. § 48(b)(5)).

18. H.R. 6, 109th Cong., 1st Sess. (2005), Pub. Law 109-58.

19. Notice 2006-40, 2006-1 C.B. 855.

20. I.R.C. § 45(b)(1) provides:

> The amount of the credit determined under subsection (a) shall be reduced by an amount which bears the same ratio to the amount of the credit (determined without regard to this paragraph) as—(A) the amount by which the reference price for the calendar year in which the sale occurs exceeds 8 cents, bears to (B) 3 cents. The phaseout threshold is adjusted for inflation. I.R.C. § 45(b)(2).

21. I.R.S. P.L.R. 200142018, 2001 PLR Lexis 1084 (July 23, 2001).

22. U.S. Energy Info. Admin., Renewable Energy Consumption and Electricity Preliminary Statistics 2008, at 2 (July 2009).

23. I.R.C. § 45(d)(2).

24. I.R.C. § 48(a)(5)(C). Wind facilities must be placed in service by the end of 2012.

25. "Subsidized energy financing means financing provided under a Federal, State, or local program a principal purpose of which is to provide subsidized financing for projects designed to conserve or produce energy." I.R.C. § 48(a)(4)(C).

26. JCX-25-09 at 36.

27. I.R.C. § 48(d).

28. I.R.C. § 48(d)(3).

29. John Dernbach, *Stabilizing and Then Reducing U.S. Energy Consumption: Legal and Policy Tools for Efficiency and Conservation*, 37 Envtl. L. Rep. 10003, 10003 (2007).

30. I.R.C. § 136.

31. I.R.C. § 48C.

32. I.R.C. § 45M.

33. The other is the deduction for soil and water conservation expenditures in I.R.C. § 175, which applies only to farmers.

34. Pub. Law No. 111-312, §§ 703 (energy efficient home credit) and 731 (research credit).

35. I.R.C. § 45L.

36. I.R.C. § 41.

37. I.R.C. §§ 167(a), 168(c).

38. Pub. Law 111-5, Div B, Title I, Subtitle B, Part I, § 1103(b)(2)(A), Part III, § 1121(a)–(e), 123 Stat. 320, 322.

39. Pub. Law 111-312, § 710.

40. A qualified fuel cell power plant is an integrated system made up of a fuel cell stack assembly and associated balance of plant components that converts a fuel into electricity by electrochemical means. I.R.C. § 48(c)(1).

41. Information available from the IRS at http://www.irs.gov/businesses/corporations/article/0,,id=214280,00.html.

42. U.S. Dep't of Energy, Energy Efficiency & Renewable Energy, Alternative and Advanced Vehicles: Fuel Cell Vehicle Availability http://www.afdc.energy.gov/afdc/vehicles/fuel_cell_availability.html (last updated Apr. 22, 2010).

43. *See* http://automobiles.honda.com/fcx-clarity/drive-fcx-clarity.aspx.

44. http://www.irs.gov/businesses/article/0,,id=219921,00.html.

45. *See* Joseph B. White, *The Surge in Electric Cars*, Wall St. J. (Dec. 16, 2009), *available at* http://online.wsj.com/article/SB10001424052748704201404574589900770542192.html.

46. Notice 2009-58, 2009-30 I.R.B. 2.

47. I.R.C. § 30C.

48. *See* Renewable Fuels Ass'n, Ethanol Industry Outlook 2007: Building New Horizons, at 8 (2007), *available at* http://ethanolrfa.3cdn.net/9591116ea271f4de76_tbm6 y72f2.pdf; *see also* Brent D. Yacobucci, Cong. Research Serv., Fuel Ethanol: Background and Public Policy Issues 1, 9 (2006) (using different numbers: 556 fuel stations with E85, 65% of which were located in the five highest ethanol-producing states—Minnesota, Illinois, Iowa, South Dakota, and Nebraska).

49. I.R.C. § 30C(b) and (c). The alternative fuel refueling property credit was originally enacted in 2005. The cost of the credit was anticipated to be just under $100 million over the

five-year period between 2006 and 2010. Staff of Joint Comm. on Taxation, 109th Cong., Estimates of Federal Tax Expenditures for Fiscal Years 2006–2010 32 (Joint Comm. Print 2006).

50. *See* Roberta F. Mann & Mona L. Hymel, *Moonshine to Motorfuel: Tax Incentives for Fuel Ethanol*, 19 Duke Envtl. L. & Pol'y F. 43, 45 (2009).

51. Am. Council for an Energy Efficient Econ. (ACEEE), The 2009 State Energy Efficiency Scorecard, Rep. No. E097, at 1 (Oct. 1, 2009), *available at* http://www.aceee.org/research-report/e097 (free log-in required to download report).

52. Comprehensive information on federal, state, and local incentives and policies is available at the Database of State Incentives for Renewables and Efficiency (DSIRE), http://www.dsireusa.org.

53. *See* http://www.dsireusa.org/summarytables/finre.cfm (last visited Dec. 30, 2010). As of December 2010, the only states without any tax incentives for renewable energy are Arkansas, Delaware, and Mississippi.

54. *Id.*

55. *Id.*

56. Eric Lantz & Elizabeth Doris, State Clean Energy Policies Analysis (SCEPA): State Tax Incentives 3, Nat'l Renewable Energy Lab. Tech. Rep. NRLE/TP-6A2-46467 (Oct. 2009).

57. *Id.*

58. This is not an exhaustive list. *See* City of Boulder, Solar Rebate and Grant Program, http://www.bouldercolorado.gov/index.php?option=com_content&task=view&id=7700&Itemid=2845.

59. I.R.C. § 136.

60. DSIRE, Financial Incentive for Energy Efficiency, http://www.dsireusa.org/summarytables/finee.cfm.

61. These alternate fuels include electricity, natural gas, E-85 (or higher blend), methanol, propane, hydrogen, and other fuels approved by the Oregon Department of Energy.

62. Ore. Dep't of Energy–Transp., Hybrid Gasoline-Electric and Alternative Fuel Vehicles, http://www.oregon.gov/ENERGY/TRANS/hybridcr.shtml (last updated Jan. 28, 2010).

63. Ore. Admin. Rule 330-090-0110 (3). *See also* http://www.oregon.gov/ENERGY/CONS/BUS/docs/Electric_ATV.pdf (BETC Application for Electric All-Terrain Vehicles.)

64. *See, e.g.*, Lantz & Doris, *supra* note 56.

65. Kelly Sims Gallagher & Erich Muehlegger, *Giving Green to Get Green: Incentives and Consumer Adoption of Hybrid Vehicle Technology* 6 (John F. Kennedy School of Government, Harvard University faculty research working paper series, Feb. 2008), *available at* http://ssrn.com/abstract=1083716.

66. *Id.*

67. *Id.*

68. *Id.*

69. *Id.* at 28.

70. *Id.*

71. Zhong Jin & Brittany Teahan, *Iowa's Tax Incentive Programs Used by Biofuel Producers: Tax Credit Evaluation Study* 4 (Tax Research & Program Analysis Section, Iowa Dep't of Revenue, Mar. 2009), *available at* http://ssrn.com/abstract=1392825.

72. *Id.*

73. *Id.*

74. Am. Council for an Energy Efficient Econ., The 2009 State Energy Efficiency Scorecard, Rep. No. E097 (Oct. 1, 2009).

75. *E.g.*, Passive Solar Space Heat, Solar Water Heat, Solar Space Heat, Photovoltaics, Wind, Biomass, Geothermal Heat Pumps.

76. DSIRE, Idaho, Residential Alternative Energy Tax Deduction, http://www.dsireusa.org/incentives/incentive.cfm?Incentive_Code=ID01F&re=1&ee=0

77. In an effort to aggressively advance large-scale wind generation in the state, South Dakota Energy Infrastructure Authority (SDEIA) produced the South Dakota Wind Power Report in 2007, which identified barriers to further wind power development. *See* www.sdeia .com/PDF/2007WindEnergyReport.pdf. The South Dakota Wind Resource Assessment Network (WRAN) operates eleven wind assessment site stations across the state to verify potential wind resource areas. *See* http://www.sdwind.com

78. Large Commercial Wind Exemption and Alternative Taxes, S.D. CODIFIED LAWS §§ 10-35-16 et seq. Commercial wind is defined as producing greater than 5 megawatts (MW) of electricity.

79. A partial rebate of this tax is available for the cost of transmission line and collector system equipment located in the state and that serves an eligible facility. The rebate is capped at 50 percent of the combined cost of the transmission lines and wind farm collector system. S.D. CODIFIED LAWS § 10-35-22. Commercial wind under 5MW is subject to the Small Commercial Wind Energy Property Tax Assessment, which only takes the base, foundation, tower, and substations into account in assessing property value. The assessment does not include the wind turbine or blades because they are considered personal property.

80. OR. REV. STAT. §§ 315–354. A trade, business, or its partners or shareholders, and rental property owners who pay taxes for a business site in Oregon are eligible for the tax credit. The applicant must be the project owner (own or be the contract buyer of the project), and the business must use the equipment in state or lease it for use in Oregon. If the project owner is an Oregon nonprofit organization, tribe, or public entity without Oregon tax liability, it may partner with an Oregon business or resident who has a state tax liability and use the pass-through option. "The Business Energy Tax Credit Pass-through Option lets a project owner transfer a tax credit to a pass-through partner in return for a lump-sum cash payment upon completion of the project." ORE. DEP'T OF ENERGY CONSERVATION, BUSINESS ENERGY TAX CREDIT PASS-THROUGH, http://www.oregon.gov/ENERGY/CONS/BUS/tax/pass-through.shtml (last updated Jan. 12, 2011).

81. ORE. ADMIN. RULES 330-090-0105; ORE. REV. STAT. § 469-200.

82. Eligible project costs are calculated based on the incremental costs of moving from standard efficiency to an increased efficiency option. Typically, this includes all costs directly related to the project, including equipment cost, engineering and design fees, materials, supplies and installation costs, loan fees, and permit costs. Costs associated with operation and maintenance and replacing worn-out equipment or equipment required to meet codes or regulations are not eligible. ORE. ADMIN. RULES 330-090-0110(17) (definition of costs).

83. *See* ORE. DEP'T OF ENERGY: INFO. FOR BUS., BUSINESS ENERGY TAX CREDITS, http://www.oregon.gov/ENERGY/CONS/BUS/BETC.shtml.

84. ORE. DEP'T OF ENERGY, BUSINESS ENERGY TAX CREDIT: FEB. 2010 RECOMMENDATIONS (ODOE RECOMMENDATIONS), at 4 (Nov. 30, 2009), *available at* http://archivedweb sites.sos.state.or.us/Governor_Kulongoski_2011/governor.oregon.gov/Gov/docs/betc_cvrltr_ report_120109.pdf.

85. ORE. REV. STAT. § 469-205.

86. ECONORTHWEST, ECONOMIC IMPACTS OF OREGON ENERGY TAX CREDIT PROGRAMS IN 2007 AND 2008 (BETC/RETC) at 28 (Feb. 2, 2009) [hereinafter ECONOMIC IMPACTS].

87. ORE. REV. STAT. §§ 469.160–469-180. *See also* ORE. ADMIN. RULE 330-070-0010.

88. "Premium-efficiency" appliances—dishwashers, clothes washers, and refrigerators— meet efficiency requirements established by the Oregon Department of Energy (ODOE). Those standards exceed federal Energy Star standards. The appliance must be located in the taxpayer's primary or secondary residence. The tax credit ranges from $60 to $180. *Id. See also* ODOE: ENERGY CONSERVATION, RESIDENTIAL ENERGY TAX CREDITS, http://www.oregon.gov/ ENERGY/CONS/RES/tax/appliances.shtml.

89. Eligible heating and cooling systems include central air systems; ductless heat pumps; duct sealing and testing; furnaces, boilers, and air handlers; geothermal heat pumps; heat pumps; heat recovery and energy recovery ventilation equipment; wood and pellet stoves. ORE. ADMIN. RULE 330-070-0021.

90. *Id.*

91. Details of the rates for each type of project are available at DSIRE, RETC, http://www .dsireusa.org/incentives/incentive.cfm?Incentive_Code=OR17F&re=1&ee=1; DSIRE, BETC, http://www.dsireusa.org/incentives/incentive.cfm?Incentive_Code=OR03F&re=1&ee=1.

92. Harry Esteve, *State Lowballed Cost of Green Tax Breaks*, THE OREGONIAN, Oct. 31, 2009, *available at* http://www.oregonlive.com/news/index.ssf/2009/10/state_lowballed_cost_ of_green.html.

93. *Id. See also* Ted Sickinger, *Oregon Business Energy Tax Credit Program Will Bring Future Liabilities*, THE OREGONIAN, Feb. 9, 2010, *available at* http://www.oregonlive.com/ business/index.ssf/2010/02/house_bill_3680_would_cut_back.html.

94. ECONOMIC IMPACTS, *supra* note 86.

95. *Id.* at 1.

96. *Id.* at 7–10.

97. *Id.* at 32.

98. *Id.*

99. *Id.*

100. *Id.* at 1.

101. *Id.* at 2.

102. *See, e.g.*, Steve Duin, *BETC Mess Just Keeps Getting Worse*, THE OREGONIAN, Nov. 3, 2009, *available at* http://www.oregonlive.com/news/oregonian/steve_duin/index.ssf/2009/11/ betc_mess_just_keeps_getting_w.html; Jeff Mapes, *BETC Taking Its Place in Oregon Pantheon of Shame*, THE OREGONIAN, Nov. 5, 2009, *available at* http://blog.oregonlive.com/ mapesonpolitics/2009/11/betc_taking_its_place_in_orego.html.

103. Press Release, Governor Ted Kulongoski (Aug. 9, 2009) (discussing veto of H.B. 2472), *available at* http://www.oregon.gov/Gov/P2009/press_080709.shtml.

104. *Id.*

105. Letter from Governor Ted Kulongoski to Secretary of State Kate Brown (Aug. 7, 2009), *available at* http://img.votesmart.org/vetotext/27243.pdf.

106. ODOE RECOMMENDATIONS, *supra* note 84, at 6.

107. *Id.* at 7–8.

108. *Id.* at 9.

109. *Id.* at 13.

110. H.B. 3680 (Mar. 18, 2010). Press Release, Governor Ted Kulongoski (Mar. 18, 2010), *available at* http://www.oregon.gov/Gov/P2010/press_031810a.shtml.

111. The legislation requires the taxpayer to provide additional information to support the application for the tax credit and modified the criteria for issuance, suspension, and revocation of certification. H.B. 3680.

112. Harry Esteve, *Kulongoski, Oregon Lawmakers Seek to Scale Back Energy Tax Credits*, THE OREGONIAN, Feb. 3, 2010, *available at* http://www.oregonlive.com/politics/index .ssf/2010/02/kulongoski_lawmakers_agree_to.html.

113. Effective January 1, 2011. *See* Jeremy Pelzer, *Wind Tax Clears House*, STAR-TRIBUNE, Feb. 19, 2010, *available at* http://trib.com/news/state-and-regional/govt-and-politics/ article_20358202-3f47-5d40-9a19-ce9c4bbe20de.html.

114. U.S. ENERGY INFO. ADMIN., ANNUAL COAL REPORT 2008, tbl. ES-2, *available at* http:// www.eia.doe.gov/cneaf/coal/page/acr/acr_sum.html.

115. *Industry Says Wyoming Wind Tax Tops in Rockies*, WYOMING ENERGY NEWS, June 23, 2010, http://wyomingenergynews.com/2010/06/industry-says-wyoming-wind-tax-tops-in -rockies/.

116. JUDY ZELIO & LISA HOULIHAN, NAT'L CONF. OF STATE LEGISLATURES, STATE ENERGY REVENUES UPDATE, *available at* http://www.ncsl.org/default.aspx?tabid=12674 (last visited Feb. 15, 2011).

117. For a more detailed analysis of the disadvantages of fuel ethanol, see Roberta F. Mann & Mona L. Hymel, *Moonshine to Motorfuel: Tax Incentives for Fuel Ethanol*, 18 DUKE ENVTL. L. & POL'Y F. 43 (2008).

118. Molly F. Sherlock, & Donald J. Marples, Cong. Research Serv. Report, Energy Tax Policy: Issues in the 111th Congress 7 (Sept. 20, 2010).

119. Steve Mufson, *An Elixir for Health Reform? Lawmakers Offer 'Black Liquor,'* Wash. Post, Nov. 8, 2009.

120. Steve Mufson, *Papermakers Dig Deep in Highway Bill to Hit Gold*, Wash. Post, Mar. 28, 2009.

121. Joint Committee on Taxation, *Estimated Revenue Effects of the Revenue Provisions Contained in the "American Workers, State and Business Relief Act of 2010,"* as passed by the Senate on Mar. 10, 2010, JCX-9-10 (Mar. 10, 2010) at 6.

122. Ted Sickinger & Harry Esteve, *Firm's Tax Credits Raise Issues: A Texas Trucking Company That Does Little Business in Oregon Has Received Millions in State Subsidies*, Eugene Register-Guard, Feb. 24, 2010, at B4, *available at* http://www.registerguard.com/csp/cms/sites/web/news/sevendays/24494156-35/oregon-tax-energy-state-cascade.csp.

123. *See* Steven Solomon, Water: The Epic Struggle for Wealth, Power, and Civilization (Harper Collins 2010). *See also* Roberta F. Mann, *Like Water for Energy: The Water-Energy Nexus Through the Lens of Tax Policy*, 82 Colo. L. Rev. 505 (2011).

124. *See, e.g.*, Roberta F. Mann, *The Case for the Carbon Tax: How to Overcome Politics and Find Our Green Destiny*, 39 Envtl. L. Rep. 10118 (2009).

chapter eight

Government Nontax Incentives for Clean Energy

John A. Herrick

Federal Incentive Programs

Types of Incentives

Financial Assistance for Clean Energy

The federal government provides assistance in many forms, financial and otherwise. Federal financial assistance programs are designed to serve a variety of purposes. Objectives may include fostering some element of national policy as directed by either the Executive or by Congress through statute; stimulating private sector involvement to achieve public purpose goals through mutually beneficial undertakings; or furnishing aid of a type or to a class of beneficiaries the private market cannot or is unwilling to otherwise accommodate.[1] The development and commercialization of clean energy technologies has been a national goal since the late 1970s through a series of overlapping and re-enforcing pieces of energy legislation.[2] Because most of these statutory regimes require the federal government to work with the private sector to advance these technologies[3] and the technologies are not solely directed for government use, the appropriate funding vehicles for these activities are financial assistance agreements rather than federal procurement contracts.[4]

Federal financial assistance was clarified by the Federal Grant and Cooperative Agreement Act in 1977,[5] which provides standards to distinguish between financial assistance and federal contracting actions and sets out the following two categories of financial assistance:

- *Grant agreements.* An agency is to use a grant agreement when the principal purpose of the relationship is to transfer a thing of value (money, property, services, etc.) to the recipient to carry out a public purpose of support or stimulation authorized by a law of the United States instead of acquiring (by purchase, lease, or barter) property or services for the direct benefit or use of the United States Government, and substantial involvement is not expected between the agency and the recipient when carrying out the contemplated activity.[6]

- *Cooperative agreements.* This type of assistance is similar to grants, as discussed above, except that substantial involvement is expected between the agency and the recipient when carrying out the contemplated activity.[7]

Notwithstanding the Federal Grant and Cooperative Agreement Act, a federal financial assistance program requires separate authorizing legislation to be able to provide the agency with the discretion to transfer federal money to a recipient for a public purpose.[8] Normally, the program's organic statute provides the agency with guidance on the public purpose goals and can contain requirements and/or conditions for the award of financial assistance under the program. While a financial assistance agreement is not considered a government contract under federal procurement law,[9] the government and the courts will usually look to contract law principles to define the rights and obligations of the parties to a federal grant.[10] In particular, a recipient must meet the conditions imposed by the federal government under the award of a financial assistance agreement in order to receive the federal funds; in this context, those conditions are analogous to contractual provisions.[11] The award of financial assistance can be accomplished through two types of financial distribution regimes. One is the categorical financial assistance agreement[12] that is awarded to a specific recipient to undertake a specific activity. The other is formula block grant awarded to a governmental unit, usually a state, allocated on a distribution formula prescribed by statute or regulation, to be used for a variety of activities within a broad functional area. Under these block grants, the state is responsible for further distribution of the money.[13]

Except for programs directed at the states, most of the clean energy funding programs discussed *infra* are discretionary and are subject to a competitive process for award.[14] The Federal Grant and Cooperative Agreement Act encourages competition in assistance programs where the type of assistance is categorical in order to fund the best possible projects and to achieve the programmatic objectives.[15] However, most agencies do not have a forum for the protest of financial assistance awards.[16] The Government Accountability Office[17] has declined to use its bid protest mechanism, which is prescribed to ensure the fairness of awards of contracts, to rule on the propriety of individual grant awards.[18] This is primarily due to the view that the award of discretionary financial assistance is left to the applicable agency's expertise in its merit determination of the technologies being supported; an administrative appeals process would unduly override that technical expertise.

U.S. Department of Energy Cooperative Agreements

Because the discretionary funding of nonfederal entities by the U.S. Department of Energy (DOE) for the research, development, and commercialization of clean energy technologies is undertaken in concert with DOE programmatic direction and priorities, the appropriate funding vehicle has been cooperative agreements rather than grant instruments. This allows DOE to have substantial involvement in the project and better assures DOE that the appropriate technology is developed and demonstrated and that public interest goals of commercialization are furthered.[19] DOE investment is done on a cost-sharing basis;[20] DOE cannot provide a cost share above 80 percent of total project costs on any applied research and development activity,[21] or above 50 percent on demonstration and commercialization projects.[22] It is within DOE's discretion to determine what category a particular project falls within.[23] DOE participation in a project through a cooperative agreement will trigger the need for a federal National Environmental Policy Act (NEPA)[24] review of the project.[25] A commitment to provide federal funds for a project is sufficient to bring that project under NEPA purview. In many instances, a multiphased project will be segmented into separate funding phases, with separate approvals. This allows the project to initiate design and permitting activity under a categorical exclusion, while allowing for a more strenuous NEPA review prior to subsequent phased funding of the developmental effort. As a general matter, formula block grants to states are an indirect use of federal funds and not subject to a federal NEPA review.[26]

Although federal cooperative agreements are not normal financing instruments in traditional energy project financing, project funds derived from this source can be treated by the project sponsor as developer equity in the project.[27] The agreements also provide confidence to other equity and debt participants of the project's technological merit and feasibility. In many instances, the involvement of DOE in the project has attracted new financial support for the project from more traditional project-financing sources. One complication of the cooperative agreement instrument in project financing is its treatment of property acquired by the recipient under the agreement. Federal regulations require that the government retain an ownership interest in property acquired by the recipient (or sub-recipient) under the agreement.[28] The government retains the right for a pro rata share of the fair market value of such property at the termination of the agreement. This could create a substantial burden on the recipient once the federal funding agreement concludes. DOE, in recognition of this problem, has revised its standard clauses to assure recipients that if they continue to use the property for similar but commercial-like purposes after expiration of the funding agreement, it will not exercise its right to realize on the property.

DOE Technology Investment Agreements

In an attempt to facilitate the commercialization of new energy technologies, Congress in 2005 provided DOE with the authority to enter into transactions other than contracts, cooperative agreements, and grants (commonly called "other transactions" authority) to advance public benefits through private sector partnerships.[29] DOE has implemented this other transactions authority by establishing a new contractual mechanism—the technology investment agreement (TIA)—as a new financing vehicle to move technologies in the clean energy marketplace.[30] TIAs are modeled after the Defense Advanced Research Projects Agency program that has spun off many successful commercial enterprises from the development of military technology. The new TIA mechanism will facilitate the financing of facilities that will commercialize innovative technologies in those cases where cooperative agreements are not well suited.

Under TIAs, the project developer and DOE provide funds on an even sharing basis to pay for the costs of moving promising clean energy technologies into the commercial marketplace.[31] TIAs join federal funds with equity or debt contributions from the developer to construct pilot or commercial production facilities or to place products in the marketplace. The developer is not obligated to pay back the federal contribution.

Congress authorized TIAs to help bring new ideas and innovations to fruition, to attract nontraditional government contractors, and to advance the clean technology sector by promoting public-private partnerships. TIAs provide for more flexible terms and conditions than normal federal financing mechanisms, and DOE has greater latitude to negotiate provisions that vary from traditional government contracts and financial assistance agreements. Traditional barriers to government-supported financing—including having to comply with federal cost accounting standards and traditional financial assistance regulations—are not applicable to TIAs. The major factor that will influence the use of this instrument is that the intellectual property statutes applicable to federal contracts and financial assistance are not applicable to TIAs. If a company that normally does not do business with the federal government has difficulty with the application of these laws on its ability to commercialize the subject technology, a TIA may provide the ability of that company to partner with DOE.

Federal Loan Guarantees

Another major form of federal financial support is federal credit assistance, which includes direct loans and, the subject of this section, guaranteed and insured loans. In essence, a federal guaranteed loan is a an advance of credit made to a borrower[32] by a participating lending institution, where the United States government, acting through the particular federal agency involved, guarantees payment of all or part of the principal amount of the loan, and often interest, in the event the borrower defaults.[33]

The primary purpose of loan guarantees is to induce private lenders to extend financial assistance to borrowers who otherwise would not be able to obtain the needed capital on reasonable terms, if at all. In other words, federal loan guarantee programs are designed to redirect capital resources by intervening in the private market decision process, in order to further objectives deemed by Congress to be in the national interest.[34] This is a major objective of the federal government in the clean energy space.[35] Specific federal loan guarantee programs in the clean energy space are discussed later in this chapter.

The authority to guarantee the repayment of indebtedness must have some statutory basis. In most cases, this takes the form of express statutory authorization. In the typical federal loan guarantee program, the borrower is charged a fee by the agency, prescribed in the program legislation. A guarantee may extend to 100 percent of the amount of the underlying loan, or some lesser percentage as specified in the program legislation. Unless otherwise provided, a maximum guarantee percentage applies only to restrict the amount the administering agency is authorized to guarantee. Typically, the statute will authorize the administering agency to establish the terms and conditions under which the guarantee will be extended, but may also impose various limitations and conditions.

When a federal agency guarantees a loan, there is no immediate cash outlay. The need for an actual cash disbursement, apart from administrative expenses, does not arise until the borrower defaults on the loan and the government is called upon to honor the guarantee. Depending on the terms of the loan, this may not happen until many years after the guarantee is made. Accordingly, loan guarantees require budgetary treatment different from ordinary government obligations and expenditures. This treatment is prescribed generally by the Federal Credit Reform Act of 1990 (FCRA).[36] The approach of the FCRA is to require federal appropriations (or other outlay) to cover the subsidy portion of a loan guarantee program, with the nonsubsidized portion (i.e., the portion expected to be repaid) financed through borrowings from the Treasury.[37] This subsidy reflects the potential borrower default contingency of the loans that the guarantees support. This credit subsidy cost plays a large role in DOE loan guarantee transactions, as discussed in more detail below.

Rights to Intellectual Property Under Federal Incentive Programs

The various parties' rights to intellectual property and data under grants and cooperative agreements are based primarily on two federal statutes: the Bayh-Dole Act[38] and the Energy Policy Act of 1992.[39] As a general matter, under the Bayh-Dole Act, the rights to intellectual property under a financial assistance agreement depend on the corporate nature of the entity that receives the federal funds.[40] Regarding patent rights, if the recipient (or sub-recipient) is a small business, university, or a not-for-profit corporation, title to subject inventions[41] under the federally funded effort becomes property of the recipient. If the recipient (or sub-recipient) is a large, for-profit corporate entity, title to inventions remains with the government, subject to a request by the recipient to the government to waive the government's title to the invention. The government almost always waives its title in favor of the private sector participants of these energy commercialization efforts. In both instances, the government retains a nonexclusive, nontransferable, royalty-free, limited-use license to use the invention for government-related purposes only.[42] The government will also retain a march-in right, i.e., authority to come in and license the invention to others if the invention is not commercialized.[43] In addition, the recipient must agree to negotiate with the government a United States preference clause encouraging a preference in the licensing and manufacturing of subject inventions.[44]

The government will not claim any rights to the recipient's proprietary intellectual property that are brought into the government-funded effort.[45] All technical data first produced under the federally funded effort will normally be unrestricted data and available for disclosure. However, the Energy Policy Act of 1992 provides recipients and sub-recipients of clean energy projects with a five-year protection from government disclosure of data first produced under the effort from the date of development of the data.[46] This is a protection most commercial recipients need to avail themselves of.

Incentive Programs for the Development and Commercialization of Renewable Energy Technologies

Technology-Specific DOE Incentive Programs

DOE's Office of Energy Efficiency and Renewable Energy

DOE's Office of Energy Efficiency and Renewable Energy (EERE) manages numerous technology-specific program areas to work cooperatively with industry and academia to develop and commercialize renewable energy electrical generation.[47] Most of EERE's activity centers on funding the research, development, and commercialization of clean energy technology. The main instrument in providing funding to nonfederal sources in EERE programs is federal financial assistance agreements awarded under competitive merit review processes. This section outlines the most important EERE programs, emphasizing each program's purpose and the budget amounts as appropriated by Congress. The American Recovery and Reinvestment Act (Recovery Act or Stimulus) included approximately $16.8 billion for EERE programs, a ten-fold increase in its previous budget. EERE was appropriated a total of $2.243 billion for fiscal year 2010.[48]

EERE's policy is to solicit discretionary financial assistance applications in a manner that provides the maximum amount of competition feasible through a merit-based selection process.[49] All of EERE's major program areas (discussed in more detail below) issue numerous program solicitations throughout the year—referred to as "funding opportunity announcements"—inviting entities to submit applications for financial assistance in specific technology areas that advance each program's mission. These announcements are placed in the Federal Business Opportunities[50] and Grants .gov[51] websites. The electronic portal for the submission of applications to EERE in response to these announcements is FedConnect.[52]

Solar Power Technologies

The mission of EERE's Solar Program is to "conduct research, development, demonstration, and deployment activities to accelerate widespread commercialization of clean solar energy technologies, which will lower greenhouse gas emissions, provide a clean and secure domestic source of energy, and create green jobs."[53] Within the Solar Program are four subprograms: Photovoltaics R&D, Concentrating Solar Power, Systems Integration, and Market Transformation.[54] Congress appropriated $225 million to the Solar Program for 2010,[55] an increase of $50 million over the 2009 appropriation.[56] The Solar Program is EERE's most funded program.

The Photovoltaics R&D and Concentrating Solar Power subprograms are the most significant. Photovoltaic (PV) technology uses light-sensitive cells or panels, usually containing silicon, to convert the sun's energy directly into electricity.[57] Photovoltaics R&D aims to develop reliable PV systems that are cost-competitive with conventional energy resources.[58]

Concentrated solar technology uses mirrors to focus the sun's energy on a fluid, creating thermal energy that can be converted to electricity.[59] The Concentrating Solar Power subprogram seeks to make concentrated solar technologies cost-competitive by 2015.[60] The program stimulates manufacturing capability for system components and proposed in 2010 to study the technical feasibility of thermal storage, which could enable concentrating solar plants to provide baseload power capacity.[61] The intermittent nature of solar energy makes this technology very attractive.

The Systems Integration subprogram centers on integrating solar systems for end use, including on the electricity grid and on buildings.[62] The Market Transformation subprogram seeks to penetrate market barriers hindering deployment of solar energy technologies, including interconnection standards, net metering, and others.[63]

Solar technologies are discussed in greater detail in chapter 17.

Wind Power Technologies

EERE's Wind Energy Program's mission is "to increase the development and deployment of reliable, affordable, and environmentally sustainable wind power and realize the benefits of domestic renewable energy production."[64] Congress appropriated to the Wind Energy Program $80 million for fiscal year 2010,[65] a significant increase over its 2009 appropriation of $55 million and $5 million more than DOE asked for.[66] The Wind Energy Program's activities are composed of two subprograms: Technology Viability and Technology Application.

The Technology Viability subprogram is divided into three technology-based components. First, Low Speed Wind Technology (LWST) seeks to decrease the cost per kilowatt of utility-scale land and offshore wind turbines.[67] Specifically, it seeks to achieve a cost of 3.6 cents/kWh for land-based systems in Class 4 winds by 2012, and 7 cents/kWh for offshore systems in Class 6 winds by 2014.[68] LWST utilizes primarily Cooperative Research and Development Agreements (CRADAs)[69] toward its goal for land-based systems, while doing basic technology and policy research toward its goal for offshore systems.[70]

The second technology-based component within the Technology Viability subprogram is Distributed Wind Technology (DWT). DWT concentrates on the development of small and medium-sized turbines through basic research, testing, and technical assistance.[71] The small and medium-sized turbines will serve markets requiring generating capacity lower than public utilities, such as residential, small commercial, farm, community, and tribal markets.[72]

The final component of the Technology Viability subprogram is Supporting Research and Testing (ST&T). The ST&T component provides technical support, expertise, and analysis tools to improve the rotor design, siting, and drivetrains of wind turbines.[73] ST&T utilizes the testing facilities of National Renewable Energy Laboratory (NREL) and Sandia National Laboratory and is slated to receive roughly half of DOE's planned expenditures for the Technology Viability subprogram, about $23 million.[74]

The second subprogram in EERE's Wind Energy Program is Technology Application, which seeks to overcome barriers to wind technology adoption through its Technology Acceptance and Systems Integration activities. The subprogram focuses on issues such as institutional resistance to wind technology, utility planning, environmental mitigation, and interconnection issues.[75]

Wind technologies are discussed in greater detail in chapter 16.

Geothermal Power Technologies

EERE's Geothermal Technology Program's mission is "to conduct research, development, and demonstration to establish Enhanced Geothermal Systems (EGS) as a major contributor for baseload electricity generation."[76] Geothermal Technology received $44 million for 2010, the same as in 2009.[77] Enhanced Geothermal Systems are artificial reservoirs of geothermal energy created by drilling wells into hot rock and circulating a fluid to generate electricity.[78] The technology allows exploitation of a geothermal resource that naturally lacks sufficient water or permeability.[79] Specific activities within the Geothermal Technology Program include basic research awards to companies and academia[80] and the creation of a national geothermal database to reduce exploration risk.[81]

Geothermal technologies are discussed in greater detail in chapter 18.

Fuel Cell Technology

EERE's Fuel Cell Technologies Program develops hydrogen fuel cell technology. Its mission is "to reduce petroleum use, greenhouse gas emissions, and criteria air pollutants, and to contribute to a more diverse energy supply and more efficient domestic energy use by enabling the widespread commercialization and application of fuel cell technologies."[82] In 2010 EERE proposed to consolidate and rename its myriad of hydrogen activities into a single fuel cell research and development subprogram;[83] however, Congress retained the same funding structure, appropriating $174 million for "Hydrogen Technology."[84] EERE has therefore retained the various hydrogen subprograms, but operates them under its Fuel Cell Technologies Program.[85]

The Fuel Cell Technologies Program continues to focus on hydrogen production, delivery, and storage, along with fuel cell stack component technology; EERE allocated $109.7 million of its 2010 appropriation to these areas.[86] The primary goal of the Hydrogen Storage subprogram is a driving range of three hundred miles for onboard light-duty vehicle systems, to facilitate eventual consumer adoption of the technology in personal vehicles.[87] The Hydrogen Production and Delivery subprograms support development of hydrogen production and infrastructure using renewable methods.[88] The Fuel Cell Stack Component subprogram aims to improve the high-temperature membranes and other components of fuel cells by reducing costs and increasing performance and durability.[89]

DOE's Office of Electricity Delivery and Energy Reliability Program

DOE's Office of Electricity Delivery and Energy Reliability (OE) was established by Congress "to lead national efforts to modernize the electric grid, to enhance the security and reliability of the energy infrastructure, and to facilitate recovery from disruptions to the energy supply."[90] OE's 2010 budget appropriation was nearly $172 million;[91] the Stimulus provided an additional $4.5 billion for OE's activities.[92] OE plans to spend the vast majority of the Stimulus money to deploy "smart grid" technologies.[93] Smart grid technologies continually monitor and report on grid conditions; this enables operators to increase grid stability and efficiency and enables consumers to better control their energy use.[94]

OE administers three programs: Research and Development; Permitting, Siting, and Analysis; and Infrastructure Security and Energy Restoration, as discussed below.

Research and Development Program. The Research and Development Program seeks to "advance technology, in partnership with industry, government, and the public, to meet America's need for a reliable, efficient, and resilient electric power grid."[95] DOE slated nearly $125 million for this program in 2010,[96] making it the best-funded program in OE. The Research and Development Program contains four subprograms.

The first subprogram is Clean Energy Transmission and Reliability (CETR). CETR seeks technological advancements that will enable grid integration of variable renewable energy sources, such as wind and solar power.[97] CETR also improves grid efficiency and capability in existing rights-of-way, possibly using superconducting power equipment.[98]

The next subprogram is Smart Grid Research and Development. The goal of this subprogram is modernizing the electric grid by integrating digital technologies; this will enhance the reliability, security, and efficiency of the electric grid.[99] Smart Grid Research and Development issues solicitations to advance its goals.[100] Specific efforts include investigating data processing capabilities, the use of advanced components, and adapting the grid to accommodate distributed electricity generation.[101]

The Energy Storage subprogram seeks to develop utility-scale energy storage systems to counteract the fluctuating nature of electricity demand, including batteries, capacitors, flywheels, compressed air energy storage, and reverse-pumped hydropower.[102] The subprogram plans to conduct economic studies on the value of such systems.[103]

Finally, the Cyber Security for Energy Delivery Systems subprogram works to improve the cyber security of electricity infrastructure through testing and deployment of new technologies.[104] The development of the smart grid makes the infrastructure much more vulnerable to cyber attack.[105]

Permitting, Siting, and Analysis. The mission of the Permitting, Siting, and Analysis Program (PSA) is "to modernize the electric grid and to enhance the reliability of the energy infrastructure."[106] PSA issues permits for international transmission lines and helps to improve policies, state laws, and programs relating to siting of electric infrastructure.[107] The program also coordinates the federal authorizations and environmental reviews for transmission lines on federal lands, in an effort to streamline the process.[108]

Infrastructure Security and Energy Restoration. The Infrastructure Security and Energy Restoration Subprogram (ISER) coordinates national efforts to secure energy infrastructure against physical and cyber disruptions and quickly restore power when these disruptions occur.[109] ISER's methods include risk analysis, stakeholder staff training, and facilitating corroboration between government agencies and industry.[110] ISER also helps industries plan for and respond to power disruptions and has emergency support responsibilities.[111]

The Advanced Research Projects Agency

The Advanced Research Projects Agency–Energy, or "ARPA–E," is an agency within DOE. ARPA–E was established by the 2007 America COMPETES Act[112] and funded by the Recovery Act, which provided $400 million in stimulus funds.[113] The agency's purpose is to overcome long-term and high-risk technological barriers associated with developing new energy technologies.[114] ARPA–E will identify and promote nascent "transformational technologies" that have the potential to drastically alter the United States' energy infrastructure.[115] Accordingly, ARPA–E is often compared to its counterpart in the Department of Defense, the Defense Advanced Research Projects Agency, or DARPA. The White House proposed to appropriate $273 million for ARPA–E projects in 2011.[116]

Power Marketing Incentive Programs for Transmission

This section briefly describes federally organized power marketing entities' activities that provide incentives for the development and commercialization of clean energy generation and transmission. The section then discusses the entities' renewable energy incentives, with particular attention to new funding provided by the 2009 Recovery Act.

Background of WAPA, BPA, and TVA, and Renewable Energy Activities

The Western Area Power Administration (WAPA) and Bonneville Power Administration (BPA) are DOE agencies that market electricity generated by federal hydropower projects in the western United States. Several similar agencies also exist in the eastern United States,[117] but are not as significant. The Tennessee Valley Authority (TVA) also markets hydropower, but is quite different from the DOE agencies. TVA is a corporation Congress created in 1933 as part of the New Deal; the purpose was economic development for the Tennessee and Mississippi River Basins, including the construction of navigation infrastructure, flood control, and hydropower generation.[118]

WAPA covers roughly fifteen western states except for the Pacific Northwest region, which is covered by BPA.[119] WAPA has approximately seven hundred electricity customers, including municipalities, rural electric cooperatives, and governmental units.[120] BPA has approximately 352 customers.[121] WAPA's and BPA's primary purposes are providing energy transmission infrastructure and marketing hydropower.[122]

Both agencies also promote renewable energy other than hydropower. As part of this focus, WAPA plans to continue studying renewable resources transmission projects and renewable energy purchases to supplement its existing hydropower projects.[123] Accordingly, on August 11, 2009, WAPA issued a request for interest to purchase electrical energy.[124] Additionally, WAPA has a Renewable Resources Program focusing on nonhydropower generation and encourages voluntary use of renewables by its wholesale customers.[125]

BPA has made more progress than WAPA in promoting renewable energy other than hydropower. Currently, BPA's largest renewable energy commitment is connection of 2,500 megawatts of wind power to its grid, with plans to continue expanding.[126] TVA has implemented a "Green Power Switch" program to add non-hydro-renewable energy to its portfolio;[127] however, its green energy incentives are limited by its corporate charter.

Recovery Act Funding

The Recovery Act provided BPA and WAPA with $3.25 billion each in borrowing authority from the United States Treasury to fund new and upgraded transmission infrastructure to facilitate the delivery of renewable generation.[128] BPA expects to complete a new, 575 kilovolt transmission line in 2012 using Recovery Act money to connect wind energy sources to its grid.[129]

WAPA announced a Transmission Infrastructure Program in May 2009 to implement its Recovery Act financing authority.[130] WAPA plans to leverage this financing with private development money to build transmission lines that will likely connect new, renewable electricity generation facilities across the West.[131] The Recovery Act provisions for WAPA appear to allow WAPA to finance transmission lines outside its service area, so long as there is one terminus within the area.[132] Accordingly, WAPA has already announced public-private funding of the Montana-Alberta Tie Limited transmission project, which will facilitate expansion of renewable energy production.[133]

DOE National Laboratory Assistance and Partnerships

DOE National Laboratories are a system of facilities and laboratories overseen by DOE for the purpose of advancing science and technology and helping promote the economic and defensive national interests of the United States. Most of the DOE national laboratories are federally funded research and development centers,[134] owned by the federal government but administered, managed, operated, and staffed by private corporations and academic universities under contract to DOE.[135] One of the primary missions of the DOE national laboratory system is to facilitate the transfer of technology, including applied clean energy technology to the private sector for commercialization purposes.[136]

Each of the DOE national laboratories has a tech transfer office[137] that coordinates its relationships with private sector entities in technology transfer activities. The following are the types of relationships and mechanisms that national laboratories enter into to transfer clean energy technologies to the private sector:

1. *Cooperative Research and Development Agreements (CRADAs)*—legal agreements between government laboratories and nonfederal parties in which both participants agree to collaborate, by providing personnel, services, facilities, or

equipment and pool the results from a particular research and development program.[138] The nonfederal parties must provide funds or in-kind contributions (no direct funding is provided by the laboratory). Rights to inventions and other intellectual property are negotiated between the laboratory and participant, and certain data that are generated may be protected for up to five years.[139]

2. *Cost-Shared Contracts/Subcontracts*—collaboration, through procurement subcontract,[140] of mutual benefit to industry and to government. Often the government can agree not to disseminate commercially valuable data that is generated under a cost-shared contract for a limited period of time.

3. *Licensing Agreements*—the transfer of less than ownership rights in intellectual property, such as a patent or software copyright, to permit its use by the licensee. Licenses can be exclusive or for a specific field of use or for a specific geographical area. The potential licensee must present plans for commercialization. Information on department-owned patents and patent applications available for license for commercial use is available from the DOE Invention Licensing Home Page and its associated databases.

4. *User Facility Agreements*—arrangements permitting private parties to conduct research and development using unique facilities or equipment at a laboratory.[141] For proprietary R&D, the laboratory is paid for the full cost of the activity. If the work will be published, cost can be adjusted.

5. *Work-for-Others Agreements*—permit DOE laboratories and facilities to conduct work for other federal agencies and nonfederal entities (including industry partners and universities) on a reimbursable basis. Intellectual property rights generally belong to the user. The work must pertain to the mission of the laboratory or facility, may not conflict or interfere with DOE programs, and cannot directly compete with capabilities that are available in the private sector. Intellectual property rights generally belong to the sponsor.

U.S. Department of Agriculture Financial Assistance Programs for Renewable Energy Generation

USDA Rural Energy for America Program Grants

Section 9007 of the 2008 Farm Bill expanded the Rural Energy for America Program (REAP) of the U.S. Department of Agriculture (USDA) to further promote energy efficiency and renewable energy development for agricultural producers and rural small businesses.[142] REAP is administered through the USDA's Rural Business-Cooperative Service. REAP has three primary components: a grant program that covers the cost of energy audits and renewable energy development assistance, a financial assistance program for producers and small business owners in the form of grants for the purchase of renewable energy systems and energy efficiency improvements, and a loan guarantee program for the purchase of these same types of systems.[143] REAP grants are awarded on a competitive basis and can be up to 25 percent of total eligible project costs. Grants are limited to $500,000 for renewable energy systems and $250,000 for energy efficiency improvements. Grant requests as low as $2,500 for renewable energy systems and $1,500 for energy efficiency improvements will be considered. At least 20 percent of the grant funds awarded must be for grants of $20,000 or less.[144]

Applicants must have projects located in a rural area, be a small business,[145] and include all environmental review documents with supporting documentation in accordance with the National Environmental Policy Act. To be eligible for funding, a proposed renewable energy system project must meet each of the following criteria: the project (1) must be for the purpose of a renewable energy system, (2) must be for a precommercial or commercially available and replicable technology, (3) must have technical merit, as determined by the agency upon review, and (4) must be located in a rural area; (5) the applicant must be the owner and have financial and physical control of the project, and (6) the site must be under the applicant's control during the term of financing; and (7) there must be satisfactory sources of revenue to operate, maintain, and service debt over the life of the project. Adverse decisions on awards of REAP grants are appealable to USDA's National Appeals Division.[146]

USDA Repowering Assistance Program

Authorized under Title IX of the 2008 Farm Bill,[147] the Repowering Assistance Program encourages the use of biomass as a replacement fuel source for fossil fuel to power and heat biorefineries by providing payments to existing biorefineries to replace the use of fossil fuels in the facility as a power source.[148] The Repowering Assistance Program is also administered by the USDA's Rural Business-Cooperative Service but in conjunction with the Rural Utilities Service. The eligibility provisions of the statute simply require that the applicant demonstrate by means of an independent study that the renewable biomass system of the eligible biorefinery is feasible, taking into account the economic, technical, and environmental aspects of the system. As of February 2011, there is no requirement that the biorefinery be located in a rural area or that an applicant needs to be a citizen to be eligible for repowering assistance.[149] A key threshold eligibility factor is that the facility be an "eligible biorefinery" in existence as of the date of enactment of the 2008 Farm Bill.[150]

Bureau of Land Management Incentives

A major source of delay for renewable energy and transmission line projects on federal lands is permitting and environmental review. The U.S. Department of Interior's Bureau of Land Management (BLM) is the primary federal land holder for property favorable for energy development.[151] As of April 2011, BLM had 241 wind projects and 199 applications for solar projects by the private sector on BLM lands in various stages of processing.[152] Recognizing this bottleneck, BLM allocated $41 million of Recovery Act funds to speed the permitting and environmental review processes for 65 renewable energy and transmission projects on public land.[153] In February 2011, Secretary of the Interior Ken Salazar implemented a coordinated approach between BLM and the Fish and Wildlife Service (FWS) to fast track renewable energy projects on public lands by improving the siting and permitting process.[154] Two FWS documents were issued that were designed to provide agency employees, developers, and state organizations the information they need to make the best possible decisions in reviewing and selecting sites for utility-scale and community-scale wind energy facilities to avoid and minimize negative impacts to fish, wildlife, plants, and their habitats.[155] In conjunction, BLM issued its final policy memoranda to provide guidance to field managers in evaluating, screening, and processing applications for utility-scale wind and solar energy projects on BLM-managed lands. This field guidance clarifies and improves National Environmental Policy Act documentation; streamlines the project application review and approval process; and strengthens development plans and due diligence requirements.[156]

To help focus BLM's resources on the processing of wind, solar, and geothermal energy applications and permitting of electrical transmission facilities on public lands, the Department of Interior has established a network of Renewable Energy Coordination Offices[157] that include multidisciplinary BLM staff and resources from other federal and state agencies to assist in the processing of applications. BLM has also identified nearly 23 million acres of public land with solar energy potential in six southwestern states and more than 20 million acres of public land with wind energy potential in 11 western states. It has completed programmatic environmental impact studies for wind and geothermal development and is working on a programmatic environmental impact study (PEIS) for solar development. The Solar PEIS has preliminarily identified 24 Solar Energy Study Areas on BLM-administered land located in six western states.[158]

Incentive Programs for the Development and Commercialization of Renewable Transportation Fuels

DOE—Office of Biomass

DOE's Biomass Program[159] in EERE works with industry, academia, and DOE's national laboratory partners on research in biomass feedstocks and conversion technologies. Its research, development, and demonstration efforts are geared toward the development of integrated biorefineries into cost-competitive, high-performance biofuels, bioproducts, and biopower.

The Biomass Program is focusing its research and development efforts to ensure that cellulosic ethanol is cost competitive by 2012. Another major effort of the program is to further develop infrastructure and opportunities for market penetration of bio-based fuels and products.

The program's technology pathways with industry under financial assistance agreements target the following areas:[160] feedstocks barriers for biofuels development; biochemical conversion technologies; thermochemical conversion technologies; integrated biorefineries; and large-scale biopower.

The various subprogram of EERE's Biomass Program are Feedstock Infrastructure, Platforms Research and Development, and Utilization of Platform Outputs.

DOE Vehicle Technology Program Office

DOE's Vehicle Technologies Program, within EERE, provides financial assistance to the automotive and transportation infrastructure sectors to develop more energy-efficient and environmentally friendly highway transportation technologies (for both cars and trucks) to reduce petroleum use and greenhouse gas emissions. Every area of activity includes industrial participation. These activities include DOE's R&D investments in vehicle energy efficiency and petroleum displacement, and Recovery Act efforts to encourage manufacturing for advanced vehicles, demonstration of advanced vehicles, and improved fuels infrastructure and utilization. The program works to improve the technologies needed for more efficient highway vehicles, such as high-energy batteries, combustion processes, lighter materials, and improved electric drives.

The Recovery Act provided an infusion into this program that resulted in investments of up to $2.8 billion in advanced efficiency technologies for highway transportation. Recovery Act funds are expected to hasten the introduction of plug-in hybrid electric vehicles and other advanced efficiency technologies in cars and trucks, and to lower their cost by establishing manufacturing capacity for batteries and electric drives. Investments are being made in higher efficiency combustion engines, commercial vehicle efficiency, ethanol and biodiesel deployment, battery and electric drive manufacturing, and vehicle electrification deployment and infrastructure development. Funds are targeted to increase the use and lower the cost of vehicles with these improvements. Motor vehicles and transportation are also covered in chapter 14.

DOE/USDA Biomass Research and Development Initiative

Reauthorized under section 9008 of the 2008 Farm Bill,[161] the Biomass Research and Development Initiative extended the program originally created under the Biomass Research and Development Act of 2000 and amended by the Energy Policy Act of 2005. This is a joint DOE/USDA program that provides competitive grants, contracts, and financial assistance to eligible entities to carry out research, development, and demonstration of biofuels and bio-based products, and the methods, practices, and technologies for their production. USDA's Cooperative State Research, Education, and Extension Service and the DOE Office of Biomass Programs competitively award grants to eligible entities to research, develop, and demonstrate biomass projects. As amended by the 2008 Farm Bill, the three main Technical Areas are: (1) Feedstocks development, (2) Biofuels & biobased products development, and (3) Biofuels development analysis.[162] The program offers an annual funding opportunity announcement that is jointly managed, but lead administration rotates between the two agencies every other year. All eligible applications are evaluated in a joint USDA/DOE technical merit review process.[163]

USDA Bioenergy Program for Advanced Biofuels

The USDA's Bioenergy Program for Advanced Biofuels, as managed by the Rural Business-Cooperative Service, provides payments to eligible advanced biofuels producers in rural areas to support and ensure an expanding production of advanced biofuels.[164] The program authorizes USDA to enter into contracts with producers for payments based on the amount of biofuels produced from renewable biomass other than corn kernel starch.[165] Eligible examples include biofuels derived from cellulose, crop residue, animal, food and yard waste material, biogas (landfill and sewage waste treatment gas), vegetable oil and animal fat, and butanol. The producer payments are intended to help eligible producers support and ensure an expanded production of advanced biofuels as necessary steps toward meeting the nation's energy needs. The amount of each payment will depend on the number of eligible advanced biofuel producers participating in the program, the amount of advanced biofuels being produced by the advanced biofuel producer, and the amount of funds available during a given yearly funding cycle.[166] As of February 2011, eligible producers did not need to be located in a rural area and could be foreign owned.[167] Decisions concerning project funding are subject to USDA's appeal process.[168]

Biofuels are covered in more detail in chapter 19.

Energy Efficiency Financial Incentive Programs

DOE Weatherization Assistance Program

DOE's Weatherization Assistance Program,[169] administered out of the Weatherization and Intergovernmental Activities Program Office of EERE, is one of the largest and most technically advanced residential energy retrofit providers. Federal funds[170] are allocated on a formula block grant basis and awarded to states, U.S. territories, the District of Columbia, and Native American tribal governments to increase the energy efficiency of homes occupied by low-income families. These agencies, in turn, contract with almost nine hundred local governmental or nonprofit agencies to deliver weatherization services to low-income clients in their areas.[171] Weatherization service providers choose the best package of efficiency measures for each home based on a comprehensive computerized energy audit. Typical energy conservation measures include installing insulation, sealing ducts, tuning and repairing heating and cooling systems, mitigating air infiltration, and reducing electric baseload consumption. The consistent delivery of quality services is addressed through active state training and technical support programs. Grant-funded training allows for the introduction of advanced assessment and installation techniques and continuing professional development for workers.

The majority of weatherization funding is allocated to the states as operating funds for this purpose, i.e., for labor, materials, equipment, and administrative systems. The Recovery Act increased the percentage (approximately twice as much as previous years) of the total program funding allocated for state-based training and technical assistance to maintain a high standard of technology application, effectiveness, and results. Most training and technical assistance is performed at state and local levels.

DOE's State Energy Program

The State Energy Program (SEP), also administered out of the Weatherization and Intergovernmental Activities Program Office of EERE,[172] is intended to help states reduce energy use and cost, increase renewable energy capacity and production, and lessen dependence on foreign oil. The program provides technical and financial resources to help states develop and manage a variety of high-impact energy programs. Financial assistance is provided through formula grants and competitive clean energy project grants. States often combine many sources of funding for their projects, including DOE and private industry. These formula grants from DOE allow state energy offices the flexibility to develop energy projects focused on the buildings, electric power, industry, and/or transportation sectors, as well as crosscutting policy initiatives and public information campaigns.[173] SEP special competitive grants[174] allow DOE to target high-impact projects geared toward critical policy and regulatory changes, including the adoption of advanced building codes, prioritization of energy efficiency in resource planning, and decoupling of utility earnings from volumetric energy sales. A portion of program funding is used for (1) outreach and technical assistance to states, such as development of state and regional best practices; (2) innovative sustainable energy initiatives; and (3) performance management.

DOE's Energy Efficiency and Conservation Block Grant Program

The Energy Efficiency and Conservation Block Grant (EECBG) Program[175] provides funds to states, U.S. territories, counties, cities, and Indian tribes to reduce their energy use and fossil fuel emissions and improve energy efficiency in the transportation, buildings and other appropriate sectors. The Recovery Act appropriated $3.2 billion for the EECBG program, with $400 million to be awarded on a competitive basis to entities that are eligible to receive formula-based funds. In addition, Section 546 of the Energy Independence and Security Act (EISA) stipulates that 2 percent of total program funding is reserved for competitive awards to units of local government (including Indian tribes) that are ineligible to receive formula-based funds, and to consortia of these ineligible entities. The EECBG is modeled after the Community Development Block Grant program administered by the Department of Housing and Urban Development.

DOE anticipates that a total of up to $453.72 million will be available for competitive grants awarded through one Funding Opportunity Announcement (FOA) with two topic areas.[176] The eligible entities for up to $390.04 million available under Topic 1 are the same as for the formula EECBG program: states, U.S. territories, counties, cities, and Indian tribes. The eligible entities for up to $63.68 million available under Topic 2 are units of local government and Indian tribes that are not eligible for the direct formula grants. The goal of this competitive FOA is to stimulate activities that move beyond traditional public awareness campaigns, program maintenance, demonstration projects, and other "one-time" strategies and projects. DOE seeks to stimulate activities and investments that can (1) fundamentally and permanently transform energy markets in a way that makes energy efficiency and renewable energy the options of first choice and (2) sustain themselves beyond the grant monies and the grant period by designing a viable strategy for program sustainability into the overall program plan.

Energy Efficiency Programs for American Energy-Intensive Industries

Energy-intensive industries are severely constrained in their ability to invest in research and development (R&D) due to their low profit margins and inability to fully appropriate R&D benefits to their companies. R&D investments in energy-intensive industries have not kept pace with the rest of the economy.[177] Process technologies that use less energy per unit of output are logical investment opportunities for energy-intensive industries, but energy-intensive manufacturers are often unable to invest in energy-related process R&D without government assistance. DOE's Industrial Technologies Program Office (ITP) in EERE supports cost-shared R&D, through financial assistance agreements with industry partners, to address energy challenges that industries face, while fostering the adoption of advanced technologies and best energy management practices.[178] To achieve this, ITP supports R&D on efficient new technologies; promotes distributed generation and fuel and feedstock flexibility; supports the commercialization of emerging technologies; assists industrial facilities to access and use proven technologies, energy assessments, software tools, and other resources; and promotes a culture of energy efficiency and carbon management in industry.[179] Current funding for partnerships with industry is $96 million. ITP received $350 million in FY 2009 with the addition of Recovery Act funds.[180]

DOE's Building Efficiency Technology Program

Buildings account for more than 70 percent of the electric energy consumed in the United States and 38 percent of total U.S. carbon dioxide emissions.[181] The purpose of DOE's Office of Building Technology, also within EERE, is to foster development of energy-efficient technologies in the American building and residential sectors. The program achieves this through partnering with nonfederal entities to develop promising R&D of energy-efficient technologies; equipment standards and analysis; and technology validation and market introduction assistance. R&D activities research the most advanced energy efficiency technologies. Equipment Standards and Analysis activities eliminate the most inefficient existing technologies in the market by establishing new, and improving existing, energy efficiency standards based on technology and product advances that frequently include technology R&D. Validation activities catalyze the introduction of new advanced technologies, and the widespread use of highly efficient technologies already in the market frequently include technology R&D. Funding levels for this program as of 2011 are $222 million.

Federal Energy Savings Performance Contracting

As the largest consumer of energy in the United States, the federal government is required by Congress to reduce federal energy consumption costs.[182] One of the major tools at the federal government's disposal is the energy savings performance contract (ESPC).[183] These long-term federal procurement contracts, first authorized by Congress in 1985,[184] have begun to be used more often by the federal government to institute energy conservation measures at federal installations.[185] The ESPC allows federal agencies to waive the federal standard requirements for up-front capital funding of infrastructure projects and one-year federal contract financing[186] and enter into contracts for up to twenty-five years with energy service companies (ESCOs)[187] for the purpose of saving energy-consumption costs at federal installations. The energy savings that result from the installation and use of the equipment by the ESCO can be shared between the government and the ESCO. An ESPC is a partnership between a federal agency and an ESCO, where the ESCO conducts a comprehensive energy audit for the federal facility and identifies improvements to save energy. In consultation with the federal agency, the ESCO then designs and constructs a project, defined as an energy conservation measure, that meets the agency's needs. The critical factor in this type of contracting is that the ESCO arranges the necessary financing for the capital improvements to the agency site. The ESCO guarantees that the improvements will generate energy cost savings sufficient to pay for the project over the term of the contract. After the contract ends, all additional cost savings accrue to the agency.

The trend has been to create more flexibility in ESPC contracting. ESPCs now can be used for developing renewable energy generation projects at federal sites. In 2007, Congress provided the authority to sell or transfer energy generated on federal sites from renewable energy sources or cogeneration in excess of federal needs to utilities or nonfederal energy users in accordance with existing federal or state laws.[188] Congress also allowed the use of any combination of appropriated funds and private financing in federal ESPCs. In addition, DOE has been active in supporting greater flexibility by encouraging the use of "Super ESPCs."[189] These "umbrella" contracts allow agencies to undertake multiple energy projects under the same contract. Using a Super ESPC, an agency can bypass cumbersome procurement procedures and partner directly with an ESCO to develop an energy efficiency or renewable energy project. As a result, Super ESPCs are being used more frequently by federal agencies, and they have largely supplanted stand-alone ESPCs.[190]

Federal Housing Authority Energy Efficient Mortgage Program

Congress created Energy Efficient Mortgages (EEMs) as a five-state pilot program in the 1992 Energy Policy Act, to be implemented by the Department of Housing and Urban Development (HUD).[191] Three years later, HUD expanded EEMs as a national program.[192] An Energy Efficient Mortgage is a mortgage loan that is funded by a traditional lending institution and is insured by the Federal Housing Administration.[193]

The EEM program encourages borrowers to install energy efficiency improvements by allowing them to add the cost of energy efficiency improvements into their FHA-insured loan, possibly exceeding National Housing Act limits.[194] Borrowers do not have to qualify for the additional funds, and no additional down payment is required.[195] There are two loan programs through which borrowers can take advantage of EEMs. The first loan program is FHA's popular Section 203(b) Mortgage Insurance[196] for the initial purchase of one- to four-bedroom single-family homes.[197] Homes that qualify for a Section 203(b) loan are eligible for up to 96.5 percent financing,[198] and borrowers are able to fold the closing costs and mortgage insurance premiums into the mortgage.[199] With the EEM program, borrowers can add to their home mortgage 100 percent of the cost of their proposed energy efficiency improvements, subject to limits based on the house's value.[200]

The other way borrowers can take advantage of the EEM program is through an FHA Section 203(k) Rehabilitation loan.[201] Section 203(k) loans are designed to provide borrowers with financing to purchase and rehabilitate "fixer-upper" single-family properties.[202] Funding for energy efficiency improvements is subject to the same limitations as a Section 203(b) loan. Drawdowns on a rehabilitation loan occur as improvements are made.[203]

Federal Loan Guarantee Programs for Clean Energy Projects

Title XVII Loan Guarantee Program—New and Innovative Clean Energy Technology Projects

DOE's clean energy loan guarantee program, authorized under Title XVII of the Energy Policy Act of 2005[204] and administered by DOE's Loan Guarantee Program Office, encourages early commercial use of new or significantly improved technologies in energy projects. Section 1703 of the Act[205] authorizes DOE to provide loan guarantees for renewable energy generation and manufacturing systems, advanced nuclear generation facilities, coal gasification, carbon sequestration, energy efficiency, and many other types of clean energy projects that use new or significantly improved[206] technologies in commercial projects that avoid, reduce, or sequester air pollutants or anthropogenic emissions of greenhouse gases, and have a reasonable prospect of repayment. The initial government response to this program was slow, but it now forms the cornerstone of the Obama administration's efforts to commercialize clean energy technologies.[207]

Under Title XVII, the face value of any debt that is supported by a DOE loan guarantee cannot be more than 80 percent of the total cost of the project.[208] DOE will require that the project sponsor(s) provide "significant equity investment in the project."[209] While the statute[210] allows for either the borrower or the government, through a direct outlay of appropriations, to pay for the project's "credit subsidy cost,"[211] DOE has required the borrower, under the 1703 program, to pay for that cost directly before closing.[212] If DOE guarantees 100 percent of the loan amount,[213] the loan must be issued by the Federal Financing Bank, a unit of the U.S. Department of Treasury.[214] If the guarantee is less than 100 percent of the loan, it must be issued by an eligible lender.[215] The guarantee portion of the loan cannot be "stripped" from the nonguaranteed portion for subsequent syndication if the DOE guarantee is above 90 percent.[216] The term of the loan that is backed by a DOE guarantee is the lesser of thirty years or 90 percent of the projected useful life of the project.[217] DOE has the flexibility to determine on a project-by-project basis the scope of the collateral package and whether *pari passu* lending is in the best interest of the government.[218] An applicant under the DOE Program is required to pay substantial administrative fees prior to closing.[219]

DOE has employed a version of the "rolling application" process for submitting applications for loan guarantees. In its solicitations,[220] DOE establishes numerous "rounds" of application periods, together extending beyond one year.

Recovery Act Loan Guarantee Program

The Recovery Act, in adding a new § 1705 to Title XVII,[221] established a temporary loan guarantee program in DOE's existing Loan Guarantee Program Office for the rapid deployment of commercial-ready renewable energy and electric power transmission projects, as well as leading-edge biofuels projects. This new program, referred to as the Section 1705 Program, increases loan guarantee funding authority, expands on the type of projects eligible for loan guarantees, and provides more flexibility to overcome barriers of the existing DOE loan guarantee program.

The Recovery Act substantially expands the categories of projects eligible for DOE loan guarantees by opening this program up to commercial projects using existing technologies in the wind, solar, and geothermal sectors, as well as commercial projects that manufacture components related to renewable energy generation. Second, the law expands eligibility to electric power transmission systems, including upgrading and reconducting projects. Third, eligibility now extends to biofuels projects that are likely candidates for full commercial use as transportation fuels. However, due to internal DOE credit restraints, it is unlikely that DOE will issue loan guarantees for biorefineries. For all of these categories, the Recovery Act imposes two major conditions on all three new categories eligible for the loan guarantee program: (1) any eligible project must commence construction before September 30, 2011, and (2) such projects must comply with the Davis Bacon Act[222] in establishing wage rate requirements for federal-like construction projects. The previous program had no such limitations. Finally, The Recovery Act also waives the burdensome requirement that the borrowers pay with their own funds the credit subsidy cost of their projects. Of the $6 billion originally appropriated for this purpose under the Recovery Act, Congress subsequently stripped the Program of $2 billion in 2009 and another $1.5 billion in 2010 for use on other Recovery Act priorities.[223]

On October 4, 2009, DOE announced its Financial Institution Partnership Program (FIPP) in conjunction with the issuance of its solicitation under the Section 1705 Program. Under FIPP, the developer of an eligible project is required to seek project construction loans from eligible FIPP financial institutions. Those financial institutions will then apply directly to DOE to obtain a loan guarantee and assume some portion of risk in the project. DOE expects the lender to conduct the necessary credit approval activities incumbent to similar senior debt, limited recourse, energy project finance transactions. DOE believes that FIPP will allow the quick and prudent implementation of the Section 1705 Loan Guarantee Program by using the resources of existing private sector financial institutions that have experience in larger-scale energy project financings. Under FIPP, a DOE loan guarantee will cover only 80 percent of the maximum aggregate loan principal and interest during the loan term for a maximum guarantee of 64 percent of the project. The other limiting factor of the FIPP Program is that developers will not be able to take advantage of federal debt financing from the Federal Financing Bank (FFB). This differs from DOE's earlier solicitations for Section 1703 projects and Section 1705 transmission projects under which the DOE guarantee can cover 100 percent of the loan amount, if that loan is through the auspices of the FFB. (This could amount to 80 percent of the total project costs.)

Advanced Technology Vehicles Manufacturing Loan Program

The Advanced Technology Vehicles Manufacturing Program Loan Program (ATVM), established by the Energy Independence and Security Act of 2007,[224] consists of both grants and direct loans of up to $25 billion in loan authority[225] to support the development of advanced technology vehicles and associated components in the United States. The ATVM Loan Program, administered out of DOE's Loan Guarantee Program Office, evaluates the technical merit of the proposed advanced technology vehicles or qualifying components. Technical Program Factors such as economic development and diversity in technology, company, risk, and geographic location are also considered. In making loans to those manufacturers that have existing facilities, priority will be given to facilities that are oldest or have been in existence for at least twenty years, even if such facilities are idle at the time of application. The program aims to help revitalize the auto industry and encourage the manufacture of environmentally responsible products through providing growth capital in an economic downturn. The loans to eligible automobile manufacturers and component suppliers are for projects that reequip, expand, and establish manufacturing facilities in the United States[226] to produce light-duty vehicles and components for such vehicles, which provide meaningful improvements in fuel economy performance beyond certain specified levels.

Department of Agriculture Loan Guarantee Programs for Biofuels

USDA Biorefinery Assistance Loan Guarantee Program

Section 9003 of the Farm Bill of 2008 authorizes a USDA loan guarantee program for the development, construction, and retrofitting of commercial-scale biorefineries that convert renewable biomass to advanced biofuels and other bioproducts using eligible technology.[227] The program is administered through USDA's Rural Business-Cooperative Service.[228] The program targets emerging technologies that are being or can be adopted by a viable commercial-scale operation that produces advanced biofuel or other bioproducts. Eligible entities under the program include individuals, entities, Indian tribes, or units of state or local government, including corporations, farm cooperatives, farmer cooperative organizations, and associations of agricultural producers, national laboratories, institutions of higher education, rural electric cooperatives, public power entities, or consortia of any of those entities. As of March 2011, USDA has issued four loan guarantees under this program. The February 2011 Program Interim Final Rule clarifies the existing USDA practice of accepting bond financing as a basis for the guaranteed debt, but only when the bond financing flows through the existing USDA-approved system of traditional lender-based credit facilities; it also extends eligible projects beyond traditional rural areas and to concerns that are foreign owned.[229]

The loans guaranteed cannot be more than 80 percent of the total project costs, and the federal guarantee for some projects can be up to 90 percent of total principal and interest,[230] with the maximum loan guarantee amount capped at $250 million for any individual project. Completed applications must be submitted by the project lender and must contain documents that address critical review areas.[231] Guarantees are awarded based on a competitive scoring system that follows the review criteria established in program regulations,[232] including whether the applicant has established a market for the advanced biofuel produced, whether other similar facilities are located in the project area, whether the applicant proposes to work with producer associations or cooperatives, the rural character of the project site, and the level of local ownership proposed in the application. In FY 2011 USDA has made $463 million available to fund up to five additional biorefinery projects under this program.[233]

USDA Rural Energy for America Loan and Loan Guarantee Program

The REAP Loan and Guaranteed Loan Program encourages the commercial financing of renewable energy (bioenergy, geothermal, hydrogen, solar, wind, and hydropower) and energy efficiency projects.[234] The program is administered through the USDA Rural Development Agency's Rural Business-Cooperative Service.[235] Under this competitive loan guarantee program, project developers will work with local lenders, who in turn can apply to USDA Rural Development for a loan guarantee up to 85 percent of the loan amount.[236] The maximum loan amount for a guarantee is $25 million, and the guaranteed portion of the loan is capped at 60 percent for loans over $10 million.[237] The loan cannot be more than 75 percent of the total project cost of the system. The agency will assess a guarantee fee equal to 1 percent of the guaranteed amount, with an annual renewal fee of 0.25 percent of the guaranteed amount. The eligible applicants are agricultural producers and small rural businesses that are at least 51 percent owned by individuals who are either U.S. citizens or legal permanent residents. USDA requires applicants to provide cash equity commitments of 15 percent of total project costs for loans of $600,000 or less and 25 percent for loans greater than $600,000. Adverse decisions on awards of guarantees are appealable to USDA's National Appeals Division.[238]

Other Federal Financial Incentives for the Development of Clean Energy Technologies

Clean Renewable Energy Bonds (CREBs)

What Are CREBs?

Clean Energy Renewable Bonds (CREBs) were created under the Energy Tax Incentives Act of 2005[239] and codified as Section 54 of the Internal Revenue Code of 1986, as amended (the Code). CREBs serve as a financing tool for public entities comparable to the production tax credit available to private developers and investor-owned utilities under Code Section 45. Qualified public entities may issue CREBs to finance renewable energy projects with the federal government providing a tax credit to bondholders in lieu of interest payments from the issuer. Recent legislation allows the CREBs issuer to elect to receive a direct payment from the federal government equal to, and in lieu of, the tax credits otherwise available.[240] Initially, the CREBs program was funded with $800 million. This amount was increased to $1.2 billion by the Tax Relief and Health Care Act of 2006.[241] The Secretary of the Treasury (the Secretary) allocated the funds among qualified projects as it deemed appropriate, except that qualified governmental borrowers were not permitted to receive more than $750 million.[242]

Entities qualified to issue CREBs include mutual or cooperative electric companies, "clean renewable energy bond lenders" (such as the National Rural Utilities Cooperative Finance Corporation), and certain governmental bodies.[243] At least 95 percent of the proceeds of a CREBs issue must be used for capital expenditures incurred by qualified borrowers for qualified projects. Only governmental bodies and mutual or cooperative electric companies are qualified CREBs borrowers.[244] Projects that qualify for CREBs financing are those energy generation projects owned by a qualified borrower that would otherwise qualify for an energy production tax credit under Section 45, including facilities that generate electricity from renewable sources such as wind, solar, closed-loop biomass, open-loop biomass, geothermal, small irrigation, qualified hydropower, landfill gas, marine renewables, and trash combustion.[245]

The Internal Revenue Service (the IRS) issues guidance and solicits applications each time Congress makes a CREBs authorization.[246] Applicants are required to identify the relevant parties, explain the project in detail, and include certifications by an independent engineer on the project's viability as well as a description of plans to obtain all necessary federal, state, and local approvals for the project. On the date of issuance, a CREBs issuer must reasonably expect that (1) at least 95 percent of the proceeds of the issue will be spent for one or more qualified projects within five years,[247] (2) a binding commitment with a third party to spend at least 10 percent of the proceeds will be incurred within six months, and (3) such projects will be completed, and the proceeds of the issue will be spent, with diligence.[248]

How CREBs Work

CREBs issuers repay principal with level annualized payments over the entire term of the bond but do not pay interest to bondholders. Instead, the federal government directly provides a tax credit against a CREBs bondholder's income tax liability in lieu of interest payments from the issuer. The tax credit thereby shifts the cost to fund renewable energy power generation projects from the issuers to the federal government and reduces the costs of the debt. Since the CREBs tax credit is included in the holder's gross income, the value of the CREBs to a bondholder is equal to the amount of the credit less the tax payable on the credit.[249] CREBs design therefore differs significantly from tax-exempt municipal bonds, which require issuers to pay cash payments to bondholders that the federal government exempts from federal taxes.

This tax-exempt design allows bond issuers to offer bond rates that are lower than corporate bonds of a similar rating.

The maximum term for CREBs is set by the Secretary based on an estimate of the present value of the cost to repay 50 percent of the principal of the CREBs using a discount rate equal to the average annual interest rate of tax-exempt obligations with a term of at least ten years that are issued during that month.[250] Generally, the maximum term for CREBs has been between fourteen and fifteen years.

Effect of 2009 Recovery Act

In 2008, the Energy Improvement and Extension Act of 2008[251] (the Energy Act) authorized $800 million of funding for New Clean Renewable Energy Bonds (New CREBs) under Code § 54C and extended the issuance deadline for CREBs by one year to December 31, 2009.[252] The Recovery Act[253] tripled the New CREBs allocation to $2.4 billion. New CREBs in the amount of $2.2 billion were awarded on October 27, 2009, to over 805 recipients nationally.

All of the available proceeds from a New CREBs issuance must be used for capital expenditures incurred by governmental bodies, public power providers, or cooperative electric companies for one or more qualified renewable energy facilities.[254] A public power provider is a "State Utility" with a "Service Obligation" (as such terms are defined in Section 217 of the Federal Power Act).[255] Entities that qualified to issue CREBs may also issue New CREBs. In addition, any not-for-profit electric utility that has received a loan or loan guarantee under the Rural Electrification Act may issue New CREBs. Projects that qualify for New CREBs are those energy generation projects that would otherwise qualify for a production tax credit under Section 45 owned by a qualified borrower, except that New CREBs cannot be used to finance certain coal production facilities.[256]

One-third of the $2.4 billion allocation for New CREBs, or $800 million, was required to be allocated to each category of applicant: governmental bodies, cooperative electric utilities, and public power providers.[257] For government bodies and cooperatives, the Secretary awarded projects from smallest to largest until $800 million for each category was exhausted or all applications were granted.[258] However, for the public power providers category, the Secretary allocated funds without regard to project size such that each project received a pro rata share of the overall allocation of funds to this category based on the fraction of total amount requested for a project to the total amount requested for all public power providers' projects.[259] Projects that receive an allocation of New CREBs have three years to issue the bonds.[260]

There are several significant differences between CREBs and New CREBs. The IRS reduced the tax credit that is paid with respect to New CREBs so that New CREBs receive a tax credit equal to 70 percent of the amount that would otherwise be available.[261] However, the tax credit may be applied against both regular and alternative minimum tax liability.[262] Also, CREBs issuers repay principal using straight-line amortization, so that an investor receives tax credit on the full amount of the bond for the entire term. In contrast, borrowers of New CREBs are repaid the entire principal in a balloon payment at the bond's maturity. Credit rate methodology was also revised. In 2006 and 2007, the Secretary set CREBs credit rates based on the market rate for AA-rated corporate bonds. However, many municipalities had credit ratings below AA. For this reason and because many investors were unfamiliar with CREBs, many issuers had to discount or pay supplementary interest to investors. As a result, the credit rate for New CREBs is determined based on yield estimates on outstanding bonds with grade ratings between A and BBB for similar maturities.[263] In addition, in order to increase liquidity, investors can strip the tax credits from New CREBs principal payments and sell them separately. Finally, CREBs, like tax-exempt bonds, are subject to investment yield restrictions and certain arbitrage requirements under Code § 148. However, the Energy Act liberalized these arbitrage rules for New CREBs, allowing issuers to set aside project revenues in equal installments annually into a sinking fund in order to accumulate funds needed to pay CREBs when due.

CREBs were created to reduce the financing challenges for states and local government to finance renewable energy projects. The amended CREBs and New CREBs program rules are intended to further attract investors for such projects. Going one step further to reduce financing challenges, the Commerce, Justice, Science, and Related Agencies Appropriations Act of 2010 (the HIRE Act), enacted on March 19, 2010, allows issuers of qualified bonds, such as New CREBs issued after the bill's enactment, and qualified issuers to elect to receive a direct payment from the federal government equal to, and in lieu of, the amount of the federal tax credit that would otherwise be provided for the bonds to bondholders. Issuers electing to receive the payments directly from the Treasury will pay taxable interest to bondholders, and bondholders cannot claim a tax credit. However, by monetizing the tax credits into a direct payment to the issuer, the HIRE Act provides direct funding to issuers for qualified renewable energy projects and reduces the total amount of debt the issuer must incur to finance a qualified project.

Qualified Energy Conservation Bonds

The Energy Act also created a credit bond program for "qualified energy conservation bonds" (QECBs) under Code § 54D. Certain provisions were later amended by the Recovery Act. QECBs are issued by states and large local governments[264] to finance certain types of qualified energy conservation projects. Like CREBs and New CREBs, the federal government directly provides a tax credit against a QECBs holder's income tax liability in lieu of interest payments from the issuer. Also, the Hire Act applies to QECBs and allows issuers to elect to receive a direct payment instead of the federal government providing a tax credit to borrowers. A total of $3.2 billion was allocated among the states for QECBs in proportion to each state's population.[265]

All available project proceeds of a QECBs issue must be used for qualified conservation purposes.[266] Qualified conservation purposes include any of the following:

1. capital expenditures incurred for the purposes of—
   - reducing energy consumption in publicly owned buildings by at least 20 percent,

- implementing green community programs (including the use of loans, grants, or other repayment mechanisms to implement such programs),
- rural development involving the production of electricity from renewable energy resources, or
- any facility that qualified for production tax credits under Code § 45(d), except refined coal and Indian coal production facilities;

2. expenditures with respect to research facilities, and research grants, to support research in—
   - development of cellulosic ethanol or other nonfossil fuels,
   - technologies for the capture and sequestration of carbon dioxide produced through the use of fossil fuels,
   - increasing the efficiency of existing technologies for producing nonfossil fuels,
   - automobile battery technologies and other technologies to reduce fossil fuel consumption in transportation, or
   - technologies to reduce energy use in buildings;

3. mass commuting facilities and related facilities that reduce the consumption of energy, including expenditures to reduce pollution from vehicles used for mass commuting;

4. demonstration projects designed to promote the commercialization of—
   - green building technology,
   - conversion of agricultural waste for use in the production of fuel or otherwise,
   - advanced battery manufacturing technologies,
   - technologies to reduce peak use electricity, or
   - technologies for the capture and sequestration of carbon dioxide emitted form combusting fossil fuels in order to produce electricity; and

5. public education campaigns to promote energy efficiency.[267]

QECBs holders receive a tax credit on quarterly credit allowance dates. The annual tax credit with respect to QECBs is 70 percent of the amount otherwise determined for qualified tax credit bonds under Code § 54A.[268] Unlike CREBs and New CREBs, there is no concept of a "qualified borrower" for QECBs, and QECBs may be private activity bonds. However, no more than 29.9 percent of each allocation to a state or large local government may be issued as private activity bonds with proceeds loaned to a nongovernmental entity, and private activity bonds may be issued only to finance capital expenditures.[269]

Carbon Credits and State Incentive Programs

Carbon Credits

In the absence of mandatory federal regulation of greenhouse gas emissions, voluntary emissions trading markets as well as regional climate change programs arose to mitigate the growth in concentration of greenhouse gases. These regional programs are a source of potential financing for U.S. renewable and efficiency measures and have provided trading partners funding to reduce greenhouse gas emissions.

The Chicago Climate Exchange (CCX) led the voluntary-offset, emissions-trading market for all six greenhouse gases.[270] CCX was a self-regulated market whose private and public sector members entered into legally binding commitments to meet annual greenhouse gas emission reduction targets. Surplus reductions were sold or banked with CCX. Members who emitted more than their target emissions complied with their CCX commitment by purchasing offsets on the CCX platform. The purchase of offset contracts funded renewable energy projects, methane capture from coal mines, livestock operations, and landfills, as well as bio-sequestration projects such as reforestation and agricultural management measures.[271] In late 2010, CCX shut down its voluntary carbon trading market in the wake of the failure of federal cap-and-trade legislation.

Many states are active partners in regional measures to regulate and reduce greenhouse gas emissions. Since 2005, a majority of the states and Canadian provinces have joined regional greenhouse gas emission reduction initiatives such as the Regional Greenhouse Gas Initiative (RGGI),[272] the Western Climate Initiative (WCI),[273] and the Midwestern Regional Greenhouse Gas Reduction Accord (MRGGA).[274] RGGI became effective in January 2009 and generated $494 million from six auctions of carbon dioxide allowances in 2009; these funds have been distributed to the ten participating states, which have been using them primarily for energy conservation and renewable energy programs.[275] Hawaii,[276] California,[277] and Minnesota[278] have adopted economy-wide measures to reduce greenhouse gas emissions.[279] These state and regional cap-and-trade programs allow states to compete to reduce greenhouse gas emissions and earn funds to invest in energy efficiency and renewable energy technology, thereby funding the transition to cleaner energy production on a local level.

State Incentives

Types of Incentives

In addition to the federal incentives, a majority of states also provide various forms of financial and educational assistance to support clean energy and energy efficiency initiatives. These initiatives typically focus on providing financial incentives for end users to reduce energy consumption. This goal is accomplished through encouraging end users to participate in energy-efficient retrofits and behavior modification. Efforts such as these advance society toward an overall reduction in energy use as well as incorporating the use of clean energy. Other state policies also require utilities and other energy businesses to provide their own enticements to their customers for the integration of renewable energy and energy efficiency, such as through rebates or electric bill credits.

In contrast to federal government incentives for energy efficiency and renewable energy, the details of state incentive policies and the amount of enticements a state provides for clean energy or energy efficiency vary widely among states. Factors contributing to state incentives include the state's political, economic, social, and geographic climate and the funds a state may have for implementation of these programs through their own budget or from other sources, including the federal government.

Clean Energy Funds and System Benefit Charges

As of April 2010, at least eighteen states had "clean energy funds."[280] Clean energy funds differ from other types of state funds for renewable energy or energy efficiency initiatives. Most other funds, as discussed in more detail in other sections, come from state or federal appropriations, federal grants, state bonds, or in the form of some type of credit. Unlike these types of funds, clean energy funds are supported by additional charges or riders on public utility bills.[281] Some clean energy funds support renewable energy or energy efficiency; some support both. The advantage of these funds is that they do not come directly from the state budget and appropriations, although they do ultimately come from taxpayers (i.e., utility payers). The authority for these funds is typically provided through the state legislature or, in some cases, the state's electricity regulation agency. Although states pass legislation for funds with objectives tailored to the inherent needs and circumstances of the state, the general framework and mechanism for the clean energy funds remain similar.

In at least fourteen states, clean energy funds are derived in an inconspicuous manner through the imposition of system benefit charges (SBC), which are taxes (or surcharges) on utility consumption.[282] It is estimated that from 1998 to 2012, $3.5 billion will be collected to endow these clean energy funds. Most state funds only fund new projects to the exclusion of retrofitting existing projects; some will run indefinitely, and others have limited life spans.[283] Variety also exists in how the states administer and disburse these funds. Some use the state energy office, an executive branch agency, while other states use a quasi-public economic development authority, third-party nonprofits, local public utilities, or self-direction in a few instances.[284] Examples of certain successful clean energy or public benefit funds are described below.

As a leader for renewable energy end energy efficiency incentives, California passed legislation dating to 1996 in California's electricity-restricting legislation.[285] The legislation directed the state's three largest public utilities to impose a surcharge on its customers, based on usage.[286] The money collected by the surcharge would fund (1) cost-effective energy efficiency and conservation activities; (2) public interest research and development not adequately provided by competitive and regulated markets; and (3) in-state operation and development of existing and new and emerging renewable resource technologies.[287] Subsequent legislation extended the program and added more funds requirements.[288]

Illinois also established a similar public benefits fund mechanism for both energy efficiency and renewable energy in 1997. Like California, Illinois also engaged in a restricting legislation for the electric industry, which established a public benefits or clean energy fund.[289] The 1997 Illinois legislation called for each state-regulated public utility, electric cooperative, and municipal utility to assess a monthly "Renewable Energy Resources and Coal Technology Development Assistance Charge" on its customer accounts.[290] The legislation prescribes that 50 percent of the funds collected pursuant to the section shall be deposited in the "Renewable Energy Resources Trust Fund" and the other 50 percent to the "Coal Technology Development Assistance Fund" for various coal capturing, research, and safety initiatives.[291] Similarly, the same legislation created an "Energy Efficiency Trust Fund" to fund projects including energy efficiency upgrades for low-income residents, retrofits, appliance upgrades, and other energy efficiency initiatives.[292]

The state of New York also requires similar clean energy funds requirements. In a series of orders, the New York State Public Service Commission (PSC), the governing body for utilities in New York State, passed the system benefits charge (SBC) to support energy efficiency, education and outreach, research and development, and low-income energy assistance.[293] To support this SBC program, the state's public utilities collect funds from customers through a surcharge on customers' bills.[294] In December 2005, the PSC extended the SBC for an additional five years and increased the funding from approximately $150 million to $175 million.[295] The order requires that from 2006 to 2011, each utility submit to the New York State Energy Research & Development Authority (NYSERDA) a sum equal to 1.42 percent of the utility's 2004 revenue for the SBC.[296] This percentage may be adjusted slightly each year based on updated utility revenue.[297]

NYSERDA published a report in March 2010 discussing and evaluating the SBC for New York.[298] The report indicated that due to the SBC, significant progress has been made for low-income energy initiatives, research and development, and other energy efficiency and renewable energy initiatives.[299]

All states administering clean energy funds encompass the membership for Clean Energy States Alliance, a nonprofit organization.[300] According to its website, the Clean Energy States Alliance opines that states with clean energy funds will administer approximately $3.5 billion from these funds to promote renewable and clean energy over the next ten years.[301] Accordingly, clean energy funds will help support the implementation of clean energy technologies and renewable energy markets by investing funds obtained through the payment of utility bills.[302]

Incentives Directly from Utilities

Utility Rebate Programs

Regulated utilities offer generous rebate programs to install energy-efficient and weatherization devices or to curb the use of energy through other avenues. Additionally, to a lesser extent, utilities offer rebate incentives for the installation and use of renewable energy. These incentives are almost always driven by the utilities' own incentive or legislatively mandated requirement to do so. A popular driver for these utilities to offer such incentives derives from Demand Side Management (DSM) requirements. DSM refers to the measures utilities can or must take in order to reduce customers' energy consumption. Many utility commissions require DSM, and many utilities must file DSM plans for submission to and approval by their jurisdictional utility commission. DSM typically encompasses three main components: performance standards, technology standards, and information provision measures.[303] Performance standards set a target reduction in energy consumption and compel a party, via incentives, to meet that target.[304] Technology standards mandate a form of action on the utilities' part, such as "command and control" regulation.[305] Finally, information provision measures allow the dissemination of information to end users so they have the knowledge to reduce their energy consumption. Such measures often impose a duty on utilities to inform their customers about their energy consumption.[306] Additionally, increasing Renewable Portfolio Standards may trigger utilities to offer these incentives.[307]

Various states or state utility commissions require utilities to provide rebate incentives for their customers for energy efficiency process, whether a part of or distinct from DSM.[308] Many of these rebates apply to small-ticket items, such as the purchase of LED light bulbs, and to more substantial items such as energy audits, energy-efficient HVAC systems, and other pricey retrofits and renewable energy equipment.[309]

The California Public Utilities Commission created the Savings by Design program for new construction or major renovations in commercial and residential buildings. The program offers up to $150,000 in financial incentives for companies investing in energy efficiency designs and goals.[310] For example, Pacific Gas & Electric Company (PG&E) participates in this program and also offers a variety of rebate programs, including the Energy Savings Bid Program, which provides rebate incentives for electric or gas efficiency programs.[311] PG&E, like many other utilities, provides various rebates for purchasing energy-efficient appliances, HVAC systems, and other related products.[312]

Additionally, other large utilities in California, such as SoCal Gas and Silicon Valley Power, offer a variety of rebates for qualifying companies that participate in energy efficiency programs. For example, SoCal Gas offers a program under the moniker "Cash for Appliances," which provides rebates for their customers' purchase of energy-efficient gas appliances and efficiency improvements.[313] For Silicon Valley Power, the rebates are capped at a total of $600,000 and range from rebates for replacing washing machines and lights to simply buying a programmable thermostat.[314]

In New York, another large energy consumption state, customers of ConEd may receive a rebate of up to 70 percent of cost for installation of efficient lighting and HVAC equipment.[315] For smaller customers, ConEd provides free energy audits and small energy efficiency measures, along with rebates for additional upgrades.[316]

Utility rebate programs, such as the ones implemented in California and New York and other states, can provide results similar to programs directly funded and implemented by states and local governments. As of February 2011, at least twenty-four states had some form of a utility-sponsored rebate incentive for energy efficiency or renewable energy.[317] These programs increase the use of energy-efficient and renewable energy equipment and can also serve to educate consumers about energy use and waste.[318] Another benefit of decreased energy consumption by utility customers, particularly in high-energy-use periods, includes the diminished change of costly brownouts and blackouts. Further, incentives by the utility for energy-efficient measures may also enhance a utility's public image to its utility customers.

Net Metering Programs

Net metering is a term that refers to the practice that utilities will offset a customer's bill and provide payments for reverse metering due to the customer's use of renewable energy sources on their property. Although this may seem like an incentive provided by an energy consumer's utility, net metering is typically mandated by a state legislature.[319] The Energy Policy Act of 2005 required state public utility commissions to consider net metering standards for utilities to implement net metering services in their territories.[320]

Net metering is discussed in greater detail in chapter 9.

Notes

1. *See generally*, Government Accountability Office, Federal Assistance: Grants and Cooperative Agreements, *in* Principles of Federal Appropriations Law Vol. 2, at 10-1 *et seq.* (3d ed. 2006) [hereinafter *Red Book*].

2. There have been over twenty separate enactments of legislation since the 1970s, still operative, that establish federal research, development, demonstration, and commercialization programs for clean energy technologies. Some of the major pieces of these congressional enactments are, e.g., the Energy Policy Act of 1992, Pub. L. No.102-486; Energy Policy Act of 2005, Pub. L. No.109-2005; Energy Independence and Security Act of 2007, Pub. L. No.111-140; Energy Policy and Conservation Act, Pub. L. No. 94-163; National Energy Conservation Policy Act, Pub. L. No. 95-619. *See also* chapter 2, *supra*.

3. *See* John A. Herrick, *Federal Project Financing Incentives for Green Industries: Renewable Energy and Beyond*, 43 Nat. Resources J. 77, 83–98 (2003).

4. Generally, federal funds can only be disbursed to nonfederal entities through two separate transactional pathways: federal procurement contracts or federal financial assistance agreements. The correct legal instrument and pathway depend on what the purpose of the activity is and the relationship of the government to the participating nonfederal entity. If the principal purpose of the activity is to acquire (by purchase, lease, or barter) property or services for the direct benefit or use of the U.S. government, the proper instrument is a procurement contract. 31 U.S.C. § 6303. If the activity is to carry out a public purpose of support or stimulation authorized by law, the proper instrument is a financial assistance agreement. 31 U.S.C. §§ 6304, 6305. *See generally* Paul G. Dembling & Malcolm S. Mason, A.L.I/A.B.A., Essentials of Grant Practice Law (1991). Accordingly, this chapter will focus on federal financial assistance except for federal shared savings performance contracting, discussed below, which are procurement contracts because they satisfy a direct need of the federal government to obtain energy efficiencies on federal installations and buildings.

5. Pub. L. No. 95-224, 31 U.S.C. §§ 6301 *et seq.* The Act was the result of the 1972 report of the Commission on Government Procurement, 3 Report of the Commission on Government Procurement chs. 1–3 (Dec. 31, 1972), which found confusion both within and outside the government over federal agency use of grant relationships versus procurement relationships. The Act was an attempt to distinguish financial assistance from procurement contracts and to further refine the concept of assistance by clearly distinguishing grants from cooperative agreements.

6. 31 U.S.C.§ 6304.

7. 31 U.S.C. § 6305.

8. *Red Book*, *supra* note 1, at 10-17.

9. In most instances the Federal Acquisition Regulation, 48 C.F.R. pts. 1–53 [hereinafter FAR], which governs federal procurement, is not applicable to federal financial assistance. Each agency formulates a separate regulatory regime for its financial assistance agreements, subject to guidance provided in Office of Management and Budget Circulars, e.g., OMB Cir., A-122. For example, the Department of Energy's financial assistance regulations, which govern all of

U.S. Department of Energy's (DOE) grant and cooperative agreements, is found at 10 C.F.R. pt. 600 (2009). Those separate regulations in some instances do incorporate certain aspects of the FAR into financial assistance. A prime example is DOE incorporation of the FAR's pt. 31 allowable costs principles into its financial assistance agreements. *See* 10 C.F.R. pt. 600.317 (2009).

10. *Red Book*, *supra* note 1, at 10-6, et seq. The U.S. Government Accountability Office (GAO) states that:

> [I]t is clear that the many varied rules and principles of contract law will not be automatically applied to grants. Nevertheless, it is equally clear that the creation of a grant relationship results in certain legal obligations flowing in both directions (grantor and grantee) that will be enforceable by the application of some basic contract rules.

Red Book at 10-12, and cases cited therein.

11. *See generally id.* at 10-34 through 10-38.

12. Normally a categorical grant is a discretionary award of the federal government under a statutorily authorized program.

13. *Id.* at 10-60, 10-61.

14. For example, the U.S. Department of Energy's policy is to use a competitive, merit-based process in its discretionary grant programs: "It is DOE policy to use competition in the award of grants and cooperative agreements to the maximum extent feasible. This policy conforms to 31 U.S.C. § 6301(3), which encourages the use of competition in awarding all grants and cooperative agreements. Contracting Officers must use merit-based, competitive procedures to award grants and cooperative agreements to the maximum extent feasible." DOE, GUIDE TO FINANCIAL ASSISTANCE § 2.1.3 (June 2008), *available at* http://management.energy.gov/documents/GuidetoFinancialAssistance.pdf. *See also* 10 C.F.R. § 600.13 (2009).

15. 31 U.S.C. § 6301(3).

16. However, a few agencies do provide a forum for the protest of grant awards. *See, e.g.*, USDA, National Appeals Division, 7 C.F.R. pt. 11, subpart A.

17. Under various statutory and regulatory authorities, GAO has served for more than eighty years as an independent forum for the resolution of disputes (commonly referred to as bid protests) concerning the award of federal contracts.

18. *See Red Book*, *supra* note 1, at 10-26.

19. It is in this context that the remaining part of this section will discuss cooperative agreements as the financial assistance vehicle. However, this discussion would be applicable to grants awarded by the federal government as the legal principles between the two remain the same.

20. Section 988 of the Energy Policy Act 0f 2005, 42 U.S.C. § 16352, mandates nonfederal cost sharing on clean energy financial assistance agreements.

21. 42 U.S.C. § 16352(b). This cost-sharing maximum for DOE can be increased on a project-by-project basis if the Secretary of Energy determines it is "necessary and appropriate." *Id.*

22. 42 U.S.C. § 16352(c). This DOE maximum can be increased if the Secretary of Energy determines on a project-by-project basis if it is "necessary and appropriate" due to "any technological risks" relating to the project. *Id.*

23. In most instances, DOE will solicit projects in a particular category in a competitive process by making Funding Opportunity Announcements (FOA) for either research and development efforts or separate FOAs for demonstration and commercialization efforts. This allows projects within a specific technology area and the same stage development to compete for the DOE funding and be able to more accurately assess the financial role DOE will play in the project.

24. Pub. L. No. 91-190, 42 U.S.C. §§ 4321 et seq. NEPA requires federal agencies to assess the environmental impact of all major federal actions significantly affecting the quality of the human environment. There are three types of review under NEPA: categorical exclusions (CX), environmental assessments (EA), and environmental impact statements (EIS). DOE's NEPA implementing regulations, 10 C.F.R.§ 1021, specify actions that normally require an EIS or an EA, and actions that can be categorically excluded.

25. *See, e.g.*, Blue Ocean Preservation Soc'y v. Watkins, 745 F. Supp. 2d 1450 (D. Haw. 1991). *See generally* DANIEL MANDELKER, NEPA LAW AND LITIGATION § 8:20 (2d ed. 2009).

26. *Id.*

27. The Energy Policy Act of 2005 states the DOE "shall not require repayment of the federal share" under the financial assistance agreement. 42 U.S.C. § 16352(e). Federal tax treatment of the federal portion of the cost share is dependent on how the federal funds will be used in the project. As a general matter, if the federal funds are authorized to be used by a corporate recipient under the agreement as a contribution to capital, it will not be treated as income for tax purposes; if the funds are not so authorized, it will be taxed as income. IRC § 118(a), 26 U.S.C. § 118; *See* IRS Revenue Procedure 2010-20 (Mar. 10, 2010).

28. 10 C.F.R. pt. 600.321 (2010).

29. Section 1007 of the Energy Policy Act of 2005, 42 U.S.C. § 4256(g). This authority is subject to reauthorization in fiscal year 2011.

30. DOE has promulgated a new part to its Assistance Regulations, 10 C.F.R. pt. 603, "Technology Investment Agreements" (May 9, 2006), modeled after Defense Advanced Research Projects Agency's (DARPA) other transactions authority regulation, Defense Grant and Regulatory System, DoD 3210.6-R, pt. 37 (1998).

31. 42 U.S.C. § 4256(g).

32. Depending on the particular federal program, the borrower may be a traditional private lending institution, private individual, business entity, the federal government through the Federal Financing Bank, a state or local government, hedge funds, or a state economic development bonding organization or other debt-like providers.

33. 2 U.S.C. § 661a(3) defines loan guarantees as follows:

> The term "loan guarantee" means any guarantee, insurance, or other pledge with respect to the payment of all or a part of the principal or interest on any debt obligation of a non-Federal borrower to a non-Federal lender, but does not include the insurance of deposits, shares, or other withdrawable accounts in financial institutions.

34. *See* Herrick, *supra* note 3, at 79–84; *see also* Red Book, *supra* note 1, *Federal Assistance: Guaranteed and Insured Loans*, 11-1 through 11-5.

35. Energy Secretary Chu, in announcing the selection of the Executive Director of DOE's Loan Guarantee Program in 2009, stated: "The loan [guarantee] programs at DOE play a critical role in spurring investment in a clean energy economy, creating new jobs, and fighting carbon pollution," Press Release, Dep't of Energy, DOE Announces New Executive Director of Loan Guarantee Program (Nov. 10, 2009), http://www.energy.gov/news/8280.htm.

36. Enacted by section 13201(a) of the Omnibus Budget Reconciliation Act of 1990, Pub. L. No. 101-508, 104 Stat. 1388, 1388-609 (Nov. 5, 1990) (codified as an amendment to title V of the Congressional Budget Act at 2 U.S.C. §§ 661–661f).

37. *See* 2 U.S.C. § 661c(b). More specifically, the cost of a loan guarantee (the "credit subsidy cost") is the—

> net present value, at the time when the guaranteed loan is disbursed, of the following estimated cash flows:
>
> (i) payments by the Government to cover defaults and delinquencies, interest subsidies, or other payments; and (ii) payments to the Government including origination and other fees, penalties and recoveries; including the effects of changes in loan terms resulting from the exercise by the guaranteed lender of an option included in the loan guarantee contract, or by the borrower of an option included in the guaranteed loan contract.

Id. § 661a(5)(C).

38. Pub. L. No. 96-517 (codified at 35 U.S.C. §§ 200–212). Office of Management and Budget Circular A-124 provides guidance to federal agencies on the implementation of the Bayh-Dole Act. Part 27 of the Federal Acquisition Regulation (FAR), Patents, Data and Copyrights, incorporates Bayh-Dole requirements, when applicable, into federal procurement contracts, and 10 C.F.R. pt. 600.325 incorporates the Act into DOE financial assistance agreements and adopts the FAR provisions when applicable.

39. Section 3001(d) of Pub. L. No. 102-486, 42 U.S.C. § 13541(d), applying 15 U.S.C. § 3710a(c)(7)'s five-year data protection to renewable energy research development and demonstration financial assistance agreements.

40. *See* 10 C.F.R. § 600.325 (2009), setting out the federal intellectual property clauses for DOE financial assistance agreements.

41. *Subject invention* means any invention of the recipient [or sub-recipients] conceived or first actually reduced to practice in the performance of work under this award. Appendix A to subpart D of 10 C.F.R. pt. 600, Patent and Data Provisions.

42. *Id.* § (b).

43. *Id.* § (j).

44. A recipient is free to negotiate with the government a satisfactory U.S. preference clause that would give a recipient the ability to grant the exclusive right to use or sell the invention to a party who agrees to substantially manufacture the subject invention in the United States. The extent of this U.S. preference clause depends on the nature of the recipient (or sub-recipient). Generally, DOE requires that universities and nonprofits limit their grant of exclusive licenses to a party that agrees to substantially manufacture in the United States; that small businesses agree to substantially manufacture in the United States for those products derived from the subject invention that will be sold or used in the United States; and that large businesses will substantially manufacture any products from the subject invention that are used or sold in any country. This clause may be negotiable, with the federal government taking into account economic reality and the benefits of worldwide use of environmental technology. Presentation of Paul Gottlieb, DOE Asst. Gen. Counsel for Tech. Transfer, ARPA–E Webinar Briefing for Selectees (Oct. 28, 2009).

45. Background intellectual property of the recipient that was funded exclusively at private expense is defined as "limited rights data," which, if provided to the government under the assistance agreement, will be protected from disclosure. 10 C.F.R. pt. 600.325. *See* FAR pt. 27.404-2 (2010). If this data is considered trade secrets of the recipient, any disclosure by the federal agency will be treated as a violation of the Trade Secrets Act, 18 U.S.C. § 1905, with associated administrative and criminal sanctions to the individual employees who disclosed such information.

46. 42 U.S.C. § 13,541(d), applying 15 U.S.C. § 3710a(c)(7). This data is defined as "protected data" under the financial assistance agreement. In most cases university and nonprofit organizations will be expected by the government not to avail themselves of this protection.

47. U.S. Dep't of Energy, Office of Energy Efficiency & Renewable Energy, Fiscal Year 2010 Budget-in-Brief 3, *available at* http://www1.eere.energy.gov/ba/pba/pdfs/fy10_budget_brief.pdf [hereinafter *2010 Budget-in-Brief*].

48. H.R. Rep. No. 111-278, 111th Cong., 1st Sess., at 17 (2009), *available at* http://www.er.doe.gov/bes/archives/budget/FY10_Conf_HRpt_111_278.pdf [hereinafter *House Report*]. The White House's proposed 2011 budget increases EERE funding to $2.355 billion. Office of Management & Budget, Budget of the United States of America Fiscal Year 2011 Appendix, Detailed Budget Estimates, at 425, *available at* http://www.whitehouse.gov/omb/budget/fy2011/assets/doe.pdf [hereinafter *2011 Proposal*].

49. *See supra* note 14. Merit review means a thorough, consistent, and independent examination of applications based on preestablished criteria by persons who are independent of those submitting the application and who are knowledgeable in the field of endeavor for which assistance is requested. Merit review is often used in conjunction with program policy evaluation factors to provide a sound basis for selection decisions. Examples of program policy factors are: geographic distribution of awards; diversity in type and size of recipients; diversity of methods, approaches, or kinds of work; and selection of projects which are complementary to other DOE programs or projects. *See* Office of Procurement & Assistance Mgmt., Federal Financial Assistance Opportunities at the Department of Energy (Mar. 2003), http://management.energy.gov/documents/finassthowto5.pdf.

50. https://www.fbo.gov/.

51. http://www.grants.gov/.

52. https://www.fedconnect.net/FedConnect/.

53. *2010 Budget-in-Brief, supra* note 47, at 37.

54. *2010 Budget-in-Brief, supra* note 47, at 37.

55. *House Report, supra* note 48, at 103.

56. *See 2010 Budget-in-Brief, supra* note 47, at 37. The White House proposed $302 million for 2011. *2011 Proposal, supra* note 48, at 425.

57. *2010 Budget-in-Brief, supra* note 47, at 37; *see also* U.S. Dep't of Energy, Solar Energy Techs. Program, http://www1.eere.energy.gov/solar/photovoltaics_program.html.

58. *2010 Budget-in-Brief, supra* note 47, at 38.

59. *Id.*

60. *2010 Budget-in-Brief, supra* note 47, at 38.

61. *2010 Budget-in-Brief, supra* note 47, at 38. The Concentrating Solar subprogram sought a substantial increase over 2009 to fund solicitations, which Congress viewed favorably. *See* U.S. Dep't of Energy, FY 2010 Congressional Budget Request 31, 149 (May 2009) [hereinafter *DOE Detailed Budget*], *available at* http://www.cfo.doe.gov/budget/10budget/ Content/Volumes/Volume3.pdf; *House Report, supra* note 48, at 103.

62. *2010 Budget-in-Brief, supra* note 47, at 39.

63. *2010 Budget-in-Brief, supra* note 47, at 39.

64. *DOE Detailed Budget, supra* note 61, at 183.

65. *House Report, supra* note 48, at 103.

66. *2010 Budget-in-Brief, supra* note 47, at 49. The White House proposed $123 million for 2011. *2011 Proposal, supra* note 48, at 425.

67. *2010 Budget-in-Brief, supra* note 47, at 49.

68. *Id.*

69. For more information on CRADAs, see *infra* this chapter.

70. *DOE Detailed Budget, supra* note 61, at 197.

71. *2010 Budget-in-Brief, supra* note 47, at 50; *DOE Detailed Budget, supra* note 61, at 198.

72. *2010 Budget-in-Brief, supra* note 47, at 50.

73. *DOE Detailed Budget, supra* note 61, at 198.

74. *See id.*; *2010 Budget-in-Brief, supra* note 47, at 49.

75. *DOE Detailed Budget, supra* note 61, at 202; *2010 Budget-in-Brief, supra* note 47, at 51.

76. *DOE Detailed Budget, supra* note 61, at 207.

77. *2010 Budget-in-Brief, supra* note 47, at 31; *House Report, supra* note 48, at 103. The White House proposed $55 million for 2011. *2011 Proposal, supra* note 48, at 425.

78. *2010 Budget-in-Brief, supra* note 47, at 31.

79. *Id.*

80. *2010 Budget-in-Brief, supra* note 47, at 32.

81. *DOE Detailed Budget, supra* note 61, at 213.

82. *DOE Detailed Budget, supra* note 61, at 63.

83. *DOE Detailed Budget, supra* note 61, at 61–63.

84. *House Report, supra* note 48, at 102. The White House proposed $137 million for 2011. *2011 Proposal, supra* note 48, at 425.

85. *See* EERA, Fuel Cell Technologies Program, Program Areas, http://www1.eere .energy.gov/hydrogenandfuelcells/program_areas.html.

86. U.S. Dep't of Energy, FY 2011 Congressional Budget Request 53 (Feb. 2010), *available at* http://www.cfo.doe.gov/budget/11budget/Content/Volume%203.pdf.

87. *See DOE Detailed Budget, supra* note 61, at 90.

88. *See DOE Detailed Budget, supra* note 61, at 88.

89. *See DOE Detailed Budget, supra* note 61, at 85, 92.

90. *See DOE Detailed Budget, supra* note 61, at 470.

91. *House Report, supra* note 48, at 18. The White House's proposed 2011 budget increased OE funding to $185.9 million. *2011 Proposal, supra* note 48, at 424.

92. *DOE Detailed Budget, supra* note 61 at 471.

93. *Id.*

94. *Id.*

95. *Id.* at 485.

96. FY 2011 Congressional Budget Request, *supra* note 86; Budget Highlights 32 (2010), *available at* http://www.cfo.doe.gov/budget/11budget/Content/FY2011Highlights.pdf.

97. *DOE Detailed Budget*, *supra* note 61, at 493.

98. *Id.* at 494.

99. *Id.* at 498.

100. *See id.* at 500, 504.

101. *Id.* at 501–02.

102. *DOE Detailed Budget*, *supra* note 61, at 505–06.

103. *Id.* at 507–08.

104. *Id.* at 509.

105. *Id.*

106. *Id.* at 534.

107. *Id.*

108. *Id.*

109. *DOE Detailed Budget*, *supra* note 61, at 538.

110. *Id.* at 538–40.

111. *Id.* at 540.

112. America COMPETES Act, Pub. L. No. 110-69, § 5012, 121 Stat. 621 (2007).

113. American Recovery and Reinvestment Act of 2009, Pub. L. No. 111-5, 123 Stat. 140 (2009).

114. *DOE Detailed Budget*, *supra* note 61, at 560.

115. *DOE Detailed Budget*, *supra* note 61, at 561.

116. *2011 Proposal*, supra note 48, at 421.

117. W. Area Power Admin., Power Marketing Administrations, http://www.wapa.gov/regions/pmadmap.htm.

118. *See* Tennessee Valley Authority Act, Pub. Law. No. 73-17, 48 Stat. 58, 59 (1933).

119. W. Area Power Admin., Power Marketing Administrations, http://www.wapa.gov/regions/pmadmap.htm.

120. W. Area Power Admin., 2009 Strategic Plan: Overview (2009), *available at* http://www.wapa.gov/newsroom/pdf/StrategicPlan09.pdf.

121. Bonneville Power Admin., 2008 BPA Facts (2009), *available at* http://www.bpa.gov/corporate/about_BPA/Facts/FactDocs/BPA_Facts_2008.pdf.

122. *Id.*; W. Area Power Admin., 2009 Strategic Plan Overview 2–5 (2009), *available at* http://www.wapa.gov/newsroom/pdf/StrategicPlan09.pdf.

123. *Id.* at 4.

124. Request for Interest for Purchase of Long-Term Firm Electrical Energy With Capacity or Non-Firm Electrical Energy, 74 Fed. Reg. 153, 40,182 (Aug. 11, 2009).

125. W. Area Power Admin., Renewable Resources Program, http://www.wapa.gov/es/renewables/default.htm.

126. Bonneville Power Admin., Wind Power, http://www.bpa.gov/corporate/WindPower/index.cfm. *See also* Bonneville Power Admin, How BPA Supports Wind Power in the Pacific Northwest (Mar. 2009), *available at* http://www.bpa.gov/corporate/pubs/fact_sheets/09fs/BPA_supports_wind_power_for_the_Pacific_Northwest_-_Mar_2009.pdf.

127. *See* Tenn. Valley Auth., Green Power Switch, http://www.tva.com/greenpowerswitch/index.htm.

128. American Recovery and Reinvestment Act of 2009, Pub. L. No. 111-5, 123 Stat. 140-41, § 401-02 (2009).

129. Press Release, Dep't of Energy, Secretary Chu Announces Progress on BPA Recovery Act Project (Aug. 10, 2009), *available at* http://www.energy.gov/news/7784.htm.

130. Western Area Power Administration Transmission Infrastructure Program, 74 Fed. Reg. 92, 22,732 (May 14, 2009).

131. *Id.* at 22,737.

132. *See* American Recovery and Reinvestment Act of 2009, Pub. L. No. 111-5, 123 Stat. 141, § 402 (2009).

133. Press Release, Dep't of Energy, Department of Energy Announces Start of Western Area Power Administration Recovery Act Project (Sept. 16, 2009), *available at* http://www .energy.gov/8017.htm.

134. Federal-funded research and development centers (FFRDCs) are government contractors who are given special status in the federal procurements system. In order to accomplish their long-term research and development responsibilities to the federal government, FFRDCs have access to government resources beyond that which is common to the normal government contractor. In consideration of this special access, FFRDCs are held to a higher standard in organizational conflicts of interest and ethics in their responsibilities to the government and to maintain currency and objectivity in its fields of expertise. FAR pt. 35.017(a).

135. DOE National Laboratories Administered by for-profit industrial firms:
- Idaho National Laboratory, administered by Battelle Energy Alliance, LLC, Idaho Falls, ID
- Lawrence Livermore National Laboratory, administered by Lawrence Livermore National Security, LLC, Livermore, CA
- Los Alamos National Laboratory, administered by Los Alamos National Security LLC, Los Alamos, NM
- Sandia National Laboratories, administered by Sandia Corporation, a subsidiary of Lockheed Martin, Albuquerque, NM
- Savannah River National Laboratory, administered by Savannah River Nuclear Solutions, LLC, a Fluor Daniel Partnership, Aiken, SC

DOE National Laboratories Administered by universities and colleges:
- Ames Laboratory, administered by Iowa State University of Science and Technology, Ames, IA
- Argonne National Laboratory, administered by UChicago Argonne, LLC, Argonne, IL
- Ernest Orlando Lawrence Berkeley National Laboratory, administered by University of California, Berkeley, CA
- Fermi National Accelerator Laboratory, administered by Universities Research Association, Inc., Batavia, IL
- Princeton Plasma Physics Laboratory, administered by Princeton University, Princeton, NJ
- Stanford Linear Accelerator Center, administered by Stanford University, Stanford, CA
- Thomas Jefferson National Accelerator Facility, administered by Southeastern Universities Research Association, Inc, Newport News, VA

DOE National Laboratories Administered by other nonprofit institutions:
- Brookhaven National Laboratory, administered by Brookhaven Science Associates, Inc, Upton, Long Island, NY
- National Renewable Energy Laboratory, administered by Midwest Research Institute; Battelle Memorial Institute; Bechtel National, Inc, Golden, CO
- Oak Ridge National Laboratory, administered by UT-Battelle, LLC, Oak Ridge, TN
- Pacific Northwest National Laboratory, administered by Battelle Memorial Institute, Richland, WA

136. *See* Title X of the Energy Policy Act of 2005, Pub. L. No. 109-58, 42 U.S.C. §§ 16,391, 16,392.

137. For web access to each laboratory technology transfer office, see http://www.er.doe .gov/Technology_Transfer/DOE_national_labs.htm.

138. CRADAs were authorized by the Federal Technology Transfer Act, Pub. L. No. 99-502, 15 U.S.C.§ 3710a(a).

139. 15 U.S.C. § 3710a(c)(7).

140. This "subcontract" is a cost-sharing contract between the private entity and the operator of the national laboratory that is entered into under authority of the DOE management and

operating contract with the operator. In this context, it is viewed as a subcontract of the DOE laboratory management contract.

141. Many specialized centers of excellence exist at DOE's laboratories and facilities. The laboratories have capabilities in state-of-the-art instrumentation for detection and measurement and analysis of a wide range of physics and atomic and nuclear science. Expertise to support innovative efforts exists in advanced materials, precision engineering, nano-technology and microfabrication, nondestructive evaluation, laser sciences, adaptive optics, chemical and biological and photon processes, healthcare and medical research, environmental and energy missions, and high-performance scientific computing. For a list of national laboratory user facilities, see DOE, Access to High Technology User Facilities at DOE National Laboratories, http://www.gc.doe.gov/1002.htm.

142. Pub. L. No. 110-234, § 9007, 122 Stat. 923, 1315–1318 (2008), 7 U.S.C. § 8107. The program regulations are at 7 C.F.R. pt. 4280, subpt. B.

143. 7 U.S.C. § 8107(c). For program specifics, see http://www.rurdev.usda.gov/rbs/busp/REAPEA.htm. The REAP loan guarantee program is discussed later in this chapter.

144. Specifics of funding and application procedures are provided by periodic Notices of Solicitation of Applications (NOSA). The current Notice was issued in 2010, Notice of Solicitation of Applications for Inviting Applications for Renewable Energy Systems and Energy Efficiency Improvements, 75 Fed. Reg. 21,584 (April 26, 2010).

145. 7 C.F.R. § 4280.108(c). A rural area is defined as any area other than a city or town of 50,000 or more and the surrounding urbanized area. 7 C.F.R. § 4280.103. The REAP small business standard adopts the North American Industry Classification System set forth in the Small Business Administration's regulations at 13 C.F.R. pt. 121. 7 C.F.R. § 4280.108(f).

146. 7 C.F.R. § 4280.105; appeal procedures can be found at 7 C.F.R. pt. 11.

147. Pub. L. No. 110-234, § 9004, 122 Stat. 923, 1313–1314 (2008), 7 U.S.C. § 8104. Program specifics can be found at 7 C.F.R. pt. 4288.

148. The program awarded $20 million in funds in FY 2009 and $28 million in FY 2010. In March 2011, $25 million was made available to this program for financial assistance. Notice of Funding Availability for Repowering Assistance Payments to Eligible Biorefineries, 76 Fed. Reg. 13,349 (Mar. 11, 2011).

149. See Repowering Assistance Payments to Eligible Biorefineries, 76 Fed. Reg. 7916 (Feb. 11, 2011).

150. The term "biorefinery" means a facility (including equipment and processes) that (A) converts renewable biomass into biofuels and biobased products; and (B) may produce electricity. 7 U.S.C. § 8101(7). The Notice of Funding Availability for Repowering Assistance Payments to Eligible Biorefineries, 74 Fed. Reg. 28,009 (June 12, 2009), further defines a biorefinery as a "producer, whose primary production is liquid transportation biofuels, that meets all requirements of this program. The biorefinery must have been in existence on or before June 18, 2008." 74 Fed. Reg. at 28,011.

151. BLM's website describes the wind, solar, geothermal, biomass resources and transmission corridors under BLM's control. See http://www.blm.gov/wo/st/en/prog/energy/renewable_energy.html.

152. Press Release, Bureau of Land Management, Secretary Salazar, Senator Reid Announce "Fast-Track" Initiatives for Solar Energy Development on Western Lands (June 29, 2009), http://www.blm.gov/wo/st/en/info/newsroom/2009/june/NR_0629_2009.html.

153. See http://recovery.doi.gov/press/bureaus/bureau-of-land-management/bureau-of-land-management-renewable-energy-authorization/.

154. Press Release, Department of Interior, Salazar Announces Additional Steps Toward Smarter Development of Renewable Energy on U.S. Public Lands (Feb. 8, 2011), http://www.doi.gov/news/pressreleases/Salazar-Announces-Additional-Steps-toward-Smarter-Development-of-Renewable-Energy-on-US-Public-Lands.cfm.

155. Draft Land-Based Wind Energy Guidelines, 76 Fed. Reg. 9590 (Feb. 18, 2011); Draft Eagle Conservation Plan Guidance, 76 Fed. Reg. 9529 (Feb. 18, 2011).

156. The BLM policy is set forth in three Instruction Memoranda dated Feb. 7, 2011: NEPA Compliance for Utility Scale Renewable Energy Right-of-Way Authorizations, No. 2011-059, *available at* http://blm.gov/yl5c; Solar and Wind Energy Applications: Due Diligence, No. 2011-060, *available at* http://blm.gov/zl5c; and Solar and Wind Energy Applications: Pre-Application Screening, No. 2011-061, *available at* http://blm.gov/xl5c.

157. As of 2010, BLM has established Renewable Energy Coordination Offices in California, Nevada, Arizona, and Wyoming, where the majority of the existing workload for renewable energy applications and projects is currently located. *See* Press Release, Department of Interior, Secretary Salazar, Director Abbey Open Renewable Energy Coordination Office in California to Speed Project Processing, http://www.doi.gov/news/pressreleases/2009_10_09_releaseC.cfm.

158. For information on the ongoing Solar PEIS process, visit http://solareis.anl.gov/.

159. The DOE Biomass Program was appropriated almost $1 billion in funds for R&D activities in fiscal year 2009, of which $777 million was funds derived from the Recovery Act. Its 2010 funding is $220 million, and it has requested $220 million for fiscal year 2011. *See* FY 2011 CONGRESSIONAL BUDGET REQUEST, *supra* note 86, at 97.

160. *Id.* at 105.

161. Section 9008(e) of Pub. L. No. 110-234, 122 Stat. 1320–1324 (2008), 7 U.S.C. § 8108(e).

162. 7 U.S.C. § 8108(e)(3).

163. Applicants must clearly demonstrate the value chain element they intend to focus on and specify whether the project is conducting research or a demonstration. The value chain can be characterized as consisting of the following elements: feedstock development and growth; feedstock harvesting and preparation; feedstock logistics and transportation; feedstock storage and handling; biomass preprocessing (as appropriate); biomass conversion; production of biofuels/bioenergy/bio-based products; product logistics and handling; and product delivery and distribution.

164. Pub. L. No. 110-234, § 9005, 122 Stat. 923, 1314 (2008), 7 U.S.C. § 8105.

165. The program rules are found at 7 C.F.R. pt. 4288 subpt. B, as amended in February 11, 2011. Additional proposal and funding information is provided in periodic Notice of Proposals. *See, e.g.*, Notice of Contract Proposal for Payments to Eligible Advanced Biofuel Producers, 76 Fed. Reg. 13,345 (Mar. 11, 2011). The Bioenergy Program for Advanced Biofuels guidelines are found at 7 C.F.R. pt. 4288 subpt. A.

166. The program received $80 million in FY 2010, $85 million in FY 2011, and is expected to receive $105 million in FY 2012. 7 U.S.C. § 8105; *see also* 7 U.S.C. § 8105(g).

167. 7 C.F.R. § 4288.110.

168. 7 C.F.R. § 4288.3.

169. Weatherization grants were first authorized under Title IV of the Energy Conservation in Existing Buildings Act of 1976, Pub. L. No. 94-385. The Weatherization Grant Program operates under regulations found at 10 C.F.R. pt. 440 (2009).

170. Recent funding for the weatherization program is as follows: FY 2009: $450 million; Recovery Act funding (FY 2009): $4.977 billion; FY 2010: $210 million; FY 2011 budget request: $300 million. DEPARTMENT OF ENERGY, FY 2011 CONGRESSIONAL BUDGET REQUEST, ENERGY EFFICIENCY AND RENEWABLE ENERGY, vol. II, 425 (2010). The FY 2011 target is to weatherize 33,484 low-income homes. *Id.*

171. *Id.* at 439.

172. The SEP was authorized by the Energy Policy and Conservation Act, Pub. L. No. 94-163, 42 U.S.C. § 7101 et seq. and operates under a regulation found at 10 C.F.R. pt. 420 (2009).

173. SEP formula grants totaled $25 million in 2010 and the same amount will be allotted in 2011. *See* FY 2011 CONGRESSIONAL BUDGET REQUEST, *supra* note 170, at 442.

174. SEP competitive grants to states totaled $25 million in FY 2010, and $37.5 million is planned for FY 2011. The most recent solicitation cycle (FY 2008) resulted in the award of $6.6 million in competitive grants for fifteen state-level projects, nine of which focused on developing policy and regulations to support gigawatt-scale clean energy capacity, six of which focused on developing advanced building codes. Future areas of interest includes encouraging:

(1) states and utilities to improve energy efficiency and renewable energy deployment; and (2) optimization of state energy planning and protocols. *Id.*

175. The current EECBG was authorized in Title V, Subtitle E of the Energy Independence and Security Act of 2007, Pub. Law No. 110-140.

176. Topic 1, the Retrofit Ramp-up Program, provides up to $390.04 million for programs of $5 to $75 million for eight to twenty awards. Topic 2, The General Innovation Fund, is for competitive grants that are reserved for units of local government and state-recognized tribes not eligible for direct formula grants, as per EISA 2007 requirements. Topic 2 provides up to $63.68 million (approximately 2 percent of $3.2 billion for projects of $1 to $5 million) for fifteen to sixty awards. *See* DOE FUNDING OPPORTUNITY ANNOUNCEMENT, DE-FOA-0000148 (Sept. 19, 2009).

177. From 1994 to 2003, R&D investments for energy-intensive industries grew by only 1.3 percent per year, compared to 4.4 percent per year for all of manufacturing. As a result, the portion of total manufacturing R&D contributed by energy-intensive industries fell from 13 percent to 10 percent. U.S. DEP'T OF ENERGY, OFFICE OF INDUSTRIAL TECHNOLOGIES.

178. ITP partnerships with key high energy use industry groups and companies support the goal of Section 106 of the Energy Policy Act of 2005 of achieving a 25 percent reduction in United States industrial energy intensity by 2017.

179. Recovery Act funding within ITP has helped to stimulate the economy and create and retain jobs through Combined Heat and Power, District Energy Systems, Waste Heat Recovery, Efficient Industrial Equipment, Information Technology Equipment Efficiency, and Pre-commercial Technology Demonstration for Information and Communication Technology Systems projects.

180. ITPs budget request for 2011 is for $100 million. DEPARTMENT OF ENERGY, FY 2011 CONGRESSIONAL BUDGET REQUEST, ENERGY EFFICIENCY AND RENEWABLE ENERGY 341 (2010).

181. U.S. DEP'T OF ENERGY, ENERGY EFFICIENCY & RENEWABLE ENERGY, 2009 BUILDINGS ENERGY DATABOOK (Nov. 2009), *available at http://*buildingsdatabook.eren.doe.gov/Default .aspx.

182. *See, e.g.,* National Energy Conservation Policy Act of 1978, Pub. L. No. 95-619 (codified as amended at 42 U.S.C. §§ 8201–8284 and in scattered sections of 12, 15, & 42 U.S.C.).

183. *See* 10 C.F.R.§ 436.34 (2009).

184. Title VIII of the National Energy Conservation Policy Act, as amended by the Consolidated Omnibus Budget Reconciliation Act of 1985, Pub. L. No. 99-272, § 7201, 100 Stat. 82, 142–143 (1986) (codified at 42 U.S.C. §§ 8260, 8287 (2000)); Energy Policy Act of 1992, Pub. L. No. 102-486, § 155, 106 Stat. 2776, 2852–2855; Energy Independence and Security Act of 2007, Pub. L. 110-140, §§ 511–518, 42 U.S.C. § 8287. *See generally* Herrick, *supra* note 3, at 96–98. For other types of ESPCs see chapter 6, *supra.* Before the 1992 amendment, these contracts were called "shared energy savings contracts."

185. Approximately $2.3 billion has been invested in federal facilities through ESPCs, saving more than 18 trillion BTU annually, equivalent to the energy used by a city of more than five hundred thousand people. DOE estimates that energy cost savings of $7.1 billion for the federal government ($5.7 billion goes to finance project investments) are due to the implementation of ESPCs. More than 460 ESPC projects have been awarded by nineteen different federal agencies in fourteen states. See ESPC QUICK FACTS at DOE Federal Energy Management Program web page, http://www1.eere.energy.gov/femp/financing/espcs.html.

186. An agency does not need a specific appropriation to cover capital costs associated with the contract activity, or specific statutory authority to contract beyond one year, to enter into an ESPC. As such, ESPCs are exempted from the federal Antideficiency Act, 31 U.S.C.§ 1342. *See Herrick, supra* note 3, at 96–98.

187. See chapter 6, *supra.* ESCOs develop, install, and finance projects designed to improve energy efficiency and reduce operation and maintenance (O&M) costs for their customers' facilities. ESCOs generally act as project developers for a wide range of tasks and assume the technical and performance risk associated with the project.

188. Pub. L. No. 110-140, §§ 512, 513.

189. Under Super ESPCs, DOE, through its Federal Energy Management Program Office, has already completed the Federal Acquisition Regulations procurement process, in compliance with all necessary requirements, and awarded contracts to selected ESCOs, who are then prequalified to undertake specific task orders. In much less time than it takes to develop a stand-alone ESPC, a federal site can implement a Super ESPC delivery order project and begin to realize energy and cost savings.

190. DOE has established two types of Super ESPs: Regional and Technology-Specific Super ESPCs. Regional Super ESPCs allow agencies in a particular U.S. region to place delivery orders with preselected ESCOs for projects using a wide variety of proven energy efficiency and conservation measures. Technology-Specific Super ESPCs encourage the use of emerging renewable energy systems to help federal agencies benefit from these promising technologies. Technology-Specific Super ESPCs currently focus on three energy systems: biomass-based fuels, geothermal heat pumps, and photovoltaic systems where the featured technology is the center of the project.

191. Pub. L. No. 102-486, § 105-06, 106 Stat. 2776, 2792 (1992) (codified at 12 U.S.C. § 1701z-16).

192. DEP'T OF HOUSING & URBAN DEV., MORTGAGEE LETTER 95-46 (Oct. 6, 1995), *available at* http://www.hud.gov/offices/adm/hudclips/letters/mortgagee/files/95-46ml.txt.

193. 12 U.S.C. § 1701z-16(a)(2).

194. 12 U.S.C. § 1701z-16(a)(3)(A).

195. *See id.* The rationale for this is that the money saved on the consumer's utility bills will offset any increase in the monthly mortgage payments.

196. National Housing Act of 1934, 74 Pub. L. No. 479, § 203(b), 48 Stat. 1246.

197. 12 U.S.C. § 1709(b)(2).

198. 12 U.S.C. § 1709(b)(9).

199. The cost of eligible energy-efficient improvements is then added to the mortgage amount and can exceed the maximum mortgage limit by the amount of the improvements. Energy-efficient upgrades are installed after the loan closes. Funds for enhancements are placed in an escrow account with either the closing company or closing attorney's office. Funds are released to the borrower or contractor after an inspection verifies that the upgrades are in place and energy savings will be reached. The cost of the rating report as well as the inspections may be financed as part of the cost of the energy improvement package.

200. 12 U.S.C. § 1701z-16(a)(2)(C), (a)(3)(A).

201. National Housing Act of 1934, 74 Pub. L. No. 479, § 203(k), 48 Stat. 1246. HUD's implementation of the EEM program is limited to mortgages and refinances and does not include its Title I Home Improvement Loan Program. *See* DEP'T OF HOUSING & URBAN DEV., ENERGY EFFICIENT MORTGAGE PROGRAM, http://www.hud.gov/offices/hsg/sfh/eem/energy-r.cfm.

202. 12 U.S.C. § 1709(k).

203. *Id.*

204. Title XVII of Pub. L. No. 109-58 (2005), 42 U.S.C.§§ 16,511 et seq., implemented under 10 C.F.R. pt. 609 (2009).

205. 42 U.S.C.§ 16513.

206. "New or significantly improved technologies" means technologies that have not been employed in the United States in three or more projects, and have not been in commercial application in those projects for more than five years, using the same general application as in the proposed project. 10 C.F.R. § 609.2 (2009).

207. From the program's inception in 2005 until 2010, only one project had received a loan guarantee. However, the pace of the Program has speeded up in 2009 and into 2010. As of March 2011, nine loan guarantees have been executed and an additional eleven conditional commitments for loan guarantees have been approved. The § 1703 program has received since 2006 over $51 billion in authority to guarantee loans, and the § 1705 program has received $ billion in subsidy cost funding, which could support up to $50 billion in loan guarantees. The 2011 DOE budget request to Congress asks for an additional $36 billion in loan guarantee authority for nuclear projects and $500 million for § 1703 subsidy costs, which could authorize up to $5 billion in national new and innovative project loan guarantees. *See*

U.S. Dep't of Energy, FY 2011 Congressional Budget Request; Budget Highlights 8 (2010), *available at* http://www.cfo.doe.gov/budget/11budget/Content/FY2011Highlights.pdf.

208. 10 C.F.R. § 609.12 sets out what DOE will considered as eligible project costs. Total project costs must fit within those guidelines.

209. 10 C.F.R. § 609.10(d)(5).

210. Section 1702(b) of Pub. L. No. 109-58, 42 U.S.C.§ 16,512(b).

211. See discussion of credit subsidy costs for federal loan guarantees *supra* this chapter.

212. 10 C.F.R. § 609.9(d)(1). The credit subsidy cost is to be paid in cash (not project equity) and cannot be rolled over into the loan as a project cost. 10 C.F.R. § 609.12(b)(8).

213. A guarantee of 80 percent of the total project cost.

214. The Federal Financing Bank was created by the Federal Financing Bank Act of 1973, Pub. L. No. 93-224, 87 Stat. 937, 12 U.S.C. §§ 2281–2296. Its purpose is to coordinate federal credit programs with overall government economic and fiscal policies. It has authority to purchase any obligation guaranteed by another federal agency to ensure that fully guaranteed obligations are financed efficiently. *Id.* It is a corporate instrumentality of the United States government, subject to the general direction and supervision of the Secretary of the Treasury. *Id.* The Bank essentially acts as an intermediary in a federal credit support transaction by purchasing the debt under a federal agency loan guarantee program.The Bank obtains funds by issuing its own securities, almost entirely to the Treasury.

215. Eligible lender qualifications are set out at 10 C.F.R. § 609.11.

216. 10 C.F.R. § 609.10(d)(4)(ii).

217. Section 1702(f) of Pub. L. No. 109-58, 42 U.S.C. § 16512(f).

218. Unlike the earlier version of DOE's loan guarantee regulations, DOE now does not have to obtain a first priority security interest in project assets. *See* 10 C.F.R.§ 609.10(d)(22).

219. A loan guarantee requires substantial fees, including an application fee, a facility fee, and maintenance fees. Up-front fees are due at closing. 10 C.F.R.§ 609.9(d)(2).

220. DE-FOA-0000140 (July 29, 2009); DE-FOA-0000166 (Oct. 7, 2009).

221. Section 406 of Pub. L. No. 111-5, 123 Stat. 115; 42 U.S.C.§ 16515.

222. 40 U.S.C. §§ 4131 et seq.

223. Pub. L. No 111-47 (2009) ($2 billion for the "Cash for Clunkers Program); Pub. L. No. 111-226, § 308 (rescinded $1.5 billion for state educational funding).

224. Pub. L. No. 110-140, § 136, 121 Stat. 1514, 42 U.S.C.§ 17013.

225. The 2009 Continuing Resolution (CR), enacted on September 30, 2008, appropriated $7.5 billion to support a maximum of $25 billion in loans under the ATVM.

226. Section 136 also allows these grants and loans to cover engineering integration costs associated with such projects. Pub. L. No. 110-140, § 136, 121 Stat. 1514, 42 U.S.C. § 17013.

227. Pub. L. No. 110-234, § 9003, 122 Stat. 923, 1310–1313 (2008), 7 U.S.C. § 8103. The term "renewable biomass" means "(A) materials, pre-commercial thinnings, or invasive species from National Forest System and other public lands (as defined [under FLPMA that meet certain definitional conditions]), or (B) any organic matter that is available on a renewable or recurring basis from non-Federal land or [certain Indian lands]." 7 U.S.C. § 8101(12). The term "advanced biofuel" means "fuel derived from renewable biomass other than corn kernel starch[, including]: (i) biofuel derived from cellulose, hemicellulose, or lignin; (ii) biofuel derived from sugar and starch (other than ethanol derived from corn kernel starch); (iii) biofuel derived from waste material, including crop residue, other vegetative waste material, animal waste, food waste, and yard waste; (iv) diesel-equivalent fuel derived from renewable biomass, including vegetable oil and animal fat; (v) biogas (including landfill gas and sewage waste treatment gas) produced through the conversion of organic matter from renewable biomass; (vi) butanol or other alcohols produced through the conversion of organic matter from renewable biomass; and (vii) other fuel derived from cellulosic biomass." 7 U.S.C. § 8101(3)(A), (B).

228. This loan guarantee program is implemented under USDA's generic loan guarantee regulations found at 7 C.F.R. §§ 4280.121–.200 (2009). On February 14, 2011, USDA published an interim final rule for the section 9003 program, 76 Fed. Reg. 8404, 8461 (Feb. 14,

2011) (effective Mar. 16, 2011), which instituted substantial changes to facilitate program participation and the availability of private sector debt instruments under the program.

229. 76 Fed. Reg. 8404, 8413, 8415, 8418 (Feb. 14, 2011).

230. *Id.* at 8466. Loans under $125 million are eligible for the 90 percent federal guarantee if the borrower also agrees to provide at least 40 percent equity in the project and other conditions are met. Otherwise the maximum guarantee is 80 percent of the loan; loans above $150 million are subject to a maximum 70 percent guarantee.

231. 7 C.F.R. § 4279.261.

232. 7 C.F.R. § 4279.265.

233. Notice of Funds Availability, Biorefinery Assistance Program, 76 Fed. Reg. 13,351 (Mar. 11, 2011).

234. Eligible purposes for loan guarantees under REAP for purchase and installation of a renewable energy system or energy efficiency improvement include: post-application purchase and installation of equipment; post-application construction or project improvements; energy audits and assessments; permit and license fees; professional service fees; feasibility study; business plan; retrofitting; construction of a new energy-efficient facility only when the facility is used for the same purpose, is approximately the same size, and based on the energy audit will provide more energy savings than improving an existing facility; and working capital and land acquisition.

235. The REAP Loan and Loan Guarantee Programs operate under 7 C.F.R. pts. 4280.101–4290.116 (loans) and 7 C.F.R. pts. 4280.121–4280.200 (loan guarantees).

236. The 85 percent maximum guarantee is for projects costing less than $600,000. The maximum for loans under $5 million but over $600,000 is 80 percent, and the maximum for loans less than $10 million but more than $5 million is 70 percent. 7 C.F.R. pt. 4280.123(c).

237. Notice of Solicitation of Applications for Inviting Applications for Renewable Energy Systems and Energy Efficiency Improvements Grants and Loan Guarantee and Feasibility Studies under REAP. 74 Fed. Reg. 2469, 24774 (May 26, 2009).

238. 7 C.F.R. pt. 11, subpart A.

239. Pub. L. No. 109-58, § 1301, 119 Stat. 594 (2005).

240. Pub. L. No. 111-147, § 301, 124 Stat. 71 (2010).

241. Pub. L. No. 109-432, § 202, 120 Stat. 2922 (2006).

242. *See* Code § 54(f).

243. *See* Code § 54(j)(4). Section 54(j) defines a "cooperative electric company" as "a mutual or cooperative electric company described in [Code] section 501(c)(12) or section 1381(a)(2)(C), or a not-for-profit electric utility which has received a loan or loan guarantee under the Rural Electrification Act"; a "clean renewable energy bond lender" as "a cooperative which is owned by, or has outstanding loans to, 100 or more cooperative electric companies and is in existence on February 1, 2002"; and "governmental body" as "any State, territory, possession of the United States, the District of Columbia, Indian tribal government, and any political subdivision thereof."

244. *See* Code Section 54(j)(5).

245. *See* Code Section 54(d)(2). *See also* IRS Notice 2006-7, which clarifies that any facility that is "functionally related and subordinate" to a qualified generation facility is also eligible for CREBs financing, including radial transmission lines, offices, storage, and so forth.

246. *See* IRS Notice 2006-7 (Mar. 6, 2006), IRS Notice 2007-26 (Apr. 2, 2007), IRS Notice 2009-15 (Jan. 22, 2009), and IRS Notice 2009-33 (Apr. 3, 2009).

247. The Secretary of the Treasury may extend the applicable five-year period if the issuer submits a request prior to the expiration of the period and establishes that the failure to meet the five-year requirement is due to reasonable cause and the related projects will continue with due diligence. However, if an issuer fails to spend 95 percent of the proceeds of the issue within the specified period, including any applicable extension period, the issuer must redeem all nonqualified bonds within ninety days after the expiration of the period. *See* Code § 54(h).

248. *See* Code § 54(h)(1).

249. *See* Code § 54(g).

250. Code § 54(e)(2).

251. Pub. L. 110-343, § 107, 122 Stat. 3765 (2008).

252. *See* Code § 54(m).

253. Pub. L. 111-5, 123 Stat. 115 (2009), Section 1111 of Title 1 of Division B.

254. *See* Section 54C(a). Two percent of the bond issue may be used for certain issuance costs.

255. *See* Code § 54C(d)(2).

256. *See* Code § 54C(d)(1).

257. *See* Code § 54C(c)(2).

258. *See* Code § 54C(c)(3)(b).

259. *See* Code § 54C(3)(a).

260. *See* IRS Notice 2009-33. Written notice must be provided to the IRS once an issuer determines that bonds will not be issued within the applicable three-year period and those bonds will be considered forfeited and available for reallocation.

261. *See* Code § 54C(b).

262. *See* Code § 54A(c).

263. *See* IRS Notice 2009-15 (Jan. 22, 2009). The Department of Treasury will determine and announce credit rates for tax credit bonds daily, based on its estimate of the yields on outstanding bonds from market sectors selected by the Treasury in its discretion that have an investment grade rating of between A and BBB. This modified IRS Notice 2007-26 (Apr. 2, 2007).

264. A "large local government" is any municipality or county with population of one hundred thousand or more. *See* Code § 54D(e)(2)(C).

265. *See* Code § 54D(e) and IRS Notice 2009-29 (Apr. 20,2009). Allocations to largest local governments are allocated a portion of the state's allocation based on the ratio of the population of large local government to the population of the state. Any unused portion can be reallocated to the state. *See* Code § 54D(e)(2).

266. *See* Code § 54D(a).

267. *See* Code § 54D(f)(1).

268. *See* Code § 54D(b).

269. *See* Code §§ 54D(e)(3) and 54(f)(2). Bonds issued to provide loans, grants, or repayment mechanisms for capital expenditures to implement green community programs are not treated as private activity bonds. *See* Code § 54D(e)(4).

270. CCX began actively trading allowances and offsets on December 12, 2003. *See* http://www.chicagoclimatex.com/content.jsf?id=821. Members' baseline emissions and annual emission reports as well as CCX offset project reports are reviewed by the Financial Regulatory Authority for accuracy. *See* http://www.chicagoclimatex.com/content.jsf?id=524.

271. *See* http://www.chicagoclimatex.com/content.jsf?id=23.

272. The RGGI program acts as a single regional compliance market for carbon emissions in the Northeast. RGGI was established in 2005 by the governors of Connecticut, Delaware, Maine, New Hampshire, New Jersey, New York, and Vermont in order to develop a regional cap-and-trade program to reduce carbon dioxide emissions from power plants. Massachusetts, Rhode Island, and Maryland later joined RGGI in 2007, and Pennsylvania and the District of Columbia have joined as observers. RGGI members require a 10 percent phased reduction in the power sector emissions by 2018, with the first annual compliance period beginning January 1, 2009.

273. The governors of Arizona, California, New Mexico, Oregon, and Washington established WCI in February of 2007. The premiers of British Columbia, Manitoba, Ontario, and Quebec, and the governors of Montana and Utah have since joined the WCI; Alaska, Colorado, Idaho, Kansas, Nevada, and Wyoming, the Canadian provinces of Nova Scotia and Saskatchewan, and the Mexican border states of Baja California, Chihuahua, Coahuila, Nuevo Leon, Sonora, and Tamaulipas are WCI observers. When fully implemented in 2015, WCI's comprehensive program will cover almost 90 percent of the greenhouse gas emissions in WCI states and provinces, including emissions from electricity, industry, transportation, and residential and commercial fuel use. WCI members' goal for regional, economy-wide greenhouse gas emissions reductions is 15 percent below 2005 levels by 2020, with the first compliance period for WCI members beginning January 1, 2012.

274. The governors of Illinois, Iowa, Kansas, Michigan, Minnesota, and Wisconsin, as well as the premier of the Canadian Province of Manitoba established MRGGA. Indiana, Ohio, and South Dakota joined MGRRA as observers. Under MRGGA, members are required to establish regional greenhouse gas targets, including a long-term target of 60 to 80 percent below current emissions levels, and develop a cap-and-trade system to help meet the targets.

275. RGGI, INC., ANNUAL REPORT ON THE MARKET FOR RGGI CO2 ALLOWANCES: 2009, at 5 (2010), *available at* http://www.rggi.org/docs/MM_2009_Annual_Report.pdf.

276. *See* Hawaii's Global Warming Solutions Act, H.B. 226.

277. *See* California Assem. B. 32 establishing a comprehensive regulatory and market-based program designed to achieve greenhouse gas reductions to 1990 levels by 2020.

278. *See* Minnesota's S.F. No. 145, 85th Legis. Session (2007–2008).

279. For a full description of each of the key state and regional initiatives, see GLOBAL CLIMATE CHANGE AND U.S. LAW 313–70 (Michael B. Gerrard ed., 2007).

280. *See* Map of Clean Energy Funds by State, http://www.dsireusa.org/documents/summarymaps/PBF_Map.ppt. The states with clean energy funds, as of April 2010, include Alaska, Arizona, California, Colorado, Connecticut, District of Columbia, Florida, Illinois, Maryland, Massachusetts, Minnesota, New Jersey, New Mexico, New York, Ohio, Oregon, Pennsylvania, Vermont, and Wisconsin.

281. In rare instances, some of these funds receive their money in lump sums either as a result of a settlement of a utility merger or sale of generation assets. *See* CLEAN ENERGY STATES ALLIANCE, http://www.cleanenergystates.org/about.html.

282. Steven Ferrey, Chad Laurent, & Cameron Ferrey, *Fire and Ice: World Renewable Energy and Carbon Control Mechanisms Confront Constitutional Barriers*, 20 DUKE ENVTL. L. & POL'Y F. 125, 136 (2010).

283. *Id.*

284. *Id.* at 137.

285. Cal. Assemb. B. 1890 (Feb. 1995).

286. *Id.* at article 7.

287. *Id.* The three major investor-owned utilities affected by this legislation included Southern California Edison, Pacific Gas & Electric Company, and San Diego Gas & Electric. The breakdown for the funds, pursuant to the bill, is as follows: renewable energy ($540 million), energy efficiency ($872 million), and research, development, and demonstration (RD&D) ($62.5 million). *See also* DATABASE OF STATE INCENTIVES FOR RENEWABLES & EFFICIENCY, CALIFORNIA PUBLIC BENEFITS FUNDS FOR RENEWABLES & EFFICIENCY, http://www.dsireusa.org/incentives/incentive.cfm?Incentive_Code=CA05R&re=1&ee=1.

288. *See* Cal. S.B. 1036 (Oct. 2007); Cal. Assemb. B. 995 (Sept. 2000); and Cal. S.B. 1194 (Sept. 2000).

289. *See* 20 Ill. Comp. Stat. 687/art. I.

290. *Id.* at § 6-5. The legislation provided for the breakdown as follows: (1) $0.05 per month on each account for residential electric service; (2) $0.50 per month on each account for nonresidential electric service; and (3) $37.50 per month on each account for nonresidential gas service.

291. *Id.*

292. *Id.* at § 6-6.

293. Order Continuing the System Benefits Charge (SBC) and the SBC-Funded Public Benefit Programs, *In re* System Benefits Charge III, Case No. 05-M-0090 (Dec. 21, 2005); Order of January 26, 2001 (extending the SBC and increasing funding from $75 million to $150 million); Opinion No. 98-3, issued January 30, 1998; and Opinion Number 96-12, issued May 20, 1996 ("In order to address the adverse environmental effects identified above on air quality, energy efficiency, and research and development, several mitigation measures will be employed as necessary. First, a system benefits charge will be used as appropriate to fund DSM and research and development in environmental and renewable resource areas during the transition to competition."), *In re* Competitive Opportunities for Electric Service, Case No. 94-E-0952. Additional PSC Orders issued during 2009 authorized New York State Energy Research & Development

Authority (NYSERDA) to further expand and add to its programs. For example, the PSC commenced a natural gas SBC for programs related to gas efficiency measures. *See* NYSERDA, New York's System Benefits Charge Programs Evaluation and Status Report for the Year Ending December 31, 2009, Report to the Public Service Commission ES-2 (Mar. 2010), *available at* http://www.nyserda.org/sbc_annual_programs_statue_2009.pdf. The "system benefits charge" is essentially a clean energy fund under a different name.

294. *See generally id.*

295. Case No. 05-M-0090, *supra* note 293, at 30.

296. *Id.* at App. A.

297. Order of January 26, 2001, *In re* Competitive Opportunities for Electric Service Case No. 94-E-0952, *supra* note 293.

298. *See* NYSERDA, New York's System Benefits Charge Programs Evaluation and Status Report for the Year Ending December 31, 2009, Report to the Public Service Commission (Mar. 2010), *available at* http://www.nyserda.org/sbc_annual_programs_statue_2009.pdf. The report was jointly prepared by staff of NYSERDA and a team of third-party evaluation contractors acting under the terms and conditions of a Memorandum of Understanding (MOU) between NYSERDA and the New York State Department of Public Service (DPS).

299. *See generally* NYSERDA, *supra* note 298.

300. Clean Energy States Alliance, http://www.cleanenergystates.org/Funds/.

301. *Id.*

302. *See id.*

303. Edan Rotenberg, *Energy Efficiency in Regulated and Deregulated Markets*, 24 UCLA J. Envtl. L. & Pol'y 259, 266 (2006).

304. *Id.*

305. *Id.*

306. *Id.*

307. Renewable Portfolio Standards are discussed at length in chapter 4.

308. *See, e.g.*, Iowa Code Ann. § 476.6(16): "The utility shall submit an energy efficiency plan which shall include economically achievable programs designed to attain these energy and capacity performance standards. . . . Energy efficiency programs include activities which lessen the amount of heating, cooling, or other forms of work which must be performed, including but not limited to energy studies or audits, general information, financial assistance, direct rebates to customers or vendors of energy-efficient products, research projects, direct installation by the utility of energy-efficient equipment, direct and indirect load control, time-of-use rates, tree planting programs, educational programs, and hot water insulation distribution programs"; Me. Rev. Stat. tit. 35A, § 3153-A-3: "Implementation of rebate structures. The Public Utilities Commission may require a transmission and distribution utility to implement rebate structures for installation or upgrade of an electric service entrance to encourage energy efficient buildings and discourage energy inefficient buildings. In designing these programs, the commission shall give due consideration to safety."

309. Richard L. Ottinger & Mindy Jayne, *Global Climate Change Kyoto Protocol Implementation: Legal Frameworks for Implementing Clean Energy Solutions*, 18 Pace Envtl. L. Rev. 19, 76 (Winter 2000).

310. Ramon Reynoso, Going Green and Adding Green to the Bottom Line, Georgetown University Law Center Continuing Legal Education, Advanced State & Local Tax Institute (May 2008), *available at* 2008 WL 2512130, at *8; *see also* DOE, Energy Efficiency & Renewable Energy, Federal Energy Management Program, Energy Incentive Programs, California, http://www1.eere.energy.gov/femp/financing/eip_ca.html. Additionally, PG&E and other California utilities also offer rebates and incentives for nonresidential customers retrofitting existing equipment. Federal Energy Management Program, *supra*.

311. *See* California PG&E website for an updated list of rebate options, http://www.pge.com/myhome/saveenergymoney/rebates/.

312. *Id.*

313. *See* SoCal Gas website, http://www.socalgas.com/rebates/residential/.

314. *See* Silicon Valley Power Corporate website, www.siliconvalleypower.com. *See also* Ramon Reynoso, *supra* note 310, 2008 WL 2512130, at *8. 315. *See* New York ConEd website for current rebates, http://coned.com/energyefficiency/forms/RHVAC%20Application.pdf.

316. ConEd offers these services pursuant to its Demand Side Management plan. *See* http://coned.com/energyefficiency/targetedDSM.asp.

317. DATABASE OF STATE INCENTIVES FOR RENEWABLES & EFFICIENCY, SUMMARY MAPS, REBATE PROGRAMS FOR RENEWABLES, *available at* http://dsireusa.org/summarymaps/index.cfm?ee=1&RE=1.

318. Richard L. Ottinger & Mindy Jayne, *supra* note 309, at 77.

319. Rule 3664 of the Colorado Public Utility Commission's rules, which implement the renewable energy legislation passed by the Colorado legislature, addresses net metering from a variety of renewable energy sources. *See* 4 COLO. CODE REGS. § 723-3-3664. The rule states that investor-owned utilities shall allow a customer's retail electrical consumption to be offset by electricity generated from "eligible energy resources" on the customer's side of the meter. Rule 3664(b) also requires that utilities compensate a customer for any accrued excess kilowatt-hour credits within sixty days of the end of a calendar year.

320. Pub. L. No. 109-58, § 1251, 16 U.S.C. § 2621(d)(11).

chapter nine

Sale of Electricity

Steven Ferrey

Introduction: The Pricing of Electricity and a Look at the Future

Electricity traditionally has been priced in a way that is atypical compared to other items in the American economy. Electricity is priced based on its reasonable cost of production. This cost is reflected in rates to retail consumers based on just and reasonable rates that reflect these costs. In a sense, it is one of the last of the "cost-plus" industries.

Regulated utilities receive an allowed percentage "rate of return" on their "ratebase," which is the undepreciated value of their capital expenditures on electric generating and distribution assets. The more that is expended and allowed into the "ratebase," the larger the base against which they earn a percentage return. This concept has been criticized as not rewarding efficiency and cost-consciousness, but rather providing incentives for additional capital expenditures at costs that may not reflect the best available bargains.

This structure of regulation emerged from the capital-intensive nature of the industry and its economies of scale, as it emerged on the American continent a century ago. Duplication of generating equipment, and particularly the poles and wires of transmission and distribution facilities, would be particularly inefficient. Therefore, the license and legal right to generate and distribute electric power were granted to various geographically confined monopolies. In return for the monopoly, the terms and prices of power were regulated by government agencies. Pursuant to the Federal Power Act,[1] the Federal Energy Regulatory Commission (FERC) regulates all terms and prices of interstate, wholesale, and transmission transactions in power; state regulatory commissions may regulate the retail prices and terms of the provision of power. Pursuant to the Filed Rate Doctrine, the application of the Supremacy Clause of the U.S. Constitution requires states to incorporate and not veto all FERC determinations into retail rates.

A 2010 report for Ceres[2] forecasts three key utility industry trends for the future:

- reducing GHG emissions by up to 80 percent
- less emphasis on fossil fuel generation of electricity
- greater implementation of smart grid and energy efficiency technologies

The Ceres report[3] foresees that utilities will:

- manage carbon reductions "across the enterprise"
- pursue all cost-effective energy efficiency
- integrate cost-effective renewable energy resources
- incorporate smart grid technologies

It notes that:[4]

- decoupling utility revenues from volumetric sales and incentive ratemaking will assist them in investing in energy efficiency
- Renewable Portfolio Standards are important policy tools
- net metering plays a critical role
- energy efficiency can cost only about 3 cents/kWh of energy saved, while new electricity costs 6 to 12 cents/kWh produced[5]

This chapter anticipates these changes and covers the adaptation of traditional regulation of the sale of electricity under somewhat modified concepts as the country moves to cleaner sources of energy. We divide the new world of clean energy into changes for greater energy efficiency and changes to promote renewable power. In the efficiency discussion, we start with the major departure of decoupling the earnings of regulated electric utilities from the amount of consumption of electricity, as a means to alter utility incentives to move away from the amount of electricity they can sell, and thereby provide incentives to control pollutants and global warming gases emitted. This is followed by discussion of demand-side management, time-sensitive pricing of power, deployment of a "smarter" grid, and submetering power. Regarding deployment of renewable power, we focus on the legality of feed-in tariffs, which several states are adopting or considering, installation and net metering of on-site power production, power purchase agreements, and green energy marketing.

A brief aside here about restructured retail electricity markets. Starting in California, Rhode Island, and Massachusetts in the late 1990s, several states sought to place their traditional monopoly utilities in the different position of remaining as power distribution monopolies, while divesting to the highest independent bidder some, or all, of their power generation assets. Thereafter, retail sale of power, which is totally within state and not federal control, was opened to competition. The monopoly distribution utilities were left in the position of purchasers, and not producers, of independently and competitively produced power. This competitive structure was expected to drive down the price of wholesale power production. While analysts disagree about whether this restructuring and/or competition has been successful, restructured retail power markets now constitute almost one-third of the states' retail power suppliers.

Progress nationwide in this direction was frustrated by the collapse of the California restructured power market in 2000–2001.[6]

Decoupling Consumption and Reward

As discussed in the section above, there is a traditional scheme of state and federal regulation of the retail and wholesale, respectively, terms and pricing of power sales. The price and terms of power sales are set by government regulatory agencies. The price is a function of assumptions regarding the number of units of power that will be sold in a future year by a utility, to allow the opportunity for the utility to earn its allowed total revenue requirement for operations. The amount of revenue earned thereon is a function, in large part, of the number of kilowatt-hours that a utility can sell and collect as payment. Quantity of sales of power is a fundamental variable in the revenues earned by regulated utilities. In this regard, financial cost breaks for larger consumers can increase the quantity sold and revenues garnered by utilities, but may be in conflict with other environmental or policy objectives.

Incentives that reward additional production and sale of power have negative environmental consequences. Approximately one-third of the states have sought to encourage third-party independent generation of power, while retaining geographic monopolies for the distribution of power. Several states have moved to decouple the amount of revenue earned by a regulated utility from lockstep with the amount of power it can produce and sell. This decoupling typically rewards the utility for doing things that the regulators suggest, apart from the volume of power produced and sold.

Such decoupling deemphasizes the accounting of utility revenues that are tracked by financial and accounting experts, and substitutes regulatory compliance as a meta-value in the profits allowed monopoly distribution utilities. Dissent has begun to surface in some decoupling states. The jury is still out on the success of decoupling, as it has, to date, been implemented in only a few states.

Decoupling to promote energy efficiency is necessary in both traditional and recently restructured energy markets. In the traditional market, profits are derived from sales over and above those projected during the utility's last rate case, creating a system where every kilowatt-hour sold after it meets the projected volume is additional profit. Restructured markets have divided utilities into separate generation, transmission, and distribution entities in order to encourage competition. Decoupling is still necessary in a restructured market because a generator's goal is to sell as much electricity as it can at as high a price as possible.[7] Retail prices to customers who are metered by time of day (also see "Submetering" section below) are highest at peak times, so any initiatives that reduce retail consumer consumption at peak times cut into the generator's profits where it is allowed to sell power reflecting these time-sensitive prices. Since incentives exist in both traditional and restructured markets, it is not possible to avoid this revenue linkage to quantity of power sold simply by restructuring the state's utilities to allow competition in retail markets to sell power.

In restructured retail markets that now characterize several states, there is competition among competitors to sell retail power. In several of these states, the regulated utility has been taken out of the business of generating electric power. In these situations, the regulated entity becomes a distribution utility, and may also be required to perform the role of the electric supplier of last resort, so that it continues to supply power where retail customers do not select an alternative supplier. To have the power to sell at retail, such regulated utilities that have divested their former generating assets must enter power purchase agreements to acquire electric power at wholesale (see section on Power Purchase Agreements, below).

Decoupling policies are more straightforward to implement in traditional markets because generation costs are passed immediately on to the captive end users, whereas in restructured markets, only transmission and distribution utilities will have their revenues decoupled from sales volume. Regulators can also create and implement efficiency programs in conjunction with the decoupling effort, further reducing demand and incentivizing efficiency.

With concern about clean energy, support is growing for new ways of regulating regulated providers to decouple ultimate revenue and earnings from the total volume of power handled, to reflect various rate recovery mechanisms tied to explicit policy incentives.[8] The names used for decoupling are varied and include "Billing Determinant Adjustment," "Volume Balancing Adjustment," and "Bill Stabilization Rider." Decoupling the revenue stream determination of regulated distribution utilities from the volume of power they sell is a critical reform that several states are trying in order to provide incentives for greater efficiency in energy supply. Incentives can be implemented by surcharges on approved rate tariffs, rate-of-return incentives decoupled from electricity sales, adjustment mechanisms for utility lost revenues from reduced power sales, or other performance incentives.

The implementation of a decoupling mechanism signals to utilities that their role as simply a power producer is changing. Under a decoupled system, utilities become energy services providers, instead of simply being a seller of electrons, with energy efficiency being one facet of their service. By recasting the role of the utility and unlinking utility sales from profit, regulators can then incentivize energy efficiency measures in a manner that makes much more sense to both shareholders and utility executives. One longtime energy efficiency and conservation advocate, Amory Lovins of the Rocky Mountain Institute, claims that the changing role of utilities is essentially "turning the utility inside out."[9]

Beginning in 1978, California started experimenting with decoupling with the goal of using energy efficiency as a resource that could prevent the construction of new power plants. By creating a robust energy efficiency industry and various incentives, California has managed to keep per capita electricity usage the same as it was almost thirty years ago, while per capita usage in the rest of the country has increased over 50 percent. The California Public Utility Commission (CPUC) also claims that its energy efficiency programs during 2004–2007 saved enough energy to prevent the construction of two new 500 megawatt power plants that would have been necessary to meet demand but for the efficiency programs.[10]

In 2007, California implemented a risk-reward incentive mechanism (RRIM) in conjunction with its four largest utilities, whereby utilities receive "rewards" if they meet specific energy efficiency goals. Under the RRIM, utilities are allowed to recover a percentage of the total net savings (savings minus costs) from energy efficiency if they achieved a minimum of 85 percent of the program goals. In this program, utilities were also subject to a penalty if performance fell below 65 percent of goals. Performance between 65 percent and 85 percent resulted in no penalties and no rewards.

There were 215 separate energy efficiency programs in California in 2004 with a combined budget of approximately $2.2 billion.[11] As an indication of the growth of these programs, by 2009, just over $3 billion was allocated for these programs.[12] The CPUC projects that these programs will save approximately 7,000 GWh annually of electricity and avoid the construction of three new 500 MW power plants for the 2010–12 program cycle.[13] Rhode Island, using a different mechanism, increased the rate of return to the utility, where it allows a utility to earn an incentive profit of 3 percent of annual contract payments under a long-term contract, in addition to its normal rate of return.[14] As of 2010, three states—California, Connecticut, and Massachusetts—fully decoupled electric utility rates, but then Connecticut backtracked somewhat, rejecting full decoupling of retail rates.[15]

Four other states have required at least one utility within their jurisdictions to decouple rates. FERC reported at the end of 2008 that ten states had adopted policies to decouple changes in utility revenue from changes in utility sales volume.

Decoupling has not been without controversy in these leading states. The Massachusetts Attorney General argued that existing utility rate-making incentives were rendered superfluous and unreasonable after decoupling.[16] In Connecticut in 2010, the state Attorney General, Wal-Mart, and other industrial consumers argued to stall decoupling, which was leading to higher rates.[17] The Attorney General charged that decoupling was not spurring greater efficiency, but was a "tool to stabilize the [utility] company's revenues" and should be abandoned.[18] The Commission disallowed full decoupling and with it, half of the requested utility rate increase, noting that utility rates in Connecticut were already among the highest in the nation. The utility favored full decoupling of its revenues from power sales. The Connecticut state legislature also diverted into other programs a $29 million annual surcharge on consumer utility bills earmarked for energy efficiency investments.[19]

California, New York, New Jersey, Maryland, and Massachusetts are the five states leading decoupling, according to one source.[20] These are the states that led electric utility restructuring and retail deregulation in the late 1990s,[21] that also led the development of renewable portfolio standards and renewable system benefit charges in the late 1990s,[22] and led state carbon regulation in 2009.[23] These states also have some of the highest consumer retail electric prices in the United States.

Decoupling for various utilities has resulted in a mixture of both increases in electricity costs and refunds to customers. Decoupling has gained momentum with the recent increased promotion of conservation and efficiency: Between 2008 and mid-2010, ten utilities decoupled rates and three states ordered decoupling.[24] Typically, decouplings tend to increase base rate returns 1–2 percent.

Originally, there was a revenue decoupling requirement in the federal 2009 stimulus proposal for states to de-link utility rate of return determinations from the volume of power sales, to garner competitively awarded funds. However, this was dropped in the enacted version of the stimulus bill[25] to only require an indication that the state is moving in the direction of decoupling quantity of sales and allowed return.[26]

Energy Efficiency, Demand-Side Management, and Response

Demand-side management (DSM) is an umbrella term used to encompass efforts of suppliers of power to manage the timing and nature of the demand for their power supplies. This becomes a unique issue with electric power because electricity cannot be efficiently stored. It must be used within a nanosecond or it is lost as grounded power or waste heat. It is possible to store electric power in batteries, but such storage is not cost-effective on a large scale. To run a laptop computer, a flashlight, or other tool, stored electricity is worth its premium cost. However, for day-to-day storage of bulk power, battery storage is not yet economical.

There also are other means to store power, such as chemical storage, compressed air, and flywheels.[27] However, by far the largest method of storing large amounts of electricity is in the form of water behind a dam. The water is held until peak times of power demand, typically on afternoons when the most electric appliances are operating, and then released through the hydroelectric water turbines to produce power. Power has more value, and the retail cost of power can be more expensive, at peak times. There are forty pumped storage projects operating in the United States, which provide more than 20 gigawatts, or nearly 2 percent, of the capacity for our nation's energy supply system.[28] Pumped storage systems also provide ancillary electrical grid services for grid network frequency control and reserve generation. Electric power storage is discussed in greater detail in chapter 22.

There are two types of DSM. Type 1 involves reshaping the load, primarily by changing the time when it occurs. Type 2 involves lowering the overall demand.

Type 1: Load Reshaping

The first type of DSM attempts to shape the demand for power (which the utility normally does not control, except for the general effect of the price of power) to fit the most cost-effective supply of power (which the utility controls, subject to governmental approval for building new generation facilities). Electric power is the most capital-intensive industry in the country.[29] A very large amount of money is invested in the generation equipment and distribution equipment. As with any capital-intensive investment, it is best from a purely economic perspective to utilize that capital equipment at or near its electric production capacity for the greatest amount of time.

To do this utilizing these Type 1 DSM tools, owners of the generating and distribution equipment want to do two primary things to shape the time and amount of demand. First, they want to shift peak-time demand to off-peak times. This allows the same amount of work to be done by electric appliances, but requires less peak-hour electric production and allows a lesser investment in total generating and transmission capacity, because capacity requirements are governed by peak demands. Among the devices that accomplish this shift are timers on certain appliances, such as dishwashers and clothes dryers. The second basic technique is to "clip" or reduce the peak demand. This causes consumers to reduce consumption at key—typically hot afternoon—times. Air-conditioning demand is a primary illustration of discretionary significant electric load at these peak times. Clipping of such peaks can be accomplished by rate incentives where peak-time pricing makes consumers pay more for this power during high-demand periods of time; by load-control devices that terminate or limit the amount of electric service at peak times to customers participating in such programs; or, in more sophisticated systems, by remotely lowering thermostat settings.

The basic procedures to implement this Type 1 DSM are:

- Establish load shape objectives for a particular utility or supply control area
- Determine which end uses can be modified to meet the load shape objectives
- Select technology options that can produce the desired end use/load shape changes
- Develop and implement an appropriate program using price incentives and/or controls

This process takes the ups and downs of electricity demand over time and attempts to level the curve. Common load shape objectives could include "peak clipping," which reduces demand at peak times and is a classic strategy; valley filling, which encompasses increasing off-peak loads; and load shifting, which moves load from on-peak to off-peak periods. Conservation is the load shape change that results from a reduction in total sales as well as a change in the pattern of use. The DSM possibilities between 2007 and 2010 were estimated to be over 230 Twh, or equivalent to about 5.5 percent of the forecast electricity power requirements in 2010.[30] This total DSM potential could trim 7.5 percent of peak period electric consumption.

A key element of DSM is load reduction that can be controlled by the grid operator or the utility, to ensure that loads are reduced at the critical times. Interruptible load is electric demand by a specific customer(s) that can be temporarily curtailed in times of power supply shortage, typically in return for annual power rate savings realized by the customer. Direct control load management denotes electric demand conservation measures that can be centrally controlled by the grid operator or utility, such as curtailment of certain nonessential circuits supplying nonessential appliances, such as air conditioners, electric clothes dryers, and so forth. The North American Electric Reliability Corporation estimates that interruptible load and direct control load management reduce national summer peak by about 2.5 percent. It is this peak reduction or peak shifting that is the ultimate goal of DSM, because it shifts the least efficiently supplied and most costly supply to more efficient and less costly periods of the day or conserves it.[31]

States have applied DSM effectively during periods of certain circumstances. During 2001 when California experienced an electricity crisis fostered by its particular form of deregulation of retail markets, one-third of all residential customers in California reduced their overall demand by 20 percent or greater and qualified for the state's 20/20 program of reduction in energy rates due to conservation in excess of 20 percent.[32] This valued total reduction, and not time-of-use reduction, because California residential consumers did not have time-sensitive demand meters at that time. Much of the discretionary power use that can be cut is during peak (typically daytime) periods, which qualifies as conservation and flexible load shaping within the DSM "toolbox."

Even though not shifting the time of demand, this broad conservation has value because in time of shortage of supply, that shortage occurs during peak periods (typically 8:00 a.m. to 8:00 p.m.). It is estimated that this conservation saved the equivalent of between fifty and one hundred and sixty hours of rolling blackouts during the summer of 2001 when California was short of electric power supply resources. Those blackouts would have occurred at peak times when the shortage of supply would be apparent. In August 2001, California ratepayers used 9 percent less electricity during peak periods than they did during August of the prior year. And 4.3 million ratepayers qualified for the California rebate program, receiving a rebate of 20 percent on their bills by using 20 percent less than they had consumed one year before. In New England, between 2005 and 2009, demand response resources offered to the grid to deal with capacity requirements increased 556 percent. These must be integrated into reliable system operation and dispatch to work effectively.

In 1978, the Public Utility Regulatory Policies Act of 1978 (PURPA) required all affected utilities in all states to consider, but not necessarily adopt, peak-time pricing.[33] The Energy Policy Act of 2005 required that within eighteen months, electric utilities shall offer certain customer classes a time-based rate schedule through such methods as time-of-use pricing, critical peak pricing, and real-time pricing.[34] Some utilities have done so.[35] Very few customers accepted these options, and surveys have shown that while residential consumers are enticed by the prospect of saving money from conservation, they are significantly dissuaded by the prospect of paying more if their consumption is during on-peak periods.

Type 2: Energy Conservation

Generic energy conservation or greater energy efficiency of power use shifts the entire demand for energy downward, at both peak and off-peak times of demand for power. Therefore, it shifts demand away from the peak-demand periods as do Type 1 load shifting techniques discussed above, but also reduces demand at other periods. In other words, these Type 2 measures tend to lower the entire curve of demand for power across the day and season.

These types of residential DSM opportunities are concentrated in the space heating, water heating, space cooling, and lighting end uses, as well as heating equipment tune-ups.[36] Commercial sector DSM energy impacts are concentrated in indoor lighting, heating, space cooling, and whole building end uses, which tend to be during on-peak times in commercial buildings, which are occupied primarily during daytime peak demand periods.[37] For further details, see chapters 2, 12 and 13 of this volume.

Financial incentives are provided to regulated utilities to pursue certain conservation and/or DSM measures (see section on Decoupling above). Incentive rate-making to manage demand and provide incentives for utilities can take various forms. Some California utilities are participating in shared savings plans, whereby achieving greater than expected baseline conservation, the utility earns 9 to 12 percent of the savings.[38] If the regulated utility companies underachieve the conservation expenditure goals, there are penalties for each kilowatt sold, or even a requirement to pay back the capital cost of conservation programs to customers, instead of customers being billed for the conservation investments. Other states provide utilities a bonus return on equity for conservation investments. The bonus is tied to utility spending on conservation, rather than power product sales.

A 1987 study found that an efficient New England home would require 35 to 57 percent less electricity in the year 2005 than was forecast, while achieving the same level of economic activity and personal comfort.[39] The American Council for an Energy-Efficient Economy ("ACEEE") reported in 2009 that the cost of energy conservation had been maintained at about 2.5 cents/kWh saved.[40] The investment in electric efficiency equipment would cost between one-quarter and one-half the price of power supplied from construction of new power plants. This could produce a kilowatt-hour of increased efficiency, thus freeing a kilowatt-hour of capacity of an existing power plant, for less than or equal to utilities' costs of producing a kilowatt-hour of electricity from new and existing generating plants. An assessment of potential electricity conservation savings, which lower the entire demand curve at both peak and off-peak times of day and season, indicated that the median technical potential is 33 percent, the median economic potential is 20 percent, and the median achievable potential is 24 percent.[41] Not all conservation savings have proved permanent changes of consumption behavior. Some are spawned by tight supplies or financial incentives for reduced demand. In 2002, about one-half of the California conservation savings initiated in 2001 persisted over time.[42]

Over the past twenty years, utility ratepayers have funded energy efficiency investments of both of these DSM types. Currently, thirty-five states implement ratepayer-funded energy efficiency programs with a budget of $3.1 billion in the most recent year surveyed.[43] Budgets have been up to 1 percent of revenues from utility retail sales, with annual savings of about 0.5 percent of retail sales. Most of these expenditures to date have been for more generic Type 2 DSM, although the deployment of "smart" meters and a smarter grid (see below) focus more on effecting Type 1 DSM. The expenditures for both are expected to rise to between $5.4 and $12 billion annually by 2020.[44]

Time-Sensitive Pricing for Electricity

As noted above, electricity produced in bulk cannot be efficiently stored in the form of electricity for more than a second, before it is lost as waste heat. Some of the Type 2

DSM potential is achieved by sending appropriate price and usage signals to consumers, and some by motivating the purchase of more efficient and lifecycle-cost-effective products. Direct feedback immediately from a meter or display monitor, where there is an instantaneous translation of consumption choices into costs incurred moment-by-moment and highlights options to alter usage, can inform and motivate consumers to achieve conservation savings in the range from 5 to 15 percent. Indirect feedback, where there is a bill received periodically that reflects total usage over a prior period, typically achieves savings of 0 to 10 percent.[45]

The typical state retail rate structure for retail residential consumers is flat, meaning these consumers pay the same for the kilowatt-hour purchased during a hot mid-summer day as they do for the kilowatt-hour consumed at 4:00 a.m. While the cost to the consumer stays the same, the cost to the utility is drastically different. When demand for electricity rises, more plants must come online to meet that demand, and these secondary generators are typically natural-gas- or oil-fired generators. Because these are relatively expensive fuels, many of these peaking plants are dispatched—allowed to operate—only at times after less-expensive-to-run plants are already operating. Price of power dictates the order of dispatch of electric supply generators in many states, as the economic operand. One type of real-time pricing for meeting peak demand now being explored is peak load pricing. This billing method would track and pass on the higher costs at peak times to the consumer, who could then adjust his or her consumption behavior accordingly to defer discretionary consumption at high-price peak times. Discretionary uses typically include air-conditioning, clothes washing and drying, dishwasher operation, and certain consumer appliances and lighting. Peak load pricing or time-of-day pricing is typically voluntary and today affects few retail residential consumers, despite the rationality of its approach of charging the real price of power at the time it is sold, to motivate Type 2 DSM actions.

San Diego Gas & Electric Co. is expected to have in place in 2011 a peak-time rebate plan for those who shift load to off-peak times, and by 2012 have a peak-pricing plan as the basic plan for all commercial and industrial customers. The Baltimore Gas & Electric smart grid plan involving almost $1 billion for universal smart meters, two-way communication, and time-of-use pricing was rejected for cost-recovery in retail rates in 2010 by Maryland's utility regulatory commission as "untenable" and not "cost-effective or serv[ing] the public interest."[46] The regulatory commission concluded that the plan would guarantee profit for the company and its shareholders and was motivated to take available federal stimulus funds.

Submetering

Submetering, sometimes also called in one variation "checkmetering," occurs when the customer of the utility is the owner or landlord of a building, and that owner or landlord installs an unofficial set of submeters to monitor consumption by individual tenants, units, or leaseholds in the building. Typically, that submetering is used, if the terms of the lease so allow, to require tenants or unit occupants to pay for individual utility consumption, although sometimes it can be used only for monitoring and information purposes without any bill presented. This can deliver the advantages of greater efficiency of centralized large-volume building heating system and cooling system services, while providing individual consumer accountability and financial incentives to building users to monitor consumption that they must pay for.[47] Individual metering or submetering of electricity generally yields savings from visiting the price signal and economic consequences of power usage directly on users, rather than the building owner.

However, by inserting the building owner or landlord into the intermediary position between the producer of power and the consumer, making a retail sale of power in the middle of the typical utility-consumer transaction, also raises legal and regulatory issues in those states that have not deregulated retail power supply. To date, slightly fewer than one-third of the states have deregulated the retail supply of electric power, allowing anyone to sell electric power to a retail consumer. Almost half of the states historically prohibited submetering of electric power to commercial or residential tenants.[48] This is because in conventionally regulated states, the reseller would become a utility in the eyes of the law. This sale would violate the exclusive retail franchise of the electric utility, as well as subject the reseller to extensive regulation as a "utility."[49] This original half of the states has shrunk, with one-third of the states since deregulating the sale of electric power within their borders.

Submetering remains a practice in flux and not without some debate. State regulatory commissions have enough to do just to monitor the sale activities of a few utilities authorized to sell energy in their states. If they had to monitor and regulate the activities of thousands of commercial and residential landlords on a monthly basis regarding every tenant lease in the state and the exact determination of its privately submetered utility charges, they would be overwhelmed. By legal requirement in most states, each retail sale of power must be done only pursuant to a state-approved tariff, to which only regulated utilities are subject, and those utilities are granted an exclusive right to sell power at retail in precisely defined geographic areas of the state. Holding regular adjudicatory hearings to approve thousands of private building retail tariffs for submeters, as opposed to a handful just for regulated utilities, would substantially increase the burden of regulatory agencies. In addition, in those two-thirds of the fifty states that have not restructured or deregulated retail power supply, allowing unregulated building owners to become *de facto* resellers of retail energy supplies would violate the exclusive retail sale monopoly granted under state statute and/or regulatory order to those utilities in return for undertaking an obligation to serve all consumers in the geographic area.[50] In actual practice, although there is legal precedent from litigation in several states, few utilities or customers choose to litigate these issues, but the theoretical potential remains.

Thus, the benefits of usage and cost signals sent to tenants though submeters run into legal barriers in several of those two-thirds of the states that have maintained conventional utility monopolies. Some landlords "mark up" what they charge their tenants for power, to reflect their often-unspecified administrative expenses. In states that allow such a mark-up,[51] this can cause disagreements between landlords and tenants regarding the financial implications of submetering.

Some states limit mark-ups by the landlord of its costs of power to a certain limit when reselling submetered power, and set up rules and procedures for tenant protections against overcharges and complaint procedures.[52] New York requires pre-approval by the New York Public Service Commission before a landlord submeters a tenant. The landlord must describe the rate plan to be used for charging for retail power, notify tenants and specify such submetered charges as a lease amendment, and put in place an enforcement mechanism to ensure tenant protection. When proposing to convert existing units to submeters in a New York condominium or cooperative unit, there must first be an affirmative vote by a majority or supermajority of the unit holders, depending on circumstances. Therefore, it is quite complicated to implement a practical system that gives tenants a financial incentive to reduce their usage while at the same time respecting regulated utilities' legal obligations and entitlements.[53]

Renewable Power and the New Grid

As discussed in detail elsewhere in this book, a great many tax benefits and incentives are being provided for the construction of renewable energy facilities utilizing wind, solar, geothermal, and other technologies. This section discusses special issues in the pricing and sale of renewable energy.

Renewable Energy Feed-In Tariffs

Feed-in tariffs are the most widely employed renewable energy policy in Europe and increasingly the rest of the world. As of 2006, seventeen European Union countries, Brazil, Indonesia, Israel, Korea, Nicaragua, Norway, Sri Lanka, Switzerland, and Turkey all used feed-in tariffs to promote and support renewable energy.[54] They are generally regarded as relatively well-supported and cost-effective means to promote renewable power in those countries.

A feed-in tariff establishes a secure contract for wholesale electricity sale at a set price that results in a rate of return attractive to investors and developers. Feed-in tariff structures are typically either fixed payments based on an electricity generator's cost to produce electricity, or a fixed premium paid above the spot market or wholesale market price of electricity.[55] These fixed payments are long-term contracts lasting from five to thirty years.[56]

These feed-in tariffs increase the price for certain renewable technologies to an amount that is deemed administratively and politically necessary to encourage their development. They typically may exceed utility-avoided costs, and therefore are justified only by their achieved objective and results, and not typically accepted rate-making methodology to minimize prudent generating costs.[57]

Costs of a feed-in tariff are passed on to consumers by purchasing energy suppliers who resell the power at retail, and reflect a public policy decision to increase the use of renewable electricity sources. Feed-in tariffs have not been sanctioned historically in the United States, unlike renewable portfolio standards (RPSs). The feed-in tariff promotes renewable power by actually linking the renewable subsidy to the price paid for renewable power, while RPSs do this by creating a separate tradable renewable attribute.

Several U.S. states have begun to propose legislation and a few to adopt policies similar to European feed-in tariffs. While state RPS programs promote renewable power, as discussed in chapter 4, states must carefully navigate around the limitations of the Commerce Clause of the U.S. Constitution, and those advocating feed-in tariffs must be aware of constitutional limitations in the Supremacy Clause of the Constitution. Feed-in tariffs, pursuant to application of the U.S. Constitution and the Federal Power Act, have been declared impermissible if mandated by states for any investor-owned utilities that are regulated.[58] The municipal utilities that serve approximately one-quarter of American consumers, and utilities in Alaska, parts of Texas, and Hawaii, which because of their lack of interconnection with other states, do not engage in interstate power sales, are not subject to the Federal Power Act, and therefore are free to adopt feed-in tariffs. Municipal utilities, such as the one in Gainesville, Florida, have done so.

The Federal Power Act, sections 205 and 206,[59] empowers FERC to regulate rates for the wholesale and interstate sale and transmission of electricity.[60] The U.S. Supreme Court has held that Congress meant to draw a "bright line," easily ascertained and not requiring case-by-case analysis, between state and federal jurisdiction.[61] Wholesale power sales fall on the *federal* side of the line.

When a transaction is subject to exclusive federal FERC jurisdiction and regulation, state regulation is preempted as a matter of federal law and the U.S. Constitution's Supremacy Clause, according to a long-standing and consistent line of rulings by the U.S. Supreme Court.[62]

FERC jurisdiction preempts all state regulation of wholesale interstate power transactions and prices. A feed-in tariff sets a price for specifically defined power sales that is above the general wholesale price of power in the region. If these renewable sources of power were competitive with general wholesale prices of power, no special higher-price intervention would be necessary. However, when states start carving out special treatment for any wholesale power sales (typically for renewable or combined heat and power sources, but some states also do so for some fossil-fuel electric generation), they cross a line reserved for exclusive federal authority: "FERC has exclusive authority to determine the reasonableness of wholesale rates."[63] If a utility or independent power producer is subject to FERC jurisdiction and regulation, state regulation of the same operational aspects is preempted as a matter of federal law.[64] This so-called "filed-rate doctrine" in 1986, and again in 1988, 2003, and 2008, was upheld emphatically by the Supreme Court.[65] This doctrine leaves open the possibility of "green pricing" options or incentives that include RPS renewable energy credits (RECs).

A careful legal analysis renders the European-used option of feed-in tariffs legally inaccessible for adoption by U.S. states for regulated investor-owned utilities under current law. A coalition of groups has continued to try to push through feed-in tariffs on a state basis without confronting constitutional issues. There has been an effort of some state attorneys general to justify a state mandate for regulated electric utilities to use ratepayer funds to pay substantially more than market rate for wholesale power purchased from independent renewable energy projects. Some, including the California Attorney General, have argued that mandating that regulated utilities only "offer" to purchase wholesale power at substantially above wholesale market rates is different than a requirement to actually "purchase" power.[66] And thereon, a few U.S. states moved ahead with mandates for promotional feed-in tariffs.

However, the basics of contract law dictate that once offered, the offeree (the wholesale renewable power seller) has the ability to accept that offer, which thereafter makes an enforceable contract. Therefore, a state requirement for utilities to take "step 1" to make a valid offer effectively gives discretion to the power seller to convert that offer into a binding contract by taking step 2. A state mandating only "step 1," knowing that it has mandated binding its regulated utilities if the power seller takes "step 2," is a fine distinction that no federal court or FERC has yet found of consequence under law. FERC in 2010 found this California argument unpersuasive, as discussed below.

The issue of constitutional authority of states to affect renewable power decisions quickly bubbled up in several formal legal challenges. In 2009, Indeck Energy, the owner of a New York cogeneration power facility, sued the state of New York regarding the constitutionality of its carbon regulation program, part of the ten-state Regional Greenhouse Gas Initiative (RGGI), which imposes additional costs on wholesale power sellers to purchase at auction carbon emission allowances. New York settled the suit, granting plaintiffs complete relief and not imposing any of these approximately $3 million annual additional costs on the specific wholesale power selling plaintiffs; the settlement stopped the court from addressing the legal issues raised in the suit, which involved state rather than federal constitutional issues. In mid-2010, Massachusetts was sued regarding the constitutionality of its renewable energy program on the grounds that it discriminated against out-of-state renewable energy projects, and similarly immediately settled the litigation, giving the plaintiffs everything they sought rather than let an independent judge address the program's legality.

In mid-2010, FERC resolved a legal dispute regarding the constitutionality of California's above-market wholesale feed-in tariff by finding it constitutionally preempted because states have no authority to set prices or terms of any wholesale power sales, and such sellers must be regulated by FERC as "utilities" (unless the seller is a "qualifying facility" (QF) pursuant to PURPA, in which case the sale price may not exceed the "avoided cost" of the utilities' alternative cost of the access of power, as discussed in detail in chapter 15). California had claimed an exemption to set above-market wholesale rates for cogeneration facilities of less than 20 MW. FERC held that wholesale generators can receive no more than system-wide avoided cost for power sales: "even if a QF has been exempted pursuant to the Commission's regulations from the ratemaking provisions of the Federal Power Act, a state still cannot impose a ratemaking regime inconsistent with the requirements of PURPA and this Commission's regulations—i.e., a state cannot impose rates in excess of avoided cost."[67]

After losing its petition for new authority, California immediately moved for a FERC rehearing or, in the alternative, a clarification of this FERC order.[68] While FERC dismissed a rehearing of its determination that state authority over wholesale power sale rates was preempted,[69] it did issue a clarification that the avoided costs determined for a QF selling power to the utility could be determined (1) with respect to actual costs incurred by the purchasing electric utility and (2) reflecting requirements or restrictions imposed under state law on the technologies eligible, thus yielding different tariffs for different technologies subject to state law supply mix requirements.[70]

Therefore, a state could require that a certain amount of a specific renewable power should be procured by a utility. The avoided cost that a utility could be ordered to pay for this technology, subject to technology supply requirements, would be the cost at which the *particular* purchasing utility could either itself construct *or* purchase such type of power. FERC turned down California's argument that avoided cost did not have to be the lowest cost for procurement of a particular type or technology of power resource.[71] None of the feed-in tariffs implemented or proposed in U.S. states, at the time of this October 2010 FERC decision, did this.

This 2010 FERC opinion clarifies the issue in FERC's 1995 decision[72] that different technologies could be subject to different avoided costs if, and only if, the amount, location, and "ability to sell to the utility" for these technologies is differentially constrained by state law.[73] FERC reaffirmed its prohibition of additions to avoided costs that reflect general environmental externality bonuses or adders, unless they "are real costs that would be incurred by utilities."[74]

While still the incentive of choice internationally for renewable power development, the popularity of above-market-price renewable feed-in tariffs in the United States is continuing to evolve. Environmental groups, renewable power developers, and officials in some states have remained enthusiastic. Some utilities, especially those that receive "incentive"-based financial rewards for following state policies, also have endorsed feed-in tariffs. On the opposite side, consumer groups and large customers, including Walmart, some utilities, and some environmental groups, have argued that these costs are yet to be quantitatively cost-justified in any state proceeding, and above-market costs are passed on to ratepayers of the utility.

Regulatory scrutiny is designed to ensure that only "necessary and prudent" costs are passed on to retail customers.[75] A decision on prudence is made in light of all the conditions and circumstances that are known at the time.[76] The states of California, New York, and Massachusetts not only have been leaders in these renewable energy efforts, but also have very significant legal staffs to sculpt programs in a careful way. When each of them is successfully sued right out of the box, and California loses while New York and Massachusetts choose to settle, it raises the profile of the legal issues in play.

This leaves RPSs, as now adopted by more than half the states, as the legally viable alternative to incentivize monetarily the adoption of renewable power technologies for power generation by independent power producers in the United States. As of 2011, approximately thirty states and the District of Columbia had some form of RPS standard. RPSs are discussed in detail in chapter 4.

Net Metering of Renewable Energy

As of 2011, forty-two states, Puerto Rico, and the District of Columbia had some form of net metering enacted.[77] "Net metering" runs the retail utility meter backward when a renewable energy generator puts power back to the grid. Net metering can pay the eligible renewable energy source approximately four times more for this power than is paid to any other independent power generators for wholesale power when it rolls backward the retail rate, and much more than the time-dependent value of this power to the purchasing utility. Some states that allow net metering put a limit on the percentage of total supply that can be net metered, to avoid the problem of net metering power back to the utility when the utility does not need the power. In Maryland, a controversy occurred in 2010 over limitations of solar output to be net metering to 125 percent of total monthly usage through the meter.[78] By turning the meter backward, net metering effectively compensates the generator at the full retail rate for transferring just the wholesale energy commodity. While most states compensate the generator for excess generation at the avoided cost or market-determined wholesale rate, some states compensate the wholesale energy seller for the excess at the fully loaded, and much higher, retail rate.

In 2001, FERC[79] held that state net metering decisions were not preempted by federal law. FERC held that no sale occurs when an individual installs distributed generation and accounts for its dealings with the utility through the practice of netting. In a somewhat ambiguous decision, it concluded that a change of title to power does not constitute a "sale."

Massachusetts has gone the furthest of all states, adopting a virtual net metering amendment[80] that looks a lot like the telecommunications "friends and family" program. One can designate anyone in the same utility service territory as someone whose metered retail electricity consumption also can be rolled backward due to sales from an unrelated net metered renewable power project. By creating a legal fiction of shared power, this ensures that the entire net wholesale distributed net generation quantity will be credited at retail rates by rolling back some retail meters.

For example, the wholesale price of power in New England was approximately $0.05/kWh during 2009–2011. Virtual net metering allows one's surplus and unused distributed renewable power to be treated as if it were produced and used on-site at another location in the same utility geographic service territory, although that power is not produced there, that other customer produces no distributed power at all, and that power physically never reaches that other customer. As a legal concept, one rolls back multiple retail meters where the retail (including transmission and distribution charges, taxes, and regulatory costs), not wholesale, price of power has been approximately $0.12 to $ 0.17/kWh over a similar period. This is approximately 300 percent of the actual market value of wholesale power through this legal convention. To date, Massachusetts and Rhode Island are the only states to allow such a virtual regulatory accounting. In both states, questions are being raised as to whether such an accounting is permissible if there is no significant host site use of power.

Power Purchase Agreements

Power purchase agreements (PPAs) are the contracts by which sellers of power sell, change ownership of, and get paid for the power they produce. This type of agreement is the essential legal document for all power projects not owned by the retail provider of power, as they link operation to a revenue stream for the power product produced and sold. Therefore, they are particularly relevant in restructured markets (see above) or in situations in traditionally regulated power markets where utilities must consider alternative sources of power. Providers of capital to all independent electricity generating stations—whether they use renewable or fossil energy—seek long-term power purchase agreements to back-stop the loan. These stabilize revenue flows, eliminate price risk, stretch out amortization of up-front capital costs, secure creditworthy buyers, and mitigate the risk of non-dispatch in deregulated markets. ("Dispatch" is the permission to operate a power plant to feed into the grid at a given day and time; "non-dispatch" denotes a situation in which, because of price of power from a unit or its geographic position in the grid, it is not signaled to operate at a given time, and therefore it sits idle.) The allocation of cash flow, tax benefits, and tax risks among project sponsors is critical. This motivates private sector investment and can be essential whenever a power project is financed using debt.

To be able to successfully structure project finance for a facility, there must be an assured market for the power that is produced for the life of any third-party financing supplied. The price of this electricity sale must be sufficient to generate adequate revenues to cover debt obligations and expected operating expenses. In addition, there must be a satisfactory return on equity investment demonstrated by cash flow from sales of electricity output. Where a cogeneration project also produces a usable thermal output, revenue from the sale of this output is important credit support.

Certain renewable energy owners are urging regulatory commissions to allow utilities to sign long-term contracts with power suppliers. Several states discourage long-term contracts with wholesale suppliers to prevent competitive markets from becoming locked in to only certain early-entrant suppliers of wholesale power. Rhode Island allows such a utility to earn an incentive profit of 3 percent of annual contract payments under such a long-term contract, in addition to its normal rate of return.[81] In addition, Rhode Island would eliminate stranded costs for the purchasing utility by allowing it to immediately resell such long-term renewable power in the wholesale spot market, which is the day-ahead and essentially instantaneous New England wholesale power market not represented by long-term power sale agreements. While there can be direct bilateral contracts for the sale of power, the bulk of restructured power markets (independent system operators (ISOs) in New England, New York, PJM (Pennsylvania-Jersey-Maryland)) operate with the day-ahead bid of offers to supply power, settled in the order of ascending cost. This creates a daily competitive market for power supply.

Massachusetts adopted long-term contracts with renewable energy suppliers to be entered by utilities. In Massachusetts, distribution companies conduct at least two separate solicitations for long-term contract proposals from renewable energy project developers between July 2009 and July 2014. Long-term contracts will be entered with renewable energy generating units in the state (expanded, after challenge, to New England) or adjacent federal waters, including the area where the Cape Wind offshore wind project was proposed, that are qualified to participate in the RPS program. This obligation is separate from the utility RPS obligation.

Many states are requiring or pressuring regulated transmission utilities to purchase certain renewable power resources at above the whole market clearing price. National Grid refused to purchase power, which otherwise sells at a wholesale price of approximately $.04/kWh in current dollars, for six times that market price. National Grid rejected a contract with Deepwater Wind for a price of $25.03/kWh.[82] The project would be located near Block Island. The utility noted that this would force customers to pay a premium price for twenty years above what wholesale power was worth: The long-term costs over this period were projected to be roughly $.09/kWh, or a fraction of what the project sought. The utility indicated that the project remained too expensive as a way to satisfy political goals of adding more renewables. Rhode Island in August 2010 approved a twenty-year contract similar to what it had rejected in March 2010, entered by its regulated utility, which was directed to purchase more renewable energy, with Deepwater Wind's 28.8 MW proposed project at $0.244/kWh beginning in 2013.[83] This price was more than other out-of-state wind energy projects that could deliver power to Rhode Island and approximately 500 percent of the then-current price of wholesale power sold in the state. The governor pushed the project, and a new statute required that the PUC factor in non-price factors such as economic development; however, no quantification of such benefits was ever established at the elevated price.[84] The Attorney General, CLF, Toray Plastics America, and Polytop Corporation filed an appeal with the Rhode Island Supreme Court, which was pending as this book went to press.

In August 2010, the CPUC approved 415 MW of above-market contracts for its utilities to purchase solar power, at what the PUC's Division of Ratepayer Advocates and a Commission identified as 50 percent above the cost of other renewable energy projects.[85] NV Energy revealed that, compelled by Nevada utility regulatory commission orders to increase renewable energy use, it agreed to pay seven renewable energy projects 40 percent more than it was paying for other renewable geothermal projects, and up to $134/MWh, or more than double the wholesale market price of power. The Virginia Corporation Commission and the Kentucky Public Service Commission denied above-market wind power PPAs; the Nevada PUC elected to reveal as public information the details of seven renewable energy PPAs.[86] PPAs are also discussed in chapter 17.

Green Energy Marketing

Pricing matters: the ability of green pricing mechanisms to promote cleaner resources will depend upon how much the customers are willing to pay for them, as well as the success of the electricity seller's marketing and promotion campaign. Green-E is an independent private consumer protection program for the sale of renewable energy credits RECs in the retail market, offering a certification of legitimate renewable generation through verification of renewable energy REC production. Ninety-five percent of the Green-E-certified RECs that were traded were purchased by nonresidential customers.[87] Commercial and institutional entities, rather than ordinary residential consumers, are the mainstay of green electricity purchasers.

The effect of green power marketing is on both the producer and consumer sides of the power market. A voluntarily accepted higher price for green power sends a price signal to power suppliers to consider adding additional renewable power capacity to be able to sell more of this distinct power commodity. This is a critical market signal regarding the preferred type of power supply. Some individual and institutional consumers want to contribute more to obtain green power, although a cost-recovering and appropriately priced green electricity purchase might be prohibitively expensive to many consumers, compared to the rates for purchase of conventional electricity.

For example, voluntary programs consisting of RPS-eligible RECs can vary in cost in different states from 1.4 cents per kWh in some states to a much higher value in states such as Massachusetts.[88] In March 2010, the price rose dramatically for those eight thousand customers electing to purchase renewable power in the greater Boston area from regulated entity NSTAR (the owner of Boston Edison Co.).[89] The premium paid for renewable energy increased from 1.4 cents/kWh to 4.4 cents/kWh because the price for generic power fell, while the price for renewable power was locked in long-term at a fixed high price, making the "renewable" component absorb the differential between the fixed price of sale and the dramatically falling price of wholesale power during the recession.[90] To one way of thinking, this overstated the true cost of renewable power by making the residual difference between current and long-term prices when the market price declined. While this was only a 16 percent increase in the total retail cost of delivered energy for these customers, it represented a much larger increase in the wholesale power commodity cost of just the power itself, before adding in transmission, distribution, tax, and regulatory elements of total retail cost.

Of that one-quarter of the nation's utilities that offer such renewable energy purchase options, it is typical that only about 1 to 2 percent of all customers, concentrated among industrial and commercial customer groups, elect this more expensive green power option, including Intel Corporation, Kohl's Department Stores, PepsiCo, Whole Foods Market, the City of Houston, Dell Inc, Pepsi Bottling Group, Inc., Cisco Systems, Inc., the Commonwealth of Pennsylvania, and Johnson & Johnson, Inc.[91] Since only about one-quarter of utilities offer this option, the overall national penetration rate is less: the 11 million MWh of these green purchases and an estimated 15 million MWh of total U.S. green energy purchases in 2008 represent less than 1 percent of the total 3,870 million MWh of electric consumption in 2008.[92]

Some have even been critical of the overall impact of green power marketing. A report by an NGO claimed that green power marketing perpetuated a hoax on retail buyers[93] by actually increasing the burning of fossil fuels. In addition, the report claims that the average $10/month paid for green power primarily goes to cover marketing and overhead costs rather than to subsidize the purchase of renewable energy.[94] This increased use of fossil fuels could occur where a supplier of power has both conventional and renewable power in its portfolio. Since renewable power has minimal operating costs, it always will be run whenever available to minimize marginal costs incurred for supply, whether or not "green" power is purchased by consumers. Renewable power, once constructed, will always operate at its maximum level with or without green power purchasers.

When a new customer asks the supplier for "green" power, to meet this increase in total power supplied, that supplier might actually on paper allocate some of the already-running green power to that purchaser, but increase the operation of its conventional power output to meet the added demand, as all renewable power is run anyway whenever possible due to its near-zero operating costs. Therefore, it is possible that a green "renewable" energy purchase actually causes a particular supplier to increase the output from its conventional, nonrenewable, generation resources. The net result, if this theoretical possibility is realized, is that conventional power is operated, while on paper a dedicated sale of green power is recorded. Nonetheless, green power purchase options do signal to the market more demand for renewable power and may spur the construction of more renewable capacity. However, there is no general complaint against voluntary green power marketing as a means for consumers to express a differentiated choice of power supply.

One-third of sales for "green" electricity is in fact the purchase of RPS RECs rather than the actual bilateral purchase by that consumer of generated renewable energy.[95] This is because of the flow of power occurring independently of the so-called "contract paths" of power negotiated by lawyers for power sellers and buyers, and reflects the easiest means of accounting for green power purchases. If the excess cost is for a green energy program in which utility customers individually voluntarily agree to higher rates covering the costs above the utility's avoided cost, this does not run afoul of the constitutional limitations discussed above because it is a voluntary, rather than a regulatory, action.

Despite the ups and downs of implementation, and the growing pains of the new renewables and conservation markets, a move to greener power is imminent. The basic technology is long-standing. Implementation and redesign of the regulatory system is the most significant challenge as we move forward. The issues that are being confronted by states and other policy makers are legal, regulatory, and institutional. In many ways this is comforting, as those issues are solvable. If proven technology did not exist, the challenge would be more daunting to adapt power markets.

Notes

1. 16 U.S.C. ch. 12.
2. CERES, THE 21ST CENTURY ELECTRIC UTILITY: POSITIONING FOR A LOW-CARBON FUTURE (2010) [hereinafter Ceres Report].
3. Ceres Report, *supra* note 2, at ix–x.

4. Ceres Report, *supra* note 2, at viii.

5. Ceres Report, *supra* note 2, at iii.

6. *See* Steven Ferrey, *Soft Paths, Hard Choices: Environmental Lessons in the Aftermath of California's Electric Deregulation Debacle*, 23 Va. Envtl. L.J. 251 (2004).

7. Pew Ctr. on Global Climate Change. Revenue Decoupling–An Overview, http://www.pewclimate.org/docUploads/Revenue_Decoupling_detail_0.pdf.

8. For a brief review of ratemaking procedure, see Steven Ferrey, Environmental Law: Examples and Explanations, ch. 12 (5th ed. 2010); for a review of legal precedent for rate-making, see Steven Ferrey, The Law of Independent Power ch. 5 (Reuters–Thomson/West, 27th ed. 2011).

9. Katherine Ling, *Rising Temps Melt Electric Utilities' Business Models*, N.Y. Times, Sept. 10, 2009.

10. Cal. Pub. Util. Comm'n, Energy Efficiency & Conservation Programs, Progress Report to the Legislature 5 (July 2009).

11. *Id.*

12. CPUC, Agenda ID #8801, Item 36, Sept. 24, 2009.

13. CPUC, Fact Sheet, California's Long-Term Energy Efficiency Strategic Plan (Sept. 24, 2009), *available at* http://www.californiaenergyefficiency.com/docs/EEFactSheet 092409.pdf.

14. *See* R.I. Gen. Laws § 39-26 (2008).

15. Lisa Wood, *Connecticut Regulators Reject Full Decoupling, Slash CL&P's Rate Increase Request by 42%*, Elec. Util. Week, July 5, 2010, at 11–12.

16. Mass. Dep't of Pub. Utils., Investigation of the Massachusetts Department of Public Utilities into Rate Structures that will Promote Efficient Deployment of Demand Resources, D.P.U. 07-50-A, 34–25 (2008).

17. Lisa Wood, *Decoupling Foes in Connecticut on the Attack as State Diverts Funds to Close Budget Gaps*, Elec, Util. Week, June 28, 2010, at 8.

18. *Id.*

19. *Id.*

20. Cathy Cash, *Decoupling Mandate Keeps the Pot Stirred as Congress Advances Stimulus Package*, Platts Elec. Util. Week, Feb. 2, 2009, at 1, 31.

21. *See* Steven Ferrey, The New Rules: A Guide to Electric Market Regulation ch. 8 (2000); Ferrey, *supra* note 8, §§ 10:6–10:12.1.

22. Steven Ferrey, *Sustainable Energy, Environmental Policy, and States' Rights: Discerning the Energy Future Through the Eye of the Dormant Commerce Clause*, 12 N.Y.U .Envtl. L.J. 507 (2004).

23. Steven Ferrey, *Goblets of Fire: State Programs on Global Warming and the Constitution*, 35 Ecology L.Q. 835 (2009).

24. Pamela Lesh, *Rate Impacts and Key Design Elements of Gas and Electric Decoupling: A Comprehensive Review*, Elec. J., Oct. 2009, at 65.

25. American Recovery and Reinvestment Act of 2009 (ARRA), Pub. L. No. 111-5, § 410(a)(1).

26. Stimulus funds can be provided if a state's governor has "obtained necessary assurances" that the state regulators will try to implement rate-making policies under which "utility financial incentives are aligned with helping their customers use energy more efficiently and that provide timely cost recovery and a timely earning opportunity for utilities associated with cost-effective measurable and verifiable efficiency savings, in a way that sustains or enhances utility customers' incentives to use energy more efficiently." The original language in the House bill included the word "decoupling," but was opposed by the National Association of Regulatory Utility Commissioners. *See* Katherine Ling, *Stimulus Does Not Require "Decoupling"—Markey*, E&E News, Feb. 24, 2009, *available at* http://www.eenews.net/public/eenewspm/2009/02/24/4.

27. *See* Ferrey, *supra* note 8, § 2:20. In 2010, the U.S. Department of Energy provided a $43 million loan guarantee for a Treasury Department loan for a 20 megawatt flywheel energy storage application owned by Beacon Power. Herman Wang, *DoE Completes $43 Million Loan*

Guarantee with Beacon for 20-Mw Flywheel Storage System, ELEC. UTIL. WEEK, Aug. 16, 2010, at 12.

28. For amount of pumped storage, see WIKIPEDIA, PUMPED-STORAGE HYDROELECTRICITY, *wikipedia.org/wiki/Pumped-storage_hydroelectricity*.

29. "Investor-owned electric utilities emerged as the most capital-intensive industry in 1990, 1.7 times more than mining and 3.3 times more than the manufacturing industries' average." *The Nation's Most Capital-Intensive Industry* (abstract), ELEC. PERSPECTIVES (Edison Elec. Inst., Inc., 1992), http://www.faqs.org/abstracts/Petroleum-energy-and-mining-industries/The-nations-most-capital-intensive-industry-Fourth-quarter-sales.html.

30. C. Gellings et al., *Assessment of U.S. Electric End-Use Energy Efficiency Potential*, ELEC. J., Nov. 2006 (quoting Keystone Institute 2003 report and 2006 Annual Energy Outlook of U.S. Department of Energy, Energy Information Administration).

31. NEW ENGLAND ENERGY POL'Y COUNCIL, POWER TO SPARE, A PLAN FOR INCREASING NEW ENGLAND'S COMPETITIVENESS THROUGH ENERGY EFFICIENCY 15 (June 1987) [hereinafter Power to Spare].

32. Charles Goldman et al., Ernest Orlando Lawrence Berkeley National Laboratory, *California Customer Load Reductions During the Electricity Crisis: Did They Help to Keep the Lights On?*, 3(4) ENV'T ENERGY TECHS. DIV. NEWS, LBNL-49733, May 2002, at 1, *available at* http://eetd.lbl.gov/ea/EMS/reports/49733.pdf.

33. 16 U.S.C. §§ 2621(b), (c)(2), & (d), and 2623(a) & (c); 15 U.S.C. §§ 3203(a) & (c).

34. Energy Policy Act of 2005, § 1252(a)(14). "Within 18 months of Commission adoption of this standard, each electric distribution utility shall offer to appropriate customer classes, and provide individual customers upon customer request, a time-based rate schedule under which the rate charged by the electric utility varies during different time periods and reflects the variance, if any, in the utility's costs of generating and purchasing electricity at the wholesale level. Within 18 months of Commission adoption of this standard, each electric distribution utility shall investigate the feasibility and cost-effectiveness of implementing advanced metering infrastructure for its service territory and shall begin implementing the technology if feasible and cost-effective."

35. For a summary of state utility activities and rate schedules including time-of-use schedules, see Smart Grid Information Clearinghouse, http://www.sgiclearing house.org/?q=node/1657.

36. Faruqui et al., *Clouds in the Future of DSM*, ELEC. J., July/Aug. 1994, at 58.

37. *Id.* at 60. Industrial-sector DSM energy impacts are concentrated in motor drive improvements and whole plant innovations.

38. Edward Comer, *Transforming the Role of Energy Efficiency*, 23 NAT'L RESOURCES & ENV'T 34 (2008).

39. Power to Spare, *supra* note 31, at 4, 6.

40. ACEEE, SAVING ENERGY COST-EFFECTIVELY: A NATIONAL REVIEW OF THE COST OF ENERGY SAVED THROUGH UTILITY-SECTOR ENERGY EFFICIENCY PROGRAMS (Sept. 1, 2009), *available at* http://www.aceee.org/research-report/u092.

41. STEVEN NADEL ET AL., ACEEE, THE TECHNICAL, ECONOMIC AND ACHIEVABLE POTENTIALS FOR ENERGY-EFFICIENCY IN THE U.S.: A META-ANALYSIS OF RECENT STUDIES (2004).

42. CAL. ENERGY COMM'N, TOTAL CONSERVATION IN THE ISO AREA (Apr. 9, 2003), *available at* http://www.energy.ca.gov/electricity/peak_demand/2002_peak_demand.html.

43. G. Barbose, C. Goldman, & J. Schlegel, *The Shifting Landscape of Ratepayer-Funded Energy Efficiency in the U.S.*, ELEC. J., Oct. 2009, at 29.

44. *Id.*

45. Sarah Darby, *The Effectiveness of Feedback on Energy Consumption*, ENVTL. CHANGE INST., UNIV. OF OXFORD (Apr. 2006), at 3.

46. *See* Press Release, Maryland Office of People's, Residential Customers Win: BGE $835 Million Smart Grid Proposal Rejected as too Risky, *available at* http://www.opc.state.md.us/LinkClick.aspx?fileticket=QVTBUqSpMtY%3D&tabid=39; Tom Tiernan & Mary Powers, *Maryland Turns Down BGE Smart Grid Plan, Stirring Surprise and Concern*, ELEC. UTIL. WEEK, June 28, 2010, at 1, 24–25; Peter Behr, *Md.'s Veto of Advanced Meter*

Deployment Stuns Smart Grid Advocates, N.Y. Times, June 23, 2010, *available at* http://www .nytimes.com/cwire/2010/06/23/23climatewire-mds-veto-of-advanced-meter-deployment- stuns-95998.html; *see also* Katherine Tweed, *Maryland PSC Reconsiders BGE Smart Grid Proposal*, Greentechgrid, July 14, 2010, http://www.greentechmedia.com/articles/read/ maryland-psc-reconsiders-bge-smart-grid-proposal/.

47. Steven Ferrey, *Energy Needs of the Poor*, Nat'l Clearinghouse Rev., Aug. 1977; S. Ferrey, *The Ghosts of Cold November: An Examination of HUD's Conservation Policy*, Nat'l Clearinghouse Rev., May 1977.

48. Quaker Bldg. Co. v. Dep't of Pub. Utils., 136 N.E.2d 246 (Mass. 1956); Ferrey, *supra* note 8, § 4:28.

49. *See supra* note 47.

50. In the various states, the utility monopoly and exclusive right to sell power at retail are granted either by act of the legislature of the state or embodied in specific regulatory orders or decisions. Steven Ferrey, Environmental Law 555 (5th ed. 2010).

51. *See, e.g.*, N.Y. Comp. Codes R. & Regs. tit. 16, § 96.2.

52. N.Y. Comp. Codes R. & Regs. tit. 16, § 96.2(b)(4)–(5).

53. *See generally* Steven Ferrey, *The Ghosts of Cold November: An Examination of HUD's Conservation Policy*, Nat'l Clearinghouse Rev., May 1977.

54. *See* Wilson Rickerson & Robert C. Grace, Heinrich Böll Found., The Debate over Fixed Price Incentives for Renewable Electricity in Europe and the United States: Fallout and Future Directions (Feb. 2007), *available at* http://www.futurepolicy .org/fileadmin/user_upload/PACT/Learn_more/Rickerson_Grace__2007_.pdf.

55. Wilson H. Rickerson, Janet L. Sawin, & Robert C. Grace, *If the Shoe FITs: Using Feed-in Tariffs to Meet U.S. Renewable Electricity Targets*, Elec. J., May 2007, at 73, 74.

56. Anne Held, Mario Ragwitz, Claus Huber, Resch, G., Thomas Faber, & Katarina Vertin, Fraunhofer Institute Systems & Innovation Research, Feed-In systems in Germany, Spain and Slovenia: A Comparison (Oct. 2007).

57. Ferrey, *supra* note 8, § 5:9.

58. FERC Order on Petitions for Declaratory Order, *In re* Cal. Pub. Utils. Comm'n, S. Cal. Edison Co., Pac. Gas & Elec. Co., San Diego Gas & Elec. Co., FERC Dockets Nos. EL10-64-000 & EL10-66-000 (July 15, 2010).

59. 16 U.S.C. §§ 824(d), (e).

60. Pub. Util. Dist. No. 1 of Snohomish Cnty. v. FERC, 471 F.3d 1053, 1058 (9th Cir. 2006), *aff'd in part and rev'd in part sub nom.* Morgan Stanley Capital Group, Inc. v. Pub. Util. Dist. No. 1, 128 S. Ct. 2733 (2008).

61. Fed. Power Comm'n v. S. Cal. Edison Co., 376 U.S. 205, 215–16 (1964).

62. Montana-Dakota Co. v. Pub. Serv. Comm'n, 341 U.S. 246, 251 (1951), Nantahala Power & Light Co. v. Thornburg, 476 U.S. 953 (1986); Miss. Power & Light Co. v. Miss. *ex rel.* Moore, 487 U.S. 354 (1988); Entergy La., Inc. v. La. Pub. Serv. Comm'n, 539 U.S. 39 (2003); New England Power Co. v. New Hampshire, 455 U.S. 331 (1982).

63. *Miss. Power & Light Co.*, *supra* note 62, at 371; *accord Pub. Util. Dist. No. 1 of Snohomish Cnty*, *supra* note 58.

64. *E.g.*, Ark. Power & Light Co. v. Fed. Power Comm'n, 368 F.2d (8th Cir. 1966); Nantahala Power & Light Co. v. Thornburg, 476 U.S. 953 (1986); New England Power Co. v. New Hampshire, 424 A.2d 807 (N.H. 1980), *rev'd and remanded*, 455 U.S. 331 (1982).

65. Nantahala Power & Light Co. v. Thornburg, 476 U.S. 953, 963 (1986) ; Miss. Power & Light Co. v. Miss. *ex rel.* Moore, 487 U.S. 354 (1988); Entergy La., Inc., v. La. Pub. Serv. Comm'n, 539 U.S. 39 (2003).

66. California Attorney General's Response to ALJ's Request for Briefs Regarding Jurisdiction to Set Prices for a Feed-In Tariff, Calif. PUC Proceeding R0808009, Rulemaking 08-08-009, June 25, 2009, *available at* http://docs.cpuc.ca.gov/efile/BRIEF/103034.pdf.

67. *In re* Connecticut Light & Power Co., 71 FERC ¶ 61,035 at 61,153 (Apr. 12, 1995).

68. Order Granting Clarification and Dismissing Rehearing, Cal. Edison Co. et al., 133 FERC 61,059 (Oct. 21, 2010).

69. *Id.* at ¶¶ 15, 19.

70. *Id.* at ¶ 20.

71. *Id.* at ¶ 13.

72. S. Cal. Edison Co. & San Diego Gas & Elec. Co., 71 FERC 61,269, at 62,078 (June 2, 1995).

73. Order Granting Clarification and Dismissing Rehearing, S. Cal, Edison Co. et al., 133 FERC 61,059, ¶ 28, 30 (Oct. 21, 2010).

74. *Id.* ¶ 31 (citing and upholding *S, Cal. Edison*, 71 FERC 61,269).

75. Midwestern Gas Transmission Co., 36 F.P.C. 61 (1966), *aff'd sub nom.* Midwestern Gas Transmission Co. v. FPC, 388 F.2d 444 (7th Cir.), *cert. denied*, 392 U.S. 928 (1968).

76. Boston Edison Co., 46 PUR 4th 431(1982), *aff'd sub nom.* Att'y Gen. v. Dep't of Pub. Utils., 455 N.E.2d 414 (Mass. 1983).

77. *See* http://www.dsireusa.org/summarymaps/index.cfm?ee=1&RE=1.

78. Mary Powers, *Maryland Regulatory Staff Takes Side of Solar Producers on Net Metering Issues*, ELEC. UTIL. WEEK, Aug. 16, 2010, 24.

79. *See* MidAmerican Energy Co., 94 FERC 61,340; 2001 FERC LEXIS 630 (2001).

80. Order Adopting Model Net Metering Tariff, Mass. D.P.U. Order 09-03-A (Aug. 20, 2009); 220 MASS. CODE REGS. 18.

81. R.I. GEN. LAWS §§ 39-26-1 et seq., 39-1-27.3, 39-1-27.8.

82. Lisa Wood, *NatGrid Refuses Pricey Deal for Off Shore Wind Project, a Blow to Fledgling Industry*, ELEC. UTIL. WEEK, Nov. 23, 2009, at 1, 23.

83. Lisa Wood, *Rhode Island Approves Deepwater Wind's Power Purchase Contract with National Grid*, ELEC. UTIL. WEEK, Aug. 16, 2010, at 25–26.

84. *Id.*

85. Lyn Corum, *California PUC Approves PG&E, SoCal Ed Renewable Power Contracts*, ELEC. UTIL. WEEK, Aug. 16, 2010, at 27.

86. Ethan Howland, *Nevada Regulators Order Renewables PPA Pricing Disclosure; OK Decoupling*, ELEC. UTIL. WEEK, July 5, 2010, at 19–20; Bob Matyi, *Wind Power Contracts Facing Tighter Scrutiny over Costs from State Regulators*, ELEC. UTIL. WEEK, July 5, 2010, at 19.

87. CTR. FOR RESOURCE SOLUTIONS, 2006 GREEN-E VERIFICATION REPORT, *available at* http://www.green-e.org/docs/06Green-e_Verification_Report.pdf.

88. *See* http://www.nstar.com/residential/customer_information/nstar_green/nstar_green .asp and http://www.newenglandgreen.org/downloads/NEWF_TermsAndConditions.pdf.

89. D. C. Denison, *NStar Green Seeks Rate Hike*, BOSTON GLOBE, Mar. 6, 2010, at B5.

90. *Id.*

91. *See* EPA data, http://www.epa.gov/greenpower/toplists/top50.htm.

92. *Id.*; U.S. Dep't of Energy, Energy Information Admin. data available at http://www.eia .doe.gov/steo/gifs/Fig22.gif.

93. PUB. CITIZEN CRITICAL MASS ENERGY PROJECT, GREEN BUYERS BEWARE: A CRITICAL REVIEW OF "GREEN ELECTRICITY" (1998).

94. Approximately 75 to 95 percent of the premium for green power went to marketing and overhead expenses, rather than the subsidy of the resource itself. *Id.*

95. CTR. FOR RESOURCE SOLUTIONS. 2006 GREEN-E VERIFICATION REPORT, *available at* http://www.green-e.org/docs/06Green-e_Verification_Report.pdf.

chapter ten

Financing Structures and Transactions

Braden W. Penhoet

Introduction

Financing structures and transactions applicable to renewable energy (RE) and energy efficiency (EE) in the United States are applied in a wide range of other contexts, particularly ones characterized by technology developments and substantial requirements of capital. RE and EE finance is distinguished by these sectors' unique risks and potential rewards and by the influence of laws, regulatory frameworks, and policy supports described below and elsewhere in this book.

This chapter focuses on the financing of private development and deployment of EE and RE technologies, products, and services, and only briefly discusses financing for customers' *acquisition* of RE and EE solutions, including by way of illustration where such revenue streams impact developers' financing options. As to RE/EE development and deployment, this chapter introduces both *corporate finance* and *project finance*.

Financing structures (and sources of capital) available to RE or EE enterprises vary according to their stage of development, capital needs, and risk profiles. The development of EE and RE solutions often starts with pre-commercial basic or applied research, and moves through initial company formation, growth phases driving toward marketable products or services, first commercial-scale installations, and, if necessary, deployment at scale. As in other sectors, financing structures and transactions at each stage balance investors' and principals' respective risks and opportunities. The particular risk and opportunity profiles of EE and RE, in light of applicable regulatory regimes and policy supports, distinguish financings in these sectors. Substantial economic opportunities will appear if support for RE and EE solutions continues to

The author gratefully acknowledges time taken for interviews by Puon Penn, Senior Vice President, head of National CleanTech and Emerging Tech Markets at Wells Fargo & Company, and Matt Maloney, Head of Cleantech Practice, Silicon Valley Bank. The author also gratefully acknowledges the helpful support of research assistants Morgan Hague and Elena Heim at the University of California, Berkeley Law School.

grow among consumers, shareholders, utilities' customers and regulators, and state and federal governments. RE and EE enterprises also face substantial risks, including, inter alia, risks related to continuing technology development and technical reliability, a still-evolving regulatory environment and marketplace, and uncertainties about the capacity of current and future infrastructure (for example, electrical grids and fuels distribution networks) to accommodate RE and EE solutions.[1] RE and EE projects and companies may take advantage of grant, equity, and debt opportunities as available, in light of these sectors' special risk and reward profiles.

As discussed below, EE and RE enterprises may progress along a financing spectrum characterized early by greater reliance on *equity* (ownership) transactions early in their life cycle, and *credit* (debt) transactions as they mature. Equity investors, as owners, buy into the upside potential of an enterprise's value, supporting the development of its technologies and/or business opportunities. Lenders, by contrast, seek predictable, defined repayments of amounts loaned, with interest, without sharing in the potential increase in a company's value (unless equity or rights to acquire it are issued in connection with a credit transaction). But lenders typically hold rights that are superior to those of equity investors as to the value of companies' assets, particularly relevant in downside scenarios, including insolvency. As we shall see, these attributes of equity and debt drive many choices regarding financing structures and transactions. Individual RE and EE companies may utilize one, some, or all of the structures and transactions described in this chapter, consistent with their individual business needs (capital-efficient or capital-intensive) and choices as to whether and when to terminate, merge, or sell up.

Finance of RE and EE, as in other sectors, reflects state and federal laws governing legal entities, securities, financial markets, commercial relationships, accounting, tax, bankruptcy, and more. In addition, RE and EE enterprises encompass a broad array of products, services, markets, and business models, implicating the generation, storage, distribution, sale, and efficient use of energy (in the form of electricity, fuels, or otherwise). Moreover, financing decisions (including as to structure) represent syntheses of judgments across many domains—not just law, but also economics, politics, technology, agency questions, administrative efficiency, and more. Comprehensive treatment of these topics—and their interplay—is beyond the scope of this chapter. Instead, this chapter provides an introductory overview of financing structures and transactions practitioners likely will encounter, highlighting elements and nuances particularly relevant to RE and EE. We hope that the reader will develop an initial basic understanding of these financing mechanisms as well as key decision-making criteria driving EE/RE finance in practice.

Early or "Seed" Stage Investments

EE/RE technologies, products, or services may stem from the independent work of individuals, research at universities, government or other research laboratories, or projects developed internally by or spun out of existing companies. Common themes in early stage funding include the likely need for further technical development and proofs-of-concept; thorough analyses of market opportunities; and the need to build both technical and business teams to bring RE/EE products and services to market.

Cash requirements at such early stages may be small relative to the total amounts of capital required to get to market. But known and unknown risks are likely at their greatest. Principals may not yet have all the information or even the full breadth of expertise required to build a company and position it in the marketplace. Intellectual property (IP) may be incompletely charted and secured, including with regard to prior inventions and international regimes, in a complex and increasingly crowded RE/EE IP landscape, complicating predictions as to ultimate IP needs. What's more, new or still-developing RE and EE sectors likely are subject to market and regulatory uncertainties, sometimes without clear precedents. And, if long-term capital requirements are expected to be substantial, as may often be the case with RE and EE, early investors risk being marginalized—their ownership reduced and diluted—in subsequent funding rounds, including pursuant to so-called "pay-to-play" structures, as discussed below.

Early Private Funding

In the entrepreneurial context (as distinct from large companies' internally generated projects, for example), committing capital to uncertain early stage RE or EE ventures often turns on special interests in a proposed business or relationships to initial leadership. Thus, early investors may include founders, their family, friends, and colleagues (including from prior ventures). The support of such initial "friends and family" investors—whether founded on fellowship or insight into character or technology—can be key to transforming ideas into ventures. Such initial, or "seed," capital may be applied to document and secure IP, form legal entities, prepare market studies, and fund proof-of-concept work on initial technologies, products, or services. Funding at these early stages—whether by direct investment or through convertible debt (as discussed below)—may be directed toward achieving near-term goals, as immediate as preparing presentations for the next round of early stage financing.

Beyond friends, family, and colleagues, so-called "angels" specialize in finding and funding promising early-stage ventures. Typically, angels invest their personal capital, and/or the capital of their individual colleagues. In many cases, angels draw on personal experience building innovative companies to uncover diamonds in the rough—business opportunities too early and speculative to attract investors deploying larger or more tightly structured pools of capital. Angels may uncover such opportunities through professional networks, technology and business plan competitions, technology transfer offices at research institutions, and myriad other avenues. Angels may operate singly or in partnership with others. As may be consistent with their prior business experience, angels may take operational roles in companies to protect their investments and help the founders develop their initial technologies, products, and/or services.

Uses of such additional seed-stage investments typically include funding early proof-of-concept work to demonstrate commercial potential; follow-up investments in IP; development of business and marketing plans; and securing the services of accountants and the like to position the venture for further funding. Such funding may take place in one or more stages, or "tranches"—allowing funders to track progress and provide founders incentives to hit initial project milestones.

Sophisticated early investors look for opportunities to minimize inherent risks and maximize opportunities for a happy outcome, or "exit" for their investments. They often also must be patient, particularly in still-developing markets such as RE and EE. Partnership agreements for angel funds may explicitly note that returns on initial investments can take time—for example, longer than the ten years most commonly contemplated by venture capital funds, as discussed below. Angels typically, though not exclusively, favor businesses for which success will not require lots of follow-on capital (that is, business concepts that are capital-efficient, rather than capital-intensive). Higher capital needs implicate the prospect of later ownership dilution as well as many kinds of risks. In the still-emerging contexts of RE and EE, with their large potential scales, substantial regulatory influence, and uncharted business models, funding such opportunities may also involve portfolio investment strategies to maximize chances of one or more successes.

Early Private Investment Structures

The simplest and most direct means of investing in an early stage venture, RE/EE or otherwise, is the outright purchase of a stake in the legal entity advancing the business opportunity. Ownership interests in corporations are reflected in shares of stock. In the case of limited liability companies, ownership may be reflected by units of membership interest.

Founders may reserve for themselves the portion of a company's equity—divided among them as they may agree—and sell further equity to initial investors. Absent arrangements or agreements to the contrary, under state laws governing legal entities, control over the company and its key employees will flow from the respective ownership positions of the founders and initial investors. To ensure that founders make intellectual or "sweat equity" contributions commensurate with their ownership positions, initial investors may seek to make founders' equity subject to vesting schedules (keyed to time of service and/or the achievement of specified milestones) or their functional equivalents, rights of repurchase that lapse with time or the achievement of milestones.

However, for several reasons, early-stage innovative ventures and/or their investors may not favor such immediate buy-in. Selling shares dilutes founders' ownership and control. Friends and family may want to help founders launch a business, but not to stay involved over the long term. Founders may appreciate angels' experience and capital, but may yet be certain who will best guide their later technical, business, and commercial development. But perhaps the greatest factor militating against such direct buy-in is the challenge of determining the value of the enterprise at such an early stage. Selling a part of a company requires coming to an agreement as to its current value. If founders underestimate the ultimate value of their enterprise, selling part of the company provides a windfall to early investors. Conversely, investors risk overestimating the value of the venture, suffering later adjustments in the value of their stakes. What is often clear is that uncertainties in early stages make assessing value difficult.

Convertible debt sidesteps such valuation issues. With convertible debt, investors make a loan rather than directly purchase equity. Such loans may be secured or unsecured.[2] Subject to a variety of negotiable nuances, such loan amounts (with accumulated interest) may later be either: (1) repaid in cash or (2) converted into ownership in a later round of financing that meets agreed criteria, when more will be known about the venture and its core technologies, products, or services, and (typically) larger amounts of capital will bring deeper investigation and analysis of anticipated opportunities and costs. Such later conversion may include a negotiated discount to reward early investors for taking early risks. An added, or alternative, compensation for such investment risks may be rights, or warrants, to acquire shares or interests in such later rounds. As will be discussed more fully below, such later-acquired ownership may take the form of preferred stock or corresponding LLC interests that carry special rights and privileges, superior to the rights attendant to ordinary, or "common" stock or interests typically on offer at the seed stage. As so used, though convertible debt is structured as a loan, it may best be understood as a means of making a deferred equity investment, with price and other key terms to be established later.

Whether RE and EE enterprises issue equity, debt, or combinations thereof, such issuances are subject to state and federal securities laws. The Securities Act of 1933 (the 1933 Act) and the Securities Exchange Act of 1934 (the 1934 Act, and together with the 1933 Act, the Federal Securities Laws) form the basis of a sweeping and multifaceted legal and federal administrative structure designed to protect investors.[3] All issuances of securities[4] in interstate commerce must comply with the information and registration requirements under the Federal Securities Laws, unless such issuances fall within one or more exemptions. Exemptions relevant to early stage and growth-stage issuances include private offerings to a limited number of persons or institutions, including, inter alia, those qualified as "accredited' investors";[5] offerings of limited size; and intrastate offerings.[6]

Early Public Funding

Investment capital in various forms is also available for early stage EE and RE ventures from public and publicly approved sources to advance a wide range of public goals. Many types of local, state, and federal support are available to companies, including particularly in EE and RE, in the form of grants, loans, loan guarantees, and other mechanisms. EE and RE ventures may obtain public support in furtherance of policy objectives not unique to these sectors—like stimulating small business, spurring robust technology development,[7] job creation, support for minority-owned businesses,[8] as well as policy objectives that specifically implicate EE and RE, including combating climate change, improving energy security, and driving technical and industrial leadership in a revamped international energy economy. Numerous forms of public financial assistance available to EE and RE projects are discussed in detail elsewhere, including in chapter 8.

RE and EE enterprises may implicate environmental, social, and/or security concerns as well as commercial objectives. For a variety of reasons, public values and private finance will not always align perfectly. Thus, private philanthropy, including foundations exempt from taxation under IRS rules, may also directly or indirectly support EE and RE enterprises. Foundations both invest and distribute capital. To avoid excise taxes on income generated through investment activities, foundations must make sufficient annual qualifying distributions of their assets.[9] The most common form of such qualifying distributions is by grant to other nonprofit charitable organizations, in furtherance of the private foundation's tax-exempt mission. Such grants may fuel technology or market developments consistent with grantees' charitable missions. In addition, program-related investing (PRI) is a tightly bounded mechanism allowing foundation dollars to be invested in for-profit entities, but still meet tax exemption requirements, so long as the primary purpose of such investments furthers the foundation's tax-exempt mission and financial return is not a significant objective. PRI may be a relevant funding mechanism in, for example, funding privately supplied efficiency improvements in low-income or financially stressed contexts. This category of finance may be of particular interest to professionals whose practices incorporate both nonprofit and for-profit clients.

Intellectual Property Transactions

The majority of this chapter focuses on equity (entity ownership) and credit (lending/ debt) structures and transactions. However, innovative companies that accumulate and protect IP have an additional set of tools at their disposal to generate working capital. Such opportunities involve the license or assignment of elements of the company's IP estate, whether in part, outright, or by dedicating some portion to a relationship with another, usually larger and more established company (so-called strategic partners or investors). Licensing, strategic research and development (R&D) investments, and joint ventures have been common in other sectors where large incumbent companies look outside for new technologies, and where market opportunities involve technology risks, high costs, and financial and regulatory hurdles to clear.

IP transactions may be attractive for several reasons. A company's IP estate may include potential applications outside the company's target markets (whether from technology, business, or geographic points of view), or which the company cannot or elects not to pursue. For example, protected biological or chemical innovations that may enable or enhance the production of biofuels may also find application in unrelated sectors, like agriculture, nutrition, medicine, or even cosmetics. Such IP may also have application in both developed and developing countries, driven by different market characteristics. Based on their business goals, capacity, and other factors, companies with such IP assets may elect to narrow their focus to one or more sets of products and markets (i.e., biofuels), and license or assign non-core IP to companies targeting such other markets, regions, or applications, for cash or equities. The company can then direct the proceeds to funding development of its core technologies and business strategies.

Alternatively, EE and RE companies may take investments from other companies where technical, business, and/or market objectives are more aligned. Such investment may fund further development of EE or RE products, services, or technologies, securing for the corporate investor rights for further development and commercialization (including through IP licensing). Careful planning and drafting regarding inventorship and project management and accounting can help to minimize later controversy as to which inventions, refinements, and commercial opportunities fall within and outside the scope of such agreements.

A more complex alternative to direct finance by one company of another company's R&D is the creation of a joint venture—an entity formed to hold, apply, develop, and perhaps commercialize assets contributed by each participant company. Such assets can include cash, personnel, IP, equipment, and so forth. Such an arrangement may make particular sense when complementary IP held by two or more entities can be usefully combined and developed together. Participating companies typically receive, in return for their respective contributions, ownership shares or interests in the joint venture, and a variety of additional rights attendant to the prospective success (e.g., minimum financial returns) or failure (e.g., reversion/assignment of IP rights) of the joint enterprise.

Growth-Phase Equity and Venture Capital Investment

The finance path for U.S.-based, innovative technology-based companies, including in RE and EE, often entails venture capital. Venture capital firms are typically partnerships investing capital raised from limited partners, which may include larger institutional investment funds. Venture funds are typically designed to provide returns to their investors after ten years. Funds tend to specialize in one or more sectors, and to target one or more phases of technology and company growth. Some funds specialize in seed-stage and early growth stage opportunities, overlapping with angel investors, while others focus on later, and typically larger, investments. Such financing phases may be described in the venture capital industry as seed-stage, growth phase, mezzanine, and presale financing. Large companies with existing, more mature platforms in relevant EE/RE sectors may also play their hands at venture investing through in-house funds deploying corporate capital.

Venture capital fills a special niche in the broader portfolio of investment management—one characterized by high risk and high potential reward—as a complement to other types of investments, including, for example, those in public companies, bonds, and currencies. The promise of high rewards is damped, however, by the passage of too much time, as opportunity costs of capital accumulate and compound. Therefore, most venture capital funds are structured to terminate after ten years.[10] As a practical matter, it can take several years after fund formation to find suitable investments for the majority of the capital raised. Allowing for unpredictable delays and changes in overall economic conditions, venture capital managers look for portfolio companies with the potential to achieve significant commercial—or at least financial—outcomes within the timeframes of their commitments to provide returns to investors.

Criteria for venture capital investing include, inter alia, size of addressable market opportunities; technology promise and technology maturity; quality of management; IP position; scalability; competition; immediate and longer-term capital requirements; regulatory matters; validation and support from outside entities, including strategic partners or government agencies (including opportunities to leverage nondilutive grants and other resources); and the prospect of an exit via public offering or acquisition by another entity.

Actual financings start with valuation—which earliest investors may have avoided through the use of convertible debt. Valuation must be agreed because what is at issue, in raw terms, is how much of the enterprise the venture investors will own, for how much money. This negotiation is typically a business matter to be addressed before lawyers begin to document the transaction, but attorneys may play key roles in the due diligence phase, identifying strengths and weaknesses in the IP estate, contracts, prior investment structures, and other legal matters. Valuation will be revisited as venture-backed companies proceed through successive rounds of financing, involving both prior and new investors. Early investors want to see valuations increase through successive rounds, to reflect progress in achieving meaningful business goals, and to avoid diluting the value of their early stakes.

Valuing EE and RE companies may pose particular challenges. Many sectors that have fueled the success of venture capital, including, for example, Internet applications or enterprise software, have combined low capital requirements and rapid scalability with clean paths to market absent significant legal or regulatory hurdles. Other venture-backed sectors, like biotechnology, present a tougher road, with high capital requirements and significant regulatory hurdles. But players in the biotech investment game still hold an ace—the prospect of selling life-saving products with pricing power afforded by patent protection. EE and RE sectors present unique challenges to the venture capital model: potentially high capital investment needs, still-evolving business models and regulatory landscapes, powerful incumbents, and the prospect of selling technologies, products, or services into electricity and fuels markets characterized by *commodity* pricing. Still, markets may be larger, and, as noted above, the venture capital industry is deeply engaged in both EE and RE, looking, like angels, for opportunities to navigate risks and generate rewards in a timeframe meeting the objectives of its limited partner investors.

Structure of Venture Capital Investments

After initial screening by one or more venture capital firms, more thorough inquiry, or due diligence, begins, for a first round of venture financing (typically called Series A in anticipation of later series B, C, etc.). Legally, distinctive features of venture capital investment include the use of preferred stock (of corporations) or preferred interests (of LLCs), and the transaction forms and norms that have been developed over the past several decades.

Under applicable state laws, companies may issue one or more series of preferred stock (or interests, but for simplicity I refer below primarily to preferred stock), which carry rights and privileges different from, and typically superior to, the rights and privileges attendant to common stock typically held by founders and initial investors. Companies may issue several series of preferred stock, with different rights and privileges vis-à-vis one another, as negotiated among existing and new investors.

Equity investors (who typically acquire minority ownership positions) are primarily interested in the upside success of the companies in which they invest. Thus, equity investors protect their investments through priority rights relating to control over a company's ownership, management, and direction. This is accomplished in part by securing the rights, preferences, and other attributes of preferred stock, as defined and described by a revised charter, negotiated and then filed with the authorities of the state in which the corporation is formed. These rights, preferences, and other attributes also justify the premium that companies charge over the price of common shares. In addition, a well-developed set of ancillary documents typically accompanies a venture transaction, reflecting decades of evolution and refinement among investors, companies, and their respective counsel. Key levers of supervision and control include supervision of management through board membership and associated influence over major decisions, managers' tenure and compensation, and the grant to managers of options to buy additional stock options tied to their continuing service and/or achievement of technical and business milestones.

Among special attributes of preferred stock are rights to dividends; rights to be repaid (sometimes at a multiple of the initial investment) upon liquidation events (e.g., merger, sale, or winding up); rights to elect one or more members of the entity's governing board; approval rights with regard to actions that may affect the value of outstanding preferred stock, issuing new classes of stock, amending the company's charter, incurring substantial debt, acquiring or selling shares in subsidiaries, and changing the size of the company's governing board; rights to convert preferred stock to common stock; and rights to address dilution of ownership arising from later issuance of lower-priced equity, through formulae that adjust the conversion of preferred stock to common stock.[11]

Transaction agreements among investors, other shareholders, and founders typically include a stock (or interest) purchase agreement controlling the terms and conditions of the sale of stock; an investors' rights agreement, specifying additional rights and obligations;[12] a first refusal/co-sale agreement, providing investors the opportunity to first purchase founders' shares offered for sale, or to sell shares along with founders; and a shareholders' agreement, committing its parties to use voting rights in favor of certain actions or outcomes, including, for example, preserving the size of the managing board and sale or other major transactions approved by the board or certain specified shareholders. So-called pay-to-play provisions require prior investors to purchase their pro rata share of future offerings of equity securities, or have their preferred stock converted to common stock.

As noted above, venture investments may involve several funds in any one round, as well as multiple, sequential rounds. A single round of venture investment may involve a phased purchase and sale of preferred stock, with later phases, or tranches, triggered, for example, by the company's achievement of certain technical or business milestones. Between rounds, or to provide working capital before a major event like a sale or public offering, venture capital firms may make convertible debt loans under the label "bridge finance." As in the seed stage, convertible debt allows funds to be deployed without triggering the pricing of stock, the implicit valuation of the enterprise as a whole, and the immediate increase in venture capital stock ownership positions.

Venture Debt

As noted above, EE and RE enterprises may progress along a financing spectrum characterized more by equity risk/equity investment on one end and credit risk/lending on the other. Certain funders apply elements of each. Venture debt is the extension of credit to early and growth-stage companies lacking sufficient revenue and/or assets to satisfy traditional lenders' risk analyses. Venture lending plays several roles in the finance of early- and growth-stage companies, and encompasses a wide range of deal structures involving loans, leases, and equity. Venture debt may be issued in connection with, between, or after rounds of venture financing, and thus may perhaps be described as credit extended on criteria more commonly associated with equity risk. Venture lenders typically receive warrants to acquire preferred stock in a subsequent venture capital financing, providing upside potential for the lender should the borrower be acquired or issue its stock publicly. That equity component, together with confidence-building relationships in key investment communities and access to dynamic and well-led borrowers, enable this hybrid business model.

Venture debt may be used for many different purposes, including, inter alia, obtaining supplies and equipment and providing working capital (through outright loans or lines of credit), which can give a company time to better position itself for further issuances of equity. Like convertible debt, this feature of venture debt enables a company to access capital without requiring concurrent valuation of its stock. This feature is particularly helpful during periods of widespread downward pressure on private companies' values, or when individual companies and their incumbent investors believe they can better position the company for valuation events later (including e.g., in a public offering) by investing the proceeds of a debt transaction.

Venture debt may be secured against borrowers' assets, either broadly (even including proprietary IP) or as financed in the particular transaction (e.g., equipment purchased with loan proceeds subject to security interests of the lender). Venture debt for early-stage companies may not feature extensive financial covenants and other contractual restrictions prevalent in larger and more traditional debt transactions. Such covenants may include requirements and restrictions as to the borrower's financial condition and assets, lenders' approval requirements related to major transactions, and the like. As borrowers progress to more mature stages of development and financing stages, such covenants and restrictions are more likely to appear in venture debt transactions, as the risk and reward scenarios converge with those of more traditional credit.[13]

Venture lenders may be banks or venture capital firms not otherwise regulated as financial institutions. As noted above, venture capital firms can use venture debt to support their portfolio companies without triggering another round of venture finance. Venture debt banks may provide ancillary services like asset and securities services; financial advisory services; cash management, including with regard to foreign exchange matters; and customized debt and syndication services.[14]

Public Equity Offerings

As EE or RE enterprises grow, they may avail themselves of public equity markets to raise additional capital, rather than seeking ever-larger investments from private equity. Doing so allows companies to diversify, rather than concentrate, their ownership structure. Also, founders may have been working for years without easy ways to realize the value of their work. Early private equity investors, including venture capital funds, need a path to liquidity to provide returns to their respective investors. Up to this point, issuances of equity to founders and early investors have generally been exempt from registration requirements under the Federal Securities Laws. Such exemptions simplified and sped early equity transactions, but at the cost of free transferability of such interests on open markets.

For these and other reasons, when their achievements and prospects point to the potential for more widespread investment interest, RE and EE companies can prepare to sell shares of stock on public exchanges, through an initial public offering (IPO).[15] Doing so also marks a company's transition from a privately held to a publicly held company, subject to the Federal Securities Laws' extensive reporting requirements. As discussed more fully below, such requirements may include disclosures of matters particularly relevant to RE and EE companies, including matters related to environmental issues and costs, and, recently, carbon emissions and climate change.

Initial Public Offerings—Business and Administrative Matters

The registration and public sale of securities is a substantial undertaking,[16] involving one or more investment banks to help guide and administer, as underwriters, the preparation for and mechanics of the public sale of the company's stock. Typically, one or two investment banks serve as lead underwriters, heading a syndicate of banks authorized to participate in the offering. Best matches for EE and RE companies may be banks with good reputations among prospective stock purchasers for research, analysis, and presentation of companies in the relevant technology and/or business sectors. Investment banks are also selective, looking for companies with attributes most likely to contribute to a successful offering. Board members from venture capital investors often play key roles brokering company–bank relationships.

Typically, IPOs involve underwriting banks' commitments to purchase all offered shares. The banks then resell the shares on the public market. Under such a firm commitment structure, banks assume the risk that the public appetite for the company's shares falls short of expectations, but keep profits generated by any price updrafts.

Effective marketing of the offering during a "road show" of presentations to prospective buyers (including institutional investors able to buy substantial blocks of shares) goes some way toward mitigating such risks by clarifying buyers' interests and questions.

Key transaction agreements and documents include a letter of intent setting the stage for work among the company and its underwriters toward the IPO; due diligence memoranda; an informational prospectus for investors; the registration statement (Form S-1)[17] to be filed with the U.S. Securities and Exchange Commission (SEC); an underwriting agreement executed immediately prior to the offering (providing details about, inter alia, pricing and allocation of proceeds); and lock-up agreements respecting the withholding of founders' and investors' shares from sale post-offering for up to six months.[18]

Initial Public Offerings—Legal Issues

As noted above, equity interests in companies[19] may only be sold in interstate commerce in compliance with registration and information requirements of the federal securities laws, unless an exemption is provided therefor. Accessing capital from the public via the widespread offering of shares on a national stock exchange requires filing a two-part registration statement with the SEC, and providing the information contained in the first part directly to prospective purchasers.

Preparing a registration statement is a complex undertaking involving the company's senior management, investment banks, counsel, and accountants/auditors, including response to comments on drafts provided by SEC staff. The full breadth of information and disclosure requirements is beyond the scope of this discussion, and is well documented elsewhere. Broadly, Form S-1 incorporates the information requirements of Regulations S-K[20] and S-X[21] promulgated under the 1933 Act. General requirements include a description of the business, its properties, legal proceedings,[22] financial statements and other information,[23] and intended uses of proceeds from the offering.[24]

Particularly relevant for RE and EE issuers may be the required discussion of risk factors that could impact the value of securities offered,[25] management's discussion and analysis of financial condition and results of operations,[26] and quantitative and qualitative disclosures about market risk.[27] RE and EE investments may present a range of unique risks, including ones related to technology risk (including product or service reliability), market adoption, financeability and insurability at scale, regulatory changes, and international factors.

In January 2010, the SEC announced new interpretive guidance for disclosures related to climate change. The guidance calls for issuers to disclose material opportunities and risks, actual and potential, that may affect their businesses and their securities, of climate-related legislation and regulation, including the potential impact of pending legislation and regulation; the impact of international accords; indirect consequences of regulation or business trends, including legal, technological, political, and scientific developments regarding climate change; and physical impacts of climate change.[28]

Subsequent Public Offerings

The disclosure regime that includes Regulations S-K and S-X remains applicable to issuers following their IPOs, through a variety of periodic and special reports required of publicly traded companies under the Federal Securities Laws, as administered by the SEC. Ongoing compliance with such requirements facilitates secondary or follow-on offerings of securities, which may involve registration of new stock to raise additional capital (including "off the shelf" registration covering issuances over a specified period of time), or companies' registration for public sale of previously unregistered stock held by prior investors and other holders.

A company that has already issued shares in public offerings can also raise money privately, through a mechanism called a PIPE—private investment in public equity. A PIPE typically involves two stages. First, a company issues equities (which may include common or preferred stock, convertible debt, warrants, and even various derivative instruments) in a private placement to one or more investors in a transaction exempt from registration requirements under the 1933 Act—typically offerings to accredited investors under Section 4(2) or pursuant to Regulation D. Prices for such equities need not be pegged to the then-current public trading value of the company's common stock. Second, often a condition to the closing of the sale of the PIPE equities, the company files with the SEC for registration of the issued securities, or common stock issuable upon conversion of such securities, to provide immediate liquidity to the PIPE investors. Advantages of PIPE transactions include speed and confidentiality, particularly appealing during times of business or market uncertainty, as may appear in RE and EE sectors due to changes in technology, markets, and/or regulatory environments. PIPE transactions allow private equity investors, including venture capital funds, to utilize the preferred mechanism of exempt offerings to make investments in companies that are already publicly traded.

Corporate Debt

Loan Transactions

As noted above in connection with both early-stage finance and venture debt, RE and EE companies may borrow rather than sell equity to finance key investments and operations, including for working capital purposes, acquiring tangible assets (e.g., equipment) and intangible assets (e.g., IP), constructing facilities, and even acquiring other entities. Making an impact at commercial scale in RE and EE often implicates the construction, installation, operation, and depreciation of large and/or widespread projects. The scale and temporal characteristics of such projects may present challenges to investors' appetite for equity finance alone.[29] Also, when RE and EE products and services near their full commercial potential, their accumulated assets and prospect of predictable revenues may allow them to access substantial pools of capital that turn on the management of credit risk. Thus, companies that have advanced to the commercial scale-up stage often turn to debt.

Lenders are primarily interested in the return of their capital with interest, and they protect their investments through restrictions, covenants, and priority rights as to the value of borrowers' assets. Thus, credit transactions rest on the careful estimation and management of borrowers' ability to repay loans with interest. Like equity, debt obligations may be issued privately or through public markets. Private debt may come from single or multiple sources and may take a number of different forms, including term loans (to be repaid by or on a certain date), loans for the purchase of equipment, and loans to finance construction of facilities that will be used for the manufacture of energy efficiency products and the production, storage, and/or transmission of electricity or fuels or other RE and EE endeavors.

Lenders may be commercial banks, investment banks, life insurance companies, pension funds, or other institutions. Examples of criteria for loans are indicia of the borrowers' ability to repay their loans, including financeable contracts for the purchase of products or services (for example, commitments to acquire energy efficiency products or services, power or fuel purchase agreements, and the like), as well as satisfaction of any concerns over legal and/or regulatory matters, such as access to required real estate or properties, and permitting processes.

Key transaction documents include loan agreements, which address the structure and repayment of loans, as well as borrowers' representations, warranties, and covenants (regarding assets, financial condition, maintenance of debt ratios, lenders' approval rights over certain actions, and transactions and events of default triggering acceleration of payment obligations); security agreements pledging borrowers' assets; and intercreditor agreements clarifying, inter alia, the hierarchy of lenders' rights.

Corporate Bonds

In addition to debt transactions with individual lenders, EE and RE companies may issue bonds to raise money for a variety of purposes, like building a new plant, purchasing equipment, or expanding the business. Corporate bonds represent rights to repayment of principal on a certain date (the date of maturity) and rights to interest (the coupon).

As with offerings of equity, corporations may sell bonds privately, to qualified institutional buyers,[30] or to the public through underwriters such as investment banks. In addition to the requirements of the 1933 Act (discussed above in connection with equity issuances), issuances of bond securities are also subject to the federal Trust Indenture Act of 1939, as subsequently amended.[31] The Trust Indenture Act provides that debt offerings (other than those exempt from registration under applicable provisions of the 1933 Act or for offerings with aggregate proceeds no greater than $10 million) must be made pursuant to an indenture of trust and a registration statement. The indenture of trust vests in third-party bond trustee (typically, a bank) rights and obligations with respect to the administration of bond repayment, events of default, and other key attributes of debt transactions for the benefit of bondholders, that may otherwise be frustrated by the wide distribution and free tradability of corporate bonds. Under the Trust Indenture Act, the registration statement filed with the SEC must include (as though required by the 1933 Act): information required by SEC rules and regulations regarding the eligibility of trustees; analysis of indenture provisions relating to default and notice to the security holders of any such default; the authentication and delivery of the bond securities and the uses of bond proceeds; matters related to the release or the release and substitution of property subject to the lien pursuant to the indenture; the satisfaction and discharge; and evidence required to be furnished by the borrower to the trustee as to compliance with indenture conditions and covenants.[32]

Key transaction documents and agreements include letters of intent and underwriter agreements, as discussed above; an offering circular and registration statement; a bond purchase agreement between the issuer and the underwriters specifying sale terms and conditions, as well as associated representations, warranties, and indemnity provisions; and the bond indenture. As with equity offerings, underwriters sell a substantial fraction of new bond issuances to institutional investors with which the underwriters have developed relationships. Successful bond offerings require prospects for and indicia of financial health that build confidence in an issuer's ability to pay obligations as they come due.

Project Finance Structures

Developers of large-scale RE and EE projects may prefer to structure equity and debt through separate entities, for many reasons. Companies may prefer to isolate substantial project-related debts from their consolidated balance sheets. Also, recall that debt obligations may be secured against the borrower's available assets, including intangible ones like IP. Commercial roll-out of a company's products or services may involve multiple similar installations, each of which may best be financed separately to limit loan security to assets related to each installation, and to facilitate individual sale transactions. Company managers may want to fund deployment of technologies that are market-ready today, while continuing to develop the company's technology platform and IP for other, future commercial opportunities, unencumbered by project debt security interests. Under such circumstances, companies may prefer not to make all of their assets, or unrelated portions, subject to the repayment and security obligations associated with debt financings.

Project finance, or off-balance sheet financing, facilitates the deployment of capital in light of these considerations, with important applications in RE and EE. Project finance may be utilized by a single corporate entity to manage risks and organize the flow of income and tax benefits, but may also allow multiple parties with different operational and economic interests and roles to come together to capitalize on a commercial opportunity, tightly allocating both risks and returns among them.

Project finance often involves creating one or more special-purpose vehicles (SPVs) to hold, develop, and deploy only those assets required for a particular commercial opportunity. Such structures also clarify roles and opportunities of each participant, assuring alignment around project success and minimizing agency problems. Separate subsidiary SPVs may be created to hold and develop assets related to specific installations, further isolating project risk and freeing up prospects of the sale of individual subprojects to provide returns to equity investors.[33]

Choices among available project finance structures are often driven by the availability of tax benefits, including federal tax incentives for EE/RE, discussed more fully in chapter 7 of this book.

Widely used project finance tools include all-equity and leveraged structures. Equity investors typically include developers of RE/EE technologies, products, or services seeking a path to market, without subjecting their other assets and activities to risks associated with project failure and equity investors primarily interested in a project's tax attributes. The simplest structures reflect financing by a single entity with both the financial capacity to fully fund a project and income characteristics enabling it to fully utilize applicable tax benefits. Investor "flip" structures (discussed in chapter 7) involve separate contributions by tax equity investors and project developers and may involve strategic or institutional investors. [34] Among many rights investors may secure are the rights to take over projects from developers should project development fail to meet specified goals.

Leveraged project finance structures introduce debt, which may fund the acquisition of land rights, equipment supply, construction services, operating capital, and the like. Because such debt is typically set up as non-recourse or limited-recourse, loan repayment must flow from project revenues. Thus, project lenders need high levels of confidence in the ability of projects to generate reliable revenue throughout the contemplated loan term. Such confidence must rest on technical, administrative, financial, and commercial grounds. Commitments from key customers, for example utilities' long-term purchase commitments in the form of power purchase agreements, are often key to both equity and lending commitments. The particular commercial arrangements and the conditions reflected in such customer commitments are therefore of great interest to equity and credit financiers alike. The value of such contracts may in turn be enhanced by regulatory supports, including renewable portfolio/electricity standards and renewable fuel standards discussed in chapters 4 and 19, respectively, as well as feed-in tariffs.[35] Similar customer commitments can support projects in other areas of RE and EE, including grid-scale energy storage.[36]

Enabling high-cost, non- or limited-recourse project finance requires a complex series of agreements and ancillary documents, starting with term sheets, which must adequately capture the full scope of ownership, tax, finance, construction, and operational issues. Agreements for execution among the participants typically include operating agreements and associated filings for SPVs; management contracts; contribution, supply, and construction agreements; interconnection agreements; loan facilities; intercreditor and security agreements; and more. Also, administratively and contractually, a range of complicating project-specific issues typically must be addressed before a project financing can close. By way of illustration (and by no means comprehensive), the manufacture of products incorporating RE or EE solutions, or the production, storage, and transport of electricity or fuels may implicate complex issues of land access, environmental protection (including species protection), and interface with applicable transmission infrastructure, as well as dealings with local, state, and federal government agencies. Several public policy initiatives aim to support private finance of EE and RE projects. At the federal level, loan guarantee authority is one such initiative, as discussed in detail in chapter 8.[37]

Summary and Conclusions

This chapter has provided an overview of primary elements of finance for private EE and RE enterprises, as well as selected discussion of applicable federal public policies and programs. It introduces the roles of grants, equity, and credit in both corporate finance and project finance, highlighting how the management of risks and potential rewards drives choices of financing structures and shapes the main elements of transactions that implement them. RE and EE encompass a broad diversity of economic activity—public and private—as well as technologies and business models designed to address them. There remain many questions as to how RE and EE will be best financed, particularly with regard to large-scale transmission and distribution infrastructure. In light of still-evolving markets and policy frameworks, combinations of public and private resources will likely continue to characterize RE and EE finance for some time.

Notes

1. For a more nuanced discussion of such risks in, e.g., power generation, see ELIOT JAMISON, CALCEF INNOVATIONS, FROM INNOVATION TO INFRASTRUCTURE: FINANCING FIRST COMMERCIAL CLEAN ENERGY PROJECTS (June 2010), www.calcef.org/innovations/activities/FirstProjFin_0610.pdf.

2. As a means of ensuring and enforcing such rights, debt repayment obligations can include security-express priority rights to the value of a wide range of valuable assets, like corporate property and equipment, IP, accounts receivable, an so forth. A lender's preference is to secure its debt against all of a company's assets, both tangible and intangible. Such security is expressed in debt transactions' contract terms, as well as evidentiary filings with state authorities where companies are incorporated and/or where their assets are located. Complexity arises as companies issue debt in multiple transactions involving more than one lender. All lenders cannot simultaneously hold first priority rights to all of a company's assets. Accordingly, ranking the priority of lenders' rights as to the value of a company's assets is a key element of debt transaction negotiations and documentation, and may involve intercreditor agreements among existing and new lenders to sort out this thicket.

3. Securities Act of 1933, 15 U.S.C. §§ 77 et seq.; Securities Exchange Act of 1934, 15 U.S.C. §§ 78 et seq.

4. The1933 Act defines "security" as follows:

> When used in this title, unless the context otherwise requires . . . [t]he term "security" means any note, stock, treasury stock, security future, bond, debenture, evidence of indebtedness, certificate of interest or participation in any profit-sharing agreement, collateral-trust certificate, preorganization certificate or subscription, transferable share, investment contract, voting-trust certificate, certificate of deposit for a security, fractional undivided interest in oil, gas, or other mineral rights, any put, call, straddle, option, or privilege on any security, certificate of deposit, or group or index of securities (including any interest therein or based on the value thereof), or any put, call, straddle, option, or privilege entered into on a

national securities exchange relating to foreign currency, or, in general, any interest or instrument commonly known as a "security," or any certificate of interest or participation in, temporary or interim certificate for, receipt for, guarantee of, or warrant or right to subscribe to or purchase, any of the foregoing.

The Securities Act of 1933, 15 U.S.C.S. § 77b(a)(1) (LEXIS 2010).

5. Rule 501 of Regulation D (as amended by the Wall Street Reform and Consumer Protection Act, July, 2010) defines accredited investors as: banks, insurance companies, registered investment companies, business development companies, or small business investment companies; certain employee benefit plans, within the meaning of the Employee Retirement Income Security Act; charitable organizations, corporations, or partnerships with assets greater than $5 million; directors, executive officers, or general partners of companies selling securities; businesses in which all equity owners are accredited investors; natural persons with individual (or joint) net worth, greater than $1 million at the time of the purchase (excluding primary residence); natural persons with income exceeding $200,000, or joint income with a spouse exceeding $300,000; or certain trusts with assets in excess of $5 million. *See, e.g.,* U.S. SEC. & EXCH. COMM'N, ACCREDITED INVESTORS, http://www.sec.gov/answers/accred.htm.

6. U.S. SEC. & EXCH. COMM'N, HOW THE SEC PROTECTS INVESTORS, MAINTAINS MARKET INTEGRITY, AND FACILITATES CAPITAL FORMATION, http://www.sec.gov/about/whatwedo.shtml. *See* 1933 Act Section (4)(1) (exempting transactions by persons not "an issuer, underwriter, or dealer"); Section (4)(2) (private offerings); Section 4(6) (offers to accredited investors). *See also* 1933 Act Section 3(b) and Regulation D (clarifying exemptions per Rules 504, 505, and 506), 17 C.F.R. §§ 230.501-230.508; 1933 Act, Section (3)(a)(11), and Rule 147; 17 C.F.R. 230.147. Rule 506 is the most frequently used of all registration exemptions. Notably, the National Securities Markets Improvement Act of 1996 declared exempt from state securities laws offerings pursuant to Rule 506. 15 U.S.C.S. § 77r (LEXIS 2010).

7. *E.g.,* Small Business Innovation Research (SBIR) Program and Small Business Technology Transfer (STTR) Program, administered by the U.S. Small Business Administration (SBA) Office of Technology. http://www.sba.gov/aboutsba/sbaprograms/sbir/index.html.

8. *E.g.,* Minority Business Development Agency, funded through grants from the U.S. Department of Commerce. http://www.mbda.gov/.

9. 26 U.S.C.S. § 4942 (LEXIS 2010).

10. Investment horizons of fifteen years are sometimes seen in venture-backed industries, for example life sciences, consistent with challenges posed by uncertain technology development and regulatory hurdles. See comments of Emily Baker, Director of Federal Policy and Political Advocacy, National Venture Capital Association, as reported in REPORT OF THE EPA-VENTURE CAPITAL COMMUNITY SUMMIT: EXPLORING PROGRAMS TO COMMERCIALIZE ENVIRONMENTAL TECHNOLOGY, NOVEMBER 12, 2008, 7 (EPA, June 2009), www.epa.gov/ncer/venturecapital/venturecapitalsummit_finaldpv_7_1_09.pdf.

11. *See, e.g.,* model transaction agreements of the National Venture Capital Association, at NAT'L VENTURE CAPITAL ASS'N, MODEL LEGAL DOCUMENTS, http://www.nvca.org/index.php?option=com_content&view=article&id=108&Itemid=136.

12. Such rights may include, inter alia, rights to compel registration of the company's stock for public sale' "lock-up" agreements with regard to the timing of sales of stock after a public offering (called "lock-ups" because they may later be required by investment bankers running such offering); making founders' stock subject to repurchase rights that extinguish over time; rights to information and reports about the company's finances and operations; rights to participate in future rounds of financing; additional approval rights of directors elected by one or more series of preferred stock; and matters relating to grants of incentive stock options.

13. MARC CADIEUX, VENTURE DEBT: A REINTRODUCTION FOR VCS AND ENTREPRENEURS 3-4 (Silicon Valley Bank 2005).

14. *See, e.g.,* SVB Corporate Finance, http://www.svb.com/corpfinance/.

15. Preferred stock held by, for example, venture capital funds is typically converted to common stock immediately prior to its sale to the public.

16. The Office of Management and Budget estimates the average investment of time required to satisfactorily complete the Securities and Exchange Commission's approved form of registration statement (Form S-1) to be 849.2 hours. SEC, Form S-1 Registration Statement Under the Securities Act of 1933, at 1, *available at* http://www.sec.gov/about/forms/forms-1.pdf.

17. SEC, Form S-1 Registration Statement Under the Securities Act of 1933, *supra* note 16.

18. Lock-up agreements serve a variety of confidence-building purposes, including keeping founders and principal investors focused on building value in the company, avoiding appearances that insiders want out, and managing the early market "float" of publicly traded shares.

19. "The term equity security is hereby defined to include any stock or similar security, certificate of interest or participation in any profit sharing agreement, preorganization certificate or subscription, transferable share, voting trust certificate or certificate of deposit for an equity security, limited partnership interest, interest in a joint venture, or certificate of interest in a business trust; any security future on any such security; or any security convertible, with or without consideration into such a security, or carrying any warrant or right to subscribe to or purchase such a security; or any such warrant or right; or any put, call, straddle, or other option or privilege of buying such a security from or selling such a security to another without being bound to do so." 17 C.F.R. § 240.3a11-1 (2010) (defining "equity security" in Sections 12(g) and 16 of the Securities Exchange Act of 1934).

20. Regulation S-K, 17 C.F.R. pt. 229 (2010).

21. Regulation S-X, 17 C.F.R. pt. 210 (2010).

22. 17 C.F.R. §§ 229.101–103.

23. This includes financial statements meeting the requirements of Regulation S-X, as well as any financial information required by Rule 3-05, 17 C.F.R. § 210.3-05, and Article 11 of Regulation S-X. 17 C.F.R. §§ 210.11-01-210.11-03. Smaller reporting companies may provide the information in Rule 8-04 and 8-05 of Regulation S-X, 17 C.F.R. §§ 210.8-04 to -05, in lieu of the financial information required by Rule 3-05 and Article 11 of Regulation S-X; selected financial data required by Item 301 of Regulation S-K, 17 C.F.R. § 229.301; and supplementary financial information required by Item 302 of Regulation S-K. 17 C.F.R. § 229.302.

24. 17 C.F.R. § 229.504.

25. 17 C.F.R. § 229.503.

26. 17 C.F.R. § 229.303.

27. 17 C.F.R. § 229.305.

28. Commission Guidance Regarding Disclosure Related to Climate Change, Securities Act Release No. 9106, Exchange Act Release No. 61469, 75 Fed. Reg. 25 (Feb. 8, 2010); *see also* Press Release, SEC, SEC Issues Interpretive Guidance on Disclosure Related to Business or Legal Developments Regarding Climate Change (Jan. 27, 2010), *available at* http://www.sec.gov/news/press/2010/2010-15.htm ("For instance, a company may face decreased demand for goods that produce significant greenhouse gas emissions or increased demand for goods that result in lower emissions than competing products. As such, a company should consider, for disclosure purposes, the actual or potential indirect consequences it may face due to climate change related regulatory or business trends.").

29. D.P Goldman, Et Al., Nat'l Renewable Energy Lab. Tech. Rep., Financing Projects That Use Clean-Energy Technologies: An Overview of Barriers and Opportunities 2 n.1 (2005).

30. 17 C.F.R. § 230.144A.

31. Trust Indenture Act of 1939, 15 U.S.C. §§ 77aaa-77bbbb (2006).

32. 15 U.S.C. § 77eee.

33. Project finance structures were first widely developed and applied in international construction contexts. For a comprehensive overview of project finance and its international application, see, for example, Graham D. Vinter, Project Finance (3d ed. 2006).

34. *See, e.g.*, E. Jamison, Calcef Innovation White Paper, from Innovation to Infrastructure: Financing First Commercial Clean Energy Projects app. A (2010). For a thorough review of project finance structures utilized for the construction and operation of wind energy projects, see John P. Harper, et al., Lawrence Berkeley Nat'l Lab, Wind Project Financing Structures: A Review & Comparative Analysis (2007).

35. *See also* Cal. Energy Comm'n, Feed-In Tariff Designs for California: Implications for Project Finance, Competitive Renewable Energy Zones, and Data Requirements (2009), http://www.energy.ca.gov/2009_energypolicy/documents/index.html#052809.

36. *See, e.g.*, Matthew Daly, Associated Press, *Salazar Vows to Speed Offshore Wind Energy*, The Boston Globe, Nov. 23, 2010.

37. For an overview of state programs, see Clean Energy States Alliance, 2010 Report: State Efforts To Advance Clean Energy, http://www.cleanenergystates.org/Publications/CESA_Members_Report_2010-Final_LR.pdf.

Part III

Energy Use Sectors

chapter eleven

Conservation of Energy in Agriculture and Forestry

Thomas P. Redick and A. Bryan Endres

This chapter concerns energy use and conservation in agriculture and forestry operations. It focuses on energy audits and energy conservation measures. Unique on-farm aspects of biofuels, wind, and solar are included in this chapter to expand on content discussed in other chapters.

2008 Farm Bill and On-Farm Energy Audits

Updated approximately every five years, the Farm Bill provides the United States Department of Agriculture (USDA) with funding for child nutrition (nearly two-thirds of its budget) and various other farm programs, from trade adjustment assistance to conservation.[1] Recent revisions have moved toward shifting funding from direct farm payments (which may be subsidies that violate international trade law) in favor of conservation payments, which provide a safe harbor from challenges at the World Trade Organization. The 2008 Farm Bill[2] also included substantial funding for energy conservation. Farmers increasingly are concerned about measuring and reducing energy use, which can enable reductions in the cost of production and environmental impacts. The USDA oversees several programs that assist farmers with energy conservation. This section reviews those government programs and also offers a broader context for voluntary standards that may lead to additional energy conservation. In addition, this section discusses developments in farm-specific energy production, such as anaerobic digesters.

Recent History and Future Options for Energy Reduction in Farming

The USDA estimates that although U.S. farms nearly doubled their energy efficiency from 1983 to 2008, high or fluctuating energy costs continue to plague producers, putting economic sustainability of farms at risk. When energy prices soar, some farms that did not plan ahead are left to struggle for their continued existence (e.g., being forced to pay cash for fertilizer that had always been offered for sale on credit). By the same token, farmers may invest capital in energy conservation projects on the assumption that energy prices will remain high and provide a return on investment within a reasonable time. Financial trouble may arise if energy prices drop.

From an energy demand perspective, farmers can conserve energy through regular equipment maintenance and, when replacing older farm equipment, by investing in increased-efficiency motors, fans, lighting, grain drying equipment, and other tools of modern farming.

Farmers can also conserve energy by conserving fertilizer. For example, fertilizer application can be controlled to avoid duplicating coverage when a tractor turns a corner, or it can be applied in varying amounts. In addition, many producers now know that ammonia fertilizer applied to soil temperature at 50 degrees Fahrenheit leads to nitrogen losses that slow crop development and leach into adjacent water.[3] Agricultural practices can also conserve energy via reduced or "no-till" farming (which may control weeds better, leading directly to fewer tractor runs later in the season). Livestock producers can use rotational grazing or drop grain-based feed for grass-fed options.

Lastly, managing water effectively (e.g., switching to drip irrigation) can reduce the energy consumption of irrigation processes. In the future, conversion to drip irrigation in water-constrained agricultural areas will also provide new ways to administer fertilizer, herbicide, and other agricultural chemicals in a manner that reduces inputs and minimizes unwanted drift or migration of agricultural chemicals, while conserving energy.

USDA Rural Energy for America Program

USDA oversees an energy conservation program through its Rural Energy for America Program (REAP) under Section 9007 of the 2008 Farm Bill. From 2003 to 2008, REAP grants provided over $140 million to 2,035 energy projects in each of the fifty states. Funded initiatives in REAP include increased support for the production of cellulosic ethanol and money for the research of pests, diseases, and other agricultural problems. Under a new version of the REAP program in 2009, USDA began funding up to 75 percent of the cost of audits to help farmers and rural small businesses assess and improve upon their energy efficiency.[4] Assisting farms and rural small businesses to determine where energy conservation is possible offers the shortest return on investment. Moreover, USDA will require such audits in any energy efficiency project funded through REAP that costs more than $50,000. USDA has funded rural electric cooperatives and public power entities to conduct these energy audits.

As of 2010, energy auditing availability spurred by USDA funding is driving an increase in demand for agronomic energy consulting. Both the level of interest and the availability of consulting make auditing somewhat limited in rural areas. While the initial impetus for an energy audit may be to qualify for USDA funding (e.g., under REAP), the demand for farm energy audits will probably continue to rise as energy prices increase and farmers recognize the benefits. For example, REAP-funded energy audit findings can help farmers find ways to make their farm buildings more energy efficient through insulation and better sealing of the enclosures.[5] Machinery energy audits and carbon footprint calculators help to assess the greenhouse gas (GHG) contributions of equipment and agronomic practices, and provide additional data to reduce on-farm energy consumption and GHG emissions. In sum, the USDA grant program should be able to demonstrate significant returns on investment as the low-hanging fruits of energy efficiency are identified and farmers reap the benefits of energy conservation.

Farm Energy Efficiency Audit Standards

Private-party adoption of voluntary standards relies on premiums paid by individuals upstream in the agricultural supply chain for these environmental values. In parallel to this industry standard, which is focusing on energy use on-farm, the Standards Committee for the SCS-001 Sustainable Agriculture Standard is also considering on-farm energy metrics in the course of setting a national standard on sustainable agriculture. This national standard depends upon input from two other processes under way outside of the American National Standards Institute (ANSI) system. First, the commodity crops of soybeans, corn, wheat, and potatoes are working together in the Keystone Field-to-Market initiative.[6] This alliance of retailers, growers, and other stakeholders created a Fieldprint Calculator that allows growers to assess how operational decisions affect overall sustainability performance. Second, the Specialty Crops Initiative, sponsored by groups including the Western Growers Association and the Natural Resources Defense Council, addresses the sustainability of specialty crop production. Subgroups within the initiative are examining energy use and conservation on farms.

The Council on Sustainable Biomass Production (CSBP) is another multi-stakeholder group, which has been working since 2007 to develop comprehensive voluntary sustainability standards for the production of biomass to use in energy production.[7] Using CSBP standards for bioenergy GHG emissions, producers of biomass and bioenergy can "maintain and enhance social, economic, and environmental well being" using a "rigorous threshold for the sustainable production of biomass,"[8] which would include energy conservation metrics.

Finally, an emerging industry standard from ANSI, in conjunction with a standard-developing organization known as the American Society of Agricultural and Biological Engineers (ASABE, formerly known as the American Society of Agricultural Engineers or ASAE) is enabling energy auditing. The ASABE Standards Project X612 on Farm Energy Audits began with a USDA grant to ASABE to help administer the consensus committee for this emerging industry standard. Specifically, the USDA's Natural Resources and Conservation Service (NRCS) conceived and promoted development of this ASABE standard, which is sometimes used as a starting point for subsequent regulation. While the standards are proprietary and use of them is not free, there is a fair use policy that ASABE uses to share copies of the standard with other standard developers.

Energy Conservation Efforts in Forestry

Forestry can be an energy-intensive operation, depending on fertilization, irrigation, and other energy inputs during production, and the methods of harvest (which can use various forms of energy-efficient equipment).

Energy can be conserved through increasingly efficient methods of harvesting and transportation. More important contributions to overall efficiency of the forestry production lifecycle will arise when wood production residues from harvesting and finishing operations are used for power generation or, in the future, cellulosic ethanol using vast supplies of wood residues. As is the case with agriculture, forestry needs to leave some residues for soil and ecosystem health.

Sustainable forestry methods include the use of soybean-based oils for lubricants in chainsaws, which leave biodegradable residues (e.g., Home Depot purchases environmentally preferred wood products based on the use of such methods). Digging deeper into the complex aspects of managing forests for optimum production of both biomass and the ecosystem services that forests provide, scientists are exploring management that is "fully systemic: it must account for, and apply to, everything."[9] The approach has to be one that, in fact, can provide specific management focus to address the variety of individual issues (e.g., the biomass that we harvest from any individual species, CO_2 production/sequestration, and harvest from ecosystems). However, each specific focus must embody an accounting for complexity that does not lose sight of either context (extrinsic factors, e.g., the environment, ecosystems, the biosphere) or content/components (intrinsic factors, e.g., chemical reactions, physiological processes, age structure, individual-based dynamics, behavior).

The social and environmental impacts of energy crop plantations may be compared unfavorably to forest residues. As the number of plantations increase, however, the amount of available wood residue is expected to decrease in coming years as forest cover is lost. Energy-efficient plantations will be more economically viable, with high productivity, efficient harvesting, and good logistics—all fundamentals of energy efficiency. Technological advancements could also improve the efficiency of biomass generation and provide significant amounts of wood energy at a moment in history when mandates to use biomass in place of coal are passing in various states.[10] In the United States and around the world, the demand for wood energy is expected to increase. As a result, demand for biomass will exceed supply in many regions, particularly if wood processing industries compete with alternative forms of bioenergy in the production of biomass.

Energy-Reduction Initiatives in Food Manufacturing That Impact the Farm

While U.S. farmers practice energy conservation in large part to maintain their economic sustainability, there are also marketplace demands emerging in the major food manufacturers. Many of the major publicly traded food manufacturers are implementing sustainability programs, hiring managers focused on sustainability and publishing annual sustainability reports. In the course of measuring and reducing their own carbon footprints, food companies will increasingly ask farmers for more information about the environmental impact of food production, especially the energy content of production methods.

For example, in the United States, Wal-Mart has a high-profile effort at setting up a "Sustainability Index" for suppliers, which will include energy conservation as an element.[11] Wal-Mart is not limiting its review of sustainability to the 10 percent of impacts that its operations cause; it is also covering the 90 percent of impacts from its supply chain, on input side, and the use and disposal of products it sells. It wants to uncover new business opportunities for its suppliers. Carbon reporting will become one of those opportunities in the food sector, with corresponding requirements at the farm-level.

The "Wal-Mart of the United Kingdom" is probably Tesco, which has reported that its current direct carbon footprint in the UK was about 2 million tons of carbon dioxide (CO_2) a year, with mass refrigeration of produce accounting for roughly a third of emissions. The firm has commissioned independent research to map the total carbon footprint of its businesses across the world and plans to use an airplane-shape symbol on all goods imported into the country by air. It is also working with key suppliers (e.g., Unilever, Nestle) to reduce its indirect carbon footprint. As these suppliers in turn take a look at their indirect footprint, the role of production agriculture in contributing—or reducing—that footprint becomes a major driver in production agriculture planning. By 2020, Tesco plans to reduce carbon emissions from stores worldwide by 50 percent and limit airplane labels to 1 percent of the firm's products.

Sustainability and energy efficiency are not limited to Wal-Mart and Tesco. There are other efforts at sustainability that could lead a broad array of food buyers to ask for energy-related information. In Canada, the major grocery trade associations are moving forward with a carbon footprint survey of their supply chain, with continued supply potentially dependent upon compliance with "voluntary" reporting (if you want to sell your product, such "voluntary" standards in contracts become a de facto legal standard).[12] In the near future, farmers will have added incentive to monitor and reduce their energy use to achieve sustainability, reporting requirements handed down further along the food supply chain.

Legal Aspects of On-Farm Energy Production

Various federal initiatives are promoting use of alternative energy sources that will allow farms to work toward more sustainable use of energy.[13] Over time, production of on-farm energy will allow many producers to cut their costs and earn more on-farm income.[14] In areas with favorable solar conditions, farmers can make use of solar energy to heat greenhouses and pump water for livestock or irrigation uses. Similarly, in areas with favorable prevailing wind patterns and minimal environmental impacts, farmers may install wind turbines. In either case, the small-scale and distributed nature of farm wind and solar power generation eliminate the need for transmission lines and the significant environmental impacts involved with installation and maintenance of those lines.[15] This section discusses the legal barriers that may arise for on-farm energy generation.

Solar Power (Photovoltaic)

Solar power is one option for farms seeking greater self-sufficiency in energy use. As the owner of photovoltaic (PV) equipment, however, a farmer may become responsible for the equipment's hazards during operation and its disposal at end of life.

Federal Laws Relating to Hazardous Waste

Environmental disposal at the end of life can be costly where the PV equipment contains substances that could be hazardous waste. Liability at this phase of the life cycle for PV equipment can arise under either state or federal law. Efforts are under way, particularly in the European Union (EU), to reduce the hazardous constituents of solar panels.[16]

To the extent that PV equipment contains cadmium and other toxic substances listed as hazardous waste under various federal statutes, product liability can arise from improper disposal, including the failure to warn a foreseeable third-party user of proper disposal practices. The U.S. regulatory framework for solar PV end of life is based on the federal Resource Conservation and Recovery Act (RCRA).

Activists monitoring the solar industry have called for product "takeback"[17] (including government mandates) to encourage recycling and avoid disposal in landfills or hazardous waste facilities.[18] If the environmental liability risks arising from improper disposal justify it, there is reason to initiate forms of take-back that encourage the return of products at end of life. Before undertaking such an initiative, however, companies should have a plan for safe storage and recycling.

State Law Liability for Release of Toxic Components of PV Equipment

States are allowed to set stricter standards for end-of-life risks from potentially hazardous products, and PV is likely to fall into the "Waste Electrical and Electronic Equipment" category of waste products. For example, California's Hazardous Waste Control Law (HWCL) and regulations in several other states may provide stricter hazardous waste designations than the federal government. Moreover, California's product liability law adds a duty to warn the public of compounds that it considers potentially harmful (often at lower levels than federal law would consider potentially harmful). An agricultural operation may be under less rigorous environmental management at the end of life of PV, compared to a solar installation or industrial facility with solar panels.

Failure to comply with a state law regulation can lead to common law product liability (e.g., for failure to warn of a toxic compound in PV), which a farmer may seek if the failure to warn of proper disposal led the farmer to incur liability for remediating contamination from PV equipment.[19]

For injuries occurring to maintenance personnel who undergo extensive training (which they ignore to their detriment), the defense of "sophisticated user" may apply to deny recovery under strict product liability.[20] As a result, the role of adequate worker training for installation, maintenance, and removal-disposal cannot be downplayed in the prevention of PV-related liability.

Emergency Personnel Hazards

While the simplest way for a farm to generate solar power is to install panels on agricultural buildings, this increases the risk to emergency personnel responding to fires.

For example, firemen working atop buildings with solar panels that are on fire may need to create holes in the roof to release smoke. If they do not see a solar panel and pierce the material, it may cause a serious electrical shock injury.[21]

Given this risk, the city of San Francisco proposed in 2010 to require prominent red warning labels on solar panels installed within the city, to ensure that firemen see the panels when providing emergency services in settings where visual observation may be impaired. San Francisco's proposed guidelines stirred controversy, and while they were withdrawn pending further discussion, they illustrate the challenges that emergency workers face in fighting fires on buildings with PV panel installations.[22]

Biomass

On-farm pelletizing of biomass (or even poultry litter) for light-industrial uses such as grain drying or heating of livestock buildings, greenhouses, or outbuildings could offset energy costs and reduce GHG emissions.[23] Although some pelletizing operations occur off-farm and mix biomass with coal or other ingredients to improve shipping efficiency,[24] on-farm pelletizing experiments[25] provide opportunities for increased value-added products at the farm-gate and diversion of product for direct use on the farm.

In addition, many small-scale biofuel (e.g., biodiesel and ethanol) projects are capable of on-farm production.[26] Locally produced energy on farms helps to keep the operating costs on a farm lower, as soybean producers who install biodiesel production equipment have learned. This biodiesel cannot be sold on the open market to third parties (or it is taxed like other fuels), but the on-farm use allows the producers to save money.

Wind Power

Wind power has arrived as an option for energy self-sufficiency and power sales on farms.[27] The legal issues raised by use of this power source include the use of easements on land for wind power development. Wind power may also raise private nuisance issues depending on the reasonableness of the installation in particular areas.[28]

While this is not the same sort of "farming" that America has seen throughout its history, the state of New Jersey recently amended its "right-to-farm" law to allow for renewable energy facilities on preserved farmland.[29] This includes "biomass, solar or wind energy"[30] that conforms to specify "agricultural management practices" recommended by a committee made up of citizens, including farmers. Compliant farms are subject to an "irrebuttable presumption" that they are not a nuisance.[31]

Some locations may be too environmentally valuable to allow wind projects, triggering another aspect of the law of wind farms. The Steens Mountain Cooperative Management and Protection Act of 2000 (legacy of Clinton-era Interior Secretary Bruce Babbitt and then Governor John Kitzhaber) has not stopped some wind developers from asking farmers on Steens Mountain in Oregon to build new wind farms, similar to the growing forest of wind towers along Interstate 84. Oregon's Energy Facility Siting Council must approve new major energy projects in the state, including large-scale wind farms. Opponents consider this area the "the crown jewel of Oregon's high desert."[32]

On the other hand, wind energy development on agricultural land presents unique challenges arising from potential nuisance-type interference with ongoing farming operations. In many areas, aerial application of pesticides is a common agronomic practice.[33] The placement of a wind development project with multiple towers more than four hundred feet high and accompanying transmission lines and meteorological towers can interfere with the ability of neighboring landowners to contract for aerial spraying, or at the very least increase costs. This also raises potential notice issues, including the duty of the wind development owner or landowner to notify crop dusting companies of the presence of wind towers with heights below Federal Aviation Administration limits or to provide markings on towers.[34] Although some states have implemented notification requirements,[35] this developing area of law requires coordination among stakeholders to arrive at reasonable limits with respect to development of wind energy resources while minimizing the impacts on agricultural lands.

On-Farm Energy Production: Anaerobic Digesters

As noted in chapter 19, in biofuels production "[t]he feedstock is produced or gathered, and from there it must be harvested, stored and transported to the biorefinery." The use of anaerobic digesters[36] on farms to convert manure to heat or power drastically shortens the bioenergy supply chain, allowing the farm to produce energy to power its operations and, depending upon state requirements, sell its excess electricity to the regional power authority. This is a winning situation at several levels as anaerobic digesters convert a potential cost to farmers (manure disposal)[37] into an income source (electricity) or carbon credits,[38] provide a source of renewable energy with potentially lower GHG emissions,[39] reduce dependence on fossil fuels, and have the potential to provide additional environmental benefits such as reduction of odors[40] or other pollutants from manure storage facilities while lowering the potential for water pollution from run-off.[41]

Anaerobic digesters offer a potential solution to two of the fundamental environmental issues facing livestock production—odors and water pollution from manure handling and storage.[42] Numerous nuisance claims lodged against existing or even proposed livestock production facilities cite these dual concerns.[43] In addition to nuisance suits, livestock facilities are subject to increasing regulatory scrutiny. Under its Clean Water Act authority, the EPA has issued rules requiring nutrient management plans to reduce the potential for water pollution from manure run-off.[44] Compliance with the new rules may result in the construction of additional waste-holding lagoons, which has the indirect effect of increasing the potential for anaerobic digesters. Strong regulatory incentives also exist for anaerobic digesters in the odor-management context. In 2005, the EPA finalized a consent decree with livestock producers to study the odors associated with manure storage.[45] In exchange for relief from potential liability arising from air emissions under the Clean Air Act, the Comprehensive Environmental Response, Compensation, and Liability Act and the Emergency Planning and

Community Right-to-Know Act, livestock operations paid EPA a civil penalty and provided $15 million for an independent study of emissions. To the extent anaerobic manure digesters can solve these air emission and water pollution issues while producing "clean" renewable energy, there is the potential for a symbiotic relationship between rural communities struggling with the intersection of environmental protection and large-scale animal agricultural operations. The following sections describe the energy potential of anaerobic digesters and the outlook for increased adoption by livestock producers.

Power Potential

Anaerobic digesters use bacteria to convert the organic compounds in manure into biogas, which is a combination of 60 to 80 percent methane, with the balance made up of carbon dioxide and trace amounts of other gases.[46] Data from mid-2008 indicated that ninety-four commercial dairy farms and seventeen hog farms had installed anaerobic digesters, and sixty-four additional dairy operations had projects in the construction, design, or planning stage.[47] This accounts for approximately 4.5 percent of dairy farms with over two thousand cows.[48] There are approximately 8.5 million cows in the United States, producing 30 cubic feet of biogas per day.[49] Biogas, with an energy value of approximately 600 to 800 BTU per cubic foot, can produce heat through direct combustion or can power internal combustion engines to power generators with cost estimates ranging from six to thirteen cents per kilowatt-hour.[50] Accordingly, anaerobic digestion of manure has the potential to replace significant amounts of fossil fuels while making productive use of a waste product.

This relatively simple technology supplies cooking or lighting for between six and eight million families in developing countries, and an additional six hundred sophisticated farm-based digesters operate in Europe.[51] There is potential for greater adoption in the United States, but research and development (R&D) and deployment of new anaerobic digester technology has been relatively small, providing only $37 million in anaerobic digester assistance funds since 2003.[52]

First instituted in the 1970s, the EPA's AgSTAR program, a collaborative effort with USDA and the Department of Energy (DOE), promotes anaerobic digestion technology adoption at the farm level through the provision of technical support and management assistance for high-visibility demonstration projects.[53] Although the program initially subsidized installation of one hundred on-farm digesters in the 1970s, most failed due to use of improper equipment or lack of capacity to handle the one to three thousand tons of manure produced on a typical dairy farm.[54] The current AgSTAR program counts 151 anaerobic digesters in operation in the United States producing 354,000 MWh equivalents of power.[55]

Outlook for the Future

Although proposed within the context of GHG emission reductions, in December 2009, the USDA pledged to work with dairy producers to increase deployment of anaerobic digesters.[56] With an average capital cost over $285,000,[57] it will be essential for dairy producers to work with existing USDA cost-sharing programs such as the Environmental Quality Incentive Program (EQIP), implemented by the USDA's Natural Resources Conservation Service and the Rural Energy for America Program (REAP), implemented by the USDA Rural Development.[58] For example, a dairy producer could secure funding for improved waste management practices through EQIP and support for the digester and electricity generation components through REAP.[59] REAP could also assist farmers in feasibility studies.[60] In addition, the USDA pledged to work with various agencies and governmental entities to assist connecting anaerobic digesters to the electrical grid in those states with net metering rules.[61]

As the enhanced environmental rules described above impact concentrated animal feeding operations and fluctuating energy prices make farm financial planning more difficult, an alternative energy source, such as anaerobic digesters, that also has the ability to reduce the risk of environmental noncompliance, provides a novel technological solution capable of immediate deployment. Farmers in Europe facing similar constraints have adopted anaerobic digesters on a larger scale, and it is likely that U.S. farmers will do the same.

Reducing Embedded Energy Costs in Inputs and Equipment

DOE currently requires testing of some product categories and may expand this regulatory initiative over time.[62] California and Canada are both moving toward greater disclosure of energy efficiency in products. Both the California Energy Commission and Natural Recovery Canada require third-party energy efficiency testing for all products. This may drive a common denominator effect as manufacturers seek to design for all markets.

Once a farmer understands the components of energy use that make up a "carbon footprint," steps can be taken to reduce it. EPA's new mandatory reporting of GHG emissions above a 25,000-ton threshold left out all but 107 of the largest agricultural operations in the United States. Washington state's 10,000-ton reporting limit, the first to take the reporting requirement to a lower tonnage level, might include some large livestock facilities and food processors and further drive the need to audit indirect energy use. Washington's reporting initiative could lead to other states following suit, with an accompanying larger impact on farming.

The potential for regulatory reporting, along with the high cost of energy, may drive more food processors to encourage farmers to seek to reduce the energy embedded in their production inputs and equipment. Suppliers of equipment have begun to design more efficient machines that use less energy in operation. Grain drying and refrigeration are two areas of energy use that are amenable to reduced energy use.

In choices of agricultural chemicals, farmers may reduce their indirect energy use (via embedded energy in fertilizers and pesticides) by practicing integrated pest management and using fertilizers in a more targeted, precise manner. The equipment used to apply fertilizer is being adapted to minimize over-application. Testing soil prior to application can tailor fertilizer use to actual needs.

Agricultural equipment manufacturers are seeing significant savings when they review their energy efficiency. For tool makers, the customer knows now that the energy-related cost of ownership is often greater than the price of the equipment, making it a valuable area of inquiry. Some equipment consumes ten times more energy during use than it took to manufacture the product.

Given the increased attention being paid to energy use as a cost center and potential regulatory or customer mandate, farmers and foresters increasingly need to measure their energy use and take conservation measures where feasible.

Notes

1. USDA, FOREIGN AGRIC. SERV., TRADE ADJUSTMENT ASSISTANCE FOR FARMERS FAQS www.fas.usda.gov/itp/taa/taafaqs.asp (last updated May 13, 2010); USDA, Natural Res. Conservation Serv., 2008 Farm Bill Brochure: Conservation Practices and Programs for Your Land, http://www.nrcs.usda.gov/programs/farmbill/2008/index.html (updated Jan. 24, 2011).

2. Food, Conservation, and Energy Act of 2008, Pub. L. No. 110-246, 121 Stat. 1768 (2008).

3. *See, e.g.*, the Nitrogen and Phosphorus Knowledge web page, http://extension.agron.iastate.edu/NPKnowledge (daily, previous-day, and three-day history of average soil temperatures in every Iowa county).

4. USDA, RURAL DEVELOPMENT, http://www.rurdev.usda.gov/rbs/busp/REAPEA.htm.

5. REAP FAQ, http://www.farmenergy.org/tools/reap.faq. *See also* Truman C. Surbrook & Aluel S. Go, Energy Savings on the Farm: MI Farm Energy Audit Program, Presentation at ACE Conference, Lansing Center (Jan. 28, 2009).

6. FIELD TO MARKET: THE KEYSTONE ALLIANCE FOR SUSTAINABLE AGRICULTURE (2008), www.fieldtomarket.org.

7. Council on Sustainable Biomass Production, Draft Standard (Sept. 11, 2009). Elements of the standard include Biofuel GHG Emissions Requirements, Indirect Land Use Change and Greenhouse Gas Emissions Requirements of Growers for Biomass CSBP. Current members of the CSBP include major environmental groups and industry representatives. See an overview of the standard at http://www.csbp.org/#Overview.

8. Council on Sustainable Biomass Production, Draft Provisional Standard for Sustainable Production of Agricultural Biomass 4 (Apr. 14, 2010), *available at* http://www.csbp.org/files/survey/CSBP_Provisional_Standard.pdf.

9. Charles W. Fowler, *Tenets, Principles, and Criteria for Management: The Basis for Systemic Management*, 65(3) Marine Fisheries Rev. 1, 4 (Mar. 22, 2003) (citing R.T. Lackey, Ecosystem Management: Implications for Fishery Management, 13 Renewable Resources J. 11 (1995–96)), *available at* http://spo.nmfs.noaa.gov/mfr652/mfr6521.pdf.

10. *See* EPA, Renewable Portfolio Standards Fact Sheet (Apr. 2009), *available at* http://www.epa.gov/chp/state-policy/renewable_fs.html.

11. WALMART, SUSTAINABILITY INDEX WORKING MODEL 2.0 (for stakeholder input), http://www.zoomerang.com/Survey/?p=WEB2289TFDQFUQ).

12. Walter Kraus, *Corporate Social Responsibility at Canada's Largest Grocery Retailer* (Apr. 12, 2010) (notes on file with author).

13. See, for example, the American Reinvestment and Recovery Act of 2009 (ARRA), which provides nearly $50 billion in direct funding, tax incentives, and loan guarantees designed to fast-track the development and implementation of renewable energy technologies. AMERICAN COUNCIL ON RENEWABLE ENERGY (ACORE), OVERVIEW: RENEWABLE ENERGY PROVISIONS: AMERICAN RECOVERY AND REINVESTMENT ACT OF 2009, www.acore.org/files/images/email/acore_stimulus_overview.pdf.

14. *See* ENVTL. LAW & POL'Y CTR., PLOW ALLOWANCES INTO LOW CARBON AG ENERGY SOLUTIONS: PROPOSAL EXPANDS AGRICULTURE BENEFITS, http://farmenergy.org/wp-content/uploads/2009/09/Ag-Energy-Carbon-Allowance-fact-sheet.2009-08.pdf.

15. *See* http://attra.ncat.org/attra-pub/farm_energy/index.php.

16. Veronica Webster, Bellona, Fighting for Clean Solar Energy in Europe (May 4, 2010), *available at* www.bellona.org/articles/articles_2010/clean_solar_in_europe.

17. One cadmium/tellurium PV manufacturer offers a take-back policy and will fund product returns and recycling with an annuity from a major international insurance company. Recovery of tellurium through recycling is important to ensure global availability. Peter Meyers, First Solar Polycrystalline CdTe Thin Film PV, Photovoltaic Energy Conversion, Conference Record of the 2006 IEEE 4th World Conference (May 2006), *available at* Texas Solar Energy Society, http://www.txses.org/solar/content/solar-photovoltaic-end-life.

18. The Silicon Valley Toxics Coalition publishes a survey called the Solar Scorecard that includes consideration of end-of-life disposal issues. *See* www.solarscorecard.com.

19. Selma Pressure Treating Co. v. Osmose Wood Preserving Co., 271 Cal. Rptr. 596 (Cal. Ct. App. 1990).

20. *See* Johnson v. Am. Standard, 179 P.3d 905 (Cal. 2008).

21. *See, e.g.*, San Francisco Fire Dep't, Solar Photovoltaic Permitting Procedures & Installation Guidelines (proposed) (withdrawn), *38.106.4.187/index.aspx?page=965* (May 19, 2010) (For example, "To limit the hazard of cutting live conduit in venting operations, DC wiring shall be run in metallic conduit or raceways when located within enclosed spaces in a building and should be run, to the maximum extent possible, along the bottom of load-bearing members").

22. *Id.*

23. Agricultural Utilization Research Initiative, AURI Looks at Biomass-Pellet Fuel's Potential for On-Farm and Light-Industrial Uses (July 2007), http://www.auri.org/agnews-section.php?sid=110&agnid=54.

24. Katie Pratt, *Switchgrass Pelletized in Kentucky Project*, Southeast Farm Press, Jan. 20, 2010, *available at* http://southeastfarmpress.com/biofuels/switchgrass-biomass-0120/?utm_source=feedburner&utm_medium=feed&utm_campaign=Feed%3A+SoutheastFarmPress+%28Southeast+Farm+Press%29.

25. Farm Pilot Project Coordination, Inc., Quarterly Report for July 1–Sept. 30, 2008: Executive Summary, *available at* http://www.fppcinc.org/pdf/FPPC_2008_Q3.pdf.

26. *See, e.g.*, Vermont Sustainable Jobs Fund, Biomass to Biofuels Resources, http://www.vsjf.org/project-details/13/biomass-to-biofuels-resources.

27. Green Energy Ohio, Wind Power for Farms, available at www.greenenergyohio.org/page.cfm?pageId=540 (citing "Wind Energy for Your Farm or Rural Land," AWEA fact sheet).

28. Roger L. Freeman & Ben Kass, *Siting Wind Energy Facilities on Private Land in Colorado: Common Legal Issues*, 39 Colo. Law. 43 (May 2010), *available at* http://www.dgslaw.com/attorneys/ReferenceDesk/Freeman-Kass_ColoLaw_SitingWindEnergy.pdf.

29. *See* New Jersey Right to Farm Act, N.J. Stat. Ann. §§ 4:1C-1 et seq., *available at* www.nj.gov/agriculture/sadc/rtfprogram/rtfact/righttofarmact.pdf.

30. *Id.* at 4:1C-2(i).

31. *Id.* at 4:1C-10.

32. Bill Marlett, Jill Workman, & Andy Kerr, *Didn't We Already Save the Steens from Wind Farms?*, OregonLive.com, June 12, 2010, http://www.oregonlive.com/opinion/index.ssf/2010/06/didnt_we_already_save_the_stee.html.

33. *See* Jay Calleja, *The Campaign for Responsible Wind Energy Development*, Agric. Aviation (May/June 2008), at 14 (published by the National Agricultural Aviation Association).

34. *See* 14 C.F.R. pt. 77; U.S. Dep't of Transp., FAA, Advisory Circular, AC 70/7460-1K, Obstruction Marking and Lighting, at 33 (Feb. 1, 2007) (providing guidance on marking wind energy projects).

35. *See* 2010 S.D. Sess. Laws ch. 229 (codified at S.D. Codified Laws § 50-9-13) (requiring marking); Wyo. Stat. Ann. § 10-4-305 (same).

36. For a description of how anaerobic digestion works, see Dep't of Energy, How Anaerobic Digestion (Methane Recovery) Works, http://www.energysavers.gov/your_workplace/farms_ranches/index.cfm/mytopic=30003.

37. USDA, Economic Research Service, Manure Use for Fertilizer and for Energy, Report to Congress IV (June 2009) [hereinafter Manure Use] (noting manure disposal costs to comply with nutrient management plans may increase production costs from 2.5 to 3.5 percent).

38. For example, the Chicago Climate Exchange (CCX) offered carbon credits to the installation of anaerobic digesters. Tony Kryzanowski, *Manure Generators with Digesters Can Earn Income from Selling Carbon Credits*, http://www.manuremanager.com/content/view/1141/132/. *See also supra* note 4; USDA, Rural Development, Cooperative Approaches for Implementation of Dairy Manure Digesters, Research Report 217, at 13–15 (Apr. 2009), *available at* http://www.rurdev.usda.gov/rbs/pub/rr217.pdf (discussing possibility of carbon credit trading).

39. EPA, The AgSTAR Program, The Accomplishments, http://www.epa.gov/agstar/accomplish.html (noting direct and indirect reductions of GHG emissions).

40. Decomposition of manure creates the odor problems associated with animal production. Because anaerobic digestion of the manure leaves few decomposable compounds, the use of an anaerobic digester can solve the odor problems. *See* USDA, Manure Use, *supra* note 37, at 32. *See also* Donald L. Van Dyne & J. Alan Weber, *Biogas Production from Animal Manures: What is the Potential*, Industrial Uses, Dec. 1994, at 21.

41. EPA, *Managing Manure with Biogas Recovery Systems: Improved Performance at Competitive Costs* 7, EPA 430F02004 (winter 2002), *available at* nepis.epa.gov/Exe/ZyPURL.cgi?Dockey=2000ZL4E.txt.

42. *See* Jody M. Endres & Margaret Rosso Grossman, *Air Emissions from Animal Feeding Operations: Can State Rules Help?* 13 Penn. St. Envtl. L. Rev. 1 (2004); Kate Celender, Note, *The Impact of Feedlot Waste on Water Pollution under the National Pollution Discharge Elimination System (NPDES)*, 33 Wm. & Mary Envtl. L. & Pol'y Rev. 947 (2009).

43. *See* Terrence J. Centner, *Nuisances from Agricultural Operations: Reconciling Agricultural Production and Neighboring Property Rights*, 11 Drake J. Agric. L. 5 (2006); Nickels v. Burnett, 798 N.E.2d 817 (Ill. App. Ct. 2003) (applying the common law doctrine of anticipatory nuisance to proposed livestock production facility despite compliance with statutory permitting regime).

44. EPA, Final Rulemaking, Revised National Pollutant Discharge Elimination System Permit Regulation and Effluent Limitations Guidelines for Concentrated Animal Feeding Operations in Response to the *Waterkeeper* Decision, 74 Fed. Reg. 70418 (2008) (codified at 40 C.F.R. § 122.23(h)). *But see* National Pork Producers Council v. EPA, 2011 WL 871736 (5th Cir. Mar. 15, 2011) (holding that EPA lacked authority to impose upon CAFOs a duty to apply for NPDES permits).

45. EPA, Animal Feeding Operations Consent Agreement and Final Order, 70 Fed. Reg. 4958 (2005).

46. Donald L. Van Dyne & J. Alan Weber, *Biogas Production from Animal Manures: What Is the Potential*, Industrial Uses, Dec. 1994, at 21; USDA, Rural Development, *supra* note 4.

47. USDA, Manure Use, *supra* note 37, at 33.

48. *Id.*

49. USDA Rural Development, *supra* note 4; USDA Rural Development, USDA Rural Development Helps Brighten California's Energy Future and Its Environment 4, *available at* http://www.rurdev.usda.gov/CA/pdf%20files%20and%20documents/methane-backgrounder.doc.

50. Steve Thompson, USDA Rural Development, Bovine Biogas, Dec. 2001, at 3, *available at* http://www.rurdev.usda.gov/rbs/pub/dec01/biogas.html; USDA Rural Development, Cooperative Approaches for Implementation of Dairy Manure Digesters, Research Report 217, at 8 (Apr. 2009).

51. USDA Rural Development, *supra* note 49, at 1.

52. *See* EPA, AgSTAR Accomplishments, http://www.epa.gov/agstar/accomplish.html.

53. Van Dyne & Weber, *supra* note 40, at 24.

54. USDA, *Bovine Biogas, supra* note 50, at 4.

55. EPA, AGSTAR ACCOMPLISHMENTS, http://www.epa.gov/agstar/accomplish.html.

56. News Release No. 0613.09, USDA, Agriculture Secretary Vilsack, Dairy Producers Sign Historic Agreement to Cut Greenhouse Gas Emissions by 25% by 2020 (Dec. 15, 2009).

57. USDA, RURAL DEVELOPMENT, COOPERATIVE APPROACHES FOR IMPLEMENTATION OF DAIRY MANURE DIGESTERS, Research Report 217, at 6 (Apr. 2009).

58. Memorandum of Understanding between UDSA and the Innovation Center for U.S. Dairy (Dec. 15, 2009), *available at* http://www.usda.gov/documents/FINAL_USDA_DAIRY_GHG_AGREEMENT.pdf.

59. *Id.*

60. *Id.*

61. *Id.*

62. Energy Conservation Program for Consumer Products: Test Procedures for Refrigerators, Refrigerator-Freezers, and Freezers (Dec. 16, 2010), *available at* http://www.federalregister.gov/articles/2010/12/16/2010-30071/energy-conservation-program-for-consumer-products-test-procedures-for-refrigerators (addressing "combination wine storage–freezer units" and potentially implicating the food supply chain).

chapter twelve

Appliances, Lighting, Computers, Data Centers, and Computer Servers

John A. Hodges

Appliances are a key element in the development of energy efficiency law. The scope of appliance rules has expanded since the oil crises in the 1970s and now includes a broad range of residential and commercial products. This includes not only traditional household appliances but also such products as lighting, computers, data centers, and computer servers.

The development of appliance efficiency law has engaged the three branches of the federal government and many other players, including industry, standards developers, efficiency conservation advocates, states, and foreign governments. The history of the law has been marked both by conflict and by instances of consensus—in which the appliance industry and energy conservation advocates have hammered out important agreements and presented them to government for adoption.

The push for appliance efficiency is further accelerating under the Obama administration. It is seeking to eliminate the backlog of rulemakings, increase enforcement, and adopt ambitious new requirements. Efforts to increase efficiency are gaining additional urgency in light of difficulties in adopting comprehensive climate change legislation. In comparison with climate change legislation, energy efficiency is relatively low-hanging fruit.

The Framework for the Federal Appliance Efficiency Program

Appliance efficiency falls within the Energy Policy and Conservation Act (EPCA), signed into law in 1975.[1] It provides for establishment of test procedures for appliances, efficiency standards, labeling, and preemption of state requirements. Standards and test procedures are administered by the Department of Energy (DOE),[2] and labeling is administered by the Federal Trade Commission (FTC).[3]

EPCA prohibits manufacturers, distributors, and retailers from making any representation concerning energy efficiency or energy use of a "covered product" for which there is a DOE test procedure unless the product has been tested in accordance with the test procedure and such representation fairly discloses the results of the testing.[4]

Mandatory efficiency standards use the DOE test procedures.[5] Labeling of products pursuant to EPCA is subject to requirements of the FTC, which are to follow DOE test procedures.[6]

EPCA contains stringent provisions for preemption of state regulations on energy efficiency, energy use, or water use of covered products.[7] Narrow exceptions to preemption are provided for certain state procurement standards and certain building code requirements.[8] There are also rules for potential waivers of preemption for state regulations under carefully defined circumstances.[9]

EPCA has extensive enforcement provisions.[10] Appliance industry third-party testing and certification programs supplement federal enforcement.[11]

EPCA also covers the voluntary Energy Star program for appliances (discussed below), which involves both DOE and the Environmental Protection Agency (EPA).[12]

History of the Federal Appliance Efficiency Program

The federal appliance efficiency program was provided for in 1975 through EPCA as part of a "comprehensive national energy policy."[13] Initially, EPCA required the Federal Energy Administration (FEA), a predecessor to DOE, to issue voluntary energy efficiency improvement targets for thirteen "covered" appliances. If FEA were to determine that manufacturers were unlikely to achieve the target for an appliance by 1980, it was to commence a proceeding to prescribe a mandatory efficiency standard for that appliance. In 1978, impatient for efficiency improvements, Congress enacted the National Energy Conservation and Policy Act (NECPA),[14] amending EPCA to abandon the target approach and require DOE to issue mandatory standards for the thirteen covered appliances, unless DOE determined that a standard was not justified.

In response, DOE, under the Reagan Administration, conducted a rulemaking resulting in the issuance of so-called "no-standard standards" for most of the covered appliances.[15] This determination was based on DOE's position that standards for these appliances were not justified. Under EPCA, the "no-standards standards" had preemptive effect against state standards.[16]

DOE's determination was overturned by the Court of Appeals for the District of Columbia Circuit.[17] The court took DOE behind the woodshed. In a highly detailed, strongly worded opinion, the court ruled that DOE had established too-stringent criteria to measure whether energy savings from an appliance standard would be "significant." It also ruled that DOE had "failed to determine the maximum technologically feasible improvements in efficiency for covered products and limited the technologies it was willing to consider for standards without sufficient explanation."[18] In addition, it ruled that DOE "made persistently pessimistic assumptions about the burdens of standards and was conspicuously reluctant to address their benefits."[19] The court sent the matter back to DOE for further rulemaking, which would require a "comprehensive reappraisal of the appliance program."[20]

The court's decision had a galvanizing effect. Energy conservation advocates had won a victory but were facing the resulting prospects of prolonged rulemaking before new DOE standards would be issued and become effective. Appliance manufacturers faced uncertainty. The court's overturning of federal standards had the effect of eliminating preemption that flowed from the standards. Even before the court's decision, states had been issuing their own requirements, and the court's decision was sure to stimulate further state activity. "Appliance manufacturers, accordingly, were confronted with the absence of Federal appliance standards for the immediate future, and a growing plethora of differing state regulations, complicating industry's long-term planning."[21]

The interests of all sides converged, and the stage was set for a legislative solution. Negotiations between appliance manufacturers and energy conservation advocates ensued. These resulted in an agreement that Congress adopted virtually intact as the National Appliance Energy Conservation Act of 1987 (NAECA) amendments to EPCA.[22] NAECA set forth congressionally established uniform national standards,[23] stronger preemption of state requirements,[24] and new and more stringent criteria, making it much more difficult for a state to obtain a waiver of preemption.[25] NAECA also provided a schedule for DOE rulemakings to periodically review and update the standards.[26] The amended standards were to set levels that achieve the maximum improvement in energy efficiency that was technologically feasible and economically justified.[27]

NAECA has provided the template for further legislative amendments expanding coverage to other products and increasing the stringency of rules for products already covered. For example, the amendments to EPCA relating to commercial and industrial equipment contained in the Energy Policy Act of 1992 (EPAct)[28] follow the approach of NAECA.

Due to dissatisfaction with DOE's procedures under EPCA, Congress enacted a moratorium on proposing or issuing energy conservation appliance standards for the remainder of fiscal year 1996.[29] In addition, the National Performance Review made recommendations on regulatory reform.[30] In light of these, DOE halted rulemaking activity and set about developing extensive new procedures for carrying out its appliance rulemakings.[31] These include such things as providing for early input from stakeholders and highly detailed analyses.

As a result of the rulemaking moratorium, the high degree of analysis involved in appliance efficiency rulemaking, and DOE's heavy workload, DOE fell behind in its rulemaking. Predictably, DOE was sued by states and energy conservation advocates, which argued that DOE was violating statutory schedules. The litigation led to a settlement in which DOE agreed to conduct further rulemakings based on an agreed-upon schedule.[32] DOE is also addressing additional standards and test procedure requirements included in the Energy Policy Act of 2005[33] and the Energy Independence and Security Act of 2007 (EISA).[34] On February 5, 2009, President Obama issued a memorandum to DOE requesting that it "take all necessary steps ... to finalize legally required standards rulemakings as expeditiously as possible consistent with all applicable judicial and statutory deadlines."[35] This all has escalated the pace of DOE appliance rulemaking. "This ambitious schedule reflects a 6-fold increase in standards activity compared to the previous 18 years."[36]

Congress has streamlined some of the time-consuming DOE rulemaking process. Under EISA, where a fairly representative group of interested persons jointly submits a recommended standard and no adverse public comments are received, DOE may issue a "direct final rule" establishing a standard.[37] In addition, Congress has removed the requirement for an Advance Notice of Proposed Rulemaking (ANOPR) for certain products.[38] In such cases, instead of an ANOPR, DOE is posting analyses on its website and holding public meetings on DOE's preliminary analyses.[39]

EISA also amends EPCA to require that DOE review test procedures at least once every seven years and amend them where warranted.[40]

EISA further provides for DOE consideration of establishing regional standards for central air conditioners, furnaces, and heat pumps.[41] This provision has caused substantial concern for manufacturers, who generally have wished to have uniform national standards, which has been a central tenet of EPCA.[42] (See further discussion of regional standards below.)

The scope of products subject to standards will inevitably increase. For example, the Waxman-Markey bill called for additional lighting standards[43] and standards for water dispensers, food handling cabinets, and electric spas.[44] While the bill was not adopted, its appliance energy efficiency provisions may well be a harbinger of things to come.

The Waxman-Markey bill would have mandated a "Best-in-Class Appliances Deployment Program."[45] This would have required DOE to establish a program to provide bonus payments to retailers or distributors for sale of best-in-class high-efficiency appliances, installed building equipment, and consumer electronics. It would have also provided for bounties to retailers and manufacturers for the replacement, retirement, and recycling of old, inefficient, and environmentally harmful products. Premium awards would have been paid for developing and producing new "Superefficient Best-in-Class Products." In carrying out these provisions, the bill would have required DOE to define product classes broadly and generally to designate as Best-in-Class Product models no more than the most efficient 10 percent of the commercially available models in a class that demonstrate, as a group, a distinctly greater energy efficiency than the average energy efficiency of that class. Thus, this would have been a way to obtain, on a voluntary basis, efficiencies beyond mandatory minimums and beyond the incentives provided by the Energy Star program.[46]

Due to the inability of Congress to pass a comprehensive energy bill, Senator Bingaman in September 2010 introduced a new bill, the "Implementation of National Consensus Appliance Agreements Act" (INCAAA).[47] INCAAA packaged a number of elements as to which there purported to be consensus, including new or amended standards negotiated between industry and energy-efficiency advocates. The bill included standard provisions for central air conditioners, heat pumps, furnaces, room air conditioners, refrigerators and freezers, clothes washers and dryers, dishwashers, portable lighting fixtures, pole-mounted outdoor lighting fixtures, drinking water dispensers, hot food holding cabinets, and electric spas. It also included provisions for accelerated rulemaking and updated decision-making criteria, and new developments such as smart-grid technologies. INCAAA died at the end of the 111th Congress. The 2010 congressional midterm elections may potentially affect the prospects for adoption of any similar bill in the next Congress.

DOE Appliance Efficiency Rulemaking

There have been extensive, highly complex DOE rulemakings to consider amendments to appliance standards, taking into account such factors as technological feasibility and economic justification.

The typical proceeding involves issuance of an ANOPR,[48] along with a draft Technical Support Document setting forth potential appliance energy efficiency standard levels; the technology configurations available to achieve each level; and the costs and benefits of achieving each level. After obtaining public comments on the ANOPR, DOE issues for public comment a Notice of Proposed Rulemaking (NOPR) with a specific proposed standard. After a further round of public comment, DOE issues a Final Rule setting forth its decision as to a standard. Lead times are provided for manufacturers to achieve the new levels, with standards to apply to products manufactured on or after a specified date. Lock-in periods help ensure that manufacturers are able to recover costs before standards are amended again.[49]

In determining whether an appliance standard is economically justified, DOE is to determine whether the benefits of the standard exceed its burdens by, to the greatest extent practicable, considering a number of factors. In brief, these include (1) the economic impact of the standard on the manufacturers and on the consumers of the products; (2) the savings in operating costs throughout the estimated average life of the covered product in the type (or class) compared to any increase in the price of, or in the initial charges for, or maintenance expenses of, the covered products that are likely to result from the imposition of the standard; (3) the total projected amount of energy savings, or as applicable, water savings likely to result directly from the imposition of the standard; (4) any lessening of the utility or the performance of the covered products likely to result from the imposition of the standard; (5) the impact of any lessening of competition, as determined by the Attorney General, that is likely to result from the imposition of the standard; (6) the need for national energy and water conservation; and (7) other factors DOE considers relevant.[50]

If DOE finds that the additional cost to the consumer of purchasing a product complying with an energy conservation standard level will be less than three times the value of the energy savings, and, as applicable, water savings during the first year that the consumer will receive as a result of the standard, as calculated under the applicable test procedure, there is a rebuttable presumption that the standard level is economically justified. A DOE determination that this criterion is not met is not to be taken into consideration in DOE's determination of whether a standard is economically justified.[51]

DOE may not prescribe an amended or new standard if, among other things, DOE determines that the establishment of the standard will not result in significant conservation of energy or, in the case of showerheads, faucets, water closets, or urinals, water, or that the establishment of the standard is not technologically feasible or economically justified.[52]

DOE may not prescribe an amended or new standard if it finds that the standard is likely to result in the unavailability in the United States in any covered product type (or class) of performance characteristics (including reliability), features, sizes, capacities, and volumes that are substantially the same as those generally available in the United States at the time of DOE's finding. The failure of some types (or classes) to meet this criterion is not to affect DOE's determination of whether to prescribe a standard for other types (or classes).[53]

A finding that a standard is not justified has the same preemptive effect as a finding that a standard is justified.[54] On this basis, the so-called "no-standard standards" of the Reagan-era DOE had preemptive effect.[55]

In November 2010, DOE announced changes to expedite its rulemaking process.[56] First, in some instances, it will speed issuance of an NOPR. Typically, DOE has not issued an NOPR until it has completed a framework document, followed by a preliminary analysis. DOE announced that henceforth in appropriate cases, it will gather the needed preliminary data informally and begin the public rulemaking process with the issuance of an NOPR. Second, DOE has typically provided, in the Federal Register standards document, extensive summarization of underlying analytical information available in other documents. DOE announced that it intends to provide references in the rulemaking documents to such analytical information. DOE says that this will shorten the rulemaking documents, allow the process to proceed more efficiently, "and allow the public to focus on the policy choices made by the rulemaking."[57] Third, DOE announced that it will use negotiated rulemakings "as a means to engage the public, gather data and information, and, attempt to reach consensus among interested parties in order to advance the rulemaking process."[58]

Rulemaking proceedings are often hard fought, reflecting the high stakes involved. But they can also involve consensus. An example is the standards for central air conditioners.

The 1987 NAECA amendments to EPCA included a standard of 10 SEER (seasonal energy efficiency ratio) for central air conditioners—a level that had been negotiated by the appliance industry and energy efficiency advocates as part of the package they presented to Congress for adoption.[59] After an extensive rulemaking, DOE in January 2001, as one of the last acts of the Clinton administration, issued a rule for central air conditioners setting an energy efficiency standard of 13 SEER.[60] DOE in the Bush administration promptly commenced further rulemaking, which resulted in DOE's rejection of 13 SEER and adoption of 12 SEER.[61] States and environmental groups sued DOE to invalidate the 12 SEER rule. The Second Circuit determined that the 12 SEER rule violated what the court deemed to be an "anti-backsliding" provision in EPCA, since it was lower than 13 SEER (even though it was higher than the 10 SEER standard provided in EPCA and even though manufacturers were not yet obliged to produce units at the 13 SEER level).[62] Industry also brought a challenge in the Fourth Circuit to the 13 SEER rule,[63] but ultimately determined to halt its challenge and accepted the 13 SEER rule. The 13 SEER standard went into effect in 2006.[64]

There have been negotiations for a further set of increases for central air conditioners. The Air-Conditioning, Heating, and Refrigeration Institute (AHRI) (formerly Air-Conditioning and Refrigeration Institute [ARI]), individual manufacturers, and numerous energy advocate organizations signed an agreement in October 2009 supporting new standards for residential central air conditioners, furnaces, and heat pumps.[65]

The agreement provides for regional standards, which are currently contemplated for these products due to the EISA amendments to EPCA.[66] Energy advocates have pushed for years for regional standards. Benefits to manufacturers from the agreement include certainty and lead times and the avoidance of rulemakings.[67] The agreement provides for standards to go into effect in 2013 for nonweatherized furnaces, and 2015 for air conditioners, heat pumps, and weatherized furnaces. The effective date for the next iteration of these standards will be 2019 for nonweatherized furnaces, and 2022 for air conditioners, heat pumps, and weatherized furnaces. The agreement also provides for amendment to EPCA's preemption provisions for building codes.[68]

DOE is moving forward with its rulemaking for central air conditioners and furnaces. This includes an NOPR for amended test procedures,[69] and steps leading toward an NOPR for amended standards.[70]

Standby Power

Standby power (also called, e.g., "sleep mode") for appliances is a subject of increasing regulation. This focus is a natural consequence of the increasing use of appliances that are controlled by remote controls and thus are usually in a standby mode rather than in an off mode.

EPCA has been amended to provide that DOE test procedures must be amended, on a scheduled basis, to include "standby mode and off mode energy consumption," taking into consideration the most current versions of Standards 62301 and 62087 of the International Electrotechnical Commission (IEC), with such energy consumption integrated into the overall energy efficiency, energy consumption, or other energy descriptor for each "covered product" unless DOE makes certain findings. DOE is generally to incorporate standby mode and off mode energy use into energy efficiency standards.[71] Congress has specifically mandated standards for certain products, such as battery chargers and external power supplies, that are to take into account existing definitions and test procedures used for measuring energy consumption in standby mode and other modes.[72]

DOE has moved to carry out these requirements. Its rules provide for regulation and measurement of standby power for various products.[73] In addition, the Energy Star program (see discussion below) has a number of provisions governing standby power. These products include, e.g., set-top boxes, audio equipment, DVD players,

VCRs, televisions, TV/VCR combos, cordless phones, battery charging systems, digital-to-analog (DTA) converters, and computer equipment.[74]

Exceptions and Waivers

One way for DOE to handle special situations prior to a general amendment of an appliance test procedure or efficiency standard is to consider requests for exceptions and waivers.

An exception petition would be appropriate for a product that contains a valuable feature, not yet recognized in the DOE rules, that requires additional energy. DOE could adjust a standard to take the feature into account.

An example of this concerns exceptions that were granted for automatic defrost refrigerator-freezers, with bottom-mounted freezer and through-the-door ice service. The exceptions created a separate class and standard for these products. The standard takes into account the additional energy involved in through-the-door ice service and adds it to the energy equation established for refrigerator-freezers—automatic defrost with bottom-mounted freezer without through-the-door ice service (Class 5).[75] Subsequently, DOE has proposed to amend its standards to establish a class (Class 5A) for automatic defrost refrigerator-freezers, with bottom-mounted freezer and through-the-door ice service.[76]

A waiver petition would be appropriate where an appliance has a characteristic that either prevents testing pursuant to the DOE test procedure, or the test procedure may evaluate the product in a way so unrepresentative of its true energy consumption characteristics as to provide materially inaccurate comparative data. DOE may provide a waiver of the DOE test procedure and impose an alternative test procedure for the product until it changes its rules to address the product.[77]

An example is so-called multi-split central air conditioners. A multi-split consists of one outdoor unit, with a compressor with variable capacity, that can connect to multiple indoor units in zoned systems and that uses variable refrigerant flow and control systems. Because numerous indoor units can be matched with each related outdoor unit and an outdoor unit can be connected with numerous separate indoor units, there may be hundreds of thousands, or even millions, of possible indoor units that can be matched in a system configuration. The regular DOE test procedure did not specify how such a product could be evaluated, and it is not practical to test each possible combination. DOE therefore granted test procedure waivers to a number of manufacturers, providing an alternative method for them to rate multi-splits.[78] DOE has sought to resolve this situation by amending the test procedure regulations to define "tested combinations" of multi-splits.[79]

Enforcement

EPCA contains stringent provisions for enforcing its appliance requirements, including fines and penalties, injunctive enforcement, and citizen suits.[80] DOE under the

Obama administration has escalated enforcement of these requirements. And it has done so in a more public manner than in prior administrations.

In October 2009, DOE issued guidance on enforcement.[81] DOE stated, for example, that under its interpretation, a failure to properly certify a covered product and retain records in conformity with its regulations may be subject to enforcement action, including fines, penalties, and injunctive relief, to prohibit distribution of an offending basic model. DOE took the position that it need not test an improperly certified product (or otherwise determine its noncompliance with an applicable efficiency standard) before seeking to enforce. At the same time, DOE stated that it intended "to exercise its enforcement authority more rigorously in the future." As part of this, DOE asserted that it would begin this effort by initiating a compliance review of certification reports and "hold manufacturers accountable for any failure to certify covered products in accordance with DOE rules."[82]

DOE announced in December 2009 a thirty-day grace period for manufacturers to submit accurate certification reports and compliance statements.[83] At the end of that period, DOE announced that it had received certifications from over 160 manufacturers for over 600,000 residential appliances in fifteen product categories. DOE then said that it will "aggressively pursue" manufacturers who fail to comply with the certification rules or whose products violate DOE efficiency standards.[84]

In May 2010, DOE issued guidance on imposition of civil penalties for energy efficiency violations.[85] DOE stated that its goals in assessing penalties are "(1) to deter future violations; (2) to ensure consistency and equity in the assessment of penalties; and (3) to encourage complete and timely resolution of any instances of noncompliance."[86] DOE's guidance stated that for knowingly distributing a product that violates a mandatory conservation standard, it will seek the maximum civil penalty—$200 per unit distributed in commerce. For failure to certify, DOE was adopting an approach of assessing a penalty of $7,300 per basic model—10 percent of the $200 maximum penalty ($20 per day) per model for one year (subject to various adjustments). It has adopted a rebuttable presumption that a model has not been reported for one year. In assessing a penalty, DOE would also take into account other factors in order to ensure the fair and reasonable application of penalties. These include, but are not limited to, the size of the violator; the extent of deviation from the EPCA requirements; the technical reason, if any, for the noncompliance; the violator's history of compliance or noncompliance; the violator's ability to pay; self-reporting of violations; and corrective actions taken. DOE may also adjust penalties as appropriate to encourage the prompt and comprehensive resolution of cases.

On September 16, 2010, DOE issued an extensive NOPR on certification, compliance, and enforcement.[87] The proposal underscores the strong enforcement orientation of DOE under the Obama administration. For example, it proposes to include an annual reporting requirement for all covered products and covered equipment. It proposes to expand the information submitted by manufacturers in certification reports. It also proposes to establish a standardized process for seeking injunctive relief, civil penalties, or other remedies for violations of conservation standards and/or certification requirements.

In November 2009, DOE announced a $13.9 million grant to the National Energy Technology Laboratory in Morgantown, West Virginia, to construct a 35,000 square foot Performance Verification Laboratory to perform nearly seventeen thousand verification tests per year on a broad range of residential and commercial appliances.[88]

In November 2010, DOE launched a new Fraud Reporting web page "to make it easier for members of the public to report suspected incidents of fraud, waste, and abuse, and to enable the Department to keep the public better informed about potential fraud involving DOE programs." DOE will examine allegations and refer matters for action, "including—where appropriate—the institution of criminal proceedings."[89]

The FTC has also been active in enforcement. For example, in November 2010, it announced penalties of over $400,000 against three retailers for failure to post EnergyGuide labels on their websites. And it notified two other online sellers that it would seek a total $640,000 in penalties from them.[90]

Energy Star

An increasingly important feature of federal appliance efficiency efforts is the voluntary Energy Star program.[91]

Begun in 1992 by EPA, Energy Star involves both EPA and DOE. The program has gathered steam over the years due to the value in the market of an Energy Star label. Manufacturers in designing products generally ask themselves not only whether a product meets a federal mandatory standard but also whether it will meet Energy Star criteria. The Energy Star program has gained substantial additional heft due to such things as Executive Order 13123, which requires federal agencies to select, where life-cycle cost-effective, Energy Star and other energy-efficient products when acquiring energy-using products[92] and utility rebate programs that key off of Energy Star.[93]

The program entails manufacturers entering into voluntary agreements with DOE or EPA, depending on the product involved, and allowing the manufacturer to use the Energy Star logo for products that meet certain criteria. These criteria generally are that a product is substantially more efficient than the applicable mandatory federal efficiency standard. Energy Star often has added criteria, and the program includes coverage of some products that are not subject to DOE mandatory standards.

Energy Star has been able to move relatively quickly in comparison with the DOE mandatory efficiency program, which is subject to extensive rules on determining whether an appliance standard is technically feasible and economically justified (see discussion above).

In response to criticisms that the program was being operated within insufficient opportunity for public comment and insufficient lead times, Congress amended EPCA to require the Energy Star program generally to obtain comments on proposed criteria and to provide lead times of 270 days before they go into effect (unless the program specifies otherwise). The effective dates are supposed to take into account the timing requirements for manufacturing, product marketing, and distribution processes of the products involved.[94]

Televisions are an example of an Energy Star program for products for which there is not a mandatory federal efficiency standard. (DOE intends to establish a standard for televisions.[95]) Energy Star had set on-mode power consumption levels for non-high definition, high definition, and full high definition televisions, and imposed a requirement that standby power consumption not exceed 1 watt.[96] New rules that took effect on May 1, 2010, and that will ramp up further on May 1, 2012, increase the stringency of the program, including new on-mode power criteria, ensure a satisfactory level of brightness, and curb energy associated with downloading program guide data.[97] Energy Star has asserted that the 2010 rules offer consumers a savings of more than 40 percent and that the 2012 rules will be as much as 65 percent more efficient than models currently on the market.[98]

In September 2009, DOE and EPA entered into a Memorandum of Understanding (MOU) making EPA the lead agency on the Energy Star program, but continuing to provide an important role for DOE.[99]

The MOU provides that the Energy Star program will be enhanced in four ways.

1. Specifications will be set so that the Energy Star logo is applied consistently with established program principles and with approximately only the top quartile of products eligible.[100]
2. Product coverage will be expanded to include new consumer products with high energy saving potential. The MOU states that "the program will aim to cover as many energy using consumer products as possible, with a focus on product categories in widespread use and with significant energy consumption." The goal is "doubling the annual addition of products from the current level, based on the availability of resources."
3. An "Energy Super Star" program will be nested within the Energy Star program to enable consumers to identify the top-performing products.
4. Verification of compliance with program requirements will be increased and efforts will be enhanced to identify and address product performance issues.

EPA is to manage the Energy Star products program and the Energy Super Star program, while DOE takes the lead in development of product testing procedures and metrics. Specifications are to be set by EPA, with technical support from DOE. Each agency is to support the other as necessary.

DOE and EPA have taken further steps to carry out the increased verification of compliance with Energy Star rules.[101] In March 2010, they announced that DOE had begun tests on six of the most common product types (freezers, refrigerator-freezers, clothes washers, dishwashers, water heaters, and room air conditioners) at third-party independent laboratories. In addition, the agencies stated that they were developing an expanded system that would require all products seeking the Energy Star label to be tested in approved laboratories and require manufacturers to participate in an ongoing verification testing program that will ensure continued compliance.[102]

Energy Star was stung by a Government Accountability Office (GAO) report in March 2010. The report found that the Energy Star product qualification process is vulnerable to fraud and abuse.[103] GAO investigators were able to obtain Energy Star qualification for fifteen bogus products (including a gasoline-powered alarm clock and a purported room air cleaner that was a space heater with a feather duster and fly strips attached to it). The problem seemed to stem primarily from Energy Star not verifying manufacturers' energy-savings data. Energy Star responded quickly, stating on March 30, 2010, that it was accelerating program enhancement efforts related to qualification and verification and was taking the following steps effective immediately:

- Products may no longer be labeled by manufacturers until qualifying product information, including a lab report, is submitted to and approved by EPA.
- EPA's automated review process was being temporarily suspended and qualified product information sheets were being held.
- New Energy Star partners would no longer be granted access to the Energy Star mark upon joining the program; going forward, the mark would be made available to partners only after a qualifying product is submitted and approved.[104]

In April 2010, EPA and DOE fleshed out the details of changes to strengthen the Energy Star program. Manufacturers wishing to qualify their products as Energy Star "must submit complete lab reports and results for review and approval by EPA prior to labeling." EPA is no longer relying on an automated approval process; all new qualification applications "will be reviewed and approved individually by EPA." By the end of 2010, all manufacturers must submit test results from "an approved, accredited lab for any product seeking the Energy Star label."[105] In October 2010, Energy Star finalized for all product categories requirements for third-party certification of product performance and testing in EPA-recognized laboratories. EPA is requiring use of revised Partnership Commitments, including participation in third-party certification, as a condition of participation in the Energy Star program. And the Energy Star program is strengthening its infrastructure of controls, audits, and other enforcement measures, such as adoption of DOE's Energy Star Verification Testing Pilot Program.[106]

Further refinements of the Energy Star program were proposed in the Waxman-Markey bill.[107] The bill would have required EPA to establish a rating system for Energy Star products, periodically review and update Energy Star product criteria, and periodically verify compliance with those criteria.[108] As discussed above, the bill was not adopted. Nonetheless, some of its concepts are being carried out, such as updating and verifying compliance with Energy Star criteria.

Lighting

Over the years, more and more lighting products have been added to the DOE energy efficiency program. The program applies to numerous lighting products, and there is a robust Energy Star lighting program.

Initially, the DOE standards program covered fluorescent lamp ballasts. The 1988 amendments to EPCA[109] established standards for certain fluorescent lamp ballasts.[110] The amendments also required DOE to conduct two rulemaking cycles to determine whether to amend the standards for these products and whether to amend the standards to apply to additional fluorescent lamp ballasts.[111] In 2000, DOE published a rule in the first rulemaking,[112] and it is moving forward with the second rulemaking.[113] Congress in the Energy Policy Act of 2005 established supplementary standards for ballasts that operate additional types of fluorescent lamps.[114] In 2007, Congress passed EISA, requiring that DOE amend its test procedures to include standby mode and off mode[115] and to include these modes in any amended or new standard adopted after July 10, 2010.[116] DOE has amended its test procedure to include these modes.[117] It has also initiated a rulemaking to amend the test procedure for active mode energy consumption.[118]

The 1992 amendments to EPCA established standards for some fluorescent lamps and incandescent lamps.[119] The amendments also provided for further rulemaking to consider broadening the standards to include additional fluorescent and incandescent lamps if warranted.[120] EISA amended EPCA in 2007 to require DOE to conduct new standards rulemakings and provided additional rules for general service fluorescent lamps, incandescent reflector lamps, and general service incandescent lamps.[121] Thus, for general service incandescent lamps, EISA requires that manufacturers improve the efficiency and lifetime requirements of these lamps over a two-year period, beginning on January 1, 2012. The National Electrical Manufacturers Association (NEMA) has stated that the EISA requirements for general service incandescent lamps "will essentially phase-out the most common incandescent light bulbs by 2012–2014."[122]

In 2009, DOE issued a final rule amending the standards for general service fluorescent lamps and incandescent reflector lamps, effective July 14, 2012. It also established standards and test procedures for additional types of general service fluorescent lamps.[123]

The DOE standards program covers a variety of additional lighting products. These include, e.g., rough service lamps, vibration service lamps, three-way incandescent lamps, 2,601–3,300 lumen general service incandescent lamps, and shatter-resistant lamps;[124] torchieres;[125] traffic signal modules and pedestrian modules;[126] medium-base compact fluorescent lamps;[127] mercury vapor lamp ballasts;[128] ceiling fans and ceiling fan light kits;[129] and metal halide lamp fixtures.[130] DOE has been working closely with standards-setting organizations to accelerate development of solid state lighting (SSL) standards.[131]

EISA also requires the FTC to conduct a rulemaking to consider the effectiveness of its current energy labeling requirements for "lamps," commonly referred to as light bulbs, and to consider alternative labeling approaches.[132] Pursuant to that directive, the FTC has issued a rule, effective in July 2011, that will require a label on the front of the package that will feature the lamp's brightness as measured in lumens, rather than a measurement of watts, and will also include an estimated yearly energy cost. The back of the package must have a "Lighting Facts" panel, including brightness, yearly energy cost, life, light appearance (ranging from warm to cool), energy used (in watts), and presence of mercury.[133]

In addition, an Energy Star program for lighting has been developed. This includes minimum efficacy (lumens/watt), life, and other criteria for compact fluorescent lamps (CFLs),[134] light fixtures,[135] SSL products;[136] and integral LED lamps.[137]

DOE, spurred by Congress, continues to push for improvement in lighting efficiency. In the Energy Policy Act of 2005, Congress directed DOE to create a Next Generation Lighting Initiative "to support research, development, demonstration, and commercial application activities related to advanced solid-state lighting technologies based on white light emitting diodes."[138] It also directed DOE to conduct a program of fundamental research to support the initiative.[139] Consistent with this, DOE has provided several rounds of funding for SSL. In January 2010, it announced more than $37 million in funding from the American Recovery and Reinvestment Act to support seventeen SSL projects, including research, product development, and improving manufacturing.[140] The Waxman-Markey bill[141] contained provisions for additional lighting standards, including outdoor luminaires, outdoor high light output lamps, and portable light fixtures. And the subsequently introduced Bingaman bill[142] contained provisions for lighting standards, including portable light fixtures,[143] GU-24 base lamps,[144] incandescent reflector lamps and reflector lamps,[145] and outdoor lighting.[146]

Computers, Monitors, Data Centers, and Computer Servers

Computers

Computers make economies more efficient.[147] At the same time, the increase in their use and their power is stimulating additional scrutiny on how they can be made more efficient.[148] And, various features such as a mouse, keyboard, or memory stick plugged into a USB port of a computer reportedly can keep a computer active.[149]

While there currently is no mandatory DOE efficiency standard for computers, there is an extensive program under Energy Star. Current eligibility criteria cover desktop computers, integrated desktop computers, notebook computers, workstations, game consoles, small-scale servers, and thin clients.[150] The products not covered by these new criteria are computer servers (as defined in Version 1.0 Computer Server specification), handhelds, PDAs, and smartphones. The eligibility criteria include power supply efficiency; typical energy consumption (TEC) levels, which take into account typical electricity consumed by a product in normal operation during a representative period of time, including power in off, sleep, and idle modes; and power management requirements, including shipping with certain settings for the sleep mode, display sleep mode, wake on LAN, and wake management. The power management is intended to put computers into a sleep mode after a designated period of inactivity.

Monitors

There currently is no mandatory DOE efficiency standard for monitors. Energy Star has a program for them.

A new set of criteria sets a more stringent level and expands the range of display products eligible for the Energy Star label. It also includes digital picture frames and larger commercial displays (up to 60 inches diagonal).[151] The criteria include rules for on mode power consumption levels, maximum sleep mode power consumption, and maximum off mode power consumption. Tier 1 criteria became effective on October 30, 2009, for diagonal screen size less than 30 inches, and on January 30, 2010, for diagonal screen size 30–60 inches. Tier 2 levels go into effect on October 30, 2011.

Data Centers and Computer Servers

There are also an increasing number of initiatives under way concerning energy-efficient data center and computer servers. In 2006, Congress directed EPA to develop a report assessing the rapid growth and energy consumption of computer data centers by the federal government and private enterprise.[152] The study was to cover data centers and computer servers. The law also included a "sense of Congress" that it is in the best interest of the United States for purchasers of computer servers to give high priority to energy efficiency as a factor in determining best value and performance for purchases of computer servers.[153]

In response, EPA in 2007 issued a report on current trends in energy use and energy costs of data centers and computer servers in the United States and emerging opportunities for improved energy efficiency.[154] The report stated that there is significant potential for energy efficiency improvement. It made a number of recommendations, including standardized performance measurements for data centers, federal leadership, private sector challenging, and information on best practices. The report stated that the federal government should work with industry to develop objective, credible energy performance metrics for this equipment. It stated that, using these metrics, the government should also investigate whether the development of Energy Star specifications for these product categories would be an effective strategy to complement whole facility approaches. The report also recommended that if and when Energy Star specifications are developed, federal procurement specifications that build on Energy Star should be implemented.

In May 2009, Energy Star issued criteria for computer servers, defined as computers that provide services and manages networked resources for client devices, such as desktop computers, notebook computers, thin clients, wireless devices, PDAs, IP telephone, other computer servers, and other networked devices.[155]

The Energy Star Tier 1 criteria, which went into effect on May 15, 2009, are limited to computer servers having at most four processor sockets. Also excluded are blade systems, including blade servers and blade chassis; fully fault-tolerant servers; server appliances; multi-node servers; storage equipment, including blade storage; and network equipment.

To qualify for an Energy Star label under Tier 1, computer servers must meet multiple criteria. Among other things, power supplies used in computer servers must meet minimum efficiency requirements. Computer servers must not exceed specified idle power levels. There are additional idle power allowances for extra components such as additional power supplies, additional hard drives, additional memories, and additional I/O devices.

Energy Star is in the process of developing Tier 2 specifications for computer servers.[156] A focus of Tier 2 development is evaluation of servers while performing actual computing work (active mode efficiency), a criterion deliberately omitted from the first set of criteria in order to allow for additional discussion of the topic.

Energy Star is also developing specifications for data centers.[157] The criteria will include power supply unit (PSU) efficiency, PSU power factor, active state efficiency, idle state efficiency, and power management.

A key event in the data centers specifications process was a meeting in January 2010 of eight organizations (including DOE and EPA) that set or use data center efficiency metrics. They developed an agreement setting forth "guiding principles" for data center energy efficiency metrics.[158]

In brief, these "guiding principles" included the following. (1) Power Usage Effectiveness (PUE) using source energy consumption is the preferred energy efficiency metric for data centers. PUE is defined as "a measurement of the total energy of the data center divided by the IT energy consumption." (2) When calculating PUE, IT energy consumption should, at a minimum, be measured at the output of the uninterruptible power supply (UPS). However, over time, measurement of IT energy directly at the IT load (i.e., servers) should become the common practice. (3) For a dedicated data center, the total energy in the PUE equation will include all energy sources at the point of utility handoff to the data center owner or operator. For a data center in a mixed-use building, the total energy will be all energy required to operate the data center and should include IT energy, cooling, lighting, and support infrastructure for the data center operations.

State Involvement in Appliance Energy Efficiency

Despite strong federal preemptive provisions,[159] some states, particularly California,[160] have remained active in energy efficiency. State involvement has included rules for products that purportedly are not covered by federal mandatory efficiency standards,[161] as well as certain activities consistent with exceptions to preemption, such as federal waivers of preemption,[162] state procurement,[163] and building code requirements meeting certain criteria.[164] State appliance efficiency regulations and preemption are discussed in further detail in chapter 3.

Full-Fuel-Cycle Measurements

DOE appliance efficiency standards are set on the basis of the energy used to operate the appliance, called "site" or "point of use" energy. This reflects the fundamental definition in EPCA of "energy use," namely, "the quantity of energy directly consumed by a consumer product," as determined in accordance with DOE test procedures.[165] Hence, standards are not set on the basis of the energy consumed in producing and distributing the power used to operate the appliances.

There has been considerable focus on whether there should be a "full-fuel-cycle" (FFC) measurement used in setting appliance standards. A congressionally mandated[166] report released by the National Academy of Sciences suggested further investigation into using an FFC measurement where more than one fuel is used in an appliance (e.g., a heating system with a gas furnace and an electric fan) or when more than one fuel can be used for the same application. The report indicated that this would provide consumers with a more complete picture of product efficiency, energy consumption, and environmental impacts.[167] The report indicated that the current use of site energy consumption is effective for setting standards for single-fueled appliances within the same class and should continue without change.

The report was not unanimous: there were two minority opinions. David H. Archer stated that the report diverts attention from the purpose of the DOE energy efficiency program: to assure that appliances are efficient, "not to compare the energy use of appliances using different energy sources on the basis of full fuel cycle energy consumption."[168] Ellen Berman stated that developing a FFC cost methodology is "fraught with complexity and controversy" and that the current measurements best serve the goals of the DOE efficiency program.[169] She further took the position that direct comparisons among fuels would favor one fuel over another, which is beyond the scope of the program.

DOE has taken the report's recommendations into account. In August 2010, it announced a proposed policy to use FFC measures of energy, greenhouse gas (GHG) emissions, and other emissions in the national impact analyses and environmental assessments included in future energy conservation standards rulemakings.[170] FFC would be used rather than the "primary energy" measures DOE currently uses. DOE also announced that it proposed to work collaboratively with the FTC to make FFC energy and GHG emissions data available to the public to enable consumers to make cross-class comparisons.

International Involvement in Appliance Efficiency

Appliance efficiency has an important international component. There are appliance efficiency rules throughout the world.[171] International initiatives on appliance energy efficiency also include the International Partnership for Energy Efficiency Cooperation (IPEEC), formed in 2008 by the G8 countries, China, India, South Korea, and the European Community. The purpose of IPEEC is "to facilitate those actions that yield high energy efficiency gains." These include, inter alia, exchanging information on standards and labeling.[172]

Of substantial interest for the North American market are the appliance standards program of Canada. The Canadian program was established pursuant to the Energy Efficiency Act of 1992.[173] The Act requires compliance with energy efficiency standards and labeling requirements.[174] It is backed by regulations imposing standards for a wide variety of products.[175] The regulations are administered by Natural Resources Canada (NRCan). In addition, there is an agreement between Canada and EPA allowing Canada to use the Energy Star logo for products in Canada. The

Energy Star program in Canada is administered by NRCan. Canadian involvement in appliance efficiency includes not only the Canadian government, but also the Canadian Standards Association (CSA), which conducts testing pursuant to NRCan rules. Mexico also has a program for mandatory and voluntary standards.[176]

The North American Energy Working Group (NAEWG)—established in 2001 by DOE, the Canadian Minister of Natural Resources, and the Mexican Secretary of Energy—seeks to enhance North American energy cooperation, including efficiency programs. NAEWG's focus includes potential harmonization of test procedures, increased mutual recognition of laboratory results, and enhanced cooperation in voluntary enforcement of labeling programs such as Energy Star.[177]

Conclusion

Appliance energy efficiency is an important federal, state, and international policy to achieve environmental, economic and strategic goals. All signs point to much more to come. DOE, EPA, and the FTC are pressing forward vigorously with programs. Mandatory standards will multiply to cover more products and to become more stringent. The Energy Star program will be an even larger carrot to induce efficiency gains above mandatory levels. Procurement rules and rebate programs keying off Energy Star will push efficiencies upward. Enactment of the "Energy Super Star" program, or a program similar to the "Best-in-Class Appliances Deployment Program," could well drive efficiencies even higher. Added to this are increasing efficiency rules throughout the world and greater levels of international cooperation and coordination.

In short, appliance efficiency has come a long way since the Oil Embargo stimulated Congress to act in 1975, and it has an exciting future.

Notes

1. Pub. L. No. 94-163, 89 Stat. 926 (1975).
2. *See* 10 C.F.R. pts. 430, 431.
3. *See* 16 C.F.R. pt. 305.
4. 42 U.S.C. § 6293(c); *see* 10 C.F.R. § 430.23 and related appendices for test procedures.
5. 42 U.S.C. § 6295; 10 C.F.R. § 430.32.
6. 42 U.S.C. § 6294(c); 16 C.F.R. pt. 305.
7. 42 U.S.C. § 6297.
8. *Id.* § 6297(e), (f).
9. *Id.* § 6297(d).
10. *Id.* §§ 6302–6305, 6316.
11. Examples are testing and certification programs for central air-conditioning and heating products managed by the Air-Conditioning, Heating, and Refrigeration Institute (AHRI) and the programs for refrigerators and freezers, room air conditioners, room air cleaners, and dehumidifiers managed by the Association of Home Appliance Manufacturers (AHAM).
12. 42 U.S.C. § 6294a.
13. S. Rep. No. 516, 95th Cong., 1st Sess. 116 (1975), U.S.C.C.A.N. 1975, p. 1762 (conference report).
14. Pub. L. No. 95-619, 92 Stat. 3288 (1978).
15. 48 Fed. Reg. 39,376 (Aug. 30, 1983); 47 Fed. Reg. 57,198 (Dec. 22, 1982).

16. 42 U.S.C. §§ 6295(o)(3), 6297.

17. Natural Res. Def. Council v. Herrington, 768 F.2d 1355 (D.C. Cir. 1985).

18. 768 F.2d at 1433.

19. *Id.*

20. *Id.*

21. H.R. Rep. No. 100-11, 100th Cong., 1st Sess., 27–28 (1987); *see* S. Rep. No. 100-6, 100th Cong., 1st Sess. 4 (1987) ("appliance manufacturers were confronted with the problem of a growing patchwork of differing state regulations").

22. Pub. L. No. 100-12, 101 Stat. 103 (1987); *see* H.R. Rep. No. 100-11, at 28.

23. 42 U.S.C. § 6295.

24. *Id.* § 6297(c).

25. *Id.* § 6297(d).

26. *Id.* § 6295.

27. *Id.* § 6295(o)(2)(A).

28. Pub. L. No. 102-486, 106 Stat. 2806 (1992).

29. *See* Department of the Interior and Related Agencies Appropriations Act for Fiscal Year 1996, contained in the Omnibus Consolidated Rescissions and Appropriations Act of 1996, Pub. L. No. 104-134, 110 Stat. 1321 (1996).

30. The National Performance Review began in 1993 when President Clinton initiated a review of the federal government. He placed Vice President Gore as head of the project.

31. 61 Fed. Reg. 36974 (July 15, 1996). These procedures appear at 10 C.F.R. pt. 430, subpart C, app. A.

32. *See* New York v. Bodman, Nos. 05 Civ. 7807 (JES), 05 Civ. 7808 (JES), 2007 U.S. Dist. LEXIS 80980 (S.D.N.Y. Nov. 1, 2007).

33. Pub. L. No. 109-58, 119 Stat. 624 (2005).

34. Pub. L. No. 110-140, 121 Stat. 1549 (2007).

35. Memorandum from President Barack Obama for Secretary of Energy (Feb. 5, 2009) on: Appliance Efficiency Standards, *available at* http://www.whitehouse.gov/the_press_office/ApplianceEfficiencyStandards/.

36. *Appliance Standards Improvement Act of 2009: Hearing Before the S. Comm. on Energy & Natural Resources*, 111th Cong. (Mar. 19, 2009) (statement of David Rodgers, Director, Strategic Planning & Analysis, DOE Office of Energy Efficiency & Renewable Energy).

37. 42 U.S.C. § 6295(p)(4).

38. *Id.* § 6295(m)(1)–(2).

39. Statement by David Rodgers, *supra,* note 36.

40. 42 U.S.C. § 6293(b)(1).

41. *Id.* § 6295(o)(6).

42. See H.R. Rep. No. 100-11, *supra* note 21, at 28 (the 1987 NAECA amendments to EPCA "realize[] a long-term objective of a rigorous, uniform standard effective in all 50 states.").

43. American Clean Energy and Security Act, H.R. 2454, 111th Cong., 1st Sess. § 211 (2009).

44. *Id.* § 212.

45. *Id.* § 214.

46. *See* www.energystar.gov.

47. S. 3925, 111th Cong., 2d Sess. (2010).

48. As previously stated, Congress has amended EPCA to eliminate the requirement for an ANOPR for certain products. *See* 42 U.S.C. § 6295(m)(1)–(2).

49. *See, e.g.,* 42 U.S.C. § 6295(d)(3) (central air conditioners).

50. *Id.* § 6295(o).

51. *Id.* § 6295(o)(2)(B)(ii).

52. *Id.* § 6295(o)(3)(B).

53. *Id.* § 6295(o)(4).

54. *Id.* §§ 6295(o)(3), 6297.

55. *See supra* text accompanying note 16.

56. DOE, Office of the Gen. Counsel, DOE Announces Changes to the Energy Conservation Standards Process (Nov. 16, 2010), http://www.gc.energy.gov/1633.htm.

57. *Id.*

58. *Id.*

59. 42 U.S.C. § 6295(d); see *supra* text accompanying notes 22–23.

60. 66 Fed. Reg. 7170 (Jan. 22, 2001).

61. 67 Fed. Reg. 36368 (May 23, 2002).

62. Natural Res. Def. Council v. Abraham, 355 F.3d 179 (2d Cir. 2004).

63. Air-Conditioning & Refrigeration Inst. v. U.S. Dep't of Energy, No. 01-1370 (4th Cir. 2004).

64. 100 C.F.R. § 430.32(c).

65. AHRI, Agreement on Legislative and Regulatory Strategy for Amending Federal Energy Efficiency Standards, Test Procedures, Metrics and Building Code Provisions for Residential Central Air Conditioners, Heat Pumps, Weatherized and Non-Weatherized Furnaces and Related Matters (Oct. 13, 2009), *available at* http://www.standardsasap.org/documents/furnace-acagreement.pdf.

66. *See* 42 U.S.C. § 6295(o)(6).

67. *See AHRI, Efficiency Advocates Ink Historic Agreement,* Air-Conditioning, Heating, Refrigeration News, Oct. 19, 2009, at 1.

68. AHRI, ACEE, ASE, Fact Sheet on Air Conditioner, Furnace, and Heat Pump Efficiency Standards Agreement, available at http://www.aceee.org/files/pdf/1009hvac_fact_0.pdf.

69. 75 Fed. Reg. 31224 (June 2, 2010).

70. *See, e.g., id.* at 27227 (May 14, 2010) (notice of extension of public comment period, residential central air conditioners and heat pumps); *id.* at 14368 (Mar. 25, 2010) (notice of public meeting and availability of preliminary technical support document, residential central air conditioners and heat pumps); *id.* at 12144 (Mar. 15, 2010) (notice of public meeting and availability of rulemaking analysis plan, furnaces).

71. 42 U.S.C. § 6295(gg).

72. *Id.* § 6295(u). In addition, in procuring appliances, federal agencies are to purchase products that use standby power devices or contain an internal standby power function, and that (if the product is available) use not more than 1 watt in the standby power consuming mode. *Id.* § 8259b(e).

73. *See, e.g.,* 10 C.F.R. § 430.23(c) (dishwashers); *id.* pt. 430, subpart B, app. C (same); *id.* pt. 430, subpart B, app. H (televisions); *id.* § 430.23(aa) (battery chargers); *id.* pt. 430, subpart B, app. Y (same); *id.* § 430.23(bb) (external power supplies); *id.* pt. 430, subpart B, app. Z (same); *see also* 75 Fed. Reg. 75290 (Dec. 2, 2010) (notice of proposed rulemaking, test procedures for residential dishwashers, dehumidifiers, and conventional cooking products (standby mode and off mode)).

74. *See* www.energystar.gov.

75. *See* Decision and Order, DOE Office of Hearings and Appeals, TEE-0022 (June 24, 2005) (Maytag); TEE-0025 (Sept. 27, 2005) (LG Electronics); TEE-0047 (July 16, 2007) (Samsung). Decisions are *available at* http://www.oha.doe.gov/eecases.asp.

76. 75 Fed. Reg. 59470, 59487–59488 (Sept. 27, 2010).

77. 10 C.F.R. § 430.27.

78. *See, e.g.,* 74 Fed. Reg. 66311 (Dec. 15, 2009) (Mitsubishi Electric & Electronics); *id.* at 66330 (Dec. 15, 2009) (LG Electronics); 70 Fed. Reg. 9629 (Feb. 28, 2005) (Samsung); 69 Fed. Reg. 52660 (Aug. 27, 2004) (Mitsubishi Electric & Electronics).

79. 10 C.F.R. § 430.2; *see id.* § 430.24(m)(2) (units to be tested).

80. *See* 42 U.S.C. §§ 6302–6305, 6316.

81. 74 Fed. Reg. 52973 (Oct. 14, 2009).

82. *Id.*

83. *Id.* at 65105 (Dec. 9, 2009).

84. DOE, DOE Steps Lead to Significant Increase in Compliance with Energy Efficiency Reporting Requirements (Jan. 12, 2010), http://www.energy.gov/news/8511.htm.

Thus, for example, DOE announced that it had resolved, for total civil penalties of $165,104, actions against four showerhead manufacturers for failure to submit required documents demonstrating compliance with federal standards. *See* DOE, CIVIL PENALTY ACTIONS FOR CERTIFICATION VIOLATIONS RESOLVED (May 6, 2010), http://www.gc.energy.gov/1572.htm. DOE also announced that a manufacturer agreed to cease distribution of certain heat pump and air conditioner models that did not meet federal efficiency standards and to pay a civil penalty of $25,000 for violating DOE's certification requirements. *See* DOE, AEROSYS AGREES TO PAY CIVIL PENALTY AND SUBMIT TEST DATA IN SETTLEMENT WITH DOE (July 6, 2010), http://www .gc.energy.gov/1589.htm.

85. DOE, GUIDANCE ON THE IMPOSITION OF CIVIL PENALTIES FOR VIOLATIONS OF EPCA CONSERVATION STANDARDS AND CERTIFICATION OBLIGATIONS (May 7, 2010), http://www .gc.energy.gov/documents/Penalty_Guidance_5_7_2010__final_(1).pdf.

86. *Id.* at 2.

87. 75 Fed. Reg. 56796 (Sept. 16, 2010); *id.* at 64173 (Oct. 19, 2010) (extension of comment period).

88. DOE, DEPARTMENT OF ENERGY ANNOUNCES MORE THAN $104 MILLION FOR NATIONAL LABORATORY FACILITIES (Nov. 18, 2009), http://www.energy.gov/8297.htm.

89. DOE, DOE LAUNCHES NEW FRAUD REPORTING WEB PAGE (Nov. 16, 2010), http:// www.gc.energy.gov/1641.htm.

90. FTC, FTC FINES ONLINE RETAILERS FOR FAILING TO POST ENERGYGUIDE INFORMATION FOR APPLIANCES (Nov. 1, 2010), http://www.ftc.gov/opa/2010/11/appliancelabel.shtm.

91. *See* www.energystar.gov.

92. Greening the Government Through Efficient Energy Management, Exec. Order No. 13123, 3 C.F.R. § 13123 (1999).

93. *See, e.g.*, PACIFIC GAS & ELECTRIC, APPLIANCE REBATES, http://www.pge.com/ myhome/saveenergymoney/rebates/appliance/; PEPCO, Appliance Rebate Program, at http:// homeener gysavings.pepco.com/dc/appliance-rebate#rebates.

94. 42 U.S.C. § 6294a.

95. 74 Fed. Reg. 53640 (Oct. 20, 2009) ("DOE will soon begin a rulemaking process to establish a new Federal test procedure and a new Federal energy-efficiency standard for televisions."); 75 Fed. Reg. 54048 (Sept. 3, 1010) (test procedure for televisions; request for information and comments). In March 2010, the FTC proposed labeling for televisions. *Id.* at 11483 (Mar. 11, 2010). And it sought further comments on labeling for cable and satellite set-top boxes, stand-alone digital video recorders (DVR), personal computers, personal computer monitors, game consoles, multifunction devices, and audio/visual equipment. *Id.* In October 2010, it announced adoption of a rule that after May 10, 2011, television manufacturers must display EnergyGuide labels for televisions. FTC, "Starting in 2011, FTC Will Require Energy-Guide Labels for Televisions"; *see* 16 C.F.R. pt. 305 (Jan. 6, 2011), *available at* http://www.ftc .gov/os/fedreg/2010/october/102710appliancelabelingrule.pdf. The FTC also said in the rule's preamble that it is continuing to consider potential labeling for the other products.

96. Energy Star Program Requirements for Televisions, Partner Commitments Versions 4.1 and 5.1, *available at* http://www.energystar.gov/ia/partners/product_specs/program_reqs/ tv_vcr_prog_req.pdf.

97. Energy Star Program Requirements for Televisions, Partner Commitments Versions 4.1 and 5.1, *available at* http://www.energystar.gov/ia/partners/product_specs/program_reqs/ tv_vcr_prog_req.pdf.

98. Letter from Katharine Kaplan, EPA, Energy Star for Consumer Electronics, to Energy Star TV Partner or Other Interested Stakeholder (Sept. 3, 2009), *available at* http://www.energy star.gov/ia/partners/prod_development/revisions/downloads/television/4-5_Cover_Memo.pdf.

99. Memorandum of Understanding on Improving the Energy Efficiency of Products and Buildings Between the U.S. Environmental Protection Agency and the U.S. Department of Energy (Sept. 30, 2009), *available at* http://www1.eere.energy.gov/office_eere/pdfs/epa_doe_ agreement.pdf.

100. For a discussion of considerations relating to periodically adjusting upward Energy Star criteria, see David A. Fahrenhold, *Wide Variance in Products That Qualify for Federal*

Energy Star Program, WASH. POST, Feb. 22, 2010, at A05, *available at* http://www.washington
post.com/wp-dyn/content/article/2010/02/21/AR2010022103688.html.

101. An example of enforcement of Energy Star's rules is DOE's notifying twenty-five manufacturers that it was withdrawing their right to use the Energy Star logo on thirty-four models
of compact fluorescent light bulbs. DOE stated that its testing revealed that the affected models
do not last as long in regular use as Energy Star certification would require. *See* DOE, OFFICE
OF THE GEN. COUNSEL, DEPARTMENT OF ENERGY WITHDRAWS THE ENERGY STAR LABEL FROM
34 COMPACT FLUORESCENT LIGHT BULBS (Jan. 26, 2010), http://www.gc.energy.gov/1241.htm.

102. Press Release, Energy.gov, EPA, DOE Announce New Steps to Strengthen ENERGY
STAR (Mar. 19, 2010), http://www.energy.gov/news/8775.htm; KATHLEEN VOKES & KATHA-
RINE KAPLAN, EPA, ENERGY STAR PRODUCTS, ENHANCED TESTING AND VERIFICATION (Mar.
26, 2010), http://www.energystar.gov/ia/partners/downloads/mou/ES_Enhanced_Testing_and_
Verification_Presentation.pdf.

103. Report to the Ranking Member, Comm. on Homeland Sec. & Governmental Affairs,
U.S. Senate, *Energy Star Program: Covert Testing Shows the Energy Star Program Certification
Process Is Vulnerable to Fraud and Abuse*, GAO-10-470, Mar. 2010, *available at* http://www
.gao.gov/new.items/d10470.pdf.

104. Letter from Energy Star to Energy Star Product Manufacturer (Mar. 30, 2010), *available at* http://www.energystar.gov/ia/partners/downloads/Letter_to_Stakeholders.pdf.

105. News Release, "EPA, U.S. EPA, DOE Announce Changes to Bolster Energy Star Program" (Apr. 14, 2010), *available at* http://yosemite.epa.gov/opa/admpress.nsf/f0d7b5b28db5b
04985257359003f533b/a1681df7e5a27357852577050058fd62!OpenDocument; see Memorandum from Cathy Zoi, Assist. Sec., DOE, and Gina McCarthy, Assist. Administrator, EPA, to
Steven Chu, Sec., DOE, and Lisa P. Jackson, Administrator, EPA, "Building a Stronger Energy
Star Program" (Apr. 2, 2010), at http://www.energystar.gov/ia/news/downloads/Joint_Letter_
with_DOE_EPA_Building_a_Stronger_Energy_Star_Program.pdf; Sonja Ryst, *U.S. Agencies
Try To Restore Faith in Energy Star Appliance Testing*, WASH. POST, July 10, 2010, at http://
www.washingtonpost.com/wp-dyn/content/article/2010/07/08/AR2010070806804.html.

106. EPA, EPA RESPONSE TO OIG EVALUATION REPORT (Oct. 2010), http://www.energy
star.gov/index.cfm?c=news.nr_news&news_id=http://www.energystar.gov/cms/default/index
.cfm/news-and-announcements/hidden-articles/epa-response-to-oig-evaluation-report/; DOE,
FAQ FOR: ENERGY STAR VERIFICATION PILOT TESTING PROGRAM (Aug. 2010), at http://
www1.eere.energy.gov/buildings/appliance_standards/pdfs/faqfinal.pdf; ENERGY STAR, FINAL
ENERGY STAR PARTNER COMMITMENTS AND PRODUCT SPECIFICATIONS, http://www.energy
star.gov/index.cfm?c=partners.draft_commitments_and_specs; Letter from Ann Bailey, Chief,
Energy Star Labeling Branch, to ENERGY STAR Manufacturing Partner or Other Interested
Party (Oct. 26, 2010), *available at* http://www.energystar.gov/ia/partners//downloads/EPA_
Cover_Letter.pdf.

107. American Clean Energy and Security Act, *supra* note 43, § 219.

108. *Id.*

109. National Appliance Energy Conservation Amendments of 1998, Pub. L. No. 100-357.

110. *See* 42 U.S.C. § 6295(g)(5). The DOE standards are set forth in 10 C.F.R. § 430.32(m).

111. 42 U.S.C. § 6295(g)(7).

112. 65 Fed. Reg. 56740 (Sept. 19, 2000).

113. On April 26, 2010, a DOE public meeting covered proposed test procedures and standards. *See* 75 Fed. Reg. 14319 (Mar. 24, 2010); *see also id.* at 14288 (Mar. 24, 2010) (notice of
proposed rulemaking for test procedures).

114. Pub. L. No. 109-58, § 135(c)(2) (codified at 42 U.S.C. § 6295(g)(8)(A)).

115. 42 U.S.C. § 6295(gg)(2)(B)(ii).

116. *Id.* § 6295(o).

117. 74 Fed. Reg. 54445 (Oct. 22, 2009).

118. *See* 75 Fed. Reg. 14288 (Mar. 24, 2010) (notice of proposed rulemaking); *id.* at 71570
(Nov. 24, 2010) (supplemental notice of proposed rulemaking).

119. Energy Policy Act of 1992, Pub. L. No. 102-486 (codified at 42 U.S.C. § 6295(i)).

120. *Id.* § 6295(i)(5).

121. *Id.*

122. NEMA SUMMARY AND ANALYSIS OF THE ENERGY INDEPENDENCE AND SECURITY ACT OF 2007, at 5, *available at* http://www.nema.org/gov/energy/upload/NEMA-Summary-and-Analysis-of-the-Energy-Independence-and-Security-Act-of-2007.pdf. NEMA has stated that these EISA initial standards for general service incandescent lamps can be met by advanced incandescent (including halogen) bulbs. *Id.*

123. 74 Fed. Reg. 34080 (July 14, 2009).

124. 42 U.S.C. § 6295(l).

125. *Id.* § 6295(x).

126. *Id.* § 6295(z).

127. *Id.* § 6295(bb).

128. *Id.* § 6295(ee).

129. *Id.* § 6295(ff).

130. *Id.* § 6295(hh).

131. *See DOE* SOLID-STATE LIGHTING RESEARCH AND DEVELOPMENT: MANUFACTURING ROADMAP 71 (July 2010), *available at* http://apps1.eere.energy.gov/buildings/publications/pdfs/ssl/ssl_manuf-roadmap_july2010.pdf.

132. 42 U.S.C. § 6294(a)(2)(D)(iii).

133. *See* 75 Fed. Reg. 41696 (July 19, 2010), *amending* 16 C.F.R. Part 305.

134. *See* Energy Star Program Requirements for CFLs, Partner Commitments (Mar. 7, 2008), *available at* http://www.energystar.gov/ia/partners/product_specs/program_reqs/cfls_prog_req.pdf.

135. *See* Energy Star Program Requirements for Residential Light Fixtures, Partner Commitments, *available at* http://www.energystar.gov/ia/partners/product_specs/program_reqs/fixtures_prog_req.pdf.

136. *See* Energy Star Program Requirements for Solid-State Lighting Products (SSL), Partner Commitments, *available at* http://www.energystar.gov/ia/partners/manuf_res/downloads/ENERGY_STAR_SSL_Program_Requirements_FINAL.pdf.

137. *See* Energy Star Program Requirements for Integral LED Lamps, Eligibility Criteria (Version 1.1) (amended March 22, 2010), at http://www.energystar.gov/ia/partners/manuf_res/downloads/IntegralLampsFINAL.pdf.

138. Codified at 42 U.S.C. § 16192.

139. Codified at *id.* § 16315.

140. Press Release, Energy.gov. Secretary Chu Announces More than $37 Million for Next Generation Lighting (Jan. 15, 2010), http://www.energy.gov/8527.htm.

141. H.R. 2454, 111th Cong., 1st Sess., § 211.

142. S. 3925, 111th Cong., 2d Sess.

143. *Id.* § 4.

144. *Id.* § 5.

145. *Id.* § 18.

146. *Id.* § 22.

147. *See, e.g.,* J.A. LAITNER, C.P. KNIGHT, V.L. MCKINNEY, & K.E. EHRHARDT-MARTINEZ, AMERICAN COUNCIL FOR AN ENERGY-EFFICIENT ECONOMY, SEMICONDUCTOR TECHNOLOGIES: THE POTENTIAL TO REVOLUTIONIZE U.S. ENERGY PRODUCTIVITY, Rep. No. E094 (May 2009), http://aceee.org/pubs/e094.pdf?CFID=4364642&CFTOKEN=24098187.

148. *See, e.g.,* INT'L ENERGY AGENCY, GADGETS AND GIGAWATTS—POLICIES FOR ENERGY EFFICIENT ELECTRONICS (OECD Pub. 2009).

149. *See* Tyler Hamilton, *Expectation of Gadgets Predicts Global Power Surge,* thestar .com, May 14, 2009, http://www.thestar.com/news/canada/article/634138.

150. Energy Star Program Requirements for Computers, (Version 5.0), *available at* http://www.energystar.gov/ia/partners/prod_development/revisions/downloads/computer/Version5.0_Computer_Spec.pdf.

151. Energy Star Program Requirements for Displays (Version 5.0), *available at* http://www.energystar.gov/ia/partners/product_specs/program_reqs/displays_spec.pdf.

152. Pub. L. No. 109-431, § 1, 120 Stat. 2920 (2006).

153. *Id.* § 2.

154. EPA, Energy Star Program, Report to Congress on Server and Data Center Energy Efficiency, Public Law 109-431 (Aug. 2, 2007), *available at* http://www.energystar.gov/ia/partners/prod_development/downloads/EPA_Datacenter_Report_Congress_Final1.pdf.

155. *See* ENERGY STAR PROGRAM REQUIREMENTS FOR COMPUTER SERVERS (VERSION 1.0), *available at* http://www.energystar.gov/ia/partners/product_specs/program_reqs/servers_prog_req.pdf.

156. *See* ENERGY STAR, COMPUTER SERVERS, http://www.energystar.gov/index.cfm?c=revisions .computer_servers.

157. ENERGY STAR, DATA CENTER STORAGE, http://www.energystar.gov/index.cfm?c=new_specs.enterprise_storage; Energy Star Program Requirements for Data Center Storage, Draft 1, Version 1.0, Partner Commitments, at http://www.energystar.gov/ia/partners/prod_develop ment/new_specs/downloads/storage/StorageDraft1Version1Specification.pdf.

158. ENERGY STAR, DATA CENTER INDUSTRY LEADERS REACH AGREEMENT ON GUIDING PRINCIPLES FOR ENERGY EFFICIENCY METRICS (Feb. 1, 2010), *available at* http://www.energy star.gov/ia/partners/prod_development/downloads/DataCenters_AgreementGuidingPrinciples .pdf.

159. *See* 42 U.S.C. § 6297.

160. *See* Cal. Energy Comm'n, Appliance Efficiency Regulations, CAL. CODE REGS., tit. 20, §§ 1601–1608.

161. *See, e.g., id.* § 1605.3(v) (consumer audio and video equipment).

162. 42 U.S.C. § 6297(d).

163. *Id.* § 6297(b)(2), (c)(1), (e).

164. *Id.* § 6297(f).

165. 42 U.S.C. § 6291(4).

166. Energy Policy Act of 2005, § 1802, Pub. L. No. 109-58 (2005), requires DOE to contract with the National Academy of Sciences "to examine whether the goals of energy efficiency standards are best served by measurement of energy consumed, and efficiency improvements, at the actual site of energy consumption, or through the full fuel cycle, beginning at the source of energy production."

167. NAT'L RESEARCH COUNCIL, REVIEW OF SITE (POINT-OF-USE) AND FULL-FUEL-CYCLE MEASUREMENT APPROACHES TO DOE/EERE BUILDING APPLIANCE ENERGY-EFFICIENCY STANDARD, LETTER REPORT (May 2009), *available for free download at* http://www.nap.edu/catalog/12670.html.

168. *Id.* attachment H, Minority Op. of David H. Archer.

169. *Id.* attachment I, Minority Op. of Ellen Berman.

170. 75 Fed. Reg. 51423 (Aug. 20, 2010).

171. A worldwide listing of standards is contained in the website of the Collaborative Labeling and Appliance Standards Program (CLASP), www.CLASPonline.org. CLASP was formed in 1999 by the International Institute for Energy Conservation, Lawrence Berkeley National Laboratory, and the Alliance to Save Energy to establish regional standards.

172. DECLARATION, INTERNATIONAL PARTNERSHIP FOR ENERGY EFFICIENCY COOPERATION (IPEEC), *available at* http://www.enecho.meti.go.jp/topics/g8/ipeecsta_eng.pdf.

173. Energy Efficiency Act, S.C. 1992, c. 36 (Can.).

174. *Id.* § 4.

175. Regulation Respecting Energy-Using Products and Requirements Pertaining to their Importation and Interprovincial Shipment (SOR/94-651).

176. *See* Ley Federal Sobre Metrología y Normalización (1992), *available at* http://www .diputados.gob.mx/LeyesBiblio/pdf/130.pdf.

177. *See* NAEWG, NORTH AMERICAN ENERGY EFFICIENCY STANDARD AND LABELING, *available at* http://www1.eere.energy.gov/buildings/appliance_standards/pdfs/naewg_report.pdf.

chapter thirteen

Buildings

J. Cullen Howe

Introduction

It should come as no surprise that buildings require massive amounts of energy for their construction and operation. The statistics are sobering. Approximately one-third of all energy generated worldwide is used in buildings.[1] In the United States, buildings use is approximately 40 percent of all energy generated[2] and three-fourths of all electricity.[3] Although green buildings on average use less energy than regular buildings, energy efficiency remains elusive even in buildings that have attained some level of certification pursuant to the U.S. Green Building Council's Leadership in Energy and Environmental Design (LEED) rating system.[4] Fortunately, there are many ways to improve a building's energy efficiency, such as installing double-paned windows, insulation, and automatic shut-off switches for lights, to name but a few. Improving the energy efficiency of buildings can be and often is mandated by local and state energy codes, which typically require that new and substantially renovated buildings comply with increasingly stringent energy efficiency requirements.[5]

This chapter discusses efforts to improve energy efficiency in buildings. The first section addresses federal, state, and municipal governmental efforts to improve building energy efficiency. The second section discusses building energy codes. The third section examines voluntary and consensus-based green building standards, most notably LEED, and how these standards address building energy efficiency. The fourth section addresses building retrofitting and weatherization. The fifth and last section explains the concept of "green leases" and how they can be used to improve energy use in buildings.[6]

Government Efforts to Improve Energy Efficiency in Buildings

The U.S. federal government owns approximately 445,000 buildings with a total floor space of over 3 billion square feet. It leases an additional 57,000 buildings comprising

374 million square feet.[7] State and local governments own and lease even more. Various initiatives have been implemented at each level of government to conserve energy in these buildings. Besides saving energy, these initiatives help to create markets for green products, materials, and sources of energy.

Federal Efforts to Promote Building Energy Efficiency

Executive Order 13123

As also discussed in chapter 6, on June 3, 1999, President Bill Clinton signed Executive Order 13123, Greening the Government Through Efficient Energy Management.[8] This Order, which was revoked in 2007,[9] directed the federal government to improve its energy efficiency. Pursuant to the Order, the federal government was directed to promote energy efficiency, water conservation, and the use of renewable energy products and to help foster markets for emerging technologies.

Executive Order 13123 set specific goals for federal agencies. Pursuant to the Order, each agency was required, through life-cycle cost-effective energy measures, to reduce energy consumption per gross square foot of its facilities by 30 percent by 2005 and 35 percent by 2010 relative to 1985.[10] Industrial and laboratory facilities were required, also through life-cycle cost-effective energy measures, to reduce energy consumption per square foot or per unit of production by 20 percent by 2005 and 25 percent by 2010 relative to 1990.[11]

The Department of Energy (DOE) and its Federal Energy Management Program (FEMP) were responsible for working with other federal agencies to ensure that they met the goals of the Executive Order.[12] DOE was also responsible for helping federal agencies in identifying products in the upper 25 percent of energy efficiency, providing technical assistance to federal agencies, issuing guidelines to clarify how agencies determine the life-cycle costs for investments, and administering and managing the Energy Service Companies (ESCOs)[13] and the Energy Savings Performance Contracts (ESPCs).[14]

Energy Policy Act of 2005

On August 8, 2005, President George W. Bush signed into law the Energy Policy Act of 2005.[15] Among other things, the Act contains provisions for commercial buildings that make improvements to their energy systems. Energy improvements completed in the years 2006–2008 were eligible for tax deductions up to $1.80 per square foot.[16] The incentives focus on improvements to lighting; heating, ventilation, and air-conditioning (HVAC); and the building envelope (the separation between the interior and the exterior environments of a building).[17] Improvements are compared to a baseline of ASHRAE Standard 90.1-2001.[18] ASHRAE Standard 90.1 is an energy conservation standard for buildings (except low-rise buildings) that was initially created by the American Society of Heating, Refrigerating and Air-Conditioning Engineers (ASHRAE) in 1975 and is updated every few years. Many buildings are eligible for tax deductions for improvements completed within the normal course of business. For municipal buildings, benefits are passed through to the primary designers/architects in an attempt to encourage innovative municipal design.[19]

Executive Order 13423

On January 24, 2007, President George W. Bush signed Executive Order 13423, Strengthening Federal Environmental, Energy, and Transportation Management.[20] Executive Order 13423 sets goals in the areas of energy efficiency, acquisition, renewable energy, toxics reductions, recycling, sustainable buildings, electronics stewardship, and fleets and water conservation.[21] The Order revoked Executive Order 13123.[22] Executive 13423 is shorter and somewhat more narrow than Executive Order 13123. For example, Order 13123 contains sections on life-cycle cost analyses when procuring goods and services and facility energy audits, as well as detailed sections on annual reports to the President and interagency coordination, while Order 13423 does not.

Executive Order 13423 directs federal agencies to implement sustainable practices for energy efficiency, greenhouse gas (GHG) emissions, and petroleum use reductions; renewable energy; acquisition of recycled content, energy efficient, biobased and environmentally preferable products and services; pollution prevention and recycling; reduction or elimination of toxics and hazardous chemicals; high performance buildings' vehicle fleet management; electronics stewardship; and water conservation.[23] Regarding energy efficiency in buildings, the Order requires each federal agency to reduce building energy consumption per square foot by 30 percent by 2015, relative to a 2003 baseline.[24]

Energy Independence and Security Act of 2007

On December 19, 2007, President Bush signed into law the Energy Independence and Security Act of 2007 (EISA).[25] Title IV of EISA contains a number of provisions related to building energy efficiency, including several designed to "green" federal and private buildings and to require more energy-efficient heating and cooling devices for buildings. These provisions include the following:

- Establishing an Office of High-Performance Green Buildings (OHPGB) in the U.S. General Services Administration (GSA) that will promote green building technology implementation in federal buildings;[26]
- requiring improved federal and commercial building energy efficiency, with green building standards for new federal buildings;[27]
- requiring that, beginning in 2010, federal buildings that are remodeled or newly constructed reduce fossil fuel generated energy consumption by 55 percent by 2010 as compared to 2003 and 100 percent by 2030;[28]
- establishing a zero-net energy initiative to develop technologies, practices, and policies to reach the goal of having all commercial buildings use no net energy by 2050;[29] and
- directing the Secretary of Energy to identify a green building certification for federal buildings.[30]

In addition, EISA contains a number of provisions that promote energy efficiency for government buildings, appliances, and the development of new efficiency standards. These provisions are located in Title III and include the following:

- requiring all general purpose lighting in federal buildings to use Energy Star products or products designated under DOE's Federal Energy Management Program by the end of fiscal year 2013;[31]

- amending the Energy Policy and Conservation Act (EPCA) to prescribe or revise standards affecting regional efficiency for heating and cooling products, and procedures for new or amended standards, energy conservation, residential boiler efficiency, electric motor efficiency, and home appliances;[32]
- requiring DOE to act on energy efficiency in a timely manner; if DOE takes more than two years to finalize new efficiency standards, states are allowed to enact their own standards;[33] and
- requiring the federal government to substitute energy-efficient lighting for incandescent bulbs.[34]

EISA also contains several provisions regarding energy efficiency in general. These are located in Title V and include the following:

- reauthorizing state energy grants to address states' energy priorities and adopt emerging renewable energy and energy efficiency technologies through 2012;[35]
- establishing an Energy and Environment Block Grant program to be used for seed money for innovative local best practices to fund local initiatives, including building and home energy conservation programs, energy audits, fuel conservation programs, building retrofits to increase energy efficiency, "smart growth" planning and zoning, and alternative energy programs;[36] and
- promoting the purchase of energy-efficient products and procurement of alternative fuels with lower carbon emissions by the federal government, with reports on the success of those efforts, along with taxpayer savings.[37]

The Emergency Economic Stabilization Act of 2008

On October 3, 2008, President Bush signed into law the Emergency Economic Stabilization Act of 2008.[38] The law contains a section entitled the Energy Improvement and Extension Act of 2008 (EIEA).[39] Among other things, EIEA extended the $1.80 tax deduction for energy efficiency improvements first created in the Energy Policy Act of 2005 for an additional five years, until 2013.[40] In addition, a law that was passed by Congress in 2004 which allowed large-scale green building and sustainable design projects to qualify for tax-free exempt facility bonds was extended by three years, such that the cut-off date for applying for the bonds is now September 30, 2012.[41]

The American Recovery and Reinvestment Act of 2009[42]

The American Recovery and Reinvestment Act (ARRA)—better known as the Obama administration's "stimulus" bill—became effective on February 17, 2009.[43] It provides some $787 billion in government spending. ARRA allocates $16.8 billion to DOE for energy efficiency and renewable energy programs.[44] A breakdown of this amount with respect to energy efficiency follows.

First, ARRA requires that $5.5 billion be deposited into the Federal Buildings Fund, which is dedicated to the upkeep of federal buildings.[45] Of this money, $4.5 billion is available for the purpose of converting GSA facilities to "High Performance Green Buildings," which are buildings that, compared to similar buildings, reduce energy and water use, improve indoor air quality, take greater advantage of natural light, make use of nontoxic materials and products, and reduce the environmental and energy impacts of transportation through building location and site design.[46]

In addition, ARRA contains $3.84 billion in supplemental appropriations spread among the various service branches for Department of Defense operations and maintenance, which is meant to both improve and modernize facilities and barracks and "invest in the energy efficiency of Department of Defense facilities."[47] ARRA makes $3.2 billion available to the Energy Efficiency and Conservation Block Grant program. This program, created by EISA, provides for federal grants to units of local government, Indian tribes, and states to reduce energy use and fossil fuel emissions, and for improvements in energy efficiency.[48] In addition, $3.1 billion is for the State Energy Program, which was created in 1996 by consolidating two other programs—the State Energy Conservation Program and the Institutional Conservation Program. The State Energy Conservation Program provided states with funding for energy efficiency and renewable energy projects, and the Institutional Conservation Program provided hospitals and schools with a technical analysis of their buildings, and identified the potential savings from proposed energy conservation measures. Through the consolidated State Energy Program, DOE provides a variety of financial and technical assistance to the states with the goal of improving energy efficiency and renewable energy on a state level.[49] A number of more detailed summaries of the law are available on the Internet.[50]

Executive Order on Sustainability

On October 5, 2009, President Barack Obama signed Executive Order 13514, which sets sustainability goals for federal agencies and focuses on making improvements in their environmental, energy, and economic performance.[51] Among other things, the Executive Order requires federal agencies to set a 2020 GHG emissions reduction target within ninety days; increase energy efficiency; reduce fleet petroleum consumption; reduce waste; support sustainable communities; and leverage federal purchasing power to promote environmentally responsible products and technologies. The Executive Order requires agencies to meet a number of energy reduction targets, including implementation by 2020 of a requirement that all federal buildings that enter the planning process are designed to achieve zero-net-energy by 2030.[52]

Selected State Efforts to Promote Building Energy Efficiency

In recent years, many states have pursued various initiatives to improve building energy efficiency through enacting legislation or by executive order.[53] Below are representative examples of some of these initiatives.

California

On December 14, 2004, Governor Arnold Schwarzenegger signed an Executive Order establishing that California considers energy- and resource-efficient high performance buildings a priority.[54] The Executive Order sets a goal of reducing energy use in state-owned buildings by 20 percent by 2015 (from a 2003 baseline) and encourages the private commercial sector to set the same goal.[55] The Executive Order assigned the California Energy Commission to: (1) develop and propose by July 2005 a simple building efficiency benchmarking system for all commercial buildings in the state;[56] (2) develop commissioning and retro-commissioning guidelines for commercial buildings; (3) further develop and refine building energy efficiency standards applicable to the commercial building sector to result in 20 percent savings by 2015 using standards adopted in 2003 as the baseline; and (4) report to the legislature on energy and peak demand savings opportunities for California's existing buildings.[57]

Florida

In 2007, Florida Governor Charlie Crist issued an Executive Order that established GHG emission reduction targets for state agencies and departments as follows: 10 percent reduction by 2012, 23 percent reduction by 2017, and 40 percent reduction by 2025.[58] To accomplish these objectives, Florida has mandated retrofitting for all government buildings owned and operated by the State Department of Management Services, which is the landlord for state agencies. Pursuant to the Executive Order, the Department is required to implement LEED-EBOM (discussed below) in all buildings it currently owns and operates.[59] Further, the Department is required to develop energy conservation measures and guidelines for new and existing office space where state agencies occupy more than twenty thousand square feet.[60]

Indiana

In June 2008, Indiana Governor Mitchell E. Daniels, Jr., signed Executive Order 08-14,[61] which requires agencies, departments, offices, boards, commissions, and public universities to be "designed, constructed, operated, and maintained" to maximum energy efficiency on a "cost effective basis" considering the life cycle of the building. The Executive Order further allows for the demonstration of efficiency through design that achieves LEED-Silver, two globes under Green Globes, Energy Star, or some other equivalent under an American National Standards Institute-accredited rating system.[62]

Massachusetts

In July 2008, Massachusetts enacted a comprehensive law entitled the Green Communities Act concerning green buildings and energy efficiency.[63] Among other things, the law provides technical and financial assistance to municipalities for energy efficiency and renewable energy efforts, and requires the State Board of Building Regulations and Standards to adopt, as its minimum standard, the latest edition of the International Conservation Code as part of the State Building Code.[64]

New York

In June 2001, New York Governor George Pataki signed Executive Order 111 entitled "Directing State Agencies to be More Energy Efficient and Environmentally Aware."[65]

Pursuant to the Executive Order, the governor established a goal for all state agencies and departments to reduce energy consumption of buildings they own, lease, or operate by 35 percent by 2010 relative to 1990 levels. The Executive Order also included a mandate to implement certain energy-efficient practices in existing buildings and to follow "to the maximum extent practicable" the green building guidelines in the state's tax code, as well as the green building guidelines established by LEED. In March 2008, Governor David A. Paterson extended this Executive Order.[66]

Selected Municipal Efforts to Increase Building Energy Efficiency

Many cities have taken steps to improve building energy efficiency through legislation or regulation. Some representative examples follow.

Aspen, Colorado

In 2000, Aspen and Pitkin County, Colorado, launched the Renewable Energy Mitigation Program, which revised the local building code to require that residential buildings meet a strict energy budget to improve energy efficiency.[67] Under the revised code, substantial renovations or additions to residences must include the installation of a 2-kilowatt solar photovoltaic system or equivalent renewable energy system, or the homeowner must pay a fee of $5,000 for a home of over 5,000 square feet and $10,000 for a home of over 10,000 square feet.[68] Homeowners who consume energy above a certain specified budget as a result of having outdoor pools, spas, or systems that melt snow must either install a renewable energy system to operate these things or pay a renewable mitigation fee of up to $100,000.[69]

Babylon, New York

In June 2008, Babylon, New York, enacted an innovative program to work with citizens to pay for energy efficiency upgrades. Under the Long Island Green Homes Program, Babylon loans residents up to $12,000 at a 3 percent interest rate to pay directly for energy efficiency improvements to their homes. Under the program, which has been funded with $2 million in town funds, residents will receive home energy audits that include recommended actions for renovations, including adding more insulation, changing out the HVAC system, and so forth. Babylon will pay for the renovations, and the homeowner then makes payments to the town based roughly on the reduction in energy bills caused by having a more efficient home. The homeowner assumes no debt, and, should the house be sold, what is remaining of the obligation is assigned to the new homeowner. According to the program's website, participants are reducing their energy bills by an average of $1,085 per year.[70]

Los Angeles, California

Los Angeles has enacted a public sector green building retrofit ordinance that requires the retrofitting of all city-owned buildings over 7,500 square feet or built before 1978 to meet LEED-Silver or higher standards.[71] The ordinance set a goal of starting one hundred retrofits annually, and priority will be given to projects with high community-impact level. A goal of the program is that, for the first five years, 50 percent of the buildings retrofitted shall be located in areas with high levels of poverty and unemployment.

New York, New York

In December 2009, New York City enacted four laws aimed at increasing energy efficiency in existing buildings over 50,000 square feet. One law requires covered buildings to conduct energy audits every ten years.[72] While the original version of the bill required both retrofitting and retro-commissioning to correct deficiencies found in an audit, the approved version requires private buildings only to carry out retro-commissioning.[73] The other laws require covered buildings to benchmark their energy use and water consumption through EPA's Portfolio Manager program;[74] to carry out lighting upgrades by 2025;[75] and create a city energy conservation construction code for building renovations that would, among other things, remove an exemption from the State Energy Code for renovations that include less than 50 percent of a building's subsystems.[76]

Building Energy Codes

A building energy code is simply a collection of energy conservation standards for buildings. Building energy codes are typically based on national model codes, which are updated every few years. As explained below, separate model energy codes exist for commercial and residential buildings. States establish actual building energy codes based on these national models by adopting them with or without amendments. States and local governments enforce these codes, but compliance can sometimes be difficult to enforce. In addition, some states have laws establishing thresholds for energy code compliance.

Federal Actions: The Energy Policy Act of 1992/IECC

In 1992, Congress passed the Energy Policy Act in an attempt to reduce the country's dependence on imported petroleum.[77] With respect to buildings, the Act required states to establish minimum commercial building energy codes and to consider minimum residential codes based on current voluntary codes.[78] It also established efficiency standards for commercial heating and air-conditioning equipment, toilets and urinals, electric motors, and light bulbs.[79] In addition, it established a program for providing federal support on a competitive basis for renewable energy technologies.[80]

The Act gave impetus to the modification of ASHRAE Standard 90.1.[81] ASHRAE 90.1 is the most commonly used energy code for commercial and other nonresidential buildings.[82] Standard 90.1 is broad in its application—in general, its requirements address the design of all building systems that affect the visual and thermal comfort of building occupants. Updated every three years, ASHRAE 90.1 was most recently updated in 2010. The Act initially required state and local governments to update their commercial building energy codes to be at least as stringent as ASHRAE

Standard 90.1-1989, the version of Standard 90.1 in place in 2010. Every time Standard 90.1 is updated, DOE is required to make a determination within one year as to whether the amended version saves energy compared to the previous version.[83] Once such a determination is made, states are required to adopt a commercial energy code at least as stringent as the national model within two years of DOE's determination.[84]

The Act also gave impetus to a new version of the Model Energy Code (MEC), referred to since 1998 as the International Energy Conservation Code (IECC).[85] The MEC/IECC contains energy efficiency criteria for new residential buildings and additions to existing buildings. It covers a building's ceilings, walls, and foundations as well as mechanical, lighting, and power systems.[86] The Act mandated that all states review and consider adopting the 1992 MEC.[87]

State Energy Codes

Most states have adopted an energy code that applies to both commercial and residential buildings. Some states have adopted the IECC without modification, while others have adopted some version of it along with state-developed amendments. Still others have adopted the IECC as recommended practice but have no statewide requirement that all new residential construction use it.[88]

A representative example of a state energy code is New York's. In 2002, the state enacted the New York State Energy Conservation Construction Code, otherwise known as the State Energy Code. The Code encompasses commercial provisions based on the text of the IECC 2003 and ASHRAE 90.1-2004. The residential provisions are based on the IECC 2004 Supplements. All building-related codes in New York are currently reviewed and updated on a three-year cycle; the most recent cycle began in 2009. Once adopted, the modifications become mandatory throughout New York, although municipalities may choose to adopt a more stringent code.[89] The previous version of the code applied to new buildings and to renovations of existing buildings only if the renovation was "substantial"—i.e., only if the renovation involved the replacement of more than 50 percent of a "building subsystem" such as exterior walls, floors, and ductwork. Thus, renovations and building system replacements that did not meet this threshold were not required to comply with it. However, the 2010 code removes this 50 percent threshold requirement.[90]

Model Energy Codes

In January 2009, the International Code Council (ICC) announced the approval of its National Green Building Standard, ICC 700.[91] ICC 700 can be used in new and renovated single-family and high-rise residential construction projects and includes provisions relating to land conservation, rainwater collection, use of low-VOC materials, and energy performance at 15 percent above the requirements of the 2006 IECC. In June 2009, the ICC announced that it was launching an International Green Construction Code (IGCC) Initiative, which would seek to create a model code that would reduce the energy usage and carbon footprint of commercial buildings by focusing on building design and performance.[92] A final version of the IGCC is expected in March 2012.[93]

ASHRAE, in collaboration with USGBC and the Illuminating Engineers Society of America (IESNA), has developed a standard for the design of high-performance green buildings, referred to as Standard 189.1.[94] It was published in January 2010.[95] This standard provides minimum criteria that apply to new buildings and major renovation projects[96] and, like LEED, addresses sustainable sites, water use efficiency, energy efficiency, materials and resources, and indoor environmental quality. However, it also provides minimum criteria for a building's GHG emissions. The standard is written in code language and contains a series of mandatory provisions applicable to all projects as well as additional prescriptive and performance options for compliance. It is designed to be adopted by jurisdictions seeking to mandate that all buildings in that jurisdiction be high-performance green buildings.

The standards described above deal with technical specifications. The Center for Climate Change Law at Columbia Law School has developed a model green building ordinance that provides the administrative, enforcement, and other legal details, and incorporates by reference certain LEED standards but provides for utilization of different standards if so desired by the municipality.[97]

Voluntary and Consensus-Based Building Energy and Green Building Rating Standards

Many green building practices are incorporated into building rating systems. One advantage of these systems is that they provide buyers, sellers, and lenders with an objective standard to measure the environmental impacts of new and existing buildings. As explained below, these rating systems typically address energy use in buildings by requiring and/or encouraging that they achieve a certain energy efficiency standard.

Leadership in Energy and Environmental Design (LEED)

The U.S. Green Building Council (USGBC), a private nonprofit organization based in Washington, DC, was formed in 1993. It is the most prominent green building rating body in the United States. In 1999, USGBC promulgated its first standard, referred to as the Leadership in Energy and Environmental Design (LEED) Standard Version 1.0.[98] The standard has been updated several times since then, most recently in 2009 with the release of LEED v3.0.

LEED Rating Systems

Different LEED rating systems are available for specific project types. LEED certification is available for new construction and major renovations (LEED-NC); existing buildings operation and maintenance (LEED-EBOM), which includes sustainable building protocols with respect to building operation and maintenance; commercial interiors (LEED-CI); core and shell design (LEED-CS), which includes building structure, building envelope, and HVAC systems; schools (LEED for Schools);

homes (LEED for Homes); and neighborhood development projects (LEED-ND).[99] There are also pilot programs for retail (LEED for Retail) and health care (LEED for Healthcare).[100]

The two most widely used rating systems are LEED-NC, which applies to both new construction and major renovations, and LEED-EBOM, which applies to existing buildings. Although LEED-NC is more widely used,[101] LEED-EBOM has by far the most potential impact given the current building stock versus the relatively small number of new buildings built each year.[102]

LEED Certification

LEED uses a points system for specific steps taken in connection with a project in six general categories: (1) site selection; (2) water efficiency; (3) energy and atmosphere; (4) materials and resources; (5) indoor environmental air quality; and (6) innovation and design quality. At the end of construction or renovation, a project must submit verification that the particular design elements were actually implemented to receive certification. In addition, project developers must satisfy a number of prerequisites in some of the six categories and achieve a certain number of points before a building can attain LEED certification. Projects are awarded specific ratings depending on the number of points achieved: (a) Certified (40–49 points), (b) Silver (50–59 points), (c) Gold (60–79 points), and (d) Platinum (80–100 points). At the end of construction or renovation, a project must submit verification that the particular design elements were actually implemented and that the mechanical systems are operating to design specifications before receiving certification.

Projects are deemed "registered" upon filing the required documentation with the USGBC during the early stages of a project.[103] Projects become "certified" once they have been fully constructed and certified by the USGBC as attaining the applicable number of credits to fulfill the desired level of LEED certification.[104] The USGBC has arranged the LEED rating systems in a reference guide format, which contains detailed descriptions of each LEED credit along with relevant background information, such as technologies and practices that can be employed to achieve the credit and further resources.[105]

The category with the most available points is "Energy and Atmosphere," with 35 points. There are three prerequisites to achieving any points in this category. First, the building's energy systems must be installed, calibrated, and perform as designed. Second, the building and building systems must meet energy efficiency standards that surpass ASHRAE Standard 90.1-2007 by at least 10 percent. Third, there must be no chlorofluorocarbon (CFC)-based refrigerants in the building. Up to 19 points can be awarded based on the overall energy savings as compared to a typical building of similar size and use. For example, a building that is 30 percent more efficient than ASHRAE 90.1-2007 is awarded 10 points.[106] Additional points are awarded for utilizing renewable energy either on-site or pursuant to an agreement with an energy provider, managing refrigerants properly, and measuring energy savings.

Criticisms of and Changes to LEED

There have been several criticisms of LEED. One criticism is the amount of money and paperwork that are required to register a project, complete the many templates and narratives required for the various points, and conduct a LEED rating audit at the end of construction. Another criticism is that all environmental improvements under LEED are assigned one value, even though some improvements cost much more and have far greater environmental benefits than others.[107] A further criticism has been that the USGBC takes too long to certify buildings, thus creating a backup of applications.[108]

Perhaps the biggest criticism, however, concerns the energy efficiency of LEED-certified buildings.[109] Many commentators have noted that a building could achieve some level of LEED certification even though it uses as much or more energy than another building of the same type and size that was not LEED-certified.[110] Before the rollout of LEED v3.0, USGBC tried to address this by requiring that, as of June 2007, all LEED-certified projects get a minimum of 2 energy points in the Energy and Atmosphere section of the credits. Practically speaking, this meant that LEED-NC projects registered after this date were required to better ASHRAE Standard 90.1-2004 by 14 percent, and LEED-EB projects had to better the standard by 7 percent.

LEED underwent substantial revisions in 2009. With respect to building energy use, energy efficiency now accounts for more than one-third of the possible points in the new rating systems. The minimum threshold for energy efficiency has been reduced from 14 percent to 10 percent, with the upgrade to ASHRAE Standard 90.1-2007.[111] Another major change is that LEED v3.0 incorporates Minimum Program Requirements (MPRs), which are minimum requirements that a project must possess in order to be eligible for certification under LEED v3.0.[112] To be eligible for certification, a project must, among other things, commit to sharing whole-building energy and water usage data. The primary goal of MPRs is to help protect the integrity of the LEED program by, inter alia, closing the gap between designed building performance and actual building performance.[113] If a project cannot or does not comply with these MPRs, the Green Building Certification Institute (GBCI), an offshoot of USGBC which is now in charge of LEED certification, reserves the right to revoke it.[114]

EPA's Energy Star Program

Perhaps the most well-known of the federal government energy efficiency initiatives is EPA's Energy Star program, administered by DOE and EPA.[115] Energy Star is "a voluntary program to identify and promote energy-efficient products and buildings in order to reduce energy consumption, improve energy security, and reduce pollution through voluntary labeling of, or other forms of communication about, products and buildings that meet the highest energy conservation standards."[116] Energy Star began in 1992 as a voluntary labeling program that was designed by EPA to "identify and promote energy-efficient products to reduce greenhouse gas emissions."[117] The program first encompassed only computers and monitors. In 1996, DOE joined EPA as a partner, and the label is now on major appliances, office equipment, lighting, home electronics, and additional items. The Energy Star program is discussed in greater detail in chapter 12.

Most significantly, the program has been extended to cover new homes and commercial and industrial buildings. In this context, the program rates commercial buildings for energy efficiency and provides Energy Star qualifications for new homes that meet their standards for energy-efficient building design.[118] EPA has created an online energy rating system for commercial buildings, referred to as "Portfolio Manager," which is an interactive energy management tool that allows users to track and assess energy and water consumption across their entire portfolio of buildings and compare them with other buildings of the same type and size across the country.[119] As of October 2007, Portfolio Manager also includes GHG emissions factors. If a building achieves an Energy Star rating of 75, meaning that it uses less energy than 74.9 percent of other buildings in its category, it receives an Energy Star designation and is listed on the EPA website as a superior user of energy.[120]

Other Green Building Rating Systems

Green Globes

Green Globes is an online building assessment tool for both residential and commercial structures. Green Globes helps both with the new construction of commercial buildings and the maintenance and improvement of existing buildings. It is questionnaire-driven and is generally acknowledged to be less cumbersome and less expensive to administer than LEED, although the standard is not as well known or rigorous. Based on a 1,000-point scale, projects can earn between one and four Globes, with four indicating the highest level of sustainability within the system.[121] Green Globes was brought to Canada from the United Kingdom in 1996. The Green Building Initiative (GBI), a nonprofit organization based in the United States, acquired the rights to distribute Green Globes to the United States in 2004.[122]

Building Research Establishment's Environmental Assessment Method

The Building Research Establishment's Environmental Assessment Method (BREEAM) green building rating system was established in 1990 by the Building Research Establishment (BRE), which is based in the United Kingdom.[123] The BREEAM scoring system is based on an accumulation of points to achieve one of the following ratings: Pass, Good, Very Good, Excellent, and Outstanding. BREEAM rating system categories include court houses, sustainable homes, EcoHomes, EcoHomesXB (existing buildings), health care, industrial, international, multifamily, prisons, office, retail, educational facilities, and communities. BRE has made a concerted effort to cover a multitude of building types and even includes the BREEAM Bespoke rating system for specialized buildings that do not conform to the aforementioned categories.

Regional and State Green Building Standards

Several regional and state green building rating standards have been developed in recent years. For example, in California, Build It Green is a nonprofit membership organization whose mission is to promote healthy, energy- and resource-efficient buildings in the state.[124] The organization has developed a rating program called

"GreenPoint Rated," which provides an objective, third-party verification system that equips consumers to find green homes, understand green benefits, and recognize green features. Under the program, homes are graded on five categories: energy efficiency, resource conservation, indoor air quality, water conservation, and community. If a home meets the minimum point requirements in each category and scores at least 50 points, it earns the right to bear the GreenPoint Rated label.[125] Similar standards have been developed in other states, such as Build Green New Mexico.[126]

Building Retrofitting and Weatherization

Building retrofitting and weatherization refer generally to the same thing—the practice of making a building more energy efficient—although weatherization can include steps to protect a building and its interior from the elements. Typical steps include sealing cracks and gaps, especially around doors, windows, and pipes that penetrate building areas with high potential for heat loss using caulk, weather-stripping, and similar materials; sealing air ducts; protecting pipes from corrosion and freezing; installing insulation in walls, floors, and ceilings, around ducts and pipes, around water heaters, and near the building foundation; and replacing older windows with low-energy, double-glazed windows, among other things. It can also include the installation of modern, energy-saving HVAC equipment, or the repair of old, inefficient equipment.

Governmental and Nonprofit Initiatives to Promote Retrofitting and Weatherization

The Obama administration has encouraged building retrofitting and weatherization programs as a way to reduce energy use, reduce GHG emissions, and create green jobs. Included in ARRA is $5 billion for the Weatherization Assistance Program. Created by the Energy Conservation and Production Act, the Weatherization Assistance Program enables low-income families to permanently reduce their energy bills by making their homes more energy efficient.[127] ARRA increases the maximum benefit per dwelling unit from $2,500 to $6,500 and expands income eligibility from 150 percent of the federal poverty level to 200 percent.[128] In addition, ARRA provides $4 billion for the Public Housing Capital Fund, a quarter of which will be distributed through a grant competition that will target energy conservation retrofit activities.[129]

States are also enacting programs to encourage building retrofits. One example is the Green Jobs-Green New York Act, enacted in New York in October 2009. The law proposes to fund residential retrofits for at least one million residential units over five years to reduce building energy use, lower housing costs, and provide green jobs.[130] The law creates a $112 million revolving loan fund for energy audits and retrofitting commercial and residential properties that is funded by proceeds from the Regional Greenhouse Gas Initiative (RGGI).[131] Loans of up to $13,000 for residential properties and $26,000 for commercial properties will be provided under the law.[132]

One noteworthy nonprofit initiative to encourage building retrofits is the Clinton Climate Initiative's Energy Efficient Building Retrofit Program.[133] This program provides cities and private building owners with access to financing to retrofit existing buildings with energy-efficient products. The Clinton Climate Initiative provides support to building owners such as city governments, commercial portfolio owners, schools, universities, and public housing authorities in identifying, designing, and implementing large-scale energy efficiency retrofit projects and brings the owner together with the necessary contracting and financial firms for implementation. The Clinton Climate Initiative has helped initiate more than 250 retrofit projects encompassing over 500 million square feet of building space in more than twenty cities around the world. The Energy Efficient Building Retrofit Program typically leads to energy savings between 20 and 50 percent.[134]

LEED for Existing Buildings: Operations and Maintenance

LEED for Existing Buildings: Operations & Maintenance, referred to as LEED-EBOM, is a well-known and widely used standard for retrofitting existing buildings.[135] LEED-EBOM focuses primarily on building operations, preventative maintenance, and system performance. To meet the prerequisites and earn a sufficient number of credits to become certified under LEED-EBOM, most buildings have to go through retrofits and make capital improvements.

The initial LEED-EBOM rating system was released in the fall of 2008. Before this release, this LEED rating system was referred to as LEED for Existing Buildings, or LEED-EB. In 2008, LEED-EB v2.0 was changed to LEED-EBOM. The focus of the rating system became the operations and maintenance of the building. In 2009, LEED v3.0 was released with minor changes to the LEED-EBOM rating system, including more stringent requirements with respect to energy performance as well as the availability of additional points for alternative transportation, water efficiency, and renewable energy and regional credits.[136]

The largest category of LEED-EBOM in terms of credits is Energy & Atmosphere. This category encourages building owners and operators to focus on conserving energy. In this category, there are three prerequisites, all of which must be satisfied to become LEED-certified, as well as six credit categories that total 35 points.

Building Energy Audits and Disclosure

Building energy audits and disclosure are geared toward addressing two issues. The first issue is that you cannot reduce what you do not measure. Thus, energy audits are simply analyses of the total amount of energy use in a building. This is important because even green buildings often use much more energy than they are designed to use. As previously mentioned, EPA's Energy Star Portfolio Manager allows buildings to upload information regarding energy use and compare it with other buildings—a process referred to as benchmarking. The second issue is that buildings are more likely to reduce the amount of energy they use if they are required to disclose it. LEED v3.0 requires that LEED-certified buildings commit to sharing whole-building energy data as a way to narrow the gap between predicted and actual energy use.[137]

States and municipalities have begun enacting laws requiring building energy audits and disclosure. For example, in 2007 California enacted a law that facilitated a building benchmarking system that provides energy consumption information for all nonresidential buildings in California, which allows building owners and operators to compare their building's performance to that of similar buildings.[138] Beginning January 1, 2009, electric and gas utilities are required to maintain records of the energy consumption data of all nonresidential buildings to which they provide service and must upload this data for the account specified for a building to EPA's Energy Star Portfolio Manager.[139] Beginning January 1, 2010, an owner or operator of a nonresidential building is required to disclose to the Energy Star Portfolio Manager, benchmarking data and ratings for the most recent twelve-month period to a prospective buyer, lessee of the entire building, or lender that would finance the entire building.[140] New York City's "Greener, Greater Buildings Plan" requires buildings subject to the law to benchmark their energy use and water consumption through EPA's Portfolio Manager program.[141] In January 2010, Seattle enacted a law that requires owners of nonresidential and multifamily buildings exceeding 50,000 square feet to provide "energy benchmarking reports" using Portfolio Manager. Under the law, building owners are required to provide copies of the energy benchmarking reports to current and prospective tenants, prospective buyers, and lenders who ask for them. Owners who provide inaccurate reports or who fail to report may be cited and fined or may receive a notice of violation.[142]

Green Leases

What Is a Green Lease?

Like the term "green building," a green lease does not have a widely accepted definition and can take many forms. A green lease typically details environmentally friendly products to be used, water and energy conservation methods and targets, the use of alternative sources of on-site energy such as solar or wind, and indoor air quality standards.

Green leases are different from normal leases in several ways. For example, a normal lease requires the landlord to construct the core and shell and the tenant to build or pay for improvements to the space. In contrast, a green lease normally requires the landlord and tenant to work together in an integrated design process to meet certain environmental goals. Second, constructing a "green" structure can cost more than a normal structure given that green materials and systems are sometimes more expensive. However, operating costs of these spaces are usually less because of energy savings. Thus, a green lease typically addresses how these costs and benefits should be allocated. Third, green spaces impact a lease's provisions relating to operations and maintenance. The HVAC and other building systems in these leased spaces may have detailed operating and maintenance requirements. A landlord may wish to prepare an operations manual and require the tenant to comply with it. Conversely, a tenant may want to impose an obligation on the landlord to operate and maintain the leased space in accordance with certain green standards. Both parties may also agree to use environmentally friendly cleaning materials. The landlord may condition approval of tenant alterations on compliance with certain green building rating criteria. These requirements should all be reflected in the lease.

Prominent Green Leasing Standards

The two most prominent green leasing standards currently available are promulgated by the USGBC and the Building Owners and Managers Association (BOMA). USGBC's LEED program utilizes widely accepted standards to certify tenant spaces through its Commercial Interiors (CI) certification process.[143] BOMA is a membership organization of building owners, managers, developers, leasing professionals, facility managers, asset managers, and the providers of the products and services necessary to operate commercial properties.[144] In the summer of 2008, BOMA released the BOMA Lease Guide, which was designed to facilitate the ongoing implementation of sustainable building practices. The BOMA Lease Guide provides both property owners and tenants with a framework for entering into a green lease without the rigidity of the USGBC certification process.[145]

The Split Incentive Problem

One of the most common barriers to implementing energy-efficient building practices and technology is the split incentive, where the landlord pays for capital improvements but the tenants, who pay the utility bills, get the benefits of energy savings. The BOMA Lease Guide emphasizes that a green lease may help overcome some of the barriers to investment in energy efficient and sustainable technologies.[146]

One approach to address the conflict between tenants and landlords is to carefully define operating costs so that landlords and tenants agree to share the cost of energy efficiency improvements. For example, annual operating costs that a tenant is required to pay can include all costs associated with registering and maintaining the building pursuant to a recognized rating system like LEED, provided that these costs can be amortized as annual operating charges under generally accepted accounting principles.[147]

Notes

1. U.N. Env't Programme, Buildings and Climate Change: Status, Challenges and Opportunities 4 (2007), *available at* http://smap.ew.eea.europa.eu/media_server/files/R/S/UNEP_Buildings_and_climate_change.pdf.

2. Dep't of Energy, Energy Info. Admin., Annual Energy Review 2007, at 74 fig. 2.1a (June 2008), *available at* http://tonto.eia.doe.gov/FTPROOT/multifuel/038407.pdf.

3. U.S. Dept. of Energy, *2008 Buildings Energy Data Book* (Sept. 2008), *available at* http://buildingsdatabook.eere.energy.gov/docs%5CDataBooks%5CSEP_2008_BEDB.pdf.

4. In fact, there is a growing debate whether buildings that achieve some level of LEED certification are more efficient in their use of energy than regular buildings. *See, e.g.,* Henry Gifford, A Better Way to Rate Green Buildings: LEED Sets the Standard for Green Building, But Do Green Buildings Actually Save Any Energy? (2008). In the new update to the four primary LEED rating systems (new construction, existing buildings, commercial

interiors, and core and shell), energy efficiency now accounts for more than one-third of all possible points. In addition, the LEED rating systems have upgraded to a more current energy efficiency standard—the American Society of Heating, Refrigeration, and Air-Conditioning Engineers (ASHRAE) Standard 90.1-2007.

5. For example, the New York State Energy Conservation and Construction Code, otherwise known as the State Energy Code and most recently updated in 2010, encompasses commercial provisions based on the text of the International Energy Conservation Code (IECC) 2009 and ASHRAE 90.1-2007. All building-related codes in New York are currently reviewed and updated on a three-year cycle, with the next cycle beginning in 2011.

6. For greater detail on all of the topics discussed in this chapter and other pertinent legal analysis, *see* The Law of Green Buildings: Regulatory and Legal Issues in Design, Construction, Operations and Financing (J. Cullen Howe & Michael B. Gerrard, eds., 2010).

7. Gen. Servs. Admin. Office of Government-Wide Policy, Federal Real Property Profile (Sept. 30, 2002).

8. Exec. Order 13123, 3 C.F.R. § 13,123 (June 3, 1999). The text of Exec. Order 13,123 is available at http://www.nepa.gov/nepa/regs/eos/eo13123.html.

9. Exec. Order 13,423, which was signed by President George W. Bush on January 24, 2007, revoked Exec. Order 13,123. This Executive Order is explained in more detail below.

10. Exec. Order 13,123, § 202.

11. *Id.* § 203.

12. *Id.* § 306(b).

13. ESCOs are companies that specialize in the analysis of energy usage and the implementation of conservation measures.

14. Exec. Order 13123, § 403. In general, an energy savings performance contract is one between a facility owner and an ESCO to reduce energy usage in buildings and facilities; the ESCO guarantees to the owner that energy savings achieved will be greater than the capital cost of the equipment being installed.

15. Pub. L. No. 109-58, 119 Stat. 594 (2005). For a complete discussion of the Energy Policy Act of 2005, see Energy Law and Transactions ch. 59 (David J. Muchow & William A. Mogel, eds., LexisNexis Matthew Bender 2009).

16. Energy Policy Act of 2005, § 1331. This was extended by the Energy Improvement and Extension Act of 2008 until 2013.

17. *Id.*

18. *Id.*

19. *Id.*

20. Exec. Order 13423 (Jan. 24, 2007), *available at* http://edocket.access.gpo.gov/2007/pdf/07-374.pdf.

21. *Id.* § 2.

22. *Id.* § 11.

23. *Id.* § 2.

24. *Id.* § 2(a).

25. Pub. L. No. 110-140, 121 Stat. 1492 (2007).

26. EISA § 436.

27. *Id.* § 433.

28. *Id.* § 431. On October 15, 2010, DOE proposed a rule (at 75 Fed. Reg. 63404) that would require new and substantially renovated federal buildings to be entirely free of fossil fuels used for energy consumption by 2030.

29. *Id.* § 422.

30. *Id.* § 437. On October 28, 2010, the U.S. General Services Administration (GSA) announced that it would require federal buildings under its jurisdiction to obtain a Gold rating from the U.S. Green Building Council's Leadership in Energy and Environmental Design (LEED) rating system, which is the second highest rating in the LEED system behind Platinum.

31. EISA § 323.

32. *Id.* § 306.

33. *Id.* § 305.

34. *Id.* § 321.

35. *Id.* § 531.

36. *Id.* § 542.

37. *Id.* §§ 525–528.

38. The Emergency Economic Stabilization Act of 2008, H.R. 1424; Pub. L. No. 110-343.

39. The Energy Improvement and Extension Act of 2008, Pub. L. No. 110-343 (EIEA). A summary of this Act is available at http://www.finance.senate.gov/sitepages/leg/LEG%20 2008/091708%20Staff%20Summary%20of%20the%20Energy%20Improvement%20 and%20Extension%20Act.pdf.

40. 26 U.S.C. § 179D.

41. *See* EIEA § 307(a).

42. This section is adapted from an article authored by Frederick R. Fucci and Joseph G. Howe III of Arnold & Porter LLP.

43. Pub. L. No. 111-5, 123 Stat.147; H.R. 1, S. 1 (2009).

44. According to the Department of Energy's 2008 Budget, a total of approximately $1.7 billion was received for implementation of its energy efficiency and renewable energy programs, and approximately $1.25 billion was requested for 2009. *See* summary of budget by appropriations, *available at* http://www.cfo.doe.gov/budget/09budget/Content/ApprSum.pdf.

45. ARRA, Title III.

46. For a complete definition of "High Performance Green Building," see EISA § 401. On October 28, 2010, GSA announced that it would require federal buildings under its jurisdiction to obtain a Gold rating from the U.S. Green Building Council's LEED rating system, which is the second highest rating in the LEED system behind Platinum.

47. ARRA, Title III. The breakdown is as follows: Army: $1.475 billion; Navy: $657 million; Marine Corps: $113 million; Air Force: $1.096 billion; Army Reserve: $98 million; Navy Reserve: $55 million.

48. EISA, Title V.

49. ARRA § 410 (Additional State Energy Grants).

50. See Press Release, U.S. Green Bldg. Council, President Signs Economic Recovery Bill with Billions for Green Building, Energy Efficiency, *available at* http://www.usgbc.org/News/ PressReleaseDetails.aspx?ID=3974, for a summary of ARRA's green construction elements.

51. A copy of the Executive Order is available at http://www.whitehouse.gov/assets/ documents/2009fedleader_eo_rel.pdf.

52. Exec. Order 13,514 § 2(g).

53. An excellent source for state initiatives concerning energy efficiency is the Database of State Initiatives for Renewables & Efficiency (DSIRE). This database is available at http://www .dsireusa.org.

54. Exec. Order S-20-04 (Cal. Dec. 14, 2004), *available at* http://www.dot.ca.gov/hq/ energy/ExecOrderS-20-04.htm.

55. *Id.* § 2.

56. Information regarding this benchmarking system is available at http://www.green .ca.gov/GreenBuildings/benchmark.htm.

57. *Id.* § 6.

58. Exec. Order 07-126 (Fla. July 13, 2007), *available at* http://www.flclimatechange.us/ ewebeditpro/items/O12F15073.pdf.

59. *Id.* § 3.3.

60. *Id.* § 3.5.

61. Exec. Order 08-14, Establishment of Energy Efficient State Building Initiative (Ind. June 24, 2008), *available at* http://www.in.gov/legislative/iac/20080709-IR-GOV080541EOA.xml .pdf.

62. *See id.*

63. Mass. Gen. Laws ch. 25A, § 10.

64. *See id.* A copy of the legislation is available at http://www.mass.gov/legis/bills/senate/185/st02pdf/st02768.pdf.

65. Exec. Order 111, Directing Agencies to Be More Energy Efficient and Environmentally Aware (N.Y. June 10, 2001), *available at* http://www.nyserda.org/programs/pdfs/exorder111.pdf.

66. Exec. Order 1, Continuation and Review of Prior Executive Orders (2008), *available at* http://www.governor.ny.gov/archive/paterson/executiveorders/eo_1.html.

67. Information about the program is available at http://www.newrules.org/environment/rules/climate-change/renewable-energy-mitigation-program-aspen-and-pitkin-county-co.

68. *See id.*

69. *See id.*

70. Additional information about the program is available at http://ligreenhomes.com/page.php?Page=home.

71. L.A. Ordinance No. 180633 (Apr. 8, 2009), *available at* http://clkrep.lacity.org/onlinedocs/2006/06-1963_ord_180633.pdf.

72. *See* File # Int. 0967-2009. This legislation is available at http://legistar.council.nyc.gov/LegislationDetail.aspx?ID=452543&GUID=AF748A00-A263-4200-A91E-316346690D2A&Options=ID|Text|&Search=Energy+audits. According to the legislation, a "covered building" includes (i) a building that exceeds 50,000 gross square feet, (ii) two or more buildings on the same tax lot that together exceed 100,000 gross square feet, or (iii) two or more buildings held in the condominium form of ownership that are governed by the same board of managers and that together exceed 100,000 gross square feet. However, it does not include "class one" property, which is defined as one, two, and three family residential property.

73. *See id.* Retrofitting involves capital alterations and installation of new equipment, while retro-commissioning includes noncapital improvements, or "fine tuning" and maintenance of existing systems.

74. File # Int. 0476-2006A. This legislation is available at http://legistar.council.nyc.gov/LegislationDetail.aspx?ID=451082&GUID=52AA7997-4F22-49E9-BDE2-A19FAA29E1C6&Options=ID|Text|&Search=476.

75. File # Int. 0973-2009A. This legislation is available at http://legistar.council.nyc.gov/LegislationDetail.aspx?ID=452544&GUID=6D5AC831-E5AD-4A26-B6CC-C46E6ED946FC&Options=ID|Text|&Search=973.

76. File # Int. 0564-2007A. This legislation is available at http://legistar.council.nyc.gov/LegislationDetail.aspx?ID=451298&GUID=B81B9B48-C100-428A-AD34-59616CC28C32&Options=ID|Text|&Search=564.

77. Pub. L. No. 102-486, 106 Stat. 2776 (1992). For a complete discussion of the Energy Policy Act of 1992, see Energy Law and Transactions ch. 58 (David J. Muchow & William A. Mogel, eds., LexisNexis Matthew Bender 2009).

78. Energy Policy Act of 1992 § 101; 42 U.S.C. § 6833 .

79. *Id.* §§ 122, 123, 124, 126; 42 U.S.C. §§ 6292, 6295.

80. *Id.* title XII.

81. This Standard is available at http://www.ashrae.org/technology/page/548.

82. *See id.*

83. Energy Policy Act of 1992 § 101(b)(2)(A).

84. *Id.* § 101(b)(2)(B)(i).

85. The most recent version of IECC, IECC-2009, is available for purchase at http://www.internationalcodes.net/2009-international-energy-conservation-codes-100-6533-09.shtml.

86. *See id.*

87. Energy Policy Act § 101(a).

88. For the status of energy codes in each state, visit http://www.energycodes.gov/states/.

89. State Energy Conservation Construction Code Act § 11-109.

90. *Id.* § 11-103(b). The "50% rule" is absent both in the International Energy Construction Code (IECC) and ASHRAE 90.1, both of which the Energy Conservation Construction Code is based on.

91. Press Release, Steve Daggers, ICC, National Green Building Standard Approved (Jan. 30, 2009), *reprint available at* http://www.igreenbuild.com/cd_3287.aspx.

92. Additional information about the IGCC Initiative is available at http://www.iccsafe .org/IGCC.

93. Information about the publication schedule for the IGCC is available at http://www .iccsafe.org/cs/IGCC/Pages/PublicVersionDevelopment.aspx.

94. Its official title is the Standard for the Design of High-Performance Green Buildings Except Low-Rise Residential Buildings.

95. The Standard is available for purchase at http://www.ashrae.org/publications/page/927.

96. However, it does not apply to residential buildings under three stories.

97. This model ordinance, together with commentaries and analyses, are available at http:// www.law.columbia.edu/centers/climatechange/resources/municipal.

98. Additional information about USGBC and LEED is available at http://www.usgbc.org.

99. Information about these LEED rating systems is available at http://www.usgbc.org/ DisplayPage.aspx?CMSPageID=222.

100. *See id.*

101. This trend may be changing given that USGBC has reduced documentation for LEED-EB and has clarified ambiguous language and cut overlap with LEED-NC. *See* Andrew C. Burr, *CoStar Green Report: The Big Skodowski*, CoStar Group (Jan. 30, 2008), *available at* http:// www.costar.com/News/Article.aspx?id=AB06F083AAD0809BB084F315F87D3425.

102. As of 2000, there were approximately 116 million residential buildings in existence. Census Bureau, General Housing Characteristics: 2000 (U.S. Dept. of Commerce). On average, 1.8 million residential buildings are built every year. Census Bureau, Annual Housing Starts (1978–2003) (U.S. Dept. of Commerce, Sept. 2004). As of 1999, 4.7 million commercial buildings existed. Energy Info. Admin., 1999 Commercial Buildings Energy Consumption Survey (U.S. Dep't of Energy 2002). It is estimated that approximately 170,000 commercial buildings are built annually. *See* Census Bureau, C-Series Reports: Mfg. & Constr. Div. (U.S. Dep't of Commerce 1999).

103. A list of all LEED registered projects is available at http://www.usgbc.org/LEED/ Project/RegisteredProjectList.aspx. Information about registering a project for LEED certification is available at http://www.gbci.org/main-nav/building-certification/certification-guide .aspx.

104. A list of all LEED certified projects is available at http://www.usgbc.org/LEED/ Project/CertifiedProjectList.aspx. Information about LEED certification is available at http:// www.usgbc.org/DisplayPage.aspx?CMSPageID=64.

105. The LEED reference guides for the various LEED rating systems as well as other USGBC publications are available at http://www.usgbc.org/Store/PublicationsList_New.aspx? CMSPageID=1518.

106. *See* USBGC, LEED 2009 for New Construction and Major Renovations 35 (USBGC member approved Nov. 2008), *available at* http://www.anjec.org/pdfs/Workshop Materials33009LEEDSChecklist.pdf.

107. Ted Bowen, *LEED Green-Building Program Confronts Critics and Growing Pains* Grist, Oct. 26, 2005,, *available at* http://www.grist.org/article/leed1.

108. *See, e.g.,* Randy Udall & Auden Schendler, LEED is Broken—Let's Fix It, iGreen-Build.com, Aug. 9, 2005, *available at* http://www.igreenbuild.com/cd_1706.aspx.

109. On October 12, 2010, a class action lawsuit was filed by Henry Gifford et al. against the USGBC in the U.S. District Court for the Southern District of New York. The lawsuit alleges violations of the Sherman and Lanham Acts for "deceiving users" of the LEED system about "whether LEED buildings use less energy than conventionally-built buildings." Gifford v. U.S. Green Bldg. Council, 10 CIV 7747 (S.D.N.Y. Oct. 8, 2010). The

complaint is available at http://www.greenrealestatelaw.com/wp-content/uploads/2010/10/Class-Action-Suit-v-USGBC-SDNY-10.12.10.pdf.

110. *See, e.g.,* Henry Gifford, A Better Way to Rate Green Buildings: LEED Sets the Standard for Green Building, But Do Green Buildings Actually Save Any Energy? (2008).

111. *See* LEED 3.0, Energy and Atmosphere Prerequisite 2.

112. *See* LEED 2009 for New Construction & Major Renovations, LEED-NC Rating System v3.0, xiv–xv, *available at* http://www.usgbc.org/ShowFile.aspx?DocumentID=5546.

113. *See* Press Release, U.S. Green Bldg. Council, Buildings Seeking LEED to Provide Performance Data (June 25, 2009), *available at* http://www.usgbc.org/Docs/News/MPRs%200609.pdf.

114. Information about GBCI is available at http://www.gbci.org.

115. More information about the Energy Star program is available at http://www.energystar.gov.

116. *See* 42 U.S.C. § 6294a(a).

117. Additional history of Energy Star is available at http://www.energystar.gov/index.cfm?c=about.ab_history.

118. Information about Energy Star for homes is available at http://www.energystar.gov/index.cfm?c=new_homes.hm_index.

119. Portfolio Manager is available at http://www.energystar.gov/index.cfm?c=evaluate_performance.bus_portfoliomanager.

120. *See id.*

121. Additional information about Green Globes is available at http://www.greenglobes.com.

122. Information about GBI is available at http://www.thegbi.org.

123. Information about BRE and BREEAM is available at http://www.bre.co.uk.

124. Information about Build It Green is available at http://www.builditgreen.org.

125. Additional information about GreenPoint Rated is available at http://www.builditgreen.org/greenpoint-rated/.

126. Information about Build Green New Mexico is available at http://www.buildgreennm.com.

127. 42 U.S.C. § 6872.

128. *See id.*

129. *Id.,* title XII.

130. 2009 N.Y. Laws chs. 487 and 488.

131. N.Y. Pub. Auth. L. Sec. § 1896.

132. *See id.*

133. Press Release, William J. Clinton Found., President Clinton Announces Landmark Program to Reduce Energy Use in Buildings Worldwide (May 16, 2007), *available at* http://www.clintonfoundation.org/news/news-media/051607-nr-cf-pr-cci-president-clinton-announces-landmark-program-to-reduce-energy-use-in-buildings-worldwide.

134. *Id.*

135. Additional information about LEED-EBOM is available at http://www.usgbc.org/DisplayPage.aspx?CMSPageID=221#v2008.

136. LEED-EBOM is available at http://www.usgbc.org/ShowFile.aspx?DocumentID=5545.

137. *See* LEED-NC Rating System v3.0, xviii, *available at* http://www.usgbc.org/ShowFile.aspx?DocumentID=5546.

138. 2007 N.Y. Laws ch. 533.

139. *See* Cal. Pub. Res. Code § 25402.10(a) & (b).

140. *See* Cal. Pub. Res. Code § 25402.10(d).

141. File # Int. 0476-2006A. This bill is available at http://legistar.council.nyc.gov/LegislationDetail.aspx?ID=451082&GUID=52AA7997-4F22-49E9-BDE2-A19FAA29E1C6&Options=ID|Text|&Search=476.

142. Seattle City Council Bill No. 116731, *available at* http://clerk.ci.seattle.wa.us/~scripts/ nph-brs.exe?d=CBOR&s1=116731.cbn.&Sect6=HITOFF&l=20&p=1&u=%2F~public%2F cbor2.htm&r=1&f=G.

143. Information about LEED for Commercial Interiors is available at http://www.usgbc .org/DisplayPage.aspx?CMSPageID=145.

144. Additional information about BOMA is available at http://www.boma.org/Pages/ default.aspx.

145. Information about the BOMA Lease Guide is available at http://shop.boma.org/ showItem.aspx?product=GL2008&session=0BFF26B48F6F4F24A0427912030ADA21.

146. STEVEN A. TEITELBAUM, BOMA's LEASE GUIDE: GUIDE TO WRITING A COMMERCIAL REAL ESTATE LEASE INCLUDING GREEN LEASE LANGUAGE (2008).

147. *Id.*

chapter fourteen

Motor Vehicles and Transportation

*Jonathan S. Martel
and Kristen Klick White*

Transportation is the second largest consumer of energy in the United States and accounts for about 69 percent of all petroleum consumption in the United States.[1] Even as energy intensity (the use of energy per dollar of gross domestic product) in the United States has declined steadily each year since 1973, consumption of transportation fuel has grown steadily.[2] According to the National Highway Traffic Safety Administration (NHTSA), half of energy consumed in the transportation sector is for passenger cars and light trucks, with the remaining uses spread among heavy trucks, aviation, public transportation, and rail and marine transportation.[3] Likewise, transportation accounts for half of all CO_2 emissions in the United States, and passenger vehicles are responsible for 60 percent of that half.[4]

This chapter will address efforts to curb the consumption of primarily petroleum-based energy in the transportation sector and to reduce greenhouse gas (GHG) emissions from transportation sources. The first section will address existing fuel economy and emissions programs and how they are being adapted to meet the newly recognized need to curb GHG emissions, as well as new federal and state legislation seeking to fill gaps left by existing programs. The second section will cover how the development of new technology and improved maintenance and operation of old technology can impact GHG emissions. Finally, the last section will address new initiatives focused on reducing demand for gasoline, such as fuel taxes and efforts to reduce vehicle miles traveled.

Regulation of Fuel Economy and Emissions: CAFE Standards and the Clean Air Act

The CAFE Standards

Historically, the primary tool for addressing fuel efficiency in passenger cars and light trucks has been the Corporate Average Fuel Economy (CAFE) standards. Although CAFE standards recently have taken center stage as a way to control carbon emissions, Congress first created the CAFE program with the Energy Policy and Conservation

Act (EPCA) of 1975 as a conservation measure designed to reduce demand for foreign oil in the wake of the Middle East oil embargo in 1973–1974 and the ensuing energy crisis and skyrocketing gas prices. Initially, the program was very successful. Fuel efficiency of cars and light trucks nearly doubled in the fifteen years after the adoption of the program and the nation's reliance on foreign oil began to fall.[5] But then, as fuel prices dropped and fuel economy grew, Americans became less interested in fuel efficiency and more interested in larger vehicles. Americans began driving more. Through most of the 1990s, Congress did not fund the CAFE program, and fuel efficiency standards stagnated just as less efficient trucks, minivans, and sports utility vehicles (SUVs) took a larger share of the market.[6] Fuel use began to grow again, and the efficiency gains of the 1970s and 1980s were offset by a shift to larger vehicles and more vehicle miles traveled.

However, renewed focus on conservation, inspired by growing concerns about dependence on foreign oil, national security, and global climate change, led Congress to amend and expand the CAFE program with the Energy Independence Security Act of 2007 (EISA), which, among other things, called for an increase in fuel efficiency across the national fleet to 35 mpg by 2020.[7] Several years later, the Obama administration called for a new purpose for the CAFE program. Not only would CAFE standards be aimed at reducing consumption and dependence on foreign oil, they would also be used to achieve the specific environmental goal of reducing carbon dioxide (CO_2) emissions.

Basic Provisions

Under EPCA, as amended by EISA, NHTSA and the Environmental Protection Agency (EPA) share responsibility for the CAFE program.[8] NHTSA sets the CAFE standards for passenger cars and light trucks, EPA calculates the average fuel economy of each manufacturer's passenger cars and light trucks, and NHTSA enforces the standards based on EPA's calculations.

NHTSA must set average fuel economy standards for each model year eighteen months in advance of the new model year (typically March 30) to give industry time to design a compliant fleet by the introduction of the new fleet in October.[9] Standards must be set at the "maximum feasible average fuel economy level" that NHTSA determines manufacturers can achieve that model year, after considering (1) technological feasibility, (2) economic practicality, (3) the effect of other motor vehicle standards of the government on fuel economy, and (4) the need of the United States to conserve energy.[10] Historically, NHTSA also has considered other factors such as safety, foreign policy, and environmental impact.

All "automobiles" (four-wheeled, highway vehicles up to 10,000 pounds) are subject to the standards, although NHTSA sets separate standards for passenger cars (designed for up to ten passengers), light trucks, and, beginning in model year (MY) 2011, medium-duty passenger vehicles (between 8,500 and 10,000 pounds) such as SUVs, passenger vans, and short-bed pickup trucks.[11] Exempted from the standards are work trucks (defined as vehicles between 8,500 and 10,000 pounds such as long-bed pickups and cargo vans, but not medium-duty passenger vehicles)[12] and "multi-stage" vehicles (built in stages by more than one manufacturer).[13]

Beginning in MY 2011, automakers must meet a specific fuel economy target based on the "footprint," or size, of each vehicle in its fleet. Smaller cars have higher targets while larger cars have lower targets. Each manufacturer's passenger car fleet must come within 92 percent of the overall standard for a given model year. Above that floor, manufacturers can earn credits for exceeding the standard in one vehicle class and assign it to a vehicle class short on compliance. Alternatively, credits may be banked for future use, or sold between manufacturers (though such inter-company transactions are not common). NHTSA expects that the fleet of passenger cars sold in MY 2011 will reach an average 30.2 mpg, while the light truck fleet will average 24.1 mpg. EISA requires that by MY 2020, NHTSA design the CAFE program so that the combined average of national fleet of all new passenger cars and light trucks is at least 35 miles per gallon. (As discussed further below, the Obama administration has called for an escalation of that goal to 35.5 mpg by 2016.)

Work trucks and commercial medium- and heavy-duty trucks also will be included in the program, as might other transportation sources, as discussed further below.

History of the CAFE Standards and SUVs

The distinction between passenger cars and light trucks is something of a historical anomaly that has outlived its usefulness and led to a large loophole in the law during the 1990s and early 2000s.[14] When Congress enacted EPCA in 1975, the use of light trucks was for the most part limited to the short trips made by agricultural and commercial vehicles. The impact of light trucks on overall fuel economy was thought to be less significant, so they were allowed to be less efficient than the far more prevalent passenger cars under the CAFE standards.[15] Congress set the average fuel economy standard for cars at 27.5 mpg in the language of the statute, while it left NHTSA to set the standard for light trucks at 20.2 mpg by 1992. The 27.5 mpg standard demanded a 75 percent increase from the 1975 fleet average of 15.8 mpg, while the light truck standard required a 50 percent increase over 1975 levels.[16] The program was a tremendous success through the early 1980s. The fuel efficiency increases, along with the high price of gas at the time, saved an estimated 55 billion gallons of gasoline each year.[17]

However, beginning in the mid-1980s, fuel prices dropped, minivans, pickup trucks, and SUVs became more prevalent, and vehicle miles traveled began to grow. Even though fuel-saving technologies were available and in use in Europe and Asia, American automakers changed their focus from the creation of more compact, efficient vehicles to the design of high-performing, heavier vehicles.[18] The structure of the CAFE standards provided an unforeseen incentive for the development of these less efficient vehicles. With their large size, load capacity, and off-road technologies, SUVs fell into the category of light trucks. Because these new light trucks were primarily designed to carry passengers, some contended the light truck standard provided an "SUV loophole" in the law.

Between 1996 and 2001, Congress denied funding for the CAFE program for six years in a row. As a result, NHTSA left the CAFE standards unchanged as automakers continued to feed the growing and profitable market for SUVs.[19] By MY 2002, SUVs and other light trucks exceeded passenger cars in sales, so a vehicle once believed to have a negligible effect on fuel consumption now dominated the new vehicle market.[20] Gradually, U.S. oil consumption, which had dropped from 18.5 million barrels per day (mmbd) in 1979 to 15.2 mmbd in 1983, increased to 20 mmbd in 2006.[21]

In 2002, as a compromise to end the stalemate over frozen CAFE standards, Congress funded a National Academy of Sciences (NAS) study of the CAFE program. The study concluded, among other things, that CAFE standards were effective in reducing fuel consumption; that technologies existed to reduce fuel consumption "significantly" in passenger cars and light trucks within fifteen years without sacrificing vehicle size, weight, utility, or performance; and that the "distinction between a car for personal use and a truck for work use/cargo transport has broken down . . . [and] stretched well beyond the original purpose."[22] Additionally, NAS concluded that the environmental impact of the accumulation of GHGs in the atmosphere and growing dependence on foreign oil were "externalities," or costs to society not reflected in what the consumer pays for fuel, that justified government-mandated fuel economy increases and should be quantified and calculated in the analysis of any new CAFE rule.[23]

After the NAS study, NHTSA in 2003 increased the long-standing 20.7 mpg light truck standard to 21 mpg in MY 2005, 21.6 mpg in MY 2006, and 22.2 mpg in MY 2007, while the standard for cars remained 27.5 mpg.[24] While NHTSA had the statutory authority to raise or lower the standard for passenger cars from the level set by Congress, it chose not to do so. In 2006, NHTSA sought to phase in reformed efficiency standards for light trucks (Reformed CAFE) that provided the industry a mechanism to increase the average fuel economy of its light truck fleet without decreasing size or compromising safety standards.[25] This "attribute-based" system was designed to address the NAS conclusion that many automakers met CAFE standards by reducing the size and weight of vehicles, making them less safe in crashes, rather than by improving technology.[26] To address the safety concern, beginning in MY 2008 through MY 2011, standards for light trucks and "medium duty passenger vehicles" (short-bed pickups, passenger vans, and SUVs) were to be based on the size of the vehicle's footprint (i.e., wheelbase), and each vehicle footprint was assigned a specific fuel economy target.[27]

However, the Ninth Circuit in the fall of 2007 held that NHTSA had failed properly to consider the rule's cumulative effects on GHG emissions in conducting the required environmental assessment of the rule under the National Environmental Policy Act (NEPA), and remanded the rule.[28] The court noted that "NHTSA may use a cost-benefit analysis to determine the 'maximum feasible' fuel economy standard, [but] it cannot put a thumb on the scale by undervaluing the benefits and overvaluing the costs of more stringent standards."[29] The rule was remanded, but not vacated, for further study of the impact on climate change and other issues. However, by the time the new environmental impact study was completed, the economy and the domestic auto industry in particular encountered severe difficulties, with General Motors and Chrysler seeking bankruptcy protection. The Bush administration decided not to issue new standards, leaving it to the new Obama administration to meet the March 30, 2009, deadline for implementation of the MY 2011 standards.[30]

Clean Air Act

The EPA is responsible for addressing air pollutants from mobile (transportation) sources under the Clean Air Act. Under Section 202(a) of the Act, EPA must set standards for the emission of any "air pollutants" from a motor vehicle "which in [EPA's] judgment cause, or contribute to, air pollution which may reasonably be anticipated to endanger public health or welfare."[31] Historically, under this provision, EPA regulated emissions of hydrocarbons, nitrogen oxide, carbon monoxide, particulate matter, and toxic chemicals from mobile sources. Each of these contaminants generally pollutes the local area, so regulations of emissions generally are focused on assisting particular regions to meet local ambient air pollution standards. CO_2, however, is pervasive and is more or less constant across the globe so that local ambient air standards are not pertinent.

Indeed, under President George W. Bush, EPA resisted enacting GHG regulations. In 1999, the International Center for Technology Assessment (ICTA) petitioned EPA to regulate GHG emissions from new motor vehicles. EPA denied the petition in 2003. ICTA appealed, and the argument eventually landed in the Supreme Court, which held, in *Massachusetts v. EPA*, that EPA's refusal to regulate GHGs was arbitrary and capricious.[32] The Court found that GHGs are "air pollutants" and that "[u]nder the clear terms of the Clean Air Act, EPA can avoid taking further action only if it determines that greenhouse gases do not contribute to climate change or if it provides some reasonable explanation as to why it cannot or will not exercise its discretion to determine whether they do."[33] Still, under President Bush, EPA did not issue its determination of whether GHGs were an endangerment to public health, the critical underpinning of any regulation of GHGs by EPA.

Then, shortly after President Obama took office, EPA on April 17, 2009, issued a proposed "endangerment finding" that GHG emissions cause or contribute to air pollution that endangers public health and welfare.[34] The rule was finalized on December 7, 2009, paving the way for EPA to regulate CO_2 and other GHGs under the Clean Air Act.[35]

The endangerment finding has continued to be highly controversial. Those who favor regulation of GHGs generally recognize that the Clean Air Act is not the ideal regulatory tool, while those who disfavor regulation do not believe EPA has the authority, in spite of the *Massachusetts* holding. In spring 2010, legislators Sen. Lisa Murkowski (R-Alaska) and Rep. Joe Barton (R-Tex.) introduced bills to strip EPA of its power to regulate GHGs until Congress adopts a comprehensive plan to address climate change.[36] Senator Murkowski's proposal was voted down by a 47–53 vote.[37] In similar bills, Sen. Jay Rockefeller (D-W. Va.) and Rep. Nick Rahall (D-W. Va.) proposed delaying EPA's regulation of GHGs from stationary sources for two years, but permitting EPA to regulate GHGs from mobile sources.[38] Senator Murkowski later adopted Senator Rockefeller's approach to delay EPA's regulation of GHGs from stationary sources, but her attempts to bring the plan to a vote were unsuccessful.[39] Additionally, on February 10, 2010, twelve House Republicans and seventeen associations and companies filed a lawsuit in federal appeals court challenging the endangerment finding.[40] The U.S. Chamber of Commerce on March 15, 2010, petitioned EPA to reconsider the endangerment finding.

Despite the challenges, two legislative proposals to control GHG emissions from motor vehicles proceeded and eventually were merged: a joint "National Plan" from NHTSA and EPA, and regulation by California that would apply to fourteen states and the District of Columbia.

California Air Resources Board

Under Title II of the Clean Air Act, EPA has sole jurisdiction to regulate new mobile sources. California historically has faced severe local air pollution problems and is the largest state by population capable of sustaining a separate market. Because it had a program in place when the Clean Air Act was enacted, it has a special waiver process under the statute. Under section 209(a), "no state or political subdivision thereof shall adopt or attempt to enforce any standard relating to the control of emissions from new motor vehicles or new motor vehicle engines."[41] However, California can regulate new mobile sources if it obtains a waiver from EPA. And EPA "shall" grant the waiver if California determines the standards "will be, in the aggregate, at least as protective of public health and welfare" as federal standards.[42] EPA "shall" deny the waiver if: (1) the protectiveness determination of California is arbitrary and capricious; (2) California does not need the standards to meet compelling and extraordinary conditions; or (3) California standards are not consistent with the Clean Air Act.[43] Under Section 177, other states may "opt in" to California's rules for new mobile sources if the state's adopted standards are identical to California's, and California and the state adopt the standards at least two years before the commencement of the applicable model year.[44]

California adopted a law in 2002 requiring the California Air Resources Board (CARB) to promulgate "regulations that achieve the maximum feasible and cost-effective reduction of greenhouse gas emissions from motor vehicles,"[45] which CARB put forth in 2004. The regulations require that vehicles reduce CO_2, methane, nitrous oxide, and hydrofluorocarbon emissions over an eight-year period.[46] As converted to terms of CO_2, passenger cars and light-duty trucks less than 3,750 pounds would have to reduce emissions to less than 323 grams per mile (gpm) in MY 2009, and less than 205 gpm in MY 2016. Larger light-duty trucks would have to decrease from 439 gpm to 332 gpm during the same time frame. Thirteen other states and the District of Columbia announced they would follow California's carbon emission rules.

In 2005, California sought a waiver from EPA, which failed to act for two years. Then, on December 19, 2007—the same day President Bush signed EISA, expanding the CAFE program—EPA denied California's waiver request to enact more stringent air emissions standards for cars and trucks. California challenged the denial in an appeal that eventually was dismissed as premature because it was filed before the EPA's official rulemaking was published.[47] Shortly after President Obama took office, he issued a Presidential Memorandum to EPA directing it to reconsider the denial.[48] On June 30, 2009, EPA granted California's waiver, explaining that the previous denial "was a substantial departure from EPA's longstanding interpretation of the Clean Air Act's waiver provision and EPA's history of granting waivers to California for its new motor vehicle emissions program."[49] The decision applied to all new passenger cars and light trucks for MY 2009 through MY 2012.

The new California regulations led to a number of court challenges, primarily on the basis of preemption under EPCA and the Clean Air Act. In *Central Valley Chrysler-Jeep Inc. v. Goldstone*,[50] automobile dealerships sought to prevent CARB from enforcing the new GHG emissions rules on the basis, among other things, that they were preempted by the Clean Air Act and EPCA. The trial court rejected the dealerships' arguments. Under the Clean Air Act, the California program was subject to the section 209 waiver process, but was not preempted. Under EPCA, the California program was not preempted by the express preemption clause of EPCA, which prohibits states from adopting laws or regulations "related to fuel economy standards."[51] Relying on *Massachusetts v. EPA*, the court found that Congress intended that there would be no conflict between EPA's duty to protect public health through emissions controls and NHTSA's duty to set fuel efficiency standards. The doctrine of conflict preemption, therefore, did not apply even where there may be overlap between emissions and fuel efficiency programs.

In a similar case, *Green Mountain Chrysler Plymouth Jeep v. Dalmasse*,[52] the trial court concluded that standards that have received the section 209 waiver are treated as federal standards and thus are not preempted. And, even if the waived program is not a federal standard, GHG rules do not precisely correlate with fuel economy standards, and thus cannot be preempted.

The National Program

Once California's waiver request was granted, automakers would be subject to three separate standards: EPA's emission controls, NHTSA's fuel efficiency standards, and California's GHG controls. In part to help the ailing auto industry avoid this regulatory tangle, the Obama administration worked to reach an agreement among the federal agencies, California, and the automakers to initiate a new national program for fuel efficiency, calling for an increase in combined average fuel efficiency of 35.5 by 2016, surpassing the EISA goal of 2020, and a reduction of 900 million metric tons of GHGs.[53] The "Obama Compromise" essentially would merge all three standards into a cohesive National Program and allow automakers to be subject to a single national standard.

EPA and NHTSA announced the proposed National Program on September 30, 2009, and issued the final rule on May 7, 2010.[54] The proposed National Program covers passenger cars, light trucks, and medium-duty passenger vehicles (together, light-duty vehicles) built in MY 2012 through MY 2016. The agencies anticipate the new standards can be met with more widespread use of existing technologies, such as improvements to engines, transmissions, and tires; increased use of start-stop technology; improvements in air-conditioning; and increased use of hybrids, electric vehicles, and plug-in hybrids.[55] Under the rule, the agencies have harmonized many elements of the program, including providing a joint definition of cars and trucks, and joint "footprint" standards. Additionally, as part of the compromise, California committed to revising its program so that compliance with the National Program will substitute for compliance with California's regulations.[56]

Some critics of EPA's regulation of GHGs have suggested that emissions from cars and trucks be regulated only through CAFE standards, but EPA and NHTSA have defended the need to issue a cohesive joint program to address all GHG emissions from passenger vehicles. CO_2 emissions from a motor vehicle are essentially a function of how much fuel that vehicle burns. Unlike other contaminants, which may be reduced by using specific technologies, CO_2 can be reduced only by reducing the amount of fuel burned. For instance, technologies that will reduce nitrogen dioxide emissions by more completely combusting fuel will only emit more CO_2. Moreover, air conditioners have GHG emissions of their own, independent of CO_2 tailpipe emissions.

The Obama Compromise offers a solution to the multi-jurisdictional governance of emissions through MY 2016. Due to the eighteen-month lead time required to give automakers notice of a new emissions rule, a new agreement must be reached between EPA, NHTSA, California, and, presumably, the automakers in time to issue a new joint rule before March 2014, to avoid renewed disputes and/or litigation over regulation of GHG emissions.

The Heavy-Duty National Program

EPA and NHTSA have proposed extending the GHG and fuel economy standards to heavy-duty vehicles, such as the largest pickup trucks, vans, semitrucks and other types of work trucks, and buses (in short, all vehicles over 8,500 pounds not including the medium-duty vehicles covered by the National Program). Under a rule proposed on October 25, 2010, manufacturers of heavy-duty vehicles would have to meet GHG standards beginning in MY 2014 and fuel economy standards by MY 2016.[57] The proposed rule divides the trucks into three categories: combination tractors (the semi-trucks that normally pull trailers), heavy-duty pickup trucks and vans, and vocational vehicles. Combination tractors and vocational trucks would have to meet varying emission and fuel consumption standards based on the size of the vehicle. Manufacturers of heavy-duty pickup trucks and vans would have to meet fleet averages, similar to the design of the light-duty vehicle program. The reductions are expected to reduce GHG emissions and fuel consumption by17 percent in diesel-powered and 12 percent in gas-powered heavy duty pickups and vans, by 7 to 20 percent in combination tractors, and by 7 to 10 percent in vocation vehicles, by MY 2017.[58]

EPA had identified a potential for up to a 40 percent reduction in GHG emissions from tractor-trailers through measures such as improvements in engine technology, eliminating aerodynamic drag on trailers, reducing rolling resistance of tires, and limiting speed.[59] Although EPA declined to regulate trailers in the October 25, 2010, proposal, it indicated that trailers likely would be regulated in a separate proposal.[60]

Potential Regulation of GHG Emissions from Other Sources

Various parties have petitioned EPA to regulate GHG emissions from other transportation sources, including ships, aircraft, non-road engines, and locomotives,[61] all of which may be regulated under the Clean Air Act. Each of these other transportation sources represent a much smaller segment of GHG emissions, as compared with on-road vehicles. However, each has significant impacts. For instance, locomotives and aircraft contribute less than 1 percent and up to 3.4 percent of total U.S. GHG emissions respectively, but they are a substantial source of soot (among other things), which could have a significant impact on global warming because of soot's ability to absorb solar radiation and reduce the reflective properties of snow and ice.[62] It is not clear whether EPA will take action in any of these areas, or whether it will first take on larger GHG emitters, such as power plants and other stationary sources.

Technological Advancements in Fuel Economy

The proposed new fuel economy and GHG emission standards for light-duty vehicles are designed to encourage more widespread use of both existing and new technologies to meet the fuel-saving requirements of the program.[63] Indeed, automakers have recognized they will need to employ a broad range of technologies to meet the required goal of 35.5 mpg by 2016. Such technology-forcing regulation has long been a cornerstone of environmental law, setting standards and then relying on industry to develop innovative ways to meet them. A Carnegie Mellon University study in 2003 looked at the success of technology-forcing provisions of the Clean Air Act in the 1970s and 1980s and found generally that while industry is not likely to invest in research and development on environmental controls that do not improve the sales of a product, assurances of enforcement can force companies to compete to develop the most efficient, cost-effective technology to meet the requirements.[64] In the context of GHG emissions, several regulations, along with significant federal investment in research, are driving the development of new fuel-efficient mobile source technologies.

In addition to the CAFE standards calling for a nearly 80 percent increase in fuel efficiency in six years, other programs are spurring new technology. In 1990, California adopted the Zero Emission Vehicle (ZEV) program with the aim to increase the use of low-emitting vehicles. Although the pace of technological advancements has not kept up with the initial goals of the program, the ZEV program has led to more than one million vehicles with near-zero or low tailpipe emissions being driven in California.[65] At the federal level, Congress in 2005 enacted a tax credit for qualified alternative vehicles of up to $3,000 to help support the market for alternative vehicles.[66] Additionally, EISA prohibits federal agencies from acquiring light-duty vehicles that are not low-GHG-emitting vehicles, requires that federal agencies increase alternative fuel consumption in vehicles by 10 percent by October 2015, and provides loans to support the retooling of domestic auto manufacturing for electric cars and battery manufacturing. The Energy Policy Act of 1992 requires that 75 percent of all new federal fleet vehicles must operate on alternative fuel, such as electric vehicles and plug-in hybrids.[67] By executive order, federal agencies must purchase plug-in hybrids when they become available at a competitive retail price.[68]

Additionally, under the American Recovery and Reinvestment Act of 2009 (ARRA), the federal government, primarily through the Department of Energy, has funded many research programs aimed at developing the technology of fuel-efficient vehicles. For instance:

- $300 million for diesel reduction grants;
- $100 million for fuel-efficient technology for heavy trucks;
- $100 million for development of new low-cost car batteries for electric vehicles and long-range plug-ins, and for "electrofuels," or new ways to make liquid transportation fuels without using petroleum or biomass;[69]
- $300 million to the General Services Administration for the purchase of fuel efficient vehicles.

In response, industry is developing a number of technologies, as described below.

Improvements to Gasoline Combustion Engines

Gasoline combustion engines are relatively inefficient compared to new vehicle technologies such as hybrid, hydrogen, and electric vehicles. In an internal combustion engine, nearly 85 percent of the fuel energy is lost to internal friction and wasted heat in the engine, idling at stop lights or in traffic, friction in the drive train, overcoming inertia of a heavy vehicle, the rolling resistance of tires, and aerodynamic drag, among other things.[70] While new technologies seek to replace the internal combustion engine, many improvements are available that would improve efficiency of traditional engines. Some existing technologies include direct fuel injection and turbo-charging to more completely mix fuel and air, six- and eight- speed automatic transmissions to allow engines to operate closer to their maximum efficiency, cylinder deactivation that shuts down part of the engine during cruising speeds, and variable valve timing that opens and closes engine valves so that they are more in sync with fuel combustion.[71] Many of these technologies have been successfully introduced in Europe. About half of the light-duty vehicles in Europe use direct injection diesel engines, with a 35 percent improvement in fuel economy compared to conventional gasoline engines.[72]

Hybrid Electric Vehicles

Hybrid electric vehicles improve on many of the inefficiencies of internal combustion engines, getting about twice the gas mileage of a vehicle of comparable size.[73] Operating under the combined power of a fuel-driven internal combustion engine and electric motor, hybrids are designed to turn off the engine when the vehicle comes to a stop and restart instantaneously when the accelerator is pressed.[74] Additionally, the hybrid motor recovers kinetic energy lost when the brakes slow a moving vehicle by capturing that energy to recharge the battery. Although hybrids continue to burn petroleum, emit CO_2 and other pollutants, and utilize batteries that may contain toxic chemicals, they provide many benefits for improved fuel economy in the near future because they are readily available, relatively affordable, and can be integrated into the national fleet without any change in the infrastructure.[75]

Plug-In Hybrid Electric Vehicles

One vehicle that shows promise in reducing GHG emissions from the transportation sector is the plug-in hybrid electric vehicle ("plug-in"). The plug-in is a hybrid that runs an electric motor by the power of a large battery. The battery is plugged into an electric socket to charge, and then discharges as the vehicle is driven. Because plug-ins can go only limited distances on one charge, the technology is likely to be most useful for local driving of light-duty vehicles, urban buses, and delivery vehicles—any use that does not require long-distance driving away from a source to plug in and recharge.[76] The benefits of plug-ins are that they do not rely on gasoline and do not create tailpipe emissions when used within their battery range. They do, however, rely on whatever source is used to create electricity where they are plugged in, so if they are recharged where electricity is supplied by coal-burning power plants, plug-ins do have a carbon cost. And there is the potential that once they become widespread, they could overwhelm an already taxed power grid.

Also, neither the technology nor the infrastructure for plug-ins is fully developed. Nickel metal hydride batteries, such as those used in conventional hybrids, store only a limited amount of energy. Manufacturers are focusing on further developing lithium ion batteries, but those can degrade after they are deeply discharged many times and are expensive to produce. Further, plug-in stations will be needed for vehicles to "refuel" while away from home and for those without access to an outlet at home, such as those who park on the street. The Department of Energy provides financial support for battery research.[77] Additionally, federal agencies are required to purchase plug-ins when they become commercially available at a competitive price.[78] The demand created by the federal buying program is expected to help reduce the cost of production by providing economies of scale for manufacturers.[79]

Hydrogen Fuel Cell

A technology that has the potential to be truly "zero emissions" is the hydrogen fuel cell vehicle.[80] The fuel cell system uses the chemical reaction between hydrogen and oxygen to power the car, producing only water and heat as by-products.[81] "Lifecycle" emissions of a hydrogen fuel cell vehicle would depend on how the hydrogen is generated. Hydrogen is not naturally available, as petroleum is, and must be extracted from other hydrogen-containing compounds, such as hydrocarbons in coal or natural gas, biomass, water, or sunlight.[82] While these sources are plentiful from domestic sources and can reduce reliance on foreign oil, the production of hydrogen from natural gas requires a lot of energy and still would generate significant CO_2 emissions. If, however, the hydrogen could be derived from water using electricity produced with renewable energy such as solar or wind, the entire system from production to tailpipe could be zero emissions.[83] Still, the technology requires years of research and development before it can be viewed as a practical alternative to the combustion engine. Onboard storage of hydrogen in amounts significant enough to allow driving of any distance is technically difficult and expensive. Also, a national fleet of hydrogen-powered cars would require a completely new refueling infrastructure.[84]

Still, hydrogen has gained significant support. Recognizing hydrogen power's promise to secure energy sources and reduce pollution, President Bush in his State of the Union address in January 2003 called for the dedication of $1.2 billion over five years to begin development of a "hydrogen economy."[85] Congress included provisions in the Energy Policy Act of 2005 (EPAct05) calling for technology research and development of the hydrogen fuels infrastructure.[86] However, by 2009, Secretary of the Department of Energy Steven Chu determined that hydrogen power was "not practical" within the next ten to twenty years and sought to withdraw funding for the program in favor of other fuel-saving technologies that were more likely to come online sooner.[87] Nonetheless, Congress continued to fund the program.

California also supports the development of hydrogen technology through its Hydrogen Highway Network Program (CaH$_2$Net).[88] As of mid-2010, California had invested or allocated $25 million toward hydrogen vehicles and fueling stations.[89] CaH$_2$Net also has funded the procurement and deployment of hydrogen buses.[90]

Alternative Fuels

Another focus of attention for reducing carbon emissions from transportation sources is on alternative fuels. EPAct05 amended the Clean Air Act provision that called on EPA to increase the use of ethanol as motor fuel[91] to require EPA to increase the amount of "renewable fuel" in the domestic transportation fuel to 7.5 billion gallons by 2012. EISA increased the Renewable Fuel Standard requirement to 36 billion gallons by 2022. Most ethanol is produced using grain or corn surplus from domestic farms, sources that have been criticized as providing a large lifetime source of GHGs due to the petroleum burned during their harvesting and production. Other potential sources for new fuels are algae-based biofuels, fuel from waste, and coal-to-liquid fuels, among others. For a more complete discussion of alternative fuels, see chapter 19.

Vehicle Operation and Maintenance

Short of replacing a vehicle or the fuel that runs it, simple operation and maintenance can reduce the amount of carbon emitted by petroleum-powered vehicles and are becoming more common targets for state regulation. For instance, twenty-eight states and the District of Columbia have laws governing idling of tractor trailers.[92] Trucks, primary movers of short-to-medium distance and time-sensitive goods, are the second largest user of oil, after passenger cars and light trucks, accounting for about 63 percent of freight energy use.[93]

CARB began phasing in the prohibition of truck idling in 2005. In California, any truck over 10,000 pounds may not idle for more than five minutes, and beginning in 2008, all new engines must be equipped with automatic systems that shut down the engine after five minutes of idling. New technology has emerged to help long-haulers cope with the stringent new rules, which apply to any truck that operates in California. Auxiliary power units are smaller, more efficient generators that power the truck's heating, cooling, and electrical devices while parked. Some trucks are now outfitted with batteries, similar to those in hybrid cars, which capture energy generated while the truck is in motion for use when it is stopped. Truck stops are beginning to offer "plug-in" stations where truck drivers can access electricity.

California has led the nation in a suite of new regulations aimed at curbing fuel use and GHG emissions of trucks. These "fleet rules" apply to all trucks that operate in California, no matter where they are based, meaning they apply to a large percentage of the national fleet. In addition to meeting the idling regulations, truck drivers in California must either replace trucks or retrofit them with verified technologies that reduce GHG emissions.[94] CARB's GHG emission rules are based on EPA's voluntary SmartWay program, which evaluates and verifies fuel savings and emissions reduction technologies for trucks, such as those that reduce idling, aerodynamic drag, tire resistance, and filter diesel exhaust.[95]

Tire inflation and design also have been targeted as ways to reduce GHG emissions. For instance, finding that underinflated tires increase fuel consumption and emissions, California required all automotive repair shops to ensure that the tires on vehicles serviced in their shops are properly inflated beginning in July 2010.[96] Similarly, NHTSA has proposed creating a new tire labeling law that would require tire manufacturers to label tires for fuel efficiency, safety, and durability based on test procedures designed by NHTSA.[97]

Other Initiatives to Reduce Gasoline Demand

Fuel Taxes

An integral part of the public debate about lowering GHG emissions of gasoline-fueled vehicles is the role of fuel prices. Many say that simply requiring the vehicles to be more efficient will not achieve meaningful reductions. While improvements in fuel economy will change what cars Americans buy, it will not change the cars they already have or the amount they drive them. And because new cars with improved emission-reduction technology are also more expensive to produce, by an average estimated $505 to $907 for cars and $322 to $961 for light trucks,[98] consumers might be more likely to keep their older, less efficient vehicles longer. Additionally, increases in CAFE standards reduce the cost of driving, which provides an incentive to drive more, thus burning more, not less, fuel. This so-called "rebound effect" is said to reduce the ability of CAFE standards and emissions controls to significantly reduce GHG emissions.[99]

What is needed, some argue, is a corresponding increase in the price of fuel that will encourage consumers to buy more efficient cars, drive less, and burn less fuel.[100] It is a matter of simple economics that increasing gas prices decreases the demand for gas. Studies have shown that consumers undervalue fuel efficiency, especially when gas prices are low and corresponding savings are not significant.[101] In 2002, the NAS concluded: "There is a marked inconsistency between pressuring automotive manu-facturers for improved fuel economy from new vehicles on the one hand and insisting on low real gasoline prices on the other. Higher real prices for gasoline—for instance, through increased gasoline taxes—would create both a demand for fuel efficient new vehicles and an incentive for owners of existing vehicles to drive them less."[102]

Some have suggested that increased fuel prices are necessary in order to create a market for low GHG-emitting alternative vehicles, such as hybrids and plug-ins. In Europe, where taxes represent 70 percent of the price of fuel, high gas prices have contributed toward the production of fuel-efficient diesel vehicles that are lightweight and use modern injection systems to improve fuel economy.[103] In the United States, where taxes comprise only 11 percent the cost of gas, low prices have contributed toward the increasing popularity of heavy, low-fuel-economy vehicles.

Another argument for increasing the price of gasoline through taxes is that higher prices reflect the reality and force drivers to pay for the "externalities" of fuel con-sumption, including the social and financial costs of the fuel that are not reflected in the price, such as the cost to secure foreign oil, the threat to the national economy of oil price shocks, and the societal cost of climate change.

Gas taxes, of course, are highly unpopular with the voting public—they tend to be flat or regressive and arguably impose a greater burden on the less wealthy[104]—and thus are not commonly advocated by politicians. Many analysts, however, propose gas taxes as the logical way to create the proper incentive for fuel conservation and to level the price of fuel at its true cost. In one proposal, two law school professors suggest implementing a gas tax to stabilize fuel prices at a sufficiently high level to encourage conservation, but not too high to reduce consumer purchasing power.[105] They would set a floor for the price of gasoline so that the price at the gas pump would never go under the floor, but would rise above the floor in accordance with the market price. If the world oil price fell below the floor, the difference between the market price and the floor would be collected by the government and refunded to consumers in a rebate, similar to tax rebates issued by the IRS. This predictable price of gasoline, they argue, would provide the proper long-term incentive necessary for consumers and manufacturers to invest in alternative energy and new technology, without taking an excessive amount of money out of the pockets of consumers. Other studies have suggested setting the price of gas as high as $7 per gallon.[106]

Efforts to Reduce Vehicle Miles Traveled

Generally, there are three ways to reduce GHG emissions from transportation sources: (1) increase fuel economy and decrease emissions per mile, such as through the CAFE program; (2) convert to low-carbon fuels or energy sources, such as through hybrids and alternative fuels; and (3) reduce vehicle miles traveled (VMT).[107] A 2009 study sponsored by a variety of stakeholders from government, industry, and the nonprofit sector identified nine strategies that can be implemented over the short and long term to reduce GHG emissions by reducing VMT, including: increasing the cost of using the transportation system through increased driving and parking tolls and fees; encouraging walking and bicycling; expanding public transportation and subsidizing fares; expanding ride-sharing programs; reducing speeds to increase fuel efficiency; reducing bottlenecking; improving efficiency of the transportation system; reducing the need for vehicle trips through improved land use and smart growth; and promoting more efficient freight movement.[108] The last three of these strategies bear more explanation.

Highway transportation efficiency improvements have been suggested by many as a method to cut down on traffic congestion and idling, and thus reduce the GHGs emitted per mile. Some strategies include ramp metering, message signs warning of disruptions, real-time traveler information, variable speed limits to help cars flow smoothly onto a highway, and advanced traffic signals that change timing based on traffic load.[109] Several states are testing programs that would use wireless communication systems to give drivers real-time information about road conditions to help them make better decisions about routes, travel times, and modes of transportation.[110] Called intelligent transportation systems (ITS), these strategies seek to make better use of existing capacity and provide better traffic flow.[111]

Also, land use strategies have been a focus for years as a way to reduce dependence on automobiles. Focusing dense, residential development around transit and mixed-use retail hubs—as opposed to the low-density development that has dominated in metropolitan suburbs over the past several decades, often referred to as sprawl—provides focal points of activity where people can easily access public transportation to work, shop, or find entertainment without the need of a car. In a study mandated by EPAct05, NAS concluded that compact, mixed-use development can shorten trips and thus VMT and GHG emissions, especially when coupled with strategies such as good neighborhood design and reduced or highly priced parking.[112] Smart Growth, however, is not without its critics. Increasing density in the suburbs often comes with protests from the existing community about increased local traffic and demand on services, and many suburban dwellers simply prefer to have more space.

Another focus of attention to reduce VMT has been to increase the use of rail for local and intercity passenger travel and for freight transportation, and to reduce the reliance on motor vehicles, including trucks. The Obama administration designated $8 billion from ARRA to support the development of high-speed, intercity rail, a move that will also improve freight travel and reduce rail-line bottlenecking, since the trains share the same rail lines.[113]

Notes

1. Nat'l Highway Transp. & Safety Admin., Final Environmental Impact Statement, Corporate Average Fuel Economy Standards, Passenger Cars and Light Trucks, Model Years 2012–2016, at 4 (Feb. 2010).

2. *Id.* at 4.

3. *Id.*

4. Brent D. Yacobucci & Robert Bamberger, Cong. Res. Serv., RL33,413, Automobile and Light Truck Fuel Economy: The CAFE Standards 10 (May 7, 2008).

5. Nat'l Acad. of Sciences, Nat'l Research Council, Transp. Research Bd., Effectiveness and Impact of Corporate Average Fuel Economy (CAFE) Standards 14 (2002) [hereinafter NAS Study].

6. Joel Ban, *NEPA Review of CAFE: A Lost Opportunity*, 23 Temp. Envtl. L. &. Tech. J. 121, 125–26 (2004).

7. *See, e.g.*, 74 Fed. Reg. 14196, 14200 (Mar. 30, 2009).

8. 42 U.S.C. §§ 32902(a), 32904(a), 32911; 49 C.F.R. § 501.2(a)(8) (delegation to NHTSA).

9. 49 U.S.C. § 32902(a).

10. 49 U.S.C. § 32902(a), (f).

11. 49 C.F.R. §§ 523, *et. seq.*

12. 74 Fed. Reg. 14196, 14215 (Mar. 30, 2009).

13. 49 C.F.R. § 523.2.

14. NAS Study, *supra* note 5, at 3.

15. Ban, *supra* note 6, at 124.

16. NAS Study, *supra* note 5, at 21.

17. NAS Study, *supra* note 5, at 19.

18. NAS Study, *supra* note 5, at 3.

19. 67 Fed. Reg. 77, 015 (Dec. 16, 2002).

20. U.S. Envtl. Protection Agency, Light-Duty Automotive Technology, Carbon Dioxide Emissions, and Fuel Economy Trends: 1975 Through 2009, at v (Nov. 2009), *available at* http://www.epa.gov/otaq/cert/mpg/fetrends/420r09014.pdf.

21. Roberta Barkman James, *Oil and the Environment: Reducing Oil Dependency in the Automotive Sector*, 15 U. Balt. J. Envtl. L. 1, 2 (2007).

22. NAS Study, *supra* note 5, at 3–5.

23. NAS Study, *supra* note 5, at 4–5,13, 83.

24. 68 Fed. Reg. 16868, 16871 (Apr. 7, 2003).

25. 71 Fed. Reg. 17,566, 17,568 (Apr. 6, 2006).

26. NAS Study, *supra* note 5, at 69–70.

27. 71 Fed. Reg. 17,566.

28. Ctr. for Biological Diversity v. NHTSA, 508 F.3d 508 (9th Cir. 2007).

29. *Id.* at 531.

30. 74 Fed. Reg. 14196, 14215 (Mar. 30, 2009).

31. 42 U.S.C. § 7521 (a)(1).

32. Massachusetts v. EPA, 549 U.S. 497 (2007).

33. *Id.* at 533.

34. 74 Fed. Reg. 18886 (Apr. 24, 2009).

35. 74 Fed. Reg. 66456 (Dec. 15, 2009).

36. S. J. Res. 26, 111th Cong. (2010).

37. 156 Cong. Rec. S4789–836 (daily ed. June 6, 2010); *see also* Dean Scott, *Murkowski Pushing for Vote on Blocking EPA Climate Rules in Small Business Bill*, Daily Env't Rep. (BNA) No. 144 at A-3 (July 29, 2010).

38. S. 3072, 111th Cong. (Mar. 4, 2010); H.R. 4753, 111th Cong. (Mar. 4, 2010). *See* Dean Scott, *House, Senate Bills Call for Two-Year Delay of EPA Greenhouse Gas Emissions Rules*, Daily Env't Rep. (BNA) No. 42 at A-1 to A-2 (Mar. 5, 2010).

39. S. Amendment 4517, 156 Cong. Rec. S6261–6262 (daily ed. July 27, 2010); Dean Scott, *With Outlook Uncertain on Energy Bill, Murkowski EPA Amendment Put Off Until Fall*, Daily Env't Rep. (BNA) No. 146 at A-5 to A-6 (Aug. 2, 2010).

40. Linder v. EPA, No. 10-1035, (D.C. Cir. Feb. 10, 2010).

41. 42 U.S.C. § 7543(a).

42. 42 U.S.C. § 7543(b)(1).

43. *Id.*

44. 42 U.S.C. § 7507.

45. Cal. Assembly Bill 1493 (codified at California Health and Safety Code, § 43,018.5).

46. CARB Res. 04-28.

47. California v. EPA, No. 08-70011 (9th Cir. July 25, 2008).

48. *See* http://www.whitehouse.gov/the_press_office/California_Request_for_Waiver_Under_the_Clean_Air_Act.

49. 74 Fed. Reg. 32744 (July 8, 2010).

50. 529 F. Supp. 2d 1151 (2007).

51. 49 U.S.C. § 32919.

52. 508 F. Supp. 2d 295 (D. Vt. 2007).

53. *See* http://www.whitehouse.gov/the-press-office/president-obama-announces-national-fuel-efficiency-policy.

54. 75 Fed. Reg. 25324 (May 7, 2010) (codified at 40 C.F.R. pts. 85, 86, 600; 49 C.F.R. pts. 531, 533, 536, et seq.).

55. 75 Fed. Reg. 25328 (May 7, 2010).

56. *Id.*

57. 75 Fed. Reg. 74152 (Nov. 30, 2010).

58. James E. McCarthy, Cong. Res. Serv., R40506, Cars, Trucks, and Climate: EPA Regulation of Greenhouse Gases from Mobile Sources 10 (Nov. 2, 2010).

59. 73 Fed. Reg. 44453 (July 30, 2008); *see also* McCarthy, *supra* note 58, at 9.

60. 75 Fed. Reg. 74152, 74157.

61. *See* McCarthy, *supra* note 58, at Table 1.

62. *Id.* at 14.

63. 74 Fed. Reg. 49454, 49460 (Sept. 28, 2009).

64. David Gerard & Lester B. Lave, Implementing Technology Forcing Policies: The 1970 Clean Air Act Amendments and the Introduction of Advance Automotive Emissions Controls 4–5 (2003).

65. Cal. Envtl. Protection Agency, Air Res. Bd., The California Zero Emission Vehicle Regulation, *available at* http://www.arb.ca.gov/msprog/zevprog/factsheets/zev_fs.pdf.

66. Energy Policy Act of 2005 § 1341.

67. *See* U.S. Gov't Accountability Office, GAO 09-493, Federal Energy and Fleet Management: Plug-in Vehicles Offer Potential Benefits, but High Costs and Limited Information Could Hinder Integration into the Federal Fleet 6–7 (June 2009), *available at* http://www.gao.gov/products/GAO-09-493 [hereinafter Federal Fleet Management].

68. Exec. Order No. 13423, 72 Fed. Reg. 3919 (Jan. 26, 2007).

69. Ari Natter, *Energy Department to Provide $100 Million for Projects Focused on New Technology*, Daily Env't Rep. (BNA) No. 233 at A-8 to A-9 (Dec. 8, 2009).

70. Shigeki Kobayashi, Steven Plotkin, & Suzana Kahn Ribeiro, *Energy Efficiency Technologies for Road Vehicles*, 2 Energy Efficiency 125, 127–28 (2009) [hereinafter Energy Efficiency].

71. Steven D. Cook, *Many Automakers to Use Gasoline Technology in Near Term to Attain Efficiency Standards*, BNA Daily Env't Rep. (BNA) No. 98 at A-4 to A-5 (May 26, 2009).

72. Energy Efficiency, *supra* note 70, at 129.

73. Energy Efficiency, *supra* note 70, at 130.

74. Energy Efficiency, *supra* note 70, at 128.

75. *See, e.g.*, Zachary W. Silverman, *Hybrid Vehicles: A Practical and Effective Short-Term Solution to Petroleum Dependence*, 19 Geo. Int'l Envtl. L. Rev. 543, 550 (2007).

76. Energy Efficiency, supra note 70, at 132.

77. Federal Fleet Management, *supra* note 67, at 8.

78. Exec. Order No. 13423; 72 Fed. Reg. 3919 (Jan. 26, 2007).

79. Federal Fleet Management, *supra* note 67, at 21.

80. Energy Efficiency, *supra* note 67, at 133.

81. Peter M. Crofton, *Emerging Issues Relating to the Burgeoning Hydrogen Economy*, 27 ENERGY L.J. 39, 39 (2006).

82. *See* NAS Study, *supra* note 5, at 54. *See also* U.S. DEP'T OF ENERGY, HYDROGEN PRODUCTION, www.hydrogen.energy.gov/production.html.

83. ENERGY EFFICIENCY, *supra* note 67, at 133.

84. *Id.*

85. PRESIDENT GEORGE W. BUSH, STATE OF THE UNION ADDRESS (Jan. 28, 2003) *available at* http://georgewbush-whitehouse.archives.gov/news/releases/2003/01/20030128-19.html.

86. Energy Policy Act 2005 § 802.

87. Matthew L. Wald, *U.S. Drops Research into Fuel Cells for Cars*, N.Y. TIMES, May 8, 2009, at A18.

88. Gov. Schwarzenegger Exec. Order S-7-04.

89. CAL. ENVTL. PROTECTION AGENCY, AIR RES. BD., CLEAN FUELS OUTLET REGULATORY CHANGES, *available at* http://www.arb.ca.gov/fuels/altfuels/cf-outlets/cfo_facts.pdf ; CAL. CODE REGS. tit. 13, § 8 (2000).

90. CAL. AIR RES. BD., HYDROGEN HIGHWAY NETWORK, CAH2NET SUMMER 2009 UPDATE, *available at* http://hydrogenhighway.ca.gov/update/summer09.pdf.

91. 42 U.S.C. § 7545(o).

92. AM. TRANSP. RESEARCH INST., COMPENDIUM OF IDLING REGULATIONS (Sept. 2010), *available at* http://www.atri-online.org/research/idling/ATRI_Idling_Compendium.pdf.

93. R. NEAL ELLIOT, THERESE LANGER, & STEVEN NADEL, AMERICAN COUNCIL FOR AN ENERGY-EFFICIENT ECONOMY, REDUCING OIL USE THROUGH ENERGY EFFICIENCY: OPPORTUNITIES BEYOND CARS AND LIGHT TRUCKS 3 (Jan. 2006).

94. CAL. CODE REGS. tit. 17, § 95,300, *et seq.*; CAL. ENVTL. PROTECTION AGENCY, AIR RES. BD., HEAVY-DUTY VEHICLE GREENHOUSE GAS EMISSION REDUCTION REGULATION, *available at* http://www.arb.ca.gov/cc/hdghg/fact_sheets/hdghg_genl_fact_sheet.pdf.

95. *See* U.S. ENVTL. PROTECTION AGENCY, SMARTWAY, http://www.epa.gov/smartway/index.htm.

96. Carolyn Whetzel, *California Regulators Adopt Rule Requiring Auto Repair Shops to Check Tire Pressure*, Daily Env't Rep. (BNA) No. 57 at A-1 (Mar. 27, 2009).

97. 74 Fed. Reg. 29542 (June 22, 2009).

98. 75 Fed. Reg. 25324, 25641–25642 (May 7, 2010).

99. YACOBUCCI & BAMBERGER, *supra* note 4, at 11.

100. Robert Stavins, *The New Auto Fuel-Efficiency Standards—Going Beyond the Headlines*, May 22, 2009, http://www.huffingtonpost.com/robert-stavins/the-new-auto-fuel-efficie_b_206682.html.

101. Testimony of David L. Greene, Senate Comm. on Energy and Natural Resources (Jan. 30, 2007).

102. NAS Study, *supra* note 5, at 4.

103. *See* FENG AN & AMANDA SAUER, PEW CTR. ON GLOBAL CLIMATE CHANGE, COMPARISON OF PASSENGER VEHICLE FUEL ECONOMY AND GREENHOUSE GAS EMISSION STANDARDS AROUND THE WORLD (Dec. 2004), *available at* http://www.pewclimate.org/docUploads/Fuel%20Economy%20and%20GHG%20Standards_010605_110719.pdf.

104. *See, e.g.*, CONGRESSIONAL BUDGET OFFICE, REDUCING GASOLINE CONSUMPTION: THREE POLICY OPTIONS 30 (Nov. 2002), *available at* http://www.cbo.gov/ftpdocs/39xx/doc3991/11-21-GasolineStudy.pdf.

105. Thomas Merrill & David Schizer, *A Proposed Petroleum Fuel Price Stabilization Plan*, 27 YALE J. ON REG. 1 (2010).

106. W. Ross Morrow, Henry Lee, Kelly Sims Gallagher, Gustavo Collantes, *Reducing the U.S. Transportation Sector's Oil Consumption and Greenhouse Gas Emissions*, 38(3) ENERGY POL'Y (Feb. 2010).

107. YACOBUCCI & BAMBERGER, *supra* note 4, at 10–11.

108. URBAN LAND INST., MOVING COOLER: AN ANALYSIS OF TRANSPORTATION STRATEGIES FOR REDUCING GREENHOUSE GAS EMISSIONS (Aug. 2009).

109. Am. Ass'n of State Highway & Transp. Officials, Real Transportation Solutions for Greenhouse Gas Emissions Reductions (July 2009), *available at* http://climatechange.transportation.org/pdf/RealSolutionsReport.pdf.

110. *See generally* Testimony on Transportation Infrastructure, House Comm. on Science and Technology, Subcomm. on Technology and Innovation (June 24, 2008).

111. Urban Land Inst., Moving Cooler: An Analysis of Transportation Strategies for Reducing Greenhouse Gas Emissions (Aug. 2009).

112. Bd. on Energy & Envtl. Sys., Driving and the Built Environment: The Effects of Compact Development on Motorized Travel, Energy Use and CO_2 Emissions (NAS 2009).

113. Press Release, The White House, President Obama, Vice President Biden to Announce $8 Billion for High-Speed Rail Projects Across the Country (Jan. 28, 2010), *available at* http://www.whitehouse.gov/the-press-office/president-obama-vice-president-biden-announce-8-billion-high-speed-rail-projects-ac.

chapter fifteen

Distributed Generation

Frederick R. Fucci

The purpose of this chapter is to set out briefly the legal and regulatory framework applicable to the generation of electric and thermal energy at the places and facilities where that energy is used, as opposed to buying power from utility distribution companies, which rely on the traditional central station model. The alternative model, where electricity and thermal energy are generated at or near the site where the energy is used, is called "distributed generation," because the generation resources are "distributed" around the grid and stand in contrast to the central generation model.

This chapter will begin by describing the main technologies for on-site power generation. It will then describe the broad outlines of the relevant federal law and how on-site generating plants generally enjoy an exemption from the federal electric regulatory scheme. It will then describe how on-site generating plants are not considered to be public utilities for purposes of state law (provided they only make sales of electricity to their hosts and in the immediate vicinity), which avoids their being subject to state public service commission oversight and rate regulation. Since a major hurdle in most distributed generation projects is the interconnection with distribution and transmission systems, this chapter will set out some considerations regarding the interconnection of distributed generation with utility distribution and transmission systems.

Introduction to Cogeneration/Combined Heat and Power

The traditional method of generating and delivering electricity in the United States is the central station model, where large power plants in relatively remote locations generate electricity, which is then transmitted long distances over high-voltage transmission lines before being stepped down in voltage for use in local distribution systems. The principal fuels used for power generation in the United States (and thus predominantly in the central station model) are coal (44.5 percent), natural gas (23.3 percent), nuclear (20.2 percent), and hydroelectric (6.8 percent).[1] Except in hydroelectric

The author acknowledges the assistance of Natara Feller in the preparation of this chapter.

plants, the process of generating electricity itself creates heat, called "waste heat" in the industry. In the United States today, most central station generating plants are single-cycle plants and thus make no use of the waste heat at all. It is either vented into the atmosphere or passed through to cooling towers or to bodies of water.[2] As a result, the average efficiency of fuel conversion for all power generation in the United States today stands today at about 34 percent, where it has been for several decades.[3] This is a striking statistic. Put another way, almost two-thirds of the fuel used for generating electricity today in the United States is wasted. Further, it takes electricity to transmit electricity, so there are losses in the process. Average "line-losses" in the United States today are between 7 and 10 percent, with greater losses during peak periods, which means that even more electricity is wasted in getting it from where it is generated to its point of use.[4] In short, the central station model, which has been the norm for decades, results in the waste of huge amounts of energy, vents a tremendous amount of heat into the atmosphere and bodies of water, and keeps the carbon footprint of power generation in the United States high, since nearly half of the electricity comes from coal.

The waste heat from power generation can be captured to make thermal energy, either in the form of steam or hot or chilled water. When steam from waste heat is used to generate more electricity, this is referred to as combined cycle generation. The most modern natural-gas-fired power plants today are combined cycle plants. Usually, they are fairly large and are designed to feed into the central station system. Since the 1990s, combined cycle plants have become the standard technology for natural gas plants. The most sophisticated ones have efficiencies approaching 60 percent. Still, on average, the overall efficiency of power generation in the United States remains at about 34 percent.

More relevant for distributed applications is cogeneration, which is the simultaneous generation of electricity and useful thermal energy. This is sometimes referred to as combined heat and power, or CHP. Cogeneration is nothing new. In fact, it is as old as power generation itself. Thomas Edison advocated it, and many of his early plants were cogeneration plants. While many companies installed cogeneration facilities on the sites of their industrial facilities, where steam was useful in the manufacturing process (one of the largest early ones was in Dearborn, Michigan, installed by Henry Ford), cogeneration did not start to become widespread in the central generation model until the 1970s when certain regulatory changes (discussed below) allowed companies that were independent of vertically integrated utilities to build cogeneration plants and sell the electrical output to electric utilities at a defined "avoided cost." Since then, many cogeneration stations have been built in the central station model, feeding power into the grid. However, a useful application must always be found for the thermal energy they produce.

Cogeneration or CHP applications can reach efficiencies over 80 percent if they are sized correctly in conjunction with the thermal loads of their hosts. Typical users of CHP plants are facilities that have significant thermal loads, like college and other types of campuses, schools, hospitals, hotels, industrial facilities, and municipal buildings. Commercial office buildings are also well suited to CHP applications. Since most CHP is for on-site applications, the plants tend to be fairly small (in the 1 to 5 MW range), although for more significant campuses they can reach sizes of 10–15 MW.

Fuel cells are another type of efficient CHP application. Fuel cells use an emissions-free chemical process to make electricity, even though they do need some sort of fuel to run. Most of the prototypes and systems in use today use natural gas, but they can also be run off of other types of gas, in particular the anaerobic digester gas that is a by-product of the wastewater treatment process. Hydrogen is also being developed as a fuel source for fuel cells, and some installations are using hydrogen now.

Since fuel cells are quiet and have no emissions other than some water, they are well suited for installation inside of buildings. Fuel cells can be configured in combined heat and power applications, particularly in on-site or campus-type situations. In this regard, they have all the advantages of combined heat and power from natural gas combustion. There are several types of fuel cells, and the differences between the technologies are complex for people who are not power engineers.[5] Some disadvantages of fuel cells are that they are rather more expensive than conventional CHP and generally less robust, thus requiring more maintenance.

Solar photovoltaic and thermal installations are also in essence small power plants on the site of the users of electricity. While various aspects of solar installations are considered in other chapters of this book, it should be kept in mind that solar installations are subject to the same broad legal and regulatory considerations as other types of on-site power generation. The same is true of on-site wind turbines, which are not in wide use yet.

The fundamental point is that every commercial and residential facility is potentially a small power plant—and this is the real alternative to the central generation model. With existing and readily available technology, every office building, apartment building, hotel, campus, hospital, and factory can generate on-site enough electricity and thermal energy to meet its own basic energy needs and export some to the grid. If configured correctly, these on-site systems can also keep the power on when the grid goes down and provide a much higher level of reliability, efficiency, and even quality than grid power.

Indeed, if broadly introduced, cogeneration technology has the potential to significantly impact energy efficiency in the United States. The Department of Energy estimated that if combined heat and power comprised 20 percent of the United States' energy-generating capacity by 2030, it would save 5.3 quadrillion BTU of fuel annually.[6] This would require, though, deployment of cogeneration technology on a utility scale, and not just as on-site generation for facilities.

Federal Regulation of Distributed Generation and CHP Facilities

Historical Background of Federal Regulation

Since 1935, the federal government has taken a very active role in regulating the electric utility industry. In response to perceived stock manipulation and shareholder abuses of power trusts, Congress enacted the Public Utility Holding Company Act of 1935 (PUHCA of 1935).[7] Under PUHCA of 1935, "holding companies" were required to register with the Securities and Exchange Commission (SEC). PUHCA of 1935 defined a holding company as any company that directly or indirectly controlled 10 percent or more of the voting securities of a public utility.[8] Among other things, PUHCA of 1935 empowered the SEC to regulate the acquisition of public utility securities and other assets, the issuance of securities, intercompany financing, and affiliate transactions.[9] PUHCA of 1935 further authorized the SEC to examine a holding company's corporate and operational structures, and empowered the SEC to simplify and integrate holding company operations, if needed, to avoid shareholder abuse.

The other base federal statute governing electricity is the Federal Power Act (FPA), initially passed by Congress in 1920 and revised in 1935 to add parts II and III, which provide the statutory foundation for regulating the business of transmitting and selling electric energy across state lines.[10] The FPA granted the Federal Power Commission (FPC) complete regulatory jurisdiction over interstate transmission of electric energy and the sale of electricity at wholesale in interstate commerce.[11] The FPC's authority was assigned to the successor Federal Energy Regulatory Commission (FERC)[12] in 1977.

Section 205 of the FPA prohibits undue preferences or discrimination and requires that any rates, charges, or classifications be "just and reasonable."[13] A public utility subject to FERC's jurisdiction must file all applicable tariffs, contracts, or rate schedules that alter the rates to be charged or the terms and conditions of service with FERC. If a public utility fails to meet its burden of demonstrating the lawfulness of its proposed rates, terms, or conditions, FERC is empowered to both determine and order a just and reasonable rate.[14] Further, §206 enables FERC to unilaterally reduce rates that were previously approved upon a demonstration that such rates have since become unjust and unreasonable.[15] The FPA also provides that FERC may make orders necessary to ensure the maintenance of adequate services.[16]

Scope of FERC Jurisdiction

Section 201 of the FPA provides the basis for FERC's jurisdiction over the electric utility industry.[17] The FPA specifically grants FERC jurisdiction over the transmission of electric energy in interstate commerce, the wholesale sale of electricity in interstate commerce, and the facilities for such sales or transmissions.[18] The FPA provides that electric energy is transmitted in interstate commerce if delivered from a state and consumed at any point outside of it.[19] Even where a local agency may also have regulatory power, FERC's reach extends to a public utility only when the company is a "public utility" because of its ownership or operation of facilities not used in local distribution.[20] Traditionally, power tariffs for electricity produced through central station power generation are subject to FERC's approval.

However, although broad, FERC's jurisdiction over electric energy production has always been limited, not general. For instance, §201 does not authorize FERC jurisdiction over facilities for electricity generation, or electric energy transmission in *intrastate* commerce.[21] In the 1970s, faced with escalating electricity rates and the monopoly power of large public utilities, Congress moved to craft another exemption to FERC's jurisdiction which appeared in the Public Utility Regulatory Policies Act of 1978 (PURPA).[22]

Public Utility Regulatory Policies Act of 1978

PURPA's primary goal was to promote energy efficiency and encourage the development of alternative sources of power, such as cogeneration and CHP.[23] To achieve these objectives, PURPA directed FERC to define a class of alternative on-site generators that "qualify" for a myriad of regulatory and financial incentives. A cogeneration or renewable energy facility that meets FERC standards is termed a "qualifying facility" (QF).

For much of the past thirty years, PURPA has provided QFs with an array of benefits within the larger regulatory scheme. PURPA required public utilities to interconnect with QFs and supply these smaller on-site facilities with supplemental or backup power at reasonable rates.[24] PURPA additionally mandated that utilities purchase excess power generated by QFs at the utility's full "avoided cost," or the price which the utility itself would pay to generate or purchase power.[25] Finally, and most important, §210(e) of PURPA exempted QFs from most state and federal utility regulations, including various sections of the FPA and PUHCA.[26] These exemptions made it possible for a QF to make sales of power (particularly to the hosts of the plant) without FERC review of the rates it charges and to operate largely free from regulatory scrutiny of its financial structure, corporate organization, and profit margin.[27] FERC, however, has recognized one notable exception for QFs that buy and sell imbalance power from an independent system operator (ISO).[28] Also, when a QF participates in an ISO competitive market transaction, the QF must comply with the jurisdictional FERC-approved tariff for the relevant ISO.[29]

In order to qualify for the foregoing benefits, the original formulation of PURPA imposed two basic requirements. First, §201 of PURPA mandated that a cogeneration or small power production facility be "owned by a person not primarily engaged in the generation or sale of electric power (other than electric power solely from cogeneration facilities or small power production facilities)."[30] Under rules promulgated by FERC, a facility violated the §201 limitations if "more than 50 percent of the equity interest in the facility [was] held by an electric utility or utilities, or by an electric utility holding company, or companies, or any combination thereof."[31] Ownership interests held by a subsidiary corporation were accounted for in the application of the 50 percent rule.[32] As noted below, this utility ownership restriction has been repealed.

Second, FERC imposed specific facility-related conditions on prospective QFs. To qualify as a QF, a facility had to be either a cogeneration facility or small power production generator. FERC's regulations defined a "cogeneration facility" as "equipment used to produce electric energy and forms of useful thermal energy (such as heat or steam), used for industrial, commercial, heating, or cooling purposes, through the sequential use of energy."[33] If a cogeneration facility's thermal output constituted a common industrial or commercial application, the FERC presumed the application was useful and refused to conduct any further inquiries.[34] The presumption of usefulness was irrebuttable.[35] To qualify as a small power production generator, a facility had to demonstrate that (1) at least 75 percent of its energy input is from biomass, waste, renewable resources, geothermal, or any combination thereof;[36] and (2) its total net power production was not greater than 80 MW[37] or that it was an "eligible solar, wind, waste, or geothermal facility" of any size.[38]

QFs are also discussed in chapter 17.

PURPA After the Energy Policy Act of 2005

Over the years, PURPA proved to be successful at fostering the growth of small, independent power generation. However, many investor-owned utilities had accepted only with great resistance the basic premise of PURPA that they had to purchase the electric output of QFs at avoided cost. They also resented plants they considered as "PURPA mills," that is to say where the thermal energy was put to some desultory use (such as to warm a greenhouse) just so the independent power producer could build a plant and force the utility to buy the power at favorable rates. These issues were hotly debated in the many attempts to arrive at energy legislation in the late 1990s and the early part of this century.[39] When final legislation emerged in the form of the Energy Policy Act of 2005 (EPAct),[40] the investor-owned utilities did succeed in trimming back somewhat the favorable treatment of QFs under PURPA, but did not succeed in eliminating the basic concepts. One thing EPAct did was eliminate PURPA's traditional limits on utility ownership.[41] The investor-owned utilities always resented that they could not own majority stakes in QFs and thus compete with true independents. In addition, pursuant to EPAct mandate, FERC has implemented regulations to ensure that the thermal output of a facility is used in a "productive and beneficial manner" by eliminating the irrebuttable presumption of usefulness. In its place, FERC now applies a rebuttable presumption, with a narrower safe harbor for facilities that can demonstrate that at least 50 percent of their aggregated energy output is used for industrial, commercial, residential, or institutional purposes.[42]

Further, EPAct and FERC's new implementing regulations have narrowed the availability of PURPA's more generous incentives. Most notably, EPAct removes the mandatory purchase requirement when a QF has nondiscriminatory access to competitive wholesale markets for both short- and long-term sales of energy and capacity.[43] As a result, in principle, many electric utilities will be able to avoid the mandatory purchase requirement under PURPA, particularly in regions of the country where FERC has created a rebuttable presumption that QFs have access to competitive short- and long-term markets. In theory, a utility may seek to terminate its QF mandatory purchase obligation in any region, but demonstrating that QFs have access to competitive short- and long-term markets can be a costly and difficult proposition. In practice, not everywhere in the country has competitive wholesale markets, so the old mandatory purchase requirements still apply in those areas. Also, in practice, when utilities need additional capacity, they do enter into PPAs with utility-scale QFs at negotiated rates.

Finally, without any specific statutory mandate, FERC has revised some of the broad regulatory exemptions that QFs had previously enjoyed. For example, FERC has eliminated the FPA exemptions from the rate regulations in §§ 205 and 206 for sales not made pursuant to a state regulatory authority's implementation of PURPA.[44] Under FERC's new rules, only facilities of 20 MW or less remain entirely exempt from §§ 205 and 206.[45]

One other aspect of EPAct is that it replaced the PUHCA of 1935 with the Public Utility Holding Company Act of 2005 (PUCHA of 2005).[46] Although the new version of PUCHA reauthorizes many of the same record-keeping and reporting requirements, PUCHA of 2005 significantly eases the traditional geographic and business pressures on the energy industry by eliminating the requirement that holding companies operate as a single integrated public utility system.[47]

Collectively, these changes are expected to make the PURPA regulatory framework less prominent and relevant in the wholesale energy market.[48] EPAct's more rigid qualification requirements will reduce the number of new cogeneration and CHP facilities that can qualify, and the diminished incentives will discourage some potential alternative power generators from even seeking certification. However, by both eliminating the restrictions on utility ownership and repealing PUCHA of 1935, some argue that QFs may come to play a more significant role in the retail market.[49]

There are two key points to retain, however, for purposes of a discussion of the potential federal regulation of distributed generation. The first is that if a host wishes to install its own on-site generation and makes no attempt to sell the power back to the grid, there is no sale of electricity and the whole transaction is exempt from federal regulation. If an energy services company owns the on-site generation and enters into a power sales agreement with the host, this transaction is also not subject to federal regulation since is not a sale in interstate commerce. If the on-site facility is interconnected to the local distribution grid or to an independent system operator or local or regional wholesale market, potentially the transaction could be subject to federal regulation under the Federal Power Act and FERC rules, but so long as the on-site generation qualifies as a QF and is under 20MW, or is a small power-generating facility, no federal regulation applies (apart from the process of qualifying as a QF). Since most on-site cogeneration systems are not as large as 20MW and almost all renewable systems used for on-site applications can qualify as small power generators, in practice, parties wishing to own or buy power from distributed generation systems are not impeded by federal legislation and regulations from doing so. The contractual relationship between an energy services company owning an on-site facility and the host buying power is not subject to federal rate or other regulation (apart from Clean Air Act permitting requirements, discussed elsewhere in this book).

State Regulation of Cogeneration and CHP Facilities

The particular position of electricity generation within the framework of the federal system is that the states and their public service commissions retain jurisdiction over electric-generating companies within their borders. This role is best observed by the states' authority to regulate the rates and other conditions of service of public utilities.

State legislatures and municipal authorities grant franchises to electric utilities and distribution companies with respect to service territories. Public service commissions grant certificates of public convenience and necessity with respect to new utility infrastructure. They are also empowered to review and approve the tariffs proposed to be charged by electric utilities and exercise numerous other powers to promote the public interest. In most states, however, cogeneration up to a certain size, distributed generation of all sorts, and many types of renewables are exempted from the jurisdiction of the public service commission. As a result, the cumbersome types of state regulation and oversight that apply to larger-scale power generation do not apply to distributed generation, first of all by the laws of the states themselves.

Further, PURPA gives FERC broad authority to exempt cogeneration and small power production facilities from state regulations that govern rates and the financial and organizational structure of energy providers.[50] FERC has aggressively exercised this power to shield QFs from numerous state electric utility regulations.[51] State laws that contradict PURPA provisions or narrow the scope of the federal QF definition are vulnerable to preemption. The Ninth Circuit, for example, has ruled that only FERC may evaluate a facility's QF status or discipline a QF that fails to comply with PURPA requirements.[52]

Many state legislatures have elected to adopt localized versions of PURPA that largely track the federal QF requirements for cogeneration and independent energy producers. In New York, for instance, Article 4 of the state's Public Service Law (PSL) requires that every electric corporation furnish safe and adequate electric service, with just and reasonable charges, and without any undue or unreasonable preferences.[53] However, to avoid conflict with PURPA, New York's Article 4 articulates a definition of "electric corporation" for rate regulation purposes that excludes a producer that generates or distributes electricity solely from cogeneration or alternate energy production facilities.[54] Consistent with federal regulations, "alternate energy production" and cogeneration facilities are exempt from New York's Article 4 rate regulations only if their electric-generating capacity does not exceed 80 MW.[55] Other states, such as New Hampshire, have largely codified the federal rules for QFs, but confined the exemptions to facilities with a generating capacity of 30 MW.[56]

According to the regulatory frameworks adopted in most states, public utility rates do not apply when a cogeneration or small power production facility sells to a host or to users on contiguous properties. For these types of transactions, the main uncertainty relates to the definition of the word "contiguous." In New Jersey, most notably, the exemption for on-site generation facilities not only extends to customers located on adjacent properties, but also reaches customers that "may be otherwise separated by an easement, public thoroughfare, transportation or utility-owned right-of-way."[57] In fact, a customer's property will always be considered "contiguous" in New Jersey if the end-use customer is purchasing thermal energy services produced by an on-site facility for heating or cooling.[58] New Jersey has perhaps the most accommodating state law in this respect. Many states still only exempt from regulation off-site power sales to properties that are in fact physically contiguous to the site where the distributed generator is located.

Interconnection

An issue in every project is interconnection to the local utility distribution grid. Most on-site generation systems are not sized to cover all of the facility's electric load. CHP systems are optimally designed to cover a facility's thermal load. In the case of photovoltaics or on-site wind, it is rarely (if ever) the case that the on-site systems can cover a commercial facility's load, given the output possibilities and the intermittency of the resource. Moreover, on-site systems have to be taken down for maintenance periodically and also can fail unexpectedly. The host will then want to revert to grid power immediately, so as to avoid interruptions.

Types and Methods of Interconnection

If an on-site generator is interconnected, the interconnection can be one of two kinds: either an induction or a synchronous generator. Induction generators cannot work without the grid—they need it to be "excited," as engineers say, to start up and continue firing. Synchronous generators run "in parallel" to the grid and do not need the grid to work (although they still need gas delivery if they are natural gas plants). If an on-site plant has induction generators, the owner may lose one of the main potential benefits of distributed generation—back-up power. Unfortunately, some utilities make it virtually impossible to synchronize a distributed plant, due to grid stability concerns—or they allow synchronization only with the installation of expensive protective relaying (to prevent fault current from going onto the grid), which makes the project uneconomic. This problem is particularly acute in cities that have so-called "network" distribution systems as opposed to "radial" distribution systems, which are common outside of urban areas.

As a result, owners need to be well informed about how grid interconnection of distributed plants is treated by their local utility company and what types of protective relaying schemes utilities have allowed in past interconnections. This will drive the type of equipment used. If synchronization is not a practical option, induction equipment can be outfitted with "black-start" capabilities, that is, a back-up diesel generator for CHP, to ensure start-up in the event grid power is lost, even if this process is not instantaneous. This could be an issue for certain kinds of industrial processes. For solar systems, battery banks need to be installed if the system is going to continue delivering electricity to the host in the event of a grid outage.

Owners also need to know how long the utility approvals for interconnection tend to take, as this will drive the schedule for ordering equipment and projecting a start-up date. Sometimes long delays become an issue in the timing of the project. It is not unheard of for a distributed plant to be built and then have to wait a long time to be tested properly because the utility is still reviewing and commenting on an interconnection application.

Indeed, interconnection problems and delays are the single greatest impediment to the successful installation of distributed generation equipment and are holding back the greater development of the distributed resources. In order to address this obstacle, several states have instituted standard interconnection procedures that local utilities must follow in response to applications from distributed generators. The rules of New York and California are summarized below.

New York

The New York Standardized Interconnection Requirements provide for an expedited approval process for distributed generation (DG) facilities up to 2 MW.[59] A DG facility wishing to interconnect to a New York utility system must first submit a detailed application to the public utility. After an application is accepted, the next steps in the process depend upon the size of the DG facility. For facilities 25 KW or less, the DG facility must then install its system according to the plans set forth in the application. The DG facility must then perform "verification testing" of the system with the utility allowed to witness the testing if it so chooses. Once the testing is complete and is proven successful, the DG facility is allowed to commence parallel operation.

For DG facilities above 25 KW and up to 2 MW, there is a more detailed review period. After an application is accepted, a "Cost Estimate for the Coordinated Electric System Interconnection Review" (CESIR) takes place. During the CESIR, the utility conducts a preliminary review as to the viability of the proposed interconnection mainly focusing on (1) the impact to the utility system associated with the proposed interconnection and (2) the proposed system's compliance with various criteria (further detailed below) by the utility. If the review is favorable, a standardized contract between the DG facility applicant and the utility is executed. The DG facility provides an advance payment for the utility's estimated costs associated with the interconnection, and construction begins. The DG facility applicant is responsible for building the facility according to the design specifications described in its application, and the utility is responsible for the construction and installation of any necessary system modifications and metering requirements. Upon completion of construction, the DG facility is tested. If satisfactory to the utility, the DG facility is then allowed to commence parallel operation. There are, however, various design and operating requirements that must be met before a proposed DG facility will be allowed to interconnect to the utility system.

A DG facility owner must provide appropriate protection and control equipment in the form of an automatic disconnect device that would instantaneously disconnect the generation in the event that the utility system serving the DG facility is de-energized for any reason or due to the fault of the DG facility operator. The specific design of this device depends on the size and characteristics of the individual DG facility.

Both synchronous and induction generation may be interconnected to the utility system. Synchronous generation requires synchronizing facilities that include: (1) automatic or manual synchronizing equipment, (2) sufficient power capability able to withstand normal voltage changes on the utility's system, and (3) a grounding mechanism. Induction generation can also be interconnected and then brought up to synchronous speed if feasible. The same requirements apply to induction generation.

Interconnected DG facilities must provide twenty-four-hour telephone contact allowing the utility to arrange access for any necessary repairs, inspections, or emergencies. They cannot supply power to the utility during any outages of the utility system that serves the point of common coupling. The DG facility's generation may be operated during an outage only with an open tie to the utility. Islanding is not permitted. A DG facility operator is not permitted to energize a de-energized utility circuit for any reason. The utility may also require the DG facility to connect to the utility system through a dedicated transformer to be provided at the expense of the DG facility owner. A disconnect switch is also required for DG facilities larger than 25 KW and must be installed, owned, and maintained by the DG facility owner. All equipment used by the DG facility must also be equipped with the minimum protective function requirements as set forth in the application materials.

California

In California, interconnection is governed by the California Public Utilities Commission (CPUC) Rule 21. As in New York, a detailed application must be submitted to the local utility for approval. The process begins with an initial review. If an applicant's interconnection equipment conforms to Commission-approved performance standards and is certified under Rule 21, the applicant does not plan to export power and the generator capacity is small compared to the facility's consumption, an applicant will most likely qualify for Simplified Interconnection.[60] If a facility does not qualify for Simplified Interconnection, a more detailed supplemental review is conducted to determine whether the facility can be made to qualify for Simplified Interconnection by meeting additional requirements.

Once it has been determined that a DG facility is eligible to interconnect to the utility's system, the applicant must sign a CPUC-approved pro forma interconnection agreement. Collateral agreements may also be necessary to address ownership, responsibility, cost, and installation issues. After the execution of these agreements, the applicant moves forward to install the DG facility and interconnect to the grid in accordance with the agreements. After installation is complete, the DG facility undergoes the final step in the interconnection process, "Commissioning Testing," whereby a well-defined set of tests is performed under the supervision of the utility to locate and correct any mistakes that may be discovered and to assure the DG operator and the utility that the DG facility functions properly. Upon successful completion of the Commissioning Testing phase, final approval is received and the DG facility can operate in parallel to the utility system.

Section D of Rule 21 describes the various technical requirements for interconnection. These include: (1) general interconnection and protection requirements; (2) the need for prevention of interference with the utility system so that the utility can be assured the interconnected DG facility will not interfere with its own power quality or operation (specific details as to voltage, power factor, frequency, and distortion are set forth); and (3) control, protective function, and safety requirements, depending on whether the DG facility is a synchronous, induction, or inverter-based system.

Relationship with the Local Utility— Standby Tariffs and Net Metering

Assuming the interconnection approvals are obtained, once a facility begins to generate a part or all of its own electricity, its relationship with the local utility changes.

While it is possible for a facility to be an "island," with no flow of power to or from the grid, for the reasons explained above, facility owners invariably wish to keep a utility service agreement in place. This changes the type of utility tariff that applies to the owner. In some places, utilities charge exit fees or impose standby tariffs. Owners need to take into account what these might be to ensure the project makes economic sense. An energy services company should be able to analyze this aspect. In some states, owners who install generation technologies using renewable fuels or fuel cells are exempt from exit fees or are required to pay less significant standby charges.

Applicable standby tariffs need to be studied carefully. Most of them are based on the idea that the distributed generator and the utility are agreeing to a type of maximum demand that the facility might need if the on-site generation is unavailable. If this demand is exceeded for some reason, the tariffs include penalties, so-called "rachet" provisions, where some multiple of the demand charge will have to be paid. Further, in some places, the new demand is set at a higher level if this happens, such that the owner has to pay more going forward. In other places, like Con Edison's service territory in New York, the facility owner can agree to pay a somewhat higher standby tariff on a steady-state basis, but will not be subject to the rachet charges. It is in essence a type of insurance policy.

One interesting approach some solar installers are using is to go behind the utility meter. In a large multi-family building, for instance, it is unlikely that solar can supply more than a certain fairly low percentage of the average load—10 to 40 percent. In this case, the inverter can be put on the customer side of the utility meter so that the AC power goes directly to the residents' submeters. No power ever goes back on the grid, so there is no need for a costly and time-consuming interconnection exercise with the utility. From the utility's point of view, all it really notices is that a certain customer is using less electricity, which, depending on how stressed its local distribution grid is, may be fine. In any case, the customer will not have to go into a standby tariff category.

Another important financial aspect of distributed generation is the practice of net metering. When a utility customer's on-site resources generate more electricity than the facility needs, the customer puts electricity back onto the grid and its meter runs in reverse. Many states regulate what the customer can be paid for the electricity it sells to the utility. Net metering is discussed further in chapter 9.

Notes

1. U.S. Energy Info. Admin., Electric Power Annual, Electric Power Industry 2009: Year in Review (statistics for 2009), (Nov. 23, 2010, revised Jan. 4, 2011), *available at* http://www.eia.doe.gov/cneaf/electricity/epa/epa_sum.html (last visited Feb. 26, 2011).

2. Facilities employing cooling towers experience further energy loss through the cooling tower's use of additional operating equipment such as pumps and fans. Estimated losses are between 2 and 4 percent, depending on the temperature and humidity of the surrounding air. U.S. Dep't of Energy, Electricity Reliability Impacts of a Mandatory Cooling Tower Rule for Existing Steam Generation Units 7 (Oct. 2008).

3. The average efficiency of utility generation has remained around 34 percent since the 1960s. U.S. Dep't of Energy, Combined Heat & Power: Effective Energy Solutions for a Sustainable Future 6 (Dec. 2008); *See* U.S. Energy Info. Admin., Table 5.4, Average

Heat Rates by Prime Mover and Energy Source (Nov. 23, 2010, revised Jan. 4, 2011), *available at* http://www.eia.doe.gov/cneaf/electricity/epa/epat5p4.html (last visited Feb. 26, 2011) (to express the average efficiency as a percentage, divide the equivalent BTU content of a kWh of electricity (3,412 BTU) by the heat rate).

4. The United States Department of Energy estimates "line losses" between 6 and 8 percent, and potentially exceeding 10 percent at peak hours. U.S. Dep't of Energy, Combined Heat & Power: Effective Energy Solutions for a Sustainable Future 19 (Dec. 2008).

5. The following is a very brief explanation, with a few notes about efficiencies, as derived from Justin Smith, *Hydrogen: The Fuel of Tomorrow?*, Energy Current (Feb. 7, 2008).

- Phosphoric acid fuel cells (PAFCs), considered the first generation of modern fuel cells with the most examples in use commercially, are typically used for stationary power generation. Efficiency is 37 to 42 percent when generating electricity alone, and up to 85 percent when used in combined heat and power applications.
- Polymer electrolyte membrane (PEM) fuel cells, also known as proton exchange membrane fuel cells, need only hydrogen, oxygen, and water to operate and are usually fed with pure hydrogen supplied from storage tanks.
- Molten carbonate fuel cells (MCFC) operate at high temperatures and are most suitable for utility and industrial applications. MCFC can be up to 60 percent efficient for electric generation alone and up to 85 percent efficient in combined heat and power applications.
- Solid oxide fuel cells (SOFC) are more experimental, operating at even higher temperatures than MCFCs, with similar efficiencies.

6. U.S. Dep't of Energy, Combined Heat and Power: A Vision for the Future 2 (Aug. 2009).

7. Public Utility Holding Company Act (PUHCA) of 1935, ch. 687, § 36, 49 Stat. 838 (repealed 2005).

8. *See* Joseph Tomain & Richard Cudahy, Energy Law 267 (2004).

9. *See, e.g.*, Kevin McIntyre et al., Energy Policy Act of 2005: Summary and Analysis of the Act's Major Provisions (LexisNexis Matthew Bender 2006).

10. Federal Power Act (FPA), 16 U.S.C. §§ 824–825r (2006).

11. *Id.* § 824(b).

12. FPA, 16 U.S.C. §§ 792 et seq. (creating Federal Power Commission), *repealed by* Department of Energy Organization Act, 42 U.S.C. § 7171, 91 Stat. 565 (2006).

13. 16 U.S.C. § 824d(a).

14. *Id.* § 824e(a).

15. *Id.* § 824e(b)–(d).

16. *Id.* § 824a.

17. *Id.* § 824.

18. *Id.* § 824(b)(1).

19. *Id.* § 824(c).

20. *Id.* § 824(e).

21. *Id.* § 824(b)(1).

22. Public Utilities Regulatory Policies Act (PURPA) of 1978, Pub. L. No. 95-617, § 210, 92 Stat. 3144 (1978) (codified as amended in scattered sections of 16 U.S.C).

23. James H. McGrew, Federal Energy Regulatory Commission (Basic Practice Series) 132 (ABA 2003).

24. 16 U.S.C. § 824a-3(a); *see* 18 C.F.R. § 292.303(a)–(c).

25. PURPA, § 210, 92 Stat. 3144 (1978), *amended by* Energy Policy Act (EPAct) of 2005, 16 U.S.C. § 824(m) (2006).

26. 16 U.S.C. § 824a-3(e); *see* 18 C.F.R. § 292.602.

27. *See id.*

28. Imbalance power refers to the discrepancy between actual energy withdrawals and scheduled energy delivery. When a generator produces less than the amount required to meet scheduled demands, the energy producer must "purchase" additional energy from an ISO to make up the balance. *See* Cent. Hudson Gas & Elec. Corp., F.E.R.C. No. ER 97-1523-011, OA

97-470-010, and ER 97 4234-008, 90 F.E.R.C. ¶ 61231, *4 (Mar. 9, 2000). In *Central Hudson*, FERC held that this "purchase" was actually an "ancillary service" provided by the ISO and therefore would not disqualify the energy producer from its QF status.

29. *See id.*

30. 16 U.S.C. §§ 796(17)(c)(ii), 796(18)(b)(ii).

31. 18 C.F.R. § 292.206(b).

32. *Id.* § 292.206(b).

33. 18 C.F.R. § 292.202(c).

34. Michael Hornstein & J.S. Gebhart Stoermer, *The Energy Policy Act of 2005: PURPA Reform, the Amendments and their Implications*, 27 ENERGY L.J. 25, 27 (2006) (citing Panda-Rosemary Ltd. P'ship, 100 F.E.R.C. P 61, 189 at P 10 (2002); Electrodyne Research Corp., 32 F.E.R.C. ¶ 61, 102 (1985)).

35. *Id.* (citing Brazos Elec. Power Coop., 83 F.E.R.C. ¶ 61, 176, at ¶ 61, 727 (1998)).

36. *Id.* § 292.204(b).

37. 16 U.S.C. § 796(17)(a)(ii); 18 C.F.R. § 292.204(a)(1).

38. Hornstein & Gebhart Stoermer, *supra* note 34, at 26 (citing FPA § 3(17)(e), 16 U.S.C. § 796(17)(e) (2006)).

39. On occasion, even FERC acknowledged that the irrebuttable presumption of the usefulness standard allowed some cogeneration facilities to qualify with "sham" uses of their thermal output. *See* Notice of Proposed Rulemaking, Revised Regulations Governing Small Power Production and Cogeneration Facilities, 70 Fed. Reg. 60456 (Oct. 18, 2005).

40. EPAct, Pub. L. No. 109-58, 119 Stat. 594 (2005) (codified as amended in scatter sections of 16 and 42 U.S.C.).

41. *See* 18 C.F.R. 292.205 (2009).

42. *Id.* § 292.205(d)(3).

43. 16 U.S.C. § 824a-3; *see* 18 C.F.R. § 292.309(a). To avoid the mandatory purchase requirement, the wholesale market must be administered independently or by a FERC-approved regional transmission entity pursuant to an open access transmission tariff. *Id.*

44. 18 C.F.R. § 292.601(c)(1).

45. *Id.*

46. PUHCA of 1935, ch. 687, § 36, 49 Stat. 838, *repealed by* EPAct, Pub. L. No. 109-58, § 1264, 119 Stat. 594 (2005).

47. *Id.*

48. *See* Hornstein, *supra* note 34, at 37.

49. *See id.* at 38.

50. 16 U.S.C. § 824a-3(e)(1).

51. 18 C.F.R. § 292.602.

52. *See* Indep. Energy Producers Ass'n, Inc. v. Cal. Pub. Utils. Comm'n, 36 F.3d 848, 854–55 (9th Cir. 1994) (striking down California's scheme of requiring utilities to monitor QF compliance with PURPA requirements).

53. N.Y. PUB. SERV. LAW § 65.

54. *Id.* § 2(13).

55. *Id.* § 2(2-b). The electric-generating capacity of any adjoining regulated facilities at the same project site will be counted toward the 80 MW limit. *Id.*

56. N.H. REV. STAT. ANN. § 362-A:1, 2.

57. N.J. STAT. ANN. § 48-3:51.

58. *Id.*

59. *See* N.Y. STATE PUB. SERV. COMM'N, NEW YORK STATE STANDARDIZED INTERCONNECTION REQUIREMENTS AND APPLICATION PROCESS FOR NEW DISTRIBUTED GENERATORS 2MW OR LESS CONNECTED IN PARALLEL WITH UTILITY DISTRIBUTION SYSTEMS (revised Dec. 16, 2010), *available at* http://www.dps.state.ny.us/distgen.htm.

60. Simplified Interconnection means that the minimum amount of review was necessary because all the thresholds set forth in the initial review process were met; it is defined in Rule 21 as interconnection conforming to the initial review requirements.

Part IV

Renewable Energy Sources

chapter sixteen

Wind

Jeremy Firestone and Jeffrey P. Kehne

Since the early 1990s, wind power in the United States has grown at an annual rate of nearly 30 percent. Steady improvement in wind power technology and the nation's abundance of untapped wind resources suggest strong potential for continued growth.

This chapter provides an overview of U.S. law and policy affecting wind power development, drawing on European experience where comparisons are instructive. The discussion examines some of the near-term drivers of U.S. wind power development, including (1) wind power technology and cost trends, (2) progress in meeting the challenges of transmission and grid integration, (3) the creation of price signals and other financial incentives for power producers that convey accurate information about the comparative social costs of different generating technologies, and (4) developers' effective resolution of leasing and permitting processes by undertaking timely, intensive outreach that involves local communities in the siting process and seeks to address local community concerns.

Wind Energy and Wind Power

The Distribution of Wind Energy

Wind power derives from uneven heating and cooling of the earth's surface and atmosphere. The resulting temperature differences generate air flows that contain vast quantities of energy. Although most of the energy flows occur at high altitudes and over the deep oceans, economically accessible wind resources still represent an enormous source of potential usable power.

A 2005 study analyzed weather station data to assess the global distribution of high-quality wind resources. The study focused on areas where class 3 or better winds (that is, winds with average wind speeds of 15.5 miles per hour or more measured at 265 feet above the surface) blow over land or shallow water. With current wind turbine technology, economically practical power generation generally requires class 3 winds over land or shallow water. The study found that wind energy in areas meeting these criteria was sufficient to generate 72 million megawatts (MW) of electrical power—roughly six times current global demand for electrical power.[1] These high-quality wind resources are distributed unevenly around the globe. They are generally concentrated in coastal areas of land masses in temperate zones. Weather station data highlighted areas with strong wind power potential along the coasts of the North Sea in Northern Europe, at the southern tip of South America, on the island of Tasmania off the coast of Australia, and in several areas of North America—specifically, the Great Lakes and central plains and the northeastern and western coasts.[2]

The abundance of high-quality wind resources in the United States creates the potential for wind power to play a significant role in U.S. electrical generating capacity. A 2010 study by the U.S. Department of Energy's National Renewable Energy Laboratory (NREL) found that overland wind energy resources in the contiguous forty-eight states could generate 37 billion megawatt-hours (MWh) of electrical power per year, or roughly ten times those states' current electrical power usage.[3] An earlier study, published in 2007, found that wind resources off the east coast from North Carolina to Massachusetts are sufficient not only to meet all existing electricity demand in those coastal states, but also to power an electrified light vehicle fleet and to replace fossil fuels used to heat buildings.[4]

Wind power development in the United States has been concentrated in the western and plains states. The top six states in installed wind power capacity, listed in descending order, are Texas, Iowa, California, Oregon, Washington, and Illinois.[5] Wind maps of the United States show an abundance of high-quality wind resources on the plains, where transmission constraints, discussed below, limit development. They also reveal that some of the United States' strongest, steadiest winds are found off the east coast, where the combination of wind resources, a gradually sloping continental shelf, and proximity to power-hungry population centers have created strong interest in offshore wind development.[6] In recent years, renewable energy developers and federal and state policy makers have also begun to focus on the potential for commercial development of winds that blow across the Great Lakes.

Wind Power Technology: Wind Turbines and Wind Farms

A wind turbine designed to produce electrical power (as opposed to purely mechanical power for pumping or milling) superficially resembles an outsized electric fan with very thin blades. However, while a fan uses an electric motor connected to a rotor to move air, converting electrical energy to kinetic energy, a wind turbine uses moving air to spin a rotor connected to a generator that produces electricity, converting kinetic energy to electrical energy.

Wind power technology has progressed rapidly over the past twenty years. In 1990, state-of-the-art wind turbines had design or "nameplate" capacities of about 0.2 MW. Today, nameplate capacities for the wind turbines most commonly installed at utility-scale wind farms range from 1.0 to 3.0 MW.[7] At offshore wind farms, where per-turbine installation and interconnection costs are higher and the size of turbine blades and rotors is not constrained by logistical limits on truck and rail transport, there is a trend toward still larger turbines. The Thornton Bank (Belgium) and Beatrice

(UK) offshore wind farms have installed 5 MW turbines, and developers of other offshore projects have announced plans to follow suit.[8] The Norwegian government stated in 2010 that it would help to fund development of a prototype 10 MW offshore turbine, scheduled for installation in 2011.[9]

Modern utility-scale wind farms, both onshore and offshore, are composed of arrays of wind turbines connected by electrical cables. Typically, medium voltage cables deliver power from turbines to transformer substations that increase the voltage for delivery onto the grid. The spacing of wind turbines within a wind farm is determined by the interplay of competing cost factors. Real estate and cable costs push in the direction of closer spacing. Turbulence effects—the tendency in multi-turbine arrays for upwind turbines to change air flows in ways that degrade the performance of downwind turbines if spacing is inadequate—push in the direction of wider spacing and increasingly sophisticated preconstruction modeling.

As the unit capacity of turbines has increased, so has the scale of wind farms. Total generating capacity at onshore wind farms is typically limited by the area of available parcels of land and the availability of transmission capacity. In the eastern and western regions of the United States, recently commissioned wind farms, typically sited on ridges, have been as large as 229 MW (the Wild Horse project in Kittitas County, Washington), and projects exceeding 100 MW have been fairly common.[10] On the plains, still larger projects have been developed. The Horse Hollow project in Taylor County, Texas, the world's largest wind farm, has an installed capacity of 735.5 MW.[11] An average coal-fired plant, by comparison, has a capacity in the 650–700 MW range.[12]

The trend toward larger wind farms is also evident offshore. The European Wind Energy Association (EWEA) reports that the average capacity of operational wind farms was 72 MW in 2009, up from less than 10 MW in 2000.[13] The average size of offshore wind farms will continue to grow as larger projects currently in the European development pipeline are completed.[14] United States offshore wind developers are also working to develop large-scale projects. First-generation U.S. projects, discussed below, include the Cape Wind project in Nantucket Sound and the NRG Bluewater Wind project off the coast of Delaware, which are expected to provide up to 468 MW and 450 MW of generating capacity, respectively.[15]

The Growth of Wind Power

The past two decades have seen rapid growth in wind-powered electrical generation, globally and in the United States. At the end of 2009, worldwide installed wind energy capacity stood at 159,000 MW. This represented nearly a sixty-four-fold increase from the end of 1992, when the global total was 2,500 MW, for an annual growth rate of just under 28 percent over this seventeen-year period.[16] Total electrical energy generated by wind turbines during 2009 was 340 million MWh, accounting for approximately 2 percent of world electricity demand.[17]

The global expansion of wind power has been broad-based. Eighty countries now have utility-scale wind farms; seventeen have installed capacity in excess of 1,000 MW.

The largest wind power generating sectors are found in the United States and China, which account respectively for 22 percent and 16 percent of global wind power capacity. In 2009, the last year for which data are available, wind farms accounted for more than 63 percent of the new electrical generating capacity that came on line in the United States.[18] The highest levels of wind power penetration (measured as the ratio of electrical energy from wind turbines to total electrical energy) have been achieved in Europe, where wind penetration rates are as high as 20 percent.[19] Among U.S. states, Texas has the most installed capacity, with over 9,000 MW, while Iowa has the highest wind penetration at 9 percent. Higher penetration of European wind as compared to the United States is most likely the result of feed-in tariffs (FITs), under which utilities are required to purchase wind energy at a guaranteed technology-based rate for a set period of time.[20]

The offshore wind sector is small but growing rapidly. In mid-2010, the total capacity of operating offshore wind farms (all but one of which was located in Northern Europe)[21] was about 1,400 MW. This represented roughly 1 percent of total wind power capacity. However, EWEA projects that offshore wind-generating capacity in the EU will increase by nearly two orders of magnitude over the next two decades, reaching 120,000 MW by 2030.[22] More than a quarter of this expansion is projected to occur in the UK, which in 2007 initiated its third round of offshore wind leasing, with a stated goal of adding within the next two decades 25,000 MW of wind-powered generating capacity to the 1,000 MW already in operation and the 7,000 MW under development in UK waters.[23] The United States trails Europe in the development of offshore wind, having yet to complete its first offshore wind project. A number of U.S. projects are moving through the development process, as will be described below.

Prospects for Continued Growth of Wind Power in the United States

In July 2008, the U.S. Department of Energy (DOE) published a report that examined U.S. wind resources and the prospects for future wind power development.[24] The report found that the United States could obtain 20 percent of its electricity from wind by 2030 by developing 300,000 MW of wind power capacity by that date, and that offshore wind could contribute 54,000 MW of this total.[25]

Whether the United States reaches the DOE's 20 percent wind power target by 2030 will depend largely on four factors: continued lowering of capital costs, progress on transmission and grid integration, financial incentives, and public policy support related to leasing and siting. The first three factors are discussed immediately below. Leasing and siting considerations are addressed at greater length subsequently.

The Cost of Wind Power

Wind power finances are dominated by capital costs. A completed wind farm requires regular operation and maintenance, but no expenditure for fuel. In 2008, DOE estimated capital costs at $1.64 million per MW of installed capacity for onshore wind farms and $2.4 million per MW for offshore projects.[26] More recent figures compiled by NREL place installed capacity costs at a capacity-weighted average of $3.5 million per MW for offshore wind projects installed between 2007 and 2009 and $4.3 million per MW for proposed projects, with wide variability among projects.[27] Wind farm capital costs vary from year to year based on exchange rates, interest rates, and conditions in markets for basic commodities such as steel, and specialized equipment such as turbines and transformers. Developments in the turbine market can be especially critical. In recent years, rapid development of wind power worldwide has outpaced the growth of the turbine supply chain, resulting in scarcity and price increases that have interrupted the long-term downward trend in installed costs of U.S. wind farms.[28]

In the long run, the costs of generating electricity from wind turbines should depend less on fluctuations in currency values, interest rates, and the prices of commodities and components than on the rate of technological improvements in key cost and performance drivers such as turbine and blade reliability, weight, and efficiency. Although predictions based on past technological advances are inherently uncertain, two decades of continuous improvements in wind power technology provide some support for projections that the cost of generating a kilowatt-hour of electrical power at a state-of-the-art wind farm will decline over the next decade.[29]

Transmission and Grid Integration

Two attributes of wind energy present significant challenges to developers and grid managers seeking to deliver wind power to consumers. First, high-quality wind resources are often found in remote locations, far from population centers, where most electricity is used. While transmission limitations can restrict the development of any new power source, they are particularly constraining in the case of wind power development. In Texas, for example, the best wind resources are located in the western part of the state. Population centers, however, are concentrated in the east, and the existing transmission system is not configured to deliver the power. In 2009, the American Wind Energy Association (AWEA) stated that "almost 300,000 MW of wind projects, more than enough to meet 20% of our electricity needs, are waiting in line to connect to the grid because there is inadequate transmission capacity to carry the electricity they would produce."[30] Indeed, proximity to load represents a key advantage for offshore wind in the United States, particularly off the eastern seaboard, which can help to offset higher construction and operating costs.

The long time line for development of new transmission adds to the challenges associated with getting wind power to market. Onshore wind farms, sited on private land, can be permitted in as little as twelve to eighteen months. Permitting time lines for transmission projects tend to be significantly longer. Transmission projects often involve multiple companies, government agencies, and permits. Moreover, efforts to site new lines frequently encounter opposition from nearby property owners, who see transmission lines as a threat to health and property or aesthetic values. Local opposition can be particularly vigorous where proposed transmission lines would cross state borders or traverse areas whose residents would derive no benefit as suppliers or consumers of the transmitted power. For these and other reasons discussed in chapter 22, transmission bottlenecks are often difficult to resolve.

The integration of wind power onto the grid is further complicated by the variability of wind energy. Even at the best sites, wind speeds sometimes fall below the minimum needed to operate the turbines. The inherent variability of wind energy means that actual power output from a wind farm, measured in MWh per year, is always lower than the theoretical maximum. The ratio of actual to theoretical output, known as the capacity factor, typically falls in the 20 to 40 percent range for wind farms.[31] In contrast, capacity factors for coal and nuclear plants, designed to operate continuously to meet base demand, are in the 70 to 95 percent range.[32] To achieve values at the upper end of the 20 to 40 percent range for wind farm capacity factors, a project needs strong, steady winds and reliable turbines that are properly matched to site conditions.

Wind power's inherent variability poses technical and economic challenges for grid managers. Although these challenges should not be understated, a number of well-informed analysts have found that the United States could accommodate significant increases in wind power penetration rates.[33] EWEA has stated that "established control methods and system reserves available for dealing with variable demand and supply are more than adequate for dealing with additional variability at wind energy penetration levels up to around 20 per cent, though the exact level depends on the nature of the specific system."[34] An extensive study by GE Energy, prepared under contract to NREL and published in May 2010, found that the grid in the western United States could accommodate 30 percent wind penetration by 2017 if specified changes were made to existing grid management practices.[35]

For a fuller discussion of grid management challenges associated with the integration of wind and solar power, including power variability, intermittency, and storage, see chapter 22.

State and Federal Financial Incentives and Policies

State and federal financial incentives and policies for the development of renewable energy development are discussed at length elsewhere in this book. For present purposes, it is sufficient to highlight a few trends and developments that are particularly important to the outlook for wind power.

In the United States, the most significant policy support for wind power development has been provided by state-level renewable electricity standards (RESs, also known as renewable portfolio standards or RPSs). An RES requires utilities to generate or acquire renewable energy or renewable energy certificates covering a specified percentage of electricity sales. The most significant federal financial support for wind power development has been provided by federal tax credits, such as the production tax credit for renewable energy projects. RESs are discussed in greater detail in chapter 4. Federal tax incentives are discussed in chapter 7.

Wind Farm Siting: Environmental, Social, and Safety Issues

Overview

Wind turbines generate electricity without emitting greenhouse gases or other air pollutants or consuming water. Moreover, a wind turbine, once built and installed, requires almost none of the mining, drilling, refining, and waste disposal that are associated with nonrenewable forms of power generation. (Although operating, maintaining, and decommissioning wind turbines involve some fossil fuel consumption, the level is insubstantial in relation to comparable activities at fossil fuel plants.) Analyses of the environmental effects of wind turbine deployment in the United States have focused primarily on bird and bat mortality. Other issues, such as infringements on scarce and fragile native ecosystems, can also affect siting in some areas. Issues involving marine mammals, particularly when a developer seeks to locate wind turbines in feeding, breeding, or calving grounds, may arise, for example, as wind farm construction moves out to sea. Recognizing that Americans will get their electricity from some source—be it fossil fuels, nuclear fuel, or renewables, that each source has social and environmental costs, and that a kilowatt-hour of wind energy substitutes for a kilowatt-hour of another form of energy, it is useful to place the environmental and social costs of wind power development in context and compare them to the effects of other means of electricity generation.

The principal human disamenities associated with wind power development involve noise and visual aesthetics. Wind turbines generate sound that can disturb sleep, and create shadows that can rotate around a room (an effect known as shadow flicker). They also change landscapes in ways that can disturb local residents' sense of place. These effects in turn may raise concern over property values and, in some areas, tourism. Human effects can be lessened through proper site planning. They are considered in the federal environmental reviews for projects that involve leasing, permitting, or financing, and in state environmental reviews where applicable. In addition, state and local efforts to control these effects are often reflected in setback requirements and height restrictions.

Where wind farm development involves action by a federal agency, that agency is required to perform a review under the National Environmental Policy Act (NEPA).[36] NEPA is discussed in chapter 5.

Lifecycle Greenhouse Gas Emissions

The discussion of environmental effects to this point has focused on wind turbine installation and operation—activities that will be examined in more detail below. However, in a full accounting one must consider life-cycle effects. For wind power, this requires attention to the carbon emissions during the manufacture of wind farm components. The National Research Council (NRC) has identified wind energy as one of the "lowest life cycle emitters" of greenhouse gases among renewable energy technologies, with emissions that range from 2 to 29 g CO_2/kWh.[37] Most of the variation arises from project-to-project differences in capacity factors.

Life-cycle CO_2 emissions, like all other environmental effects, must be considered in relation to alternative actions. For the analysis of a wind farm project, the relevant comparison is to the effects of generating electricity using other alternatives, including coal-, gas-, and oil-fired plants, nuclear reactors, and other renewable technologies such as hydroelectric and solar, as well as to the reduction of the need for electricity through energy conservation.[38]

Avian and Bat Impacts

In this section,[39] we consider the effects of wind turbines on birds and bats, which vary by species and location. Offshore wind development also can be expected to have some adverse effects on marine species, such as whales, dolphins, and turtles, at least during construction. However, given that no offshore wind project has yet been built in the Americas and that the impacts may be different in U.S. Atlantic Ocean coastal waters, which are populated by great whales, than in the North Sea, we are limiting consideration here for the most part to birds and bats.[40]

Wind turbines cause two types of injuries to birds—fatalities from blade collisions and habitat displacement. When looking broadly at the industry, the National Research Council found "no evidence of significant [avian] impacts as a result of wind power production."[41] The NRC estimated bird collisions at between 20,000 and 37,000 in 2003. Separately, the Government Accountability Office (GAO), extrapolating from then-current figures, noted that the United States would need 78,000 wind turbines to obtain 5 percent of its electricity from wind, and that these turbines would cause 200,000 bird fatalities. This is a small fraction of the annual number of avian deaths caused by collisions with existing structures. As Erickson has noted, even if the United States were to install one million wind turbines, wind power would still most likely "cause no more than a few percent of all [avian] collision deaths related to human structures."[42]

Thus, the issue is not so much total wildlife kills as it is population-level impacts based on local wind projects. While night-migrating passerines (also known as perching birds and sometimes as songbirds) are the most frequent fatalities at wind farms, the most controversy over bird kills has arisen at Altamont Pass, part of the Diablo Range in Central California, home to raptors and other birds of prey. The Altamont Pass wind farm, which kills over one thousand raptors annually, is one of the oldest wind farms in the world. Regrettably, it was sited without an adequate understanding of the interactions among birds, terrain, and wind turbines. Raptor mortality may be reduced in the future, however, since repowering at Altamont Pass is expected to substitute in newer, larger turbines with slower moving blades and to expand distances between towers. Altamont Pass provides a cautionary tale that highlights the need to undertake appropriate wildlife analysis as part of the NEPA process.

Data on avian impacts of offshore wind farms are relatively limited. However, initial indications from the first wave of European projects suggest that these impacts are not likely to be biologically significant. Postconstruction studies at the Nysted and Horns Rev wind farms off the coast of Denmark indicate that habitat displacement may be a greater threat to seabirds than collision. Indeed, Danish researchers observed that most avian species have avoided these sites, with only 1 percent of ducks and geese that migrate in the vicinity of the wind farm flying close enough to a wind turbine to be at risk of collision.[43] Even that low figure is conservative, because it assumes that the ducks and geese were flying at the height of the blade sweep, when in fact they tend to fly either below or above the blades, depending on whether it is day or night. Continuing studies of long-term avian impacts are required, however, to improve understanding of factors such as the artificial reef effect associated with wind turbine foundations, which may attract migrating species in search of food.

More recently, large numbers of bats have been killed at wind farms in Appalachia—for example, over two thousand bats carcasses were recovered during sixty-one days of surveying during spring, summer, and fall 2003 at a sixty-four-turbine wind farm in West Virginia.[44] Because bats are long-lived and have low reproductive rates, relatively low increases in mortality can have significant population-level effects. A study published in 2008 suggests that bat deaths at wind farms may result from barotrauma—pressure-related damage to internal organs—more often than from collisions. The trauma occurs as a result of changes in air pressure from the movement of wind turbine blades.[45] Encouragingly, another 2008–2009 study suggests that wind farm operators may be able to achieve sharp reductions in bat fatalities with little loss in power production by raising the cut-in speed (the wind speed at which the wind turbine blades begin to spin) during late summer and early fall nights.[46]

To minimize bird and bat mortality from wind farms, states such as New York and New Jersey have begun to provide guidance to wind power developers on the conduct of wildlife studies in support of proposed wind power projects.[47]

Comparative Wildlife Impacts

Experience indicates that wind farms will have some negative environmental impacts on birds and bats, and that in the case of poorly located wind farms, those impacts may be locally significant. In evaluating the effects of wind farms on local wildlife, it is important to consider comparative impacts—just as we earlier did in reviewing life-cycle carbon emissions of wind farms and other sources of electrical power. The wildlife impacts of generating power from wind farms must be compared to the impacts of other types of electrical power plants. Because we are ultimately concerned with electricity generation, and different means of generation have different capacity factors and availabilities because of scheduled and unscheduled maintenance, the best metric on which to base such a comparison is the impact per MWh of electricity produced.

One study has made a preliminary comparative analysis of avian and bat mortality at fossil fuel, nuclear, and wind energy projects using just such a metric.[48] That study finds avian mortality of 0.279, 0.416, and 5.18 fatalities/GWh respectively at wind, nuclear, and fossil fuel power plants, although it should be noted that, excluding fatalities attributed to climate change effects, fossil fuel avian mortality is 0.20/GWh.[49]

Other technologies generally thought of as "clean," such as hydropower, also pose threats to wildlife. With hydropower, we can make a "fish to avian" comparison. Six related hydropower projects on Michigan's Au Sable river were found to have entrained fish from thirty-seven different species, with an average mortality rate of 24.2 percent. This resulted in 365.5 fish killed/GWh of electricity produced.[50] This figure is conservative because it considered only mortality that resulted from entrainment (neglecting, for example, the effects of reduced recruitment, increased water temperature, decreased dissolved oxygen levels, and reduced food and habitat). Although the ability to extrapolate to all hydropower dams is limited given that this calculation is based on six related dams on one river system, the more than a thousandfold greater wildlife mortalities/GWh in comparison to average avian mortality is instructive.

Even a brief comparative review of the environmental impacts of wind power and alternative generating technologies, including comparative effects on greenhouse gas emissions and wildlife, raises some important public policy questions. For example, should the Council on Environmental Quality (CEQ), which promulgates government-wide NEPA regulations and policies, have required federal agencies to evaluate potential alternatives to the 130 wind-turbine Cape Wind project in Nantucket Sound, Massachusetts, that included not only no action, a smaller wind project in the same location, and wind farms at other offshore locations (e.g., on the far side of Nantucket Island), but also construction and operation of a coal, natural gas, or nuclear power plant?[51] Similarly, in determining how much preconstruction analysis to require for a proposed wind farm—in deciding, for example, whether to require three years of bird or bat surveys for a wind farm Environmental Impact Statement (EIS) or only two—should federal permitting agencies and CEQ (and ultimately the courts) weigh the benefits of hoped-for improvements in preconstruction understanding against the costs of delaying renewable energy production that will yield significant environmental benefits?

Noise, Visual, Aesthetic, and Economic Issues

Noise can be thought of as unwelcome sound. Wind turbines generate sound primarily through the rotation of the blades, which make a "whooshing" sound. To prevent sound disturbance from wind turbines, some communities have setback requirements that specify a uniform distance from residences (e.g., one-half mile) or a range of distances that vary with turbine height. However, distance is only one of several relevant factors. Sound levels at a given distance can vary with the height of the wind turbine, topography, land use in the vicinity, and local atmospheric effects. Sound from multiple turbines is also typically louder than from a single wind turbine and sensitivity to sound varies from person to person. The stress and annoyance that can arise as a result of these influences can lead to controversy even at wind farms that have enjoyed widespread community support. Wind turbine noise is most likely to annoy neighbors at night, when other ambient noises subside and people are trying to sleep. A controversy surrounding the operation of the Fox Islands Wind Project in Vinalhaven, Maine, completed in 2009, provides an illustration.[52] However, much of the discussion more generally of sound associated with wind turbines has concerned allegations of the health effects of infrasound—that is, sound that is inaudible. While there have been a number of reports of such complaints, no study has been subject to scientific peer review, and government health agencies that have reviewed those claims have found no scientific evidence to substantiate or support them.[53] Because wind turbines will be placed many miles from residences at sea and the ocean environment is comparatively noisy, offshore wind development is unlikely to generate sound that would impact humans in their residences.[54]

Another concern of people who live near wind turbines is a phenomenon known as "shadow flicker." Like any object, a wind turbine blade can cast a shadow. A moving, rotating blade, however, creates a flickering, strobe-like effect. Shadow flicker occurs only when the sun is shining and wind speeds fall within the operating range for the relevant turbine (that is, between the cut-in speed below which it will not operate (7 to 8 mph) and the cut-out speed at which it shuts down to avoid damage, approximately 55 mph). In addition, flicker is generally not noticeable at a distance of more than 10 rotor diameters (generally 3,000 feet for utility-scale land-based wind turbines). To be at its most pronounced, the wind has to be blowing directly toward or away from the sun. Shadow flicker tends to be most pronounced in the hours after sunrise and before sunset, when the sun is low in the sky and blades cast longer shadows. It also becomes more manifest as distance from the equator increases, and thus has been more of an issue in northern Europe than in the United States. Employing conservative assumptions such as zero cloud cover and constant operating wind speeds during daylight hours, software programs are used to generate worst-case predictions of shadow flicker on nearby receptors (windows). The National Wind Coordinating Collaborative, an association of representatives from government, the wind industry, utilities, and environmental and consumer organizations, has suggested that an estimate of twenty to thirty hours of shadow flicker per year, generated by such models, is a reasonable threshold of concern in the siting process.[55]

To address annoyances such as noise and shadow flicker as well as turbine lighting and aesthetic and safety concerns such as appearance and safety, many states and communities have enacted laws and ordinances establishing minimum setbacks from homes and streets, maximum heights, and noise restrictions.[56] Local wind project opponents are often described as being motivated by selfishness—of supporting wind power elsewhere while opposing it in their backyards. Research suggests, however, that the NIMBY ("not in my backyard") label incorrectly describes many project opponents, provides little insight into the underlying reasons for opposition, and conflates attitudes toward wind power with attitudes toward wind power projects. Indeed, personal attachment to particular places, including associations with landscapes and seascapes, and expectations that these places and related ecosystems such as tall grass prairies would remain unchanged, appear to be better predictors of opposition to wind power projects than the objective qualities of the affected viewshed.[57] Research also suggests that individuals may regard seascapes differently than they do landscapes. On land, wind farms are perceived as more obtrusive when sited in pristine natural areas (such as unspoiled ridge lines) than when sited in areas that are already developed. At sea, the opposite may be true—place attachment is most strongly felt to semi-enclosed seas (sounds and bays), which are arguably less pristine than the open ocean.[58]

In a study of Delaware residents, including those living near the Atlantic Ocean and near Delaware Bay, researchers found that residents have a preference for wind turbines to be located farther offshore and are willing to pay for the increased distance. The more salient finding however is that disamenity values rapidly descend after six to nine miles from the shore.[59]

In some locations, concerns about the sight and sound of wind turbines are linked to tourism. Studies of tourism effects to date have been limited, but fall into two categories—studies of observed behavior in response to installed wind turbines and studies examining expected behavior in response to a proposed or hypothetical wind project. Studies of actual projects find either no effect or a positive effect on tourism. Studies of proposed and hypothetical projects report more mixed results, with some suggesting an expected increase in tourism, others little to no effect, and others indicating a potential decline in tourism. In a 2007 study of expected behavior, a substantial minority of beachgoers reported that they would avoid beaches with visible offshore turbines, but their reported aversion diminished as the location of the proposed wind turbines moved farther offshore. A larger countervailing effect was also noted.[60] Respondents reported an interest in offshore wind boat tours and an attraction to beaches that they have infrequently or never visited where wind turbines would be visible. Finally, it is important to distinguish the potential for *local* tourism effects from the effect on tourism more generally. If a wind power project decreases tourism in a given locality, tourism would presumably increase in another location. Nevertheless, these broader tourism effects also need to be considered. Indeed, even if overall tourism revenues do not change, those individuals who switch beaches would experience a loss in consumer surplus (by presumably switching to less desired locations).

Finally, there are concerns that sound, shadow flicker, and visual aesthetic impacts will depress property values. In 2009, Hoen and others published a comprehensive study of some 7,500 real estate transactions that occurred within ten miles of twenty-four wind power projects. The study examined the potential for view, area, and nuisance stigmas associated with wind power projects to reduce property values. Using a hedonic pricing model, which essentially treated houses as bundles of utility-generating attributes (such as square feet and number of bathrooms and bedrooms), the researchers controlled for those attributes and focused on measuring the marginal effect of other factors, such as distance from a wind power project. Their research found that neither the view of nor the proximity to the project had a statistically significant impact on sales price.[61]

Aviation and Maritime Safety Concerns

The Federal Aviation Administration (FAA) evaluates wind turbine structures to determine whether they constitute an aeronautical hazard.[62] In reviewing proposed projects, the FAA considers not only risks of aircraft collisions with blades, turbines, or towers, but also the potential for wind farms to degrade radar performance. The FAA has issued a number of Notices of Presumed Hazard, stopping or delaying development work on projects accounting for several thousand MWs of power.[63] The Department of Homeland Security has issued an interim policy calling for federal opposition to the establishment of any wind farm "within radar line of sight" of a Department of Defense (DOD) or Homeland Security radar installation.[64] On several occasions, DOD concerns about possible effects of wind turbines on military radar have stalled construction of wind farms. For example, objections from DOD have delayed the 845 MW Sheperd's Flat Wind Farm in Oregon.[65]

Offshore wind projects also must take into account navigational safety. This requires developers to avoid locating in designated navigational shipping lanes, and also to provide a margin of safety between the wind project and shipping lanes.[66] The required margin of safety can vary based on vessel traffic patterns and the characteristics of the wind project. For the NRG Bluewater project off the coast of Delaware, the U.S. Coast Guard has established an initial buffer of 500 meters.[67]

Wind on and in Federal, State, and Tribal Lands and Waters

Wind Farms on Federal, State, and Tribal Lands

Federally Managed Lands

Section 211 of the Energy Policy Act of 2005 recited "the sense of the Congress" that the Secretary of the Interior should, by 2015, "seek to have approved non-hydropower renewable energy projects located on the public lands with a generation capacity of at least 10,000 megawatts of electricity."[68] The agencies principally responsible for meeting this objective are the Bureau of Land Management (BLM) within the Department of the Interior and the U.S. Forest Service (USFS) within the Department of Agriculture.

In 2005, BLM published a record of decision explaining its adoption of a comprehensive Wind Energy Development Program in eleven western states and its amendment of fifty-two land use plans in light of that new program.[69] Environmental effects of the program were evaluated in an accompanying programmatic EIS. The BLM program excludes highly protected areas, such as Wilderness and Wilderness Study Areas, National Monuments, and Wild and Scenic Rivers, from wind energy site monitoring and testing and development. The program also provides that, to the extent possible, wind energy projects will be developed in a manner that permits other land uses, such as mineral extraction, livestock grazing, and recreational use.

In September 2007, the USFS issued draft directives governing wind development on Forest Service land.[70] The draft directives propose adding a new chapter 70, concerning "Wind Energy Use," to the USFS Special Uses Handbook, and a new chapter 80, "Monitoring at Wind Energy Sites," to the Wildlife Monitoring Handbook, FSH 2609.13. Various USFS units across the nation have received applications for meteorological testing tower (met tower) installation. Pending adoption of final revisions to the handbooks, these applications will be evaluated under existing special uses regulations.

Tribal Lands

A number of federal agencies encourage wind energy development on tribal lands. The Department of the Interior's Division of Energy and Minerals Development (DEMD) has developed the Native American Lands National Wind Resource Atlas.

The Atlas provides wind energy resource maps for seventeen Indian reservations spanning ten states. It also seeks to encourage wind power development on Indian lands by providing economic advice, technical assistance, and engineering support. DOE has instituted the Tribal Energy Program and the Wind Power for Native Americans Program. As of 2007, DOE had awarded funds related to twenty-four potential wind energy projects on Native American lands—projects that for the most part are subject to tribal rather than state regulation. DOE funds have generally been used for feasibility and environmental studies, although some grants have supported the installation of small wind turbines.

In addition to seeking renewable energy self-sufficiency, tribes also have sought to diversify the income they receive from their lands by entering into leases with wind developers. For example, in late 2005, the privately developed and owned 50 MW Kumeyaay project, located on the Campo Indian Reservation, began generating electricity to serve San Diego Gas and Electric customers. The project leases the wind farm site from the tribe and pays rents and royalties, much as if the project had been developed on BLM land.

Offshore Wind

Projects Proposed to Date

Several offshore wind projects have been proposed for sites off the Atlantic and Gulf coasts and in the Great Lakes. The following relatively advanced, large-scale projects are particularly noteworthy:

- *Cape Wind's Nantucket Sound Wind Farm*—up to 468 MW on Horseshoe Shoals in federal waters surrounded by Cape Cod, Martha's Vineyard, and Nantucket Island. In 2001, EMI Energy began efforts to permit and construct the first offshore wind project in U.S. coastal waters. In April 2010, following nearly a decade of administrative battles, the Secretary of the Interior issued a decision that ended a National Historic Preservation Act dispute and approved the Cape Wind lease. Following the lease approval, opponents of the Cape Wind project filed a suit to block the project. (Some highlights of the Cape Wind leasing and permitting effort are summarized at the end of this chapter.)
- *NRG Bluewater Wind's Delaware Wind Farm*—up to 450 MW fourteen miles off Rehoboth Beach, Delaware. In 2007, Bluewater Wind, now a subsidiary of NRG Energy, prevailed in a competition administered by the State of Delaware. (Competing proposals included plans to construct a natural gas and advanced coal plant.) In 2007, the Delaware Public Service Commission approved the first Power Purchase Agreement (PPA) for offshore wind energy in the United States, guaranteeing Bluewater a twenty-five-year stream of revenue in exchange for the energy produced by 200 MW from the wind project.[71] In April 2010, the first round of offshore wind leasing pursuant to federal regulations promulgated under the Energy Policy Act of 2005 was initiated by the issuance of a Request for Interest (RFI) at an offshore wind site with boundaries that encompass

Bluewater's proposed development. The RFI seeks to gauge whether there are entities other than Bluewater that wish to develop in this same area.[72]

- *New Jersey Projects*—approximately 1,000 MW in three projects off the coast of New Jersey: New Jersey is subsidizing the installation of met towers to facilitate the development of three 300–350 MW projects. The New Jersey projects would be roughly seventeen miles off the coast in the general vicinity of Atlantic City. In 2010, New Jersey adopted a 1,100 MW set aside for off-shore wind power in its renewable portfolio standards and provided $100M in tax credits.[73] Fishermen's Energy of New Jersey has announced plans to build a demonstration scale (six-turbine) wind farm, just under three miles off the beach at Atlantic City, New Jersey.

- *Deepwater Wind's Rhode Island Projects*—the State of Rhode Island selected Deepwater in an offshore-wind-only competition held in 2008. In 2009, Deepwater signed a twenty-year PPA with National Grid to deliver power from an initial 30 MW wind farm off the coast of Block Island. Initially, the Rhode Island Public Utility Commission rejected the proposed agreement on the ground that its price (24.4 cents/kWh with a 3.5 percent yearly escalator) was too expensive.[74] Subsequently, the Rhode Island legislature amended state law to require reconsideration of the PPA under different criteria, and the Commission approved the PPA.[75] Appeals of the Commission's decision, filed by an environmental group and two power consumers, are pending.[76]

Leasing and Permitting Offshore Wind Projects in State Waters

The Submerged Lands Act of 1953[77] granted states ownership of submerged lands and waters within three nautical miles of their oceanic coasts. (State ownership extends farther, out to nine nautical miles, off the coasts of Puerto Rico, Texas, and the Gulf Coast of Florida.) On the landward side of the state-federal boundary, the adjacent state exercises control over natural resources, subject to reserved federal authority over navigation, commerce, foreign affairs, and national security. On the seaward side of the state-federal boundary, leasing authority resides with the federal government. States also exercise leasing authority in the Great Lakes, where the boundaries of the adjoining states extend to the international border between the United States and Canada.

An offshore wind developer seeking to site a project in state waters will first need a state lease or permit, such as a Great Lakes Submerged Lands Act[78] permit in Michigan. In addition to state authorization, the developer of an offshore wind project in state waters will also need a permit from the U.S. Army Corps of Engineers (the Corps). Section 10 of the Rivers and Harbors Act of 1899 makes it unlawful "to excavate or fill, or in any manner to alter or modify the course, location, condition, or capacity of, any port, roadstead, haven, harbor, canal, lake, harbor of refuge, or inclosure within the limits of any breakwater, or of the channel of any navigable water," without a permit.[79] Both the extraction of core samples, which is essential to the proper design of met tower and wind turbine foundations, and the installation of the structures themselves are activities for which section 10 permits are required. The Corps also administers section 404 of the Clean Water Act,[80] which requires a permit for dredge and fill activities in state waters. By virtue of these permitting functions, the Corps will need to initiate an Endangered Species Act (ESA)[81] consultation, and will likely serve as lead federal agency for NEPA review of these projects.[82]

Leasing and Permitting Offshore Wind Projects in Federal Waters

On the seaward side of the state-federal boundary, leasing for offshore wind development is administered by the Bureau of Ocean Energy Management, Regulation and Enforcement (BOEMRE, formerly known as the Minerals Management Service or MMS)[83] under § 8(p) of the Outer Continental Shelf Lands Act (OCSLA),[84] as added by § 388 of the Energy Policy Act of 2005. Section 8(p) authorizes the Secretary of the Interior to grant leases, easements, and rights-of-way for alternative energy development on the OCS.

On April 9, 2009, the Department of the Interior and the Federal Energy Regulatory Commission (FERC) entered into a Memorandum of Understanding (MOU) clarifying their jurisdiction and responsibilities for renewable energy projects on the OCS. The agreement resolved a long-standing jurisdictional dispute between BOEMRE and FERC concerning the relationship between BOEMRE's leasing authority under § 8(p) of OCSLA and FERC's authority to license hydrokinetic energy projects under § 23 of the Federal Power Act (FPA).[85] Although FERC does not exercise jurisdiction over offshore wind projects, the dispute over hydrokinetic projects delayed BOEMRE's issuance of a final rule implementing its new authority, which governs not only offshore wind power, but hydrokinetic projects (wave, tidal, and current) as well. BOEMRE published its offshore renewable energy rule in April 2009,[86] nearly three years after the rulemaking deadline established in the Energy Policy Act of 2005.[87]

The rule sets out "baseline" leasing standards and procedures, which define BOEMRE's default approach to OCS leasing for offshore wind development. Under the baseline approach, offshore wind developers will be required to make three types of payments in order to obtain and hold a BOEMRE operating lease: (a) acquisition fee; (b) rental payment; and (c) operating fees/royalties. Developers must also make easement rental payments.[88]

For a handful of offshore wind projects, where developers are working to construct the first generation of U.S. offshore wind farms, the leasing and permitting timeline may be shortened somewhat by a pre-rule program that BOEMRE established to expedite wind testing. To minimize the effect of its rulemaking delay, BOEMRE established an interim mechanism for authorization of met towers, which are used to measure wind speed at hub height and thus facilitate financing and serve as a platform for measuring environmental data such as wave loading and avian populations. In November 2007, BOEMRE announced its plan to authorize alternative energy resource assessment and technology testing on a case-by-case basis pending promulgation of the alternative energy rule, and invited offshore alternative energy developers to propose sites and activities for authorization by interim policy lease.[89] In April 2008, BOEMRE identified sixteen potential locations for interim policy leases, including nine locations specified in applications for leases to install and operate wind testing equipment.[90] BOEMRE has issued four interim policy leases for met towers off the coasts of Delaware and New Jersey.

On June 4, 2009, BOEMRE and FWS signed an MOU to enhance collaboration with the goal of strengthening the conservation of migratory birds and their habitat.[91]

The Obama Administration's Marine Spatial Planning Initiative

Another complication confronting the nascent U.S. offshore wind industry is the Obama administration's campaign to implement a comprehensive system of coastal and marine spatial planning. In June 2009, President Obama issued a memorandum creating an Ocean Policy Task Force and instructing that Task Force to produce a series of reports. In July 2010, the Task Force published its Final Recommendations to the President,[92] which adopted most of the recommendations of the Task Force and directed executive agencies "to implement those recommendations under the guidance of a National Ocean Council."[93]

The intent of the Final Recommendations, as described by CEQ, which led the Task Force, is to move federal agencies away from "the current sector-by-sector approach" to permitting for offshore activities, shaped by statutes that generally focus on "a limited range of management tools and outcomes," and toward "a more integrated, comprehensive, ecosystem-based, flexible, and proactive approach to planning and managing these uses and activities."[94] To achieve these objectives, the Final Recommendations and Executive Order create a series of new governance structures. Key elements include a newly constituted National Ocean Council to oversee the creation of nine regional planning bodies—one for the Great Lakes and eight for various stretches of the U.S. coastline—populated by federal, state, tribal, and local authorities. Each Regional Council will formulate and execute, in succession, a development agreement, a work plan, a draft plan, an environmental review document evaluating the draft plan, and a final plan. Each draft plan will be reviewed by the National Ocean Council for consistency with established national policies and principles and compatibility with plans for adjoining regions. Where existing regulatory or statutory requirements constrain the ability of an agency to fully implement the plan, the agency will be encouraged to consider whether to seek regulatory or legislative changes to provide needed authority.[95]

Public Trust Doctrine

The public trust doctrine also may provide a constraint or a basis for regulating offshore wind power in certain circumstances. The doctrine, which can be traced back to the sixth-century Institutes of Justinian, has deep roots in English common law. "In England, from the time of Lord Hale it has been treated as settled that the title in the soil of the sea, or of arms of the sea, below ordinary high water mark is in the King

. . . [and] is held subject to the public right, *jus publicum*, of navigation and fishing."[96] The U.S. Supreme Court has affirmed that the public trust doctrine applies in the Great Lakes,[97] as well as in non-navigable tidally influenced streams.[98] However, the specific content of the doctrine is determined by the states, which retain the right to limit lands held in trust and define private rights to those lands.

The core of the doctrine was set forth in *Illinois Central Railroad v. Illinois*, where the Supreme Court analogized state responsibilities for administration of this trust to state police powers. The Court recognized state authority to alienate public trust lands where the affected parcels are "used in promoting the interests of the public therein or can be disposed of without any substantial impairment of the public interest in the lands and waters remaining."[99] Thus, the public trust doctrine imposes a clear legal duty on states to protect navigation and perhaps recreation and wildlife values.[100]

As noted by Charles Wilkinson, courts have been reluctant to recognize a federal public trust doctrine, and thus its principal applicability will be on state-controlled bottomlands.[101] In light of the fact that the states did not assume ownership of what are now referred to as state offshore waters (generally a three-mile coastal band but extended to nine miles off Texas, Gulf Coast of Florida, and Puerto Rico, which have wider state waters) until the passage of the Submerged Lands Act of 1953, the public trust doctrine's applicability to these waters varies on a state-by-state basis. It is thus likely to play its most prominent role in regard to the siting of wind turbines in the Great Lakes, although as we shall see later, the doctrine is flexible enough to include impacts on birds and other wildlife. It appears that offshore wind leases will fit neatly within the ambit of the public trust doctrine and indeed will enhance the remaining waters through non-CO_2, pollution-free generation (e.g., no loading of mercury to the Lakes), yet the doctrine may result in greater scrutiny of wildlife impacts of Great Lakes projects and provide an impetus for rents and royalties.[102]

Overview of Litigation and Administrative Proceedings

Takings of Protected Species

State and local governments have been largely responsible for regulating land-based wind facilities because the majority of wind energy development has occurred on nonfederal lands. However, regardless of where an activity takes place (on federal or nonfederal land or in state or federal waters), any "taking" (which includes not only killing, but also harming or harassing) of protected species would only be lawful if the person responsible was in possession of an incidental-take permit.

"Take" is broadly defined as "harass, hunt, capture or kill" or to attempt the same under the Marine Mammal Protection Act (MMPA),[103] and as "harass, harm, pursue, hunt, shoot, wound, kill, trap, capture, or collect, or to attempt to engage in any such conduct" under the ESA.[104] Further, the subsidiary terms of the take definitions are themselves defined broadly. For example, the MMPA defines "harassment" to encompass "any act of pursuit, torment, or annoyance" that has either the "potential to injure" or the potential to disrupt "behavioral patterns, including, but not limited to, migration, breathing, nursing, breeding, feeding, or sheltering. . . ."[105]

The ESA defines "harm" in similarly broad terms to include any act that results in "significant habitat modification or degradation where it actually kills or injures wildlife by significantly impairing essential behavioral patterns, including breeding, feeding or sheltering."[106] These take prohibitions establish important substantive constraints on private actions that may affect protected species, regardless of whether those actions occur on federal property.[107]

The MMPA and ESA do, however, provide exceptions to their otherwise sweeping takings prohibitions, including, most notably, provisions for the issuance of "incidental take permits." Under the MMPA, an applicant may obtain authorization for potential takes within a specified geographical region based on a showing that the proposed undertaking will have negligible impacts.[108] Under the ESA, an applicant must show that the potential taking is "incidental to, and not the purpose of, the carrying out of an otherwise lawful activity."[109]

Under the ESA, the unauthorized taking of a protected species can give rise to civil and criminal penalties. Moreover, the ESA (unlike the MMPA) contains a citizen suit provision that authorizes citizen plaintiffs to seek injunctions to prevent or halt violations. Citizen plaintiffs have used the ESA citizen suit provision to impose important limits on activities affecting protected species, including logging in spotted owl habitat, and water diversions in rivers and streams where protected salmon breed.

The potential for ESA litigation to delay, curtail, or derail wind energy development was illustrated in *Animal Welfare Institute v. Beech Ridge Energy*.[110] In that case, plaintiff alleged that a partially completed wind farm in West Virginia violated the ESA's prohibition against takes of the endangered Indiana bat, even though no take had yet occurred. The court held that the ESA's citizen suit provision protects against "wholly future" violations, despite Congress's use of the present tense to authorize civil actions against a person "who is alleged to be in violation of any provision of this Act. . . ."[111] The court concluded that "requiring that a listed species be harmed, wounded, killed, or harassed before conferring jurisdiction would thwart" a central goal of the ESA.[112]

The court next addressed the question of the probability of a taking that a plaintiff must prove in order to prevail. The court rejected the defendants' argument for an "absolute certainty" standard, noting that it would frustrate Congress's purpose of protecting endangered species before they are injured. Reasoning that plaintiffs must meet a higher burden to establish "harm" than "harassment," and that by regulation "harassment" requires proof of a "likelihood" of injury, the court held that a plaintiff must establish that the "challenged activity is reasonably certain to imminently harm, kill, or wound the listed species."[113]

Based on the record before it, the court concluded that it was a "virtual certainty" that the Beech Ridge wind project would imminently harm, wound, or kill Indiana bats in violation of the ESA.[114] As a result, the court issued an injunction limiting the operation of those wind turbines that were then under construction to the time period when Indiana bats hibernate (November 16 to March 31) and prohibiting the construction of additional turbines until the defendants had obtained an incidental take permit.

On January 26, 2010, the parties entered into a stipulation that requires Beech Ridge to abandon (neither construct nor operate) some thirty-one wind turbines, to prepare a habitat conservation plan and seek an incidental take permit, and curtail operations at forty other wind turbines to protect the Indiana bat pending receipt of the incidental take permit. The stipulation does allow Beech Ridge to install twenty-seven additional wind turbines and operate them under the agreed curtailed schedule.

The Beech Ridge litigation takes on added significance because the current range of the Indiana bat includes approximately twenty states in the midwestern and eastern United States. In February 2010, one month after the district court entered the stipulation that ended the Beech Ridge litigation, Pattern Energy abandoned its attempt to develop a proposed fifty-turbine project in Ohio because of concern over impacts to the Indiana bat.

The conservation status of Indiana bats is not the only wildlife issue posed by wind farm development. The proposed 825 MW Daggert Ridge wind power project in California has been called into question because part of the project would be located within an area designated as Desert Tortoise critical habitat by FWS. An avenue to slow or stop wind power development that is perhaps even more promising for wind power opponents is the public trust doctrine. In *Center for Biological Diversity v. FPL Group, Inc.*,[115] a California appellate court found that all birds and other wildlife are a public trust resource. The court nevertheless dismissed the claim because the plaintiffs had improperly asserted their claims against the owners and operators of the wind turbines at Altamont Pass rather than against the public agency with permitting authority. Although the claim was dismissed on technical grounds, the court's analysis suggests that the public trust doctrine may provide another avenue for plaintiffs who seek to enjoin wind power projects to prevent harm to wildlife.

Federal protection of wildlife under the Migratory Bird Treaty Act of 1918 (MBTA) differs from protections afforded by the ESA and MMPA in important respects. Although the MBTA's definition of "take" is significantly narrower than the ESA's, being limited in the wind turbine context to killing,[116] the statute provides for strict criminal liability. The owner or operator of a structure that causes the death of a migratory bird can, in theory, be convicted of a misdemeanor and imprisoned for up to six months. Moreover, the MBTA lacks an incidental take provision, and FWS has so far not promulgated an incidental take rule that could serve as a safe harbor for wind developers.[117] As a result, the MBTA creates a dilemma for project developers and regulators alike. On one hand, owners and operators of wind farms—like owners and operators of oil wells,[118] cell phone and radio towers, and even office buildings—risk jail time despite any good faith efforts they may take to avoid killing migratory birds while engaging in otherwise lawful activities. On the other hand, regulators have few tools under the MBTA as presently constituted—beyond the threat of criminal prosecution under a statute that, on its face, criminalizes ownership and operation of virtually every tower and office building in the country—to minimize takes of migratory birds.

Given the strict liability nature of the MBTA and federal prosecutors' broad discretion to determine which offenses to prosecute, it is worthwhile considering whether incidental takings of birds at wind farms could plausibly lead to criminal prosecutions under the MBTA (and, if so, under what circumstances). To date, there appears to be no record of an MBTA prosecution arising out of a wind farm collision. Is avian mortality that results from collisions with wind turbines more like mortality from pesticide application (which has resulted in a handful of MBTA prosecutions) or from collisions with automobiles or living room picture windows (which has not)?[119]

The Prolonged Dispute over the Cape Wind Project

The Cape Wind project, announced in 2001, calls for construction of an offshore wind farm on Horseshoe Shoals within Nantucket Sound. The proposed project site extends to within six miles of the towns of Hyannis Port and Osterville. Project opponents have pursued all available means to block it, including administrative challenges and litigation in state and federal court. The history of this project illustrates the obstacles that determined, well-financed opponents can create under existing federal and state leasing and permitting regimes. Some highlights include the following.

- *Met Tower Litigation: NEPA and Rivers and Harbors.* In *Alliance to Protect Nantucket Sound, Inc. v. U.S. Department of the Army*, project opponents challenged the Corps' approval of a met tower that Cape Wind sought to install to obtain an accurate assessment of the wind resource.[120] Opponents argued that the Corps lacked authority under section 10 of the Rivers and Harbors Act to permit the met tower because Cape Wind lacked the property interest allegedly required under Corps rules. The court found that OCSLA (as it existed prior to the 2005 amendment that authorized BOEMRE leasing for alternative energy development) extended the Corps' jurisdiction to all artificial islands and all installations for exploring, developing, or producing resources or other installations of devices. The Alliance also attacked the Corps' refusal to prepare an EIS under NEPA, arguing that the Corps' finding that the met tower would have no significant impact was unlawful because the project was "without precedent."
- *State Permitting Disputes.* The Massachusetts Supreme Court rejected an appeal by the town of Barnstable, the Cape Cod Commission, and the Alliance contesting the state Energy Facilities Siting Board's decision to issue a so-called "super permit" for the project. That permit overrode the Cape Cod Commission's 2008 rejection of Cape Wind's plan on procedural grounds.
- *National Historic Preservation Act Dispute.* In early April 2010, the Advisory Council on Historic Preservation (ACHP) recommended against approval of the project because of its impacts on the Wampanoag tribe and historic properties and districts, including Nantucket Islands (given its association with the whaling industry) and the Kennedy Compound.[121] The ACHP stated that there would be a significant "adverse effect to the Wampanoag tribes' traditional cultural practices" and noted that the "uninterrupted view across Nantucket Sound of the rising eastern sun ... is a defining feature of ... tribal culture and history."[122] It summarized its views, describing Nantucket Sound and the

surrounding land areas as a "rich and unique tapestry of American prehistory, history, and culture" and went so far as to proclaim that the destruction of the seabed through the placing of wind turbine foundation would result in permanent adverse effects even though the project would be decommissioned at some point.[123] Despite these concerns, Secretary Salazar announced that a lease would be issued to Cape Wind. Secretary Salazar did, however, require the array to be painted off-white and to be reconfigured to diminish the visual impact on the Kennedy Compound and on Nantucket Island and required additional archaeological surveys.[124] A coalition of organizations, including the Alliance, announced their intention to file suit.[125]

- *Federal Leasing Litigation: ESA, MBTA, and NEPA claims.* In June 2010, opponents of the Cape Wind project filed suit in federal district court for the District of Columbia to block construction of the project. The complaint asserts that BOEMRE and FWS violated the ESA, MBTA, and NEPA in reaching decisions that allowed the Cape Wind project to proceed.[126]
- *Dispute of Power Purchase Agreement.* In May 2010, National Grid announced that it had entered a fifteen-year PPA with Cape Wind to buy power from at least half of the project for 20.7 cents/kWh beginning in 2013 and increasing by 3.5 percent per year thereafter. Opponents of the project objected to the PPA as being too expensive. On July 30, 2010, the Massachusetts Attorney General announced a tentative agreement with National Grid and Cape Wind, whereby the parties would revise the PPA in several respects, including capping the initial price at 18.7 cents/kWh if the entire project is built and 19.3 cents/kWh if only a portion of the project is built.[127] On November 22, 2010, the Massachusetts Department of Public Utilities (DPU) approved the PPA between Cape Wind and National Grid for 50 percent of the project output, concluding that the project's benefits exceeded its costs, that it would moderate electric peak loads, and that the agreement was in the public interest.[128] The DPU rejected the proposed PPA for the other half of the project because it had not specified a buyer.

Notes

1. Cristina L. Archer & Mark Z. Jacobson, *Evaluation of Global Wind Power*, 110 J. Geophysical Res. D12110 (2005), *available in manuscript form at* http://www.stanford.edu/group/efmh/winds/global_winds.html (last visited Aug. 2, 2010).

2. *Id.*

3. NREL & AWS Truewind, Estimates of Windy Land Area and Wind Energy Potential by State for Areas >= 30% Capacity Factor at 80m (Feb. 4, 2010), *available at* http://www.windpoweringamerica.gov/pdfs/wind_maps/wind_potential_80m_30percent.pdf (last visited Aug. 2, 2010).

4. Willett Kempton, Cristina L. Archer, Amardeep Dhanju, Richard W. Garvine & Mark Z. Jacobson, *Large CO2 Reductions Via Offshore Wind Power Matched to Inherent Storage in Energy End-Uses,* 34 Geophysical Res. Letters L02847 (2007), *available at* http://www.windri.org/conference/Session_1_Vision_Future_of_Wind_Power/Kempton_Article_Mab_Resource_2007.pdf (last visited Aug. 2, 2010).

5. Am. Wind Energy Ass'n, U.S. Wind Energy Projects (through Sept. 30, 2010), *available at* http://archive.awea.org/projects/ (last visited Mar. 11, 2011).

6. Marc Schwartz, Donna Heimiller, Steve Haymes & Walt Musial, NREL, Assessment of Offshore Wind Energy Resources for the United States, Technical Report NREL/TP-500-45889 (June 2010), *available at* http://www.nrel.gov/docs/fy10osti/45889.pdf (last visited Aug. 2010).

7. AWEA, Size Specifications of Common Industrial Wind Turbines (undated), *available at* http://www.aweo.org/windmodels.html (last visited Aug. 2, 2010).

8. European Wind Energy Ass'n, Wind in Power: 2009 European Statistics (Feb. 2010), *available at* http://www.ewea.org/fileadmin/emag/statistics/2009generalstats/#/0/ (2009).

9. Rolleiv Solholm, *Grants for New Wind Turbine Project*, Norway Post, Feb. 13, 2010 (describing joint venture between Norwegian agency Enova and manufacturing firm Sway), *available at* http://www.norwaypost.no/genbus/grants-for-new-wind-turbine-project.html (last visited Aug. 2, 2010).

10. Am. Wind Energy Ass'n, U.S. Wind Energy Projects (through Dec. 31, 2009), *available at* http://archive.awea.org/projects/ (last visited Aug. 2, 2010).

11. Am. Wind Energy Ass'n, U.S. Wind Energy Projects (through Dec. 31, 2009), *available at* http://www.awea.org/projects/Projects.aspx?s=Texas (last visited Aug. 2, 2010). In 2008, T. Boone Pickens announced plans to build a 4,000 MW wind farm in four Texas counties, but those plans were later scaled back in response to tightening credit and falling natural gas prices. *T. Boone Pickens Suspends Mega-Wind Farm in Texas*, Power, July 8, 2009, *available at* http://www.powermag.com/POWERnews/T-Boone-Pickens-Suspends-Mega-Wind-Farm-in-Texas_2037.html (last visited Aug. 2, 2010).

12. U.S. Dep't of Energy, Energy Info. Admin., Form EIA-860 Data Base, Annual Electric Generator Report (Mar. 2010), *available at* http://www.eia.doe.gov/cneaf/electricity/page/eia860.html (last visited Aug. 2, 2010). Because coal-fired plants typically operate closer to their rated capacities, they generally produce more power per MW of nameplate capacity than wind farms.

13. European Wind Energy Ass'n, The European Offshore Wind Industry: Key Trends and Statistics 2009, at 9 (Jan. 2010), *available at* http://www.ewea.org/fileadmin/emag/statistics/2009offshore/pdf/offshore%20stats%2020092.pdf (last visited Aug. 2, 2010).

14. European projects currently under construction are as large as 500 MW (the Greater Gabbard project in the UK). Projects currently in development with planned completion dates in 2015 or earlier are as large as 1,150 MW (the Tromp project in the Netherlands). European Wind Energy Ass'n, Offshore Statistics 2008, *available at* http://www.ewea.org/fileadmin/ewea_documents/documents/publications/statistics/Offshore_Statistics_2008.pdf (last visited Aug. 2, 2010). *See also* European Offshore Wind Industry: Key Trends and Statistics 2009, supra note 13.

15. For the developers' descriptions of these projects, see Cape Wind's FAQ page, *available at* http://www.capewind.org/FAQ-Category4-Cape+Wind+Basics-Parent0-myfaq-yes.htm (last visited Aug. 2, 2010), and Bluewater Wind's Delaware Project Facts, *available at* http://www.bluewaterwind.com/facts.htm?cat=delaware (last visited Aug. 2, 2010).

16. The 2009 figure is from World Wind Energy Ass'n, World Wind Energy Report 2009 (Feb. 2010), *available at* http://www.wwindea.org/home/images/stories/worldwindenergyreport2009_s.pdf (last visited Aug. 2, 2010). The 1992 figure is from European Wind Energy Ass'n, Wind Energy: The Facts, Executive Summary (2009), *available at* http://www.ewea.org/fileadmin/ewea_documents/documents/publications/WETF/1565_ExSum_ENG.pdf (last visited Aug. 2, 2010). *See also* http://www.gwec.net/fileadmin/documents/Publications/Global%20Wind%202008%20Report.pdf (last visited Aug. 2, 2010).

17. *Id.*

18. *See* U.S. Dep't of Energy, Energy Info. Admin., Electric Power Annual 2009 (Apr. 2011), *available at* http://www.eia.doe.gov/cneaf/electricity/epa/epa_sum.html (last visited Apr. 7, 2011).

19. During 2009, wind power produced 20 percent of the electricity generated in Denmark, 15 percent in Portugal, 14 percent in Spain, and 9 percent in Germany. World Wind Energy Report 2009, *supra* note 16, at 9.

20. For a discussion of FIT design, see TOBY D. COUTURE, KARLYNN CORY, CLAIRE KREYCIK & EMILY WILLIAMS, A POLICYMAKERS GUIDE TO FEED-IN TARIFF DESIGN, TECHNICAL REPORT NREL/TP-6A2-44849 (July 2010), *available at* http://www.nrel.gov/docs/fy10osti/44849.pdf.

21. The only operating offshore wind farm outside Europe is the 102 MW Shanghai Dong-hai Bridge project in eastern China, which reportedly began generating power from its first three turbines earlier this year. INSTALLATION COMPLETE FOR FIRST OFFSHORE WIND FARM OUTSIDE EUROPE, ALTERNATIVE ENERGY (Mar. 4, 2010), *available at* http://www.instalbiz .com/news/3-full-news-installation-complete-for-first-offshore-wind-farm-outside-europe_444 .html (last visited Aug. 2, 2010).

22. EUROPEAN WIND ENERGY ASS'N, SEAS OF CHANGE: OFFSHORE WIND ENERGY 1 (Feb. 2009), *available at* http://www.ewea.org/fileadmin/ewea_documents/documents/publications/ factsheets/EWEA_FS_Offshore.pdf (last visited Aug. 2, 2010).

23. Nao Nakanishi, *UK Expects $160 Billion Offshore Wind Investment*, REUTERS, Oct. 7, 2009, *available at* http://www.reuters.com/article/idUSTRE5961V820091007 (last visited Aug. 2, 2010).

24. U.S. DEP'T OF ENERGY, 20% WIND ENERGY BY 2030: INCREASING WIND ENERGY'S CON-TRIBUTION TO U.S. ELECTRICITY SUPPLY (July 2008), *available at* http://www.20percentwind .org (last visited Aug. 2, 2010).

25. *Id.* at 9–10, 107. Other studies of U.S. offshore wind resources indicate that offshore wind could exceed this contribution. The National Renewable Energy Laboratory has esti-mated that offshore wind resources located five to fifty nautical miles off the U.S. coast could provide up to 1 million MW of wind energy. WALT MUSIAL, SANDY BUTTERFIELD & BONNIE RAM, NAT'L RENEWABLE ENERGY LAB., ENERGY FROM OFFSHORE WIND 1–2 (2006) (Confer-ence Paper NREL/CP-500-39450), *available at* http://www.nrel.gov/wind/pdfs/39450.pdf (last visited Aug. 2, 2010).

26. 20% WIND ENERGY BY 2030, *supra* note 24. These figures are in 2006 U.S. dollars.

27. WALT MUSIAL & BONNIE RAM, NAT'L RENEWABLE ENERGY LAB., LARGE-SCALE OFF-SHORE WIND POWER IN THE UNITED STATES, EXECUTIVE SUMMARY, NREL/TP-500-40745 (Sept. 2010), *available at* http://www.nrel.gov/docs/fy10osti/49229.pdf. These figures are in 2008 U.S. dollars. *See also* U.S. OFFSHORE WIND COLLABORATIVE, U.S OFFSHORE WIND ENERGY: A PATH FORWARD 28 (Oct. 2009), *available at* http://www.usowc.org/pdfs/PathForwardfinal.pdf (last visited Aug. 2, 2010) (citing higher estimates—$2.4 million per MW for land-based instal-lations and $4.6 million per MW offshore—from David Milborrow & Lynn Harrison, *Wind Rock Solid as Uncertainty Reigns*, WINDPOWER MONTHLY (Jan. 2009)).

28. RYAN WEISER & MARK BOLLINGER, U.S. DEP'T OF ENERGY, OFFICE OF ENERGY EFFI-CIENCY & RENEWABLE ENERGY, 2008 WIND TECHNOLOGIES MARKET REPORT 33–36 (July 2009), *available at* http://www1.eere.energy.gov/windandhydro/pdfs/46026.pdf (last visited Aug. 2, 2010) (steady declines in installed project for U.S. wind farms, from a weighted average of $3,500/kilowatt in 1985 to less than $1,500 in 2004, interrupted by turbine price increases).

29. In 2008, the European Commission estimated then current and projected costs of pro-ducing electrical power from utility-scale wind farms. For onshore wind farms, the costs of generating power using state-of-the-art (2007) technology were estimated at $93 to $137 per MWh. For offshore wind farms, the corresponding estimate was somewhat higher—$106 to $174 per MWh. Based on past technological improvements and innovations under develop-ment, the Commission projected significant cost decreases. By 2030, costs were projected to decline to $62 to $106 per MWh at onshore sites and $62 to $118 per MWh at offshore sites. COMM'N OF THE EUR. CMTYS., SECOND STRATEGIC ENERGY REVIEW, AN EU ENERGY SECURITY AND SOLIDARITY ACTION PLAN: ENERGY SOURCES, PRODUCTION COSTS AND PERFORMANCE OF TECHNOLOGIES FOR POWER GENERATION, HEATING AND TRANSPORT (COMMISSION STAFF WORKING DOCUMENT), at 4, Table 2.1 (Nov. 13, 2008), *available at* http://eur-lex.europa.eu/ LexUriServ/LexUriServ.do?uri=SEC:2008:2872:FIN:EN:PDF (last visited Aug. 2, 2010) (cost estimates presented here are in 2005 dollars, converted from Commission figures presented in 2005 euros, at an exchange rate of 1.245 dollars per euro).

30. AM. WIND ENERGY ASS'N & SOLAR ENERGY INDUS. ASS'N, GREEN POWER SUPERHIGH-WAYS: BUILDING A PATH TO AMERICA'S CLEAN ENERGY FUTURE 1 (Feb. 2009), *available at* http://www.awea.org/documents/GreenPowerSuperhighways.pdf (last visited Feb. 27, 2011).

31. Renewable Energy Res. Lab., Univ. of Mass. at Amherst, Wind Power: Capacity Factor, Intermittency, and What Happens When the Wind Doesn't Blow? (undated), *available at* http://www.ceere.org/rerl/about_wind/RERL_Fact_Sheet_2a_Capacity_Factor.pdf (last visited Aug. 2, 2010).

32. The DOE's Energy Information Administration reported average capacity factors in 2007 of 73.6 percent for coal plants and 91.8 percent for nuclear plants. U.S. Dep't of Energy, Energy Info. Admin., Average Capacity Factors by Energy Source (Nov. 23, 2010, revised Jan. 4, 2011), *available at* http://www.eia.doe.gov/cneaf/electricity/epa/epata6 .html (last visited Feb. 27, 2011).

33. Michael Milligan & Brendan Kirby, Nat'l Renewable Energy Lab., and Robert Gramlich & Michael Goggin, Am. Wind Energy Ass'n, Impact of Electric Industry Structure on High Wind Penetration Potential 7 (July 2009), *available at* http://www .nrel.gov/wind/pdfs/46273.pdf (last visited Aug. 2, 2010) ("Economically dealing with wind's variability and predictability requires a large, flexible power system. Physical size is important because the correlation between production from multiple wind plants diminishes as those plants are geographically farther apart."). A 2007 study, published in the Journal of Applied Meteorology and Climatology, found that connecting multiple wind farms can substantially increase the reliability of wind power at a system-wide level. A 2010 study in the Proceedings of the National Academy of Sciences found significant benefits in terms of wind leveling from an offshore transmission trunk line in the Atlantic. Willett Kempton, Felipe M. Pimenta, Dana E. Veron, & Brian A. Colle, *Electric Power from Offshore Wind via Synoptic-Scale Interconnection*, PNAS, (Apr. 2010), *available at* www.pnas.org/cgi/doi/10.1073/pnas.0909075107 (last visited Aug. 2, 2010).

34. Eur. Wind Energy Ass'n, Wind Energy, the Facts, Part II: Grid Integration (undated), *available at* http://www.wind-energy-the-facts.org/en/executive-summary/part-iigrid -integration.html (last visited Dec. 1, 2010). Denmark currently relies on wind for 20 percent of its electrical power and plans to increase wind penetration to 32.5 percent by 2012. Danish Wind Indus. Ass'n, Denmark—Wind Power Hub 7 (2008), *available at* http://www .windpower.org/download/378/profilbrochure_2008.pdf (last visited Aug. 2, 2010).

35. GE Energy, Nat'l Renewable Energy Lab., Western Wind and Solar Integration Study at ES-1 (May 2010), *available at* http://www.nrel.gov/wind/systemsintegration/ pdfs/2010/wwsis_final_report.pdf.

36. 42 U.S.C. §§ 4321 et seq. Many states have their own state EPAs for evaluating the environmental impacts of projects when federal action (permitting, licensing, and funding) are not involved. *See, e.g.*, California Environmental Quality Act (CEQA), Cal. Pub. Res. Code §§ 21000–21177; *see* http://opr.ca.gov/index.php?a=ceqa/index.html (last visited Aug. 2, 2010).

37. Nat'l Research Council, Nat'l Acad. of Sciences, Electricity from Renewable Resources: Status, Prospects, and Impediments 138 (2009), *available at* http://www .nap.edu/openbook.php?record_id=12619&page=1(last visited Aug. 2, 2010); *see also* Eur. Comm'n Cmty. Research, External Costs: Research Results of Socio-Environmental Damages Due to Electricity and Transport, EUR 20198 (2003), *available at* http://www .externe.info/externpr.pdf (last visited Aug. 2, 2010).

38. Nat'l Research Council, Nat'l Acad. of Sciences, Hidden Costs of Energy: Unpriced Consequences of Energy Production and Use (2009); *see also* Bureau of Land Management (BLM), Programmatic Wind Energy EIS § 6.4.2 (2005), *available at* http://windeis.anl.gov/documents/fpeis/maintext/Vol1/Vol1Ch6.pdf (last visited Aug. 2, 2010); U.S. Dep't of the Interior, Minerals Mgmt. Serv., Cape Wind Energy Project, Final Environmental Impact Statement 3–37 (Jan. 2009), *available at* http://www.mms .gov/offshore/AlternativeEnergy/PDFs/FEIS/Cape%20Wind%20Energy%20Project%20FEIS .pdf (last visited Aug. 2, 2010) (defining the no action alternative as building a comparably sized fossil fuel plant).

39. This section is drawn from Meredith Blaydes Lilley & Jeremy Firestone, *Wind Power, Wildlife, and the Migratory Bird Treaty Act: A Way Forward*, 38(4) Envtl. L. 1167 (2008).

40. Steven Degraer & Robin Brabant, eds., Offshore Wind Farms in the Belgian Part of the North Sea, Royal Belgian Institute for Natural Sciences (2009); Danish Energy Auth., Danish Offshore Wind—Key Environmental Issues (2006), *available at*

http://193.88.185.141/Graphics/Publikationer/Havvindmoeller/index.htm (last visited Aug. 2, 2010).

41. NAT'L RESEARCH COUNCIL, NAT'L ACAD. OF SCIENCES, ENVIRONMENTAL IMPACTS OF WIND-ENERGY PROJECTS (2007), *available at* http://www.nap.edu/catalog.php?record_id=11935 (last visited Aug. 3, 2010).

42. WALLACE P. ERICKSON ET AL., NAT'L WIND COORDINATING COMM., AVIAN COLLISIONS WITH WIND TURBINES: A SUMMARY OF EXISTING STUDIES AND COMPARISONS TO OTHER SOURCES OF AVIAN COLLISION MORTALITY IN THE UNITED STATES (2001), *available at* http://www.west-inc.com/reports/avian_collisions.pdf (last visited Aug. 3, 2010).

43. Mark Desholm & Johnny Kahlert, *Avian Collision Risk at an Offshore Wind Farm*, 1 BIOLOGY LETTERS 296, 297 (2005).

44. JESSICA KERNS & PAUL KERLINGER, A STUDY OF BIRD AND BAT COLLISION FATALITIES AT THE MOUNTAINEER WIND ENERGY CENTER, TUCKER COUNTY, WEST VIRGINIA: ANNUAL REPORT FOR 2003 (Feb. 14, 2004), *available at* http://www.wvhighlands.org/Birds/Mountain eerFinalAvianRpt-%203-15-04PKJK.pdf (last visited Aug. 3, 2010).

45. Erin F. Baerwald, Genevieve H. D'Amours, Brandon J. Klug & Robert M.R. Barclay, *Barotrauma Is a Significant Cause of Bat Fatalities at Wind Turbines*, 18 CURRENT BIOLOGY 695, 695 (2008).

46. Edward B. Arnett, Manuela M.P. Huso, Michael R. Schirmacher & John P. Hayes, *Altering Turbine Speed Reduces Bat Mortality at Wind-Energy Facilities*, FRONTIERS IN ECOLOGY & THE ENVIRONMENT (2010). Relatively small changes to wind turbine cut-in speeds resulted in reductions in bat mortality of 44 percent to 93 percent, with annual power losses of less than 1 percent.

47. *See e.g.*, N.J. DEP'T OF ENVTL. PROTECTION, TECHNICAL MANUAL FOR EVALUATING WILDLIFE IMPACTS OF TURBINES REQUIRING COASTAL PERMITS (Sept. 8, 2009), *available at* http://www.nj.gov/dep/landuse/forms/wind_manual090908f.pdf (last visited Aug. 2, 2010); and N.Y. STATE DEP'T OF ENVTL. CONSERVATION, GUIDELINES FOR CONDUCTING BIRD AND BAT STUDIES AT COMMERCIAL WIND ENERGY PROJECTS (Aug. 2009), *available at* http://www .dec.ny.gov/docs/wildlife_pdf/finwindguide.pdf (last visited Aug. 2, 2010).

48. Benjamin K. Sovacool, *Contextualizing Avian Mortality: A Preliminary Appraisal of Bird and Bat Fatalities from Wind, Fossil-Fuel, and Nuclear Electricity*, 37 ENERGY POL'Y 2241 (2009).

49. *Id.* at 2244–46.

50. Lilley & Firestone, *supra* note 39, at 1203.

51. In a non-NEPA context, Delaware recently required its regulated utilities to incorporate the environmental benefits and externalities associated with methods of electricity production on a life-cycle basis into their long-term integrated resources plans. DEL. CODE tit. 26, ch. 3010, §6.1.4.

52. Fox Islands Electric Coop, *Update on the Fox Islands Wind Project*, July 7, 2010, *available at* http://www.foxislandswind.com/pdf/July2010FIECWindPowerUpdate.pdf (last visited Aug. 3, 2010).

53. AUSTL. NAT'L HEALTH & MED. COUNCIL, WIND TURBINES AND HEALTH: A RAPID REVIEW OF THE EVIDENCE (July 2010), *available at* http://www.nhmrc.gov.au/_files_nhmrc/ file/publications/synopses/evidence_review__wind_turbines_and_health.pdf (last visited Aug. 3, 2010); ONTARIO CHIEF MED. OFFICER OF HEALTH, THE POTENTIAL HEALTH IMPACTS OF WIND TURBINES (May 2010), *available at* http://www.health.gov.on.ca/en/public/publications/ ministry_reports/wind_turbine/wind_turbine.pdf (last visited Aug. 3, 2010).

54. *See generally* MINN. DEP'T OF HEALTH, PUBLIC HEALTH IMPACTS OF WIND TURBINES (May 22, 2009), *available at* http://energyfacilities.puc.state.mn.us/documents/Public%20 Health%20Impacts%20of%20Wind%20Turbines,%205.22.09%20Revised.pdf (last visited Aug. 2, 2010).

55. Technical Considerations for Siting Wind Developments: NWCC Research Meeting, Dec. 1–2, 2005, Washington, DC (March 2006), *available at* http://www.nationalwind.org/ assets/blog/FINAL_Proceedings.pdf (last visited Aug. 3, 2010).

56. A good compilation of these is found in Nat'l Renewable Energy Lab., An Overview of Existing Wind Energy Ordinances, Technical Report NREL/TP-500-44439 (Dec. 2008), *available at* http://www.nrel.gov/docs/fy09osti/44439.pdf (last visited Aug. 2, 2010).

57. Willett Kempton, Jeremy Firestone, Jonathan Lilley, Tracey Rouleau & Phillip Whitaker, *The Offshore Wind Power Debate: Views from Cape Cod*, 33(2) Coastal Mgmt. 121 (2005); Martin J. Pasqualetti, *Living with Wind Power in a Hostile Landscape, in* Wind Power in View: Energy Landscapes in a Crowded World 153–72 (Martin Pasqualetti, Paul Gipe & Robert Righter eds., 2002).

58. Jeremy Firestone, Willett Kempton & Andrew Krueger, *Public Acceptance of Offshore Wind Power Projects in the United States*, 12(2) Wind Energy 183 (2009); *see* www.ceoe.udel.edu/windpower (last visited Aug. 2, 2010).

59. Jeremy Firestone, Willett Kempton & Andrew Krueger, Delaware Opinion on Offshore Wind Power, Final Report (Jan. 2008) (prepared pursuant to a grant from the Delaware Energy Office); *see* http://www.ceoe.udel.edu/windpower (last visited Aug. 2, 2010).

60. Meredith Blaydes Lilley, Jeremy Firestone & Willett Kempton, *The Effect of Wind Power Installations on Coastal Tourism*, 3(1) Energies 1 (2010), *available at* http://www.mdpi.com/1996-1073/3/1/1/.

61. Ben Hoen, Ryan Wiser, Peter Cappers, Mark Thayer & Gautam Sethi, Nat'l Renewable Energy Lab., The Impact of Wind Power Projects, on Residential Property Values in the United States: A Multi-Site Hedonic Analysis (Dec. 2009), *available at* http://eetd.lbl.gov/ea/EMS/reports/lbnl-2829e.pdf (last visited Aug. 2, 2010).

62. *See* 49 U.S.C. § 44,718; 14 C.F.R. pt. 77 (standards and notification requirements for objects affecting navigable airspace).

63. The FAA has no power to prohibit construction activities. Instead, it evaluates proposed structures and works with local zoning authorities and project developers to eliminate or mitigate hazards. The adverse effect of an FAA hazard determination on the availability and price of insurance provides an incentive for project developers to cooperate with the FAA in addressing potential hazards.

64. DOD/DHS Joint Program Office, Interim Policy on Proposed Wind Farm Locations (Mar. 1, 2006), *available at* http://www1.eere.energy.gov/windandhydro/federalwindsiting/pdfs/windmill_policy_letter_032106.pdf (last visited Aug. 2, 2010). A "radar line of sight" is similar to a visual line of sight. However, radar propagates through the atmosphere differently from visual light, and a radar installation can therefore "see" objects that the horizon would hide from a visual observer. For an explanation, see U.S. Dep't of Defense, Office of the Dir. of Defense Research & Eng'g, The Effect of Windmill Farms on Military Readiness: Report to the Congressional Defense Committees 12–13 (2006), *available at* http://www1.eere.energy.gov/windandhydro/federalwindsiting/pdfs/dod_windfarms.pdf (last visited Aug. 2, 2010). For a broader description of the effects of wind farms on radar and the range of technical fixes, see Michael Brenner et al., The Mitre Corp., Wind Farms and Radar (Jan. 2008) (report for Department of Homeland Security), *available at* http://fas.org/irp/agency/dod/jason/wind.pdf (last visited Aug. 2, 2010).

65. Juliet Eilperin, *Pentagon Objections Hold Up Oregon Wind Farm*, Wash. Post, Apr. 15, 2010, *available at* http://www.washingtonpost.com/wp-dyn/content/article/2010/04/15/AR2010041503120.html (last visited Aug. 2, 2010).

66. 33 C.F.R. pts. 62, 64, 66; *see also* U.S. Coast Guard, Navigation and Vessel Inspection Circular No. 02-07, at 5 (Mar. 9, 2007), *available at* http://www.uscg.mil/hq/cg5/nvic/pdf/2007/NVIC02-07.pdf (last visited Aug. 2, 2010) (Coast Guard, as cooperating agency in NEPA review of leases for offshore renewable energy installations, will seek to ensure that review documents address reasonably foreseeable navigational issues involving the "siting, construction, establishment, operations, maintenance, and or decommissioning" of such an installation).

67. 75 Fed. Reg. 21,653, 21,656 (Apr. 26, 2010).

68. Energy Policy Act of 2005, Pub. L. No. 109-58 § 211, 119 Stat. 660 (2005).

69. 33 U.S.C. § 403.

70. Proposed Directive: Wind Energy, 72 Fed. Reg. 54,233 (Sept. 24, 2007).

71. Order No. 7440, Delaware PSC Docket No. 06-241, *available at* http://depsc.delaware
.gov/orders/7440.pdf (last visited Feb. 28, 2011).

72. 75 Fed. Reg. 21,653–21,657 (Apr. 26, 2010).

73. Offshore Wind Economic Development Act, S. 2036 (second reprint, with amendments)
(June 2010), *available at* http://www.njleg.state.nj.us/2010/Bills/S2500/2036_R2.PDF (last visited Aug. 2, 2010).

74. Docket No. 4111, National Grid—Review of Proposed Town of New Shoreham Project
Pursuant to R.I.G.L. § 39-26.1-7 (filed Oct. 15, 2009), *available at* http://www.ripuc.org/event
sactions/docket/4111page.html (last visited Aug. 2, 2010).

75. Press Release, Governor Donald L. Carcieri Signs Offshore Wind Project Legislation
Paving the Way for the Block Island Offshore Wind Project (June 16, 2010). The Rhode Island
PUC issued its decision approving the revised contract in August 2010. *See In re* Amended
Power Purchase Agreement Between Narragansett Electric Co. and Deepwater Wind B.I., No.
4185 (R.I. Pub. Util. Comm'n Aug. 16, 2010).

76. The case is captioned *In re* Review of Amended Power Purchase Agreement, Nos.
10-272-M.P., 10-273-M.P., and 10-274-M.P. (R.I.). Opening petitions were filed on November
22, 2010.

77. 43 U.S.C. §§ 1301–1315.

78. 1955 Mich. Pub. Acts 247 (codified at Mich. Comp. Laws §§ 324.32501 et seq.).

79. 33 U.S.C. § 403.

80. 33 U.S.C. § 1344.

81. Under 16 U.S.C. § 1536, each federal agency that proposes to authorize, fund, or carry
out an action must consult with the appropriate resource agency (NMFS or FWS), and undertake a "biological assessment" if directed by that resource agency to ensure its proposed action
will not "jeopardize the continued existence" of a species or destroy or adversely modify that
species critical habitat.

82. In both federal and state waters, the Coast Guard and FAA (*see supra* notes 62–67) also
play a role in ensuring maritime and air safety.

83. After the April 2010 BP Deepwater Horizon explosion and oil spill in the Gulf of Mexico, MMS regulatory authorities were reassigned to three new offices within the Department
of the Interior. Leasing authority was assigned to BOEMRE. Dep't of the Interior, Secretarial Order No. 3302 (June 18, 2010), *available at* http://www.doi.gov/deepwaterhorizon/
loader.cfm?csModule=security/getfile&PageID=35872 (last visited Aug. 2, 2010). For simplicity, this chapter generally refers to BOEMRE as the federal offshore wind leasing authority even
for periods pre-dating the Secretarial Order.

84. 43 U.S.C. § 1337(p). Relevant regulations are promulgated at 30 C.F.R. §§ 285.502–
285.507.

85. 16 U.S.C. § 817. The Corps also exercises jurisdiction over met towers and wind turbines
under provisions of OCSLA that extend the Corps' Rivers and Harbors Act authority (discussed
in text accompanying notes 79–82, *supra*) to structures placed on the seabed beyond the territorial seas. 43 U.S.C. § 1333(f). However, the exercise of concurrent jurisdiction by BOEMRE
and the Corps has not raised the same issues as the BOEMRE-FERC overlap. In addition, the
United State Environmental Protection Agency (EPA) regulates air quality related to structures
placed on the OCS. *See* 40 C.F.R. pt. 55. Delaware was the first state delegated authority to
implement and enforce offshore wind air permitting on July 22, 2010. *See* http://www.dnrec
.delaware.gov/News/Pages/Delaware_becomes_first_state_to_receive_delegation_from_EPA_
for_offshore_wind_permitting.aspx (last visited Dec. 2, 2010).

86. 74 Fed Reg. 19,638–19,871 (Apr. 29, 2009), to be codified primarily at 30 C.F.R. pt. 285.

87. 43 U.S.C. § 1337(p) (setting 270-day deadline for issuance of "any necessary regulations to carry out this subsection"). MMS's leasing authority under § 8(p) does not extend to
certain protected areas on the OCS, such as Marine Sanctuaries.

88. 72 Fed. Reg. 62,673 (Nov. 6, 2007).

89. 72 Fed. Reg. 71,152 (Dec. 14, 2007). One month later, BOEMRE published a draft
lease for resource assessment and technology testing activities under the interim policy. 73 Fed.
Reg. 21,152 (Apr. 18, 2008), *revised at* 73 Fed. Reg. 21,363 (Apr. 21, 2008) (revised notice).

90. Press Release, The White House, Memorandum for the Heads of Executive Departments and Agencies: National Policy for the Oceans, Our Coasts, and the Great Lakes (June 12, 2009), *available at* http://www.whitehouse.gov/sites/default/files/page/files/2009ocean_mem_rel.pdf (last visited Aug. 2, 2010).

91. *See* Memorandum of Understanding Between MMS and FWS Regarding Migratory Bird Protection, http://www.fws.gov/migratorybirds/PartnershipsAndIniatives.html (last visited Aug. 2, 2010). *See also* Exec. Order No. 13,186, Responsibilities of Federal Agencies to Protect Migratory Birds, 66 Fed. Reg. 3853 (Jan. 10, 2001) (directing each federal agency whose actions may negatively impact migratory birds to a measurable extent to enter into an MOU with U.S. FWS).

92. White House Council on Envtl. Quality, Final Recommendations of the Interagency Ocean Policy Task Force (July 19, 2010) (Task Force Final Recommendations), *available at* http://www.whitehouse.gov/files/documents/OPTF_FinalRecs.pdf (last visited Aug. 3, 2010).

93. Exec. Order No. 13,547, Stewardship of the Ocean, Our Coasts, and the Great Lakes, 75 Fed. Reg. 43,023 (July 22, 2010).

94. Task Force Final Recommendations at 42–43.

95. Noteworthy state efforts to engage in comprehensive planning for activities in state waters have been undertaken in Massachusetts and Rhode Island. *See* Final Massachusetts Ocean Management Plan, *available at* http://www.mass.gov/?pageID=eoeeaterminal&L=3&L0=Home&L1=Ocean+%26+Coastal+Management&L2=Massachusetts+Ocean+Plan&sid=Eoeea&b=terminalcontent&f=eea_oceans_mop&csid=Eoeea (last visited Aug. 2, 2010) and Rhode Island Ocean Special Area Management Plan, *available at* http://seagrant.gso.uri.edu/oceansamp/samp.html (last visited Aug, 2, 2010).

96. Shively v. Bowlby, 152 U.S. 1, 13 (1894) (citations omitted).

97. Ill. Cent. R.R. v. Illinois, 146 U.S. 387 (1892).

98. Phillips Petroleum Co. v. Mississippi, 484 U.S. 469 (1988).

99. *Ill. Cent. R.R.*, 146 U.S. at 453.

100. *See generally* Joseph L. Sax, *The Public Trust Doctrine in Natural Resource Law: Effective Judicial Intervention*, 68 Mich. L. Rev. 471 (1970).

101. Charles F. Wilkinson, *The Public Trust Doctrine in Public Land Law*, 14 U.C. Davis L. Rev. 269 (1980).

102. *See* David C. Slade et al., Putting the Public Trust Doctrine to Work (2d ed. 1997).

103. 16 U.S.C. § 1362(13).

104. 16 U.S.C. §1532(19). Some states have their own ESA laws. For example, a violation of Michigan's ESA or failure to obtain a state ESA permit subjects the violator to a misdemeanor punishable by up to ninety days of imprisonment or a fine of up to $1,000. Mich. Comp. Laws § 324.36507.

105. 16 U.S.C. § 13,62(18)(A).

106. *See* 50 C.F.R. §§ 17.3 & 222.102. *See* Babbitt v. Sweet Home Chapter of Cmtys. for a Great Or., 515 U.S. 687 (1995) (rejecting a facial challenge to regulation).

107. The listing of a species as threatened or endangered also triggers a federal obligation to designate "critical habitat" for the protected species, subspecies, or discrete population segment and a requirement that any federal agency seeking to authorize or fund any activity affecting that species first consult with the appropriate federal resource agency (USFWS or NMFS, depending on the species at issue).

Under the MMPA, marine mammals receive a degree of protection irrespective of the health of the population of a given marine mammal stock—indeed, there is a general moratorium prohibiting all nonauthorized or permitted takes. "Depleted" marine mammals stocks, which by definition are those stocks that are either below optimum sustainable population or listed as threatened or endangered under the ESA, receive heightened protection, 16 U.S.C. § 1362(1).

108. 16 U.S.C. § 1371.

109. 16 U.S.C. § 1539(a). To obtain an incidental take permit, an applicant must submit a conservation plan that specifies, among other things, the steps that will be taken to minimize and mitigate impacts to protected species. *Id.*

110. 675 F. Supp. 2d 540 (D. Md. 2009).

111. 16 U.S.C. § 1540(g)(1)(A).

112. *Animal Welfare Inst.*, 675 F. Supp. 2d at 561.

113. *Id.* at 564.

114. *Id.* at 575.

115. 83 Cal. Rptr. 3d 588 (Cal. Ct. App. 2008).

116. 16 U.S.C. § 703(a); 50 C.F.R. § 10.12.

117. This is in contrast to the Bald and Golden Eagle Protection Act, 16 U.S.C. §§ 668–668d, under which the FWS adopted a rule in 2009 authorizing the incidental take of bald eagles and golden eagles in appropriate circumstances. U.S. FWS, Eagle Permits, Take Necessary to Protect Interests in Particular Localities, 74 Fed Reg. 46836–47879 (Sept. 11, 2009) (to be codified at 50 C.F.R. pts. 13 & 22).

118. In 2009, Exxon Mobil pled guilty to MBTA violations that resulted in the deaths of eighty-five migratory birds at oil drilling and production facilities in five states. The company agreed to pay $400,000 in fines and $200,000 in community service payments, and was placed on probation for three years. Jennifer Koons, *Exxon Mobil Pleads Guilty to Killing Migratory Birds*, GREENWIRE, Aug. 13, 2009, *available at* http://www.nytimes.com/gwire/2009/08/13/13greenwire-exxon-mobil-pleads-guilty-to-killing-migratory-90137.html.

119. Lilley & Firestone, *supra* note 39.

120. 398 F.3d 105 (1st Cir. 2005), *aff'g* 288 F. Supp. 2d 64, 80–81 (D. Mass. 2003).

121. ADVISORY COUNCIL ON HISTORIC PRESERVATION, COMMENTS OF THE ADVISORY COUNCIL ON HISTORIC PRESERVATION ON THE PROPOSED AUTHORIZATION BY THE MINERALS MANAGEMENT SERVICE FOR CAPE WIND ASSOCIATES, LLC TO CONSTRUCT THE CAPE WIND ENERGY PROJECT ON HORSESHOE SHOAL IN NANTUCKET SOUND, MASSACHUSETTS (Apr. 2, 2010), *available at* http://www.achp.gov/docs/CapeWindComments.pdf (last visited Aug. 2, 2010).

122. *Id.* at 3.

123. *Id.* at 3–4.

124. Press Release, U.S. Dep't of the Interior, Secretary Salazar Announces Approval of Cape Wind Energy Project on Outer Continental Shelf off Massachusetts (Apr. 28, 2010), *available at* http://www.doi.gov/news/doinews/Secretary-Salazar-Announces-Approval-of-Cape-Wind-Energy-Project-on-Outer-Continental-Shelf-off-Massachusetts.cfm (last visited Aug. 2, 2010).

125. Coalition of Stakeholder Groups Announce Cape Wind Lawsuits (Apr. 28, 2010), *available at* http://pointmass.org/profiles/blogs/coalition-of-stakeholder (last visited Feb. 28, 2011).

126. Pub. Employees for Envtl. Responsibility v. Bromwich, No. 10-cv-01067 (D.D.C. filed June 25, 2010), *available at* http://peer.org/docs/ma/6_25_10_Cape_Wind_Wildlife_Complaint.pdf (last visited August 3, 2010).

127. Press Release, Attorney Gen. Martha Coakley, AG Coakley's Office Reaches Agreement in Principle with Cape Wind to Reduce Costs for Ratepayers (July 30, 2010), *available at* http://www.mass.gov/?pageID=cagopressrelease&L=1&L0=Home&sid=Cago&b=pressrelease&f=2010_07_30_cape_wind&csid=Cago (last visited Aug. 3, 2010).

128. *In re* Mass. Elec. Co. & Nantucket Elec. Co., Docket No. 10-54 (Mass. Bd. of Public Utils.).

chapter seventeen

Solar

Craig M. Kline

Introduction

Although the technology to generate electricity from the sun has existed for some time,[1] only recently has the United States begun to embrace solar electricity as an integral part of our energy mix. This shift is fueled in part by the rising cost of traditional nonrenewable energy and in part by increased social acceptance that fossil fuels are causing irreparable harm to our environment. Recently, during the "Great Recession," the budding renewable energy industry provided an ideal place for the government to allocate recovery money to stimulate the economy and job growth. Investing in renewable energy allowed the government to claim multiple accomplishments—specifically, (i) reducing the United States' dependence on foreign oil, (ii) creating new jobs, (iii) stimulating the economy, and (iv) promoting a sustainable and clean environment.[2]

Solar energy continues to require government subsidies to be competitive with traditional sources of electricity. This could very well change with the enactment of carbon legislation that would internalize the cost of carbon on the emitter of fossil-fuel-generated energy. Short of a comprehensive energy bill that would price carbon, much of the recent solar activity in the United States has been a direct result of increased federal, state, and local incentives made available to consumers and developers.[3] Such government incentives have been quite successful in promoting the development of renewable energy, reflected in the 29.2 percent increase in solar energy capacity in the United States in 2007 and 28.2 percent increase in 2008.[4] As the solar energy market matures and solar technology, particularly photovoltaic technology, evolves to become increasingly affordable and/or efficient, the lower development costs will allow solar energy to become an economically attractive alternative to fossil fuels notwithstanding the costs of carbon or government subsidies.[5]

While there are a variety of solar technologies available to consumers in the market today, the two main technologies used commercially for generating solar energy are concentrated solar power and photovoltaics.[6]

1. Concentrated solar power (CSP) uses mirrors or lenses to reflect and concentrate solar radiation onto a receiver that collects the solar energy and then converts it into thermal energy.[7] The solar radiation collected is used to heat a working fluid, which at high temperatures creates steam to spin a turbine that produces electricity.[8] The most cost-effective size for a CSP plant is one with a large capacity of megawatts (MW), making CSP plants mostly attractive to energy suppliers to utilities or to utilities themselves.[9] There is also a growing market of behind-the-meter CSP that could be used in conjunction with conventional energy generation.[10] As of September 2009, the Solar Energy Industries Association reports that over 400 MW of CSP plants operate in the United States, with more than 8,000 MW currently under development.[11]

2. Photovoltaics (PV) is the most common and recognizable method of utilizing solar radiation. Sunlight is directly converted into energy when solar radiation strikes the semiconductor material and electrons are released from their atomic bonds.[12] PV material can be several individual solar cells or a single thin layer that makes up a larger solar panel. Materials used for solar cells include, among others, silicon,[13] polycrystalline thin films,[14] and single-crystalline thin films.[15] PV panels can be either ground mounted or roof mounted and contain no moving parts (other than sun-tracking hardware) or fluids. PV panels typically have a lifetime of twenty years or more and, once installed, require minimal maintenance to run properly. The versatility and longevity of PV panels, along with relatively low maintenance requirements, make them very popular among developers, consumers, and investors for behind-the-meter applications.[16] PV creates DC electricity and requires inverters to convert to AC electricity, which we use in our homes. Inverters are more prone to failure and require more maintenance than PV panels.

By 2008, concentrated solar power and PV capacity installed in the United States was approximately 1,500 MW.[17] The vast majority of this installed capacity directly benefited from government subsidies. The U.S. federal Investment Tax Credit (ITC), which is described in more detail below, in conjunction with state-level rebate and incentive programs, has been integral to the continued growth of this domestic solar energy market. It is important to note, however, that financial incentives vary tremendously from state to state. Currently, the states with the most attractive renewable energy incentive programs include California, New Jersey, Colorado, and Nevada. These four states represented 82 percent of the market share in 2008 for grid-connected PV systems in the United States, with California claiming the lion's share of the installed PV capacity.[18]

PV capacity in the United States has shown steady growth since 2000; however, the past several years have seen a particularly dramatic rise in PV capacity as a result of the federal ITC.[19] Concentrated solar power installations stalled in the early 1990s due to a lack of government-supported incentives. There has been a several fold increase in planned concentrated solar power installations since 2006.[20] Total concentrated solar power capacity reached approximately 419 megawatts in 2008, with approximately 60 megawatts installed during 2006 and 2007.[21] No concentrated solar plants came online in 2008; however, of the 8,000 MWs in development, approximately 80 MWs of capacity are currently under construction or have secured financing.[22]

This chapter will provide a general discussion of the issues arising from the development and financing of solar energy generation facilities. Since each project site will be subject to various state, local, and utility regulations and procedures, and because utilities may offer incentives in addition to available state incentives, it is important that additional real-time legal diligence be conducted to ensure that the project is in compliance with all applicable requirements and is benefiting from all available incentive programs.

Government Role in Solar

Tax Incentives Available for Solar Project Investments

Eligible solar energy projects generally provide developers a federal investment tax credit (ITC) and accelerated depreciation deductions. Under a government grant program enacted pursuant to the 2009 stimulus legislation, developers may elect to forgo the ITC and receive an equivalent cash payment.[23] Various financing structures are also available to developers in order to obtain capital from and transfer federal tax benefits to tax equity investors. The predominant structures for accommodating tax equity investors are so-called "partnership flips" and sale-leasebacks. Notably, federal tax incentives, including tax credits and accelerated depreciation deductions, have had the most significant impact on making the financing of solar power projects competitive with more traditional energy projects.

Section 48 Investment Tax Credit

Qualifying solar property under the ITC rules refers to property that uses solar energy to generate electricity, to heat or cool a structure, or to provide solar process heat. Virtually any photovoltaic or concentrated solar project, whether used to provide energy to a particular building or to supply energy to the electric grid, should qualify for the ITC.[24] Except with respect to certain specially designed solar systems, supporting structures, including roof materials, generally do not qualify for the ITC.

The amount of the ITC is 30 percent of the cost of qualifying solar equipment, including related assembly and installation costs. The ITC generally may only be taken by the owner or lessee of a solar power plant, and except in the case of a sale-leaseback transaction, the owner must have originally placed the project in service. Although an oversimplification, a solar power plant will be considered to be "placed in service" when the equipment is delivered and assembled at the host site, interconnected in the case of utility-scale projects, and in commercial operation. Qualifying solar property must be placed in service by December 31, 2016, in order to be eligible for the ITC.

In general, the ITC may not be claimed with respect to property that is used predominantly outside the United States. Additionally, the ITC is not allowed with respect to solar equipment that is leased to a tax-exempt organization, including governmental entities like schools, municipal utilities, and charitable organizations. However, the ITC may be claimed where a power plant, although installed on-site, merely sells electricity to a tax-exempt customer.

If the solar power plant is sold (or otherwise disposed of), or if the plant equipment otherwise ceases to be eligible for the ITC, before the end of five full years following the placed-in-service date, the "unvested" portion of the credit will be recaptured. The ITC "vests" over a five-year period at a rate of 20 percent per year. The recapture amount, therefore, would be determined by multiplying the ITC amount by the number of years remaining in the five-year period multiplied by 20 percent. In the event of a recapture, one-half of the income recognized as a consequence of the recaptured ITC will be added to basis and deducted as additional depreciation according to the project's depreciation schedule or effectively reduce the resulting gain from a sale of the project.

Accelerated Depreciation

Solar power plant equipment may be depreciated for tax purposes over a five-year period using the double declining (200 percent) balance method (which converts to the straight line method for the first taxable year for which using the straight line method will yield a larger depreciation deductions).[25] If the ITC is claimed or the cash grant is received with respect to a solar power plant, depreciation is reduced by one-half of the ITC or grant amount.[26] Therefore, 85 percent of the eligible costs of the power plant may be deducted as depreciation.

Solar power plants also may be eligible for so-called "bonus" depreciation—an additional deduction in the first year of a power plant's operation of a percentage of its cost.

Cash Grant Program

The American Recovery and Reinvestment Act of 2009 (ARRA) provides developers and owners of ITC-qualified (and ITC-in-lieu-of-PTC-qualified) facilities with the option of receiving a direct cash payment instead of claiming the ITC.[27] The purpose of the cash grant program was to address a temporary lack of profitable tax equity investors that could utilize the credits. By allowing the monetization of the ITC into a cash payment, the immediate benefit of the ITC is obtained, whether or not the investor would have been able to currently utilize the ITC against its tax liability. The grant amount is equal to the ITC amount (30 percent of the costs of the project) and is calculated on the same cost basis that would have been used to calculate the ITC.[28] The cash grant option is available for (1) qualified renewable energy projects placed in service during 2009, 2010, or 2011, or (2) projects that are not placed in service in 2009, 2010, or 2011, but commence construction in 2009, 2010, or 2011 and are completed before January 1, 2017, for solar projects, January 1, 2013, for large wind projects, and January 1, 2014, for biomass, marine energy, and landfill gas projects.[29]

In the event that the property is disposed of to a disqualified person and/or ceases to qualify as specified energy property within five years from the date the property is placed in service, the applicant will be subject to recapture.[30] The cash grant will vest ratably over a five-year period.[31] Notably, contrary to the usual investment tax credit rule, the cash grant will not be recaptured if the applicant sells the project to a transferee that would have been a qualified grant applicant.[32] Neither the grant nor the credit will be subject to recapture if the project ceases to generate electricity temporarily, provided the owner of the property intends to resume production at the time production ceases.[33]

Unlike the ITC, the grant is allowed for property leased to a tax-exempt entity, but such a lease would result in a reduction of tax depreciation benefits.[34] Such a reduction would not occur if the project is leased to a taxable entity that sells the power to a tax-exempt entity under a power purchase agreement that qualifies as a service contract for tax purposes.[35] Unlike the ITC, individual investors can claim the grant notwithstanding that they would have been subject to "passive loss" limitations had they claimed the ITC rather than the grant.

In order to apply for the cash grant, certain documentation must be submitted with the application to demonstrate that the property is eligible property that has been placed in service (or, if placed in service after 2011, that construction began in 2009, 2010, or 2011).[36] The type of documentation that must be submitted depends on the type of project and other facts relating to the property.[37]

Applicants to the grant may choose to assign the payments to a third party, provided that the applicant complies with the Federal Assignment of Claims Act, which restricts the assignment of a claim against the United States unless certain criteria are met. These conditions are as follows: (1) the contract must specify payments totaling at least $1,000; (2) the contract must not prohibit assignment; (3) the assignment is for the entire amount not already paid; (4) the assignment is not subject to further assignment; and (5) the assignment is made to one party, and such party participates directly in the financing (there is an exception to this requirement for assignments made to an agent or trustee for more than one party participating in the financing).[38]

The tax incentives described above are also discussed in chapter 7.

Renewable Portfolio Standards

A variety of state and federal governmental incentives promote the generation of electricity from renewable resources. Many such incentives go directly to developers of renewable energy projects, including direct subsidies, tax benefits, low-interest loans, net metering, and simplified interconnection procedures.[39] Increasingly, states have been encouraging retail electric utilities to increase their use of renewable energy generation by imposing renewable energy quotas known as renewable portfolio standard (RPS) programs. RPS programs are discussed in greater detail in chapter 4.

Many RPS programs include solar carve-outs, which require utilities to satisfy a specific percentage of its RPS from solar energy. This policy has provided significant encouragement to solar power development.

Renewable Energy Certificates

One outgrowth from the emphasis on renewable energy is the development of markets for renewable energy credits or certificates (RECs).[40] RECs are generally transacted on a standardized basis where one REC represents the environmental attributes associated with the production of one megawatt-hour (MWh) of electricity from a renewable resource.[41] Such attributes include the tangible benefits of renewable energy generation, notably the avoidance of carbon and other emission types associated with fossil fuel consumption, as well as intangible attributes such as green marketing rights. RECs allow electric consumers, wholesalers, and utilities to purchase "green power" on a notional basis without regard to the specific source of the generation.[42] Additionally many states also permit utilities to purchase RECs to satisfy their RPS requirements.

The premise underlying REC markets is that users of electricity may support and derive benefit from renewable resources on a basis that is uncoupled from the physical flow of electricity. Generally, the RECs are retained by the solar system owner; however, if the solar system is installed by a solar developer and the solar electricity is sold to a customer through a power purchase agreement, then the solar developer remains the system owner and may or may not retain the benefit of the RECs, depending on the terms of the power purchase agreement (please see below for a more detailed discussion on power purchase agreements). The power purchase agreements may be beneficial to the purchaser even without the benefits of the RECs since they generally offer the customers electricity at a long-term fixed price without the customer bearing the up-front cost of the solar system installation.

Under the state RPS programs, after the RECs for a solar system are sold to a third party, the system owner can no longer make any claims that they are using or generating solar or renewable electricity.[43] The rights to make such statements have been passed on to the purchaser of the RECs. In an effort to provide some clarification with respect to environmental marketing, the Federal Trade Commission (the FTC) and the National Association of Attorneys General (the NAAG) have both issued guidelines addressing marketing claims that are permissible under the law. The FTC guidelines apply to all "environmental marketing claims included in labeling, promotional materials and other forms of marketing, whether asserted directly or by implication, through words, symbols, emblems, logos, depictions, product brand names, or through any other means. . . ." (FTC Guidelines).[44] The guideline issued by the NAAG provides similar guidance, except it applies specifically to marketing claims related to the attributes of electricity products (the NAAG Guidelines).[45] Although the FTC Guidelines do not have the effect of law, they allow the FTC to initiate enforcement actions under § 5 of the Federal Trade Commission Act (the FTCA), which prohibits entities from engaging in unfair or deceptive acts or practices in interstate commerce.[46] Section 5 of the FTCA authorizes the FTC to seek injunctive and other equitable relief for violations under the FTCA, and provides a basis for enforcement actions by the FTC for failure to comply with its rules and guidelines.[47]

In an effort to "strengthen the FTC's guidance on those marketing claims that are already addressed in the current Guides as well as to provide new guidance on marketing claims that were not common when the Guides were last reviewed [in 1998]," on October 6, 2010, the FTC proposed revisions to the FTC Guidelines that specifically address what marketers can say in advertising the use of renewable materials, renewable energy, and carbon offsets (Proposed Guidelines).[48] Since the last revision of the FTC Guidelines, environmental awareness by the consumer and, as a result, the use of environmental marketing claims in advertising have increased dramatically. The FTC acknowledges these changes in the marketplace and issued the Proposed Guidelines, in part, to "keep pace with evolving consumer perceptions and new environmental claims."

Among other provisions, the Proposed Guidelines state that it is not necessary for companies to disclose whether renewable energy claims made by the company are based on the purchase of RECs or the purchase of actual renewable energy, since there was no indication to the FTC that this distinction would be material to consumers.[49] Unsurprisingly, the Proposed Guidelines confirm that "companies should not sell RECs for renewable energy they generate onsite . . . and then tout their renewable energy facilities or equipment in advertising."[50] Notably, however, the Proposed Guidelines also provide that a company may not claim that they "host a renewable energy facility" if the RECs related to such facility have been sold to another party, as such a claim, according to the FTC, would likely mislead consumers.[51]

There are two distinct markets for RECs: a voluntary market driven by consumer demand and a compliance market driven by RPS programs and other legislative mandates. The voluntary market includes consumers that are willing to pay a green energy premium in connection with their energy consumption. For individuals, a REC purchase typically takes the form of a premium or surcharge on their electricity bills. Similar programs exist for industrial and commercial users of electricity, but such users may also buy RECs in bulk (individually or through consortiums) from renewable energy generators or marketers.[52]

Voluntary REC purchases are often made by either energy-intensive industries, those seeking to offset greenhouse emissions in environmentally sensitive areas (e.g., ski resorts), individuals who wish to promote the adoption of renewable energy, or companies that wish to fulfill corporate goals of using cleaner energy. The purchase of RECs is a major technique used by companies that wish to declare themselves "carbon neutral"—a phrase that is frequently used in marketing efforts, but that lacks a clear legal definition. RECs may be supplied from a variety of renewable energy sources throughout the country and sold to customers nationally, or they may be supplied from sources in a particular region or locality and marketed as such to local customers. Because most RECs are unbundled from the physical generation of electricity, they are fungible and free from any inherent geographical and temporal limitations (although such limitations may arise as a result of certification requirements or state mandates).

Compliance-driven REC purchases are generally made to satisfy state-level RPS requirements or other similar mandates. The detailed requirements of such programs vary considerably among states, and certain states may exclude or limit the use of RECs as a compliance mechanism. In New Jersey, for example, electricity suppliers may meet their requirements under New Jersey's RPS by purchasing RECs. The RECs used to satisfy RPS requirements must come from certain types of renewable electricity (solar, wind, biomass, etc.). As a general rule, RECs that are used in the compliance market cannot be used again in the voluntary market and vice versa, a practice known as double-counting.

As discussed above, a REC is a tradable commodity that reflects the environmental attributes associated with one MWh of renewable energy generation, which is typically purchased by energy utilities to satisfy requirements imposed by the state's RPS program. Certain RPS programs around the country also includes a solar carve-out, which requires that a certain percentage of RPS be satisfied using solar energy.[53] As a result, in those states with a solar carve-out, solar-RECs or S-RECs can be sold for a much higher price than RECs generated through other renewable resources and can play a key role in the financing of a solar project. REC pricing can vary greatly from state to state and is subject to market and regulatory influences.

In the constantly evolving regulatory landscape, the buyer and seller of RECs should be particularly concerned with how regulatory changes may impact each party's rights and obligations in the REC purchase agreement. In the event that a governmental authority repeals or modifies the RPS program, such regulatory change may adversely affect the value of RECs or may eliminate the REC commodity altogether. This change-in-law risk arises since REC purchase agreements are typically long-term contracts for the future delivery of RECs; and, similar to other commodities to be delivered in the future, the RECs are subject to future events that impact their value at the time of delivery. As a result, the allocation of the change-in-law risk is often a heavily negotiated point between the parties. A sale of "environmental attributes" as opposed to a sale of defined RECs puts greater risk on the buyer. Likewise, it gives the buyer the upside of any future undefined environmental attributes created as a result of a change in law.

If neither the buyer nor the seller has an appetite for the change-in-law risk, the parties could seek to transfer the risk of a change in law to a third party through a financial swap with a financial counterparty. Whether the seller or buyer would be the counterparty (the REC counterparty) to the swap, the payment of costs associated with the swap would be subject to the parties' needs and to negotiation. The REC counterparty would pay a periodic or up-front fee to the financial counterparty, and in return, the financial counterparty would agree to pay the REC counterparty a set amount if an event outside the control of the parties occurred causing the environmental attributes to be ineligible under the RPS program. The swap agreement mitigates risk by transferring the risk of delivery or receipt of noneligible RECs from one party to another without transferring the underlying RECs.

RECs are also discussed in chapter 4.

Commerce Clause Implications

Most state RPS programs require that all or some of the renewable energy or RECs generated to satisfy the RPS goal be generated from facilities located within the state. The imposition of this requirement has opened up the question of whether such a requirement violates the dormant commerce clause of the United States Constitution. The dormant commerce clause is derived from the negative implication of Article I, Section 8 of the United States Constitution, which provides that "the Congress shall have Power . . . to regulate Commerce . . . among the several States. . . . ."[54] It is settled law that the dormant commerce clause limits the authority of states to enact regulations that burden interstate commerce.[55] Specifically in *Wyoming v. Oklahoma*,[56] the Court held that "when a state statute clearly discriminates against interstate commerce, it will be struck down unless the discrimination is demonstrably justified by a valid factor unrelated to economic protectionism."[57]

A state that only permits a utility to use renewable energy or RECs purchased from in-state generators to satisfy their requirements under an RPS program could be considered to have discriminated against interstate commerce since it treats the same type of commodity differently based solely on where the renewable energy or REC is produced. As a result, a renewable energy generator who produces energy or RECs in one state may not be able to sell to a utility in a neighboring state, which has the effect of decreasing competition and lowering prices the generator may be able to obtain for their product.

In *Pike v. Bruce Church, Inc.*,[58] the Court indicated that there is no bright line rule in determining whether a state statute is unconstitutionally interfering with interstate commerce.[59] The courts must weigh the benefits of the legitimate local purpose against the extent that impact may have on interstate commerce.[60] Certainly, encouraging renewable energy production within the state is a legitimate state purpose; however, whether such a state purpose can be achieved through an alternative nondiscriminatory method and whether the state purpose justifies the impact on interstate commerce remain novel issues.

Although the constitutionality of such restrictions has not yet been tested in the courts, a complaint filed in April of 2010 by TransCanada Power Marketing Ltd. (TransCanada) against the Commonwealth of Massachusetts provided some insight on how these restrictions will be viewed vis-à-vis the Commerce Clause.[61] In its complaint, TransCanada argues that Massachusetts is unconstitutionally discriminating against out-of-state renewable energy producers by requiring that (i) energy distribution companies solicit proposals for long-term renewable energy contracts only from renewable energy developers who are generating within the state and (ii) RECs purchased in connection with the state's solar carve-out program come solely from generators within the state.[62]

Rather than litigating the issue, the Massachusetts Department of Public Utilities (MA DPU) agreed to suspend the provision in its regulations that required energy distribution companies to solicit proposals for long-term renewable energy contracts only from within the state.[63] The MA DPU relied on a provision in the original rule that allows the MA DPU to "suspend the applicability of the challenged provision" if it became subject to a judicial challenge.[64] In an order issued by the MA DPU, it stated that the suspension of the requirement is needed "to provide certainty concerning the ability of electric distribution companies to enter into long-term contracts with renewable energy developers to facilitate the financing of renewable energy generation sources . . . [and] [t]o ensure that long-term contracting pursuant to [the rule] proceeds expeditiously in accordance with [its] legislative purpose. . . ."[65]

The second element of TransCanada's complaint was settled in a separate agreement between TransCanada and Massachusetts. In the settlement, TransCanada agreed to drop its claims against the Massachusetts solar carve-out program since state officials agreed to revise the provision to allow the alternative compliance payment rate for "that portion of a Retail Supplier's Solar Renewable Energy Credit obligations that were contractually committed or renewed prior to January 1, 2010" to be equal to the Class I rate, as opposed to the much higher Solar Carve-Out rate.[66] This revision allows TransCanada to avoid paying the higher Solar Carve-Out alternative compliance payments in the event that they are unable to meet their Solar Carve-Out compliance obligations.[67]

State Subsidies and Incentives

Many states encourage solar energy development by creating financial incentives for consumers or developers who are investing money into developing solar energy generation facilities. The amount and type of incentive can vary significantly by state. For example, the financial incentive may come in the form of a one-time payment based on the system size of the facility, or it can be in the form of a monthly payment based on the amount of energy that is produced by the facility. In relying on state subsidies or incentive payments to develop a project, consumers and developers should be aware that each program will have its own requirements, application procedures, and funding limitations; therefore a thorough investigation should be conducted early in the development process.

In the event that the solar facility is financed, lenders will typically want to be assigned the subsidy or incentive payments or, as an alternative, will require that the incentives be collaterally assigned to them. Perfecting a security interest in a state subsidy or incentive payment poses a unique issue for many lenders with respect to how the incentive payments should be categorized under the revised Article 9 of the Uniform Commercial Code (the UCC). The UCC does not address the issue specifically, but notes in the official comments that the UCC "does not contain a defined term that encompasses specifically rights to payment or performance under the many and varied government entitlement programs. Depending on the nature of a right under a program, it could be an account, a payment intangible, a general intangible other than a payment intangible, or another type of collateral."[68]

Prior to the system achieving commercial operation, but after the facility has been approved to receive the subsidy or incentive payment, the collateral would most likely be considered a General Intangible.[69] However, once the system achieves commercial operation and starts generating solar electricity, the collateral changes from a General Intangible to an Account since at that point in the development process the project will have a "right to payment of a monetary obligation."[70] In either situation, the

Lender may perfect its security interest by filing a UCC-1 financing statement in the proper jurisdiction.[71] Be aware that certain states allow for designation of third-party payees as well.

U.S. Department of Energy's Loan Guarantees

Another program available for clean energy projects in the United States is the U.S. Department of Energy's Loan Guarantee program, which provides loan guarantees for (1) projects that employ new or significantly improved technologies that avoid, reduce, or sequester air pollutants or anthropogenic emissions of greenhouse gases or (2) renewable energy systems that commence construction not later than September 30, 2011.[72] The program, established under Title XVII of the Energy Policy Act of 2005 (Title XVII) and later expanded through the ARRA,[73] was created to promote domestic economic growth, secure a more stable energy supply, and encourage environmentally friendly benefits.[74]

The Title XVII loan guarantee program and its expansion through ARRA are discussed in detail in chapter 8 of this book.

Clean Renewable Energy Bonds

Clean Renewable Energy Bonds (CREBs) were initially created as part of the Energy Policy Act of 2005 to finance public sector renewable energy projects.[75] The stimulus package provided for $1.6 billion in new CREBs to finance wind, closed-loop biomass, open-loop biomass, geothermal, small irrigation, hydropower, landfill gas, marine renewable, and trash combustion facilities.[76] Each participant must first apply and receive approval from the IRS for a CREB allocation.[77] In 2009, this program allocated $800 million in funding for 739 projects and has proven to be a ripe source of funding. Currently, however, the IRS has no open funding announcements, and it is unclear whether authorization for CREBs will continue and, if so, on what terms.[78]

CREBS are discussed in detail in chapter 8 of this book.

Regulatory Issues

Federal Energy Regulatory Commission

Before a project can start producing energy, it must first satisfy all regulatory requirements at the federal, state, and utility levels. The Federal Energy Regulatory Commission (FERC) regulates all interstate transmissions of electricity, natural gas, and oil in the United States, including having jurisdiction over all public electric and natural gas utilities.[79] Since the majority of solar energy facilities will be interconnected to their local utilities' grid, the facilities will also be subject to the jurisdiction of FERC.[80] Only those facilities that generate power solely for the owner's use (and not interconnected with the electrical grid) are not subject to FERC rules. A 2009 declaratory order from FERC clarified that the sale of solar power by a developer to an end-use customer will also not fall under FERC's jurisdiction when the facility does not produce more energy than it needs over the applicable billing period since there is no net sale to the utility.[81] For those facilities that do put net positive energy onto the grid, the facility will be deemed to have made a sale for resale in interstate commerce, and such system would be required to meet FERC's regulations applicable to "public utilities" (i.e., reporting requirements, accounting standards, standards of conduct, and a panoply of other requirements).[82]

Qualifying Facilities

As a way to "encourage, among other things . . . the conservation of electric energy, increased efficiency in the use of facilities and resources by electric utilities, [and] equitable retail rates for electric consumers," the Public Utility Regulatory Policies Act of 1978 (PURPA) created a class of facilities known as "qualifying facilities" (or QFs) that would receive special rate and regulatory treatment.[83] QFs enjoy three types of benefits, "(1) the right to sell energy or capacity to a utility, (2) the right to purchase certain services from utilities, and (3) relief from certain regulatory burdens."[84] To accomplish these purposes, PURPA established two categories of QFs: qualifying small power production facilities and qualifying cogeneration facilities.[85]

1. A small power production facility is a facility generating "80 MW or less whose primary energy source is renewable (hydro, wind or solar), biomass, waste, or geothermal resources. . . . In order to be considered a qualifying small power production facility, a facility must meet all of the requirements of 18 C.F.R. §§ 292.203(a), 292.203(c) and 292.204 for size and fuel use, and be certified as a QF pursuant to 18 C.F.R. § 292.207."[86]
2. A cogeneration facility is a facility that "sequentially produces electricity and another form of useful thermal energy (such as heat or steam) in a way that is more efficient than the separate production of both forms of energy. . . . In order to be considered a qualifying cogeneration facility, a facility must meet all of the requirements of 18 C.F.R. §§ 292.203(b) and 292.205 for operation, efficiency and use of energy output, and be certified as a QF pursuant to 18 C.F.R. § 292.207. There is no size limitation for qualifying cogeneration facilities."[87]

In order to obtain QF status, the owner or operator of the facility may either submit a self-certification or apply for a FERC certification of QF status.[88] Self-certification status can be obtained by the applicant by completing a Form No. 556 and submitting it to FERC.[89] For cogeneration facilities that were "either not certified as a QF on or before August 8, 2005, or that had not filed a notice of self-certification, self-recertification or an application for FERC certification or FERC recertification as a qualifying cogeneration facility on or before February 1, 2006," the self-certifications must be accompanied by a draft notice suitable for publication in the Federal Register.[90]

On March 19, 2010, FERC issued a final rule that confirmed, among other things, an exemption for "generating facilities with net power production capacities of 1 MW or less" from the requirement that the facility file a notice of self-certification or apply for FERC certification in order to be a qualifying facility.[91] Notably, FERC did not specifically define "net power production" in the final rule. Previous FERC cases indicate that net power production is not merely the solar system's name plate capacity, thus, the power producer must determine what comprises net power production. This exemption seems to be a signal that FERC is encouraging the development of small renewable facilities by lowering the regulatory burdens imposed on them.

FERC has also indicated that it will not exercise its authority over small power producers with only a *de minimis* amount of activity.[92] In a declaratory order issued on November 19, 2009, FERC determined that "where the net metering participant . . . does not . . . make a net sale to the utility, the sale of electric energy" is not subject to FERC jurisdiction.[93] In the order, FERC stated that net metering is a "method of measuring sales of electricity" and that only when the consumer "produces more energy than it needs over the applicable billing period" will FERC consider it a net sale of energy to a utility.[94] As a result of these two decisions, small power producers should carefully analyze whether they fall into either of the two exemptions provided by FERC to determine whether they can be relieved of the regulatory burdens that are imposed on typical energy generation facilities.

PURPA is also discussed in chapter 15.

Interconnection and Net Metering

Since interconnection and net metering are both related to a facility's connection to the grid, they are often discussed in tandem with each other. Interconnection refers to the technical, contractual, and metering issues between the system owner and the local utility to which the system is connected. Most utilities have a standardized interconnection agreement that system owners must enter into before they can connect their system to the grid. Because the utilities are subject to the jurisdiction of FERC, interconnection agreements are also generally governed by FERC.[95] A typical interconnection agreement includes provisions on testing and inspection, term and termination, access rights, disconnection, risk and cost allocation, billing and payment, and insurance requirements. Each utility establishes its own procedures and requirements in approving a generating facility for interconnection. As a matter of practice, most investors and/or lenders will require a project to achieve interconnection with the local utility as a condition precedent to financing.

Once interconnection is obtained, the process of net metering enables customers to obtain full retail credits on their utility bill for energy produced by their solar system in excess of the amount of electricity used by the purchaser. Net metering rules typically provide restrictions on the amount of electricity that can be sold to the utility and the rate at which the utility will purchase the electricity. Since net metering rules vary from state to state, each project owner should investigate the rules of the state where the project is located prior to the installation of a solar system.

Interconnection and net metering are discussed in greater detail in chapters 22 and 9, respectively.

Davis-Bacon Act

The Davis-Bacon Act, established in 1931, specifies that every public works contract in excess of $2,000 entered into with the United States or District of Columbia, "which requires or involves the employment of mechanics or laborers shall contain a provision stating the minimum wages to be paid various classes of laborers and mechanics."[96] The minimum wages are determined by the Secretary of Labor for the "corresponding classes of laborers and mechanics employed on projects of a character similar to the contract work in the civil subdivision of the State in which the work is to be performed."[97]

The American Recovery and Reinvestment Act of 2009, which has allocated $16.7 billion to the Department of Energy's Office of Energy Efficiency and Renewable Energy for its programs and initiatives, specifically requires that all laborers and mechanics employed by contractors and subcontracts on any project "funded directly by or assisted in whole or in part by" ARRA funds be paid prevailing wages as determined by the Secretary of Labor.[98] Therefore, any project that involves the United States or the District of Columbia or has received funds from the ARRA has an obligation to comply with all prevailing wage laws.

Development

Distributed Generation versus Utility Scale Generation

Solar energy generation can occur in varying scales. Solar energy projects are generally distinguished between distributed generation projects and utility scale projects. Distributed generation arises from smaller scale projects that are installed on-site in which the purchaser utilizes the energy that is being generated. Any excess electricity is typically sold to the local utility and distributed to other customers. Relative to distributed generation projects, utility scale projects are much larger projects that are typically developed on a big swath of land. All of the energy produced by the system is then sold to a utility to be distributed to its customers. The acreage and sunlight requirement of a utility-scale project makes such projects particularly feasible in desert regions.

Predictably, utility-scale projects are much more complex than typical distributed generation projects. In addition to significantly larger amounts of financing necessary to build a utility-scale project, almost all aspects of developing a solar system are amplified when a project is utility scale, including obtaining easements and site access; transportation of materials; installation; maintaining site security; overcoming regulatory hurdles; and conducting ordinary operations and maintenance on the solar system. Distributed generation projects, on the other hand, are typically streamlined by the local utility to encourage home owners and small businesses to install solar systems on their home or business. Additionally, many states and local utilities offer substantial financial incentives to consumers who choose to install solar panels on their homes or business. Numerous private companies provide one-stop shopping to consumers, including purchase and installation of the equipment, interconnection with the local utility system, and completion of the paperwork for available financial incentives.

Environmental Due Diligence

Particularly, with respect to ground-mounted PV or CSP projects, environmental due diligence (including a Phase I environmental assessment) is a critical component in determining whether any potential environmental risks exist on the land where the solar system is located. Those who purchase or build on land that has preexisting contamination may find themselves liable for its cleanup, even if they played no role in the initial pollution. Numerous techniques have been established to search for potential contamination and to employ various regulatory and transactional techniques to reduce liability exposure. These techniques are beyond the scope of this book, but are discussed in detail in several other works.[99]

Building Codes, Zoning Restrictions, and Site Approvals

When determining where to install a solar system, a thorough investigation of the local building codes, zoning ordinances, and subdivision covenants, as well as any special regulations pertaining to the site, should be conducted. The issue of building codes and zoning compliance for a solar system installation is typically a local issue. Almost every locality has its own building and zoning codes and regulations; many of these have provisions specifically addressing where and how solar facilities can be installed. If not, residential installations are typically considered accessory uses, while utility-scale installations are typically covered by the locality's rules on utilities. Common problems developers may have with building codes include exceeding roof load, improper wiring, and unlawful tampering with potable water supplies.[100] Potential zoning issues include erecting unlawful protrusions on roofs or siting the system too close to streets or lot boundaries.[101] Various building permits are also likely to be required by the site's locality in order to install a solar energy system onto an existing building. For large projects, additional siting approval may be required from the state's siting board before the project can proceed. Whether a project will be subject to siting approval may depend on the project size. Although the scope of the review will vary depending on the state, it will typically cover issues such as environmental effects of the project, transmission issues; financial, technical, and managerial capabilities of applicant; noise and landscape impact of the project; and public need for the project. Since most site approval procedures require comment periods and public hearings, the process can take from six months to a year to complete.

Solar Easements

A solar easement prohibits neighboring property owners from building or planting anything on their property that would obstruct the amount of sunlight to which the solar facility is exposed. A typical solar easement will normally contain a description of the dimensions of the easement, including vertical and horizontal angles measured in the degrees or the hours of the day during which direct sunlight to a specified surface or structural design feature may not be obstructed and terms and conditions for revision and termination of the easement. Additionally, the solar easement is required to be recorded with the office of the recorder of the county where the easement is granted.

Before construction begins, the developer should determine whether obtaining a solar easement from the site's neighbors is necessary in order to protect the viability of the solar project. In the event that a neighboring property owner refuses to grant a solar easement, the developer may want to reconsider whether that particular site is suitable for a solar facility. Although many states statutorily permit solar easements, generally there is no requirement that a neighbor grant one.[102] Several western states, however, have enacted legislation in order to help secure solar rights for those attempting to develop solar energy facilities.

One example of such legislation is the Solar Rights Act and Solar Recordation Act enacted in New Mexico (the NM Solar Rights Act).[103] The NM Solar Rights Act was enacted in order to manage situations in which agreements for express easements could not be reached.[104] The statute provides that the owner of a property adjacent to one containing a solar system may develop that property so long as it does not impede the previously existing system's access to sunlight.[105] This statute was later revised to provide greater protection to neighboring property owners by limiting the hours of the solar easement to 9:00 a.m. and 3:00 p.m.[106] and allows the neighboring property owners to contest the solar easement upon notification by the property owner seeking the solar easement.[107]

A different approach taken by Iowa gives a property owner a right to acquire a solar easement from its neighbor at market value when the parties are unable to come to an agreement through voluntary bargaining.[108] The property owner wishing to obtain a solar easement is required to submit an application to the locally designated solar access regulatory board for an order granting the easement.[109] In order to protect neighboring property owners, the applicant must make certain affirmative statements certifying that the location of the solar equipment is designed in order to minimize its impact on neighboring properties and that the applicant has attempted, but has been unable to negotiate, a voluntary solar easement from its neighbor.[110]

A third approach is taken by California in its enactment of the Solar Shade Control Act.[111] Rather than using solar easements to protect a solar system's access to the sun, the statute allows the solar system owner to sue a neighboring property owner in tort by declaring any tree or shrub that shades more than 10 percent of any solar device a private nuisance.[112] The statute exempts any trees or shrubs planted before the installation of the solar system, even if such plant or shrub eventually grows to cover the solar panels.[113]

Effect of Solar Installations on Water Resources

One additional consideration when developing a CSP facility is the significant amount of water that is required to operate a CSP plant. Since sites most attractive for solar plants are also often in the hottest and driest parts of the country, the availability of water, or lack thereof, can be a major hurdle in the development of a CSP plant. As discussed earlier in the chapter, CSP technology uses solar radiation to heat a transfer medium in order to generate steam to spin a turbine. While some water is consumed during the steaming process, the majority of water is consumed during the cooling process.[114] By comparison, a typical CSP plant consumes approximately 800 gallons per MWh of electricity generated, whereas a typical nuclear plant consumes approximately 500 gallons of water per MWh of electricity generated.[115] Although technology exists to cool the system without water, it is not often utilized since it is less efficient and requires more energy.[116]

There is clearly tension between the benefits of solar energy and the need to conserve water in the regions where the solar energy is being generated.[117] This tension was documented in a report issued in May 2010 by Senator Jon Kyl of Arizona, which discusses the harmful impact of CSP projects on Arizona's limited water supply.[118] The report criticizes solar developers for being too focused "on securing access to greater supplies of water rather than looking at more water-efficient ways to produce energy" and even goes as far as stating that "it is not in the public interest for the state to approve, or . . . encourage, solar thermal power plants when Arizona's water supplies are so constrained. . . ."[119] The water usage issue for CSP plants is a significant one; therefore, CSP developers should carefully consider and research local water laws and restrictions, permitting and environmental review requirements, and availability of local water resources early in the development process.

Construction and Installation

The installation of a solar energy system, whether on a roof or on the ground, requires engineering expertise that incorporates structural and electrical design and engineering aspects. The designers of the solar energy system must weigh a number of factors including, for example, the energy needs of the purchaser, weather patterns in the region, structural integrity of the building, the angle and elevation of the sun, present or anticipated obstructions to sunlight, and access and security to the solar system.

The development of any solar energy system requires several elements: design and engineering of the system, procurement of the equipment, and construction and installation of the solar system. These services are typically covered in one agreement referred to as an Engineering, Procurement and Construction Agreement, or EPC Agreement (sometimes also referred to as an Installation Agreement). The EPC Agreement will govern all aspects related to the design and installation of the solar system, and for large facilities can be a heavily negotiated document (unless the contractor is a subsidiary of the developer). Typical provisions in an EPC Agreement include: responsibilities of the developer and contractor; pricing and terms of payment; commencement of work and progress report requirements; insurance requirements; inspection and testing; changes in work; damages; and warranties concerning the installed system.

Properly defining the contractor's scope of work in the EPC Agreement is critical for the developer so that the solar system delivered by the contractor is the one that is expected by the developer and its investors. Scope of work provisions should describe in detail the actual design, engineering, and construction obligations of the contractor, including the system's performance and design specifications. Other services that the parties may want to include in the definition of scope of work are management of suppliers and subcontractors, site security during installation, testing and inspection of solar equipment, site restoration after completion of installation, and obtaining necessary permits and approvals. Typically, the contractor is also required to prepare an operations and maintenance manual for the system, which describes the proper operations and maintenance procedures that should be taken during the useful life of the solar system.

Other provisions in the EPC Agreement that are negotiated between the developer and contractor include, among others: delay damages and liquidated damages for failure to meet certain construction milestones, limitation of the contractor's liability, allocation of the change-in-law risk, performance and payment bonds, insurance requirements, force majeure, and indemnification. Since many solar projects rely heavily on third-party financing, liquidated damages are typically subject to heavy negotiation between the developer and contractor. As with other typical service contracts, requiring the contractor to obtain a performance bond will protect the developer in the event that the contractor fails to perform is obligations under the EPC Agreement. Likewise, payment bonds protect certain subcontractors and suppliers against nonpayment. Because of the emerging nature of solar technology, developers should require the contractor to provide an intellectual property indemnity in addition to the mutual indemnities that are typically given. Solar equipment is constantly evolving, and it should be the contractor's responsibility to ensure that their work and use of certain equipment does not infringe against a third party's intellectual property right.

Another important aspect of the EPC Agreement is the system warranty provided by the contractor upon completion of the installation. The contractor will typically warrant that the installed system (1) will be free from defect in materials and workmanship; (2) complies with requirements of applicable laws and regulations; and (3) conforms to all previously approved design and engineering specifications. Issues that may arise during the negotiation of the system warranty include term of the warranty and the definition of defect and limitations on the warranty. The contractor warranty period for EPC Agreements will vary depending on the type of technology being installed; however, once the system warranty expires, the developer may still have recourse through the equipment's original manufacturer's warranty.

In the event that the solar system is financed, the financing party will commonly ask to review the EPC Agreement as part of their due diligence process in order to ensure that their interests would be protected in the event that the developer defaults. Once the system is completed, the developer will often enter into a separate agreement governing the operations and maintenance of the system. The operations and maintenance agreement, or O&M Agreement, will ensure that the equipment is operated and maintained in accordance with industry standards and manufacturers' recommendations to guarantee optimal energy generation through the life of the system. The operations and maintenance of the solar system are discussed in further detail below.

Power Purchase Agreements

The power purchase agreement (PPA) is the agreement between an electricity generator and a power purchaser (sometimes referred to as the "host" in distributed generation facilities) setting forth the obligations of the electricity generator to deliver power to a specified point and of the power purchaser to buy the power, and the price the purchaser will pay for the power. Typical provisions negotiated between the parties in a PPA include billing and payment, operation and maintenance of the system, allocation of environmental attributes, interconnection, access rights, scheduled outages, assignment rights, force majeure provisions, and purchase options. The solar developer will typically be required to satisfy a number of requirements before it is able to enter into a PPA or be bound by such PPA, including obtaining interconnection approval from the local utility; obtaining adequate financing to develop the solar system; obtaining consent from the purchaser's landlord to install a solar system on the premises, which will typically include an acknowledgment that the solar system is the property of the developer and may be subject to a security interest of a lender or investor; and obtaining preliminary approval for the application of certain state or local subsidies in connection with the solar system.

A purchaser may elect to enter into a PPA as opposed to purchasing energy from their local utility through conventional means because the purchaser is able to receive stable, renewable energy from the solar system (and occasionally at a discount), while the responsibility of operating the solar system is passed on to a third party. The revenue stream in the PPA from the purchaser is a key asset in the solar project and an important element to obtaining project financing. As a result, the creditworthiness of the purchaser will play a crucial factor during an investor's or lender's risk analysis and ultimately their decision to invest money in the solar project. This section provides a brief summary on the critical elements to look for when negotiating a PPA. Although there are many similarities between negotiating a renewable energy PPA and a traditional PPA, renewable energy generation is typically intermittent and somewhat unpredictable and generally unable to be adjusted based on the power purchaser's needs. As a result, a renewable energy PPA should be negotiated accordingly.

Payment Structures

In the majority of cases, the power purchaser will agree to purchase all electricity generated by the system. The PPA will provide an electricity rate that the power purchaser will pay for each kilowatt-hour of energy generated by the system. Several pricing structures can be used in the PPA. The electricity rate can be fixed throughout the entire term of the PPA, increase based on an annual escalator, fluctuate based on utility rates, or be renegotiated by the parties at certain intervals during the PPA. Rarely, a capacity payment structure may be employed. Each structure has its own advantages and disadvantages, and each party will need to determine how much risk it is willing to take when negotiating the pricing terms. In instances in which the purchaser's energy needs are disproportionate to the size of the system, or if the purchaser's energy needs are seasonal, the parties may want to limit the power purchase requirement as applicable.

Term

The term of a PPA typically begins on the "commercial operation date," which is the day the installation of the solar energy system is completed, all permits and approvals have been obtained, all testing and inspection have been completed, and the system is capable of delivering electricity to the power purchaser. Typical distributed generation PPAs range anywhere from ten to twenty years, while utility-scale PPAs have longer terms ranging from twenty to thirty.[120] At the end of the PPA term, the PPA will provide three options to the parties: (1) the developer removes the system from the site, (2) the PPA is renewed or extended, or (3) the power purchaser purchases the system from the developer. A more detailed discussion on the power purchaser's purchase option can be found below.

Allocation of Environmental Attributes

As discussed above, the generation of renewable energy also creates other valuable intangible attributes in the form of RECs or carbon credits. Such environmental attributes may be sold to the purchaser bundled with the energy or may be kept by the solar developer and sold separately. When negotiating the environmental attributes provision of the PPA, it is important that the definition of environmental attributes used in the PPA be sufficient to cover all possible environmental attributes that may be associated with the solar energy system.[121] Tax benefits are typically excluded in such definitions.

Relocation

In smaller distributed generation systems, the purchaser is typically given the right to relocate the solar energy system to a substitute site so long as such a move would not materially alter the financial aspects of the PPA. For example, the substitute location would need to (i) be within the same utility, or with another utility that has similar utility rates; (ii) have similar solar insolation (i.e., the amount of solar radiation received) as the original location so that the system will generate a similar amount of solar energy; and (iii) retain similar benefits from the environmental attributes and environmental financial incentives that the original location enjoyed. The power purchaser may choose to exercise those rights in the event it ceases the operation of its business or sells its business on the site where the PV system is located and would therefore no longer have a need to purchase electricity.

Early Termination

Many PPAs allow for early termination in case of a default by the other party. Any failure by either party to perform its obligations under the PPA or declaration of bankruptcy by either party would be an event of default that would give rise to the other party's right to early termination. If the power provider defaults and the power purchaser is permitted to terminate the PPA early, the provider may be required to pay for the difference in energy costs incurred by the purchaser as a result of the PPA termination. If the purchaser defaults, the provider may be entitled to receive a termination payment from the purchaser. The termination payment is typically calculated when the PPA is entered into and is equal to the provider's expected income from the PPA (and may include lost tax benefits to the provider or its financing partners). In either event, the solar system would be returned to the provider since they are the system owner.

Certain events outside the control of either party may also give rise to one or both parties' right to early termination of the PPA. One example is a change in law that would affect the right of the power provider to obtain certain financial incentives or tax benefits, which has a materially adverse economic impact on the developer or the finances of the solar system. Since such an event is outside the control of the power purchaser, it should not be required to pay termination value for the system and will simply be relieved of its obligations under the PPA. Other events that may result in an early termination of a PPA include force majeure; change in solar insolation with respect to the area that the solar system is located; change in law that would subject energy pricing to federal or state regulation; or a casualty event that would take an extended time to repair (usually one year).

Purchase Options

Most PPAs provide that a power purchaser has an option to purchase the solar facility at certain points during the term of the PPA. Several considerations must be weighed by the solar developer when negotiating when to grant such purchase options to the power purchaser. Particularly if the solar system is eligible for the investment tax credit, if it is purchased too early in the PPA term, certain tax benefits received by the solar developer (or its financing partners) may be subject to recapture or the solar developer may not have had sufficient time to realize its expected returns. Although a purchase option is usually given at the end of the PPA term, the parties may agree to periodic purchase options after the fifth anniversary of the placed-in-service date. So as not to cause the PPA to be deemed a sale of the facility by taxing authorities, the parties should not provide for bargain purchase options at the end of the term.

Tax Issues

The key tax issues that arise in solar installations, including the numerous available tax incentives, are discussed in detail in chapter 7.

Operations and Maintenance

Almost all solar PPAs will include provisions requiring the solar developer to operate and maintain (also referred to as "O&M") the solar system in accordance with the manufacturer's requirements and prudent solar industry practices. Those duties would include, among others, regular inspection of the equipment (including any metering equipment), module cleaning and repair, and conducting scheduled maintenance of the solar system. Conducting regular preventative maintenance can significantly increase the productivity and extend the life of the solar energy system. Most solar developers subcontract this obligation to an outside contractor or a subsidiary. The agreement that governs the relationship between the solar developer and the O&M contractor is referred to as the Operations and Maintenance Agreement. If the developer chooses to subcontract this responsibility to an outside contractor, the PPA should require that the third-party contractor maintain similar levels of insurance as required of the developer.

The equipment used in the solar energy system typically also comes with a limited manufacturer's warranty that will guarantee the equipment against defects in materials and workmanship for a certain period of time. In addition, PV module warranties will most likely provide a two-tier power output warranty. Typically, the output warranties warrant that the PV modules will provide a power output of at least 90 percent or better of the module's specified power rating for a period of ten years, and at least 80 percent or better for a period of twenty-five years. Since the system will be located on the premises that the power purchaser owns or leases, the PPA will also need to include provisions that provide access rights for the O&M personnel and security personnel.

Force Majeure

All PPAs will include provisions relating to a force majeure event. Should a force majeure occur, the affected party will be excused from performance of its obligations under the PPA to the extent the force majeure event has interfered with such performance. The inability to obtain the governmental approval necessary to enable the parties to fulfill their obligations in accordance with the PPA is often a negotiated point between the solar developer and power purchaser. A prolonged force majeure event will typically give rise to the right for either party to terminate the agreement. It is important to note that a party's inability to make payments under the PPA should not be included as a force majeure event.

Assignment

Since the revenue stream in the PPA is a key factor in financing a solar deal, investors and lenders will conduct a thorough evaluation of the purchaser's creditworthiness before investing or lending money to a particular project. In most cases, the purchaser is permitted to assign the PPA to an affiliate or to a third party with similar creditworthiness only with the consent of the developer.

Conversely, the developer is typically permitted to assign its rights to payments under the PPA without any consent rights by the purchaser upon written notice by the developer. Additionally, with respect to the collateral assignment of the PPA to the lender, to the extent it is not provided for in the PPA, lenders will request that the purchaser provide lender accommodations or an acknowledgment from the purchaser of such collateral assignment, including the right of the lender to step in and cure during a default by the developer.

Permitting and Insurance

It will be the solar developer's responsibility to obtain any necessary permits or government approvals related to the operation of the solar system. Since most permits and approvals require information from the power purchaser, particularly with on-site PV systems, the PPA should require the purchaser to provide assistance, as required, in obtaining such approvals.

The PPA will generally require the solar developer to obtain and maintain adequate property and casualty insurance as required by applicable law and sufficient to cover any losses that may arise out of damages to the solar energy system for affected property. Due to the fact that any damage to the solar system affects the ability of the system to produce energy, and inevitably the financeability of the PPA, obtaining sufficient insurance is a crucial component to protect both parties as well as lenders.

In the event the solar energy system is financed, lenders (and any owner trustee) will want to be included as additional insureds and loss payees for any insurance policy and may require a lender's loss payable endorsement. The loss payee will receive any proceeds from an insurance loss.[122] If the solar energy project is financed through a sale-leaseback transaction (as described below), where there is no recourse beyond the special purpose entity created to run the solar energy system, it is also common for the lessor to require the developer to obtain sufficient business interruption coverage to cover any unscheduled outages and to ensure that the lessee has sufficient funds to pay any rent owed under the lease.

PPAs are also discussed in chapter 9.

Partnership versus Lease

Basic Structures

Similar to other renewable energy projects, solar power projects are driven by a number of unique energy pricing, policy, and tax considerations. Significant advances in solar energy technology over the last twenty-five years have resulted in reductions in the cost of energy at productive solar sites. When tax credits are taken into account, the pricing for solar power financing compares favorably with natural gas, particularly during times when natural gas prices are high.

As also discussed in chapter 7, two popular financing techniques are used to finance renewable energy projects, a sale-leaseback structure, and a partnership "flip" structure. A sale-lease back structure involves the developer selling a project to a bank or a tax equity investor, which leases the project back to the developer under a long-term net lease. This financing structure is popular for solar projects since the 30 percent ITC is available to the owner of a facility even if the owner is not producing electricity.[123] In a partnership "flip" structure, the developer and one or more tax equity investors form a tax partnership in which the tax equity investor is allocated the majority of the cash and tax benefits before the flip point. This financing structure is predominantly found in wind projects eligible for the PTC. Below are more complete descriptions of both the sale-leaseback structure and the partnership "flip" structure.

Because the ITC is available to the owner of a solar facility whether the owner produces electricity (as discussed above) or not, traditional secured financing techniques, including leasing, can be used to finance solar projects. Typically, the type of financing used with a solar project involves project finance, meaning a long-term investment in which liability for the investment does not go beyond the project company. In these structures, a project company is set up as a subsidiary of an operating development company to collect revenues under the PPA with recourse limited to such project company and its revenues.

Commercial Risks to Investor

An equity investment in a solar power project, whether structured as a direct investment or as a lease, carries with it certain identifiable commercial risks. Such risks include operational risk, electricity transmission risk, and power purchase agreement risk, as well as credit risk of other participants, asset warranty risk, and asset residual value risk.

Solar plants generally have much lower environmental risks and impacts and require less maintenance than conventional power plants and other renewable sources such as wind. A performance study may be useful to quantify typical risks such as shading, dust, conversion losses, and annual standard deviations in sunlight. Operational risks and costs may be further managed by an experienced operator, the use of trusted technologies, and a modular design that allows some portion of the facility to be operational, even while other parts may be down.

In addition to the value of the solar equipment itself, the key asset in the investment is the revenue stream under the PPA. In a lease structure, the lessor would look to the credit of the power purchaser under the PPA in addition to the credit of the lessee. Likewise, in a partnership structure, both the sponsor and power-purchaser credit are relevant. In the event of a default by the provider, the PPA may have termination provisions that would require an investor to consider certain step-in rights to prevent such a termination. The PPA normally would not require payment unless energy has been delivered. Furthermore, interconnection issues should be identified. As a practical matter, the risk of nonpayment resulting from failure to deliver power is mitigated by the fact that solar projects typically have less downtime and fewer maintenance issues than conventional power generation facilities due to the nature of the equipment.

Financiers should negotiate for full inspection rights and rights to receive the reports under the PPA and other agreements. Refer to the discussion above on PPAs for a more in-depth look into the material provisions of a PPA.

Sale-Leaseback

Because the 30 percent ITC is available to the owner of a facility whether or not the owner produces electricity, traditional secured financing techniques, including leasing, can be used to finance qualifying projects.[124] Pursuant to the American Recovery and Reinvestment Act, signed by President Obama on February 17, 2009, qualifying projects include solar and fuel cell projects placed in service by 2016, and wind, biomass, geothermal, hydroelectric, and marine energy projects where an election is made to claim the ITC instead of the PTC and the project is placed in service after 2008 and by 2012 (for wind) or 2013 (for other qualifying assets).[125]

Under a sale-leaseback structure, a developer and operator of solar assets constructs and agrees to operate a solar facility and agrees to sell the electricity produced to a utility or to a business or institution on whose property the solar project is built (e.g., a retail "big box" store or a school) under a long-term PPA. The PPA would require the store or the school (the power purchaser) to buy all of the power produced, generally at a fixed price, thereby ensuring a stream of revenue over the term of the PPA.

The developer sells the solar property to a bank or a tax equity investor (the lessor) which leases the property back to the developer (the lessee) under a long-term net lease. A lessor investor may also enter into a direct lease, where the lessee is the direct user of the solar property (subject to certain limitations noted earlier in this chapter). A net lease (sometimes referred to as a "hell or high water" lease) is one where the lessee is responsible for all the risks that are related to the ownership and maintenance of the asset—in this case the solar equipment—while the lessor's only responsibility is to provide the asset free of interference from third parties it controls.[126] The "hell or high water" reference derives from the lessee's obligation to perform its duties under the lease "come hell or high water."[127] When a lease agreement is being drafted, many issues are negotiated between the parties, including, among others, the term of the lease; the lessee's option to purchase the equipment at the end of the term; the lessee's option for an early buyout; the lessee's renewal options; termination provisions; risk allocation; third-party liability; tax liability; and events of default.[128]

In structuring the lease, the bank or tax equity investor (the lessor investor) will often establish a trust to take legal title to the property for the benefit of the lessor (in effect, making the trust the lessor in the lease). By establishing a trust, the lessor investor obtains several benefits, namely: "(a) ease of handling money; (b) ease of transferability of equity interest . . . (c) protection of the [investor] from third party liability; (d) protection of the lessee . . . from consequences of an [investor] bankruptcy; and (e) avoidance of the necessity for the [investor] to qualify as a foreign corporation . . . in the jurisdiction in which the asset is located."[129] As a general rule, the lease cannot run longer than 80 percent of the expected life and value of the project.

The developer-lessee shares in the ITC and depreciation tax benefits through reduced rents. To secure its rent payment obligations, the lessee grants to the lessor a collateral assignment of the PPA and other revenues (such as funds from the sale of RECs). To qualify for the ITC, the sale-leaseback transaction must be completed within three months after the project is placed in service.

Since the lessor is relying on the revenues generated through the solar system, in addition to financial incentives and tax credits, to satisfy the lease rent payments, it is important that the lessor ensure that the lessee has not entered into additional arrangements with other parties who would receive the benefit of the revenues generated by the solar system. By requiring the lessee to establish a special-purpose entity whose operations are limited to the acquisition and financing of the specific solar project, the lessor can minimize the potential risk of the lessee engaging in other activities that may put the project revenues at risk. Furthermore, the lessor should conduct additional due diligence to ensure that it (or the special-purpose entity) will be the beneficiary of all revenues generated by the system, including REC sales, federal, state, or local subsidies, PPA payments, and insurance proceeds.

If the developer-lessee wants to continue using the project after the lease ends, then it must either negotiate an extension at then-current market rent or buy the project at fair market value. From the tax equity–lessor's perspective, the residual value of the property at the end of the lease term, combined with the rents, the ITC, and the tax depreciation deductions, will generate a target after-tax yield to the lessor. The transaction can be structured to also generate a positive pretax yield and cash-on-cash return without regard to tax benefits.

The main advantage of a sale-leaseback is it provides 100 percent financing. The lessor investor pays the full market value for the project at the time it is placed in service. The downside of entering into a sale-leaseback versus a partnership flip is that it costs more for the developer to retake possession of the project. After the lease ends, the developer can only continue using the project by purchasing it from the investor for fair market value. Another advantage of the sale-leaseback is that it divorces project ownership from project operations, and largely insulates the investor from operational risk.

Partnership "Flip" Structure

The partnership structure maximizes the tax benefits by using the partnership tax rules to allocate the tax benefits to tax equity investors. The developer and the equity investor form a partnership or limited liability company (a project company) that owns the project. Partnerships and limited liability companies are "pass-through" entities for tax purposes (rather than separate taxable entities), so the members of the partnership are treated as the owners of the project. The construction of the project is financed by funding commitments from the developer (and/or third-party construction period debt providers). Once the project is placed in service, the tax equity contribution repays all or a portion of the construction period financing.

The partnership agreement allocates between the parties taxable income or loss and cash distributions in a manner designed to optimize the after-tax economics. Once the project is placed in service and the tax equity has funded its contribution pursuant to Department of Treasury Rev. Proc. 2007-65,[130] up to 99 percent of the tax benefits and cash flow are allocated to the tax equity investor. Rev. Proc. 2007-65 provides certain acceptable parameters with respect to the production tax credit in the context of wind energy partnerships. Although not technically applicable to solar power projects involving the ITC or cash grant, the standards prescribed in Rev. Proc. 2007-65 should likewise apply to partnership flip structures used for solar transactions. Those allocations remain in place until the tax equity investor has achieved an agreed yield on its investment (generally this occurs when most of the tax benefits have been accrued). At that point, the allocations "flip," with the developer taking up to 95 percent of the cash and tax attributes. The developer then has a fair market value option to buy out the tax equity's remaining 5 percent interest in the project.

Unlike the sale-leaseback structure, where the back-end residual in the project can be retained by the tax equity, the "flip" structure reserves to the developer the upside potential and downside risk in the residual. By the same token, the developer's return on its investment is delayed and more dependent on the residual in the partnership, whereas in the sale-leaseback, the developer may realize an up-front profit on the sale of the project to the tax equity (and that sale steps up the basis of the project in the hands of the tax equity for ITC and depreciation purposes).

Notes

1. The photovoltaic effect was first discovered in the late 1800s by the French scientist, Henri Bacquerel. *See* SOLAR ENERGY INDUS. ASS'N, ABOUT SOLAR ENERGY, http://www.seia .org/cs/about_solar_energy/history (last visited Aug. 13, 2010).

2. The American Recovery and Reinvestment Act of 2009 has awarded over $16.8 billion to the U.S. Department of Energy Efficiency and Renewable Energy for its programs and initiatives. U.S. Dept. of Energy Office of Energy Efficiency & Renewable Energy, http://www.eere .energy.gov/recovery/ (last visited August 13, 2010).

3. U.S. ENERGY INFO. ADMIN., INTERNATIONAL ENERGY OUTLOOK 2010, http://www.eia .doe.gov/oiaf/ieo/electricity.html (last visited Feb. 28, 2011).

4. U.S. DEP'T OF ENERGY, OFFICE OF ENERGY EFFICIENCY & RENEWABLE ENERGY, 2008 RENEWABLE ENERGY DATA BOOK 66 (Michelle Kubik ed., 2009) [hereinafter 2008 Renewable Energy Data Book], http://www.nrel.gov/docs/fy09osti/45654.pdf (the report indicates that at the end of 2008, there was approximately 1,106 MWs of PV capacity and 419 MWs of concentrated solar capacity in the United States).

5. U.S. ENERGY INFO. ADMIN., HOW MUCH OF OUR ELECTRICITY IS GENERATED FROM RENEWABLE SOURCES (Dec. 8, 2009, last updated Sept. 1, 2010), http://tonto.eia.doe.gov/ energy_in_brief/renewable_energy.cfm. From 2004 to 2007, the total investment made in the solar industry in the United States increased to approximately $3.2 billon from $215 million during the 2000 to 2004 period. CHARLES E. JENNINGS ET AL., NAT'L RENEWABLE ENERGY LAB., A HISTORICAL ANALYSIS OF INVESTMENT IN SOLAR ENERGY TECHNOLOGIES (2000–2007), TECHNICAL REPORT NREL/TP-6A2-43602 (Dec. 2008), *available at* http://www.nrel.gov/docs/ fy09osti/43602.pdf.

6. SOLAR ENERGY INDUS. ASS'N, SOLAR TECHNOLOGY & PRODUCTS (2009), *available at* http://www.seia.org/cs/solar_technology_and_products.

7. SOLAR ENERGY INDUS. ASS'N, CONCENTRATING SOLAR POWER: UTILITY-SCALE SOLUTIONS FOR POLLUTION-FREE ELECTRICITY 1 (2009), http://seia.org/galleries/pdf/factsheet_csp .pdf [hereinafter SEIA CSP].

8. *Id.*

9. *Id.*

10. *See* Ausra home page, http://www.ausra.com/ (last visited Aug. 13, 2010); *see also* Areva home page, http://www.areva.com/ (last visited Aug. 13, 2010).

11. SEIA CSP, *supra* note 7, at 10. *See also* SOLAR ENERGY INDUS. ASS'N, UTILITY-SCALE SOLAR PROJECTS IN THE UNITED STATES OPERATIONAL, UNDER CONSTRUCTION, AND UNDER DEVELOPMENT (2010, updated Feb. 8, 2011), *available at* http://www.seia.org/galleries/pdf/ Major%20Solar%20Projects.pdf.

12. Solar Energy Indus. Ass'n, Photovoltaic Solar Technology: Creating Electricity from Sunlight 1 (Feb. 4, 2010), *available at* http://www.seia.org/galleries/pdf/SEIA_PV_Factsheet.pdf.

13. Silicon is a primary solar cell semiconductor material and comes in crystalline, multicrystalline, and amorphous forms. U.S. Dep't of Energy, Office of Energy Efficiency and Renewable Energy, Energy Basics: Photovoltaic Cell Materials, http://www.eere.energy.gov/basics/renewable_energy/pv_cell_materials.html.

14. Polycrystalline thin film includes specific discussion of copper indium diselenide, cadmium telluride, and thin-film silicon. *Id.*

15. Single-crystalline thin film includes material such as gallium arsenide. *Id.*

16. *Id.*

17. Solar Energy Indus. Ass'n, U.S. Solar Industry Year in Review 2008, at 11 (2009), *available at* http://www.seia.org/galleries/pdf/2008_Year_in_Review-small.pdf [hereinafter SEIA 2008 Review]. According to a report issued by the Solar Energy Industries Association, photovoltaic and concentrated solar power represents 1,547 megawatts of capacity, while solar thermal power represents 7,636 megawatts of capacity. *Id.*

18. *Id.* at 3–4. In 2008, PV installations in California represented 62 percent of the market share, with New Jersey coming in second at 8 percent of the market share. *Id.*

19. *Id.*

20. *See id.* at 10.

21. 2008 Renewable Energy Data Book, *supra* note 4, at 66.

22. *Id.* at 65.

23. American Recovery and Reinvestment Act of 2009, Pub. L. No. 111-5, 123 Stat. 140 (2009).

24. 26 U.S.C. § 48(a)(3)(2009).

25. 26 U.S.C. §§ 167, 168.

26. 26 U.S.C. § 50(c).

27. AARA, § 1603.

28. *Id.* at § 1603(b).

29. *Id.* at § 1603(a). Projects that are owned wholly or partly by government agencies, municipal utilities, electric cooperatives, or other tax-exempt entities (so-called "disqualified persons") are not eligible for the cash grant option. *Id.* at § 1603(g). In addition, partnerships in which a disqualified person owns an interest, regardless of how small or remote, are not eligible for the grant. *Id.* The original deadlines, which were set to expire on December 31, 2010, were extended by one year, through December 31, 2011, by the Tax Relief, Unemployment Insurance Reauthorization, and Job Creation Act of 2010 (the Tax Relief Act), signed into law by President Obama on December 17, 2010. Tax Relief Act, § 707, Pub. L. No. 111-312.

30. U.S. Dep't of Treasury, 1603 Program: Payments for Specified Energy Property in Lieu of Tax Credits (2010), http://www.ustreas.gov/recovery/1603.shtml [hereinafter 1603 Guidance].

31. *Id.*

32. *Id.*

33. *Id.*

34. ARRA, § 1603(d).

35. *Id.*

36. 1603 Guidance, *supra* note 30, at 3. The application form requires, among other items, the applicant's Data Universal Numbering System (DUNS) number from Dun and Bradstreet. If an applicant does not already have a DUNS number, it must request one by calling 1-866-705-5711. Applicants are also required to register with the Central Contractor Registration (CCR) by going to www.ccr.gov/startregistration.aspx. *Id.* at 4.

37. Examples of the pertinent documentation include (1) final engineering design documents; (2) a commissioning report from the project engineer, equipment vendor, or the third party that has installed and tested the equipment; and (3) an interconnection agreement. Documentation must also be submitted to support the cost basis of the property. For properties with a cost basis in excess of $500,000, an independent accountant's certification regarding the accuracy of the claimed cost basis must also be submitted. *Id.* at 17.

38. 1603 Guidance, *supra* note 30.

39. Examples of various state incentive programs include: Go Solar California (http://www.gosolarcalifornia.org/), New Jersey Renewable Energy Incentive Program (http://www.njcleanenergy.com/), Connecticut Clean Energy Fund (http://www.ctcleanenergy.com/).

40. RECs are typically traded via a registry or regional tracking system that provides a reliable and transparent method to track and certify REC ownership. Although several regional tracking systems are operational and active, there is currently no national registry of RECs. Three established regional systems include (1) the Western Renewable Energy Generation Information System (http://www.wregis.org/); (2) NEPOOL Generation Information System (http://www.nepoolgis.com/); and (3) PJM Environmental Information Services' Generation Attribute Tracking System (http://www.pjm-eis.com/).

41. A megawatt-hour is a commonly used term when describing how much energy a solar system produces. One megawatt-hour means one megawatt of electricity is supplied for a period of one hour.

42. In certain jurisdictions, the state's RPS requires that the renewable energy generation goals be met through "bundled" transactions in which both the RECs from an eligible renewable facility and associated energy are acquired together by the utility.

43. *See, e.g.*, 4 COLO. CODE REGS. § 723-3, Rule 3659 (2010) (RECs shall be used for a single purpose only, and shall expire or be retired upon use for that purpose).

44. *See* 16 C.F.R. pt. 260 (2009).

45. NAT'L ASS'N OF ATTORNEYS GEN., ENVIRONMENTAL MARKETING GUIDELINES FOR ELECTRICITY (Dec. 1999) [hereinafter NAAG Guidelines].

46. *See* 16 C.F.R. pt. 260; *see* 15 U.S.C. §§ 41–58 (2009).

47. 15 U.S.C. § 45.

48. *See* Guides for the Use of Environmental Marketing Claims, FTC File No. P954501 (proposed Oct. 6, 2010), http://www.ftc.gov/os/fedreg/2010/october/101006greenguidesfrn.pdf.

49. *Id.* at 164.

50. *Id.* at 165.

51. *Id.* at 166.

52. Frito-Lay has purchased enough RECs through the voluntary market to advertise their SunChips® brand as "made with the help of solar energy." SunChips, *Healthier Planet*, http://www.sunchips.com/healthier_planet.shtml (last visited Aug. 13, 2010).

53. Examples of states with solar carve-outs in their RPS programs include New Jersey, Massachusetts, Maryland, and Oregon. *See generally* N.J. STAT. §§ 48:3–49 et seq. (2009); MASS. GEN LAWS ch. 25A, § 11F (2008); MD. CODE ANN., Pub. Util. Cos. § 7-701 et seq (2010); OR. REV. STAT. § 469A.

54. U.S. Const. art. I, § 8, cl. 3.

55. Hughes v. Oklahoma, 441 U.S. 322, 326 (1979); Dean Milk Co. v. City of Madison, 340 U.S. 349 (1951).

56. 502 U.S. 437, 454–55 (1992).

57. Wyoming v. Oklahoma, 502 U.S. 437, 454 (1992) (citations omitted).

58. 397 U.S. 137 (1970).

59. Pike v. Bruce Church Inc., 397 U.S. at 142 (citing Huron Cement Co. v. Detroit, 362 U.S. 440, 443 (1960)).

60. *Id.*

61. Complaint, TransCanada Power Mktg, Ltd. v. Bowles, No. 2010cv40070 (D. Mass. Apr. 16, 2010).

62. *Id.*

63. Order Adopting Emergency Regulations, Mass. Dep't of Pub. Utils., D.P.U. 10-58 (June 9, 2010), *available at* http://www.env.state.ma.us/dpu/docs/electric/10-58/6910dpuord.pdf [hereinafter June 9, 2010, Order].

64. 2008 Mass. Acts. ch. 169, § 83.

65. June 9, 2010, Order, *supra* note 63, at 5.

66. *See* Partial Settlement Agreement, ¶ 8, *available at* http://www.mass.gov/Eoeea/docs/doer/renewables/solar/Settlement-Agreement.pdf.

67. In 2010, the Class I alternative compliance rate was $60.93 and the Solar Carve-Out alternative compliance rate was $600.00. DATABASE OF STATE INCENTIVES FOR RENEWABLES & EFFICIENCY, MASSACHUSETTS INCENTIVES/POLICIES FOR RENEWABLES & EFFICIENCY, RENEWABLE Portfolio Standard (June 11, 2010, revised Feb. 2, 2011), *available at* http://www.dsire usa.org/incentives/incentive.cfm?Incentive_Code=MA05R&re=1&ee=1.

68. U.C.C. § 9-102 (2010), official cmts. § 9-102 5(i).

69. *Id.* at § 9-102 5(d).

70. *Id.* at § 9-102(a)(2).

71. UCC § 9-501.

72. 42 U.S.C. §§ 16,511–16,514 (2006); ARRA, H.R. 1-20, Title IV (2009). The original legislation was amended by the ARRA to § 1705, which allows certain projects that commence construction no later than September 30, 2011, to participate in the program. Qualifying projects under § 1705 include: (1) renewable energy systems, including incremental hydropower, that generate electricity or thermal energy, and facilities that manufacture related components; (2) electric power transmission systems, including upgrading and reconductoring projects; and (3) leading edge biofuel projects that will use technologies performing at the pilot or demonstration scale that the Secretary determines are likely to become commercial technologies and will produce transportation fuels that substantially reduce life-cycle greenhouse gas emissions compared to other transportation fuels. *Id.* The ARRA appropriated approximately $6 billion to pay the costs of the guarantees made under § 1705.

73. *Id.*

74. Loan Guarantees for Projects that Employ Innovative Technologies; Guidelines for Proposals Submitted in Response to the First Solicitation, 71 Fed. Reg. 156, 46,451 (Aug. 14, 2006).

75. Energy Policy Act, Pub. L. No. 109-58, 119 Stat. 594 (2005) (the Energy Policy Act of 2005 was passed by Congress on July 29, 2005, and signed into law by President George W. Bush on August 8, 2005).

76. ARRA, § 1111.

77. 26 U.S.C. § 54(f).

78. Press Release, Internal Revenue Service, IRS Announces New Clean Renewable Energy Bonds Allocations (Oct. 27, 2009), http://www.irs.gov/taxexemptbond/article/0,,id=214748,00 .html (last visited Aug. 13, 2010).

79. FED. ENERGY REGULATORY COMM'N, WHAT FERC DOES (2009), http://www.ferc.gov/ about/ferc-does.asp.

80. We note that the Electric Reliability Council of Texas (ERCOT) is generally not subject to the jurisdiction of FERC. Jared M. Fleisher, *ERCOT's Jurisdictional Status: A Legal History and Contemporary Appraisal*, 3 TEX. J. OIL, GAS & ENERGY 6 (2008).

81. Declaratory Order, Fed. Energy Regulatory Comm'n, Docket No. EL09-31-000 (Nov. 19, 2009), http://www.ferc.gov/whats-new/comm-meet/2009/111909/E-29.pdf. In its petition, SunEdison argued that there is no sale of electric energy at wholesale in interstate commerce for the purposes of § 201 of the Federal Power Act because its power sales agreements require that each of SunEdison's on-site end-use customers purchase 100 percent of the electrical output of a SunEdison Retail Operations facility. *Id.*

82. FERC clarified on November 19, 2009, that only if the end-use customer participating in the net metering program produces more energy than it needs over the applicable billing period, and thus is considered to have made a net sale of energy to a utility over the applicable billing period, does the Commission assert jurisdiction. *See id.*

83. FED. ENERGY REGULATORY COMM'N, WHAT IS A QUALIFYING FACILITY?, http://www .ferc.gov/industries/electric/gen-info/qual-fac/what-is.asp. On March 19, 2010, FERC issued an order that exempted QFs with a net power production capacity of less than 1 MW from the requirement to self-certify or request FERC certification of QF status. 130 F.E.R.C. ¶ 61,214 (Mar. 19, 2010), *available at* http://www.ferc.gov/whats-new/comm-meet/2010/031810/E-31 .pdf.

84. FED. ENERGY REGULATORY COMM'N, WHAT ARE THE BENEFITS OF QF STATUS? (2010), http://www.ferc.gov/industries/electric/gen-info/qual-fac/benefits.asp.

85. FED. ENERGY REGULATORY COMM'N, WHAT IS A QUALIFYING FACILITY? (2010), http://www.ferc.gov/industries/electric/gen-info/qual-fac/what-is.asp.

86. *Id.*

87. *Id.*

88. FED. ENERGY REGULATORY COMM'N, HOW TO OBTAIN QF STATUS FOR YOUR FACILITIES (2010), http://www.ferc.gov/industries/electric/gen-info/qual-fac/obtain.asp.

89. *Id.*

90. FED. ENERGY REGULATORY COMM'N, SELF-CERTIFICATION (2010), http://www.ferc.gov/industries/electric/gen-info/qual-fac/self-cert.asp.

91. Order No. 732 Final Rule, Fed. Energy Regulatory Comm'n, Docket No. RM09-23-000 (Mar. 19, 2010). Other revisions made in the final rule include, providing "that an applicant seeking to certify qualifying facility status of a small power production or cogeneration facility must complete, and electronically file, the Form No. 556 that is in effect at the time of filing. . . ." *Id.*

92. Declaratory Order, Fed. Energy Regulatory Comm'n, Docket No. EL09-31-000 (Nov. 19, 2010).

93. *Id.* at 8.

94. *Id.*

95. FERC has issued standard interconnection agreements and procedures for generators greater than 20 MW and less than 20 MW. FED. ENERGY REGULATORY COMM'N, GENERATOR INTERCONNECTION (2010), http://www.ferc.gov/industries/electric/indus-act/gi.asp.

96. 40 U.S.C. § 3142(a) (2009).

97. 40 U.S.C. § 3142(b) (2009). The wage rates can be found at www.wdol.gov.

98. ARRA, § 1606.

99. *E.g.*, ENVIRONMENTAL ASPECTS OF REAL ESTATE AND COMMERCIAL TRANSACTIONS (James B. Witkin ed., 4th ed. ABA 2011); BROWNFIELDS LAW AND PRACTICE: THE CLEANUP AND REDEVELOPMENT OF CONTAMINATED LAND (Michael B. Gerrard, ed., Matthew Bender LexisNexis 1998 & Supp. 2010).

100. U.S. DEP'T OF ENERGY, ENERGY EFFICIENCY & RENEWABLE ENERGY, BUILDING CODES, COVENANTS, AND REGULATIONS FOR SOLAR WATER HEATING SYSTEMS (2009), http://www.energysavers.gov/your_home/water_heating/index.cfm/mytopic=12920.

101. *Id.*

102. DATABASE OF STATE INCENTIVES FOR RENEWABLES & EFFICIENCY, DIRECT CASH INCENTIVES, http://www.dsireusa.org/solar/solarpolicyguide/?id=10 (last visited Aug. 13, 2010).

103. N.M. STAT. § 47-3-1 (1978).

104. The statute follows a prior appropriation doctrine that was originally used by western states to govern access to water rights. Wyoming v. Colorado, 259 U.S. 419 (1922). This doctrine allows the first person to use a quantity of water source for a valuable purpose to continue using that quantity of water for that purpose. Subsequent users could draw from the same water source provided they do not impede on the first user's established rights. *Id.*

105. *See generally* N.M. STAT. § 47-3-2.

106. *Id.* at § 47-3-11.

107. *Id.* at § 47-3-9.

108. IOWA CODE ANN. § 562A.5 (1992).

109. *Id.* at § 562A.4. The application requires, among other items, a legal description of the two properties, proposed easement areas, and proposed location of the solar equipment. *Id.*

110. *Id.*

111. CAL. PUB. RES. CODE §§ 25980–25986 (1978).

112. *Id.*

113. *Id.* at § 25982.

114. Since most of the water consumption occurs during the cooling process, the choice of cooling technology largely determines how much water is actually being used at the CSP facility. NICHOLE T. CARTER & RICHARD J. CAMPBELL, CONG. RES. SERV., R40631 WATER ISSUES OF CONCENTRATING SOLAR POWER (CSP) ELECTRICITY IN THE U.S. SOUTHWEST (June 8, 2009), *available at* http://www.circleofblue.org/waternews/wp-content/uploads/2010/08/

Solar-Water-Use-Issues-in-Southwest.pdf. The steam produced is cooled back to a liquid state in a condenser, water is then used to cool the condenser—a technique that is referred to as "wet cooling." *Id.*

115. U.S. Dep't of Energy, Concentrating Solar Power Commercial Application Study: Reducing Water Consumption of Concentrating Solar Power Electricity Generation (2010), *available at* http://www1.eere.energy.gov/solar/pdfs/csp_water_study.pdf.

116. Currently, no CSP plants in the United States utilize a "dry cooling" process. *Id.*

117. Rhone Resch, *Kyl's Solar Article Omitted Point*, Ariz. Republic, June 11, 2010, *available at* http://www.azcentral.com/arizonarepublic/opinions/articles/2010/06/11/20100611 voices111.html; Kris Mayes, *Solar Projects Will Protect Arizona's Water Supply, Not Threaten It*, Ariz. Republic, June 21, 2010, *available at* http://www.azcentral.com/arizonarepublic/opinions/articles/2010/06/21/20100621mayes21.html.

118. Office of Senator Jon Kyl, Deploying Solar Power in the State of Arizona: A Brief Overview of the Solar-Water Nexus (May 2010), *available at* http://www.circleof-blue.org/waternews/wp-content/uploads/2010/08/solar-water1.pdf.

119. *Id.* at 12, 15.

120. Stoel Rives LLP, "Power Purchase Agreements: Distributed Generation Projects," *in* Lex Helius: The Law of Solar Energy—A Guide to Business and Legal Issues ch. 2. at 5(2008).

121. A sample definition used for environmental attributes in a PPA is: "Environmental Attributes" includes, without limitation, Tradable Renewable Certificates, green-e tags, allowances, reductions or other transferable indicia denoting carbon offset credits or indicating generation of a particular quantity of energy from a renewable energy source by a renewable energy facility attributed to the Energy during the Term created under a renewable energy, emission reduction, or other reporting program adopted by a Governmental Authority, or for which a registry and a market exists (which, as of the Effective Date are certificates issued by Green-e in accordance with the Green-e Renewable Electric Certification Program, National Standard Version 1.3 administered by the Center of Resource Solutions) or for which a market may exist at a future time.

122. Ian Shrank & Arnold Gough, *Equipment Leasing—Leveraged Leasing*, 12 Practising L. Inst. 5 (4th ed. 2010) (1977). An additional insured under an insurance policy has direct rights against the insurance company in the event of a loss or third-party claim; however, only the named insured has the obligation to pay the policy premiums. *Id.*

123. *See supra* notes 28–36.

124. Shrank & Gough, *supra* note 122, at 2:3.3.

125. *Id.*

126. *Id.* at 2:3.2.

127. *Id.*

128. *Id.*

129. *Id.* at 2:5.3.

130. Rev. Proc. 2007-65, 2007-2 C.B. 967.

chapter eighteen

Geothermal Resources

Sylvia Harrison

Introduction

Geothermal energy, simply and literally, means energy from the heat of the earth. Planet Earth is a heat engine, perpetually producing heat from the disintegration of radioactive elements. The temperature gradient of the earth increases with depth. The relatively cool "crust" of the earth is divided into "plates," which ride the convective currents generated in the mantle. The slow movement of these tectonic plates sets up collisions at plate boundaries, which can force one plate beneath the other, creating temperature and pressure conditions that result in the melting of the "subducted" plate rocks and the formation of magma. The relative buoyancy of magma allows it to rise though subsurface weakness zones or faults, where it can move relatively near the surface, or even reach the surface, forming volcanoes or surface flows. Where tectonic plates move apart, subsurface magma can also reach the surface or near-surface in these rift zones.[1]

The same weakness zones that allow the rise of magma can also allow the deep percolation of rainwater and snowmelt into the subsurface. This water becomes heated as it descends and comes into proximity with the molten rock, finally reaching a temperature that causes it to recirculate upward, where it can eventually be expressed as hot springs or geysers. However, if this heated water is trapped below the surface by an impermeable layer of rock, it will continue to build temperature and pressure, sometimes reaching a temperature of up to 700°F.[2] These subsurface reservoirs of geothermally heated fluids can be accessed by drilled production wells and exploited for their energy potential.

Geothermal energy is used in one of two ways, either direct use of the geothermal heat, or the production of electrical energy, chiefly through one of three primary technologies: dry steam plants, flash plants, and binary plants. In the United States, currently, geothermal energy produces more than 3,000 megawatt electrical (MWe) annually, and a 2008 United States Geological Survey report estimates 39,090 MWe of potential from conventional geothermal resources.[3]

Generation of Electricity

Dry Steam

The simplest and oldest technology using geothermal energy for electrical generation is the dry steam plant. This technology is possible where the geothermal resource consists primarily of steam, without significant quantities of liquid water. Under these conditions, the steam can be conveyed to the surface through production wells as high-pressure "dry steam" and directed to steam turbines for electric energy generation. In the simplest configuration of a dry steam plant, once the geothermal steam passes through the turbine, it is vented to the atmosphere. Today, most dry steam plants capture the steam, condense it, and reinject it into the subsurface through injection wells.

Flash Plants

A flash plant can be used where geothermal fluids have temperatures above 360°F, but do not consist of dry steam. The boiling point of water is normally 212°F at sea-level pressures, but increases with pressure. Water confined to high pressures in a geothermal reservoir will remain in a liquid state at temperatures well in excess of the surface boiling point. In a flash plant facility, superheated geothermal water is brought to the surface and introduced into a low-pressure chamber where it "flashes" into steam. As in a dry steam plant, this steam then turns turbines that generate electricity. The steam is then condensed and reinjected.

Binary Plants

The third method for electrical generation utilizes geothermal resources to heat a fluid that has a much lower boiling point than water, such as pentane. Vapors produced by boiling this fluid turn a turbine in the same manner as steam. The "working" fluid is condensed and recycled, while the geothermal resources are reinjected. The use of this binary fluid system allows electrical energy production from moderate temperature resources, 400°F or less. Because this is the temperature range for most known accessible geothermal resources, binary plants are becoming increasingly important in electrical generation.

Cooling Geothermal Resources

Each of these three technologies requires cooling of the working fluid. Geothermal steam must be cooled and condensed for recirculation or reinjection. In a binary plant, the working fluid is cooled, condensed, and recycled. Cooling can require large quantities of water, often requiring augmentation from nongeothermal resources. Air cooling is a viable alternative to water cooling but results in reduced plant efficiency when ambient temperatures are relatively high. Under high temperature conditions, a small amount of water vapor is often introduced to enhance cooling efficiency.

Enhanced Geothermal Systems

Enhanced Geothermal Systems, or EGS, is a term referring to technologies for recovering heat from dry rock, usually through some form of forcible fluid injection deep into dry nonporous rock. The injection is intended to create fractures to make the rock permeable while at the same time heating the fluid at depth. The heated fluid can then be accessed from a recovery well and used for conventional geothermal power generation. Some EGS programs are also experimenting with the use of supercritical carbon dioxide, which has properties of both a gas and liquid, as the working fluid.

Currently, at least one commercial-scale EGS facility and several pilot EGS projects are in operation, but the technology has encountered problems, such as the permanent loss of large quantities of the injected fluid and induced seismicity. The process of fracturing the subsurface rocks and injecting fluids can have the unintended consequence of creating earthquakes of sufficient magnitude to be felt at the surface. For example, a commercial-scale EGS project near Basel, Switzerland, ten years in development, was shut down indefinitely in 2006 after a magnitude 3.4 earthquake occurred shortly after high-pressure fluids were introduced into the deep injection well.[4] Given the huge potential for energy production from EGS, estimated to be as much as 517,800 MWe of generation in the United States alone,[5] solving the technical challenges of EGS systems is a critical area for research and investment.

Direct Use

Where the temperature of geothermal resources is insufficient for the production of electrical energy, geothermal heat energy can be used directly in residential and commercial applications. In a typical direct use application, geothermal fluids are piped from a near-surface reservoir or surface hot springs to a heat exchanger. The heated secondary fluid can then be used in heating processes, while the geothermal fluid is directed to a cooling pond or reinjected to the subsurface through an injection well. Typical uses are residential or commercial space heating, or agricultural applications, such as dehydration of fruits and vegetables, heating greenhouses, and aquaculture.

Low-temperature geothermal resources are plentiful in the United States; the U.S. Geological Survey has identified more than 120,000 MW of untapped low-temperature resources.[6] Several western communities use geothermal heat for heating districts comprising individual residences and commercial buildings. The state capitol building in Boise, Idaho, is heated with geothermal energy. Reno, Nevada, has several neighborhood developments heated by "district" heating. Klamath Falls, Oregon, employs geothermal heat to melt snow on 50,000 square feet of its sidewalks and crosswalks. Several projects funded by the American Recovery and Reinvestment Act of 2009 are currently exploring ways to enhance the use of these low-temperature resources, including an experimental desalination plant making use of osmotic heat engines.[7]

Heat pumps are a related direct application of geothermal energy. These devices rely on the difference between ambient air temperature and the relatively constant temperature of the shallow subsurface. During winter months, heat can be transferred to a building using air or water heated by the earth; the transfer is reversed during the summer months for cooling, when the earth acts as a heat sink. Heat pump technologies are improving to allow institutional and commercial applications and enhancements such as hot water heating. These nonresidential applications are gaining interest in parts of the United States that lack geothermal resources as they are conventionally defined. For example, Ball State University in Indiana has embarked on a program to convert its campus to geothermal heat pump heating and cooling,[8] and Columbia University in New York City recently completed a similar system relying on deep wells for heating and cooling a hundred-year-old classroom building.[9]

Direct-use geothermal applications are estimated to save as much as 50 percent of the cost of heating and cooling relative to natural gas, in addition to the benefits of reduced carbon emissions. Because of the wide variety of applications, the actual energy value of direct-use systems is difficult to quantify. Installed capacity, excluding heat pumps, was estimated at 704 megawatt thermal (MWt) in 2008, while installed capacity for heat pumps in the United States was equivalent to 12,031 MWt, with a capacity factor of 10 percent.[10]

The Definition and Regulatory Classification of Geothermal Resources

Despite the simple definition of geothermal energy discussed in the Introduction above, there is no single, universally recognized definition of "geothermal resources." In the United States, geothermal resources are regulated under one of three classifications: as a mineral, as water, or as something unique (*sui generis*). Statutory definitions have generally been developed in connection with laws regulating geothermal resources in an attempt to describe *what* is being regulated, but considered alone, do not usually describe *how* the resource is regulated.

Regulation as a Mineral

The federal government and many states regulate geothermal resources as a mineral. Describing "heat energy" as a mineral makes little scientific or technical sense, but the regulation of geothermal resources as a "mineral" has a logical basis. Oil and gas resources are generally regulated under some form of "mineral" management, and the development of geothermal resources has many similarities to the development of oil and gas and raises similar regulatory issues. Moreover, as discussed in the next section, the character of geothermal resources as a source of energy like oil and gas has been a persuasive factor in resolving questions of title.

The federal definition of geothermal resources is found in the Geothermal Steam Act of 1970:

> (c) "geothermal resources" means
>
> (i) all products of geothermal processes, embracing indigenous steam, hot water and hot brines;

(ii) steam and other gases, hot water and hot brines resulting from water, gas, or other fluids artificially introduced into geothermal formations;

(iii) heat or other associated energy found in geothermal formations; and

(iv) any byproduct derived from them.[11]

The Geothermal Steam Act of 1970 provided that laws reserving any mineral to the United States shall "hereafter" be construed to embrace geothermal resources. Texas also regulates geothermal resources as a mineral, regulating them similarly to oil and gas.

Hawaii explicitly characterizes geothermal resources as a mineral[12] and defines them as follows:

"Geothermal resources" means the natural heat of the earth, the energy, in whatever form, below the surface of the earth present in, resulting from, or created by, or which may be extracted from the natural heat, and all minerals in solution or other products obtained from naturally heated fluids, brines, associated gases and steam, in whatever form, found below the surface of the earth, but excluding oil, hydrocarbon gas or other hydrocarbon substances, and any water, mineral in solution, or other product obtained from naturally heated fluids, brines, associated gases, and steam, in whatever form, found below the surface of the earth, having a temperature of 150 degrees Fahrenheit or less, and not used for electrical power generation.[13]

This definition is similar to that adopted by California[14] and New Mexico,[15] but neither state embraces a purely "mineral" system of regulation.

Regulation as Water

Wyoming and Utah regulate geothermal resources as water. Utah's definition of geothermal resources explicitly excludes "geothermal fluids."[16] Wyoming has amended its groundwater appropriation code to include hot water and geothermal steam.[17] Both Utah and Wyoming require an application to appropriate geothermal water through their respective water rights systems.

Sui Generis

Recognizing the unique character of geothermal resources, a number of states have classified geothermal resources as *sui generis*. For example, Idaho's definition states "[g]eothermal resources are found and hereby declared to be sui generis, being neither a mineral resource nor a water resource, but they are also found and hereby declared to be closely related to and possibly affecting and affected by water and mineral resources in many instances."[18] Montana[19] and Washington[20] also use this classification.

Dual Regulation Systems

A number of states have attempted a pragmatic approach of defining a threshold water temperature to distinguish groundwater from geothermal resources. Idaho defines two temperature regimes: between 85°F and 212°F, the groundwater is characterized as a low-temperature geothermal resource and is governed under the state's appropriation laws; groundwater above that temperature is administered as a geothermal resource.[21] New Mexico takes a similar approach.[22] Oregon excludes geothermal resources below 250°F from the well permitting regulations of its Geothermal Act, but subjects these to regulation of its Water Resources Department.[23]

Nevada and Arizona have taken another approach to dual regulation. In Nevada, geothermal wells are permitted through the Commission on Minerals, and the state's groundwater appropriation laws are applied only to the consumptive uses of water in geothermal operations, except for water reinjected into the resource or lost through temporary conditions such as testing.[24] Arizona exempts geothermal resources from water laws unless they are commingled with or can impair groundwater.[25]

Water Rights in Relation to Geothermal Resources

Where geothermal fluids are regulated as groundwater, how a state defines the right to use groundwater will bear directly on the right to use this resource. In those states that do not regulate geothermal fluids under water laws, availability of nongeothermal waters for purposes such as cooling and EGS applications will be governed and constrained by the water rights systems.[26]

At traditional common law, a landowner whose property bordered surface waters was entitled to the reasonable use of that water as an incident of ownership. This riparian doctrine applies in most eastern states and is recognized in some form in the western coastal states (except Alaska) and the Midwest.

In most interior arid western states, the riparian system was ultimately abandoned in favor of the appropriation doctrine. In appropriation states, water is a public resource, either "owned" by the state or held by the state in trust for the public. Some appropriation states characterize water rights as real property, while others characterize them as a usufruct. Most appropriation states now apply the doctrine to groundwater as well as surface water.

Under the appropriation doctrine, a water right can be established by diverting water from its source and putting the water to a beneficial use. The first appropriator has a superior right to junior appropriators. The quantity of the water right is measured by the amount of water used for a beneficial purpose. An appropriator generally has the right of reasonable access and use of property necessary for the diversion of the water right, regardless of property ownership. Water rights are generally administered through a permit system requiring various stages of proofs of diversion and beneficial use before the water right is accorded a "vested" status. An application for a water right is subject to public notice and protest, and will not be granted if the appropriation is contrary to the public interest or interferes with the rights of prior appropriators. A water right can be abandoned and may be subject to forfeiture as a result of a continuous period of non-use, usually five years.

California, Oregon, and Washington and most of the midwestern states recognize riparian rights but have integrated an appropriation system into their water laws to varying degrees. In California, landowners overlying the same aquifer have a preferential right to use the water, and must use it on an equal and correlative basis. "Surplus" groundwater is subject to appropriation. In contrast, Oregon requires groundwater to be appropriated under its permit system.

Ownership Presumptions and Title Issues

The complex question of classification of geothermal resources can become even more convoluted when ownership is at issue. Although statutory clarifications and court decisions have largely settled questions of federal rights, private rights to geothermal resources vary from state to state. Adding to the confusion, states do not always follow the logic of their classification systems in recognizing private ownership.

Federal Rights

Congress settled any question of federal rights to geothermal resources underlying federal lands in enacting the Geothermal Steam Act of 1970, which provided for the administration of federal geothermal resources as a mineral, available for private development through a leasing program similar to those established for oil and gas.[27] Congress recognized the potential for conflicts as to the ownership of geothermal rights in those cases where the surface rights had been granted to private owners with a reservation of mineral rights. The Act provides that *future* United States mineral reservations would be deemed to include geothermal resources, but left to the courts to decide the issue as to prior reservations.[28]

During the initial phases of the disposition of public lands, the federal government attempted to segregate "mineral lands" from agricultural lands, allowing homesteading only on the latter. This distinction ignored geologic and geographic realities and was subject to widespread abuse. When the Stock-Raising Homestead Act (the SRHA)[29] was enacted in 1916, Congress opted to include a general mineral reservation in the patents, stating that the land patented under the act "shall be subject to and contain a reservation to the United States of all the coal and other minerals in the lands so entered and patented, together with the right to prospect for, mine and remove the same."[30] Today, the United States Bureau of Land Management (the BLM)—the federal agency charged with managing federal minerals—manages about 58 million acres of split estate lands with private surface and federal minerals.[31]

Whether these reserved minerals included geothermal resources was decided by the Ninth Circuit in the case, *United States v. Union Oil Co. of California*.[32] The court held that the Act applied to mineral reservations in patents issued under the SRHA, finding the clear intent of Congress was to reserve energy resources to the United States.[33] It should be noted that federal reservations vary from Act to Act, and the specific statutory language may not always support such a broad construction.

Private Ownership

Jurisdictions that classify geothermal resources as a mineral generally recognize the surface owner as the presumptive owner of those geothermal resources, as an incident of the mineral estate. Those regulating geothermal fluids under groundwater appropriation systems require an appropriation permit to develop these fluids and may or may not recognize ownership interests of the surface owner. For example, Colorado and Utah recognize the interest of the surface owner in "hot dry rock" or geothermal resources exclusive of geothermal fluids, but require appropriation of the associated fluids.[34] Wyoming, which classifies geothermal resources as water, treats them as a "public resource" available for appropriation,[35] apparently without regard to surface ownership. By statute, Nevada and Oregon recognize the surface owner as the owner of geothermal resources, unless the geothermal resources have been reserved or conveyed to another person.[36]

State Ownership

Most states assert ownership of geothermal resources on lands under state ownership and administer these through leasing programs. Idaho, for example, asserts ownership of geothermal resources on state lands as a reserved "mineral deposit,"[37] notwithstanding Idaho's classification of geothermal resources as *sui generis*. Alaska goes further and asserts state ownership of geothermal resources, including those under private lands, giving a preferential right to the surface owner for exploration and leasing.[38]

Split Estates and Private Reservations

In jurisdictions recognizing a private property right in geothermal resources, even more ownership complexities can arise from private reservations, particularly in jurisdictions treating geothermal resources as a mineral. In western states with a rich history of mining and mineral development, landowners recognize the potential value of subsurface rights and frequently reserve or sever these rights from the surface estate. Language used in mineral reservations or grants is highly variable and commonly includes general reservations of "all minerals" without specifically naming geothermal resources. As in the case of the federal reservation at issue in *Union Oil*, whether these general private mineral reservations include geothermal resources can be a contentious issue.

One of the first cases considering this question is *Geothermal Kinetics, Inc. v. Union Oil Co. of California*,[39] which considered whether the surface owner or the owner of a 1951 grant of "extractable minerals" was the owner of the geothermal resources. Relying in part on the rationale of *Union Oil*, the court found that in "[e]xamining both the broad purpose of the 1951 conveyance of the mineral estate and the expected manner of enjoyment of this property interest, it appears that the rights to the geothermal resources are part of the [mineral] grant."[40] Further, the court stated that "the fact that the presence of geothermal resources may not have been known to one or both parties to the 1951 conveyance is of no consequence."[41]

In the majority of jurisdictions, courts attempt to determine the intent of the parties in construing an ambiguous mineral reservation. The factors cited in *Geothermal Kinetics*, including the court's analysis of the purposes of the grant and of general versus specific intent, are likely persuasive guidelines in jurisdictions treating geothermal resources as a mineral, but may be less instructive, or irrelevant, in a jurisdiction like Wyoming that treats geothermal resources as a public water resource. An equally problematic question could arise in jurisdictions that simply treat low-temperature geothermal resources as groundwater that can be appropriated under general water rights appropriation laws (see the discussion of the *Rosette* cases below). Given that appropriated water rights can be severed from the surface estate, will geothermal resources be included in grants or reservations of such water rights?

Fractional Interests

Multiple owners, or "cotenants," may hold title to undivided fractional interests in geothermal resources, particularly where the resources are construed as part of the surface or mineral estates. Under the majority common law rule, each cotenant has the nonexclusive right to develop a mineral resource without the consent of other cotenants. If developing unilaterally, the developing cotenant will bear all costs in connection with the development and must account to the nondeveloping cotenant for its share of the profits. The developing cotenant is only entitled to reimbursement from the nondeveloping tenant's pro rata share of subsequent revenue generated from the development. If the development does not result in production, or does not produce sufficient revenue to cover the nondeveloping cotenant's proportionate share of the costs, the nondeveloping cotenant has no reimbursement obligation. In jurisdictions where the majority rule is not followed, the cotenant developing the mineral may be liable for trespass and waste, sometimes carrying penalties of treble damages. Competing and incompatible mineral developments complicate the application of these rules. To avoid these issues, geothermal developers will usually attempt to control all of the rights to all of the minerals.

Other Property Interests and Royalties

Private property rights in geothermal resources can theoretically be held in any of the numerous arcane species of present, future, possessory, nonpossessory, and executory property interests. In addition, one of the rights commonly associated with mineral rights, particularly oil and gas development, is an "executive right" (not to be confused with an executory interest), which means the right to control decisions about the mineral estate, independently from any possessory interest. For example, a landowner may convey away ownership of all or a portion of the mineral estate, but retain the executive right, and thus be in a position to determine whether the minerals can be leased for development. Another common right is a royalty interest, or a right to a percentage of the profits from mineral production. A royalty holder has no executive powers and is simply the passive recipient of proceeds generated from the mineral estate. In the context of oil and gas development, sorting through these various rights has resulted in a large body of law that may be directly applicable to geothermal resources in states such as Texas that have clearly determined these resources to be part of the mineral estate. In states with more ambiguous classifications, determining the application of these various property rights to geothermal resources will be less straightforward.

Relative Rights of Surface and Geothermal Resource Owners

At common law, the mineral estate is the dominant estate, and ownership of this interest includes an implied right of access and reasonable use of the surface as necessary for operation. Federal laws explicitly recognize this right. For example, the SRHA provides that any person who acquired from the United States the right to mine and remove the mineral deposits "may reenter and occupy so much of the surface thereof as may be required for all purposes reasonably incident to the mining or removal of the coal or other minerals," without the consent of the surface owner, upon the execution of a bond or undertaking to secure the payment of the amount of damages "to the crops or tangible improvements of the entryman or owner. . . ."[42]

What is the reasonable use of the surface? In the case of *Occidental Geothermal, Inc. v. Simmons*, the court determined that siting a geothermal power plant on the property was a reasonable use of the surface and was among the rights granted by a federal geothermal lease.[43] The property in question was a split estate patented under the SRHA. The court reasoned that geothermal resources could not be transported long distances without losing their practical utility.[44] The court stated: "To hold that geothermal lessees own the rights to geothermal resources and yet do not have the right to exploit those resources without the consent of the owners of surface interests would reduce the holding of *Union Oil* to an empty theoretical exercise."[45]

In recent years, the BLM has developed explicit policies[46] to protect the relative rights of parties to split estate lands, generally requiring the mineral developer to attempt in good faith to reach a surface use agreement with the surface owner as to access rights and compensation. If an agreement cannot be reached, the mineral owner can post a bond to protect the legitimate interests of the surface owner.

In determining relative rights between private parties to split estates, many jurisdictions have adopted the "accommodation doctrine," which requires "due regard" for the rights of the surface owner.[47] In addition, many states have enacted surface damage acts, but these were developed to resolve conflicts between surface owners and oil and gas developers and do not explicitly apply to geothermal development.

Pooling, Unitization, and Participation Agreements

Geothermal resources extend over large areas of the subsurface, irrespective of property boundaries. Maximizing the energy potential of these resources depends on careful attention to production and reinjection well spacing. Improper well spacing can lead to the depletion of subsurface pressure necessary for optimal recovery of geothermal fluids, while poorly planned placement of injection wells can lead to cooling of the resource. Configuring a geothermal well field to protect and preserve the resource commonly requires cooperation among adjoining landowners or leaseholders. "Pooling" is a term usually used to denote the combination of adjoining properties into a single block to meet well spacing requirements. "Unitization" is a similar concept, but implies the cooperation among the adjoining owners to operate the entire "pool" of properties overlying a geothermal resource under an agreement providing for the distribution of costs and revenues among the separate owners, and usually, designating a single operator for the unit.

In a typical unitization or participation agreement, large tracts of adjoining leases or properties are unitized for exploration purposes, and once the subsurface geothermal resources have been adequately delineated, the unit is contracted to exclude property not overlying the resource. The "participating area" then forms the basis for the allocation of costs and revenues based upon the pro rata ownership of the participants.

Federal geothermal leasing regulations include a provision for the cooperative formation of units, which may include owners of nonfederal interests.[48] The regulations also allow the BLM to require unitization of federal leases in the public interest.[49] Several states, including Arizona,[50] Idaho,[51] New Mexico,[52] and Oregon,[53] have also enacted laws allowing the state to mandate unitization to protect geothermal resources.

Federal Geothermal Leases and Site Permitting

Federal Leases

According to some estimates, up to 90 percent of geothermal resources in the United States are located on federal lands.[54] Federal geothermal resources are available for private development under a leasing program first enabled by the Geothermal Steam Act of 1970, and amended by the Energy Policy Act of 2005.[55] The BLM is the delegated authority to issue these leases for federal lands, including those administered by the United States Forest Service (USFS).

Under the Geothermal Steam Act of 1970, leases were made available through a competitive bid process for so-called Known Geothermal Resource Areas (KGRAs). These leases have a primary term of ten years and can be held by production for forty years. If the property is still in production at the end of this term, the lessee has a preferential right to renew the lease for an additional forty years. Outside KGRAs, geothermal leases could be obtained on a non-competitive basis.

Under the Energy Policy Act of 2005 (the Energy Policy Act), all leases are issued on a competitive basis through an auction process.[56] Private entities or individuals may nominate designated federal lands for leasing, or the BLM may nominate available lease blocks on its own initiative. The BLM evaluates the nominated lands for critical resources and may disqualify certain parcels, or impose predetermined stipulations (such as "no surface occupancy" provisions) for specific areas of the proposed leases.[57]

Nominated lands cannot be included in a lease sale until National Environmental Policy Act (NEPA) requirements are met and the leasing conforms to the applicable land use plan. Leases are awarded to the highest qualified bidder. The bid consists of a one-time per-acre payment or "bonus bid." Recent auctions have garnered bids as high as $14,000 per acre for a 470-acre parcel in The Geysers geothermal field of California.[58] An auction held in Reno, Nevada, in August 2008 brought in bids totaling $28.2 million for a total of 105,211 acres.[59]

Under the Energy Policy Act, a single lease may be as large as 5,120 acres. The leases have a primary term of ten years, can be held by making minimum payments or meeting work requirements for two additional five-year terms, and can be held by production or diligent development for up to an additional thirty-five years.[60] Under commercial production, the lease may be held for up to fifty-five years longer. Rents escalate from $2 to $5 per acre during the various lease terms, and the Energy Policy Act authorizes royalties to be set between 1 percent and 5 percent of gross proceeds. Under the Energy Policy Act, 50 percent of revenues from the lease sale (including bonus bids, rentals, and royalties) is distributed to the state in which the leased lands are located, 25 percent is distributed to the counties where the leases are located, and 25 percent is distributed to the BLM for use in processing geothermal leases and use authorizations.

Federal Site Permitting

The decision to issue a geothermal lease is a federal action requiring compliance with NEPA. During the last two decades, the time-consuming, site-specific reviews required by NEPA, the National Historic Preservation Act (NHPA), and the Clean Water Act, coupled with increasing interest in geothermal development, resulted in a huge backlog of unprocessed lease applications. By 2005, there were at least 194 pending applications, some of which had been pending for more than ten years.[61] The Energy Policy Act mandated a 90 percent reduction of this backlog by August 2010. To accomplish this goal, the BLM and USFS jointly prepared a Programmatic Environmental Impact Statement (PEIS) to assess the impacts of federal geothermal leasing. Under the preferred alternative, approved by the Record of Decision issued in December 2008, approximately 197 million acres of federal lands and split federal mineral estates are identified as open for geothermal leasing.[62] The PEIS develops a list of stipulations, best management practices, and procedures for leasing, and amends BLM land use plans to adopt these provisions. The PEIS is intended to allow the BLM to issue leases without further NEPA analysis, but contemplates that the agencies can conduct additional review under the Endangered Species Act, NHPA, or other laws, as appropriate.

The PEIS covers only the lease issuance and land use decisions associated with geothermal development. Site-specific ground disturbing activities, e.g., exploration, drilling, and site utilization (project construction and operation) are each subject to additional federal permits and additional environmental review. A new geothermal electrical generation facility will almost always require new interconnection and transmission facilities, requiring additional surface occupancy permits and rights of way and additional environmental analysis.

Although the PEIS has greatly facilitated the issuance of federal geothermal leases, cultural resource inventories and tribal consultation mandated by § 106 of NHPA[63] are still creating a backlog in geothermal permitting. Consultation under the Endangered Species Act and the determination of federal jurisdiction over "waters of the United States" under the Clean Water Act[64] are additional bottlenecks. These issues are particularly problematic for geothermal development, because the location of the resource dictates the location of the surface disturbance, and the developer has relatively little flexibility to avoid sensitive sites.

In addition to the environmental reviews, full development of a geothermal facility will require the usual surface disturbance permits for dust control, air quality permits, storm water control permits, possible NPDES permits depending on the discharge of fluids, and public water system permits.

The siting and permitting of renewable energy facilities, including geothermal facilities, are discussed in greater detail in chapter 5.

Private and State Leases and Permitting Regimes

The basic structure of leases of private geothermal rights is similar to federal leases, requiring payment to the lessor of rents (sometimes as advance minimum royalties) and royalties, providing the lessee a right to pool and unitize the lease, the right to abandon nonproductive portions of the leased property, and to extend the lease term indefinitely by commercial production. Lessees will typically seek to control all minerals within the leased property to prevent mineral development incompatible with use and protection of the geothermal resource. Leases usually delineate the rights of the lessee to the use of the surface, and rights to water resources owned or controlled by the lessor.

As discussed above, states regulate state and private geothermal resources as a mineral, as water, or through dual systems. All western states, other than Wyoming, have specific laws requiring permits for geothermal wells, administered by either or both of their respective water resources and minerals agencies. Most of these states also have laws or regulations relating to the conservation and protection of the geothermal resource, such as well spacing laws, and laws recognizing or mandating unit development. In addition, most states have specific well casing requirements to protect near-surface groundwater. Wyoming simply administers geothermal resources through its water rights system.

State environmental laws applicable to geothermal projects vary widely. For example, the California Environmental Quality Act[65] is similar in complexity and rigor to NEPA. By contrast, neighboring Nevada has no comparable law and little environmental regulation of geothermal facilities, other than its implementation of federal acts such as the Clean Air Act and Clean Water Act (likely because most geothermal development occurs on federal land and is subject to federal environmental laws).

Application of Federal and State Energy Laws to Geothermal Projects

Federal Energy Regulatory Commission Jurisdiction

As discussed in chapter 4, most renewable energy electrical generation facilities can obtain exemption from Federal Energy Regulatory Commission (FERC) jurisdiction as a "qualifying facility." However, the commercial viability of a geothermal generator almost always depends on securing not only a power purchase agreement, but also an interconnection and transmission agreement, both of which are usually subject to FERC jurisdiction.

Renewable Portfolio Standards and Tax Incentives

As discussed in greater detail in chapter 4, renewable portfolio standards, now mandated in many states, have created a significant impetus for the development of renewable energy. As one of the only renewable technologies to supply baseload power, geothermal energy has particularly benefited from these programs, as utilities seeking to balance their renewable portfolios are eager to negotiate power purchase agreements with geothermal developers.

Tax and other incentives at both the federal and state levels (discussed in detail in chapters 7 and 8) have also been particularly beneficial to geothermal projects. Because of the high cost and high risk of geothermal exploration and development, smaller companies have struggled with financing projects, especially during the recent credit crisis. The extension of tax credits in the American Recovery and Reinvestment Act of 2009 and newly enacted state laws offering local tax incentives[66] have helped spur project financing.

Common Environmental Issues

Because of the broad range of geothermal technologies and differing characteristics of geothermal fluids and geothermal development sites, the environmental impacts of geothermal energy projects vary widely from one project to another. Relative to other sources of electrical generation, most geothermal plants operating under today's regulatory regimes have minimal air emissions and impacts to water resources.

Air Quality

Geothermal fluids commonly contain small amounts of entrained gases such as methane (CH_4), hydrogen sulfide (H_2S), and ammonia (NH_3), as well as trace amounts of mercury and arsenic. When geothermal steam is released to the atmosphere, as in open dry steam and flashed-steam plants, these pollutants can negatively impact air quality. H_2S oxidizes quickly to sulfur dioxide (SO_2). Both forms are injurious in sufficient quantities and contribute to acid rain and other environmental degradation. These substances are regulated under the Clean Air Act, and geothermal plants now routinely use abatement systems to convert the gases to elemental sulfur. Mercury emissions have also been a problem at some projects, such as The Geysers, but these emissions are now carefully controlled at most geothermal plants.[67] In binary and air-cooled systems, atmospheric emissions are minimal because the geothermal fluids are not released to the atmosphere, but reinjected to the subsurface or collected and chemically altered for safe disposal.

Water Quality

Geothermal fluids can have as little as 0.1 to as much as 25 weight percent dissolved solutes. Upon cooling, many of the dissolved chemicals will precipitate. Some of these precipitates, such as silica, are removed from the fluids prior to reinjection to prevent clogging reinjection wells or the geothermal reservoir.[68] Unless these precipitates and the resulting brines are appropriately managed, they are potential sources of water pollution. Today, geothermal fluids are reinjected back into the deep reservoir rocks through steel-cased wells, usually regulated under state casing standards, preventing communication with near-surface groundwater.

Depletion of Water Resources

Because of the huge variability in water requirements from one geothermal facility to another, it is difficult to make reliable generalizations regarding geothermal water use. Obviously, plants that vent steam to the atmosphere use large quantities of water consumptively, but since much of this water consists of nonpotable geothermal fluids, the impact on "water resources" can be easily overstated. Nonetheless, most geothermal generation facilities require a large amount of water for cooling. According to U.S. Department of Energy estimates, a closed-loop binary cycle geothermal power plant requires 450 to 600 gpm to generate 1MW from a 300°F fluid given an ambient air temperature of 60°F. The water requirements more than double if the temperature of the geothermal fluid is only 210°F. Note that these volumes assume recirculation of the water. If evaporative cooling is used, an additional 45 to 75 gpm would be needed for make-up water (consumptive use).[69] Dedicating potable or nongeothermal waters for cooling water will inevitably conflict with existing or competing uses for such water. Given that much of the current geothermal development is occurring in arid western states like Nevada, air-cooled facilities are more and more common, but generally require some consumptive water use during summer months to prevent unacceptable losses of efficiency.

On the other hand, geothermal development can provide new opportunities for water resource management. The City of Santa Rosa, in California, delivers 11 million gallons of treated wastewater from its water reclamation facility to The Geysers geothermal field, forty miles away, for subsurface reinjection to prevent the deterioration of geothermal resource pressures.[70]

Site Conflicts—Species Habitat and Cultural Resources

As discussed above, geothermal resources are where you find them. Although geothermal resources do not always have a surface expression, they are frequently associated with hot springs, which in turn are often sites of historic cultural resources or provide habitat for rare or unique species. Conflicts over these sites can be irreconcilable.[71]

Although geothermal power plants extend over hundreds of acres, the actual use of the surface is relatively small, allowing preservation of habitat over much of the project. However, noise and extensive pipelines can cause disruption of wildlife and may be incompatible with other land uses.

Advantages and Disadvantages of Geothermal Energy

Geothermal power plants, in contrast to solar and wind-generating facilities, are capable of producing electricity continuously. This makes geothermal generation an important source for baseload power, increasingly important to allow utilities to meet renewable portfolio standards with an appropriate mix of peaking and baseload generation. Geothermal plants are becoming extremely efficient, with capacity factors (actual generation relative to nameplate capacity) sometimes in excess of 95 percent, compared with 30 percent for typical solar and wind projects.[72] In addition, the plants are relatively simple and inexpensive to operate, and free from the challenges of fluctuating fuel prices.[73] As discussed above, the environmental impacts of modern geothermal projects are relatively small compared with other forms of energy generation.

Offsetting these advantages are the long lead time and high up-front exploration costs required to adequately delineate a geothermal resource and design the geothermal field.[74] In addition, control of a large amount of property, commonly thousands of acres, is required for optimum exploration and development of a geothermal resource. Ambiguities in state laws, uncertain title, multiple owners, and fractional interests can make acquisition of this control a challenging task. While federal leases avoid these title questions, federal environmental requirements can be onerous and time-consuming. Inflexibility of facility siting adds to the risk. In addition, because potential geothermal power plants are commonly in remote locations, but will generate relatively small amounts of electricity, the cost-benefit analysis for a long, dedicated transmission line required to connect geothermal generation to the grid may weigh in favor of no development.

Significant improvements in the management of geothermal reservoirs and geothermal fluids have reduced the environmental impact of geothermal power plants and helped ensure that geothermal resources are truly renewable. The rapid evolution of geothermal technologies is expanding the potential for both thermal and electrical energy production from geothermal resources. Improved drilling techniques allow access to deeper resources, while new heat transfer technologies enhance electrical generation from lower-temperature fluids. Low-temperature geothermal fluids coproduced with oil and gas have an estimated generation potential of 3,000 to 14,000 MWe.[75] A recent report estimated the energy potential for EGS to be as much as 100,000 MWe within the next fifty years.[76] These new developments will be accompanied by new environmental and legal challenges as regulators and property owners sort through the consequences of exploiting these unanticipated resources.

Litigation: Representative Cases

Ownership Issues: The *Rosette* Cases

Despite the confusion over the character of geothermal resources, relatively few cases concerning ownership have been reported in the last decade. A line of cases from New Mexico accounts for the bulk of these and illustrates how contentious questions of title can become.

Rosette, Inc. is a commercial rose producer, growing roses in greenhouses on property patented under the SRHA.[77] The land is subject to United States mineral reservations, and the United States had leased geothermal resources to several leaseholders. In 1978, Rosette entered into an agreement with the leaseholders to use the geothermal resources to heat the greenhouses, and, as the designated operator of the leases, agreed to pay royalties to the United States. Rosette also holds groundwater rights appropriated under New Mexico law, and extracts water from separate wells for irrigating the roses.[78]

In 1993, Rosette filed suit against the United States, contending that the geothermal resources were not reserved minerals under the SRHA. Rosette's suit was dismissed on procedural grounds,[79] but the litigation continued over the ownership issue.[80] Ultimately, the Tenth Circuit affirmed the decision of the district court in favor of the United States, which had distinguished "heat" as a reserved mineral from the water which carried the heat.[81]

Rosette then attempted an end run around the federal decisions, filing a petition in state court for an adjudication of groundwater rights, contending that Rosette, not the United States, owned the water rights to the hot water.[82] Rosette relied on New Mexico's dual regulation system, which regulates groundwater with a temperature below 250°F as groundwater subject to appropriation under its water laws, and not as a geothermal resource.[83] The state court declined jurisdiction on the basis that the true issue was the ownership of a United States mineral resource. The New Mexico Court of Appeals affirmed on a number of grounds, including its finding that the Supremacy Clause prevented New Mexico law from defining geothermal resources more narrowly than the applicable federal law.[84] This decision includes a clear synopsis of the federal cases and a thorough discussion of the interplay among state and federal geothermal laws and water rights decisions.

NEPA and NHPA: *Pit River Tribe v. U.S. Forest Service*

Pit River Tribe v. US Forest Service is representative of the conflict between geothermal development and culturally significant sites.[85] The Pit River Tribe, the Native Coalition for Medicine Lake Highlands Defense, and the Mount Shasta Bioregional Ecology Center (collectively, Pit River) sued the United States Forestry Service (USFS), BLM, and the Department of Interior (collectively, the Agencies) regarding the Agencies' decision extending the terms of geothermal leases for the Medicine Lake Highlands area in California and approving the construction of a geothermal plant by Calpine Corporation (Calpine).[86] Pit River contended the decisions violated NEPA,

NHPA, the National Forest Management Act (NFMA), the Administrative Procedure Act (APA), and the Agencies' fiduciary obligations to Native American tribes.[87]

Geothermal leases were initially issued to Calpine's predecessor in 1988 after the preparation of an Environmental Assessment (EA) and supplemental EAs tiered to the 1973 Programmatic Environmental Impact Statement (EIS) prepared for the Geothermal Steam Act of 1970. The NEPA process had elicited virtually no public interest until the Agencies began preparing an EIS in June 1996 for a geothermal power plant.[88] The Pit River Tribe was highly critical of the draft EIS. In May 1998, the BLM extended Calpine's leases for five more years without any further environmental review. In September 1998, the Agencies issued a final EIS for the power plant.[89] The EIS rejected the no-action alternative because it would not meet the purpose of developing the geothermal resource on Calpine's federal geothermal leases. In June, Pit River filed suit in the Eastern District of California, and the district court entered summary judgment for the Agencies on all claims. Pit River appealed to the Ninth Circuit.

Since the statute of limitations had run on the 1988 leasing decision, Pit River argued that the Agencies violated NEPA, NHPA, and their fiduciary trust obligations to the Pit River Tribe by extending the leases in 1998 without completing an EIS. The Ninth Circuit rejected the Agencies' argument that the 1998 lease extensions were merely a continuation of the status quo that did not require a separate assessment.[90] The court reasoned that if it were not for the extension in 1998, Calpine would have lost its right to develop the leases and commence construction of the power plant, and accordingly, the Agencies were required to conduct an EIS prior to extending the 1998 leases.[91] The court also concluded that NHPA had been violated because the Agencies had failed to give the tribe an adequate opportunity to participate in the decision to extend the leases.[92]

Interior Board of Land Appeal Decisions

Because the first stop in most appeals from BLM decisions is the Interior Board of Land Appeals (IBLA), these administrative decisions should not be overlooked as sources of helpful authority, particularly for NEPA decisions and management of federal leases. See Vulcan Power Company[93] (applications for geothermal leases, which had been pending since 1992 without environmental review, were rejected by the BLM in 2008 after USFS refused to consent to the leases).

Unitization Disputes

A growing field of litigation involves disputes over the delineation of participating areas. See Wagner v. Chevron Oil Company[94] (lessor sued after her properties were omitted from the participating area; a federal court determined that it lacked jurisdiction over disputes concerning private minerals, even though the unit included federal leases).

Notes

1. GEOTHERMAL EDUCATION OFFICE, GEOTHERMAL ENERGY FACTS: ADVANCED LEVEL (2004), http://www.geothermal.marin.org/geoenergy.html.
2. *Id.*

3. U.S. Dept. of Energy, Geothermal Techs. Program, Energy Efficiency & Renewable Energy, 2008 Geothermal Technologies Market Report 14 (2009), *available at* http://www.eere.energy.gov/geothermal/pdfs/2008_market_report.pdf [hereinafter 2008 Geothermal Report].

4. Domenico Giardini, Opinion, *Geothermal Quake Risks Must Be Faced*, 462 Nature 848, 848–49 (Dec. 17, 2009).

5. 2008 Geothermal Report, *supra* note 3, at 14.

6. U.S. Dep't of Energy, Energy Efficiency & Renewable Energy, Nat'l Renewable Energy Lab., Low-Temperature Geothermal Resources 1 (2010), *available at* http://www.eere.energy.gov/geothermal/pdfs/low_temp_overview.pdf.

7. *Id.* at 2.

8. Ball State University, Going Geothermal: FAQ (last visited Jul. 30, 2010), http://cms.bsu.edu/About/Geothermal/FAQ.aspx.

9. Press Release, Columbia University, Knox Hall Receives Green Preservation and Renovation Work (Sept. 21, 2009), *available at* http://facilities.columbia.edu/knox-hall-receives-green-preservation-and-renovation-work.

10. 2008 Geothermal Report, *supra* note 3, at 28–29.

11. 30 U.S.C. § 1001(c).

12. Haw. Rev. Stat. § 182-1.

13. *Id.*

14. Cal. Pub. Res. Code § 6903.

15. N.M. Stat. Ann. § 71-5-3(A).

16. Utah Code Ann. § 73-22-3.

17. Wyo. Stat. Ann. § 41-3-901.

18. Idaho Code Ann. §§ 42-4002(c); 47-1602.

19. Mont. Code Ann. § 77-4-104.

20. Wash. Rev. Code § 78.60.040.

21. Idaho Code Ann. § 42-230(a).

22. N.M. Stat. Ann. § 71-5-2.1.

23. Or. Rev. Stat. § 522.025.

24. Nev. Rev. Stat. 534A.040.

25. Ariz. Rev. Stat. § 27-667.

26. See Owen Olpin, A. Dan Tarlock & Carl F. Austin, *Geothermal Development and Western Water Law*, 1979 Utah L. Rev. 773, for an excellent discussion of the evolution of geothermal resource regulation relative to western water law. Although the paper was written more than thirty years ago and cannot be relied on for the current status of state laws, it provides a thorough discussion of the general principles of western water law and the difficulties states have faced in integrating geothermal resources into that framework.

27. 30 U.S.C. §§ 1001 et seq.

28. 30 U.S.C. § 1002.

29. 43 U.S.C. §§ 291 et seq.

30. 43 U.S.C. § 299.

31. *See* U.S. Dep't of the Interior, Bureau of Land Mgmt., Split Estate (Oct. 20, 2009), http://www.blm.gov/wo/st/en/prog/energy/oil_and_gas/best_management_practices/split_estate.html.

32. 549 F.2d 1271 (9th Cir. 1977).

33. *Id.* at 1274.

34. Colo. Rev. Stat. § 37-90.5-104(2); Utah Code Ann. § 73-22-8.

35. Wyo. Stat. Ann. § 41-3-901.

36. Nev. Rev. Stat. 534A.050; Or. Rev. Stat. § 522.035.

37. Idaho Code Ann. § 47-701.

38. Alaska Stat. 38.05.181.

39. 75 Cal. App. 3d 56, 141 Cal. Rptr. 879 (Cal. Ct. App. 1977).

40. 75 Cal. App. 3d at 64.

41. *Id.* at 61.

42. 43 U.S.C. § 299.

43. 543 F. Supp. 870 (N.D. Cal. 1982).

44. *Id.* at 874.

45. *Id.* at 877.

46. 72 Fed. Reg. 10,308 (Mar. 7, 2007); *see also* Bureau of Land Mgmt., Split Estate: Rights, Responsibilities, and Opportunities, *available at* http://www.blm.gov/pgdata/etc/medialib/blm/wo/MINERALS__REALTY__AND_RESOURCE_PROTECTION_/bmps.Par.57486.File.dat/SplitEstate07.pdf.

47. For an excellent discussion of this issue in the context of oil and gas operations, where the law is well developed, see Christopher M. Alspach, *Surface Use by the Mineral Owner: How Much Accommodation Is Required under Current Oil and Gas Law*, 55 Okla L. Rev. 89 (2002).

48. 43 C.F.R § 3280.3.

49. 43 C.F.R § 3280.4.

50. Ariz. Rev. Stat. Ann. § 27-665.

51. Idaho Code Ann. § 42-4013(b).

52. N.M. Stat. Ann. § 71-5-11.

53. Or. Rev. Stat. § 522.405(2).

54. *See* News Release, U.S. Dep't of the Interior, Kempthorne Launches Initiative to Spur Geothermal Energy and Power Generation on Federal Lands (Oct. 22, 2008), *available at* http://www.blm.gov/or/news/files/Geothermal_Initiative_Wed22Oct2008.pdf.

55. Energy Policy Act of 2005, Pub. L. No. 109-58, 119 Stat. 594 (2005) (codified as amended in scattered sections of 16 and 42 U.S.C.).

56. There are a few exceptions. For example, a lease nominated for sale but not sold during the auction may be held open for noncompetitive leasing for up to two years. *See* 43 C.F.R. § 3204.5(a).

57. 43 C.F.R. § 3203.

58. U.S. Dep't of the Interior, Bureau of Land Mgmt., BLM Geothermal Lease Auction Signals New Trend in Renewable Energy: Leasing Implements Clean Energy Goals in Energy Policy Act, *available at* http://www.blm.gov/wo/st/en/info/newsroom/2007/august/NR_0708_04.html.

59. News Release, U.S. Dep't of the Interior, Record Geothermal Lease Sale Generates $28 Million in Bids: Sale Underscores Commitment to Renewable Energy (Aug. 8, 2008), *available at* http://www.doi.gov/archive/news/08_News_Releases/080808b.html.

60. 30 U.S.C. § 1005.

61. *See* Record of Decision and Resource Management Plan Amendments for Geothermal Leasing in the Western United States *available at* http://www.blm.gov/pgdata/etc/medialib/blm/wo/MINERALS__REALTY__AND_RESOURCE_PROTECTION_/energy/geothermal_eis/final_programmatic.Par.90935.File.dat/ROD_Geothermal_12-17-08.pdf.

62. *Id.*

63. 16 U.S.C. § 470.

64. Under § 404 of the Clean Water Act (33 U.S.C. § 1344), the "discharge of dredged or fill material" into "navigable waters" requires a permit from the United States Army Corps of Engineers (subject to oversight by the U.S. Environmental Protection Agency (EPA)). Through a complex history of regulations and court decisions, the definition of waters subject to federal jurisdiction under this law has become ever murkier. In the consolidated cases *Rapanos v. United States* and *Carabell v. United States*, 547 U.S. 715 (2006) ("*Rapanos*"), the Supreme Court rendered a 4-4-1 decision regarding the reach of federal jurisdiction, resulting in a new guidance issued by the U.S. Army Corps of Engineers and EPA, but no certainty. The definition of "jurisdictional waters" is particularly perplexing in arid regions where a normally dry drainage may be "jurisdictional" if it is tributary to an interstate water.

65. Cal. Pub. Res. Code §§ 21,000–21,177.

66. *See e.g.*, Nev. Rev. Stat. § 701A.300-390 (2009).

67. *See* Alyssa Kagel, Diana Bates & Karl Gawell, Geothermal Energy Ass'n, A Guide to Geothermal Energy and the Environment (2007), *available at* http://www.geo-energy.org/reports/Environmental%20Guide.pdf.

68. Frances S. Sterrett, Alternative Fuels and the Environment (1995).

69. See U.S. Dep't of Energy, Energy Efficiency & Renewable Energy, Geothermal Technologies Program FAQs (2006), http://www.eere.energy.gov/geothermal/faqs.html.

70. *See* http://www.geysers.com/history.htm.

71. See discussion of *Pit River Tribe v. U.S. Forest Service*, 469 F.3d 768 (9th Cir. 2006), in the following section of this chapter.

72. *See* http://www.nevadageothermal.com/s/Company.asp.

73. See 2008 Geothermal Report, *supra* note 3, at 19–25, for a thorough discussion of costs of construction and operation of geothermal generation facilities.

74. *Id.*

75. *Id.* at 16.

76. *Id.* at 5.

77. Rosette, Inc. v. United States, 169 P.3d 704 (N.M. Ct. App. 2007).

78. *Id.* at 708.

79. Rosette, Inc. v. United States (*Rosette I*), 141 F.3d 1394, 1395 (10th Cir. 1998).

80. Rosette, Inc. v. United States (*Rosette II*), 64 F. Supp. 2d 1116 (D.N.M. 1999).

81. Rosette, Inc. v. United States (*Rosette III*), 277 F.3d 1222, 1230–34 (10th Cir. 2002).

82. *Rosette*, 169 P.3d at 709.

83. *Id.*

84. *Id.* at 722.

85. 469 F.3d 768 (9th Cir. 2006).

86. *Id.* at 772–73.

87. *Id.* at 772.

88. *Id.* at 773–74.

89. *Id.* at 777.

90. *Id.* at 784.

91. *Id.*

92. *Id.* at 787.

93. 178 IBLA 210 (Nov. 5, 2009).

94. 321 F. Supp. 2d 1195 (D. Nev. 2004).

chapter nineteen

Biofuels

James M. Van Nostrand
and Anne Marie Hirschberger

Introduction

The use of biofuels in transportation fuels is nothing new. During the late nineteenth and early twentieth centuries, Rudolf Diesel, inventor of the diesel engine, promoted vegetable oil as a fuel source and designed a small prototype engine capable of running on peanut oil.[1] Henry Ford's Model T could run on either straight gasoline or pure ethanol.[2] Pre–World War II, 18 million gallons of ethanol were produced annually from an ethanol plant in Kansas.[3] With the reduced price of petroleum-based fuels that followed after the war, however, biofuels took a backseat until the 1970s when the oil crisis struck the U.S.[4] Soaring gas prices and shortages spurred the nation toward promoting biofuels, among other renewables, as a means of achieving energy security.

Since then, a new challenge has arisen that continues to drive U.S. biofuels policy: climate change. In addition to energy security objectives, the use of biofuels as a means of reducing greenhouse gases (GHGs) that contribute to climate change has become an increasingly important goal. While biofuels can have positive contributions in reducing GHG emissions in the transportation sector, there are also potentially negative effects associated with biofuels, such as impacts on water quality and quantity, and land use change.

In this chapter, we will review the complex set of policy issues and laws that have developed over recent years to increase the use of biofuels and to make them cost-competitive with petroleum-based fuels. After covering the basic technical aspects of biofuel production, we will explore some of the legal drivers behind biofuels production, such as federal incentives, flexible fuel vehicle requirements, the renewable fuel standard (RFS), and the low-carbon fuel standard (LCFS). Finally, we will examine recent and potential sources of future litigation.

What Are Biofuels?

The Process of Producing Biofuels

The biofuels supply chain generally consists of the following elements: (1) feedstock production, (2) feedstock logistics, (3) biofuels production, (4) biofuels distribution, and (5) biofuels end use.[5]

Feedstock refers to the material that will be converted into the biofuel. The feedstock is produced or gathered, and from there it must be harvested, stored, and transported to the biorefinery. Once there, the feedstock undergoes a conversion process that transforms the feedstock into a biofuel. This biofuel must then be blended into gasoline at a blending facility in order to be used for transportation fuel. From there, it is distributed and used to fuel vehicles. For purposes of this chapter, we will focus on feedstock production and biofuels production.

Feedstock Production

Feedstocks[6] for biofuels include a variety of materials, such as corn, grain, grasses, forest residue, crop residue, waste biomass (including yard waste, municipal solid waste, and construction and demolition debris), willow, soy, sugarcane, soybean oil, vegetable oil, and recycled grease. The type of feedstock used, in turn, depends upon a wide range of factors, including the climate in the growing region, land availability, landowner preferences, the laws addressing feedstocks, market conditions, and current subsidies and incentives. According to a 2005 study, the United States has the ability to produce over 1.3 billion dry tons[7] of biomass annually from forest and agricultural resources.[8]

Biofuels Production

Once the feedstocks arrive at the biorefinery, they undergo certain processes that convert them into one of the two main types of biofuels used as transportation fuels: ethanol and biodiesel.[9]

Current Technologies

Ethanol, like other alcohols, is made through the fermentation of sugar. In the United States, corn is the primary feedstock used for ethanol production. To produce ethanol, the corn undergoes either dry mill or wet mill processing to release the sugars. This means that the corn is either ground into flour (dry mill) or "steeped" in water where the corn grain components are separated (wet mill). Next, the fermentation process begins, where by-products (such as dried distillers grains and solubles (DDGS)[10] under the dry mill process) are separated, the ethanol is concentrated, and it is ultimately blended with gasoline.

Biodiesel is created from oil feedstocks, such as soybean oil or recycled grease. To produce biodiesel, these feedstocks undergo a process called transesterification. Here, the oil reacts with an alcohol such as methanol, and this produces biodiesel, which is then separated and refined into transportation fuel.

Advanced Technologies

Current U.S. biofuels policy is predominantly focused on developing a robust cellulosic ethanol industry. Cellulosic ethanol differs from traditional ethanol in that the feedstock is not cornstarch, but rather structural, nonedible plant materials. Such materials include certain forestry and agricultural residues and grasses, including switchgrass. There are several benefits to cellulosic ethanol, such as reduced GHG emissions during the life cycle of the fuel as well as the elimination of competition with food crops. Currently, however, there are only demonstration plants producing cellulosic ethanol in the United States.

Several complex conversion processes convert cellulosic material into ethanol, such as fermentation and gasification. Under fermentation, pretreatment is required in order to break the cell walls and access the sugars inside. Under gasification, the feedstock is converted into synthetic gas (syngas), which is purified and then converted back to liquid fuel.

Calculating GHG Emissions from Biofuels

Life Cycle Analysis

Biofuels are effective as a strategy to reduce GHG emissions from transportation fuels only insofar as their GHG emissions are actually lower than that of petroleum-based fuels. In order to calculate the total GHG emissions that result from biofuels, a complete life-cycle analysis (LCA) must be performed.[11] An LCA involves calculating GHG emissions at each step of the process of taking feedstock to a vehicle fuel tank. This is also known as a "well to wheels," or, more aptly, "field to wheels" analysis.[12] Typical stages of the analysis include the following: land use change; electricity generation necessary for fertilizer production; feedstock production; soil emissions from the application of fertilizers (which contain nitrogen, and from which nitrogen oxides (NO_x) are emitted); emissions from biorefineries; the transportation of refined fuel; and end use combustion of fuel.[13] Furthermore, there are different paths that could be taken—corn to ethanol, for example, will have different GHG emissions than soybean oil to biodiesel. These different paths are referred to as "fuel pathways." Once the LCA is complete, the total emissions are compared to those of a corresponding petroleum-based fuel in order to determine whether that particular biofuel's emissions are indeed less.

Land Use Change

Land use change is a crucial, and often controversial, element of an LCA. There are two types of land use change—direct and indirect. Direct land use change involves the effects directly associated with biofuel production activities when land not previously used for biofuel production is converted to such use, potentially resulting in a loss of carbon sequestration capacity and a release of carbon through tilling the land (soil stores carbon) or burning existing plants to clear the land. Indirect land use change (ILUC), on the other hand, occurs when biofuel production "displace[s] crops or pasture from current agricultural lands, indirectly causing GHG release via conversion of native habitat to cropland elsewhere."[14]

Another issue related to land use change is the "food versus fuel" debate. If an inedible energy crop is grown on prime agricultural land, food supplies will be reduced and food prices may rise.[15] Between April 2007 and April 2008, for example, the price of corn rose by over 50 percent.[16] During this same time, ethanol production increased 42 percent, due in large part to federal incentives designed to support increased production in order to achieve RFS goals.[17] Confirming an obvious correlation between increased ethanol production and increases in corn prices, a congressional study found that increased use of corn for ethanol in the United States contributed between 10 and 15 percent of the price increases.[18] The correlation between food prices and using corn as an energy crop is an important driver toward the increased production of cellulosic biofuel, which does not use food products as feedstock.

Impacts on Water

Evaluating the significance of the large amounts of water used in the biofuels supply chain requires a focus on local and regional considerations, because the effects of biofuels production on water supplies will be highly localized in nature.[19] The Ogallala Aquifer in the Midwest, for example, is "being drawn down at record rates, with an average drawdown of 4 m across the 8-state region it underlies, and water levels have dropped by over 40 m in some areas."[20] Biorefineries also use large amounts of water—a corn ethanol plant that produces 100 million gallons per year might use about 400 million gallons of water per year.[21]

Water quality is also affected due to increased fertilizer usage and soil erosion. Fertilizers such as nitrogen and phosphorous, in addition to seeping into groundwater, run off the land into surface waterways. Once in the surface water, these nutrients serve as food for plants such as algae, leading to tremendous growth in population called algae blooms. When the algae die, the decomposition process removes oxygen from the water (eutrophication), creating hypoxic zones (also known as dead zones), which are unable to sustain aquatic life.[22] Corn requires the most fertilizers and pesticides per hectare as compared to other common feedstocks,[23] so it is likely that increased demand of biofuels may increase demand for corn, thereby leading to more nutrient loading in U.S. waterways. Biorefineries also affect water quality, with both corn and cellulosic ethanol plants releasing acidic water with substances such as salts and chlorine, as well as high biochemical oxygen demand (BOD).[24]

Water quality also deteriorates from erosion, which increases as land is used for agricultural practices, especially row cropping.[25] In fact, the biofuels mandates have increased erosion by converting land that was formerly set aside under the federal conservation resource program (CRP) back into production.[26] Under the CRP, "highly erodible and minimally productive lands" are protected by giving farmers financial incentives and binding them under ten- to fifteen-year contracts to ensure they do not use such land for farming.[27] Once the second renewable fuel standard (RFS2) and other federal incentives came out, farmers began seeking early release from these contracts, and enrollment in the CRP program has substantially decreased.[28]

There are ways to mitigate these impacts, however. Different types of crops, for example, use different amounts of water. Corn requires more water than switchgrass, and jatropha (a type of succulent) requires even less. Some biorefineries have installed systems that allow them to reuse wastewater. Planting perennial crops helps stabilize the soil, preventing erosion. The responsible conduct of feedstock production is increasingly important in achieving sustainability objectives. While definitions of sustainability vary greatly, one report highlighted four areas of sustainability in the production of biofuels: "(1) soil resources and greenhouse gas emissions; (2) water quality, demand, and supply; (3) biodiversity and ecosystem services; and (4) integrated landscape ecology and feedstock production analysis."[29] In addition, a November 2009 government report found that further research is required in the areas of "water effects of feedstock cultivation and conversion and . . . better data on local and regional water resources" in order to "evaluate and understand the effects of increased biofuel production on water resources."[30]

Federal Incentives and Subsidies

Introduction

While biofuels have been strongly promoted through the implementation of RFS programs, LCFS programs, and other measures, there are some competitive disadvantages that remain in relation to petroleum-based fuels, including higher production costs and lack of technological infrastructure. Two of the major factors influencing the cost-competitiveness of biofuels are the cost of feedstocks and the cost of oil.[31] In order to overcome these barriers, the federal government has developed supportive policies—primarily tax incentives and grant/loan programs—that have enabled the rapid growth of the biofuels industry.[32] Indeed, federal incentives helped boost domestic ethanol production from 175 million gallons in 1980 to 6.8 billion gallons in 2007.[33] Given the steep fuel mandates imposed under RFS2, there is also a noticeable increase in new incentives designed to support the burgeoning advanced biofuels industry, especially cellulosic ethanol.[34]

Tax incentives have been the primary, and perhaps the most powerful, driver of the U.S. biofuels industry to date.[35] The Volumetric Ethanol Excise Tax Credit, for example, is credited with "helping to create a profitable cornstarch ethanol industry when the industry had to fund investment in new facilities."[36]

In addition, grant and loan programs that stimulate research and development (R&D) of new biofuels-related technologies have played a critical role in reducing the risk of investment in cutting-edge projects. According to one report, "[g]overnment cost sharing of pilot-scale, demonstration-scale, and pioneering commercial-scale integrated biorefineries is needed to reduce investment risks and provide the reliability and performance data required to foster rapid commercialization."[37] Further, R&D support is a major focus of current strategies to promote further development of the biofuels industry. Indeed, the President's "Growing America's Fuels" strategy, which is geared toward spurring growth in the biofuels industry, stresses the importance of collaborative R&D, and through the 2011 budget, the United States "will develop five USDA regional feedstock research and demonstration centers with robust partnerships."[38] The 2011 budget proposes $220 million for R&D in biomass/biofuels as well as $325 million in R&D for advanced vehicles.[39]

Examples of Federal Legislation Promoting Biofuels

Below are examples of federal legislation promoting biofuels. For further details on federal tax incentives, grant/loan programs, and other nontax incentives for clean energy sources, including biofuels, see chapters 7 and 8.

The American Recovery and Reinvestment Act of 2009

In order to stimulate the economy after the impact of the recession in the second half of 2008, Congress passed the American Recovery and Reinvestment Act of 2009 (ARRA) on February 17, 2009.[40] Below are select provisions from sections of ARRA that promote biofuels.[41]

Energy Efficiency and Renewable Energy. The Department of Energy (DOE) was given $2.5 billion to go toward "applied research, development, demonstration and deployment activities" and $800 million to go to projects related to the development of biomass.[42]

Alternative Fueled Vehicles. ARRA provides $300 million for competitive grants to promote "the purchase of alternative fuel and advanced technology vehicles" as well as associated infrastructure.[43] These grants are based on the framework provided under the Energy Policy Act of 2005 (EPAct 2005) § 721, which established "a competitive grant pilot program . . . to be administered through the Clean Cities Program of the Department [of Energy]."

Extension of Production Tax Credit (PTC). A renewable energy production tax credit of $0.015 cents/kWh[44] is available for electricity generated from specified renewable energy sources, including biomass systems.[45] ARRA extends these tax credits to 2014 and provides additional flexibility options to ease the difficulties associated with financing PTC projects.[46]

Clean Renewable Energy Bonds (CREBs). CREBs are designed to promote the construction of facilities that generate energy from renewable sources, including biomass.[47]

Energy Conservation Bonds (ECBs). The Emergency Economic Stabilization Act of 2008 initially created the ECB program, which is designed to allow local governments to finance renewable energy projects. Among the qualifying projects under this program are expenditures "to support research in . . . the development of cellulosic ethanol and other nonfossil fuels."[48]

Alternative Fuel Infrastructure Tax Credit. The alternative fuel infrastructure tax credit allows a property owner to recover up to 30 percent of the cost of installing fueling infrastructure that dispenses specified renewable fuels, including E85 and certain biodiesel blends.[49]

The Food, Conservation, and Energy Act of 2008

The Food, Conservation, and Energy Act of 2008, more commonly known as the Farm Bill of 2008, has roots dating back to the 1930s.[50] The Farm Security and Rural Investment Act of 2002 (FSRIA or Farm Bill of 2002) was the first farm bill to contain a separate title dedicated to energy.[51] The Farm Bill of 2008 substantially builds upon the foundations laid by the 2002 bill and expands upon the incentives available for biofuels.

Agricultural Bioenergy Feedstock and Energy Efficiency Research and Extension Initiative. This program, to be operated by the U.S. Department of Agriculture (USDA), focuses on "improving agricultural biomass production, biomass conversion in biorefineries, and biomass use by . . . supporting on-farm research" and "supporting the development and operation of on-farm, integrated biomass feedstock production systems."[52]

Biorefinery Assistance. A prominent section, the Biorefinery Assistance Program, seeks "to assist in the development of new and emerging technologies for the development of advanced biofuels, so as to . . . increase the energy independence of the United States; promote resource conservation, public health, and the environment; . . . [and] diversify markets for agricultural and forestry products and agriculture waste material. . . ."[53] Grants are provided on a competitive basis for parties "to assist in paying the costs of the development and construction of demonstration-scale biorefineries,"[54] and loan guarantees are provided for funding "the development, construction, and retrofitting of commercial-scale biorefineries. . . ."[55]

Biomass Research and Development Initiative. The Farm Bill of 2008 "provides competitive funding for research, development, and demonstration projects on biofuels and bio-based chemicals and products."[56] This joint effort between the USDA and the DOE incorporates advisory boards and technical guidance from multiple government agencies. Between 2002 and 2007, this initiative provided over $159 million in funding for nearly one hundred biofuels R&D projects.[57]

Rural Energy for America Program (REAP). This program provides a wide variety of support for renewable energy and energy incentives, including loan guarantees and grants, as well as feasibility studies and energy audits.[58] Eligible renewable energy projects include biorefineries and electricity generators that run on biomass.

Biomass Crop Assistance Program (BCAP). The BCAP was designed to "support the establishment and production of eligible crops for conversion to bioenergy in selected BCAP project areas; and . . . assist agricultural and forest land owners and operators with collection, harvest, storage, and transportation of eligible material for use in a biomass conversion facility."[59] Eligible parties under this program will have coverage for up to 75 percent of their costs related to establishing a crop.[60] In addition, payments made by a biomass conversion facility for crops will be matched dollar-for-dollar up to $45/ton.[61]

Credit for Production of Cellulosic Biofuel. This tax credit amends the Internal Revenue Code (IRC) to provide any taxpayer with $1.01 for each gallon of cellulosic ethanol produced.[62]

Modification of Alcohol Credit. The tax credit for traditional ethanol is reduced from $0.51/gallon to $0.45/gallon.[63] If the U.S. Environmental Protection Agency (EPA) determines that the total amount of ethanol (including cellulosic) in the United States is under 7.5 million gallons, however, the credit will remain at $0.51.[64]

Flexible Fuel Vehicles and Fleet Acquisition Requirements

Flexible fuel vehicles (also known as flex fuel vehicles or FFVs) are alternative-fuel vehicles that are capable of running on gasoline, E85 (meaning a blend of 85 percent ethanol and 15 percent gasoline), or any combination of gasoline and E85.[65] E85 has a lower energy content than regular gasoline, meaning that compared to a vehicle running on gasoline, FFVs may get 20 to 30 percent fewer miles to the gallon.[66] Even with the fewer miles per gallon, however, E85 is reported to reduce GHG emissions by between 17 percent and 23 percent on a per-mile basis as compared to gasoline.[67]

Aside from the components that handle the fuel, FFVs are structurally identical to gasoline-powered vehicles.[68] Today, there are roughly 6 million FFVs on the road in the United States[69] and 1,980 fueling stations that offer E85.[70] These numbers are expected to increase in response to the higher renewable fuel mandates required under the Energy Independence and Security Act of 2007 (EISA).[71]

In order to reduce GHG and other polluting emissions resulting from vehicle use, the federal government and some state governments mandate that a certain percentage of the vehicles purchased in their fleets must be capable of running on alternative fuels. These are generally known as acquisition requirements. They often require that these vehicles must run on an alternative fuel at all times (subject to certain waivers) or a certain percentage of the time.

Federal Requirements

Under the Energy and Policy Act of 1992 (EPAct 1992), 75 percent of the vehicles in the fleets acquired by federal agencies must be capable of running on alternative fuel[72] and must actually operate on that fuel unless the waiver provisions apply.[73] EPAct 1992 considers "dual fueled vehicles," such as FFVs, to qualify under this mandate.[74] Guidance provided by DOE in September 2009 indicates that over 90 percent of the alternative-fuel vehicles acquired under this mandate have been FFVs.[75] EPAct 1992 also set acquisition requirements for state fleets that have been implemented through DOE rulemaking.[76] These regulations require that 75 percent of the vehicle acquisitions made by states (excluding municipalities) must be alternative-fueled vehicles,[77] including FFVs.[78] Federal acquisition requirements are discussed in greater detail in chapter 6.

State Requirements

As of July 2009, forty-five states and the District of Columbia had laws imposing acquisition or fuel use requirements for fleets under their jurisdiction.[79] Examples of select state laws include the following:

Arizona. Under Arizona law, the governing board of certain school districts is required to ensure that at least 50 percent of the school-district-owned vehicles weighing over 17,500 pounds are able to operate on alternative fuels, including E85.[80] Arizona mandates that 75 percent of all annual state vehicles must be able to run on alternative fuels.[81] Buses operating in certain cities, towns, and counties must be able to run on alternative fuel or clean-burning fuel.[82]

California. In California, every city, county, and special district awarding a procurement contract may require that 75 percent of the purchases run on alternative fuels such as E85.[83] The Department of General Services is required to study energy-efficient vehicles and rank them according to class in terms of their efficiency and their purpose for the state.[84] State fleet procurements will be based upon these rankings, and, if the vehicles are capable of running on alternative fuels, they should do so "to the maximum extent practicable."[85]

Iowa. Iowa's "State Government E85 Use Plan" as well as Executive Order 3 (2007) both promote the use of E85, and the Executive Order specifically mandated that use of E85 in FFVs be increased to 60 percent by June 30, 2009.[86] Executive Order No. 41 (2005) also requires that 100 percent of all state fleet acquisitions must be either alternative-fuel vehicles (including FFVs) or hybrids.[87] At least 10 percent of all light-duty vehicle acquisitions made by various state-run institutions must be composed of fuel-efficient vehicles, including FFVs.[88]

Massachusetts. Massachusetts law requires that every year, 5 percent of all vehicles purchased by the state must be either hybrids or alternative-fuel vehicles, including FFVs, such that by 2018, at least 50 percent of the fleet owned by the state are either hybrids or alternative-fuel vehicles.[89]

New York. In 2008, New York's governor continued Executive Order No. 111 (2001), which mandated that by 2010, "100 percent of all new light-duty vehicles [procured by the state] shall be alternative-fueled vehicles," with certain exceptions.[90] In New York City, at least 80 percent of all vehicles purchased must be alternative-fuel vehicles, including FFVs.[91]

North Carolina. North Carolina requires that "at least seventy-five percent (75%) of the new or replacement light duty cars and trucks purchased by the State will be alternative-fueled vehicles or low emission vehicles."[92]

Renewable Fuel Standard

The Beginnings of the Renewable Fuels Program

The Energy Policy Act of 2005

The foundation of the RFS was laid in EPAct 2005. In response to growing concerns over domestic energy security, high energy prices, and the need for clean energy sources, EPAct 2005 sought "[t]o ensure jobs for our future with secure, afford-able, and reliable energy."[93] Some of the most significant provisions were those that amended the Clean Air Act (CAA) by adding §211(o), a section implementing what is referred to as the "renewable fuel program."[94] This program, or RFS program, requires that an increasing amount of the "gasoline sold or introduced into commerce in the United States" must be blended with designated renewable fuels according to a specific timeline.[95] It called for 7.5 billion gallons to be blended by 2012 and, there-after, that 250 million gallons of renewable fuel be derived from cellulosic biomass.[96] Under EPAct 2005, renewable fuel was defined as "motor vehicle fuel" produced from several sources, including grain, natural gas, and greases; cellulosic ethanol and biodiesel were also considered renewable fuels.[97]

The EPA Administrator was given primary responsibility for developing a pro-gram that would ensure that the RFS program achieved these goals. In order for these renewable fuel volume targets to be met, the Administrator was required to consult with the Energy Information Administration (EIA) and determine the "applicable percentages" of renewable fuel that must be blended each year and make that infor-mation known each November.[98] These applicable percentage requirements apply to "refineries, blenders, and importers, as appropriate,"[99] and compliance would be determined by a credit-tracking system to be developed by EPA.[100]

The Initial RFS Regulations—Not Enough Time

According to EPAct 2005, the Administrator was to promulgate regulations and essentially have the program up and running by August 8, 2006.[101] EPA determined, however, that a properly designed RFS program capable of providing regulatory cer-tainty to the affected parties could not be crafted by August 2006, and therefore issued a direct final rule, meaning that it did not seek public comment before final-izing the rule because it believed it would not receive any adverse comments. In doing so, EPA relied on a default provision provided in EPAct 2005, which stated that if the Administrator has not yet promulgated regulations to implement the RFS program, the applicable percentage for the year 2006 would be 2.78 percent.[102] In addition, EPA developed a more lenient set of regulations to apply during the interim period while the actual RFS program was structured.[103]

Implementing the Renewable Fuel Standard Program

Final Rulemaking Comes to Pass

After the 2006 direct final rule was promulgated, EPA proceeded to develop regula-tions that would fully implement the RFS program. It began by engaging stakeholders, including refiners, producers, distributors, marketers, and environmental groups,[104] in the development of the rules, using the following principles as guidelines:

> [T]hat the compliance and trading program should provide certainty to the
> marketplace and minimize cost to the consumers; that the program should
> preserve existing business practices for the production, distribution, and

use of both conventional and renewable fuels; that the program should be designed to accommodate all qualifying renewable fuels; that all renewable volumes produced are made available to obligated parties for compliance; and that the Agency should have the ability to easily verify compliance to ensure that the volume obligations are in fact met.[105]

EPA issued a Notice of Proposed Rulemaking (NPRM)[106] on September 22, 2006, and then issued the Final Rule on the structure of the RFS program effective for 2007 and thereafter on May 1, 2007.[107] It refined some aspects of the 2006 rule and developed several new regulations to ensure clarity and effectiveness.

Overview of the RFS

Renewable Volume Obligations

As of the May 2007 rulemaking, the RFS was 4.7 billion gallons. EPA determined in the rulemaking that the required percentage of renewable fuel for each obligated party (as defined below) would be 4.02 percent.[108] Once this percentage is established, each obligated party must determine its renewable volume obligation, or RVO.[109] The RVO is calculated by multiplying the party's projected annual gasoline volume (in gallons) that will either be produced or imported during the compliance year by the applicable percentage (plus any deficit from the prior year).[110] For example, if a party expects to produce 100,000 gallons of gasoline, and the applicable percentage is 4.02 percent, it will have to ensure that 4,020 gallons are considered renewable.

Obligated Parties

Obligated parties are required to demonstrate that a certain volume of their fuel, based on the regulatory percentage for that particular year, is considered renewable fuel. Under these regulations, "[a]n obligated party is a refiner that produces gasoline within the 48 contiguous states, or an importer that imports gasoline into the 48 contiguous states."[111] Certain blenders are also considered obligated parties.[112]

Renewable Fuels

The May 2007 rulemaking promulgated regulations that provided greater specificity as to the types of fuels that would qualify as renewable under EPAct 2005.[113] EPA interpreted the definition of "renewable fuel" in EPAct 2005 as being "broad in scope, and [covering] a wide range of fuels," and providing for more flexibility and practicality.[114] It is also important to note that different renewable fuels have different "equivalence values" for purposes of compliance with the RFS, based on energy content. For example, EPAct 2005 "stipulates that every gallon of waste-derived ethanol and cellulosic biomass ethanol should count as if it were 2.5 gallons for RFS compliance purposes."[115]

Ensuring Compliance with the RFS

Tracking gallons of renewable fuels through the complex network of production, refinement, and distribution operations raises a host of challenges in terms of ensuring that each obligated party's RVO is met. In response to this, EPA developed a tracking system involving a tradable commodity called a Renewable Identification Number, or an RIN, which is a series of numbers that provides information unique to that particular volume of renewable fuel. Generally speaking, in order for an obligated party to demonstrate that it has met its RVO, the party must obtain the required number of RINs by the end of the compliance period. To meet this requirement, obligated parties may engage in the trading of RINs much like other environmental commodities (i.e., parties in need of RINs may purchase them from those with excess RINS, and those with excess RINs may sell them). Such a system not only allows EPA to ensure compliance with the RFS, but it also gives the obligated parties flexibility in terms of meeting their respective RVOs. EPA has established a trading platform called the EPA Moderated Transaction System, or EMTS, to manage these trades and ensure the validity of the RINS being traded.[116]

When renewable fuel is produced or imported, the producer or importer of that fuel must generate and assign an RIN to that fuel before transferring ownership of the RIN and volume of renewable fuel to which it corresponds.[117] An RIN may represent one gallon of fuel, or it may represent a batch of renewable fuel, meaning multiple gallons (but no more than 99,999,999 gallons).[118] In order to obtain an RIN for compliance purposes, the RIN must be "separated" from the renewable fuel with which it is associated. EPA regulations mandate specific circumstances that must exist in order for RINs to be separated from the renewable fuel volumes. For purposes of this discussion, the most important circumstance occurs when an obligated party obtains ownership of the renewable fuel.[119] This means that a refiner/importer of gasoline must separate the RIN from the renewable fuel, and at that point, the refiner/importer may keep the RIN for compliance, bank it for the following year, or sell it on the market.[120] At the end of a compliance period, each obligated party must have enough RINs to meet its RVO.

The Energy Independence and Security Act of 2007 and the Creation of RFS2

EISA was signed into law on December 19, 2007.[121] Much like EPAct 2005, EISA is intended to reduce dependence on foreign fuel and promote energy security. However, EISA features a more ambitious plan for achieving energy security that includes a sharp focus on GHG reduction as well.[122] Ultimately, these changes would be referred to as RFS2 since it is effectively the second renewable fuel standard.

Senate Hearings on EISA

Well before EPA proposed regulations to implement RFS2, there was concern over the impacts EISA would have on the energy market and related infrastructure. On February 7, 2008, the Senate Energy and Natural Resources Committee held a hearing on this subject. Government witnesses, though supportive of the goals and optimistic about achieving them, acknowledged that significant infrastructure changes would be required in order to support the growing biofuel industry. Such changes include improved distribution networks and an increase in the number of pumps that can dispense higher blends such as E15, E20, and E85.[123]

Witnesses from the biofuels industry were supportive of the mandates as well, though they expressed concern over the life-cycle analyses, GHG thresholds, and consideration of ILUC because it "unfairly penalizes domestic grain-based ethanol."[124] An environmental group, on the other hand, was quite supportive of the inclusion of ILUC in life-cycle analyses, but encouraged an expansion of what constitutes "renewable biomass" in order to include "feedstocks that do not induce land use changes."[125]

Implementing RFS2: Notice of Proposed Rulemaking

EPA issued its NPRM on RFS2 on May 26, 2009.[126] EISA required several changes to the RFS program, including: (1) substantial increases in renewable fuel volumes; (2) the introduction of four discrete categories of renewable fuels with unique volumes to be met; (3) new feedstock definitions; and (4) the requirement of a life-cycle GHG analysis to determining eligibility of a renewable fuel.

Volume Increases and New Categories

The following table illustrates the substantial increases in renewable fuel volumes, as well as the new categories of fuel, required under EISA.[127] The four categories are cellulosic biofuel, biomass-based diesel, advanced biofuels, and renewable fuels.

Renewable Fuel Volume (billions of gallons)

Calendar Year	Cellulosic Biofuel	Biomass-based Diesel	Advanced Biofuels	Total Requirement
2008	n/a	n/a	n/a	9.0
2009	n/a	0.5	0.6	11.1
2010	0.1	0.65	0.95	12.95
2011	0.25	0.80	1.35	13.95
2012	0.5	1.0	2.0	15.2
2013	1.0	a	2.75	16.55
2014	1.75	a	3.75	18.15
2015	3.0	a	5.5	20.5
2016	4.25	a	7.25	22.25
2017	5.5	a	9.0	24.0
2018	7.0	a	11.0	26.0
2019	8.5	a	13.0	28.0
2020	10.5	a	15.0	30.0
2021	13.5	a	18.0	33.0
2022	16.0	a	21.0	36.0
2023+	b	b	b	b

a: To be determined by EPA through a future rulemaking, but no less than 1.0 billion gallons.

b: To be determined by EPA through a future rulemaking.

These increases in the amounts of these fuels were expected to have profound effects on the biofuels market and biofuels-related infrastructure. According to EPA, they "will push the market to new levels—far beyond what current market conditions would achieve alone."[128] The push for cellulosic biofuel in particular "will provide a strong foundation for investment in cellulosic production and position cellulosic fuel to become a major portion of the renewable fuel pool over the next decade."[129]

Life Cycle GHG Emissions

As mentioned above, the introduction of these new renewable fuel categories is in part a response to a growing concern over GHG emissions. For each category, EPA established a life-cycle GHG emissions threshold that must be met in order for a particular fuel to be counted toward the RFS. Under EISA, "lifecycle greenhouse gas emissions" are defined as:

> [T]he aggregate quantity of greenhouse gas emissions (including direct emissions and significant indirect emissions such as significant emissions from land use changes), as determined by the Administrator, related to the full fuel lifecycle, including all stages of fuel and feedstock production and distribution, from feedstock generation or extraction through the distribution and delivery and use of the finished fuel to the ultimate consumer, where the mass values for all greenhouse gases are adjusted to account for their relative global warming potential.[130]

Further, these GHG thresholds are relative to "baseline lifecycle greenhouse gas emissions," which are defined as "the average lifecycle greenhouse gas emissions . . . for gasoline or diesel . . . sold or distributed as transportation fuel in 2005."[131] In order to ensure that the GHG emission thresholds are met for the renewable fuels, EPA is required to analyze the various fuel pathways.[132]

Based on these factors, a renewable fuel may be considered an "advanced biofuel" if the "lifecycle greenhouse gas emissions . . . are at least 50 percent less than baseline lifecycle greenhouse gas emissions."[133] The standards for cellulosic biofuel and bio-based diesel are 60 percent and 50 percent, respectively.[134] One source of future contention, as discussed below, was the requirement that any renewable fuel, including cornstarch ethanol, must meet a 20 percent threshold if it is produced at a facility constructed after the enactment of EISA.[135]

Feedstock Definitions

Under EISA, renewable fuels must meet more stringent requirements in terms of the feedstock from which the fuel is made. EISA defines "renewable fuel" as "fuel that is produced from renewable biomass and that is used to replace or reduce the quantity of fossil fuel present in a transportation fuel."[136] "Renewable biomass," in turn, not only specifies which sources are permissible, but also "limits many of these feedstocks according to the management practices for the land from which they are derived."[137] In addition, "[t]he statutory definition of 'renewable biomass' in EISA does not include a reference to municipal solid waste (MSW) as did the definition of 'cellulosic biomass ethanol' in EPAct [2005], but instead includes 'separated yard waste and food waste.'"[138]

The Indirect Land Use Change Dilemma

By far the greatest source of controversy raised by the proposed rule was indirect land use change, or ILUC—especially as it relates to the corn ethanol industry. Under the proposed rule, EPA, as required by EISA, included international ILUC in determining the GHG emissions from corn ethanol, which is significant given that the fuel must meet a 20 percent GHG reduction relative to the 2005 gasoline baseline. When ILUC was included in the analysis, corn ethanol showed a 16 percent reduction in GHG over a one hundred-year period and a 5 percent increase in GHG over a thirty-year period.[139] When ILUC was not included in the analysis, corn ethanol showed a 60 percent reduction in GHG, regardless of the period of analysis.[140] While many believed this placed corn ethanol at a disadvantage compared to the other renewable fuels, others noted the importance of including land use change impacts in the life-cycle analyses.[141]

Final Rule Issued

On March 26, 2010, EPA issued the final rule implementing RFS2.[142] This rule reflects essentially the same changes that were suggested in the NPRM, namely, increases in renewable fuel volume, the creation of four categories of fuel with unique volumetric requirements that must be met under the RFS, incorporation of life-cycle GHG considerations in assessing whether a renewable fuel qualifies under the RFS, and the "renewable biomass" definition. There are some key points, however, that are important to note.

EPA's final rule reflected new life-cycle GHG emission analyses it performed based on input from stakeholders and experts. Regarding corn ethanol, EPA "found less overall indirect land use change (less land needed), thereby improving the life-cycle GHG performance of corn ethanol."[143] This was primarily due to increased crop yields, the use of dried distillers grains and soluble (DDGS) for feed instead of corn, and improved satellite data on the types of land converted due to ILUC.[144] Similar reductions in the ILUC impacts of soybean production were also found.[145] In addition, "EPA plans to continue to improve upon its analyses, and will update it in the future as appropriate."[146] These findings have, at least temporarily, quelled the concerns cited by those in the ethanol industry and the environmental community alike.[147]

In addition, the final rule clarified and expanded the definition of "renewable biomass" as compared to the version in the NPRM. It alleviated some of the restrictions on the "planted trees and tree residue" portion, and, by reference, included "separated municipal solid waste," which includes "material remaining after separation actions have been taken."[148]

Is 36 Billion Gallons by 2022 Achievable?

One lingering question is whether the United States will be capable of meeting the volumetric targets set by EISA. As of January 2010, there are 187 ethanol plants in the United States with the ability to produce over 1.3 billion gallons per year.[149] While this production is expected to increase over the years, the blend wall issue presents a particular challenge. The blend wall is "the point where all of the nation's gasoline supply is blended as E10 and extra volumes of ethanol cannot be readily consumed."[150] Because currently the vast majority of the nation's cars can run only on E10, there may come a point when the additional ethanol production simply lacks a market for the required output.[151]

Cellulosic ethanol also faces significant problems, including market uncertainty, potentially limited availability of agricultural residues, and the conflicting definitions of "renewable biomass" found in EISA and the 2008 Farm Bill.[152] In addition, there are no commercially scaled cellulosic ethanol plants in the United States, though, according to the Renewable Fuels Association, there are twenty-eight plants under construction.[153] The EIA's Annual Energy Outlook 2010 Early Release Overview gives a bleak forecast:

> Although the situation is uncertain, the current state of the industry and EIA's present view of the projected rates of technology development and market penetration of cellulosic biofuel technologies suggest that available quantities of cellulosic biofuels will be insufficient to meet the new RFS targets for cellulosic biofuels before 2022. . . . [154]

To address such problems with achieving the RFS2 targets, DOE has proposed an extensive action plan targeting all segments of the biofuels supply chain.[155] In addition, the President's Biofuels Interagency Working Group has devised a plan to stimulate and improve the efficiency of the biofuels industry. Both plans have similar strategies, including extensive R&D, public-private partnerships, and integration among government agencies.

Low Carbon Fuel Standards

Introduction

An LCFS is a policy aimed at reducing GHG emissions from the transportation sector. The following excerpt from a recent report from the National Renewable Energy Laboratory (NREL) explains the general principles behind LCFS programs:

> An LCFS is an intensity target for the amount of carbon and other greenhouse gases (GHGs) emitted per unit of energy obtained from the fuel (i.e., gCO2e/MJ). The LCFS regulatory strategy is varied: it can require measuring all fuel consumption or partial amounts and regulation can take place at a number of points in the supply chain, most commonly at the level of oil refineries and importers. For an LCFS, some kind of valuing carbon intensity and trading system for carbon credits must be designed and implemented. The strategy may effectively encourage development of innovative low-carbon fuels and better transportation options.
>
> An LCFS is similar to an RFS in that they both are market-based approaches dealing with the transportation energy sector. The goal of an

LCFS is to reduce the carbon intensity of the transportation sector through three strategies: increasing the efficiency of vehicle technologies; reducing fuel-related GHGs (this can be achieved in several ways, one of which is increasing the use of renewable fuels); and, finally, decreasing the amount and use of vehicles and fuels by increasing the availability and use of alternative transportation. . . . [156]

Attempts at a Federal Standard

While there are not currently any federal LCFS, there have been several attempts to implement such a program through congressional bills. According to a report by the Congressional Research Service, seven bills were introduced in the 110th Congress that included provisions for an LCFS.[157] One of those bills was the National Low-Carbon Fuel Standard Act of 2007, sponsored by then Senator Obama and cosponsored by Senator Durbin and Senator Harkin, which called for a 10 percent reduction by 2020.[158] It eventually stalled in a Senate subcommittee. In addition, the discussion draft of the American Clean Energy and Security Act of 2009 introduced by Representatives Waxman and Markey on March 31, 2009, contained a more modest low carbon fuel standard provision (5 percent reduction below the gasoline baseline between 2023 and 2030 and a 10 percent reduction after 2030), though it was later removed.[159]

State-Implemented Standards

California

The California LCFS seeks to reduce the carbon intensity of transportation fuel by 10 percent by 2020, and in doing so will prevent 16 million metric tons of GHG from being emitted.[160] According to the California Air Resources Board (CARB), the LCFS was "designed to capture the diverse fuel portfolio available today and in the near future, while offering a fuel-neutral platform in which alternative fuels can be incentivized without choosing winners or losers."[161] Despite these attempts at creating an even playing field, however, several groups have sued California because of claims that the LCFS discriminates against certain types of fuel sources.[162]

Background

The foundation for California's LCFS was laid by the California Global Warming Solutions Act of 2006 (AB 32), which mandated a reduction in California's GHG emissions to 1990 levels by 2020.[163] Then, on January 18, 2007, Governor Schwarzenegger signed Executive Order No. S-01-07,[164] which placed CARB in charge of implementing an LCFS to reduce the carbon intensity of California's transportation fuel by 10 percent by the year 2020.[165] After several public meetings and comment periods, the first part of the regulations was adopted on November 25, 2009,[166] and they were approved by the Office of Administrative Law on January 12, 2010;[167] the second part was adopted on March 4, 2010,[168] and the LCFS became effective on April 15, 2010.[169]

Elements of the California LCFS

The LCFS established a comprehensive framework of regulations governing various elements of the transportation fuel industry, including carbon intensity standards of fuel, compliance obligations of regulated parties, and market-based credit/deficit mechanisms.

Unlike the RFS, the LCFS seeks to reduce GHG emissions from transportation fuels by requiring reductions in the carbon intensity of those fuels rather than by specifying which types of fuels may be used. The LCFS provides for two different standards: one for gasoline and the fuels used to replace it, and another for diesel fuel and the fuels used to replace it. For each one, the carbon intensity is based on the amount of carbon released for each unit of energy (mega joule).[170] Over time, the amount of carbon dioxide equivalent released for each mega joule is required to be decreased until it reaches a level that is 10 percent less than that emitted in 2010.

Under the LCFS, regulated parties generally include refiners and importers of fuel.[171] To comply with the LCFS, they must demonstrate that the carbon intensity of the fuel they are refining or importing meets or falls below the average carbon intensity permitted for that particular year. Regulated parties may review tables containing the carbon intensities for numerous fuel pathways which were determined through computer-modeled life-cycle analyses accounting for direct and indirect land use change.[172] If the carbon intensity for its fuel is at or below the average required under the LCFS for that year, the regulated party will generate credits; if the intensity is above the average, the party will generate a deficit.[173] The LCFS is also intended to provide flexibility for regulated parties in meeting their compliance obligations.[174]

Indirect Land Use Change

Much like the controversy surrounding ILUC in terms of its impact on the RFS life-cycle analysis, there are groups opposed to the inclusion of ILUC in analyzing the carbon intensity of ethanol as a transportation fuel because they believe that (1) the science behind ILUC is not yet sufficient to warrant its application, and (2) the application as it stands now unfairly targets the ethanol industry. During the public comment periods, hundreds of comments were received, and many of them were concerned with the treatment of ILUC.[175] In order to address ILUC concerns and other technical issues, CARB created an Expert Workgroup comprising various experts that will meet publicly to develop policy recommendations on these matters.[176]

Northeast and Mid-Atlantic States

On December 31, 2008, the Commissioners of the environmental agencies of eleven Northeastern and Mid-Atlantic states—Connecticut, Delaware, Maine, Maryland, Massachusetts, New Jersey, New Hampshire, New York, Pennsylvania, Rhode Island, and Vermont—signed a letter of intent signifying their commitment to draft a Memorandum of Understanding (MOU) creating an LCFS for their region.[177] Throughout the process of developing an LCFS program for this region, the interested states have been "closely following" the development of California's LCFS and are looking to it as a model.[178]

After conducting stakeholder meetings and soliciting public comments, the eleven states signed an MOU on December 30, 2009.[179] In this document, they committed to developing a proposed framework by 2011 that would address (1) compliance goals to be met by reduced carbon intensity, specifically seeking to achieve a 10 percent reduction; (2) what entities would be regulated; (3) the possibility of including heating fuels under the LCFS; (4) market-based mechanisms to drive the program; and (5) compliance and enforcement options.[180] In addition, they agreed "to determine the lifecycle carbon intensity of fuels based on the best available science and analyses, and to include *non–de minimis* direct and indirect emissions, such as those from land use changes attributable to food production."[181]

Currently, the Northeast States for Coordinated Air Use Management (NESCAUM), which has been taking a lead role in developing the LCFS along with Delaware, Maryland, and Pennsylvania,[182] is working to develop strategies for conducting a comprehensive economic analysis and determining the best methods for establishing carbon intensity values.[183]

Washington

On May 21, 2009, Governor Christine Gregoire signed Executive Order No. 09-05, entitled "Washington's Leadership on Climate Change," which required the Department of Ecology to determine whether an LCFS such as California's would further Washington's GHG reduction goals.[184] After receiving public comment, the Department of Ecology plans to have draft recommendations ready for presentation and discussion at a final workshop in order for a final report to be presented to the Governor by July 2010.

Oregon

Oregon passed House Bill 2186 on July 22, 2009, declaring an emergency because of the urgency associated with reducing GHGs. This declaration permits the Oregon Environmental Quality Commission to adopt rules implementing a low-carbon fuel standard for transportation fuels.[185] Much like Washington, Oregon plans on using California's LCFS as a model for developing its own LCFS.[186] A report issued by the Oregon Department of Environmental Quality states that the LCFS program should replace the average carbon intensity of conventional gasoline and diesel fuel by 10 percent over a ten-year period, and that Oregon plans to have a proposed low-carbon fuel standard rule drafted for public comment by summer 2011.[187]

Midwestern Governors Association

In its publication, "Energy Security and Climate Stewardship Platform for the Midwest 2007," the Midwestern Governors Association (MGA) discusses developing an LCFS.[188] According to the MGA, stakeholders have agreed that an LCFS should "[c]reate a framework and incentives for development of, and demand for, low carbon fuels in the Midwest; [d]ecrease the GHG intensity of transportation fuels; [t]ake advantage of our agricultural and industrial strengths to benefit our regional economy while protecting our natural resources; and [c]omplement other policies focused on improving transportation efficiency and reducing GHG emissions in the region."[189] In December 2010, the Low Carbon Fuel Policy Advisory Group proposed a goal of at least 10 percent reduction in carbon intensity of fuels within ten years.[190] The overall program is structured much like the California model, with special attention paid to the Midwest's unique agricultural opportunities and natural resources.[191]

Recent Litigation

Introduction

Litigation related to biofuels touches upon several different practice areas. Currently, however, the majority of cases address biofuels only tangentially. For example, there are many cases regarding contract disputes, including delivery contracts,[192] joint ventures/start-ups,[193] and breach of construction/financing contracts,[194] as well as fraud.[195] There is also an increasing amount of litigation regarding technology transfer agreements and patents,[196] so many that the President directly addressed this issue in his "Growing America's Fuel" plan on achieving the biofuels mandates.[197] There are some specific areas, however, that are worth addressing individually as they have greater implications on the growth of the biofuels industry as a whole and are therefore likely to become more prevalent as the mandates take hold.

Federalism Issues

Federalism issues are likely to arise because of the nature of the RFS2 mandates. These requirements contain specific definitions of what types of fuel will qualify, and they apply equally across the entire nation. Meanwhile, states not only have unique sources of renewable fuel, but also unique laws regarding what constitutes renewable fuels. All of these interactions will continue to reveal themselves as the states, as well as the federal government, move forward with implementing these mandates.

Because of the controversial issues raised by the California LCFS with respect to life-cycle analyses, two lawsuits have been filed. The first is *Rocky Mountain Farmers Union v. Goldstene.*[198] The basis for the suit is plaintiffs' claim that the LCFS is preempted by EISA because the California LCFS effectively excludes midwestern ethanol and favors local ethanol, whereas EISA's goal was to promote investment in and development of the domestic ethanol industry nationwide and to ensure that ethanol may be sold anywhere.[199] Plaintiffs similarly claim that the California LCFS improperly interferes with interstate commerce by discriminating against midwestern ethanol in favor of local ethanol and by requiring out-of-state producers to first obtain California's approval of the delivery methods before it may be sold there.[200] Plaintiffs are seeking declaratory and injunctive relief.

The second case is *National Petrochemicals & Refiners Association v. Goldstene.*[201] Plaintiffs in this case claim that the California LCFS interferes with the Commerce Clause because it imposes excessive burdens on interstate commerce and discriminates in favor of local production.[202] Plaintiffs further claim that the California

LCFS violates the Supremacy Clause because it conflicts with EPAct 2005, EISA, and the RFS.[203] Plaintiffs seek declaratory and injunctive relief. This case has been consolidated with *Rocky Mountain Farmers Union v. Goldstene*.

In *Construction Materials Recycling Association Issues and Education Fund, Inc. v. Burack*, New Hampshire passed several laws prohibiting the combustion of construction and demolition debris (C&D debris), one of which excluded C&D debris from being considered a "biomass fuel," which could satisfy the state's laws regarding electricity generation from renewable sources.[204] Recycling groups selling C&D debris sued the New Hampshire Department of Environmental Services (DES) alleging, among other things, that the legislation violated the dormant Commerce Clause by discriminating against out-of-state C&D debris fuel-producers in favor of the in-state virgin wood industry.[205] The court granted DES's motion for summary judgment, finding that "[p]laintiffs have failed to present a triable case either that the C&D legislation is discriminatory or that it excessively burdens interstate commerce."[206]

Finally, *American Petroleum Institute v. Cooper* concerns North Carolina's enactment of the Ethanol Blending Statute, which requires those importing gasoline into North Carolina to offer retailers and distributors "the option to both *buy* and *blend* unblended gasoline" (emphasis in original) to enable retailers and distributors to participate in the RFS program.[207] Plaintiffs contend that the Ethanol Blending Statute is preempted by EISA, and that the Ethanol Blending Statute's restrictions on a refiner's ability to choose between either blending fuels themselves or purchasing RINs under the RFS serve as an obstacle to fulfilling EISA; plaintiffs also contend that the North Carolina statute violates the dormant Commerce Clause because it discriminates against out-of-state importers.[208] The court held that the Ethanol Blending Statute is not preempted by EISA because refiners will still be able to blend in North Carolina, and Congress intended for retailers and distributors to participate in this program as well, a goal that is advanced by the North Carolina statute.[209] The court also held that there was no dormant Commerce Clause violation given that *all* gasoline supplies were imported into the state, thus eliminating the possibility of discrimination between in-state and out-of-state producers.[210]

Violations of Environmental Laws

Even though increased use of biofuels is intended to reduce GHG emissions and thereby improve environmental conditions, biorefineries and other related infrastructure will still need to comply fully with environmental laws and regulations. Of particular note are the requirements under the Clean Air Act (CAA) and the Clean Water Act (CWA).

In *LaFleur v. Whitman*, the New York State Department of Environmental Conservation (NYSDEC) concluded that a waste-to-ethanol plant did not fall under the CAA's prevention of significant deterioration (PSD) provisions, which would have put more stringent requirements on its emissions, a determination to which EPA did not object.[211] Petitioner challenged EPA's failure to object based on "(a) her improper classification of the facility's primary activity as 'refuse processing' rather than 'chemical processing,' which has the effect of raising the threshold (in terms of the quantity of pollutant emitted per year) for the applicability of the PSD program; (b) her improper allocation of certain of the facility's emissions to the activity of refuse processing; and (c) her failure to consider important factors relevant to the facility's classification."[212] The court rejected the claim on all three grounds. First, the Administrator's decision to classify the facility as "refuse processing" was not arbitrary and capricious because she was justified in considering other factors in addition to the "primary activity" standard, such as projected revenue and the reason for the facility.[213] Regarding the second ground, the emissions from the gasifier were not counted toward the determination of whether the PSD rules should apply; if they had been, the plant would have been subject to PSD.[214] The Administrator concluded that these emissions should not apply because they were steam generated by waste lignin, which she did not consider to be a fuel source.[215] The court agreed with this position. Finally, the court also found that the Administrator properly considered other relevant factors, namely relative value added, patents, and the possibility of two sources.[216]

There will also be significant implications for laws regulating water quality and use.[217] If increased biofuels mandates have adverse impacts on water, laws governing water issues will come into play. Under the fundamental principles of water law, surface water is governed by the riparian system (applied in most of the states affected by biofuels), which is generally based on the right of a riparian landowner to make reasonable use of the water. Groundwater laws vary significantly, with some states applying a reasonable use standard and others harm or malice-based standards. The CWA regulates water pollution through the use of permits and enforcement mechanisms. The conversion of more land to agricultural use and the increases in the numbers of biorefineries to meet federal mandates will likely result in increases in water pollution as well as strains on already stressed surface and groundwater supplies. These will raise conflicts among riparians as to what constitutes reasonable use, among other things, and compliance with CWA permits may become impaired.

Zoning

As the United States gears up to meet the biofuels mandates required under RFS2, it will be necessary to construct a large number of biorefineries in order to produce the fuel. As is the case with many industrial projects, the zoning of these facilities will become an increasingly important issue. While zoning is obviously a local issue resolved by local laws, the general types of challenges brought and the conclusions reached are worth exploring.

In *North Iredell Neighbors for Rural Life v. Iredell County*,[218] Iredell County adopted a zoning ordinance which rezoned a portion of a lot from single-family residential to a heavy manufacturing conditional use district, allowing the farmer who applied for that rezoning to construct a biorefinery producing biodiesel. A community group sued the county, seeking a declaration that rezoning was void and alleging, among other things, that it constituted illegal spot zoning.[219] The trial court entered an order stating that biorefineries are a bona fide farm use and therefore not subject to zoning.[220] This finding was reversed on interlocutory appeal, where the Court of Appeals held on the basis of state law that a landowner's intended use of land for large-scale biodiesel production was not a bona fide farm use and, accordingly, was subject to zoning.[221]

In *Step Now Citizens Group v. Town of Utica Planning and Zoning Committee*,[222] the Town of Utica rezoned property from agricultural to industrial in order for a $36 million ethanol refinery to be constructed.[223] A citizens group brought an action against the landowner, town zoning board, and others, seeking a declaratory judgment that, among other things, the rezoning constituted illegal spot zoning.[224] The court held that although the action technically constituted spot zoning, it was not illegal because it was part of a long-range plan for development, and the Town had taken testimony regarding advantages and disadvantages of building the plant.[225] (Even though the Town had not adopted a comprehensive plan, a comprehensive plan is not necessary under state law in order to adopt zoning ordinances.[226])

Looking Ahead

Scaling up the use of biofuels use can significantly reduce GHG emissions and improve the nation's energy security. At the same time, doing so will require the resolution of several challenges in order for the benefits of increased biofuels production to be captured. The ambitious mandates required under RFS2, for example, are intended to stimulate the development of an advanced biofuels industry. The United States currently does not have the technological ability to meet these targets, however, and the existing infrastructure does not have the capacity to absorb these levels of biofuels even if they were to be produced. In addition, international issues, such as ILUC, pose significant hurdles that will require candid discourse and dedicated scientific and political research.

In response to these challenges, the federal government is focusing on R&D and properly structured incentives to help move the industry forward. Various states and regions are also in the process of developing laws and regulations governing the characteristics of transportation fuel. In order to implement an effective network of policies that will propel the nation toward a future where biofuels play a key role in confronting climate change and energy challenges, it will be necessary for all of these activities to be well coordinated to avoid redundancy and to ensure efficiency and clarity.

As these issues unfold, lawyers will be tasked with navigating and understanding a wide array of subjects in addition to law—such as science, technology, and economics—at the local, state, regional, and international levels. It is also likely that litigation will increase as the government and various stakeholders exercise their rights to have their interests fully considered and protected. Biofuels policy is constantly evolving, so it will be critical for lawyers to keep abreast of statutory and regulatory developments.

Notes

1. Robert Scott Norman, *Powered by Grease: The Case for Straight Vegetable Oil in the New Fuel Economy*, 44 CAL. W. L. REV. 257, 264 (2007).

2. Christine C. Benson, *Putting Your Money Where Your Mouth Is: The Varied Success of Biofuel Incentive Policies in the United States and the European Union*, 16 TRANSNAT'L L. & CONTEMP. PROBS. 663, 636 (2007).

3. *Id.*

4. *Id.*

5. U.S. Dep't of Energy, Biomass Program (2009), http://www1.eere.energy.gov/biomass/deployment.html.

6. According to the National Renewable Energy Laboratory (NREL), "feedstock" is defined as "any material used as a fuel directly or converted to another form of fuel or energy product." Biomass, in turn, is defined as "any plant-derived organic matter." This means that biomass is not necessarily a feedstock, but biomass used for biofuel production is a feedstock. In biofuels parlance, these terms are often used interchangeably, but it is important to note the distinction. *See* U.S. Dep't of Energy, Nat'l Renewable Energy Lab., Glossary of Biomass Terms (2009), http://www.nrel.gov/biomass/glossary.html.

7. "Dry ton" means that the 2000 pounds of biomass has had the moisture removed.

8. Robert D. Perlack et al., Biomass as a Feedstock for a Bioenergy and Bioproducts Industry: The Technical Feasibility of a Billion-Ton Annual Supply, Executive Summary (2005). It is currently in the process of being updated.

9. *See generally* Renewable Fuels Association, How Ethanol Is Made (2010), http://www.ethanolrfa.org/resource/made/; U.S. Dep't of Energy, ABC's of Biofuels (2009), http://www1.eere.energy.gov/biomass/abcs_biofuels.html#feed; U.S. Dep't of Energy, Nat'l Renewable Energy Lab., Capabilities (2009), http://www.nrel.gov/biomass/capabilities .html.

10. DDGS is an important source of animal feed and plays a large role in configuring biofuels policy.

11. These LCAs are performed through the use of computer models that are programmed to calculate various types of emissions from various sources for different fuel pathways. One of the most widely known is the GREET model, which stands for "Greenhouse gases, Regulated Emissions, and Energy use in Transportation," and which is currently capable of modeling over one hundred fuel pathways. *See generally* Argonne Nat'l Lab., Transp. Tech. R&D Ctr., The Greenhouse Gases, Regulated Emissions, and Energy Use in Transportation (GREET) Model, http://www.transportation.anl.gov/modeling_simulation/GREET/.

12. Michael Wang et al., *Life-Cycle Energy and Greenhouse Gas Emission Impacts of Different Corn Ethanol Plant Types*, 2 Envtl. Research Letter 024001, at 3 (2007).

13. Brent D. Yacobucci & Kelsi S. Bracmort, Cong. Research Serv., R40460, Calculation of Lifecycle Greenhouse Gas Emissions for the Renewable Fuel Standard 7 (2009) (citing Jason Hill, Stephen Polasky, Erik Nelson et al., *Climate Change and Health Costs of Air Emissions from Biofuels and Gasoline*, Proceedings of the Nat'l Acad. of Sciences, vol. 106(6) at 2082 (Feb. 10, 2009), and U.S. Dep't of Energy, Energy Efficiency & Renewable Energy, Biomass Program, Ethanol: The Complete Lifecycle Energy Picture (Mar. 2007), http://www1.eere.energy.gov/vehiclesandfuels/pdfs/program/ethanol_brochure_color .pdf).

14. Joseph Fargione, et al., *Land Clearing and the Biofuel Carbon Debt*, Science 1237 (Feb. 2008).

15. Bruce A. Babcock, *Breaking the Link between Food and Biofuels*, Iowa Ag Rev. 2 (Summer 2008).

16. Cong. Budget Office, The Impact of Ethanol Use on Food Prices and Greenhouse-Gas Emissions, Summary (Apr. 2009).

17. *Id.* at 1.

18. Other factors contributing to the price increases include higher global demand for meat (therefore increased demand for feed), depreciation of the U.S. dollar, and expectations of a poor growing season in spring 2008. *Id.* at 7–8.

19. Yi-Wen Chiu et al., *Water Embodied in Bioethanol in the United States*, Envtl. Sci. & Technol. (2009); R. Dominguez-Faus et al., *The Water Footprint of Biofuels: A Drink or Drive Issue?*, Envtl. Sci. & Technol. (2009); Nat'l Research Council, Water Implications of Biofuels Production in the United States 21 (2008).

20. R. Dominguez-Faus et al., *supra* note 19, at 3006.

21. Nat'l Research Council, *supra* note 19, at 46.

22. This is currently happening where nutrient runoff in the Mississippi River flows downstream into the Gulf of Mexico, producing a hypoxic zone sized at more than 20,700 km² in 2008 and growing. R. Dominguez-Faus et al., *supra* note 19, at 3007.

23. Nat'l Research Council, *supra* note 19, at 21.

24. *Id*. at 51–52. BOD refers to "the oxygen used when organic matter is decomposed by microbes."

25. R. Dominguez-Faus et al., *supra* note 19, at 3007.

26. *Id*. at 3008; Nat'l Research Council, *supra* note 19, at 30. The CRP provides financial incentives to farmers to ensure they do not use "highly erodible and minimally productive lands" for farming. This had the effect of preventing "187 million [tons] of sediment erosion, 218,000 [tons] of N, and 23,000 [tons] of P" from entering waterways. R. Dominguez-Faus et al., *supra* note 19, at 3008.

27. R. Dominguez-Faus et al., *supra* note 19, at 3008.

28. *Id*. 29. U.S. Dep't of Energy & U.S. Dep't of Agric., Sustainability of Biofuels: Future Research Opportunities, Report from the October 2008 Workshop 1 (2008).

30. U.S. Gov't Accountability Office, Many Uncertainties Remain about National and Regional Effects of Increased Biofuel Production on Water Resources 31 (Nov. 2009).

31. U.S. Dep't of Energy, Office of the Biomass Program, Biomass: Multi-Year Program Plan 1–6 (Dec. 2009) [hereinafter Biomass Multi-Year Program Plan].

32. Biomass Multi-Year Program Plan, *supra* note 31, at 1–7.

33. Roberta F. Mann & Mona M. Hymel, *Moonshine to Motorfuel: Tax Incentives for Fuel Ethanol*, 19 Duke Envtl. L. & Pol'y F. 43, 52 (2008) (citing Brent D. Yacobucci, Cong. Research Serv., RL30,369, Fuel Ethanol: Background and Public Policy Issues 24 (2008)).

34. Biomass Multi-Year Program Plan, *supra* note 31, at ii, 1–4.; U.S. Gov't Accountability Office, Biofuels: Potential Effects and Challenges of Required Increases in Production and Use 8 (Aug. 2009) [hereinafter Biofuels: Potential Effects and Challenges].

35. Biofuels: Potential Effects and Challenges, *supra* note 34, at 8; Brent D. Yacobucci, Cong. Research. Serv., RL33,572, Biofuels Incentives: A Summary of Federal Programs, Summary (Jan. 2009).

36. Biofuels: Potential Effects and Challenges, *supra* note 34, at 95.

37. Biomass Multi-Year Program Plan, *supra* note 31, at 1–20.

38. Biofuels Interagency Working Group, Growing America's Fuels 3 (2009).

39. Office of Mgmt. & Budget, Budget of the U.S. Government: Fiscal Year 2011, Department of Energy 70 (2009), *available at* http://www.gpoaccess.gov/usbudget/fy11/pdf/budget/energy.pdf.

40. American Recovery and Reinvestment Act of 2009, Pub. L. No. 111-5, 123 Stat. 115 (2009).

41. *See generally* Fred Sissne et al., Cong. Research Serv., R40412, Energy Provisions in the American Recovery and Reinvestment Act of 2009 (P.L. 111-5) (2009).

42. H.R. Rep. 111-16, Conference Report to Accompany H.R. 1 (American Recovery and Reinvestment Act of 2009), at 426–27 (2009).

43. Fred Sissne et al., *supra* note 41, at 8.

44. 26 U.S.C. § 45(b)(2) (2009) (subject to adjustment for inflation).

45. 26 U.S.C. § 45(d)(2)(3) (2009).

46. American Recovery and Reinvestment Act of 2009, 123 Stat. 319 (2009). The ARRA permits "facilities that qualify for the PTC to opt instead to take the federal business energy investment credit (ITC) or an equivalent cash grant from the U.S. Department of Treasury." Database of Incentives for Renewables & Efficiency (DSIRE), Renewable Electricity Production Tax Credit (PTC), http://dsireusa.org/incentives/incentive.cfm?Incentive_Code=US13F&State=federal&currentpageid=1&ee=1&re=1%20(. This provision is intended to provide flexibility because "[t]he renewable energy industry found that current market conditions

have created an uncertain future tax position for potential investors in PTC-supported projects, making financing difficult." Fred Sissne et al., *supra* note 41, at 18.

47. 26 U.S.C. § 54C(d)(1) (2009).

48. 26 U.S.C. § 54D(f)(1)(B)(i) (2009).

49. 26 U.S.C. § 30C (2009).

50. Traditionally, farm practices, such as commodity pricing, rural development, and agricultural credit, are governed by several different statutes that are updated periodically by an omnibus bill; other farm laws are considered freestanding legislation that are updated individually. GEOFFREY S. BECKER & JASPER WOMACH, CONG. RESEARCH SERV., RL31,195, THE 2002 FARM BILL: OVERVIEW AND STATUS 1 (Sept. 3, 2002); JASPER WOMACH, THE 2002 FARM BILL: COMPARISON OF COMMODITY SUPPORT PROVISIONS WITH THE HOUSE AND SENATE PROPOSALS AND PRIOR LAW 1 (Aug. 1, 2002).

51. TOM CAPEHART, RENEWABLE ENERGY POLICY IN THE 2008 FARM BILL 1 (Aug. 1, 2008).

52. Food, Conservation and Energy Act of 2008, Pub. L. No. 110-234, 122 Stat. 923, H.R. 2419 110th Cong. (2007–2008) (enacted), § 1672C(c)(1), amending § 7207 of Title XVI of the Food, Agriculture, Conservation, and Trade Act of 1990; Tom Capehart, *supra* note 51, at 9.

53. Food, Conservation and Energy Act of 2008, § 9003(a), 122 Stat. 2072.

54. *Id.* at sec. § 9003(c)(1), 122 Stat. 2072.

55. *Id.* at sec. § 9003(c)(2), 122 Stat. 2072.

56. Tom Capehart, *supra* note 541, at 17; Food, Conservation and Energy Act of 2008, § 9008(e)(1)(A), (B), 122 Stat. 2082.

57. BIOMASS RESEARCH & DEVELOPMENT INITIATIVE, MATRIX OF PROJECTS AWARDED UNDER THE JOINT SOLICITATION, http://www.brdisolutions.com/default.aspx?rdr=http://www.brdisolutions.com/publications/default.aspx#Joint.

58. Food, Conservation and Energy Act of 2008, § 9007, 122 Stat. 2078.

59. *Id.* § 9011(b)(1),(2), 122 Stat. 2090.

60. *Id.* § 9011(c)(5)(B), 122 Stat. 2092.

61. *Id.* § 9011(d)(2)(B), 122 Stat. 2093.

62. *Id.* at § 15321, § 40(b)(6)(A), (B), 122 Stat. 2274.

63. *Id.* at § 15331, § 40(h)(3)(A), (B), 122 Stat. 2277.

64. *Id.* at § 15331, § 40(h)(3)(A), (B), 122 Stat. 2277.

65. U.S. DEP'T OF ENERGY, ENERGY EFFICIENCY & RENEWABLE ENERGY, CLEAN CITIES FACT SHEET, FLEXIBLE FUEL VEHICLES: PROVIDING A RENEWABLE FUEL CHOICE (June 2008) [hereinafter CLEAN CITIES FACT SHEET].

66. *See* www.fueleconomy.gov and FLEX FUEL VEHICLES, http://www.fueleconomy.gov/feg/flextech.shtml.

67. MICHAEL WANG, ARGONNE NAT'L LAB., ENERGY AND GREENHOUSE GAS EMISSIONS IMPACTS OF FUEL ETHANOL, slide 14 (Aug. 23, 2005), *available at* www.anl.gov/Media_Center/News/2005/NCGA_Ethanol_Meeting_050823.ppt; U.S. DEP'T OF ENERGY, ENERGY EFFICIENCY & RENEWABLE ENERGY, ALTERNATIVE FUEL & ADVANCED VEHICLES DATA CENTER, ALTERNATIVE & ADVANCED VEHICLES, E85 EMISSIONS, http://www.afdc.energy.gov/afdc/vehicles/emissions_e85.html.

68. CLEAN CITIES FACT SHEET, *supra* note 65.

69. *Id.*

70. U.S. DEP'T OF ENERGY, ENERGY EFFICIENCY & RENEWABLE ENERGY, ALTERNATIVE FUEL AND ADVANCED VEHICLES DATA CENTER, ALTERNATIVE AND ADVANCED FUELS, ALTERNATIVE FUELING STATION TOTAL COUNTS BY STATE AND FUEL TYPE, http://www.afdc.energy.gov/afdc/fuels/stations_counts.html.

71. According to a recent report, "The Energy Independence and Security Act of 2007 mandates renewable fuel levels of more than 10% of total gasoline consumption in the United States. Therefore, the ethanol surplus may result in an increase in the use of high-percentage ethanol fuels in FFVs, particularly E85, which currently represents only a small fraction of the U.S." Janet Yanowitz & Robert L. McCormick, *Effect of E85 on Tailpipe Emissions from Light-Duty Vehicles*, 59(2) J. AIR & WASTE MGMT. ASS'N 172 (Feb. 2009).

72. 42 U.S.C. § 13,212(b)(1)(D) (2007).

73. 42 U.S.C. § 6374(a) (2005). However, if alternative fuel is "not reasonably available" or "is unreasonably more expensive than gasoline," dual fueled vehicles (including FFVs) may apply for a waiver from the Secretary of the U.S. Department of Energy. 42 U.S.C. § 6374(a)(3)(E)(i)(I), (II) (2005).

74. 42 U.S.C. § 13,211(8) (2007); U.S. Dep't of Energy, Fed. Fleet Mgmt. Program, Draft Guidance: Documentation Requirements for Waiver Requests under EPACT 2005 Section 701, at 2 (Sept. 2009) [hereinafter Federal Fleet Management Program].

75. 42 U.S.C. § 13,211(8) (2007); Federal Fleet Management Program, *supra* note 74, at 2.

76. Energy Policy Act of 1992, Pub. L. No. 102-486, § 507(o), 106 Stat. 2776, 2897 (1992).

77. 10 C.F.R. § 490.201(a)(5) (2007).

78. 10 C.F.R. § 490.2 (2007).

79. U.S. Dep't of Energy, Energy Efficiency & Renewable Energy, Alternative Fuel & Advanced Vehicles Data Center, Federal & State Incentives and Laws, All Incentives and Laws Sorted by Type (July 10, 2009), http://www.afdc.energy.gov/afdc/laws/matrix/reg. This site was used to find the acquisition requirements discussed. The states currently without acquisition or fuel use requirements are Alaska, Delaware, North Dakota, Pennsylvania, and Wyoming.

80. Ariz. Rev. Stat. §§ 1-215, 15-349 (2010).

81. Ariz. Rev. Stat. § 4-803 (2010).

82. Ariz. Rev. Stat. § 49-571 (2010).

83. Cal. Pub. Res. Code § 25726 (2010).

84. Cal. Pub. Res. Code § 25,722.6(a),(b) (2010).

85. Cal. Pub. Res. Code § 25,722.6(c)(1),(2)(A),(e) (2010).

86. Iowa Office of Energy Independence, State Gov't E85 Use Plan (Dec 31, 2007); Iowa Exec. Order No. 3 (2007).

87. Iowa Exec. Order No. 41 (2005).

88. Iowa Code §§ 216B.3, 260C.19A, 262.25A, 307.21 & 904.312A (2010).

89. Mass. Gen. Laws ch. 7, § 9A & ch. 90, §1 (2010).

90. New York Exec. Order No. 111, "Green and Clean State Buildings and Vehicles" (directing state agencies to be more energy-efficient and environmentally aware (2001)).

91. N.Y. City Admin. Code § 24-163.1(b)(4) (2010).

92. N.C. Gen. Stat. § 143-215.107C(b) (2010).

93. Energy Policy Act of 2005, Pub. L. No. 102-58, 119 Stat. 594.

94. *Id.* § 1501(a), § 211(o), 119 Stat. 594, 1067–1074.

95. *Id.* § 1501(a), § 211(o)(2)(A)(i), 119 Stat. 594, 1068.

96. *Id.* § 1501(a), § 211(o)(2)(B)(iii)(I), 119 Stat. 594, 1070.

97. More specifically, renewable fuel was defined as "motor vehicle fuel that (I)(aa) is produced from grain, starch, oilseeds, vegetable, animal, or fish materials including fats, greases, and oils, sugarcane, sugar beets, sugar components, tobacco, potatoes, or other biomass; or (bb) is natural gas produced from a biogas source, including a landfill, sewage waste treatment plant, feedlot, or other place where decaying organic material is found; and (II) is used to replace or reduce the quantity of fossil fuel present in a fuel mixture used to operate a motor vehicle." *Id.* § 1501(a), § 211(o)(1)(C)(i) & (ii), 119 Stat. 594, 1067–1068.

98. *Id.* § 1501(a), § 211(o)(3)(A)–(B)(i), 119 Stat. 594, 1070.

99. *Id.*

100. *Id.* § 1501(a), § 211(o)(5), 119 Stat. 594, 1071.

101. *Id.* § 1501(a), § 211(o)(2)(A)(i), 119 Stat. 594, 1068.

102. *Id.* § 1501(a), § 211(o)(2)(A)(iv), 119 Stat. 594, 1069.

103. In its direct final rule and notice of proposed rulemaking regarding these "temporary" rules, EPA stated:

> The issues that need to be resolved in adopting regulations to establish the comprehensive compliance and credit trading program are complex, making it important

for EPA to receive input from the various stakeholders. . . . This work cannot be completed in the context of a final rulemaking by August, 2006, which must be preceded by a notice and comment process. At the same time, it is critical that industry be informed of how to demonstrate compliance prior to August, 2006, since the program defined by the Act begins in January 2006. The default provisions in the Act are not self explanatory, neither identifying the responsible parties nor the method by which they must demonstrate compliance. EPA is therefore proposing a limited set of regulations that would interpret and clarify the statutory default provision for 2006. The rule would provide certainty to the parties involved as to their responsibilities for 2006, and will help to provide a smooth transition to the long-term RFS program.

Regulation of Fuels and Fuel Additives: Renewable Fuel Standard Requirements for 2006, 70 Fed. Reg. 77,351-01, 77,353 (direct final rule and notice of proposed rulemaking) (Dec. 30, 2005) (codified at 40 C.F.R. pt. 80).

It decided on a "collective liability" standard for determining compliance. Under the rule, responsible parties included refiners/blenders and importers since EPA determined that they were in a better position to ensure that the blending requirement was met. 40 C.F.R. § 80.1100(c); 70 Fed. Reg. 77,351-01, 77355. The collective liability standard dictates that as long as the 2.78 percent standard was met nationwide, all of these parties would be deemed in compliance, even if they did not blend at all. 70 Fed. Reg. 77,351-01, 77,355–77,356. If the 2.78 percent standard was not met, the only effect was that the deficit would carry over to the following year. 40 C.F.R. § 80.1100(e).

104. George Lawrence & Scott Christian, Renewable Fuels Ass'n, Overview of the RFS Program Requirements (PowerPoint) (2007), *available at* http://www.ethanolrfa. org/page/-/rfa-association-site/studies/Overview8.22.07.pdf?nocdn=1.

105. Regulation of Fuels and Fuel Additives: Renewable Fuel Standard Program, 72 Fed. Reg. 23,900-01, 23904 (May 1, 2007).

106. Regulation of Fuels and Fuel Additives: Renewable Fuel Standard Program, 71 Fed. Reg. 55,552-01 (Sept. 22, 2006).

107. Regulation of Fuels and Fuel Additives: Renewable Fuel Standard Program, 72 Fed. Reg. 23,900-01, 23904 (May 1, 2007).

108. 72 Fed. Reg. 23900, 23908. Because of the time constraints associated with bringing the RFS program online, EPA released the 2007 compliance percentage in May, with a start date of September 1, 2007. EPA acknowledged that this time line was not entirely consistent with the EPAct, but it was the best they could do. In addition, EPA was confident that a sufficient amount of renewable fuels would be used in 2007: "We are confident that the combined effect of the regulatory requirements for 2007 and the expected market demand for renewable fuels will lead to greater renewable fuel use in 2007 than is called for under the Act. Current renewable production already exceeds the rate required for all of 2007, and . . . capacity is expected to continue to grow." 72 Fed. Reg. 23,900, 23913–23914.

109. 40 C.F.R. § 80.1107 (2007).

110. *Id.*

111. 40 C.F.R. § 80.1106(a)(1) (2007).

112. While blenders of fuel are generally not considered obligated parties since they are not technically producing renewable fuel or introducing it into the market but are rather mixing it "downstream" from the refiners and importers, those blenders who produce "gasoline by combining blendstocks [materials which are blended together to make gasoline] or blending blendstocks into finished gasoline" are also considered obligated parties. 72 Fed. Reg. 23900, 23924.

113. "(1) Renewable fuel is any motor vehicle fuel that is used to replace or reduce the quantity of fossil fuel present in a fuel mixture used to fuel a motor vehicle, and is produced from any of the following: (i) Grain. (ii) Starch. (iii) Oilseeds. (iv) Vegetable, animal or fish materials including fats, greases, and oils. (v) Sugarcane. (vi) Sugar beets. (vii) Sugar components. (viii) Tobacco. (ix) Potatoes. (x) Other biomass. (xi) Natural gas produced from a biogas source, including a landfill, sewage waste treatment plant, feedlot, or other place where there is

decaying organic material. (2) The term 'Renewable fuel' includes cellulosic biomass ethanol, waste derived ethanol, biodiesel (mono-alky ester), non-ester renewable diesel, and blending components derived from renewable fuel." 40 C.F.R. § 80.1101(1)–(2) (2007).

114. This perspective is illustrated as EPA describes generally what sorts of fuels may qualify as renewable:

> EPA interprets the Act as allowing regulated parties to demonstrate compliance based on any fuel that meets the statutory definition for renewable fuel, whether it is directly blended with gasoline or not. This would include neat alternative fuels such as ethanol, methanol, and natural gas that meet the definition of renewable fuel. This is appropriate for several reasons. First, it promotes the use of all renewable fuels, which will further the achievement of the purposes behind this provision. Congress did not intend to limit the program to only gasoline components, as evidenced by the provision for biodiesel, and the broad definition of renewable fuel evidences an intention to address more renewable fuels than those used with gasoline. . . . Finally . . . , EPA's compliance program is based on assigning volumes at the point of production, and not at the point of blending into motor vehicle fuel. This interpretation avoids the need to track renewable fuels downstream to ensure they are blended with gasoline and not used in their neat form. . . . EPA continues to believe, therefore, that this approach is consistent with the intent of Congress and is a reasonable interpretation of the Act.

72 Fed. Reg. 23,900, 23915.

115. 72 Fed. Reg. 23,900, 23,918; 40 C.F.R. § 80.1115(b)(1) (2007). EPA established equivalence values for other fuels as well; for example, one gallon of corn ethanol counts simply as 1.0 gallon for RFS compliance, one gallon of biodiesel counts as 1.5 gallons, and one gallon of biobutanol counts as 1.3 gallons. 40 C.F.R. § 80.1115(b)(2)–(4) (2007).

116. U.S. ENVTL. PROTECTION AGENCY, RENEWABLE FUELS: EPA MODERATED TRANSACTION SYSTEM (EMTS), http://www.epa.gov/otaq/fuels/renewablefuels/epamts.htm.

117. 40 C.F.R. § 80.1126(d)(1), (e)(1), (2) (2007).

118. 40 C.F.R. § 80.1126(c)(1) (2007).

119. 40 C.F.R. § 80.1129(b)(1) (2007). EPA noted one particular problem related to how obligated parties would have access to RINs to meet their RVOs. The producer/importer of a renewable fuel must generate and assign an RIN to each volume of fuel it produces/imports. However, there are several parties that might have opportunities to trade the RINs associated with a volume of renewable fuel as the fuel makes its way through the complex distribution networks before the obligated parties, i.e., refiners or importers of gasoline have a chance to obtain those RINs for compliance. This is why separation typically occurs only when a refiner/importer takes ownership. 72 Fed. Reg. 23,900, 23,937.

120. The regulations promulgated under this rulemaking also provide for flexibility mechanisms that allow nonobligated parties to transfer ownership of volumes of renewable fuel without assigned RINs, as well assigned RINs that may not have corresponding volumes of renewable fuel. For greater discussion of this situation, see 72 Fed. Reg. 23,900, 23,940–23,942.

121. Energy Independence and Security Act of 2007, Pub. L. No. 110-140, 121 Stat 1492.

122. Among President George W. Bush's policy initiatives featured in his 2007 State of the Union Address is the "Twenty in Ten" initiative, meaning that gasoline usage should decrease by 20 percent in ten years. In order to meet this goal, he proposed expanding the RFS to include a diverse array of fuels which would also achieve reductions in CO_2. WHITE HOUSE OFFICE OF COMMUNICATIONS, PRESIDENT GEORGE W. BUSH, STATE OF THE UNION ADDRESS: POLICY INITIATIVES 6–11 (Jan 23, 2007), http://georgewbush-whitehouse.archives .gov/stateoftheunion/2007/initiatives/sotu2007.pdf.

123. *The Energy Market Effects of the Recently-Passed Renewable Fuel Standard*, Hearing on S. Rep. 110-362, 110th Cong. (2008) [hereinafter *Energy Market Effects*] (statement of Robert J. Meyers, Principal Deputy Assistant Administrator, Office of Air and Radiation, U.S. EPA, and statement of Alexander Karsner, Assistant Secretary, Energy Efficiency and Renewable Energy, U.S. EPA).

124. *Energy Market Effects, supra* note 123 (statement of Bob Dineen, President and CEO Renewable Fuels Association and statement of Brian Jennings, Executive Vice President, American Coalition for Ethanol (ACE)).

125. *Energy Market Effects, supra* note 123 (statement of Carol Werner, Executive Director, Environmental and Energy Study Institute).

126. Regulation of Fuels and Fuel Additives: Changes to Renewable Fuel Standard Program, 74 Fed. Reg. 24904 (May 26, 2009).

127. Table adapted from the U.S. ENVTL. PROTECTION AGENCY, EPA PROPOSES NEW REGULATIONS FOR THE NATIONAL RENEWABLE FUEL STANDARD PROGRAM FOR 2010 AND BEYOND, EPA-420-F-09-023 (May 2009), http://www.epa.gov/OMS/renewablefuels/420f09023.htm.

128. Regulation of Fuels and Fuel Additives: Changes to Renewable Fuel Standard Program; Proposed Rule, 74 Fed. Reg. 24,904, 24,908 (May 26, 2009).

129. 74 Fed. Reg. 24,904, 24,908.

130. Energy Independence and Security Act of 2007, §201, §211(o)(1)(H), 121 Stat 1492, 1520. EPA defines global warming potential, or GWP, as "the ratio of heat trapped by one unit mass of the greenhouse gas to that of one unit mass of CO_2 over a specified time period." For example, sulfur hexafluoride (SF_6) has a GWP of 23,900. U.S. ENVTL. PROTECTION AGENCY, HIGH GLOBAL WARMING POTENTIAL (GWP) GASES, http://www.epa.gov/highgwp/scientific .html.

131. Energy Independence and Security Act of 2007, §201, §211(o)(1)(C), 121 Stat 1492, 1520.

132. 74 Fed. Reg. 24,904, 24908.

133. Energy Independence and Security Act of 2007, §201, §211(o)(1)(B)(i), 121 Stat 1492, 1519.

134. *Id.* §201, §211(o)(1)(D), (E), 121 Stat 1492, 1520.

135. *Id.* §202(a)(1), §211(o)(2)(A)(i), 121 Stat 1492, 1521–1522. Plants built before EISA or that commenced construction before EISA were considered to be "grandfathered" in and thus exempt from the 20 percent requirement.

136. Energy Independence and Security Act of 2007, §201, §211(o)(1)(J), 121 Stat 1492, 1521.

137. "For example, planted crops and crop residue must be harvested from agricultural land cleared or cultivated at any time prior to December 19, 2007, that is actively managed or fallow, and non-forested. Therefore, planted crops and crop residue derived from land that does not meet this definition cannot be used to produce renewable fuel for credit under RFS2." 74 Fed. Reg. 24,904, 24,911.

138. 74 Fed. Reg. 24,904, 24,911; Energy Policy Act of 2005, §1501(a), §211(o)(1)(A)(viii), 119 Stat. 594, 1067.

139. 74 Fed. Reg. 24,904, 25042.

140. 74 Fed. Reg. 24,904, 25042.

141. EPA's analysis "came under heavy fire from the ethanol industry, farm groups, and farm-state members of Congress." *EPA Issues Final Rule Outlining Fuels That Qualify as Renewable Under Energy Law*, DAILY ENV'T REP. (BNA) (Feb. 4, 2010). According to the Union of Concerned Scientists: "If EPA were to ignore emissions from land use changes, biofuels could easily produce paper gains within the RFS program that would be negated, off the balance sheet, by increased emissions from deforestation and other emissions of carbon stored in soils and trees." UNION OF CONCERNED SCIENTISTS, INDIRECT LAND USE CHANGE AND THE RENEWABLE FUEL STANDARD (June 2009).

142. Regulation of Fuels and Fuel Additives: Changes to Renewable Fuel Standard Program; Final Rule, 75 Fed. Reg. 14670–14904 (codified at 40 C.F.R. pt. 80 (Mar. 26, 2010)).

143. *Id.* at 14678.

144. *Id.*

145. *Id.*

146. *Id.* at 14,874.

147. The Renewable Fuels Association stated: "As structured, the RFS is a workable program that will achieve the stated policy goals of reduced oil dependence, economic opportunity,

and environmental stewardship," though it was still disappointed about the inclusion of ILUC. Press Release, Renewable Fuels Association, RFS Rules "Workable"—ILUC Inclusion Still Problematic (Feb. 3, 2010), *available at* http://renewablefuelsassociation.cmail1.com/T/ViewEmail/y/78B3C6C380747C63. The Union of Concerned Scientists, who supported the inclusion of ILUC, "praised the agency for a transparent process that accurately accounted for biofuels' lifecycle heat-trapping emissions by including so-called 'indirect-land-use emissions.'" Press Release, Union of Concerned Scientists, New Renewable Fuel Standard, Which Sets First Heat Trapping Emissions Requirements for Biofuels, Gets Favorable Review From UCS (Feb. 3, 2010), http://www.ucsusa.org/news/press_release/new-renewable-fuel-standard-favorable-review-from-UCS-0345.html.

148. Pre-publication regulation, 40 C.F.R. § 80.1426(f)(5)(i)(C) (2010).

149. RENEWABLE FUELS ASS'N, ETHANOL INDUSTRY OVERVIEW, http://www.ethanolrfa.org/pages/statistics#EIO.

150. BIOFUELS: POTENTIAL EFFECTS AND CHALLENGES, *supra* note 34, at 18.

151. This concern was echoed during the February 2008 hearings on EISA discussed earlier where several stakeholders stressed the need for increased blending limits. *Energy Market Effects*, *supra* note 123 (testimony of Robert Meyers, Principal Deputy Assistant Administrator for Air and Radiation, U.S. EPA, and Charles Dravena, President, National Petrochemical and Refiners Association).

152. BIOFUELS: POTENTIAL EFFECTS AND CHALLENGES, *supra* note 34, at 114–15.

153. RENEWABLE FUELS ASS'N, CLIMATE OF OPPORTUNITY: 2010 ETHANOL INDUSTRY OUTLOOK 9 (2010).

154. U.S. ENERGY INFO. ADMIN., ANNUAL ENERGY OUTLOOK EARLY RELEASE, http://www.eia.doe.gov/oiaf/aeo/overview.html#4 (Outlook 2010 archived at *AEO2010*).

155. BIOMASS: MULTI-YEAR PROGRAM PLAN, *supra* note 31.

156. GAIL MOSEY & CLAIRE KREYCIK, NAT'L RENEWABLE ENERGY LAB., STATE CLEAN ENERGY PRACTICES: RENEWABLE FUEL STANDARDS 7 (July 2008).

157. BRENT D. YACOBUCCI, CONG. RESEARCH SERV., R40078, A LOW CARBON FUEL STANDARD: STATE AND FEDERAL LEGISLATION AND REGULATIONS 9 (Dec. 23, 2008).

158. National Low-Carbon Fuel Standard Act of 2007, S. 1324, 110th Cong. (2007).

159. WORLD RESOURCES INSTITUTE, BRIEF SUMMARY OF THE WAXMAN-MARKEY DISCUSSION DRAFT (Apr. 20, 2009), *available at* http://www.wri.org/stories/2009/04/brief-summary-waxman-markey-discussion-draft. Its mandates were slightly more modest than the earlier standards mentioned, calling for a 5 percent reduction below the gasoline baseline between 2023 and 2030 and a 10 percent reduction after 2030. The current version pending on the Senate calendar has no such LCFS provision because it was reportedly removed as a "concession[] to moderate and conservative lawmakers." Alison Winter, *Ethanol Advocates Call for Intervention on Low-Carbon Fuels*, ENV'T & ENERGY DAILY (May 22, 2009).

160. CAL. AIR RES. BD., PROPOSED REGULATION TO IMPLEMENT THE LOW CARBON FUEL STANDARD, VOLUME I, STAFF REPORT: INITIAL STATEMENT OF REASONS, ES-1 (Mar. 5, 2009) [hereinafter INITIAL STATEMENT OF REASONS].

161. *Id.* at V-2.

162. *See infra* in this chapter, "Recent Litigation," for more information.

163. Cal. Assembly Bill 32 (2006).

164. Cal. Exec. Order No. S-01-07 (Jan. 18, 2007).

165. Cal. Exec. Order No. S-01-07 (Jan. 18, 2007). The University of California wrote two reports on the LCFS which provide good background information. *See* ALEXANDER E. FARRELL & DANIEL SPERLING, A LOW-CARBON FUEL STANDARD FOR CALIFORNIA, PART 1: TECHNICAL ANALYSIS (May 29, 2007) and ALEXANDER E. FARRELL & DANIEL SPERLING, A LOW-CARBON FUEL STANDARD FOR CALIFORNIA, PART 2: POLICY ANALYSIS (Aug 1, 2007).

166. CAL. AIR RES. BD. EXEC. ORDER NO. R-09-014, RELATING TO THE PUBLIC HEARING TO ADOPT A REGULATION TO IMPLEMENT THE CALIFORNIA LOW CARBON FUEL STANDARD (Nov. 25, 2009).

167. Cal. Office of Admin. Law, Notice of Approval of Regulatory Action, No. 2009-1125-05-S (Jan. 12, 2010).

168. Cal. Air Res. Bd. Exec. Order No. R-10-003, Relating to the Public Hearing to Adopt a Regulation to Implement the California Low Carbon Fuel Standard (Mar. 4, 2010).

169. Cal. Air Res. Bd., Low Carbon Fuel Standard, Rulemaking to Consider the Proposed Regulation to Implement the Low Carbon Fuel Standard, *available at* http://www.arb.ca.gov/regact/2009/lcfs09/oalapplcfs.pdf.

170. The unit gCO2e/MJ means "grams of carbon dioxide equivalent per mega joule."

171. CAL. CODE REGS. tit. 7, § 95,484 (2010).

172. CAL. CODE REGS. tit. 7, § 95,486(b) (2010).

173. *See generally* CAL. CODE REGS. tit. 7, § 95485 (2010) and INITIAL STATEMENT OF REASONS, *supra* note 160, at ES-2. According to the Air Resources Board, "A regulated party meets its compliance obligation by ensuring that the amount of credits it earns (or otherwise acquires from another party) is equal to, or greater than, the deficits it has incurred. Credits and deficits are generally determined based on the amount of fuel sold, the carbon intensity of the fuel, and the efficiency by which a vehicle converts the fuel into useable energy." INITIAL STATEMENT OF REASONS, *supra* note 160, at ES-2.

174. "The regulation is performance-based, and fuel providers have several options. First, they may supply a mix of fuels above and below the standard that, on average, equal the required carbon intensity. Second, they can choose to only provide fuels that have lower carbon intensity than the standard. . . . Third, they may purchase credits generated by other fuel providers to offset any accumulated deficits from their own production. . . . Fourth, a fuel provider may bank excess credits generated in a previous year and use those credits when needed." INITIAL STATEMENT OF REASONS, *supra* note 160, at ES-2–ES-3.

175. *See* CAL. AIR RES. BD., BOARD MEETING COMMENTS LOG, *available at* http://www.arb.ca.gov/lispub/comm/bccommlog.php?listname=lcfs09. A group of roughly one hundred scientists, academics, and industry leaders signed a March 2009 letter written to Governor Schwarzenegger stating that the science surrounding ILUC is too uncertain at this point "and should not be enforced selectively," and further, that "[a]dding an iLUC penalty to biofuels will hold the sector accountable to decision-making far outside of its control . . . [and] will chill investment in both conventional and advanced biofuel production." Letter from Blake A. Simmons et al., Vice-President, Deconstruction Division, Joint BioEnergy Institute, to Gov. Arnold Schwarzenegger (Mar. 2, 2009). There were also several letters supportive of the inclusion of ILUC in life-cycle analysis. A letter from the Union of Concerned Scientists, signed by 177 scientists, economists, and academics, stated: "There are uncertainties inherent in estimating the magnitude of indirect land use emissions from biofuels, but assigning a value of zero is clearly not supported by the science," and that the "[f]ailure to include a major source of pollution, like indirect land use emissions, will distort the carbon market, suppress investment in truly low carbon fuels, and ultimately result in higher emissions." Letter from Pam Matson et al., Chester Naramore Dean of the School of Earth Sciences, Stanford University, to Mary D. Nichols, Chair of the California Air Resources Board (Apr. 21, 2009).

176. CAL. AIR RES. BD., LOW CARBON FUEL STANDARD PROPOSAL FOR AN EXPERT WORKGROUP (Sept. 17, 2009), *available at* http://www.arb.ca.gov/fuels/lcfs/expert_workgroup_propsl.pdf.

177. NORTHEAST STATES FOR COORDINATED AIR USE MANAGEMENT (NESCAUM), LETTER OF INTENT, NORTHEAST/MID-ATLANTIC STATES LOW CARBON FUEL STANDARD PROGRAM (Dec. 31, 2008), *available at* http://www.nescaum.org/topics/low-carbon-fuels.

178. NESCAUM, LETTER FROM NE/MID-ATLANTIC COMMISSIONERS TO MARY D. NICHOLS, CHAIRMAN, CALIFORNIA AIR RESOURCES BOARD (Apr. 17, 2009), *available at* http://www.nescaum.org/topics/low-carbon-fuels.

179. NESCAUM, MEMORANDUM OF UNDERSTANDING, NORTHEAST AND MID-ATLANTIC LOW CARBON FUEL STANDARD (Dec. 30, 2009), http://www.nescaum.org/topics/low-carbon-fuels.

180. *Id.*

181. *Id.*

182. NESCAUM effectively represents the other eight Northeast and Mid-Atlantic LCFS states in terms of assisting with the development of the LCFS.

183. NESCAUM, The Northeast/Mid-Atlantic Low Carbon Fuel Standard: Plan for the LCFS Economic Analysis (PowerPoint) (Feb. 23, 2010), http://www.nescaum.org/topics/low-carbon-fuels.

184. Washington Exec. Order No. 09-05, Washington's Leadership on Climate Change, §(1)(f) (May 21, 2009).

185. Or. H.B. 2186, 75th Oregon Legislative Assembly (2009).

186. Or. Dep't of Envtl. Quality, Oregon Low Carbon Fuel Standard, http://www.deq.state.or.us/aq/committees/lowcarbon.htm.

187. Or. Dep't of Envtl. Quality, Oregon Low Carbon Fuel Standards, Advisory Committee Process and Program Design 8–9 (Jan. 25, 2011), http://www.deq.state.or.us/aq/committees/docs/lcfs/reportFinal.pdf.

188. Midwestern Governors Ass'n, Energy Security and Climate Stewardship Platform for the Midwest 2007, at 13.

189. Midwestern Governors Ass'n, Low Carbon Fuel Standard, http://www.midwesterngovernors.org/LCFS.htm.

190. Midwestern Governors Ass'n, Energy Security and Climate Stewardship Platform for the Midwest: Low Carbon Fuel Policy Advisory Recommendations 2 (Dec. 2010), http://www.midwesterngovernors.org/Publications/LCFPagDoc.pdf.

191. Id.

192. Lansing Trade Group, LLC v. 3B Biofuels GmbH & Co., 612 F. Supp. 2d 813 (S.D. Texas 2009); Cargill Inc. v. Biodiesel of Las Vegas, No. 09-672, 2009 WL 3164761 (D. Minn. Sept. 28, 2009).

193. GAGE, Inc. v. Bioconversion Tech., LLC, No. 2:08CV57 DB, WL 3181940 (D. Utah Sept. 30, 2009); Transocean Group Holdings Party Ltd. v. S. Dak. Soybean Processors, LLC, 663 F. Supp. 2d 731 (D. Minn. 2009); SunOpta, Inc. v. Abengoa Bioenergy New Techs., Inc., No. 4:2008cv78, 2008 WL 782704 (E.D. Mo. Jan. 18, 2008).

194. Agri-Process Innovations, Inc. v. Greenline Indus., Inc., No. 4:08CV00558, 2008 WL 4126909 (E.D. Ark. Sept. 4, 2008); Renerglobe, Inc. v. Northeast Biofuels, LLC, 24 Misc. 3d 1212(A), 2009 WL 1929090 (N.Y. Sup. Ct. June 24, 2009).

195. Borneo Energy Sendirian Berhad v. Sustainable Power Corp, No. H-09-06122009, WL 2498596 (S.D. Tex. Aug. 12, 2009); SRS Energy, Inc. v. Bio-Products International, Inc., No. 4:08 CV 285 HEA, 2008 WL 2224803 (E.D. Mo. May 27, 2008).

196. Idaho Energy, LP v. Harris Contracting Co., No. CV07-423-N-EJL, 2008 WL 4498809 (D. Idaho Sept. 30, 2008); Novozymes v. Genencor Int'l, Inc., 474 F. Supp. 2d 592 (D. Del. 2007).

197. Biofuels Interagency Working Group, "Up-Front Shared Intellectual Property Rights Will Establish Guiding Principles on Protection, Ownership and Dissemination of Intellectual Property," Growing America's Fuels 4 (2009).

198. Rocky Mountain Farmers Union v. Goldstene, No. 1:09-cv-02234-LJO-DLB (E.D. Cal. 2009).

199. Id., Complaint at ¶¶ 65–73.

200. Id., Complaint at ¶¶ 82–88.

201. Nat'l Petrochemicals & Refiners Ass'n v. Goldstene, CV-F-10-163 LJO DLB (E.D. Cal. 2010 filed Feb. 2, 2010).

202. Id., Complaint at ¶¶ 38–69.

203. Id., Complaint at ¶¶ 75–83.

204. Constr. Materials Recycling Ass'n Issues & Educ. Fund, Inc. v. Burack, 686 F. Supp. 2d 162, 165 (D.N.H. 2010).

205. Id. at 166.

206. Id. at 173.

207. Am. Petroleum Inst. v. Cooper, 681 F. Supp. 2d 635, 645 (E.D.N.C. 2010); see also N.C. Gen. Stat. §75-90 (2008).

208. Cooper, 681 F. Supp. 2d at 642–643.

209. Id. at 642–645.

210. *Id.* at 655–656. Certain of plaintiffs' other claims remain pending in this case.

211. Under the CAA, EPA must review every Title V permit proposed by a state, and here, the waste-to-ethanol plant was a Title V facility. LaFleur v. Whitman, 300 F.3d 256, 262 (2d Cir. 2002).

212. *Id.* at 259.

213. *Id.* at 276.

214. *Id.* at 278.

215. *Id.* at 278–79.

216. *Id.* at 279–81.

217. For more thorough discussion of these issues, see Jacqueline M. Wilkosz, *Thirsting for Change: How the Growth of the Biofuel Industry Can Stimulate Advancements in Water Law*, 2009 U. ILL. L. REV. 583, 593.

218. 674 S.E.2d 436 (N.C. Ct. App. 2009).

219. 674 S.E.2d at 438.

220. *Id.* at 439.

221. *Id.* at 442.

222. 663 N.W.2d 833 (Wis. Ct. App. 2003).

223. 663 N.W.2d at XXX.

224. *Id.* at 840.

225. *Id.* at 842–43.

226. *Id.* at 845.

chapter twenty

Hydropower

Charles R. Sensiba

Introduction

This chapter surveys regulatory requirements associated with the construction, operation, and maintenance of hydropower projects in the United States.[1] The chapter begins with a brief discussion of hydropower's significance as the nation's largest, most mature, and most reliable source of renewable, clean energy, as well as some of the current challenges and opportunities associated with hydropower development. Next, the chapter examines the regulatory framework associated with nonfederal hydropower projects in the United States, including the jurisdictional reach of the Federal Power Act (FPA); the various forms of authorizations issued by the Federal Energy Regulatory Commission (FERC) under the FPA; environmental requirements that are specific to, or of particular significance in, the licensing of hydropower projects; and FERC's compliance and license reopener authorities. Following a brief discussion of regulatory requirements associated with federal hydropower facilities, the chapter concludes with a description of current and emerging issues in the hydropower industry, including economic incentives for new development, renewable energy standards, and ongoing efforts to promote expansion of hydropower resources in the United States.

Hydropower's Contribution to Clean, Renewable Energy Development

Hydropower is the largest and most mature renewable source of electric energy in the United States and worldwide. Since its earliest beginnings in the late 1800s, hydropower has been a major contributor to the electric grid. In the early 1900s, approximately 25 percent of the electric supply in the United States was generated from hydropower facilities, a figure that increased to about 40 percent by the 1940s.[2] While hydropower's relative contribution to the electric grid has decreased in recent decades due to the proliferation of fossil fuel power plants and development of nuclear facilities, today the approximately 2,400 conventional hydropower facilities in the United States provide nearly 80,000 megawatts (MW) of installed capacity—accounting for over 7.5 percent of total installed capacity from all sources of electricity nationwide.[3] The forty pumped storage facilities in the United States—hydropower projects that, through the use of two bodies of water at different elevations and reversible pump-generators, can store energy by pumping water into the elevated reservoir during periods of low demand, and then generate hydropower by releasing water back through the pump-generators to the lower water body—add another 22,000 MW in domestic capacity,[4] and hydropower projects in operation or construction worldwide account for 808,000 MW of installed capacity as of 2008.[5]

As a long-understood energy resource and technology, hydropower helps reduce greenhouse gas emissions and combat global climate change more than any other renewable resource. In 2009, the 272 terawatt hours of conventional hydropower production in the United States accounted for over 65 percent of all renewable energy generation—nearly doubling the generation of all other renewable energy resources combined.[6] Conventional hydropower generation in the United States displaces some 530 million barrels of oil annually[7] and avoids approximately 184 million metric tons of carbon dioxide emissions each year.[8]

Hydropower offers other benefits as well. Following initial capital costs of development, conventional hydropower projects are among the least expensive power sources, as operating and maintenance costs tend to be low, fuel costs (water) are generally minimal or zero and not sensitive to market fluctuations, and facilities are designed and constructed to operate indefinitely. Hydropower projects provide stable sources of energy, in some cases peaking power,[9] and promote security and reliability to the transmission grid by providing significant ancillary benefits such as frequency control,[10] reserve generation,[11] load following[12] and balancing,[13] and black start capabilities.[14] Pumped storage projects, moreover, provide energy storage and help to firm and integrate variable sources of renewable energy, such as wind and solar.[15] In addition to providing these and other "developmental" benefits, such as flood control, irrigation, and water supply,[16] hydropower projects are statutorily required to offer recreational opportunities, "protect, mitigate damages to, and enhance" fish and wildlife resources affected by the construction and operation of these facilities,[17] and "preserv[e] other aspects of environmental quality."[18]

Despite these immense benefits, hydropower projects are among the most heavily regulated energy facilities in the United States.[19] As described in more detail below, most hydropower projects not owned and operated by the federal government must be federally licensed—a requirement for electric generating facilities that is shared only with nuclear projects.[20] Nonfederal hydropower projects are licensed and regulated by FERC under the auspices of Part I of the FPA.[21] Originally enacted in 1920 as the Federal Water Power Act (FWPA),[22] the FPA was intended to promote hydropower development in the United States by centralizing federal licensing and regulatory authority of hydropower projects in the Federal Power Commission (FPC), FERC's predecessor agency,[23] and by establishing fixed license terms. As subsequently amended and applied today, however, the FPA arguably impedes development as compared to other energy sources by requiring fractured decision-making at the federal and state levels, imposing lengthy, complex administrative processes, and effectively stripping FERC's ability to consider the developmental and nondevelopmental values of a river basin and craft license conditions that best balance these values in the public interest.[24]

Because many of the nation's largest hydropower facilities were initially licensed and constructed beginning in the New Deal era through the early 1960s,[25] the expiration of the original fifty-year licenses for these projects requires relicensing before FERC in accordance with the suite of modern federal environmental programs that now apply to federal licensing and permitting actions. Today's FERC licensing process is an extraordinarily complex, multiyear proceeding to satisfy multiple federal and state requirements and involves a host of federal and state resource agencies, Indian tribes, the environmental community, and members of the public,[26] and the relicensing process provides an opportunity to ensure that existing hydropower facilities meet current federal environmental requirements. While not subject to the FPA, federally owned hydropower projects are also heavily regulated in accordance with project-specific authorizing legislation, federal environmental requirements, and planning mandates.

Nonetheless, interest in preserving existing hydropower projects and developing new projects remains high. It is a competitively priced generation resource relative to the price of oil and other fossil fuels. With the current administration and Congress focused on transitioning the United States to a clean energy economy, hydropower—an emissions-free, proven technology—has been targeted as a major contributor to meeting policy objectives of reducing greenhouse gas emissions and decreasing our reliance on fossil fuels. Accordingly, hydropower is quickly regaining prominence in the United States. As discussed in greater detail below, federal and state regulators—recognizing the numerous benefits provided by hydropower—have started to respond by extending economic incentives for new development, requiring regulators to equally consider developmental and nondevelopmental factors when authorizing hydropower facilities, classifying many hydropower projects as renewable resources under state and proposed federal renewable energy standards, and committing to explore other ways to promote efficient development of this valuable resource in an environmentally responsible manner.

And the potential for additional hydropower development is substantial. As of 2010, it is the fastest-growing major energy source worldwide,[27] and in the United States only about 3 percent of the estimated 80,000 existing dams are outfitted as hydropower facilities.[28] Much of the domestic potential for new development of hydropower projects, therefore, could be realized without any new dam construction. In fact, recent studies have concluded that the nation's hydropower capacity has the potential to nearly double by 2025 from current levels of approximately 80,000 MW, even when accounting for environmental feasibility and constraints.[29] According to these studies, between 4,000 and 9,000 MW of new capacity is available through expansion of and efficiency improvements at existing hydropower facilities, with another 10,000 to 17,000 MW available through construction of new hydropower facilities at existing dams.[30] With regard to new project development, studies have concluded that the potential for development of small projects (i.e., projects less than 30 MW in installed capacity) is about 40,000 MW,[31] and the potential for new pumped storage projects stands at approximately 24,000 MW.[32]

Regulation of Nonfederal Hydropower Projects

Regulatory Jurisdiction over Nonfederal Hydropower Projects Under the Federal Power Act

The vast majority of hydropower projects in the United States are owned and operated by nonfederal entities, such as investor-owned utilities, independent power producers, state and local governments, and water districts. As of 2010, approximately 1,600 nonfederal hydropower projects operated throughout the United States. These projects are diverse, incorporating conventional impoundment, diversion, and pumped storage projects, and ranging from generating capacities of nearly 3,000 MW—rivaling the largest electric power generating facilities in the United States—down to less than 1 kilowatt.[33] In terms of scale, these nonfederal projects range from large dams and expansive reservoirs occupying tens of thousands of acres, down to "microhydro" projects that consist of little more than a small turbine and generator.

Despite these vast differences, with very few exceptions, all these projects—together with the approximately three hundred projects that currently are being studied for potential development[34]—are licensed and regulated by FERC pursuant to the FPA.

Scope of FERC Jurisdiction Under the FPA

Enacted in 1920 as the nation's first comprehensive energy regulatory program, the FWPA was intended to establish a complete scheme of federal regulation and control of water power projects.[35] Its overarching framework centralized and consolidated federal jurisdiction over hydropower development in the FPC—an agency with technical expertise that issued and regulated licenses for hydropower projects according to "a comprehensive plan for improving or developing" the nation's waterways.[36] Under this structure, the FPC was able to "establish a uniform policy and . . . coordinate more effectively the activities of the several agencies hitherto charged with individual responsibility."[37]

To carry out the designs of the FWPA, Congress placed nearly all nonfederal hydropower facilities under the FPC's jurisdiction. Under the original 1920 legislation, Congress mandated that the construction, operation, or maintenance of a hydropower project requires licensing if the project: (1) is located "across, along, or in any of the navigable waters of the United States"; (2) occupies "any part of the public lands or reservations of the United States"; or (3) "utilize[s] the surplus water or water power from any Government dam."[38] While the FWPA grandfathered projects operating "under and in accordance with" a permit or right-of-way granted prior to the 1920 legislation,[39] Congress—as part of the Public Utility Act of 1935 that amended the FWPA and retitled it as Part I of the FPA—expanded the FPA's jurisdictional reach to include hydropower projects that: (1) are located on non-navigable waterways that are subject to Congress's Commerce Clause jurisdiction; (2) affect interstate or foreign commerce; and (3) have undergone construction or major modification after August 26, 1935, the date of the amendment.[40] With the passage of the Department of Energy Organization Act of 1977, FERC assumed the functions of the FPC.[41]

As a result, today the FPA contains a fairly complex set of jurisdictional requirements that are highly dependent on the facts and circumstances of each case, requiring FERC to apply terms such as "navigable waters,"[42] "reservations,"[43] and "public lands,"[44] as well as extensive FERC and judicial precedent regarding Commerce Clause waterways,[45] a project's effect on commerce,[46] and "post-1935 construction."[47] As a practical matter, nearly all hydropower projects in the United States—except, perhaps, for those located on nonfederal lands along non-navigable creeks and streams in remote areas unconnected to the interstate transmission grid—are subject to FERC's jurisdiction.[48] And if FERC's jurisdiction is at all in question with respect to an identified project, the FPA provides for project proponents to file a "declaration of intent" with FERC to ascertain a project's jurisdictional status.[49]

FERC Licenses, Exemptions, Permits, and Approvals

FERC carries out its statutory responsibilities under the FPA and other federal statutory programs by issuing and regulating various authorizations to project proponents. At the initial stage of project development, FERC issues preliminary permits to establish priority for licensing[50] and facilitate the proponent's study of the environmental and technical feasibility of the project. To authorize the construction and operation of a hydropower facility, FERC issues various types of licenses and is authorized under certain circumstances to grant "exemptions." Finally, various FERC authorizations facilitate the decommissioning of a hydropower project. FERC's decisions in carrying out its responsibilities under the FPA are reviewable exclusively before the U.S. courts of appeals, following a mandatory rehearing before FERC in most instances.[51]

Preliminary Permits

Section 4(f) of the FPA authorizes FERC "[t]o issue preliminary permits for the purpose of enabling applicants for a license . . . to secure the data" and to prepare the maps, plans, specifications, and estimates required for its license application.[52] Preliminary permits are limited to a term of three years,[53] and the permit does not authorize the permittee to construct or operate the proposed project, or even to access the proposed project site.[54] Rather, the "sole purpose" of a preliminary permit is to facilitate the permittee's study of the proposed site by preserving its priority status in any subsequent competitive licensing process.[55]

Licenses

A FERC-issued license is the central authorization under the FPA to construct and operate a hydropower project.[56] Section 4(e) of the FPA authorizes FERC to issue licenses:

> for the purpose of constructing, operating, and maintaining dams, water conduits, reservoirs, power houses, transmission lines, or other project works necessary or convenient for the development and improvement of navigation and for the development, transmission, and utilization of power. . . . [57]

In addition, § 10 of the FPA directs FERC to include certain conditions in the license as required by the FPA—such as to ensure a comprehensive development of the waterway;[58] to protect fish and wildlife resources as recommended or prescribed by certain resource agencies;[59] to adequately protect and utilize federal reservations occupied by the project, as directed by the federal agency that manages the reservation;[60] to establish annual charges to be paid by the licensee;[61] and to set the term of the license, which can be for up to fifty years.[62] Aside from these statutorily required conditions, FPA § 6 authorizes FERC to include license conditions "in conformity with this Act, which said terms and conditions and the acceptance thereof shall be expressed in said license."[63] Typically, FERC includes conditions related to environmental and recreational standards, such as drawdown restrictions, fish screening and ramping, minimum flows, dissolved oxygen content, and recreational access. FERC's licenses also include more standard-form conditions related to land management and ownership requirements, dam safety, and authorization for FERC to reopen the license and reestablish a licensee's obligations under certain circumstances.[64]

While FERC has broad authority to include certain conditions in its licenses, the FPA balances that authority by protecting licensees' pecuniary interests. The FPA specifically provides that a license is conditioned "upon acceptance by the licensee of all of the terms and conditions,"[65] so the license is not operative unless and until it is accepted by the license applicant. Moreover, the FPA protects the security to attract investment by providing fixed license terms for up to fifty years that "may be altered or surrendered only upon mutual agreement between the licensee and [FERC]."[66]

Finally, the FPA authorizes FERC to relicense a project at the end of the original license term. Section 15 of the FPA provides that new licenses be issued on "reasonable terms" and for terms of thirty to fifty years.[67] If FERC, at the end of a license term, has not yet issued a new license, the FPA requires it to "issue from year to year an annual license to the then licensee under the terms and conditions of the existing license until . . . a new license is issued."[68] Since the mid-1990s, much of FERC's regulatory focus on hydropower projects has been on relicensing, as many of the original licenses for large hydropower projects constructed in the mid-twentieth century have expired. Because the relicensing process, including the attendant federal environmental programs discussed below, requires a renewed evaluation of the project and its environs, many projects emerge from the relicensing process with different operational, recreational, and environmental conditions, such as: operational constraints to benefit resident and migratory fisheries; construction and operation of fish passage facilities; greater recreational opportunities, including whitewater rafting; enhanced land management practices; and management of historic properties.

Exemptions

In an effort to promote renewable, environmentally beneficial domestic energy resources, Congress in the 1978 Public Utility Regulatory Practices Act (PURPA) and 1980 Energy Security Act encouraged "small scale"[69] hydropower development by making certain projects eligible for exemptions from the licensing requirements of the FPA.[70] Under PURPA, Congress authorized exemptions from licensing for small conduit projects up to 15 MW for nonmunicipal developers and 40 MW for municipalities.[71] Under the Energy Security Act, Congress extended the exemption program to include projects up to 5 MW at "existing dams"[72] and those using "natural water features" to generate electricity "without the need for any dam or impoundment."[73]

Although an exemption, like a license, allows the holder to develop and operate a hydropower project, exemptions differ significantly from licenses in several important ways. First, while FERC's issuance of both licenses and exemptions is subject to National Environmental Policy Act (NEPA) requirements, exemptions typically qualify for expedited review and in some instances are categorically excluded from review.[74] Second, FERC-issued exemptions must contain conditions set by federal and state fish and wildlife agencies,[75] whereas in the licensing context, these conditions are set by FERC upon recommendation of these agencies.[76] Third, unlike a license, an exemption does not grant the holder a federal right of eminent domain.[77] Finally, unlike licenses, exemptions are not issued for specific terms and upon fixed conditions; rather, exemptions—although perpetual—do not enjoy the protections offered by § 6 of the FPA.

License Surrender and Project Decommissioning

Finally, the FPA establishes several avenues for retiring and decommissioning hydropower projects. To begin with, decommissioning a project during the license term requires a license surrender application. Section 6 of the FPA provides that a license "may be . . . surrendered only upon mutual agreement between the licensee and the Commission after thirty days' public notice,"[78] and FERC applies "a broad 'public interest' standard" when ruling on surrender applications.[79] Under this standard, FERC accepts license surrenders for any number of reasons, most often technical infeasibility of an unconstructed project or escalating operational and repair costs at an existing facility.[80] Relatedly, FERC can terminate the license during the license term if the licensee fails to commence construction by the deadline established under the license,[81] or if it finds that the licensee impliedly surrendered its license.[82] FERC also has approved surrender applications where mitigation measures required as part of the relicensing effort render the project uneconomic.[83]

In the relicensing context, a licensee has additional options for decommissioning a project. Although a license expires at the end of its stated term, FERC has interpreted the FPA as requiring it to issue an "annual license" that indefinitely extends the license terms until it issues a new license[84]—even where the licensee informs FERC that it will not be seeking to relicense the project.[85] Thus, FERC has allowed licensees to seek a surrender of an "annual license" in lieu of obtaining a new license.[86] In addition, § 15(f) of the FPA authorizes FERC to issue "nonpower" licenses upon the expiration of an existing power license if it determines that "in conformity with a comprehensive plan for improving or developing a waterway or waterways for beneficial public uses all or part of any licensed project should no longer be used or adapted for use for power purposes."[87] A nonpower license serves the sole purpose of facilitating FERC's continued oversight of the project site for a short period until an agency with regulatory authority over the site is willing to assume responsibility over the lands and facilities covered by the nonpower license. While § 15(f) allows FERC to grant a nonpower license *sua sponte* or upon the motion of "any licensee, person, State, municipality, or State Commission,"[88] in practice FERC has "never issued a nonpower license over the objection of a licensee,"[89] and has limited use of nonpower licenses to narrow circumstances where such action is specifically contemplated in a settlement agreement among the project owner, the agency assuming regulatory authority over the site, and other participants in the relicensing process.[90]

FERC has, however, asserted authority to decommission a project at relicensing over the objection of the licensee. In 1994, FERC issued a policy statement that asserts authority to force a licensee to cease operation and pay for decommissioning costs of a hydropower facility—even where the incumbent licensee seeks to relicense and continue operation of the project.[91] Under the policy, FERC will deny new licenses if it determines that no license could be issued consistent with its FPA licensing authority and the requirements of other applicable law.[92]

FERC has mandated project decommissioning at the licensee's expense in only one case—which, due to a subsequent settlement, was never judicially tested.[93] In *City of Tacoma v. FERC*, however, the D.C. Circuit held that FPA § 15's mandate that FERC relicense projects "upon reasonable terms"[94] does not require FERC to impose environmental conditions in a manner that protects the economic viability of a project. "The obligation [under § 4(e) of the FPA] to give 'equal consideration' to wildlife protection and the environment," the court held, "implies that, at least in some cases, these environmental concerns will prevail."[95] Thus, *Tacoma* holds that "Congress implicitly extended to FERC the power to shut down projects either directly, by denying a new license, or indirectly, by imposing reasonable and necessary conditions that cause the licensee to reject the new license,"[96] although the issue of payment of decommissioning costs remains unresolved.[97]

State Regulation of Hydropower Projects

The FPA establishes a federal licensing and regulatory scheme for nonfederal hydropower projects. While the FPA specifically carves out the authority of states to regulate matters "relating to the control, appropriation, use, or distribution of water used in irrigation or for municipal or other uses, or any vested right acquired therein,"[98] and other federal statutory programs grant significant authority to the states to participate in licensing processes and condition FERC-issued licenses,[99] the federal scheme under the FPA preempts state regulation of other aspects of hydropower projects subject to FERC's jurisdiction.

The Supreme Court's 1946 ruling in *First Iowa Hydro-Electric Cooperative v. FPC* is the seminal case establishing federal preemption of the licensing of projects within FERC's jurisdiction.[100] In that case, the Court concluded that the federal policy expressed in the FPA preempted a state-imposed requirement in Iowa that a developer obtain a state permit prior to constructing a dam and hydropower power plant.[101] Noting that "[a] dual final authority, with a duplicative system of state permits and federal licenses required for each project, would be unworkable,"[102] the Court held that the detailed national regulation scheme under the FPA should not be obstructed by conflicting state laws.[103]

In its 1990 decision in *California v. FERC*, the Supreme Court unanimously reaffirmed *First Iowa*, noting that "the FPA establishes a broad and paramount federal regulatory role" in the licensing and regulation of hydropower projects.[104] Under these Supreme Court rulings, the FPA has been found to preempt various conflicting state requirements,[105] including fish protection programs,[106] eminent domain statutes,[107] land-use requirements,[108] and payment of annual charges.[109] Thus, with the exception of the few hydropower projects falling outside FERC's jurisdiction, states do not license or directly regulate hydropower projects,[110] although as discussed in detail below, the FPA itself and other federal statutes grant states significant involvement and authority in FERC's licensing efforts.

Licensing and Environmental Requirements

Because the construction and operation of a hydropower facility requires a FERC-issued license or exemption, FERC must comply with a host of environmental review requirements before issuing its authorization, including review under NEPA,[111] consultation pursuant to § 7 of the Endangered Species Act (ESA),[112] water quality certification under § 401 of the Clean Water Act (CWA),[113] consistency review under the Coastal Zone Management Act (CZMA),[114] and consultation under § 106 of the National Historic Preservation Act (NHPA).[115] Depending on the facts and circumstances at each project, other federal reviews and requirements may apply,[116] and FERC has developed several different licensing processes designed to meet these numerous and complex requirements.[117] Even after FERC grants the license, certain license amendment proposals trigger subsequent consultation and environmental review.[118]

While numerous federal programs apply to FERC's licensing and regulation of nonfederal hydropower projects, several have exclusive applicability or particular significance in the licensing of these facilities. These are discussed below.

FPA §§ 4(e) and 10(a): "Comprehensive Development/Public Interest" Conditions

When licensing or relicensing a hydropower project, FERC is required under FPA § 10(a)(1) to impose license conditions that ensure the project is "best adapted" to a comprehensive plan for improving or developing the waterway at issue for a number of beneficial public purposes, including interstate and foreign commerce, power development, fish and wildlife protection, enhancement and mitigation, irrigation, flood control, water supply, and recreation.[119] FPA § 4(e), in turn, requires FERC to give "equal consideration" to developmental and nondevelopmental values when issuing licenses.[120]

In discharging this "comprehensive development/public interest" standard, FERC considers comprehensive plans prepared by federal and state entities,[121] as well as the recommendations of resource agencies, Indian tribes, and members of the public.[122] FERC's conditioning authority under this standard is quite broad, requiring FERC's "'consideration of all factors affecting the public interest,'" and empowering FERC "with the flexibility to weight different public-interest factors differently on a case-by-case basis, so that '[a]s the public interest changes over time, [FERC's] considerations under the section 10(a) standard likewise change, encompassing new criteria or reevaluating the weight given established criteria.'"[123]

FPA § 4(e): Federal Reservation Conditions

While FERC is authorized under FPA § 4(e) to issue licenses for hydropower projects located on federal reservations, that section also provides that any such license "shall be subject to and contain such conditions as the Secretary of the department under whose supervision such reservation falls shall deem necessary for the adequate protection and utilization of such reservation."[124] Thus, for a hydropower project located on a federal reservation[125]—such as a National Forest, Indian reservation, or military reservation[126]—§ 4(e) extends considerable authority to the federal land management agency that administers the reservation.

Indeed, the Supreme Court in *Escondido Mutual Water Co. v. La Jolla Band of Mission Indians* held that § 4(e) conditions submitted by land management agencies are mandatory, and that FERC is required to include them in the license without modification—even if it disagrees with the submitted conditions.[127] In that case, the Court determined that while Congress, under the FPA, clearly intended for FERC to have exclusive authority to issue all licenses, it wanted the individual Secretaries to determine what conditions would be included in the license to protect the resources under their respective jurisdictions. While these conditions are to be narrowly tailored to the adequate protection and utilization of the resource, the Court concluded that the courts of appeals—not FERC—have authority to decide when a Secretary's conditions exceed the permissible limits. A little over a decade after *Escondido*, which involved the initial licensing of a proposed project, the D.C. Circuit upheld FERC's determination that mandatory § 4(e) conditioning authority applies in the relicensing context as well.[128]

Following *Escondido*, FERC narrowly interpreted § 4(e) as requiring it to include mandatory conditions only insofar as they address project works located within the reservation.[129] In *City of Tacoma v. FERC*, however, the D.C. Circuit in 2006 determined that § 4(e) is not so limited, holding that § 4(e) "nowhere limits [the agency's] regulatory authority to those portions of the project that are on the reservation. On the contrary, so long as some portion of the project is on the reservation, the Secretary is authorized to impose any conditions that will protect the reservation. . . ."[130] While the court narrowly confined federal land management agencies' § 4(e) mandatory authority as extending to conditions "to mitigate the effect of the project . . . to the extent doing so is reasonably related to protecting the reservation,"[131] the court rejected FERC's rigid geographic application of § 4(e).

Responding to the concern that federal land management agencies' mandatory conditions imposed under § 4(e) did not balance environmental protection with air quality, energy, and economic factors in the overall public interest as provided under the FPA,[132] Congress, as part of the Energy Policy Act of 2005 (EPAct 2005), made three significant amendments to the FPA in an attempt to restore balance in agencies' § 4(e) conditions. First, Congress added § 33 of the FPA, which requires federal land management agencies to consider the effects of their § 4(e) conditions on the developmental purposes of the hydropower facility.[133] The agency must demonstrate that it gave "equal consideration" to the impacts of the § 4(e) condition on "energy supply, distribution, cost, and use; flood control; navigation; water supply; and air quality (in addition to the preservation of other aspects of environmental quality)."[134] When submitting their § 4(e) conditions to FERC, moreover, agencies must provide a rationale and submit all data and information relevant to the condition, whether supportive of the condition or not.[135]

Second, the new FPA § 33 allows license applicants and other parties to FERC licensing proceedings to submit alternative § 4(e) conditions. If an alternative § 4(e) condition "provides for the adequate protection and utilization of the reservation" and is either more economical or improves electrical production as compared to the agencies' original condition, § 33 requires the federal land management agency to accept that condition in lieu of its own.[136]

Finally, Congress in EPAct 2005 amended § 4(e) itself to entitle the license applicant or any other party to the FERC proceeding to a trial-type hearing of up to ninety days "on any disputed issues of material fact with respect to such conditions."[137] Trial-type hearings include opportunities for discovery and cross-examination,[138] and in 2005, federal resource agencies issued interim final regulations governing the hearing process for § 4(e) conditions.[139]

Collectively, these and other amendments to the FPA under EPAct 2005[140] represented Congress's belief that since § 4(e) conditions are mandatory, federal land management agencies issuing such conditions must—like FERC—balance developmental and nondevelopmental values in the overall public interest. While § 4(e) continues to be a considerable source of power to federal land management agencies in the licensing of nonfederal hydropower projects, since EPAct 2005, these agencies can no longer take the parochial view that their sole responsibility is to protect riverine natural resources.

FPA § 18: Fishway Prescriptions

FPA § 18 requires FERC to "require the construction, maintenance, and operation by a licensee at its own expense of . . . such fishways as may be prescribed by the Secretary of the Interior or the Secretary of Commerce, as appropriate."[141] The purpose of § 18 "is to provide for 'safe and timely' fish passage . . . as well as other 'fish and wildlife benefits both downstream and upstream of a project.'"[142]

Like § 4(e) federal reservation conditions, § 18 prescriptions submitted by the Secretary of the Interior, through the U.S. Fish and Wildlife Service (USFWS), and the Secretary of Commerce, through National Marine Fisheries Service (NMFS), are mandatory. FERC "may not modify, reject, or reclassify any prescriptions submitted by the Secretaries under color of section 18."[143] Instead, if FERC disagrees with a fishway prescription, its only choices are to not issue the license at all, or to issue the license with the prescription and raise its concerns with the reviewing court.[144]

Like all other license conditions, however, § 18 prescriptions must be supported by "substantial evidence,"[145] which has been interpreted to require the prescribing agency "to show that fishery resources will be adversely affected by a particular project as well as to support the particular solutions for protecting those resources."[146] Upon review, the D.C. Circuit has struck down fishway prescriptions that lack any evidentiary support in FERC's administrative record,[147] although the court has found that the "substantial evidence" standard does not always require project-level studies, but can be met through "official notice of matters of common knowledge, of evidence available to [the Secretary] from other proceedings, and of matters known to the agency through its cumulative experience and consequent expertise."[148]

In EPAct 2005, Congress extended the same reform measures that apply to § 4(e) conditions to the Secretaries' submittal of § 18 prescriptions.[149] When preparing their prescriptions, USFWS and NMFS must give "equal consideration" to developmental and nondevelopmental values, and they must provide a rationale and relevant data and information to FERC.[150] License applicants and other parties in the FERC process are authorized to submit alternative § 18 prescriptions, which the agencies must accept if the alternative: (1) "will be no less protective" than the agencies' initial prescription; and (2) will either "cost significantly less to implement; or . . . result in improved operation of the project works for electricity production."[151] And applicants and other parties are entitled to trial-type hearings of "any disputed issues of material fact with respect to such fishways."[152]

FPA § 10(j): Fish and Wildlife Agency Recommendations

Section 10(j) of the FPA, which Congress added to the FPA as part of the Electric Consumers Protection Act of 1986,[153] requires FERC to impose license conditions, "based on recommendations" of federal and state fish and wildlife agencies, that "adequately and equitably protect, mitigate damages to, and enhance" fish, wildlife, and habitat affected by licensed projects.[154] Unlike § 4(e) conditions and § 18 prescriptions, agencies' authority under § 10(j) is not mandatory; it does, however, provide a greater role for federal and state resource agencies in FERC's licensing proceedings.

The FPA authorizes FERC to reject recommendations submitted under § 10(j) only if it determines them to be "inconsistent with the purposes and requirements" of the FPA or other applicable law, and only after FERC: (1) attempts to resolve the inconsistency, "giving due weight to the recommendations, expertise, and statutory responsibilities of such agencies"; and (2) publishes its findings as to why the recommended § 10(j) measures are inconsistent with the FPA or other applicable law.[155] FERC's regulations set forth a multistep consultation process for implementing § 10(j) requirements.[156]

In practice, FERC accepts a majority of filed § 10(j) recommendations.[157] FERC has declined, however, to accept recommendations that only propose a study, as opposed to actual protection, mitigation, and enhancement measures,[158] or recommendations addressing recreational issues instead of fish and wildlife.[159]

CWA § 401: Water Quality Certification

CWA § 401 requires "[a]ny applicant for a Federal license or permit to conduct any activity . . . which may result in any discharge into the navigable waters" to "provide the licensing or permitting agency a certification from the State in which the discharge originates . . . that any such discharge will comply" with state water quality standards.[160] FERC's licensing and relicensing of hydropower projects trigger water quality certification requirements under § 401,[161] and FERC may not grant the license application until the state grants certification, unless the certification requirements are deemed to be waived by the state's failure or refusal to act on a request for certification within a reasonable time (not to exceed one year).[162]

Water quality certification under § 401 confers significant and broad authority to the states in the FERC licensing process. Section 401(d) provides:

> Any certification provided under this section shall set forth any effluent limitations and other limitations, and monitoring requirements necessary to assure that any applicant for a Federal license or permit will comply with any applicable effluent limitations and other limitations, . . . standard of performance . . . , or prohibition, effluent standard, or pretreatment standard . . . , and with any other appropriate requirement of State law set forth in such certification, and shall become a condition on any Federal license or permit subject to the provisions of this section.[163]

In issuing § 401 certification, therefore, the states are authorized to impose conditions they consider necessary to ensure compliance with state water quality standards, as well as any other "appropriate requirement of State law," which become conditions of the FERC-issued license.[164] And—like FPA § 4(e) conditions and § 18 prescriptions—FERC has no authority to reject or modify § 401 conditions.[165] If a state denies certification, moreover, FERC will not issue the license.[166]

While it is generally recognized that § 401 conditions must address "water quality in one manner or another,"[167] the Supreme Court in *Public Utility District No. 1 of Jefferson County v. Washington Department of Ecology (Dosewallips)* endorsed a broad interpretation of state conditioning authority under § 401.[168] In *Dosewallips*, the Court held that a minimum streamflow condition, which the state deemed necessary to preserve the designated use of the river as salmon habitat, was an appropriate means to ensure compliance with the state's water quality standards.[169] The Court upheld the state's authority to impose conditions designed to meet a state's numerical water quality criteria, but also to meet qualitative, subjective, narrative standards, designated uses, and the state's antidegradation policy.[170] Accordingly, the Court held that the state may properly impose instream flow requirements, and even protect recreational and aesthetic values, as part of the § 401 certification.[171]

As a result of *Dosewallips*, states wield tremendous authority to shape the operational constraints of FERC-licensed hydropower projects, as well as required protection, mitigation, and enhancement measures. In 2006, the Supreme Court in *S.D. Warren Co. v. Maine Board of Environmental Protection* broadly defined the type of activity that constitutes a "discharge" for purposes of triggering § 401 certification.[172] The unanimous Court held that a "discharge" under § 401 encompasses any "flowing or issuing" and therefore does not require—unlike CWA § 402—the addition of any "pollutant" in order to apply.[173]

License Compliance, Enforcement, and Reopeners

Once FERC issues a license or exemption authorizing the construction, operation, and maintenance of a hydropower facility, it has significant authority to ensure compliance with the required terms and conditions.[174] Under certain circumstances where it has reserved authority under the license, moreover, FERC may revisit and modify license conditions during the license term.[175]

FPA § 31 authorizes FERC to monitor and investigate compliance with hydropower licenses, permits, and exemptions, and to issue orders as necessary to require compliance with those licenses, permits, and exemptions.[176] Under § 31, FERC is empowered to impose civil penalties—up to $11,000 per violation per day[177]—upon a licensee, permittee, and exemptee for violations of FERC rules or regulations or of the terms and conditions of a license, permit, or exemption.[178] Section 31 also authorizes FERC to revoke a license or exemption when a licensee or exemptee violates a compliance order after being given a reasonable time in which to comply with the order, and after notice and an opportunity for hearing.[179]

In addition to enforcing license and exemption requirements, FERC in certain circumstances is authorized to adjust license terms and conditions over the license term. FPA § 6 prohibits FERC from unilaterally altering the terms of a license by requiring that license amendments be "only upon mutual agreement between the licensee and [FERC]."[180] However, FERC has adopted several standard conditions—called "L-Forms"—that it includes in all its licenses, several of which reserve authority for FERC to "reopen" the license during the license term to adjust requirements related to project structures, project operations, fish and wildlife resources, and recreation.[181] FERC's policy on addressing cumulative impacts of multiple hydropower projects in a river basin also recognizes the difficulty of identifying and studying all potential impacts in the basin during the relatively short relicensing period and provides that FERC will include specific license articles reserving its authority to examine and address such impacts at a later date after the new licenses have issued.[182] Before reopening a license in any instance, however, FERC must give notice and provide an opportunity for hearing by the licensee and any interested parties.[183]

Regulation of Federal Hydropower Facilities

In addition to the large number of hydropower facilities owned and operated by non-federal entities, the federal government owns significant hydropower assets in many parts of the United States (other than the Midwest through the Northeast), as part of multipurpose dams authorized in specific federal statutes. Among these are some of the largest and most well-known projects in the country, such as Hoover Dam on the Colorado River in Arizona and Nevada, Grand Coulee Dam in Washington State, Glen Canyon Dam on the Colorado River in Arizona, Oahe Dam on the Missouri River in South Dakota, and the four dams—Bonneville, The Dalles, John Day, and McNary—on the main stem Lower Columbia River in Oregon and Washington. The U.S. Army Corps of Engineers (the Corps) operates seventy-five hydropower dams nationwide, with a total installed capacity of 20,720 MW,[184] while the Bureau of Reclamation (the Bureau) operates fifty-eight hydropower dams in seventeen western states, with a total installed capacity of 14,808 MW.[185] In addition, the Tennessee Valley Authority (TVA)—a federally owned corporation—is the largest electric utility in the United States, whose numerous generation assets include twenty-nine hydropower plants, which have a combined installed capacity of 5,576 MW, including its pumped storage facility.[186]

Power and energy generated from plants operated by the Bureau and the Corps are marketed on a regional, river system basis, by four Power Marketing Administrations (PMAs) established within the Department of Energy: Bonneville Power Administration, Southeastern Power Administration, Southwestern Power Administration, and Western Area Power Administration.[187] The power from each dam or group of dams on a particular river system, in the case of the PMAs, and within a defined multistate area, in the case of TVA, can be marketed only within the geographic regions specified by the authorizing federal statutes.

With respect to the regulation of the federal hydropower projects themselves, these facilities—unlike nonfederal projects—are not licensed and regulated by FERC pursuant to the FPA.[188] Rather, federal hydropower facilities are governed in accordance with regulations and manuals adopted pursuant to the congressional legislation authorizing the specific facility[189] and the operating entities' organic statute(s).[190]

With regard to water resource planning, decisions by the Bureau, the Corps, and TVA (as well as the Natural Resources Conservation Service (NRCS), which does not operate any federal hydropower facilities) are governed by the Economic and Environmental Principles and Guidelines for Water and Related Land Resources Implementation Studies (Principles and Guidelines), developed under the Water Resources Planning Act of 1965.[191] The Principles and Guidelines document, which was last amended in 1983,[192] is "intended to ensure proper and consistent planning by Federal agencies in the formulation and evaluation of water and related land resources implementation studies."[193] Its overall objective is "to contribute to national economic development consistent with protecting the Nation's environment, pursuant to national environmental statutes, applicable executive orders, and other Federal planning requirements."[194] The Principles and Guidelines directs agencies' planning and decision-making by requiring planning decisions to be coordinated with affected states and interested individuals and groups,[195] mandating an interdisciplinary approach to technical and environmental studies,[196] requiring an environmental scoping process similar to NEPA requirements,[197] establishing forecasting and risk assessment requirements,[198] and requiring agencies to consider alternatives.[199] At the conclusion of the planning process, agencies' decisions are to be governed primarily by which alternative provides the greatest national economic benefit (NEB).[200] The Principles and Guidelines document sets forth detailed procedures for evaluating NEB benefits for many different types of water projects, including proposed hydropower facilities.[201]

As part of the Water Resources Planning Act of 2007 (WRPA), Congress articulated a shift in policy to expand federal planning beyond the economic focus of the Principles and Guidelines document by providing that:

> all water resources projects should reflect national priorities, encourage economic development, and protect the environment by—
>
> (1) seeking to maximize sustainable economic development;
>
> (2) seeking to avoid the unwise use of floodplains and flood-prone areas and minimizing adverse impacts and vulnerabilities in any case in which a floodplain or flood-prone area must be used; and
>
> (3) protecting and restoring the functions of natural systems and mitigating any unavoidable damage to natural systems.[202]

In light of this shift in policy, the WRPA directed the Secretary of the Army—after public comment and in consultation with various departmental secretaries, the Council on Environmental Quality (CEQ), and National Academy of Sciences (NAS)—to revise the Principles and Guidelines "for use by the Secretary in the formulation, evaluation, and implementation of water resources projects."[203] In September 2008, the Corps issued a proposed revised Principles and Guidelines document for public review and comment,[204] and in 2009 the Obama administration decided to consider "developing uniform planning standards for the development of water resources that would apply government-wide, including agencies other than" the Bureau, the Corps, TVA, and NRCS.[205] As such, CEQ was tasked with "facilitat[ing] an interagency drafting of revised Principles and Guidelines for planning water resources projects that could be applied government-wide."[206] CEQ released a proposed draft revised Principles and Guidelines document in December 2009, which, as of 2010, was under review by NAS.[207]

Finally, certain actions of federal entities such as the Bureau, the Corps, and TVA trigger review and consultation under federal statutory environmental programs. For instance, the Corps' decision to review its Master Water Control Manual governing the regulation of its six reservoirs on the Missouri River main stem in Montana,

North Dakota, and South Dakota triggered environmental review under NEPA and consultation under ESA and led to numerous challenges in federal court.[208] Similarly, NMFS's listing of salmon and steelhead species as threatened or endangered species under the ESA, beginning with the agency's listing of Snake River sockeye salmon as an endangered species in 1991, led to protracted litigation—which continues today—regarding the Bureau's and Corps's management and operation of numerous federal hydropower facilities comprising the Federal Columbia River Power System.[209] And in arguably the most well-known case involving the ESA, the Supreme Court in *TVA v. Hill* enjoined TVA's completion of construction of a federal dam on the basis that the proposed reservoir would have destroyed critical habitat of the snail darter—a fish species listed as endangered under the ESA.[210]

Current and Emerging Issues

Since the 1990s, the predominant issue facing the hydropower industry in the United States has been project relicensing, as many of the fifty-year licenses originally issued for most nonfederal projects—including some of the largest projects constructed during a significant build-up period during the mid-twentieth century—have expired.[211] During this period, FERC twice implemented major changes to its licensing regulations,[212] and Congress stepped in several times to reform the FPA and other applicable statutes.[213]

While project relicensing continues to be a significant issue within the industry, the recent focus on clean energy has promoted the emergence of marine and hydrokinetic technologies,[214] as well as renewed interest in new conventional hydropower development in the United States—particularly at locations of minimal environmental impact. Furthermore, transmission planners and project developers have a renewed interest in developing additional pumped storage projects, as these projects offer the most cost-effective means for large-scale energy storage and—of particular importance to renewable energy—have the inherent ability to firm and integrate variable renewable energy sources.[215]

As a result, over the past several years, FERC has experienced a near unprecedented surge in the filing of preliminary permit applications, and federal and state policy makers have started to respond. Over half the states, for example, have enacted either voluntary or mandatory Renewable Portfolio Standards (RPS), as discussed in detail in chapter 4. While state RPS programs vary widely in their requirements, limitations, and applicability, all recognize at least some forms of hydropower as a renewable resource. Most state RPS programs, for example, include incremental increases of generation at existing hydropower facilities—attained through installation of new capacity, efficiency improvements, or other equipment upgrades—as renewable. And while some states have defined generation from all existing conventional hydropower projects as renewable,[216] other states have imposed restrictions. For example, some state RPS programs broadly exclude generation from all existing larger-scale hydropower projects over a specified installed capacity, such as 100 or 200 MW,[217] and some states categorically exclude smaller projects, such as those as small as 30 MW or even 5 MW.[218] Other states have developed a process to certify existing hydropower projects as low impact, and therefore eligible to be treated as a renewable resource.[219] With regard to new project development, some state RPS programs allow only certain types of hydropower projects to be counted as renewable, such as small projects at existing, nonpowered dams; low-head micro hydro projects; generating stations along water supply and irrigation conduits and canals; and marine and hydrokinetic projects.[220]

While these restrictions and exclusions apparently are based on the assumption that certain classes of hydropower projects have greater environmental impacts than others, they have proven to be controversial. For example, the United States imports over 50 million MW hours of electricity from Canada annually, which constitutes over 97 percent of all electricity imports into the United States.[221] Because most electricity imported from Canada is generated at large-scale hydropower facilities, these imports do not qualify as renewable resources under many state RPS programs. As such, Canada has expressed concern that RPS programs impede access of Canadian-generated hydropower to markets in the United States, in violation of the North American Free Trade Agreement.[222] This issue—together with others that seek to account for and balance hydropower's benefits and environmental effects—inevitably will receive more attention and debate as Congress considers a national RPS.

In addition, Congress has promoted development of hydropower projects through economic incentives. Many of the incentives that are extended to other renewable energy sources—Production Tax Credits, Investment Tax Credits, Clean Renewable Energy Bonds, loan guarantees, grant programs under the American Recovery and Reinvestment Act, and funding opportunities offered by the U.S. Department of Energy[223]—are available to developers of hydropower facilities.

Finally, federal regulatory agencies are actively looking for ways to promote and spur development of new hydropower projects. In late 2009, FERC held a workshop, soliciting public comment on improving procedures for small hydropower project development,[224] and has implemented measures to improve and streamline the licensing process.[225] In early 2010, the Department of Energy, Department of the Interior, and the Corps sent a strong signal in support of hydropower growth in the United States by entering into a Memorandum of Understanding that establishes broad-based goals and designates specific action items with the intent of increasing hydropower project development at federal facilities and on federal lands in an environmentally responsible manner.[226]

As the nation grapples with greenhouse gas emissions and other adverse effects and risks of fossil fuel extraction and generation, and continues to seek solutions to effectively transition to a clean energy economy, hydropower is well positioned to help meet the challenge. It offers tremendous growth potential, is a well-understood, mature technology, is competitively priced, improves reliability to the transmission grid, and even supports other, more variable and intermittent renewable energy sources. While hydropower development will continue to be heavily regulated to ensure equal consideration and balancing of resources supported by our nation's waterways, the next decade could potentially experience expansion of hydropower resources at a pace that has not been seen for over half a century.

Notes

1. For a more in-depth discussion of the matters discussed in this chapter, see MICHAEL A. SWIGER ET AL., "Hydroelectric Regulation Under the Federal Power Act," in WATERS AND WATER RIGHTS ch. 40 (2009), MICHAEL A. SWIGER ET AL., HYDROELECTRIC POWER IN ENERGY LAW AND TRANSACTIONS ch. 53 (2009), and JAMES H. MCGREW, FERC: FEDERAL ENERGY REGULATORY COMMISSION 217–25 (2d ed. 2009). Other helpful resources include ENDANGERED SPECIES ACT: LAW, POLICY, AND PERSPECTIVES (Donald C. Baur & Wm. Robert Irvin eds., 2d ed. 2010), TONY A. SULLINS, ESA: ENDANGERED SPECIES ACT (2001), THE CLEAN WATER HANDBOOK (Mark A. Ryan ed., 2d. ed. 2003), JOEL M. GROSS & LYNN DODGE, CLEAN WATER ACT (2005), and SHERRY HUTT ET AL., CULTURAL PROPERTY LAW (2004).

2. U.S. DEP'T OF ENERGY, ENERGY EFFICIENCY & RENEWABLE ENERGY, HISTORY OF HYDROPOWER, http://www1.eere.energy.gov/windandhydro/hydro_history.html; U.S. DEP'T OF INTERIOR, BUREAU OF RECLAMATION, THE HISTORY OF HYDROPOWER DEVELOPMENT IN THE UNITED STATES, http://www.usbr.gov/power/edu/history.html.

3. U.S. ENERGY INFO. ADMIN., U.S. ELECTRIC NET SUMMER CAPACITY (2009), http://www .eia.doe.gov/cneaf/solar.renewables/page/table4.html; ELEC. POWER RESEARCH INST., ASSESSMENT OF WATERPOWER POTENTIAL AND DEVELOPMENT NEEDS 3-1 (2007), http://www.aaas .org/spp/cstc/docs/07_06_1ERPI_report.pdf [hereinafter EPRI ASSESSMENT].

4. U.S. ENERGY INFO. ADMIN., ELECTRIC POWER ANNUAL, ELECTRIC POWER INDUSTRY 2009: YEAR IN REVIEW, http://www.eia.doe.gov/cneaf/electricity/epa/epa_sum.html.

5. INT'L ENERGY AGENCY, ENERGY TECHNOLOGY PERSPECTIVES IN SUPPORT OF THE G8 PLAN OF ACTION: SCENARIOS AND STRATEGIES TO 2050, at 390 (2008), *available at* http://www .iea.org/textbase/nppdf/free/2008/etp2008.pdf.

6. U.S. ENERGY INFO. ADMIN., NET GENERATION BY ENERGY SOURCE: TOTAL (ALL SECTORS), http://www.eia.doe.gov/cneaf/electricity/epm/table1_1.html.

7. BP, BP STATISTICAL REVIEW OF WORLD ENERGY 38 (June 2010) (estimating the equivalent of 62.2 million tons of hydropower generation in the United States during 2009), *available at* http://www.bp.com/liveassets/bp_internet/globalbp/globalbp_uk_english/reports_and_publications/statistical_energy_review_2008/STAGING/local_assets/2010_downloads/statistical_ review_of_world_energy_full_report_2010.pdf.

8. *See* U.S. ENERGY INFO. ADMIN., VOLUNTARY REPORTING OF GREENHOUSE GASES, Form EIA-1605 2007, App. F (calculating a national average of 0.676 metric tons of carbon dioxide emissions per MW hour of electricity generation), *available at* http://www.eia.doe.gov/ oiaf/1605/pdf/Appendix%20F_r071023.pdf.

9. Peaking power refers to generating plants that can be brought online quickly to meet high, or peaking, demand.

10. Alternating current is transmitted from the power generating source to the end user at a standard frequency, 60 Hertz (Hz) in the United States and 50 Hz in most other parts of the world. Frequency control refers to the maintenance of frequency within a normal band and control time error and is attained through adjustment of the mechanical power of the generators using speed governor feedback and area generation control.

11. Reserve generation refers to available capacity in the system that can be brought online to avert a system collapse when system load and generation are significantly imbalanced, such as when a generating unit or interconnection to a neighboring system fails.

12. Load following refers to a power plant that can quickly adjust its power output as demand for electricity fluctuates throughout the day.

13. Load balancing refers to the process and measures for controlling system generation to match the prevailing load throughout the daily and weekly cycle of demand in the electrical distribution system.

14. Black start refers to the capability of a generating station to begin operation independently, without reliance on external energy sources, and to power up other generating stations on the associated interconnected grid in the event of a blackout.

15. For an in-depth discussion on energy transmission and storage, see chapter 22.

16. *See* 16 U.S.C. §§ 797(e), 803(a)(1).

17. *Id.* § 803(j)(1); *see also id.* § 797(e).

18. *Id.* § 797(e).

19. *See, e.g.,* Charles R. Sensiba, *Who's in Charge Here? The Shrinking Role of the Federal Energy Regulatory Commission in Hydropower Relicensing,* 70 U. COLO. L. REV. 603, 633 & n.194 (1999) (listing "approximately forty federal statutes [that] apply to hydropower licensing").

20. 16 U.S.C. §§ 797(e), 817(1); 42 U.S.C. § 2133.

21. 16 U.S.C. §§ 791a–823d.

22. Pub. L. No. 66-280, 41 Stat. 1063 (codified as amended at 16 U.S.C. § 791a–823d). In the Public Utility Act of 1935, the hydropower licensing provisions of the Federal Water Power Act of 1920 were amended and retitled as Part I of the FPA. Pub. L. No. 74-333, §§ 201–213, 49 Stat. 803, 838–863 (codified as amended in 16 U.S.C. §§ 791a–823d).

23. As part of the Department of Energy Organization Act of 1977, FERC assumed the functions of the Federal Power Commission. Pub. L. No. 95-91, § 401, 91 Stat. 565, 582.

24. *See generally* Michael C. Blumm & Viki A. Nadol, *The Decline of the Hydropower Czar and the Rise of Agency Pluralism in Hydroelectric Licensing,* 26 COLUM. J. ENVTL. L. 81(2001); Sensiba, *supra* note 19.

25. *See* MARC REISNER, CADILLAC DESERT 145–68 (1993).

26. *See generally* 18 C.F.R. pt. 5.

27. BP, BP STATISTICAL REVIEW OF WORLD ENERGY 5 (June 2010), *available at* http://www .bp.com/liveassets/bp_internet/globalbp/globalbp_uk_english/reports_and_publications/statistical_energy_review_2008/STAGING/local_assets/2010_downloads/statistical_review_of_world_energy_full_report_2010.pdf.

28. *See* U.S. ARMY ENG'R RESEARCH & DEV. CTR., NATIONAL INVENTORY OF DAMS (last updated May 11, 2009), http://www.erdc.usace.army.mil/pls/erdcpub/www_welcome .navigation_page?tmp_next_page=88255.

29. U.S. DEP'T OF ENERGY, DOE-ID-11263, FEASIBILITY ASSESSMENT OF THE WATER ENERGY RESOURCES OF THE UNITED STATES FOR NEW LOW POWER AND SMALL HYDRO CLASSES OF HYDROELECTRIC PLANTS 21–24, 35 (Jan. 2006), http://hydropower.inel.gov/resourceassessment/pdfs/main_report_appendix_a_final.pdf [hereinafter DOE FEASIBILITY ASSESSMENT]; EPRI ASSESSMENT, *supra* note 3, at vii; NAT'L HYDROPOWER ASS'N, NAVIGANT CONSULTING, JOB CREATION OPPORTUNITIES IN HYDROPOWER, EXECUTIVE SUMMARY 17 (2010), http:// www.hydro.org/Jobs%20Study/NHA_JobsStudy_ExecSummary%20Final%20Sept%2020 .pdf [hereinafter NAVIGANT STUDY].

30. EPRI ASSESSMENT, *supra* note 3, at 3-2 to 3-3; NAVIGANT STUDY, *supra* note 29, EXECUTIVE SUMMARY at 17.

31. EPRI ASSESSMENT, *supra* note 3, at 3-2 to 3-3; *see also* DOE FEASIBILITY ASSESSMENT, *supra* note 29, at 21–24, 35.

32. NAVIGANT STUDY, *supra* note 29, EXECUTIVE SUMMARY at 17.

33. FERC maintains a listing of projects licensed and exempted under the Federal Power Act. *See* http://www.ferc.gov/industries/hydropower.asp.

34. As of 2010, approximately 260 proposed conventional hydropower projects were subject to a preliminary permit issued by FERC, with an additional sixty projects under consideration by FERC for preliminary permits. *See id.*

35. Originally enacted in 1920 as the FWPA, Pub. L. No. 66-280, 41 Stat. 1063, the hydropower licensing and regulation provisions of the FWPA were amended and retitled as Part I of the FPA under the Public Utility Act of 1935. Pub. L. No. 74-333, §§ 201–213, 49 Stat. 803, 838–863. For a detailed account of the history and politics leading to the FWPA, see JEROME G. KERWIN, FEDERAL WATER-POWER LEGISLATION (1926); Gifford Pinchot, *The Long Struggle for Effective Federal Water Power Legislation,* 14 GEO. WASH. L. REV. 9 (1945).

36. 16 U.S.C. § 803(a)(1).

37. 1 F.P.C. Ann. Rep. 10 (1921).

38. 16 U.S.C. § 817(1).

39. *Id*. This grandfathering clause has been narrowly applied, such that FPA jurisdiction is triggered when the pre-1920 permit requires reauthorization, when the project is expanded beyond its pre-1920 authorization, or when the power is used differently than contemplated under the pre-1920 permit. *E.g.*, Minn. Power & Light Co. v. FPC, 344 F.2d 53 (8th Cir. 1965); Nw. Paper Co. v. FPC, 344 F.2d 47 (8th Cir. 1965); Homestake Mining Co., 98 FERC ¶ 61,236 at 61,958–61,959, *reh'g denied*, 99 FERC ¶ 61,332, *reh'g denied*, 101 FERC ¶ 61,159 (2002).

40. 16 U.S.C. § 817(1).

41. Pub. L. No. 95-91, § 401, 91 Stat. 565, 582.

42. 16 U.S.C. § 817(1). The term "navigable waters" is specifically defined in the FPA, *see id*. § 796(8), and the test for determining navigability for FPA purposes is different than under other federal statutes, such as the Clean Water Act. *Cf*. 33 U.S.C. § 1362(7). The FPA adopts a navigability-in-fact test, where the reach of the waterway at issue must form a highway for commerce with other states or foreign countries by itself or by connecting with other waters, or waters that could be made navigable by reasonable improvements. *E.g.*, United States v. Appalachian Elec. Power Co., 311 U.S. 377 (1940); Sierra Pac. Power Co. v. FERC, 681 F.2d 1134 (9th Cir. 1982), *cert. denied*, 460 U.S. 1082 (1983).

43. 16 U.S.C. § 796(2). The FPA specifically prohibits FERC from issuing licenses for hydropower projects within national parks and national monuments. *Id*. §§ 796(2), 797(e). Under the Energy Policy Act of 1992, Congress extended this prohibition to any project within the boundaries of any unit of the national park system "that would have a direct adverse effect on Federal lands within any such unit." *Id*. § 797c.

44. *Id*. § 796(1).

45. Commerce Clause streams are non-navigable tributaries to navigable waterways. FPC v. Union Elec. Co., 381 U.S. 90 (1965); *see* Murphy, 98 FERC ¶ 61,302 (2002).

46. 16 U.S.C. § 817(1). The project must have a "real and substantial effect" on interstate or foreign commerce. City of Centralia v. FERC, 661 F.2d 787, 791–92 (9th Cir. 1981). A project affects interstate commerce if it is interconnected to the interstate electric grid, even if the project's power is entirely consumed by the project owner. Habersham Mills v. FERC, 976 F.2d 1381 (11th Cir. 1992); Fairfax County Water Auth., 43 FERC ¶ 61,062 at 61,166–61,167 (1988). In some instances, moreover, a project's effect on commercial fisheries constitutes an effect on interstate commerce for the purposes of establishing jurisdiction under the FPA. U.S. Dep't of Commerce v. FERC, 36 F.3d 893 (9th Cir. 1994); Alaska Power & Tel. Co., 101 FERC ¶ 61,191 (2002).

47. Not all construction activities at an existing hydropower project qualify as "post-1935 construction" for the purposes of triggering FERC's jurisdiction under the FPA. Substantial repairs or work that restores a damaged project to its former specifications does not constitute post-1935 construction for purposes of jurisdiction. Puget Sound Power & Light v. FPC, 557 F.2d 1311, 1315–16 (9th Cir. 1977). Generally, to qualify as post-1935 construction, the activity must enlarge the project's generating capacity, diversion, or physical plant. Thomas Hodgson & Sons, Inc. v. FERC, 49 F.3d 822 (1st Cir. 1995). If a project was abandoned prior to rehabilitation, however, even minor maintenance can constitute post-1935 construction. Aquenergy Sys. Inc. v. FERC, 857 F.2d 227 (4th Cir. 1988).

48. *E.g.*, Noland, 130 FERC ¶ 62,267 (2010); Schofield, 128 FERC ¶ 62,091 (2009); Werner, 126 FERC ¶ 62,018 (2009).

49. 16 U.S.C. § 817(1).

50. The FPA and FERC's implementing regulations promote competition among applicants to encourage them to develop applications that "are best adapted to develop, conserve, and utilize in the public interest the water resources of the region." 16 U.S.C. § 800(a). In instances where FERC cannot determine, based on information in the record, whether one project is better adapted than a competing application, FERC's regulations and orders establish a set of tie-breaker preferences, including development applications over preliminary permit applications, municipal applicants over nonmunicipal applicants, and first filed applications. *See generally*

18 C.F.R. §4.37. More recently, FERC introduced a lottery system where none of these other factors break the tie among competing applicants, *e.g.*, *City of Angoon*, 129 FERC ¶ 62,101 (2009), *aff'd*, Petersburg Mun. Power & Light v. FERC, No. 10-1096 (D.C. Cir. Feb. 25, 2011).

51. 16 U.S.C. §825*l*; 18 C.F.R. §385.713.

52. 16 U.S.C. §797(f).

53. *Id.* §798.

54. *E.g.*, Williamson, 96 FERC ¶ 62,333 at 64,643 (2001); Continental Lands, Inc., 90 FERC ¶ 61,355 at 62,178 (2000).

55. 16 U.S.C. §798.

56. FERC has established different licensing requirements for different types of hydropower projects, depending on the generating capacity of the project, and whether the licensing would involve an unconstructed or existing dam. *See* 18 C.F.R. §§4.40–4.61.

57. 16 U.S.C. §797(e).

58. *Id.* §803(a)(1).

59. *Id.* §§797(e), 803(j), 811.

60. *Id.* §797(e).

61. *Id.* §803(e), (f).

62. *Id.* §799. FERC's well-established policies provide that projects located at the site of an existing federal dam, *e.g.*, *Idaho Water Res. Bd.*, 84 FERC ¶ 61,146 at 61,797 (1998), or that entail construction of a new dam generally will receive fifty-year licenses. City of Danville, 58 FERC ¶ 61,318 at 62,020 (1992). Unconstructed projects at an existing nonfederal dam will receive a thirty-year license if very little new construction is involved, a forty-year license where there is a moderate amount of new construction, and a fifty-year license for a substantial amount of new construction. *Id.*

63. 16 U.S.C. §799.

64. *See infra* this chapter, section on "Regulation of Nonfederal Hydropower Projects: License Compliance, Enforcement, and Reopeners"; 18 C.F.R. §2.9 (identifying FERC's standard-form license conditions).

65. 16 U.S.C. §799.

66. *Id.*; *see infra* this chapter, section on "Regulation of Nonfederal Hydropower Projects: License Compliance, Enforcement, and Reopeners."

67. 16 U.S.C. §808. FERC's policy for establishing the length of the license term at relicensing is set forth in *Mead Corp.*, 72 FERC ¶ 61,027 at 61,077 (1995).

68. 16 U.S.C. §808(a)(1). Several cases address the issue of whether FERC's issuance of an annual license triggers environmental review or other statutory requirements, or whether FERC can impose new license conditions during the annual license term. *See* Cal. Trout, Inc. v. FERC, 313 F.3d 1131 (9th Cir. 2002), *cert. denied*, 540 U.S. 818 (2003); Hoopa Valley Tribe v. FERC, 629 F.3d 209 (D.C. Cir. 2010); Platte River Whooping Crane Critical Habitat Maint. Trust v. FERC, 962 F.2d 27 (D.C. Cir. 1992); Platte River Whooping Crane Critical Habitat Maint. Trust v. FERC, 876 F.2d 109 (D.C. Cir. 1989).

69. "Small scale" includes "small hydroelectric projects" at existing dams with a total installed capacity of not more than 5 MW; "small conduit hydroelectric facilities" not part of a dam with an installed capacity of 15 MW or less (40 MW for municipalities); and "minor water projects" with a total installed capacity of 1.5 MW or less. 18 C.F.R. §§4.30(b)(17), 4.30(b)(28), 4.30(b)(29). The first two categories qualify for exemptions from licensing, *see id.* §§4.90–4.96, 4.101–4.108, while the third category qualifies for short-form licensing. *Id.* §§4.60–4.61. In addition, "small" hydropower projects up to 80 MW qualify for guaranteed purchase under §210 of PURPA. 16 U.S.C. §824a-3.

70. *See* 16 U.S.C. §§2701–2708.

71. *Id.* §823a. Conduits are tunnels, canals, pipelines, and other such facilities, which are operated primarily for water distribution, not hydropower generation. 18 C.F.R. §4.30(b)(2).

72. To qualify as an "existing dam," construction of the project must have been completed on or before July 22, 2005. 18 C.F.R. §4.30(b)(6).

73. 16 U.S.C. §§2705(d), 2708; *see* 18 C.F.R. §§4.101–4.108.

74. Some exemptions are categorically excluded from NEPA review. *See* 18 C.F.R. §§ 380.4(a)(12), 380.4(a)(13). Other exemption applications require preparation of an Environmental Assessment. *See* 18 C.F.R. § 380.5(b)(7).

75. 16 U.S.C. §§ 823a(c), 2705(b), 2705(d).

76. *Id.* § 803(j). As discussed below, projects occupying a federal reservation are subject to mandatory conditions imposed by the federal agency that manages the reservation. *See id.* § 797(e); *infra* this chapter, section on "Regulation of Nonfederal Hydropower Projects, Licensing and Environmental Requirements, FPA § 4(e): Federal Reservation Conditions."

77. 16 U.S.C. § 814; *see* 18 C.F.R. § 4.31(b)(2); Phoenix Hydro Corp. v. FERC, 775 F.2d 1187 (D.C. Cir. 1985). The exemption applicant must have exclusive control of the necessary interest in land at the time the application is accepted for filing with FERC. 18 C.F.R. § 4.31(c)(2).

78. 16 U.S.C. § 799; *see* 18 C.F.R. §§ 6.1–6.5.

79. FPL Energy Maine Hydro, LLC, 106 FERC ¶ 61,038 at P 20 (2004). FERC has held that a license surrender proceeding is not subject to the requirements of §§ 10(a), 10(j), 15(b), and 18 of the FPA. N.Y. State Elec. & Gas Corp., 105 FERC ¶ 61,381 at P 15 n.13 (2003).

80. *E.g.*, Fairfax County Water Auth., 129 FERC ¶ 62,085 (2009); Idaho Power Co., 38 FERC ¶ 61,126 (1987).

81. 18 C.F.R. § 6.3.

82. *Id.* § 6.4. In general, FERC will find an implied surrender of a minor project if "essential project property" is removed, destroyed, or becomes unfit for use. *Id.* FERC also will find an implied surrender if the licensee, for a period of three years, abandons the project or discontinues good faith operation. *Id.*

83. *E.g.*, FPL Energy Maine Hydro, LLC, 106 FERC ¶ 61,038 (granting approval of a surrender application, which was filed, in part, because the capital costs to install the license-imposed fish lift at the 1.4 MW facility were estimated at $4.1 million, with an additional $130,000 in annual operation and maintenance expenses).

84. 16 U.S.C. § 808(a)(1).

85. *E.g.*, S. Cal. Edison Co., 105 FERC ¶ 61,046 (2003), *on reh'g*, 106 FERC ¶ 61,212 (2004).

86. *E.g.*, Penobscot River Restoration Trust, 131 FERC ¶ 62,238 (2010); Duke Energy Carolinas, LLC, 120 FERC ¶ 61,054 (2007); Portland Gen. Elec. Co., 107 FERC ¶ 61,158 (2004).

87. 16 U.S.C. § 808(f).

88. *Id.*

89. Green Island Power Auth., 110 FERC ¶ 61,331 at P 12 n.16 (2005).

90. *E.g.*, N.Y. State Elec. & Gas Corp., 105 FERC ¶ 61,381 (2003); Wis. Elec. Power Co., 96 FERC ¶ 61,009, *on reh'g*, 96 FERC ¶ 61,218 (2001).

91. Policy Statement on Project Decommissioning at Relicensing, FERC Stats. & Regs., Regs. Preambles 1991–1996 ¶ 31,011 (1995). Where the incumbent licensee does not seek to relicense the project, and no other entity files a relicensing application, FERC's regulations require the licensee to file a schedule for the filing of a surrender application with FERC. 18 C.F.R. § 16.25(c).

92. FERC later explained that modern amendments to the FPA, which require it "to give greater attention to environmental concerns[,] . . . have made it increasingly possible that a project might need to be decommissioned rather than continue to operate for the term of a new license." S. Cal. Edison Co., 106 FERC ¶ 61,212 at P 29 (2004).

93. Edwards Mfg. Co., 81 FERC ¶ 61,255 (1997); Edwards Mfg. Co., 84 FERC ¶ 61,227 (1998), *reh'g denied sub nom.* State of Maine, 91 FERC ¶ 61,213 (2000); Edwards Mfg. Co., 84 FERC ¶ 61,228 (1998), *reh'g denied sub nom.* State of Maine, 91 FERC ¶ 61,213 (2000). "The validity of this policy has never been tested in the courts." City of Tacoma v. FERC, 460 F.3d 53, 72 (D.C. Cir. 2006).

94. 16 U.S.C. § 808(a)(1).

95. *City of Tacoma*, 460 F.3d at 74.

96. *Id.* It should be noted that subsequent to the *Tacoma* decision, the licensee and resource agencies in that case reached settlement, which provided for the continued operation of the

project. FERC approved the settlement and incorporated its terms into the license. *City of Tacoma*, 132 FERC ¶ 61,037 (2010).

97. "We have no cause to decide in this case whether, and in what circumstances, FERC can impose decommissioning obligations or costs on a former licensee." *Id.*

98. 16 U.S.C. § 821.

99. *See infra* this chapter, section on "Regulation of Nonfederal Hydropower Projects: Licensing and Environmental Requirements."

100. 328 U.S. 152 (1946).

101. *Id.* at 171, 178–81.

102. *Id.* at 168.

103. *Id.* at 181–83.

104. 495 U.S. 490, 499 (1990).

105. While *California v. FERC* appears to hold that the FPA preempts state law only where it conflicts with FERC regulation, *id.* at 506–07, the Ninth Circuit has interpreted the case as holding that the FPA "occupies the field" of hydropower regulation, except to the extent that proprietary water rights are at issue. Sayles Hydro Assocs. v. Maughan, 985 F.2d 451 (9th Cir. 1993).

106. *E.g.*, FPC v. Oregon, 349 U.S. 435, 449–50 (1955); Wash. Dep't of Game v. FPC, 207 F.2d 391, 395 (9th Cir. 1953), *cert. denied*, 347 U.S. 936 (1954).

107. *E.g.*, City of Tacoma v. Taxpayers of Tacoma, 357 U.S. 320, 339–40 (1958).

108. *E.g.*, Town of Springfield v. Vermont, 549 F. Supp. 1134, 1154–57 (D. Vt. 1982), *aff'd*, 722 F.2d 728 (2d Cir.), *cert. denied*, 464 U.S. 942 (1983).

109. *E.g.*, Albany Eng'g Corp. v. FERC, 548 F.3d 1071 (D.C. Cir. 2008); Wis. Valley Improvement Co. v. Meyer, 910 F. Supp. 1375 (W.D. Wis. 1995).

110. Because of the broad reach of the FPA and its preemptive effect, most states have not enacted hydropower licensing and permitting programs. *But see*, *e.g.*, OR. REV. STAT. §§ 543.010–543.990. In most instances, nonfederal hydropower projects not subject to FERC's jurisdiction are regulated under states' zoning laws, dam safety programs, and environmental permitting requirements, although other federal permits may be necessary, such as dredge and fill permits under § 404 of the Clean Water Act. 33 U.S.C. § 1344.

111. 42 U.S.C. §§ 4321–4370d. FERC regulations provide guidelines regarding actions that are categorically excluded from environmental review under NEPA, actions that usually involve the initial preparation of an environmental assessment, and actions that typically require an environmental impact statement. 18 C.F.R. §§ 380.4–380.6. Also, with regard to the relicensing of existing projects, FERC has determined that the appropriate environmental baseline for its NEPA analysis is the existing environment at the time of relicensing, and both the D.C. and Ninth Circuits have upheld this determination. Am. Rivers v. FERC, 201 F.3d 1186 (9th Cir. 1999); Conservation Law Found. v. FERC, 216 F.3d 41 (D.C. Cir. 2000).

112. 16 U.S.C. § 1536; *see* 18 C.F.R. § 380.13. In the context of FERC's licensing actions, challenges to a biological opinion issued as part of the § 7 consultation must be to the U.S. courts of appeals, in accordance with § 313(b) of the FPA, 16 U.S.C. § 825*l*(b). City of Tacoma v. FERC, 460 F.3d 53 (D.C. Cir. 2006). Outside the licensing context, there has been some controversy as to whether ESA § 7 is triggered as a result of FERC's ongoing administration and regulation of hydropower licenses. FERC has held that its continuing authority over a project's operation alone does not constitute ongoing agency action that automatically triggers consultation under ESA whenever operation of a project may affect a newly listed species. Cal. Sportfishing Protection Alliance v. FERC, 472 F.3d 593 (9th Cir. 2006); Phelps-Dodge Morenci, Inc., 94 FERC ¶ 61,202 (2001). Rather, FERC has explained that the necessary federal agency action would be present, and therefore formal consultation would be required for actions adversely affecting listed species or their critical habitat, if a change in the terms and conditions of the license became necessary and FERC takes some action to amend the license, either in response to a licensee's request for a license amendment or pursuant to FERC's authority reserved in the license. Puget Sound Energy, Inc., 95 FERC ¶ 61,015, *reh'g denied*, 95 FERC ¶ 61,319 (2001).

113. 33 U.S.C. § 1341.

114. 16 U.S.C. § 1456(c)(3)(A). Because the CZMA provides that FERC can issue a license only if the applicable state agency concurs that the proposed project is consistent with the state's approved coastal management program, the statute provides significant opportunity for state involvement in the FERC licensing process. *E.g.*, Mountain Rhythm Res. v. FERC, 302 F.3d 958 (9th Cir. 2002) (upholding FERC's dismissal of a license application where the license applicants for several projects in Washington State failed to obtain permits under Washington's Shoreline Management Act, which is required under Washington's approved coastal zone management program).

115. 16 U.S.C. § 470f; *see also* 18 C.F.R. § 380.14; 36 C.F.R. §§ 800.1–800.16. FERC's issuance of a license is considered an "undertaking" for NHPA purposes, 36 C.F.R. § 800.16(y), and FERC usually satisfies its obligations under § 106 by entering into a programmatic agreement or memorandum of agreement with the state historic preservation officer, which typically provides for the licensee to develop and implement a Historic Properties Management Plan (HPMP) that governs operation and maintenance activities through the license term. In 2002, FERC and the Advisory Council on Historic Preservation developed a joint guidelines document for developing HPMPs. *See* Guidelines for the Development of Historic Properties Management Plans for FERC Hydroelectric Projects (May 20, 2002), *available at* http://www.ferc.gov/industries/hydropower/gen-info/guidelines/hpmp.pdf.

116. Some have estimated that up to forty separate federal statutory programs apply to the licensing and regulation of hydroelectric projects. *See* Sensiba, *supra* note 19, at 633 & n.194.

117. These processes are referred to as the "Integrated Licensing Process," which is FERC's default licensing process, the "Alternative Licensing Process," and the "Traditional Licensing Process." *See* 18 C.F.R. §§ 4.34(i), 4.38, 5.1–5.31, 16.8.

118. *See* 18 C.F.R. § 4.38(a).

119. 16 U.S.C. § 803(a)(1).

120. *Id.* § 797(e). "Equal consideration" does not require "equal treatment," but instead requires FERC to "balance the public interest in all of its stated dimensions, give equal consideration to conflicting interests, and reach a reasoned factual decision." California v. FERC, 966 F.2d 1541, 1550 (9th Cir. 1992).

121. 16 U.S.C. § 803(a)(2)(A). FERC maintains a list of approved comprehensive plans at http://www.ferc.gov/industries/hydropower/gen-info/licensing/complan.pdf.

122. 16 U.S.C. § 803(a)(2)(B).

123. Green Island Power Auth. v. FERC, 577 F.3d 148, 166 (2d Cir. 2009) (quoting H.R. Rep. No. 99-507, at 12 (1986), *as reprinted in* 1986 U.S.C.C.A.N. 2496, 2499); *see also* Udall v. FPC, 387 U.S. 428 (1967); Scenic Hudson Preservation Conference v. FPC, 354 F.2d 608 (2d Cir. 1965), *cert. denied*, 384 U.S. 941 (1966).

124. 16 U.S.C. § 797(e).

125. Section 4(e) conditioning authority does not extend "to reservations that may somehow be affected by, but will contain no part of, the licensed project works." Escondido Mut. Water Co. v. La Jolla Band of Mission Indians, 466 U.S. 765 (1984).

126. 16 U.S.C. § 796(2).

127. 466 U.S. at 772, 779.

128. S. Cal. Edison Co. v. FERC, 116 F.3d 507 (D.C. Cir. 1997).

129. *E.g.*, City & County of Denver, 94 FERC ¶ 61,313, *on reh'g*, 95 FERC ¶ 61,222 (2001); Minn. Power & Light Co., 72 FERC ¶ 61,028 (1995), *on reh'g*, 75 FERC ¶ 61,131 (1996).

130. 460 F.3d 53, 66–67 (D.C. Cir. 2006).

131. *Id.* at 67.

132. *See* S. Rep. No. 109-78, at 2–3 (2005).

133. 16 U.S.C. § 823d(a)(4).

134. *Id.*

135. *Id.*

136. *Id.* § 823d(a)(2).

137. *Id.* § 797(e).

138. *Id.*

139. Resource Agency Procedures for Conditions and Prescriptions in Hydropower Licenses; Interim Final Rule, 70 Fed. Reg. 69,803 (Nov. 17, 2005); *see also* U.S. Gov't Accountability Office, GAO-10-770, Hydropower Relicensing: Stakeholders' Views on the Energy Policy Act Varied, but More Consistent Information Needed (2010), *available at* http://www.gao.gov/new.items/d10770.pdf.

140. *See* 16 U.S.C. §§ 823d(a)(5) (authorizing FERC, if it determines that any final § 4(e) condition would be inconsistent with the purposes of the FPA or other applicable law, to refer the matter to its Dispute Resolution Service, which will consult with the parties and issue an advisory opinion that the federal land management agency "may" accept).

141. 16 U.S.C. § 811.

142. Wis. Power & Light Co. v. FERC, 363 F.3d 453, 461 (D.C. Cir. 2004) (quoting Pub. L. No. 102-486, § 1701(b), 106 Stat. 2776, 3008 (1992); H.R. Conf. Rep. No. 99-934, at 23 (1986)).

143. Am. Rivers v. FERC, 187 F.3d 1007, 1030 (9th Cir. 1999).

144. *Id.* In practice, USFWS and NMFS often do not impose fishway prescriptions during the FERC licensing process, and FERC's established policy is to allow these agencies to reserve authority to exercise this authority throughout the license term. *E.g.*, N.Y. Power Auth., 105 FERC ¶ 61,102 (2003), *on reh'g*, 107 FERC ¶ 61,259 (2004); *see also* Wis. Pub. Serv. Corp. v. FERC, 32 F.3d 1165 (7th Cir. 1994).

145. 16 U.S.C. § 825*l*(b); *see* Bangor Hydro-Elec. Co. v. FERC, 78 F.3d 659 (D.C. Cir. 1996).

146. *Wis. Power & Light Co.*, 363 F.3d at 462.

147. *Bangor Hydro-Elec. Co.*, 78 F.3d at 664.

148. *Wis. Power & Light Co.*, 363 F.3d at 463.

149. *See supra* this chapter, section on "Regulation of Nonfederal Hydropower Projects: Licensing and Environmental Requirements, FPA § 4(e): Federal Reservation Conditions."

150. 16 U.S.C. § 823d(b)(4).

151. *Id.* § 823d(b)(2).

152. *Id.* § 811.

153. Pub. L. No. 99-495, § 3(b), 100 Stat. 1243 (codified at 16 U.S.C. § 803(j)).

154. 16 U.S.C. § 803(j)(1).

155. *Id.* § 803(j)(2).

156. 18 C.F.R. § 4.34(e).

157. U.S. Gen. Accounting Office, GAO/RCED-92-246, Electricity Regulation: Electric Consumers Protection Act's Effects on Licensing Hydroelectric Dams 18 (1992), *available at* http://archive.gao.gov/d35t11/147885.pdf.

158. *E.g.*, City of LeClaire, 74 FERC ¶ 61,127 (1996).

159. *E.g.*, Allegheny Elec. Coop., 48 FERC ¶ 61,363 (1989).

160. 33 U.S.C. § 1341. With regard to the origination of the discharge, the D.C. Circuit has held that a state whose waters would be inundated by a FERC-licensed reservoir, but in which the discharge would not originate, has no § 401 authority. Nat'l Wildlife Fed'n v. FERC, 912 F.2d 1471, 1483–84 (D.C. Cir. 1990).

161. *See* 18 C.F.R. § 4.34(b)(5). In some instances, FERC's orders amending licenses triggers § 401 certification as well. *See* Ala. Rivers Alliance v. FERC, 325 F.3d 290 (D.C. Cir. 2003); *cf.* North Carolina v. FERC, 112 F.3d 1175 (D.C. Cir. 1997); 18 C.F.R. §§ 4.34(b)(5)(iv), 5.23(b)(3). Section 401 certification is not required, however, with respect to FERC's issuance of annual licenses for existing projects. Cal. Trout, Inc. v. FERC, 313 F.3d 1131 (9th Cir. 2002), *cert. denied*, 540 U.S. 818 (2003).

162. 33 U.S.C. § 1341(a)(1); 18 C.F.R. §§ 4.34(b)(5)(iii), 5.23(b)(2).

163. 33 U.S.C. § 1341(d).

164. *Id.*

165. Am. Rivers v. FERC, 129 F.3d 99 (2d Cir. 1997).

166. 33 U.S.C. § 1341(a)(1).

167. Am. Rivers v. FERC, 129 F.3d at 107.

168. 511 U.S. 700 (1994).

169. *Id*. at 714–21.

170. *Id*. at 715–18.

171. *Id*. at 719–20. Relatedly, the Ninth Circuit has held that FERC may require stream-flows above and beyond those required by the § 401 certification, so long as they do not conflict with or weaken the protections provided in the certification. Snoqualmie Indian Tribe v. FERC, 545 F.3d 1207 (9th Cir. 2008).

172. 547 U.S. 370 (2006).

173. *Id*. at 376; *cf*. 33 U.S.C. § 1342; S. Fla. Water Mgmt. Dist. v. Miccosukee Tribe, 541 U.S. 95 (2004).

174. FERC's authority to enforce the requirements of the FPA upon a non-licensee owner of a hydropower project is more limited. 16 U.S.C. §§ 825m, 825p; *e.g.*, FERC v. Keck, 818 F. Supp. 792 (M.D. Pa. 1993); *see also* Wolverine Power Co. v. FERC, 963 F.2d 446 (D.C. Cir. 1992).

175. *Cf*. Platte River Whooping Crane Critical Habitat Maint. Trust v. FERC, 876 F.2d 109 (D.C. Cir. 1989); Platte River Whooping Crane Critical Habitat Maint. Trust v. FERC, 962 F.2d 27 (D.C. Cir. 1992) (Platte River II).

176. 16 U.S.C. § 823b(a).

177. *Id*. § 823b(c); Pub. L. No. 101-410, 104 Stat. 890 (1990), as amended by Pub. L. No. 104-134, title III, § 31001(s)(1), 110 Stat. 1321, 1321–1373 (1996), and Pub. L. No. 105-362, title XIII, § 1301(a), 112 Stat. 3293 (1998) (28 U.S.C. § 2461 note); Order No. 692, FERC Stats. & Regs., Regs. Preambles 2001–2005 ¶ 31,131 (2002).

178. FERC must provide prior notice and opportunity for public hearing before assessing the civil penalty, and must consider several factors in determining the amount of the penalty. 16 U.S.C. § 823b(c); 18 C.F.R. § 385.1505. FERC must also provide prior notice of the proposed penalty. 16 U.S.C. § 823b(d). Special procedures apply to the review of FERC's orders imposing civil penalties. *Id*.

179. 16 U.S.C. § 823b(b); *e.g.*, Turnbull Hydro, LLC, 126 FERC ¶ 62,141 (2009). At the revocation hearing, FERC must take into consideration the nature and seriousness of the violation and the efforts of the licensee to remedy the violation. 16 U.S.C. § 823b(b).

180. 16 U.S.C. § 799.

181. *See generally* 18 C.F.R. § 2.9.

182. *Id*. § 2.23. FERC must describe in such license articles the "reasonably foreseeable future resource concerns that may warrant" project modifications. *Id*.

183. *Id*. FERC has stated that a reopener provision "is not self-executing, and it does not give the Commission any ongoing discretionary involvement or control over the licensee's day-to-day operation of its project pursuant to the license. Rather, a reopener clause provides the Commission with the necessary authority, after notice and an opportunity for a hearing, to reopen the license and require changes to project facilities and operation, provided that those changes have a nexus to project effects and are supported by substantial evidence, as required by Section 313 of the FPA." Pac. Gas & Elec. Co., 110 FERC ¶ 61,323 at P 15 (2005).

184. U.S. ARMY CORPS OF ENG'RS, HYDROPOWER: VALUE TO THE NATION 2 (2001), *available at* http://www.spn.usace.army.mil/value_to_the_nation/Hydropower.pdf.

185. BUREAU OF RECLAMATION POWER FACILITIES (2005), http://www.usbr.gov/power/facil/fy05fac.pdf.

186. TVA, ENERGY VISION 2020, INTEGRATED RESOURCES PLAN ENVIRONMENTAL IMPACT STATEMENT 4.2 (1995), http://www.tva.gov/environment/reports/energyvision2020.

187. PMAs are required to market their power with a preference for public and cooperatively owned utilities at "the lowest possible rates . . . consistent with sound business principles." 16 U.S.C. § 825s; *see also* 16 U.S.C. §§ 832c, 837–837h, 839c(a).

188. In this regard, it is important to distinguish between federal dams and federal hydropower projects. In some instances where Congress authorizes construction of a federal dam, it reserves exclusive authority to the federal government to develop the hydropower resources

at the dam; in other instances, Congress does not include such a reservation. *See, e.g.,* Uncompahgre Valley Water Users Ass'n v. FERC, 785 F.2d 269 (10th Cir. 1986). Where Congress does not reserve federal authority to develop hydropower resources at a federal dam, the site may be open to development by nonfederal entities, subject to FERC's jurisdiction under the FPA. *See* 16 U.S.C. §§ 797(e), 817(1). FERC and the Bureau have entered into a Memorandum of Understanding that establishes criteria and guidelines for determining whether a proposed nonfederal project at a Bureau facility is subject to FERC's jurisdiction. *See* Memorandum of Understanding between the Federal Energy Regulatory Commission and the Bureau of Reclamation Department of the Interior for Establishment of Processes for the Early Resolution of Issues Related to the Timely Development of Non-Federal Hydroelectric Power at Bureau of Reclamation Facilities (1992), *available at* http://www.ferc.gov/legal/maj-ord-reg/mou/mou-6.pdf.

189. *See, e.g.,* Boulder Canyon Project Act, 43 U.S.C. § 617.

190. *See, e.g.,* Reclamation Act of 1902, ch. 1093, 32 Stat. 388 (codified as amended in scattered sections of 43 U.S.C.); Reclamation Project Act of 1939, ch. 418, 53 Stat. 1187 (codified as amended in scattered sections of 43 U.S.C.); Reclamation Reform Act of 1982, 43 U.S.C. §§ 390aa–390zz-1.

191. Pub. L. No. 89-80, 79 Stat. 245 (codified as amended at 42 U.S.C. §§ 1962, 1962-1, 1962a–1962d-3).

192. Economic and Environmental Principles and Guidelines for Water and Related Land Resources Implementation Studies (Mar. 10, 1983), *available at* http://www.usace.army.mil/CECW/Documents/pgr/pg_1983.pdf.

193. *Id.* at iv.

194. *Id.*

195. *Id.* at 3.

196. *Id.*

197. *Id.* at 4.

198. *Id.* at 5–6.

199. *Id.* at 6.

200. *Id.* at iv; *see also id.* at 15.

201. *Id.* at 41–49.

202. 42 U.S.C. § 1962-3(a).

203. *Id.* § 1962-3(b).

204. 73 Fed. Reg. 52,960 (Sept. 12, 2008).

205. 74 Fed. Reg. 31,415, 31,415 (July 1, 2009).

206. *Id.*

207. Proposed National Objectives, Principles and Standards for Water and Related Resources Implementation Studies (Dec. 3, 2009), *available at* http://www.whitehouse.gov/sites/default/files/microsites/091203-ceq-revised-principles-guidelines-water-resources.pdf.

208. *In re* Operation of the Missouri River Sys. Litig., 421 F.3d 618 (8th Cir. 2005).

209. Nat'l Wildlife Fed'n v. NMFS, 254 F. Supp. 2d 1196 (D. Or. 2003). NMFS's 2010 Supplemental Biological Opinion for the Federal Columbia River Power System can be viewed at https://pcts.nmfs.noaa.gov/pls/pcts-pub/sxn7.pcts_upload.download?p_file=F25013/201002096_FCRPS%20Supplemental_2010_05-20.pdf.

210. TVA v. Hill, 437 U.S. 153 (1978).

211. Between the period 2000 to 2010 alone, in fact, the licenses of approximately 220 projects, representing almost one-third of FERC-licensed hydropower capacity in the United States, expired.

212. In 1997, FERC implemented the "Alternative Licensing Process" regulations, 18 C.F.R. § 4.34(i), and in 2003 it promulgated the "Integrated Licensing Process" regulations. 18 C.F.R. §§ 5.1–5.31.

213. *E.g.,* Energy Policy Act of 1992, Pub. L. No. 102-486, §§ 1701, 2401–2403, 106 Stat. 2776, 3008, 3096–3097; Energy Policy Act of 2005, Pub. L. No. 109-58, §§ 203, 241–243, 1301(c), 119 Stat. 594, 652, 674–678, 987–988.

214. Marine and hydrokinetic technologies are discussed in chapter 21.

215. *See* Jenny Mandel, *DOE Promotes Pumped Hydro as Option for Renewable Power Storage*, N.Y. TIMES, Oct. 15, 2010, *available at* http://www.nytimes.com/gwire/2010/10/15/15green wire-doe-promotes-pumped-hydro-as-option-for-renewa-51805.html?pagewanted=all.

216. *See* D.C. CODE § 34-1431(16)(A); HAW. REV. STAT. § 269-91; KAN. STAT. ANN. § 66-1257(f)(9)(A); OKLA. STAT. tit. 17, § 801.4(D)(4); TEX. UTIL. CODE ANN. § 39.904(d); VA. CODE ANN. § 56-576.

217. *E.g.*, VT. STAT. ANN. tit. 30, § 8002(2)(C) (maximum capacity of 200 MW); ME. REV. STAT. tit. 35-A, § 3210(2)(C)(2)(f) (maximum capacity of 100 MW).

218. *E.g.*, MASS. GEN. LAWS ch. 25A, § 11F(d) (maximum capacity of 5 MW); NEV. REV. STAT. § 704.7811(3) (maximum capacity of 30 MW); N.H. REV. STAT. ANN. § 362-F:4(IV)(a) (maximum capacity of 5 MW); N.C. GEN. STAT. § 62-133.8(5), (7) (maximum capacity of 10 MW); R.I. GEN. LAWS § 39-26-2(26) (maximum capacity of 30 MW).

219. *E.g.*, N.J. STAT. ANN. § 48:3-51; 73 PA. CONS. STAT. § 1648.2(5); CONN. GEN. STAT. § 16-245n; UTAH CODE ANN. § 10-19-102(11)(b)(i).

220. *E.g.*, ARIZ. ADMIN. CODE § R14-2-1802(A)(9); DEL. CODE. ANN. tit. 26, § 352(6)(c), (g).

221. U.S. ENERGY INFO. ADMIN., ELECTRIC POWER INDUSTRY—U.S. ELECTRICITY IMPORTS FROM AND ELECTRICITY EXPORTS TO CANADA AND MEXICO, http://www.eia.doe.gov/cneaf/ electricity/epa/epat6p3.html.

222. *See* FOREIGN AFFAIRS & INT'L TRADE CANADA, TRADE BARRIER FICHE, RENEWABLE ENERGY (2009), http://w01.international.gc.ca/CIMAR-RCAMI/fiche-detail.aspx?id=1333& lang=eng; Robert K. Strundberg, *NAFTA Services and Climate Change* at 18-19, *in* THE FUTURE OF NORTH AMERICAN TRADE POLICY: LESSONS LEARNED FROM NAFTA (2009).

223. 26 U.S.C. §§ 45, 48, 54; American Recovery and Reinvestment Act of 2009, § 1603, Pub. L. No. 111-5, 123 Stat. 115, 364. For a detailed discussion on incentives for development of clean energy projects, see chapters 7 and 8.

224. *See* Notice of Technical Conference, FERC Docket No. AD09-9-000 (issued Aug. 14, 2009).

225. For example, in 2010, FERC entered into a Memorandum of Understanding with the State of Colorado to promote small-scale hydropower project development while safeguarding environmental values. Memorandum of Understanding between the Federal Energy Regulatory Commission and the State of Colorado through the Governor's Energy Office to Streamline and Simplify the Authorization of Small Scale Hydropower Projects, *available at* http://www.ferc .gov/legal/maj-ord-reg/mou/mou-co.pdf. In 2010, FERC also enhanced its website with tools intended to assist in preparing applications for small hydropower projects. *See* http://www.ferc .gov/industries/hydropower/gen-info/licensing/small-low-impact.asp.

226. *See* Memorandum of Understanding for Hydropower among the Department of Energy, Department of the Interior, and the Department of the Army (2010), *available at* http:// www.usbr.gov/power/SignedHydropowerMOU.pdf.

chapter twenty-one

Tides, Waves, and Ocean Currents

Judith Wallace

The Potential of Marine and Hydrokinetic Energy

Marine and hydrokinetic power projects use kinetic energy from the movement of ocean and river water to generate electricity. Unlike conventional hydropower, marine and hydrokinetic power projects do not rely on dams or diversions to capture energy from waves, tides, ocean currents, the natural flow of water in rivers, and marine thermal gradients.[1] Instead, marine and hydrokinetic projects capture the power of the tides, currents, or ocean thermal energy with devices incorporating turbines, pumps, oscillation, and hydraulics.[2] The Federal Energy Regulatory Commission (FERC) estimates that "[n]ew hydrokinetic technologies, if fully developed, have the potential to double hydropower production in the United States, bringing it from just below 10% to close to 20% of the national supply."[3] Some estimate that 10,000 to 20,000 megawatts (MW) are available from ocean energy.[4] In locations such as the Pacific Northwest and Hawaii, these technologies are expected to have the potential to be economically competitive with other renewables.[5]

Ocean energy technologies have numerous advantages. Ocean waves, currents, and tides are predictable to the day or even the hour and are not as variable as wind or solar energy.[6] Population centers are located near coasts. Because water is more than eight hundred times denser than air, turbines can be effective in slow-flowing water and can use far smaller turbines than wind projects.[7] However, these projects and their transmission lines are also challenging and expensive to install and maintain in the ocean environment, where they are corroded by salt water, buffeted by storms, and fouled by marine life.

Thus, marine and hydrokinetic power technologies remain at an early stage of development when compared to wind and solar projects, which have been providing utility-scale grid-connected electric power for decades.[8] In the United States, as of this writing, wave, current, and tidal projects are in the planning, demonstration, and pilot phases. In New York's East River, the six-turbine demonstration phase has been completed for a project that the developer, Verdant Power, seeks to build out, in phases, to a 300-turbine 10 MW total.[9] In 2008, the first of a planned group of 12-foot wide and 55-foot long modular point absorbers, which use wave energy to raise and lower a buoy in a hydraulic system that powers a generator, was placed one mile offshore of the Kaneohe Bay Marine Corps base in Oahu. In February 2010, construction began on the first of ten point absorbers, in a planned 1.5 MW commercial project off the Oregon coast.[10] In the United Kingdom, which is estimated to have the capacity to produce an even greater proportion of its electricity from wave, current, and tidal energy,[11] the government has advanced further in this process and in March 2010 completed a competitive round of leasing for 1.2 gigawatts (GW) of tidal and wave energy projects in waters in Scotland's Pentland Firth and Orkney waters.[12] In Northern Ireland, the SeaGen tidal energy project is delivering 1.2 MW to the electrical grid, and off the Isle of Lewis in Scotland, the Siadar Wave Energy project has obtained government approval for a 4 MW wave energy system.[13]

Leasing and Licensing

Whether they are located in federal or state waters, ocean, wave, and tidal power projects generally require a lease for access to the outer continental shelf or state submerged lands and licenses to construct and operate the project and to transmit power to the grid.

Department of Interior Leasing Authority on the Outer Continental Shelf

The Outer Continental Shelf (OCS) is the approximately 1.7 billion acres of submerged lands, subsoil, and seabed from the seaward limit of state jurisdiction (generally, approximately three nautical miles from shore, and nine nautical miles for Texas, the Gulf coast of Florida, and Puerto Rico) to the limit of the federal Exclusive Economic Zone (approximately 200 nautical miles offshore) in the Atlantic and Pacific Oceans and the Gulf of Mexico.[14]

Historically, the Minerals Management Service (MMS) of the Department of the Interior (DOI), renamed in June 2010 the Bureau of Ocean Energy Management, Regulation and Enforcement (BOEMRE),[15] has managed gas, oil, and mineral resources on the OCS. The Energy and Policy Act (EPAct) of 2005[16] amended the Outer Continental Shelf Lands Act (OCSLA)[17] to provide of the Department of the Interior with exclusive jurisdiction to issue leases, easements, and rights of way for the use of the OCS for renewable energy.[18] DOI delegated that authority to MMS (as noted above, now known as BOEMRE), which already had authority over granting access to the OCS for oil and gas leasing.

As discussed below, as the result of a compromise, DOI has leasing authority over hydrokinetic projects on the OCS, and FERC has licensing authority. Geological and geophysical and related site assessment surveys are the responsibility of the U.S. Army Corps of Engineers.[19] In a long-awaited April 2009 final rule, DOI promulgated a new Part 285[20] to its regulations to provide a leasing and licensing process for all alternative energy projects on the OCS.

The DOI leasing process can begin with either a DOI request for interest in an area or an unsolicited proposal, but in either case involves a public competitive sale process (unless DOI determines there is no competitive interest in an area) and environmental review under the National Environmental Policy Act (NEPA), a coastal zone consistency determination, and coordination with relevant federal agencies and affected states and Indian tribes.[21]

DOI can issue either (a) commercial leases (which allow for phased development with a five-year site assessment term and twenty-five-year operations term) or (b) "limited leases" for site assessment and technology testing only (generally for a five-year term), which may allow for the sale of power, but which will not provide any right to convert the limited lease into a commercial one.[22]

Lease terms include rent for both commercial and limited leases, and for operating fees and financial assurances.[23] Generally, a lessee would have six months to submit either a Site Assessment Plan (SAP) for a commercial lease or a General Activities Plan (GAP) for limited lease.[24] Review of environmental impacts under NEPA, discussed in more detail below, is required at several points in this process, including at the time of the lease and the approval of the SAP or GAP. Hydrokinetic projects must obtain a FERC license, which replaces the need for a Commercial Operating Plan (COP) required by DOI for renewable projects other than hydrokinetic projects (i.e., wind, over which DOI has exclusive jurisdiction), and NEPA review is required in connection with that license.[25]

FERC Licensing of Hydrokinetic Projects on the Outer Continental Shelf

Resolution of Jurisdictional Dispute with DOI

While DOI has exclusive authority to issue leases for access to the OCS, the authority to issue operating licenses for renewable energy projects located on the OCS is divided between DOI and the Federal Energy Regulatory Commission (FERC). As the result of an April 2009 compromise, leasing authority belongs to DOI, but licensing authority for hydrokinetic projects belongs to FERC.[26]

Prior to April 2009, there was a long-running interagency dispute that had created uncertainty over the licensing process and may have deterred projects.[27] In 2003, in the *AquaEnergy* proceeding, FERC asserted its licensing authority over a wave energy project under §§ 23(b)(1) and 8(1) of the Federal Power Act, regardless of whether it was located within state waters or on the OCS, on the grounds that all such waters constituted "navigable waters" subject to the requirement for a FERC hydropower license.[28] DOI, for its part, asserted authority over licensing as well as leasing of such projects under the 2005 amendments to the Outer Continental Shelf Lands Act in the EPAct, noted above.[29] FERC, citing the *AquaEnergy* decisions, repeatedly objected to DOI's proposed rulemaking and recommended an integrated licensing process.[30]

Coordination with DOI Leasing Process

Under an April 2009 FERC-DOI Memorandum of Understanding (MOU), private parties, states, and municipalities developing hydrokinetic projects must first obtain a DOI lease and then a FERC license for projects located on the OCS.[31] (Federal agencies are not subject to the requirement for a FERC license but would require a lease.[32]) Typically, the entire process should take three to five years—DOI anticipates that it will take two to two and a half years to complete the lease sale process where there is competitive interest and one to two years where there is no competitive interest; FERC expects to be able to issue a license in one to two years after a complete application is filed.[33]

Under the Federal Power Act, FERC has exclusive licensing authority over hydropower projects located in federal or navigable waters or connected to the interstate power grid.[34] The regulations governing the issuance of such licenses and alternative application and review procedures are set forth at 18 C.F.R. Subchapter B.[35]

On the OCS, FERC licensing is coordinated with the DOI leasing process. DOI leases will not take effect until FERC issues its project license.[36] FERC agreed not to issue "preliminary" licenses that would take effect upon issuance of a lease, but rather to hold off on review of an application until after the lease has been granted. FERC licenses will incorporate any conditions in the DOI lease. Finally, while DOI and FERC each are required to conduct any environmental review required by NEPA for their respective actions, FERC can participate as a cooperating agency in DOI's environmental review and vice versa.[37]

While the MOU and regulations do not provide for a single coordinated environmental review process, the DOI Guidelines note that the DOI applications have many common elements and that FERC and DOI might be able to coordinate on a single scoping process.[38] For noncompetitive leases, a joint NEPA document and consultations for both agencies are possible if an applicant files a complete license application and DOI lease application simultaneously.[39] In addition, in FERC licensing, there is an independent obligation to consult with state and federal fish and wildlife agencies under §§ 10(j) and 18 of the Federal Power Act.[40]

Expedited Review for "Experimental" Hydrokinetic Projects

Although this staggered process with separate actions by the two agencies may appear duplicative and cumbersome, FERC has issued decisions and policies that expedite its licensing for experimental hydrokinetic technologies.

First, in certain circumstances a FERC license is not needed at all. In 2005, FERC held in the proceeding for Verdant's New York tidal energy project that a FERC license is not needed for certain experimental projects, for a (1) short-term testing or study of (2) experimental technology (3) for a project that is not transmitting to the grid and does not displace power from the grid.[41] However, it would be difficult to test the project without providing power to anyone. Thus, FERC later clarified that it would be permissible for Verdant to provide power to an end user at no charge, and to make Consolidated Edison and the New York Power Authority whole by reimbursing them for the cost of that power.[42] An exemption from the FERC licensing for experimental projects does not exempt the project from any required state approvals or environmental reviews.[43]

In 2007, FERC proposed a Pilot Project Policy for short-term licenses usually for five-year terms, compared with the usual thirty-year term. These pilot licenses are only available for small projects less than 5MW that are removable or that can be shut down on short notice, not in waters with sensitive designation, and for the purpose of testing technologies or determining project sites. In contrast to the exception from the need for a FERC license recognized in the *Verdant* decision, the pilot permit process can lead to a long-term FERC license, is overseen by FERC, allows for the transmission of electricity into the power grid, and is available to developers whether or not they intend to seek a standard FERC license to follow the pilot permit. In addition to being for a shorter term, pilot project licenses provide for post-license monitoring, removal if the project has unacceptable impacts, and a condition requiring project removal and site restoration before license expiration if a standard license is not obtained.[44]

FERC's generally applicable regulations also provide for "Preliminary Permits," allowing a developer to maintain priority on a site for a three-year term while studying the project's feasibility and developing a FERC license application.[45] FERC has sought comment on preliminary permits for hydrokinetic power.[46] In the interim, FERC has adopted a policy of "strict scrutiny" in which FERC seeks to minimize the size of preliminary permit areas and prevent site banking. FERC requires developers holding preliminary permits to submit reports every six months and may revoke the permit for failure to file those reports.[47]

FERC Licensing of Hydrokinetic Projects in State Waters

While the Federal Power Act preempts state and local licensing law for projects under FERC jurisdiction,[48] under FERC's "equal consideration" standard, FERC may not consider only power and development benefits. FERC is also required to give "equal consideration" to other values, such as fish and wildlife, visual resources, cultural resources, recreation, and other aspects of environmental quality.[49]

In fact, FERC has already issued approvals for projects in state waters. FERC issued its first approval of a hydrokinetic project in 2007 for the Makah Bay Offshore Wave Pilot Project, which is located in state waters off the coast of Washington state.[50] FERC has also approved a small hydrokinetic device on a tethered barge in the Mississippi River operated by the City of Hastings, Minnesota, downstream from its FERC-licensed dam.[51]

NOAA Jurisdiction over Ocean Thermal Energy Projects

Despite the DOI-FERC accord over most ocean energy projects, the National Oceanic and Atmospheric Administration (NOAA) has jurisdiction over one category of ocean energy projects—ocean thermal energy.

The oceans cover 70 percent of the earth's surface and are the planet's largest solar energy collector and storage system.[52] Ocean thermal energy technology uses the thermal gradient of the oceans—the disparity in temperature between warm surface water and colder, deeper water—to generate electricity.

Ocean thermal energy projects are excluded from the DOI regulations for ocean renewable energy.[53] Under the Ocean Thermal Energy Conversion (OTEC) Act,[54] and the Ocean Thermal Energy Conversion Research, Development, and Demonstration Act,[55] NOAA has authority over the licensing, construction, and operation of thermal energy facilities. The U.S. Coast Guard also has jurisdiction, with authority to ensure safe construction and operation, prevent pollution, require cleanup of discharged pollutants, and ensure that the discharged pollutants do not change the thermal gradient of the ocean region.[56]

Over the past thirty years, there have been small-scale projects of the Natural Renewable Energy of Hawaii Authority to test electricity generation and assess environmental impacts, and also in the Republic of Nauru.[57] NOAA promulgated regulations for OTEC licenses in 1981, only to renew them in 1996 due to a lack of applicants.[58] Nevertheless, in 1998, because of the high cost and risk of interruptions in the supply of imported fossil fuels in Hawaii, the DOE and the State of Hawaii entered into an MOU to promote ocean thermal energy and other renewable energy projects.[59]

Federal Ocean Energy Planning Process

A comprehensive planning process for oceans, starting with identification of ecologically important ocean resources and with opportunities for public participation, can also play an important role in identifying the most suitable locations for leasing and licensing hydrokinetic projects.[60]

The new DOI regulations contemplate both a federal assessment process to determine areas suitable for renewable energy leasing and federal participation with state and local governments in task forces and joint planning agreements.[61] The federal Ocean Policy Task Force created in 2009 has begun this process, and in December 2009 released a draft marine spatial planning framework to set forth principles and a timeline for this effort to balance multiple uses of the ocean.[62] While no specific zones have been identified for renewable energy development, some areas are off-limits—DOI rules prohibit leases in national parks, national monuments, national marine sanctuaries, and wildlife refuges.[63]

Some have criticized the joint DOI-FERC approach, with its sequential reviews, as too lengthy, and as a reason to site projects in state waters.[64] The dual reviews may mean that approvals may take longer in the United States than in nations with a more centralized approach. Nevertheless, the new approach resolves uncertainty and may prevent some litigation, which put some projects over the tipping point for feasibility. Finally, if this new regulatory process can help all the involved parties to identify projects that have the support of all the relevant agencies with decision-making authority, it has the potential to speed the development of ocean energy.

State Proprietary and Regulatory Authority

Although FERC has exclusive jurisdiction to issue licenses for hydrokinetic projects in "navigable waters," including those within the state three-mile limit, states have proprietary authority as landowners and limited regulatory authority over state waters and submerged lands.[65]

State waters can be attractive sites for ocean power projects. The optimal location for wave power generation is at depths of 40 to 100 meters. In shallower waters, wave energy tends to dissipate through interaction with the seabed, and in deeper waters, the projects are challenging to install and maintain.[66]

Several states have enacted legislation or promulgated regulations to specify a process for allowing renewable energy projects in state waters. Some states, such as New Jersey and Rhode Island, have also begun a state planning process for ocean energy development.[67] In November 2009, Oregon's Department of State Lands, which has long engaged in "ocean" and "territorial sea" planning,[68] promulgated rules for the placement of ocean energy on, in, or over submerged lands within the three-mile limit from its shores.[69] Through this framework, Oregon will grant access and charge fees for demonstration projects, grant leases and charge royalties for commercial projects, and ensure consistency with its planning goals and management of marine and ecological resources. In any event, project developers will need a lease. For example, Verdant Power obtained its underwater lands lease for its experimental project in New York's East River from the state Office of General Services.[70]

States also have limited authority under federal law over projects that require federal approvals. State determinations are required for projects in federal waters that affect state coastal resources to confirm consistency with state coastal zone policies, under the Coastal Zone Management Act;[71] to certify that the project is consistent with state water quality regulations, pursuant to Section 401 of the Clean Water Act;[72] and to ensure that federal undertakings do not have negative effects on historic resources, pursuant to the National Historic Preservation Act.[73]

FERC has abandoned its practice of "conditional licenses," which sought to partially circumvent the need for these state determinations. Because state approvals can hold up federal approvals, sometimes indefinitely, FERC initially sought to craft a "conditional license" that would allow planning and consultation while the necessary state approvals were pending.[74] FERC issued its first conditional license for the Makah Bay project in Washington State, before the state had issued a Clean Water Act Section 401 certification or Coastal Zone Management Act consistency determination.[75] Washington petitioned for review in the U.S. Court of Appeals for the District of Columbia.[76] Ultimately, this federal-state conflict was resolved in 2008 through MOUs with Oregon,[77] Maine,[78] Washington,[79] and California[80] that allow for FERC's expedited pilot and short-term license programs and set timeframes for environmental review and state approvals. For example, Maine promises a decision on water quality certification within sixty days of applications. Through this system, Ocean Renewable Power Company received a preliminary FERC permit for tidal energy sites in Eastport, Maine.[81] The MOUs also provide for coordination with state comprehensive planning[82] and river management.[83]

Environmental Impacts

Environmental Review Under the National Environmental Policy Act

Ocean energy projects have the potential to strike, entrain, and entangle fish and wildlife; to create noise and vibration; to release contaminants and oils; and to alter currents and waves, thermal gradients, ocean bottoms, sediments, seafloor habitats, and marine life. The National Environmental Policy Act (NEPA) requires federal agencies to consider these potential environmental impacts of federal actions, such as issuance of a lease or license, and to consider a reasonable range of alternatives to those actions.[84] Review of environmental impacts under NEPA is also often coordinated with review required by other applicable statutes and consultation with other agencies, as discussed below.

DOI-FERC NEPA Coordination of NEPA Review

The DOI-FERC MOU and regulations do not provide for a single coordinated environmental review process. DOI and FERC each are required to comply with NEPA for their respective agency actions. DOI's issuance of a lease will typically precede FERC's issuance of a license for ocean energy projects, and environmental reviews will also be staggered.

A joint DOI-FERC NEPA review appears to be possible only for noncompetitive leases where an applicant files a complete license application and DOI lease application simultaneously.[85] Nevertheless, FERC and DOI can coordinate on a single scoping process that considers common elements of each agency's application, and each agency can participate as a cooperating agency in the other agency's NEPA review.[86]

In a run-of-the-mill land-based project, this separate and staggered environmental review might not require more than an examination of project changes. However, because the state of information is so limited for ocean energy projects, there is a greater likelihood that significant new information about the environmental impacts of commercial-scale projects or cumulative impacts of multiple projects will come to light, or that agencies will reach different conclusions about the scope of analysis, the significance of information, or the type of follow-up monitoring that will be required in response to scanty data. At this point, it is unclear whether this potentially duplicative process will be more challenging to project developers or to opponents. Multiple reviews will provide opportunities to parties with concerns about a project to submit multiple challenges. On the other hand, the process could be burdensome and challenging for project opponents if they are penalized for failure to raise concerns early and often in the DOI process—perhaps before all project information and environmental analyses are available.

Completed Environmental Review Efforts

Despite the developing state of the ocean energy industry and the lack of data about the impacts of commercial-scale projects, a number of federal, state, and private industry studies of environmental impacts have been completed. These provide insight into key issues that will need to be considered for individual projects and identify research and information needs.

The most comprehensive of these is a 2007 Programmatic EIS prepared by DOI,[87] which provides a broad analysis of the environmental impacts of DOI's overall program and is designed to be followed with narrower site-specific analyses for individual projects. This tiered analysis is designed to lead to a more streamlined, consistent, and predictable review process. The DOI programmatic review analyzed wind, wave, and ocean current energy, identified the range of potential environmental impacts, included guidelines for analysis, analyzed possible mitigation strategies, and set forth best management practices.

State agencies and other federal agencies are also potentially required to undertake environmental review for their approvals and leases.[88] Thus, the large-scale studies prepared by states (such as California)[89] and other federal agencies (such as the Department of Energy)[90] provide further confirmation of environmental issues that require analysis under other federal and state law.

Finally, there have also been a few project-specific reviews completed, such as the FERC review of the Makah Bay project in 2007. These are illustrative of the site-specific analysis, consultation process, and conditions required for an ocean energy project that requires federal approvals, although their conclusions, which are often based on the small size and short life span of these pilot projects, cannot necessarily be relied upon for commercial-scale projects.[91] For example, the Makah Bay project will consist of four buoys in a 60-by-240-foot area, but a large-scale commercial wave farm could occupy several square miles of ocean.[92] Because of this lack of knowledge about large-scale and cumulative impacts of multiple projects, some have advocated adaptive management of impacts during project operations, in which the protective measures would be revised as information about those impacts develops.[93]

These early reviews have indicated which aspects of construction of projects, construction of transmission lines, operation, maintenance, and decommissioning are thought to be most likely to have the potential for significant environmental impacts. The DOI Programmatic EIS, for example, considered alteration of ocean surface and sediments, air quality, alteration of ocean currents and movements, water quality, acoustic environment, hazardous materials and waste management, electromagnetic fields, marine and coastal birds, marine mammals, terrestrial biota, fish resources and essential fish habitat, sea turtles, coastal habitats, seafloor habitats, areas of special concerns such as visual impacts from coastal parks, military use areas, transportation, socioeconomic resources, land use and existing infrastructure, visual resources, tourism and recreation, fisheries, and other nonroutine conditions such as storms and terrorism. The key areas of concern are discussed below.

Fish and Wildlife

The major risks to fish and wildlife are strikes or entanglement in equipment or transmission lines, vessel strikes, and noise and vibration from blasting and pile driving during construction.

The chief concern with ocean energy is with the impact of turbines. Ocean power projects have unique characteristics that make it difficult to reach firm conclusions about impacts based on either land-based energy projects or marine nonenergy activities. Rotor blades in turbines used in ocean energy projects operate at a relatively slow speed. Some turbines operate at 10 to 20 revolutions per minute (rpm), compared to 100 to 200 rpm for conventional hydropower or 80 to 100 rpm for boat propellers, which should make it easier for fish to avoid collisions with the equipment.[94] In addition, when turbine blades are open to the surrounding ocean, without a housing structure on the sides of the turbine, like the model used in the Verdant New York project, it is easier for fish to swim away and not become caught in the rotor blades, though such a rotor may pose greater risks to navigation.[95] However, although it might be comparatively easy to avoid a single turbine, it is unclear how fish and marine mammals will respond to large fields of turbines, especially extremely large mammals that may not be able to maneuver quickly or pass between units. The DOI programmatic EIS recommended constructing components onshore, avoiding construction in sensitive habitats, requiring reduced vessel speeds, avoiding fish and wildlife by halting work when wildlife is present and scheduling work to avoid migration seasons, and using measures such as horn blasts to deter wildlife from construction areas before blasting or pile driving.[96]

In addition to impacts they may experience from the energy-collecting devices, birds may become entangled in equipment and cables when they dive for fish, or disoriented by lights needed for navigational safety.[97] Sea turtles and shore birds, and their nesting sites and hatchlings, can be affected by transmission lines and onshore facilities such as substations, transmission lines, and access roads. Thus, the DOI Programmatic EIS recommended siting onshore facilities to avoid sensitive areas and timing onshore construction to avoid nesting periods.[98]

To ensure that appropriate project-specific conditions are included in leases and licenses, numerous federal statutes require consultation with state and federal fish and wildlife management agencies to incorporate appropriate conditions in leases, licenses, or other approvals, as discussed below.

Endangered Species

Ocean energy projects potentially affect endangered species, such as certain kinds of whales, sea turtles, birds, and fish.

Section 9 of the Endangered Species Act (ESA) prohibits the "taking" of endangered or threatened species by harming or killing the species or causing habitat modification that significantly impairs activities such as breeding, feeding, or sheltering.[99] If a federal agency determines that its action "may affect" endangered or threatened species or their critical habitat, § 7 of the Endangered Species Act requires informal and potentially formal consultation with the U.S. Fish and Wildlife Service (FWS) and the National Marine Fisheries Service (NMFS), depending on which species is at issue, to ensure that the federal action is not likely to jeopardize listed species or destroy or adversely modify critical habitat.[100] This consultation, which potentially requires a biological assessment by the agency proposing the action and a biological opinion by the wildlife management agency, can be folded into environmental review under NEPA.[101]

If the project is likely to result in a take of listed species "incidental to" its otherwise lawful activities, the project can still proceed, but the developer must obtain an Incidental Take Permit authorizing the take, and must mitigate harmful effects through a conservation plan.[102] Renewable energy developers that fail to survey potential listed species impacts to the satisfaction of the relevant wildlife management agency or fail to obtain an Incidental Take Permit may find that they are enjoined from operating their facilities—as was the case in 2009 for one wind project developer that disregarded directions from FWS about proper survey times and locations, and therefore inaccurately concluded that the turbines would not harm Indiana Bats and failed to obtain the required Incidental Take Permit.[103]

Consultation with FWS is also required for migratory birds pursuant to the Migratory Bird Treaty Act,[104] and with state and federal fish and wildlife agencies under the Fish and Wildlife Coordination Act.[105]

Marine Mammals

Marine mammals are at risk from construction noise and vibration and from strikes by equipment and vessels. Some species can hear pile driving from 80 kilometers away and experience permanent hearing loss from severe noises as much as 1.8 kilometers away.[106] Noise also interferes with marine mammal communications and can cause them to abandon habitat.[107] Populations of certain marine mammals are already so critically low (such as right whales, approximately three hundred of which remain along the Atlantic coast) that further loss of individuals can have population-level impacts.[108]

Under the Marine Mammal Protection Act (MMPA), developers are responsible for complying with the requirements of FWS or the Department of Commerce, depending on the species, and obtaining an incidental take permit (also known as a letter of authorization in MMPA parlance) or incidental harm authorization.[109] If the marine mammal is also an endangered species, the MMPA process must be completed first, before an incidental take permit under the Endangered Species Act can be obtained.[110]

In its programmatic EIS, to mitigate impacts on marine mammals, DOI recommended avoiding mating, feeding, and calving areas and migration routes; halting construction when marine mammals are nearby; and minimizing the use of explosives.[111] The Department of Energy recommended the use of sound insulation, noise barriers, aversive sounds to drive away sensitive species, and attention to design of rotor blades, among other measures.[112] It has also been found that cables that are thick and taut are less likely to cause entanglements and lacerations in marine mammals.[113]

Ocean energy projects may also alter conditions in ways that are not necessarily negative, but about which there is not yet much data and which will be difficult to evaluate. Pilings and other equipment may become artificial reefs colonized by marine life, which in turn attract predators such as seals or sea otters, as well as predatory fish and birds, to the area. The exclusion of bottom trawling or fishing may also increase biodiversity, at least in the immediate project area. Birds, seals, and sea lions may use above-water structures to haul out or roost.[114] These developments may benefit some species to the detriment of others.

Fish

The impact on fish is also a major focus of environmental analysis, especially for projects involving turbines. Agencies must consult with NMFS regarding any proposed action that may adversely affect Essential Fish Habitats identified under the Magnuson Stevens Fishery Conservation and Management Act.[115] In FERC licensing, there is an independent obligation under Federal Power Act § 10(j) to include license conditions based on recommendations of the federal National Marine Fisheries Service and Fish and Wildlife Service and state fish and wildlife agencies.[116] Section 18 of the Federal Power Act authorizes the Department of Commerce or Interior, as appropriate, depending on the fish species, to prescribe the construction of fishways.[117]

The design and placement of turbines will be a factor. For Verdant's New York East River project, where the endangered shortnose sturgeon is a major concern, the developer, working with the environmental group Riverkeeper, used hydroacoustic transducers and ultrasound imaging to monitor fish behavior and found that nearly all fish swam around or through its turbine.[118] In Hastings, Minnesota, a short-term study for a pilot project used balloon- and radio-tagged fish, and found that 97.5 percent of fish survived its in-river turbine.[119] However, it is not clear how fish will respond to large arrays of turbines. Furthermore, the impacts of turbines on aquatic life will vary depending on the turbine design and the fish species. For example, some tidal systems are open on the sides and do not have a confined forebay or penstock into which fish may be drawn, unlike conventional hydropower turbines.[120]

Analyses of ocean energy impacts have also noted that electromagnetic fields from transmission lines may impact orientation and behavior, particularly in sharks, rays, and skates, which have specialized tissues to detect electric fields in competitors and prey, and in sea turtles and other species that use magnetic fields for long-distance migration.[121]

Cables, moorings and anchors will impact the seabed and aquatic life that lives on the seabed. For transmission cables, the installation method is the critical factor. Cables that are not buried will sweep along the seabed and be a constant source of disturbance.[122] Burying a cable by plowing can require disturbing an area only one meter wide, while air jetting requires disturbing an area 1.5 meters to 4 meters wide, and horizontal directional drilling does not require any open trenching.[123] These impacts are potentially significant because commercial-scale projects can involve many miles of underground cable. For example, the Cape Wind project in Nantucket Sound involves the installation of seventy-eight miles of buried underwater transmission cable.[124] The use of concrete anchors and heavy, less mobile chains can reduce the impact from chain sweep on the seabed.[125] In the Makah Bay project, NMFS recommended, and FERC agreed, not to install mooring and anchoring systems in the rocky substrate that was essential habitat for groundfish.

Water Quality and Pollution

Disposal of Dredged Materials and Pollutants

Dumping of dredged materials—for example, during construction of devices or anchors affixed to the ocean floor—requires a permit from the U.S. Army Corps of Engineers, pursuant to §404 of the Clean Water Act.[126] If the dredged materials are contaminated, the Marine Protection, Research, and Sanctuaries Act[127] prohibits dumping of certain materials and waste into ocean waters without a permit from the EPA. Hydraulic fluids and lubricating oils can leak, and chemicals may be used to prevent encrustation of equipment and cables with marine organisms.[128] For discharges of pollutants, a Clean Water Act permit is required.[129]

Impact on Wave Heights, Tides, and Currents

By harnessing wave and tidal energy and by placing nongenerating structures in the water, ocean energy projects have the potential to create wave shadows and affect patterns of sediment transport and beach building.[130] Reduction in wave energy may also affect plant and animal species that have adapted to a wave-swept environment and that rely on water movement for an influx of food or nutrients, fertilization, dispersal, or settlement.[131] Such reductions could permanently reduce the tidal range and mean high water level in estuaries and lagoons.[132] Estimates of the reduction in wave height range from 1 percent to 13 percent on the landward side of wave farms, but at this early stage in the development of the industry, the overall effects of large-scale development can only be estimated through modeling.[133] This impact can be addressed by the choice of ocean energy technology, streamlining components, burying cables, reducing size and surface areas, and altering the location of equipment.[134] Similarly, ocean thermal projects may alter the thermal structure of water, turbidity, salinity, and distribution of nutrients in ways that can only be estimated based on incomplete knowledge.[135]

Visual Impacts

Ocean energy projects tend to be close to the surface or submerged and therefore do not raise the same level of concern about aesthetic impacts as fields of offshore wind turbines that are hundreds of feet in height and visible from the shore. In fact, wave energy converters are typically invisible from shore.[136] Buoy-style point absorbers protrude only a few feet above the surface and resemble navigational buoys that are an accepted part of the marine visual environment. Long and cylindrical attenuators, which are long, multisegment floating structures that use the differing heights of waves along their length to flex the area between segments, driving hydraulic pumps or other converters, also barely protrude above the ocean surface. Terminators, which are located perpendicular to wave travel to capture or reflect wave energy, and overtopping devices, which create reservoirs higher than surrounding water and release that water through turbines, also have very low profiles.[137]

Historic Resources

Ocean energy projects have the potential to impact historic resources. One concern is the effect on shipwrecks. In addition, as the coastline has changed over time, the archaeological remains of some coastal communities have become submerged off-shore. When a proposed undertaking may affect historic resources, federal agencies are required to consult with the federal Advisory Council on Historic Preservation and with state or tribal historic preservation officers under § 106 of the National Historic Preservation Act to determine whether any historic properties may be affected and to seek ways to avoid or minimize adverse effects.[138] For the Makah Bay project, the state historic preservation officer requested a professional archaeologist to critique the seabed survey performed by the developer and to implement a cultural resources management plan.[139]

Other Regulatory Requirements

Other federal laws may require permits or approvals for construction and operation of ocean energy projects.

Navigation

One potential concern with respect to navigation is entanglement with mooring and transmission cables. For the Verdant New York project, recreational boaters and longshoremen expressed concerns that underwater cables close to the surface pose a navigation hazard.[140] Several federal statutes contain requirements that address these concerns.

The U.S. Coast Guard has authority over marking obstructions such as renewable energy infrastructure on navigable waters and on the OCS,[141] and may impose operating and other requirements under the Ports and Waterways Safety Act.[142] The Federal Power Act also imposes separate requirements for FERC licensing. Section 18 of the FPA requires FERC to include lights and signals prescribed by the Coast Guard.[143] In contrast, FERC approval pursuant to § 4(e) of the Federal Power Act "normally will obviate" the need for a Corps of Engineers permit for an obstruction of navigable waters under § 10 of the Rivers and Harbors Act.[144]

Coastal Zone Consistency

Under the Coastal Zone Management Act (CZMA), federal agencies may act on particular projects in coastal waters and adjacent shore lands subject to the CZMA only after making a finding of consistency with the affected state's federally approved coastal zone management plan, and obtaining the state's concurrence or presumed concurrence with such a finding.[145] Projects that exclude fishing, navigation, and recreation can pose conflicts with coastal zone plans if they interfere with commercial or recreational fishing, port operations, and tourism. California's study, for example, noted the dearth of information about the economic value of tourism due to surfing and the potential impact of a reduction in wave heights.[146]

Other Environmental Statutes and Findings

Other federal natural resources and land management statutes also apply in some circumstances.[147]

When a project is located within a "reservation" such as an Indian reservation or a marine sanctuary, § 4(e) of the Federal Power Act requires a finding by FERC that any project located within that reservation will not interfere with or be inconsistent with the purpose of the reservation and must contain such conditions as the secretary of the department responsible for the reservation (e.g., the Secretary of the Interior) deems necessary for the adequate protection and utilization of the reservation.[148] In its evaluation of the Makah Bay project, FERC found the project consistent with the National Marine Sanctuaries Act, 16 U.S.C. §§ 1431 et seq., because of its limited scope and size.[149] FERC also examined the consistency of the project with the terms of the U.S. treaty with the Makah tribe.[150] Larger-scale projects that exclude fishing and recreation may be in conflict with the purposes of such reservations.

Financing Hydrokinetic Projects

Some provisions of the tax code and requirements for renewable energy that provide economic incentives for renewable energy have been extended in recent years to apply to hydrokinetic projects, although these incentives have limits in what they can accomplish at this stage of development in the ocean and tidal energy.

Federal Incentives

While there is a grab bag of federal financial incentives that in 2005 were extended to include ocean energy, these provisions are of limited utility to ocean and tidal energy.[151] The Energy Policy Act of 2005 (EPAct) amended the definition of renewable energy to include tidal, wave, current, and thermal ocean energy.[152] However, projects must still meet deadlines to be in construction or in service, depending on the incentive program, and some of these programs, such as federal production incentives, are dependent on annual appropriations to continue.[153] Because demonstration and pilot projects still prevail in this developing industry, grant programs may be more critical than revisions to the tax code. Thus, the U.S. Department of Energy, for example, provides direct financial assistance to enhance commercial viability, market acceptance, and environmental performance through funding for grid studies, environmental impact review, and device design and development.[154] In addition, in June 2010, the Department of the Interior and the U.S. Department of Energy entered into a Memorandum of Understanding to exchange information, develop standards and guidelines, and perform research on offshore renewable energy, which should help to identify joint research, development, and funding priorities.[155]

State Incentives

While state tax incentives and grant programs can also contribute to the development of ocean energy, states have a unique role in promoting development of renewable energy technology through a state renewable portfolio standard (RPS). Renewable portfolio standards, which are discussed in detail in chapter 4, require retail electricity suppliers to provide a certain amount of their power from renewable sources, either by owning generating facilities, by purchasing power, or by purchasing renewable energy credits. Each state sets its own RPS for the amount of renewable energy required, the types of energy that qualify (e.g., some exclude waste-to-energy or large-scale hydropower), and the types that are required.[156] Some states already have included ocean energy among the qualifying renewables in their state policies.[157] In addition, to promote technologies that might not yet be economically competitive with other renewables, some state RPSs also have set-asides that require a set proportion to come from a specific source, such as solar.[158] Once hydrokinetic energy is commercially available, this mechanism can be used to provide an advantage to this developing industry.

Conclusion

In sum, ocean and tidal energy is governed by a newly established regulatory process that requires actions by DOI and FERC, along with numerous other determinations by federal and state agencies. Because only pilot and demonstration projects have been installed in the United States, the full and cumulative impacts of these projects, and the requirements that state and federal agencies will impose to address those impacts, are still largely unknown. Nevertheless, now that at least some regulatory uncertainty and friction have been resolved with the agreements between FERC and DOI and between FERC and several coastal states, it can be hoped that the projects will become more economically feasible, and we can learn if it is practicable and safe to harness the ocean's tides, waves, and currents for electrical power.

Notes

1. U.S. Dep't of Energy, Energy Efficiency & Renewable Energy, Wind & Water Program, Program Areas, http://www1.eere.energy.gov/windandhydro/marine_hydrokinetic _tech.html (last visited July 28, 2010).

2. U.S. Dep't of Energy, Energy Efficiency & Renewable Energy, Wind & Water Program, Technologies, Marine & Hydrokinetic Technology Glossary, http://www1 .eere.energy.gov/windandhydro/hydrokinetic/techTutorial.aspx (last visited July 28, 2010); John W. Lavrakas & Jedediah M. Smith, Infrastructure Assessment in Oregon 9–10 (2009), available at http://oregonarc.com/blog/wp-content/uploads/2010/03/20100305-Final Report-small.pdf (describing current technologies).

3. Fed. Energy Regulatory Comm'n, Licensing Hydrokinetic Pilot Projects 3 (2008), available at http://www.ferc.gov/industries/hydropower/indus-act/hydrokinetics/pdf/ white_paper.pdf.

4. Elec. Power Research Inst., Assessment of Water Power Potential and Dev. Needs 3-2 (2007), available at http://bakser.aaas.org/spp/cstc/docs/07_06_1ERPI_report.pdf.

5. Jeff Scruggs & Paul Jacob, Harvesting Ocean Wave Energy, Science, Feb. 27, 2009, at 1176.

6. Elec. Power Research Inst., supra note 4.

7. Michael B. Walsh, A Rising Tide in Renewable Energy: The Future of Tidal In-Stream Energy, 19 Vill. Envtl. L. J. 193 (2008).

8. See Colin Sullivan, Marine Power Not Ready for Prime Time, Experts Say, N.Y. Times, Apr. 14, 200.

9. Verdant Power, The RITE Project, http://verdantpower.com/what-initiative/ (last visited July 28, 2010).

10. RenewableEnergyWorld.com, Ocean Power Technologies Begins Wave Power Farm Development Off Oregon Coast (Feb. 22, 2010), http://www.renewableenergyworld

.com/rea/news/article/2010/02/ocean-power-technologies-begins-wave-power-farm-develop ment-off-oregon-coast (last visited Aug. 9, 2010).

11. Scruggs & Jacob, *supra* note 5.

12. Press Release, The Crown Estate, World's First Wave and Tidal Energy Leasing Round to Power UP to Three Quarters of a Million Homes (March 16, 2010), *available at* http://www .thecrownestate.co.uk/newscontent/92-pentland-firth-developers.htm.

13. A comprehensive list of projects in the United States and overseas is available on the Department of Energy's (DOE) marine and hydrokinetic energy website. U.S. DEP'T OF ENERGY, ENERGY EFFICIENCY & RENEWABLE ENERGY, WIND & WATER POWER PROGRAM, MARINE & HYDROKINETIC TECHNOLOGY PROJECT LISTINGS, http://www1.eere.energy.gov/windandhydro/ hydrokinetic/listings.aspx?type=Project (last visited July 28, 2010).

14. U.S. DEP'T OF INTERIOR, MINERALS MGMT. SERV., GUIDELINES FOR THE MINERALS MANAGEMENT SERVICE: RENEWABLE ENERGY FRAMEWORK 34 (2009) [hereinafter DOI GUIDE-LINES] (*see also* joint DOI-FERC Guidelines on Regulation of Hydrokinetic Projects on the OCS, annexed as Appendix A to the DOI Guidelines, at 31) [hereinafter DOI-FERC GUIDE-LINES]; *see also* U.S. COMM'N ON OCEAN POLICY, AN OCEAN BLUEPRINT FOR THE 21ST CEN-TURY, FINAL REPORT 70–73 (2004) (primer on ocean jurisdictions), *available at* http://ocean commission.gov/documents/full_color_rpt/000_ocean_full_report.pdf.

15. Dep't of Interior Order No. 3302 (June 18, 2010), *available at* http://www.doi.gov/ deepwaterhorizon/loader.cfm?csModule=security/getfile&PageID=35872.

16. Energy Policy Act of 2005, Pub. L. No. 109-58, 119 Stat. 597 (codified as amended in scattered sections of 42 U.S.C.).

17. 43 U.S.C. § 1337(p).

18. Press Release, DOI, President Obama, Secretary Salazar Announce Framework for Renewable Energy Development on the U.S. Outer Continental Shelf (April 22, 2009), *avail-able at* http://www.DOI.gov/initiatives/documents/April%202009%20NewsWave.pdf.

19. Renewable Energy and Alternate Uses of Existing Facilities on the Outer Continental Shelf, 74 Fed. Reg. 19638-01 (Apr. 29, 2009) (codified at 30 C.F.R. pts. 250, 285, & 290) [hereinafter DOI Final Rule].

20. *Id.* (promulgating 30 C.F.R. § 285).

21. *Id.* at 19,658–19,870.

22. 30 C.F.R. § 285.235; DOI GUIDELINES at 22–23, 38 (DOI-FERC GUIDELINES).

23. *See* DOI GUIDELINES at 28–29; 74 Fed. Reg. 19657; *see also* 30 C.F.R. §§ 285.505 (rent), 285.506 (operating fee), 511–537 (financial assurances).

24. DOI GUIDELINES at 21–22.

25. *See* DOI GUIDELINES at 37 (DOI-FERC GUIDELINES).

26. *See id.* at 33 (DOI-FERC GUIDELINES).

27. Sarah McQuillen Tran, *Why Have Developers Been Powerless to Develop Ocean Power?*, 4 TEX. J. OIL GAS & ENERGY L. 195 (2008–2009) (describing jurisdictional dispute).

28. 101 FERC ¶ 62,009 (Oct. 3, 2002) (reviewing project proposed for 1.9 miles off Wash-ington coast), *on reh'g*, 102 FERC ¶ 61,242 (Feb. 28, 2003) (reviewing revised proposal relo-cating project to more than 3 miles offshore) (citing 16 U.S.C. §§ 817(1) & 797(8)).

29. Advance Notice of Proposed Rulemaking, 70 Fed. Reg. 77,345 (Dec. 30, 2005) (describ-ing alternative energy-related uses on the OCS).

30. Comments of the FERC Staff on the Advanced Notice of Proposed Rulemaking on Alternative Energy-Related Uses on the OCS (Feb. 28, 2006), *available at* http://www.ferc .gov/industries/hydropower/indus-act/hydrokinetics/pdf/DOI020806.pdf; Pacific Gas & Elec. Co., Project Nos. 12781-001, 12781-002, 12779-001, 12779-002, 125 FERC ¶ 61,045, Oct. 16, 2008 (order on rehearing).

31. Memorandum of Understanding between the U.S. Dep't of the Interior and Fed. Energy Regulatory Comm'n, Apr. 9, 2009 (hereafter, DOI-FERC MOU), *available at* http://www.ferc .gov/legal/maj-ord-reg/mou/mou-doi.pdf.

32. DOI GUIDELINES at 34 (DOI-FERC GUIDELINES).

33. Alan Koviski, *Interior, FERC Issue Guidance on Gaining Approval for Wave, Tide, Current Projects*, 148 DAILY ENV'T REP. (BNA), at A8, Aug. 5, 2009.

34. 16 U.S.C. §§ 792–823a (FPA); 16 U.S.C. §§ 2705 & 2708 (exemptions).

35. *See* FERC, Handbook for Hydroelectric Project Licensing and 5 MW Exemptions from Licensing (Apr. 2004), *available at* http://www.ferc.gov/industries/hydropower/gen-info/handbooks/licensing_handbook.pdf.

36. This is true unless a FERC license is not required, e.g., because the developer is a federal agency.

37. DOI-FERC MOU.

38. DOI GUIDELINES at 37 (DOI-FERC GUIDELINES).

39. *Id.* at 38 (DOI-FERC GUIDELINES).

40. 16 U.S.C. §§ 803(j), 811.

41. Verdant Power LLC, Docket No. P-12178-001, 111 FERC ¶ 61,024, at 3 (Apr. 14, 2005) (declaratory order).

42. Order on Clarification and Dismissing Request for Rehearing, Project No. 12178-2002 (July 27, 2005), *available at* http://www.ferc.gov/whats-new/comm-meet/072105/H-4.pdf.

43. Verdant Power LLC, Project No. 12178-001, 111 FERC ¶ 61,024, at 3.

44. *See FERC White Paper on Licensing Hydrokinetic Pilot Projects*, Apr. 14, 2008, *available at* http://www.ferc.gov/industries/hydropower/indus-act/hydrokinetics/pdf/white_paper.pdf.

45. 18 C.F.R. § 4.30 et seq.

46. FERC, Notice of Inquiry and Interim Statement of Policy, Docket No. RM07-08-000, 118 FERC ¶ 61,112 (Feb. 15, 2007), *available at* http://www.ferc.gov/whats-new/comm-meet/2007/021507/H-1.pdf.

47. Reedsport OPT Wave Park, LLC, Project No. 12713-000, 118 FERC 61,118 (Feb. 16, 2007), *available at* http://www.ferc.gov/industries/hydropower/indus-act/hydrokinetics.asp#timeline (timeline, containing link to order).

48. 16 U.S.C. §§ 791a et seq.

49. 16 U.S.C. § 797(e), 16 U.S.C. § 803(a)(1) (FPA § 4(e)).

50. Finavera Ocean Energy, Ltd., Project No. 12751-000, 121 FERC ¶ 61,288 (Dec. 21, 2007), *available at* http://www.ferc.gov/whats-new/comm-meet/2007/122007/H-1.pdf.

51. City of Hastings, Project No. 4306-017, 125 FERC ¶ 61,287 (Dec. 13, 2008), *available at* http://www.ferc.gov/EventCalendar/Files/20081213163047-P-4306-017.pdf.

52. NAT'L RENEWABLE ENERGY LAB., OCEAN THERMAL ENERGY CONVERSION, WHAT IS OCEAN THERMAL ENERGY CONVERSION?, http://www.nrel.gov/otec/what.html (last visited August 9, 2010).

53. 74 Fed. Reg. 19638.

54. 42 U.S.C. §§ 9101–9168.

55. 42 U.S.C. §§ 9001–9009.

56. 42 U.S.C. § 9118.

57. STATE OF HAWAII, DEP'T OF BUS., ECON. DEV. & TOURISM, OCEAN THERMAL ENERGY, http://hawaii.gov/dbedt/info/energy/renewable/otec; L.A. Vega, *Ocean Thermal Energy Conversion*, OTEC NEWS, at http://www.otecnews.org/articles/vega/01_background.html.

58. *See* 15 C.F.R. pt. 981 (repealed); 61 Fed. Reg. 21073 (May 9, 1996) (repealing regulations).

59. *See* Memorandum of Understanding between the state of Hawaii and the U.S. Department of Energy, Jan. 31, 2008, *available at* http://hawaii.gov/dbedt/info/energy/hcei/hawaii_mou.pdf.

60. *See* Tundi Agardy, *Is Ocean Zoning the Solution to Dying Marine Ecosystems?* SCI. AM., June 2009.

61. *See* DOI Final Rule at 19653, 19662.

62. WHITE HOUSE COUNCIL ON ENVTL. QUALITY, INTERAGENCY OCEAN POL'Y TASK FORCE, INTERIM FRAMEWORK FOR EFFECTIVE COASTAL AND MARINE SPATIAL PLANNING (Dec. 9, 2009), *available at* http://www.whitehouse.gov/sites/default/files/microsites/091209-Interim-CMSP-Framework-Task-Force.pdf.

63. DOI Final Rule at 19662; but see DOI GUIDELINES (DOI-FERC GUIDELINES), at 34 (FERC may be able to issue some licenses in sanctuaries and refuges).

64. Danielle Murray, *Dual Federal Regulation Slowing Public Wave Power Project Development*, TRENDS: A.B.A. SEC. ENV'T, ENERGY & RES. NEWSLETTER 14 (July/August 2010).

65. 16 U.S.C. § 797.

66. Scruggs & Jacob, *supra* note 5, at 1176.

67. DOI Final Rule at 19643.

68. Or. Coastal Mgmt. Program, Territorial Sea Plan: Part Five, Uses of the Territorial Sea for the Development of Renewable Energy Facilities and Other Related Structures, Equipment, or Facilities (2009), http://www.oregon.gov/LCD/OCMP/Ocean_TSP.shtml (last visited August 9, 2010).

69. Or. Admin. R., 141-140-0010, *available at* http://arcweb.sos.state.or.us/rules/OARS_100/OAR_141/141_140.html.

70. Roosevelt Island Tidal Energy Project, FERC No. 12611, Draft Kinetic Hydropower Pilot License Application, at C-4 (Nov. 2008), *available at* http://www.theriteproject.com/uploads/VerdantDLA_Vol1.pdf.

71. 16 U.S.C. §§ 1451 et seq.

72. 33 U.S.C. § 1341.

73. 16 U.S.C. §§ 470 et seq.

74. FERC, Policy Statement on Conditioned Licenses for Hydrokinetic Projects, 121 FERC ¶ 61,221 (Nov. 30, 2007). *See also* FERC, Conditioned Licenses, FAQ (Apr. 14, 2008), http://www.ferc.gov/industries/hydropower/indus-act/hydrokinetics/pdf/faq.pdf (last visited Aug. 9, 2010).

75. Finavera Renewables Ocean Energy Ltd., 121 FERC 61,288 (Dec. 21, 2007), *available at* http://www.ferc.gov/whats-new/comm-meet/2007/122007/H-1.pdf (amended at 122 FERC ¶ 61,248 (Mar. 20, 2008) to incorporate such state approvals, *available at* http://www.ferc.gov/whats-new/comm-meet/2008/032008/H-2.pdf).

76. State of Washington Dept. of Ecology v. FERC, No. 08-1191 (D.C. Cir. filed May 15, 2008).

77. Memorandum of Understanding between FERC and the State of Oregon, Mar. 26, 2008, *available at* http://www.ferc.gov/legal/maj-ord-reg/mou/mou-or-final.pdf.

78. Memorandum of Understanding between FERC and the State of Maine, Aug. 19, 2009, *available at* http://www.ferc.gov/legal/maj-ord-reg/mou/mou-ma.pdf.

79. Memorandum of Understanding between FERC and the State of Washington, June 4, 2009, *available at* http://www.ferc.gov/legal/maj-ord-reg/mou/mou-wa.pdf.

80. Memorandum of Understanding between FERC and the State of California, May 13, 2010, *available at* http://www.ferc.gov/legal/maj-ord-reg/mou/mou-ca.pdf.

81. Kevin Miller, *Baldacci, FERC Head Sign Agreement on Tidal Power*, Bangor Daily News (Aug. 20, 2009), *available at* http://www.bangordailynews.com/detail/116912.html?print=1.

82. Developers must also identify and comply with such plans under the Federal Power Act. FPA § 10(a), 18 C.F.R. § 4.38, 18 C.F.R. § 2.19.

83. Memorandum of Understanding between FERC and the State of Maine, Aug. 19, 2009.

84. 42 U.S.C. §§ 4321 et seq.

85. DOI Guidelines at 38 (DOI-FERC Guidelines).

86. *Id.* at 37 (DOI-FERC Guidelines).

87. Minerals Management Service, OCS Alternative Energy & Alternate Use Programmatic EIS Info. Ctr., Guide to the OCS Alternate Energy Final Programmatic Environmental Impact Statement (EIS) (Oct. 2007), *available at* http://ocsenergy.anl.gov/eis/guide/index.cfm; Minerals Management Service, 73 Fed. Reg. 1894 (Jan. 10, 2008) (record of decision) [hereinafter DOI FPEIS].

88. *See, e.g.*, N.Y. Envt'l Conserv. L ¶¶ 3-0301(1)(b), 3-0301(2)(m) & 8-0113; N.Y. Comp. Codes R. & Regs. tit. 6, § 617; Cal. Pub. Res. Code, §§ 21000–21178, and Cal. Code Regs. tit. 14, § 753, and tit. 3, §§ 15000–15387.

89. *See* Cal. Energy Comm'n, Public Interest Energy Research Program, Developing Wave Energy in Coastal California: Potential Socio-Economic and Environmental Impacts (Nov. 2008) [hereinafter California Energy Commission].

90. U.S. Dep't of Energy, Energy Efficiency & Renewable Energy, Department of Energy Releases Report on Potential Environmental Effects of Marine and Hydrokinetic Energy Technologies (Feb. 23, 2010), *available at* http://apps1.eere.energy.gov/

news/progress_alerts.cfm/pa_id=302; *see* Pub. L. No. 110-140 (Dec. 19, 2007) (prepared in response to the Energy Independence and Security Act of 2007, §633(B)).

91. Finavera Ocean Energy, Ltd., Project No. 12751-000, 121 FERC ¶ 61,288 (Dec. 21, 2007), *available at* http://www.ferc.gov/whats-new/comm-meet/2007/122007/H-1.pdf (describing Environmental Assessment prepared by FERC).

92. *See* California Energy Commission 24.

93. *See, e.g.,* Dep't of Energy, Wind & Hydropower Techs. Program, Report to Congress 49–52.

94. *See* Elec. Power Research Inst., Instream Tidal Power in North America: Environmental and Permitting Issues (June 2006) at p. 2-11, 2-13 n.5, *available at* http://ocean energy.epri.com/attachments/streamenergy/reports/007_Env_and_Reg_Issues_Report_060906 .pdf.

95. *See id.* at p. 2-32 to 2-33.

96. *See generally* DOI FPEIS Chapters 5, 7.

97. *See* California Energy Commission 129.

98. *See generally* DOI FPEIS Chapters 5, 7.

99. 16 U.S.C. §15,38(a)(1)(B); 16 U.S.C. §1532(19); 50 C.F.R. §17.3 (FWS regulations defining harm).

100. 16 U.S.C. §1371.

101. U.S. Fish & Wildlife Serv. & Nat'l Marine Fisheries Serv., Endangered Species Consultation Handbook: Procedures for Conducting Consultation and Conference Activities Under Section 7 of the Endangered Species Act (Mar. 1998), *available at* http://www.nmfs.noaa.gov/pr/pdfs/laws/esa_section7_handbook.pdf.

102. 16 U.S.C. §1539.

103. Animal Welfare Inst. v. Beech Ridge Energy LLC, 675 F. Supp. 2d 540 (D. Md. 2009) (enjoining operation of wind turbines under construction except during winter when bats are in hibernation).

104. Exec. Order No. 13,186; 16 U.S.C. §§703–712.

105. 16 U.S.C. §§661 et seq.; 16 U.S.C. §803(j)(1) (requiring FERC to include license conditions based on recommendations by state and federal wildlife agencies).

106. *See* California Energy Commission 129.

107. U.S. Dep't of Energy, Wind and Hydropower Technologies Program, Report to Congress 24.

108. DOI FPEIS at 4–57.

109. 16 U.S.C. §§1361–1407.

110. 16 U.S.C. §1536(b)(4)(C).

111. *See generally* DOI FPEIS Chapters 5, 7.

112. U.S. Dep't of Energy, Wind and Hydropower Technologies Program, Report to Congress 25–26.

113. *See id.* at 36.

114. Elec. Power Research Inst., Instream Tidal Power in North America, *supra* note 94, at 2-15 to 2-16.

115. 16 U.S.C. §1855.

116. *See* 16 U.S.C. §803(j) (requiring FERC consultation with NMFS).

117. *See* 16 U.S.C. §811.

118. Hashim Rahman, *Turbines May Carpet More of E. River Floor*, City Limits Weekly, Feb. 23, 2009, *available at* http://www.citylimits.org/news/articles/3702/turbines-may-carpet.

119. Project No. 4306-017, 125 FERC ¶ 61,287 (Dec. 13, 2008), *available at* http://www .ferc.gov/EventCalendar/Files/20081213163047-P-4306-017.pdf.

120. *See* Elec. Power Research Inst., Instream Tidal Power in North America, *supra* note 94, at 2-13.

121. *See id.* at 2-19; U.S. Dep't of Energy, Wind & Hydropower Techs. Program, Report to Congress D-5 to D-7.

122. *See* U.S. Dep't of Energy, Wind & Hydropower Techs. Program, Report to Congress 16.

123. *See* Elec. Power Research Inst., Instream Tidal Power in North America, *supra* note 94, at 2-4 to 2-5.

124. *See id.*

125. *See* U.S. Dep't of Energy, Wind & Hydropower Techs. Program, Report to Congress 23.

126. 33 U.S.C. § 1344.

127. 33 U.S.C. §§ 1401 et seq. (also known as the Ocean Dumping Act).

128. U.S. Dep't of Energy, Wind & Hydropower Techs. Program, Report to Congress 31.

129. 33 U.S.C. §§ 1342 (National Pollutant Discharge Elimination System) and 1343 (Ocean Discharge Criteria Evaluation).

130. *See* California Energy Commission 1.

131. *See id.* at 87–89.

132. U.S. Dep't of Energy, Wind & Hydropower Techs. Program, Report to Congress 17.

133. *See* California Energy Commission 27, 53–70; U.S. Dep't of Energy, Wind & Hydropower Techs. Program, Report to Congress 15.

134. U.S. Dep't of Energy, Wind & Hydropower Techs. Program, Report to Congress 16.

135. *Id.* at 44.

136. Jeff Scruggs & Paul Jacob, *Harvesting Ocean Wave Energy*, Science, Feb. 27, 2009, at 1176.

137. U.S. Dep't of Energy, Wind & Hydropower Techs. Program, Report to Congress 6 (listing and describing current technologies).

138. 16 U.S.C. §§ 470–470(t).

139. Makah Bay FERC Decision at ¶ 52.

140. Hashim Rahman, *Turbines May Carpet More of E. River Floor*, City Limits Weekly, Feb. 23, 2009.

141. 14 U.S.C. § 28.

142. 33 U.S.C. §§ 1221 et seq.

143. *See* 16 U.S.C. § 811.

144. 33 C.F.R. § 221.1(f)(1).

145. 16 U.S.C. § 1456; DOI Final Rule at 19659. The "coastal zone" subject to the CZMA is defined at 16 U.S.C. § 1453.

146. *See* California Energy Commission.

147. *See* DOI Final Rule at 19648–19651, listing applicable federal laws. *See* FERC, Handbook for Hydroelectric Project Licensing and 5 MW Exemptions from Licensing 121 (Apr. 2004) *available at* http://www.ferc.gov/industries/hydropower/gen-info/handbooks/licensing_handbook.pdf. (listing applicable statutes and reviews).

148. 16 U.S.C. § 797(e).

149. *See* Finavera Ocean Energy, Ltd., Project No. 12751-000, 121 FERC ¶ 61,288 at ¶¶ 20, 23–28.

150. *See id.* at ¶¶ 29–32.

151. *See, e.g.*, U.S. Treasury Department, Payments for Specified Energy Property in Lieu of Tax Credits Under the American Recovery and Reinvestment Act of 2009 5 (July 2009). For a detailed discussion of this and other tax incentives, see Chapter 7.

152. *See* 42 U.S.C. § 15851 (EPAct § 201(a); Pub. L. No. 109-58).

153. *See* 42 U.S.C. § 13317; U.S. Dep't of Energy, Database of State Incentives for Renewables & Efficiency (DSIRE), Renewable Energy Production Incentive (REPI), http:// www.dsireusa.org/incentives/incentive.cfm?Incentive_Code=US33F&re=1&ee=0 (last visited Aug. 9, 2010).

154. Press Release, U.S. Department of Energy, DOE Awards Up to $14.6 Million to Support Development of Advanced Water Power Technologies (Sept. 15, 2009), *available at* http://www.energy.gov/news/8012.htm.

155. Memorandum of Understanding between the U.S. Department of the Interior, Bureau of Ocean Energy Management, Regulation, and Enforcement and the U.S. Department of Energy, Office of Energy Efficiency and Renewable Energy, dated June 29, 2010, *available at* http://www.doi.gov/whatwedo/energy/loader.cfm?csModule=security/getfile&PageID=37040.

156. *See* PEW CTR. ON GLOBAL CLIMATE CHANGE, RENEWABLE & ALTERNATIVE ENERGY PORTFOLIO STANDARDS, *available at* http://www.pewclimate.org/what_s_being_done/in_the_states/rps.cfm (fifty-state survey map); U.S. DEP'T OF ENERGY, ENERGY EFFICIENCY & RENEWABLE ENERGY, STATES WITH RENEWABLE PORTFOLIO STANDARDS, http://apps1.eere.energy.gov/states/maps/renewable_portfolio_states.cfm#chart.

157. *See, e.g.*, Proceeding on a Motion of the Commission Regarding a Retail Renewable Portfolio Standard, Case 03-E-0188 (N.Y. Pub. Serv. Comm'n Sept. 24, 2004) (Order regarding retail renewable portfolio standard, excluding most "mature" hydropower and waste-to-energy, and including ocean and tidal power).

158. *See, e.g.*, NEV. REV. STAT. § 704.7821 (portfolio standard with minimum solar energy requirement).

chapter twenty-two

Energy Transmission and Storage

Michael Dworkin,
Javier García-Lomas Gago,
Clay Francis, Paul Foley,
Anna Skubikowski, and Shahin Milani

Introduction: Why Transmission Matters to Clean Energy

The Context from Which Renewable Energy Sources See Transmission

Modern societies depend on a reliable supply of electricity, and since electricity is a form of energy that cannot be readily stored, utilities must provide adequate supply 24 hours a day and 8,760 hours per year. This constant need to balance supply and demand adds to the complexity of the electric transmission system. The transmission network's reliability has received greater attention since the rolling blackouts in California and the New York mid-Atlantic cascading blackout of 2003. Indeed, Congress has taken several actions to develop a more reliable and integrated transmission system. Since 2005, the federal government has increased its presence in the regulation of the transmission system.

Why is transmission so important in the energy industry? First, as many authors, scientists, and regulators explain, a strong transmission system improves the overall reliability of the grid. Second, increased transmission capabilities can enable customers to choose the fuel mix that provides electricity to their homes. Finally, an open transmission system enables competition among power suppliers, thus creating a competitive market.

These features are important for all generating stations, but they are particularly so for sources relying on renewable energy. This is due to a simple but fundamental physical reason: many renewable energy sources, such as wind, hydro, and biomass, are more difficult to transport than fossil or nuclear fuels. As with all forms of demand for energy, the use of renewable energy on a large scale means either moving the sources of demand to places where the renewable energy resources are strong, or bringing energy from those places to where demand exists.

This is often more difficult for renewable resources than for other fuels. With traditional fuels like coal, petroleum variants, or natural gas, billions of calories of potential energy can be carried in small, tight spaces such as rail cars, ships, or pipelines. Nuclear reactions draw even vaster energy yields from quite small and dense fuel rods. In sharp contrast, wind energy cannot be transported; moving water tends to exhaust the hydraulic head that yields power; biomass requires larger mass and volume than fossil fuels containing comparable amounts of power; and even sunlight is far more intensive in some areas than in others, and solar power generation requires more land mass. Indeed, the most energy-efficient and economically attractive way of delivering energy from renewable sources to demanding customers is usually to convert it into electricity at or close to its source and then to use electricity-transmission lines to transport the energy to customers. Thus, the growth of renewables to strategically significant levels will depend heavily upon the availability and terms of use for current—and emerging—transmission systems.

The Context from Which the Transmission Industry Sees Renewables

For the reasons just noted, a strong and redundant transmission system is vital to the deployment of renewable generation at a societally significant level. However, the inverse is less obvious. From the point of view of transmission investors, regulators, builders, or operators, the promotion of renewable energy is a challenge and an opportunity, but it may not be seen as vital because it is only one of several imminent issues. Ensuring that America's transmission grid meets the needs of the emerging renewable energy industry will be possible only if we recognize the issues faced by transmission investors, owners, operators, and regulators—and the operational challenges that arise from those issues.

The foremost of these issues is reliability, i.e., whether "the lights go on" when expected, and stay on as expected. This issue is often taken for granted by the consuming public, but it actually requires serious attention by providers. Indeed the need for improving that attention was highlighted by a series of outages of increasing scale and frequency, the most striking of which was the 2003 blackout that lasted almost four days, affecting up to 50 million Americans and Canadians. That event played a critical role in legitimating the passage of the mandatory reliability provisions of the Energy Policy Act of 2005, which, for the first time, authorized nationwide minimum standards of reliability for transmission and related services.[1]

After reliability, the second issue that is regarded as vital by transmission regulators, operators, and builders is the ability to allow efficient selection of different generation and end user resources, telling each of hundreds of large power plants when to turn on and when to turn off. This "dispatch" function is similar to a musical conductor's role with a symphony, ensuring that that total system acts in harmony, so that energy services can be offered more efficiently and at lower cost.

A third factor is the integration of smart grid technology into the existing system. That system is decades old and was not designed to take advantage of, or even to allow, the general benefits of far greater situational awareness, which can now be provided through digital enhancement.

These three concerns, together, feed into three operational challenges faced by many transmission systems. The first of these is "the cap-x requirement," i.e., access to the capital investment that will be required for major retrofit and upgrade of a decades-old system.

A second operational problem is access to the land upon which new or enhanced transmission facilities will be sited. While private action can achieve some of the access that is needed, the ability of "hold-outs" on predefined lines to extract monopoly rents or to deny access altogether has meant that, for a century, transmission builders have relied on the threat or actuality of eminent domain to ensure the siting of facilities perceived as necessary for the general public good. For a century, this has been done through petitions for favorable decisions by state regulatory agencies. However, industry concern that state agencies might act too slowly led Congress, in the Energy Policy Act of 2005, to grant the Federal Energy Regulatory Commission (FERC) the authority to authorize new transmission construction in geographic areas of compelling national interest and under circumstances where state inaction had persisted for a year or more.

The third operational challenge in this area is clarifying and rationalizing the federal/state jurisdictional boundary in regard to fees and charges for the use of the transmission operating system.

Finally, a fourth area (of particular significance to the renewable energy facilities) is the tension between the long-standing governmental policies of "open access" for transmission and the reliance upon promotion of renewable energy as a rationale for new transmission facilities. This tension is serious, because there is a great risk that the rationale for building new facilities may be to serve renewable generation, but that the actual use that occurs may be to serve traditional sources. This can happen if the traditional sources have lower short-term financial costs and, thus, can more readily gain priority to use the newly built transmission infrastructure.

America's Electricity Transmission System: Jurisdiction, Challenges, and Potentials

This chapter offers an overview of America's transmission system. We start by reviewing the regulatory framework at both the federal and state levels, considering the jurisdictional problems between the two levels. Next, we confront the problems the aging transmission system presents for renewable energy facilities. Last, we consider the possibility for energy storage to serve as a means to improve system reliability and the technological improvements that would transform our network into a smart grid.

To understand how the transmission sector sees things, it is important to remember that transmission is a central component of a more complex integrated system and to recognize that the overall system is consciously operated on a "real-time" basis for purposes of reliability. Legal mandates for "deregulation" or "restructuring" may separate the ownership of various components of the overall electricity grid; however, on a minute-to-minute and hour-to-hour basis, system operators must treat it, functionally, as a unified system, explicitly considering hundreds of generation options and dozens of transmission connection choices on an ongoing and integrated basis.

When the scale for decision-making moves from immediate operational decisions to planning and investment and construction, the next key fact arises. Transmission lines connect generation to distribution networks, forming a critical link between the main components of the electricity grid.[2] In many states and regions, transmission lines are the key "bottleneck facility," with fewer than a dozen large transmission lines in place to link hundreds or thousands of generation sites with millions of electricity users.

The success of efforts to integrate greater renewable energy generation into the electric system depends on both the efficient use of existing lines and the development of new transmission lines that connect remote renewable generation facilities with major population centers. Thus, maximizing the interconnection between the grid and renewable sources is a key to the successful deployment of renewable technologies. This, however, will create tensions among competing policies. For example, a centuries-old concept of "common carriage" on ferries, bridges, railroads, telephone wires, and other public utilities means that providers of bottleneck facilities have generally not inquired into the purpose for which their facilities are used. In addition, for more than a decade now, FERC has pushed for "open access transmission tariffs," explicitly seeking to allow all generating facilities equal access to the grid, regardless of whether they are owned by the same investors who own transmission facilities or not. These policies will be hard to reconcile with preferential treatment for renewable generation or other energy resources with lower externalized costs.

It is also important to recognize that the successful "greening" of our transmission system hinges upon the research, development, and deployment of several emerging technologies. While there are policy measures that could reduce the need for future transmission capacity, any serious clean energy agenda should include updates and additions to the current system. Maximizing interconnection between the transmission system and renewable power sources—both through regulatory and structural developments—is a necessary step toward making clean power sources a strategically meaningful proportion of our fuel mix.

Federal Roles

Brief History of Transmission Regulation and Its Tensions

The legal regulation of electric transmission is one of the most complex issues in energy law because it involves at least five players: regulated utilities, nonutility generators, and local, state, and federal authorities. The complexity of the regulatory scheme creates inherent conflicts among those players.

Although the first transmission systems were rudimentary (based on copper lines, using direct current (DC)) and predicted a distributed generation system, the subsequent development of high-voltage power transmission lines using alternating current (AC)[3] allowed for power transmission over much longer distances. This spurred the industry to build larger generators to serve larger loads and populations, creating large companies. State governments reacted by extending the jurisdiction of their regulatory commissions to electric companies. This is the origin of state authority over transmission lines. Moreover, the continuous growth of these vertically integrated electric companies created the need for federal regulation.

Major Statutes

The Federal Power Act

The 1920 Federal Power Act[4] (FPA) was the first statute that regulated electric transmission at the federal level. The FPA created the regulatory framework needed to assure a reliable transmission grid by creating and vesting the Federal Power Commission (FPC), today's Federal Energy Regulatory Commission or FERC, with authority over interstate wholesale electricity trade and its associated transmission interconnections and rate-making practices. This statutory framework lasted for more than fifty years without serious change, and although it began to be modified to some degree in the 1970s, it was the basis for much of the system network architecture and physical and financial investments that are still in place.

The Public Utility Regulatory Policy Act

The Public Utility Regulatory Policy Act[5] (PURPA) was passed in 1978. In response to the OPEC boycotts of the 1970s, Congress acted to reduce dependence on foreign oil, to promote alternative energy sources and energy efficiency, and to diversify the electric power industry. One of the most important effects of this law has been its creation of a market for power generated by nonutility generators (NUGs), which now provide 7 percent of the country's power.[6] Before PURPA, only utilities could own and operate electric generating plants. PURPA required utilities to buy power from independent companies, called qualifying facilities (QFs), which could produce power for less than what it would have cost for the utility to generate the power, called the "avoided cost."[7] These provisions of PURPA affected the transmission system and required independent access to the power grid. As nonutility generators began to provide power through the grid, it became essential to offer them physical access to the system. This led to a need to explicitly and transparently define both the needed physical facilities and the interconnection obligations of generators and transmission operators. PURPA is discussed in further detail in chapter 15.

The Energy Policy Acts

The different Energy Policy Acts (1992 and 2005) have substantively altered the transmission market. For example, before the Energy Policy Act of 1992 (EPAct 1992)[8] authorized individual utility access to all interstate transmission systems, each utility that wanted to move electricity across another system had to first obtain FERC approval. Furthermore, the Energy Policy Act of 2005 (EPAct 2005) added § 216[9] to the FPA, strengthening FERC's authority by creating national transmission corridors. EPAct 2005 also extended FERC authority with the charge "to oversee mandatory reliability standards governing the nation's electricity grid."[10]

EPAct 2005 amended and repealed several important provisions of PURPA. First, EPAct 2005 added a section to PURPA requiring utilities to provide net metering services and other smart metering practices that would allow for more distributed uses of the transmission system.[11] Similarly, the Act included a requirement that a utility must provide interconnection services to any customer in that utility's service area.[12] Finally, EPAct 2005 repealed the obligation in PURPA that utilities purchase electricity from certain qualifying facilities (QFs).[13]

The Energy Independence and Security Act

Passed by Congress in 2007, the Energy Independence and Security Act[14] (EISA) included several mandates related to the modernization of the transmission system. Federal policy now explicitly declared that transmission upgrades were needed to maintain system reliability and ensure infrastructure protection.[15] Additionally, EISA required that the Department of Energy oversee and report to Congress on the development and deployment of the smart grid, with special considerations given to the potential impacts the smart grid might have on the security of the electricity infrastructure and operating capability.[16]

FERC's Authority over Transmission

FERC's authority over electric transmission is grounded in Part II and Part III of the FPA. Section 201[17] provides the authority over transmission of electricity in interstate commerce. Thus, FERC's authority extends to terms and conditions for the use of transmission facilities that are, or may be, used for interstate commerce, but does not encompass transmission facilities used solely for intrastate transmission. This is in contrast to federal authority over the terms and conditions of wholesale sales of electricity ("sales for resale"), which are subject to FERC regulation even if both buyer and seller are within a single state.

Rate Setting

Sections 205, 206, and 212 of the FPA are the bases for FERC's authority to set rates. Section 205[18] covers rate filings by public utilities engaged in the wholesale market, and § 206[19] contains provisions for rate changes initiated by FERC. In both cases, the test for compliance is the "just and reasonable rate" standard. Both sections prohibit terms of service that are unduly discriminatory or preferential. Section 212[20] allows transmission utilities to recover their costs through rates with the same conditions of nondiscrimination.

In order to achieve implementation of the 1992 EPAct, in 1996, FERC issued Order 888,[21] which required all public utilities that own, control, or operate facilities used for transmitting electric energy in interstate commerce to file nondiscriminatory open access transmission tariffs (OATTs), which contain minimum terms and conditions of service. Order 888 also permitted public utilities and transmitting utilities to seek recovery of legitimate, prudent, and verifiable stranded costs associated with providing open access transmission services under FPA § 211.[22]

Siting Transmission Projects

EPAct 2005 created federal roles in transmission siting by adding § 216[23] of the FPA. However, the main siting authorities have historically been the states; therefore this issue will be discussed in the next subsection.

Recent Issues in Federal Authority over Transmission

By amending the FPA, the EPAct 2005 gave DOE and FERC authority over electric transmission siting. These new roles consist basically of the following:

- The expansion of a DOE study about electric transmission congestion, mandated by § 1221(a).
- The grant of authority to DOE to "designate any geographic area experiencing electric energy transmission capacity constraints or congestion that adversely affects consumers as a national interest electric transmission corridor (NIETC)."[24] In designating these areas, the DOE will follow a source-and-sink approach—thus, DOE will attempt to link sources of excess generation capacity to sinks where there is currently a drain on the grid.[25] DOE has, however, recognized "that determining the exact perimeters for a National Corridor under a source-and-sink approach is more of an art than a science, and there will rarely be a clear reason to draw a boundary in one place as opposed to some number of miles to the left or right."[26]

In addition, EPAct 2005 gave FERC backstop authority over some transmission facilities in the context of the NIETCs.[27] This has improved FERC's role in transmission in cases when the authority of states and their siting processes are overly draconian or difficult to meet. For example, in the context of an NIETC, FERC may issue a construction or modification permit for a transmission facility if the state takes longer than one year after the filing of the application to act. This is especially important for renewable power sources because it limits the risk that a state might effectively deny a renewable power siting option by *delaying* action on the transmission-upgrade permits needed to make the new project viable.

However, delaying a permit is different from denying one, and in cases of denial by a state, FERC cannot use its backstop authority. For example, the Fourth Circuit Court of Appeals has held that the FPA[28] does not "give FERC permitting authority when [a] state has affirmatively denied [a new transmission] permit application within [the] one-year deadline."[29] Thus, while FERC's jurisdiction in this area has expanded, it is not without limit—the states still hold the authority to block new transmission projects by issuing a clear rejection. FERC's authority is also subordinate to some conditions that the transmission facility must meet, such as demonstrated reduction of transmission congestion and consistency with the public interest.

State Roles

The Diversity of State Regulation

One of the biggest challenges for an integrated transmission network is the authority vested in the states to regulate the transmission system. Each state has its own statutes and regulations for transmission siting, with varying transmission and distribution policies. For example, in California, all thermal generation facilities of 50 MW or more must be certified by the California Energy Commission. In Connecticut, a Certificate of Environmental Compatibility and Public Need issued by the Public Utility Commission is needed for the construction or major modification of transmission lines with more than 69 kV. Florida's transmission regulatory framework creates three different categories of siting authorizations, which are determined by the size and capacity of the transmission line. Depending on the line being built, multiple agencies can become involved, including the Department of Environmental Protection.

This scattered regulatory framework is one reason some regulators and policy makers have called for increased federal authority in this field. Moreover, the deregulation of some wholesale markets and the parochialism of most state statutes, which do not consider interstate effects or the possibilities for regional coordination, have made state regulation inefficient in the interstate context. However, it is important to note that the lack of interconnected transmission policies makes sense in the classic world of regulated, vertically integrated utilities.

Transmission Siting

Despite these disparate state policies, the diversity of state regulation does not preclude the existence of some common considerations in the world of traditional state regulation of transmission. First, most of the states vest Public Utility Commissions (PUCs) with the power to approve the construction of a new transmission line, although a significant number of states use multi-agency panels to review such requests.[30] These siting laws focus on the need for the transmission line to be built and the line's effects on system reliability. However, state regulation varies with respect to interstate transmission lines and the possibility of multistate coordination. Some states are silent, while others explicitly authorize cooperating in joint investigations or hearings.

The siting procedure usually involves other agencies, as discussed above. There is also a very prominent land use component that involves local community input into the siting process, which can contribute to lengthy and contested proceedings.

One of the recurring elements of the siting procedure has been the issue of eminent domain. Under the vertically integrated model, the utility could use eminent domain to obtain land as soon as the regulators approve the transmission line on that land. The first problem with this model is that PUCs are legally constrained in their judgment about the need for a transmission line. Sometimes these regulatory bodies apply a legal standard such as "the general good of the state" in ways that treat a healthy regional system as beneficial to their own state.[31] In other cases, they may feel constrained to consider intrastate issues without regard for the total regional picture. In a world where reliability and grid coordination are so important, there is a real need for interstate coordination. Thus, the threat of "backstop" federal authority after EPAct 2005 may play a role toward improving state siting coordination even if no federal order actually is issued. A second problem is that the model of siting review based on demonstrated need tends to lead to presentations focused on usage by specific expected generators, a conceptual model that is not fully consistent with the deregulated wholesale market.

Regional Transmission Organizations

In Order 2000,[32] FERC in 1999 encouraged the formation of Regional Transmission Organizations (RTOs) as one mechanism to ensure that the transmission grid is operated in a nondiscriminatory manner. Order 2000 prescribed twelve criteria required for FERC to grant an organization RTO status, in addition to a requirement that the organization have open architecture that will allow for the future integration of efficiency improvements that are consistent with these criteria.[33] Indeed, FERC defines an RTO as an entity that "satisfies" these requirements.[34] The terminology and substance differentiating "Independent System Operators" and RTOs is sadly confusing. Ironically, each of the two terms, read literally, seems to describe the elements of the other. In fact, the key characteristic of an RTO is FERC-certified *independence* from market participants in decision-making, while the essence of being an ISO is being a "given region's designated '*transmission operator.*'"[35]

The twelve required criteria to achieve FERC RTO status consist of four "characteristics" and eight "functions." The required characteristics are:

1. independence from market participants,
2. sufficient regional scope,
3. operational authority over all transmission facilities, and
4. exclusive authority over short-term reliability.[36]

The transmission entity must perform the following functions:

1. sole tariff administration,
2. management of transmission congestion,
3. parallel path flow,
4. ancillary services,
5. calculation of available transmission,
6. independent market monitoring,
7. transmission planning, and
8. coordination with other transmission regions.[37]

Regional Transmission Jurisdiction

There are six RTOs under FERC jurisdiction nationwide.[38] The New York ISO[39] (NYISO) and the California ISO[40] (CAISO) are the only single-state RTOs under FERC jurisdiction. The territory of the PJM Interconnection RTO[41] (PJM) extends over the mid-Atlantic region, southward to Virginia and westward to the northern portion of Illinois. The Midwest ISO[42] (MISO), which also spans westward to include most of North Dakota and the western portion of Montana, serves most of Illinois and the Midwest. All six New England states form the ISO New England[43] (ISO NE). Meanwhile, the Southwest Power Pool RTO[44] (SPP) serves the Great Plains states (excluding South Dakota) and a small portion of territory over their borders, including the Texas panhandle, western Louisiana, and western Missouri.

There are no RTOs in the northwestern states, and, likewise, no RTO serves the Southeast. The western states, which rely heavily on federal hydroelectric power, are not likely to achieve RTO status under the current regulatory regime. However, the federal power marketer, the Bonneville Power Administration (BPA), which owns the majority of transmission lines in the Pacific Northwest, carries out many similar functions. In that region, states are not inclined to disrupt a status quo of low retail electric rates.[45] Also, an RTO does not seem imminent in the mountain and desert Southwest (as distinct from the SPP of the Great Plains states), which similarly benefits from low rates and a strong federal hydroelectric presence. Utilities in the Southeast, meanwhile, have abandoned their efforts at RTO status for their organization, seTrans.

The Electric Reliability Council of Texas (ERCOT) functions as an ISO to administer a transmission grid that is located solely within Texas and only asynchronously (DC current) connected to the interstate grid. Thus, ERCOT is not subject to FERC's jurisdiction over electric utilities engaging in interstate commerce under the FPA.[46] As FERC described in a declaratory order, ERCOT's "jurisdictional status quo" is not disturbed so long as electric energy does not flow over transmission lines "between ERCOT and the rest of the continental United States."[47]

Jurisdictional Tension Between States and RTOs

A growing jurisdictional tension exists between the environmental policies of individual states and the RTOs' exercise of federal authority over transmission lines. Insufficient private investment in new generation facilities has encouraged RTOs to create capacity markets aimed at ensuring sufficient future generation capacity. These capacity markets compensate generators for making their future output available to meet system reliability needs, irrespective of whether the underlying energy will ultimately be used. At the same time, many states in RTO regions have adopted increasingly stringent renewable portfolio standards (RPS).[48] RTO-supervised capacity markets therefore mark an expansion of FERC jurisdiction at the very time when there exists neither a federal RPS nor federal regulation of greenhouse gases from generating facilities. As a 2009 D.C. Circuit decision, *Connecticut Department of Public Utility Con-*

trol v. Federal Energy Regulatory Commission,[49] makes clear, such an expansion of RTO authority could engender a severe clipping of states' environmental policy wings.

In *Connecticut PUC*, the D.C. Circuit held that FERC had jurisdiction over ISO NE's installed capacity requirements. The Connecticut PUC had argued that installed capacity requirements mandate that new generation be built—the domain of state retail jurisdiction under the FPA—while FERC had argued that these requirements were necessary for it to regulate transmission.[50] The D.C. Circuit upheld ISO NE's installed capacity requirements on grounds that they did not "directly" regulate generation facilities because no actual requirement existed that new in-state facilities be built. If the Connecticut PUC objected to the heaviness of this "incidental" regulation, the D.C. Circuit reasoned, the state could separate itself from the New England power grid.[51]

Not analyzed in the D.C. Circuit opinion is the fact that the fulfillment of state RPS requirements ultimately will require the addition of significant *new* renewable generation capacity. But the market clearing price in an RTO-run capacity market—the price bid for the final increment of capacity needed to meet reliability requirements—creates a disincentive to the construction of more costly renewable generation. The market clearing price is the price signal designed to encourage that new generation be built; new generation is thereby assured of receiving the market clearing price for its output. However, the market clearing price is typically set by natural gas—not by more costly renewables. Thus, taken to the extreme, RTOs' "incidental" regulation in the form of installed capacity requirements could preclude states from meeting their own RPS mandates. For this reason, the ongoing jurisdictional tension between RTOs and those states now at the forefront of imposing environmental regulations on the energy sector is only expected to worsen throughout the next decade.

While investor-owned utilities (IOUs) own the transmission lines operated by RTOs, nonutility generators (NUGs) own an increasing portion of generation assets in RTO territories. NUGs include the following power generators, which lack a designated service area: qualifying facilities (QFs) under PURPA; independent power producers (IPPs), which sell electricity wholesale; and cogeneration facilities that are often attached to industrial plants. OATTs for RTOs aim (largely successfully) to ensure that NUGs have "equal access" to transmission lines, i.e., access on terms that are substantially similar among differing NUGs and competitively equal to access by utility-owned generating stations.

NUGs have the status of "market participants" in the governance structure of RTOs. FERC defines a market participant as "[a]ny entity that, either directly or through an affiliate, sells or brokers electric energy, or provides transmission or ancillary services to the [RTO]."[52] FERC appears to conflate the terms "stakeholder" and "market participant."[53] Most RTO boards are comprised entirely of nonstakeholders.[54] The fact that stakeholders or market participants may contribute to the formulation of RTO policies does not ensure that RTOs are "legally accountable."[55] Rather, "it tends to operate as a check against bad decisions—the RTO staff obviously would not want to bring many issues to the stakeholders only to have their proposals rejected."[56]

Interconnection Standards

EPAct 1992 authorized FERC to require that utilities allow open and nondiscriminatory access to the transmission grid.[57] FERC initially decided whether to mandate open access to the grid on a case-by-case basis, but this proved "too costly and time consuming to provide an adequate remedy for undue discrimination throughout the market."[58] Accordingly, FERC issued Order 888 in 1996, which requires that all transmission utilities "file open access non-discriminatory transmission tariffs (OATTs) that contain minimum terms and conditions of non-discriminatory service."[59] Among these conditions is the requirement that all generators incur the same interconnection costs as would a transmission utility's affiliates.

Both RTO and non-RTO transmission providers are required to have an OATT approved by FERC. These individual OATTs are based on the updated pro forma OATT that FERC issued in Order 890.[60] The pro forma OATT prescribes the standards and procedures for a generator to obtain and receive transmission and ancillary services.[61] Service terms and conditions, including billing and payment procedures, are made available on a company's public website and are posted on the Open Access Same-Time Information System (OASIS).[62] The pro forma OATT requires that the transmission provider offer standard "point-to-point" agreements for respective short- and long-term transmission customers.[63] A point-to-point agreement refers to a contract for the provision of transmission service that is reserved or scheduled between specified points of receipt and delivery.[64] If the transmission provider has conducted a System Impact Study, and if that study concludes that additional transmission capacity is needed, then the transmission customer "shall be responsible for such costs to the extent consistent with [FERC] policy."[65]

Transmission providers are required by FERC Order 2003 to include a large generator interconnection procedure (LGIP) and a large generator interconnection agreement (LGIA) in their respective OATTs.[66] Order 2003 contains a standard LGIP and LGIA for large generating facilities, which are defined as those facilities with greater than 20 MW in generating capacity.[67] FERC issued a standard small generator interconnection procedure (SGIP) and a small generator interconnection agreement (SGIA) in Order 2006.[68] The small generator interconnection standards prescribe a more streamlined procedure for the interconnection of facilities with less than or equal to 20 MW in generating capacity. Meanwhile, FERC addressed the distinct transmission requirements of wind generation in Order 661, which is applicable to wind facilities exceeding 20 MW in generating capacity.[69] Order 661 contains a standard LGIP and LGIA for wind projects that requires facilities to remain online during low-level voltage disturbances in areas where transmission providers have demonstrated a reliability need.[70] From the point of view of a wind-generating facility, the existence of—and incorporation of—preexisting agreements is an important benefit, avoiding an indefinite time period for negotiating such an agreement; however, the substantive terms of such agreements force intermittent resources to face some of the costs of assuring coverage during low-wind periods.

Dispatch

Dispatch can be defined as (1) ordering generators and generating facilities to begin or end the delivery of electricity to a coordinated electricity grid, plus (2) the inclusion of generator output into the transmission grid.[71] Dispatch is accomplished through a planned schedule of operation. Customer loads vary greatly over the course of a day, week, and year; some generators are therefore in constant use, while others are on occasionally or only operated on days with very high loads.[72] Scheduling dispatch requires a utility to control all plants and monitor transmission lines for each control area, gathering minute-to-minute data on the operating cost of each generator and load flow. Based on collected data, the utility system planners develop a schedule for the generation and transmission of electricity.

The scheduling and dispatch of electricity is a complex process dependent on a variety of interrelated factors, including electricity market conditions, generation levels of individual units, the cost of generation (including fuel prices), the emissions generated by units, and forecasted load and transmission conditions in individual areas. Dispatch and scheduling considerations can be divided into three categories based on different priorities for generation: economic dispatch, reliability must-run dispatch, and environmental dispatch.

Economic dispatch concerns which generation units operate, at what time, and at what levels so as to minimize overall costs.[73] In practice, this means turning on generators producing the lowest-cost units first.[74] Today, most electric power systems dispatch their own generating units and their own purchased power in a way that may be said to meet these definitions. Responsibility for the key economic decisions is typically assigned to a scheduling coordinator—a generation group or an independent market operator who functions as a separate entity from the system operator.[75] Scheduling generation units to match the forecast load is done on a daily and hourly basis, in a central scheduling process by means of an economic dispatch algorithm.[76] To minimize costs, the algorithm takes into account the marginal cost of each unit's output in dollars of fuel and operational expense per additional megawatt-hour, as well as the approximate line losses associated with supplying power from each location.[77] According to DOE, economic dispatch can lead to better fuel utilization, lower fuel usage, and reduced air emissions than would result from using less efficient generation.[78]

Reliability must-run dispatch takes into consideration that a unit should be turned on in order to ensure transmission voltage control.[79] While economic dispatch requires operators to pay close attention to system conditions and to maintain secure grid operation, thus increasing operational reliability without increasing costs, in practice, increased grid reliability may not always be accomplished through economic dispatch.[80] Reliability must-run dispatch generates the power that the RTO determines is required to be on line to meet applicable reliability requirements, to meet load demand in constrained areas, or to provide voltage or security support. Reliability must-run generation requires a contract between the RTO and a generator, giving the RTO the right to call on the generator to provide energy as required to ensure the reliability of the RTO-controlled grid.

Environmental (or emissions) dispatch takes into consideration fuel cost in terms of emissions produced from a unit, as well as other environmental externalities not typically included in economic dispatch cost calculations. Environmental dispatch is not commonly practiced, having generally been ignored by RTOs in favor of economic or "reliability must-run" dispatch. As a theory of dispatch, however, it remains topical—by encompassing the "true cost" of electric generation (such as negative health implications), environmental dispatch could cause RTOs to send consumers a price signal that discourages overconsumption. And some application of environmental dispatch theory may be one path for ensuring that the renewable generating stations that are cited to justify the siting and construction of new transmission lines actually result in delivering power over those facilities.

The Effects of Renewable Energy on Transmission Needs

The Old System

The United States electricity infrastructure was not originally built to support power sharing over long distances. Initially, vertically integrated utilities developed generation and transmission systems to sell power to neighboring utilities and meet customer demand at a local level.[81] Rapid population growth and increased suburbanization resulted in a fragmented transmission system that lacked regional planning and connections. Fuel source location and proximity to load centers also play a principal role in the construction of transmission lines. Today, the success of renewable energy depends on developing new transmission lines to connect large cities and renewable power sources.[82]

Geographic constraints in the transmission system currently limit the amount of renewable power that can reach large load centers.[83] For example, wind power off the coast of Maine cannot meet the energy needs of New York because there is not currently a means to transport the electrons.[84] Similarly, areas in the Southwest that receive the most sunlight cannot readily share solar power with the Southeast on a hot day in August. The old system's limitations teach us that regional planning for new transmission lines will be an essential part of connecting renewable power to the grid.[85] However, determining the best location for new transmission connections to renewable power sources is not easy.

According to a recent ANBARIC study, there are several proposed transmission additions that would maximize the use of renewable power sources. Terrestrial and offshore wind resources on both the East and West coast could provide power to major population centers along the coastline.[86] Likewise, wind resources in the Midwest could supply power as far west as Las Vegas and as far east as Chicago. Solar and wind resources in Texas could serve the needs of large cities in the South. Unfortunately, geographic constraints and the need for new transmission lines are not the only problems that renewable energy must overcome.

Power Variability and Intermittency

In order to function properly, the electricity system must constantly balance supply and demand "in accordance with established operating criteria such as maintaining system voltages and frequency within acceptable limits."[87] Thus, maintaining this balance requires that the electric supply be constant and available at all times.[88] Unlike traditional coal and natural gas plants, renewable energy sources like wind and solar cannot always deliver predetermined levels of energy at a specified time.[89] Variability in sunlight and wind gives rise to inconsistent power generation from photovoltaics and wind turbines. While electricity systems generally manage supply variability in response to quick changes in demand, plants fueled by traditional power sources can still go offline for a variety of reasons like inclement weather, fuel interruptions (such as drought for hydro sites or rail problems for coal facilities), or operational failures. Thus, renewable power source variability is not an unprecedented issue, but may be at a scale that is more difficult to manage than other changes in supply and demand.

Supply Side Flexibility

Increasing supply flexibility, or the ability to vary output in response to changing demand,[90] can help reduce the negative effects of renewable power intermittency. This is because some of the interruptions in renewable generation can be predicted in advance (for example, a storm front may increase wind above safe levels for generation and may be forecast reliably some hours in advance, thus allowing time to bring online an alternative generator—but only if transmission paths to that source are already in existence). Building more physical transmission links between electricity systems provides utilities with more options for the exchange of power, contractually or operationally.[91] Indeed, renewable power source variability can be managed more effectively to the degree that system operators can more readily purchase and sell power over longer distances. Greater transmission availability also ensures that nonrenewable power sources can step in when the sun is not shining or when the wind is not blowing. Finally, combining power generated from several renewable energy plants could decrease overall power variability.[92]

Demand Response and Eliminating the Need for New Transmission

Managing the demand side of the electric power system can also help absorb some of the inherent variability of renewable power sources. Electric utilities already respond to spikes in demand by asking large customers to limit or cut energy consumption.[93] Conceptually, renewable power intermittency presents some of the same reliability problems as does a hot day in August.[94] Implementing demand response through nonwire options—that is, without building new transmission—is "a cost-effective way to manage both sources of variability."[95] The nonwire options include expanding efficiency programs, developing electric power storage, and promoting the smart grid.[96] Successful integration of elements from all of these emerging technologies will allow renewable energy sources to connect to end users without the need for new transmission.

The Effects of Transmission Capacity on Renewable Energy

The drive to increase renewable energy generation will undoubtedly be a principal cause for future transmission construction. Correspondingly, it is also important to consider the complement to this phenomenon: how transmission capacity—or lack thereof—has shaped the development of renewable energy. Because transmission investments and corresponding upgrades are generally bunched together,[97] regulators, utilities, and investors must attempt to predict what transmission needs will be for many years into the future. Substantive transmission upgrades in the latter half of the twentieth century did not properly consider how renewable energy would connect to the grid. Currently, imminent transmission investments offer a chance to be more forward-looking; if so, renewable energy sources will be a more viable option for utility scale implementation.

It is difficult to quantify how much a lack of available transmission has hindered renewable energy's growth, but the overall effect is clearly material. Other obstacles limiting renewable generation sources—like consumer, investor, and regulatory uncertainty—have a much less tangible presence than the physical lack of transmission. As a business matter, the first requirement for every major generating station—renewable or otherwise—has been interconnection to the grid and to potential customers. The dearth of available transmission capacity, combined with renewable energy's unfavorable economics, has been an important influence limiting the range of those who could even begin to consider the expansion of renewable energy. More recently, technological improvements have caused many consumers to change previously held notions concerning the viability of renewable energy. Now the task falls to convincing investors and regulators that connecting renewable energy to the grid will be both environmentally and economically profitable. This task requires both a willingness for existing operators to accept new prospects and a recognition of the legitimate concerns of existing operators.

Electric Power Storage

Electricity generation from renewable power sources is limited by the relative inability to store power. While some electric power storage (EPS) is possible, current technologies limit the amount of energy that utilities can store and later return to the grid.[98] Furthermore, high costs for development and deployment of EPS technology could deter investment by regulated IOUs.[99] Despite these obstacles, successful implementation of EPS will be necessary for the widespread use of renewable power sources.[100] EPS increases bidirectional energy flow by allowing energy to be produced at off-peak hours and then used when demand is highest.[101] Storing nonrenewable energy would also generally improve our aging system's reliability while increasing effective transmission capacity.[102] Additionally, a greater ability to store power—whether from fossil fuels or renewable power—would reduce the need for both transmission capacity and generating capacity, because it would provide an alternative method of meeting peak loads.

Centralized and Distributed Power Storage

There are two broad categories of EPS technology: centralized (bulk) power storage and distributed power storage.[103] Centralized power storage technologies include complex storage mechanisms "designed to store large amounts of energy."[104] Distributed power storage technologies, on the other hand, store less energy and are typically smaller than centralized units; however, distributed storage units can be combined to create a larger network of electricity storage. Each technology will play an important role in bolstering transmission reliability. The following metrics are useful for evaluating the benefits of—and potential challenges to—centralized and distributive power storage: representative application, energy discharge time span, status, capacity, and recovery rate.

Representative application describes the potential use for a given storage technology. Applications range from load shifting and peak shaving during times of high demand to frequency regulation for intermittent power sources. Energy discharge time span explains how long the storage technology can produce energy. The status metric lists current and expected developments for each storage technology. Capacity is a measure of "potential instantaneous output of a . . . storage unit, measured in watts."[105] Finally, recovery rate indicates the net power gain after subtracting the energy needed for the storage process. The table on the next page lists the major electric power storage technologies and their relationship to these metrics.

Special Storage Considerations

Three of the above technologies warrant special attention for their current and potential uses: hydroelectric pumped storage (HPS), compressed air energy storage (CAES), and plug-in hybrid electric vehicles (PHEV). Hydroelectric pumped storage is noteworthy for being the only type of storage currently used on a widespread, commercial level. As with hydroelectric generation sources, geological constraints on available water sources and environmental considerations limit the expansion of HPS. Some sources say that "it is unlikely that many more HPS facilities will be built."[106] Even if some are built, it seems clear that the United States should expect few large new areas of land to be flooded for electricity storage sites and that most of the best sites have already been developed. In contrast, according to DOE's Electricity Advisory Committee, CAES is poised to take a more substantial role in utility-scale EPS.[107] In this type of storage system, "compressors are used to inject air into a cavern developed within a salt dome or into another suitable geological formation. To recover the power, the compressed air is released, heated using a natural gas-fired combustion turbine, and used to help drive a turbine generator."[108] Energy research institutes, municipal utilities, and commercial developers have all expressed interest in further developing CAES pilot programs.[109] Whatever the emerging technology, the need is clear, because most current generating systems respond slowly to requests to increase output in response to interruptions of renewable resources.

Finally, PHEV technology offers the opportunity "to improve grid utilization, levelize demand, and improve reliability."[110] By facilitating bidirectional communication

Summary of Current Electric Power Storage Technology

Technology	Representative Applications	Energy Discharge Time Span	Status	Capacity	Recovery Rate
Hydroelectric Pumped Storage (Centralized)	Peak shaving and load shifting; future applications for wind and solar	Hours	Commercial: 37 facilities in the U.S.	Tens to hundreds of megawatts	70–75%
Compressed Air Energy Storage (Centralized)	Peak shaving and load shifting; future applications for wind and solar	Hours	Commercial: one unit apiece in Germany and Alabama; improved technology proposed	Tens to hundreds of megawatts	35–55%
Stationary Batteries (Distributed)	Frequency regulation, peak shaving and load shifting; backup power supply	Milliseconds to minutes to a few hours, depending on technology and application	Pilot projects being installed	Currently up to about one megawatt; units can be combined for larger output	Depends on scale and number of units combined
Plug-In Hybrid Electric Vehicles (Distributed)	Could be used to meet emergency and peak demand power	Hours	Research and Development	Individually kilowatt scale, but cumulatively could amount to thousands of megawatts	Depends on scale and number of units combined
Flywheels (Distributed)	Frequency regulation; emergency backup	Milliseconds to minutes depending on application	Pilot projects being installed	About 25 kilowatts per unit; combined units could be as large as 20 megawatts	85–90%

Source: Adapted from STAN KAPLAN, CONG. RESEARCH SERV., R40797, ELECTRIC POWER STORAGE 4, 5, & 9 table 1 (2009).

between utilities and end users, PHEVs can actually discharge electricity back into the grid at times of high demand. This vehicle-to-grid (V2G) concept benefits both the end user and the electricity provider.[111] Thus, PHEVs have the potential to drastically change local energy generation, consumption, and storage. Local integration of PHEVs would certainly have larger global ramifications as well: distributed power generation and storage reduces dependence on the volatile oil-producing regions of the world.

| Michael Dworkin, Javier García-Lomas Gago, Clay Francis, Paul Foley, Anna Skubikowski, and Shahin Milani

With the proper storage and interconnection technology, PHEVs could supplement renewable energy as a viable source of clean energy. When "fueled" by clean electricity, PHEVs drastically reduce the variability inherent to renewable energy sources. V2G technology is also important for the development of the smart grid. Increased communication and energy flow between user and provider, coupled with storage technology and demand response initiatives, improve the chances for smart grid success. Nonetheless, PHEV technology, along with other means of EPS, must overcome technological, regulatory, and financial barriers before utility scale implementation can be realized.

Smart Grid

What Is a Smart Grid?

The smart grid can be defined as a proposed transformation to the U.S. power grid that will apply different technologies to route power in ways that increase the efficiency of the grid, prevent blackouts, respond to a wider range of conditions, and prepare the grid to handle ever-increasing demand. Support for the development of a smart grid system became federal policy with the passage of the Energy Independence and Security Act of 2007, which set aside $100 million per fiscal year between 2008 and 2012, and established a matching program for states, utilities, and consumers to build smart grid capabilities.[112] The EISA additionally directs the National Institute of Standards and Technology (NIST) to coordinate the development of smart grid standards, which FERC would promulgate through rulemaking.[113]

How a Smart Grid Works

To better understand the advantages of a smart grid over what is currently in place, it is useful to think about what would happen when a large power line goes into outage. Currently, in the event of an outage, sensors would send signals to control area operators. The control area operators' response would be partly automatic and partly manual.[114] Their response would include increasing power plant output in some locations, stopping new transmission transactions, and otherwise containing the outage.

A smart grid would respond differently. Instead of few centralized actions, which might take longer to implement, a smart grid would respond to any changes in power generation, distribution, and the demand chain with hundreds of automatic decentralized actions.[115] Simultaneously, the generation side could respond by automatically increasing the output of generators, connecting superconducting storage devices to the system, and adjusting loads and breaker-points on power lines.[116] Generator failures are only one example. A smart grid could be designed to rapidly respond to natural disasters and even adjust for environmental events, such as clouds blocking the sun, which would hamper electricity generation from solar cells.

Once the smart grid is in place, electricity consumers and suppliers would be able to communicate and coordinate with each other. In other words, electricity generation and consumption would no longer be a one-way street between electricity generators and consumers. Consider how the Internet has enabled ordinary citizens to become citizen journalists by posting videos on YouTube, writing on their blogs, or sharing links with each other on Facebook. The word "interactive" is the best definition for today's Internet. A smart grid would also be an interactive network, and, like the Internet, it would be decentralized. The grid that is used today was designed for a time when electricity flowed from large suppliers to consumers. Now, any person possessing a solar panel could be both a consumer and a generator of electricity, and could sell his surplus energy back to the utility. With a smart grid, people will no longer be passive recipients of electricity.[117]

Smart meters, advanced electrical meters that track consumption, would make it possible for energy suppliers to charge variable electric rates that reflect these differences in the cost of generating electricity during peak or off-peak periods. A smart grid would also allow generating consumers to take advantage of different electricity rates, using relatively cheaper electricity during nonpeak hours, and selling back expensive electricity during peak hours. Smart meters would not only have the ability to communicate with the network in real time, but would also be designed to show the time at which electricity is consumed. As a result, a consumer who possesses a smart meter could better identify and adapt his or her consumption habits. Additionally, individual consumers could use load control switches to control large energy-consuming devices, such as domestic appliances, so that they could consume electricity when it is cheaper.

Functions of the Smart Grid

While regulators and policy makers agree generally about the functions of the smart grid, there is some debate about the specifics. For a point of reference, DOE outlines the following functions that are required of the smart grid in its Modern Grid Initiative Report:[118]

1. Intelligence. A smart grid system is capable of sensing system overloads and rerouting power to prevent or minimize a potential outage.
2. Efficiency. A smart grid system should be able to meet increasing consumer demand without adding infrastructure.
3. Accommodation. It should be able to accept energy from virtually any fuel source, including solar and wind, as easily and transparently as coal and natural gas.
4. Motivation. It should enable real-time communication between the consumer and utility so consumers can tailor their energy consumption based on individual preferences.
5. Opportunism. It should create new opportunities and markets by means of its ability to capitalize on plug and play innovation whenever and wherever.
6. Quality-Focused. It should be able to deliver power free of sags, spikes, disturbances, and interruptions.
7. Resilience. It should become resilient to attacks and natural disasters as it becomes more decentralized.
8. Green. A smart grid system should reduce greenhouse gas emissions through smarter consumption.

Benefits of the Smart Grid

The development of the smart grid has been driven by the desire to increase the reliability and safety of the power grid, as well as the desire to enable decentralized power so homes can be both energy clients and suppliers. Additionally, the smart grid can increase the flexibility of power consumption to clients, allowing for more selection between alternative sources such as solar, wind, and biomass, and allow for more efficiency in the generation, transmission, and consumption of electricity.

Renewable energy sources will play an important part in the implementation of the smart grid. Nonetheless, studies have questioned how reliable the smart grid can be if it depends heavily on input from renewable sources.[119] Since many renewable energy sources are intermittent, as we already know, a power infrastructure using renewable energy resources must be capable of coping with variable generation. Utilizing a variety of renewable sources within a smart grid system can overcome this problem. Stormy weather, while bad for direct solar collection, is generally good for windmills and small hydropower plants; dry, sunny weather, which is bad for hydropower, is ideal for photovoltaics.[120] The challenge of variable power supply may be further alleviated by energy storage.[121] Additionally, electricity prices can be increased at times when the sun or wind is not present, providing an incentive for consumers to decrease their energy consumption at those times.

A smart grid could also play a very important role in reducing overall energy consumption. A study by the Electric Power Research Institute estimated that smart grid technologies could help America reduce its future electricity needs by 200 billion kilowatt-hours, or 4.3 percent, by 2030.[122] The smart grid could additionally help reduce the sizable amount of energy that is wasted every year in the transmission process. A smart grid would not eliminate all inefficiencies, but rather enable suppliers to track where loss occurs and enable suppliers to watch load capacity and line use.[123] Once all this information is available to the supplier, it can optimize daily loading requirements and find ways to improve grid efficiency. Studies have shown that switching to a smart grid could save Europe $16.6 billion.[124] These savings will come from loading optimization, micro-power generation, and energy network monitoring. In Europe, 500 million machine-to-machine wireless connections would be needed to achieve this goal.[125] A recent DOE study states that a smart grid could increase electricity generation efficiency by 12 percent in the United States.[126] Another calculated that internal modernization of U.S. grids with smart grid capabilities would save between $46 and $117 billion over the next twenty years.[127]

How Smart Is the Smart Grid?

Ultimately, the true test of smart grid intelligence will be how it handles fluctuations and changes in supply of energy to and consumer demand from the grid. At every moment the supply of electricity must equal demand.[128] Otherwise, wires overheat, voltage drops, and circuit breakers snap open to protect other portions of the grid.[129] The problem is that the current system is capable of handling fluctuations that span hours or several minutes. Fluctuations from solar and wind sources, for example, occur in seconds. Therefore, the smart grid must be able to respond within seconds, or a few minutes at the most.[130] A number of solutions have been introduced that can help solve this problem. One is using sensors that monitor high-voltage transmission lines. These sensors are designed to react instantly when conditions worsen.[131] Another is using precise weather forecasts.[132] These solutions can prove very expensive, and they might not work as the utilities expect them to.

Where Should We Go from Here?

The previous sections have reviewed the most important issues concerning energy transmission by reviewing the legal framework and the jurisdictional problems associated with transmission development. Additionally, the transmission system and its future have been explored with regard to emerging technologies, including renewable energy, energy storage, and the smart grid.

What lessons can be learned from these relationships between the transmission system's past and potential? Several important issues for consideration arise from this analysis:

- First, there is a great need for a more coherent regulatory framework. The evolution of the regulation of electric transmission has shown that there is a very important need for a broader federal authority in order to assure a more reliable grid. Siting issues should be solved in a way that allows states to cooperate among themselves and with the federal authorities.
- Second, the roles of ISOs and their responsibilities for securing a reliable transmission system and market should be clarified to avoid jurisdictional problems and interference with state policy. RPSs must be encouraged and coordinated since renewables are so dependent on transmission.
- Third, the role of renewables in the transmission grid must be encouraged, even though this may entail the construction of new transmission lines. There is clear tension between two different legislative trends. The first one is reflected in FERC Orders 888 and 890 and is inspired by the idea of open access to transmission systems to all fuel sources. The second trend is the need to encourage a preference for renewables and their dispatch and transmission.
- Fourth, environmental dispatch should be encouraged in ISO's practices.
- Fifth, technological progress is intrinsically associated with electric transmission. Thus, a smarter grid is a key concept in the future of energy transmission and the role of renewable energy sources in that transmission—accordingly, research and development in this field must be encouraged. However, research, development, and deployment have to be encouraged not only in the smart grid field, but also in the energy storage field.

Transmission and Renewables: FERC Initiatives Leading the Way

Much of the renewable energy potential in the United States is located in areas that are remote from the transmission grid. FERC is acting to encourage increased grid investment, improve regional transmission planning, and remove regulatory barriers at the wholesale level to address development of renewable energy.[133]

FERC is exploring options to end the cyclical response to bunched investments through more efficient integration of variable energy resources (VER) into the grid.[134] According to FERC Chairman Jon Wellinghoff, FERC will "examine whether existing rules, regulations, tariffs or practices within the Commission's jurisdiction hinder such efficient integration."[135] Additionally, FERC Commissioner Phillip Moeller noted that FERC is resolved to overcoming the technological and regulatory barriers inherent to variable energy resource generation.[136] By "bolster[ing] investment in the nation's transmission infrastructure . . . and reduc[ing] transmission congestion," FERC will ensure that the next wave of transmission investment will be transformational.[137]

FERC has also supported initiatives aimed at the future development of the smart grid.[138] In December of 2009, FERC "agreed that Pacific Gas and Electric Company (PG&E) [could] recover a portion of its costs in transmission rates for a regional project . . . ensur[ing] electric power reliability for consumers and integrat[ing] variable renewable resources into its system."[139] FERC Chairman Wellinghoff explained, "[o]ne goal of [FERC's] smart grid policy is to protect consumers while providing early-moving utilities that invest in smart grid technologies with the cost recovery assurances they need to take that important first step."[140] In the end, FERC's willingness to balance consumer and utility interest will benefit both groups: transmission upgrades will ultimately lower costs to consumers and increase utility productivity. It is not yet clear how Regional Transmission Organizations or Independent System Operators will act to support increased growth of renewable resources; and state commitments to renewable resource portfolios will be reflected in not yet achieved transmission siting policies if they are to be successful.

Balancing "Neutral" Regulated Utilities against a Priority for Most-Needed Resources

Even with substantial regulatory and financial support from FERC, bridging the transmission gap will not be an easy task. If regulators and utilities respectively approve and build transmission to extend renewable energy's reach, then ratepayers will want some type of assurance that more renewable power actually flows through the lines. Adding a new transmission line through someone's backyard to transport more dirty electrons will seldom be a socially tolerable practice. Indeed, renewable energy's rise to mainstream use hinges on the realization that carbon-based fuels are destroying our atmosphere, just as particulates are destroying lungs. Accordingly, using renewable power to justify new transmission construction raises the following question: should FERC continue to grant open access to new transmission or should it limit new lines for use by renewable power sources? To abate the imminent dangers of global climate change, FERC should seriously consider the latter option. Without some type of green power preference, cheap, unhealthful fuels will continue to clog our atmosphere and our transmission lines.

The path ahead will not be easy. It requires both enhanced use of existing transmission facilities and introduction of new ones. This means a significant capital investment requirement. At the same time, it requires changing rules for a system that is already in flux as it tries to integrate increased wholesale sales over longer distances, greater reliability obligations, and multi-owner use of systems that were once designed for vertically integrated single-company operations. Ensuring that new, renewable, generating resources have adequate use of existing infrastructure and that they actually do get a chance to use the new systems constructed in their name will require conscious attention from both FERC and state utility commissions. However, new technologies, such as digitally assisted system operations, offer the chance to make this transition; and America's needs for reliability, environmental sustainability, and financially efficient energy sources also all require the change. Knowing that it can be done, it is time to make sure the transition occurs.

Notes

1. Zhen Zhang & Matthew Stern, *NERC Today and Tomorrow: Living in the New World of Mandatory Reliability Standards*, PUB. UTILS FORTNIGHTLY, Mar. 2010.

2. For an illustration of the basic structure of an electric system, see U.S.-CANADA POWER SYSTEM OUTAGE TASK FORCE, FINAL REPORT ON THE AUGUST 14, 2003 BLACKOUT IN THE UNITED STATES AND CANADA: CAUSES AND RECOMMENDATIONS 5 fig. 2.1 (Apr. 2004), *available at* https://reports.energy.gov/BlackoutFinal-Web.pdf.

3. This method of transmission was discovered in the late 1880s by Nikola Tesla, who sold the patent to George Westinghouse.

4. 16 U.S.C. §§ 791a–823d.

5. 16 U.S.C. §§ 2601–26045.

6. U.S. DEP'T OF ENERGY, U.S. ENERGY INFO. ADMIN., U.S. STATES, http://www.eia.doe.gov/overview_hd.html (last visited Oct. 24, 2010).

7. 18 C.F.R. § 292.304(b)(2).

8. Pub. L. No. 102-486, 106 Stat. 2776 (1992).

9. 16 U.S.C. § 824p.

10. FACT SHEET: ENERGY POLICY ACT OF 2005, FEDERAL ENERGY REGULATORY COMMISSION 2 (2006).

11. 16 U.S.C. § 2621(d)(11). *See also* 16 U.S.C. § 2621(d)(14).

12. 16 U.S.C. § 2621(d)(15).

13. 16 U.S.C. § 824(a-3)(m)(1).

14. 42 U.S.C. § 17000.

15. 42 U.S.C. § 17381.

16. FRED SISSINE, CONG. RESEARCH SERV., RL34294, ENERGY INDEPENDENCE AND SECURITY ACT OF 2007: A SUMMARY OF MAJOR PROVISIONS 20 (2007).

17. 16 U.S.C. § 824.

18. *Id.* § 824d.

19. *Id.* § 824e.

20. *Id.* § 824k.

21. Order No. 888, Promoting Wholesale Competition Through Open Access Non-Discriminatory Transmission Services by Public Utilities, 61 Fed. Reg. 21,540 (May 10, 1996) [hereinafter Order 888]; *reh'g*, Order No. 888-A, 62 Fed. Reg.12,274 (Jan. 21, 1997); *reh'g*, Order No. 888-B, 81 FERC ¶ 61,248 (1997).

22. 16 U.S.C. § 824j.

23. *Id.* § 824p.

24. *Id.* § 824p(a)(1).

25. U.S. DEP'T OF ENERGY, NATIONAL ELECTRIC TRANSMISSION CONGESTION REPORT AND FINAL NATIONAL CORRIDOR DESIGNATIONS, FREQUENTLY ASKED QUESTIONS 2–3 (2007), *available at* http://nietc.anl.gov/documents/docs/FAQs_re_National_Corridors_10_02_07.pdf.

26. *Id.* at 3.

27. 16 U.S.C. § 824p(a)(2).

28. *Id.* § 824p(b)(1)(C)(i).

29. Piedmont Envtl. Council v. FERC, 558 F.3d 304 (4th Cir. 2009).

30. *See, e.g.*, 30 Vt. Stat. Ann. § 248. *See also* Michael Dworkin et al., *Revisiting "The Environmental Duties of Public Utility Commissions,"* 7 Vt. J. Envtl. L. 1 (2006); Michael Dworkin et al., *The Environmental Duties of Public Utility Commissions*, 18 Pace Envtl. L. Rev. 325 (2001).

31. 30 Vt. Stat. Ann. § 248.

32. Regional Transmission Organizations, 89 FERC ¶ 61,285, 65 Fed. Reg. 809 (1996) (codified at 18 C.F.R. pt. 2).

33. 18 C.F.R. § 35.34(l). 34. *Id.* § 35.34(b)(1).

35. Michael H. Dworkin & Rachel Aslin Goldwasser, *Ensuring Consideration of the Public Interest in the Governance and Accountability of Regional Transmission Organizations*, 28 Energy L.J. 552 (2007).

36. 18 C.F.R § 35.34(j).

37. *Id.* § 35.34(k).

38. *See* FERC, RSO/ITO Map, http://www.ferc.gov/industries/electric/indus-act/rto/rto-map.asp.

39. Regional Transmission Organizations, 89 FERC ¶ 61,285 (1999) [hereinafter Order No. 2000]; *order on reh'g*, Order No. 2000-A, FERC Stats. & Regs. ¶ 31,092 (2000), *aff'd sub nom.* Pub. Util. Dist. No. 1 of Snohomish Cnty. v. FERC, 272 F.3d 607 (D.C. Cir. 2001).

40. Cal. Indep. Sys. Operator Corp., 107 FERC ¶ 61,274 (2004).

41. PJM Interconnection, LLC, 96 FERC ¶ 61,061 (2001).

42. Midwest Indep. Transmission Sys. Operator, Inc., 97 FERC ¶ 61, 326 (2001), *reh'g denied*, 103 FERC ¶ 61,169.

43. ISO New Eng., Inc., 106 FERC ¶ 61,280 (2004).

44. Southwest Power Pool, Inc., 106 FERC ¶ 61,110 (2004).

45. In 2005, these states succeeded in persuading BPA not to join Grid West—which would have been FERC jurisdictional. *See* Bonneville Power Admin., 112 FERC ¶ 61,012 (2005).

46. 16 U.S.C. § 824(a).

47. ISO-NE Proposed Elimination of the Peaking Unit Safe Harbor Mechanism, 118 FERC ¶ 61,108 (2007).

48. A national map with RPS data for each state is available at http://www.dsireusa.org. *See also* chapter 4, *supra*, for a discussion on RPSs.

49. Conn. Dep't of Pub. Util. Control v. FERC, 569 F.3d 477 (D.C. Cir. 2009).

50. *Id.* at 481.

51. *Id.* at 482.

52. 18 C.F.R. § 35.34(b)(2).

53. Dworkin & Goldwasser, *supra* note 35, at 558 n.59.

54. *Id.* at 563–65. Other RTO boards are comprised exclusively of nonstakeholder interests or, increasingly, a hybrid of the two. Each type of board presents problems of accountability.

55. *Id.* at 570.

56. *Id.*

57. Federal Power Act, 16 U.S.C. §§ 211(a), 213(a) (as amended).

58. New York v. FERC, 535 U.S. 1, 3 (2002).

59. Order 888, *supra* note 21, ¶ 61,080.

60. Preventing Undue Discrimination and Preference in Transmission Service, RM05-25-000, FERC Stats. & Regs. ¶ 31,241 att. C (2007), *amended by* RM05-17-003, 123 FERC ¶ 61,299 att. B (2008).

61. *Id.*, 123 FERC ¶ 61,299 att. B, § 3.

62. *Id.* § 4.

63. *Id.* § 13.4.

64. *Id.* § 1.14.

65. *Id.* § 27.

66. Standardization of Generator Interconnection Agreements and Procedures, RM02-1-000, 104 FERC ¶ 61,103 (2003), *amended by* RM02-1-006, 111 FERC ¶ 61,401 (2005).

67. *Id.* app. B, § 1.

68. Standardization of Small Generator Interconnection Agreements and Procedures, RM02-12-000, FERC Stats. & Regs. ¶ 31,180 apps. E–F (2005).

69. Interconnection for Wind Energy, RM05-4-000, 111 FERC ¶ 61,353 (2005).

70. *Id.* at 12, app. G.

71. *See* Michael H. Brown & Richard P. Sedano, Nat'l Council on Elec. Pol'y, Electricity Transmission: A Primer 60 (2004); Sarah McKinley, Natural Gas and Electricity Glossary 17 (2001).

72. Peter S. Fox-Penner, Electric Power Transmission and Wheeling: A Technical Primer 19 (1990).

73. Alexandra Von Meier, Electric Power Systems: A Conceptual Introduction 264 (2006).

74. Fox-Penner, *supra* note 72, at 20. The 2005 EPAct defines "economic dispatch" to mean "the operation of generation facilities to produce energy at the lowest cost to reliably serve consumers, recognizing any operational limits of generation and transmission facilities." 42 U.S.C. § 16,432(b) (2005).

75. Von Meier, *supra* note 73, at 264.

76. *Id.*

77. *Id.*

78. U.S. Dep't of Energy, The Value of Economic Dispatch: A Report to Congress Pursuant to Section 1234 of the Energy Policy Act of 2005, at 3–4 (2005), *available at* http://www.oe.energy.gov/DocumentsandMedia/value.pdf.

79. Robert H. Sarikas, Introduction to Electrical Theory and Power Transmission 73 (1995).

80. DOE, The Value of Economic Dispatch, *supra* note 78.

81. Elec. Advisory Council, Keeping the Lights On in a New World 3 (2009), *available at* http://www.oe.energy.gov/DocumentsandMedia/adequacy_report_01-09-09.pdf.

82. *Id.* at 16.

83. Paul Komor, Pew Ctr. on Global Climate Change, Wind and Solar Electricity: Challenges and Opportunities 13 (2009), *available at* http://www.pewclimate.org/docUploads/wind-solar-electricity-report.pdf.

84. *See* Brown & Sedano, *supra* note 71, at 37 (noting that bottlenecks preventing the flow of electrons are prevalent in New England, with specific reference to constraints on Maine's connection to the grid). The effect of those transmission constraints is already visible when comparing the locational marginal price (LMP) costs for Maine to those for other New England States. *See LMP Map*, ISO-NE.com, http://www.iso-ne.com/portal/jsp/lmpmap/Index.jsp (last visited Oct. 28, 2010).

85. Elec. Advisory Council, *supra* note 81, at 48.

86. Ed Krapels & John M. Edwards, ANBARIC Transmission, Integrating 200,000 MWs of Renewable Energy into the US Power Grid: A Practical Proposal 16, 17 (2009), *available at* http://anbarictransmission.com/wp-content/uploads/2009/03/integrating-200000mws-december_2009.pdf.

87. N. Am. Elec. Reliability Corp., Accommodating High Levels of Variable Generation 3 (2009) *available at* http://www.nerc.com/files/IVGTF_Report_041609.pdf.

88. Joseph P. Tomain & Richard D. Cudahy, Energy Law in a Nutshell 257 (2004).

89. Elec. Advisory Council, *supra* note 81, at 12–13.

90. Komor, *supra* note 83, at 24.

91. *Id.*

92. For example, combing a windy night with a sunny but still day creates a power source that is more reliable than wind or solar alone.

93. Komor, *supra* note 83, at 25.

94. *Id.*

95. *Id.*

96. Of the available demand response instruments, many legal scholars and regulators have declared efficiency programs to be the most important tool for increasing reliability while reducing the need for new transmission. *See generally* Michael Dworkin, Kari Twaite, & Dan York, *A Driving Need, A Vital Tool: The Rebirth of Efficiency Programs for Electric Customers, in* Capturing the Power of Electric Restructuring (Joey Lee Miranda ed., 2009).

97. These investments are bunched together in the sense that transmission upgrades occur infrequently. Indeed, regulators and utilities look to improve transmission capacity with completed projects having a multidecadal lifespan.

98. Stan Kaplan, Cong. Research Serv., R40797, Electric Power Storage 1 (2009).

99. U.S. Dep't of Energy, Elec. Advisory Council, Bottling Electricity: Storage as a Strategic Tool for Managing Variability and Capacity Concerns in the Modern Grid 16 (2009) [hereinafter Bottling Electricity], *available at* http://www.oe.energy.gov/DocumentsandMedia/final-energy-storage_12-16-08.pdf.

100. *Id.* at 6.

101. Wind, for example, often blows strongest at night when demand is lowest. EPS technology could put that electricity into the grid later the next day when demand is higher, thus compensating for wind power's intermittency and variable generation.

102. Bottling Electricity, *supra* note 99, at 6.

103. Kaplan, *supra* note 98, at 5.

104. *Id.*

105. *Id.* at 2.

106. *Id.* at 5. Interestingly, one of the first major cases in environmental law, *Scenic Hudson Preservation Conference v. Federal Power Commission*, 354 F.2d 608 (1965), arose from a dispute over a proposed pumped storage plant.

107. Bottling Electricity, *supra* note 99, at 1.

108. Kaplan, *supra* note 98, at 6.

109. Bottling Electricity, *supra* note 99, at 1.

110. *Id.* at 7.

111. *Id.* at 21.

112. Energy Independence and Security Act § 422, 42 U.S.C. § 17082 (2007).

113. *Id.* § 130; 42 U.S.C. §17385.

114. Peter Fox-Penner, *Reinventing the Grid: The Electrical Distribution Grid Is an Antiquated Hodgepodge. How Do We Restructure It?*, Energy, June 24, 2004, at 9.

115. *Id.*

116. *Id.*

117. *Europe Electricity: A Smart Approach*, Energy & Electricity Forecast, Nov. 12, 2009, at 1.

118. *See* U.S. Dep't of Energy, Nat'l Energy Tech. Lab, The NETL Smart Grid Implementation Strategy (SGIS), *available at* http://www.netl.doe.gov/moderngrid/docs/A%20Vision%20for%20the%20Modern%20Grid_Final_v1_0.pdf.

119. *See* Dan Charles, *Renewables Test IQ of the Grid*, Science, Apr. 10, 2009.

120. Meir Shargal & Doug Houseman, *Myths and Realities of Renewable Energy*, SmartGridNews.com (Apr. 3, 2009), http://www.smartgridnews.com/artman/publish/commentary/Myths_and_Realities_of_Renewable_Energy-556.html.

121. *Id.*

122. Jeff St. John, *EPRI Plugs Smart Grid for Energy Savings*, greentechmedia (Dec. 4, 2008), http://www.greentechmedia.com/articles/read/epri-plugs-smart-grid-for-energy-savings-5308/.

123. *Id.*

124. *Id.*

125. *Id.*

126. R.G. Prat et al., Pac. Nw. Lab., The Smart Grid: An Estimation of the Energy and CO₂ Benefits (2010), *available at* http://energyenvironment.pnl.gov/news/pdf/PNNL-19112_Revision_1_Final.pdf.

127. L.D. Kannberg et al., Pac. Nw. Lab., GridWise: The Benefits of a Transformed Energy System 25 (2003) (under contract with the United States Department of Energy), *available at* http://www.pnl.gov/main/publications/external/technical_reports/PNNL-14396.pdf.

128. Charles, *supra* note 119, at 172–75.

129. *Id.*

130. *Id.*

131. *Id.*

132. *Id.*

133. Fed. Energy Regulatory Comm'n, Integration of Renewables, http://www.ferc.gov/industries/electric/indus-act/integration-renew.asp (last visited Oct. 28, 2010).

134. Integration of Variable Energy Resources, 130 FERC ¶ 61,053 (2010), *available at* http://www.ferc.gov/whats-new/comm-meet/2010/012110/E-4.pdf.

135. Fed. Energy Regulatory Comm'n, Statement of Chairman Jon Wellinghoff on Efficient Integration of Renewables into the Grid (Jan. 21, 2010), http://www.ferc.gov/media/statements-speeches/wellinghoff/2010/01-21-10-wellinghoff-E-4.pdf.

136. Fed. Energy Regulatory Comm'n, Statement of Commissioner Philip D. Moeller on Efficient Integration of Renewables into the Grid (Jan. 21, 2010), http://www.ferc.gov/media/statements-speeches/moeller/2010/01-21-10-moeller-E-4.pdf.

> The challenges facing us are significant, but not insurmountable. Besides the critical need for new transmission lines to deliver these clean domestic resources, we also need to address the difficulties of integrating into the grid an energy supply that is variable, which by its very nature has characteristics unlike those of traditional generation sources that are easily controlled and dispatched.

137. W. Grid Dev., LLC, 130 FERC ¶ 61,056 (2010), *available at* http://www.ferc.gov/whats-new/comm-meet/2010/012110/E-6.pdf.

138. *See* Smart Grid Policy, 128 FERC ¶ 61,060 (2009), *available at* www.ferc.gov/whats-new/comm-meet/2009/071609/E-3.pdf.

139. News Release, Fed. Energy Regulatory Comm'n, FERC Approves First Smart Grid Proposal Using New Policy, (Dec. 17, 2009), http://www.ferc.gov/media/news-releases/2009/2009-4/12-17-09-E-4.pdf.

140. *Id.*

State Actions on Clean Energy: A Fifty-State Survey

This appendix briefly summarizes the laws of each of the fifty states relating to energy efficiency and renewable energy. More detailed coverage, with full citations and periodic updates, can be found in a website maintained by Columbia Law School's Center for Climate Change Law, www.columbiaenergylaw.com. Much of the information presented in this summary is drawn from the Database of State Incentives for Renewable Energy (DSIRE), http://www.dsireusa .org/, and the U.S. Department of Energy's Office of Energy Efficiency and Renewable Energy's Alternative Fuels & Advanced Vehicles Data Center, http://www.afdc.energy.gov/afdc/laws/. Abbreviations are spelled out in the list of abbreviations on pp. xxxvii–xlii.

Alabama

Financial Incentives

Loan Programs: Alabama's Local Government Energy Loan Program offers zero-interest loans to local governments, schools, and public colleges and universities for renewable energy systems and energy efficiency improvements.

Grants: The Biomass Energy Program assists businesses, up to $75,000 in interest subsidy payments, in installing biomass energy systems. The Alabama Biofuels for Schools Grant Program provides grants up to $2,500 to cover the costs of cleaning existing fuel tanks to prepare for the use of biodiesel blends in school buses.

Rebates: Rebates are available for select Energy Star appliances installed in households in Alabama.

Rules and Regulations

Building Codes, Appliance, and Equipment Standards: All new public buildings are subject to the 2006 International Energy Conservation Code (IECC), though residential and commercial

---

The appendix was put together by Kelly Cataldo, Jerry Chen, Michael Dreibelbis, Michael Panfil, Mark Popovsky, and Ben Schifman, all of the Environmental Law Clinic at Columbia Law School, and by Julia Ciardullo, of the Center for Climate Change Law at Columbia Law School.

construction is not yet required to comply. The Residential Energy Code for Alabama is a voluntary code based on the 2000 IECC.

Government Procurement: State departments and agencies have a goal of reducing energy consumption in conditioned facilities by 20 percent by 2010, relative to 2005 levels, and must purchase Energy Star equipment when cost-effective. State departments and agencies must also designate an Energy Officer to be given the authority to study, investigate, and recommend potential energy saving procedures within the agency.

Policies, Plans, and Governmental Affiliations

Policies and Plans: Alabama has released a final report, Policy Planning to Reduce Greenhouse Gas Emissions in Alabama, which includes a number of recommended greenhouse gas (GHG) reduction strategy options.

Government Entities: Alabama Department of Economic and Community Affairs.

Regional Memberships: Alabama is a member of the Southern Governors Association (SGA), which has issued an economic analysis and report to identify cost-effective policies and strategies that could be implemented independently at the state level to address concerns about the impacts of climate change.

Alaska

Financial Incentives

Tax Benefits: In certain areas of Alaska, the tax rate on fuel blended with ethanol is reduced by $0.06 per gallon as compared to the tax rate on other motor fuels.

Loan Programs: Alaska offers interest rate reductions to home buyers purchasing energy-efficient homes and offers loans to make energy-efficient home improvements. The Alaska Power Project Loan Fund provides loans for small-scale power production facilities, conservation facilities, and bulk fuel storage facilities. Loans are also available to state and local governments and schools for energy efficiency improvements through the Alaska Energy Efficiency Revolving Loan Fund Program. Alaska requires financial institutions to take into consideration the economic benefits of alternative energy systems, life-cycle energy costs, energy-efficient building design, and energy conservation when financing homes and buildings with state financial assistance.

Grants: Alaska provides funds for energy conservation improvements in residential buildings, grants to utilities, independent power producers, and local governments for renewable energy projects, and grants for projects deploying technology that is expected to be commercially viable within five years.

Rebates: Alaska offers rebates to homeowners who make energy efficiency improvements to an existing home and to purchasers of a newly constructed 5 Star Plus home. Alaska's Residential Energy-Efficient Appliance Rebate Program offers rebates for select Energy Star appliances installed in disabled Alaskans' households.

Bonds: $250 million in bond financing is available for energy efficiency projects through the Alaska Housing and Finance Corporation.

Rules and Regulations

Renewable Portfolio Standard: Alaska has established a target of producing 50 percent of its electricity from renewable resources by 2025.

Facility Siting and Permitting: Parties in Alaska may enter into solar easement contracts.

Building Codes, Appliance, and Equipment Standards: Alaska has adopted the residential provisions of the 2006 IECC, with Alaska-specific amendments.

Electricity Transmission, Interconnection, and Storage: All electric utilities subject to economic regulation are required to offer net metering to renewable energy facilities up to 25 kilowatts (kW) in capacity.

Policies, Plans, and Governmental Affiliations

Policies and Plans: The Alaska Climate Change Mitigation Advisory Group released a final report in 2009 with thirty-two policy recommendations for further study that could reduce GHG emissions in Alaska. In November 2010, the Alaska Department of Fish and Game released its Climate Change Strategy, describing the potential impacts of climate change and outlining an approach to statewide adaptation.

Government Entities: Alaska Climate Change Mitigation Advisory Group, Alaska Climate Impact Assessment Commission, Alaska Department of Fish and Game, Alaska Energy Authority, Alaska Housing Finance Corporation, Regulatory Commission of Alaska.

Regional Memberships: Alaska is an observer of the Western Climate Initiative (WCI) and a member of the Western Governors' Association (WGA), which has adopted a number of policy resolutions and initiatives in support of clean energy.

Arizona

Financial Incentives

Tax Benefits: Arizona's Renewable Energy Tax Incentives Program provides tax incentives to renewable energy companies expanding in or locating to Arizona. The program offers a refundable income tax credit of up to 10 percent and a reduction on real and personal property taxes of up to 75 percent. Arizona's Commercial/Industrial Solar Energy Tax Credit Program subsidizes the initial cost of solar energy devices by providing businesses a tax credit worth 10 percent of the installed cost of the solar energy device. An income tax credit is available to taxpayers who install a residential solar or wind energy device. In addition, the Arizona Department of Revenue is authorized to provide $20 million annually in tax credits to qualified renewable energy systems installed on or after December 31, 2010, based on the amount of electricity produced. Arizona also offers an individual income tax subtraction to taxpayers who sell one or more energy-efficient single-family residences, condominiums, or town houses, or convert an existing wood fireplace to a qualifying wood stove. The retail sale of solar energy devices to contractors is exempt from sales tax. Renewable energy technologies, combined heat and power (CHP) systems, and energy-efficient building components are considered to add no value to the property for property tax assessment purposes, and renewable energy equipment owned by utilities is assessed at 20 percent of its depreciated cost for the purpose of determining property tax.

Grants: The Arizona Biofuel Conversion Program provides grants of up to $75,000 for the cost of projects that result in new or converted biofuel storage and dispensing infrastructure.

Rules and Regulations

Renewable Portfolio Standard: Arizona's renewable portfolio standard (RPS) requires utilities to obtain renewable energy credits (RECs) from eligible renewable resources to meet 15 percent of their retail electric load by 2025. Eligible sources include solar photovoltaics (PV), solar thermal, landfill gas, wind, biomass, anaerobic digestion, hydro, geothermal electric and heat pumps, CHP and cogeneration, fuel cells using renewable fuels, and certain energy efficiency technologies. In addition, utilities must procure 20 percent of their RPS-eligible power from distributed renewable (DR) sources in 2010, 25 percent from DR in 2011, and 30 percent from DR in 2012 and thereafter.

Facility Siting and Permitting: Owners of solar PV systems and solar water heating systems in Arizona are required to obtain a building permit before their systems may be installed. Individual property owners in Arizona have a right to solar energy access protected by state law, but a homeowners' association may adopt reasonable rules governing the placement of solar installations, provided that such rules do not preclude such installations. New thermal electric, nuclear, and hydroelectric generation projects greater than 100 megawatts (MW) must receive a Certificate of Environmental Compatibility from the Arizona State Power Plant and Transmission Lines Siting Committee and approval from the Arizona Corporation Committee before construction.

Building Codes, Appliance, and Equipment Standards: Arizona has established minimum energy efficiency standards for appliances (however, some have been superseded by subsequent federal standards). Solar systems sold in Arizona must comply with certain standards adopted by the Arizona Department of Commerce.

Electricity Transmission, Interconnection, and Storage: The Arizona Corporation Commission initiated a rulemaking process to establish statewide interconnection standards for distributed generation (DG). This proceeding is still in progress, and draft guidelines have been established in the interim, which apply to systems up to 10 MW in capacity. Net metering is available to customers who generate electricity from certain renewable energy technologies.

Government Procurement: Arizona law requires that all new state-funded buildings procure at least 10 percent of their energy from renewable resources and meet the Leadership in Energy and Environmental Design (LEED) Silver standard. Arizona law also requires that new state building projects over 6,000 square feet follow prescribed solar design standards and that solar improvements be evaluated on the basis of life cycle costs. State agencies must purchase hybrid electric vehicles (HEVs), alternative fuel vehicles (AFVs), and/or vehicles that meet low-GHG emissions standards.

Policies, Plans, and Governmental Affiliations

Policies and Plans: Former Governor Napolitano established a statewide goal to reduce Arizona's GHG emissions to 2000 levels by 2020, and 50 percent below 2000 levels by 2040.

Government Entities: Arizona Corporation Commission, Arizona Department of Commerce, Arizona Department of Revenue, Arizona Power Plant and Transmission Lines Siting Committee.

Regional Memberships: Arizona is a member of the Southwest Climate Change Initiative, the WGA, WCI, and the International Carbon Action Partnership (ICAP).

Arkansas

Financial Incentives

Tax Benefits: Arkansas provides a tax exemption for windmill blade and component manufacturers.

Loan Programs: The Arkansas Industrial Energy Technology Loan Program provides low-interest loans to industries in Arkansas to implement energy efficiency retrofits or install renewable energy technologies. The Sustainable Building Design Revolving Loan Fund provides loans for energy efficiency improvements made to state buildings. Arkansas also offers low-interest loans of up to $45,000 to small businesses for pollution control and energy efficiency measures.

Grants: The Arkansas Alternative Fuels Development Fund provides grants and other financial incentives to alternative fuel producers and distributors.

Rebates: Arkansas offers rebates of up to $200 for the purchase of certain Energy Star appliances. Each household is eligible for one rebate in each of several categories. Arkansas also offers rebates for newly installed residential and commercial renewable energy systems and solar water heating systems.

Rules and Regulations

Building Codes, Appliance, and Equipment Standards: Residential and commercial buildings in Arkansas are subject to the 2004 Arkansas Energy Code for New Building Construction, which is based on the 2003 IECC and incorporates by reference the American Society of Heating, Refrigerating and Air-Conditioning Engineers (ASHRAE) Standard 90.1-2001 for buildings other than low-rise residential buildings.

Electricity Transmission, Interconnection, and Storage: Residential renewable energy systems, microturbines, and fuel cells of fewer than 25 kW and commercial systems of fewer than 300 kW are eligible for interconnection and net metering. For net metering, customers' net excess generation (NEG) is credited to their account, and any remaining excess generation at the end of an annualized period is returned to the utility.

Government Procurement: The Arkansas Energy Office must develop a plan for a 20 percent reduction from 2008 energy use levels in all existing major state-owned facilities by 2014 and a 30 percent reduction by 2017. New state-owned constructions must be at least 10 percent more efficient than required by ASHRAE Standard 90.1-2007. Arkansas must also complete an energy audit of every public agency by 2014. All diesel-powered motor vehicles, light trucks, and equipment owned or leased by state agencies are required to use diesel fuel that contains a minimum of 2 percent biofuel, with certain exceptions.

Policies, Plans, and Governmental Affiliations

Policies and Plans: The Governor's Commission on Global Warming issued a final report in October 2008 recommending that Arkansas adopt a goal of reducing the state's GHG emissions below 2000 levels according to the following schedule: 20 percent by 2020; 35 percent by 2025; and 50 percent by 2035. The report also proposed a set of fifty-four policies to meet this goal.

Government Entities: Arkansas Department of Environmental Quality, Arkansas Economic Development Commission, Arkansas Energy Office, Arkansas Public Service Commission, Governors Commission on Global Warming.

Regional Memberships: Arkansas is a member of the SGA.

California

Financial Incentives

Tax Benefits: California has established an exemption from the state's sales and use tax for expenses related to the design, manufacture, production, and assembly of renewable energy, CHP, and alternative transportation equipment. Projects must apply for the exemption through the California Alternative Energy and Advanced Transportation Financing Authority (CAEATFA). CAEATFA may give out $100 million in such exemptions per year, and then must provide the California legislature with notice of any further exemptions. Solar systems are also completely exempt from California's property tax until 2017.

Grants: The School Facility Program provides grants to school districts for the modernization of school facilities, including energy efficiency improvements.

Rebates: California has committed approximately $3.2 billion toward rebates for new solar systems through 2016. Recipients receive rebates on either a per-watt or per-kWh basis, depending on the size of the system. Of that $3.2 billion, California has dedicated $216 million to rebates for PV installations on low-income housing. Half of that $216 million is funding the Multi-Family Affordable Solar Housing (MASH) program, and the other half is funding the Single-Family Affordable Solar Housing (SASH) Program. California's New Solar Homes Partnership has committed $400 million over ten years to promote the incorporation of energy efficiency measures and solar systems into new residential construction. Wind systems up to 50 kW and fuel cell systems up to 30 kW using renewable fuels are eligible for rebates on a per-watt basis, up to 30 kW. A total of $83 million has been designated for the Self-Generation Incentive Program, through which customers of several of California's utilities who generate electricity through wind turbines or fuel cells are eligible for rebates.

Other Financial Incentives: California has authorized a feed-in tariff for small renewable energy generators that are interconnected to the grid. The feed-in tariff law was amended in 2009, but will not take effect until new regulations are promulgated. The current program requires certain utilities to pay a tariff to generators up to 1.5 MW in capacity and other utilities to pay a tariff to generators up to 1.0 MW in capacity. The new rules will require all utilities serving 75,000 or more customers to pay tariffs to generators up to 3 MW in capacity. There is a cap on the program: 228.447 MW of total capacity under the existing program, to be raised to 750 MW under the new rules. Rates are based on the length of the contract between the generator and the utility, the year in which the contract was made, which utility is purchasing the power, and the time of day and month during which the power was produced. California has created a public benefits fund for renewable energy, energy efficiency, and energy research and development programs. The fund is authorized until 2012, with annual funding of about $65.5 million for renewable energy, $228 million for energy efficiency, and $62.5 million for R&D.

Rules and Regulations

Renewable Portfolio Standard: All utilities, including investor-owned utilities (IOUs) and publicly owned utilities, are obligated to comply with California's RPS. The standard currently requires obligated entities to procure 20 percent of the electricity they sell in California from eligible renewable resources by 2010, and 33 percent from renewable resources by 2020. Eligible renewable resources include biomass, solar thermal, solar PV, wind, geothermal, fuel cells using renewable fuels, anaerobic digestion, certain municipal solid waste, certain small hydro, landfill gas, wave, ocean thermal, and tidal. To be eligible, the energy must be generated in California or meet certain interconnection and delivery requirements. California has also established electricity savings and demand reduction goals for the state's IOUs.

Facility Siting and Permitting: Developers of a power plant greater than 50 MW in capacity must receive certification from the California Energy Commission. However, wind, hydroelectric, and solar PV facilities are specifically excluded from this definition. California has authorized counties to adopt ordinances governing installation of wind systems up to 50 kW. California allows its citizens to create solar easements. Subdivisions in California may include in their plans solar easements applicable to all of their plots. Homeowners' associations and other public entities may not bar the installation of solar systems. California regulates the extent to which trees or shrubbery may cast shade on solar panels.

Building Codes, Appliance, and Equipment Standards: California's 2008 Building Energy Efficiency Standards are mandatory for residential and commercial buildings. The residential component meets or exceeds the stringency of the 2009 IECC, and the commercial component meets or exceeds the stringency of ASHRAE Standard 90.1-2007. The CALGREEN Code, the nation's first mandatory green building code, went into effect on January 1, 2011. California's 2009 Appliance Efficiency Regulations set standards for twenty-three categories of appliances (however, some have been superseded by subsequent federal standards).

Electricity Transmission, Interconnection, and Storage: California has established standard interconnection requirements for DG systems up to 10 MW in capacity. Small PV and wind energy systems less than 10 kW in capacity are subject to simplified rules, i.e., do not require interconnection studies or supplemental review. California requires all but one of its utilities to offer net metering to customers with solar and wind energy systems up to 1 MW, and requires all IOUs to offer net metering to customers generating electricity from biogas or fuel cells. Customer-owned generation facilities that generate more power than the customer consumes receive the NEG as a credit to their account with the utility. At the end of an annualized period, customers can choose to roll over any remaining NEG from month to month indefinitely or receive financial compensation from the utility for the remaining NEG.

Fuel Standards and Transportation: The California Air Resources Board (CARB) has issued a Low Carbon Fuel Standard (LCFS) for California. The LCFS will require fuel manufacturers to reduce the carbon intensity of transportation fuel sold in California by 10 percent by 2020, with certain exceptions for fuel type and fuel application. Carbon intensity refers to the quantity of GHG emissions per unit of fuel delivered.

Government Procurement: California has established a Green Building Action Plan for state-owned buildings to improve energy efficiency and reduce energy consumption in state buildings by 20 percent relative to 2003 levels by 2015. The Plan requires all new and renovated state buildings to be rated at least LEED Silver. State agencies must take certain measures to reduce or mitigate energy consumption. California also requires feasibility assessments of energy efficiency and onsite generation potential for public buildings.

Policies, Plans, and Governmental Affiliations

Policies and Plans: California's Global Warming Solutions Act mandates a reduction in GHG emissions to 1990 levels by 2020, and includes penalties for noncompliance. In December 2010, CARB approved proposed regulations to establish a statewide cap-and-trade program for GHGs.

Government Entities: California Air Resources Board, California Alternative Energy and Advanced Transportation Financing Authority, California Energy Commission, California Public Utilities Commission, California State Board of Equalization.

Regional Memberships: California is a member of WCI, the West Coast Governors' Global Warming Initiative, the WGA, and ICAP.

Colorado

Financial Incentives

Tax Benefits: Colorado provides an exemption from the state's sales and use tax for certain renewable energy equipment. Colorado also exempts residential renewable energy systems from property taxes. When assessing the value of a commercial renewable energy facility for property tax purposes, the incremental value of the facility compared to a nonrenewable energy facility is disregarded. AFV and HEV users qualify for an income tax credit.

Grants: Colorado, through the Governor's Energy Office (GEO), provides grant opportunities for renewable energy projects to businesses and individuals.

Rebates: The GEO offers rebates to certain businesses and homeowners who purchase and install a qualifying renewable energy system. Rebates are also available to homeowners who purchase and install certain energy-efficient appliances and weatherization products.

Rules and Regulations

Renewable Portfolio Standard: An RPS is currently in place, with a 30 percent requirement by 2020. The Colorado Public Utilities Commission currently acts as the executing agency for this policy. Eligible technologies include solar thermal electric, PV, landfill gas, wind, biomass, hydroelectric, geothermal electric, "recycled energy," anaerobic digestion, and fuel cells using renewable fuels.

Facility Siting and Permitting: Colorado has enacted a statewide cap on building permit fees for solar PV systems and solar water heating systems. Colorado prohibits residential agreements that restrict solar and wind turbine installation access. Solar easements are allowed to provide access to direct sunlight.

Building Codes, Appliance, and Equipment Standards: Colorado has adopted the 2003 IECC as its residential and commercial building codes. Builders must provide prospective homebuyers with solar installation and water-efficient products as standard options. New construction and major renovations of state buildings must meet LEED Gold standards.

Electricity Transmission, Interconnection, and Storage: Net metering is available for qualifying renewable energy systems. This electricity generation can be applied toward the utility's RPS obligation. A three-tiered interconnection policy is also in place, with interconnection levels based upon system complexity. Municipal electric utilities providing service to more than 40,000 customers must offer a green power program to customers.

Fuel Standards and Transportation: The Colorado Division of Oil and Public Safety is required to promulgate regulations so that the process of obtaining a permit for an underground storage tank that contains renewable fuel is more efficient and affordable.

Government Procurement: State facilities must reduce energy consumption 20 percent by fiscal year 2011–2012, compared to 2005–2006. All state agency vehicles using diesel must use biodiesel.

Policies, Plans, and Governmental Affiliations

Policies and Plans: The governor has set a goal of reducing statewide GHG emissions to 20 percent below 2005 levels by 2020, and 80 percent below 2005 levels by 2050.

Government Entities: Colorado Department of Local Affairs, Colorado Department of Public Health and Environment, Colorado Department of Revenue, Colorado Governor's Energy Office, Colorado Office of Economic Development and International Trade, Colorado Public Utilities Commission.

Regional Memberships: Colorado is a member of the WGA and an observer of WCI.

Connecticut

Financial Incentives

Tax Benefits: Connecticut provides a property tax exemption for approved renewable energy systems and hydropower facilities that generate electricity for private residential use. Solar energy and geothermal systems and weatherization products purchased for residential use are exempt from the state's sales and use tax.

Loan Programs: Loans are available through the Connecticut Housing Investment Fund, Inc. to single- and multifamily property owners who meet established income limits for the purchase and installation of energy efficiency improvements. Financing is also available to retail end-use customers for the installation of customer-side electric generating equipment.

Grants: The Connecticut Energy Efficiency Fund and the Connecticut Clean Energy Fund provide grants, rebates, loans, and other financial incentives to residents and business undertaking projects to increase energy efficiency or develop renewable energy technologies. Grants are also available through Connecticut's New Energy Technology program to applicants who design energy-efficient and renewable energy technologies. The Connecticut Clean Fuel Program provides grants to municipalities and public agencies that purchase, operate, and maintain alternative fuel and advanced technology vehicles.

Rebates: Electricity customers who install energy efficiency equipment and reduce their energy use during peak hours may be eligible for a rebate based on the amount of kW-hours (kWh) saved during peak hours.

Rules and Regulations

Renewable Portfolio Standard: Connecticut's RPS requires that IOUs, certain municipal utilities, and retail suppliers provide 10 percent of their electricity from renewable sources by 2010, increasing to 23 percent by 2020. Eligible energy sources are divided into two tiers. Class I energy sources include solar, wind, fuel cells, landfill gas, certain biomass, tidal or wave energy, and certain hydro facilities up to 5 MW in capacity. Class II resources include certain hydro and biomass facilities not included in Class I, as well as trash-to-energy facilities. For the purposes of RPS compliance, RPS-obligated entities may only obtain up to 3 percent of their renewable energy from Class II resources in each compliance year. Obligated entities must also satisfy a CHP and energy efficiency requirement.

Building Codes, Appliance, and Equipment Standards: Connecticut's current residential and commercial building codes are based on the 2006 IECC. Connecticut is required to adopt the 2012 version of the IECC within eighteen months of its publication. Building projects and renovation projects meeting certain cost thresholds, as well as state building projects, must achieve a Silver rating from LEED or a comparable standard. The base minimum energy performance for all building projects subject to this requirement must be 21 percent better than the Connecticut State Building Code or ASHRAE Standard 90.1-2004, whichever is more stringent. Connecticut enforces efficiency standards for over thirty different commercial appliances sold in the state (although some have been superseded by subsequent federal standards).

Electricity Transmission, Interconnection, and Storage: Connecticut has established interconnection guidelines for DG systems up to 20 MW in capacity. Utilities must provide net metering to customers that generate electricity using Class I renewable energy resources.

Government Procurement: The state government has a goal of providing 20 percent of its electricity from Class I renewable-energy sources by 2010, 50 percent by 2020, and 100 percent by 2050. In 2009, the governor ordered the state's fleet of automobiles to be reduced by 20 percent from 2009 levels. In addition, at least 50 percent of all cars and light-duty trucks the state purchases or leases must be HEVs, plug-in HEVs, or AFVs. This requirement increases to 100 percent on January 1, 2012.

Policies, Plans, and Governmental Affiliations

Policies and Plans: Connecticut has set a statewide GHG emissions reduction target of 10 percent below 1990 levels by 2020, and 80 percent below 2001 levels by 2050. The state's Climate Change Action Plan contains fifty-five recommendations for reducing the state's GHG emissions.

Government Entities: Connecticut Department of Consumer Protection, Connecticut Department of Economic and Community Development, Connecticut Department of Public Utility Control, Connecticut Department of Revenue Services, Connecticut Office of Policy and Management, the Governor's Steering Committee on Climate Change.

Regional Memberships: Connecticut is a member of the Regional Greenhouse Gas Initiative (RGGI).

Delaware

Financial Incentives

Grants: Delaware's Green Energy Program provides cash incentives to Delaware residents for the installation of renewable energy systems, and for research and development of projects that develop or improve renewable energy technology in Delaware.

Rules and Regulations

Renewable Portfolio Standard: Delaware's RPS is 5 percent for compliance year 2010–2011 and increases to 25 percent for 2025–2026. Specific standards are set for PV sources. Delaware's rural electric cooperatives and municipal utilities may opt out of the RPS if they establish a green energy fund and a voluntary green power program. Eligible renewable sources include solar electric and PV, wind, ocean tidal, ocean thermal, fuel cells powered by renewable fuels, small hydro, biomass, anaerobic digestion, and landfill gas.

Facility Siting and Permitting: Unreasonable restrictions on the installation of wind energy systems on single-family residential properties are prohibited, as are private covenants that restrict the use of solar energy systems on residential rooftops. However, Delaware allows some restrictions on setbacks, noise, and other features of residential wind energy systems.

Building Codes, Appliance, and Equipment Standards: Newly constructed small residential buildings must comply with the 2009 IECC. All other residential buildings must comply with ASHRAE 90.1-2007. Commercial buildings must comply with the 2000 IECC and the 2001 IECC Supplement, which references ASHRAE 90.1-1999. LEED Silver certification is required for new construction and renovation of state buildings.

Electricity Transmission, Interconnection, and Storage: Delaware's only IOU has established three categories of interconnection guidelines based on system size and system type. Net metering is available to any customer that generates electricity using solar, wind, or hydro resources, anaerobic digesters, or fuel cells powered by renewable fuels.

Government Procurement: State agencies are required to reduce energy consumption by 30 percent below 2008 levels by 2015 and purchase Energy Star products when cost-effective. State agencies are also required to reduce petroleum consumption by 25 percent, vehicle emissions by 25 percent, and vehicle miles traveled by 15 percent below 2008 levels by 2013.

Policies, Plans, and Governmental Affiliations

Policies and Plans: The Delaware State Energy Office sponsored the Delaware Climate Change Action Plan, which details a number of policy options to reduce Delaware's GHG emissions by 7 percent below 1990 levels by 2010.

Government Entities: Delaware Department of Natural Resources and Environmental Control, Delaware Public Service Commission.

Regional Memberships: Delaware is a member of RGGI.

Florida

Financial Incentives

Tax Benefits: Florida provides an annual tax credit of up to 5 percent of eligible capital costs generated by new or expanding clean energy manufacturing facilities. Tax credits are also available for corporations that invest in (1) hydrogen-powered vehicles and hydrogen vehicle fueling stations; (2) commercial stationary hydrogen fuel cells; and (3) the production, storage, and distribution of biodiesel and ethanol. Florida also provides a sales tax exemption for purchasers of equipment, machinery, and other material for certain renewable energy technologies, including solar energy systems, hydrogen-powered vehicles, hydrogen-fueling stations, commercial stationary hydrogen fuel cells, and materials used in the distribution of biodiesel and ethanol.

Rules and Regulations

Facility Siting and Permitting: Florida law forbids ordinances, deed restrictions, covenants, declarations, or similar binding agreements from prohibiting the use of solar collectors (including clotheslines) or "other energy devices based on renewable resources." Florida law also allows easements for the purpose of maintaining exposure of a solar energy system to sunlight.

Building Codes, Appliance, and Equipment Standards: The Florida Building Code, which applies to residential and commercial developments, meets or exceeds the 2006 IECC and ASHRAE 90.1-2004. Florida also has adopted standards for public buildings, including the installation of solar technologies and energy-efficient measures when determined to be economically feasible. In addition, buildings constructed and financed by the state must comply with LEED standards or a nationally recognized, high-performance green building rating system, and new educational facilities must include passive solar design.

Electricity Transmission, Interconnection, and Storage: The Florida Public Service Commission has established net metering and interconnection rules for renewable energy systems up to 2 MW in capacity.

Government Procurement: Florida has established a goal for all state agencies and departments to reduce GHG emissions by 40 percent from 2007 levels by 2025 and to increase the energy efficiency of state buildings.

Policies, Plans, and Governmental Affiliations

Policies and Plans: In July 2007, Florida Governor Charlie Crist issued an executive order establishing a statewide GHG emission reduction target of 2000 levels by 2017, 1990 levels by 2025, and 80 percent below 1990 levels by 2050.

Government Entities: Florida Department of Revenue, Florida Energy & Climate Commission, Florida Public Service Commission.

Regional Memberships: Florida is a member of the SGA.

Georgia

Financial Incentives

Tax Benefits: Georgia offers personal and corporate tax credits for clean energy equipment installed and placed into service. Georgia also offers a sales tax exemption for biomass materials utilized in the production of energy and an income tax credit to purchase or lease a new AFV or zero emission vehicle.

Rebates: Georgia's Residential Energy-Efficient Appliance Rebate Program offers rebates for select Energy Star appliances installed in residences.

Rules and Regulations

Facility Siting and Permitting: The Georgia Public Service Commission regulates IOUs but has no siting responsibility for any independent power producer, co-op, or municipal utility. Solar easements may be established to allow owners of solar energy systems continued access to sunlight.

Building Codes, Appliance, and Equipment Standards: The Georgia State Energy Code for Buildings, which applies to residential and commercial developments, is based on the 2006 IECC and ASHRAE 90.1-2004.

Electricity Transmission, Interconnection, and Storage: Georgia allows residential electricity customers with PV systems, wind energy systems, or fuel cells up to 10 kW in capacity, and commercial facilities up to 100 kW, to connect to the grid. There is no provision in Georgia's interconnection standards requiring customers to install a manual external disconnect device, and utilities may not require additional tests or additional liability insurance.

Government Procurement: In 2008, the governor signed an executive order creating the Governor's Energy Challenge 2020, which requires state agencies and departments to reduce energy consumption 15 percent by 2020, compared to 2007.

Policies, Plans, and Governmental Affiliations

Government Entities: Georgia Department of Revenue, Georgia Environmental Finance Authority, Georgia Environmental Protection Division, Georgia Public Services Commission.

Regional Memberships: Georgia is a member of the SGA.

Hawaii

Financial Incentives

Tax Benefits: The Hawaii Energy Tax Credits allow individuals and corporations to claim an income tax credit of 20 percent of the cost of a wind system and 35 percent of the cost of a solar thermal or PV system if certain circumstances are satisfied. Hawaii also offers a credit to taxpayers who invest in businesses that develop renewable energy technologies.

Loan Programs: Hawaii offers low-interest loans to farmers and aquaculturists for 85 percent of the project costs or $1.5 million, whichever is less, for the production of renewable energy through PV, hydroelectric, wind, methane, biodiesel, or ethanol.

Other Financial Incentives: Hawaii has created a public benefits fund, which provides various financial incentives for energy efficiency programs.

Rules and Regulations

Renewable Portfolio Standard: Hawaii's RPS requires utilities to generate 10 percent of their electricity from renewable energy sources by 2010, gradually increasing to 40 percent by 2030. Eligible technologies include solar thermal and PV, landfill gas, wind, biomass (including municipal solid waste), hydro, geothermal electric and heat pumps, wave and ocean thermal energy, biofuels, renewable hydrogen, and fuels cells using renewable fuels. Certain electricity savings also count.

Facility Siting and Permitting: County agencies issuing development-related permits must give priority to projects incorporating energy and environmental design building standards. Subject to several exceptions, building permits may not be issued for new single-family homes that do not include a solar water heating system. Hawaii prohibits the creation of any covenant or restriction on the installation or use of a solar energy system on a residential dwelling.

Building Codes, Appliance and Equipment Standards: The Hawaii Building Code Council has adopted the 2006 IECC, with amendments, as the state energy code. The code will become law once an Administrative Directive is approved. Each state agency must, to the extent possible, meet the LEED Silver standard or another similar guideline approved by the state, and follow other energy conservation practices. By the end of 2010, state agencies must evaluate the energy efficiency of all existing public buildings that are larger than 5,000 square feet or use more than 8,000 kW-hours annually and identify opportunities for increased energy efficiency.

Electricity Transmission, Interconnection, and Storage: Hawaii has established various simplified interconnection rules for small renewable energy facilities and separate rules for all other DG. The Hawaii Public Utilities Commission has established a feed-in tariff, and net metering is available on a first-come, first-served basis to residential and "small commercial" customers that generate electricity using solar, wind, biomass, or hydroelectric systems.

Fuel Standards and Transportation: Hawaii has enacted extensive energy efficiency and environmental standards for motor vehicles and transportation fuels.

Policies, Plans, and Governmental Affiliations

Policies and Plans: The Global Warming Solutions Act of 2007 mandates that Hawaii reduce its GHG emissions to 1990 levels by 2020. By the end of 2011, the Department of Health must promulgate regulations that include mandatory reductions for large emitters, as well as reporting and monitoring requirements.

Government Entities: Hawaii Department of Agriculture, Hawaii Department of Business, Economic Development, & Tourism, Hawaii Department of Commerce & Community Affairs, Hawaii Department of Health, Hawaii Department of Taxation, Hawaii Public Utilities Commission.

Regional Memberships: Hawaii is a member of the WGA.

Idaho

Financial Incentives

Tax Benefits: Idaho gives taxpayers an income tax deduction of 40 percent of the cost of certain renewable systems. Certain commercial wind and geothermal operators are exempt from property taxes associated with their systems. Instead, they pay a tax of 3 percent of their gross energy earnings. Idaho also offers an income tax credit for capital investment in biofuel infrastructure. Idaho residents with homes built or under construction before 1976, or who had a building permit issued before 1976, qualify for an income tax deduction for 100 percent of the costs of installing new insulation.

Loan Programs: The Idaho Office of Energy Resources provides low-interest loans for energy efficiency projects and renewable energy generation projects.

Grants: Developers of biofuels infrastructure are entitled to grants for up to 50 percent of the cost of installing new fueling infrastructure dedicated to offering biofuel for retail sale, or for upgrading existing fueling infrastructure that is certified as incompatible with biofuel, including cleaning existing storage tanks for the purpose of offering biofuel for retail sale.

Rebates: Purchases of equipment used to develop renewable energy systems capable of generating at least 25 kW of electricity qualify for a sales and use tax rebate. Idaho's Residential Energy-Efficient Appliance Rebate Program also offers rebates for certain Energy Star appliances.

Bonds: Independent renewable energy producers that are not "qualifying facilities" under the federal Public Utility Regulatory Policies Act of 1978 can request financing from the Idaho

Energy Resources Authority, a state bonding authority, for the development of renewable energy projects in the state.

Rules and Regulations

Facility Siting and Permitting: Idaho's solar easement provisions allow a solar energy device access rights to sunlight.

Building Codes, Appliance, and Equipment Standards: Idaho's statewide building code requires that all residential and commercial buildings comply with the 2006 IECC. Idaho requires all major state facility projects to be at least 10 percent to 30 percent more efficient than a comparable building on a similar site.

Electricity Transmission, Interconnection, and Storage: Idaho does not have a statewide net-metering policy, but each of the state's three IOUs have developed a net-metering tariff that has been approved by the Idaho Public Utilities Commission.

Policies, Plans, and Governmental Affiliations

Policies and Plans: In 2007, the governor of Idaho, by executive order, instructed the Director of the Department of Environmental Quality to develop a GHG emission inventory and to provide recommendations for reducing the state's GHG emissions.

Government Entities: Idaho Department of Environmental Quality, Idaho Office of Energy Resources, Idaho Public Utilities Commission, Idaho Tax Commission.

Regional Memberships: Idaho is an observer of WCI and a member of the WGA.

Illinois

Financial Incentives

Tax Benefits: Illinois employs an alternate taxation structure for solar and wind systems. Building materials used in the construction of certain wind power facilities are eligible for a sales tax exemption.

Grants: Affordable housing developers, state and local governments, and public schools are eligible for grants for energy-efficient construction and renovation projects. Low-income households are eligible for grants for the installation of energy efficiency measures.

Rebates: Rebates for state-funded technical assessments and energy efficiency planning studies are available. Rebates are also available for wind and solar system construction and energy efficiency improvements made to public sector buildings. The Illinois Alternate Fuels Rebate Program provides rebates for 80 percent of the cost, up to $4,000, of purchasing an AFV or converting a conventional vehicle or an HEV to an AFV, as well as for purchasing alternative fuels.

Bonds: Tax-exempt bonds are available for the financing of commercial and nonprofit renewable energy and energy efficiency projects through the Illinois Finance Authority.

Other Financial Incentives: Illinois has established the Renewable Energy Resources Trust Fund and the Energy Efficiency Trust Fund, which support renewable energy and residential energy efficiency initiatives through grants, loans, and other financial incentives.

Rules and Regulations

Renewable Portfolio Standard: Illinois's retail electricity suppliers and major IOUs must supply 25 percent of their customers' electricity from renewable sources by 2025. Seventy-five percent of IOU's electricity obligation and 60 percent of retail suppliers' must be met through wind. Other eligible systems include solar thermal and PV, landfill gas, wind, biomass, non-newly created hydropower, and other unspecified sources.

Facility Siting and Permitting: Local governments may not require wind turbines to be set back from the property line a distance of more than 1.1 times the height of the system. Homeowners' associations, common interest community associations, and condominium unit owners' associations may not prevent homeowners from using or installing solar energy systems.

Building Codes, Appliance, and Equipment Standards: The Illinois Energy Conservation Code requires residential buildings to comply with the 2009 IECC. Privately funded commercial buildings must comply with the 2009 IECC and ASHRAE 90.1-2007. Publicly funded commercial buildings must comply with ASHRAE 90.1-2007. All new state-funded construction or major renovations are required to seek LEED or equivalent certification.

Electricity Transmission, Interconnection, and Storage: Illinois has established four-tiered interconnection standards for DG facilities up to 10 MW and a separate set of rules for DG facilities over 10 MW. IOUs are required to provide net metering to certain customer-generators up to 40 kW in capacity. Any NEG carries over to the next billing period and expires at the end of an annualized period.

Government Procurement: Illinois has established a goal for state agencies to purchase at least 15 percent of their power from renewable energy sources by 2020. State agencies are also required to reduce energy use by 10 percent by 2018 and to purchase Energy Star equipment if cost-effective. Illinois created an Energy Efficiency Committee to coordinate energy savings activities in state government. Illinois also set a goal for state agencies to reduce petroleum use by 20 percent by July 1, 2012, compared to 2008 levels.

Policies, Plans, and Governmental Affiliations

Policies and Plans: Former Governor Rod Blagojevich set a goal of reducing statewide GHG emissions to 1990 levels by 2020 and 60 percent below 1990 levels by 2050.

Government Entities: Illinois Commerce Commission, Illinois Department of Central Management Services, Illinois Department of Commerce and Economic Opportunity, Illinois Department of Revenue, Illinois Power Agency.

Regional Memberships: Illinois is a member of the Midwestern Greenhouse Gas Reduction Accord (MGGRA) and the Midwestern Governors Association (MGA).

Indiana

Financial Incentives

Tax Benefits: Individuals and small businesses that purchase certain Energy Star heating and cooling equipment are eligible for a tax credit worth the lesser of $100 or 20 percent of the equipment's cost. Taxpayers who install a solar-powered roof vent or fan on their homes are eligible for a tax deduction worth the lesser of $1,000 or 50 percent of the installation cost. Solar, wind, hydro, and geothermal systems are exempt from Indiana property taxes.

Grants: Grants of up to $20,000 are available to purchase, convert, or retrofit an existing fueling station for the purpose of dispensing fuel blended with ethanol, and for 50 percent of the cost, up to $100,000, to install infrastructure used to produce or distribute biofuels.

Rebates: Homeowners are eligible for a rebate of up to $1,000 for the purchase of certain Energy Star heating and cooling equipment.

Rules and Regulations

Facility Siting and Permitting: State law prohibits local municipalities from unreasonably restricting the use of solar energy. Indiana residents may create enforceable solar easements.

Building Codes, Appliance, and Equipment Standards: Indiana's residential and commercial building codes are based on the 1992 Model Energy Code (MEC). Commercial buildings must also comply with ASHRAE 90.1-2007. New state buildings must earn the LEED Silver rating or an equivalent rating.

Electricity Transmission, Interconnection, and Storage: Indiana has adopted a three-tiered system of rules for the interconnection of DG systems. IOUs must offer net metering to certain residential customers and schools with a valid interconnection agreement with the utility. Any NEG is credited to the customer's next monthly bill.

Government Procurement: State entities in Marion County are required to purchase 10 percent of their energy from renewable sources by 2010, increasing to 25 percent by 2025.

Policies, Plans, and Governmental Affiliations

Policies and Plans: Indiana's strategic energy plan, Hoosier Homegrown Energy, calls for a number of measures to create jobs through the adoption of energy efficiency measures and the further development of in-state energy resources, including clean coal and biomass.

Government Entities: Indiana Department of Administration, Indiana Department of Local Government Finance, Indiana Department of Revenue, Indiana Office of Energy Development, Indiana State Department of Agriculture, Indiana Utility Regulatory Commission.

Regional Memberships: Indiana is an observer of the MGGRA and a member of the MGA.

Iowa

Financial Incentives

Tax Benefits: Certain methane gas, wind, and large hydro generators are exempt from Iowa's replacement generation tax on electricity. Up to 330 MW of wind systems and up to 20 MW total of solar, hydrogen, and biomass generators are eligible for a production tax credit. Certain wind facilities are eligible for a separate production tax credit. Property used to generate methane gas from waste or convert methane gas to energy are exempt from property tax, and the market value added to a property by a solar or wind energy generator is exempt from property tax for five years after construction. Iowa does not levy a sales tax against the equipment or materials used to manufacture or install wind or solar energy systems. Iowa also provides a tax credit of $0.065 per gallon of ethanol that has been blended into gasoline sold by any retailer that sells a certain percentage of renewable fuels as part of its total gasoline sales.

Loan Programs: Iowa provides loans of up to 50 percent of the cost, up to $1 million, of the construction of solar, landfill gas, wind, biomass, and small hydro facilities.

Grants: Grants are available for research projects related to renewable energy and energy efficiency.

Rules and Regulations

Renewable Portfolio Standard: Iowa's two IOUs must own or contract for a total of 105 MW of biomass, hydro, wind, solar, landfill gas, municipal solid waste, or anaerobic digestion generation capacity.

Facility Siting and Permitting: Iowa residents can voluntarily agree to create an easement for access to sunlight to operate a solar energy system. Persons unable to obtain a voluntary solar easement can apply to the solar access regulatory board. The Department of Natural Resources has designated areas of concern for wind siting and established guidelines for wind developers.

Building Codes, Appliance, and Equipment Standards: Iowa's residential and commercial building codes are based on the 2009 IECC and incorporate ASHRAE 90.1-2004 for commercial buildings.

Electricity Transmission, Interconnection, and Storage: The Iowa Utilities Board has established interconnection standards for certain DG facilities up to 10 MW. Renewable energy systems up to 500 kW can benefit from net metering with Iowa's two IOUs. NEG is credited toward future utility payments. All utilities must provide their consumers with alternative energy options.

Government Procurement: State agencies must reduce their natural gas and electricity consumption by 15 percent from 2008 levels by 2015.

Policies, Plans, and Governmental Affiliations

Policies and Plans: In December 2008, the Iowa Climate Change Advisory Council released its final report, which presents two scenarios designed to reduce statewide GHG emissions by 50 percent and 90 percent from a 2005 baseline by 2050. The report also identifies fifty-six policy options to achieve the more stringent emissions reduction scenario. The Iowa Office of Energy Independence developed a renewable fuels marketing plan to promote the state's biofuels industry.

Government Entities: Iowa Climate Change Advisory Council, Iowa Department of Economic Development, Iowa Department of Natural Resources, Iowa Department of Revenue, Iowa Energy Center, Iowa Office of Energy Independence, Iowa Utilities Board.

Regional Memberships: Iowa is a member of the MGGRA and the MGA.

Kansas

Financial Incentives

Tax Benefits: Kansas provides an income tax credit to businesses and individuals for the construction of certain renewable energy facilities. Kansas also provides a property tax exemption to businesses and individuals for certain renewable energy equipment. An income tax credit is also available to individuals and businesses who own or operate AFVs or who install alternative fueling infrastructure. Tax incentives are also offered to producers and blenders of biofuels.

Loan Programs: Homeowners and small businesses are eligible to receive loans for energy improvements and renewable energy systems.

Bonds: Manufacturing companies building solar or wind equipment are eligible for up to $5 million in bond financing from the Kansas Department of Commerce.

Rules and Regulations

Renewable Portfolio Standard: Kansas utilities, other than cooperatives with 15,000 or fewer customers, must generate or purchase 20 percent of their electricity from renewable energy resources by 2020. Eligible resources for compliance include wind, solar thermal, PV, methane gas, hydropower, biomass, and fuel cells using renewable resources.

Facility Siting and Permitting: Easements are allowed to provide a party's solar energy system proper exposure.

Building Codes, Appliance, and Equipment Standards: The Kansas commercial building code is based on the 2006 IECC. Although Kansas does not have a statewide residential building code, builders and sellers of new residential buildings are required to provide an energy efficiency disclosure form to potential buyers.

Electricity Transmission, Interconnection, and Storage: Kansas has established interconnection guidelines and net metering for customers of IOUs generating qualifying renewable energy. Residential systems up to 25 kW and nonresidential systems up to 200 kW are eligible.

Government Procurement: Kansas requires 75 percent of state-owned light-duty vehicles to be AFVs. Fuel purchased by the state must contain a certain percentage of biofuel.

Policies, Plans, and Governmental Affiliations

Policies and Plans: In March 2008, Governor Kathleen Sebelius issued an executive order establishing the Kansas Energy and Environmental Planning Advisory Group (KEEP) to develop a plan to reduce GHG emissions in Kansas. KEEP submitted its interim report in January 2009.

Government Entities: Kansas Corporation Commission, Kansas Department of Commerce, Kansas Department of Health and Environment, Kansas Electric Transmission Authority, Kansas Energy and Environmental Planning Advisory Group.

Regional Memberships: Kansas is a member of the MGGRA, the MGA, and the WGA. Kansas is an observer of WCI.

Kentucky

Financial Incentives

Tax Benefits: Certain energy efficiency measures and renewable energy installations allow residential and commercial owners to take a 30 percent state income tax credit. Kentucky also provides companies a tax credit of up to 100 percent of the Kentucky income tax for building or renovating certain facilities that utilize renewable energy, as well as a sales tax exemption for equipment purchased for such projects. Biodiesel and ethanol producers can receive a $1 per gallon tax credit. Liquefied petroleum gas is exempt from the state excise tax when used to operate motor vehicles on public highways.

Loan Programs: Kentucky offers loans for residential energy efficiency improvements through the KY Home Performance program. The state also provides, through the Green Bank of Kentucky, loans to state agencies for energy efficiency improvements.

Grants: Kentucky provides grants to farmers for energy efficiency and renewable energy technologies. Funding is also available to companies for research and development of alternative fuels and renewable energy.

Rebates: Kentucky also offers rebates for residential energy efficiency improvements through the KY Home Performance program.

Rules and Regulations

Facility Siting and Permitting: Solar easements may be obtained to provide access to direct sunlight.

Building Codes, Appliance, and Equipment Standards: Kentucky's residential building code is based on the 2006 IECC and the 2006 International Residential Code (IRC). Kentucky's commercial building code is based on the 2006 IECC and the 2006 International Building Code (IBC). New construction and major renovations of public buildings must meet LEED certification and must incorporate Energy Star appliances if cost-effective. Moreover, public schools in Kentucky are required to implement an energy efficiency management program.

Electricity Transmission, Interconnection, and Storage: Utilities are required to offer net metering for certain renewable energy systems up to 30 kW. Kentucky has also developed interconnection standards for both inverter- and non-inverter-based systems.

Fuel Standards and Transportation: Service rates, terms, and conditions for natural gas for use as a motor vehicle fuel are exempt from Kentucky Public Service Commission regulation.

Government Procurement: At least 50 percent of state-owned light-duty vehicles must be replaced with energy-efficient vehicles. Vehicles in the Kentucky Transportation Cabinet's fleet must use fuel blended with either ethanol or biodiesel.

Policies, Plans, and Governmental Affiliations

Policies and Plans: Kentucky has established the Kentucky Climate Action Plan Council (KCAPC) to develop a climate action plan to reduce the state's GHG emissions. KCAPC submitted its interim report in July 2010. The Kentucky Department for Energy Development and Independence has been tasked with developing and implementing a strategy for the production of alternative transportation fuels and synthetic natural gas from fossil energy and biomass resources.

Government Entities: Governor's Office of Agricultural Policy, Kentucky Climate Action Plan Council, Kentucky Department for Energy Development and Independence, Kentucky Department for Environmental Protection, Kentucky Department for Natural Resources, Kentucky Environmental Quality Commission, Kentucky Public Service Commission.

Regional Memberships: Kentucky is a member of the SGA.

Louisiana

Financial Incentives

Tax Benefits: Louisiana provides a tax credit for the purchase and installation of residential solar and wind energy systems. This credit may be applied to personal, corporate, or franchise taxes, depending on the entity that purchases and installs the system. In Louisiana, any equipment attached to an owner-occupied residential building or swimming pool as part of a solar energy system is considered personal property that is exempt from *ad valorem* taxation.

Loan Programs: The Home Energy Loan Program allows homeowners to get a five-year loan to improve the energy efficiency of their existing home.

Rebates: The Home Energy Rebate Option Program offered by the Louisiana Department of Natural Resources provides a number of cash rebates to residents and businesses for energy efficient improvements made to existing homes and buildings, as well as for new homes that meet a certain energy efficiency rating. Rebates are also available for select Energy Star appliances installed in households in Louisiana.

Rules and Regulations

Facility Siting and Permitting: Louisiana's solar access law prohibits unreasonable restrictions on property owners from installing solar collectors.

Building Codes, Appliance, and Equipment Standards: Louisiana's building codes for residential and commercial developments are based on the 2006 IRC and ASHRAE 90.1-2004, respectively. Louisiana has also adopted standards for public buildings, requiring energy efficiency measures to be incorporated in the construction and renovation of major facility projects funded by the state.

Electricity Transmission, Interconnection, and Storage: The Louisiana Public Service Commission has established rules for net metering and interconnection. Louisiana's rules, based on those in place in Arkansas, require publicly owned utilities and rural electric cooperatives to offer net metering to customers with systems that generate electricity using solar, wind, hydropower, geothermal or biomass resources, or fuel cells or microturbines that generate electricity from renewable resources.

Fuel Standards and Transportation: Six months after the annual production of ethanol equals 50 million gallons or the annual production of biodiesel equals 10 million gallons, all gasoline must contain 2 percent ethanol or all diesel must be 2 percent biodiesel, respectively, unless it is determined that supply or distribution capabilities are insufficient.

Policies, Plans, and Governmental Affiliations

Government Entities: Division of Administration, Louisiana Department of Environmental Quality, Louisiana Department of Natural Resources, Louisiana Department of Revenue, Louisiana Public Service Commission.

Regional Memberships: Louisiana is a member of the SGA.

Maine

Financial Incentives

Tax Benefits: Maine offers a sales and use tax refund for qualified wind energy generation projects of 10 MW or less. Certified producers of ethanol, biodiesel, hydrogen, or methanol derived from biomass are eligible for an income tax credit of $0.05 per gallon for the commercial production of biofuels for use in motor vehicles or otherwise used as a substitute for liquid fuels.

Loan Programs: Low-interest loans of up to $35,000 are available to small businesses for certain energy efficiency measures.

Grants: Maine provides funding for small-scale demonstration projects that educate the public on the value of renewable energy. The Efficiency Maine Business Program provides cash incentives and free, independent technical advice to help grid-tied nonresidential electric customers save energy and money. Each applicant is eligible for incentives up to $300,000 per calendar year. The incentive may be up to 75 percent of the incremental cost of high-efficiency equipment over standard equipment.

Rebates: Maine offers rebates of up to $1,500 to homeowners who receive preapproval for energy efficiency upgrades. Maine separately offers rebates for certain Energy Star appliances and energy-efficient lighting. Maine also offers rebates for PV, solar water heating, and residential wind energy systems.

Other Financial Incentives: Maine offers incentives to small, community-based renewable energy generating facilities, including long-term contracts with the state's IOUs and REC multipliers.

Rules and Regulations

Renewable Portfolio Standard: Maine's Renewable Resource Portfolio Requirement mandates that the state's IOUs and retail suppliers meet 40 percent of the state's energy needs from renewable resources and energy efficiency measures by 2017. Thirty percent of that total may come from Class II resources, which include electricity generated by facilities no greater than 100 MW in capacity that use fuel cells, tidal power, solar arrays and installations, wind power, geothermal power, hydropower, biomass power, or generators fueled by municipal solid waste in conjunction with recycling or by CHP facilities that qualify as "small power production facilities." The remaining 10 percent must be met through Class I resources, which include renewable generation facilities that commenced operation after September 1, 2005. Eligible Class I resources include all resources in Class II except for CHP systems, certain municipal solid waste facilities, and certain hydro facilities. Wind systems larger than 100 MW are also eligible Class I resources.

Facility Siting and Permitting: Maine allows for the creation of easements to ensure access to direct sunlight. In addition, municipalities and homeowners' associations may not unreasonably restrict residents from installing or using a solar energy device (including clotheslines) on their property. Maine has also developed a model wind ordinance.

Building Codes, Appliance, and Equipment Standards: The Maine Uniform Building and Energy Code, setting the 2009 versions of the IECC, IBC, IRC, the International Existing Building Code (IEBC), and ASHRAE 90.1 as the mandatory building code standards for residential and commercial buildings, goes into effect in certain cities and towns in 2010 and statewide in 2012. LEED standards are required in new and existing state buildings, if cost-effective.

Electricity Transmission, Interconnection, and Storage: The Interstate Renewable Energy Council 2006 Model Interconnection Procedures provide the basis for the state's interconnection procedures and regulations. IOUs are required to offer net metering to eligible renewable energy facilities with capacity limits up to 660 kW. The Maine Public Utilities Commission is in the process of developing a program to offer green power as an option to residential and small commercial customers.

Government Procurement: State agencies are required to purchase 100 percent of their electricity from renewable energy sources.

Policies, Plans, and Governmental Affiliations

Policies and Plans: Maine has established a goal of reducing GHG emissions to 10 percent below 1990 levels by 2020, and 75 to 80 percent below 2003 levels in the long term.

Government Entities: Energy Resources Council, Finance Authority of Maine, Maine Department of Environmental Protection, Maine Public Utilities Commission.

Regional Memberships: Maine is a member of RGGI and ICAP.

Maryland

Financial Incentives

Tax Benefits: Maryland offers individuals and corporations tax credits for purchases of biodiesel used for space or water heating. Tax credits are also available for individual and corporate producers of renewable energy, and nonresidential and residential multifamily buildings that are constructed or rehabilitated to meet U.S. Green Building Council criteria. Maryland has also established an excise tax credit of up to $2,000 for the purchase of qualified plug-in vehicles. Maryland has a real property tax exemption for solar PV, solar hot water, solar thermal, and residential wind energy systems. Solar and geothermal heating and cooling systems are granted a special assessment that makes their assessed value equivalent to a conventional system. Geothermal, solar, and residential wind energy equipment is exempted from the state sales and use tax, and wood or "refuse-derived" fuel used for heating purposes is exempted from the state sales tax. Maryland will also offer a sales tax holiday to purchasers of certain energy-efficient appliances beginning in 2011.

Loan Programs: Maryland provides loans to nonprofits, local governments, and businesses for energy efficiency improvements. Maryland also provides loans to state agencies for energy efficiency improvements in state facilities. The Maryland Agricultural and Resource Based Industry Development Corporation offers low-interest loans for energy efficiency improvements to farms and rural businesses through the Rural Business Energy Efficiency Improvement Loan Program, which receives funding from the state.

Grants: Maryland offers grants for the installation of solar PV systems and solar water heating systems, as well as for certain nonresidential wind energy systems.

Rebates: Maryland offers rebates for the installation of geothermal heat pump systems, and for the installation of certain types of energy-efficient equipment by agricultural producers.

Rules and Regulations

Renewable Portfolio Standard: Maryland's RPS requires electricity suppliers to use renewable energy sources to generate a certain percentage of retail electricity sales in the state from Tier 1 sources (solar, wind, biomass, methane, geothermal, ocean, and small hydroelectric power plants) and 2.5 percent from Tier 2 sources (other hydroelectric power plants). The Tier 1 requirement increases gradually, reaching a level of 20 percent in 2022. The Tier 2 requirement sunsets in 2019. In addition, Maryland separately requires that electricity suppliers derive at least 0.5 percent of their energy from solar electric sources in 2011, increasing to 2 percent in 2022.

Facility Siting and Permitting: Maryland protects the right of property owners to enter into solar easement agreements. Maryland also prohibits covenants that unreasonably restrict the installation of solar collection systems.

Building Codes, Appliance, and Equipment Standards: The Maryland Building Performance Standards are mandatory statewide and based on the 2009 IECC. The Maryland High Performance Buildings Act requires the construction and major renovation of state buildings to meet the LEED Silver rating or a comparable rating. The state has adopted minimum energy efficiency standards for several appliances (however, some have been superseded by subsequent federal standards).

Electricity Transmission, Interconnection, and Storage: Maryland's interconnection rules apply to DG systems of less than 10 MW for all types of utilities. The state's net metering law applies to all utilities and is available until the aggregate capacity of all net-metered systems reaches 1,500 MW. System size is generally limited to 2 MW.

Government Procurement: Maryland law requires a 10 percent reduction in energy consumption in state buildings by 2010, compared to 2005, and requires agencies to conduct an energy consumption analysis for each building under their jurisdiction each year. In addition, Maryland has set a goal for state agencies to procure at least 6 percent of their electricity from renewable energy sources, including wind, solar PV, solar thermal, biomass, landfill gas, and specified amounts of municipal solid waste. At least 50 percent of state vehicles must use a minimum biodiesel blend of 5 percent.

Policies, Plans, and Governmental Affiliations

Policies and Plans: Maryland's Greenhouse Gas Emissions Reduction Act of 2009 sets a target of reducing GHG emissions to 25 percent below 2006 levels by 2020 and requires that a task force create and submit a plan for achieving this target.

Government Entities: Maryland Commission on Climate Change, Maryland Department of the Environment, Maryland Department of General Services, Maryland Energy Administration, Maryland Public Services Commission.

Regional Memberships: Maryland is a member of RGGI, ICAP, and the SGA.

Massachusetts

Financial Incentives

Tax Benefits: Massachusetts grants gas tax exemptions for certain biofuels. Businesses may deduct the cost of installing a wind or solar climate control or water heating unit. Such units are also exempt from the state's corporate excise tax. A 15 percent credit—up to $1,000—is provided against the state income tax for the purchase and installation of a residential renewable energy system. Massachusetts offers a corporate and personal excise tax deduction for any income received from the sale or lease of a U.S. patent for energy conservation or alternative energy development, and a corporate excise tax deduction for any income received from the sale or lease of personal or real property or materials manufactured in Massachusetts and subject to the approved patent. The value added by eligible solar, wind and hydropower systems is exempt from local property tax. Certain solar, wind, and heat pump systems are also exempt from the state's sales tax.

Grants: The state provides up to $10 million per year to municipalities for the development of clean energy programs.

Rebates: Residents are eligible for up to $2,000 in rebates for certain energy-efficient home improvements. Home builders can receive up to $8,000 in rebates for building a new home to the most stringent Energy Star standards.

Other Financial Incentives: Massachusetts supports a number of different clean energy incentives through the Renewable Energy Trust Fund (RETF) and the Energy Efficiency Fund. For example, RETF funds the Massachusetts Sustainable Energy Economic Development (SEED) initiative, which provides convertible loans to renewable energy companies in the early stage of development, and various other wind, solar, and hydropower projects.

Rules and Regulations

Renewable Portfolio Standard: IOUs and retail electricity suppliers must provide 5 percent of their retail sales from Class I renewable sources by 2010, increasing to 15 percent by 2020. Class I resources include any of the following that have begun production or incrementally expanded production since 1998: solar PV or thermal electric, wind, ocean thermal, wave, tidal, fuel cells using renewable fuels, landfill gas, certain biomass, hydrokinetic, certain hydroelectric, and geothermal. Obligated entities must also provide 3.6 percent of their retail sales from Class II sources each year. Class II sources may be any of the types in Class I, but from facilities that came online prior to 1998. Obligated entities must also provide 3.5 percent of their retail sales from municipal solid waste each year. Massachusetts has also established an alternative energy portfolio standard. Under this standard, obligated entities must provide a certain percentage of their retail sales from technologies that incorporate carbon capture and storage, CHP, flywheel energy storage, paper-derived fuel source substitute, energy-efficient steam technology, or other technologies, as approved.

Facility Siting and Permitting: The state has created model siting ordinances for wind and large-scale solar facilities. Massachusetts allows for the creation of voluntary solar easements to protect solar exposure and authorizes zoning rules that prohibit unreasonable infringements on solar access. Solar access contracts are voluntary and solar access is not an automatic right, but zoning boards may create solar rights.

Building Codes, Appliance, and Equipment Standards: Massachusetts has adopted the 2009 IECC, with amendments, for new residential and commercial buildings. The state has also developed a "stretch" code, which mandates a percentage reduction in total building energy use and is approximately 20 percent more efficient than the 2009 IECC. The Green Communities Act of 2008 (GCA) establishes a goal that fossil fuel use in buildings be cut to 10 percent below 2007 levels by 2020. Certain state construction and renovation projects must meet the Massachusetts LEED Plus standard. Massachusetts has set minimum energy efficiency standards for a number of appliances (however, some have been superseded by subsequent federal standards).

Electricity Transmission, Interconnection, and Storage: Massachusetts has adopted the Model Interconnection Tariff, which includes provisions for three levels of interconnection. For small renewables and larger DG systems, technical requirements are based on the IEEE 1547 and UL 1741 standards. The state's IOUs must offer net metering. The aggregate capacity of net metering is limited to 1 percent of each utility's peak load.

Government Procurement: The state government must procure 15 percent of agency annual electricity consumption from renewable sources by 2012 and 30 percent by 2020. GCA requires that half of the state government vehicles be comprised of hybrid or alternative use vehicles by 2018.

Policies, Plans, and Governmental Affiliations

Policies and Plans: In 2008, the governor established a task force of industry experts charged with designing a plan to reach Zero Net Energy building by 2030. The Global Warming Solutions Act of 2008 has the ultimate goal of reducing statewide GHG emissions to 80 percent below 1990 levels by 2050. In December 2010, the state released its Clean Energy and Climate Plan for 2020, which includes an interim target of reducing GHG emissions to 25 percent below 1990 levels by 2020, along with a plan to achieve that target.

Government Entities: Energy Efficiency Advisory Council, Executive Office of Energy and Environmental Affairs, Massachusetts Clean Energy Center, Massachusetts Department of Agricultural Resources, Massachusetts Department of Energy Resources, Massachusetts Department of Housing & Community Development, Massachusetts Department of Public Utilities, Massachusetts Department of Revenue, Massachusetts Energy Facilities Siting Board, Massachusetts Sustainable Design Roundtable.

Regional Memberships: Massachusetts is a member of RGGI and ICAP.

Michigan

Financial Incentives

Tax Benefits: Michigan allows for a personal property tax exemption for a wide range of renewable energy technologies. The state also exempts farmers from real and personal property taxes when certain renewable energy technologies are used. Qualified individuals are entitled to a tax credit when purchasing or installing eligible energy-efficient residential improvements. A tax credit is also available to station owners installing new infrastructure or converting existing infrastructure to sell biofuels. Biofuel is taxed at a lower rate than standard gasoline. Qualifying advanced vehicle battery manufacturers and businesses researching and developing hybrid systems for motor vehicles are eligible for a tax credit. Tax credits are also available to businesses engaged in alternative energy research, development, and manufacturing. Businesses located within a state-designated "renewable energy renaissance zone" are exempt from the state business tax, the state education tax, personal and real property taxes, and local income taxes.

Grants: Michigan's public benefits fund, the Low-Income and Energy Efficiency Fund, provides grants to businesses, nonprofits, government agencies, and schools for energy efficiency projects. The Michigan Biomass Energy Program provides funding to government agencies and nonprofits for biofuel and bioenergy projects.

Rules and Regulations

Renewable Portfolio Standard: Under Michigan's RPS, IOUs, alternative retail suppliers, electric cooperatives, and municipal electric utilities are required to supply 10 percent of their retail load from renewable sources by 2015. Eligible resources include solar thermal and PV, wind, geothermal, municipal solid waste, landfill gas, certain types of hydropower, and biomass. Utilities are permitted to use energy efficiency measures and advanced cleaner energy systems to meet a limited portion of the RPS requirement.

Facility Siting and Permitting: Michigan has developed a model wind ordinance for local governments.

Building Codes, Appliance, and Equipment Standards: Michigan has adopted the 2003 IRC and the 2004 IECC Supplement for residential buildings, and ASHRAE 90.1-1999 for commercial buildings.

Electricity Transmission, Interconnection, and Storage: Utilities must provide renewable energy customer-generators with net metering. For net-metered customers, service rates must match those of customers not participating in net metering. This net metering system was implemented alongside a five-tiered interconnection scheme, with levels based on a system's generation capability.

Fuel Standards and Transportation: AFVs using qualifying sources of energy are exempt from emissions inspection requirements. The Michigan Department of Transportation is directed to promote the transition of transit bus fleets to hybrid vehicles.

Government Procurement: Michigan has set a goal of reducing energy usage in state buildings 25 percent by 2015, compared to 2002, and requires state agencies to purchase energy-efficient products whenever possible.

Policies, Plans, and Governmental Affiliations

Policies and Plans: Michigan has set a goal of reducing GHG emissions to 20 percent below 2005 levels by 2020 and 80 percent by 2050.

Government Entities: Michigan Department of Environmental Quality, Michigan Department of Transportation, Michigan Energy Office, Michigan Public Service Commission.

Regional Memberships: Michigan is a member of the MGGRA and the MGA.

Minnesota

Financial Incentives

Tax Benefits: Solar and wind energy systems are exempt from Minnesota's sales tax. The real and personal property of wind energy systems and the value added by solar PV systems are not subject to the state's property tax. However, large wind energy systems are subject to a separate production tax in lieu of the property tax.

Loan Programs: Certain Minnesota farmers are eligible for loans to install wind energy systems and anaerobic digesters, for stock purchases of wind energy and anaerobic digestion cooperatives, and for other energy efficiency projects. Minnesota also provides low-interest loans for energy efficiency improvements made to homes and residential rental properties. The Public Buildings Enhanced Energy Efficiency Program identifies, helps finance, and implements energy efficiency improvements in public buildings.

Grants: Low-income families are eligible for grants to install solar air or biofuel heating systems. Minnesota also provides grants to local governments for the installation of solar energy systems within parks and on trails of regional or statewide significance.

Rebates: Rebates are available for the installation costs of small residential and commercial wind systems, solar hot water heating systems designed primarily to provide domestic hot water, and solar air heating systems.

Other Financial Incentives: Certain hydro facilities and anaerobic digesters are eligible to receive a production incentive of 1 to 1.5 cents per kWh generated through the Renewable Development Fund. Xcel Energy is required by statute to fund and administer the fund for the development of renewable energy resources and research into renewable energy technology.

Rules and Regulations

Renewable Portfolio Standard: Minnesota's RPS requires Xcel Energy to generate 30 percent of its total retail electricity sales from renewable sources by 2020. Other utilities must generate 25 percent of their total retail electricity sales from renewable sources by 2025. Eligible resources include solar thermal and PV, wind, hydrogen, small hydropower, landfill gas, anaerobic digestion, municipal solid waste, and other biomass. Of the 30 percent required of Xcel Energy in 2020, at least 25 percent must be generated by wind energy or solar energy systems, with solar limited to no more than 1 percent. In addition, Xcel Energy is specifically required by statute to build or contract for 825 MW of wind generation capacity, as well as 110 MW of biomass.

Facility Siting and Permitting: Local building officials may only issue permits for the installation of solar water heating systems and solar space heating systems that have been certified by the Solar Rating and Certification Corporation. Wind systems larger than 5 MW must receive a siting permit from the Minnesota Public Utilities Commission (MPUC) rather than comply with local land use rules. The MPUC has developed standardized siting rules for projects between 5 and 25 MW. Certain wind projects of 50 MW or more must receive a Certificate of Need from MPUC. Minnesota law provides for the creation of solar and wind easements for solar and wind energy systems.

Building Codes, Appliance, and Equipment Standards: Minnesota's residential building code is based on the 2006 IRC, and the commercial building code is based on ASHRAE 90.1-2004. New construction and major renovations of state buildings must comply with the Sustainable Building Guidelines.

Electricity Transmission, Interconnection, and Storage: Qualifying facilities of less than 40 kW are eligible for net metering. Compensation may take the form of an actual payment for NEG or as a credit on the customer's bill. Interconnection standards for DG systems of up to 10 MW have been established. Public utilities are required to create a twenty-year power purchase agreement for community-owned renewable energy projects.

Fuel Standards and Transportation: All gasoline sold in Minnesota must contain at least 10 percent ethanol or the maximum percent of denatured ethanol allowed by the U.S. Environmental Protection Agency regardless of model year. Diesel fuel sold or offered for sale in the state for use in internal combustion engines must contain at least 5 percent biodiesel.

Policies, Plans, and Governmental Affiliations

Policies and Plans: Minnesota has established a goal of reducing statewide GHG emissions 15 percent by 2015, 30 percent by 2025, and 80 percent by 2050, based on 2005 levels.

Government Entities: Center for Energy and Environment, Minnesota Department of Administration, Minnesota Department of Agriculture, Minnesota Department of Commerce, Minnesota Department of Natural Resources, Minnesota Housing Finance Agency, Minnesota Office of Energy Security, Minnesota Pollution Control Agency, Minnesota Public Utilities Commission.

Regional Memberships: Minnesota is a member of the MGGRA and the MGA.

Mississippi

Financial Incentives

Tax Benefits: The Mississippi Clean Energy Initiative provides a tax exemption to companies that manufacture renewable energy systems or components.

Loan Programs: Mississippi offers loans to businesses for renewable energy and energy efficiency projects.

Other Financial Incentives: Mississippi's Energy-Efficiency Lease Program allows public institutions and private, nonprofit hospitals to lease-purchase energy-efficient services and equipment. Mississippi provides a production incentive to ethanol and biodiesel producers located in Mississippi.

Rules and Regulations

Building Codes, Appliance, and Equipment Standards: Mississippi's state energy code, which applies to residential and commercial developments, is based on ASHRAE 90-1975. The code is mandatory for state-owned buildings, public buildings, and high-rise buildings, and is voluntary for residential buildings.

Policies, Plans, and Governmental Affiliations

Government Entities: Mississippi Department of Agriculture and Commerce, Mississippi Development Authority, Mississippi Public Service Commission.

Regional Memberships: Mississippi is a member of the SGA.

Missouri

Financial Incentives

Tax Benefits: Missouri offers an income tax deduction for the cost of home energy audits and certain energy efficiency home improvements. Missouri provides a tax credit to individuals and businesses processing Missouri forestry industry residues into fuels. An income tax credit is also available for 20 percent of the cost, up to $20,000, of the purchase and installation of any alternative fuel storage and dispensing equipment. Missouri also offers an annual sales tax holiday to purchasers of qualified Energy Star appliances.

Loan Programs: Public schools and local governments are eligible for low-interest loans for energy efficiency and renewable energy projects.

Rebates: Consumers purchasing certain Energy Star appliances are eligible for a rebate of up to $575 through the state's Energize Missouri Appliance Rebate Program.

Other Financial Incentives: The Missouri Agricultural and Energy Saving Team—A Revolutionary Opportunity (MAESTRO) program provides a variety of incentives to livestock farmers to implement energy efficiency improvements, including energy audits, rebates for the cost of energy audits, loan guarantees, interest rate buy-downs, and down payment grants.

Rules and Regulations

Renewable Portfolio Standard: Missouri has established a mandatory RPS for IOUs. The standard requires renewable energy generation to account for 2 percent of annual retail electricity sales in 2011, increasing incrementally to 15 percent in 2021. Solar energy must account for 2 percent of each interim requirement (thus, in 2021, solar must account for 0.3 percent of retail electricity sales). The remainder may come from any combination of solar PV, solar thermal, methane, landfill gas, wind, biomass, small hydroelectric, municipal solid waste, anaerobic digestion, and fuel cells using renewable fuels.

Facility Siting and Permitting: In Missouri, the right to utilize solar energy is a property right, and property owners may grant solar easements.

Building Codes, Appliance, and Equipment Standards: State-owned single-family and multi-family residential buildings must comply with the latest edition of the MEC or ASHRAE Standard 90.2-1993. State-owned commercial buildings must comply with the 2006 IECC.

Electricity Transmission, Interconnection, and Storage: IOUs must offer net metering to renewable energy customer-generators of up to 100 kW. A customer's NEG is credited to the customer each month, and at the end of an annualized period, the remaining excess generation is credited to the utility without compensation.

Fuel Standards and Transportation: All gasoline sold at retail stations within the state must contain 10 percent ethanol.

Government Procurement: All state agencies under the Missouri Office of Administration are required to adopt policies to reduce energy consumption by 2 percent each year until 2019. Appliances purchased with state funds must be Energy Star if cost-effective.

Policies, Plans, and Governmental Affiliations

Government Entities: Missouri Department of Natural Resources, Missouri Department of Revenue, Missouri Office of Administration, Missouri Public Service Commission.

Regional Memberships: Missouri is a member of the MGA and the SGA.

Montana

Financial Incentives

Tax Benefits: Montana provides a corporate tax deduction and an individual tax credit for the cost of capital investments made to buildings for energy conservation purposes. Individuals may also claim a tax credit for the purchase and installation of residential renewable energy systems. Commercial alternative energy systems are eligible for a tax credit of up to 35 percent of the income generated by the investment. Commercial renewable energy facilities are assessed at 50 percent of their taxable value. New commercial renewable electricity generation facilities with a capacity of less than 1 MW are exempt from property taxes for five years. Buildings using renewable energy generation equipment are exempt from property taxes for ten years following installation. Montana has made up to $6 million a year available to provide tax incentives to three ethanol companies that will build plants and produce ethanol in Montana.

Loan Programs: Montana's Alternative Energy Revolving Loan Program provides loans to individuals, small businesses, nonprofits, universities, and government agencies to install renewable energy systems.

Bonds: Montana's State Buildings Energy Conservation Bond program finances energy improvement projects on state-owned buildings.

Other Financial Incentives: Montana's Universal System Benefits Program supports low-income assistance and weatherization, energy efficiency, renewable energy, research and development, and other programs.

Rules and Regulations

Renewable Portfolio Standard: Montana requires public utilities and competitive electricity suppliers to obtain 10 percent of their retail electricity sales from eligible renewable resources by 2010, increasing to 15 percent by 2015. Eligible energy sources include solar thermal, PV, landfill gas, biomass, anaerobic digestion, wind, geothermal electric, small hydro, and fuel cells using renewable fuels.

Facility Siting and Permitting: Property owners may create solar and wind easements.

Building Codes, Appliance, and Equipment Standards: Montana's statewide building code is based on the 2009 IECC. New construction and major renovation projects for state-owned buildings and new construction projects for state-leased buildings must exceed the effective IECC by 20 percent, to the extent that it is cost-effective.

Electricity Transmission, Interconnection, and Storage: Montana's net metering rules apply to systems up to 50 kW that generate electricity using hydropower, wind, or solar energy, and require interconnected facilities to comply with all national safety, equipment, and power-quality standards. All regulated electric utilities are required to offer customers the option of purchasing electricity generated by renewable energy resources.

Fuel Standards and Transportation: Montana has passed a law that requires low- and mid-grade gasoline sold in the state to contain 10 percent ethanol within twelve months after the Department of Transportation has certified that the state has produced 40 million gallons of denatured ethanol and has maintained that level of production on an annualized basis for at least three months.

Policies, Plans, and Governmental Affiliations

Policies and Plans: The Montana Climate Change Action Plan includes a goal of reducing Montana's GHG emissions to 1990 levels by 2020, and contains fifty-four policy suggestions to meet that goal.

Government Entities: Montana Department of Environmental Quality, Montana Department of Labor and Industry, Montana Department of Revenue.

Regional Memberships: Montana is a member of WCI and the WGA.

Nebraska

Financial Incentives

Tax Benefits: Nebraska exempts from the state sales and use tax the gross receipts from the sale, lease, or rental of personal property used in community-based wind energy development projects. Investors in Nebraska biodiesel production facilities are eligible to receive a tax credit of up to 30 percent of the amount invested, up to $250,000.

Loan Programs: The Nebraska Energy Office offers low-interest loans for energy efficiency improvements made to existing residential and commercial buildings that are at least five years old.

Rules and Regulations

Facility Siting and Permitting: Nebraska property owners may create binding easements for access to sunlight and wind.

Building Codes, Appliance, and Equipment Standards: The Nebraska Energy Code, which is based on the 2003 IECC, applies to all new buildings and all renovations of existing buildings, as long as the renovations cost more than 50 percent of the replacement cost of the building.

Electricity Transmission, Interconnection, and Storage: Qualifying renewable energy systems of up to 25 kW are eligible for net metering and interconnection to the distribution grid. Customers may offset their monthly bills through their own generation, and any surplus generation will be credited at the utility's avoided cost rate for that month and carried over to the next billing period. At the end of an annualized period, the excess is paid to the customer.

Government Procurement: All state employees operating flexible fuel or diesel vehicles as part of the state fleet must use ethanol or biodiesel blends whenever reasonably available.

Policies, Plans, and Governmental Affiliations

Government Entities: Nebraska Energy Office, Nebraska State Electrical Division.

Regional Memberships: Nebraska is a member of the WGA.

Nevada

Financial Incentives

Tax Benefits: Nonresidential buildings and multifamily residential buildings that earn LEED certification may be eligible for a partial abatement of property taxes. New or expanded businesses may apply for a property tax abatement of up to 55 percent for up to 20 years for personal property used to generate renewable energy, as well as a sales and use tax abatement for qualifying renewable energy technologies. Any value added by a qualifying renewable energy system will be subtracted from the assessed value of any residential, commercial, or industrial building for property tax purposes.

Rebates: Rebates are available for grid-connected PV systems installed on residences, small businesses, public buildings, nonprofits, and schools; small wind systems installed on residences, small businesses, agricultural sites, schools, and public buildings; and small hydroelectric systems installed at grid-connected agricultural sites. Nevada also offers rebates for select Energy Star appliances installed in homes.

Rules and Regulations

Renewable Portfolio Standard: Nevada's RPS requires that utilities provide 12 percent of their retail electricity sales from renewable energy sources by 2009, increasing to 25 percent in 2025. Solar energy resources must account for 5 percent of the annual requirement through 2015, increasing to 6 percent in 2016 (thus, in 2016, solar must account for 1.5 percent of retail sales). In addition to solar, eligible renewable resources include wind, biomass, geothermal, waste tires, certain hydro, and certain "energy recovery processes" at facilities 15 MW in capacity or less. Efficiency measures may also be used to satisfy a portion of the requirement.

Facility Siting and Permitting: Nevada prohibits the adoption of any legal instrument that unreasonably restricts a landowner from installing solar or wind energy systems. Renewable energy generation facilities up to 70 MW in capacity do not require a permit from the Public Utilities Commission of Nevada prior to construction.

Building Codes, Appliance, and Equipment Standards: Nevada's mandatory state residential and commercial building codes are based on the 2006 IECC and ASHRAE 90.1-2004. Nevada is now in the process of adopting the 2009 IECC. Nevada has established efficacy standards for general-purpose lights.

Electricity Transmission, Interconnection, and Storage: The Public Utilities Commission of Nevada has adopted interconnection standards for customers of NVEnergy with renewable energy systems up to 20 MW in capacity. Nevada law also provides for net metering for renewable energy systems up to 1 MW in capacity. For all net-metered systems, if the cost of purchasing and installing a net-metered system is paid for in whole or in part by a utility, then the electricity generated by the system will be considered to be generated by the utility or acquired from a renewable energy system for the purpose of complying with the state's RPS.

Fuel Standards and Transportation: AFVs are exempt from the state's emissions testing requirements. HEVs are exempt from emissions inspection testing for the first five model years. HEVs operating as taxicabs may remain in operation for an additional twenty-four months beyond the limits for conventional vehicles.

Government Procurement: Nevada's state energy reduction plan requires state agencies to reduce energy purchases for state-owned buildings by 20 percent by 2015. The Department of Administration is required to establish standards that favor Energy Star purchases, and the State Public Works Board must implement guidelines for renewable energy and efficient energy use in all state buildings.

Policies, Plans, and Governmental Affiliations

Policies and Plans: In 2008, the Nevada Climate Change Advisory Committee produced its final report, which included twenty-eight recommendations for reducing GHG emissions in Nevada.

Government Entities: Public Utilities Commission of Nevada, Nevada Climate Change Advisory Committee, Nevada Department of Administration, Nevada Department of Conservation and Natural Resources, Nevada Department of Taxation, Nevada Renewable Energy and Energy Efficiency Authority, Nevada State Office of Energy.

Regional Memberships: Nevada is a member of the WGA and an observer of WCI.

New Hampshire

Financial Incentives

Loan Programs: The New Hampshire Business Finance Authority oversees a revolving loan program for businesses in the state to finance energy efficiency upgrades. All businesses, including nonprofits, are eligible to apply for loans of $100,000 or more. The New Hampshire Community Development Finance Authority administers two revolving loan programs, the Enterprise Energy Fund, which helps business owners and nonprofits make energy improvements on their buildings, and the Municipal Energy Reduction Fund, which helps municipal governments invest in energy-efficient technology. Low-interest loans of $10,000 or more are available through the New Hampshire Business Resource Center to small businesses to finance energy efficiency projects.

Rebates: Rebates for $1.25 per watt of generation capacity per residential owner are available for certain renewable energy systems, up to the lesser of $4,500 or 50 percent of system costs. New Hampshire also provides rebates for new residential hot water heaters, boilers, and furnaces that replace existing, less efficient systems; solar water heaters that replace existing hot water heaters; and residential bulk-fed, wood-pellet central heater boilers or furnaces. Rebates are available for nonresidential solar PV and solar thermal installations served by an IOU or rural electric utility that is required to comply with the state's RPS.

Other Financial Incentives: New Hampshire has created a systems benefit charge on electric customers' bills to fund commercial and residential energy efficiency programs, as well as programs for low-income residents.

Rules and Regulations

Renewable Portfolio Standard: Electricity providers other than municipal utilities must comply with New Hampshire's Electric Renewable Portfolio Standard. New Hampshire has designated four classes of renewable resources, each with their own compliance schedules. Class I resources include wind, geothermal, ocean thermal, wave, current, tidal, methane, certain biomass, and hydrogen derived from biomass or methane, as well as energy efficiency savings from solar hot water heating. Class I resources must have been installed in 2006 or later to be eligible for compliance. Class II resources include solar generation facilities, which began production in 2006 or later. Class III resources include biomass and methane facilities, which began production prior to 2006. Class IV resources include certain hydro facilities up to 5 MW, which began production prior to 2006. By 2025, RPS-obligated entities must procure 16 percent of their retail load from Class I resources, 0.3 percent from Class II resources, 6.5 percent from Class III resources, and 1 percent from Class IV resources.

Facility Siting and Permitting: Property owners may create solar easements for access to solar energy. New Hampshire has created a model solar easement form.

Building Codes, Appliance, and Equipment Standards: The New Hampshire Energy Code for residential and commercial buildings is a mandatory, statewide code that is based on the 2009 IECC.

Electricity Transmission, Interconnection, and Storage: All utilities selling power in New Hampshire must provide net metering to homeowners and small businesses that generate electricity using renewable energy systems with a capacity of up to 100 kW.

Fuel Standards and Transportation: Each school district must develop and implement a policy to minimize or eliminate emissions from buses, cars, delivery vehicles, maintenance vehicles, and other motor vehicles used on school property.

Government Procurement: State agencies must reduce energy use in buildings by 10 percent, purchase Energy Star equipment, and ensure that all state-funded new construction and renovation projects exceed the state energy code by 20 percent in terms of energy efficiency. State agencies must also implement a Clean Fleets program requiring highway fuel economy ratings of at least 27.5 mpg for cars and 20 mpg for light-duty trucks.

Policies, Plans, and Governmental Affiliations

Policies and Plans: The New Hampshire Climate Action Plan recommends a long-term reduction in GHG emissions of 80 percent below 1990 levels by 2050.

Government Entities: Energy Planning Advisory Board, New Hampshire Business Finance Authority, New Hampshire Community Development Finance Authority, New Hampshire

Department of Environmental Services, New Hampshire State Building Code Review Board, New Hampshire Public Utilities Commission.

Regional Memberships: New Hampshire is a member of RGGI.

New Jersey

Financial Incentives

Tax Benefits: New Jersey exempts renewable energy systems used to meet on-site electricity, heating, cooling, or general energy needs from local property taxes. Solar energy equipment is also exempt from sales taxes. Businesses that invest in qualified wind energy facilities are eligible for a tax credit equal to 100 percent of their capital investment. Zero emissions vehicles sold, rented, or leased in New Jersey are exempt from state sales and use tax.

Loan Programs: The New Jersey Clean Energy Solutions Capital Investment program provides grants and loans to businesses for CHP, energy efficiency, and state-of-the-art electricity production projects. Businesses may apply for loans and grants for the commercialization and development of renewable energy and energy efficiency technologies. Low-interest loans and rebates are available to homeowners for certain energy efficiency improvements.

Grants: The New Jersey Commission on Science and Technology administers the Edison Innovation Clean Energy Fund, which provides grants of $100,000 to $500,000 to New Jersey companies for demonstration projects involving renewable energy technology and energy efficiency.

Rebates: New Jersey offers a wide variety of rebates, including rebates to utility customers who purchase and install new energy-efficient electric air conditioners and heat pumps; builders who construct homes that are 15 percent more efficient than homes built to the 2006 IECC; residents who purchase heating systems, water heaters, or certain energy-efficient home appliances; individuals, businesses, public entities, and nonprofits who install small wind energy systems or biomass energy technologies; and homeowners and businesses who install PV system components manufactured in New Jersey.

Other Financial Incentives: New Jersey offers financial incentives, primarily in the form of payments for each kWh of energy produced and grants for onshore wind and biomass electricity generation projects larger than 1 MW. New Jersey also provides direct installation of energy efficiency measures in low-income residences. New Jersey's societal benefits charge supports investments in energy efficiency and renewable energy through various programs, including the Pay for Performance program, which provides incentives for energy efficiency improvements made to new construction projects greater than 50,000 square feet and existing buildings with an annual peak electricity demand greater than 200 kW.

Rules and Regulations

Renewable Portfolio Standard: New Jersey's RPS requires each IOU and retail electricity supplier to procure 22.5 percent of its electricity from qualifying renewable sources by 2021. Eligible sources include solar thermal and PV, wind, biomass, landfill gas, anaerobic digestion, hydro, geothermal, wave and tidal, approved resource-recovery facilities, and fuel cells using renewable fuels. The standard also contains a separate solar-specific provision, which requires suppliers to procure at least 2,518 gigawatt-hours (GWh) from in-state solar electric generators by 2021 and 5,316 GWh by 2026. The New Jersey Board of Public Utilities is in the process of developing a percentage-based standard for offshore wind.

Facility Siting and Permitting: New Jersey municipalities may not place unreasonable limits on small wind energy systems. Solar and wind systems are permitted in areas zoned for industrial uses. Homeowners' associations may not prohibit the installation of solar collectors on certain types of residential properties. New Jersey law also provides for the creation of solar easements.

Building Codes, Appliance, and Equipment Standards: New Jersey has adopted the 2006 IECC with amendments as its code for residential buildings, and ASHRAE/IESNA 90.1-2004 with amendments as its commercial code. New Jersey law also requires that developers of residential developments with twenty-five or more dwelling units offer prospective purchasers the option of installing a solar energy system on the dwelling. Newly designed schools must incorporate LEED guidelines. With several exceptions, new state buildings larger than 15,000 square feet must achieve a LEED Silver certification or a comparable rating.

Electricity Transmission, Interconnection, and Storage: New Jersey's net-metering and interconnection rules allow renewable electricity generators to obtain a credit on their utility bill for each kWh of electricity produced. Electric suppliers must offer net metering to residential, commercial, and industrial customers who produce electricity using solar, wind, geothermal, wave, tidal, landfill gas, or sustainable biomass resources, as well as fuel cells using renewable fuels.

Policies, Plans, and Governmental Affiliations

Policies and Plans: New Jersey's Global Warming Response Act calls for a reduction in the level of statewide GHG emissions, and GHG emissions from electricity generated outside the state but consumed in the state, to 1990 levels by 2020 and 80 percent below 2006 levels by 2050.

Government Entities: New Jersey Board of Public Utilities, New Jersey Department of Community Affairs, New Jersey Department of Environmental Protection, New Jersey Economic Development Authority, New Jersey Office of Clean Energy.

Regional Memberships: New Jersey is a member of RGGI and ICAP.

New Mexico

Financial Incentives

Tax Benefits: Tax credits are available for the development and construction costs of any commercial solar thermal electric, PV, or geothermal electric generating facility; the purchase and installation of a geothermal heat pump; companies that generate electricity from solar, wind, or biomass technologies; the purchase and installation of PV and solar thermal systems; LEED Silver-certified buildings; and each gallon of diesel fuel blended with a minimum of 2 percent biodiesel. Businesses can deduct the revenue generated from selling and installing certain geothermal, solar, and recycled energy systems, as well as the revenue generated from the sale of certain wind turbine equipment and solar thermal and PV systems to government entities, from their gross receipts before state taxes are calculated. Businesses using biomass equipment or materials are eligible for a tax deduction. Solar energy systems are exempt from property tax at the time of installation.

Bonds: Through the Energy Efficiency and Renewable Energy Bonding Act, state school systems and government agencies can use bonds to finance energy efficiency and renewable energy improvements.

Other Financial Incentives: New Mexico has created a public benefits fund to support the implementation of energy-reduction programs.

Rules and Regulations

Renewable Portfolio Standard: By 2020, IOUs must generate 20 percent, and rural cooperatives must generate 10 percent, of their total retail sales from renewable energy sources. The New Mexico Public Regulation Commission (NMPRC) currently acts as the executing agency for this policy. Eligible systems include solar thermal and PV, wind, landfill gas, biomass, anaerobic digestion, new hydro, geothermal electric, and fuel cells using renewable fuels. IOUs are specifically required to meet their RPS requirement using 20 percent solar, 20 percent wind, 10 percent geothermal, biomass, new hydro, and/or other renewable sources, and 3 percent distributed renewables.

Facility Siting and Permitting: The New Mexico Game and Fish Department has created wildlife impact guidelines for all wind system developers. Solar easements are allowed to provide access to direct sunlight.

Building Codes, Appliance, and Equipment Standards: The 2006 New Mexico Energy Conservation Code adopts the 2006 IECC for residential buildings and ASHRAE 90.1-2004 for commercial buildings. New construction of public buildings over 15,000 square feet or using over 50 kW peak electrical demand and renovations involving the replacement of more than three major systems must achieve a LEED Silver rating.

Electricity Transmission, Interconnection, and Storage: IOUs and electric cooperatives are required to offer net metering to all renewable energy and CHP systems generating up to 80 MW. NMPRC oversees this policy. NMPRC likewise oversees the state's interconnection policy, which provides a four-tiered approach based upon kW production.

Government Procurement: All state agencies must reduce energy consumption 10 percent by 2012 and 20 percent by 2015, compared to 2005. All diesel fuel used by state agencies and public schools must contain at least 5 percent biodiesel.

Policies, Plans, and Governmental Affiliations

Policies and Plans: New Mexico has set a target of reducing statewide GHG emissions to 2000 levels by 2012, 10 percent below 2000 levels by 2020, and 75 percent below 2000 levels by 2050.

Government Entities: New Mexico Energy, Minerals and Natural Resources Department, New Mexico Environment Department, New Mexico Public Regulation Commission.

Regional Memberships: New Mexico is a member of the WGA, ICAP, and WCI.

New York

Financial Incentives

Tax Benefits: The Green Building Tax Credit is available to corporate and residential taxpayers who construct a green building or rehabilitate a building to be a green building. A tax credit is also available for biodiesel purchased for residential space and water heating equal to $0.01 per gallon for each percent of biodiesel blended with conventional home heating oil, up to a maximum of $0.20 per gallon. A personal income tax credit is available for 25 percent of the cost of the purchase and installation of solar PV and solar thermal equipment, capped at $5,000, and 20 percent of the cost of the purchase and installation of fuel cells, capped at $1,500. Certain energy conservation improvements made to homes are exempt from real property taxation to the extent that the improvement increases the value of the home. The purchase and installation of qualifying residential solar energy systems is exempt from the state's sales and compensating use taxes.

Loan Programs: New York's System Benefits Charge (SBC) annually generates approximately $175 million for renewable energy and energy efficiency projects, including the New York Residential Loan Fund, which provides reduced-interest rate loans through participating lenders to finance renovation or construction projects that improve a home's energy efficiency, and the Green Jobs—Green New York Loan Program, which provides loans for the installation of energy-efficient measures in homes. The SBC is authorized until June 2011. SBC programs are administered by the New York State Energy Research and Development Authority (NYSERDA).

Grants: The SBC also funds grant programs such as the Clean Energy Business Growth and Development program, which provides clean energy business projects with grants of up to 50 percent of a project's cost, with a maximum of $200,000 per project; direct cash incentives of $750 to $1,500 for certified builders who build an Energy Star Standard Home; grants to manufacturers to develop or expand facilities that produce renewable, clean, and energy-efficient products; the Assisted Home Performance Program, which provides grants to low-income homeowners for up to 50 percent of the costs of energy-efficient improvements; and EmPower New York, which provides grants for electricity reduction measures in homes.

Rebates: NYSERDA offers rebates through the SBC for the implementation of prequalified performance-based energy efficiency measures; the operation of demand-side, energy efficiency, and CHP systems; the construction or substantial renovation of residential buildings that meet certain green building requirements; energy efficiency measures in single- and multifamily homes; and PV and wind systems. New York also offers rebates for the purchase and installation of certain energy-efficient appliances that replace existing appliances in residences.

Rules and Regulations

Renewable Portfolio Standard: IOUs must generate 30 percent of the state's electricity from renewable energy sources by 2015. Of this 30 percent, about 20.7 percent will be generated from existing facilities and 1 percent will be generated through voluntary green power sales. The remainder will be divided into two types: Main Tier, which accounts for about 93 percent of the remaining requirement, and Customer-Sited Tier (CST), which accounts for about 7 percent. Eligible Main Tier resources include solar PV, ocean, tidal, wind, hydro, methane digesters, biomass (including clean wood sourced from mixed demolition debris), liquid biofuels, and fuel cells. Eligible CST resources include PV, solar hot water, wind, methane digesters, and fuel cells.

Facility Siting and Permitting: NYSERDA has created a wind energy toolkit to provide information on various aspects of wind energy development. New York's real property laws allow for the creation of solar easements to ensure uninterrupted solar access for solar energy devices.

Building Codes, Appliance, and Equipment Standards: New York's residential and commercial building codes are based on the 2009 IECC. New York also requires compliance with ASHRAE 90.1-2007 for commercial buildings. New York has set minimum energy efficiency standards for certain appliances (however, some have been superseded by subsequent federal standards).

Electricity Transmission, Interconnection, and Storage: The New York Public Service Commission's Standard Interconnection Requirements apply to all DG systems up to 2MW. Simplified rules exist for systems up to 25 kW. IOUs must offer net metering on a first-come, first-served basis to renewable energy systems. System size and aggregate capacity limitations vary by technology. NEG is credited to the customer's account at the utility's retail rate, except for small CHP and fuel cell systems, where it is credited at the utility's cost-avoided rate.

Government Procurement: All state agencies and departments are required to reduce energy consumption by 35 percent, relative to 1990 levels, in all buildings that they own, lease, or operate, by 2010. State agencies must also procure 20 percent of their electricity from PV, solar thermal, wind, biomass, geothermal, methane waste, and fuel cells by 2010. State agencies must follow green building guidelines when constructing or substantially renovating state buildings, and select Energy Star-labeled products when acquiring or replacing energy-using equipment. All new light-duty vehicles procured by state agencies must be AFVs or HEVs, with exceptions for designated police and emergency vehicles.

Policies, Plans, and Governmental Affiliations

Policies and Plans: In November 2010, New York released its Climate Action Plan, which calls for a 40 percent reduction in GHG emissions below 1990 levels by 2030, increasing to 80 percent by 2050.

Government Entities: New York Climate Action Council, New York Public Service Commission, New York State Department of Environmental Conservation, New York State Department of Public Service, New York State Department of Taxation and Finance, NYSERDA.

Regional Memberships: New York is a member of RGGI and ICAP.

North Carolina

Financial Incentives

Tax Benefits: North Carolina offers a tax credit to individuals and businesses that construct, purchase, or lease renewable energy property. Starting January 1, 2011, North Carolina will also offer a tax credit to businesses for the costs of constructing or retooling a facility to manufacture renewable energy property. The state exempts 80 percent of the appraised value of PV systems from property tax, and all active solar heating and cooling systems may not be assessed at more than the value of a conventional system for property tax purposes. North Carolina also has a sales tax holiday for certain Energy Star appliances.

Loan Programs: North Carolina's Energy Improvement Loan Program is available to businesses, local governments, public schools and colleges, and nonprofits for projects that include energy efficiency improvements and renewable energy systems.

Grants: The North Carolina Green Business Fund provides grants of up to $500,000 to small and mid-size businesses, nonprofits, state agencies, and local governments to encourage the development of renewable energy and green building technologies.

Rebates: The North Carolina Housing Finance Agency (HFA) encourages the construction of energy-efficient affordable housing through their SystemVision Energy Guarantee Program. Through this program, HFA provides a $4,000 subsidy to nonprofits and local governments for each home they develop that follows specific energy efficiency standards. North Carolina provides a $500 rebate to residents who purchase a new Energy Star certified home. North Carolina also offers rebates for certain Energy Star appliances.

Rules and Regulations

Renewable Portfolio Standard: North Carolina's Renewable Energy and Energy Efficiency Portfolio Standard requires IOUs to supply 12.5 percent of retail electricity sales from renewable energy resources by 2021. Municipal utilities and electric cooperatives must meet a 10 percent target by 2018. Eligible energy resources include solar electric, solar thermal, wind, hydropower up to 10 MW, ocean current or wave energy, biomass, landfill gas, CHP using waste heat from renewables, and hydrogen derived from renewables. A percentage of the standard may also be met through energy efficiency measures.

Facility Siting and Permitting: The North Carolina Wind Working Group has published a model wind ordinance to provide guidance for communities seeking to promote wind energy. Subject to certain exceptions, cities and counties may not adopt ordinances prohibiting the installation of solar collectors, and restrictive covenants prohibiting the installation of solar collectors are unenforceable.

Building Codes, Appliance, and Equipment Standards: The 2009 North Carolina Energy Conservation Code, which applies to residential and commercial developments, is mandatory statewide. The code is based on the 2006 IECC and references ASHRAE 90.1-2004 for commercial buildings. State-owned buildings must exceed the energy efficiency requirements of ASHRAE 90.1-2004.

Electricity Transmission, Interconnection, and Storage: The North Carolina Utilities Commission (NCUC) requires the state's IOUs to make net metering available to customers that operate systems that generate electricity from renewable resources. The individual system capacity limit is 1 MW, but there is no aggregate capacity limit. NCUC has also adopted interconnection standards that apply to all state-jurisdictional interconnections.

Fuel Standards and Transportation: School buses capable of operating on diesel fuel must use fuel blended with biodiesel.

Government Procurement: Total energy consumption in state buildings must be reduced by 20 percent by 2010 and 30 percent by 2015 based on consumption during the 2003–2004 fiscal year. At least 75 percent of new or replacement state government light-duty cars and trucks must be AFVs or low-emission vehicles.

Policies, Plans, and Governmental Affiliations

Policies and Plans: The Climate Action Plan Advisory Group released a final report and recommendations in 2008 detailing fifty-six mitigation options for addressing climate change.

Government Entities: Climate Action Plan Advisory Group, North Carolina Department of Commerce, North Carolina Housing Finance Agency, North Carolina Utilities Commission.

Regional Memberships: North Carolina is a member of the SGA.

North Dakota

Financial Incentives

Tax Benefits: Corporate income tax credits are available for the cost of purchasing and installing geothermal, biomass, wind, and solar energy systems. Individuals are eligible for an income tax credit for the cost of purchasing and installing geothermal systems. Commercial wind turbines over 100 kW receive a special property tax assessment, and locally assessed solar, wind, and geothermal systems are exempt from local property taxes for five years after installation. Licensed fuel suppliers who blend biodiesel with diesel fuel are entitled to an income tax credit of $0.05 per gallon of fuel containing at least 5 percent biodiesel. Equipment purchased by a facility that enables the facility to sell diesel fuel containing at least 2 percent biodiesel is exempt from sales tax.

Grants: State institutions and agencies are eligible for grants for energy efficiency improvements through the State Facility Energy Improvement Program.

Rules and Regulations

Renewable Portfolio Standard: North Dakota has established a voluntary goal that 10 percent of the retail electricity sold in the state will come from solar, wind, biomass, geothermal, hydropower, hydrogen, or recycled energy systems by 2015.

Facility Siting and Permitting: Solar and wind system operators may obtain an easement for access to sunlight and wind from other property owners.

Electricity Transmission, Interconnection, and Storage: Renewable energy and CHP systems of up to 100 kW are eligible for net metering through North Dakota's IOUs. Such utilities must purchase a system's NEG at their cost-avoided rate.

Policies, Plans, and Governmental Affiliations

Government Entities: North Dakota Department of Commerce, North Dakota Public Service Commission.

Regional Memberships: North Dakota is a member of the WGA.

Ohio

Financial Incentives

Tax Benefits: Property used in energy conversion, thermal-efficiency improvements, and the conversion of solid waste to energy is exempt from the state sales and use tax and the state's corporate franchise tax. Qualified energy projects of 250 kW or less are exempt from public utility tangible personal property taxes and real property taxes. Businesses that undertake new energy efficiency or renewable energy projects may also be eligible for an exemption from the state's tangible personal property tax, real property tax, a portion of the corporate franchise tax, and the sales and use tax. A tax credit is available to taxpayers that invest in a certified ethanol production facility.

Loan Programs: Low-interest loans are available to residents for energy-efficient home upgrades and renewable energy systems.

Grants: Ohio's public benefits fund, the Advanced Energy Fund, provides a variety of grants to residents, low-income housing developers, businesses, industry, local governments, schools, nonprofits, and farmers for the design and implementation of renewable energy and energy-efficient programs. Grants and loans are available to support biofuel development in the state. Grants are also available to retrofit older school buses operating on diesel fuel in order to reduce emissions.

Other Financial Incentives: Ohio has created the Advanced Energy Job Stimulus Fund to support projects that increase the development, production, and use of advanced energy technologies in the state. Qualified businesses are eligible for a variety of financial incentives, including grants, low-interest loans, and conduit bonds.

Rules and Regulations

Renewable Portfolio Standard: Ohio's RPS requires that utilities provide 25 percent of their retail electricity supply from alternative energy resources by 2025. Of this 25 percent, 12.5 percent must come from renewable resources by 2024. Of this 12.5 percent, 0.5 percent must come from solar resources by 2024. The Public Utilities Commission of Ohio (PUCO) currently acts as the executing agency for this policy.

Facility Siting and Permitting: Ohio has a streamlined permitting process for wind energy projects. Wind facilities of 5 MW or more must only obtain a certificate of environmental compatibility and public need from the Ohio Power Siting Board within PUCO. The certificate satisfies all siting and permitting requirements for state agencies and local governments. Solar easements are allowed to provide access to direct sunlight.

Building Codes, Appliance, and Equipment Standards: Residential buildings must comply with the 2006 IECC, the Residential Code of Ohio, or the state's Prescriptive Energy Requirements. Commercial buildings must comply with the 2006 IECC and ASHRAE 90.1-2004. New public schools must achieve LEED Silver certification, with a goal of achieving LEED Gold certification. State agencies are also required to perform life-cycle cost analyses before construction, as well as energy consumption analyses prior to new leases.

Electricity Transmission, Interconnection, and Storage: Ohio's IOUs and retail electricity suppliers are required to provide net metering to customers generating electricity through qualified renewable energy sources. The state has also adopted a three-tiered interconnection standard applicable to IOUs for all DG systems up to 20 MW in capacity, with PUCO acting to implement and oversee the program.

Government Procurement: Newly acquired state agency vehicles, other than law enforcement vehicles, must be equipped to use alternative fuels and must use alternative fuels if reasonably available and priced.

Policies, Plans, and Governmental Affiliations

Government Entities: Ohio Air Quality Development Authority, Ohio Power Siting Board, Ohio Treasury, Public Utilities Commission of Ohio.

Regional Memberships: Ohio is an observer of the MGGRA and a member of the MGA.

Oklahoma

Financial Incentives

Tax Benefits: Businesses producing renewable energy from a zero emissions facility are eligible for a state income tax credit. Oklahoma also offers an income tax credit to contractors who build energy-efficient homes and manufacturers of small wind turbines; however, due to a moratorium on certain state tax incentives, these tax credits are unavailable for projects completed on or after July 1, 2010, and before July 1, 2012. Tax credits are available for 50 percent of the cost of purchasing a new AFV or converting a vehicle to operate on an alternative fuel, as well as for up to 75 percent of the cost of installing alternative fueling infrastructure. Tax credits are also available to producers of biodiesel.

Loan Programs: The Oklahoma Department of Commerce provides loans to local governments, public schools, and institutes of higher education for energy efficiency improvements.

Rules and Regulations

Renewable Portfolio Standard: Oklahoma has established a goal that 15 percent of the electricity generated in Oklahoma be derived from renewable sources by 2015. Eligible resources include wind, solar, hydropower, hydrogen, geothermal, and biomass. Energy efficiency may be used to meet up to 25 percent of the goal.

Facility Siting and Permitting: The Oklahoma Wind Energy Development Act provides a set of rules for owners of wind energy facilities related to decommissioning, payments, and insurance.

Building Codes, Appliance, and Equipment Standards: Oklahoma has adopted the 2003 IECC as its statewide residential and commercial building code, although each jurisdiction in the state can choose to adopt another nationally recognized model code in lieu of the 2003 IECC. New construction and major renovations of state buildings larger than 10,000 square feet must be developed to meet the requirements of the LEED or GreenGlobes systems.

Electricity Transmission, Interconnection, and Storage: Oklahoma requires the state's IOUs and regulated electric cooperatives to provide net metering to all customers who generate electricity from renewable energy and CHP systems up to 100 kW in capacity. Utilities are prohibited from creating additional charges for net-metered customers.

Fuel Standards and Transportation: School districts should, when feasible, purchase vehicles that utilize alternative fuel. The Oklahoma Department of Commerce has established the Oklahoma Bioenergy Center, with the goal of becoming a leader in the field of biofuel production and research.

Government Procurement: State agencies are required to create and implement energy efficiency and conservation plans, and are urged to include purchasing preferences for AFVs in such plans.

Policies, Plans, and Governmental Affiliations

Government Entities: Oklahoma Conservation Commission, Oklahoma Corporation Commission, Oklahoma Department of Central Services, Oklahoma Department of Commerce, Oklahoma Department of Environmental Quality.

Regional Memberships: Oklahoma is a member of the WGA and the SGA.

Oregon

Financial Incentives

Tax Benefits: Oregon provides a variety of tax credits to businesses for investments in energy conservation, recycling, renewable energy resources, sustainable buildings, and less-polluting transportation fuels. Homeowners and renters can receive a tax credit if they purchase certain energy efficiency or renewable energy systems. The added value to any property from the installation of a renewable energy system is not included in the assessment of the property's value for property tax purposes. Individuals are allowed a credit against income taxes otherwise due for costs paid or incurred to purchase fuel blended with biofuel for use in an AFV. Residents and businesses that purchase a new AFV, convert a vehicle to operate on an alternative fuel, or purchase alternative fuel infrastructure may also qualify for a tax credit.

Loan Programs: The Oregon Small-Scale Energy Loan Program offers low-interest loans and bonds to finance small-scale, local renewable energy, energy efficiency, and alternative fuel projects.

Grants: The Oregon Department of Energy provides grants for feasibility studies for renewable energy, heat, and fuel projects.

Rebates: Oregon homeowners and renters are eligible for home weatherization rebates of up to $500 through the State Home Oil Weatherization Program. Oregon also offers rebates for select Energy Star appliances installed in low-income households.

Other Financial Incentives: Oregon has established a solar volumetric incentive rate and payment program for PV systems up to 500 kW in capacity. Oregon's public benefits fund, the Energy Trust of Oregon, provides financial incentives for energy efficiency and renewable energy programs, low-income housing energy assistance, and school energy-conservation efforts. The fund is supported by a 3 percent charge on utility customers' bills.

Rules and Regulations

Renewable Portfolio Standard: Oregon has an RPS for electric utilities and retail electricity suppliers that varies, depending on the utility's size. Large utilities must generate 5 percent of their energy from renewable energy sources by 2011, increasing to 25 percent by 2025. Smaller utilities are subject to lower standards. Eligible renewable resources include wind, solar, hydro, ocean thermal, wave, tidal, geothermal, certain types of hydrogen power, biomass, biogas, and municipal solid waste.

Facility Siting and Permitting: Oregon's solar access law forbids the prohibition of solar energy systems when conveying a property, and property owners may create solar and wind easements. Oregon state law also allows municipalities and local authorities to establish solar access laws. The Oregon Department of Energy has issued a model ordinance for energy projects, which includes guidance for local governments siting wind, solar, geothermal, biomass, and cogeneration projects.

Building Codes, Appliance, and Equipment Standards: Oregon has developed its own residential and commercial building codes for energy efficiency, based on the 2006 IRC and the 2009 IECC, respectively. New state facilities must exceed the energy conservation requirements in Oregon's building code by at least 20 percent. Oregon also requires all public building projects for which the total contract price is $1 million or more to include solar technologies. Oregon has set minimum energy efficiency standards for eleven appliances (however, some have been superseded by subsequent federal standards).

Electricity Transmission, Interconnection, and Storage: Oregon has three separate interconnection standards: one for net-metered systems; one for small generator facilities that are not net metered; and one for large generator facilities that are not net metered. Net metering is available to utility customers generating electricity using renewable energy resources. The individual system limit is 2 MW for nonresidential and 25 kW for residential customers of the state's primary IOUs, and 25 kW for nonresidential and 10 kW for residential customers of the state's municipal utilities and electric cooperatives. Oregon has also established separate net-metering requirements and interconnection standards for the state's utilities. All electric utilities must offer customers an optional green power program.

Government Procurement: Existing state buildings must reduce energy use by 20 percent compared to the building's baseline energy use in 2000. State agencies and transit districts must purchase AFVs and use alternative fuels to operate those vehicles to the maximum extent possible.

Policies, Plans, and Governmental Affiliations

Policies and Plans: Oregon's Global Warming Commission is charged with developing and implementing the state's GHG emissions reduction goals. Oregon has established a target of stopping the growth of GHG emissions by 2010, and reducing emissions 10 percent below 1990 levels by 2020 and 75 percent below 1990 levels by 2050.

Government Entities: Department of Consumer and Business Services, Oregon Department of Energy, Oregon Public Utility Commission.

Regional Memberships: Oregon is a member of ICAP, the West Coast Governors' Global Warming Initiative, the WGA, and WCI.

Pennsylvania

Financial Incentives

Tax Benefits: Tax credits are available for projects related to the production of alternative fuels, as well as the research and development of technology to provide alternative fuels. Wind turbines and related equipment may not be counted by tax assessors when setting property values.

Loan Programs: Businesses, multifamily residential homeowners, nonprofits, and government entities are eligible for loans of up to $2.5 million for energy efficiency improvements in existing buildings. Loans of up to $35,000 are available to homeowners who improve energy efficiency through high-efficiency heating, air-conditioning, insulation, windows, doors, and geothermal and "whole house" improvements. Pennsylvania also provides loans and grants to small businesses that implement energy efficiency and pollution prevention measures.

Grants: Grants are available for the purchase of AFVs or HEVs, or the conversion of conventional fuel vehicles to operate on alternative fuels. Grants are also available for new schools to be built according to green building standards.

Rebates: Rebates are available to individuals and small businesses for the installation of solar PV and solar thermal systems.

Other Financial Incentives: Pennsylvania enacted a broad $650 million alternative energy bill in 2008 to provide a variety of financial incentives, including loans, grants and loan guarantees to businesses, nonprofits, economic development organizations, local governments, and schools for alternative energy and clean energy projects, wind and geothermal energy technologies, and high-performance buildings.

Rules and Regulations

Renewable Portfolio Standard: Pennsylvania's Alternative Energy Portfolio Standard requires retail electricity suppliers to supply 18 percent of their electricity from alternative forms of energy by 2020. Of that 18 percent, 8 percent must come from "Tier I" sources and 10 percent from "Tier II" sources. Tier I sources include solar thermal, solar PV, wind, low-impact hydro, geothermal, biomass, certain methane gas, and fuel cells. Tier II sources include waste coal, DG systems, demand-side management increasing energy efficiency, large hydro, municipal solid waste generation, wood pulping, and integrated gasification combined cycle coal. Pennsylvania has also specified that 5 percent of the Tier I requirement must come from solar PV by 2020.

Facility Siting and Permitting: Pennsylvania has developed a model local ordinance for wind energy facilities.

Building Codes, Appliance, and Equipment Standards: Residential buildings in Pennsylvania must comply with the 2009 IECC, the 2009 IRC, or the 2009 Pennsylvania Alternative Residential Energy Provisions. Commercial buildings must comply with the 2009 IECC and ASHRAE 90.1 2007.

Electricity Transmission, Interconnection, and Storage: Interconnection standards have been adopted for net-metered systems and other forms of DG up to 5 MW in capacity. The state's IOUs must offer net metering to customers that generate electricity with renewable energy systems. The individual system limit is 50 kW for residential customers, 3 MW for nonresidential customers, and 5 MW for customers who make their systems available during emergencies or in order to maintain critical infrastructure.

Government Procurement: State agencies are required to reduce energy use in state buildings 10 percent from 2008 levels by 2010. The state government is also required to purchase 50 percent of its total electricity from wind and biomass resources by mid-2010. State agencies are also subject to a number of energy-efficiency-related requirements, including the requirement to procure Energy Star or other energy efficiency products when economically feasible.

Policies, Plans, and Governmental Affiliations

Policies and Plans: Pennsylvania's Climate Change Action Plan calls for a 30 percent reduction in GHG emissions below 2002 levels by 2020 and outlines fifty-two recommendations for reducing GHG emissions in the state.

Government Entities: Climate Change Advisory Committee, Pennsylvania Department of Community and Economic Development, Pennsylvania Department of Environmental Protection,

Pennsylvania Department of General Services, Pennsylvania Department of Labor and Industry, Pennsylvania Department of Revenue, Pennsylvania Energy Development Authority, Pennsylvania Public Utilities Commission.

Regional Memberships: Pennsylvania is an observer of RGGI.

Rhode Island

Financial Incentives

Tax Benefits: Rhode Island offers a tax credit of up to 25 percent of the cost of residential solar, wind, and geothermal energy systems. For the purposes of local property tax assessments, certain residential solar energy systems cannot be assessed at a value more than that of a conventional electric generator. Certain solar, wind, and geothermal equipment is also exempt from the state's sales-and-use tax. Biodiesel is exempt from the state motor fuel tax.

Loan Programs/Grants: Rhode Island's public benefits fund, the Rhode Island Renewable Energy Fund, provides up to $750,000 annually in grants and loans to support a variety of renewable energy projects. Nonprofit affordable housing developers and agencies are eligible for $100,000 per award per year, with total funding of $200,000 available. Municipalities are eligible for $500,000 per award per year, with a total of $1 million available. Also available to businesses, nonprofits, municipalities, schools, and civic institutions is $200,000 per award per year to fund technical feasibility studies. The balance of the fund is available for renewable energy development projects.

Rules and Regulations

Renewable Portfolio Standard: IOUs and retail suppliers of electricity must supply 16 percent of their retail electricity sales from renewable sources by 2019. Eligible renewable resources include solar radiation, wind, ocean heat, ocean movement, small hydro, geothermal, certain biomass facilities, and fuel cells using renewable fuels. Waste-to-energy combustion is specifically excluded from the RPS. In addition, electric distribution companies must enter into long-term contracts for 90 MW in capacity from new renewable energy facilities, of which 3 MW must be solar, in-state generation by 2014.

Facility Siting and Permitting: Rhode Island allows property owners to grant solar easements.

Building Codes, Appliance, and Equipment Standards: Rhode Island recently adopted the 2009 IECC and ASHRAE 90.1-2007 as the state building code, and is required by law to develop a plan to achieve compliance with these standards in 90 percent of new and renovated building space by February 2017. Rhode Island has set minimum efficiency standards for seventeen appliances (however, some have been superseded by subsequent federal standards). Public building construction projects of at least 5,000 square feet and public building renovation projects of at least 10,000 square feet must be designed and built to achieve LEED or equivalent certification.

Electricity Transmission, Interconnection, and Storage: The Rhode Island Public Utilities Commission has approved an interconnection tariff for customers of the state's primary IOUs that generate electricity using net-metered systems and certain other forms of DG. Net metering is available to customers that generate electricity using solar or wind resources. The maximum individual system capacity is limited to 3.5 MW for systems owned by cities and towns, and 1.65 MW for other customers.

Government Procurement: At least 75 percent of state motor vehicle acquisitions must be AFVs, and the remaining 25 percent must be HEVs to the greatest extent possible. In addition, all new passenger vehicles and light-duty trucks in the state's fleet must achieve a minimum city fuel economy of 23 mpg and 19 mpg, respectively.

Policies, Plans, and Governmental Affiliations

Policies and Plans: Rhode Island signed on to the Climate Change Action Plan developed by the New England Governors and the Eastern Canadian Premiers, which requires the state to reduce its GHG emissions to 1990 levels by 2010, 10 percent below 1990 levels by 2020, and 75 to 85 percent below 2001 levels in the long term.

Government Entities: Rhode Island Department of Administration, Rhode Island Department of Environmental Management, Rhode Island Economic Development Corporation, Rhode Island Office of Energy Resources, Rhode Island Public Utilities Commission.

Regional Memberships: Rhode Island is a member of RGGI.

South Carolina

Financial Incentives

Tax Benefits: In South Carolina, individual and corporate taxpayers may claim a tax credit of up to 25 percent of the costs of purchasing and installing a solar energy system or small hydropower system for heating water, space heating, air cooling, energy-efficient daylighting, heat reclamation, energy-efficient demand response, or the generation of electricity. The state also offers a corporate tax credit for the purchase and installation of equipment used to create energy from fuels consisting of at least 90 percent biomass. South Carolina provides a $750 tax credit to individuals who purchase a manufactured home that meets or exceeds certain energy efficiency standards. There is also a $300 sales tax cap on manufactured homes that meet these energy efficiency standards. South Carolina offers a sales tax exemption for any device, equipment, or machinery operated by or used to produce hydrogen fuel cells. Residents that claim the federal fuel cell, advanced lean burn, HEV, or AFV tax credit are eligible for a state income tax credit equal to 20 percent of the federal credit.

Loan Programs: South Carolina's ConserFund Loan Program funds energy efficiency improvements in state agencies, local governments, public schools, and nonprofits.

Other Financial Incentives: A production incentive is available for certain biomass energy facilities.

Rules and Regulations

Building Codes, Appliance, and Equipment Standards: South Carolina's Energy Standard Act, which applies to residential and commercial developments, is mandatory statewide and based on the 2006 IECC. Major state facility projects must be designed and constructed to meet the LEED Silver standard or two globes using the Green Globes rating system.

Electricity Transmission, Interconnection, and Storage: South Carolina has developed simplified interconnection standards for small DG systems. The standards apply to three of the state's four IOUs and cover residential renewable energy systems up to 20 kW and nonresidential renewable energy systems up to 100 kW.

Government Procurement: South Carolina requires state agencies and public school districts to develop energy conservation plans toward an ultimate goal of a 20 percent reduction in energy use by 2020, relative to 2000 levels.

Policies, Plans, and Governmental Affiliations

Policies and Plans: The South Carolina Climate, Energy, and Commerce Committee released its final report in 2008, setting forth fifty-one policy recommendations for reducing GHG emissions in the state, including a voluntary goal of reducing GHG emissions to 5 percent below 1990 levels by 2020.

Government Entities: South Carolina Climate, Energy, and Commerce Committee, South Carolina Department of Revenue, South Carolina Energy Office, South Carolina Office of Regulatory Staff, South Carolina Public Service Commission.

Regional Memberships: South Carolina is a member of the SGA.

South Dakota

Financial Incentives

Tax Benefits: Wind farms that are 5 MW or larger are subject to an alternative taxation structure. Renewable energy facilities smaller than 5 MW are exempt from real property tax, up to $50,000 or 70 percent of the assessed value of the property, whichever is greater. New or expanded wind energy systems are eligible for a sales tax refund of up to 55 percent. Licensed biodiesel blenders are eligible for a tax credit for each gallon of fuel blended with biodiesel. Ethanol producers are eligible for a $0.20 per gallon production incentive for ethanol that is fully distilled and produced in South Dakota.

Rules and Regulations

Renewable Portfolio Standard: South Dakota has established a voluntary objective for retail electricity providers to supply at least 10 percent of their retail sales from renewable, recycled, and conserved energy by 2015.

Facility Siting and Permitting: Property owners may grant wind easements. The South Dakota Public Utilities Commission has developed a model ordinance for the siting of wind energy systems.

Building Codes, Appliance, and Equipment Standards: The South Dakota Residential Energy Standard is a voluntary code based on the 2006 IECC. There is no mandatory statewide commercial building code. All state facilities must comply with ASHRAE 90.1-1999. Large new state construction and renovation projects must achieve a LEED Silver certification or a comparable accreditation.

Electricity Transmission, Interconnection, and Storage: South Dakota allows customers of IOUs that generate electricity from renewable energy systems up to 10 MW to interconnect to the grid.

Policies, Plans, and Governmental Affiliations

Government Entities: Bureau of Administration, Energy Management Office, South Dakota Public Utilities Commission.

Regional Memberships: South Dakota is member of the MGA and the WGA, and an observer of the MGGRA.

Tennessee

Financial Incentives

Tax Benefits: Wind energy systems operated by public utilities, businesses, or industrial facilities cannot be taxed in excess of one-third of their total installed cost. Tax credits of up to $1.5 million are available to manufacturers of clean energy technologies that invest $250 million or more in the state. Manufacturers of clean energy technologies that invest $100 million or more in the state and create fifty full-time jobs at 150 percent the rate of Tennessee's average occupational wage are also eligible for a reduced sales and use tax on certain building materials, machinery, and equipment.

Loan Programs: Through the Energy Efficient Schools Initiative, public schools are eligible to receive loans and grants to implement energy efficiency improvements. Small businesses implementing energy efficiency projects are eligible for low-interest loans of up to $300,000. Additionally, the state provides low-interest loans to municipal and county governments implementing energy efficiency building projects.

Grants: Businesses seeking to implement renewable energy technologies are eligible for the Tennessee Clean Energy Technology Grant for up to 40 percent of the total installed system cost, up to $75,000. The Biofuel Green Island Corridor grant is also available to businesses purchasing or installing biofuel storage tanks and fuel pumps at commercial fuel stations.

Rebates: Tennessee offers rebates for certain Energy Star appliances installed in residences.

Rules and Regulations

Facility Siting and Permitting: Solar easements are allowed to provide access to direct sunlight.

Building Codes, Appliance, and Equipment Standards: The 2006 IECC is mandatory for new residential buildings. ASHRAE 90A-1980 and 90B-1975 is voluntary for commercial buildings.

Government Procurement: New public building office equipment, appliances, lighting, heating, and cooling systems must meet Energy Star requirements unless unavailable. All state agencies are urged to purchase energy-efficient vehicles and to use alternative fuels whenever possible.

Policies, Plans, and Governmental Affiliations

Policies and Plans: Tennessee's climate action plan includes a number of policy recommendations for reducing GHG emissions in the state. The Governor's Task Force on Energy Policy was created to develop an energy-efficient usage plan to be implemented throughout the state.

Government Entities: Tennessee Regulatory Authority, Tennessee Department of Economic and Community Development, Tennessee Department of Environment and Conservation.

Regional Memberships: Tennessee is a member of the SGA.

Texas

Financial Incentives

Tax Benefits: Texas allows a corporation or other entity subject to the state franchise tax to deduct the cost of a solar energy device from the franchise tax. In addition, companies in Texas engaged solely in the business of manufacturing, selling, or installing solar energy devices are exempted from the franchise tax. The Texas property tax code allows an exemption of the amount of the appraised property value that arises from the installation or construction of a solar- or wind-powered energy device that is primarily for the production and distribution of thermal, mechanical, or electrical energy for on-site use, or devices used to store that energy. The state also offers a sales tax holiday to purchasers of certain energy-efficient products during Memorial Day weekend.

Loan Programs: Through the State Energy Conservation Office, the LoanSTAR Program offers low-interest loans to public entities for certain energy cost reduction measures.

Grants: The Texas Department of Rural Affairs (TDRA) offers the Renewable Energy Demonstration Pilot Program, which provides grants to local governments for the installation of renewable energy projects. TDRA also offers grants of up to $1.5 million to qualified local governments that use wind turbines to desalinate brackish ground water. The Texas Commission on Environmental Quality provides grants for various types of clean air projects, including heavy-duty vehicle replacement and retrofits, and alternative fuel dispensing infrastructure.

Rebates: Texas provides rebates to homeowners who replace older, less efficient appliances with Energy Star appliances.

Rules and Regulations

Renewable Portfolio Standard: The Public Utility Commission of Texas has adopted rules for the state's Renewable Energy Mandate, which establishes an RPS, an REC trading program, and renewable energy purchase requirements for competitive retailers in Texas. The rules require 5,880 MW of new renewables to be installed in the state by 2015, including a goal of 500 MW from resources other than wind. The rules also set a goal of reaching 10,000 MW of renewable energy capacity by 2025. Qualifying renewable energy sources include solar, wind, geothermal, hydroelectric, wave, tidal, biomass, and biomass-based waste products, including landfill gas.

Building Codes, Appliance, and Equipment Standards: The Texas Building Energy Performance Standards, which apply to residential and commercial developments, are mandatory and based on the 2000 IECC and 2001 Supplement, and reference ASHRAE 90.1-2001 for commercial buildings. For single-family homes, the 2009 IRC goes into effect on January 1, 2012. For other residential, commercial, and industrial buildings, the 2009 IECC goes into effect on April 1, 2011. All state-funded residential construction must comply with the 2003 IECC, and all state-funded commercial construction must comply with ASHRAE 90.1-2004. Texas law prescribes energy efficiency standards for new and rehabilitated single- and multifamily dwellings that receive assistance from the Texas Department of Housing and Community Affairs.

Electricity Transmission, Interconnection, and Storage: Texas has established interconnection rules for distributed renewable energy generation systems with a maximum capacity of 10 MW and connected at a voltage of less than 60 kilovolts. Retail electricity providers are permitted, but not required, to provide net metering.

Government Procurement: Texas has adopted energy standards for public buildings, requiring state government departments to compare the cost of providing energy alternatives for new and reconstructed state buildings and for certain construction or repair to energy systems and equipment. State agencies and political subdivisions have a goal of reducing electricity consumption by 5 percent each year for six years, beginning September 1, 2007. Texas law requires state-owned or leased buildings to use Energy Star appliances and equipment, as well as low-wattage light bulbs. State agency fleets with more than fifteen vehicles, other than emergency and law enforcement vehicles, must consist of at least 50 percent AFVs and use alternative fuels at least 80 percent of the time.

Policies, Plans, and Governmental Affiliations

Government Entities: Texas Commission on Environmental Quality, Texas Department of Rural Affairs, Texas State Energy Conservation Office, Public Utility Commission of Texas.

Regional Memberships: Texas is a member of the SGA and the WGA.

Utah

Financial Incentives

Tax Benefits: Residential and commercial taxpayers are eligible to receive an income tax credit for the costs of installing certain renewable energy systems. Utah also exempts equipment used to generate renewable energy from the state sales tax. The state also provides a tax credit to certain businesses that construct renewable electricity generation facilities or manufacture equipment used in the generation of alternative energy in a designated alternative energy development zone in Utah. Qualifying compressed natural gas vehicle purchasers can claim a tax credit of 35 percent of the vehicle's purchase price, up to $2,500.

Loan Programs: School districts and political subdivisions are eligible to receive interest-free loans from the state to implement energy-efficient projects. Government entities and businesses can apply to receive loans and grants to cover a portion of the cost of purchasing clean fuel vehicles, converting vehicles to operate on clean fuels, or retrofitting diesel vehicles. The state has also created a loan program for state agencies working to implement energy efficiency improvements in state buildings.

Rebates: Utah provides rebates of 50 percent or 80 percent of the cost (depending on income level), up to $2,000, for energy efficiency improvements made to homes constructed prior to 2000.

Rules and Regulations

Renewable Portfolio Standard: A voluntary RPS policy is currently in place for the state's utilities, with a goal of providing 20 percent of adjusted retail sales from renewable forms of energy by 2025, if cost-effective. The Utah Department of Environmental Quality currently acts as the executing agency for this policy.

Facility Siting and Permitting: Solar easements are allowed to provide access to direct sunlight.

Building Codes, Appliance, and Equipment Standards: Utah has adopted the 2009 IECC for residential buildings and the 2009 IECC and ASHRAE 90.1-2004 for commercial buildings. New state building projects must be certified LEED Silver.

Electricity Transmission, Interconnection, and Storage: The state's only IOU and most electric cooperatives must provide net metering to customers generating qualifying renewable energy. Residential systems up to 25 kW and nonresidential systems up to 2 MW are eligible. The Utah Public Service Commission oversees both this policy and the state's interconnection system.

Fuel Standards and Transportation: All state school buses must meet idle reduction requirements.

Government Procurement: The Utah Air Quality Board has the ability to require clean fuel use in the state's fleet of vehicles if necessary to meet national air quality standards.

Policies, Plans, and Governmental Affiliations

Policies and Plans: The Utah Department of Environmental Quality has set a goal of reducing statewide GHG emissions to 2005 levels by 2020.

Government Entities: Division of Facilities Construction and Management, Governor's Office of Economic Development, Utah Air Quality Board, Utah Department of Environmental Quality, Utah Public Service Commission, Utah State Tax Commission.

Regional Memberships: Utah is a member of the WGA and WCI.

Vermont

Financial Incentives

Tax Benefits: The Business Solar Tax Credit is available to C corporations prior to 2012 for up to 30 percent of the cost of installations of solar energy systems of up to 150 kW on business properties. The tax credit stays in effect for individual tax payers through 2016 at a reduced rate of 7.2 percent. Vermont exempts from its sales tax the cost of certain renewable energy, CHP, and solar water heating systems.

Loan Programs: Vermont requires payments from utilities to be paid to the Clean Energy Development Fund (CEDF) in order to promote the development of renewable energy and CHP technologies. The fund will provide approximately $6 to $7.2 million annually through March 2012. The CEDF Loan Program seeks to promote the development of clean electric energy technologies by providing funding for purchasing land and buildings (when specific to qualifying projects), purchasing and installing machinery and equipment, and working capital. Low-interest loans with a fixed rate of 2 percent are available to individuals, companies, nonprofits, and municipalities. The minimum loan amount is $50,000; the maximum amount is $750,000. The Vermont Business Energy Conservation Loan Program provides low-interest loans of up to $150,000 to certain businesses and nonprofits for projects that improve the energy efficiency of a building.

Rebates: Efficiency Vermont, administered by the Vermont Public Services Board (PSB), offers a number of rebates to a range of sectors through funding from a volumetric charge on electric customers' bills. Vermont's Small Scale Renewable Energy Incentive Program provides rebates for certain new solar water heating, PV, wind, and micro-hydro energy system installations.

Other Financial Incentives: Vermont requires retail electricity providers to purchase electricity generated by eligible renewable energy facilities through the Sustainably Priced Energy Enterprise Development (SPEED) program via long-term contracts with fixed standard offer rates.

Rules and Regulations

Renewable Portfolio Standard: The SPEED program established a voluntary goal that 20 percent of total statewide electric retail sales be generated by SPEED projects by July 1, 2017. In addition, PSB has the authority to require Vermont utilities and cooperatives to comply with a mandatory RPS if a minimum obligation established by the SPEED program is not met. The minimum obligation requires that either (1) the amount of qualifying SPEED resources that came into service between January 1, 2005, and July 1, 2012, is equal to or greater than total statewide growth in retail electric sales during that same time period, and at least 5 percent of the 2005 total retail electric sales in the state are provided by qualified SPEED resources; or (2) the amount of qualifying SPEED resources equals or exceeds 10 percent of the retail electric sales in 2005 for the state of Vermont.

Facility Siting and Permitting: Vermont law forbids ordinances, deed restrictions, or covenants that prohibit the use of solar collectors, clotheslines, or other renewable energy devices.

Building Codes, Appliance, and Equipment Standards: The Vermont Residential Building Energy Standards are based on the 2000 IECC with state-specific amendments. The Vermont Commercial Building Energy Standards are based on the 2004 IECC and ASHRAE 90.1-2004 with state-specific amendments. The Vermont Department of Public Service is currently required to develop a new statewide energy code that would mandate compliance with the 2009 IECC and ASHRAE 90.1-2007. State buildings must be designed to be "highly efficient" and to exceed state efficiency codes for existing buildings by 30 percent. Vermont has established minimum energy efficiency standards for certain appliances.

Electricity Transmission, Interconnection, and Storage: Net metering is available for renewable energy systems of up to 250 kW and CHP systems of up to 20 kW on a first-come, first-served basis until the cumulative capacity of net-metered systems equals 2 percent of a utility's peak demand during 1996 or the previous year, whichever is greater. NEG is credited to the customer's next billing period. Any excess left after an annualized period reverts to the utility, without compensation to the customer-generator. Vermont has established separate interconnection standards for net-metered systems of 150 kW or less, net-metered systems less than 250 kW but more than 150 kW, and systems that are not net metered.

Government Procurement: State agencies may only purchase Energy Star or comparable products and use them in a manner that maximizes their energy efficiency potential. Vermont's "Energy Efficiency and Affordability Act" promotes the use of biodiesel in state vehicle fleets.

Policies, Plans, and Governmental Affiliations

Policies and Plans: In 2005, the governor issued an executive order setting goals for the reduction of GHG emissions by 25 percent from 1990 levels by 2012, by 50 percent by 2028 and, "if practical using reasonable efforts," by 75 percent by 2050. The Governor's Commission on Climate Change approved a report on October 26, 2007, that sets forth a strategy to address climate change and achieve these goals.

Government Entities: Vermont Climate Change Oversight Committee, Vermont Department of Public Service, Vermont Economic Development Authority, Vermont Governor's Commission on Climate Change, Vermont Public Services Board.

Regional Memberships: Vermont is a member of RGGI.

Virginia

Financial Incentives

Tax Benefits: Individuals may claim a deduction of 20 percent, up to $500, for sales taxes paid to purchase certain energy-efficient products. Virginia has also created a four-day sales tax holiday on Energy Star appliances. The state provides a green jobs tax credit; for every green job created with a yearly salary of $50,000 or more, the company will earn a $500 income tax credit for five years. Qualifying biodiesel producers are eligible for a tax credit of $0.01 per gallon, up to $5,000, of biodiesel produced.

Loan Programs: Virginia provides funding for energy efficiency projects in state facilities.

Grants: Manufacturers of PV panels are eligible for grants of up to $0.75 per watt for panels sold in a calendar year for up to five years, with a total maximum of 6 MW per year. Grants are also available to producers of advanced biofuels.

Rebates: Virginia offers rebates to homeowners who install certain Energy Star appliances.

Rules and Regulations

Renewable Portfolio Standard: IOUs are encouraged, but not required, to procure a percentage of their retail electricity from renewable energy sources. Eligible energy resources include solar, wind, geothermal, hydropower, wave, tidal, and biomass energy.

Facility Siting and Permitting: Virginia generally bars community associations from prohibiting a homeowner from installing a solar energy collection device on his or her property. The state allows property owners to create binding solar easements for the purpose of protecting and maintaining proper access to sunlight.

Building Codes, Appliance, and Equipment Standards: The Virginia Uniform Statewide Building Code, which applies to residential and commercial developments, is mandatory statewide and based on the 2009 IECC. New state buildings over 5,000 square feet and major renovations of existing state-owned facilities are required to follow certain energy performance standards at least as stringent as the LEED Silver or the Green Globes 2 Globes standards.

Electricity Transmission, Interconnection, and Storage: Virginia's net-metering law applies to residential generating systems up to 10 kW in capacity and nonresidential systems up to 500 kW in capacity. Net metering is available until the rated generating capacity owned and operated by customer-generators reaches 1 percent of an electric distribution company's adjusted peak-load forecast for the previous year. Net metering is available to customers of IOUs and electric cooperatives, but not to customers of municipal utilities. Customer-generators that are net metered must comply with the state's interconnection rules. Systems that are not net metered must follow rules based on the FERC Small Generator Interconnection Procedure. Utilities must offer customers the option to purchase 100 percent of their electricity from renewable energy sources.

Government Procurement: State agencies and institutions must purchase or lease Energy Star-rated appliances and equipment, if available.

Policies, Plans, and Governmental Affiliations

Policies and Plans: On December 21, 2007, the governor issued an executive order creating the Governor's Commission on Climate Change and setting a target of reducing statewide GHG emissions by 30 percent by 2025.

Government Entities: Governor's Commission on Climate Change, Virginia Department of Mines, Minerals and Energy, Virginia Department of Taxation, Virginia Department of Treasury.

Regional Memberships: Virginia is a member of the SGA.

Washington

Financial Incentives

Tax Benefits: Washington offers a reduced business and occupation tax rate for manufacturers and wholesale marketers of solar PV modules or silicon components of those systems. Equipment used to generate electricity using fuel cells, wind, sun, biomass energy, tidal or wave energy, geothermal, anaerobic digestion, or landfill gas is exempt from the state's sales and use tax.

Other Financial Incentives: Washington has established a production incentive of $0.12 to $1.08 per kWh (depending on project type, technology type, and where the equipment was manufactured), up to $5,000 per year, for individuals, businesses, and local governments that generate electricity from solar power, wind power, or anaerobic digesters.

Rules and Regulations

Renewable Portfolio Standard: Washington's RPS requires utilities to procure at least 3 percent of their loads by 2012, and at least 15 percent of their loads by 2020. Eligible renewable resources include wind, hydro, solar, geothermal, wave, ocean, tidal, landfill gas, sewage treatment gas, biodiesel fuel, and certain types of biomass.

Facility Siting and Permitting: Washington's solar easement law allows parties to enter into solar easement contracts voluntarily, and homeowners' associations may not prohibit the installation of solar energy panels.

Building Codes, Appliance, and Equipment Standards: Washington's current state energy code exceeds the 2006 IECC's stringency for low-rise residential buildings, exceeds ASHRAE 90.1-2007's stringency for high-rise residential buildings, and is roughly equivalent to ASHRAE 90.1-2004 for commercial buildings. The 2009 version of the state energy code becomes effective in 2011. The Evergreen Sustainable Development Standard is a set of green building criteria that is required for any affordable housing project applying for state funds through the Washington State Housing Trust Fund. An executive order has been issued directing state agencies to adopt green building practices in the construction of all new buildings and in major renovations of existing buildings. State building projects over 25,000 square feet must meet the LEED Silver standard. Washington has established unique minimum efficiency standards for certain products (however, some have been superseded by subsequent federal standards).

Electricity Transmission, Interconnection, and Storage: The Washington Utilities and Transportation Commission has adopted interconnection standards for DG systems up to 20 MW in capacity. Net metering is available to renewable energy and CHP systems up to 100 kW in capacity on a first-come, first-served basis until the cumulative generating capacity of net-metered systems equals 0.25 percent of a utility's peak demand during 1996. This cap will increase to 0.5 percent on January 1, 2014. All electric utilities serving more than 25,000 customers must offer customers the option of purchasing renewable energy.

Government Procurement: State agencies must use all practicable and cost-effective means available to reduce energy purchases by 10 percent from fiscal year 2003 levels by 2009. Washington requires at least 30 percent of all new vehicles purchased through a state contract to be clean fuel vehicles.

Policies, Plans, and Governmental Affiliations

Policies and Plans: It is the policy of Washington to establish the state as a leader in clean energy research, development, manufacturing, and marketing. Washington has adopted a target of reducing GHG emissions to 1990 levels by 2020, 25 percent below 1990 levels by 2035, and 50 percent below 1990 levels by 2050. The Department of Ecology is to develop a system for monitoring and reporting Washington's GHG emissions. Washington also has a carbon dioxide mitigation plan for fossil-fueled thermal electric generation facilities.

Government Entities: State of Washington Energy Facility Site Evaluation Council, Washington State Department of Commerce, Washington State Department of Ecology, Washington State Department of General Administration, Washington State Department of Revenue, Washington Utilities and Transportation Commission.

Regional Memberships: Washington is a member of WCI, ICAP, the WGA, and the West Coast Governors' Global Warming Initiative.

West Virginia

Financial Incentives

Tax Benefits: West Virginia has increased the taxable value of wind turbine generating capacity, resulting in a business and operation tax rate on wind-powered turbines that is about 30 percent of the effective tax rate of most other types of newly constructed generating units. The state has also authorized a solar energy tax credit of 30 percent of the cost of purchasing and installing a residential system, which is capped at $2,000. For the purposes of property tax assessment, utility-owned wind projects are considered to have a value equal to their salvage value, with certain limitations. Additionally, West Virginia's annual sales tax holiday on Energy Star products provides a sales tax exemption on qualified products of $5,000 or less that are purchased for home or personal use.

Rebates: West Virginia provides rebates to residents who replace an existing appliance with a new Energy Star–qualified appliance.

Rules and Regulations

Renewable Portfolio Standard: West Virginia has enacted an Alternative and Renewable Energy Portfolio Standard that requires IOUs with more than 30,000 residential customers to supply 25 percent of retail electric sales from eligible alternative and renewable energy resources by 2025. Alternative energy resources include coal technology, coal bed methane, natural gas, fuel produced by a coal gasification or liquefaction facility, synthetic gas, integrated gasification combined cycle technologies, waste coal, tire-derived fuel, pumped storage hydroelectric projects, and recycled energy. Renewable energy resources include solar electric, solar thermal energy, wind power, run-of-river hydropower, geothermal energy, fuel cells, and certain biomass energy and biologically derived fuels.

Building Codes, Appliance, and Equipment Standards: The West Virginia building code, which is voluntary for residential and commercial developments, is based on the 2003 IECC.

Electricity Transmission, Interconnection, and Storage: The West Virginia Public Service Commission has established interconnection and net-metering rules applicable to systems that generate electricity using alternative or renewable energy resources. The interconnection standards are applicable to systems up to 2 MW in capacity. The system capacity for net metering ranges from 25 kW to 2 MW (depending on the size of the utility and the customer-generator).

Fuel Standards and Transportation: West Virginia law prohibits any commercial motor vehicle with a gross vehicle weight rating of 10,000 pounds or more from idling for more than fifteen minutes in any sixty-minute period.

Policies, Plans, and Governmental Affiliations

Government Entities: West Virginia Department of Environmental Protection, West Virginia Department of Commerce, West Virginia Public Service Commission, West Virginia State Tax Department.

Regional Memberships: West Virginia is a member of the SGA.

Wisconsin

Financial Incentives

Tax Benefits: Taxpayers are eligible for a tax credit of up to 10 percent of the cost of equipment used to process woody biomass for fuel. Any value added by a solar or wind energy system is exempt from property taxes. Biomass sold for residential or commercial energy production is exempt from Wisconsin's sales and use tax. Starting on July 1, 2011, wind, solar, and anaerobic digester systems will also be exempt from the sales and use tax. A tax credit is available for 25 percent of the cost to install or retrofit fueling stations in Wisconsin that dispense motor vehicle fuel blends of at least 85 percent ethanol or 20 percent biodiesel.

Loan Programs: Wisconsin provides low-interest loans for renewable energy commercialization and supply chain development projects for up to 25 percent of the project cost. The Focus on Energy program offers low-interest loans for qualifying Home Performance with Energy Star evaluations and efficient heating and cooling home improvements. The $100 million Green to Gold Fund offers loans to manufacturers for projects related to energy efficiency and renewable energy.

Grants: Renewable energy research and development projects are eligible for grants. The Focus on Energy program also offers grants to eligible businesses that install qualifying renewable energy systems.

Rebates: The Focus on Energy program offers a number of rebates to a range of sectors to support energy efficiency and renewable energy projects.

Rules and Regulations

Renewable Portfolio Standard: Wisconsin has set a goal of meeting 10 percent of its statewide energy needs through renewable energy sources by 2015. Utilities must meet mandatory requirements each year en route to achieving this target. Eligible systems include fuel cells using renewable fuels, solar thermal and PV, wind, geothermal, small hydro, tidal, wave, biomass, and biogas. Additionally, energy derived from solar, geothermal, biomass, biogas, waste gasification, and fuel pellets may count toward the standard only if their use results in a verifiable and measurable displacement of conventional energy use.

Facility Siting and Permitting: Wisconsin has several laws that protect a resident's right to install and operate a solar or wind energy system. These laws cover zoning restrictions by local governments, private land use restrictions, and system owner rights to unobstructed access to resources. The Public Service Commission of Wisconsin (PSC) is also in the process of establishing statewide wind energy system siting rules.

Building Codes, Appliance, and Equipment Standards: Wisconsin's residential and commercial building codes are based on the 2006 IECC, with amendments. New state facilities are required to be 30 percent more efficient than the commercial code.

Electricity Transmission, Interconnection, and Storage: The PSC has adopted a four-tiered interconnection standard for DG systems of up to 15 MW. All DG systems of up to 20 kW are eligible for net metering.

Government Procurement: The Wisconsin Department of Administration has set energy efficiency goals for state facilities to reduce overall energy use per square foot by 10 percent by 2008 and 20 percent by 2010, based on fiscal year 2005, adjusted for weather. Wisconsin's Departments of Administration, Corrections, Health and Family Services, Public Instruction, Veterans Affairs, and the Board of Regents of the University of Wisconsin System have a goal of purchasing or generating 10 percent of their power from renewable energy by December 31, 2007, and 20 percent by December 31, 2011. All motor vehicles owned or leased by the state must be HEVs or operate on alternative fuels whenever feasible.

Policies, Plans, and Governmental Affiliations

Policies and Plans: Wisconsin's Strategy for Reducing Global Warming, released in 2008, sets a goal of reducing GHG emissions to 2005 levels by 2014, 22 percent below 2005 levels by 2022, and 75 percent below 2005 levels by 2050.

Government Entities: Governor's Task Force on Global Warming, Public Service Commission of Wisconsin, Wisconsin Department of Administration, Wisconsin Department of Commerce, Wisconsin Department of Natural Resources.

Regional Memberships: Wisconsin is a member of the MGGRA and the MGA.

Wyoming

Financial Incentives

Tax Benefits: The sale, purchase, or lease of equipment used to generate renewable energy is exempted from Wyoming's state sales tax.

Loan Programs: The state, through the Wyoming Community Development Authority, provides low-interest loans to low-income residents for energy efficiency home retrofits.

Grants: Wyoming provides grants of 75 percent of the cost, up to $5,000, to small business owners executing a level two energy audit.

Rebates: State residents installing PV, small wind, or geothermal systems may be eligible to receive rebates through the State Energy Office. In addition, Wyoming provides rebates to residents who replace an existing appliance with a new Energy Star–qualified appliance.

Rules and Regulations

Facility Siting and Permitting: Wyoming law requires wind facilities larger than 0.5 MW that begin construction after July 1, 2010, to obtain a permit from the county in which the facility is located. Facilities must also obtain permits for any enlargements. Prior to submitting an application for a permit, certain notification procedures must be followed. Wyoming has also enacted siting rules for wind facilities. The base of any tower must be at least 110 percent of the maximum height of the tower away from any property line or public road. Towers must be at least 1,000 feet from any platted subdivision, residential dwelling, or occupied structure, and at least one-half mile from any city limits. These rules may be waived with permission from residents or owners.

Building Codes, Appliance, and Equipment Standards: Wyoming does not have a mandatory statewide code. Local jurisdictions may, but are not required to, adopt the 1989 MEC.

Electricity Transmission, Interconnection, and Storage: Wyoming's net-metering law mandates coverage for systems up to 25 kW in capacity that generate electricity using solar, wind, hydropower, or biomass resources. This law is applicable only to IOUs, electric cooperatives, and irrigation districts. The law also provides for interconnection requirements. The Wyoming Public Service Commission oversees both net metering and interconnection.

Policies, Plans, and Governmental Affiliations

Government Entities: State Energy Office, Wyoming Community Development Authority, Wyoming Department of Environmental Quality, Wyoming Public Service Commission.

Regional Memberships: Wyoming is a member of the WGA and an observer of WCI.

Table of Cases

New Mexico Industrial Energy Consumers v. New Mexico Public Regulation Commission, 168 P.3d 105 (N.M. 2007), 88

New York v. Bodman, Nos. 05 Civ. 7807 (JES) & 05 Civ. 7808 (JES), (S.D.N.Y. Nov. 6, 2006), 51n96

New York v. Bodman, Nos. 05 Civ. 7807 (JES) & 05 Civ. 7808 (JES), 2007 U.S. Dist. LEXIS 80980 (S.D.N.Y. Nov. 1, 2007), 295n32

New York v. FERC, 535 U.S. 1 (2002), 555n58

North Carolina v. FERC, 112 F.3d 1175 (D.C. Cir. 1997), 504n161

North Iredell Neighbors for Rural Life v. Iredell County, 674 S.E.2d 436 (N.C. Ct. App. 2009), 466

Novozymes v. Genencor Int'l, Inc., 474 F. Supp. 2d 592 (D. Del. 2007), 477n196

Nw. Paper Co. v. FPC, 344 F.2d 47 (8th Cir. 1965), 499n39

Occidental Geothermal, Inc. v. Simmons, 543 F. Supp. 870 (N.D. Cal. 1982), 432

Operation of the Missouri River Sys. Litig., In re, 421 F.3d 618 (8th Cir. 2005), 506n208

Ownership of Renewable Energy Certificates, In re, 913 A.2d 825 (N.J. Super. Ct. App. Div. 2007), 93n95

Pac. Coast Fed'n of Fishermen's Ass'n v. Gutierrez, 606 F. Supp. 2d 1122 (E.D. Cal. 2008), 108n31

Petersburg Mun. Power & Light v. FERC, No. 10-1096 (D.C. Cir. Feb. 25, 2011), 500n50

Phillips Petroleum Co. v. Mississippi, 484 U.S. 469 (1988), 389n98

Phoenix Hydro Corp. v. FERC, 775 F.2d 1187 (D.C. Cir. 1985), 501n77

Piedmont Envtl. Council v. FERC, 558 F.3d 304 (4th Cir. 2009), 555n29

Pike v. Bruce Church Inc., 397 U.S. 137 (1970), 399, 419n59

Pit River Tribe v. U.S. Forest Service, 469 F.3d 768 (9th Cir. 2006), 106n12, 110n51, 439

Platte River Whooping Crane Critical Habitat Maint. Trust v. FERC, 876 F.2d 109 (D.C. Cir. 1989), 500n68, 505n175

Platte River Whooping Crane Critical Habitat Maint. Trust v. FERC, 962 F.2d 27 (D.C. Cir. 1992), 500n68, 505n175

Plaxton v. Lycoming Cnty. Zoning Hearing Bd., 986 A.2d 199 (Pa. Commw. Ct. 2009), 113n106

Pub. Employees for Envtl. Responsibility v. Bromwich, No. 10-cv-01067 (D.D.C. filed June 25, 2010), 390n126

Pub. Util. Dist. No. 1 of Snohomish Cnty. v. FERC, 471 F.3d 1053 (9th Cir. 2006), aff'd in part and rev'd in part sub nom. Morgan Stanley Capital Group, Inc. v. Pub. Util. Dist. No. 1, 128 S. Ct. 2733 (2008), 63, 239n60

Public Utility District No. 1 of Jefferson County v. Washington Department of Ecology (Dosewallips), 511 U.S. 700 (1994), 491–492

Puget Sound Power & Light v. FPC, 557 F.2d 1311 (9th Cir. 1977), 499n47

Quaker Bldg. v. Dep't of Pub. Utils., 136 N.E.2d 246 (Mass. 1956), 239n48

Rankin v. FPL Energy, LLC, 266 S.W.3d 506 (Tex. App. 2008), 109n45

Rapanos v. United States, 547 U.S. 715 (2006), 442n64

Renerglobe, Inc. v. Northeast Biofuels, LLC, 24 Misc. 3d 1212(A), 2009 WL 1929090 (N.Y. Sup. Ct. June 24, 2009), 477n194

Residents Opposed to Kittitas Turbines v. State Energy Facility Site Evaluation Council, 197 P.3d 1153 (Wash. 2008), 107n18

Roberts v. Manitowoc Cnty. Bd. of Adjustment, 2006 WI App. 169, 295 Wis. 2d 522, 721 N.W.2d 499 (2006), 114n113

Rocky Mountain Farmers Union v. Goldstene, No. 1:09-cv-02234-LJO-DLB (E.D. Cal. 2009), 464–465

Rosette cases, 431, 439. See also Rosette, Inc. v. United States

Rosette, Inc. v. United States (Rosette I), 141 F.3d 1394 (10th Cir. 1998), 443n79

Rosette, Inc. v. United States (Rosette II), 64 F. Supp. 2d 1116 (D.N.M. 1999), 443n80

Rosette, Inc. v. United States (Rosette III), 277 F.3d 1222 (10th Cir. 2002), 443n81

Rosette, Inc. v. United States, 169 P.3d 704 (N.M. Ct. App. 2007), 82–84, 443n77

S. Cal. Edison Co. v. FERC, 116 F.3d 507 (D.C. Cir. 1997), 503n128

S. Fla. Water Mgmt. Dist. v. Miccosukee Tribe, 541 U.S. 95 (2004), 505n173

Index

advanced energy property, tax credits
for, 150

Advanced Research Projects Agency-Energy
(ARPA–E), 38, 178

Advanced Technology Vehicles
Manufacturing Program Loan Program
(ATVM), 190

Advance Notice of Proposed Rulemaking
(ANOPR), 280

aesthetic impact, wind energy and, 370–372

affluence, energy consumption and, 3–8

Agricultural Bioenergy Feedstock and Energy
Efficiency Research and Extension
Initiative (USDA), 451

agriculture sector, conservation of energy,
263–276. *See also* Farm Bill (2008); U.S.
Department of Agriculture (USDA)

AgSTAR (EPA), 271

Air-Conditioning, Heating, and Refrigeration
Institute (ACHRI), 70, 283

air quality, geothermal energy and,
436–437

Alabama, state actions on clean energy,
559–560

Alaska
sale of electricity, 229
state actions on clean energy, 560–561

Albuquerque (New Mexico), appliance
efficiency standards, 70

algae blooms, biofuels and, 448

Alliance to Save Energy, 132

alternative fuels, 336
alternative fuel infrastructure tax credit,
450–451
biofuels, 450
federal incentives for, 154–160

alternative fuel vehicles (AFV)
alternative motor vehicle credit,
152–153
government procurement, 136

American Clean Energy and Security Act of
2009, 16, 35, 39, 42–43, 280

American Council for an Energy-Efficient
Economy, 41–42, 225
utility cost and revenue recovery, 62
utility shareholder incentives, 63–64

American National Standards Institute
(ANSI), 265

American Petroleum Institute v. Cooper, 465

American Recovery and Reinvestment Act of
2009 (ARRA), 15
appliance rebates, 61
biofuels, 450–451
building sector, 66, 304–305, 314
federal energy efficiency and conservation
laws and, 28, 34, 37
government procurement, 130
motor vehicles and transportation
sector, 334
nontax incentives, 179, 181–182, 183,
184, 185, 189–190, 193
solar energy, 394–395, 404
state and municipal government
procurement, 138–139
tax incentives, 147, 150, 152

American Society of Agricultural and
Biological Engineers (ASABE), 265

American Society of Heating, Refrigerating,
and Air-Conditioning Engineers
(ASHRAE) Code, 35, 66, 302, 308–309,
310, 312

American Solar Energy Society, 18

American Wind Energy Association
(AWEA), 365

anaerobic digesters, 270–272

angel investors, 243–244, 247

*Animal Welfare Institute v. Beech Ridge
Energy*, 379–380

Anti-Deficiency Act, 118

appliance and equipment efficiency
standards, 277–300
computers or monitors or data centers or
computer servers and, 290–292
DOE appliance efficiency rulemaking,
281–283
energy efficient appliance credit, 150
Energy Star, 286–288
enforcement, 284–286
exceptions or waivers, 284
Federal Appliance Efficiency Program,
277–281
federal energy efficiency and conservation
laws and policies for specific economic
sectors, 32–34
full-fuel-cycle measurements, 292–293
generally, 277
international involvement in, 293–294
lighting, 288–290

investment tax credits (ITC), 146–147, 149, 392–395. *See also* financial issues

Iowa
   biofuels, 453
   facility siting and permitting and, 112n92
   hydropower, 487
   state actions on clean energy, 575–576
   tax incentives, 157

ISO New England, 86, 233–234, 540

Jacobson, Mark C., 18

Kansas
   facility siting and permitting and, 99
   state actions on clean energy, 576–577

Kennedy, Robert F., Jr., 99

Kentucky
   personal energy efficiency tax incentives, 59
   state actions on clean energy, 577–578

Keystone Field-to-Market initiative, 265

Kitzhaber, John, 269

Kyoto Protocol, 43–45

LaFleur v. Whitman, 465–466

land acquisition, facility siting and permitting and, 102–103

land use change, biofuels and, 447–448

large generator interconnection procedure (LGIP), 542

Lawrence Livermore National Laboratory, 6

lead agency, 95

Leadership in Energy and Environmental Design (LEED), 66, 301, 310
   certification, 311
   criticism, 312
   LEED for Existing Buildings: Operations & Maintenance (LEED-EBOM), 315
   rating systems, 310–311

leasing issues
   buildings and green leases, 316–317
   geothermal energy, 433–435
   marine and hydrokinetic energy, 510–515
   solar energy, 413–417

LEED. *See* Leadership in Energy and Environmental Design (LEED)

licensing issues
   agreements as nontax incentives, 180
   hydropower, 487–493
   intellectual property transactions, 246
   marine and hydrokinetic energy, 510–515

life-cycle costs, 141n56, 447, 458

lifecycle greenhouse gas emissions, 367

lighting, 288–290

load reshaping, electric power and, 222–224

Loan Guarantee Program Office (DOE), 188–190, 401

loan guarantee programs, federal, 172–173

Los Angeles (California), building sector and, 307–308

Louisiana, state actions on clean energy, 578–579

Lovins, Amory, 38

low carbon fuel standards (LCFS), 460–464

Magnuson Stevens Fishery Conservation and Management Act, 520

Maine
   biofuels, 462–463
   marine and hydrokinetic energy, 515
   RPS, 79–80
   state actions on clean energy, 579–581
   wind energy, 370

Makah Bay Offshore Wave Pilot Project (Washington), 513, 515, 517, 520, 522–523

marine energy. *See* tides, waves, and ocean currents

Marine Mammal Protection Act (MMPA), 378, 519–520

marine spatial planning initiative, 377

maritime safety, wind energy and, 372–373

Maryland
   biofuels, 462–463
   property taxes, 60
   sale of electricity, 221, 232
   state actions on clean energy, 581–582

Massachusetts
   ASHRAE Code and, 35
   biofuels, 453, 462–463
   building sector, 306
   Energy Efficiency Resource Standards (EERS), 64
   RPS, 83
   sale of electricity, 218, 221, 230, 231, 232, 234, 235
   solar energy, 399–400
   state actions on clean energy, 582–584
   state appliance efficiency standards, 68
   utility shareholder incentives, 63
   wind energy, 370, 374, 381–382, 520

Massachusetts v. EPA, 29, 329

McKinsey (consulting firm), reports by, 7

merit review, 203n49

Metcalf, Gilbert E., 145

Michigan, 369–370
   appliance rebates, 62